Principles of Finance with Excel

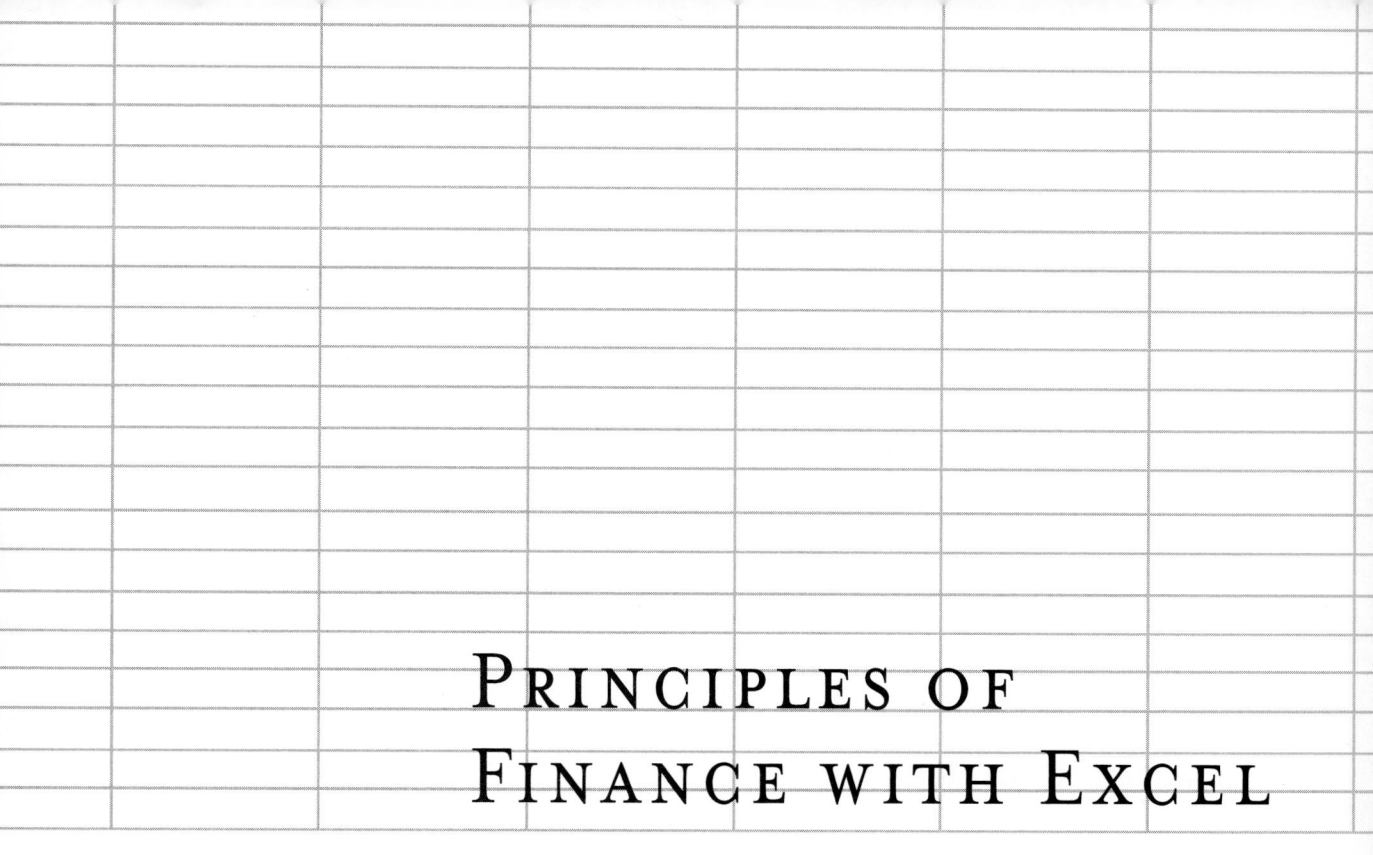

PRINCIPLES OF
FINANCE WITH EXCEL

Simon Benninga
Faculty of Management, Tel Aviv University
The Wharton School, University of Pennsylvania

New York   Oxford
OXFORD UNIVERSITY PRESS
2006

Oxford University Press, Inc., publishes works that further Oxford University's objective of excellence in research, scholarship, and education.

Oxford New York
Auckland   Cape Town   Dar es Salaam   Hong Kong   Karachi
Kuala Lumpur   Madrid   Melbourne   Mexico City   Nairobi
New Delhi   Shanghai   Taipei   Toronto

With offices in
Argentina   Austria   Brazil   Chile   Czech Republic   France   Greece
Guatemala   Hungary   Italy   Japan Poland   Portugal   Singapore
South Korea   Switzerland   Thailand   Turkey   Ukraine   Vietnam

Copyright © 2006 by Oxford University Press, Inc.

Published by Oxford University Press, Inc.
198 Madison Avenue, New York, New York 10016
http://www.oup.com

Oxford is a registered trademark of Oxford University Press

Library of Congress Cataloging-in-Publication Data
Benninga, Simon.
    Principles of finance with Excel / by Simon Benninga.
      p. cm.
    Includes index.
    ISBN-13: 978-0-19-530150-2

    1. Finance—Data processing.   2. Microsoft Excel (Computer file)
3. Capital assets pricing model.   I. Title.
HG173.B463 2005
332'.0285—dc22

                                  2005011411

Printing number: 9 8 7 6

Printed in the United States of America
on acid-free paper

To Terry, Noah, Sara, and Zvi

CONTENTS

PREFACE

Finance is the study of financial decision making. Individuals and companies make financial decisions every day, and it's important to make them wisely. *Principles of Finance with Excel* (PFE) will teach you how to make these decisions—both the theory and the implementation of wise financial decision making—and how to express your decisions using Excel.

Learning to do finance with Excel serves two purposes: It teaches you an important academic and practical subject (finance), and it teaches you how to implement financial analysis using the most important tool (in most cases, the *only* tool) for financial analysis (Excel). Your knowledge of both finance and Excel will be enhanced by carefully working through the examples and exercises in each chapter.

Finance is a very practical discipline. Most readers of this book will be studying finance not only to increase their understanding of the valuation process, but also to get answers to practical problems. You will find that the extensive computation required in this book will not only enable you to get numerical answers to important problems (though that alone would justify the Excel-centered focus of this book)—it will also deepen your understanding of the concepts involved.

Prerequisites—What Excel Background Is Required
for *Principles of Finance with Excel?*

This book teaches you—together with finance—all the Excel concepts needed for finance. However, you should not expect the book to be a complete Excel text. I expect that, before you start your finance course, you will know how to do the following things in Excel (just in case—many of these topics are covered in Chapter 27):

- Open and save an Excel workbook.
- Use basic Excel functions, for example, **Sum( )**.
- Format numbers. Here's an example of something that is usually not explained in the text:

	C	D	E	F	G
6	($6,144.57)	<-- =PV(10%,10,1000)			
7					
8					
9	-6,144.57	<-- In many cases I prefer this format			

- Use absolute and relative values in copying and formulas.
- Graphing—building the basic Excel charts. The favorite chart format in this book is Excel's XY graph. You should know how to do the basics of graphing in Excel: label axes, put in chart titles, format axes.

Somewhat More Advanced Excel Concepts

Chapters 28–34 cover a grab bag of other Excel concepts used in this book. You can refer to these chapters as you need them. Topics covered in Chapters 28–34 include the following:

- **Charts in Excel:** More advanced charting techniques are explained in Chapter 28.
- **Excel functions:** Most of the Excel functions required for this book are explained the first time they occur. Chapter 29 is a compendium of these explanations and may be useful for reference.
- **Data tables:** "Data table" is Excel jargon for "sensitivity table." The data table technique is a little tricky, but it is well-worth learning (for some reason, data tables are often not covered in introductory Excel courses). Although the early chapters avoid the use of data tables, their use is required in later chapters of the book. Chapter 30 teaches you how to use data tables.
- **Dates in Excel:** Many finance computations require the use of dates. This topic is covered in Chapter 31.
- **Goal Seek and Solver:** These two Excel tools allow you to fine-tune your spreadsheets. Most students will have learned to use **Goal Seek**, but in many cases **Solver** is more useful. Both topics are discussed in Chapter 32.
- **Data manipulation:** While not often used in this book, data manipulation is an important topic (Chapter 33) for many financial analysts.
- **Word and Excel:** Most financial analysis is done in Excel and written in Word. Chapter 34 shows you how to combine the two programs for best results.

CD-ROM Accompanying This Book

Each chapter is accompanied by two spreadsheets, which are on the enclosed CD-ROM. One spreadsheet, typically called **pfe_chap01.xls** or **pfe_chap15.xls**, presents all the examples covered in Chapter 1 or Chapter 15. A second spreadsheet, called something like **pfe_exer15.xls**, gives the answers to the end-of-chapter exercises. Instructors can contact the author for a separate set of exercises to use in classes or for exams. Powerpoints for most chapters are also available.

When you open a PFE spreadsheet, you will see the following message informing you that there is a macro attached to the spreadsheet:

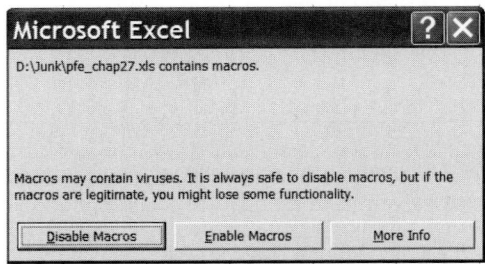

This message refers to a little program (in Excel jargon: a "macro") that dynamically updates cell references, so that output like the following will automatically retain the correct cell references even if you move things around or add rows:

	A	B	C	D
1	**CALCULATING PRESENT VALUES WITH EXCEL**			
2				
3	X, future payment	100		
4	n, time of future payment	3		
5	r, interest rate	6%		
6	Present value, $X/(1+r)^n$	83.96	<-- =B3/(1+B5)^B4	
7				
8	**Proof**			
9	Payment today	83.96		
10	Future value in *n* years	100	<-- =B9*(1+B5)^B4	

You can safely enable this macro. There is a document (**GetFormula.doc**) on the CD-ROM showing you how to put this macro into any spreadsheet you want to create.

A Final Word from the Author

Writing *Principles of Finance with Excel* was a lot of fun! I hope you enjoy the book. If you have comments or suggestions, feel free to contact me.

Acknowledgments

During the years of writing *Principles of Finance with Excel,* I've gotten many wonderful comments from readers of the many versions of the Web draft of the book. University instructors, financial professionals, and students have all chipped in to make PFE a better book.

I've tried to carefully note all the readers who've been helpful in the editorial/writing process (if I've forgotten someone, there's always the next printing of the book . . .): Meni Aboudy, Ilan Adam, Gil Aharony, Mazin A. M. Al Janabi, Thomas C. Altman, Clifford S. Ang, Tom Arnold, Chana Arnon, Naftali Arnon, Almaz Asylbek, Dan Atzmon, Erik Austin, Daniel Bachner, Robert Balik, Keshav Baljee, Naomi Belfer, Helen Benninga, Ricardo Botero, Reider Bratvold, Lucas Brown, Yoshua Carhuamaca, P. J. Carroll, Lydia Cassorla, Elizabeth Caulk, David Centeno, Le Chang, Peter Chepets, Nikolai Chuvakhin, Marcus Cole, Daniel Diamant, Ian Dickson, Bjarne Eggesbo, Patricia A. Ellenburg, Etune Emelieze, Rune Enge, Jon Fantell, Yiktat Fung, Brian Fusco, Denis Gaiovy, Terry Garden, Glenn Gaston, Fan Ge, Gary Glassie, Kobi Glazer, Randy Gordon, Kenji Goto, Michael Grant, Jonathan Gray, Pallav Gupta, George Guzzi, Kim Hale, Mark Helmantel, Raoul Hermens, Charlyn Ho, Reginald Holden, James W. B. Hole, Cesar Hurtado, Mafaz Ishaq, Ryan Scott Jackson, Youngsoo Kim, Itzik Kleschelski, Pierre Kohn, Timo Korkeamaki, Kevin Kretzschmar, Krushna Kumaar, Jeff S. Lee, Rowan Legg, Ross Leimberg, Björn Leonardz, Shai Leshkowitz, Daniel Leung, Hui Li, Shulin Liu, Paul Malherbe, Ariela Markel, Carlos Martinez, William Matthaei, Walter McGuire, Steve Medwin, Michael Miles, Tal Mofkadi, Kirill Mokh, Igor Morais, Eran Mordechai, Sviatoslav Moskalev, Joshua Nabatian, Bharat Pardasani, Dror Parnes, Jayesh Patel, Langston Payne, David Piccardi, Yong-Xuan Qiu, Justin Rapp, Ravinder Rayu, Roberto Rivalta, Jamie Adler Rodriguez, Bas Röling, Yashwant Sankpal, Roderik Schlösser, Jason Scott, Hanan Shahaf, Yaffa Shalit, Benny Sharvit, Teslim K. Shitta-Bey, Dmitry Shklovsky, Wayne Smith, José Arnaldo Ribeiro Soares, Nagaratnam Sreedharan, Yossi Steinblatt, Nathaniel V. Stevens, Lisa Sun, Maurry Tamarkin, Zoltan Till, Masahiro Tokoro, Efrat Tolkowsky, Jake Vachal, Rafael Paschoarelli Veiga, Shally Venugopal, Torben Voetmann, Simon Wang, Michael Wassermann, James L. Williams, Jared Work, Mark Yoffe, Jumana Zahalka, Aziza Zakhidova, Fan Zhang.

Finally, my thanks go to Christina Dellabartolomea, copyeditor, and to Catherine Rae, Karen Shapiro, and Terry Vaughn, the wonderful staff at Oxford University Press.

Simon Benninga
Benninga@wharton.upenn.edu

Principles of Finance with Excel

PART I

INTRODUCTORY CHAPTERS

Chapters 1–4 of *Principles of Finance with Excel* introduce the basic framework of the book.

Chapter 1 tries to answer the question, "What is finance all about?" This is not an easy task, given that you are most likely reading this book because you're trying to learn finance! Nevertheless, Chapter 1 tries to give you some feel for the questions addressed in this book.

Chapter 2 discusses the basic forms of business organization and gives you some background on how taxes—both personal income taxes and corporate taxes—are calculated. When you finish this chapter, you will understand the difference between a solely owned company, a partnership, and a corporation. It will not surprise you that Excel is a great aid in computing taxes and integrating tax tables into the calculations.

Chapter 3 provides the necessary accounting background for *Principles of Finance with Excel*. Although most readers of the book will have some basic accounting grounding, Chapter 3 is for readers wanting to brush up or to learn accounting basics.

Chapter 4 shows you how to use Excel for cash management for a business. Cash management—a somewhat more sophisticated version of checkbook balancing—involves the prediction of the future cash balances available to a business. As this chapter illustrates, Excel can be used to build highly flexible cash management models.

INTRODUCTION TO FINANCE

1.1 What Is Finance?

Finance is the study of financial decision making. Individuals and companies make financial decisions every day, and it's important to make them wisely. *Principles of Finance with Excel* will teach you how to make these decisions—both the theory and the implementation of wise financial decision making—and how to express your decisions using Excel.

Learning to do finance with Excel serves two purposes: It teaches you an important academic and practical subject (finance), and it teaches you how to implement financial analysis using the most important tool (in most cases, the *only* tool) for financial analysis (Excel).

Individual Financial Decision Making

People are constantly called on to make financial decisions in their personal lives. Here are examples of decisions we examine in this book:

- How much should you save to attain a specific goal in the future? For example: You're starting a savings plan today to save for your college education. How much should you put away each month in order to have the money to pay for your education?

- You're thinking about buying a house and renting it out for the income. How should you evaluate this decision?

- You have some money saved from working, and you'd like to invest it. How should you choose your financial portfolio? Investors big and small have to decide whether to invest in stocks, bonds, or other assets such as real estate, art, and gold. They also have to decide how to choose the *investment proportions*. What percentage of your financial portfolio should you invest in stocks (and what percentage in *which* stocks), what percentage in bonds, real estate, and so on?

- How should you finance a purchase, a project, or some other undertaking? Here are some examples. You're about to buy a new car. Should you borrow the money from the bank or should you accept the car dealer's "zero interest loan" alternative? That piece of real estate you're buying—should you finance it with a mortgage? If so, how large should the mortgage be?

- What is financial risk and how can it be measured? Financial risk can be measured using statistical tools. This book shows you which tools you need and how to apply them. When you're comfortable applying these tools, you'll be much better at comparing the riskiness of two assets or two investments. Comparing risks is critical to making optimal financial decisions.

- What is the fair value for stocks and bonds and other financial assets? This book shows you how to compute the value of stocks and bonds. It also discusses the role of financial markets in incorporating available financial information into prices. If financial markets do this well, you may not need to determine these values yourself: You can let the financial markets tell you what the value should be.

- How can you value options? Options are securities that give you the right to buy a stock in the future. If you work in a corporate environment, your employers are likely, at some point, to offer you some options on the company's stock instead of a regular salary. If you're trying to regulate the risk of your financial portfolio, your investment advisor may try to sell you some options. This book explains what an option is, how to use it to regulate financial risk, and how to value it.

As these examples show, the study of finance can benefit you in many areas of your personal life by enabling you to make better financial decisions.

Financial Decisions in a Business Environment

You only have to turn on the TV, log onto the Internet, or read a newspaper to hear about the financial decisions that businesses make every day. Some of these financial decisions are huge and dramatic, like Comcast's $54 billion bid to buy Disney; some are smaller but nonetheless very important for the company, like Courier Corporation's purchase of Dover Publications for $39 million (Figure 1.1).

Dramatic business decisions like mergers and acquisitions make the news, but "run-of-the-mill" business financial decisions critical to the financial health of the firm are made by all businesses, big or small. Here are some typical decisions that businesses make:

- A company wants to replace its current production line with a line of new, improved machines. The new machines cost more but are more efficient. Should the company buy the new machines or leave the old ones in place?

- A firm needs to acquire a particular kind of machine. Should it buy a cheap machine with a relatively short life or an expensive machine with a longer life span?

- When a company wants to develop and produce a new product, how can it integrate the marketing forecasts for the new product with the financial requirements of the development and production processes? How can the company deal with the fact that the biggest costs of

Courier To Acquire Dover Publications For $39 Million - Courier Corp., Dover Publications Inc - Brief Article

Courier Corp. (North Chelmsford, MA) continues to branch out from its book manufacturing roots with the acquisition of Mineola, NY-based Dover Publications, a longtime client it bought last month for $39 million.

The deal is expected to close by Sept. 30. Dover, which has 170 employees, will operate as a subsidiary. No changes will be made in management. Dover has more than 7,000 in-print titles in over 30 specialty categories, including fine and commercial art, children's activity books, mathematics, science, history, classic literature for children and adults, puzzles and games.

Figure 1.1 Two corporate financial decisions.

development and production will be incurred before any revenues have been realized from the sale of the product?

- How should the financial officers of a corporation plan for a new or existing business? A *financial planning model* can provide a systematic approach to making many of the financial decisions in a new or existing business. Perhaps you're thinking of setting up a laundromat on the corner of Main and Pine streets. Perhaps you're starting a real estate business. Or perhaps you're trying to finance a new high-tech idea. In each case your ability to get financing from financial institutions—whether banks or venture capital funds or your Uncle Joe—will depend on your ability to make a financial model for the new business. This financial model will show your thoughts about how the business will develop, how much equipment you'll need to purchase, and how you will finance sales. Most importantly, the financial model will project future earnings from the business.

- All companies must decide how to finance their activities. This is true for multinational conglomerates, mom-and-pop convenience stores, and the new taxi company you're about to start with your cousin Sarah. In all cases someone has to decide whether to borrow the money from others or whether to use shareholder funds (equity, in the terminology of finance) to finance the company.

Wealth Maximization and Risk

This book is primarily about making *sensible financial decisions.* Sometimes a sensible financial decision is also an *optimal* financial decision. Optimal financial decisions make you better off than all the other relevant alternatives, including doing nothing at all. Economists call this property of optimal financial decisions *wealth maximization.* Not every case of money management boils down to making a wealth-maximizing decision; sometimes we are only able to point to a *sensible set of financial alternatives* from which you can choose a final decision.

Making sensible or wealth-maximizing financial decisions always involves two elements:

- **Defining the parameters of the decision:** Financial decisions can always be defined in terms of numbers. The outcomes of a financial decision almost always depend on the *decision parameters,* the inputs that define the results of the financial decision.

  Here's an example: You've been given $100 for your birthday, and you decide to save it toward your summer vacation next year. You have two choices—leave the money in your checking account or put the money in a savings account. The two parameters of this decision are the amount you're saving ($100) and the interest paid on the account—the checking account pays 1% interest, whereas the savings account pays 4% interest. The *financial outcomes* are that, one year from now, you will have $101 if you leave the money in your checking account and $104 if you put the money in a savings account. This decision is, of course, a no-brainer: You always prefer earning 4% to earning 1% on your money.

  This book helps you distinguish between the parameters of financial decisions and the outcomes of financial decisions.

- **Recognizing the risks of financial decisions**: Financial decisions should be made within a framework that takes into account the risks associated with them.

  Let's go back to the $100 you intend to save for your summer vacation. In addition to the two alternatives (1% on your checking account and 4% on your savings account), your Uncle Joe suggests that you might want to buy shares in his new hot dog stand. Investors in Joe's previous hot dog stands have earned as much as 40% on their investment.

  If you put your money in Uncle Joe's hot dog stand, you *might* have $140 at the end of the year, instead of $104, but if the hot dog stand does poorly, you could lose your $100 investment and end up with nothing. Uncle Joe's hot dog stand is *much riskier* than a bank account—although some investors have made as much as 40%, others have lost all their money with Joe. Comparing an investment in the hot dog stand with a deposit in a savings account must take into account the differences in their risks. This book shows you how to account for risks inherent in making financial decisions.

1.2 Microsoft Excel: Why This Book and Not Another?

There are dozens of introductory finance texts out there. Many of them are very good. So why this one? In a word: **Excel.** Finance is the study of financial decision making and is therefore inherently a topic requiring lots of computation. In this book the computation is done in, and illustrated with, Excel, the premier business computational tool. Excel gives you the flexibility to change the elements of an example and to immediately get a new answer. We use this flexibility extensively throughout *Principles of Finance with Excel*.

Finance is a very practical discipline. Most of you are studying finance not only to increase your understanding of the valuation process, but also to *get answers to practical problems*. You will find that the extensive computation required in this book not only enables you to get numerical answers to important problems (though that alone would justify the Excel-centered focus of this book)—it also deepens your understanding of the concepts involved.

Using Excel enables us to discuss many more real-life examples than is possible by using a calculator. Your knowledge of both finance and Excel will be enhanced by carefully working through the examples and exercises in each chapter.[1]

Most college students will be coming to a finance course after having taken an initial computing course that covers the basics of Excel used in this book. If you want an Excel review, the last eight chapters of this book cover the essential Excel concepts used in this book. In addition, throughout the book you will find explanations of Excel functions and their application to financial problems. When things get really rough, you'll find little boxes called "Excel Notes," which explain difficult concepts. Here is an example of such a box:

EXCEL NOTE

The Excel function **Sum** can often be used to simplify calculations. Here's an example based on the computation of a profit and loss statement:

	A	B	C
1	**USING SUM TO COMPUTE THE PROFIT AND LOSS**		
2	Profit and loss		
3	Sales	1,000	
4	Cost of goods sold	-500	
5	Depreciation	-100	
6	Interest	-35	
7	Profit before taxes	365	<-- =SUM(B3:B6)
8	Taxes (40%)	-146	<-- =-40%*B7
9	Profit after taxes	219	<-- =SUM(B7:B8)

Cells B7 and B9 use the **Sum** function to add multiple cells. An alternative to using **Sum** in cell B7 is to use the formula **=B3+B4+B5+B6**. As you can see, **Sum** is more concise.

What Are the Excel Prerequisites for This Book?

You do not have to be an Excel expert to use this book. Almost all the Excel concepts needed to do finance are explained in the text itself. While this book teaches you the Excel concepts needed for finance, it is not a complete Excel text. Before you start Chapter 2, you should know how to

---

[1]If you're a finance student at a college or university, this combination of Excel and finance will also enhance your employment opportunities. Excel is practically the only financial tool used by business today.

do the following in Excel (all are covered in Chapter 27):

- Open and save an Excel notebook.
- Format numbers. Using the command **Format|Cells|Number,** you can make numbers appear in different forms. In the example below, the number 2313.88 is shown in three different ways.

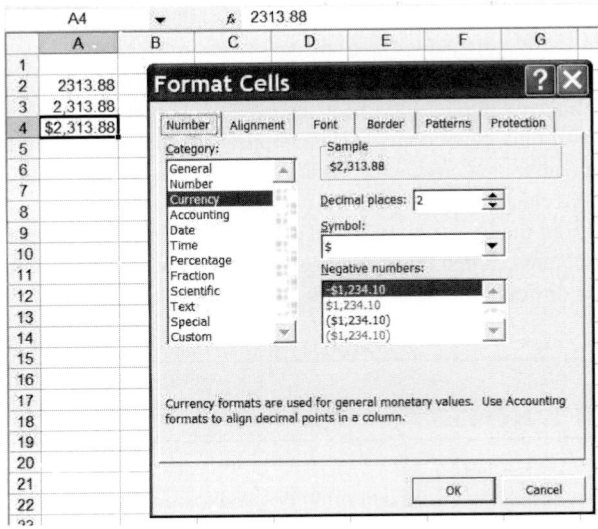

- Use absolute and relative values in copying and formulas. When you copy in Excel, you can use either *relative* or *absolute* copying. As explained in Chapter 27, relative copying changes the cell addresses, whereas absolute copying leaves them the same.[2]
- Build basic Excel charts to graph data. You should know how to label axes, put in chart titles, format axes, and so on.

1.3 Eight Principles of Finance

In this section we look at eight unifying principles of finance. At this stage you may not understand them all or even find them convincing, but we introduce them here to give you an overview of what finance is all about. They are explained more fully in the rest of *Principles of Finance with Excel.*

Principle 1: Buy Assets That Add Value; Avoid Buying Assets That Don't

On the simplest level, making optimal financial decisions has to do with buying assets that add value and avoiding those that don't. For example, you need to decide whether to keep using your old, inefficient photocopying machine or buy an expensive new one that works faster, doesn't break down as often, and uses less ink and energy. The finance question about these two alternatives is: Which—keeping the old photocopier or buying a new one—adds more value to your business? To make a determination about how valuable things (such as stocks, bonds, machines, companies) are, you need to be sure that you are comparing apples with apples and oranges with oranges. This sounds like a simple principle to follow, but it can be surprisingly tricky to implement!

---

[2]If you find this sentence mysterious, look at Section 27.3.

Principle 2: Cash Is King

The value of an asset is determined by the *cash flows it produces over its life*. The cash flow of an asset is the *after-tax cash* the asset produces at a given point in time.

While it is too early in the book to give you the full flavor of the difference between a cash flow and a profit number, we can give a small example. Suppose your pizza parlor sells $500 of pizzas on Tuesday night, and suppose the same day you bought $300 worth of ingredients. Looking in the cash register at the end of the day, you expect to find $200, but instead you're surprised to find $300. The explanation: Of the $500 of pizzas sold, you collected only $400—the other $100 of pizzas were sold to a campus fraternity that maintains an account with you and settles at the end of each month. Of the $300 of ingredients you bought, you paid for only $100—the other $200 will be billed to you for payment in ten days.

Cash flows are different from accounting profits or sales receipts. The pizza parlor's *accounting profit* for the day is $200, but its *cash flow* for the day is $300 (= $400 collected from sales minus $100 paid for supplies). The difference between the two is due to the *timing difference* between inflows and outflows. (Of course, ten days from now the pizza parlor will have a negative cash flow of $200 as a result of paying for the ingredients.)

In finance, *cash flow is all-important*. Most corporate financial data comes from accountants, who—despite the bad press they've gotten in the past few years—do a very good job at representing the economic realities of corporate activities. When making financial decisions, we have to translate the accounting data to their cash equivalents. Much of finance involves first translating accounting information into cash flows.

Principle 3: The Time Dimension of Financial Decisions is Important

Many financial decisions have to do with comparing cash flows at different points in time. As an example: You pay for that new photocopy machine *today* (a cash *outflow*), but you save money in the *future* (a cash *inflow*). Finance has to do with correctly dealing with this time dimension of cash flows.

Principle 4: Know How to Compute the Cost of Financial Alternatives

Financial alternatives are often bewildering: Is it more expensive to buy or lease a photocopier? When your credit card charges you "daily interest," is it more or less expensive than the bank loan, which charges you "monthly interest?" In making financial decisions, you need to know how to compute the cost of two or more competing alternatives. This book teaches you how.

Principle 5: Minimize the Cost of Financing

Many financial decisions have to do with choosing the right alternative. Should you finance that photocopier with a loan from the dealer or with a loan from the bank? Should you invest in a real estate project or leave your money in the stock market?

Choosing the right financial alternative is, in many cases, a decision made separately from the investment decision: You've decided to purchase the copier (the investment decision), and now you have to choose whether to finance it through a bank loan or through the dealer's "zero interest financing" (the financing decision).

Principle 6: Take Risk into Account

Many financial alternatives cannot be compared directly without taking into account their risk. Should you take money out of the bank and invest it in the stock market? On the one hand, people who invest in the stock market *on average* earn more than those who leave their money in the bank. On the other hand, a bank deposit is safe, whereas a stock market investment is much less safe (riskier).

"Risk" is the magic word in finance. This book shows you how to quantify risk so that you can compare financial alternatives.

Principle 7: Markets Are Efficient and Deal Well with Information

Financial markets are awash in information. In making a financial decision, how can we possibly know or obtain all the information we need to make a sensible, well-informed decision? The bad news is that we probably can't incorporate all available information into our decision-making process. The good news is that we may not have to: The confluence of many market participants striving to make use of what information they have leads markets to work to eliminate profitable opportunities. In many cases financial markets work so well that we can't add anything to their information-gathering abilities. In short: It may well be that the stock market's valuation of XYZ stock is correct given all the information available about the stock. This *market efficiency* can simplify the way you think about assets and their prices when making financial decisions.

Principle 8: Diversification Is Important

"Don't put all your eggs in one basket." The financial equivalent of this hackneyed expression is: Diversify the assets you hold; don't hold just a few stocks or bonds—buy a portfolio. *Principles of Finance with Excel* shows you how to analyze portfolios of assets and how to choose the individual assets in your portfolio wisely.

CONCLUSION

The combination of finance concepts with an Excel implementation is a "killer app!" *Principles of Finance with Excel* is the only finance principles book on the market that contains this combination.

Enjoy!

BUSINESS ORGANIZATION AND TAXES

OVERVIEW

This chapter very generally introduces two interrelated topics that form the background for the rest of the book: the forms of business organization and the taxation of business income.

- Business forms: The simplest form of a business is the sole proprietorship, a business owned by a single person. More complicated forms of business organization are partnerships, corporations, or limited liability companies. Section 2.1 discusses these various methods of organization and the differences among them.

- Business taxation: Taxes are a fact of life. In this book you will learn how to integrate taxes into optimal financial decision making. As you will see, taxes affect the paybacks you can expect from assets and hence affect optimal financial decision making. One of the primary ways in which the organizational form affects a business is in the taxation of the business income. Sections 2.2 and 2.3 discuss income taxation in the United States. These sections show you how income is taxed at both the personal and the corporate levels.

- To incorporate or not? Section 2.4 compares the taxation of a sole proprietorship/partnership/ limited liability company with the taxation of a corporation.

Finance Concepts Discussed

- Sole proprietorship
- Partnership
- Corporation
- Limited liability company
- Shareholders
- Taxation
- Double taxation of corporate income

Excel Functions Used

- **Sum**
- **If**

2.1 Different Forms of Financial Organization

The way a business is organized affects its taxes. It also affects the liability situation of the business's owners—the way a business is organized can affect who pays the business's debts.

In Section 2.1 we discuss briefly four different forms of business ownership: sole proprietorship, partnership, corporation, and limited liability company (Figure 2.1).

Sole Proprietorship

A **sole proprietorship** is a business owned by a single person. It is the simplest form of business organization. From the organizational point of view, a sole proprietorship requires no paperwork—you simply start your business and that's it.

The income and expenses of a sole proprietorship are reported by the owner on his/her own personal income tax return. This means that there is no legal separation between the business and the owner. This lack of legal separation differentiates sole proprietorships from corporations. It has its good points (simplicity, primarily) and bad points. The biggest disadvantage of the lack of legal separation is that the liabilities of the sole proprietorship are the personal liabilities of its owner. In principle, all the sole proprietor's assets (both personal and business-related) can be used to pay off the business's debts.[1]

---

[1]The general rule that in a sole proprietorship there is no distinction between personal and business assets has many exceptions. Two typical examples: In some states, homes up to a certain value are exempt (the so-called "homestead exemption") and personal property up to a certain amount is also exempt (the "wildcard exemption").

Sole proprietorship	Expenses recognized as business costs?	Advantages	Disadvantages
All income is reported as personal income.	Most expenses—medical, insurance—are not expenses for tax purposes.	Simplicity. No need for registration or other complex organizational details.	Owner is personally liable for all claims on the business.

Good websites:
http://www.nolo.com/lawcenter/ency/article.cfm/ObjectID/3FD19141-DB91-4FCA-BDB93416A4D05479/catID/ 3FED35C1-7BBA-4468-901354F101CBEBE2
http://www.irs.gov/businesses/small/article/0,,id=99336,00.html. This is a good place to look if starting a small business.

Partnership	Expenses recognized as business costs?	Advantages	Disadvantages
Income is split between the partners and reported as personal income.	Most expenses—medical, insurance—are not expenses for tax purposes.	Simplicity. No need for registration or other complex organizational details.	Owners are personally liable for all claims on the business.

Good websites:
http://www.nolo.com/lawcenter/ency/article.cfm/ObjectID/D2C7200B-28A8-49FB-9EA5E2B7E7F15CB5/catID/ DA9428C8-2E99-47F2-A24C1190FE5F24E7#9F61FCB5-91B1-4FBF-839BFF095AB1CB8D

Corporations	Expenses recognized as business costs?	Advantages	Disadvantages
A separate legal entity whose income is taxed separately.	All the costs of doing business are expenses of the corporation. This includes employee medical expenses and insurance the business buys for employees.	Limited liability.	Complicated to run and organize. Two levels of income taxation—corporate and personal. Profits that are passed through to the corporation's owners are taxed at the owners' personal tax rates.

Good websites:
http://www.nolo.com/lawcenter/ency/article.cfm/ObjectID/B6061AF8-E1FE-43D9-B3117C83BD1CCA82/catID/ B491956E-A152-424B-A2342A5861B5EACF

Limited liability company (LLC)	Expenses recognized as business costs?	Advantages	Disadvantages
Combines the limited liability feature of corporations with the single-tax feature of corporations.	As in the case of a sole proprietorship, most LLC expenses are not recognized for tax purposes.	Limited liability. No double taxation of income. LLC income is passed through to the owners and taxed at the owners' personal tax rates.	Though less complicated to organize and run than a corporation, a limited liability company must be formally organized.

Good websites:
http://www.nolo.com/lawcenter/ency/article.cfm/ObjectID/ED01121A-B4BF-498A-8BC0DBD121A0C869/catID/BAAE1B67-F54A-41B4-91943A51F56C3F79

Figure 2.1 Forms of business organization. (All PFE web references can be accessed through the book's web page http://pfe.wharton.upenn.edu.)

Partnership

A **partnership** is a business owned by two or more people. Usually the partners split the management and the profits of the business, though there are many exceptions to this rule. Partnerships are almost as easy to start as sole proprietorships: They require no formal paperwork (though many partners wisely choose to record the formalities of ownership, management, and profit sharing). There are few organizational formalities involved in partnerships: Although they may choose to elect officers, hold meetings, and make formal records of business relationships, partnerships are not required by law to do so.

From the tax point of view, the income of a partnership is reported by each partner on his/her personal income tax return. In the terminology of financial markets, the partnership income is "passed through" to the partners. As in the case of a sole proprietorship, the personal and business-related assets of the partners can be used to pay off the partnership debts.

Corporation

A **corporation** is a separate legal entity established for doing business. From a legal point of view, the corporation is a separate legal "person." This means that corporations can make contractual arrangements, borrow money, sell shares, and buy other businesses. Corporations also pay taxes. Whereas neither sole proprietorships nor partnerships can be sued (you can sue the owners, but not the business, since it has no separate legal standing), corporations can be sued. On the other hand, the legal liabilities of the corporation do not, in general, extend to become the liabilities of the corporation's owners.

Whereas the organization of a sole proprietorship or a partnership is quite simple, the organization of a corporation requires some legal formalities. Corporations are separate legal entities that must be registered in a particular state. The owners of a corporation are called its **shareholders.**

The **limited liability** of a corporation generally means that only the corporation's assets can be claimed in payment for a corporate debt and not the personal assets of the corporation's owners (unless that corporate debt has been personally guaranteed by an owner or employee of the corporation). Generally, this limited liability covers all judgments entered against the corporation, as long as the owners and/or employees involved were acting in their corporate capacity and without the intention to defraud. Limited liability is the primary reason why corporate structure is so widespread.

The Taxation of Corporate Income

Corporate income is subject to two levels of taxation: First, income of the corporation is taxed at the corporate income tax rate. Then, if shareholders of the corporation are paid dividends, the shareholders must pay taxes on their dividends at their personal income tax rates.

Here's an example: The Garden family owns Brass Tacks Inc., a business that makes picture frames. Estelle Garden and her daughter Terry are the only shareholders of Brass Tacks. Estelle owns 90% of the shares of Brass Tacks, and her daughter Terry owns the other 10% of the shares.

In 2006, Brass Tacks had a profit before taxes of $1 million. The company pays a corporate income tax of 35% on this income, leaving it with $650,000 of after-corporate-tax income. Of this income, the company decided to pay a dividend of $400,000 to its shareholders. Since Estelle owns 90% of the shares, she got $360,000 of this dividend; Terry got the other $40,000.

The dividend income received by Estelle and Terry is taxable as personal income. If Estelle's tax rate is 40%, she will end up with $216,000 of after-personal-tax income from the dividend [$216,000 = (1 − 0.40) * $360,000]. If Terry's personal income tax rate is 25%, she will have $30,000 of after-personal-tax income from the dividend [$30,000 = (1 − 0.25) * $40,000].

There's one other thing to notice about this example: Each of the owners—Estelle and Terry—is taxed twice on her income from the corporation, once through the corporate tax and a second time through her personal tax. In Section 2.3 we return to this "double taxation" of corporate income.

S Corporations and Limited Liability Companies

S Corporations and **limited liability companies (LLCs)** combine some features of sole proprietorships and partnerships with the limited liability enjoyed by corporations. In particular, both corporate structures maintain the traditional corporation's limited liability status, but avoid the two-tier tax structure of traditional corporations (often called C Corporations). S Corporations and LLCs generally do not pay federal income tax, but instead pass through their income to the corporation's owners, resulting in one level of taxation. Note that LLCs are usually more flexible than S Corporations, as the latter's many restrictions result in compliance difficulties.

2.2 Personal Income Taxes in the United States

This section presents a brief overview of how income taxes—both individual and corporate—work in the United States. If you live in the United States, your income will be taxed, possibly several times. Your income will certainly be liable to federal income taxes and, depending on where you live, it may also be liable to state and local income taxes. This section presents some insights into the complexities of personal income taxation.

Federal Income Taxes in the United States

Suppose that you live in Nevada, that you're single, and that your taxable income in 2004 was $32,000. We've chosen Nevada for this example because it has neither state nor local income taxes, so that the only taxes due on your income are U.S. federal taxes. The U.S. tax schedule for single taxpayers is given in Figure 2.2. Using this tax table, you can compute that you owe $4,738 in taxes:

- Ten percent tax on the first $7,150 of income = $715.
- Fifteen percent tax on income between $7,150 and $29,050. This works out to $3,285 = 15% * ($29,050 − $7,150).
- Twenty-five percent tax on income over $29,050. As you can see from the tax table, this income is taxed at a 25% rate. This works out to $738 = 25% * ($32,000 − $29,050).

U.S. PERSONAL TAX SCHEDULES FOR SINGLE TAXPAYERS--2004				
Taxable income				
Over	But not over		Tax rate	On amount over
$0	$7,150		10%	$0
$7,150	$29,050		15%	$7,150
$29,050	$70,350		25%	$29,050
$70,350	$146,750		28%	$70,350
$146,750	$319,100		33%	$146,750
$319,100			35%	$319,100

Figure 2.2 U.S. federal income tax table for a single taxpayer.

This tax calculation can be done easily in Excel, as illustrated in cells B14 to B17 below:

	A	B	C
1	**U.S. FEDERAL INCOME TAX SCHEDULES FOR SINGLE INDIVIDUALS, 2004**		
2	**Taxable income**		
3	Over	But not over	Tax rate on bracket
4	$ -	$ 7,150.00	10%
5	$ 7,150.00	$ 29,050.00	15%
6	$ 29,050.00	$ 70,350.00	25%
7	$ 70,350.00	$ 146,750.00	28%
8	$ 146,750.00	$ 319,100.00	33%
9	$ 319,100.00		35%
10			
11	**Your income**	$ 32,000	
12			
13	**Tax computation**		
14	Tax on first $7,150	$ 715	<-- =10%*7150
15	Tax on income to $29,050	$ 3,285	<-- =15%*(29050-7150)
16	Tax on income over $29,050	$ 738	<-- =25%*(B11-29050)
17	Total tax	$ 4,738	<-- =B14+B15+B16
18			
19	Average tax rate	14.80%	<-- =B17/B11
20	Marginal tax rate	25%	

The **average tax rate** paid is 14.80% (cell B19: 14.80% = *total taxes paid/income* = $4,738/$32,000). The **marginal tax rate** is the rate paid on the last dollar of income earned; in this example, the marginal tax rate is 25%, the rate that applies to income between $29,050 and $70,350.

State and Local Income Taxes

In the United States, the federal income tax is only part of the story. Almost all states and many municipalities have their own income tax. In our personal income tax story above, we purposely picked Nevada as your home—the state of Nevada has no personal income tax, and Nevada localities have no local income tax.

If, instead of Nevada, you lived in Philadelphia, Pennsylvania, you would pay a Pennsylvania state income tax of 2.8% and a city wage tax of 4.4625%. These state and local income taxes would amount to $2,324 (cell B5 below). State and local income taxes are subtracted from your income before computing your federal income tax. Your taxable income for federal taxes would be $29,676 (cell B6) and your total tax bill—state, local, and federal—would be $6,481 (cell B16).

	A	B	C
1	**HOW MUCH WOULD YOU PAY IN TAXES?** **Single taxpayer, living in Philadelphia, PA**		
2	Income	$ 32,000	
3	Philadelphia wage tax	$ 1,428	<-- =4.4625%*B2
4	Pennsylvania state income tax	$ 896	<-- =2.8%*B2
5	Total state and local taxes	$ 2,324	<-- =B4+B3
6	Income liable for federal taxes	$ 29,676	<-- =B2-B5
7	Federal income tax		
8	Tax on first $7,150 (10%)	$ 715	<-- =10%*7150
9	Tax on income to $29,050 (15%)	$ 3,285	<-- =15%*(29050-7150)
10	Tax on income over $29,050 (25%)	$ 157	<-- =25%*(B6-29050)
11	Tax on income over $70,350 (28%)	$ -	
12	Tax on income over $146,750 (33%)	$ -	
13	Tax on income over $319,100 (35%)	$ -	
14			
15	Total federal taxes	$ 4,157	<-- =SUM(B8:B13)
16	Total income taxes paid	$ 6,481	<-- =B15+B5
17	Average tax rate	20.25%	<-- =B16/B2

Living in Philadelphia, your average tax rate is 20.25% (cell B17).

If you lived in Philadelphia and your income were $100,000, your average tax rate would be 27.86%:

	A	B	C
1	**HOW MUCH WOULD YOU PAY IN TAXES?** **Single taxpayer, living in Philadelphia, PA**		
2	Income	$ 100,000	
3	Philadelphia wage tax	$ 4,463	<-- =4.4625%*B2
4	Pennsylvania state income tax	$ 2,800	<-- =2.8%*B2
5	Total state and local taxes	$ 7,263	<-- =B4+B3
6	Income liable for federal taxes	$ 92,738	<-- =B2-B5
7	Federal income tax		
8	Tax on first $7,150 (10%)	$ 715	<-- =10%*7150
9	Tax on income to $29,050 (15%)	$ 3,285	<-- =15%*(29050-7150)
10	Tax on income over $29,050 (25%)	$ 10,325	<-- =25%*(70350-29050)
11	Tax on income over $70,350 (28%)	$ 6,269	<-- =28%*(B6-70350)
12	Tax on income over $146,750 (33%)	$ -	
13	Tax on income over $319,100 (35%)	$ -	
14			
15	Total federal taxes	$ 20,594	<-- =SUM(B8:B13)
16	Total income taxes paid	$ 27,856	<-- =B15+B5
17	Average tax rate	27.86%	<-- =B16/B2

Income Taxes Depend on Your Filing Status

The United States federal tax regulations admit four different filing statuses:

- A **single taxpayer** is an individual who pays taxes only on his/her own income.
- A **married individual filing jointly** reports his/her income and his/her spouse's income on the same income tax form.
- A **married individual filing separately** reports only his/her own income. The spouse reports his/her income separately. The tax rates that apply to a married individual filing separately are the same as those that apply to a single taxpayer.
- A **head of household** is a taxpayer who supports some other individual. This individual could be a child, a parent, a spouse, or a nonrelative who permanently resides in the household.

As you can see in Figure 2.3, income tax rates depend on the filing status of the individual.

	A	B	C
2	**Single Taxpayer**		
3	Taxable income		
4	Over	But not over	Tax rate on current bracket
5	$ -	$ 7,150.00	10%
6	$ 7,150.00	$ 29,050.00	15%
7	$ 29,050.00	$ 70,350.00	25%
8	$ 70,350.00	$ 146,750.00	28%
9	$ 146,750.00	$ 319,100.00	33%
10	$ 319,100.00		35%
11			
12	Income	$32,000	
13	**Tax computation**		
14	Tax on first $7,150	$ 715	<-- =C5*B5
15	Tax on income to $29,050	$ 3,285	<-- =C6*(B6-B5)
16	Income over $29,050	$ 2,950	<-- =B12-B6
17	Tax on income over $29,050	$ 738	<-- =C7*B16
18	Total tax	$ 4,738	<-- =B14+B15+B17
19			
20	**Married Individuals Filing Jointly**		
21	Taxable income		
22	Over	But not over	Tax rate on current bracket
23	$ -	$ 14,300	10%
24	$ 14,300	$ 58,100	15%
25	$ 58,100	$ 117,250	25%
26	$ 117,250	$ 178,650	28%
27	$ 178,650	$ 319,100	33%
28	$ 319,100		35%
29			
30	Income	$32,000	
31	**Tax computation**		
32	Tax on first $14,300	$ 1,430	<-- =C23*B23
33	Tax on income over $14,300	$ 2,655	<-- =C24*(B30-B23)
34	Total tax	$ 4,085	<-- =B32+B33

	A	B	C
36	**Married Individuals Filing Separately**		
37	Taxable income		
38	Over	But not over	Tax rate on current bracket
39	$ -	$ 7,150	10%
40	$ 7,150	$ 29,050	15%
41	$ 29,050	$ 58,625	25%
42	$ 58,625	$ 89,325	28%
43	$ 89,325	$ 159,550	33%
44	$ 159,550		35%
45			
46	Income	$32,000	
47	**Tax computation**		
48	Tax on first $7,150	$ 715	<-- =C39*B39
49	Tax on income to $29,050	$ 3,285	<-- =C40*(B40-B39)
50	Income over $29,050	$ 2,950	<-- =B46-B40
51	Tax on income over $29,050	$ 738	<-- =C41*B50
52	Total tax	$ 4,738	<-- =B48+B49+B51
53			
54	**Heads of Households**		
55	Taxable income		
56	Over	But not over	Tax rate on current bracket
57	$ -	$ 10,200	10%
58	$ 10,200	$ 38,900	15%
59	$ 38,900	$ 100,500	25%
60	$ 100,500	$ 162,700	28%
61	$ 162,700	$ 319,100	33%
62	$ 319,100		35%
63			
64	Income	$32,000	
65	**Tax computation**		
66	Tax on first $10,200	$ 1,020	<-- =C57*B57
67	Tax on income over $10,200	$ 3,270	<-- =C58*(B64-B57)
68	Total tax	$ 4,290	<-- =B66+B67

Figure 2.3 Tax tables for four kinds of filers in the United States, showing taxes payable on $32,000 of annual income. Single taxpayers and married individuals filing separately pay the most tax; married individuals filing jointly pay the least tax.

2.3 Corporate Taxation in the United States

Corporate taxation in the United States is in some ways similar to personal taxation—there are eight corporate tax brackets, ranging from 15% to 39%, as shown below:

	A	B	C
1	U.S. FEDERAL INCOME TAX SCHEDULES FOR CORPORATIONS 2004 rates were applicable in 2000-2004		
2	Taxable income over	Not over	Tax rate
3	$ -	$ 50,000	15%
4	$ 50,000	$ 75,000	25%
5	$ 75,000	$ 100,000	34%
6	$ 100,000	$ 335,000	39%
7	$ 335,000	$ 10,000,000	34%
8	$ 10,000,000	$ 15,000,000	35%
9	$ 15,000,000	$ 18,333,333	38%
10	$ 18,333,333		35%
11			
12	Corporate income	$ 500,000	
13	Tax on first $50,000 (15%)	$ 7,500	<-- =15%*50000
14	Tax on income over $50,000 less than $75,000 (25%)	$ 6,250	<-- =25%*(75000-50000)
15	Tax on income over $75,000 less than $100,000 (34%)	$ 8,500	<-- =34%*(100000-75000)
16	Tax on income over $100,000 less than $335,000 (39%)	$ 91,650	<-- =39%*(335000-100000)
17	Tax on income over $335,000 less than $10,000,000 (34%)	$ 56,100	<-- =34%*(500000-335000)
18	Tax on income over $10,000,000 less than $15,000,000 (35%)	$ -	
19	Tax on income over $15,000,000 less than $18,333,333 (38%)	$ -	
20	Tax on income over $18,333,333 (35%)	$ -	
21	U.S. corporate income tax	$ 170,000	
22			
23	Average corporate tax rate	34%	<-- =B21/B12

A corporation with $500,000 of annual income (cell B12) pays federal income taxes of $170,000. The company's average tax rate is 34% = $170,000/$500,000 (cell B23).

The corporate tax rate schedule is designed so that companies with income over $18,333,333 pay an average tax rate of 35%.

2.4 What's Better—Being a Corporation or a Sole Proprietorship?

The owner of a corporation has his income taxed twice. His income is first taxed as corporate income and subsequently, when part of the income is paid out as salary, it is taxed again as personal income.[2] This section discusses this "double taxation" of corporate income and compares it to the taxation of a sole proprietorship, whose income is taxed only at the personal level.

---

[2]In an attempt to be gender inclusive, "he" and "she" are used throughout *Principles of Finance with Excel* in situations that in fact include people of both genders.

An Example: Rob and Jennifer Smith

Jennifer Smith has a business. Last year Jennifer earned $500,000 from her business, which she reported as a sole proprietorship. As you can see from the spreadsheet below, Jennifer paid $155,908 in federal income taxes on this income, leaving her with $344,093 income after taxes.

	A	B	C
1	SINGLE TAXATION: INDIVIDUAL EARNS $500,000 FROM BUSINESS PAYS TAXES AS SOLE PROPRIETORSHIP		
2	Taxable income		
3	Over	But not over	Tax rate on bracket
4	$ -	$ 7,150.00	10%
5	$ 7,150.00	$ 29,050.00	15%
6	$ 29,050.00	$ 70,350.00	25%
7	$ 70,350.00	$ 146,750.00	28%
8	$ 146,750.00	$ 319,100.00	33%
9	$ 319,100.00		35%
10			
11	Your income	$ 500,000	
12			
13	Tax computation		
14	Tax on first $7,150 (10%)	$ 715	<-- =10%*7150
15	Tax on income to $29,050 (15%)	$ 3,285	<-- =15%*(29050-7150)
16	Tax on income to $70,350 (25%)	$ 10,325	<-- =25%*(70350-29050)
17	Tax on income to $146,750 (28%)	$ 21,392	<-- =28%*(146750-70350)
18	Tax on income to $319,100 (33%)	$ 56,876	<-- =33%*(319100-146750)
19	Tax on income over $319,100 (35%)	$ 63,315	<-- =35%*(B11-319100)
20	Total tax	$ 155,908	<-- =SUM(B14:B19)
21			
22	Net income after taxes	$ 344,093	<-- =B11-B20

Jennifer's brother, Rob Smith, has the same kind of business, but he chose to incorporate. Rob's corporation is called RobSmith Inc. This means that RobSmith Inc. first has to pay corporate income taxes of $170,000 on the $500,000 income (cell B22 on p. 21). This leaves RobSmith Inc. with $330,000 of after-tax income (B24), which it then pays as a dividend to Rob Smith. This dividend is liable to federal personal income taxes. When all is said and done, Rob will have $233,593 as after-tax income (cell B49 below).

Double Taxation of Business Income

As you can see, Jennifer Smith is a lot better off than her brother Rob—her after-tax income is about $110,000 more than Rob's. Jennifer pays about half the taxes that Rob pays on his income.

If incorporation causes the total tax bill of the final beneficiaries of the income to increase, why incorporate? There are several reasons:

- Corporations can take more expenses for tax purposes than individuals. For example, it may be that Rob's corporation can buy him a car and legally report the purchase of the car as an expense. If Rob has employees, it may be that his corporation can pay for their child-care expenses and pensions and deduct these payments as an expense. Figure 2.4 shows a large range of corporate expenses that the state of Arizona allows its corporations. These expenses are available only to corporations and not to sole proprietorships.

	A	B	C
1	**DOUBLE TAXATION: FIRST CORPORATE INCOME TAX THEN PERSONAL TAXES**		
2	**Corporate tax**		
3	Taxable income over	Not over	Tax rate
4	$ -	$ 50,000	15%
5	$ 50,000	$ 75,000	25%
6	$ 75,000	$ 100,000	34%
7	$ 100,000	$ 335,000	39%
8	$ 335,000	$ 10,000,000	34%
9	$ 10,000,000	$ 15,000,000	35%
10	$ 15,000,000	$ 18,333,333	38%
11	$ 18,333,333		35%
12			
13	**Corporate income**	$ 500,000	
14	Tax on first $50,000 (15%)	$ 7,500	<-- =15%*50000
15	Tax on income over $50,000 less than $75,000 (25%)	$ 6,250	<-- =25%*(75000-50000)
16	Tax on income over $75,000 less than $100,000 (34%)	$ 8,500	<-- =34%*(100000-75000)
17	Tax on income over $100,000 less than $335,000 (39%)	$ 91,650	<-- =39%*(335000-100000)
18	Tax on income over $335,000 less than $10,000,000 (34%)	$ 56,100	<-- =34%*(B13-335000)
19	Tax on income over $10,000,000 less than $15,000,000 (35%)	$ -	
20	Tax on income over $15,000,000 less than $18,333,333 (38%)	$ -	
21	Tax on income over $18,333,333 (35%)	$ -	
22	U.S. corporate income tax	$ 170,000	<-- =SUM(B14:B21)
23			
24	Net after corporate tax	$ 330,000	<-- =B13-B22
25			
26			
27	**Personal tax**		
28	**Taxable income**		
29	Over	But not over	Tax rate on bracket
30	$ -	$ 7,150.00	10%
31	$ 7,150.00	$ 29,050.00	15%
32	$ 29,050.00	$ 70,350.00	25%
33	$ 70,350.00	$ 146,750.00	28%
34	$ 146,750.00	$ 319,100.00	33%
35	$ 319,100.00		35%
36			
37	**Your income**	$ 330,000	<-- =B24
38			
39	**Tax computation**		
40	Tax on first $7,150 (10%)	$ 715	<-- =10%*7150
41	Tax on income to $29,050 (15%)	$ 3,285	<-- =15%*(29050-7150)
42	Tax on income to $70,350 (25%)	$ 10,325	<-- =25%*(70350-29050)
43	Tax on income to $146,750 (28%)	$ 21,392	<-- =28%*(146750-70350)
44	Tax on income to $319,100 (33%)	$ 56,876	<-- =33%*(319100-146750)
45	Tax on income over $319,100 (35%)	$ 3,815	<-- =35%*(B37-319100)
46	Total tax	$ 96,408	<-- =SUM(B40:B45)
47			
48	Total taxes paid	$ 266,408	<-- =B22+B46
49	**Net income after all taxes**	$ 233,593	<-- =B13-B48

Corporate Tax Incentives & Credits

The following tax credits apply to corporate income tax. Arizona has a flat rate corporate income tax that was lowered in January 2001 to 6.968 percent. Income tax incentive for items such as construction materials can provide significant benefit to businesses that are building or expanding in Greater Phoenix. There are also a number of programs to benefit and encourage development of specific types of industries, as described below.

Increased Research Activities. Corporations may claim a credit for qualified expenses associated with research conducted in Arizona, including research conducted at a state university and funded by the company. For tax years beginning in 2002, the tax credit cap is $2,500,000. If the allowable expenses under the federal regular credit computation method do not exceed $2,500,000, the allowable credit is 20 percent of this amount. If the allowable expenses under the federal regular credit computation method exceed $2,500,000, the allowable credit amount is $500,000 plus 11 percent of the amount of expenses over $2,500,000, subject to certain limitations. The taxpayer may carry forward any unused credit over the next 15 consecutive taxable years.

Pollution Control Tax Credit. The purchase of real or personal property used to control or prevent pollution is applicable for a 10 percent income tax credit.

Agricultural Pollution Control Equipment. A taxpayer may claim a credit for 25 percent of the cost of agricultural pollution control equipment up to a maximum of $25,000 annually. The taxpayer must be engaged in agricultural production, livestock, horticulture, viticulture, or floriculture.

Environmental Technology. A corporation can claim a tax credit for expenses incurred during the construction of any qualified environmental technology manufacturing or processing facilities. The credit is equal to 10% of the amount spent in the taxable year. This includes: land acquisition, improvements, building improvements, machinery, and equipment. The credit can not exceed 75% of Arizona tax income liability.

Defense Contractors. Qualified defense contractors may claim tax credits for net employment increases under defense related contracts or net employment increases from transferring jobs from exclusively defense related activities to commercial activities.

Military Reuse Zones. The Arizona Legislature designated the former Williams Air Force Base, now known as Williams Gateway Airport, as a Military Reuse Zone. Companies locating within this zone will have their personal property classified as class 8, representing an 80 percent property tax savings, for five years. Additionally, there exists a transaction privilege tax exemption for many types of construction performed for an eligible company located in the Military Reuse Zone.

Technology Training. Qualified employers are awarded tax credits for expenses incurred while providing technology skills training. The maximum benefit is $1,500 per employee.

Arizona Enterprise Zones. Firms are eligible to receive income tax credit for a net increase in qualified employment positions located within an enterprise zone, which are determined by the Arizona Department of Commerce. 35% of the net new eligible employees must live within the enterprise zone, and the sale of tangible personal property at retail can make up no more than 10% of the activity.

Figure 2.4 Why incorporate? Here is a list of corporate expenses valid under the Arizona tax code. These tax breaks are available only to corporations. Despite the "double taxation" of corporate income, it may be worthwhile for a company to incorporate. *Source:* http://www.gpec.org/InfoCenter/Topics/Incentives/CorporateIncomeTaxIncentives&Credits.html

- Corporations can have shareholders. If Rob wants his company to grow and wants to have many people invest in RobSmith Inc., he will need to become a corporation and issue shares. Jennifer's sole proprietorship is not legally able to sell shares.
- Corporations have limited liability. If RobSmith Inc. gets sued for more than the corporation is worth, the litigants will not have access to Rob's personal property—his house, his car, his investments. On the other hand, if Jennifer gets sued, all her personal property is fair game.

- Corporations have a choice about what to do with their income. RobSmith Inc. can choose to pay out *some* of its income as a salary to Rob and can choose to retain the rest of the income in the corporation to finance future growth. Only that part of the income paid out to Rob is subject to double taxation. Jennifer has no such choice.

CONCLUSION

Taxes are extremely important. This chapter relates the taxes of businesses to the form of business organization. At this point you should have a better concept of how the income tax system works to tax both personal and corporate incomes.

EXERCISES

1. John Doe lives in Anycity, Anystate, USA. Mr. Doe works as a vice president in a high-tech firm and his annual salary is $125,000. Federal income tax in Anystate is based on the tax schedules given in Section 2.2. The state income taxes in Anystate depend on the tax bracket:
   - On income between $0 and $15,000, the Anystate tax is 4%.
   - From $15,001 to $30,000, the Anystate tax rate is 6%.
   - Above $30,000, the rate is 8%.

   Additionally, Mr. Doe has to pay 3.2% for the municipality. Assuming that Mr. Doe is single, compute his federal, state, and local taxes. What will be his net income?

2. Mr. Doe just turned 55 this year. In Anystate, residents between the ages of 55 and 65 can declare $20,000 savings for pension without paying income taxes on them. However, the remainder of the income is fully taxable. Compute Mr. Doe's taxes, assuming that he saves the $20,000. What is the tax advantage of his being over 55?

3. In this chapter the tax codes for both Nevada and Philadelphia, Pennsylvania, are specified. Calculate the difference in tax payment between Nevada and Philadelphia for different earning levels (at least three).

4. Last year the "ABC" Corporation had a total profit of $25,000,000. Calculate the tax payment of the company, according to the federal corporate tax brackets in Section 2.3.

5. Assume that you earn $25,000,000 annually (lucky you!). Compute your federal tax payments, assuming no state or local taxes. Compare these payments to the federal corporate tax payment you computed in the previous question. How do you explain the fact that the tax payments are similar although the tax brackets are different?

6. After finishing your Ph.D. in finance, you decided to open a consulting business for companies in Nevada. According to your estimation, your annual income will be $200,000 in the first few years. You are considering two options—being a corporation or a sole proprietorship. Your accountant estimated that being a corporation will enable you to deduct an additional $30,000 as expenses. Calculate in which alternative you will pay less tax.

7. Janice Jane Johnson (JJJ) is a famous writer living in Nevada. Every six years JJJ finishes a new novel, which she then sells to her publisher for the sum of $750,000. Until now JJJ was a sole proprietorship, but her accountant has advised her to become a corporation. The accountant argues that there are two advantages to this move:
   - JJJ can write off $25,000 annually as additional expenses.
   - JJJ can smooth her income over the six-year cycle (meaning $125,000 annually), thus enjoying lower tax brackets.

In which alternative will JJJ pay fewer total taxes over the six-year span?

8. Go back to Estelle and Terry, the owners of Brass Tacks (Section 2.1). Estelle owns 90% of the shares, and Terry owns the rest. Brass Tacks has a tax rate of 35%, Estelle has a tax rate of 40% on her dividend income, and Terry has a tax rate of 25%. Suppose Brass Tacks pays out all its after-tax profits as dividends. What are the total taxes (corporate + personal) that Estelle and Terry pay on their dividends? What is the total tax rate of each?

APPENDIX 2.1: THREE EXCEL FUNCTIONS THAT CAN SIMPLIFY TAX COMPUTATIONS

In this appendix we explain how you can use three Excel functions to automate the tax computations in this chapter. The three functions are **Sum, If,** and **VLookup.** By combining two **If** statements, you can write a clever little spreadsheet that completely automates the income tax computations. A somewhat more complicated use of Excel (which you can skip on first reading) involves **VLookup.** Using this function, you can simplify the tax computation even further.

SUM

The Excel function **Sum** adds a series of numbers. We have used this function to add a series of numbers, as in the example below:

	A	B	C
1	**U.S. FEDERAL INCOME TAX SCHEDULES FOR SINGLE INDIVIDUALS, 2004**		
2	**Taxable income**		
3	Over	But not over	Tax rate on bracket
4	$ -	$ 7,150.00	10%
5	$ 7,150.00	$ 29,050.00	15%
6	$ 29,050.00	$ 70,350.00	25%
7	$ 70,350.00	$ 146,750.00	28%
8	$ 146,750.00	$ 319,100.00	33%
9	$ 319,100.00		35%
10			
11	**Your income**	$ 32,000	
12			
13	**Tax computation**		
14	Tax on first $7,150	$ 715	<-- =10%*7150
15	Tax on income to $29,050	$ 3,285	<-- =15%*(29050-7150)
16	Tax on income over $29,050	$ 738	<-- =25%*(B11-29050)
17	Total tax	$ 4,738	<-- =SUM(B14:B16)

In cell B17 we have used the **Sum** function instead of the simple addition **=B14+ B15+B16.**

IF

The Excel function **If** allows you to condition your answer in a particular cell based on other information.

Here's an example: WeNeverCrash Airlines is running a "youth special" on airfares from St. Louis to Chicago. If you're under 23, you can get a standby fare for $75, whereas the regular fare on the route is $200. In the spreadsheet below we use the **If** function to compute your fare:

	A	B	C
1	**USING EXCEL'S IF FUNCTION** **do you get the youth airfare discount?**		
2	Your age	25	
3	Your airfare from St. Louis to Chicago	$ 200	<-- =IF(B2<23,75,200)

The structure of **If** is as follows:

If(question, result if answer to question is yes, result if answer to question is no)

In our case the question is, "Is your age (cell B2) < 23?" If the answer is "yes," then the fare is $75; if the answer is "no," then the fare is $200.

	A	B	C
1	**USING EXCEL'S IF FUNCTION** **do you get the youth airfare discount?**		
2	Your age	25	
3	Your airfare from St. Louis to Chicago	$ 200	<-- =IF(B2<23,75,200)
4			
5			
6	=IF(B2<23,75,200)		
7			
8	Is your age (cell B2) less than 23?		
9			
10	Age < 23, airfare = 75		
11			
12	Age ≥ 23, airfare = 200		

USING THE IF FUNCTION TO COMPUTE TAXES

We can use Excel's **If** function to compute taxes. In the spreadsheet below, we've used two **If** statements to compute the tax in each tax bracket. It's a bit complicated but worth the effort (for a discussion of the programming, see the next subsection).

	A	B	C
1	U.S. FEDERAL INCOME TAX SCHEDULES FOR SINGLE INDIVIDUALS, 2004 using Excel's IF function		
2	Taxable income		
3	Over	But not over	Tax rate on bracket
4	$ -	$ 7,150.00	10%
5	$ 7,150.00	$ 29,050.00	15%
6	$ 29,050.00	$ 70,350.00	25%
7	$ 70,350.00	$ 146,750.00	28%
8	$ 146,750.00	$ 319,100.00	33%
9	$ 319,100.00		35%
10			
11	Your income	$ 32,000	
12			
13	Tax computation		
14	Tax on income to $7,150	$ 715	<-- =IF($B$11<A4,0,IF($B$11>B4,(B4-A4)*C4,($B$11-A4)*C4))
15	Tax on income between $7,150 and $29,050	$ 3,285	<-- =IF($B$11<A5,0,IF($B$11>B5,(B5-A5)*C5,($B$11-A5)*C5))
16	Tax on income between $29,050 and $70,350	$ 738	<-- =IF($B$11<A6,0,IF($B$11>B6,(B6-A6)*C6,($B$11-A6)*C6))
17	Tax on income between $70,350 and $146,750	$ -	<-- =IF($B$11<A7,0,IF($B$11>B7,(B7-A7)*C7,($B$11-A7)*C7))
18	Tax on income between $146,750 and $319,100	$ -	<-- =IF($B$11<A8,0,IF($B$11>B8,(B8-A8)*C8,($B$11-A8)*C8))
19	Tax on income over $319,100	$ -	<-- =IF($B$11<A9,0,($B$11-A9)*C9)
20	Total tax	$ 4,738	

The advantage of this spreadsheet is that it is *completely automated*—if you put in the income in cell B11, the spreadsheet correctly computes the income tax in cell B20. For example, if taxable income is $100,000, then U.S. federal taxes are $22,627:

	A	B	C
1	U.S. FEDERAL INCOME TAX SCHEDULES FOR SINGLE INDIVIDUALS, 2004 using Excel's IF function		
2	Taxable income		
3	Over	But not over	Tax rate on bracket
4	$ -	$ 7,150.00	10%
5	$ 7,150.00	$ 29,050.00	15%
6	$ 29,050.00	$ 70,350.00	25%
7	$ 70,350.00	$ 146,750.00	28%
8	$ 146,750.00	$ 319,100.00	33%
9	$ 319,100.00		35%
10			
11	Your income	$ 100,000	
12			
13	Tax computation		
14	Tax on income to $7,150	$ 715	<-- =IF($B$11<A4,0,IF($B$11>B4,(B4-A4)*C4,($B$11-A4)*C4))
15	Tax on income between $7,150 and $29,050	$ 3,285	<-- =IF($B$11<A5,0,IF($B$11>B5,(B5-A5)*C5,($B$11-A5)*C5))
16	Tax on income between $29,050 and $70,350	$ 10,325	<-- =IF($B$11<A6,0,IF($B$11>B6,(B6-A6)*C6,($B$11-A6)*C6))
17	Tax on income between $70,350 and $146,750	$ 8,302	<-- =IF($B$11<A7,0,IF($B$11>B7,(B7-A7)*C7,($B$11-A7)*C7))
18	Tax on income between $146,750 and $319,100	$ -	<-- =IF($B$11<A8,0,IF($B$11>B8,(B8-A8)*C8,($B$11-A8)*C8))
19	Tax on income over $319,100	$ -	<-- =IF($B$11<A9,0,($B$11-A9)*C9)
20	Total tax	$ 22,627	

HOW DOES IT WORK?

The spreadsheet above works by using two **If** statements. Here's how this works:

- Each tax bracket has a lower limit (in column A) and an upper limit (column B). For example, the first tax bracket has lower limit $0 (cell A4) and upper limit $7,150 (cell B4).

- The first **If** statement asks whether the income is less than the bracket's lower limit. If the answer is "yes," then the tax for this bracket is zero.
- If the answer to the first **If** statement is "no," then there is a second **If** statement. This statement asks whether the income is greater than the bracket's upper limit.
  - If the answer to this question is "yes," then the tax on the bracket is the **bracket size** times the **bracket tax rate.** For example, if income (cell B11) is greater than \$7,150 (cell B4), then the tax on the bracket is $10\% * (7150 - 0) = C4 * (B4 - A4)$.
  - If the answer to this question is "no," then the tax on the bracket is the **amount of income in the bracket** times the **bracket tax rate.** For example, if income (cell B11) is less than \$7,150 (cell B4), then the tax on the bracket is $10\% * (\text{income} - 0) = C4 * (B11 - A4)$.

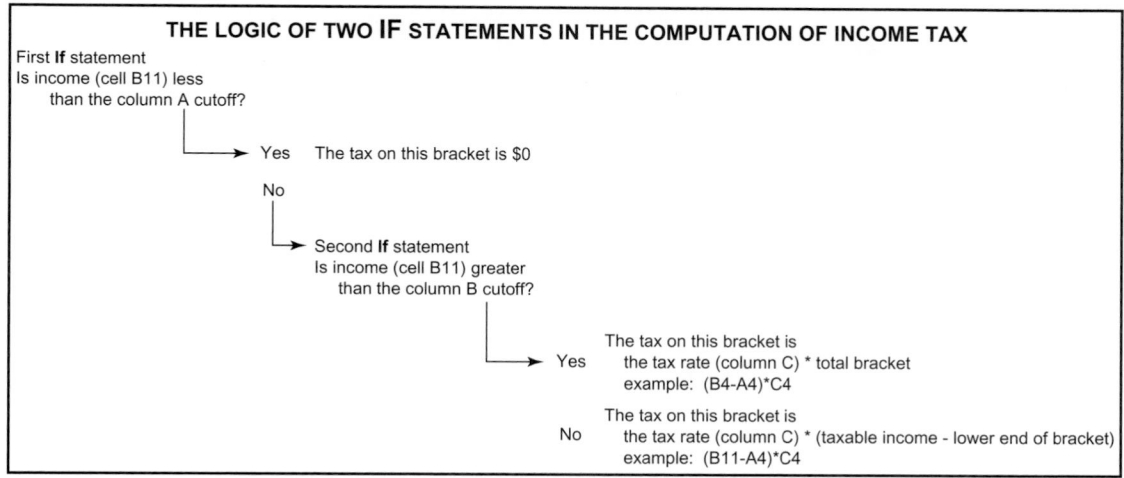

Figure A.1 Graphical representation of the computation of income taxes using two **If** statements.

ADVANCED EXCEL NOTE: USING VLOOKUP TO COMPUTE THE TAXES

If you know a bit more Excel, you can simplify the calculation by using the Excel function **VLookup** (see Chapter 29). Here's the tax calculation using **VLookup:**

	A	B	C	D	E
1			U.S. FEDERAL INCOME TAX	SCHEDULES FOR SINGLE INDIVIDUALS, 2004	
2	**Taxable income**		**Tax**		
3	Over	But not over	Tax rate on current bracket	Tax on previous brackets	
4	$ -	$ 7,150.00	10%	$ -	
5	$ 7,150.00	$ 29,050.00	15%	$ 715.00	<-- =C4*A5
6	$ 29,050.00	$ 70,350.00	25%	$ 4,000.00	<-- =D5+C5*(A6-A5)
7	$ 70,350.00	$ 146,750.00	28%	$ 14,325.00	<-- =D6+C6*(A7-A6)
8	$ 146,750.00	$ 319,100.00	33%	$ 35,717.00	
9	$ 319,100.00		35%	$ 92,592.50	
10					
11	Income	$ 32,000			
12	Tax	$ 4,738	<-- =VLOOKUP(B11,A4:D9,4)+VLOOKUP(B11,A4:C9,3)*(B11-VLOOKUP(B11,A4:C9,1))		

The advantage of using **VLookup** is that it enables you to do a concise calculation of the taxes. Inserting any number into cell B11 above will produce a correct tax calculation in cell B12. Suppose, for example, that your income is $175,000:

	A	B	C	D	E
1			**U.S. FEDERAL INCOME TAX SCHEDULES FOR SINGLE INDIVIDUALS, 2004**		
2	**Taxable income**		**Tax**		
3	Over	But not over	Tax rate on current bracket	Tax on previous brackets	
4	$ -	$ 7,150.00	10%	$ -	
5	$ 7,150.00	$ 29,050.00	15%	$ 715.00	<-- =C4*A5
6	$ 29,050.00	$ 70,350.00	25%	$ 4,000.00	<-- =D5+C5*(A6-A5)
7	$ 70,350.00	$ 146,750.00	28%	$ 14,325.00	<-- =D6+C6*(A7-A6)
8	$ 146,750.00	$ 319,100.00	33%	$ 35,717.00	
9	$ 319,100.00		35%	$ 92,592.50	
10					
11	Income	$ 175,000			
12	Tax	$ 45,040			<-- =VLOOKUP(B11,A4:D9,4)+VLOOKUP(B11,A4:C9,3)*(B11-VLOOKUP(B11,A4:C9,1))

An Accounting Primer

OVERVIEW

Accounting is an important component of financial analysis. Although you've probably had an accounting course, you may have forgotten some basic accounting principles. In this chapter we remind you of these accounting principles, using a series of simple examples.

One of the things you will notice is that—with the exception of this sentence—we never refer to *debits* and *credits*. This is an accounting chapter for finance students: We write all our accounts and information directly onto the balance sheet.

This chapter will help you understand three basic accounting statements: the balance sheet, the profit and loss statement, and the consolidated statement of cash flows. In addition, we explain in detail the concept of free cash flow, an important finance concept that plays a central role in the valuation of companies.

Accounting Concepts Discussed

- Balance sheet, profit and loss statement, consolidated statement of cash flows
- Assets, liabilities
- Equity, debt
- Fixed assets, depreciation
- Accounts receivable, accounts payable
- Accrual accounting

Finance Concepts Discussed

- Free cash flow (FCF)

Excel Functions Used

- This chapter uses only the most basic Excel functions.

3.1 Three Basic Accounting Statements

The three basic accounting statements you need to understand if you're to do financial accounting are summarized in this section. If you do not understand this summary, skip this section and read on—more explanations follow (if you *do* understand everything, perhaps this section is superfluous for you).

The Balance Sheet

The balance sheet (see next page) is a *double-columned* statement.

- The left-hand column ("Assets") gives details of what the company owns. It includes items such as cash on hand, inventories, and equipment. It also includes items such as the billings the company has sent out for which it has not received payment (accounts receivable).
- The right-hand column ("Liabilities and Equity") gives details of how the company's assets are financed—the sources of the money used to finance the assets. This column includes items like borrowing from banks and other debtholders, money raised from shareholders (equity), and bills not yet paid (accounts payable).

The Profit and Loss (P&L) Statement

The profit and loss statement (also called an "income statement") is a statement of how much the firm has earned over a given period. This period is most often a year, but it can also be a quarter or a month. The accountant's aim in the P&L statement is to provide a statement of earnings that accurately reflects the underlying economics of the firm's operations. Many readers of P&L statements view them as providing a statement of the amount of cash left in the company's till at the end of the period. However, the firm's earnings are not equivalent to the amount of cash

Basic Balance Sheet—What assets does the firm own and how are these assets financed?

Assets:	Liabilities and Equity:
What the company owns	Who put up the money for the assets

Short-term assets—assets with a short life (generally less than one year)
    Cash
    Marketable securities
    Inventories
    Accounts receivable: Customer
        billings that are not yet paid
	Short-term liabilities—financing the company will repay in the short term (generally within one year)
	        Short-term borrowing from banks
	        Accounts payable: Bills that the
	            company must pay
	        Taxes payable: Taxes that the company
	
	            knows it will have to pay in the short term

Fixed assets—assets with a longer life
    Land
    Plant, property, and equipment
        net of depreciation
	Long-term liabilities—debt financing that has to be repaid over a period of more than one year
	Equity—money provided by shareholders
	        Stock: Money paid by shareholders to
	            the company for shares in the company
	        Accrued retained earnings: Firm profits
	            not paid out to shareholders

Total Assets	**Total Liabilities and Equity**

Note: Total assets and total liabilities and equity are *always equal.*

generated. The divergence between these two concepts provides much material for the conflict between accountants and finance professionals. In Section 3.3, we show the accounting profession's solution to this problem—the consolidated statement of cash flows. In Section 3.4 we discuss the free cash flow (FCF), which is the finance profession's answer.

But these issues are for later! In the meantime, here's a typical profit and loss statement:

Profit and Loss—How much money did the firm make?

Sales
Subtract **costs of goods sold (COGS)**—the direct cost of producing the sales
Subtract **selling, general, and administrative expenses (SG&A)**—the overheads
    involved in producing the sales
Subtract **depreciation**—the cost of using the firm's fixed assets
Subtract **interest expenses**—the cost of the firm's borrowings
Add **interest income** and **other income** from cash and marketable securities

Profits before taxes (PBT)
Subtract **taxes**

Profits after taxes (PAT)
Subtract **dividends paid to shareholders**

Retained earnings—firm profits not paid to shareholders
    These are added to the "accrued retained earnings" item on the Liabilities and
        Equity side of the balance sheet

A BASIC MISUNDERSTANDING—THE CORNER GROCERY STORE VERSUS IBM, OR ACCRUAL VERSUS CASH ACCOUNTING

Why is it that the amount of cash left in the company's till at the end of a day (or at the end of an accounting period) may not give a complete picture about the firm's profitability? The following example will help clarify this question.

"My grandparents operated a corner grocery store. Gramps gave no credit and paid all his bills in cash. At the end of every day he walked to the bank and deposited whatever he had in the cash register drawer ("the till"). This was his profit for the day. I don't understand all this b.s. about the profit and loss not reflecting the cash realities of a business. Why can't everyone be like Gramps?"

If you have a simple business, you can still be like Gramps. You can do your accounting using the **cash accounting method**—whatever remains in the till (or in your bank account) is your profit over a given period. But most businesses use the **accrual accounting method** discussed in this chapter. In this method, certain noncash items count as either income or expenses. The system applies economic logic to make the income/expense determination. Here are some examples even Gramps would agree with:

- On January 15, 1953, Gramps took in $1,000 and paid out bills of $600. But when writing down the profit at the end of the day, he saw that Mrs. Smith, one of his best and most reliable clients, had promised to pay him her $25 grocery bill tomorrow. By the logic of cash accounting, Gramps had made $400 for the day, but by any other logic, his actual profits for the day were $425.
- On the next day, the milkman came by before the store opened and left $50 of dairy products on the stoop. Gramps will pay him a day later. By economic logic, the unpaid bill of $50 should be attributed to today (and lower today's profits), even if only paid the next day.

These examples can be multiplied, until even Gramps would agree that **accrual accounting,** though more complicated than cash accounting, is a more logical way to determine his profits.

The Consolidated Statement of Cash Flows

The firm's consolidated statement of cash flows explains *where the money came from and where it went*. Because the profit and loss statement does not necessarily reflect the realities of how cash flows into and out of the firm as a result of its activities, the cash flow statement is necessary to close the loop.

Consolidated Statement of Cash Flows—Where did the cash come from and where did it go?

Operating cash flows—cash implications of the firm's activities
  Profits after taxes
  Add back depreciation (this is an expense on the P&L but doesn't cost cash)
  Subtract increases in inventories, accounts receivable, etc. (these don't appear on the P&L, but they require cash)
  Add increases in accounts payable, taxes payable, etc. (these appear on the P&L as expenses, but they weren't actually paid, and so they supply cash)

Investment cash flows—cash implications of the firm's investment activities
  Subtract purchases of equipment
  Subtract purchases of subsidiaries, other companies, etc.
  Add back sales of equipment, subsidiaries, etc.
  Add or subtract sales or purchases of financial investments (such as securities) by the firm

Financing cash flows—cash implications of the firm's financing activities
  Add new debt financing
  Subtract repayment of debts
  Add sales of new shares (and subtract repurchases of shares by the firm)
  Subtract dividends paid to shareholders

Adding all these items together should give the *change in the firm's cash balances* over the accounting period

In the following sections, we show how to construct these three statements for Anytown Travel Services (ATS), a new company that is just being started in Anytown, USA.

3.2 Starting a Firm

Brother and Sister live in Anytown, USA. They've just graduated from college and have decided to start a taxi service. There's no taxi company in Anytown, and they think it will be a great success. They've got $25,000 in cash with which to start the business.

It's 2 January 2003. Brother and Sister

- Go to a lawyer and incorporate themselves as Anytown Travel Services (ATS).
- They open a bank account and deposit $25,000.

At this point their balance sheet looks like this:

	A	B	C	D	E
2	**ANYTOWN TRAVEL SERVICES (ATS), Inc.**				
3	**Balance Sheet, 2 January 2003**				
4	**Assets**			**Liabilities and equity**	
5	Cash	25,000		Equity	25,000
6	Total assets	25,000		Total liabilities and equity	25,000

Now they need a taxi. On 3 January 2003, Brother and Sister go to a local used-car dealer and pick out a nice car. Along with the taxi sign on top of the car, some minor repairs, and a tank of gas, the car costs $18,000. They pay for the car in cash. Here's their new balance sheet:

	A	B	C	D	E
9	**ANYTOWN TRAVEL SERVICES (ATS), Inc.**				
10	**Balance Sheet, 3 January 2003**				
11	**Assets**			**Liabilities and equity**	
12	Cash	7,000		Equity	25,000
13	Taxi	18,000			
14	Total assets	25,000		Total liabilities and equity	25,000

Notice that the purchase of the taxi involves only a shift on the asset side of the balance sheet: The cash account decreased by $18,000, and the new "Taxi" account increased by the same amount. There is no change on the liabilities and equity side of the balance sheet.

31 January 2003

During January 2003, their first month of operation, Brother and Sister have

- Collected $12,000 in taxi fares.
- Paid $4,000 in gasoline and other costs.
- Paid themselves $1,000 each as a salary.[1]

This means that the balance sheet on 31 January 2003 looks like this:

	A	B	C	D	E
17	**ANYTOWN TRAVEL SERVICES (ATS), Inc.**				
18	**Balance Sheet, 31 January 2003**				
19	**Assets**			**Liabilities and equity**	
20	Cash			Equity	25,000
21	Cash at beginning of month	7,000			
22	Fares	12,000			
23	Gas, etc.	-4,000			
24	Salaries	-2,000			
25	Cash at end of month	13,000			
26					
27	Taxi	18,000			
28	Total assets	31,000		Total liabilities and equity	25,000

Unfortunately, this balance sheet doesn't *balance*—the total assets don't equal the total liabilities and equity. This is probably the worst transgression you can make in an accounting framework! In this case the solution to the problem is easy—ATS has actually made $6,000 during the month ($12,000 in receipts minus $6,000 in costs).

In the picture below we include the ATS profit and loss (P&L) statement for the period to the right of the ATS balance sheet. The profit of $6,000 is added to the initial equity of the firm as *retained earnings* (meaning profits not paid out):

---

[1]Do Anytown residents give tips? Yes, but Brother and Sister decided that whoever's driving can keep the tips.

	A	B	C	D	E	F	G	H
31		**ANYTOWN TRAVEL SERVICES (ATS), Inc.**						
32		**Balance Sheet, 31 January 2003**					**Profit and Loss, 31 January 2003**	
33	**Assets**			**Liabilities and equity**				
34	Cash						Sales	12,000
35	Cash at beginning of month	7,000					Owner salaries	-2,000
36	Fares	12,000					Fuel	-4,000
37	Gas, etc.	-4,000		**Equity**			Profit	6,000
38	Salaries	-2,000		Initial stock	25,000		Dividends	0
39	Cash at end of month	13,000		Accumulated retained earnings			Retained earnings	6,000
40				January 2003	6,000 ←			
41	Taxi	18,000						
42	**Total assets**	**31,000**		**Total liabilities and equity**	**31,000**			

The retained earnings from the profit and loss—that part of the profits that ATS doesn't pay out as dividends—ends up on the balance sheet in "accumulated retained earnings." This means that we've now got two equity accounts—"initial stock" is the amount of money Brother and Sister initially put into the firm, and "accumulated retained earnings" is that part of profits they've decided not to pay out.

A NOTE ON TERMINOLOGY

Almost every accounting item in our example has another (equally valid) name. For example:

- Profit is also called Income or Earnings, and a Profit and Loss statement is often called an Income Statement or an Earnings Statement.
- Initial Stock is also called "Stock issued at par" or sometimes "Stock issued at par and additional premium" or "Paid-in capital" (in this book we often use just "Stock").

We'll try to be consistent in this book, but we can't always keep our promise!

28 February 2003

Receipts, costs, and salaries during the month were the same as those in January. On the last day of February, however, ATS underwent a dramatic expansion: Brother and Sister bought another taxi. Like the first, this one cost $18,000. They paid for this taxi by using $10,000 of their cash and borrowing $8,000 from the bank. The loan has to be paid off over the next 10 months ($800 per month) and ATS has to pay 1% interest per month on the outstanding loan balance. Because the loan has to be paid back in the short term, it is classified as a *current liability*—an obligation of the firm that has to be paid back within a year.

Here's what the balance sheet looks like:

	A	B	C	D	E	F	G	H
45		**ANYTOWN TRAVEL SERVICES (ATS), Inc.**						
46		**Balance Sheet, 28 February 2003**					**Profit and Loss, 28 February 2003**	
47	**Assets**			**Liabilities and equity**				
48	Cash			**Current liabilities**			Sales	12,000
49	Cash at beginning of month	13,000		Taxi loan from bank	8,000		Owner salaries	-2,000
50	Fares	12,000					Fuel	-4,000
51	Gas	-4,000					Profit	6,000
52	Salaries	-2,000		**Equity**			Dividends	0
53	Used to buy new taxi	-10,000		Initial stock	25,000		Retained earnings	6,000
54	Cash at end of month	9,000		Accumulated retained earnings				
55				January 2003	6,000		Highlighted items relate to new taxi	
56	Taxis (2 taxis, each costing $18,000)			February 2003	6,000		purchase. Note that these items	
57	Taxi purchased in January 2003	18,000					balance: $8,000 is added to Assets and	
58	Taxi purchased in February 2003	18,000					$8,000 to the Liabilities and equity	
59	**Total assets**	**45,000**		**Total liabilities and equity**	**45,000**			

Notice that on the right-hand side of the balance sheet, we've started to distinguish between "liabilities" and "equity." The former represents financing from outside sources, while "equity" is financing by the owners of the company.

31 March 2003

ATS had another very successful month:

- They hired an extra driver for each of the two taxis (Brother and Sister still drive a couple of hours per day, but the drivers bear the brunt of it). The drivers are getting a salary of $1,500 each. Each taxi brought in $20,000 for the month. However, $8,000 of this derives from a contract signed to provide transportation for the local flour mill and its executives and guests. The flour mill hasn't paid this money yet; it pays its bills on the 15th of the month following. As you will see below, this unpaid bill generates an *account receivable* on ATS's balance sheet—a bill to customers which is outstanding and is anticipated to be paid within a year. An account receivable is an asset of the firm (some firms sell their accounts receivable—if you can sell it, it must be an asset).

- One of the drivers was promised a signing bonus of $800, which would be paid only if she proved herself for a reasonable period of time. If she's still working for ATS by 20 May 2003, this driver will be paid the $800 bonus. The bonus (as yet unpaid) is listed as a *current liability;* this is accounting terminology for an unpaid bill that will be paid within a year.

- Brother and Sister bought a computer for the office (still located in the spare room of their house). The computer cost $2,000.

- Other expenses: Gas $6,000; Brother and Sister raised their salaries to $2,000 each, for a total of $4,000.

- They paid off $800 on the car loan. The bank charges them 1% per month, so that they also paid $80 interest.

	A	B	C	D	E	F	G	H
62	**ANYTOWN TRAVEL SERVICES (ATS), Inc.**							
63	**Balance Sheet, 31 March 2003**						**Profit and Loss, 31 March 2003**	
64	**Assets**			**Liabilities and equity**				
65	**Current assets**			**Current liabilities**			Sales	40,000
66	Cash			Unpaid signing bonus	800		Driver salaries	-3,000
67	Cash at beginning of month	9,000		Taxi loan from bank			Owner salaries	-4,000
68	Fares paid in cash ($40,000 - $8,000)	32,000		Initial loan	8,000		Signing bonus	-800
69	Driver salaries	-3,000		This month's repayment	-800		Fuel	-6,000
70	Owner salaries	-4,000		Net loan priniciple outstanding	7,200		Interest	-80
71	Fuel	-6,000					Profit	26,120
72	Interest	-80					Dividends	0
73	Repayment of principal	-800					Retained earnings	26,120
74	Computer	-2,000						
75	Cash at end of month	25,120					Of $40,000 sales, $8,000 were on credit	
76				**Equity**				
77	Accounts receivable	8,000		Initial stock	25,000			
78				Retained earnings			Unpaid signing bonus is listed as a cost on	
79	**Fixed assets**			January 2003	6,000		the P&L and as a current liability on balance	
80	Computer	2,000		February 2003	6,000		sheet.	
81	Taxis	36,000		March 2003	26,120			
82								
83	**Total assets**	71,120		**Total liabilities and equity**	71,120			

Here are some notes on the balance sheet:

- Look at how the computer is listed (cells B74 and B80). On the one hand, it was paid for out of cash and therefore there's a −$2,000 item in the cash lines (B74). On the other hand, the computer is *not* an expense—instead, it's a capital investment (like the two taxis) and is listed under fixed assets (cell B80). Accountants (and the tax authorities) define a capital asset as an asset that (1) has a life longer than a year and (2) produces income over its lifetime. Capital assets are not immediately listed on the profit and loss statement as expenses; instead, their costs are written off over their lifetimes as depreciation.[2]

- Notice that the $880 paid to the bank is *fully deducted* from the cash in the balance sheet (cells B72 and B73) but that only $80 of this amount (the interest payment) is an expense on the profit and loss statement (cell H70). Repayment of loan principal is not an expense (you're only paying back what you got—it's not a cost, although it is a negative cash flow; see below). The $800 repayment of the loan also appears on the right-hand side of the balance sheet as a reduction in the auto loan under current liabilities (cell E69). At the end of the month, the remaining taxi loan debt to the bank is $7,200.

- We've started to distinguish between *current assets* and *fixed assets* on the left-hand side of the balance sheet. "Current assets" are short-lived assets, which can or will be liquidated at short notice, usually a year or less. The cash account on the balance sheet is obviously a current asset. ATS's accounts receivable are also current assets because they relate to the unpaid bills of the flour mill, which will be paid off within the month.

- Note that the accounts receivable of $8,000 is part of the sales of the firm on the profit and loss statement (cell H65). That is—not all the firm's sales are in cash. Any *reasonably anticipated receipt* should be put in the profit and loss statement as a sale. Similarly, any reasonably anticipated expense should be recorded in the profit and loss statement as a cost (see next bullet). On the other hand, the repayment of this $8,000 receivable in the coming month will not affect the profit and loss statement.

- In a similar way, the $800 unpaid signing bonus is listed as a *current liability* (cell E66) and reduces the month's profits (cell H68), even though it has not yet actually been paid. In the next statement, the company will pay this $800 bonus, and at that point it will not affect the profit and loss statement.

April–June 2003

The following events occurred during this three-month period:

- The two taxis produced sales of $25,000/month each, $150,000 for the whole period. Of this figure, $30,000 ($10,000 per month) is for the transportation contract with the local flour mill. This company always pays one month in arrears, so that at the end of June, they still have a $10,000 bill outstanding.[3]

- The drivers were paid $1,500 each per month = $9,000.

- Salaries for Brother and Sister stayed the same as in March ($2,000 each per month) = $12,000.

---

[2]As we write this chapter, a financial scandal in the United States involves WorldCom, which misclassified some expenses of doing business as the purchase of long-term assets. (This would be similar to ATS listing the salaries of their taxi drivers as the purchase of a fixed asset.) By doing this, WorldCom *over reported* its income.

[3]During the April–June period, the flour mill (1) paid off the $8,000 bill left from March, (2) was billed $10,000 per month, and (3) paid off April's $10,000 bill in May and paid off May's $10,000 bill in June. At the end of the period, the company still owed ATS $10,000 for services rendered in June.

- Gasoline for the two taxis cost $7,000 per month per taxi = $42,000. The gas station has agreed to extend credit to ATS—the company can now pay its gasoline bills on the 10th of the month following. At the end of June, $14,000 in gasoline bills remained to be paid (this will be recorded as an account payable on the liabilities side of the balance sheet).

- In each of the three months, ATS paid $800 off on the taxi loan, so that the total loan outstanding at the end of June is $4,800 (this is the initial $8,000 loan, minus repayments of $800/month for March–June). The interest payments (1% per month on outstanding balances) during the April–June period were
  - $72 for April (1% of $7200)
  - $64 for May (1% of $6400)
  - $56 for June (1% of $5600)

- ATS was billed by its insurance company for a policy that has been in force since January. The cost is $12,000. They paid this whole amount in May 2003. At the end of June, $6,000 of this amount relates to insurance for the period January–June; this will be included in the profit and loss statement as an expense. The other $6,000 relates to insurance for the rest of the year. As you will see below, the *unused portion* of the insurance ($6,000) is recorded as a *prepaid expense* on the asset side of the balance sheet.

- On 30 June 2003, Brother and Sister bought a small building to house the ATS offices. The building (an old gas station) includes a garage, some office space, and fuel pumps for the taxis. The cost of the building was $80,000. They financed the purchase with $20,000 in cash and a $60,000, ten-year mortgage from the bank. The mortgage conditions are
  - Monthly principal repayment: $\dfrac{\$60,000}{\underbrace{10 * 12}_{\text{10 years} * \text{12 months/year}}} = \$500.$

  - Monthly interest payment: 0.5% on outstanding mortgage balance.

- They paid the signing bonus to the driver ($800).

Here are the new balance sheet and profit and loss statement:

	A	B	C	D	E	F	G	H
86	**ANYTOWN TRAVEL SERVICES (ATS), Inc., Jan-June 2003** **Financial statements not including depreciation and taxes**							
87		**Balance Sheet, 30 June 2003**					**Profit and Loss, 30 June 2003**	
88	**Assets**			**Liabilities and equity**				
89	**Current assets**			**Current liabilities**			Sales	150,000
90	Cash			Taxi loan from bank	4,800		Driver salaries	-9,000
91	Cash at beginning of April	25,120		Unpaid signing bonus	0		Owner salaries	-12,000
92	Fares paid	140,000		Accounts payable (gasoline)	14,000		Fuel	-42,000
93	Payment of outstanding receivable	8,000		Total current liabilities	18,800		Interest	-192
94	Driver salaries	-9,000					Insurance	-6,000
95	Owner salaries	-12,000		**Long-term liabilities**			Profit	80,808
96	Fuel	-28,000		Mortgage to buy building	60,000		Dividends	0
97	Interest	-192					Retained earnings	80,808
98	Repayment of principal	-2,400						
99	Insurance	-12,000						
100	Building, cash payment	-20,000					**Highlighting:**	
101	Signing bonus	-800					$12,000 insurance premium is divided	
102	Cash at end of June	88,728					between cost of $6,000 on profit and loss	
103							and prepaid expense on balance sheet	
104	Accounts receivable	10,000		**Equity**				
105	Prepaid expenses (insurance)	6,000		Initial stock	25,000		Building bought with $20,000 cash and	
106	Total current assets	104,728		Retained earnings			$60,000 mortgage.	
107				January 2003	6,000			
108	**Fixed assets**			February 2003	6,000		Signing bonus finally paid off. Note that	
109	Computer	2,000		March 2003	26,120		it does not appear on this period's profit	
110	Taxis	36,000		April-June 2003	80,808		and loss-- it was already listed as a cost	
111	Building	80,000		Total equity	143,928		in March profit and loss.	
112	Total fixed assets	118,000						
113								
114	**Total assets**	222,728		**Total liabilities and equity**	222,728			

In columns G and H we've given a profit and loss statement for the period which ignores depreciation and taxes (we'll get to these in a moment). An outlay is recorded as an expense only if it is required in the current period to produce income. Here are some examples:

- The $20,000 paid in cash for the building is balanced by an asset of $80,000 (the building itself) and the $60,000 mortgage, which is recorded as a liability. Thus, the $20,000 is not an expense, even though it's a cash outlay. When the building starts to be depreciated, this depreciation will be recorded as an expense, which represents the cost of the building in producing the current period's income.

- The $800 for the signing bonus is a cash outlay balanced by a reduction in a corresponding current liability. The signing bonus was an expense in the April accounting period.

- The $12,000 spent for insurance is partially offset by a $6,000 prepaid expense. Thus, only $6,000 of the insurance outlay is an expense on the profit and loss statement.

Preparing a Profit and Loss Statement for January–June 2003

Their accountant insists that Brother and Sister prepare a profit and loss statement for the first half-year of the company's operations. The accountant explains that

- It is important to know how the new company has performed thus far.
- Brother and Sister have to pay an estimated tax payment to the IRS on July 15 based on their profit for the first half-year.

The main difference between the profit and loss statements shown thus far and the statement that the accountant prepares is *depreciation*. There are several different interpretations of depreciation:

- Depreciation is a cost that the tax authorities allow for the use of a fixed asset. Since we have not thus far included the costs of fixed assets (the taxis, the computer, and the building) in our profit and loss statements, depreciation is a way to spread out these costs over the useful lifetimes of the assets.

- Depreciation represents the *economic cost* of using a fixed asset over the life of the asset.
    - The accountant depreciates the computer over a two-year useful life. The monthly depreciation of the computer is therefore $2,000/24 = $83.33. Since they've owned the computer for three months, the total depreciation on the computer for the period is 3 * $83.33 = $250.
    - The taxis are depreciated over a three-year useful life; this works out to $18,000/(3 * 12) = $500 per month. They bought the first taxi on 3 January, so that it has six months of depreciation (= $3,000). The second taxi is four months old (it was purchased the last day of February), so that its depreciation is $2,000. Thus, total depreciation on the taxis is $5,000.
    - Finally, the building, bought on 30 June 2003, is going to be depreciated over ten years. However, since it has just been put on the balance sheet, there is no depreciation to be taken for this building yet.

The corporate tax rates applicable to ATS are 5% state tax and 36% federal tax. For purposes of computing the federal tax, the state tax is an expense.[4] Here's the way the balance sheet

---

[4]In plain English, here's what this means: ATS's profits before taxes are $113,678 (cell H128). The 5% state income tax on this amount is $5,684 (cell H129). Profits for the computation of the federal income tax are $113,678 − $5,684 = $107,994 (cell H130). The 36% federal tax on these profits is $38,878 (cell H131).

and the profit and loss statement look after taking into account depreciation and the tax rates:

	A	B	C	D	E	F	G	H
117	ANYTOWN TRAVEL SERVICES (ATS), Inc., Jan-June 2003							
118	Financial statements including depreciation and taxes							
	Balance Sheet, 30 June 2003						Profit and Loss, 30 June 2003	
119	**Assets**			**Liabilities and equity**				
120	**Current assets**			**Current liabilities**			Sales	214,000
121	Cash			Taxi loan from bank	4,800		Driver salaries	-12,000
122	Cash at beginning of period	25,000		Unpaid signing bonus	0		Owner salaries	-20,000
123	Cash sales	204,000		Accounts payable (gasoline)	14,000		Signing bonus	-800
124	Driver salaries	-12,000		Taxes payable	44,562		Fuel	-56,000
125	Owner salaries	-20,000		Total current liabilities	63,362		Interest	-272
126	Signing bonus	-800					Insurance	-6,000
127	Fuel	-42,000		**Long-term liabilities**			Depreciation	-5,250
128	Interest	-272		Mortgage to buy building	60,000		Profit before taxes	113,678
129	Repayment of car loan principal	-3,200					State income tax (5%)	-5,684
130	Insurance	-12,000					Profit subject to Federal tax	107,994
131	Building, cash payment	-20,000					Federal income tax (36%)	-38,878
132	Cash paid for taxis	-28,000					Profit after taxes	69,116
133	Cash paid for computer	-2,000					Dividends	0
134	Cash at end of period	88,728					Retained earnings	69,116
135								
136	Accounts receivable	10,000						
137	Prepaid expenses (insurance)	6,000						
138	Current assets	104,728					**Highlighting**	
139							Tax bill for first half year is unpaid and	
140	**Fixed assets**			**Equity**			listed as taxes payable.	
141	Computer	2,000		Initial stock	25,000		Accumulated retained earnings now	
142	Minus accumulated depreciation	-250		Accumulated retained earnings	69,116		reflect the impact of taxes.	
143	Taxis	36,000		Total equity	94,116			
144	Minus accumulated depreciation	-5,000					Profit and loss includes total depreciation	
145	Building	80,000					on assets as an expense for tax	
146	Minus accumulated depreciation	0					purposes.	
147	Net fixed assets	112,750						
148								
149	**Total assets**	217,478		**Total liabilities and equity**	217,478			

Note that on 1 July 2003, ATS hasn't actually paid the taxes (they're due on 15 July). To take care of this, the accountant creates a category called *taxes payable;* this is a current liability for taxes (1) due within a short period of time, (2) that have already been accounted for in the profit and loss statement, and (3) that have not yet been paid. The taxes payable account (cell E124) of $44,562 is the sum of the state and federal taxes owed ($5,684 + $38,878).

3.3 The Consolidated Statement of Cash Flows

This is the third accounting statement we're mastering in this chapter. The purpose of the consolidated statement of cash flows is to explain the growth over the period of the cash balances on the balance sheet. The statement of cash flows accomplishes this by classifying all the firm's cash inflows and outflows into three categories: cash flow from operating activities, cash flow from investing activities, and cash flow from financing activities.

Cash Flow from Operating Activities

Cash flow from operating activities includes the profit after taxes for the period minus increases in operating current assets plus increases in operating current liabilities:

	A	B	C	D	E
153	**Cash flow from operating activities**				
154	Profit after taxes	69,116			
155	Add back depreciation	5,250			
156	Subtract increase in operating current assets	-16,000	<--	$10,000 receivables + $6,000 prepaid expenses	
157	Add increases in operating current liabilities	58,562	<--	$14,000 unpaid gas bills + $44,562 unpaid taxes	
158	**Cash provided from operating activities**	116,928	<--	=SUM(B154:B157)	

- In the period January–June, ATS had profits of $69,116. It recorded depreciation of $5,250 on its taxis and computer; this depreciation is not a cash expense, and it is added back in the cash flow statement.

- In addition, the company's current assets excluding cash grew by $16,000. This is the sum of the end-June account receivable from the flour mill plus the prepaid insurance expenses. This $16,000 is a cost of business not recorded in the profit and loss; the cash flow statement subtracts this amount.

- At the end of June, the company had $44,562 of unpaid taxes and $14,000 of unpaid gasoline bills. This *increase in operating current liabilities* is an expense that was recorded on the P&L but that has (as yet—ultimately these bills will, of course, be paid) no cash implications. Therefore, we add it back.[5]

Cash Flow from Investing Activities

Cash flow from investing activities includes acquisition of fixed assets (land, property, machines) and investments made by the company in marketable securities (ATS has neither bought nor sold such securities during its first half-year of existence, but we've shown these items anyway):

	A	B	C	D	E
160	**Cash flow from investing activities**				
161	Payments for fixed assets				
162	Taxis	-36,000	<--	Two taxis purchased	
163	Computer	-2,000			
164	Building	-80,000			
165	Purchases of marketable securities	0			
166	Proceeds from sales of marketable securities	0			
167	**Cash used in investing activities**	-118,000			

Cash Flow from Financing Activities

This item includes money raised by the company from sale of stock, from taking loans, and so on.

	A	B	C	D	E
169	**Cash flow from financing activities**				
170	Proceeds from new debt	68,000	<--	Taxi loan of $8,000 + mortgage of $60,000	
171	Debt repayments	-3,200	<--	Partial repayment of taxi loan	
172	Cash dividends paid	0			
173	New stock sold	0			
174	Stock repurchased	0			
175	**Cash used in financing activities**	64,800			

---

[5]Note that current liabilities also include the taxi loan. This loan is included in the cash flow from financing activities, the third section of the consolidated statement of cash flows.

Here's the whole consolidated statement of cash flows:

	A	B	C	D	E
152	Consolidated statement of cash flows, 30 June 2003				
153	**Cash flow from operating activities**				
154	Profit after taxes	69,116			
155	Add back depreciation	5,250			
156	Subtract increase in operating current assets	-16,000	<--	$10,000 receivables + $6,000 prepaid expenses	
157	Add increases in operating current liabilities	58,562	<--	$14,000 unpaid gas bills + $44,562 unpaid taxes	
158	**Cash provided from operating activities**	116,928	<--	=SUM(B154:B157)	
159					
160	**Cash flow from investing activities**				
161	Payments for fixed assets				
162	Taxis	-36,000	<--	Two taxis purchased	
163	Computer	-2,000			
164	Building	-80,000			
165	Purchases of marketable securities	0			
166	Proceeds from sales of marketable securities	0			
167	**Cash used in investing activities**	-118,000			
168					
169	**Cash flow from financing activities**				
170	Proceeds from new debt	68,000	<--	Taxi loan of $8,000 + mortgage of $60,000	
171	Debt repayments	-3,200	<--	Partial repayment of taxi loan	
172	Cash dividends paid	0			
173	New stock sold	0			
174	Stock repurchased	0			
175	**Cash used in financing activities**	64,800			
176					
177	**Net change in cash over period**	63,728	<--	=B158+B167+B175	
178	Initial cash balances	25,000			
179	**Ending cash balance**	88,728	<--	=B178+B177	

During the period January–June, ATS had a net cash inflow of $63,728 (cell B177). Added to the initial cash balance of the company over this period, $25,000, the ending cash balance should be $88,728. And indeed they are—this is the cash balance listed on the company's end-June balance sheet (cell B134).

3.4 Computing the Free Cash Flow (FCF)

The consolidated statement of cash flows gives the amount of cash generated by ATS during its first half-year of existence. For finance purposes (recall, dear reader, that this is a finance and not an accounting book!), it is useful to know *how much cash was generated by the firm's operations*. Our measure of this is the *free cash flow* (FCF). The consolidated statement of cash flows does not give this information, since it mixes operational and financial cash flows.

The FCF is defined as

Definition of the Free Cash Flow (FCF)

	Explanation
Profit after taxes Add back depreciation	Depreciation is a noncash expense and is therefore added back.
Subtract increase in current assets used for operations	For purposes of the FCF, this item does not include cash or marketable securities.
Add increase in current liabilities from operations	Accounting current liabilities include items like short-term debt and current portion of long-term debt. These financial items are not included in the FCF.
Subtract increase in fixed assets at cost	This represents the amount spent on new assets over the period. In the jargon of Wall Street, it is often called "capital expenditures" (CAPEX).
Add back after-tax interest expenses	The FCF is an *operating concept:* It relates to cash generated by the firm's operations. Interest expenses are a financial (nonoperating) item and should therefore be added back. On the other hand, the profit after taxes includes only *after-tax interest*; this is the amount added back in the FCF calculation. Note that in our case the firm's *effective tax rate* is $$\underbrace{36\%}_{\substack{\text{Federal} \\ \text{tax rate}}} + \underbrace{(1-36\%)}_{\substack{\text{Federal tax} \\ \text{deductability} \\ \text{of state tax}}} * \underbrace{5\%}_{\substack{\text{State tax} \\ \text{rate}}} = 39.2\%.$$
FCF	The free cash flow is the amount of cash generated by the firm's operations or business activities. Another way of looking at this is that the FCF is the amount of cash generated by the firm if everything were financed with equity.

To compute the FCF, it is handy to put the profit and loss and the balance sheet in two side-by-side columns, one for the start of the period (1 January 2003) and one for the end of the period (30 June 2003).

	A	B	C	D
1	ANYTOWN TRAVEL SERVICES (ATS), Inc. Calculating the free cash flow (FCF)			
2	**Profit and loss for period ending**	1-Jan-03	30-Jun-03	
3	Sales		214,000	
4	Cost of sales		-94,800	
5	Interest		-272	
6	Depreciation		-5,250	
7	Profit		113,678	
8	State income tax (5%)		-5,684	
9	Federal income tax (36%)		-38,878	
10	Profit after taxes		69,116	
11	Dividends		0	
12	**Retained earnings**		69,116	
13				
14	**Balance sheet--Assets**	1-Jan-03	30-Jun-03	
15	Current assets			
16	Cash	25,000	88,728	
17	Accounts receivable	0	10,000	
18	Prepaid expenses (insurance)	0	6,000	
19	Total current assets	25,000	104,728	
20				
21	Fixed assets			
22	At cost	0	118,000	
23	Accumulated depreciation	0	-5,250	
24	Net fixed assets	0	112,750	
25	**Total assets**	**25,000**	**217,478**	
26				
27	**Balance sheet--Liabilities and equity**	1-Jan-03	30-Jun-03	
28	Current liabilities			
29	Short-term loan from bank (taxi loan)		4,800	
30	Taxes payable	0	44,562	
31	Accounts payable (gasoline)	0	14,000	
32	Total current liabilities	0	63,362	
33				
34	Long-term liabilities			
35	Mortgage to buy building	0	60,000	
36				
37	Equity			
38	Stock	25,000	25,000	
39	Retained earnings	0	69,116	
40	Total equity	25,000	94,116	
41	**Total liabilities and equity**	**25,000**	**217,478**	
42				
43	**Free cash flow (FCF)**			
44	Profit after taxes		69,116	<-- =C10
45	Add back depreciation		5,250	<-- =-C6
46				
47	Change in net working capital			
48	Subtract increase in operating current assets		-16,000	<-- =-SUM(C17:C18)-SUM(B17:B18). Changes in cash and marketable securities are not included
49	Add increase in operating current liabilities		58,562	<-- =C32-C29-B32. The taxi loan is financing and not operational
50	Change in net working capital		42,562	<-- =C49+C48
51				
52	Change in fixed assets at cost		-118,000	<-- =-(C22-B22)
53				
54	Add back after-tax net interest paid		165	<-- =-(1-39.2%)*C5
55	**Free cash flow**		**-907**	<-- =C44+C45+C50+C52+C54

So what does the FCF (cell C55) of −$907 mean? If ATS had paid all its operating expenses in cash and collected all its operating payments in cash during the first six months of its existence, it would be "in the hole" $907.

Evaluating ATS's Performance during January–June 2003

So . . . did Brother and Sister do well this half-year? Or should we be worried by their negative free cash flow?

- The negative FCF tells us that the business did not produce enough cash to pay all its expenses and capital costs. But, of course, the "changes in fixed asset at cost" item of $118,000 (cell C52) includes several long-term investments (two taxis, a computer, and a building), which are expected to produce revenues over a long period of time.

- The accounting profits of $69,116 deal with these long-term investments by including only their *depreciation* as a cost of operating the business. Conceptually, this depreciation attributes the cost of having a long-term asset to the current period's income.

3.5 Evaluating ATS's Performance for Its First Year of Operation

The months July–December 2003 were a period of stabilization for ATS. During this period, the company bought no more new assets. Here's what happened:

- Sales continued at $50,000 per month, for a total of $300,000.
- The flour mill continued to rack up $10,000 in fares per month. It paid its bills faithfully at the end of each month, so that at end-December 2003 it had only December's $10,000 outstanding.
- The two drivers continued to make $1,500 per month each. This made their total salaries for the period $18,000.
- The two owners continued to take $2,000 per month salary, for a total of $24,000 for these six months.
- Gasoline bills continued to be $7,000 per taxi per month. Total fuel bills for the period were $7 * \$14,000 = \$98,000$. ATS was paying its gasoline bill at the end of the following month, so that at year end it had $14,000 in gasoline bills outstanding. The remainder ($84,000) had been paid in full.
- The "prepaid expense (insurance)" became an actual expense:
  - The balance sheet line called "prepaid expense" became 0 instead of $6,000.
  - The $6,000 of insurance expenses were charged against profits as an expense.
- The company continued to pay off its taxi loan to the bank. During the period July–December, it paid off the loan in full and paid $168 in interest on the loan (1% per month on the outstanding balance).

	A	B	C	D
		Principal outstanding, beginning of month	Principal paid, end of month	Interest (1% per month)
39	**Taxi loan**			
40	31-Jul-03	4,800	800	48
41	31-Aug-03	4,000	800	40
42	30-Sep-03	3,200	800	32
43	31-Oct-03	2,400	800	24
44	30-Nov-03	1,600	800	16
45	31-Dec-03	800	800	8
46	1-Jan-04	0		
47	**Total**		4,800	168

- The company started to pay off its mortgage. The mortgage payments were $500 per month, with 0.5% interest on the outstanding balance:

	A	B	C	D
		Principal outstanding, beginning of month	**Principal paid, end of month**	**Interest (0.5% per month) numbers rounded**
49	**Mortgage**			
50	31-Jul-03	60,000	500	300
51	31-Aug-03	59,500	500	298
52	30-Sep-03	59,000	500	295
53	31-Oct-03	58,500	500	293
54	30-Nov-03	58,000	500	290
55	31-Dec-03	57,500	500	288
56	1-Jan-04	57,000		
57	**Total**		3,000	1,763

- At the end of the year, when the owners saw that the business was profitable, they declared a $30,000 dividend. In order not to stress the business, they decided to pay out $15,000 of this dividend immediately and the remainder at the end of March 2004. This created
  - A charge of $15,000 against the cash accounts of the business.
  - An item called "dividends payable" in the current liabilities of the firm.

Putting all these numbers together, here are the company's financial statements for the second half-year:

	A	B	C	D	E	F	G	H
1	**ANYTOWN TRAVEL SERVICES (ATS), Inc., July - December 2003**							
	Financial statements including depreciation and taxes							
2	**Balance Sheet, 31 December 2003**						**Profit and Loss, 31 December 2003**	
3	**Assets**			**Liabilities and equity**				
4	**Current assets**			**Current liabilities**				
5	Cash			Taxi loan from bank	0		Sales	300,000
6	Cash at beginning of period	88,728		Accounts payable (gasoline)	14,000		Driver salaries	-18,000
7	Cash sales	290,000		Taxes payable			Owner salaries	-24,000
8	Driver salaries	-18,000		For Jan - June			Fuel	-98,000
9	Owner salaries	-24,000		For July - Dec	55,103		Interest	-1,931
10	Receivable paid	10,000		Dividend payable	15,000		Insurance	-6,000
11	Fuel	-84,000		Total current liabilities	84,103		Depreciation	
12	Interest						Computer	-500
13	Auto loan	-168		**Long-term liabilities**			Building	-4,000
14	Mortgage	-1,763		Mortgage to buy building	57,000		Taxis	-7,000
15	Repayment of principal							
16	Auto loan	-4,800					Profit before taxes	140,570
17	Mortgage	-3,000					State income tax (5%)	-7,028
18	Taxes paid, 15 Jul 2003	-44,562					Profit subject to Federal tax	133,541
19	Payment of outstanding gas bill	-14,000					Federal income tax (36%)	-48,075
20	Dividend paid	-15,000					Profit after taxes	85,466
21	Cash at end of period	179,436					Dividends	-30,000
22							Retained earnings	55,466
23	Accounts receivable	10,000						
24	Prepaid expenses (insurance)	0						
25	Current assets	189,436					**Highlighting**	
26							Of $30,000 dividends declared, half were	
27	**Fixed assets**			**Equity**			paid and half remained unpaid at year end.	
28	Computer	2,000		Initial stock	25,000			
29	Minus accumulated depreciation	-750		Accumulated retained earnings			Building depreciation is $8,000 per year.	
30	Taxis	36,000		Jan - June	69,116		Building has been on the books since end-	
31	Minus accumulated depreciation	-12,000		July - December	55,466		June, so that depreciation for this year	
32	Building	80,000		Total equity	149,582		is $4,000.	
33	Minus accumulated depreciation	-4,000						
34	Net fixed assets	101,250						
35								
36	Total assets	290,686		Total liabilities and equity	290,686			

3.6 Computing the Free Cash Flow for the Second Half-Year

In rows 44–58 below, we calculate the free cash flow for the company at the end of December 2003:

	A	B	C	D	E
1	**ANYTOWN TRAVEL SERVICES (ATS), Inc.** **Free cash flow for 2003**				
2	**Profit and loss for period ending**	**1-Jan-03**	**30-Jun-03**	**31-Dec-03**	
3	Sales		214,000	300,000	
4	Cost of sales		-94,800	-146,000	
5	Interest		-272	-1,931	
6	Depreciation		-5,250	-11,500	
7	Profit		113,678	140,570	
8	State income tax (5%)		-5,684	-7,028	
9	Federal income tax (36%)		-38,878	-48,075	
10	Profit after taxes		69,116	85,466	
11	Dividends		0	-30,000	
12	**Retained earnings**		**69,116**	**55,466**	<-- =D10+D11
13					
14	**Balance sheet--Assets**	**1-Jan-03**	**30-Jun-03**	**31-Dec-03**	
15	Current assets				
16	Cash	25,000	88,728	179,436	
17	Accounts receivable	0	10,000	10,000	
18	Prepaid expenses (insurance)	0	6,000	0	
19	Total current assets	25,000	104,728	189,436	
20					
21	Fixed assets				
22	At cost	0	118,000	118,000	
23	Accumulated depreciation	0	-5,250	-16,750	
24	Net fixed assets	0	112,750	101,250	
25	**Total assets**	**25,000**	**217,478**	**290,686**	
26					
27	**Balance sheet--Liabilities and equity**	**1-Jan-03**	**30-Jun-03**	**31-Dec-03**	
28	Current liabilities				
29	Short-term loan from bank (taxi loan)		4,800	0	
30	Taxes payable	0	44,562	55,103	
31	Accounts payable (gasoline)	0	14,000	14,000	
32	Dividend payable			15,000	
33	Total current liabilities	0	63,362	84,103	
34					
35	Long-term liabilities				
36	Mortgage to buy building	0	60,000	57,000	
37					
38	Equity				
39	Stock	25,000	25,000	25,000	
40	Retained earnings	0	69,116	124,582	
41	Total equity	25,000	94,116	149,582	
42	**Total liabilities and equity**	**25,000**	**217,478**	**290,686**	
43					
44	**Free cash flow (FCF)**				
45	Profit after taxes		69,116	85,466	<-- =D10
46	Add back depreciation		5,250	11,500	<-- =-D6
47					
48	Change in net working capital				
49	Subtract increase in operating current assets		-16,000	6,000	<-- =-(SUM(D17:D18)-SUM(C17:C18))
50	Add increase in operating current liabilities		58,562	25,541	<-- =(D33-D29)-(C33-C29)
51	Change in net working capital		42,562	31,541	<-- =D50+D49
52					
53	Change in fixed assets at cost		-118,000	0	
54					
55	Add back after-tax net interest paid		165	1,174	
56	**Free cash flow**		**-907**	**129,681**	<-- =D45+D46+D51+D53+D55
57					
58	**Year total FCF**			**128,775**	<-- =C56+D56

During the year, the company had a total FCF of $128,775. Not bad for a new company!

WHICH DEPRECIATION DO YOU ADD BACK IN THE CASH FLOW?

When calculating the free cash flow (FCF) for ATS for the period July–December 2003, the depreciation we add back in the free cash flow (cell D46) computation is the depreciation that appears in the profit and loss statement for the period (cell D6), and not the accumulated depreciation that appears on the balance sheet (cell D23) for the same period. The reason for this is that cell D6 refers to the depreciation applied to the profits of the period, whereas cell D23 refers to the accumulated depreciation for all of the fixed assets that appear on the balance sheet.

CONCLUSION

In this chapter we've reviewed the basic methodology of financial accounting. We've reviewed the construction of the balance sheet, the profit and loss statement, and the statement of cash flows of a business. In addition, we showed how to construct a free cash flow statement and how to use this statement to value a business.

EXERCISES

1. Use the following data to calculate the cash at the end of the period:
   - The company's cash at the end of the previous year was $135,000.
   - Its shareholders invested $600,000 more in the company.
   - The company bought a machine for $200,000 at the beginning of the year. Half of this amount was financed by a loan. At the end of the year, the company paid $5,000 of this principal and $1,500 interest.
   - The company paid to its suppliers $10,000 and received $25,000 from its clients from the previous year's accounts receivable.
   - The company's sales during the year were $170,000. Of this amount, only 70% was paid. It paid salaries of $50,000, bought materials for $35,000 (but paid only 80% of this amount), and at the end of the year had inventory of $5,000. In addition, the company paid $3,000 for a license. It also owed taxes of $10,000 but paid only half of this amount.
   - The company sold its old vehicles for $15,000.
   - The company paid rent of $14,000.
   - The company paid dividends of $15,000.
2. Use the following data to prepare a balance sheet and profit and loss statement:
   - The company started its activity at the beginning of the year.
   - Its shareholders invested $400,000 in it.
   - The company bought a machine for $250,000 at the beginning of the year. The machine is not depreciated.
   - The company's income during the year was $90,000. Its expenses were $35,000.
   - The company paid $10,000 for rent.

3. Repeat Exercise 2, assuming that the machine purchased at the beginning of the year is being depreciated over five years. Present the consolidated statements of cash flows and free cash flow (FCF) estimation.

4. Use the following data to prepare a balance sheet and profit and loss statement:
   - The company was founded at the beginning of the year, and its shareholders invested $600,000 in it.
   - The company bought a machine for $300,000.
   - The company's sales for the year were $150,000.
   - The company paid salaries of $50,000, paid $25,000 to its suppliers, and remained with an inventory of $5,000 at the end of the year.
   - The company paid $10,000 in rent.

5. Use the following data to compute a balance sheet and a profit and loss statement:
   - The company was founded a year ago with a shareholder investment of $50,000.
   - The company immediately purchased two computers for $4,000 total.
   - At the end of the first year, the company's profit was $2,000. All these sales and costs for the year were in cash.
   - In the current period, the company's income (from selling software) was $10,000. From this amount, $2,000 shall be paid in the following year.
   - The company paid salaries of $3,000. Other expenses paid are rent ($1,000) and the purchase of another computer ($2,000), half of it still unpaid.
   - The company paid a dividend of $1,000.

6. Repeat Exercise 5, assuming that the depreciation period on the company's computers is two years. Compute the cash balances for both years.

7. Crystal Clear Company (CCC) started its activity—distributing mineral water—on 1 January 2002. The initial investment in the company was $500,000. The following data describe its activity in year 2002:
   - On 1 January 2002, the company bought vehicles for $100,000, paid in cash. On the same day it also bought a building for $600,000 to house its inventory and offices. It paid 20% in cash, and the remaining 80% was financed by a fifteen-year mortgage, with monthly repayments of the principal plus 0.5% interest rate per month (at the end of each month).
   - The company's revenue was $400,000. However, $75,000 from this amount will be paid next year, due to a special sale that CCC offered its clients.
   - CCC paid salaries of $130,000 to its employees. It also announced that if the revenue shall be more than $300,000 in the first year, all employees will receive a bonus of 10% of their salary, which will be paid in January of the following year.
   - Other expenses paid are office equipment ($15,000) and the purchase of a computer system ($6,000), half of it still unpaid. The inventory at the end of the year was estimated in the amount of $15,000.
   - The company paid $130,000 to its supplier. The agreement between the two parties was that the payments will be at the end of the following month. CCC estimated that the payment for the last month will be $20,000.
   - CCC paid the electricity bill of $300 per month. It also paid in advance $500 to the electricity company, a fixed payment for 2003.

   Present CCC's balance sheet and profit and loss statement.

8. Pretty Me Company (PMC) started its activity—selling cosmetic items—on 1 January 2002. The initial investment in the company was $1,000,000. The following data describe its activity in the year 2002:

   - The company bought a building for manufacturing, inventory, and housing its offices for $800,000. It paid half in cash and the rest was financed by a ten-year mortgage, with monthly repayments of the principal plus 0.5% interest rate per month.

   - The company's revenue was $700,000, while $55,000 from this amount will be paid next year.

   - PMC bought a manufacturing line for $400,000. The company borrowed the whole amount and repays it in four annual payments of the principal plus an 8% interest rate. The payments are at the end of each year.

   - PMC paid salaries of $200,000. Other expenses paid during 2002 are: office equipment—$20,000; computer purchases—$10,000; advertising—$50,000, of which $10,000 hasn't been paid yet. The inventory at the end of the year was estimated in the amount of $25,000.

   - PMC paid $180,000 to its supplier. The agreement between the two parties was that the payments will be at the end of the following month. The payment for December 2002 is $25,000.

   - The company also rented several marketing places at major malls. Each mall charges annual rent of $12,000. PMC signed an agreement with six malls for a period of five years each and paid the whole amount in advance.

   - PMC signed an agreement with a mobile company to distribute the products from the factory to the selling points. According to the agreement, each shipment costs $300 and each selling point needs two shipments each month. The payments are made two months after the shipments were made (for example, the shipments of January are paid in March).

   - PMC also paid $5,000 for the years 2002–2003 for a cosmetics manufacturing license.

   Present PMC's balance sheet and profit and loss statement.

9. Repeat Exercise 7, regarding Crystal Clear Company (CCC), adding the following data:

   - Computers—the depreciation period is two years.

   - Office equipment—the depreciation period is four years.

   - Vehicle depreciation—the depreciation period is three years.

   - Building depreciation—the depreciation period is twenty years.

   - Taxes—there is 10% state tax and 25% federal tax. For purposes of computing the federal tax, the state tax is an expense. In our case, the state tax has been paid. The federal tax hasn't been paid yet.

10. Repeat Exercise 8, regarding Pretty Me Company, adding the following data:

    - Computers—the depreciation period is two years.

    - Operation machine depreciation—the depreciation period is eight years.

    - Building depreciation—the depreciation period is twenty years.

    - Office equipment—the depreciation period is four years.

    - Taxes—there is 10% state tax and 30% federal tax. For purposes of computing the federal tax, the state tax is an expense. Both taxes have been paid.

11. Present the consolidated statements of cash flows for the statements you have found in Exercises 8 and 9.

12. Calculate the free cash flow (FCF) estimation according to the statements of Exercise 10. Explain why the FCF in both cases is negative.

13. The following is the 2001 balance sheet of the Easy Find Company, which manufactures home indoor intercoms.

	A	B	C	D	E
1	EASY FIND BALANCE SHEET				
2	**Assets**			**Liabilities and equity**	
3	Current assets			Current liabilities	
4	Cash	300,500		Accounts payable	40,500
5	Prepaid expenses	40,000		Total current liabilities	40,500
6	Receivables	50,000			
7	Total current assets	390,500		Long-term liabilities	0
8					
9	Fixed assets			Equity	
10	At cost	800,000		Stock	850,000
11	Accumulated depreciation	-250,000		Accumulated retained earnings	50,000
12	Net fixed assets	550,000		Total equity	900,000
13					
14	**Total assets**	**940,500**		**Total liabilities and equity**	**940,500**

Additional data regarding the balance sheet: The fixed asset is an operating machine bought on 1 January 1997 for $500,000 and which has a ten-year depreciation and vehicles that cost $300,000 and were bought on 30 December 2001. The vehicles' depreciation period is three years. In addition, all the payments from 1999 were paid.

The following activities were made by the company in the year 2002:

- The company's revenue was $1,500,000. From this amount, 15% is still unpaid.

- The company replaced its production line, paying $900,000 on the last day of 2002. The company borrowed $500,000 for this purpose and plans to repay it in four annual payments of the principal plus 5% interest rate. The payments are at the end of each year. The previous production line was sold at its book value, $200,000.

- Easy Find Company paid $400,000 in salaries. Other expenses paid during 2002 are factory rent—$10,000 per month, with half of 2003's rent paid in advance, and advertising—$80,000, only half of which was paid.

- Due to cash distress during the year, Easy Find took out a short-term loan of $20,000 in March 2002. It repaid the loan in six monthly payments of the principal plus 0.8% interest rate.

- Easy Find paid its supplier $250,000 for materials (20% of which is still unpaid). The company also rents two selling places. Each place charges an annual rent of $10,000. Easy Find paid a year in advance.

- On 7 January 2002, the company bought a store in order to open a third selling point. The store's cost is $80,000 with a ten-year depreciation. It was financed by a $50,000 mortgage for five years with monthly payments of the principal plus 0.5% interest rate. The rest was paid in cash.

- The company paid $60,000 in dividends.

- The company's tax rate is 36% and the taxes were paid in cash.

Calculate Easy Find Company's free cash flow.

14. The following is the 1999 balance sheet of Another Round Company, which manufactures little flags for election campaigns:

	A	B	C	D	E
1	**ANOTHER ROUND BALANCE SHEET**				
2	**Assets**			**Liabilities and equity**	
3	Current assets			Current liabilities	
4	Cash	10,000		Accounts payable	50,000
5	Prepaid expenses	18,000		Taxes payable	10,000
6	Receivables	90,000		Total current liabilities	60,000
7	Total current assets	118,000			
8				Bonds	150,000
9	Fixed assets				
10	At cost	250,000		Equity	
11	Accumulated depreciation	-75,000		Stock	70,000
12	Net fixed assets	175,000		Accumulated retained earnings	13,000
13				Total equity	83,000
14	**Total assets**	**293,000**		**Total liabilities and equity**	**293,000**

Additional data regarding the balance sheet: The operating machine was bought on 1 January 1997, and it has a ten-year depreciation. Furthermore, the company's bonds pay an annual interest of 8% every 30 December, and all the payments from 1999 were paid.

The following activities were made by the company in the year 2000:

- On 7 January 2000, the company paid $100,000 for a vehicle for distributing. The vehicle depreciation period is five years, with a terminal value of $10,000.
- The employee's salary was $80,000. The management's salary was $40,000.
- The company sales were $600,000 ($50,000 of which is still unpaid), and its material cost was $150,000 ($20,000 of which is still unpaid).
- The company paid rent of $35,000 and $20,000 for advertising.
- On 30 December 2000, the company paid the coupon to the bondholders. The company also paid $30,000 of the principal to its debt holders on 30 December 2000.
- The company tax rate is 40%. The company did not pay any tax in 2000.
- The company paid a dividend of $25,000.

Calculate the company's FCF.

CASH MANAGEMENT WITH EXCEL

OVERVIEW

In this chapter we show you how a business can build a cash management model. The purpose of building a cash management model (also called a cash budget) is to predict how much cash a business will have on hand at the end of each day, week, month, and so on. By tracking the inflows and outflows of cash, a business can predict its cash shortfalls or surpluses: It will know how much additional cash it needs to pay bills or how much cash it will have available for short-term investments.

The primary reason why businesses fail is insolvency—the lack of cash to pay bills. It follows that cash management is a topic of great importance to every business. By making a cash budget, a business can see where its money comes from and where it goes.

Excel is probably the most widely used tool for business cash management. In this chapter we illustrate how to use Excel to build a model for a simple business. We also illustrate the connection between our model and the profit and loss statement of the business. From our simple example you'll understand why cash management is so important.

What Is a Cash Management Model?

Underlying a cash management model is a simple "checkbook balancing" exercise:

Cash balance at the beginning of the period
$+$. Cash inflows from sales during the period
$-$ Cash costs during the period
$=$ Cash balances at the end of the period

Data Required for Cash Management

The data required for a cash management model include the following:

- Sales forecast: Cash management models are based on predictions of how much the business will sell during each prediction period (day, week, month).

- Cash receipts: Not all sales result in immediate cash receipts to the business. For example, a business may sell on credit, in which case some of the sales will result in cash only at a later date.

- Forecast of purchases and other expenses: In order to predict cash balances, we need a prediction of the business's purchases during each prediction period. Additional expenses include wages, taxes, utilities, and so on.

- Forecast of cash expenses: Not all expenses result in immediate cash outlays. If a business buys on credit, then it may only have to pay this month's expenses at some future date.

- Payment terms: As we have already noted, not every sale is made in cash and not every purchase is immediately paid for. Cash management models include these delays to predict the cash balances.

- Initial cash on hand: Every cash management model starts with some initial data on the business's cash balances.

Finance Concepts Discussed

- Cash flow
- Forecasting
- Cash management
- Profit and loss statement

Excel Functions Used

- **Sum**

4.1 Simple Example of a Cash Management Model

Before we start with a business example, let's consider a simple personal cash management model. During Christmas vacation of 2005, Jonathan decides to project his financial situation for the next six months. Jonathan currently has $800 in the bank. He is going to college and has a part-time job in Crazy Jim's Hamburger Stand (Jim's motto: "Crazy Jim's is cheaper than food"). Jonathan makes $700 a month, pays no taxes, has rent of $200, and has food expenses of $300. He estimates his monthly entertainment expenses at $100. Here's Jonathan's model:

	A	B	C	D	E	F	G	H
1	JONATHAN'S CASH MANAGEMENT MODEL							
2		Jan-05	Feb-05	Mar-05	Apr-05	May-05	Jun-05	Jul-05
3	Initial bank balance	$ 800	$ 900	<-- =B12				
4	Earned at Crazy Jim's	$ 700						
5								
6	**Expenses**							
7	Rent	$ 200						
8	Food	$ 300						
9	Other	$ 100						
10	Total expenses	$ 600	<-- =SUM(B7:B9)					
11								
12	Ending bank balance	$ 900	<-- =B3+B4-B10					

Jonathan predicts that at the end of January 2005, he will have $900 in the bank (cell B12). This is his initial bank balance for February 2005 (cell C3).

Continuing this model for the first six months of 2005 allows him to estimate that at the end of June 2005 he will have $1,400 in the bank (cells G12 and H3):

	A	B	C	D	E	F	G	H
1	JONATHAN'S CASH MANAGEMENT MODEL							
2		Jan-05	Feb-05	Mar-05	Apr-05	May-05	Jun-05	Jul-05
3	Initial bank balance	$ 800	$ 900	$ 1,000	$ 1,100	$ 1,200	$ 1,300	$ 1,400
4	Earned at Crazy Jim's	$ 700	$ 700	$ 700	$ 700	$ 700	$ 700	
5								
6	**Expenses**							
7	Rent	$ 200	$ 200	$ 200	$ 200	$ 200	$ 200	
8	Food	$ 300	$ 300	$ 300	$ 300	$ 300	$ 300	
9	Other	$ 100	$ 100	$ 100	$ 100	$ 100	$ 100	
10	Total expenses	$ 600	$ 600	$ 600	$ 600	$ 600	$ 600	
11								
12	Ending bank balance	$ 900	$ 1,000	$ 1,100	$ 1,200	$ 1,300	$ 1,400	

Thinking about this model, Jonathan realizes that his life is somewhat more complicated than the model indicates:

- He intends to quit his job at Crazy Jim's at the end of March in order to prepare for his end-of-semester exams in April. Thus, he'll have no income during April.

- During May and June he will work at Crazy Jim's full time, earning $1,600 per month.
- In May he intends to buy a cheap car. He thinks this will cost him $2,000. Gas and insurance for the car will cost him $150 per month.

Putting this into his model, Jonathan realizes that he's going to have a cash flow problem in May. He'll have to find a way to finance his predicted cash shortfall of $650:

	A	B	C	D	E	F	G	H
1	JONATHAN'S CASH MANAGEMENT MODEL							
2		Jan-05	Feb-05	Mar-05	Apr-05	May-05	Jun-05	Jul-05
3	Initial bank balance	$ 800	$ 900	$ 1,000	$ 1,100	$ 500	$ -650	$ 200
4	Earned at Crazy Jim's	$ 700	$ 700	$ 700		$ 1,600	$ 1,600	
5								
6	**Expenses**							
7	Rent	$ 200	$ 200	$ 200	$ 200	$ 200	$ 200	
8	Food	$ 300	$ 300	$ 300	$ 300	$ 300	$ 300	
9	Other	$ 100	$ 100	$ 100	$ 100	$ 100	$ 100	
10	Car					$ 2,000		
11	Gas/insurance					$ 150	$ 150	
12	Total expenses	$ 600	$ 600	$ 600	$ 600	$ 2,750	$ 750	
13								
14	Ending bank balance	$ 900	$ 1,000	$ 1,100	$ 500	$ -650	$ 200	

This simple story illustrates the uses of a cash management model in financial planning. We could, of course, make the model more complicated. For example, perhaps Jonathan will finance his temporary cash problem in May with a car loan from the bank. He could include the loan and the interest on the loan in the model.

However, assuming that you've gotten the point of cash management modeling, here's a somewhat more complicated business version of the model.

4.2 Bob's Bikes: A Business Cash Management Example

We now look at a cash management model for a small business. Bob Schwartz owns a bicycle shop in downtown Nowhere. It is New Year's Eve, 31 December 2006, and Bob is trying to build a model to predict his bike shop's cash balances. Bob has developed a simple cash management model, which he built in Excel. He started December with $3,000 in the bank, and he is using the model to explain his end-December cash balance of $28,293.

Bob's **cash management model** has four parts:

Part 1 of the Cash Management Model: Model Parameters

Bob sells only two kinds of bikes. Cheap bikes sell for $100 and expensive bikes for $250 each. The wholesale price of each kind of bike is 60% of its retail price. Bob's arrangement with the bike manufacturer is that any bike he orders during a given month has to be paid for in the following month.

In addition to bicycles, Bob also sells bike parts. His markup on these parts is 100%—that is, he sells them at double their cost. The payment arrangement for the parts is the same as that for the bicycles—Bob has to pay for parts a month after he orders them. Bob's formula for ordering bike parts is related to his bicycle order: Each month he orders parts worth 20% of the retail price of the bikes he orders during the same month. For example, if in a given month Bob orders bikes that will sell for $1,000 retail, he will order $200 of parts. Given the 100% markup on parts, they will sell for $400.

Bob makes only credit card sales (he's had too many bounced checks . . .). The credit card companies charge him 3% of his charges. Thus, $100 charged on a credit card results in an immediate payment to Bob's bank account of $97.

Bob's Bikes pays monthly rent of $5,000. Bob has an assistant, Mary, who makes $1,000 per month. Bob pays himself a salary of $2,000 per month.

Here are these numbers in Excel format:

	A	B	C	D
1		BOB'S BIKES--CASH MANAGEMENT MODEL		
2	**Model parameters**			
3	Bicycle prices, retail			
4	Cheap bikes	$ 100		
5	Expensive bikes	$ 250		
6	Wholesale price as percent of retail	60%	<-- Bikes ordered during the month are paid for during following month	
7	Parts ordered, as percentage of bikes	20%	<-- Parts ordered = 20% of monthly bike orders	
8	Markup on parts	100%	<-- Parts are sold at double their cost, paid for during following month	
9	Credit card discount	3%	<-- The credit card company takes 3% of credit card sales	
10	Monthly rental, store	$ 5,000		
11	Mary's salary	$ 1,000		
12	Bob's salary	$ 2,000		

Part 2 of the Cash Management Model: Sales Forecasts, Cash Receipts, and Inventories

Each month Bob forecasts his sales and orders bicycles and parts based on these forecasts. He also computes the end-of-month bike and parts inventories.

Bob started December with 10 cheap bikes and 5 expensive ones. Anticipating a busy Christmas season, he ordered 125 cheapies and 100 expensive bikes (cells C21 and C22 in the spreadsheet below). The sales price of the December bikes ordered is $125 * \$100 + 100 * \$250 = \$37,500$. Actual December sales of bikes were a bit disappointing: Bob sold 100 cheap bikes and 75 expensive ones, so that the value of the bikes sold was $100 * \$100 + 75 * \$250 = \$28,750$ (cell C36). Bob ended the month with 35 cheap bikes in inventory (10 on hand at the beginning of the month + 125 ordered − 100 sold = 35) and 30 expensive ones (cells C24 and C25).[1]

---

[1] The number of bikes ordered in a particular month is a very tricky business. Bob doesn't want to end the month with too many bikes on hand, but, on the other hand, he doesn't want to sell out of bikes. His strategy is to predict monthly sales and then order enough bikes so that the end-of-month inventories will be slightly positive.

Bob's parts inventory at the beginning of December was $300. Each month Bob orders parts equal to 20% of the retail price of the bikes ordered that month. Actual parts sales are 20% of the value of the bikes actually sold. Thus, Bob ordered parts worth 20% ∗ $37,500 = $7,500 (cell C28) and sold $5,750 parts (20% ∗ bike sales of $28,750, cell C29), leaving him with an ending parts inventory of $2,050 (cell C30).

	A	B	C	D
16	**Sales: forecasts and actuals**	30-Nov-06	31-Dec-06	
17	Bicycles sold during December			
18	Cheap bikes		100	
19	Expensive bikes		75	
20	Bikes ordered at beginning of December			
21	Cheap bikes		125	
22	Expensive bikes		100	
23	Inventory: Bikes on hand at end of month			
24	Cheap bikes	10	35	<-- =B24+C21-C18
25	Expensive bikes	5	30	<-- =B25+C22-C19
26				
27	Parts inventory: (wholesale $ value)			
28	Parts ordered		$ 7,500	<-- =$B$7*(C21*$B$4+C22*$B$5)
29	Parts sold		$ 5,750	<-- =$B$7*(C18*$B$4+C19*$B$5)
30	Ending parts inventory	$300	$ 2,050	<-- =B30+C28-C29
31				
32	**Sales**			
33	Bikes sold			
34	Cheap bikes		$ 10,000	<-- =C18*$B$4
35	Expensive bikes		$ 18,750	<-- =C19*$B$5
36	Total bikes sold during month		$ 28,750	<-- =C34+C35
37	Parts sold		$ 11,500	<-- =$B$7*C36*(1+$B$8)
38	Monthly sales		$ 40,250	<-- =C37+C36
39	Less amount paid to credit card company		$ 1,208	<-- =$B$9*C38
40	Total cash receipts for month		$ 39,043	<-- =C38-C39

Total sales for December were $28,750 (bikes) + $11,500 (parts) = $40,250 (cell C38). Since the credit card company takes 3%, this gives December cash receipts of $39,043 (cell B40).

EXCEL NOTE

DO EXCEL'S NUMBERS ALWAYS ADD UP?

Sometimes it may seem that Excel makes simple adding and subtracting mistakes. In the example above, monthly sales for December (cell C38) are $40,250 and Jonathan pays $1,208 to the credit card company (cell C39). Shouldn't his cash receipts for the month be $39,042?

	A	B	C	D
38	Monthly sales		$ 40,250	<-- =C37+C36
39	Less amount paid to credit card company		$ 1,208	<-- =$B$9*C38
40	Total cash receipts for month		$ 39,043	<-- =C38-C39

contd.

The answer has to do with how we represent the numbers in Excel. In our example we have represented all the dollar figures as whole numbers. By clicking the **Increase decimal** icon on the toolbar, we can see that the actual numbers are slightly different:

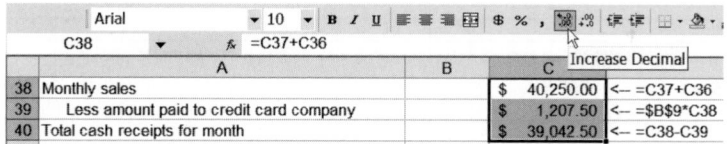

In Excel changing the format of numbers does not change the actual numbers; it just changes the way they look. Sometimes this can cause confusion.

A Further Note

Another way to change the formatting of the numbers is to use the **Format|Cells|Number** command, discussed in Chapter 27.

Part 3 of the Cash Management Model: Cash Expenses

The expenses are based on the following assumptions:

- Each month Bob pays rent of $5,000 on the store. During some months of the year he also pays city taxes and a quarterly estimated income tax payment. However, in December, he has neither of these payments.
- Bob pays for the bikes and parts one month after ordering them. December's payment for November's bike sales was $5,000 and for November's part sales was $750 (cells C46 and C47).
- Each month Bob pays himself a salary of $2,000 and pays his assistant, Mary, a salary of $1,000 (cells C49 and C48).

  This makes December's expenses $13,750.

	A	B	C	D
42	**Expenses**			
43	Rent		$ 5,000	<-- =$B$10
44	City taxes			
45	Quarterly estimated tax payment			
46	Payment for bicycles from previous month		$ 5,000	<-- Based on November sales (not shown)
47	Payment for parts from previous month		$ 750	<-- Based on November sales (not shown)
48	Mary's salary		$ 1,000	<-- =$B$11
49	Bob's salary		$ 2,000	<-- =$B$12
50	Total cash expenses for month		$ 13,750	<-- =SUM(C43:C49)

Part 4 of the Cash Management Model: Ending Cash Balances

The ending cash balances for the month are the sum of the initial cash balances (December's initial balances were $3,000) plus sales minus expenses. Thus, December's ending cash balances are $28,293 (cell C52):

	A	B	C	D
1	BOB'S BIKES--CASH MANAGEMENT MODEL			
2	Model parameters			
3	Bicycle prices, retail			
4	Cheap bikes	$100		
5	Expensive bikes	$250		
6	Wholesale price as percent of retail	60%		<-- Bikes ordered during the month are paid for during following month
7	Parts ordered, as percentage of bikes	20%		<-- Parts ordered = 20% of monthly bike orders
8	Markup on parts	100%		<-- Parts are sold at double their cost, paid for during following month
9	Credit card discount	3%		<-- The credit card company takes 3% of credit card sales
10	Monthly rental, store	$5,000		
11	Mary's salary	$1,000		
12	Bob's salary	$2,000		
13				
14	Bank balance at beginning of month		$ 3,000	
15				
16	Sales: forecasts and actuals	30-Nov-06	31-Dec-06	
17	Bicycles sold during December			
18	Cheap bikes		100	
19	Expensive bikes		75	
20	Bikes ordered at beginning of December			
21	Cheap bikes		125	
22	Expensive bikes		100	
23	Inventory: Bikes on hand at end of month			
24	Cheap bikes	10	35	<-- =B24+C21-C18
25	Expensive bikes	5	30	<-- =B25+C22-C19
26				
27	Parts inventory: (wholesale $ value)			
28	Parts ordered		$ 7,500	<-- =$B$7*(C21*$B$4+C22*$B$5)
29	Parts sold		$ 5,750	<-- =$B$7*(C18*$B$4+C19*$B$5)
30	Ending parts inventory	$300	$ 2,050	<-- =B30+C28-C29
31				
32	Sales			
33	Bikes sold			
34	Cheap bikes		$ 10,000	<-- =C18*$B$4
35	Expensive bikes		$ 18,750	<-- =C19*$B$5
36	Total bikes sold during month		$ 28,750	<-- =C34+C35
37	Parts sold		$ 11,500	<-- =$B$7*C36*(1+$B$8)
38	Monthly sales		$ 40,250	<-- =C37+C36
39	Less amount paid to credit card company		$ 1,208	<-- =$B$9*C38
40	Total cash receipts for month		$ 39,043	<-- =C38-C39
41				
42	Expenses			
43	Rent		$ 5,000	<-- =$B$10
44	City taxes			
45	Quarterly estimated tax payment			
46	Payment for bicycles from previous month		$ 5,000	<-- Based on November sales (not shown)
47	Payment for parts from previous month		$ 750	<-- Based on November sales (not shown)
48	Mary's salary		$ 1,000	<-- =$B$11
49	Bob's salary		$ 2,000	<-- =$B$12
50	Total cash expenses for month		$ 13,750	<-- =SUM(C43:C49)
51				
52	Cash at end of month		$ 28,293	<-- =C14+C40-C50
53				
54	Monthly cash flow = Cash receipts - cash expenses		$ 25,293	<-- =C40-C50

The last line of the spreadsheet shows the month's **cash flow,** the actual cash that flows into the bike shop bank account during the month. December's cash flow of $25,293 equals December cash receipts ($39,043, cell C40) minus December cash expenses ($13,750, cell C50).

Bob realizes that December's highly positive cash flow may be somewhat misleading: The December cash flow does not yet reflect the cost of the bikes sold in December (Bob will only pay for these bikes in January). In the next section we show how the cash management model can be extended to produce cash forecasts for the next year.

4.3 Extending the Model to Produce Cash Forecasts for the Year

January is usually a slow month, and Bob forecasts that he will sell only 50 cheap and 50 expensive bikes during the month. From a cash budget point of view, January is not an easy month:

- Bob has to pay for the bikes and the parts he ordered in December. Bikes cost him 60% (cell B6) of their retail price. Since he ordered $37,500 of bikes in December (C21 $*$ $B$4 + C22 $*$ $B$5 = $37,500), this means that the expense for these bikes is $22,500 in January (cell D48). December's parts sales of $11,500 cost Bob $5,750 (cell C29).
- On 15 January Bob has to pay his estimated income taxes. He does this four times per year (January, April, June, and September), and the estimated taxes are based on his previous year's income. January's estimated taxes are $10,000 (cell C47).
- Bob's monthly orders of bikes (cells D18 and D19) are computed so that his forecasted end-month bike inventory will be 30 cheap and 30 expensive bicycles.

As you can see, at the end of the month Bob will have $5,808 in his bank account. The projected cash flow for the month is a whopping −$22,485! The negative cash flow largely results from the fact that Bob has to pay for his December sales in January and that he has a large estimated tax bill.[2]

---

[2]At the end of January, Bob will update his model, replacing his forecasted sales (cells D18 and D19) with his actual monthly sales. He will also replace the estimated parts sales (D29 and D39) with actual parts sold. This way he updates the model each month, tracking actual performance.

Here are Bob's forecasts for January in Excel form:

	A	B	C	D	E
1	**BOB'S BIKES--CASH MANAGEMENT MODEL** **December - January**				
2	**Model parameters**				
3	Bicycle prices, retail				
4	Cheap bikes	$ 100			
5	Expensive bikes	$ 250			
6	Wholesale price as percent of retail	60%			
7	Parts ordered, as percentage of bikes	20%			
8	Markup on parts	100%			
9	Credit card discount	3%			
10	Monthly rental, store	$ 5,000			
11	Mary's salary	$ 1,000			
12	Bob's salary	$ 2,000			
13					
14	Bank balance at beginning of month		$ 3,000	$ 28,293	<-- =C52
15					
16	**Sales: forecasts and actuals**	30-Nov-06	31-Dec-06	31-Jan-07	
17	Bicycles sold				
18	Cheap bikes		100	50	
19	Expensive bikes		75	50	
20	Bikes ordered at beginning of the month				
21	Cheap bikes		125	45	<-- =30+D18-C24
22	Expensive bikes		100	50	<-- =30+D19-C25
23	Inventory: Bikes on hand at end of month				
24	Cheap bikes	10	35	30	<-- =C24+D21-D18
25	Expensive bikes	5	30	30	<-- =C25+D22-D19
26					
27	Inventory: (wholesale $ value)				
28	Parts ordered		$ 7,500	$ 3,400	<-- =$B$7*(D21*$B$4+D22*$B$5)
29	Parts sold		$ 5,750	$ 3,500	<-- =$B$7*(D18*$B$4+D19*$B$5)
30	Ending parts inventory	$ 300	$ 2,050	$ 1,950	<-- =C30+D28-D29
31					
32	**Sales**				
33	Bikes sold				
34	Cheap bikes		$ 10,000	$ 5,000	<-- =D18*$B$4
35	Expensive bikes		$ 18,750	$ 12,500	<-- =D19*$B$5
36	Total bikes sold during month		$ 28,750	$ 17,500	<-- =D34+D35
37	Parts sold		$ 11,500	$ 7,000	<-- =$B$7*D36*(1+$B$8)
38	Monthly sales		$ 40,250	$ 24,500	<-- =D37+D36
39	Less amount paid to credit card company		$ 1,208	$ 735	<-- =$B$9*D38
40	Total cash receipts for month		$ 39,043	$ 23,765	<-- =D38-D39
41					
42	**Expenses**				
43	Rent		$ 5,000	$ 5,000	<-- =$B$10
44	City taxes				<-- Estimated taxes paid 4 times per year:
45	Estimated tax payment			$ 10,000	January, April, June, September
46	Payment for bicycles from previous month		$ 5,000	$ 22,500	<-- =(C21*$B$4+C22*$B$5)*$B$6
47	Payment for parts from previous month		$ 750	$ 5,750	<-- =C29
48	Mary's salary		$ 1,000	$ 1,000	<-- =$B$11
49	Bob's salary		$ 2,000	$ 2,000	<-- =$B$12
50	Total cash expenses for month		$ 13,750	$ 46,250	<-- =SUM(D43:D49)
51					
52	Cash at end of month		$ 28,293	$ 5,808	<-- =D14+D40-D50
53					
54	Monthly cash flow = Cash receipts - cash expenses		$ 25,293	$ -22,485	<-- =D40-D50

4.4 One Year of Forecasts

One of the uses for Bob's model is to project the year's performance of the bike shop throughout the year. Page 64 gives the forecasted model for the whole year.

Although the months January–April 2007 will not be easy ones, Bob projects an end-of-year bank account balance of $98,303 (cell O52).[3]

Notice that in addition to the estimated income tax payments in January, April, June, and September, Bob has to pay city taxes of $40,000 in April (cell G44).

Presented graphically, here are Bob's projected end-of-month bank balances:

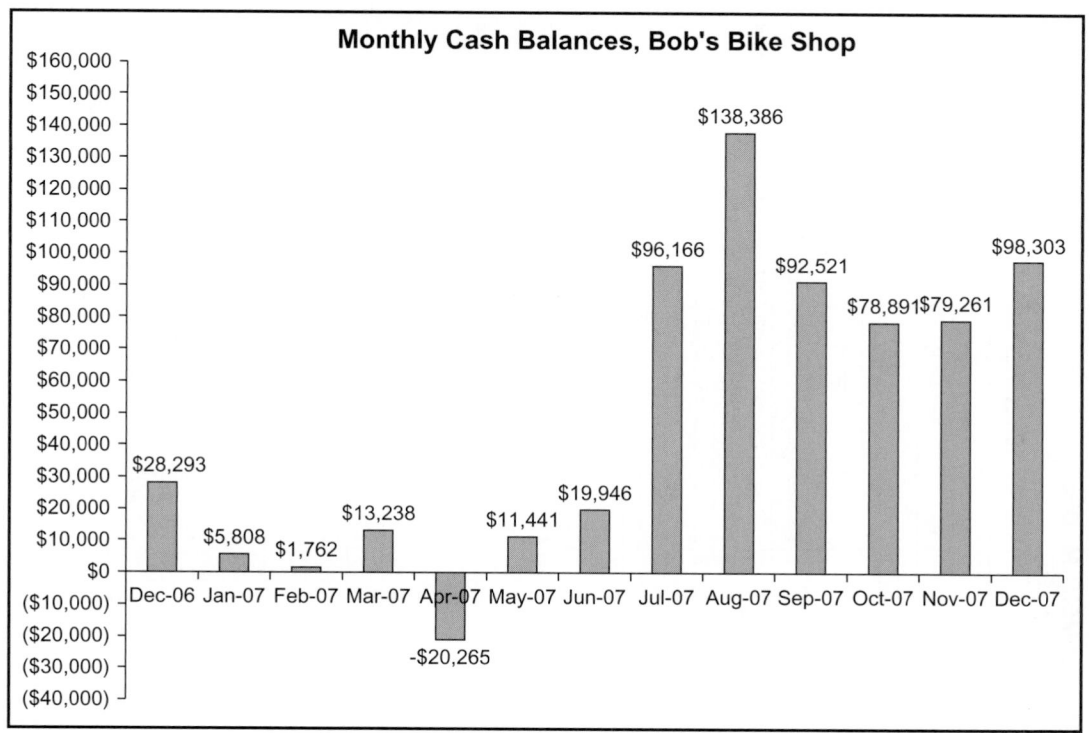

_____

[3]Bob realizes that one of the things his model ignores is the cost of having negative cash balances and the interest he can earn on positive bank balances. We've left this as an exercise for the end of the chapter.

BOB'S BIKES--CASH MANAGEMENT MODEL
December 2006 - December 2007

	B	C	D	E	F	G	H	I	J	K	L	M	N	O
Model parameters														
Bicycle prices, retail														
Cheap bikes	$ 100													
Expensive bikes	$ 250													
Wholesale price as percent of retail	60%													
Parts ordered, as percentage of bikes	20%													
Markup on parts	100%													
Credit card discount	3%													
Monthly rental, store	$ 5,000													
Mary's salary	$ 1,000													
Bob's salary	$ 2,000													
Bank balance at beginning of month		$ 3,000	$ 28,293	$ 5,808	$ 1,762	$ 13,238	$ (20,265)	$ 11,441	$ 19,946	$ 96,166	$ 138,386	$ 92,521	$ 78,891	$ 79,261
	30-Nov-06	31-Dec-06	31-Jan-07	28-Feb-07	31-Mar-07	30-Apr-07	31-May-07	30-Jun-07	31-Jul-07	31-Aug-07	30-Sep-07	31-Oct-07	30-Nov-07	31-Dec-07
Sales: forecasts and actuals														
Bicycles sold														
Cheap bikes		100	50	30	45	60	100	100	150	150	75	25	25	100
Expensive bikes		75	50	40	70	100	150	150	300	300	100	50	50	75
Bikes ordered at beginning of the month														
Cheap bikes		125	45	30	45	60	100	100	150	150	75	25	25	100
Expensive bikes		100	50	40	70	100	150	150	300	300	100	50	50	75
Inventory: Bikes on hand at end of month														
Cheap bikes	10	35	30	30	30	30	30	30	30	30	30	30	30	30
Expensive bikes	5	30	30	30	30	30	30	30	30	30	30	30	30	30
Inventory: (wholesale $ value)														
Parts ordered		$ 7,500	3,400	2,600	4,400	6,200	9,500	9,500	18,000	18,000	6,500	3,000	3,000	5,750
Parts sold		$ 5,750	3,500	2,600	4,400	6,200	9,500	9,500	18,000	18,000	6,500	3,000	3,000	5,750
Ending parts inventory	$ 300	$ 2,050	1,950	1,950	1,950	1,950	1,950	1,950	1,950	1,950	1,950	1,950	1,950	1,950
Sales														
Bikes sold														
Cheap bikes		$ 10,000	$ 5,000	$ 3,000	$ 4,500	$ 6,000	$ 10,000	$ 10,000	$ 15,000	$ 15,000	$ 7,500	$ 2,500	$ 2,500	$ 10,000
Expensive bikes		$ 18,750	12,500	10,000	17,500	25,000	37,500	37,500	75,000	75,000	25,000	12,500	12,500	18,750
Total bikes sold during month		$ 28,750	17,500	13,000	22,000	31,000	47,500	47,500	90,000	90,000	32,500	15,000	15,000	28,750
Parts sold		$ 11,500	7,000	5,200	8,800	12,400	19,000	19,000	36,000	36,000	13,000	6,000	6,000	11,500
Monthly sales		$ 40,250	24,500	18,200	30,800	43,400	66,500	66,500	126,000	126,000	45,500	21,000	21,000	40,250
Less amount paid to credit card company		$ 1,208	735	546	924	1,302	1,995	1,995	3,780	3,780	1,365	630	630	1,208
Total cash receipts for the month		$ 39,043	23,765	17,654	29,876	42,098	64,505	64,505	122,220	122,220	44,135	20,370	20,370	39,043
Expenses														
Rent		$ 5,000	$ 5,000	$ 5,000	$ 5,000	$ 5,000	$ 5,000	$ 5,000	$ 5,000	$ 5,000	$ 5,000	$ 5,000	$ 5,000	$ 5,000
City taxes						$ 40,000								
Estimated tax payment			10,000			10,000		10,000			10,000			
Payment for bicycles from previous month		$ 5,000	22,500	10,200	7,800	13,200	18,600	28,500	28,500	54,000	54,000	19,500	9,000	9,000
Payment for parts from previous month		$ 750	5,750	3,500	2,600	4,400	6,200	9,500	9,500	18,000	18,000	6,500	3,000	3,000
Mary's salary		$ 1,000	1,000	1,000	1,000	1,000	1,000	1,000	1,000	1,000	1,000	1,000	1,000	1,000
Bob's salary		$ 2,000	2,000	2,000	2,000	2,000	2,000	2,000	2,000	2,000	2,000	2,000	2,000	2,000
Total cash expenses for month		$ 13,750	46,250	21,700	18,400	75,600	32,800	56,000	46,000	80,000	90,000	34,000	20,000	20,000
Cash at end of month		$ 28,293	5,808	1,762	13,238	-20,265	11,441	19,946	96,166	138,386	92,521	78,891	79,261	98,303
Monthly cash flow = Cash receipts - cash expenses		$ 25,293	-22,485	-4,046	11,476	-33,502	31,705	8,505	76,220	42,220	-45,865	-13,630	370	19,043
Total annual cash flow January - December 2007		$ 70,011	<-- =SUM(D54:O54)											

64

Cash Flow Analysis

Bob's monthly cash flows are very different from his account balances:

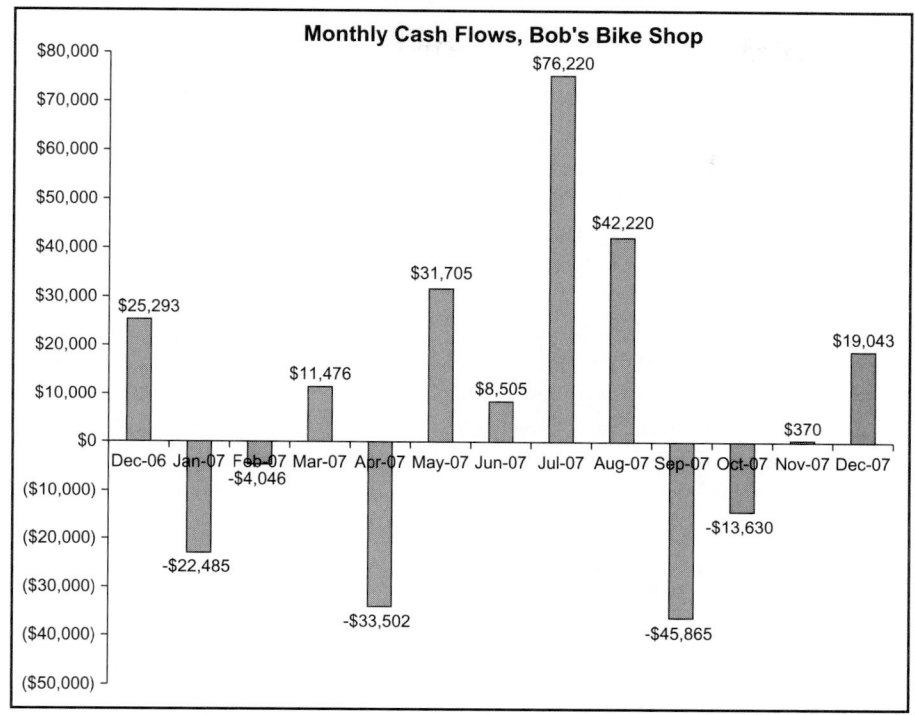

As you can see from the cash flow pattern, three of the months in which Bob pays taxes (January, April, and September) are very bad months. September is also a highly negative cash flow month because August is such a good month—this means that Bob has to pay for the bikes ordered in August in September.

4.5 Computing a Pro Forma Profit and Loss Statement

Bob can use the cash flow model to project an end-of-year profit and loss statement:

	A	B	C	D
59	**Pro Forma Profit and Loss for the Year**			
60	Sales	$ 610,761	<-- =SUM(D40:O40)	
61	Expenses			
62	Rent	$ 60,000	<-- =SUM(D43:O43)	
63	City taxes	$ 40,000	<-- =SUM(D44:O44)	
64	Bicycles	$ 274,800	<-- =SUM(D46:O46)	
65	Parts	$ 89,950	<-- =SUM(D47:O47)	
66	Mary's salary	$ 12,000	<-- =SUM(D48:O48)	
67	Profit before taxes	$ 134,011	<-- =B60-SUM(B62:B66)	
68	Income tax (25%)	$ 33,503	<-- =25%*B67	
69	Profit after tax	$ 100,508	<-- =B67-B68	
70				
71	Taxes already paid	$ 40,000	<-- =SUM(C45:O45)	
72	Taxes owing	$ -6,497	<-- =B68-B71	

This statement requires a bit of explanation:

- Bob's Bike Shop is not separately incorporated: All the cash from the shop is reported on his personal tax returns. Thus, the bike store's tax rate is Bob's own personal tax rate. In this model we've assumed that Bob pays a flat tax of 25% on his income. In actual fact, of course, the tax schedule would be graduated (see Exercise 5 at end of chapter).
- Cash versus accrual accounting. The profit and loss statement assumes that Bob pays taxes only on his *net cash receipts* during the course of the year. This is called *cash basis accounting* and is acceptable for small businesses. The most common accounting method for most companies, however, is accrual accounting (see Chapter 3).
- No depreciation? Most accounting statements include write-offs for depreciation (see Chapter 3). In the case of Bob's Bikes, there is no depreciation, since the bike store has no fixed assets.
- For tax purposes, Mary's salary is an expense to Bob's Bikes. However, since Bob is the owner, his salary is not an expense of the business. The pretax business profits of $134,011 are his personal income, on which he pays a 25% tax of $33,503 (cell B68).
- Bob's projected taxes for the year are $33,503 (cell B68), but he paid estimated quarterly taxes of $40,000. Thus, he can expect a tax refund of $6,497 (cell B72). Consequently, he could—after consulting his accountant—lower his estimated tax payments a bit.

4.6 Cash Management in a More Complex Business

The principles of cash management in a more complex business are similar to those illustrated for Bob's Bike Shop. A cash management model can still be built using Excel, though usually you will want to program each business or production unit separately. Figure 4.1 gives an

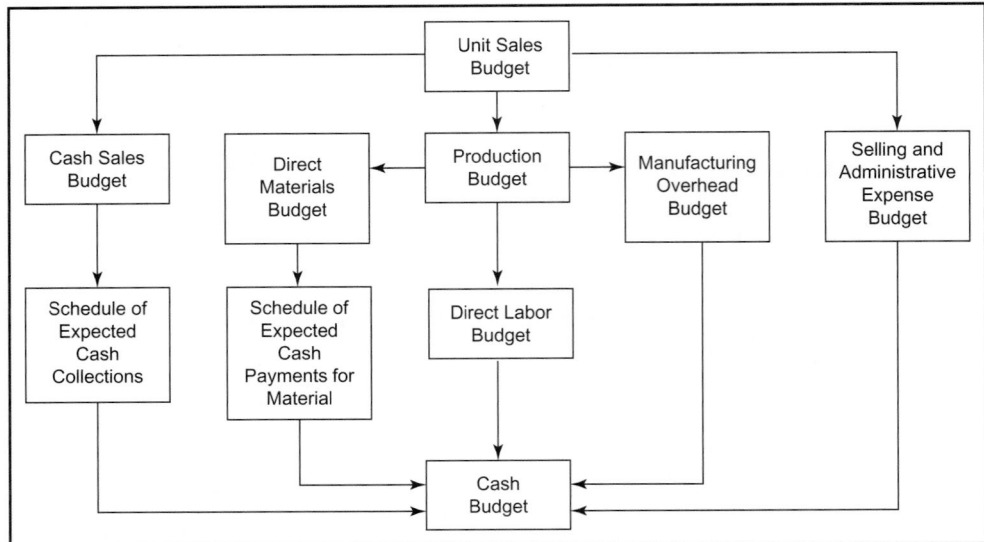

Figure 4.1 Constructing the cash budget in a large business. *Source:* Reprinted by permission from "Assessing New Venture Risk and Cash Budgeting with Simulation" (http://www.decisioneering. com/articles/barker.html) by David C. Barker, Supply Chain Management, Nevada, Inc. Charles R. Harrell (harrellc@byu.edu), Brigham Young University, Robert H. Todd (todd@byu.edu), Brigham Young University. http://www.decisioneering.com/articles/barker.html

illustration for a larger business. By following the reference, you can find an Excel spreadsheet that implements the model.

CONCLUSION

A cash management model is a vital tool to track the inflows and outflows of cash to the business. A cash management model makes it possible to predict the future cash balances of the business and so avoid crises caused by insolvency. Needless to say, Excel is the best tool available for building such a model!

EXERCISES

1. Use the following information and the spreadsheet to fill in the ??? for the Hotel California:
   - The hotel wishes to redecorate the penthouse floor. For this purpose, it will use its cash to finance a $350,000 investment in the second quarter.
   - The hotel will pay dividends of $200,000 to its shareholders at the last quarter of 2004.

	A	B	C	D	E	F
1	HOTEL CALIFORNIA CASH BUDGET					
2	Period	Q1	Q2	Q3	Q4	Year
3	Cash balance - beginning of the period	$ 220,000	???	???	???	???
4						
5	Cash income					
6	Cash payments during the period	$ 750,000	???	$ 760,000	$ 710,000	???
7	Total cash receipts	$ 970,000	$ 1,050,000	???	???	???
8						
9	Cash Expenses					
10	Payment to suppliers	$ 275,000	$ 300,000	???	$ 285,000	$ 1,150,000
11	Salary payments	$ 155,000	$ 175,000	???	???	$ 680,000
12	Other expenses	$ 70,000	$ 80,000	$ 81,000	???	$ 330,000
13	Redecoration expenses					
14	Taxes	$ 72,000	$ 66,000	???	$ 60,000	$ 280,000
15	Dividends	???	???	???	???	???
16	Total cash expenses	???	???	$ 646,000	???	???
17						
18	Net cash balance during the period	???	???	???	???	???

2. On 1 January you moved into an apartment. Calculate your monthly cash budget for the next year using the following information:
   - Your income is $8,000 each month.
   - Rent is $1,800 a month.
   - Food costs $1,200 a month. You are interested in organic food, which is more expensive; you estimate that your food expenses will grow by 2% each month.
   - You have to pay the following bills, payable every two months: city taxes, $675; electricity bill, $290; phone bill, $245; cable TV, $220.
   - Dog food costs $155 every three months. Every four months the dog goes to the veterinarian, who charges $130 for a visit.

- You own a car. Gas costs $450 each month. In addition, the car license and insurance cost $4,000 every year (paid in mid-July). The car goes to the garage every four months, which costs $460.
- You like to buy clothes, and you estimate that your monthly expenditure on clothes is $370.
- Every year your parents give you $2,000 for your birthday, which is in May.
- You go to night school, which costs $2,000 per month for the first eight months of the year.
- You estimate that your expenses for movies, restaurants, theater, and other entertainment are $420 each month.
- Your yearly vacation is in August, and you estimate its cost at $1,400.
- You have $500 in your bank account at the beginning of the year.

3. Repeat the previous exercise with the following assumptions:
   - Instead of renting an apartment, you decided to buy one. You found a lovely place and to finance the purchase you took a mortgage of $200,000 for fifteen years, with 8% annual interest rate paid monthly.
   - The bank pays you 0.5% interest on your cash balances and charges you 0.8% if you're in a cash deficit in your account. Assume the interest is paid on your cash balances at the beginning of each month.
   - After a closer look, you decided that the expense on clothes is too big. It's actually only $210 per month.

4. Let's go back to the Bob's Bike Shop example from the chapter. Bob realizes that one of the things his model ignores is the cost of having negative cash balances and the interest he can earn on positive cash balances. Adapt Bob's cash budget to this change, assuming he's paying 12% annual interest on his negative cash balances and that he gets 8% annual interest for his positive cash balances. Assume also that the interest is calculated each month on the average balances of that month and is paid at the beginning of the following month.

5. Let's take another look at Bob's Bike Shop. In the model presented in the chapter, we've assumed that Bob pays a flat tax rate of 25% on his income. In actual fact, the tax schedule is graduated. Assuming the tax schedule is like the one presented below, adapt Bob's model to this change.

	A	B
1	**TAX SCHEDULE, BOB'S BIKE SHOP**	
2	**Monthly income less than**	**Tax rate**
3	1,499	15%
4	2,499	25%
5	3,999	30%
6	5,999	35%
7	over 5,999	40%

6. The following Excel sheet presents the 2004 cash budget of Small-Town College. All the numbers are in thousands.

	A	B	C	D	E	F
1	SMALL-TOWN COLLEGE, CASH BUDGET					
2		Q1	Q2	Q3	Q4	Year
3	Beginning cash balance	$ 7,000				
4						
5	**Cash receipts**					
6	Cash collections	$ 390,000		$ 320,000		$ 1,410,000
7	**Cash on hand before payments**					
8						
9	**Cash payments**					
10	Salaries - administrative staff		$ 112,000	$ 105,000	$ 107,000	$ 437,000
11	Salaries - academic staff	$ 160,000		$ 140,000	$ 142,000	$ 605,000
12	Other costs	$ 50,000			$ 46,000	$ 177,000
13	Interest expense (on loan)					
14	Building construction					$ 70,000
15	Income taxes	$ 12,000	$ 16,000		$ 11,000	
16	**Total cash payments**		$ 321,000	$ 296,000		
17						
18	**Ending cash balance**					

Complete the college's cash budget using the following information:
- In the first quarter, the college plans a long-term investment of $70 million cash in new buildings for management and medicine studies.
- The college has an existing $40 million long-term loan, with a 10% interest rate. The interest rate is paid quarterly, and there are no payments of principal.

7. In 2005, a year after you successfully completed Small-Town College's cash budget, the college management turned to you again, requesting a cash budget for 2005. This time the management also mentioned it wishes to maintain a minimum quarterly cash balance of $5 million. In case of cash deficiency, the management policy is to borrow the amount needed in order to return to the minimum cash balance required. The interest rate on such a loan is 8% annually and calculated from the beginning of the quarter in which it's borrowed until the end of the fiscal year, as the principal and the interest rate are repaid. Use this information with the following adjusted cash balance to complete the college's cash budget for the year 2005.

	A	B	C	D	E	F
1	SMALL-TOWN COLLEGE, CASH BUDGET					
2		Q1	Q2	Q3	Q4	Year
3	Beginning Cash Balance	$ 5,000				
4						
5	**Cash receipts**					
6	Cash collections	$ 390,000		$ 320,000		$ 1,330,000
7	**Cash on hand before payments**	$ 395,000	$ 325,000			
8						
9	**Cash payments**					
10	Salaries - administrative staff		$ 112,000	$ 105,000	$ 107,000	$ 434,000
11	Salaries - academic staff	$ 160,000		$ 140,000	$ 142,000	$ 597,000
12	Other costs	$ 50,000			$ 46,000	$ 174,000
13	Interest expense (on loan)					
14	Building construction					$ 70,000
15	Income taxes	$ 12,000	$ 16,000		$ 11,000	
16	**Total cash payments**		$ 321,000	$ 296,000		
17						
18	**Net cash inflow**			$ 29,000		
19	Minimum cash balance	$ 5,000	$ 5,000	$ 5,000	$ 5,000	$ 5,000
20	**Cash surplus (deficit)**	$ -13,000		$ 24,000	$ 17,000	
21						
22	**Financing**					
23	Borrowing (beginning of quarter)			$ 0	$ 0	$ 14,000
24	Repayment of principal	$ 0	$ 0	$ 0	$ -14,000	$ -14,000
25	Interest (8% annually)					$ -1,100
26	**Net cost of financing**		$ 1,000	$ 0	$ -15,100	$ -1,100
27						
28	**Ending cash balance**					

8. You were asked by your cousin to help him prepare a cash budget for his family business, Amadeus Supermarket. In order to build the budget, he gave you the following information.

- The supermarket sales are 80% in cash, 20% in credit. You assume that credit accounts are all collected within 30 days from sale in the following month. For example, the accounts receivables of March are the result of the credit sales for February (20% of $40,000).

- Amadeus Supermarket treats cash discounts on purchases in the income statement as "other income."

- Amadeus's operating costs: Salaries are 18% of monthly sales, rent 7%, and other operating costs (excluding depreciation) 5%. Assume that these costs are paid each month. Depreciation is $1,500 per month.

- Purchases are 70% of next month's sales. A 2% discount is available if the payment is made within three days after purchase, and the supermarket policy is to take advantage of this discount.

- In March, $1,000 is spent for equipment and an additional $800 is to be spent in April.

- A minimum cash balance of $6,000 must be maintained. You assume that borrowing is effective at the beginning of the month and all repayments are made at the end of the month of repayment. Loans are repaid at the end of the quarter, and the interest rate is repaid at the same time. The interest rate is 12% per year.

Based on the information above, complete the tables in the following Excel sheet:

	A	B	C	D	E
1	**Cash Budget - Amadeus Supermarket**				
2	**Data**				
3	Sales in cash	80%			
4	Credit sales	20%			
5	Salaries as percentage of sales	18%			
6	Rent as percentage of sales	7%			
7	Operating costs as percentage of sales	5%			
8	Purchases as percentage of **next** month forecasted sales	70%			
9	Discount for cash payments of materials	2%			
10	Annual interest rate for minimum cash balance loans	12%			
11	Monthly interest rate	1.0%	<-- =B10/12		
12					
13	**Forecasted sales**				
14	February	$ 40,000			
15	March	$ 52,000			
16	April	$ 61,000			
17	May	$ 68,000			
18	June	$ 80,000			
19	July	$ 60,000			
20					
21	**Table 1: Monthly cash payments**	September	October	November	December
22	Forecasted sales		$ 61,000		
23	Credit sales		$ 12,200		
24	Cash sales				
25	Cash receipts				
26	Cash sales				
27	Collections from credit sales of previous month		$ 10,400		
28	Total cash receipts		$ 59,200		
29					
30	**Table 2: Monthly cash expenses from purchases**	October	November	December	Quarter
31	Purchases	$ 47,600			
32	2% cash discount	$ 952			
33	Total	$ 46,648			
34					
35	**Table 3: Cash expenses for operating costs**	October	November	December	Quarter
36	Salaries			$ 14,400	
37	Rent			$ 5,600	
38	Other operating costs			$ 4,000	
39	Total operating costs			$ 24,000	
40					
41	**Table 4: Total monthly cash expenses**	October	November	December	Quarter
42	Purchases	$ 46,648			
43	Cash operating costs	$ 18,300			
44	Equipment purchases	$ 1,000			
45	Total expenses	$ 65,948			
46					
47	**Table 5: Cash balance calculation**	October	November	December	Quarter
48	Cash receipts	$ 59,200			
49	Cash disbursements	$ 65,948			
50	Cash balance	$ -6,748			
51					
52	**Table 6: Financing requirement calculations**	October	November	December	Quarter
53	Beginning cash balance	$ 12,000			
54	+ Cash balance from operations				
55	Total cash				
56	Minimum cash balance	$ 6,000			
57	Surplus (deficit)				
58	Borrowing required				
59	Interest payments				
60	Borrowing repaid				
61	Ending cash balance				

9. (Continuation of previous exercise) Based on the information above, prepare an income statement for the second quarter using the income statement below:

	A	B
63	**INCOME STATEMENT--AMADEUS SUPERMARKET**	
64	**Sales**	
65	Cost of goods sold (70% of Sales)	
66	**Gross profit**	
67		
68	Operating expenses:	
69	Salaries	
70	Rent	
71	Other operating costs	
72	Depreciation (1,500 * 3 months)	
73		
74		
75	**Operating Income**	
76	Less: interest expense	
77	Add: purchase discounts	
78	**Income before Taxes**	

PART II

CAPITAL BUDGETING AND VALUATION

Chapters 5–10 contain the core of most introductory finance courses. These chapters are wholly self-contained. They teach

- Time value of money—net present value (NPV), internal rate of return (IRR)
- Pricing using IRR—real-world examples
- Capital budgeting
- Determining the discount rate
- Using the weighted average cost of capital (WACC)
- Financial planning models and valuation

Details and Outline

Chapter 5 addresses the basics of time value of money. We introduce the concepts of present and future value, net present value (NPV), and internal rate of return (IRR). Excel has functions that make all these calculations easier to do, and Chapter 5 both illustrates the concepts and shows you how to use the relevant Excel functions.

Chapter 6 stresses the uses of discounting and present value in making effective financial decisions. The examples are taken primarily from consumer math and cover credit cards, mortgages, and auto leasing. Along the way we also discuss multiple IRR and continuous compounding—all motivated by simple examples.

"Capital budgeting" is finance jargon for spending money on a specific project. Chapter 7 covers basic capital budgeting calculations. This chapter deals with the classic questions: making decisions using IRR versus NPV, choosing between projects with different life spans, mid-year versus end-year discounting, sunk costs, and reinvestment rates.

Chapter 8 discusses more advanced issues in capital budgeting, including several problems with using IRR as a decision criterion. It also shows you how to choose between projects with different lifetimes and how to discount cash flows that don't occur at year end (we call this "mid-year discounting"). Chapter 8 shows you how to incorporate taxes and inflation into the capital budgeting process.

A critical factor in time-value-of-money computations is the choice of the discount rate. Chapter 9 discusses how to compute a discount rate appropriate to both risk and tax considerations. This chapter shows you how to use the weighted average discount rate to calculate the value of a project.

Chapter 10 shows how to construct a financial planning model and how to use this model to value a firm. This is a topic that integrates much of the material in Chapters 2–9: A financial planning model combines both accounting and finance concepts to arrive at the valuation of the firm and its shares. This highly useful tool is the core of most business plans and valuations.

The Time Value of Money

OVERVIEW

This chapter deals with the most basic concepts in finance: future value, present value, net present value, and internal rate of return. These concepts tell you how much your money will grow if deposited in a bank (future value), how much promised future payments are worth today (present value), what an investment is worth (net present value), and what percentage rate of return you're getting on your investments (internal rate of return).

Financial assets and financial planning always have a time dimension. Here are some simple examples:

- You put $100 in the bank today in a savings account. How much will you have in three years?
- You put $100 in the bank today in a savings account and plan to add $100 every year for the next ten years. How much will you have in the account in twenty years?
- XYZ Corporation just sold a bond to your mother for $860. The bond will pay her $20 per year for the next five years. In six years she gets a payment of $1,020. Has she paid a fair price for the bond?
- Your Aunt Sara is considering making an investment. The investment costs $1,000 and will pay back $50 per month in each of the next 36 months. Should she do this or should she leave her money in the bank, where it earns 5%?

This chapter discusses these and similar issues, all of which fall under the general topic of *time value of money*. You will learn how compound interest causes invested income to grow (*future value*) and how money to be received at future dates can be related to money in hand today (*present value* and *net present value*). You will also learn how to calculate the compound rate of return earned by an investment (*internal rate of return*). The concepts of future value, present value, net present value, and internal rate of return underlie much of the financial analysis that appears in the following chapters.

As always, we use Excel, the best financial analysis tool!

Finance Concepts Discussed

- Future value
- Present value
- Net present value
- Internal rate of return
- Pension and savings plans and other accumulation problems

Excel Functions Used

- **PV, NPV, IRR, PMT, NPER**
- **Goal Seek**

5.1 Future Value

Future value is the value at some future date of a payment (or payments) made before this future date. The future value includes the interest earned on the payments.

Future value (FV) is a concept that relates the value in the future of money deposited in a bank account today and over time and left in the account to draw interest. Suppose, for example, that you put $100 in a savings account in your bank today and that the bank pays you 6% interest at the end of every year. If you leave the money in the bank for one year, you will have $106 after one year: $100 of the original savings balance + $6 in interest. The $106 is the *future value after one year of the initial deposit of $100 at 6% annual interest.*

Now suppose you leave the money in the account for a second year: At the end of this year, you will have

$106	The savings account balance at the end of the first year
+	
6% * $106 = $6.36	The interest on this balance for the second year
= $112.36	Total in account after two years

The $112.36 is the *future value after two years of the initial deposit of $100 at 6% annual interest.* Another way to express this is $112.36 = \$100 * (1 + 6\%)^2$:

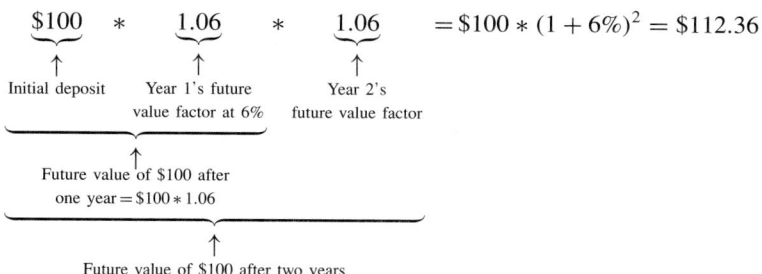

Notice that the future value uses the concept of *compound interest:* The interest earned in the first year ($6) itself earns interest in the second year. To sum up:

The future value of $X deposited today in an account paying $r\%$ interest annually and left in the account for n years is $FV = X * (1 + r)^n$.

NOTATION

In this book we often match our mathematical notation to that used by Excel. Since in Excel, multiplication is indicated by a star (*), we sometimes write $6\% * \$106 = \$6.36$, even though this is not necessary. Similarly, we sometimes write $(1.10)^3$ as 1.10^3.

Future value calculations are easily done in Excel:

	A	B	C
1	**CALCULATING FUTURE VALUES WITH EXCEL**		
2	Initial deposit	100	
3	Interest rate	6%	
4	Number of years, n	2	
5			
6	Account balance after n years	112.36	<-- =B2*(1+B3)^B4

Notice the use of the carat (^) to denote the exponent: In Excel, $(1 + 6\%)^2$ is written as **(1+B3)^B4**, where cell **B3** contains the interest rate and cell **B4** the number of years.

We can use Excel to make a table of how the future value grows with the years and then use Excel's graphing abilities to graph this growth:

	A	B	C	D	E	F	G
1	THE FUTURE VALUE OF A SINGLE $100 DEPOSIT						
2	Initial deposit	100					
3	Interest rate	6%					
4	Number of years, n	2					
5							
6	Account balance after n years	112.36	<-- =B2*(1+B3)^B4				
7							
8	Year	Future value					
9	0	100.00	<-- =$B$2*(1+$B$3)^A9				
10	1	106.00	<-- =$B$2*(1+$B$3)^A10				
11	2	112.36	<-- =$B$2*(1+$B$3)^A11				
12	3	119.10	<-- =$B$2*(1+$B$3)^A12				
13	4	126.25	<-- =$B$2*(1+$B$3)^A13				
14	5	133.82					
15	6	141.85					
16	7	150.36					
17	8	159.38					
18	9	168.95					
19	10	179.08					
20	11	189.83					
21	12	201.22					
22	13	213.29					
23	14	226.09					
24	15	239.66					
25	16	254.04					
26	17	269.28					
27	18	285.43					
28	19	302.56					
29	20	320.71					

Future Value of $100 at 6% Annual Interest

EXCEL NOTE

Notice that the formulas in cells B9 to B29 in the table have $ signs on the cell references (for example, $= \$B\$2 * (1 + \$B\$3)^{A9}$). This use of the *absolute copying* feature of Excel is explained in Chapter 27.

In the spreadsheet below, we present a table and graph that show the future value of a $100 deposit for three different interest rates: 0%, 6%, and 12%. As the spreadsheet shows, future value is *very* sensitive to the interest rate! Note that when the interest rate is 0%, the future value doesn't grow.

	A	B	C	D	E
1	**FUTURE VALUE OF A SINGLE DEPOSIT AT DIFFERENT INTEREST RATES** **How $100 at time 0 grows at 0%, 6%, 12%**				
2	Initial deposit	100			
3	Interest rate	0%	6%	12%	
4					
5	**Year**	**FV at 0%**	**FV at 6%**	**FV at 12%**	
6	0	100.00	100.00	100.00	<-- =$B$2*(1+D$3)^$A6
7	1	100.00	106.00	112.00	<-- =$B$2*(1+D$3)^$A7
8	2	100.00	112.36	125.44	
9	3	100.00	119.10	140.49	
10	4	100.00	126.25	157.35	
11	5	100.00	133.82	176.23	
12	6	100.00	141.85	197.38	
13	7	100.00	150.36	221.07	
14	8	100.00	159.38	247.60	
15	9	100.00	168.95	277.31	
16	10	100.00	179.08	310.58	
17	11	100.00	189.83	347.85	
18	12	100.00	201.22	389.60	
19	13	100.00	213.29	436.35	
20	14	100.00	226.09	488.71	
21	15	100.00	239.66	547.36	
22	16	100.00	254.04	613.04	
23	17	100.00	269.28	686.60	
24	18	100.00	285.43	769.00	
25	19	100.00	302.56	861.28	
26	20	100.00	320.71	964.63	
27					

Terminology: What's a Year? When Does It Begin?

While these questions may seem obvious, this is not the case. There's a lot of semantic confusion on this subject in finance courses and texts.

Throughout this book, we use the following as synonyms:

Year 0	Year 1	Year 2		
	End of	End of		
Today	year 1	year 2		
Beginning	**Beginning**	**Beginning**		
of year 1	**of year 2**	**of year 3**		
0	1	2	3	

To reiterate, the words "Year 0," "Today," and "Beginning of year 1" are synonyms. For example, "$100 at the beginning of year 2" is the same as "$100 at the end of year 1." If you're at a loss to understand what someone means, ask for a drawing; better yet, ask for an Excel spreadsheet.

Accumulation—Savings Plans and Future Value

In the previous example you deposited $100 and left it in your bank. Suppose that you intend to make ten annual deposits of $100, with the first deposit made in year 0 (today) and each succeeding deposit made at the end of years 1, 2, . . . , 9. The *future value* of all these deposits at the end of year 10 tells you how much you will have accumulated in the account. If you are saving for the future (whether to buy a car at the end of your college years or to finance a pension at the end of your working life), this is obviously an important and interesting calculation.

So how much will you have accumulated at the end of year 10? There's an Excel function for calculating this answer, which we discuss later; for the moment we set this problem up in Excel and do our calculation the long way, by showing how much we will have at the end of each year:

	A	B	C	D	E	F
1		**FUTURE VALUE WITH ANNUAL DEPOSITS** at beginning of year				
2	Interest	6%				
3					=$B$2*(C6+B6)	
4	=E5 / Year	**Account balance, beg. year**	**Deposit at beginning of year**	**Interest earned during year**	**Total in account at end of year**	
5	1	0.00	100.00	6.00	106.00	<-- =B5+C5+D5
6	2	106.00	100.00	12.36	218.36	<-- =B6+C6+D6
7	3	218.36	100.00	19.10	337.46	
8	4	337.46	100.00	26.25	463.71	
9	5	463.71	100.00	33.82	597.53	
10	6	597.53	100.00	41.85	739.38	
11	7	739.38	100.00	50.36	889.75	
12	8	889.75	100.00	59.38	1,049.13	
13	9	1,049.13	100.00	68.95	1,218.08	
14	10	1,218.08	100.00	79.08	1,397.16	
15						
16		Future value using Excel's FV function		$1,397.16	<-- =FV(B2,A14,-100,,1)	

For clarity, let's analyze a specific year: At the end of year 1 (cell E5), you've got $106 in the account. This is also the amount in the account at the beginning of year 2 (cell B6). If you now deposit another $100 and let the whole amount of $206 draw interest during the year, it will earn $12.36 interest. You will have $218.36 = (106 + 100) * 1.06 at the end of year 2.

	A	B	C	D	E
6	2	106.00	100.00	12.36	218.36

Finally, look at rows 13 and 14: At the end of year 9 (cell E13), you have $1,218.08 in the account; this is also the amount in the account at the beginning of year 10 (cell B14). You then deposited $100 and the resulting $1,318.08 earns $79.08 interest during the year, accumulating to $1,397.16 by the end of year 10.

	A	B	C	D	E
13	9	1,049.13	100.00	68.95	1,218.08
14	10	1,218.08	100.00	79.08	1,397.16

The Excel FV (Future Value) Function

The spreadsheet of the previous subsection illustrates in a step-by-step manner how money accumulates in a typical savings plan. To simplify this series of calculations, Excel has a **FV** function, which computes the future value of any series of constant payments. This function is illustrated in cell C16:

	B	C	D	E
16	Future value using Excel's FV function	$1,397.16 <-- =FV(B2,A14,-100,,1)		

The **FV** function and the inputs required can be computed using a dialog box—an important feature that comes with each Excel function. The Excel note that follows illustrates how to generate the dialog box for the computation in cell C16. If you already know how to use dialog boxes, here it is for this example:

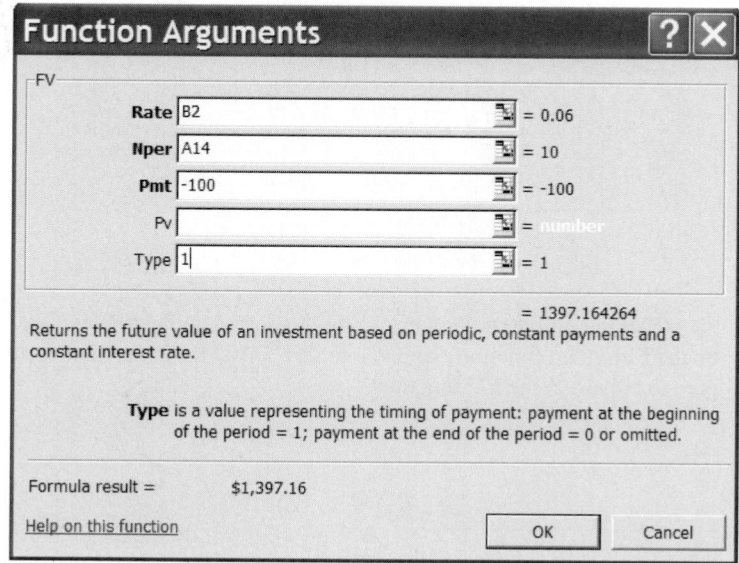

The **FV** function requires as inputs the **Rate** of interest, the number of periods **Nper,** and the annual payment **Pmt.** You can also indicate the **Type,** which tells Excel whether payments are made at the beginning of the period (type **1** as in our example) or at the end of the period (type **0**).[1] A detailed explanation of how to use the **FV** function is given in the Excel note which follows.

EXCEL NOTE

FUNCTIONS AND DIALOG BOXES

Cell C16 of the previous example contains the function **FV(B2,A14,-100,,1)**. In this note we illustrate the use of the dialog box for **FV** to generate this function.

The last part of this Excel note discusses why the payment of $100 is entered into this function as a negative number. This is a peculiarity of the **FV** function shared by many other Excel financial functions.

Going Through the Function Wizard

Suppose you're in cell C16 and you want to put the Excel function for future value in the cell. With the cursor in C16, you move your mouse to the f_x icon on the tool bar:

	A	B	C	D	E	F
		FUTURE VALUE WITH ANNUAL DEPOSITS				
1		at beginning of year				
2	Interest	6%			=$B$2*(C6+B6)	
3						
4	Year	Account balance, beg. year	Deposit at beginning of year	Interest earned during year	Total in account at end of year	
5	1	0.00	100.00	6.00	106.00	<-- =B5+C5+D5
6	2	106.00	100.00	12.36	218.36	<-- =B6+C6+D6
7	3	218.36	100.00	19.10	337.46	
8	4	337.46	100.00	26.25	463.71	
9	5	463.71	100.00	33.82	597.53	
10	6	597.53	100.00	41.85	739.38	
11	7	739.38	100.00	50.36	889.75	
12	8	889.75	100.00	59.38	1,049.13	
13	9	1,049.13	100.00	68.95	1,218.08	
14	10	1,218.08	100.00	79.08	1,397.16	
15						
16		Future value using Excel's FV function				

Clicking on the f_x icon brings up the dialog box below. We've chosen the **category** to be the **Financial** functions, and we've scrolled down in the next section of the dialog box to put the cursor on the **FV** function.

---

[1]Exercises 2 and 3 at the end of the chapter illustrate both cases.

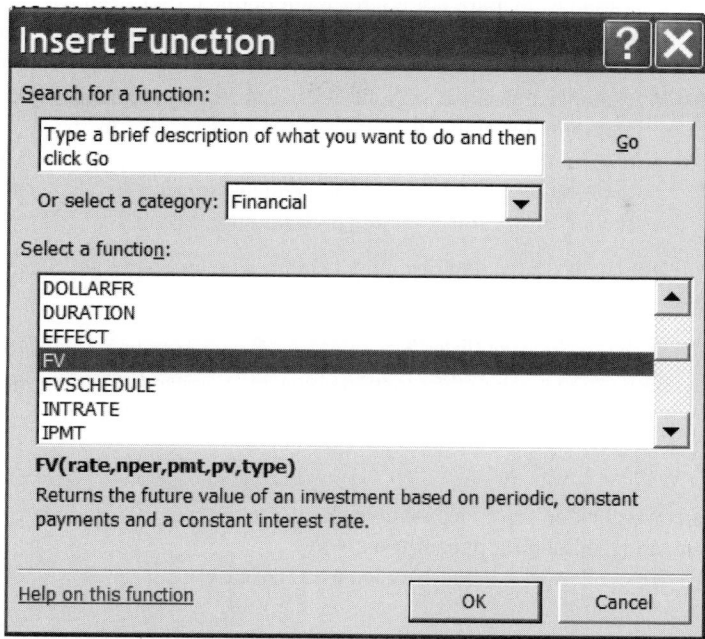

Clicking on **OK** brings up the dialog box for the **FV** function, which can now be filled in as illustrated below:

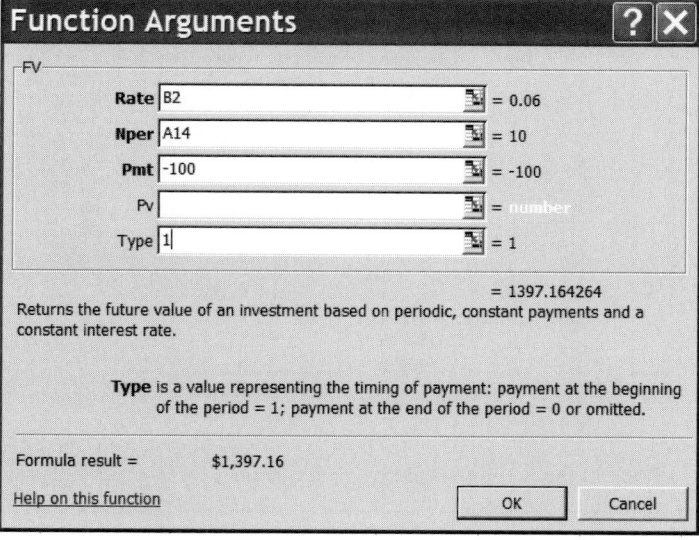

Excel's function dialog boxes have room for two types of variables.

- **Boldface** variables must be filled in—in the **FV** dialog box, these are the interest **Rate,** the number of periods **Nper,** and the payment **Pmt.** (Read on to see why we wrote a negative payment.)

contd.

- Variables that are not boldface are optional. For example, **Type** refers to when the payments are made and so has only two options—**1** when the payments are made at the beginning of the period and **0** when they are made at the end of the period. In the example above, we've indicated a **1** for the **Type;** this indicates (as shown in the dialog box itself) that the future value is calculated for payments made at the beginning of the period. Had we *omitted this variable* or put in **0**, Excel would compute the future value for a series of payments made at the end of the period; see the subsection of Section 5.1 entitled "Beginning Versus End of Period" for an illustration.

Notice that the dialog box already tells us (even before we click on **OK**) that the future value of $100 per year for ten years compounded at 6% is $1397.16.

A Short Way to Get to the Dialog Box

If you know the name of the function you want, you can just write it in the cell and then click the 𝑓ₓ icon on the tool bar. As illustrated below, you have to write

$$=\mathbf{FV(}$$

and then click on the 𝑓ₓ icon—note that we've written an **equal sign,** the **name of the function,** and the **opening parenthesis.**

Here's how the spreadsheet looks in this case:

	A	B	C	D	E	F
			FUTURE VALUE WITH ANNUAL DEPOSITS			
1			at beginning of year			
2	Interest	6%				
3					=$B$2*(C6+B6)	
4	=E5 → Year	Account balance, beg. year	Deposit at beginning of year	Interest earned during year	Total in account at end of year	
5	1	0.00	100.00	6.00	106.00	<-- =B5+C5+D5
6	2	106.00	100.00	12.36	218.36	<-- =B6+C6+D6
7	3	218.36	100.00	19.10	337.46	
8	4	337.46	100.00	26.25	463.71	
9	5	463.71	100.00	33.82	597.53	
10	6	597.53	100.00	41.85	739.38	
11	7	739.38	100.00	50.36	889.75	
12	8	889.75	100.00	59.38	1,049.13	
13	9	1,049.13	100.00	68.95	1,218.08	
14	10	1,218.08	100.00	79.08	1,397.16	
15						
16		Future value using Excel's FV function	=FV(			
17			FV(**rate**, nper, pmt, [pv], [type])			

Look in the text displayed by Excel below cell C16: As illustrated here, some versions of Excel show the format of the function when you type it in a cell.

One Further Option

You don't have to use a dialog box! If you know the format of the function, then just type in its variables and you're all set. In the example of Section 5.1, you could just type **=FV(B2,A14,−100,,1)** in the cell. Pressing Enter would give the answer.

Why Is the Pmt Variable a Negative Number?

In the **FV** dialog box, we've entered in the payment **Pmt** as a negative number, -100. The **FV** function has the peculiarity (shared by some other Excel financial functions) that a *positive* deposit generates a *negative* answer. We won't go into the (strange?) logic that produced this thinking; whenever we encounter it, we just put in a negative deposit.

Beginning Versus End of Period

In the example above, you make deposits of $100 at the *beginning* of each year. In terms of timing, your deposits are made at dates 0, 1, 2, 3, ... , 9. Here's a schematic way of looking at this, showing the future value of each deposit at the end of year 10:

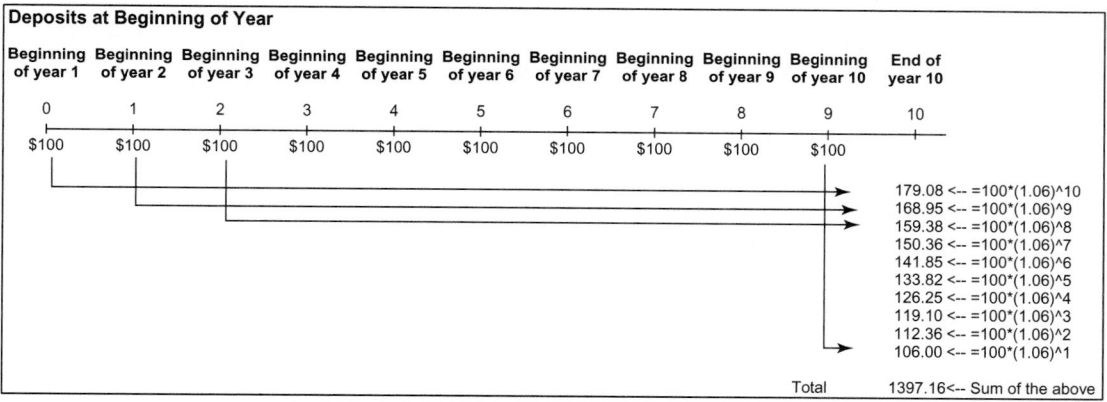

Suppose you made ten deposits of $100 at the *end of each year*. How would this affect the accumulation in the account at the end of ten years? The schematic diagram below illustrates the timing and accumulation of the payments:

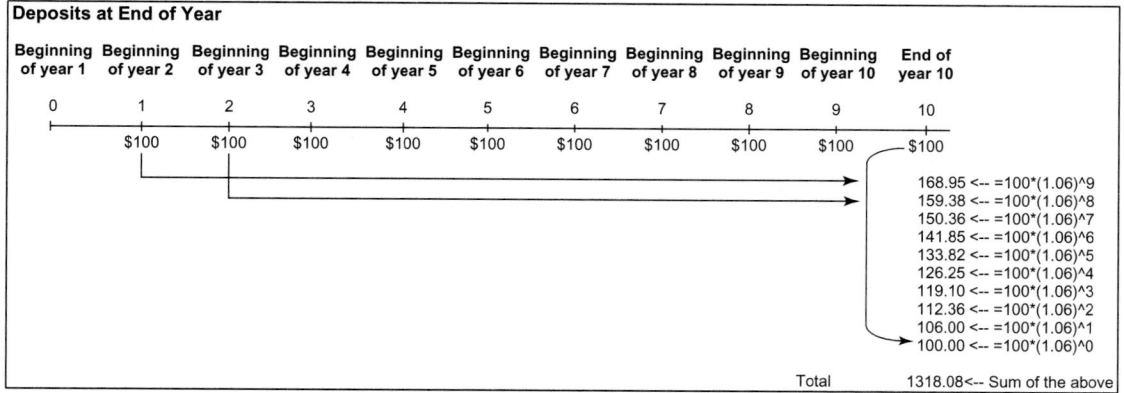

The account accumulation is less when you deposit at the end of each year than when you deposit at the beginning of the year. When you deposit at the end of each year, each deposit is in the account one year less and consequently earns one year's less interest. In a spreadsheet, this looks like the following:

	A	B	C	D	E	F
1		**FUTURE VALUE WITH ANNUAL DEPOSITS** **at end of year**				
2	Interest	6%			=$B$2*B6	
3						
4	=E5 Year	Account balance, beg. year	Deposit at end of year	Interest earned during year	Total in account at end of year	
5	1	0.00	100.00	0.00	100.00	<-- =B5+C5+D5
6	2	100.00	100.00	6.00	206.00	<-- =B6+C6+D6
7	3	206.00	100.00	12.36	318.36	
8	4	318.36	100.00	19.10	437.46	
9	5	437.46	100.00	26.25	563.71	
10	6	563.71	100.00	33.82	697.53	
11	7	697.53	100.00	41.85	839.38	
12	8	839.38	100.00	50.36	989.75	
13	9	989.75	100.00	59.38	1,149.13	
14	10	1,149.13	100.00	68.95	1,318.08	
15						
16		Future value	$1,318.08	<-- =FV(B2,A14,-100)		

Cell C16 illustrates the use of the Excel **FV** function to solve this problem. Here's the dialog box for the **FV** function in cell C16:

EXCEL NOTE

DIALOG BOX FOR FV WITH END-PERIOD PAYMENTS

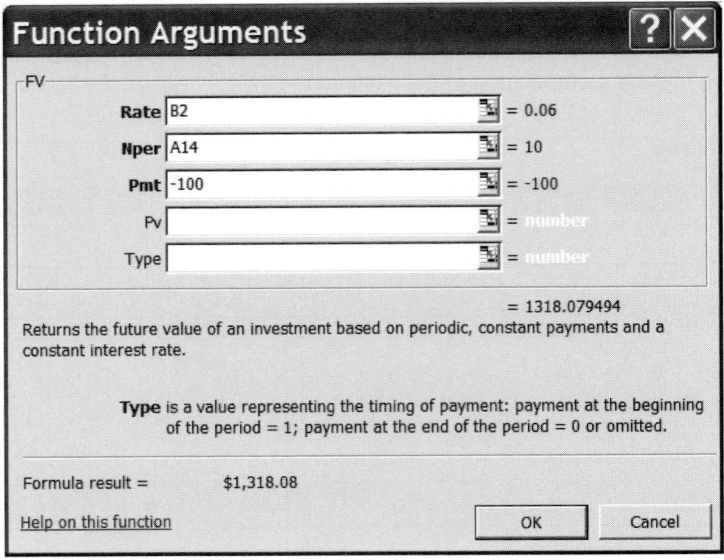

In the example above, we've omitted any entry in the **Type** box. We could have put a **0** in the **Type** box and gotten the same result.

Some Finance Jargon and the Excel FV Function

An *annuity* is a series of *equal* periodic payments made over a specified amount of time. Examples of annuities are widespread:

- The allowance your parents give you ($1,000 per month, for your next four years of college) is a monthly annuity with 48 payments.
- Pension plans often give the retiree a fixed annual payment for as long as he/she lives. This is a more complicated annuity, since the number of payments is uncertain.
- Certain kinds of loans are paid off in fixed, periodic (usually monthly, sometimes annual) installments. Mortgages and student loans are two examples.

An annuity with payments at the end of each period is often called a *regular annuity*. As you've seen in this section, the value of a regular annuity is calculated with **=FV(B2,A14,−100)**. An annuity with payments at the beginning of each period is often called an *annuity due,* and its value is calculated with the Excel function **=FV(B2,A14,−100,,1)**.

5.2 Present Value

The present value is the value today of a payment (or payments) that will be made in the future.

Here's a simple example: Suppose that you anticipate getting $100 in three years from your Uncle Simon, whose word is as good as a bank's. Suppose that the bank pays 6% interest on savings accounts. *How much is the anticipated future payment worth today?* The answer is $83.96 = $100/(1.06)^3$; if you put $83.96 in the bank today at 6% annual interest, then in three years you would have $100 (see the "proof" in rows 9 and 10).[2] The $83.96 is also called the *discounted or present value of $100 in three years at 6% interest.*

	A	B	C
1	**SIMPLE PRESENT VALUE CALCULATION**		
2	X, future payment	100	
3	n, time of future payment	3	
4	r, interest rate	6%	
5	Present value, $X/(1+r)^n$	83.96	<-- =B2/(1+B4)^B3
6			
7	**Proof**		
8	Payment today	83.96	
9	Future value in n years	100	<-- =B8*(1+B4)^B3

To summarize:

The present value of $X to be received in n years when the appropriate interest rate is $r\%$ is $X/(1+r)^n$.

The interest rate r is also called the *discount rate*. We can use Excel to make a table of how the present value decreases with the discount rate. As you can see—higher discount rates make

---

[2]Actually, $100/(1.06)^3 = 83.96193$, but we've used **Format|Cells|Number** to show only two decimals.

for lower present values:

	A	B	C	D	E	F	G	H
1	THE PRESENT VALUE OF $100 IN 3 YEARS in this example we vary the discount rate r							
2	X, future payment	100						
3	n, time of future payment	3						
4	r, interest rate	6%						
5	Present value, X/(1+r)^n	83.96	<-- =B2/(1+B4)^B3					
6								
7	Discount rate	Present value						
8	0%	100.00	<-- =100/(1+A8)^3					
9	1%	97.06	<-- =100/(1+A9)^3					
10	2%	94.23	<-- =100/(1+A10)^3					
11	3%	91.51	<-- =100/(1+A11)^3					
12	4%	88.90	<-- =100/(1+A12)^3					
13	5%	86.38						
14	6%	83.96						
15	7%	81.63						
16	8%	79.38						
17	9%	77.22						
18	12%	71.18						
19	15%	65.75						
20	18%	60.86						
21	20%	57.87						
22	22%	55.07						
23	25%	51.20						
24	30%	45.52						
25	35%	40.64						
26	40%	36.44						
27	45%	32.80						
28	50%	29.63						

Present Value of $100 to be Paid in 3 Years when Discount Rate Varies

Why Does PV Decrease as the Discount Rate Increases?

The Excel table above shows that the $100 Uncle Simon promises you in three years is worth $83.96 today if the discount rate is 6% but worth only $40.64 if the discount rate is 35%. The mechanical reason for this is that taking the present value at 6% means dividing by a smaller denominator than taking the present value at 35%:

$$83.96 = \frac{100}{(1.06)^3} > \frac{100}{(1.35)^3} = 40.64$$

The economic reason relates to future values: If the bank is paying you 6% interest on your savings account, you would have to deposit $83.96 today in order to have $100 in three years. If the bank pays 35% interest, then $40.64 today will grow to $100 in three years, since $40.64 * (1.35)^3 = $100.

What this short discussion shows is that the *present value is the inverse of the future value:*

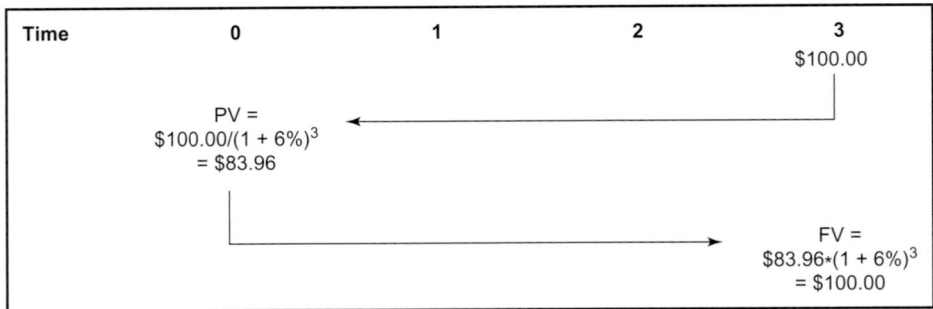

Present Value of an Annuity

Recall that an *annuity* is a series of equal periodic payments. The *present value* of an annuity tells you *the value today* of all the future payments on the annuity. Suppose you've been promised $100 at the end of each of the next five years. Assuming that you can get 6% at the bank, this promise is worth $421.24 today:

	A	B	C	D
1	**CALCULATING PRESENT VALUES WITH EXCEL**			
2	Annual payment	100		
3	r, interest rate	6%		
4				
5	Year	Payment at end of year	Present value of payment	
6	1	100	94.34	<-- =B6/(1+$B$3)^A6
7	2	100	89.00	<-- =B7/(1+$B$3)^A7
8	3	100	83.96	
9	4	100	79.21	
10	5	100	74.73	
11				
12	**Present value of all payments**			
13	Summing the present values		421.24	<-- =SUM(C6:C10)
14	Using Excel's PV function		421.24	<-- =PV(B3,5,-100)
15	Using Excel's NPV function		421.24	<-- =NPV(B3,B6:B10)

The example above shows three ways of getting the present value of $421.24:

- You can sum the individual discounted values. This is done in cell C13.
- You can use Excel's **PV** function, which calculates the present value of an annuity (cell C14).
- You can use Excel's **NPV** function (cell C15). This function calculates the present value of any series of periodic payments (whether they're flat payments, as in an annuity, or nonequal payments).

We devote separate subsections to the **PV** function and the **NPV** function.

The Excel PV Function

The **PV** function calculates the present value of an *annuity* (a series of equal payments). It looks a lot like the **FV** function discussed above, and, like **FV**, it also has the peculiarity that positive payments give negative results (which is why we set **Pmt** equal to −100). As in the case of the **FV** function, **Type** denotes whether the payments are made at the beginning or the end of the year. Because end-year is the default, you can either enter **0** or leave the **Type** entry blank (if the payment is at the beginning of the period, you have to enter **1** in the **Type** box):

EXCEL NOTE

DIALOG BOX FOR THE PV FUNCTION

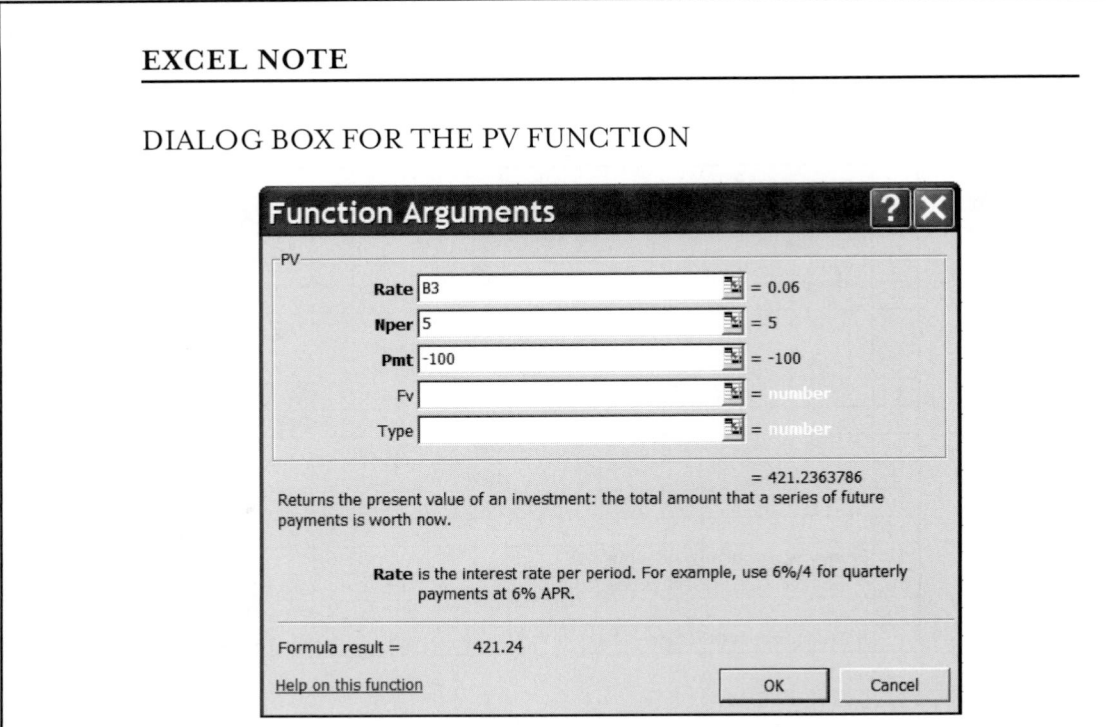

The "Formula result" in the dialog box shows that the answer is $421.24.

The Excel NPV Function

The **NPV** function computes the present value of a series of payments. The payments need not be equal, though in the current example they are. The ability of the **NPV** function to handle non-equal payments makes it one of the most useful of all Excel's financial functions. We make extensive use of this function throughout this book. In the current example, since the annual payments are equal, the result is the same ($421.24) whether we use the **PV** function or the **NPV** function.

Choosing a Discount Rate

We've defined the present value of $X to be received in n years as $X/(1 + r)^n$. The interest rate r in the denominator of this expression is also known as the *discount rate*. Why is 6% an appropriate discount rate for the money that Uncle Simon promised you? The basic principle is to choose a discount rate that is appropriate to the *riskiness* and the duration of the cash flows being discounted. Uncle Simon's promise of $100 per year for five years is assumed to be as good as the promise of your local bank, which pays 6% on its savings accounts. Therefore, 6% is an appropriate discount rate.[3]

---

[3]There's more to be said on the choice of a discount rate, but we postpone the discussion until Chapter 9.

EXCEL NOTE

DIALOG BOX FOR THE NPV FUNCTION

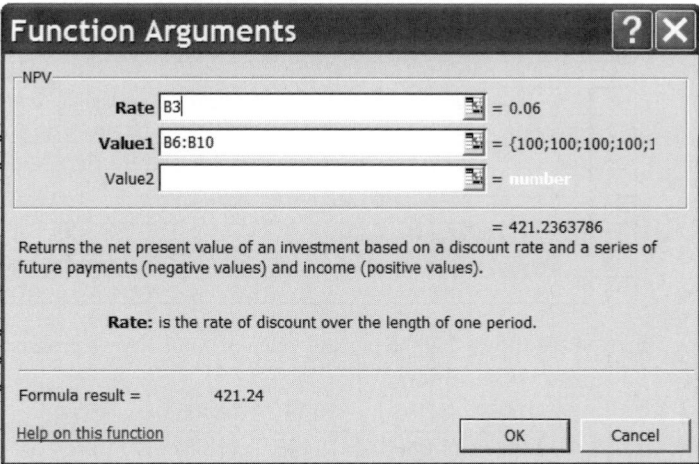

Excel's **NPV** function computes the present value of a series of payments. You can either enter the payments separately (as **Value1**, **Value2**, . . .) or—as illustrated above—enter a range of payments into the **Value1** box.

IMPORTANT NOTATION NOTE

Finance professionals use "NPV" to mean "net present value," a concept we explain in the next section. Excel's **NPV** function actually calculates the *present value* of a series of payments. Almost all finance professionals and textbooks would call the number computed by the Excel **NPV** function "PV." Thus, the Excel use of "NPV" differs from the standard usage in finance, which is explained in Section 5.3.

The Present Value of Nonannuity (Meaning Nonconstant) Cash Flows

The present value concept can also be applied to nonannuity cash flow streams, meaning cash flows that are not the same every period. Suppose, for example, that your Aunt Terry has promised to pay you $100 at the end of year 1, $200 at the end of year 2, $300 at the end of year 3, $400 at the end of year 4, and $500 at the end of year 5. This is not an annuity, and so it cannot be accommodated by the **PV** function. But we can find the present value of this promise by using the **NPV** function:

	A	B	C	D
1	**CALCULATING PRESENT VALUES WITH EXCEL**			
2	r, interest rate		6%	
3				
4	Year	**Payment at end of year**	**Present value**	
5	1	100	94.34	<-- =B5/(1+$B$2)^A5
6	2	200	178.00	<-- =B6/(1+$B$2)^A6
7	3	300	251.89	
8	4	400	316.84	
9	5	500	373.63	
10				
11	**Present value of all payments**			
12	Summing the present values		1,214.69	<-- =SUM(C5:C9)
13	Using Excel's NPV function		1,214.69	<-- =NPV($B$2,B5:B9)

The example shows that the present value of Aunt Terry's promised series of payments over the next five years is $1,214.69:

$$\frac{\$100}{1.06} + \frac{\$200}{(1.06)^2} + \frac{\$300}{(1.06)^3} + \frac{\$400}{(1.06)^4} + \frac{\$500}{(1.06)^5} = \$1,214.69$$

EXCEL NOTE

In the example above, we input the cash flows as a range B5:B9. We could also input the cash flows directly. Excel's **NPV** function allows you to input up to 29 payments directly in the function dialog box. Here's an illustration for the example above:

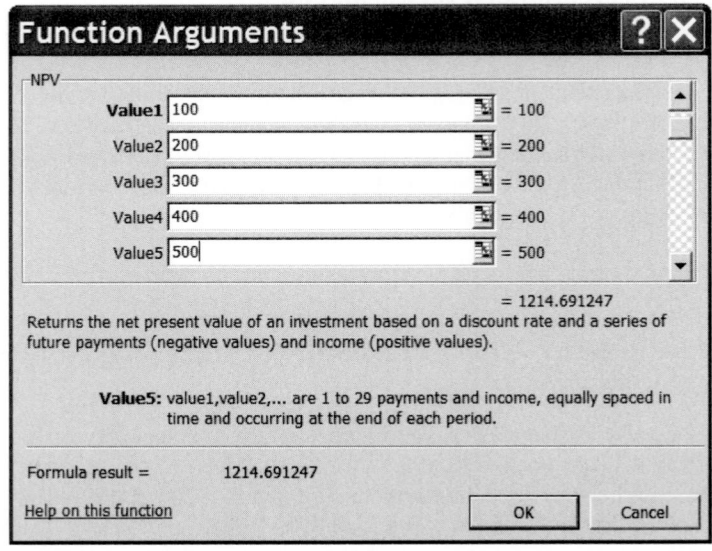

5.3 Net Present Value

The net present value (*NPV*) of a series of future cash flows is their present value minus the initial investment required to obtain the future cash flows. The *NPV* = *PV* of future cash flows − initial investment. The *NPV* of an investment represents the increase in wealth that you get if you make the investment.

Here's an example based on the spreadsheet on page 92. Would you pay $1,500 today to get the series of future cash flows in cells B5:B9? Certainly not—they're worth only $1,214.69, so why pay $1,500? If you were asked to pay $1,500, the NPV of the investment would be

$$NPV = \underbrace{-\$1,500}_{\substack{\uparrow \\ \text{Cost of the} \\ \text{investment}}} + \underbrace{\frac{100}{1.06} + \frac{200}{(1.06)^2} + \frac{300}{(1.06)^3} + \frac{400}{(1.06)^4} + \frac{500}{(1.06)^5}}_{\substack{\uparrow \\ \text{Present value of} \\ \text{investment's future} \\ \text{cash flows at discount} \\ \text{rate of 6\%}}}$$

$$= -\$1,500 + \quad\quad\quad\quad \$1,214.69 \quad\quad\quad\quad = \underbrace{-\$285.31}_{\substack{\uparrow \\ \text{Net present value}}}$$

If you paid $1,500 for this investment, you would be overpaying $285.31 for the investment, and you would be poorer by the same amount. That's a bad deal!

On the other hand, if you were offered the same future cash flows for $1,000, you'd snap up the offer, since you would be paying $214.69 less for the investment than its worth:

$$NPV = \underbrace{-\$1,000}_{\substack{\uparrow \\ \text{Cost of the} \\ \text{investment}}} + \underbrace{\$1,214.69}_{\substack{\uparrow \\ \text{Present value of} \\ \text{investment's future} \\ \text{cash flows at discount} \\ \text{rate of 6\%}}} = \underbrace{\$214.69}_{\substack{\uparrow \\ \text{Net present value}}}$$

In this case, the investment would make you $214.69 richer. As we said before, the NPV of an investment represents the increase in your wealth if you make the investment.

To summarize:

The net present value (NPV) of a series of cash flows is used to make investment decisions: An investment with a positive NPV is a good investment, and an investment with a negative NPV is a bad investment. An investment with a zero NPV is a "fair game"—the future cash flows of the investment exactly compensate you for the investment's initial cost.

Net present value (NPV) is a basic tool of financial analysis. It is used to determine whether a particular investment ought to be undertaken; in cases where we can make only one of several investments, it is the tool-of-choice to determine which investment to undertake.

Here's another NPV example: You've found an interesting investment—if you pay $800 today to your local pawnshop, the owner promises to pay you $100 at the end of year 1, $150 at the end of year 2, $200 at the end of year 3, . . . , $300 at the end of year 5. You feel that the pawnshop owner is as reliable as your local bank, which is currently paying 5% interest. The following spreadsheet shows the NPV of this $800 investment:

	A	B	C	D
1	CALCULATING NET PRESENT VALUE (NPV) WITH EXCEL			
2	r, interest rate	5%		
3				
4	Year	Payment	Present value	
5	0	-800	-800.00	
6	1	100	95.24	<-- =B6/(1+$B$2)^A6
7	2	150	136.05	<-- =B7/(1+$B$2)^A7
8	3	200	172.77	
9	4	250	205.68	
10	5	300	235.06	
11				
12	NPV			
13	Summing the present values		44.79	<-- =SUM(C5:C10)
14	Using Excel's NPV function		44.79	<-- =NPV($B$2,B6:B10)+C5

The spreadsheet shows that the value of the investment—the *net present value* (*NPV*) of its payments, including the initial payment of $-\$800$—is \$44.79:

$$NPV = -800 + \underbrace{\frac{100}{(1.05)} + \frac{150}{(1.05)^2} + \frac{200}{(1.05)^3} + \frac{250}{(1.05)^4} + \frac{300}{(1.05)^5}}_{\substack{\text{The } present\ value \text{ of the future payments:} \\ \text{Calculated with Excel } \textbf{NPV} \text{ function} = 844.79}} = 44.79$$

At a 5% discount rate, you should make the investment, since its NPV is \$44.79, which is positive.

EXCEL NOTE

As mentioned on page 91, the Excel **NPV** function's name does **not correspond** to the standard finance use of the term "net present value."[4] In finance, "present value" usually refers to the value today of future payments (in the previous example, the present value is

$$\frac{100}{(1.05)} + \frac{150}{(1.05)^2} + \frac{200}{(1.05)^3} + \frac{250}{(1.05)^4} + \frac{300}{(1.05)^5} = 844.79).$$ Finance professionals use

net present value (NPV) to mean the *present value* of future payments *minus the cost of the initial payment;* in the previous example, this is \$844.79 − \$800 = \$44.79. In this book, we use the term "net present value" (NPV) to mean its true finance sense. The Excel function **NPV** will always appear in boldface. We trust that you will rarely be confused.

---

[4]There's a long history to this confusion, and it doesn't start with Microsoft. The original spreadsheet—Visicalc—(mistakenly) used "NPV" in the sense Excel still uses today; this misnomer has been copied ever since by all other spreadsheets: Lotus, Quattro, and Excel.

NPV Depends on the Discount Rate

Let's revisit the pawnshop example on page 94 and use Excel to create a table that shows the relation between the discount rate and the NPV. As the graph below shows, the higher the discount rate, the lower the net present value of the investment:

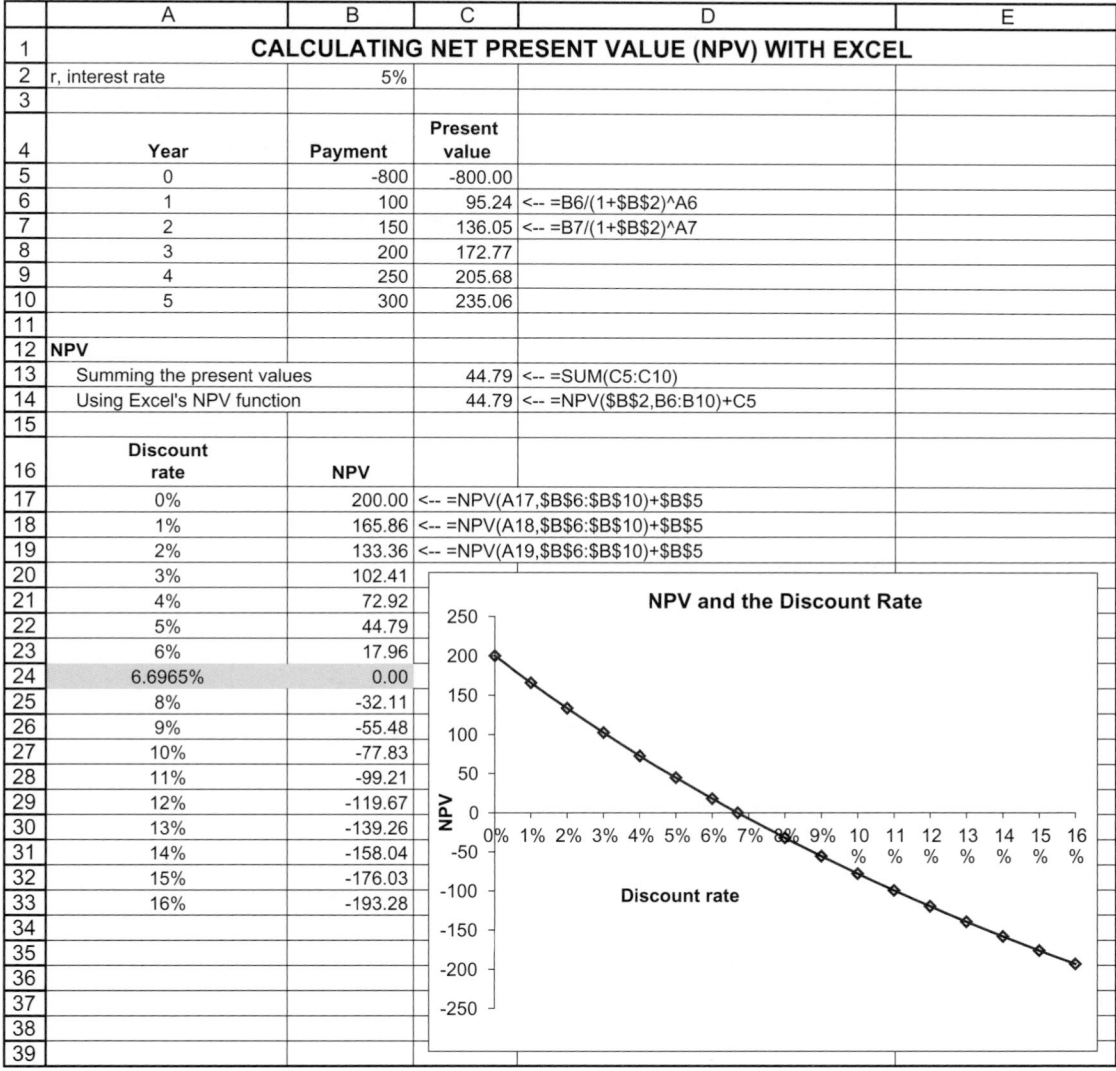

	A	B	C	D	E
1	CALCULATING NET PRESENT VALUE (NPV) WITH EXCEL				
2	r, interest rate	5%			
3					
4	Year	Payment	Present value		
5	0	-800	-800.00		
6	1	100	95.24	<-- =B6/(1+$B$2)^A6	
7	2	150	136.05	<-- =B7/(1+$B$2)^A7	
8	3	200	172.77		
9	4	250	205.68		
10	5	300	235.06		
11					
12	NPV				
13	Summing the present values		44.79	<-- =SUM(C5:C10)	
14	Using Excel's NPV function		44.79	<-- =NPV($B$2,B6:B10)+C5	
15					
16	Discount rate		NPV		
17	0%		200.00	<-- =NPV(A17,$B$6:$B$10)+$B$5	
18	1%		165.86	<-- =NPV(A18,$B$6:$B$10)+$B$5	
19	2%		133.36	<-- =NPV(A19,$B$6:$B$10)+$B$5	
20	3%		102.41		
21	4%		72.92		
22	5%		44.79		
23	6%		17.96		
24	6.6965%		0.00		
25	8%		-32.11		
26	9%		-55.48		
27	10%		-77.83		
28	11%		-99.21		
29	12%		-119.67		
30	13%		-139.26		
31	14%		-158.04		
32	15%		-176.03		
33	16%		-193.28		
34					
35					
36					
37					
38					
39					

Note that we've highlighted a special discount rate: When the discount rate is 6.6965%, the net present value of the investment is zero. The 6.6965% rate is referred to as the *internal rate of return (IRR)*. For discount rates less than the IRR, the net present value is positive; for discount rates greater than the IRR, the net present value is negative. We discuss the IRR in more detail in Section 5.4.

Using NPV to Choose Between Investments

In the examples discussed thus far, we've used NPV only to choose whether or not to undertake a particular investment. But NPV can also be used to choose between investments. Look at the following spreadsheet: You have $800 to invest, and you've been offered the choice between Investment A and Investment B. The spreadsheet below shows that at an interest rate of 15%, you should choose Investment B because it has a higher net present value. Investment A will increase your wealth by $219.06, whereas Investment B increases your wealth by $373.75.

	A	B	C	D
1	USING NPV TO CHOOSE BETWEEN INVESTMENTS			
2	Discount rate	15%		
3				
4	Year	Investment A	Investment B	
5	0	-800	-800	
6	1	250	600	
7	2	500	200	
8	3	200	100	
9	4	250	500	
10	5	300	300	
11				
12	NPV	219.06	373.75	<-- =NPV(B2,C6:C10)+C5

To summarize:

In using the NPV to choose between two positive-NPV investments, we choose the investment with the higher NPV.

TERMINOLOGY–IS IT A *DISCOUNT RATE* OR AN *INTEREST RATE?*

In some of the examples above, we've used *discount rate* instead of *interest rate* to describe the rate used in the net present value calculation. As you will see in further chapters of this book, the rate used in the NPV has several synonyms: discount rate, interest rate, cost of capital, opportunity cost—these are but a few of the names for the rate that appears in the denominator of the NPV:

$$\frac{Cash\ flow\ in\ year\ t}{(1+r)^t}$$

$\uparrow$

Discount rate
Interest rate
Cost of capital
Opportunity cost

5.4 Internal Rate of Return (IRR)

The IRR of a series of cash flows is the discount rate that sets the net present value of the cash flows equal to zero.

Before we explain in depth (in the next section) why you want to know the IRR, we explain how to compute it. Let's go back to the example on page 94: If you pay $800 today to your local pawnshop, the owner promises to pay you $100 at the end of year 1, $150 at the end of year 2, $200 at the end of year 3, $250 at the end of year 4, and $300 at the end of year 5. Discounting these cash flows at rate r, the NPV can be written

$$NPV = -800 + \frac{100}{(1+r)} + \frac{150}{(1+r)^2} + \frac{200}{(1+r)^3} + \frac{250}{(1+r)^4} + \frac{300}{(1+r)^5}$$

In cells B16 to B32 of the spreadsheet below, we calculate the NPV for various discount rates. As you can see, somewhere between $r = 6\%$ and $r = 7\%$, the NPV becomes negative.

	A	B	C	D
1		CALCULATING THE IRR WITH EXCEL		
2	r, interest rate	6.6965%		
3				
4	Year	Payment		
5	0	-800		
6	1	100		
7	2	150		
8	3	200		
9	4	250		
10	5	300		
11				
12	NPV	0.00	<-- =NPV(B2,B6:B10)+B5	
13	IRR	6.6965%	<-- =IRR(B5:B10)	
14				
15	Discount rate	NPV		
16	0%	200.00	<-- =NPV(A16,$B$6:$B$10)+$B$5	
17	1%	165.86	<-- =NPV(A17,$B$6:$B$10)+$B$5	
18	2%	133.36	<-- =NPV(A18,$B$6:$B$10)+$B$5	
19	3%	102.41		
20	4%	72.92		
21	5%	44.79		
22	6%	17.96		
23	7%	-7.65		
24	8%	-32.11		
25	9%	-55.48		
26	10%	-77.83		
27	11%	-99.21		
28	12%	-119.67		
29	13%	-139.26		
30	14%	-158.04		
31	15%	-176.03		
32	16%	-193.28		
33				
34				
35				

NPV and the Discount Rate

In cell B13, we use Excel's **IRR** function to calculate the exact discount rate at which the NPV becomes 0. The answer is 6.6965%; at this interest rate, the NPV of the cash flows equals zero (look at cell B12). We can use the dialog box for the Excel **IRR** function.

EXCEL NOTE

DIALOG BOX FOR **IRR** FUNCTION

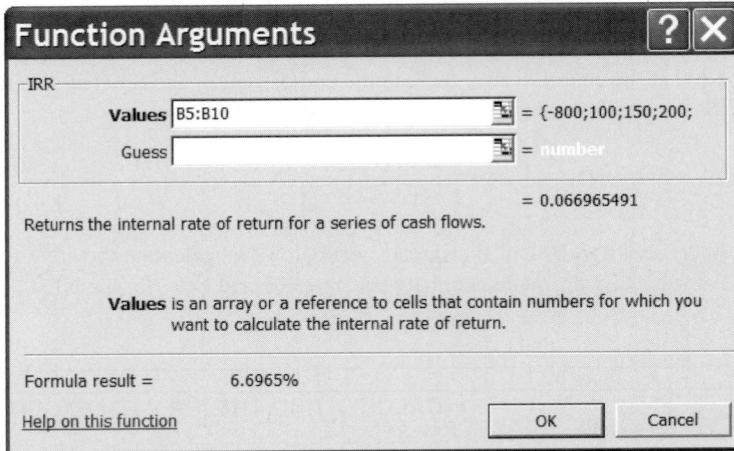

Notice that we haven't used the second option ("Guess") to calculate our IRR. We discuss this option in Chapter 8.

What Does the IRR Mean?

Suppose you could get 6.6965% interest at the bank and suppose you wanted to save today to provide yourself with the future cash flows of the example on page 94:

- To get $100 at the end of year 1, you would have to put the present value $100/1.06965 = $93.72 in the bank today.
- To get $150 at the end of year 2, you would have to put its present value $150/(1.06965)^2 = $131.76 in the bank today.
- And so on . . . (see the picture below).

The total amount you would have to save is $800, exactly the cost of this investment opportunity. This is what we mean when we say that

The internal rate of return is the compound interest rate you earn on an investment.

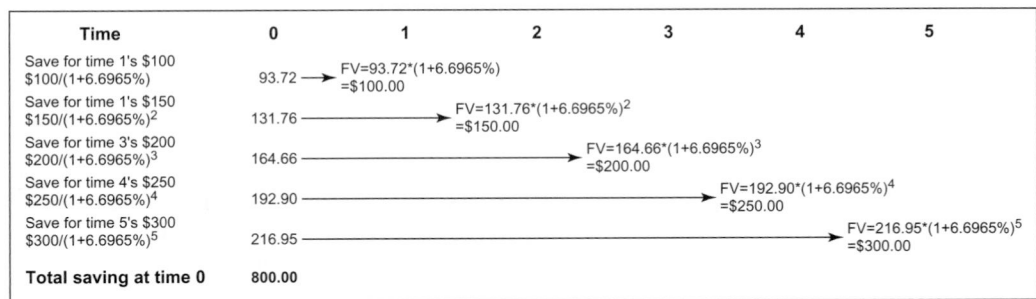

Using IRR to Make Investment Decisions

The IRR is often used to make investment decisions. Suppose your Aunt Sara has been offered the following investment by her broker: For a payment of $1,000, a reputable finance company will pay her $300 at the end of each of the next four years. Aunt Sara is currently getting 5% on her bank savings account. Should she withdraw her money from the bank to make the investment? To answer the question, we compute the IRR of the investment and compare it to the bank interest rate:

	A	B	C
1	**USING IRR TO MAKE INVESTMENT DECISIONS**		
2	Year	Cash flow	
3	0	-1,000	
4	1	300	
5	2	300	
6	3	300	
7	4	300	
8			
9	IRR	7.71%	<-- =IRR(B3:B7)

The IRR of the investment, 7.71%, is greater than the 5% Sara can earn on her alternative investment (the bank account). Thus, she should make the investment.

To summarize:

In using the IRR to make investment decisions, an investment with an IRR greater than the alternative rate of return is a good investment, and an investment with an IRR less than the alternative rate of return is a bad investment.

Using IRR to Choose Between Two Investments

We can also use the internal rate of return to choose between two investments. Suppose you've been offered two investments. Both Investment A and Investment B cost $1,000, but they have different cash flows. If you're using the IRR to make the investment decision, then you would choose the investment with the *higher* IRR. Here's an example:

	A	B	C	D
1	**USING IRR TO CHOOSE BETWEEN INVESTMENTS**			
2	Year	**Investment A cash flows**	**Investment B cash flows**	
3	0	-1,000.00	-1,000.00	
4	1	450.00	550.00	
5	2	425.00	300.00	
6	3	350.00	475.00	
7	4	450.00	200.00	
8				
9	IRR	24.74%	22.26%	<-- =IRR(C3:C7)

You should choose Investment A, which has the higher IRR.

To summarize:

In using the IRR to choose between two comparable investments, we choose the investment that has the higher IRR. This assumes that (1) both investments have an IRR greater than the alternative rate, and (2) the investments are of comparable risk.

USING NPV AND IRR TO MAKE INVESTMENT DECISIONS

In this chapter we have now developed two tools, NPV and IRR, for making investment decisions. We've also discussed two kinds of investment decisions. Here's a summary:

	"Yes or No": Choosing Whether to Undertake a Single Investment	"Investment Ranking": Comparing Two Investments That Are Mutually Exclusive
NPV criterion	The investment should be undertaken if its NPV > 0.	Investment A is preferred to Investment B if NPV(A) > NPV(B).
IRR criterion	The investment should be undertaken if its IRR > r, where r is the appropriate discount rate.	Investment A is preferred to Investment B if IRR(A) > IRR(B).

In Chapter 7 we discuss further implementation of these two rules and two decision problems.

5.5 What Does IRR Mean? Loan Tables and Investment Amortization

In the previous section we gave a simple illustration of what we meant when we said that *the internal rate of return (IRR) is the compound interest rate that you earn on an asset.* This short sentence underlies a slew of finance applications: When finance professionals discuss the "rate of return" on an investment or the "effective interest rate" on a loan, they are almost always refering to the IRR. In this section we explore some meanings of the IRR. Almost the whole of Chapter 6 is devoted to this topic.

A Simple Example

Suppose you buy an asset for $200 today, and suppose that the asset will pay you $300 in one year. Then the asset's IRR is 50%. To see this, recall that the IRR is the interest rate that makes the NPV zero. Since the investment NPV $= -200 + 300/(1 + r)$, this means that the NPV is zero when $1 + r = 300/200 = 1.5$. Solving this equation gives $r = 50\%$.

Here's another way to think about this investment and its 50% IRR:

- At time zero, you pay $200 for the investment.
- At time one, the $300 investment cash flow repays the initial $200. The remaining $100 represents a 50% return on the initial $200 investment. This is the IRR.

The IRR is the rate of return on an investment; it is the rate that repays, over the life of the asset, the initial investment in the asset and pays interest on the outstanding investment balances.

A More Complicated Example

We now give a more complicated example that illustrates the same point. This time, you buy an asset costing $200. The asset's cash flows are $130.91 at the end of year 1 and $130.91 at the end of year 2. Here's our IRR analysis of this investment:

	A	B	C	D	E	F
1	THE IRR AS A RATE OF RETURN ON AN INVESTMENT					
2	IRR	20.00%	<-- =IRR({-200,130.91,130.91})			
3	Year	Investment at beginning of year	Payment at end of year	Part of payment which is interest	Part of payment which is repayment of principal	
4	1	200.00	130.91	40.00	90.91	
5	2	109.09	130.91	21.82	109.09	
6	3	0.00				
7						
8	=B4-E4			=$B$2*B4	=C4-D4	
9						
10			=B5-E5			
11				=$B$2*B5		=C5-D5

- The IRR for the investment is 20.00%. Note how we calculated this—we simply typed into cell B2 the formula **=IRR({−200,130.91,130.91})** (if you're going to use this method of calculating the IRR in Excel, you have to put the cash flows in the curly brackets).
- Using the 20% IRR, $40.00 (= 20% ∗ $200) of the first year's payment is interest, and the remainder—$90.91—is repayment of principal. Another way to think of the $40.00 is to consider that to buy the asset, you gave the seller the $200 cost of the asset. When he pays you $130.91 at the end of the year, $40 (= 20% ∗ $200) is interest—your payment for allowing someone else to use your money. The remainder, $90.91, is a partial repayment of the money lent out.
- This leaves the outstanding principal at the beginning of year 2 as $109.09. Of the $130.91 paid out by the investment at the end of year 2, $21.82 (= 20% ∗ 109.09) is interest, and the rest (*exactly* $109.09) is repayment of principal.
- The outstanding principal at the beginning of year 3 (the year *after* the investment finishes paying out) is *zero*.

As in the first example of this section, the IRR is the rate of return on the investment—defined as the rate that repays, over the life of the asset, the initial investment in the asset and pays interest on the outstanding investment balances.

USING FUTURE VALUE, NET PRESENT VALUE, AND INTERNAL RATE OF RETURN—THE REST OF THE CHAPTER

In the remaining sections, we apply the concepts learned in the chapter to solve several common problems:

- Sections 5.6–5.8: Saving for the future
- Section 5.9: Paying off a loan with "flat" payments of interest and principal
- Section 5.10: How long does it take to pay off a loan?

5.6 Saving for the Future: Buying a Car for Mario

Mario has his eye on a car that costs $20,000. He wants to buy a car in two years. He plans to open a bank account and to deposit $X today and $X in one year. Balances in the account will earn 8%. How much does Mario need to deposit so that he has $20,000 in two years? In this section we'll show you that

> In order to finance future consumption with a savings plan, the net present value of all the cash flows has to be zero. In the jargon of finance—the future consumption plan is <u>fully funded</u> if the net present value of all the cash flows is zero.

In order to see this, start with a graphical representation of what happens:

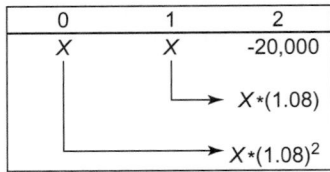

In year 2, Mario will have accumulated $X * (1.08) + X * (1.08)^2$. This should finance the $20,000 car, so that

$$\underbrace{X * (1.08) + X * (1.08)^2}_{\substack{\uparrow \\ \text{Future value of} \\ \text{deposits in 2 years}}} = \underbrace{20{,}000}_{\substack{\uparrow \\ \text{Desired accumulation}}}$$

Now subtract the $20,000 from both sides of the equation and divide by $(1.08)^2$:

$$\underbrace{X + \frac{X}{(1.08)} - \frac{20{,}000}{(1.08)^2}}_{\substack{\uparrow \\ \text{Net present value} \\ \text{of all cash flows}}} = 0$$

If you were to actually solve this equation, you would find that $X = \$8,903.13$. In order to fully fund the future purchase of the car, Mario has to deposit $8,903.13 today and another $8,903.13 one year from now. If he does this, the net present value of all the payments is zero:

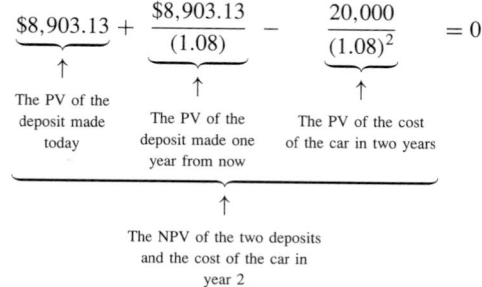

$$\underbrace{\$8,903.13}_{\substack{\uparrow \\ \text{The PV of the} \\ \text{deposit made} \\ \text{today}}} + \underbrace{\frac{\$8,903.13}{(1.08)}}_{\substack{\uparrow \\ \text{The PV of the} \\ \text{deposit made one} \\ \text{year from now}}} - \underbrace{\frac{20,000}{(1.08)^2}}_{\substack{\uparrow \\ \text{The PV of the cost} \\ \text{of the car in two years}}} = 0$$

The NPV of the two deposits
and the cost of the car in
year 2

Excel Solution

Of course, this same solution is easily reached using Excel:

	A	B	C	D	E
1	**HELPING MARIO SAVE FOR A CAR**				
2	Deposit, X	8,903.13			
3	Interest rate	8.00%			
4	**Year**	**In bank, before deposit**	**Deposit or withdrawal**	**Total at beginning of year**	**End of year with interest**
5	0	0.00	8,903.13	8,903.13	9,615.38
6	1	9,615.38	8,903.13	18,518.52	20,000.00
7	2	20,000.00	(20,000.00)	0.00	0.00
8					
9		NPV of all deposits and payments		$0.00	<-- =C5+NPV(B3,C6:C7)

If Mario deposits $8,903.13 in years 0 and 1, then the accumulation in the account at the beginning of year 2 will be exactly $20,000 (cell B7). The NPV of all the payments (cell C9) is zero.

In the next section, we discuss three methods for solving Mario's savings problem.

5.7 Solving Mario's Savings Problem: Three Solutions

We can solve Mario's savings problem by using one of three methods: trial and error, Excel's **Goal Seek,** and a formula set up in Excel. These three methods are illustrated in this section.

Method 1: Trial and Error

You can "play" with the spreadsheet, adjusting cell B2 until cell C9 equals zero. For example, if you put $5,000 into cell B2, you see that the NPV in cell C9 is negative, indicating that

Mario is saving too little:

	A	B	C	D	E
1			**HELPING MARIO SAVE FOR A CAR**		
2	Deposit, X	5,000.00			
3	Interest rate	8.00%			
4	**Year**	**In bank, before deposit**	**Deposit or withdrawal**	**Total at beginning of year**	**End of year with interest**
5	0	0.00	5,000.00	5,000.00	5,400.00
6	1	5,400.00	5,000.00	10,400.00	11,232.00
7	2	11,232.00	(20,000.00)	(8,768.00)	(9,469.44)
8					
9		NPV of all deposits and payments	($7,517.15)	<-- =C5+NPV(B3,C6:C7)	

If you put $10,000 into cell B2, cell C9 will be positive; this indicates that the answer is somewhere between $5,000 and $10,000. By trial and error you can reach the correct solution.

Method 2: Excel's Goal Seek

Goal Seek is an Excel function that looks for a specific number in one cell by adjusting the value of a different cell (for a discussion of how to use **Goal Seek**, see Chapter 32). To solve Mario's problem, we can use **Goal Seek** to set cell C9 equal to 0. After selecting **Tools|Goal Seek**, we fill in the dialog box as shown below:

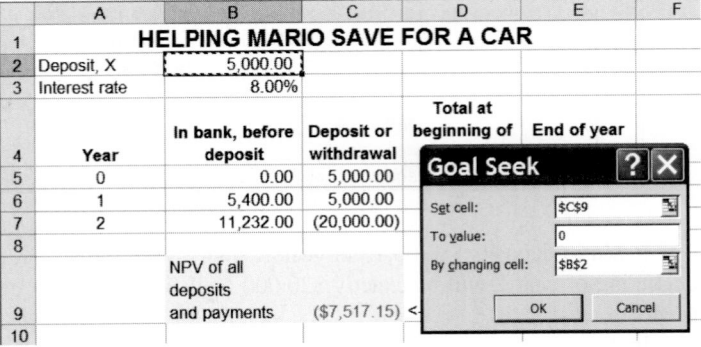

When we press **OK, Goal Seek** will find the solution of $8,903.13.

Method 3: Excel's PV Function

Method 3 is more theoretical than either Method 1 or 2. It is also the most compact. If you deal with many problems of this type, you will certainly want to understand it and use it.

As shown in Section 5.6, to solve Mario's problem, we have to solve the equation

$$\underbrace{X + \frac{X}{(1.08)} - \frac{20,000}{(1.08)^2}}_{\substack{\text{Net present value} \\ \text{of all cash flows}}} = 0$$

Solving this equation for X gives

$$X = \frac{20{,}000}{(1.08)^2} \bigg/ \left(1 + \frac{1}{1.08}\right)$$

The first term on the right-hand side, $20{,}000/(1.08)^2$, is the present value of the cost of the car. The second term, $(1 + 1/1.08)$, is the present value of an annuity of $1 per year for two years, with the first deposit made today. This present value can be computed using the Excel **PV** function.

Putting these formulas into a spreadsheet gives the answer:

	A	B	C
1	**HELPING MARIO SAVE FOR A CAR**		
		using Excel's PV function	
2	Goal	20,000.00	<-- The cost of the car
3	When to reach the goal?	2	<-- The year in which Mario wants to buy the car
4	Interest rate	8.00%	
5	Deposit, X	8,903.13	<-- =B2/(1+B4)^B3/PV(B4,B3,-1,,1)

Notice that we have written the spreadsheet so that if the cost of the car (cell B2), the year in which Mario wants to buy the car (cell B3), or the interest rate (cell B4) change, the answer automatically changes (no need to do trial and error or **Goal Seek**). For example, if Mario wants to buy the car in five years and the interest rate is 6%, then the annual payment is $3,347.10:

	A	B	C
1	**HELPING MARIO SAVE FOR A CAR**		
		using Excel's PV function	
2	Goal	20,000.00	<-- The cost of the car
3	When to reach the goal?	5	<-- The year in which Mario wants to buy the car
4	Interest rate	6.00%	
5	Deposit, X	3,347.10	<-- =B2/(1+B4)^B3/PV(B4,B3,-1,,1)

5.8 Saving for the Future: More Complicated Problems

In this section we present two more complicated versions of Mario's problem from Section 5.6. We start by trying to determine whether a young girl's parents are putting enough money aside to save for her college education. Here's the problem:

- On her 10th birthday, Linda Jones's parents decide to deposit $4,000 in a savings account for their daughter. They intend to put an additional $4,000 in the account each year on her 11th, 12th, . . . , 17th birthdays.
- All account balances will earn 8% per year.
- On Linda's 18th, 19th, 20th, and 21st birthdays, her parents will withdraw $20,000 to pay for Linda's college education.

Is the $4,000 per year sufficient to cover the anticipated college expenses? We can easily solve this problem in a spreadsheet:

	A	B	C	D	E
1		SAVING FOR COLLEGE				
2	Interest rate	8%			
3	Annual deposit	4,000.00			
4	Annual cost of college	20,000			
5					
6	Birthday	In bank on birthday, before deposit/withdrawal	Deposit or withdrawal at beginning of year	Total	End of year with interest
7	10	0.00	4,000.00	4,000.00	4,320.00
8	11	4,320.00	4,000.00	8,320.00	8,985.60
9	12	8,985.60	4,000.00	12,985.60	14,024.45
10	13	14,024.45	4,000.00	18,024.45	19,466.40
11	14	19,466.40	4,000.00	23,466.40	25,343.72
12	15	25,343.72	4,000.00	29,343.72	31,691.21
13	16	31,691.21	4,000.00	35,691.21	38,546.51
14	17	38,546.51	4,000.00	42,546.51	45,950.23
15	18	45,950.23	-20,000.00	25,950.23	28,026.25
16	19	28,026.25	-20,000.00	8,026.25	8,668.35
17	20	8,668.35	-20,000.00	-11,331.65	-12,238.18
18	21	-12,238.18	-20,000.00	-32,238.18	-34,817.24
19					
20		NPV of all payments	-13,826.4037	<-- =NPV(B2,C8:C18)+C7	

By looking at the end-year balances in column E, the $4,000 is *not* enough—Linda and her parents will run out of money somewhere between her 19th and 20th birthdays.[5] By the end of her college career, they will be $34,817 "in the hole" (cell E18). Another way to see this is to look at the net present value calculation in cell C20: As we saw in the previous section, a combination savings/withdrawal plan is fully funded when the NPV of all the payments/withdrawals is zero. In cell C20 we see that the NPV is negative—Linda's plan is *underfunded*.

How much should Linda's parents put aside each year? There are several ways to answer this question, which we explore below. These methods are basically the same as the three methods for solving Mario's problem presented in the previous section, but for completeness we present them again.

Method 1: Trial and Error

Assuming that you have put the correct formulas in the spreadsheet, you can "play" with cell B3 until cell E18 or cell C20 equals zero. Doing this shows that Linda's parents should have planned to deposit $6,227.78 annually:

[5]At the end of Linda's 19th year (row 16), there is $8,668.35 remaining in the account. At the end of the following year, there is a negative amount in the account.

	A	B	C	D	E
1		**SAVING FOR COLLEGE**			
2	Interest rate	8%			
3	Annual deposit	6,227.78			
4	Annual cost of college	20,000			
5					
6	Birthday	In bank on birthday, before deposit/withdrawal	Deposit or withdrawal at beginning of year	Total	End of year with interest
7	10	0.00	6,227.78	6,227.78	6,726.00
8	11	6,726.00	6,227.78	12,953.77	13,990.08
9	12	13,990.08	6,227.78	20,217.85	21,835.28
10	13	21,835.28	6,227.78	28,063.06	30,308.10
11	14	30,308.10	6,227.78	36,535.88	39,458.75
12	15	39,458.75	6,227.78	45,686.52	49,341.45
13	16	49,341.45	6,227.78	55,569.22	60,014.76
14	17	60,014.76	6,227.78	66,242.54	71,541.94
15	18	71,541.94	-20,000.00	51,541.94	55,665.29
16	19	55,665.29	-20,000.00	35,665.29	38,518.52
17	20	38,518.52	-20,000.00	18,518.52	20,000.00
18	21	20,000.00	-20,000.00	0.00	0.00
19					
20		NPV of all payments		0.0000	<-- =NPV(B2,C8:C18)+C7

Notice that the net present value of all the payments (cell C20) is zero when the solution is reached. The future payouts are fully funded when the NPV of all the cash flows is zero.

Method 2: Excel's Goal Seek

We can use **Goal Seek** to set cell E18 equal to zero. After selecting **Tools|Goal Seek,** we fill in the dialog box:

	A	B	C	D	E
1		**SAVING FOR COLLEGE**			
2	Interest rate	8%			
3	Annual deposit	4,000.00			
4	Annual cost of college	20,000			
5					
6	Birthday	In bank on birthday, before deposit/withdrawal	Deposit or withdrawal at begin. of year	Total	End of year with interest
7	10	0.00	4,0		
8	11	4,320.00	4,0		
9	12	8,985.60	4,0		
10	13	14,024.45	4,0		
11	14	19,466.40	4,0		
12	15	25,343.72	4,0		
13	16	31,691.21	4,0		
14	17	38,546.51	4,0		
15	18	45,950.23	-20,000.00	25,950.23	28,020.25
16	19	28,026.25	-20,000.00	8,026.25	8,668.35
17	20	8,668.35	-20,000.00	-11,331.65	-12,238.18
18	21	-12,238.18	-20,000.00	-32,238.18	-34,817.24
19					
20		NPV of all payments		-13,826.4037	<-- =NPV(B2,C8:C18)+C7

Goal Seek dialog:
Set cell: $E$18
To value: 0
By changing cell: $B$3
[OK] [Cancel]

When we press **OK, Goal Seek** looks for the solution. The result is the same as before: $6,227.78.

Method 3: Excel's PV Formula

The method in this subsection involves the most preparation. Its advantage is that it leads to a very compact solution to the problem—a solution that doesn't require a long Excel table for its implementation. On the other hand, the formulas required are somewhat intricate (if you really hate formulas, skip this method!).

Linda's parents are going to make eight deposits of X each, starting today. The present value of these deposits is

$$X + \frac{X}{(1.08)} + \frac{X}{(1.08)^2} + \cdots + \frac{X}{(1.08)^7} = X\left(1 + \frac{1}{(1.08)} + \frac{1}{(1.08)^2} + \cdots + \frac{1}{(1.08)^7}\right)$$

The account created will then have four withdrawals of $20,000, starting in year 8. The present value of these withdrawals is

$$\frac{20{,}000}{(1.08)^8} + \frac{20{,}000}{(1.08)^9} + \frac{20{,}000}{(1.08)^{10}} + \frac{20{,}000}{(1.08)^{11}} = \frac{20{,}000}{1.08^7} * \left(\frac{1}{(1.08)} + \frac{1}{(1.08)^2} + \frac{1}{(1.08)^3} + \frac{1}{(1.08)^4}\right)$$

Setting these two equations equal allows us to solve for X:

$$X = \frac{\frac{20{,}000}{1.08^7} * \left(\frac{1}{(1.08)} + \frac{1}{(1.08)^2} + \frac{1}{(1.08)^3} + \frac{1}{(1.08)^4}\right)}{1 + \frac{1}{(1.08)} + \frac{1}{(1.08)^2} + \cdots + \frac{1}{(1.08)^7}}$$

In Excel, both the numerator and the denominator are computed by filling in the dialog box for the **PV** function:

EXCEL NOTE

DIALOG BOX FOR **PV** FUNCTION

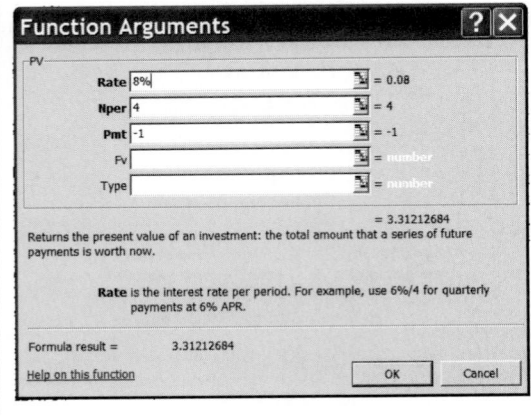

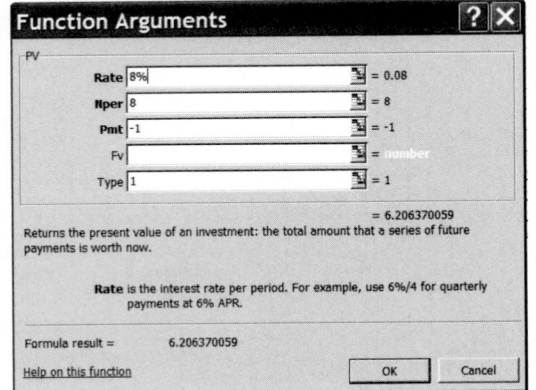

The numerator:

$$\frac{1}{(1.08)} + \frac{1}{(1.08)^2} + \frac{1}{(1.08)^3} + \frac{1}{(1.08)^4}$$
$$= 3.1212684$$

To complete the numerator, we have to multiply by $20{,}000/(1.08)^7$.

Note that **Type** is empty (payments at the end of the period). We could have also put in a 0.

The denominator:

$$1 + \frac{1}{(1.08)} + \frac{1}{(1.08)^2} + \cdots + \frac{1}{(1.08)^7}$$
$$= 6.206370059$$

Note that **Type** is 1 (payments at beginning of period).

Recall from page 85 that **Pmt** must be expressed as a negative number in order to get a positive answer.

Rows 2–9 of the following spreadsheet show how we use these two **PV** functions to solve for the annual deposit required:

	A	B	C
1		**SAVING FOR COLLEGE--USING EXCEL FORMULAS ONLY**	
2	Linda's age when plan started	10	
3	Linda's age at last deposit	17	
4	Number of deposits	8	<-- =B3-B2+1
5	Number of withdrawals	4	
6	Annual cost of college	20,000	
7	Interest rate	8%	
8			
9	Annual deposit	6,227.78	<-- =(B6/(1+B7)^(B4-1))*PV(B7,4,-1)/PV(B7,B4,-1,,1)
10			
11	**Linda's age today**	**Annual amount deposited**	
12	0	1,768.81	<-- =($B$6/(1+$B$7)^($B$3-A12))*PV($B$7,4,-1)/PV($B$7,$B$3-A12+1,-1,,1)
13	1	1,962.73	<-- =($B$6/(1+$B$7)^($B$3-A13))*PV($B$7,4,-1)/PV($B$7,$B$3-A13+1,-1,,1)
14	2	2,184.47	<-- =($B$6/(1+$B$7)^($B$3-A14))*PV($B$7,4,-1)/PV($B$7,$B$3-A14+1,-1,,1)
15	3	2,439.68	
16	4	2,735.61	
17	5	3,081.72	
18	6	3,490.65	
19	7	3,979.61	
20	8	4,572.69	
21	9	5,304.68	
22	10	6,227.78	
23	11	7,423.96	
24	12	9,029.88	
25	13	11,291.47	
26	14	14,700.60	
27	15	20,404.92	
28			
29			
30			
31			

Annual Deposit Required to Fund 4 Years of $20,000 When Linda is 18

The formula in cell B9 is the solution:

$$= \underbrace{(B6/(1 + B7)^{\wedge}(B4 - 1))}_{\frac{20{,}000}{(1.08)^7}} * \quad \underbrace{PV(B7, B5, -1)}_{\frac{1}{1.08} + \frac{1}{(1.08)^2} + \cdots + \frac{1}{(1.08)^4}} \quad / \quad \underbrace{PV(B7, B4, -1, , 1)}_{1 + \frac{1}{1.08} + \frac{1}{(1.08)^2} + \cdots + \frac{1}{(1.08)^7}}$$

The problem as initially set out assumes that Linda is 10 years old today. Rows 12–27 in the table show the problem solutions for other starting ages.[6]

Pension Plans

The savings problem of Linda's parents is exactly the same as that faced by an individual who wishes to save for retirement. Suppose that Joe is 20 today and wishes to start saving so that

---

[6]Rows 12–27 in the table would be simpler to compute if we used **Data Table.** This advanced feature of Excel is explained in Chapter 30. The file **pfe_chap05.xls** on the disk accompanying *Principles of Finance with Excel* shows how to use **Data Table** to do the calculations in rows 12–27.

when he's 65 he can have twenty years of $100,000 annual withdrawals. Adapting the previous spreadsheet, we get

	A	B	C
1			**SAVING FOR RETIREMENT**
2	Joe's age today	20	
3	Joe's age at last deposit	64	
4	Number of deposits	45	<-- =B3-B2+1
5	Number of withdrawals	20	
6	Annual withdrawal from age 65	100,000	
7	Interest rate	8%	
8			
9	Annual deposit	2,540.23	<-- =(B6/(1+B7)^(B4-1))*PV(B7,B5,-1)/PV(B7,B4,-1,,1)
10			
11	**Joe's age today**	**Annual amount deposited**	
12	20	2,540.23	<-- =($B$6/(1+$B$7)^($B$3-A12))*PV($B$7,$B$5,-1)/PV($B$7,$B$3-A12+1,-1,,1)
13	22	2,978.96	<-- =($B$6/(1+$B$7)^($B$3-A13))*PV($B$7,$B$5,-1)/PV($B$7,$B$3-A13+1,-1,,1)
14	24	3,496.73	<-- =($B$6/(1+$B$7)^($B$3-A14))*PV($B$7,$B$5,-1)/PV($B$7,$B$3-A14+1,-1,,1)
15	26	4,109.02	
16	28	4,834.85	
17	30	5,697.73	
18	32	6,727.03	
19	34	7,959.85	
20	35	8,666.90	
21	38	11,239.91	
22	40	13,430.03	
23	42	16,123.53	
24	44	19,471.60	
25	46	23,688.86	
26	48	29,090.61	
27	50	36,159.79	
28			
29			

Annual Deposit Required to Fund 20 Years of $100,000 When Joe is 65

In the table, rows 12–27 show the power of compound interest: If Joe starts saving at age 20 for his retirement, an annual deposit of $2,540.23 will grow to provide him with his retirement needs of $100,000 per year for twenty years at age 65. On the other hand, if he starts saving at age 35, it will require $8,666.90 per year.

5.9 Computing Annual "Flat" Payments on a Loan: Excel's PMT Function

You've just graduated from college, and the balance on your student loan is $100,000. You now have to pay off the loan over ten years at an annual interest rate of 10%. The payment is in "even payments"—meaning that you pay the same amount each year. How much will you have to pay off?

Suppose we denote the annual payment by X. The correct X has the property that the present value of all the payments equals the loan principal:

$$100,000 = \frac{X}{1.10} + \frac{X}{(1.10)^2} + \frac{X}{(1.10)^3} + \cdots + \frac{X}{(1.10)^{10}}$$

Rewriting the right-hand side slightly, you can see that

$$X = \underbrace{\frac{100,000}{\frac{1}{1.10} + \frac{1}{(1.10)^2} + \frac{1}{(1.10)^3} + \cdots + \frac{1}{(1.10)^{10}}}}_{}$$

This expression can be calculated using Excel's **PV** function

Here's all this in an Excel spreadsheet:

	A	B	C
1		**LOAN PAYMENT**	
2	Loan principal	100,000	
3	Loan interest	10%	
4	Years to pay off loan	10	
5	Annual payment	16,274.54	<-- =B2/PV(B3,B4,-1)
6		16,274.54	<-- =PMT(B3,B4,-B2)

In cell B6 we use Excel's **PMT** function, which does the calculation of the loan payment directly (see box below).

EXCEL NOTE

DIALOG BOX FOR **PMT** FUNCTION

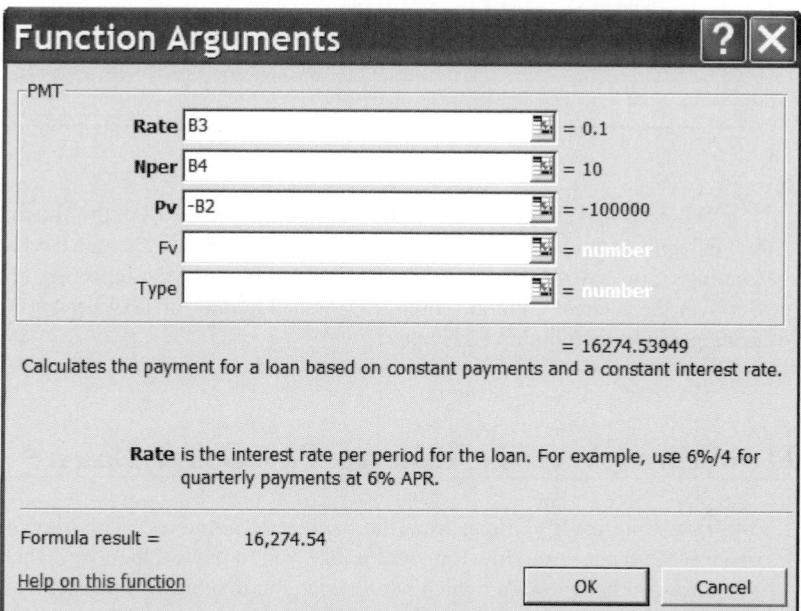

Like some other Excel financial functions, **PMT** generates positive answers for negative entries in the **Pv** box. We therefore write −B2 as **Pv** to generate a positive **PMT**.

Loan Amortization Tables

"Amortize" means to pay off something over time. A *loan amortization table* shows how the payments on a loan are split between interest and repayment of the loan principal. Here's the previous example, with the amortization table attached (rows 9–18):

	A	B	C	D	E	F
1		**LOAN PAYMENT**				
2	Loan principal	100,000				
3	Loan interest	10%				
4	Years to pay off loan	10				
5	Annual payment	16,274.54	<-- =B2/PV(B3,B4,-1)			
6		16,274.54	<-- =PMT(B3,B4,-B2)			
7						
8	**Year**	**Principal at beginning of year**	**Payment at end of year**	**Part of payment that is interest**	**Part of payment that is principal**	=$B$3*B9
9	1	100,000.00	16,274.54	10,000.00	6,274.54	<-- =C9-D9
10	2	93,725.46	16,274.54	9,372.55	6,901.99	
11	3	86,823.47	16,274.54	8,682.35	7,592.19	
12	4	79,231.27	16,274.54	7,923.13	8,351.41	
13	5	70,879.86	16,274.54	7,087.99	9,186.55	
14	6	61,693.31	16,274.54	6,169.33	10,105.21	
15	7	51,588.10	16,274.54	5,158.81	11,115.73	
16	8	40,472.37	16,274.54	4,047.24	12,227.30	
17	9	28,245.07	16,274.54	2,824.51	13,450.03	
18	10	14,795.04	16,274.54	1,479.50	14,795.04	
19	=B9-E9					
20			The principal due at the beginning of year 10			
21			equals the principal paid off at the end of the			
22			year. **Meaning**: The loan is paid off over 10			
23			years.			
24						

When we put all the payments in a loan table (rows 9–18 of the above spreadsheet), you can see the split of each end-year payment between interest on the outstanding principal at the beginning of the year and repayment of principal. If you were reporting to the Internal Revenue Service, the interest column (column D) is deductible for tax purposes; the repayment of the principal column (column E) is not.

5.10 How Long Will It Take to Pay Off a Loan?

You're getting a $1,000 loan from the bank at 10% interest. The maximum payment you can make is $250 per year. How long will it take you to pay off the loan? There's an Excel function that answers this question, which we'll show you in a bit. But first let's do this the long way so we can understand the question. In the spreadsheet below we look at a loan table like the one considered in Section 5.5:

	A	B	C	D	E
1	HOW LONG TO PAY OFF THIS LOAN?				
2	Loan amount	1,000			
3	Interest rate	10%			
4	Annual payment	250			
5					
6	Year	Principal at beginning of year	Payment at end of year	Interest	Return of principal
7	1	1,000.00	250.00	100.00	150.00
8	2	850.00	250.00	85.00	165.00
9	3	685.00	250.00	68.50	181.50
10	4	503.50	250.00	50.35	199.65
11	5	303.85	250.00	30.39	219.62
12	6	84.24	250.00	8.42	241.58
13					
14					
15		Year 6 is the first year in which the return			
16		of principal at the end of the year			
17		> principal at the beginning of the year--			
18		meaning that sometime during year 6			
19		you will have paid off the loan.			
20					

As you can see from row 12, year 6 is the first year in which the return of principal at the end of the year is bigger than the principal at the beginning of the year. Thus, sometime between years 5 and 6 you pay off the loan.

Excel's **NPER** function, illustrated in cell B22, provides an exact answer to this question:

EXCEL NOTE

DIALOG BOX FOR NPER FUNCTION

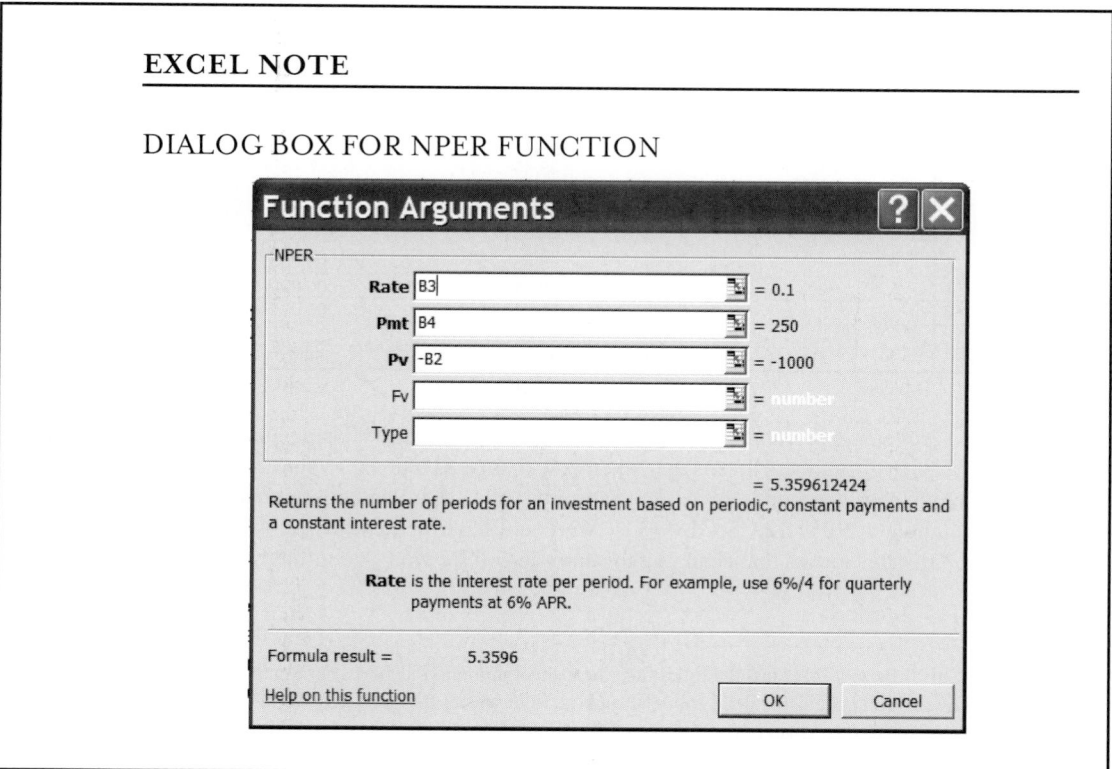

Like the functions **PMT, PV,** and **FV** discussed elsewhere in this chapter, the **NPER** function requires you to make the amount owed negative in order to get a positive answer.

5.11 An Excel Note: Building Good Financial Models[7]

If you've gotten this far in Chapter 5, you've probably put together a few basic Excel spreadsheets. You'll be doing lots more in the rest of this book, and you'll be amazed at the insights Excel gives you over complicated financial problems.

We've chosen this place in the chapter to tell you a bit about financial modeling (that's what you've actually been doing).

Here are three important rules for good Excel modeling:

- Put all the important variables (the fashionable jargon is "value drivers") at the top of your spreadsheet. In the "Saving for College" spreadsheet on page 106, the three value drivers—interest rate, annual deposit, and annual cost of college—are in the top left-hand corner of the spreadsheet:

	A	B	C	D	E
1		SAVING FOR COLLEGE			
2	Interest rate	8%			
3	Annual deposit	6,227.78			
4	Annual cost of college	20,000			
5					
6	Birthday	In bank on birthday, before deposit/withdrawal	Deposit or withdrawal at beginning of year	Total	End of year with interest
7	10	0.00	6,227.78	6,227.78	6,726.00
8	11	6,726.00	6,227.78	12,953.77	13,990.08
9	12	13,990.08	6,227.78	20,217.85	21,835.28
10	13	21,835.28	6,227.78	28,063.06	30,308.10
11	14	30,308.10	6,227.78	36,535.88	39,458.75
12	15	39,458.75	6,227.78	45,686.52	49,341.45
13	16	49,341.45	6,227.78	55,569.22	60,014.76
14	17	60,014.76	6,227.78	66,242.54	71,541.94
15	18	71,541.94	-20,000.00	51,541.94	55,665.29
16	19	55,665.29	-20,000.00	35,665.29	38,518.52
17	20	38,518.52	-20,000.00	18,518.52	20,000.00
18	21	20,000.00	-20,000.00	0.00	0.00
19					
20		NPV of all payments		0.0000 <-- =NPV(B2,C8:C18)+C7	

- Never use a number where a formula will also work. Using formulas instead of "hard-wiring" numbers means that when you change a parameter value, the rest of the spreadsheet changes appropriately. As an example—cell C20 in the above spreadsheet contains the formula **=NPV(B2,C8:C18)+C7**. We could have written this as **=NPV(8%,C8:C18)+C7**. But this means that changing the entry in cell B2 won't go through the whole model.

---

[7]This little section is just the tip of the spreadsheet modeling iceberg. For much more useful information on how to build lucid financial models, look at John Raffensperger's wonderful website: http://www.mang.canterbury.ac.nz/people/jfraffen/spreadsheets/index.html.

- Avoid the use of blank columns to accommodate cell "spillovers." Here's an example of a potentially bad model:

	A	B	C
1	Interest rate		6%

Because "Interest rate" has spilled over to column B, the author of this spreadsheet has decided to put the "6%" in column C. He's going to end up getting confused (don't ask why); he should have made column A wider and put the 6% in column B:

	A	B
1	Interest rate	6%

EXCEL NOTE

MAKING A COLUMN WIDER

Widening the column is simple: Put the cursor on the break between columns A and B:

B3		▼	*fx*
	A ┿ B		C
1	Interest rat	6%	
2			
3			

Clicking the left mouse button will expand the column to accommodate the widest cell. You can also "stretch" the column by holding the left mouse button down and moving the column width to the right.

CONCLUSION

In this chapter we have covered the basic concepts of the time value of money:

- Future value (FV): the amount you will accumulate at some future date from deposits made in the present.
- Present value (PV): the value today of future anticipated cash flows.
- Net present value (NPV): the value today of a series of future cash flows, including the cost of acquiring these cash flows.
- We've gone to great pains to point out the difference between the finance concept of net present value (NPV) and the Excel **NPV** function. The Excel **NPV** function calculates the present value of the future cash flows, whereas the finance concept of NPV computes the present value of the future cash flows *minus* the initial cash flow.
- Internal rate of return (IRR): the compound interest rate paid by a series of cash flows, including the cost of their acquisition.

We have also showed you the Excel functions (**FV, PV, NPV, IRR**) that do these calculations and discussed some of their peculiarities. Finally, we have showed you how to do these calculations using formulas.

EXERCISES

1. You just put $600 in the bank and you intend to leave it there for ten years. If the bank pays you 15% interest per year, how much will you have at the end of ten years?

2. Your generous grandmother has just announced that she's opened a savings account for you with a deposit of $10,000. Moreover, she intends to make nine more similar gifts, at the end of this year, next year, and so on. If the savings account pays 8% interest, how much will you have accumulated at the end of ten years (one year after the last gift)?

   Suggestion: Solve this problem two ways, as shown below: (a) Take each amount and calculate its future value in year 10 (as illustrated in cells C4:C13) and then sum them; (b) use Excel's **FV** function, noting that here the amounts come at the *beginning* of the year (you'll need to enter "1" in the **Type** option as described in Section 5.1).

	A	B	C	D
1	Interest rate		8.00%	
2				
3	Year		Gift	Future value in year 10
4		0	10,000	21,589.25	<--=B4*(1+$B$1)^(10-A4)
5		1	10,000		
6		2	10,000		
7		3	10,000		
8		4	10,000		
9		5	10,000		
10		6	10,000		
11		7	10,000		
12		8	10,000		
13		9	10,000		
14					
15	Total (summing C4:C13)			
16	Using FV function			

3. Your uncle has just announced that he's going to give you $10,000 per year at the end of each of the next four years (he's less generous than your grandmother). If the relevant interest rate is 7%, what's the value today of this promise? (If you're going to use **PV** to do this problem, note that the **Type** option is 0 or omitted.)

4. What is the present value of a series of four payments, each $1,000, to be made at the end of years 1, 2, 3, 4? Assume that the interest rate is 14%.

   Suggestion: Solve this problem two ways, as shown in rows 9 and 10 below.

	A	B	C	D
1	Interest rate	14%		
2				
3	Year	Payment	PV	
4	1	1,000	877.19	<-- =B4/(1+$B$1)^A4
5	2	1,000		
6	3	1,000		
7	4	1,000		
8				
9	Total of C4:C7			
10	Using NPV function			

5. Screw-'Em-Good (SEG) Corp. has just announced a revolutionary security: If you pay SEG $1,000 now, you will get back $150 at the end of each of the next 15 years. What is the IRR of this investment?

Suggestion: Solve this problem two ways—once using Excel's **IRR** function and once using Excel's **RATE** function (illustrated below).

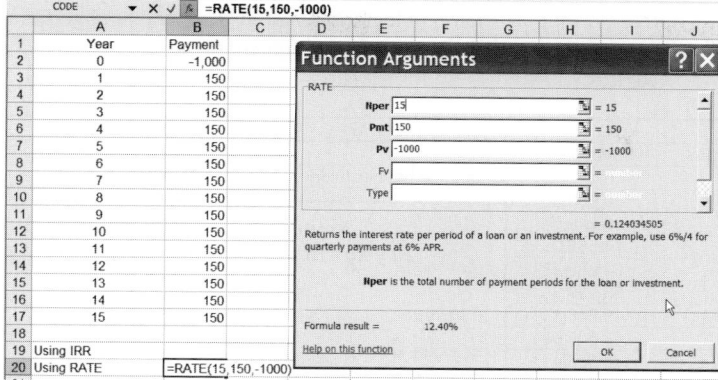

6. Make-'Em-Happy (MEH) Corp. has a different security for sale: You pay MEH $1,000 today and the company will give you back $100 at the end of the first year, $200 at the end of year 2, ..., $1,000 at the end of year 10.
   (a) Calculate the IRR of this investment.
   (b) Show an amortization table for the investment.

7. You are thinking about buying a $1,000 bond issued by the Appalachian Development Authority (ADA). The bond will pay $120 interest at the end of each of the next five years. At the end of year 6, the bond will pay $1,120 (this is its face value of $1,000 plus the interest). If the relevant discount rate is 7%, how much is the present value of the bond's future payments?

8. Look at the pension problem in Section 5.8, page 110, Answer the following questions:
   (a) What if the desired annual pension is $100,000? How much does a 55-year-old have to save annually? The CD-ROM that accompanies this book contains the following template:

	A	B	C	D	E
1	SAVING FOR THE FUTURE				
2	Your age today	35			
3	Retirement age	65			
4	Planned age of demise	85			
5					
6	Annual desired pension payout	100,000			
7	Annual payment	???			
8	Interest rate	8%			
9					
10	Your age	Account balance, beginning of year	Deposit or withdrawal beginning of year	Interest earned during year	Total in account end of year
11	55				
12	56				
13	57				
14	58				
15	59				
16	60				
17	61				
18	62				
19	63				
20	64				
21	65				

(b) Suppose you are 35 years old and you wish to save until you are 65. You wish to withdraw $50,000 per year at the beginning of your 65th, 66th, . . . , 89th years. How much would you have to save if the interest rate is 10%?

9. Return to the pension problem discussed in Section 5.8, page 110, Use Excel to make a graph showing the relationship between the amount saved and the interest rate. Your graph should look like this:

	B	C	D	E	F	G	H	I
20	Interest rate	Saving						
21			<-- Data table header (hidden)					
22	0%	100,000.00						
23	1%	86,241.57		Annual Savings Required to Fund				
24	2%	74,665.98		20 years of $50,000 Pension Starting at Age 65				
25	3%	64,888.48						
26	4%	56,597.56						
27	5%	49,540.14		120,000				
28	6%	43,509.98						
29	7%	38,338.41		100,000				
30	8%	33,887.08		80,000				
31	9%	30,042.08						
32	10%	26,709.35		60,000				
33	11%	23,810.92						
34	12%	21,282.00		40,000				
35	13%	19,068.53						
36	14%	17,125.28		20,000				
37	15%	15,414.25						
38	16%	13,903.45		0				
39	17%	12,565.85		0% 5% 10% 15% 20%				
40	18%	11,378.50						
41	19%	10,321.93						
42	20%	9,379.48						

Note: If you're going to use the formula approach used in the book, you have to modify the formula a bit to make it work for interest = 0%. The existing formula in Section 5.8 is

$$X = \frac{\left(\begin{array}{c} annual \\ pension \\ payout \end{array}\right) * \left(1 - \left(\frac{1}{1+r}\right)^{20}\right)}{(1+r)^{10}\left(1 - \left(\frac{1}{1+r}\right)^{10}\right)}$$

but when $r = 0$, the denominator in this expression becomes 0. On the other hand, when $r = 0$, it is clear that the payout is

$$X = \frac{\left(\begin{array}{c} annual \\ pension \\ payout \end{array}\right) * \left(\begin{array}{c} number \\ of\ payout \\ years \end{array}\right)}{\left(\begin{array}{c} number \\ of\ payment \\ years \end{array}\right)}$$

Use Excel's **If** function to modify the formula in the Section 5.8 spreadsheet.

10. If you deposit $25,000 today, Union Bank offers to pay you $50,000 at the end of ten years. What is the interest rate?

11. Assuming that the interest rate is 5%, which of the following is more valuable?
    (a) $5,000 today.
    (b) $10,000 at the end of five years.

(c) $9,000 at the end of four years.

(d) $300 a year in perpetuity (meaning forever), with the first payment at the end of this year.

12. You receive a $15,000 signing bonus from your new employer and decide to invest it for two years. Your banker suggests two alternatives, both requiring a commitment for the full two years. The first alternative will earn 8% per year for both years. The second alternative earns 6% for the first year, and 10% for the second year. Interest compounds annually. Which should you choose?

13. Your annual salary is $100,000. You are offered two options for a severance package. Option 1 pays you six months' salary now. Option 2 pays you and your heirs $6,000 per year forever (first payment at the end of this year). If your required return is 11%, which option should you choose?

14. Today is your 40th birthday. You expect to retire at age 65, and actuarial tables suggest that you will live to be 100. You want to move to Hawaii when you retire. You estimate that it will cost you $200,000 to make the move (on your 65th birthday), and that your annual living expenses will be $25,000 a year after that. You expect to earn an annual return of 7% on your savings.
(a) How much will you need to have saved by your retirement date?
(b) You already have $50,000 in savings. How much would you need to save at the end of each of the next twenty-five years to be able to afford this retirement plan?
(c) If you did not have any current savings and did not expect to be able to start saving money for the next five years (that is, your first savings payment will be made on your 45th birthday), how much would you have to set aside each year after that to be able to afford this retirement plan?

15. You have just invested $10,000 in a new fund that pays $1,500 at the end of the next ten years. What is the compound rate of interest being offered by the fund? (**Suggestion:** Solve this problem two ways: using Excel's **IRR** function and using Excel's **Rate** function.)

16. John is turning 13 today. His birthday resolution is to start saving toward the purchase of a car that he wants to buy on his 18th birthday. The car costs $15,000 today, and he expects the price to grow at 2% per year.

John has heard that a local bank offers a savings account that pays an interest rate of 5% per year. He plans to make six contributions of $1,000 each to the savings account (the first contribution to be made today); he will use the funds in the account on his 18th birthday as a down payment for the car, financing the balance through the car dealer.

He expects the dealer to offer the following terms for financing: seven equal yearly payments (with the first payment due one year after he takes possession of the car) and an annual interest rate of 7%.
(a) How much will John need to finance through the dealer?
(b) What will be the amount of his yearly payment to the dealer?
(Hint: This is like the college savings problem discussed in Section 5.8.)

17. Mary has just completed her undergraduate degree from Northwestern University and is already planning to enter an MBA program four years from today. The MBA tuition will be $20,000 per year for two years, paid at the beginning of each year. In addition, Mary would like to retire fifteen years from today and receive a pension of $60,000 every year for twenty years, with the first pension payment paid out fifteen years from today. Mary can borrow and lend as much as she likes at a rate of 7%, compounded annually. In order to fund her expenditures, Mary will save money at the end of years 0–3 and at the end of years 6–14.
  • Calculate the constant annual dollar amount that Mary must save at the end of each of these years to cover all her expenditures (tuition and retirement). (It might be helpful to use **Goal Seek**.)

Note: Just to remove all doubts, here are the cash flows:

	A	B	C	D	E	F
1			**MARY**			
2	Year	Balance at beginning of year before withdrawal	Withdrawal beginning of year	Net balance beginning of year	Savings at end of year	Account end of year
3	0	0			$X	
4	1				$X	
5	2				$X	
6	3				$X	
7	4		$ (20,000.00)			
8	5		$ (20,000.00)			
9	6				$X	
10	7				$X	
11	8				$X	
12	9				$X	
13	10				$X	
14	11				$X	
15	12				$X	
16	13				$X	
17	14				$X	
18	15		$ (60,000.00)			
19	16		$ (60,000.00)			
20	17		$ (60,000.00)			
21	18		$ (60,000.00)			
22	19		$ (60,000.00)			
23	20		$ (60,000.00)			
24	21		$ (60,000.00)			
25	22		$ (60,000.00)			
26	23		$ (60,000.00)			
27	24		$ (60,000.00)			
28	25		$ (60,000.00)			
29	26		$ (60,000.00)			
30	27		$ (60,000.00)			
31	28		$ (60,000.00)			
32	29		$ (60,000.00)			
33	30		$ (60,000.00)			
34	31		$ (60,000.00)			
35	32		$ (60,000.00)			
36	33		$ (60,000.00)			
37	34		$ (60,000.00)			0

18. You are the CFO of Termination, Inc. Your company has 40 employees, each earning $40,000 per year. Employee salaries grow at 4% per year. Starting from next year, and every second year thereafter, eight employees retire and no new employees are recruited. Your company has in place a retirement plan that entitles retired workers to an annual pension equal to their annual salary at the moment of retirement. Life expectancy is twenty years after retirement, and the annual pension is paid at year-end. The return on investment is 10% per year. What is the total value of your pension liabilities?

19. You are 30 today and are considering studying for an MBA. You just received your annual salary of $50,000 and expect it to grow by 3% per year. MBAs typically earn $60,000 upon graduation, with salaries growing by 4% per year.

     The MBA program you're considering is a full-time, two-year program that costs $20,000 per year, payable at the end of each study year. You want to retire on your 65th birthday. The relevant discount rate is 8%.[8] Is it worthwhile for you to quit your job in order to do an MBA (ignore income taxes)? What is the internal rate of return of the MBA?

20. You're 55 years old today, and you wish to start saving for your pension. Here are the parameters:
   - You intend to make a deposit today and at the beginning of each of the next nine years (that is, on your 55th, 56th, . . . , 64th birthdays).
   - Starting from your 65th birthday until your 84th, you would like to withdraw $50,000 per year (no plans for after that).
   - The interest rate is 12%.

   (a) How much should you deposit in each of the initial years in order to fully fund the withdrawals?

   (b) If you start saving at age 45, what is the answer?

   (c) (More difficult) Set up the formula for the savings amount so that you can solve for various starting ages. Do a sensitivity analysis, which shows the amount you need to save as a function of the age at which you start saving.

21. Section 5.8 of this chapter discusses the problem of Linda Jones's parents, who wish to save for Linda's college education. The setup of the problem implicitly assumes that the bank will let the Jones family borrow from their savings account and will charge them the same 8% it was paying on positive balances. This is unlikely!

   In this problem you are asked to program the following spreadsheet: In it you will assume that the bank pays Linda's parents 8% on positive account balances but charges them 10% on negative balances.

   If Linda's parents can only deposit $4,000 per year in the years preceding college, how much will they owe the bank at the beginning of year 22 (the year after Linda finishes college)?

	A	B	C	D	E
1		**SAVING FOR COLLEGE**			
2	Interest rates				
3	On positive balances	8%			
4	On negative balances	10%			
5	Annual deposit	4,000.00			
6	Annual cost of college	20,000			
7					
8	Birthday	In bank on birthday, before deposit/withdrawal	Deposit or withdrawal at beginning of year	Total	End of year with interest
9	10		4,000.00		
10	11		4,000.00		
11	12		4,000.00		
12	13		4,000.00		
13	14		4,000.00		
14	15		4,000.00		
15	16		4,000.00		
16	17		4,000.00		
17	18		-20,000.00		
18	19		-20,000.00		
19	20		-20,000.00		
20	21		-20,000.00		
21	22				

   Excel note: In order to set up this spreadsheet, you will need to use the Excel **If** function (if you are not familiar with this function, see Chapter 28).

---

[8]Meaning: Your MBA is an investment like any other investment. On other investments you can earn 8% per year; the MBA has to be judged against this standard.

22. A fund of $10,000 is set up to pay $250 at the end of each year indefinitely. What is the fund's IRR? (There's no Excel function that answers this question—use some logic!)

23. In the spreadsheet below we calculate the future value of five deposits of $100, with the first deposit made at time 0. As shown in Section 5.1, this calculation can also be made using the Excel function =**FV(interest,periods,−amount,,1)**.
    (a) Show that you can also compute this by =**FV(interest,periods,−amount)* (1+ interest)**.
    (b) Can you explain why **FV(r,5,−100,,1)=FV(r,5,−100)*(1+r)**?

	A	B	C	D	E	F
1			**FUTURE VALUE**			
2	Interest		6%			
3						
4	Year	Account balance, beginning of year	Deposit at beginning of year	Interest earned during year	Total in account at end of year	
5	1	0.00	100.00	6.00	106.00	<-- =B5+C5+D5
6	2	106.00	100.00	12.36	218.36	<-- =B6+C6+D6
7	3	218.36	100.00	19.10	337.46	
8	4	337.46	100.00	26.25	463.71	
9	5	463.71	100.00	33.82	597.53	

24. Abner and Maude are both in their 80s. They're thinking of selling their house for $500,000 and moving into an apartment complex for seniors. The apartment rent is $50,000 per year, payable in full at the beginning of each year.
    (a) If they can earn 6% annually on the proceeds from their house, and if they live for ten more years, how much will they be able to leave their children as inheritance?
    (b) What is the longest they can live from the house proceeds before the money runs out?

25. What are your answers to the questions in Exercise 24 assuming that the interest rate is 7%? 5%?

26. Michael is considering his consumption habits, trying to figure out how to save money. He realizes that he could save $2 every day by ordering regular coffee instead of latte at the local coffee shop. Since he buys a cup of coffee every workday, this works out to $10 per week, which amounts to a saving of $520 per year.
    (a) If Michael is 25 today and retires at age 65, how much money will he have accumulated from savings on coffee versus latte? Assume that the annual interest rate is 4% and that the $520 savings occur at the end of each year.
    (b) Michael was astounded at the answer to part (a) of this problem. He realized he had more wasteful habits, and he made a list of possible savings to see how much richer he could be at age 65. What are the rewards for Michael's frugality?

	A	B	C	D
	MICHAEL SAVES MONEY			
1	**By changing his consumption habits**			
2	Annual interest rate	4%		
3	Item	Weekly savings	Yearly savings	Future value at age 65
4				
5	Latte versus regular coffee	$ 10.00	$ 520.00	
6	Deli versus brown bag lunch	$ 25.00	$ 1,300.00	
7	Excess alcohol	$ 10.00	$ 520.00	
8	Cigarettes	$ 11.00	$ 572.00	
9	Candy	$ 5.00	$ 260.00	
10	Excess junk food	$ 10.00	$ 520.00	
11	Cell phone (chat vs. needed calls)	$ 6.00	$ 312.00	
12	Wasted groceries	$ 7.00	$ 364.00	
13	Restaurants.fast food vs. eat at home	$ 30.00	$ 1,560.00	
14	Wasted energy: heat, AC, lights	$ 12.00	$ 624.00	
15	Movies versus books	$ 10.00	$ 520.00	
16	Expensive cable TV	$ 13.00	$ 676.00	
17	Wasted gasoline on excessive trips, etc.	$ 8.00	$ 416.00	
18	Wasteful spending at mall	$ 10.00	$ 520.00	
19	**Money saved by time Michael is 65**			

APPENDIX 5.1: ALGEBRAIC PRESENT VALUE FORMULAS

Most of the computations in this chapter can also be done with one basic bit of high-school algebra relating to the sum of a geometric series. Suppose you want to find the sum of a geometric series of n numbers $a + aq + aq^2 + aq^3 + \cdots + aq^{n-1}$. In the jargon of geometric series:

a is the *first term*

q is the *ratio* between terms (the number by which the previous term is multiplied to get the next term)

n is the *number of terms*

Denote the sum of the series by S: $S = a + aq + aq^2 + aq^3 + \cdots + aq^{n-1}$. In high school you learned a trick to find the value of S:

1. Multiply S by q:

$$qS = \quad aq \;+\; aq^2 \;+\; aq^3 \;+\; \cdots \;+\; aq^{n-1} \;+\; aq^n$$

2. Subtract qS from S:

$$
\begin{aligned}
S = \;& a \;+\; aq \;+\; aq^2 \;+\; aq^3 \;+\; \cdots \;+\; aq^{n-1} \\
-qS = -(\;& \quad\;\; aq \;+\; aq^2 \;+\; aq^3 \;+\; \cdots \;+\; aq^{n-1} \;+\; aq^n)
\end{aligned}
$$

$$(1-q)S = a - aq^n \Rightarrow S = \frac{a\,(1-q^n)}{1-q}$$

In the remainder of this appendix we apply this formula to a variety of situations covered in the chapter.

FUTURE VALUE OF A CONSTANT PAYMENT

This topic is covered in Section 5.1. The problem there is to find the value of $100 deposited annually over ten years, with the first payment today:

$$S = 100 * (1.06)^{10} + 100 * (1.06)^9 + \cdots + 100 * (1.06) = ???$$

For this geometric series:

$$a = first\ term = 100 * 1.06^{10}$$

$$q = ratio = \frac{1}{1.06}$$

$$n = number\ of\ terms = 10$$

The formula gives

$$S = \frac{a(1 - q^n)}{1 - q} = \frac{100 * 1.06^{10}\left(1 - \left(\frac{1}{1.06}\right)^{10}\right)}{1 - \frac{1}{1.06}} = 1397.16$$

where we have done the calculation in Excel:

	A	B	C
1	**FUTURE VALUE FORMULA**		
2	First term, a	179.0848	<-- =100*1.06^10
3	Ratio, q	0.943396	<-- =1/1.06
4	Number of terms, n	10	
5			
6	Sum	1,397.16	<-- =B2*(1-B3^B4)/(1-B3)
7	Excel PV function	1,397.16	<-- =FV(6%,B4,-100,,1)

Substituting symbols for the numerical values, we get

$$\begin{array}{c}\text{Future value of } n \text{ payments} \\ \text{at end of year } n, \text{ at interest } r, \\ \text{first payment today}\end{array} = \frac{payment * (1 + r)^n\left(1 - \left(\frac{1}{1 + r}\right)^n\right)}{1 - \frac{1}{1 + r}} = \underbrace{\mathbf{FV(r, n, -1, 1)}}_{\uparrow \text{ The Excel function}}$$

PRESENT VALUE OF AN ANNUITY

We can also apply the formula to find the present value of an annuity. Suppose, for example, that we want to calculate the present value of an annuity of $150 per year for five years:

$$\frac{150}{(1.06)} + \frac{150}{(1.06)^2} + \frac{150}{(1.06)^3} + \frac{150}{(1.06)^4} + \frac{150}{(1.06)^5}$$

For this annuity:

$$a = first\ term = \frac{150}{1.06} \quad \text{(see footnote 9)}$$

$$q = ratio = \frac{1}{1.06}$$

$$n = number\ of\ terms = 5$$

Thus, the present value of the annuity becomes

$$S = \frac{a(1 - q^n)}{1 - q} = \frac{\frac{150}{1.06}\left(1 - \left(\frac{1}{1.06}\right)^5\right)}{1 - \frac{1}{1.06}} = 631.85 = \underbrace{\mathbf{PV(6\%,5,-150)}}$$

$\uparrow$
The Excel function

We can work this out in a spreadsheet:

	A	B	C
1		**ANNUITY FORMULAS**	
2	First term, a	141.509434	<-- =150/1.06
3	Ratio, q	0.943396226	<-- =1/1.06
4	Number of terms, n	5	
5			
6	Sum	631.85	<-- =B2*(1-B3^B4)/(1-B3)
7	Excel PV function	631.85	<-- =PV(6%,5,-150)

CLEANING UP THE FORMULA (A BIT)

Standard textbooks often manipulate the annuity formula to make it look "better." Here's an example of something you might see in a textbook:

$$S = \frac{a(1 - q^n)}{1 - q} = \frac{\frac{annual\ payment}{(1 + r)}\left(1 - \left(\frac{1}{1 + r}\right)^n\right)}{1 - \frac{1}{1 + r}}$$

$$= \frac{annual\ payment}{r}\left(1 - \left(\frac{1}{1 + r}\right)^n\right)$$

This is not a different annuity formula—it's just an algebraic simplification of the formula we've been using. If you put it in Excel, you'll get the same answer (and in our opinion, there's no point in the simplification).

---

[9] If you're like most of humanity, you (mistakenly) thought that the first term was $a = 150$. But look at the series—the first term actually is 150/1.06. So there you are.

PRESENT VALUE OF A SERIES OF GROWING PAYMENTS

Suppose we're trying to apply the formula to the following series:

$$\frac{150}{(1.06)} + \frac{150*(1.10)}{(1.06)^2} + \frac{150*(1.10)^2}{(1.06)^3} + \frac{150*(1.10)^3}{(1.06)^4} + \frac{150*(1.10)^4}{(1.06)^5}$$

Here there are five payments, the first of which is $150; this payment grows at an annual rate of 10%. We can apply the formula:

$$a = \textit{first term} = \frac{150}{1.06}$$

$$q = \textit{ratio} = \frac{1.10}{1.06}$$

$$n = \textit{number of terms} = 5$$

In the following spreadsheet, you can see that the formula and the Excel **NPV** function give the same answer for the present value:

	A	B	C
1	**A CONSTANT-GROWTH CASH FLOW**		
2	First term, a	141.5094	<-- =150/1.06
3	Ratio, q	1.037736	<-- =1.1/1.06
4	Number of terms, n	5	
5			
6	Sum	763.00	<-- =B2*(1-B3^B4)/(1-B3)
7			
8	Year	Payment	
9	1	150.00	
10	2	165.00	<-- =B9*1.1
11	3	181.50	<-- =B10*1.1
12	4	199.65	
13	5	219.62	
14			
15	Present value	763.00	<-- =NPV(6%,B9:B13)

Notice that the formula in cell B6 is more compact than Excel's **NPV** function. **NPV** requires you to list all the payments, whereas the formula in cell B6 requires only several lines. (Think about finding the present value of a very long series of growing payments—clearly, the formula is more efficient.)

PRESENT VALUE OF A CONSTANT-GROWTH ANNUITY

An annuity is a series of annual payments; a constant-growth annuity is an annuity whose payments grow at a constant rate. Here's an example of such a series:

$$\frac{20}{(1.10)} + \frac{20*(1.05)}{(1.10)^2} + \frac{20*(1.05)^2}{(1.10)^3} + \frac{20*(1.05)^3}{(1.10)^4} + \frac{20*(1.05)^4}{(1.10)^5} + \cdots$$

We can fit this into our formula:

$$a = first\ term = \frac{20}{1.10}$$

$$q = ratio = \frac{1.05}{1.10}$$

$$n = number\ of\ terms = \infty$$

The formula gives

$$S = \frac{a(1-q^n)}{1-q} = \frac{\frac{20}{1.10}\left(1 - \left(\frac{1.05}{1.10}\right)^n\right)}{1 - \frac{1.05}{1.10}}$$

When $n \to \infty$, $(1.05/1.10)^n \to 0$, so that

$$S = \frac{a(1-q^n)}{1-q} = \frac{\frac{20}{1.10}\left(1 - \left(\frac{1.05}{1.10}\right)^n\right)}{1 - \frac{1.05}{1.10}} = \frac{\frac{20}{1.10}}{1 - \frac{1.05}{1.10}} = \frac{20}{0.10 - 0.05} = 400$$

Warning: You have to be careful! This version of the formula works only because the growth rate of 5% is smaller than the discount rate of 10%. The discounted sum of an infinite series of constantly growing payments exists only when the growth rate g is less than the discount rate r.

Here's a general formula:

$$\begin{array}{c} \text{Sum of} \\ \text{constant-growth} \\ \text{annuity} \end{array} = \frac{CF}{(1+r)} + \frac{CF * (1+g)}{(1+r)^2} + \frac{CF * (1+g)^2}{(1+r)^3} + \cdots$$

$$= \frac{\frac{CF}{(1+r)}\left(1 - \left(\frac{1+g}{1+r}\right)^\infty\right)}{1 - \frac{1+g}{1+r}}$$

$$= \begin{cases} \dfrac{CF}{r - g} & \text{when}|g| < |r| \\ \text{undefined} & \text{otherwise} \end{cases}$$

To summarize:

The present value of a constant-growth annuity—a series of cash flows with first term CF, which grows at rate g—that is discounted at rate r is $CF/(r-g)$, provided g, r.

We use this formula in Chapter 9, when we discuss the valuation of stocks using discounted dividends (the "Gordon dividend model").

CHAPTER 6

What Does It Cost? Applications of the Time Value of Money

OVERVIEW

In Chapter 5 we introduced the basic tools of financial analysis—present value (PV), net present value (NPV), and internal rate of return (IRR). In Chapters 6–10 we use these tools to answer two basic types of questions:

•   *What is it worth?* Presented with an asset—this could be a stock, a bond, a real estate investment, a computer, or a used car—we would like to know *how to value* the asset. The finance tools used to answer this question are mostly related to the concept of present value (PV) and net present value (NPV). The basic principle is that the value of an asset is the present value of its future cash flows. Comparing this present value to the asset's price tells us whether or not we should buy it. We introduced PV and NPV in Chapter 5 and we return to them and their applications in Chapter 7.

- *What does it cost?* This sounds like an innocuous question—after all, you usually know the price of the stock, bond, real estate investment, or used car that you're trying to value. But many interesting questions of *financing alternatives* depend on the relative cost of each alternative. For example, should you pay cash for a car or borrow money to pay for it (and hence make a series of payments over time)? Should you lease that new computer you want or buy it outright? Or should you borrow money from the bank to buy it? It's all clearly a question of *cost*—you'd like to pick the alternative that costs the least.

The tools used for the second question—What does it cost?—are mostly derived from the concept of internal rate of return (IRR). This concept, introduced in Chapter 5, measures the compound rate of return of a series of cash flows. In this chapter we show you that rate of return, when properly used, can be used to measure the cost of a financing alternatives. The main concept presented in this chapter is the *effective annual interest rate* (EAIR), a concept based on the annualized internal rate of return that you can use to compare financing alternatives.

Much of the discussion in this chapter relates to calculating the EAIR and showing its relation to the IRR. We show that the EAIR is a much better gauge of the financing costs than the *annualized percentage rate* (APR), the financing cost often quoted by many lenders such as banks and credit card companies. We show you how to apply this concept to credit card borrowing, mortgages, and auto leasing.

Finance Concepts Discussed

- Effective annual interest rate (EAIR)
- Internal rate of return (IRR)
- Annual percentage rate (APR)
- Loan tables
- Mortgage points
- Lease versus purchase

Excel Functions Used

- **IRR**
- **PMT**
- **Rate**
- **NPV**
- **PV**
- **Sum**
- **Goal Seek**

6.1 Don't Trust the Quoted Interest Rate: Three Examples

In order to set the stage for the somewhat more complicated examples in the rest of the chapter, we start with three simple examples. Each example shows why *quoted interest rates* are not necessarily representative of costs.

We use the three examples in this section to introduce the concept of *effective annual interest rate* (EAIR).

> The effective annual interest rate (EAIR) is the annualized internal rate of return (IRR) of the cash flows of a particular credit arrangement or security.

Example 1: Borrowing From a Bank

In finance, "cost" often refers to an interest rate: "I'm taking a loan from the West Hampton Bank because it's cheaper—West Hampton charges 8% instead of the 9% charged by the East Hampton Bank." This is a sentence we all understand—8% interest results in lower payments than 9% interest.

But now consider the following alternatives. You want to borrow $100 for one year, and you've investigated both the West Hampton Bank and East Hampton Bank:

- West Hampton Bank is lending at 8% interest. If you borrow $100 from them today, you'll have to repay them $108 in one year.
- East Hampton Bank is willing to lend you any amount you want at a 6% rate. BUT: East Hampton Bank has a "loan initiation charge" of 4%. This means that for each $100 you borrow, you'll get only $96, even though you'll pay interest on the full $100.[1]

Obviously the cost of West Hampton's loan is 8%. But is this cheaper or more expensive than the East Hampton loan? You reason as follows: To actually get $100 in your hands from East Hampton, you'll have to borrow $104.17; after they deduct their 4% charge, you'll be left with $100 in hand, which is exactly what you need ($96 * $104.17 = 100). At the end of a year, you'll owe East Hampton Bank $104.17 + 6%$ interest $= 110.42. So the actual interest rate they're charging you (we'll call it the *effective annual interest rate,* EAIR) is $(110.42/100)-1 = 10.42\%$.

This makes everything easier—West Hampton's 8% loan (EAIR = 8%) is actually cheaper than East Hampton's "6%" loan (EAIR = 10.42%).

	A	B	C	D
1	CHEAPER LOAN: WEST HAMPTON OR EAST HAMPTON?			
2		West Hampton	East Hampton	
3	Quoted interest rate	8%	6%	
4	Initial charges	0%	4%	
5	Amount borrowed to get $100 today	100.00	104.17	<-- =100/(1-C4)
6				
7	Date	Cash flow	Cash flow	
8	Date 1, get loan	100.00	100.00	
9	Date 2, pay it back	-108.00	-110.42	<-- =-C5*(1+C3)
10	Effective annual interest rate, EAIR	8.00%	10.42%	<-- =IRR(C8:C9)

---

[1]Such charges are common in many kinds of bank loans, especially mortgages. They're obviously a way to increase the cost of the loan and to befuddle the customer.

Notice in this example that the EAIR is just an IRR, adjusted for the cost of taking the loan from East Hampton Bank. EAIR is *always an interest rate*, but usually with some kind of adjustment.

The lesson of Example 1: When calculating the cost of financial alternatives, *you must include the fees*, even if the lender (in our case East Hampton Bank) does not include the fees.

Example 2: Monthly Versus Annual Interest

You want to buy a computer for $1,000. You don't have any money, so you'll have to finance the computer by taking out a loan for $1,000. You've got two financing alternatives:

- Your bank will lend you the money for 15% annual interest. When you ask the bank what this means, the loan officer assures you that the bank will give you $1,000 today and ask you to repay $1,150 at the end of one year.
- Loan Shark Financing Company will also lend you the $1,000. Its ad says "14.4% annual percentage rate (APR) on a monthly basis." When you ask them what this means, it turns out that Loan Shark charges 1.2% *per month* (they explain to you that 14.4%/12 = 1.2%). This means that each month Loan Shark adds 1.2% to the loan balance outstanding at the end of the previous month:

	A	B	C	D	E	F	G	H
1	HOW LOAN SHARK CHARGES: 14.4% PER YEAR ON A MONTHLY BASIS = 1.2% PER MONTH							
2								
3	Loan balance outstanding at the end of each month							
4	Month 0	Month 1	Month 2	Month 3	Month 4	Month 5	Month 6	
5	$ 1,000.00							
6		$ 1,012.00 <-- =A5*(1+1.2%)						
7			$ 1,024.14 <-- =B6*(1+1.2%)					
8				$ 1,036.43 <-- =C7*(1+1.2%)				
9					$ 1,048.87 <-- =D8*(1+1.2%)			
10						$ 1,061.46 <-- =E9*(1+1.2%)		
11							$ 1,074.19 <-- =F10*(1+1.2%)	
12								
13	Month 7	Month 8	Month 9	Month 10	Month 11	Month 12		
14	$ 1,087.09 <-- =G11*(1+1.2%)							
15		$ 1,100.13 <-- =A14*(1+1.2%)						
16			$ 1,113.33 <-- =B15*(1+1.2%)					
17				$ 1,126.69 <-- =C16*(1+1.2%)				
18					$ 1,140.21 <-- =D17*(1+1.2%)			
19						$ 1,153.89 <-- =E18*(1+1.2%)		

By the end of the year, you will owe Loan Shark $1,153.89.

$$\$1,153.89 = \$1,500 * \left(1 + \underbrace{\frac{14.4\%}{12}}\right)^{12}$$

Loan Shark's loan is "compounded monthly," meaning that the 14.4% annual interest rate translates to 1.2% per month

Since this is more than the $1,150 you will owe the bank, you should prefer the bank loan.

The effective annual interest rate (EAIR) of each loan is the *annualized interest rate* charged by the loan. The bank charges you 15% annually and Loan Shark charges you 15.39% annually:

	A	B	C	D
1	THE BANK OR LOAN SHARK?			
2		**Bank**	**Loan Shark**	
3	Quoted interest rate	15.0%	14.4%	
4	Borrow today	$ 1,000.00	$ 1,000.00	
5	Repay in one year	-$1,150.00	-$1,153.89	<-- =-C4*(1+C3/12)^12
6	Effective annual interest rate, EAIR	15.00%	15.39%	<-- =IRR(C4:C5)
7				
8	A second way to compute the EAIR			
9	Monthly interest rate		1.20%	<-- =C3/12
10	EAIR Annualized monthly rate		15.39%	<-- =(1+C9)^12-1

Cells C9 and C10 show another way to compute the 15.39% EAIR charged by Loan Shark. Cell C9 computes the monthly rate charged by Loan Shark as 1.20%, and cell C10 annualizes this rate $(1 + 14.4\%/12)^{12} - 1 = 15.39\%$ Thus, there are two ways to compute the EAIR:

$$EAIR = 15.39\% = \begin{cases} \dfrac{\text{payment at end of year}}{\text{loan taken out beginning of year}} - 1 = \dfrac{\$1,153.89}{\$1,000.00} - 1 \quad \leftarrow \text{Cell C6} \\[2em] \left(1 + \dfrac{14.4\%}{12}\right)^{12} - 1 \qquad\qquad\qquad\qquad\qquad \leftarrow \text{Cell C10} \end{cases}$$

The lesson of Example 2: Annual percentage rate (APR) does not always correctly reflect the cost of borrowing. To compute the true cost, calculate the effective annual interest rate (EAIR).

Example 3: An "Interest-Free" Loan

You're buying a used car. The Junkmobile your heart desires has a price tag of $2,000. You have two financing options:

- The dealer explains that if you pay cash you'll get a 15% discount. In this case you'll pay $1,700 for the car today. Since you don't have any money now, you intend to borrow the $1,700 from your Uncle Frank, who charges 10% interest.
- On the other hand, the dealer will give you "0% financing": You don't pay anything now, and you can pay the dealer the full cost of the Junkmobile at the end of the year.

Thus you have two choices: the dealer's 0% financing and Uncle Frank's 10% rate. Which is cheaper?

A little thought will show that the dealer is actually charging you an effective annual interest rate (EAIR) of 17.65%: His "0% financing" essentially involves a loan to you of $1,700 with an end-year repayment of $2,000:

	A	B	C	D	E
1	FINANCING THE JUNKMOBILE				
2		**Cash**	**Dealer**	**Difference**	
3	Today, get loan	-1,700.00	0.00	1,700.00	<-- =C3-B3
4	End of year, repay loan		-2,000.00	-2,000.00	<-- =C4-B4
5	Effective Annual Interest Rate (EAIR) charged by dealer			17.65%	<-- =IRR(D3:D4)

Uncle Frank's EAIR is 10%: He will loan you $1,700 and have you repay only $1,870. So you're better off borrowing from him.

The lesson of Example 3: Free loans are usually not free! To compute the cost of a "free" loan, calculate the EAIR of the differential cash flows.

6.2 Calculating the Cost of a Mortgage

Now that we've set the stage, we proceed to a series of somewhat more complicated examples. We start with a mortgage. Housing is most often the largest personal asset an individual owns. Financing housing with a mortgage is something almost every reader of this book will do in his/her lifetime. Calculating the cost of a mortgage is thus a useful exercise. In this chapter mortgages are one of the examples we use to illustrate the problems encountered in computing the cost of financial assets.

A Simple Mortgage

We start with a simple example. Your bank has agreed to give you a $100,000 mortgage, to be repaid over ten years at 8% interest. For simplicity, we assume that the payments on the mortgage are annual.[2] The bank calculates the annual payment as $14,902.95, using Excel's **PMT** function:

EXCEL NOTE
_____

DIALOG BOX FOR **PMT** FUNCTION

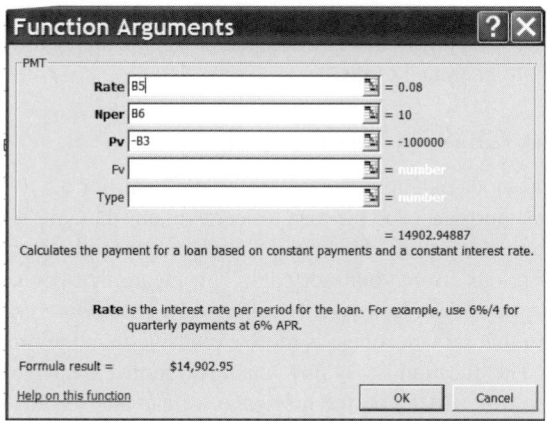

In the dialog box for Excel's **PMT** function, **Rate** is the interest rate on the loan, **Nper** is the number of repayment periods, and **Pv** is the loan principal. As discussed in Chapter 5, if the loan principal is written as a positive number, Excel presents the payment as a negative number; to avoid this, we write **Pv** as a negative number.

---

[2]In the real world, payments are probably monthly; see the example in Section 6.3.

The **PMT** function calculates an annuity payment (a constant periodic payment), which pays off a loan:

$$100,000 = \sum_{t=1}^{10} \frac{14,902.95}{(1.08)^t} = \frac{14,902.95}{(1.08)} + \frac{14,902.95}{(1.08)^2} + \frac{14,902.95}{(1.08)^3} + \cdots + \frac{14,902.95}{(1.08)^{10}}$$

We can summarize all of this in an Excel spreadsheet:

	A	B	C
1	**A SIMPLE MORTGAGE**		
2	Mortgage principal	100,000	
3	Interest rate	8%	
4	Mortgage term (years)	10	
5	Annual payment	$14,902.95	<-- =PMT(B3,B4,-B2)
6			
7	Year	Mortgage cash flow	
8	0	100,000.00	
9	1	-14,902.95	<-- =-$B$5
10	2	-14,902.95	
11	3	-14,902.95	
12	4	-14,902.95	
13	5	-14,902.95	
14	6	-14,902.95	
15	7	-14,902.95	
16	8	-14,902.95	
17	9	-14,902.95	
18	10	-14,902.95	
19			
20	Effective annual interest rate (EAIR)	8.00%	<-- =IRR(B8:B18)

The *effective annual interest rate* (*EAIR*) of this particular mortgage is simply the internal rate of return of its payments. Because the payments on the mortgage are annual, the IRR in cell B20 is already in annual terms.

The Bank Charges "Mortgage Points"

As in the previous example, you've asked the bank for a $100,000 mortgage. It has agreed to give you this mortgage, and the loan officer explains that you'll be asked to repay $14,902.95 per year for the next ten years. However, when you get to the bank, you learn that the bank has deducted "1.5 points" from your mortgage. This means that you get only $98,500 ($100,000 minus 1.5%). Your payments, however, continue to be based on a principal of $100,000.[3] You realize immediately that this mortgage is more expensive than the mortgage discussed in the previous subsection. The question is: By *how much* is it more expensive? By calculating the *effective annual interest rate* (*EAIR*) on the mortgage we can answer this question. The calculation below shows that you're actually paying 8.34% interest annually.

Notice that the effective annual interest rate (EAIR) of 8.34% is the internal rate of return of the stream of payments consisting of the actual loan amount ($98,500) versus the actual

---

[3]Some banks and mortgage brokers also charge an "origination fee," defined as a payment to cover the initial cost of processing the mortgage. The net effect of "points" and the "origination fee" is the same—you are charged interest on more money than you actually get in hand.

	A	B	C
1	**A MORTGAGE WITH POINTS**		
2	Mortgage principal	100,000	
3	"Points"	1.50%	
4	Quoted interest	8%	
5	Mortgage term (years)	10	
6	Annual payment	$14,902.95	
7			
8	Year	Mortgage cash flow	
9	0	98,500.00	<-- =B2*(1-B3)
10	1	-14,902.95	<-- =-$B$6
11	2	-14,902.95	
12	3	-14,902.95	
13	4	-14,902.95	
14	5	-14,902.95	
15	6	-14,902.95	
16	7	-14,902.95	
17	8	-14,902.95	
18	9	-14,902.95	
19	10	-14,902.95	
20			
21	Effective annual interest rate	8.34%	<-- =IRR(B9:B19)

payments you're making ($14,902.95 annually). Here's the calculation:

$$98,500 = \sum_{t=1}^{10} \frac{14,902.95}{(1.0834)^t} = \frac{14,902.95}{(1.0834)} + \frac{14,902.95}{(1.0834)^2} + \frac{14,902.95}{(1.0834)^3} + \cdots + \frac{14,902.95}{(1.0834)^{10}}$$

At the end of each year, you will report to the Internal Revenue Service the amount of interest paid on the mortgage. Because this interest is an expense for tax purposes, it's important to get it right. To calculate this interest, we need a loan table, which allocates each year's payment made between interest and repayment of principal (see Section 5.5, p. 112). This table is sometimes called an "amortization table" ("amortize" means to repay with a series of periodic payments):

	A	B	C	D	E	F
21	Effective annual interest rate	8.34%	<-- =IRR(B9:B19)			
22						
23	**MORTGAGE AMORTIZATION TABLE**					
24	Year	Mortgage principal at beginning of year	Payment at end of year	Part of payment that is interest (expense for taxes!)	Part of payment that is repayment of principal (not an expense for tax purposes)	
25	1	98,500.00	$14,902.95	$8,211.41	6,691.54	<-- =C25-D25
26	2	91,808.46	$14,902.95	$7,653.58	7,249.37	
27	3	84,559.09	$14,902.95	$7,049.23	7,853.71	
28	4	76,705.38	$14,902.95	$6,394.51	8,508.44	
29	5	68,196.94	$14,902.95	$5,685.21	9,217.74	
30	6	58,979.20	$14,902.95	$4,916.78	9,986.17	
31	7	48,993.03	$14,902.95	$4,084.28	10,818.66	
32	8	38,174.37	$14,902.95	$3,182.39	11,720.56	
33	9	26,453.81	$14,902.95	$2,205.31	12,697.64	
34	10	13,756.17	$14,902.95	$1,146.78	13,756.17	

Annotations above columns: B25-E25 (pointing to column C), $B$21*B25 (pointing to column D).

Column D of the table gives the interest expense for tax purposes. If you report interest payments on your tax return, this is the payment you'd be allowed to report. Notice that the interest portion of the annual $14,902.95 payments gets smaller over the years, while the repayment of principal portion (which is not deductible for tax purposes) gets larger.

6.3 Mortgages With Monthly Payments

We continue with the mortgage examples from Section 6.2. This time we introduce the concept of monthly payments. Suppose you get a $100,000 mortgage with an 8% interest rate, payable monthly, and suppose you have to pay the mortgage back over one year (twelve months).[4] Many banks interpret the combination of 8% annual interest and "payable monthly" to mean that the monthly interest on the mortgage is $8\%/12 = 0.667\%$. This is often referred to as "monthly compounding," although the usage of this term is not uniform. To compute the monthly repayment on the mortgage, we use Excel's **PMT** function:

	A	B	C
1	**MORTGAGE WITH MONTHLY PAYMENTS**		
2	Loan principal	100,000	
3	Loan term (years)	1	
4	Quoted interest rate	8%	
5			
6	**Month**	**Cash flow**	
7	0	100,000.00	
8	1	-8,698.84	<-- =PMT($B$4/12,$B$3*12,$B$2)
9	2	-8,698.84	
10	3	-8,698.84	
11	4	-8,698.84	
12	5	-8,698.84	
13	6	-8,698.84	
14	7	-8,698.84	
15	8	-8,698.84	
16	9	-8,698.84	
17	10	-8,698.84	
18	11	-8,698.84	
19	12	-8,698.84	
20			
21	Monthly IRR	0.667%	<-- =IRR(B7:B19)
22	Effective annual interest rate, EAIR	8.30%	<-- =(1+B21)^12-1

The EAIR on the mortgage in the example is computed by using Excel's **IRR** function (cell B21). In our case, the **IRR** function gives a monthly interest rate of 0.667% (we already knew this, since $8\%/12 = 0.667\%$). Annualizing this gives $8.30\% = (1 + 8\%/12)^{12} - 1$ (cell B22).

---

[4]Most mortgages are, of course, for much longer term. But twelve months enables us to fit the example comfortably within a page. Later, we'll consider longer terms, but the principles will be the same.

Mortgages—More Complicated Example

As we saw in Section 6.2, many mortgages in the United States have "origination fees" or "discount points" (the latter are often just called "points"). All of these fees reduce the initial amount given to you by the bank, *without reducing* the principal on which the bank computes its payments (sounds misleading, doesn't it?).

As an example, consider the above twelve-month mortgage with an 8% annual rate, payable monthly, but with an origination fee of 0.5% and 1 point. This means that you actually get $98,500 ($100,000 minus $500 for the origination fee and $1,000 for the point), but that your monthly repayment remains $8,698.84:

	A	B	C
1	**MORTGAGE EXAMPLE WITH POINTS AND ORIGINATION FEE**		
2	Loan principal	100,000.00	
3	Loan term (years)	1	
4	Quoted interest rate	8%	
5	Discount points	1	
6	Origination fee	0.5%	
7			
8	**Month**	**Cash flow**	
9	0	98,500.00	<-- =B2*(1-B5/100-B6)
10	1	-8,698.84	<-- =PMT($B$4/12,$B$3*12,$B$2)
11	2	-8,698.84	
12	3	-8,698.84	
13	4	-8,698.84	
14	5	-8,698.84	
15	6	-8,698.84	
16	7	-8,698.84	
17	8	-8,698.84	
18	9	-8,698.84	
19	10	-8,698.84	
20	11	-8,698.84	
21	12	-8,698.84	
22			
23	Monthly IRR	0.9044%	<-- =IRR(B9:B21)
24	EAIR	11.41%	<-- =(1+B23)^12-1
25			
26	Monthly IRR using Excel's **Rate** function	0.9044%	<-- =RATE(12,8698.84,-98500)

The monthly IRR (cell B23) is the interest rate that sets the present value of the monthly payments equal to the initial $98,500 received:

$$\$98,500 = \frac{\$8,698.94}{(1+0.9044\%)} + \frac{\$8,698.94}{(1+0.9044\%)^2} + \frac{\$8,698.94}{(1+0.9044\%)^3} + \cdots + \frac{\$8,698.94}{(1+0.9044\%)^{12}}$$

The effective annual interest rate $EAIR = 11.41\% = (1+0.9044\%)^{12} - 1$ is the annualized cost of the mortgage payments.

As you can see in cell B26, Excel's **Rate** function also calculates the monthly IRR that we calculated in cell B23:

EXCEL NOTE

CALCULATING THE MONTHLY IRR WITH **RATE**

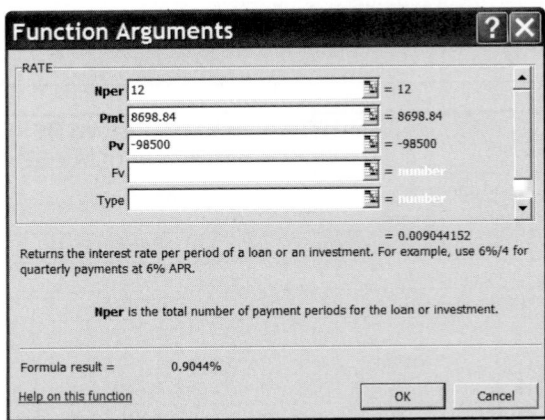

The **Rate** function computes the IRR of a series of constant (the financial jargon is "flat" or "even") payments so that the discounted value equals the **Pv** indicated. Notice that in the **Rate** function the signs of the payments (indicated by **Pmt**) and the present value **Pv** of these payments must be different. This is a feature that **Rate** shares with Excel functions like **PMT** and **Pv** discussed in Chapter 5.

Longer-Term Mortgages

Suppose the mortgage in the previous example has a thirty-year term (meaning: $360 = 30*12$ repayments). Each repayment would be \$733.76 and the EAIR would be 8.4721%:

	A	B	C
1	**30-YEAR MORTGAGE** **with points and origination fee**		
2	Loan principal	100,000.00	
3	Loan term (years)	30	
4	Quoted interest rate	8%	
5	Discount points	1	
6	Origination fee	0.5%	
7			
8	Initial amount of loan, net of fees	98,500.00	<-- =B2*(1-B5/100-B6)
9	Monthly repayment	733.76	<-- =PMT(B4/12,B3*12,-B2)
10			
11	**Calculating the EAIR**		
12	Monthly interest rate	0.6800%	<-- =RATE(B3*12,B9,-B8)
13	Effective annual interest rate (EAIR)	8.4721%	<-- =(1+B12)^12-1

We use **PMT** to calculate the payment and **Rate** to compute the monthly interest rate. The EAIR is computed in the usual manner—by compounding the monthly payments (cell B13).

Note that the effect of the initial mortgage fees on mortgage EAIR declines when the mortgage is longer term:

- For the one-year mortgage discussed previously, the 1.5% initial fee increased the EAIR of the mortgage from 8% to 11.41%.

- For the thirty-year mortgage discussed above, the same initial fees increase the EAIR from 8% to 8.4721%.

- The reason that the fees have a smaller effect for the second mortgage is that they are spread out over a much longer term.

6.4 Lease or Purchase?

This section uses the concepts of present value and internal rate of return to explore the relative advantages of leasing versus buying an asset. As you will see, the choice between leasing and buying basically comes down to choosing the cheaper of two methods of financing.

Here's our terminology: A *lease* is a rental agreement; in our examples leases are usually for equipment (we discuss a computer lease and a car lease), but the analysis for real estate is virtually the same. The party that rents the asset and uses it is called the *lessee* and the owner of the asset is called the *lessor*.

A Simple Lease Example

You need a new computer, but you can't decide whether you should buy it or lease it. The computer costs $4,000. The lessor is your neighborhood computer leasing company, which offers to lease you the computer for $1,500 per year. The lessor's conditions are that you make four payments of $1,500: the first payment at the start of the lease (time 0) and subsequent payments at the end of years 1, 2, and 3. Based on past experience, you know that you will keep your new computer for about three years. One additional fact: You can borrow from your bank at 15%.

Here is a spreadsheet with the cash flows for the lease and for the purchase:

	A	B	C	D
1		BASIC LEASE VERSUS PURCHASE		
2	Asset cost	4,000.00		
3	Annual lease payment	1,500.00		
4	Bank rate	15%		
5				
6	Year	Purchase cash flow	Lease cash flow	
7	0	4,000.00	1,500.00	
8	1		1,500.00	
9	2		1,500.00	
10	3		1,500.00	
11				
12	PV of costs	4,000.00	4,924.84	<-- =C7+NPV($B$4,C8:C10)
13	Lease or purchase?	purchase		<-- =IF(B12<C12,"purchase","lease")

To decide whether the lease is preferable, we discount the cash flows from both the lease and the purchase at the 15% bank lending rate. We write the outflows as positive numbers, so that the PV in row 12 is the *present value of the costs*. As you can see in cell B12, the present value of the lease costs is $4,924.84, which is more than the $4,000 cost of purchasing the computer. Thus, you prefer the purchase, which is less costly.

There's another way of doing this same calculation. We compute the IRR of the *differential cash flows*—subtracting the lease cash flow from the purchase cash flow in each of the years:

	A	B	C	D	E
1			BASIC LEASE VERSUS PURCHASE THE DIFFERENTIAL CASH FLOWS		
2	Asset cost	4,000			
3	Annual lease payment	1,500			
4	Bank rate	15%			
5					
6	Year	Purchase cash flow	Lease cash flow	Differential cash flow	
7	0	4,000	1,500	2,500	<-- =B7-C7
8	1		1,500	-1,500	<-- =B8-C8
9	2		1,500	-1,500	<-- =B9-C9
10	3		1,500	-1,500	<-- =B10-C10
11					
12	IRR of differential cash flows			36.31%	<-- =IRR(D7:D10)
13	Lease or purchase?			purchase	<-- =IF(D12>B4,"purchase","lease")
14					
15	Explanation: The lease is like a loan--you save 2,500 in year 0 and pay back 1,500 in each of years 1-3. The IRR of this "loan" is 36.31%.				

The computer lease is equivalent to paying $1,500 for the computer in year 0 and taking a loan of $2,500 from the computer leasing company. The computer leasing "loan" has three equal repayments of $1,500 and an internal rate of return (IRR) of 36.31%. Because you can borrow money from the bank at 15%, you would prefer to purchase the computer with borrowed money from the bank (at 15%) rather than "borrowing" $2,500 from the leasing company, which charges 36.31%.

In the spreadsheet below you can see another way to make this same point. If you borrow $2,500 from the bank at 15%, you have to pay back $1,094.94 per year for each of the next three years (assuming the bank asked for a flat repayment schedule). This is substantially less than the $1,500 that the computer lessor asks for on the same loan.

$$2,500 = \frac{1,094.94}{1.15} + \frac{1,094.94}{(1.15)^2} + \frac{1,094.94}{(1.15)^3}$$

The conclusion is that if you decide to borrow $2,500 to purchase the computer, you should do so from the bank rather than from the computer leasing company. In the spreadsheet, we used the Excel **PMT** function to compute the repayment:

	A	B	C	D	E
17	What if you borrowed $2,500 from the bank?				
18	Year	Money saved by leasing		Same amount from bank	
19	0	2,500		2,500.00	
20	1	-1,500		-1,094.94	<-- =PMT($B$4,3,$D$19)
21	2	-1,500		-1,094.94	
22	3	-1,500		-1,094.94	

What Have We Assumed About Leasing Versus Purchasing?

The leasing example considered above illustrates the spirit of lease/purchase analysis. The example makes some simplifying assumptions that are worth noting:

- No taxes: When corporations lease equipment, the lease payments are expenses for tax purposes; when these corporations buy assets, the depreciation on the asset is an expense for tax purposes. Taxes complicate the analysis somewhat; the case of leasing with taxes is considered in Chapter 8.
- Operational equivalence of lease and purchase: In our analysis we don't ask whether you need a computer—we assume that you've already answered this question positively, so that only the method of acquisition is in question. Our analysis also assumes that any maintenance or repairs that need to be done on the computer will be done by you, whether you lease or buy the computer.
- No residual value: We've assumed that the asset (in this case, the computer) is worthless at the end of the lease term.

We explore the last point briefly. Suppose you think that the computer will be worth $800 at the end of year 3. Then, as shown below, the purchase cash flows change, so that owning the computer gives you an inflow of $800 in year 3.[5] The cost of purchasing the computer is reduced (the present value of the purchase is now $3,304) and the lease alternative becomes even less attractive than the purchase. Another way of seeing this is to look at the IRR of the differential cash flows, which is now 45.07% (cell B23).[6]

	A	B	C	D
1	**LEASE VERSUS PURCHASE WITH RESIDUAL VALUE**			
2	Asset cost	4,000.00		
3	Annual lease payment	1,500.00		
4	Residual value, yr. 3	800	<-- Value of computer at end year 3	
5	Bank rate	15%		
6				
7	Year	Purchase cash flow	Lease cash flow	
8	0	4,000.00	1,500.00	
9	1		1,500.00	
10	2		1,500.00	
11	3	-800.00	1,500.00	
12				
13	PV of costs	3,304.35	4,924.84	<-- =C8+NPV($B$5,C9:C11)
14	Lease or purchase?		purchase	<-- =IF(B13<C13,"purchase","lease")
15				
16	Calculating the IRR of the differential cash flow			
17	Year		Money saved by leasing	
18	0		2,500.00	<-- =B8-C8
19	1		-1,500.00	<-- =B9-C9
20	2		-1,500.00	
21	3		-2,300.00	
22				
23	IRR of differential		45.07%	<-- =IRR(C18:C21)
24	Lease or purchase?		purchase	<-- =IF(C23>B5,"purchase","lease")

---

[5] Note that since we're writing *outflows* (like the cost of the computer) as *positive numbers,* we have to write the inflows as negative numbers.

[6] A caveat is in order here: We're treating the computer's residual value as if it has the same certainty as the rest of the cash flows, whereas clearly it is less certain. The finance literature has a technical solution to this: We find the *certainty equivalent* of the residual value. For example, it may be that we expect the residual value to be $1,200, but that—recognizing the uncertainty of getting this value—we treat this as equivalent to getting an $800 residual with certainty.

6.5 Auto Lease Example

Here's a slightly more realistic (and more complicated) example of leasing: You've decided to get a new car. You can either lease the car or buy it (perhaps financing it with an auto loan from your bank—something we'll look at later). The relevant facts are given in the spreadsheet below, but we summarize them here:

- The manufacturer's suggested retail price (MSRP) for the car is $24,550, but you've been able to negotiate a price of $22,490 with the dealer.[7] In the jargon of the car leasing business, the $22,490 is referred to as the "capitalized cost." To this price must be added a destination charge of $415, so that you end up paying $22,905 if you purchase the car. This price represents your alternative purchase cost if you decide to buy instead of lease the car.
- The dealer has offered you the following lease terms:
  - You pay $1,315 at the signing of the lease. This includes a $450 security deposit that will be refunded when the lease is up.
  - You'll pay $373.43 per month for the next 24 months. In month 24 you get your security deposit of $450 back.
  - You guarantee that the car will have a residual value of $13,994 at the end of the lease. The dealer has based this value on 57% of the MSRP. What this means is that if the car is worth less than $13,994 at the end of the 24th month, the lessee (you) will make up the difference.[8] The end-lease payment associated with this residual can be written as

$$\text{end-lease residual payment} = \begin{cases} 13{,}994 - \text{market value} & \text{if } \text{market value} < 13{,}994 \\ 0 & \text{otherwise} \end{cases}$$

    Another way of writing this payment is as *Max* (13,994 – *market value*, 0). The *Max(A,B)* notation means that you pay the larger of *A* or *B*. Conveniently, **Max** is also a function in Excel.

The residual value turns out to be an important factor in the way you view leasing versus purchase. We'll devote more time to it later. For the moment, let's assume that you think the car will actually be worth $15,000 at the end of two years so your last payment on the lease is zero:

$$\text{end-lease residual payment} = Max(13{,}994 - \text{market value}, 0)$$
$$= Max(13{,}994 - 15{,}000, 0) = Max(-1{,}006, 0) = 0$$

All of the lease costs are listed in column C of the spreadsheet below. To evaluate these costs, look at column D, which shows the costs associated with buying the car. There are only two of these: the initial purchase price of the car ($22,490 + the destination cost of $415 = $22,905) and what you anticipate will be the market value of the car at the end of the lease term

---

[7]The (MSRP—also referred to as the car's "sticker price"—is price the auto manufacturer suggests as an appropriate price for the car. In reality it's a kind of official fiction and forms the basis for negotiation between the dealer and the car purchaser. In our example, the MSRP is used in the residual value computation, but the actual price paid for the car is less.

[8]According to www.edmunds.com: "The lease-end fees are generally reasonable, unless the car has 100,000 miles on it, a busted-up grille, and melted chocolate smeared into the upholstery. Dealers and financial institutions want you to buy or lease another car from them and can be rather lenient regarding excess mileage and abnormal wear. After all, if they hit you with a bunch of trumped-up charges you're not going to remain a loyal customer, are you? . . . But keep in mind that if you take your business elsewhere, you're going to be facing a bill for items like worn tires, paint chips, door dings, and the like."

(in this example, you think the car will actually be worth $15,000). Since we use the convention of making costs positive numbers, the inflow from selling the car is a negative number.

This last number bears some examination: If you lease, your last payment is

$$last\ lease\ payment = last\ month's\ rental - return\ of\ security\ deposit$$
$$+ end\text{-}of\text{-}lease\ residual\ payment$$
$$= 373.43 - 450 + Max(13,994 - market\ value, 0)$$

If you're right, and the actual market value of the car is $15,000, then your last "payment" is −$76.57 (meaning that you'll get $76.57 back from the lease company).

Column E in the spreadsheet subtracts the lease from the purchase cash flows. Initially, the lease saves you $21,590; in months 1–23, the lease costs you $373.43 more than the purchase, and at the end of month 24 the lease costs you $14,923.43 more than the purchase.

	A	B	C	D	E	F
1		**AUTO LEASE VERSUS PURCHASE**				
2	MSRP	24,550	<-- Manufacturer's suggested retail price			
3	Capitalized cost	22,490	<-- Negotiated price			
4	Destination charge	415	<-- Paid both by the lessee and the buyer			
5	Acquisition fee	450	<-- Paid only by the lessee			
6	Security deposit	450	<-- refunded at end of lease			
7						
8	Payment due at signing	1,315	<-- =SUM(B4:B6)			
9	Monthly payment	373.43	<-- Dealer's lease offer			
10						
11						
12	Residual value after 2 years as % of MSRP	57%				
13	Lease residual value after 2 years	13,994	<-- =B12*B2--lessee guarantees this value			
14	Your estimated residual value	15,000	<-- Your guess			
15					=B3+B4	
16						
17			**Month**	**Payment**	**Purchase**	**Difference**	
18			0	1,315.00	22,905.00	21,590.00	<-- =D18-C18
19		=B8	1	373.43		-373.43	<-- =D19-C19
20			2	373.43		-373.43	<-- =D20-C20
21			3	373.43		-373.43	
22			4	373.43		-373.43	
23			5	373.43		-373.43	
24			6	373.43		-373.43	
25			7	373.43		-373.43	
26			8	373.43		-373.43	
27			9	373.43		-373.43	
28			10	373.43		-373.43	
29			11	373.43		-373.43	
30			12	373.43		-373.43	
31			13	373.43		-373.43	
32			14	373.43		-373.43	
33			15	373.43		-373.43	
34			16	373.43		-373.43	
35			17	373.43		-373.43	
36			18	373.43		-373.43	
37			19	373.43		-373.43	
38			20	373.43		-373.43	
39			21	373.43		-373.43	
40			22	373.43		-373.43	
41			23	373.43		-373.43	
42			24	-76.57	-15,000.00	-14,923.43	<-- =D42-C42
43						
44		=$B$9-B6+MAX(B13-B14,0)		Monthly IRR		0.44%	<-- =IRR(E18:E42)
45				EAIR		5.39%	<-- =(1+E44)^12-1
46						
47				**Buy or lease?**		
48				Alternative financing		7%	
49				Buy or lease?		lease	<-- =IF(E48>E45,"lease","buy")

The monthly IRR of the differential cash flows is 0.44% (cell E44), which gives an EAIR of 5.39% (cell E45).

Should you buy or should you lease? It depends on your alternative cost of financing. If you can finance at a bank for less than 5.39%, then you should buy the car; otherwise, the lease looks like a good deal.

Role of the Residual

The residual value of the car is very important in determining the cost of the lease. To illustrate this, we use the **Data|Table** feature of Excel (see Chapter 30) to run a sensitivity table, which shows the EAIR and the lease/buy decision as a function of your estimated end-lease market value of the car:

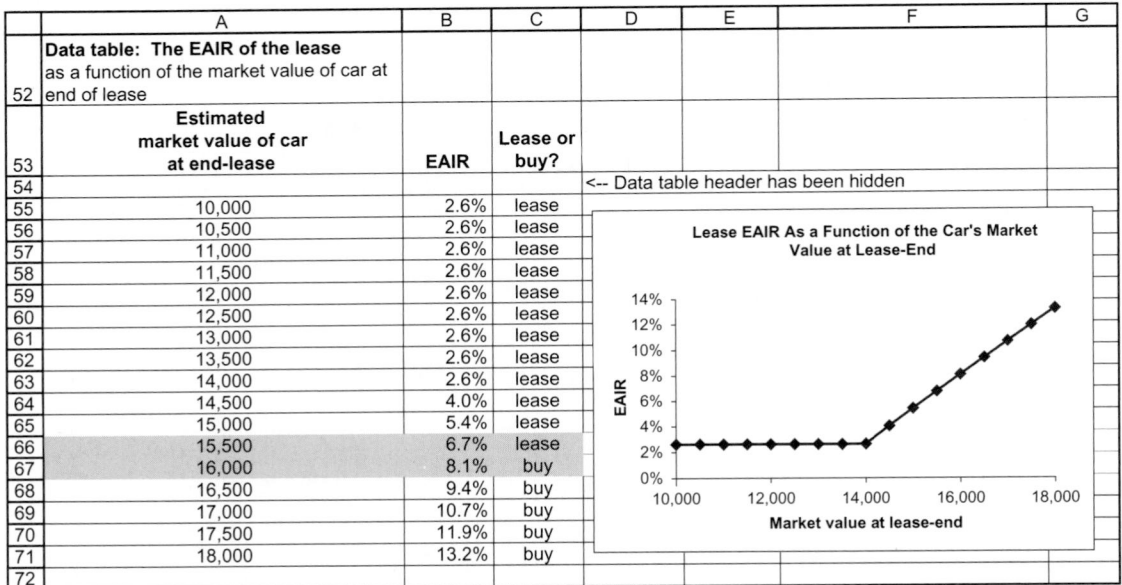

	A	B	C	D	E	F	G
52	Data table: The EAIR of the lease as a function of the market value of car at end of lease						
53	Estimated market value of car at end-lease	EAIR	Lease or buy?				
54				<-- Data table header has been hidden			
55	10,000	2.6%	lease				
56	10,500	2.6%	lease				
57	11,000	2.6%	lease				
58	11,500	2.6%	lease				
59	12,000	2.6%	lease				
60	12,500	2.6%	lease				
61	13,000	2.6%	lease				
62	13,500	2.6%	lease				
63	14,000	2.6%	lease				
64	14,500	4.0%	lease				
65	15,000	5.4%	lease				
66	15,500	6.7%	lease				
67	16,000	8.1%	buy				
68	16,500	9.4%	buy				
69	17,000	10.7%	buy				
70	17,500	11.9%	buy				
71	18,000	13.2%	buy				
72							

As the data table shows, leasing is preferable if you think that the actual market value at the end of the lease term will be low relative to the lease residual of $13,994. The lease is based on your "reselling" the car to the dealer for $13,994; if you think that the actual market value of the car will be much higher, then you would be selling it to the dealer at a loss, and you're better off buying the car and reselling it yourself.[9] The breakeven market value—the estimated market value for which you are indifferent between leasing the car or financing it at the bank at 7%—is somewhere between $15,500 and $16,000; in this range the EAIR of the lease is 7%, which is equal to the cost of the alternative financing.[10]

---

[9]Some leases actually give you the option of buying the car for the residual value at the end of the lease term. This effectively locks in the lease EIAR, since if the car is worth more than the lease residual value, you can always buy it for the residual and resell the car on the open market.

[10]The exact residual value for which you are indifferent is $15,594.

Financing the Purchase of a Car With a Bank Loan: Cheaper or More Expensive?

In our analysis above, we concluded that the annual cost of the two-year lease (cell E45) is an EAIR of 5.39%. So it stands to reason that if you can get a cheaper loan from a bank, you should take the bank loan and use the proceeds to buy the car. And yet . . . suppose the bank offers you a 3% loan (with monthly compounding, so that the monthly interest rate is $3\%/12 = 0.25\%$), and suppose that you have the same amount to finance (namely, the car cost of $22,905 minus the money down of $1,315). The spreadsheet below shows that the monthly payments on this bank loan are much *larger* than those of the car lease:

	H	I	J
2	**Financing with a bank loan**		
3	Cost of car	22,905	<-- =B3+B4
4	Money down	1,315	
5	Amount to finance	21,590	<-- =I3-I4
6			
7	Bank rate	3%	
8	Monthly loan payment	927.96	<-- =-PMT(I7/12,24,I5)
9	Monthly lease payment	373.43	
10			
11	**Note**: The PMT function in cell H8 calculates the		
12	monthly payment on a $21,590 loan (cell H5) given for 24		
13	months at monthly interest 0.25% (cell H7/12).		

Now this is confusing: Borrowing from the bank at 3% to buy the car involves a much higher monthly payment ($926.96) than the monthly lease payment ($373.43). Yet in our first analysis of the lease on page 144, we concluded that a loan rate of 3% is preferable to the lease EAIR of 5.39%. To resolve this apparent contradiction, recall that the difference between the two—the lease and the loan—is the residual value built into the lease: This residual value—essentially a guarantee that you, the lessee, extend to the lender—both reduces your monthly lease payments *and* increases your stake in the residual value of the car. Compared to the bank loan, the lease gives you lower payments in return for bearing the higher risk of guaranteeing the residual value of the car. There is no free lunch.

   To see that the loan is actually cheaper, assume that you take a separate bank loan to finance the car's residual value of $15,000 in two years:

$$PV \text{ of residual value} = \frac{\$15,000}{\left(1 + \frac{3\%}{12}\right)^{24}} = \$14,127.53$$

We can now divide the purchase price of $22,905 into two parts:

$$\$22,905 = \underbrace{\$14,127.53}_{\substack{\uparrow \\ \frac{\$15,000}{\left(1+\frac{3\%}{12}\right)^{24}}}} + \$8,777.47$$

   The $8,777.47 is the cost of using the car for the next two years. Of this amount, you have to pay an immediate down payment of $1,315, which leaves $7,462.47 to finance. Financing this amount with a lease will cost $373.43 per month, whereas financing with a bank loan will cost

$320.75 per month:

	A	B	C
1	AUTO LEASE VERSUS PURCHASE COMPARING BANK LOAN TO LEASE PAYMENT		
2	MSRP	24,550.00	<-- Manufacturer's suggested retail price
3	Capitalized cost	22,490.00	<-- Negotiated price
4	Destination charge	415.00	<-- Paid both by the lessee and the buyer
5	Acquisition fee	450.00	<-- Paid only by the lessee
6	Security deposit	450.00	<-- refunded at end of lease
7			
8	Payment due at signing	1,315.00	<-- =SUM(B4:B6)
9	Monthly payment	373.43	<-- Dealer's lease offer
10			
11	Residual value after 2 years as % of MSRP	57%	
12	Lease residual value after 3 years	13,993.50	<-- =B11*B2--lessee guarantees this value
13	Your estimated residual value	15,000.00	<-- Your guess
14			
15	**Financing with a bank loan**		
16	Bank rate	3%	
17	Monthly rate	0.25%	<-- =B16/12
18			
19	Cost of car	22,905.00	<-- =B3+B4
20	Money down	1,315.00	
21	Amount to finance	21,590.00	<-- =B19-B20
22			
23	Loan principal to finance residual in 2 years	14,127.53	<-- =B13/(1+B17)^24
24	Loan principal to finance car lease for 2 years	7,462.47	<-- =B19-B20-B23
25			
26	Monthly loan payment to finance car lease for 2 years	320.75	<-- =PMT(B17,24,-B24)
27	Monthly lease payment	373.43	

The bank loan is cheaper. We've summarized our logic in Figure 6.1.

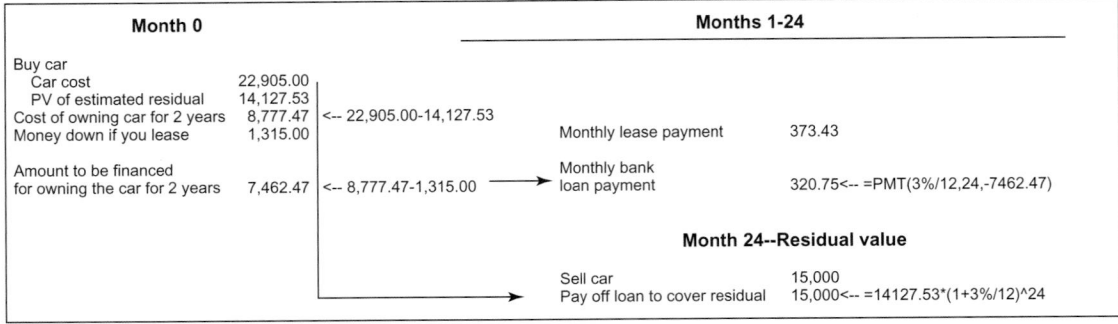

Figure 6.1 Car lease versus car loan from a bank. Explanation: The cost of the car is $22,905. You estimate the residual value of the car in two years at $15,000, which has a present value of $14,127.53. The cost of owning the car for two years is therefore $8,777.47. If you lease the car you are required to put down $1,315. Assume that you finance the remaining cost of $7,462.47 with a bank loan. This loan will cost you $320.75 per month, compared with the $373.43 per month for the car lease. It's thus cheaper to finance with a car loan from the bank.

6.6 More-Than-Once-a-Year Compounding and the Effective Annual Interest Rate (EAIR)

Suppose you are charged interest on a monthly basis, but you want to compute the annual interest cost. Here's an example. XYZ Bank says that it charges an annual percentage rate (APR) of 18% on your credit card balances, with "interest computed monthly." Suppose that what the bank means is that it charges 1.5% per month on the outstanding balance at the beginning of the month. To determine what this means in practice, you should ask yourself, "If I have a credit balance of $100 outstanding for twelve months, how much will I owe at the end of the twelve-month period?" If we set this up in Excel, we get:

	A	B	C	D
1	MONTHLY COMPOUNDING OF CREDIT CARD BALANCES			
2	"Annual" rate	18%		
3	Monthly rate	1.5%	<-- =B2/12	
4				
5	Month	Balance at beginning of month	Interest for month	Balance at end of month
6	1	100.00	1.50	101.50
7	2	101.50	1.52	103.02
8	3	103.02	1.55	104.57
9	4	104.57	1.57	106.14
10	5	106.14	1.59	107.73
11	6	107.73	1.62	109.34
12	7	109.34	1.64	110.98
13	8	110.98	1.66	112.65
14	9	112.65	1.69	114.34
15	10	114.34	1.72	116.05
16	11	116.05	1.74	117.79
17	12	117.79	1.77	119.56
18				
19	Effective annual interest rate (EAIR)	19.56%	<-- =D17/B6-1	
20		19.56%	<-- =(1+B3)^12-1	

At the end of twelve months you would owe $119.56—the initial $100 balance plus $19.56 in interest. Cells B19 and B20 show two ways of calculating the effective annual interest rate:

- In cell B19, we take the end-year balance that results from the initial $100 credit card balance and divide it by the initial balance to calculate the interest rate:

$$EAIR = \frac{end\text{-}year\ balance}{initial\ balance} - 1$$

$$= \frac{119.56}{100} - 1 = 19.56\%$$

- In cell B20 we take the monthly interest rate and compound it:

$$EAIR = (1 + monthly\ rate)^{12} - 1$$
$$= (1.015)^{12} - 1 = 19.56\%$$

When the annual interest rate r is compounded n times per year, the $EAIR = \left(1 + \dfrac{r}{n}\right)^n - 1$.

APR and EAIR

By an act of Congress (The Federal Truth in Lending Act), lenders are required to specify the *annual percentage rate* (APR) charged on loans. Unfortunately, the Truth in Lending Act does not specify how the APR is to be computed, and the use of the term by lenders is not uniform. Although "APR" is legal terminology designed to help the consumer understand the true cost of borrowing, in practice the APR is not well-defined and may not represent the actual cost of borrowing. Sometimes the APR is the actual effective annual interest rate (EAIR), but in other cases—like the credit card example of this section—the APR is something else. The result is much convoluted wording and a lot of confusion.[11]

EAIR and the Number of Compounding Periods Per Year *n*

In the previous example, the credit card company takes its 18% "annual" interest rate charge and turns it into a 1.5% monthly interest rate. As we saw, the resulting effective annual interest rate (EAIR) is 19.56%.

In Figure 6.2 we compute the effect of the number of compounding periods on the EAIR. The EAIR grows with the number of compounding periods:

$$EAIR = \left(1 + \frac{\text{stated annual interest rate}}{\text{number of annual compounding periods}}\right)^{\text{annual compounding periods}} - 1$$

Number of compounding periods per year	Effective annual interest rate formula	Effective annual interest rate EAIR
1	$(1 + 18\%) - 1$	18.00%
2 (semiannual compounding)	$\left(1 + \frac{18\%}{2}\right)^2 - 1$	18.81%
4 (quarterly compounding)	$\left(1 + \frac{18\%}{4}\right)^4 - 1$	19.252%
12 (monthly compounding)	$\left(1 + \frac{18\%}{12}\right)^{12} - 1$	19.562%
24 (semimonthly compounding)	$\left(1 + \frac{18\%}{24}\right)^{24} - 1$	19.641%
52 (weekly compounding)	$\left(1 + \frac{18\%}{52}\right)^{52} - 1$	19.685%
365 (daily compounding)	$\left(1 + \frac{18\%}{365}\right)^{365} - 1$	19.716%

Figure 6.2 The effective annual interest rate (EAIR) when an annual interest rate of 18% is compounded for various times per year.

---

[11]A case that accompanies this book gives three actual APR examples and the resulting EAIR. In each case the definition of APR used by the lender is different. In only one of the three cases does the APR correspond to the EAIR.

When we do this in Excel, we see that the EAIR grows as the number of compounding periods increases. For a very large number of compounding periods, the EAIR approaches a limit of 19.722% (cell C20 below):

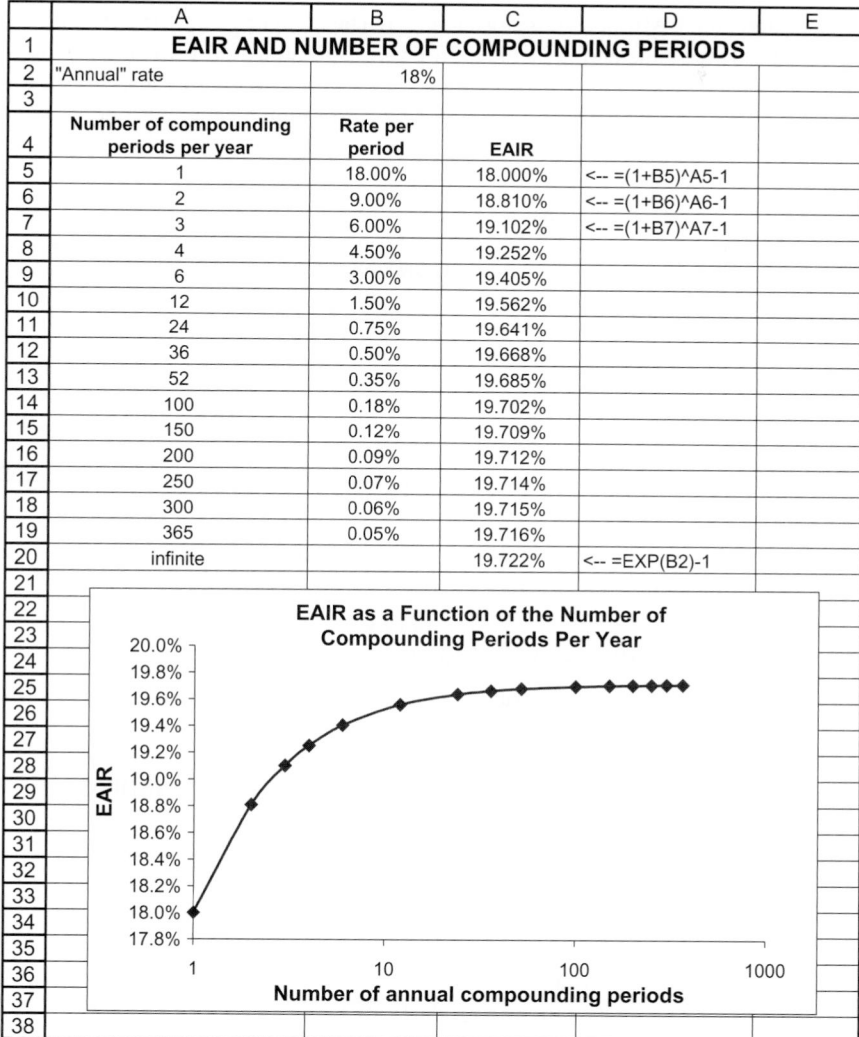

	A	B	C	D	E
1	**EAIR AND NUMBER OF COMPOUNDING PERIODS**				
2	"Annual" rate	18%			
3					
4	**Number of compounding periods per year**	**Rate per period**	**EAIR**		
5	1	18.00%	18.000%	<-- =(1+B5)^A5-1	
6	2	9.00%	18.810%	<-- =(1+B6)^A6-1	
7	3	6.00%	19.102%	<-- =(1+B7)^A7-1	
8	4	4.50%	19.252%		
9	6	3.00%	19.405%		
10	12	1.50%	19.562%		
11	24	0.75%	19.641%		
12	36	0.50%	19.668%		
13	52	0.35%	19.685%		
14	100	0.18%	19.702%		
15	150	0.12%	19.709%		
16	200	0.09%	19.712%		
17	250	0.07%	19.714%		
18	300	0.06%	19.715%		
19	365	0.05%	19.716%		
20	infinite		19.722%	<-- =EXP(B2)-1	
21					

EAIR as a Function of the Number of Compounding Periods Per Year

There are two important things to notice about the EAIR computation:

- As the number of compounding periods per year n increases, the $EAIR = (1 + r/n)^n - 1$ gets higher.
- The rate at which the EAIR increases gets smaller as the number of annual compounding periods gets larger. There is very little difference between the EAIR when interest is compounded 36 times per year (EAIR = 19.668%) and the EAIR when we compound 365 times per year (EAIR = 19.716%).

6.7 Continuous Compounding (Advanced Topic)

In cell C20 we compute the limit of the EAIR when the number of compounding periods gets very large. This limit is called *continuous compounding*. For n annual compounding periods per year, the $EAIR = (1 + r/n)^n - 1$. When the number of annual compounding periods n gets very large, the EAIR becomes close to $e^r - 1$. The number $e = 2.71828182845904$ is the base of natural logarithms and is included in Excel as the function **Exp( )**. In the jargon of finance, e^r is called the *continuously compounded future value*. In the spreadsheet below you can see the difference between the *discretely compounded* future value and the *continuously compounded* future value:

	A	B	C
1	**CONTINUOUS COMPOUNDING**		
2	"Annual" rate	18%	
3	Number of compounding periods per year	250	
4			
5	Discretely compounded future value =1+EAIR	1.1971	<-- =(1+B2/B3)^B3
6	Continuously compounded future value =e^r	1.1972	<-- =EXP(B2)

When the number of compounding periods gets very large, the difference between the discrete and continuous interest rate becomes very small.

The Continuously Compounded Discount Factor

In Chapter 5 we saw that future value and present value are closely related:

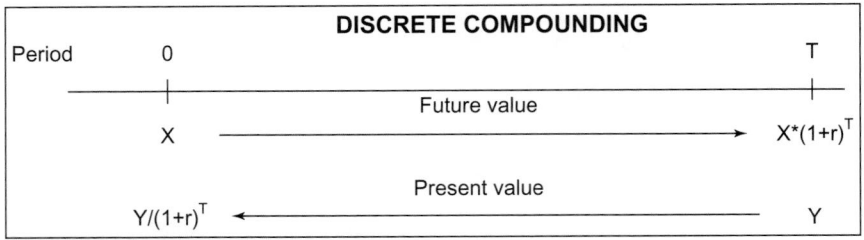

A similar relation holds for continuous compounding:

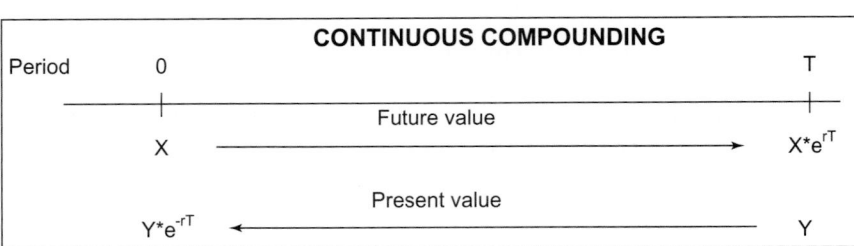

The following spreadsheet summarizes these relations:

	A	B	C
1	**DISCRETE AND CONTINUOUS COMPOUNDING**		
2	Interest rate	10%	
3	Initial amount, X	100	
4	Terminal date, T	3	
5	Discretely compounded future value, $X*(1+r)^T$	133.100	<-- =B3*(1+B2)^B4
6	Continuously compounded future value, $X*e^{rT}$	134.986	<-- =B3*EXP(B2*B4)
7			
8	Interest rate	10%	
9	Terminal amount, Y	100	
10	Terminal date, T	3	
11	Discretely compounded present value, $Y/(1+r)^T$	75.131	<-- =B9/(1+B8)^B10
12	Continuously compounded present value, $Y*e^{-rT}$	74.082	<-- =B9*EXP(-B10*B8)

An Actual Credit Card Example

Continuously compounded interest may seem like an ethereal concept—highly theoretical but not very useful. The example in this subsection shows how useful continuously compounded interest can actually be. The Exxon credit card in the ad below charges an annual percentage rate (APR) of 19.34%. The explanation in parentheses in the ad makes it clear that the company is actually charging 0.05299% *per day* on outstanding balances. This rate is calculated by Exxon by taking 19.34% and dividing it by the number of days per year: 0.05299% = 19.34%/365.

If you carried a $100 balance throughout the year, you would owe $100 * (1.0005299)^{365}$ at the end of the year. As the spreadsheet shows, this translates into a 21.331% EAIR (cell B5):

	A	B	C
1	**EXXON CREDIT CARD EXAMPLE**		
2	APR	19.34%	
3	Daily	0.05299%	<-- =B2/365
4			
5	Effective annual interest rate (EAIR)	21.331%	<-- =(1+B3)^365-1
6	Continuously compounded interest	21.337%	<-- =EXP(B2)-1

As you can see in cell B6, essentially the same interest rate can be computed by using continuous compounding. From a computational point of view, using continuous compounding is simpler than discretely compounding a daily interest rate.

CONTINUOUS COMPOUNDING IN THIS BOOK

We rarely use continuous compounding in this book, except in the options chapters (Chapters 23–26). In other cases, we use only discrete compounding, although we may occasionally point out in a footnote the continuously compounded counterpart of a discretely compounded calculation.

CONCLUSION

In this chapter we've applied the time value of money (PV, NPV, and IRR) to a number of relevant problems:

- Finding the effective annual interest rate (EAIR): This is the compound annual interest rate implicit in a specific financial asset; another way to think about this is that it's the annualized IRR. We've given a number of examples—leases, mortgages, credit cards—all of which illustrate that the only way to evaluate the financing cost is by calculating the EAIR.
- The effect of nonannual compounding periods: Many interest rates are calculated on a monthly or even a daily basis. The EAIR demands that we annualize these interest rates so that we can compare them. When the number of compounding periods gets very large (like our Exxon Mastercard example), the EAIR $= e^r$, where $e = 2.71828182845905$ (computed by =**Exp( )** in Excel) and r is the stated interest rate.

EXERCISES

1. You are considering buying the latest stereo system model. The dealer in The Stereo World store has offered you two payment options. You can either pay $10,000 now or take advantage of their special deal and "buy now and pay a year from today," in which case you will pay $11,100 in one year. Calculate the effective annual interest rate (EAIR) of the store's special deal.

2. You have two options of paying for your new dishwasher: You can either make a single payment of $400 today or pay $70 for the next six months, with the first payment made today. What is the effective annual interest rate (EAIR) of the second option?

3. Your lovely wife has decided to buy you a vacuum cleaner for your birthday (she always supports you in your hobbies . . .). She called your best friend, a manager of a vacuum cleaner store, and he has suggested one of two payment plans: She can either pay $100 now or make 12 monthly payments of $10 each, starting from today. What are the monthly IRR and the EAIR of the payment-over-time plan?

4. Your local bank has offered you a mortgage of $100,000. There are no points, no origination fees, and no extra initial costs (meaning: you get the full $100,000). The mortgage is to be paid back over ten years in annual payments, and the bank charges 12% annual interest.
   (a) Calculate the monthly mortgage payments.
   (b) What the mortgage EAIR?

5. Your local bank has offered you a twenty-year, $100,000 mortgage. The bank is charging 1.5 points and "processing" costs of $750. Payments on the mortgage are annual and are based on a 10% interest rate on the full amount of the mortgage (that is, $100,000).
   (a) Calculate the annual mortgage payment.
   (b) Calculate the EAIR.
   (c) Compute an amortization table showing the amount of interest you can report for tax purposes each year.

6. (a) Repeat Exercise 5, assuming the bank's offer is 12% annual interest, compounded monthly.
   (b) Will the IRR and the EAIR of the mortgage change if the loan period is six years? Answer without doing any calculations.

7. You just bought the first floor of the famous Egg-Plant Building for $250,000. You plan to rent the space to convenience stores. Your banker has offered you a mortgage with the following terms:
   - The mortgage is for the full amount of $250,000.
   - The mortgage will be repaid in equal monthly payments over 36 months, starting one month from now.
   - The annual interest rate on the mortgage is 8%, compounded monthly (meaning: $8\%/12 = \frac{2}{3}\%$ per month).
   - You have to pay the bank an initiation charge of $1,500 and 1 point.

   (a) What is your monthly payment to the bank?
   (b) What is the EAIR of the mortgage?
   (c) Compute an amortization table showing the amount of interest you can report for tax purposes each month.

8. Your local bank has offered you a five-year, $100,000 mortgage. The bank is charging 1.5 points and "processing" costs of $750. The interest rate is 12% compounded monthly (meaning: 1% per month).
   (a) Calculate the monthly mortgage payment.
   (b) Calculate the EAIR.
   (c) Compute an amortization table showing the amount of interest you can report for tax purposes each month and use it to compute the annual mortgage interest you can report for tax purposes.

9. You're considering buying an asset that has a three-year life and costs $15,000. As an alternative to buying the asset, you can lease it for $4,000 per year (four annual payments, the first due on the day you sign the lease). If you can borrow from your bank at 10%, should you lease or buy?

10. You're considering buying an asset that has a three-year life and costs $2,000. As an alternative to buying the asset, you can lease it for $600 per year (four annual payments, the first due today). Your bank is willing to lend you money for 15%.
    (a)   Should you lease or purchase the asset?
    (b)   What is the largest lease payment you would be willing to make?

11. You're considering leasing or purchasing an asset with the following cash flows.

	A	B	C	D
1	LEASE VERSUS PURCHASE WITH RESIDUAL VALUE			
2	Asset cost	20,000		
3	Annual lease payment	5,500		
4	Residual value, year 3	3,000	<-- Value of asset at end year 3	
5	Bank rate	15%		
6				
7	Year	Purchase cash flow	Lease cash flow	
8	0	20,000	5,500	
9	1		5,500	
10	2		5,500	
11	3	-3,000	5,500	

    (a)   Calculate the present value of the lease versus the purchase. Which is preferable?
    (b)   What is the largest annual lease payment you would be willing to pay?

12. You intend to buy a new laptop computer. Its price at electronic shops is $2,000, but your next door neighbor offered to lease you the same computer for monthly payments of $70 for a 24-month period, with the first payment made today. Assuming you can sell the computer at the end of two years for $500, and the interest rate in the market is 20%, should you buy or lease?

13. You're considering leasing or purchasing a car. The details of each method of financing are given below. The lease is for 24 months. What should you do?

	A	B	C	D	E	F
1	AUTO LEASE VERSUS PURCHASE					
2	MSRP	15,000.00	<-- Manufacturer's suggested retail price			
3	Capitalized cost	14,000.00	<-- Negotiated price			
4	Destination charge	415.00	<-- Paid both by the lessee and the buyer			
5	Acquisition fee	450.00	<-- Paid only by the lessee			
6	Security deposit	450.00	<-- refunded at end of lease			
7						
8	Payment due at signing	1,000.00				
9	Monthly payment	200.00	<-- Dealer's lease offer			
10						
11						
12	Residual value after 2 years as % of MSRP	65%				
13	Lease residual value after 3 years	9,750.00	<-- =B12*B2			
14	Your estimated residual value	5,000.00	<-- Your guess			

14. You are considering buying a new, very expensive, FancyCar. The details of your negotiation for a 48-month lease are given below.
    (a)   If your alternative cost of financing is 6%, should you buy or lease?
    (b)   If you financed the purchase through the bank at 6%, what would be your monthly loan payment?

(c) As your estimated residual value (cell B15) gets larger, does leasing or buying become more advantageous? Explain.

(d) What is the estimated residual value for which you are indifferent between buying and leasing?

	A	B	C
1	AUTO LEASE VERSUS PURCHASE: 48 MONTH LEASE		
2	MSRP	50,000	<-- Manufacturer's suggested retail price
3	Capitalized cost	45,000	<-- Negotiated price
4	Destination charge	415	<-- Paid both by the lessee and the buyer
5	Acquisition fee	450	<-- Paid only by the lessee
6	Security deposit	450	<-- refunded at end of lease
7			
8	Payment due at signing	1,315	
9	Monthly payment	400	<-- Dealer's lease offer
10			
11			
12	Residual value after 4 years as % of MSRP	60%	
13	Lease residual value after 4 years	30,000	
14	Your estimated residual value	35,000	<-- Your guess

15. You're considering buying a new top-of-the-line luxury car. The car's list price is $99,000. The dealer has offered you two alternatives for purchasing the car:

   - You can buy the car for $90,000 in cash and get a $9,000 discount in the bargain.
   - You can buy the car for the list of $99,000. In this case the dealer is willing to take $39,000 as an initial payment. The remainder of $60,000 is a "zero-interest loan" to be paid back in equal installments over 36 months.

   Alternatively, your local bank is willing to give you a car loan at an annual interest rate of 10%, compounded monthly (that is, 10%/12 per month).

   Decide how to finance the car: bank loan, zero-interest loan with the dealer, or cash payment.

16. You've been offered three credit cards:

   - Credit card 1 charges 19% annually, on a monthly basis.
   - Credit card 2 charges 19% annually, on a weekly basis.
   - Credit card 3 charges 18.90% annually, on a daily basis.

   Rank the cards on the basis of EAIR.

17. You plan to put $1,000 in a savings plan and leave it there for five years. You can choose between various alternatives. How much will you have in five years under each alternative?

   (a) Bellon Bank is offering 12% stated annual interest rate, compounded once a year.

   (b) WNC Bank is offering 11% stated annual interest rate, compounded twice a year.

   (c) Plebian Bank is offering 10% stated annual interest rate, compounded monthly.

   (d) Byfus Bank is offering 11.5% stated annual interest rate, compounded continuously.

18. Assuming that the interest rate is 5%, compounded semiannually, which of the following is more valuable?

   (a) $5,000 today.

   (b) $10,000 at the end of five years.

   (c) $9,000 at the end of four years.

   (d) $450 at the end of each year (in perpetuity) commencing in one year.

19. You plan to put $10,000 in a saving plan for two years. How much will you have at the end of two years with each of the following options?
    (a) Receive 12% stated annual interest rate, compounded monthly.
    (b) Receive 12.5% stated annual interest rate, compounded annually.
    (c) Receive 11.5% stated annual interest rate, compounded daily.
    (d) Receive 10% stated annual interest rate in the first year and 15% stated annual interest rate in the second year, compounded annually.

20. Michael Smith was in trouble: He was unemployed and living on his monthly disability pay of $1,200. His credit card debts of $19,000 were threatening to overwhelm this puny income. Every month in which he delayed paying the credit card debt cost him 1.5% on the remaining balance. His only asset was his house, on which he had a $67,000 mortgage.

    Then Michael got a phone call from Uranus Financial Corporation: The company offered to refinance Michael's mortgage. The Uranus representative explained to Michael that, with the rise in real estate values, Michael's house could now be remortgaged for $90,000. This amount would allow Michael to repay his credit card debts and even leave him with some money.

    Here are some additional facts:
    • The new mortgage would be for 25 years and would have an annual interest rate of 9.23%. The mortgage would be repayable in equal monthly payments over this term, at a monthly interest rate of $9.23\%/12 = 0.76917\%$. The fees on the mortgage are $8,000.
    • There are no penalties involved in repaying the $67,000 existing mortgage.

    Answer the following questions:
    (a) What will Michael's monthly payments be on the new mortgage?
    (b) After repaying his credit card debts how much money will Michael have left?
    (c) What is the effective annual interest rate on the Uranus mortgage?

21. A recent notice from the author's credit card company included the following statement.

    Annual Percentage Rate for Cash Advances:
    Your annual percentage rate for cash advances is the U.S. Prime Rate plus 14.99%, but such cash advance rate will never be lower than 19.99%. As of August 1, 2004, this cash advance **ANNUAL PERCENTAGE RATE** is 19.99%, which corresponds to a daily periodic rate of 0.0548%. A daily periodic rate is the applicable annual percentage rate divided by 365. Please see the section of your Card Agreement entitled "Variable Annual Percentage Rates for Purchases and Cash Advances" for details relating to how this cash advances rate may change, including if you default under any Card Agreement that you have with us.

    As of August 1, 2004, what is the effective annual interest rate (EAIR) charged by the credit card company on cash advances?

22. WindyRoad is an investment company that has two mutual funds. The WindyRoad Dull Fund invests in boring corporate bonds while its Lively Fund invests in "high risk, high return" companies. The returns for the two funds in the five-year period 2001–2005 are given below.
    (a) Suppose you had invested $100 in each of the two funds at the beginning of 2001. How much would you have at the end of 2005?
    (b) What was the effective annual interest rate paid by each of the funds over the five-year period 2001–2005?
    (c) Is there a conclusion you can draw from this example?

	A	B	C	D
1	**DULL FUND OR LIVELY FUND?**			
2	Year	**Dull Fund return**	**Lively Fund return**	
3	2001	9.20%	11.50%	
4	2002	5.20%	-14.50%	
5	2003	4.30%	-23.40%	
6	2004	3.30%	42.40%	
7	2005	7.00%	13.60%	
8				
9	Average return	5.80%	5.92%	<-- =AVERAGE(C3:C7)

23. (Advanced).

(a) Compute the annual continuous returns for Dull Fund and Lively Fund (Exercise 22) for each of the years 2001–2005. What is the average continuous return $r_{average}^{continuous}$ for each fund?

(b) Suppose you had invested \$100 in each of the two funds at the beginning of 2001. Show that the total amount you would have in each fund (see Exercise 22(a)) can be written as $\$100 * e^{5 * r_{average}^{continuous}}$. Notice that this makes computations much simpler.

INTRODUCTION TO CAPITAL BUDGETING

OVERVIEW

Capital budgeting is finance terminology for the process of deciding whether or not to undertake an investment project. There are two standard concepts used in capital budgeting: net present value (NPV) and internal rate of return (IRR). Both of these concepts were introduced in Chapter 5; in this chapter we discuss their application to capital budgeting. Here are some of the topics covered:

- Should you undertake a specific project? We call this the "yes–no" decision, and we show how both NPV and IRR answer this question.
- Ranking projects: If you have several alternative investments, only one of which you can choose, which should you undertake?
- Should you use IRR or NPV? Sometimes the IRR and NPV decision criteria give different answers to the yes–no and the ranking decisions. We discuss why this happens and which criterion should be used for capital budgeting (if there's disagreement).
- Sunk costs. How should you account for costs incurred in the past?
- The cost of foregone opportunities.
- Salvage values and terminal values.
- Incorporating taxes into the valuation decision. This issue is dealt with briefly in Section 7.7. We return to it at greater length in Chapters 8–10.

Finance Concepts Discussed

- IRR
- NPV
- Project ranking using NPV and IRR
- Terminal value
- Taxation and calculation of cash flows
- Cost of foregone opportunities
- Sunk costs

Excel Functions Used

- **NPV**
- **IRR**
- **Data Tables**

7.1 The NPV Rule for Judging Investments and Projects

In preceding chapters we introduced the basic NPV and IRR concepts and their application to capital budgeting. We start off this chapter by summarizing each of these rules—the NPV rule in this section and the IRR rule in the following section.

Here's a summary of the decision criteria for investments implied by the net present value:

The NPV rule for deciding whether or not a specific project is worthwhile: Suppose you are considering a project that has cash flows $CF_0, CF_1, CF_2, \ldots, CF_N$. Suppose that the appropriate discount rate for this project is r. Then the NPV of the project is

$$NPV = CF_0 + \frac{CF_1}{(1+r)} + \frac{CF_2}{(1+r)^2} + \cdots + \frac{CF_N}{(1+r)^N} = CF_0 + \sum_{t=1}^{N} \frac{CF_t}{(1+r)^t}$$

Rule: A project is worthwhile by the NPV rule if its NPV > 0.

The NPV rule for deciding between two mutually exclusive projects: Suppose you are trying to decide between two projects A and B, each of which can achieve the same objective. For example, your company needs a new widget machine, and the choice is between widget machine A and machine B. You will buy either A or B (or perhaps neither machine, but you will certainly not buy both machines). In finance jargon, these projects are "mutually exclusive."

Suppose project A has cash flows $CF_0^A, CF_1^A, CF_2^A, \ldots, CF_N^A$ and that project B has cash flows $CF_0^B, CF_1^B, CF_2^B, \ldots, CF_N^B$.

Rule: Project A is preferred to project B if

$$NPV(A) = CF_0^A + \sum_{t=1}^{N} \frac{CF_t^A}{(1+r)^t} > CF_0^B + \sum_{t=1}^{N} \frac{CF_t^B}{(1+r)^t} = NPV(B)$$

The logic of both NPV rules presented above is that the *present value* of a project's cash flows—$PV = \sum_{t=1}^{N} [CF_t/(1+r)^t]$—is the economic value today of the project. Thus, if we have correctly chosen the discount rate r for the project, the PV is what we ought to be able to sell the project for in the market.[1] The net present value is the *wealth increment* produced by the project, so that NPV > 0 means that a project adds to our wealth:

$$NPV = \underbrace{CF_0}_{\substack{\text{Initial cash}\\ \text{flow required}\\ \text{to implement}\\ \text{the project.}\\ \text{This is usually}\\ \text{a negative number.}}} + \underbrace{\sum_{t=1}^{N} \frac{CF_t}{(1+r)^t}}_{\substack{\text{Market value}\\ \text{of future cash}\\ \text{flows.}}}$$

An Initial Example

To set the stage, let's assume that you're trying to decide whether to undertake one of two projects. Project A involves buying expensive machinery that produces a better product at a lower cost. The machines for project A cost $1,000 and, if purchased, you anticipate that the project will produce cash flows of $500 per year for the next five years. Project B's machines are cheaper, costing $800, but they produce smaller annual cash flows of $420 per year for the next five years. We'll assume that the correct discount rate is 12%.

---

[1]This assumes that the discount rate is "correctly chosen," by which we mean that it is appropriate to the riskiness of the project's cash flows. For the moment, we fudge the question of how to choose discount rates; this topic is discussed in Chapter 9.

Suppose we apply the NPV criterion to projects A and B:

	A	B	C	D
1		**TWO PROJECTS**		
2	Discount rate	12%		
3				
4	**Year**	**Project A**	**Project B**	
5	0	-1000	-800	
6	1	500	420	
7	2	500	420	
8	3	500	420	
9	4	500	420	
10	5	500	420	
11				
12	NPV	802.39	714.01	<-- =NPV($B$2,C6:C10)+C5

Both projects are worthwhile, since each has a positive NPV. If we have to choose between the projects, then project A is preferred to project B because it has the higher NPV.

EXCEL NOTE

EXCEL'S NPV FUNCTION VERSUS THE FINANCE DEFINITION OF NPV

We reiterate our Excel note from Chapter 5 (p. 94): Excel's **NPV** function computes the present value of *future* cash flows; this does not correspond to the *finance notion* of NPV, which includes the initial cash flow. To calculate the finance NPV concept in the spreadsheet, we have to include the initial cash flow. Hence, in cell B12, the NPV is calculated as **=NPV($B$2,B6:B10)+B5** and in cell C12 the calculation is **=NPV($B$2,C6:C10)+C5**.

7.2 The IRR Rule for Judging Investments

An alternative to using the NPV criterion for capital budgeting is to use the internal rate of return (IRR). Recall from Chapter 5 that the IRR is defined as the discount rate for which the NPV equals zero. It is the compound rate of return that you get from a series of cash flows.

Here are the two decision rules for using the IRR in capital budgeting.

The IRR rule for deciding whether or not a specific investment is worthwhile: Suppose we are considering a project that has cash flows $CF_0, CF_1, CF_2, \ldots, CF_N$. *IRR is an interest rate such that*

$$CF_0 + \frac{CF_1}{(1+IRR)} + \frac{CF_2}{(1+IRR)^2} + \cdots + \frac{CF_N}{(1+IRR)^N} = CF_0 + \sum_{t=1}^{N} \frac{CF_t}{(1+k)^t} = 0$$

Rule: If the appropriate discount rate for a project is r, you should accept the project if its IRR $> r$ and reject it if its IRR $< r$.

The logic behind the IRR rule is that the IRR is the compound return you get from the project. Since r is the project's required rate of return, it follows that if the IRR $> r$, you get more than you require.

The IRR rule for deciding between two competing projects: Suppose you are trying to decide between two mutually exclusive projects A and B (meaning: both projects are ways of achieving the same objective, and you will choose at most one of the projects). Suppose project A has cash flows $CF_0^A, CF_1^A, CF_2^A, \ldots, CF_N^A$ and that project B has cash flows $CF_0^B, CF_1^B, CF_2^B, \ldots, CF_N^B$.
Rule: Project A is preferred to project B if IRR(A) $>$ IRR(B).

Again the logic is clear: Since the IRR gives a project's compound rate of return, if we choose between two projects using the IRR rule, we prefer the higher compound rate of return.
Applying the IRR rule to our projects A and B, we get:

	A	B	C	D
1		**TWO PROJECTS**		
2	Discount rate	12%		
3				
4	**Year**	**Project A**	**Project B**	
5	0	-1000	-800	
6	1	500	420	
7	2	500	420	
8	3	500	420	
9	4	500	420	
10	5	500	420	
11				
12	IRR	41%	44%	<-- =IRR(C5:C10)

Both project A and project B are worthwhile, since each has an IRR $> 12\%$, which is our relevant discount rate. If we have to choose between the two projects by using the IRR rule, project B is preferred to project A because it has a higher IRR.

7.3 NPV or IRR, Which to Use?

We can sum up the NPV and IRR rules as follows:

Criterion	"Yes or No": Choosing Whether or Not to Undertake a Single Project	"Project Ranking": Comparing Two Mutually Exclusive Projects
NPV criterion	The project should be undertaken if its NPV > 0.	Project A is preferred to project B if NPV(A) $>$ NPV(B).
IRR criterion	The project should be undertaken if its IRR $> r$, where r is the appropriate discount rate.	Project A is preferred to project B if IRR(A) $>$ IRR(B).

Both the NPV rules and the IRR rules look logical. In many cases your investment decision—to undertake a project or not, or which of two competing projects to choose—will be the same whether you use NPV or IRR. There are some cases, however (such as that of projects A and B illustrated above), where NPV and IRR give different answers. In our present value analysis, project A won out because its NPV is greater than project B's. In our IRR analysis of the same projects, project B was chosen because it had the higher IRR. In such cases, you should always use the NPV to decide between projects. The logic is that if individuals are interested in maximizing their wealth, they should use NPV, which measures the incremental wealth from undertaking a project.

7.4 The "Yes–No" Criterion: When Do IRR and NPV Give the Same Answer?

Consider the following project. The initial cash flow of −$1,000 represents the cost of the project today, and the remaining cash flows for years 1–6 are projected future cash flows. The discount rate is 15%.

	A	B	C
1	SIMPLE CAPITAL BUDGETING EXAMPLE		
2	Discount rate	15%	
3			
4	Year	Cash flow	
5	0	-1,000	
6	1	100	
7	2	200	
8	3	300	
9	4	400	
10	5	500	
11	6	600	
12			
13	PV of future cash flows	1,172.13	<-- =NPV(B2,B6:B11)
14	NPV	172.13	<-- =B5+NPV(B2,B6:B11)
15	IRR	19.71%	<-- =IRR(B5:B11)

The NPV of the project is $172.13, meaning that the present value of the project's future cash flows ($1,172.13) is greater than the project's cost of $1,000.00. Thus, the project is worthwhile.

If we graph the project's NPV we can see that the IRR—the point where the NPV curve crosses the *x*-axis—is very close to 20%. As you can see in cell B15, the actual IRR is 19.71%.

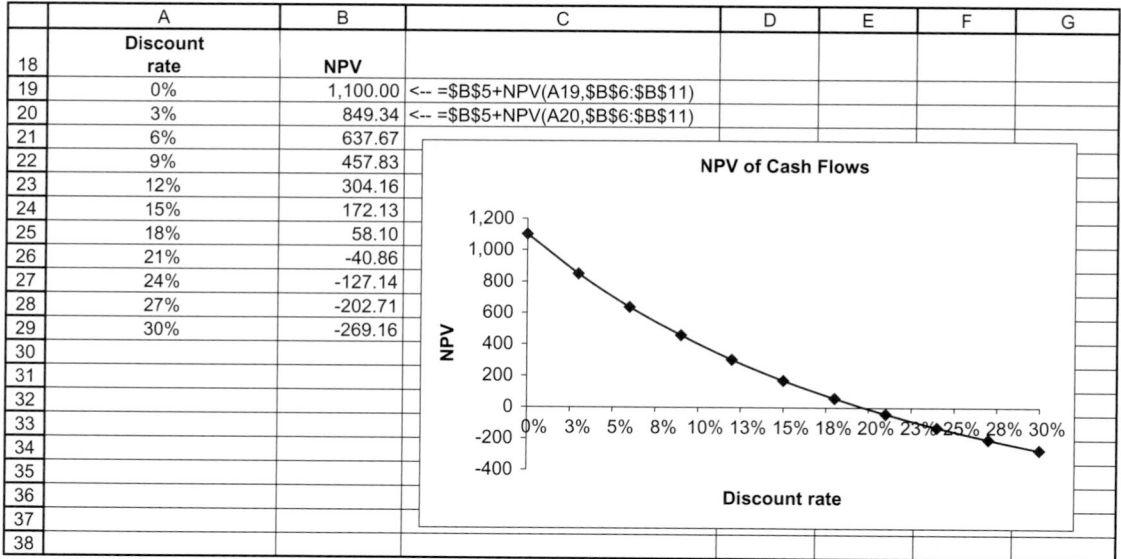

	A	B	C	D	E	F	G
18	Discount rate	**NPV**					
19	0%	1,100.00	<-- =$B$5+NPV(A19,$B$6:$B$11)				
20	3%	849.34	<-- =$B$5+NPV(A20,$B$6:$B$11)				
21	6%	637.67					
22	9%	457.83					
23	12%	304.16					
24	15%	172.13					
25	18%	58.10					
26	21%	-40.86					
27	24%	-127.14					
28	27%	-202.71					
29	30%	-269.16					
30							
31							
32							
33							
34							
35							
36							
37							
38							

Accept or Reject? Should We Undertake the Project?

It is clear that the above project is worthwhile:

- Its NPV > 0, so that by the NPV criterion the project should be accepted.
- Its IRR of 19.71% is greater than the project discount rate of 15%, so that by the IRR criterion the project should be accepted.

A General Principle

We can derive a general principle from this example:

> For conventional projects, projects with an initial negative cash flow and subsequent nonnegative cash flows ($CF_0 < 0, CF_1 \geq 0, CF_2 \geq 0, \ldots, CF_N \geq 0$), the *NPV* and *IRR* criteria lead to the same "Yes–No" decision: If the NPV criterion indicates a "Yes" decision, then so will the IRR criterion (and vice versa).

7.5 Do NPV and IRR Produce the Same Project Rankings?

In the previous section we saw that, for conventional projects, NPV and IRR give the same "Yes–No" answer about whether to invest in a project. In this section we see that NPV and IRR do not necessarily *rank* projects the same, even if the projects are both conventional.

Suppose we have two projects and can choose to invest in only one. The projects are *mutually exclusive:* They are both ways to achieve the same end, and thus we would choose only one. In this section we discuss the use of NPV and IRR to rank the projects. To sum up our results before we start:

- Ranking projects by NPV and IRR can lead to possibly contradictory results. Using the NPV criterion may lead us to prefer one project whereas using the IRR criterion may lead us to prefer the other project.

- Where a conflict exists between NPV and IRR, the project with the larger NPV is preferred. That is, the NPV criterion is the correct criterion to use for capital budgeting. This is not to impugn the IRR criterion, which is often very useful. However, NPV is preferred over IRR because it indicates the *increase in wealth* that the project produces.

An Example

Below we show the cash flows for project A and project B. Both projects have the same initial cost of $500 but have different cash flow patterns. The relevant discount rate is 15%.

	A	B	C	D
1	**RANKING PROJECTS WITH NPV AND IRR**			
2	Discount rate	15%		
3				
4	**Year**	**Project A**	**Project B**	
5	0	-500	-500	
6	1	100	250	
7	2	100	250	
8	3	150	200	
9	4	200	100	
10	5	400	50	
11				
12	NPV	74.42	119.96	<-- =C5+NPV(B2,C6:C10)
13	IRR	19.77%	27.38%	<-- =IRR(C5:C10)

Comparing the Projects Using IRR: If we use the IRR rule to choose between the projects, then B is preferred to A, since the IRR of project B is higher than that of project A.

Comparing the Projects Using NPV: Here the choice is more complicated. When the discount rate is 15% (as illustrated above), the NPV of project B is higher than that of project A. In this case the IRR and the NPV agree: Both indicate that project B should be chosen. Now suppose that the discount rate is 8%; in this case the NPV and IRR rankings conflict:

	A	B	C	D
1	**RANKING PROJECTS WITH NPV AND IRR**			
2	Discount rate	8%		
3				
4	**Year**	**Project A**	**Project B**	
5	0	-500	-500	
6	1	100	250	
7	2	100	250	
8	3	150	200	
9	4	200	100	
10	5	400	50	
11				
12	NPV	216.64	212.11	<-- =C5+NPV(B2,C6:C10)
13	IRR	19.77%	27.38%	<-- =IRR(C5:C10)

In this case we have to resolve the conflict between the ranking on the basis of NPV (project A is preferred) and the ranking on the basis of IRR (project B is preferred). As we stated in the introduction to this section, the solution to this conflict is that you should choose on the basis of NPV. We explore the reasons for this later on, but first we discuss a technical question.

Why Do NPV and IRR Give Different Rankings?

Below we build a table and graph that show the NPV for each project as a function of the discount rate:

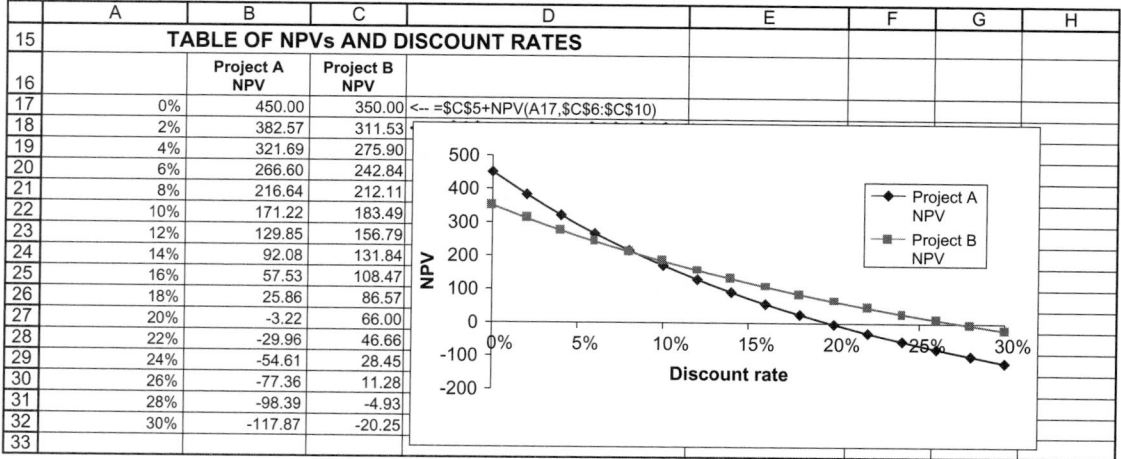

	A	B	C	D	E	F	G	H
15		**TABLE OF NPVs AND DISCOUNT RATES**						
16		**Project A NPV**	**Project B NPV**					
17	0%	450.00	350.00	<-- =$C$5+NPV(A17,$C$6:$C$10)				
18	2%	382.57	311.53					
19	4%	321.69	275.90					
20	6%	266.60	242.84					
21	8%	216.64	212.11					
22	10%	171.22	183.49					
23	12%	129.85	156.79					
24	14%	92.08	131.84					
25	16%	57.53	108.47					
26	18%	25.86	86.57					
27	20%	-3.22	66.00					
28	22%	-29.96	46.66					
29	24%	-54.61	28.45					
30	26%	-77.36	11.28					
31	28%	-98.39	-4.93					
32	30%	-117.87	-20.25					
33								

From the graph you can see why contradictory rankings occur:

- Project B has a higher IRR (27.38%) than project A (19.77%). (Remember that the IRR is the point at which the NPV curve crosses the *x*-axis.)

- When the discount rate is low, project A has a higher NPV than project B, but when the discount rate is high, project B has a higher NPV. There is a crossover point (in the next subsection you will see that this point is 8.51%) that marks the disagreement/agreement range.

- Project A's NPV is more sensitive to changes in the discount rate than project B's NPV. The reason for this is that project A's cash flows are more spread out over time than those of project B; another way of saying this is that project A has substantially more of its cash flows at later dates than project B.

To summarize:

Criterion	Discount Rate < 8.51%	Discount Rate = 8.51%	Discount Rate > 8.51%
NPV criterion	Project A preferred: NPV(A) > NPV(B)	Indifferent between projects A and B: NPV(A) = NPV(B)	Project B preferred: NPV(B) > NPV(A)
IRR criterion		Project B is always preferred to project A, since IRR(B) > IRR(A)	

Calculating the Crossover Point

The crossover point—which we claimed earlier was 8.51%—is the discount rate at which the NPVs of the two projects are equal. A bit of formula manipulation will show you that *the crossover point is the IRR of the differential cash flows.* To see what this means, consider the following example:

	A	B	C	D	E
34	**Calculating the crossover point**				
35	Year	Project A	Project B	Differential cash flows: cash flow(A) - cash flow(B)	
36	0	-500	-500	0	<-- =B36-C36
37	1	100	250	-150	<-- =B37-C37
38	2	100	250	-150	
39	3	150	200	-50	
40	4	200	100	100	
41	5	400	50	350	
42					
43	IRR			8.51%	<-- =IRR(D36:D41)

Column D in the above example contains the differential cash flows—the difference between the cash flows of project A and project B. In cell D43 we use the Excel **IRR** function to compute the crossover point.

A bit of theory (can be skipped): To see why the crossover point is the IRR of the differential cash flows, suppose that for some rate r, NPV(A) = NPV(B):

$$NPV(A) = CF_0^A + \frac{CF_1^A}{(1+r)} + \frac{CF_2^A}{(1+r)^2} + \cdots + \frac{CF_N^A}{(1+r)^N}$$

$$= CF_0^B + \frac{CF_1^B}{(1+r)} + \frac{CF_2^B}{(1+r)^2} + \cdots + \frac{CF_N^B}{(1+r)^N} = NPV(B)$$

Subtracting and rearranging shows that r must be the IRR of the differential cash flows:

$$CF_0^A - CF_0^B + \frac{CF_1^A - CF_1^B}{(1+r)} + \frac{CF_2^A - CF_2^B}{(1+r)^2} + \cdots + \frac{CF_N^A - CF_N^B}{(1+r)^N} = 0$$

What to Use? NPV or IRR?

Let's go back to the initial example and suppose that the discount rate is 8%:

	A	B	C	D
1	**RANKING PROJECTS WITH NPV AND IRR**			
2	Discount rate	8%		
3				
4	Year	Project A	Project B	
5	0	-500	-500	
6	1	100	250	
7	2	100	250	
8	3	150	200	
9	4	200	100	
10	5	400	50	
11				
12	NPV	216.64	212.11	<-- =C5+NPV(B2,C6:C10)
13	IRR	19.77%	27.38%	<-- =IRR(C5:C10)

In this case, we know there is disagreement between the NPV (which would lead us to choose project A) and the IRR (by which we choose project B). Which is correct?

The answer to this question—for the case where the discount rate is 8%—is that we should choose based on the NPV (that is, choose project A). This is just one example of the general principle discussed in Section 7.3: *Using the NPV is always preferred,* since the NPV is the additional *wealth* that you get, whereas IRR is the compound rate of return. The economic assumption is that consumers maximize their wealth, not their rate of return.

WHERE IS THIS CHAPTER GOING?

Until this point in the chapter, we've discussed general principles of project choice using the NPV and IRR criteria. The following sections discuss some specifics:

- Ignoring sunk costs and using marginal cash flows (Section 7.6)
- Incorporating taxes and tax shields into capital budgeting calculations (Section 7.7)
- Incorporating the cost of foregone opportunities (Section 7.9)
- Incorporating salvage values and terminal values (Section 7.11)

7.6 Capital Budgeting Principle: Ignore Sunk Costs and Consider Only Marginal Cash Flows

This is an important principle of capital budgeting and project evaluation: Ignore the cash flows you can't control and look only at the *marginal cash flows*—the outcomes of financial decisions you can still make. In the jargon of finance: Ignore *sunk costs,* costs that have already been incurred and thus are not affected by future capital budgeting decisions.

Here's an example: You recently bought a plot of land and built a house on it. Your intention was to sell the house immediately, but it turns out that the house is really badly built and cannot be sold in its current state. The house and land cost you $100,000, and a friendly local contractor has offered to make the necessary repairs, which will cost $20,000. Your real estate broker estimates that even with these repairs you'll never sell the house for more than $90,000. What should you do? There are two approaches to answering this question:

- "My father always said 'Don't throw good money after bad.'" If this is your approach, you won't do anything. This attitude is typified in column B below, which shows that if you make the repairs you will have lost 25% on your money.
- "My mother was a finance professor, and she said, 'Don't cry over spilt milk. Look only at the marginal cash flows.'" These turn out to be pretty good. In column C below you see that making the repairs will give you a 350% return on your $20,000.

	A	B	C	D
1	**IGNORE SUNK COSTS**			
2	House cost	100,000		
3	Fix up cost	20,000		
4				
5	Year	Cash flow wrong!	Cash flow right!	
6	0	-120,000	-20,000	
7	1	90,000	90,000	
8	IRR	-25%	350%	<-- =IRR(C6:C7)

Of course, your father was wrong and your mother right (this often happens): Even though you made some disastrous mistakes (you never should have built the house in the first place), you should—at this point—ignore the sunk cost of $100,000 and make the necessary repairs.

7.7 Capital Budgeting Principle: Don't Forget the Effects of Taxes—Sally and Dave's Condo Investment

In this section we discuss the capital budgeting problem faced by Sally and Dave, two business school grads who are considering buying a condominium apartment and renting it out for the income.

We use Sally and Dave and their condo to emphasize the place of taxes in the capital budgeting process. No one needs to be told that taxes are very important.[2] In the capital budgeting process, the cash flows that are to be discounted are *after-tax cash flows*. We postpone a fuller discussion of this topic to Chapters 9 and 10, where we define the concept of *free cash flow*. For the moment, we concentrate on a few obvious principles, which we illustrate with the example of Sally and Dave's condo investment.

Sally and Dave—fresh out of business school with a little cash to spare—are considering buying a nifty condo as a rental property. The condo will cost $100,000, and (in this example at least) they're planning to buy it with all cash. Here are some additional facts:

- Sally and Dave figure they can rent out the condo for $24,000 per year. They'll have to pay property taxes of $1,500 annually and they're figuring on additional miscellaneous expenses of $1,000 per year.

- All the income from the condo has to be reported on their annual tax return. Currently, Sally and Dave have a tax rate of 30%, and they think this rate will continue for the foreseeable future.

- Their accountant has explained to them that they can depreciate the full cost of the condo over ten years—each year they can charge $10,000 depreciation (= *(condo cost)/* *(10-year depreciable life)*) against the income from the condo.[3] This means that they can expect to pay $3,450 in income taxes per year if they buy the condo and rent it out and have a net income from the condo of $8,050:

	A	B	C
1	**SALLY & DAVE'S CONDO**		
2	Cost of condo	100,000	
3	Sally & Dave's tax rate	30%	
4			
5	Annual reportable income calculation		
6	Rent	24,000	
7	Expenses		
8	Property taxes	-1,500	
9	Miscellaneous expenses	-1,000	
10	Depreciation	-10,000	
11	Reportable income	11,500	<-- =SUM(B6:B10)
12	Taxes (rate = 30%)	-3,450	<-- =-B3*B11
13	Net income	8,050	<-- =B11+B12

---

[2]Will Rogers said, "The difference between death and taxes is death doesn't get worse every time Congress meets."

[3]You may want to read the box on depreciation on the next page before going on.

WHAT IS DEPRECIATION?

In computing the taxes they owe, Sally and Dave get to subtract expenses from their income. Taxes are computed on the basis of the *income before taxes* (= income − expenses − depreciation − interest). When Sally and Dave get the rent from their condo, this is *income*—money earned from their asset. When Sally and Dave pay to fix the faucet in their condo, this is an *expense*—a cost of doing business.

The cost of the condo is neither income nor an expense. It's a *capital investment*—money paid for an asset that will be used over many years. Tax rules specify that each year part of the capital investments can be taken off the income ("expensed," in accounting jargon). This reduces the taxes paid by the owners of the asset and takes account of the fact that the asset has a limited life.

There are many depreciation methods in use. The simplest method is *straight-line depreciation*. In this method the asset's annual depreciation is a percentage of its initial cost. In the case of Sally and Dave, for example, we've specified that the asset is depreciated over ten years. This results in annual depreciation charges of

$$straight\text{-}line\ depreciation = \frac{initial\ asset\ cost}{depreciable\ life\ span} = \frac{\$100,000}{10} = \$10,000\ annually$$

In some cases depreciation is taken on the asset cost minus its salvage value: If you think that the asset will be worth $20,000 at the end of its life (this is the salvage value), then the annual straight-line depreciation might be $8,000:

$$\begin{aligned} straight\text{-}line\ depreciation \atop with\ salvage\ value &= \frac{initial\ asset\ cost - salvage\ value}{depreciable\ life\ span} \\ &= \frac{\$100,000 - \$20,000}{10} = \$8,000\ annually \end{aligned}$$

ACCELERATED DEPRECIATION

Although historically depreciation charges are related to the life span of the asset, in many cases this connection has been lost. Under United States tax rules, for example, an asset classified as having a five-year depreciable life (trucks, cars, and some computer equipment are in this category) will be depreciated over six years (yes *six*) at 20%, 32%, 19.2%, 11.52%, 11.52%, and 5.76% in each of the years 1, 2, ..., 6. Notice that this method *accelerates* the depreciation charges—more than one-sixth of the depreciation is taken annually in years 1–3 and less in later years. Since, as we show in the text, depreciation ultimately saves taxes, this benefits the asset's owner, who now gets to take more of the depreciation in the early years of the asset's life.

Two Ways to Calculate the Cash Flow

In the previous spreadsheet you saw that Sally and Dave's net income was $8,050. In this section you'll see that the *cash flow produced by the condo* is much more than this amount. It all has to do with depreciation: Because the depreciation is an expense for tax purposes but not a cash expense, the *cash flow* from the condo rental is different. So even though the net income from the condo is $8,050, the annual cash flow is $18,050—you have to add back the depreciation to the net income to get the cash flow generated by the property.

	A	B	C
16	**Cash flow, method 1:** **Add back depreciation**		
17	Net income	8,050	<-- =B13
18	Add back depreciation	10,000	<-- =-B10
19	Cash flow	18,050	<-- =B18+B17

In the above calculation, we've added back the depreciation to the net income to get the cash flow.

An asset's *cash flow* (the amount of cash produced by an asset during a particular period) is computed by taking the asset's net income (also called profit after taxes or sometimes just "income") and adding back noncash expenses like depreciation.[4]

Tax Shields

There's another way of calculating the cash flow, which involves a discussion of *tax shields*. A tax shield is a tax saving that results from being able to report an expense for tax purposes. In general, a tax shield just reduces the cash cost of an expense: In the above example, since Sally and Dave's property taxes of $1,500 are an expense for tax purposes, the after-tax cost of the property taxes is

$$(1 - 30\%) * \$1,500 = \$1,500 - \underbrace{30\% * 1,500}_{\substack{\uparrow \\ \text{This } \$450 \text{ is the} \\ \text{tax shield}}} = \$1,050$$

The tax shield of $450 (= 30% * $1,500) has reduced the cost of the property taxes.

Depreciation is a special case of a *noncash expense* that generates a tax shield. A little thought will show you that the $10,000 depreciation on the condo generates $3,000 of cash. Because depreciation reduces Sally and Dave's reported income, each dollar of depreciation saves them $0.30 of taxes, without actually costing them anything in out-of-pocket expenses (the $0.30 comes from the fact that Sally and Dave's tax rate is 30%). Thus, $10,000 of depreciation is worth $3,000 of cash. This $3,000 *depreciation tax shield* is a cash flow for Sally and Dave.

In the spreadsheet below we calculate the cash flow in two stages:

- We first calculate Sally and Dave's net income ignoring depreciation (cell B29). If depreciation were not an expense for tax purposes, Sally and Dave's net income would be $15,050.
- We then add to this figure the depreciation tax shield of $3,000. The result (cell B32) gives the cash flow for the condo.

---

[4]In Chapter 3 we introduced the concept of *free cash flow,* which is an extension of the cash flow concept discussed here.

	A	B	C	D
21	**Cash flow, method 2:** **Compute after-tax income without depreciation, then add depreciation tax shield**			
22	Rent	24,000		
23	Expenses			This is what the net income would have been if depreciation were not an expense for tax purposes.
24	Property taxes	-1,500		
25	Miscellaneous expenses	-1,000		
26	Depreciation	0		
27	Reportable income	21,500	<-- =SUM(B22:B26)	
28	Taxes (rate = 30%)	-6,450	<-- =-B3*B27	
29	Net income without depreciation	15,050	<-- =B27+B28	
30				The effect of depreciation is to add a $3,000 tax shield.
31	Depreciation tax shield	3,000	<-- =B3*10000	
32	Cash flow	18,050	<-- =B31+B29	
33				

Is Sally and Dave's Condo Investment Profitable?—A Preliminary Calculation

At this point Sally and Dave can make a preliminary calculation of the net present value and internal rate of return on their condo investment. Assuming a discount rate of 12% and assuming that they hold the condo for only ten years, the NPV of the condo investment is $1,987 and its IRR is 12.48%:

	A	B	C
1	**SALLY & DAVE'S CONDO--PRELIMINARY VALUATION**		
2	Discount rate	12%	
3			
4	Year	Cash flow	
5	0	-100,000	
6	1	18,050	
7	2	18,050	
8	3	18,050	
9	4	18,050	
10	5	18,050	
11	6	18,050	
12	7	18,050	
13	8	18,050	
14	9	18,050	
15	10	18,050	
16			
17	Net present value, NPV	1,987	<-- =B5+NPV(B2,B6:B15)
18	Internal rate of return, IRR	12.48%	<-- =IRR(B5:B15)

Is Sally and Dave's Condo Investment Profitable?—Incorporating Terminal Value into the Calculations

A little thought about the previous spreadsheet reveals that we've left out an important factor: the value of the condo at the end of the ten-year horizon. In finance an asset's value at the end of the investment horizon is called the asset's *salvage value* or *terminal value*. In the above spreadsheet, we've assumed that the terminal value of the condo is zero, but this assumption is implausible.

To make a better calculation about their investment, Sally and Dave will have to make an assumption about the condo's terminal value. Suppose they assume that at the end of the ten years they'll be able to sell the condo for $80,000. The taxable gain relating to the sale of the condo is the difference between the condo's sale price and its book value at the time of sale—the initial price minus the sum of all the depreciation since Sally and Dave bought it. Since Sally and Dave have been depreciating the condo by $10,000 per year over a ten-year period, its book value at the end of ten years will be zero.

In cell E10 below, you can see that the sale of the condo for $80,000 will generate a cash flow of $56,000:

	A	B	C	D	E	F
1	SALLY & DAVE'S CONDO: PROFITABILITY AND TERMINAL VALUE					
2	Cost of condo	100,000				
3	Sally & Dave's tax rate	30%				
4						
5	Annual reportable income calculation			Terminal value		
6	Rent	24,000		Estimated resale value, year 10	80,000	
7	Expenses			Book value	0	
8	Property taxes	-1,500		Taxable gain	80,000	<-- =E6-E7
9	Miscellaneous expenses	-1,000		Taxes	24,000	<-- =B3*E8
10	Depreciation	-10,000		Net after-tax cash flow from terminal value	56,000	<-- =E8-E9
11	Reportable income	11,500	<-- =SUM(B6:B10)			
12	Taxes (rate = 30%)	-3,450	<-- =-B3*B11			
13	Net income	8,050	<-- =B11+B12			
14						
15	Cash flow, method 1 Add back depreciation					
16	Net income	8,050	<-- =B13			
17	Add back depreciation	10,000	<-- =-B10			
18	Cash flow	18,050	<-- =B17+B16			

To compute the rate of return on Sally and Dave's condo investment, we put all the numbers together:

	A	B	C	D
20	Discount rate	12%		
21				
22	Year	Cash flow		
23	0	-100,000		
24	1	18,050	<-- =B18, Annual cash flow from rental	
25	2	18,050		
26	3	18,050		
27	4	18,050		
28	5	18,050		
29	6	18,050		
30	7	18,050		
31	8	18,050		
32	9	18,050		
33	10	74,050	<-- =B32+E10	
34				
35	NPV of condo investment	20,017	<-- =B23+NPV(B20,B24:B33)	
36	IRR of investment	15.98%	<-- =IRR(B23:B33)	

Assuming that the 12% discount rate is the correct rate, the condo investment is worthwhile: Its NPV is positive and its IRR exceeds the discount rate.[5]

[5]When we say that a discount rate is "correct," we usually mean that it is appropriate to the riskiness of the cash flows being discounted. In Chapter 9 we have our first discussion in this book on how to determine a correct discount rate. For the moment, let's assume that the discount rate is appropriate to the riskiness of the condo's cash flows.

BOOK VALUE VERSUS TERMINAL VALUE

The *book value* of an asset is its initial purchase price minus the accumulated depreciation. The *terminal value* of an asset is its assumed market value at the time you "stop writing down the asset's cash flows." This sounds like a weird definition of terminal value, but often when we do present value calculations for a long-lived asset (like Sally and Dave's condo, or like the company valuations we discuss in Chapters 9 and 10), we write down only a limited number of cash flows.

Sally and Dave are reluctant to make predictions about condo rents and expenses beyond a ten-year horizon. Past this point, they're worried about the accuracy of their guesses. So they write down ten years of cash flows; the terminal value is their best guess of the condo's value at the end of year 10. Their thinking is, "Let's examine the profitability of the condo if we hold on to it for ten years and sell it."

This is what we mean when we say that "the terminal value is what the asset is worth when we stop writing down the cash flows."

Taxes: If Sally and Dave are right in their terminal value assumption, they will have to take account of taxes. The tax rules for selling an asset specify that the tax bill is computed on the *gain over the book value*. So, in the example of Sally and Dave,

$$terminal\ value - taxes\ on\ gain\ over\ book$$
$$= terminal\ value - tax\ rate * (terminal\ value - book\ value)$$
$$= 80,000 - 30\% * (80,000 - 0) = 56,000$$

Doing Some Sensitivity Analysis (Advanced Topic)

A sensitivity analysis can show how the IRR of the condo investment varies as a function of the annual rent and the terminal value. Using Excel's **Data Table** (see Chapter 30), we build a sensitivity table:

	A	B	C	D	E	F	G	H
38	Data table--Condo IRR as function of annual rent and terminal value							
39		Rent						
40		15.98%	**18,000**	**20,000**	**22,000**	**24,000**	**26,000**	**28,000**
41	Terminal value -->	50,000	9.72%	11.45%	13.15%	14.82%	16.47%	18.10%
42		60,000	10.26%	11.93%	13.59%	15.22%	16.84%	18.44%
43		70,000	10.77%	12.40%	14.01%	15.61%	17.19%	18.76%
44	=B36	80,000	11.25%	12.84%	14.42%	15.98%	17.54%	19.08%
45		90,000	11.71%	13.27%	14.81%	16.34%	17.87%	19.38%
46		100,000	12.15%	13.67%	15.19%	16.69%	18.19%	19.68%
47		110,000	12.58%	14.06%	15.55%	17.02%	18.50%	19.96%
48		120,000	12.98%	14.44%	15.90%	17.35%	18.80%	20.24%
49		130,000	13.37%	14.80%	16.23%	17.66%	19.09%	20.51%
50		140,000	13.75%	15.15%	16.56%	17.96%	19.37%	20.78%
51		150,000	14.11%	15.49%	16.87%	18.26%	19.65%	21.03%
52		160,000	14.46%	15.82%	17.18%	18.55%	19.91%	21.28%
53								
54		Note: The data table above computes the IRR of the condo investment for combinations of rent (from $18,000 to						
55		$26,000 per year) and terminal value (from $50,000 to $160,000).						
56		Data tables are very useful though not trivial to compute. See Chapter 30 for more information.						

The calculations in the data table aren't that surprising: For a given rent, the IRR is higher when the terminal value is higher, and for a given terminal value, the IRR is higher given a higher rent.

Building the Data Table[6]

Here's how the data table was set up:

- We build a table with terminal values in the left-hand column and rent in the top row.

---

[6]This subsection doesn't replace Chapter 30, but it may help reinforce what we say there.

- In the top left-hand corner of the table (cell B40), we refer to the IRR calculation in the spreadsheet example (this calculation occurs in cell B36).

At this point the table looks like this:

	A	B	C	D	E	F	G	H
38	Data table--Condo IRR as function of annual rent and terminal value							
39			Rent					
40		15.98%	18,000	20,000	22,000	24,000	26,000	28,000
41	Terminal value -->	50,000						
42		60,000						
43		70,000						
44	=B36	80,000						
45		90,000						
46		100,000						
47		110,000						
48		120,000						
49		130,000						
50		140,000						
51		150,000						
52		160,000						

Using the mouse, we now mark the whole table. We use the **Data|Table** command and fill in the cell references from the original example:

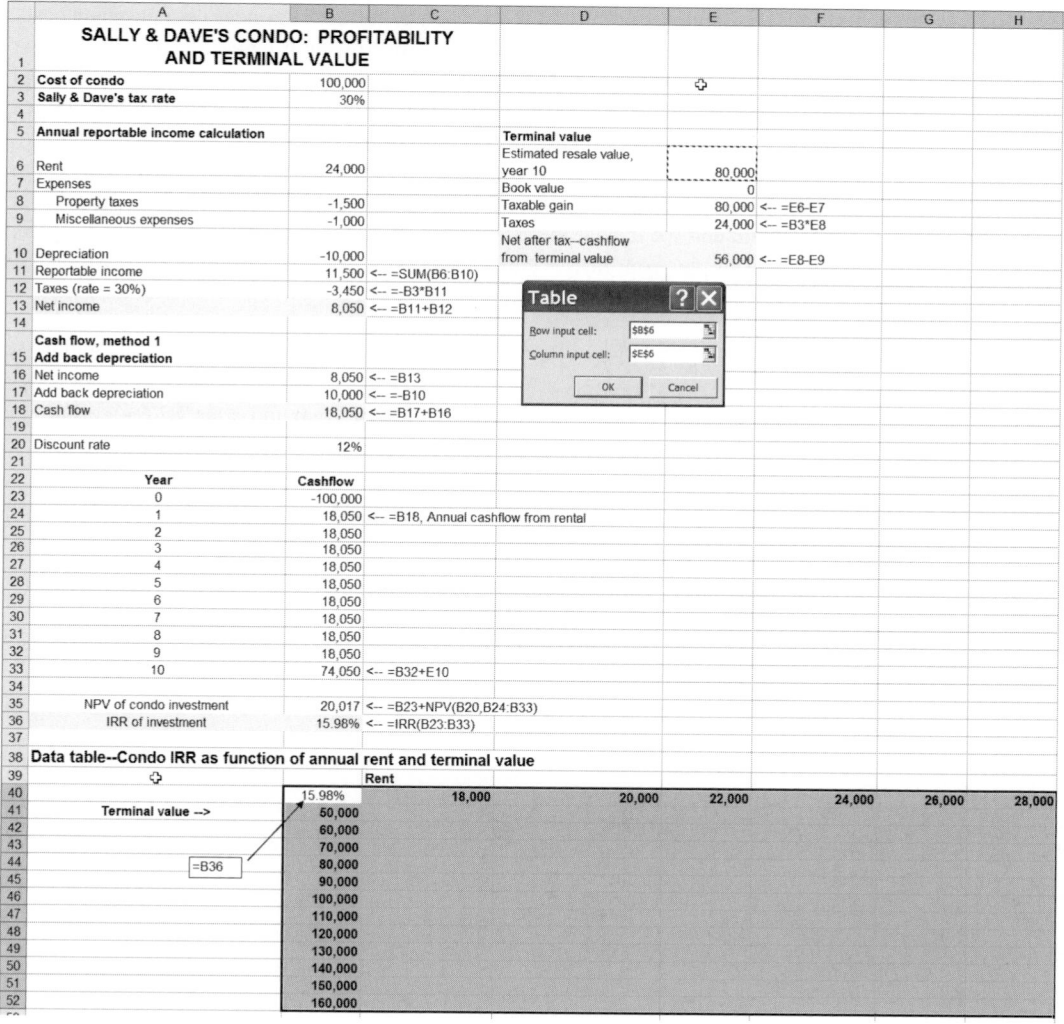

The dialog box tells Excel to repeat the calculation in cell B36, varying the rent number in cell B6 and varying the terminal value number in cell E6. Pressing **OK** does the rest.

MINI-CASE

A mini-case for this chapter looks at Sally and Dave's condo once more—this time under the assumption that they take out a mortgage to buy the condo. Highly recommended!

7.8 Capital Budgeting and Salvage Values

In the Sally–Dave condo example, we focused on the effect of noncash expenses on cash flows: Accountants and the tax authorities compute earnings by subtracting certain kinds of expenses from sales, even though these expenses are *noncash expenses*. In order to compute the cash flow, we add back these noncash expenses to accounting earnings. We showed that these noncash expenses create *tax shields*—they create cash by saving taxes.

In this section, we consider a capital budgeting example in which a firm sells its asset before it is fully depreciated. We show that the asset's book value at the date of the terminal value creates a tax shield and we look at the effect of this tax shield on the capital budgeting decision.

Here's the example. Your firm is considering buying a new machine. Here are the facts:

- The machine costs $800.
- Over the next eight years (the life of the machine) the machine will generate annual sales of $1,000.
- The annual cost of the goods sold (COGS) is $400 per year and other costs—selling, general, and administrative expenses (SG&A)—are $300 per year.
- Depreciation on the machine is straight-line over eight years (that is, $100 per year).
- At the end of eight years, the machine's salvage value (or terminal value) is zero.
- The firm's tax rate is 40%.
- The firm's discount rate for projects of this kind is 15%.

Should the firm buy the machine? Here's the analysis in Excel:

	A	B	C	D	E	F	G
1			BUYING A MACHINE--NPV ANALYSIS				
2	Cost of the machine	800					
3	Annual anticipated sales	1,000					
4	Annual COGS	400					
5	Annual SG&A	300			NPV Analysis		
6	Annual depreciation	100			Year	Cash flow	
7					0	-800	<-- =-B2
8	Tax rate	40%			1	220	<-- =$B$23
9	Discount rate	15%			2	220	
10					3	220	
11	Annual profit and loss (P&L)				4	220	
12	Sales	1,000			5	220	
13	Minus COGS	-400			6	220	
14	Minus SG&A	-300			7	220	
15	Minus depreciation	-100			8	220	
16	Profit before taxes	200	<-- =SUM(B12:B15)				
17	Subtract taxes	-80	<-- =-B8*B16		NPV	187	<-- =F7+NPV(B9,F8:F15)
18	Profit after taxes	120	<-- =B16+B17				
19							
20	Calculating the annual cash flow						
21	Profit after taxes	120					
22	Add back depreciation	100					
23	Cash flow	220					

Notice that we first calculate the profit and loss (P&L) statement for the machine (cells B12 to B18) and then turn this P&L into a cash flow calculation (cells B21 to B23). The annual cash flow is $220. Cells F7 to F15 show the table of cash flows, and cell F17 gives the NPV of the project. The NPV is positive, and the firm should therefore buy the machine.

Salvage Value—A Variation on the Theme

Suppose the firm can sell the machine for $300 at the end of year 8. To compute the cash flow produced by this salvage value, we must make the distinction between *book value* and *market value:*

Book value	An accounting concept: The book value of the machine is its initial cost minus the accumulated depreciation (the sum of the depreciation taken on the machine since its purchase). In our example, the book value of the machine in year 0 is $800, in year 1 it is $700, . . . , and at the end of year 8 it is zero.
Market value	The market value is the price at which the machine can be sold. In our example, the market value of the machine at the end of year 8 is $300.
Taxable gain	The taxable gain on the machine at the time of sale is the difference between the market value and the book value. In our case, the taxable gain is positive ($300), but it can also be negative (see an example on p. 180).

Here's the NPV calculation including the salvage value:

	A	B	C	D	E	F	G
1			BUYING A MACHINE--NPV ANALYSIS with salvage value				
2	Cost of the machine	800					
3	Annual anticipated sales	1,000					
4	Annual COGS	400					
5	Annual SG&A	300			NPV Analysis		
6	Annual depreciation	100			Year	Cash flow	
7					0	-800	<-- =-B2
8	Tax rate	40%			1	220	<-- =$B$23
9	Discount rate	15%			2	220	
10					3	220	
11	Annual profit and loss (P&L)				4	220	
12	Sales	1,000			5	220	
13	Minus COGS	-400			6	220	
14	Minus SG&A	-300			7	220	
15	Minus depreciation	-100			8	400	<-- =$B$23+B30
16	Profit before taxes	200	<-- =SUM(B12:B15)				
17	Subtract taxes	-80	<-- =-B8*B16		NPV	246	<-- =F7+NPV(B9,F8:F15)
18	Profit after taxes	120	<-- =B16+B17				
19							
20	Calculating the annual cash flow						
21	Profit after taxes	120					
22	Add back depreciation	100					
23	Cash flow	220					
24							
25	Calculating the cash flow from salvage value						
26	Machine market value, year 8	300					
27	Book value, year 8	0					
28	Taxable gain	300	<-- =B26-B27				
29	Taxes paid on gain	120	<-- =B8*B28				
30	Cash flow from salvage value	180	<-- =B26-B29				

Note the calculation of the cash flow from the salvage value (cell B30) and the change in the year 8 cash flow (cell F15).

One More Example

Suppose we change the example slightly:

- The annual sales, SG&A, COGS, and depreciation are still as specified in the original example. The machine will still be depreciated on a straight-line basis over eight years.
- However, you think you may sell the machine at the *end of year 7* for an estimated salvage value of $450. At the end of year 7 the book value of the machine is $100.

Here's how the calculations look now:

	A	B	C	D	E	F	G
1			BUYING A MACHINE--NPV ANALYSIS with salvage value Machine sold at end of year 7				
2	Cost of the machine	800					
3	Annual anticipated sales	1,000					
4	Annual COGS	400					
5	Annual SG&A	300		NPV Analysis			
6	Annual depreciation	100		Year	Cash flow		
7				0		-800	<-- =-B2
8	Tax rate	40%		1		220	<-- =$B$23
9	Discount rate	15%		2		220	
10				3		220	
11	Annual profit and loss (P&L)			4		220	
12	Sales	1,000		5		220	
13	Minus COGS	-400		6		220	
14	Minus SG&A	-300		7		530	<-- =$B$23+B30
15	Minus depreciation	-100					
16	Profit before taxes	200	<-- =SUM(B12:B15)		NPV	232	<-- =F7+NPV(B9,F8:F15)
17	Subtract taxes	-80	<-- =-B8*B16				
18	Profit after taxes	120	<-- =B16+B17				
19							
20	Calculating the annual cash flow						
21	Profit after taxes	120					
22	Add back depreciation	100					
23	Cash flow	220					
24							
25	Calculating the cash flow from salvage value						
26	Machine market value, year 7	450					
27	Book value, year 7	100					
28	Taxable gain	350	<-- =B26-B27				
29	Taxes paid on gain	140	<-- =B8*B28				
30	Cash flow from salvage value	310	<-- =B26-B29				

Note the subtle changes from the previous example:

- The *cash flow from salvage value* is

$$salvage\ value - \underbrace{tax * (salvage\ value - book\ value)}_{\substack{\text{Taxable gain at time} \\ \text{of machine sale}}}$$

In our example this is $310 (cell B30).

- Another way to write the cash flow from the salvage value is

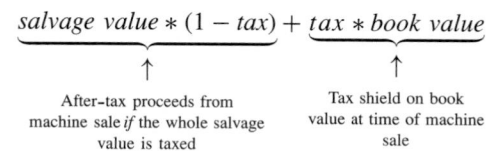

$$\underbrace{salvage\ value * (1 - tax)}_{\substack{\text{After-tax proceeds from} \\ \text{machine sale } if \text{ the whole salvage} \\ \text{value is taxed}}} + \underbrace{tax * book\ value}_{\substack{\text{Tax shield on book} \\ \text{value at time of machine} \\ \text{sale}}}$$

Using this example, you can see the role taxes play even if the machine is sold at a loss. Suppose, for example, that the machine is sold in year 7 for $50, which is less than the book value:

	A	B	C	D	E	F	G
1			**BUYING A MACHINE--NPV ANALYSIS** with salvage value Machine sold at end of year 7				
2	Cost of the machine	800					
3	Annual anticipated sales	1,000					
4	Annual COGS	400					
5	Annual SG&A	300			**NPV Analysis**		
6	Annual depreciation	100			Year	Cash flow	
7					0	-800	<-- =-B2
8	Tax rate	40%			1	220	<-- =$B$23
9	Discount rate	15%			2	220	
10					3	220	
11	**Annual profit and loss (P&L)**				4	220	
12	Sales	1,000			5	220	
13	Minus COGS	-400			6	220	
14	Minus SG&A	-300			7	290	<-- =$B$23+B30
15	Minus depreciation	-100					
16	Profit before taxes	200	<-- =SUM(B12:B15)		NPV	142	<-- =F7+NPV(B9,F8:F15)
17	Subtract taxes	-80	<-- =-B8*B16				
18	Profit after taxes	120	<-- =B16+B17				
19							
20	**Calculating the annual cash flow**						
21	Profit after taxes	120					
22	Add back depreciation	100					
23	Cash flow	220					
24							
25	**Calculating the cash flow from salvage value**						
26	Machine market value, year 7	50					
27	Book value, year 7	100					
28	Taxable gain	-50	<-- =B26-B27				
29	Taxes paid on gain	-20	<-- =B8*B28				
30	Cash flow from salvage value	70	<-- =B26-B29				

In this case, the negative taxable gain (cell B28, the jargon often heard is "loss over book") produces a tax shield—the negative taxes of −$20 in cell B29. This tax shield is added to the market value to produce a salvage value cash flow of $70 (cell B30). Thus, even selling an asset at a loss can produce a positive cash flow.

7.9 Capital Budgeting Principle: Don't Forget the Cost of Foregone Opportunities

This is another important principle of capital budgeting. An example: You've been offered the project below, which involves buying a widget-making machine for $300 to make a new product. The cash flows in years 1–5 have been calculated by your financial analysts:

	A	B	C
1	**DON'T FORGET THE COST OF FOREGONE OPPORTUNITIES**		
2	Discount rate	12%	
3			
4	**Year**	**Cash flow**	
5	0	-300	
6	1	185	
7	2	249	
8	3	155	
9	4	135	
10	5	420	
11			
12	NPV	498.12	<-- =NPV(B2,B6:B10)+B5
13	IRR	62.67%	<-- =IRR(B5:B10)

Looks like a fine project! But now someone remembers that the widget process makes use of some already existing but underused equipment. Should the value of this equipment be somehow taken into account?

The answer to this question has to do with whether the equipment has an alternative use. For example, suppose that, if you don't buy the widget machine, you can sell the equipment for $200. Then the true year 0 cost for the project is $500, and the project has a lower NPV:

	A	B	C
16	Discount rate	12%	
17			
18	**Year**	**Cash flow**	
19	0	-500	The $300 direct cost + $200 <-- value of the existing machines
20	1	185	
21	2	249	
22	3	155	
23	4	135	
24	5	420	
25			
26	NPV	298.12	
27	IRR	31.97%	

While the logic here is clear, the implementation can be murky: What if the machine is to occupy space in a building that is currently unused? Should the cost of this space be taken into account? It all depends on whether there are alternative uses, now or in the future.[7]

7.10 In-House Copying or Outsourcing? A Mini-case Illustrating Foregone Opportunity Costs

Your company is trying to decide whether to outsource its photocopying or continue to do it in-house. The current photocopier won't do anymore—it either has to be sold or thoroughly

[7]There's a fine Harvard case on this topic: "The Super Project," Harvard Business School case 9-112-034.

fixed up. Here are some details about the two alternatives:

- The company's tax rate is 40%.
- Doing the copying in-house requires an investment of $17,000 to fix up the existing photo-copy machine. Your accountant estimates that this $17,000 can immediately be booked as an expense, so that its after-tax cost is $(1 - 40\%) * \$17,000 = \$10,200$. Given this investment, the copier will be good for another five years. Annual copying costs are estimated to be $25,000 on a before-tax basis; after-tax this is $(1 - 40\%) * \$25,000 = \$15,000$.
- The photocopy machine is on your books for $15,000, but its market value is in fact much less—it could be sold today for only $5,000. This means that the sale of the copier will generate a loss for tax purposes of $10,000; at your tax rate of 40%, this loss gives a tax shield of $4,000. Thus, the sale of the copier will generate a cash flow of $9,000.
- If you decide to keep doing the photocopying in-house, the remaining book value of the copier will be depreciated over five years at $3,000 per year. Since your tax rate is 40%, this will produce a tax shield of $40\% * \$3,000 = \$1,200$ per year.
- Outsourcing the copying will cost $33,000 per year—$8,000 more expensive than doing it in-house on the rehabilitated copier. Of course, this $33,000 is an expense for tax purposes, so that the net savings from doing the copying in-house are

$$(1 - tax\ rate) * outsourcing\ costs = (1 - 40\%) * \$33,000 = \$19,800$$

- The relevant discount rate is 12%.

We show two ways to analyze this decision. The first method values each of the alternatives separately. The second method looks only at the differential cash flows. We recommend the first method—it's simpler and leads to fewer mistakes. The second method produces a somewhat "cleaner" set of cash flows that take explicit account of foregone opportunity costs.

Method 1: Write Down the Cash Flows of Each Alternative

This is often the simplest way to do things; if you do it correctly, this method takes care of all the foregone opportunity costs without your thinking about them. Below we write down the cash flows for each alternative:

	In-House	Outsourcing
Year 0	$-(1 - tax\ rate) * machine\ rehab\ cost$ $= -(1 - 40\%) * 17,000$ $= -\$10,200$	*Sale price of machine* $+ tax\ rate * loss\ over\ book\ value$ $= \$5,000 + 40\% * (\$15,000 - \$5,000)$ $= \$9,000$
Years 1–5 Annual Cash Flow	$-(1 - tax\ rate) * in\text{-}house\ costs$ $+ tax\ rate * depreciation$ $= -(1 - 40\%) * \$25,000$ $+ 40\% * \$3,000 = -\$13,800$	$-(1 - tax\ rate) * outsourcing\ costs$ $= -(1 - 40\%) * \$33,000$ $= -\$19,800$

Putting these data in a spreadsheet and discounting at the discount rate of 12% shows that it is cheaper to do the in-house copying. The NPV of the in-house cash flows is $-\$59{,}946$, whereas the NPV of the outsourcing cash flows is $-\$62{,}375$. Note that both NPVs are negative; but the in-house alternative is less negative (meaning: more positive) than the outsourcing alternative; therefore, the in-house alternative is preferred:

	A	B	C
1	**SELL THE PHOTOCOPIER OR FIX IT UP?**		
2	Annual cost savings (before tax) after fixing up the machine	8,000	
3	Book value of machine	15,000	
4	Market value of machine	5,000	
5	Rehab cost of machine	17,000	
6	Tax rate	40%	
7	Annual depreciation if machine is retained	3,000	
8	Annual copying costs		
9	In-house	25,000	
10	Outsourcing	33,000	
11	Discount rate	12%	
12			
13	**Alternative 1: Fix up machine and do copying in-house**		
14	Year	Cash flow	
15	0	-10,200	<-- =-B5*(1-B6)
16	1	-13,800	<-- =-$B$9*(1-$B$6)+$B$6*$B$7
17	2	-13,800	
18	3	-13,800	
19	4	-13,800	
20	5	-13,800	
21	NPV of fixing up machine and in-house copying	-59,946	<-- =B15+NPV(B11,B16:B20)
22			
23	**Alternative 2: Sell machine and outsource copying**		
24	Year	Cash flow	
25	0	9,000	<-- =B4+B6*(B3-B4)
26	1	-19,800	<-- =-(1-$B$6)*$B$10
27	2	-19,800	
28	3	-19,800	
29	4	-19,800	
30	5	-19,800	
31	NPV of selling machine and outsourcing	-62,375	<-- =B25+NPV(B11,B26:B30)

Method 2: Discounting the Differential Cash Flows

In this method we subtract the cash flows of Alternative 2 from those of Alternative 1:

	A	B	C
34	**Subtract Alternative 2 CFs from Alternative 1 CFs**		
35	Year	Cash flow	
36	0	-19,200	<-- =B15-B25
37	1	6,000	<-- =B16-B26
38	2	6,000	
39	3	6,000	
40	4	6,000	
41	5	6,000	
42	NPV(Alternative 1 - Alternative 2)	2,429	<-- =B36+NPV(B11,B37:B41)

The NPV of the differential cash flows is positive. This means that Alternative 1 (in-house) is better than Alternative 2 (outsourcing):

$$NPV(in\text{-}house - outsourcing) = NPV(in\text{-}house) - NPV(outsourcing) > 0$$

This means that

$$NPV(in\text{-}house) > NPV(outsourcing)$$

If you look carefully at the differential cash flows, you'll see that they take into account the cost of the foregone opportunities:

Year	Differential Cash Flow	Explanation
Year 0	−$19,200	This is the after-tax cost of rehabilitating the old copier (−$10,200) and the foregone opportunity cost of selling the copier (−$9,000). In other words: This is the cost in year 0 of deciding to do the copying in-house.
Years 1–5	$6,000	This is the after-tax saving of doing the copying in-house: If you do it in-house, you save $8,000 pretax (=$4,800 after tax) and you get to take depreciation on the existing copier (=tax shield of $1,200). Relative to in-house copying, the outsourcing alternative has a foregone opportunity cost of theloss of the depreciation tax shield.

If you examine the convoluted prose in the table above ("the outsourcing alternative has a foregone opportunity cost of the loss of the depreciation tax shield"), you'll agree that it may just be simpler to list each alternative's cash flows separately.

7.11 Accelerated Depreciation

As you know by now, the *salvage value* for an asset is its value at the end of its life; another term sometimes used is *terminal value*. Here's a capital budgeting example that illustrates the importance of accelerated depreciation in computing the Net present value:

- Your company is considering buying a machine for $10,000.
- If bought, the machine will produce annual cost savings of $3,000 for the next five years; these cash flows will be taxed at the company's tax rate of 40%.
- The machine will be depreciated over the five-year period using the accelerated depreciation percentages allowable in the United States. At the end of year 6, the machine will be sold; your estimate of its salvage value at this point is $4,000, even though for accounting purposes its book value is $576 (cell B19 below).

You have to decide what the NPV of the project is, using a discount rate of 12%. Here are the relevant calculations:

	A	B	C	D	E	F	G
1	**CAPITAL BUDGETING WITH ACCELERATED DEPRECIATION**						
2	Machine cost	10,000					
3	Annual materials savings, before tax	3,000					
4	Salvage value, end of year 5	4,000					
5	Tax rate	40%					
6	Discount rate	12%					
7							
8	**Accelerated depreciation schedule (ACRS)**						
9	Year	ACRS depreciation percentage	Actual depreciation	Depreciation tax shield			
10	1	20.00%	2,000	800	<-- =$B$5*C10		
11	2	32.00%	3,200	1,280	<-- =$B$5*C11		
12	3	19.20%	1,920	768	<-- =$B$5*C12		
13	4	11.52%	1,152	461	<-- =$B$5*C13		
14	5	11.52%	1,152	461			
15	6	5.76%	576	230	The book value at the end of year 6 is the initial cost of the machine ($10,000) *minus* the sum of all the depreciation taken on the machine through year 6 ($9,424).		
16							
17	**Terminal value**						
18	Year 6 sale price, estimated	4,000	<-- =B4				
19	Year 6 book value	576	<-- =B2-SUM(C10:C14)				
20	Taxable gain	3,424	<-- =B18-B19				
21	Taxes	1,370	<-- =B5*B20				
22	Net cash flow from terminal value	2,630	<-- =B18-B21		The net cash flow from the terminal value equals the year 6 sale price minus applicable taxes.		
23							
24							
25	**Net present value calculation**						
26	Year	Cost	After-tax cost savings	Depreciation tax shield	Terminal value	Total cash flow	
27	0	-10,000				-10,000	
28	1		1,800	800		2,600	<-- =SUM(B28:E28)
29	2		1,800	1,280		3,080	
30	3		1,800	768		2,568	
31	4		1,800	461		2,261	
32	5		1,800	461		2,261	
33	6				2,630	2,630	
34							
35	Net present value	657	<-- =F27+NPV(B6,F28:F33)				
36	IRR	14.36%	<-- =IRR(F27:F33)				

The annual after-tax cost saving is $1,800 = (1 − 40\%) * \$3,000$. The depreciation tax shields are determined by the accelerated depreciation schedule (rows 10–15), When the asset is sold at the end of year 6, its book value is $576. This leads to a taxable gain of $3,424 (cell B20) and to taxes of $1,370 (cell B21). The net cash flow from selling the asset at the end of year 6 is its sale price of $4,000 minus the taxes (cell B22).

The NPV of the asset is $657 and the IRR is 14.36% (cell B35 and B36).

CONCLUSION

In this chapter we've discussed the basics of capital budgeting using NPV and IRR. Capital budgeting decisions can be separated crudely into "Yes–No" decisions ("Should we undertake a given project?") and into "ranking" decisions ("Which of the following list of projects do we prefer?"). We've concentrated on two important areas of capital budgeting:

- The difference between NPV and IRR in making the capital budgeting decision. In many cases these two criteria give the same answer to the capital budgeting question. However, there are cases—especially when we rank projects—where NPV and IRR give different answers. Where they differ, NPV is the preferable criterion to use because the NPV is the additional wealth derived from a project.

- Every capital budgeting decision ultimately involves a set of anticipated cash flows, so when you do capital budgeting, it's important to get these cash flows right. We've illustrated the importance of sunk costs, taxes, foregone opportunities, and salvage values in determining the cash flows.

EXERCISES

1. You are considering a project whose cash flows are given below:

	A	B
3	Discount rate	25%
4		
5	**Year**	**Cash flow**
6	0	-1,000
7	1	100
8	2	200
9	3	300
10	4	400
11	5	500
12	6	600

   (a) Calculate the present values of the future cash flows of the project.
   (b) Calculate the project's net present value.
   (c) Calculate the internal rate of return.
   (d) Should you undertake the project?

2. Your firm is considering two projects with the following cash flows:

	A	B	C
5	Year	Project A	Project B
6	0	-500	-500
7	1	167	200
8	2	180	250
9	3	160	170
10	4	100	25
11	5	100	30

   (a) If the appropriate discount rate is 12%, rank the two projects.
   (b) Which project is preferred if you rank by IRR?
   (c) Calculate the crossover rate—the discount rate r for which the NPVs of both projects are equal.
   (d) Should you use NPV or IRR to choose between the two projects? Give a brief discussion.

3. Your uncle is the proud owner of an up-market clothing store. Because business is down, he is considering replacing the languishing tie department with a new sportswear department. In order to examine the profitability of such a move, he hired a financial advisor to estimate the cash flows of the new department. After six months of hard work, the financial advisor came up with the

following calculations:

Investment (at $t = 0$)	
Rearranging the shop	40,000
Loss of business during renovation	15,000
Payment for financial advisor	12,000
Total	67,000

Profits (from $t = 1$ to infinity)	
Annual earnings from the sport department	75,000
Loss of earnings from the tie department	−20,000
Loss of earnings from other departments*	−15,000
Additional worker for the sport department	−18,000
Municipal taxes	−15,000
Total	7,000

*Some of your uncle's stuck-up clients will not buy in a shop that sells sportswear.

The discount rate is 12%, and there are no additional taxes. Thus, the financial advisor calculated the NPV as follows:

$$-67,000 + \frac{7,000}{0.12} = -8,667$$

Your surprised uncle asked you (a promising finance student) to go over the calculation. What are the correct NPV and IRR of the project?

4. You are the owner of a factory that supplies chairs and tables to schools in Denver. You sell each chair for $1.76 and each table for $4.40 based on the following calculation:

	Chair Department	Table Department
Number of units	100,000	20,000
Cost of material	80,000	35,000
Cost of labor	40,000	20,000
Fixed cost	40,000	25,000
Total cost	160,000	80,000
Cost per unit	1.60	4.00
Plus 10% profit	1.76	4.40

You have received an offer from a school in Colorado Springs to supply an additional 10,000 chairs and 2,000 tables for the price of $1.50 and $3.50, respectively. Your financial advisor advises you not to take up the offer because the price does not even cover the cost of production. Is the financial advisor correct?

5. A factory's management is considering the purchase of a new machine for one of its units. The machine costs $100,000. The machine will be depreciated on a straight-line basis over its ten-year life to a salvage value of zero. The machine is expected to save the company $50,000 annually,

but in order to operate it the factory will have to transfer an employee (with a salary of $40,000 a year) from one of its other units. A new employee (with a salary of $20,000 a year) will be required to replace the transferred employee. What is the NPV of the purchase of the new machine if the relevant discount rate is 8% and the corporate tax rate is 35%?

6. You are considering the following investment:

Year	EBDT (Earnings Before Depreciation and Taxes)
0	−10,500
1	3,000
2	3,000
3	3,000
4	2,500
5	2,500
6	2,500
7	2,500

The discount rate is 11% and the corporate tax rate is 34%.

(a) Calculate the project NPV using straight-line depreciation.

(b) What will be the company's gain if it uses the ACRS depreciation schedule of Section 7.11?

7. A company is considering buying a new machine for one of its factories. The cost of the machine is $60,000 and its expected life span is five years. The machine will save the cost of a worker estimated at $22,500 annually. The book value of the machine at the end of year 5 is $10,000 but the company estimates that the market value will be only $5,000. Calculate the NPV of the machine if the discount rate is 12% and the tax rate is 30%. Assume straight-line depreciation over the five-year life of the machine.

8. The ABD Company is considering buying a new machine for one of its factories. The machine cost is $100,000 and its expected life span is eight years. The machine is expected to reduce the production cost by $15,000 annually. The terminal value of the machine is $20,000 but the company believes that it would only manage to sell it for $10,000. If the appropriate discount rate is 15% and the corporate tax is 40%:

(a) Calculate the project NPV.

(b) Calculate the project IRR.

9. You are the owner of a factory located in a hot tropical climate. The monthly production of the factory is $100,000 except during June–September when it falls to $80,000 due to the heat in the factory. In January 2003 you get an offer to install an air-conditioning system in your factory. The cost of the air-conditioning system is $150,000 and its expected life span is ten years. If you install the air-conditioning system, the production in the summer months will equal the production in the winter months. However, the cost of operating the system is $9,000 per month (only in the four months that you operate the system). You will also need to pay a maintenance fee of $5,000 annually in October. What is the NPV of the air-conditioning system if the discount rate is 12% and the corporate tax rate is 35% (the depreciation costs are recognized in December of each year)?

10. The Cold and Sweet (C&S) Company manufactures ice-cream bars. The company is considering the purchase of a new machine that will top the bar with high quality chocolate. The cost of the machine is $900,000.

Depreciation and terminal value: The machine will be depreciated over ten years to zero salvage value. However, management intends to use the machine for only five years. Management thinks that the sale price of the machine at the end of five years will be $100,000.

The machine can produce up to one million ice-cream bars annually. The marketing director of C&S believes that if the company will spend $30,000 on advertising in the first year and another $10,000 in each of the following years, the company will be able to sell 400,000 bars for $1.30 each. The cost of producing each bar is $0.50; and other costs related to the new products are $40,000 annually. C&S's cost of capital is 14% and the corporate tax rate is 30%.

(a)   What is the NPV of the project if the marketing director's projections are correct?

(b)   What is the minimum price that the company should charge for each bar if the project is to be profitable? Assume that the price of the bar does not affect sales.

(c)   The C&S Marketing Vice President suggested canceling the advertising campaign. In her opinion, the company sales will not be reduced significantly due to the cancellation. What is the minimum quantity that the company needs to sell in order to be profitable if the Vice President's suggestion is accepted.

(d)   Extra: Use a two-dimensional data table to determine the sensitivity of the profitability to the price and quantity sold.

11. The Less Is More Company manufactures swimsuits. The company is considering expanding into the bathrobe market. The proposed investment plan includes:

   - Purchase of a new machine: The cost of the machine is $150,000 and its expected life span is five years. The terminal value of the machine is 0, but the chief economist of the company estimates that it can be sold for $10,000.

   - Advertising campaign: The head of the marketing department estimates that the campaign will cost $80,000 annually.

   - Fixed cost of the new department will be $40,000 annually.

   - Variable costs are estimated at $30 per bathrobe but due to the expected rise in labor costs they are expected to rise at 5% per year.

   - Each of the bathrobes will be sold at a price of $45 at the first year. Management estimates that it can raise the price of the bathrobes by 10% in each of the following years.

The Less Is More Company discount rate is 10% and the corporate tax rate is 36%.

(a)   What is the break-even point of the bathrobe department?

(b)   Plot a graph in which the NPV is the dependent variable of the annual production.

12. The Car Clean Company operates a car wash business. The company bought a machine two years ago at the price of $60,000. The life span of the machine is six years and the machine has no disposal value; the current market value of the machine is $20,000. The company is considering buying a new machine. The cost of the new machine is $100,000 and its life span is four years. The new machine has a disposal value of $20,000. The new machine is faster than the old one; thus, management believes the revenue will increase from $1 million annually to $1.03 million. In addition, the new machine is expected to save the company $10,000 in water and electricity costs. The discount rate of the Car Clean Company is 15% and the corporate tax rate is 40%. What is the NPV of replacing the old machine?

13. A company is considering whether to buy a regular or color photocopier for the office. The cost of the regular machine is $10,000, its life span is five years, and the company has to pay another $1,500 annually in maintenance costs. The color photocopier's price is $30,000, its life span is also five years, and the annual maintenance costs are $4,500. The color photocopier is expected to increase the revenue of the office by $8,500 annually. Assume that the company is profitable and pays 40% corporate tax; the relevant discount rate is 11%. Which photocopy machine should the firm buy?

14. The Coka Company is a soft drink company. Until today, the company bought empty cans from an outside supplier that charges Coka $0.20 per can. In addition, the transportation cost is $1,000

per truck that transports 10,000 cans. The Coka Company's management is considering whether to start manufacturing cans in its plant. The cost of a can machine is $1,000,000 and its life span is twelve years. The terminal value of the machine is $160,000. Maintenance and repair costs will be $150,000 for every three-year period. The additional space for the new operation will cost the company $100,000 annually. The cost of producing a can in the factory will be $0.17.

The cost of capital for Coka is 11% and the corporate tax rate is 40%.

(a)   What is the minimum number of cans that the company has to sell annually in order to justify self-production of cans?

(b)   Advanced: Use data tables to show the NPV and IRR of the project as a function of the number of cans.

15. The ZZZ Company is considering investing in a new machine for one of its factories. The company has two alternatives from which to choose:

Considerations	Machine A	Machine B
Cost	$4,000,000	$10,000,000
Annual fixed cost per machine	$300,000	$210,000
Variable cost per unit	$1.20	$0.80
Annual production	400,000	550,000

The life span of each machine is five years. ZZZ sells each unit for a price of $6. The company has a cost of capital of 12% and its tax rate is 35%.

(a)   If the company manufactures 1,000,000 units per year, which machine should it buy?

(b)   Plot a graph showing the profitability of investment in each machine type depending on the annual production.

16. The Easy Sight Company manufactures sunglasses. The company has two machines, each of which produces 1,000 sunglasses per month. The book value of each of the old machines is $10,000 and their expected life span is five years. The machines are being depreciated on a straight-line basis to zero salvage value. The company assumes it will be able to sell a machine today (January 2006) for the price of $6,000. The price of a new machine is $20,000 and its expected life span is five years. The new machine will save the company $0.85 for every pair of sunglasses produced.

Demand for sunglasses is seasonal. During the five months of the summer (May–September) demand is 2,000 sunglasses per month, while during the winter months it falls down to 1,000 per month.

Assume that due to insurance and storage costs it is uneconomical to store sunglasses at the factory. How many new machines should Easy Sight buy if the discount rate is 10% and the corporate tax rate is 40%?

17. Poseidon is considering opening a shipping line from Athens to Rhodes. In order to open the shipping line, Poseidon will have to purchase two ships that cost 1,000 gold coins each. The life span of each ship is ten years, and Poseidon estimates that he will earn 300 gold coins in the first year and that the earnings will increase by 5% per year. The annual costs of the shipping line are estimated at 60 gold coins annually, Poseidon's interest rate is 8%, and Zeus's tax rate is 50%.

(a)   Will the shipping line be profitable?

(b)   Due to Poseidon's good connections on Olympus, he can get a tax reduction. What is the maximum tax rate at which the project will be profitable?

18. At the board meeting on Olympus, Hera tried to convince Zeus to keep the 50% tax rate intact due to the budget deficit. According to Hera's calculations, the shipping line will be more profitable if Poseidon buys only one ship and sells tickets only to first class passengers. Hera estimated that Poseidon's annual costs will be 40 gold coins.

    (a) What are the minimum annual average earnings required for the shipping line to be profitable, assuming that earnings are constant throughout the ten years?

    (b) Zeus, who is an old fashioned god, believes that "blood is thicker than money." He agrees to give Poseidon a tax reduction if he buys only one ship. Use data tables to show the profitability of the project, dependent on the annual earnings and the tax rate.

19. Kane Running Shoes is considering the manufacture of a special shoe for race walking, which will indicate if an athlete is running (that is, both legs are not touching the ground). The chief economist of the company presented the following calculation for the Smart Walking Shoe (SWS):

    • R&D: $200,000 annually in each of the next four years

    For the manufacturing project:

    • Expected life span: ten years
    • Investment in machinery: $250,000 (at $t = 4$) expected life span of the machine ten years
    • Expected annual sales: 5,000 pairs of shoes at the expected price of $150 per pair
    • Fixed cost: $300,000 annually
    • Variable cost: $50 per pair of shoes

    Kane's discount rate is 12%, the corporate tax rate is 40%, and R&D expenses are tax deductible against other profits of the company. Assume that at the end of project (that is, after fourteen years) the new technology will have been superseded by other technologies and therefore will have no value.

    (a) What is the NPV of the project?

    (b) The International Olympic Committee (IOC) decided to give Kane a loan without interest for six years in order to encourage the company to take on the project. The loan will have to be paid back in six equal annual payments. What is the minimum loan that the IOC should give in order that the project will be profitable?

20. (Continuation of previous problem) After long negotiations, the IOC decided to lend Kane $600,000 at $t = 0$. The project went ahead. After the research and development stage was completed (at $t = 4$) but before the investment was made, the IOC decided to cancel race walking as an Olympic event. As a result, Kane is expecting a large drop in sales of the SWS shoes. What is the minimum number of shoes Kane has to sell annually for the project to be profitable in each of the following two cases:

    (a) If, in the event of cancellation, the original loan term continues?

    (b) If, in the event of cancellation, the company has to return the outstanding debt to the IOC immediately?

21. The Aphrodite Company is a manufacturer of perfume. The company is about to launch a new line of products. The marketing department has to decide whether to use an aggressive or regular campaign.

Aggressive Campaign

Initial cost (production of commercial advertisement using a top model): $400,000

First month profit: $20,000

Monthly growth in profit (months 2–12): 10%

After 12 months the company is going to launch a new line of products and it is expected that the monthly profits from the current line would be $20,000 forever.

Regular Campaign

Initial cost (using a less famous model): $150,000

First month profit: $10,000

Monthly growth in profits (months 2–12): 6%

Monthly profit (months $13–\infty$): $20,000

(a) The cost of capital is 7%. Calculate the NPV of each campaign and decide which campaign the company should undertake.

(b) The manager of the company believes that, due to the recession expected next year, the profit figures for the aggressive campaign (both first month profit and monthly growth in profits for months 2–12) are too optimistic. Use a data table to show the differential NPV as a function of first month payment and growth rate of the aggressive campaign.

22. The Long-Life Company has a ten-year monopoly for selling a new vaccine that is capable of curing all known cancers. The price at which the company can sell the new drug is given by the following equation:

$$P = 10,000 - 0.3 * X \qquad 0 \leq X < 25,000$$

where P is the price per vaccine and X is the quantity. In order to mass-produce the new drug, the company needs to purchase new machines. Each machine costs $70,000,000 and is capable of producing 150,000 vaccines per year. The expected life span of each machine is five years; over this time it will be depreciated on a straight-line basis to zero salvage value. The R&D cost for the new drug is $1,500,000,000, the variable costs are $1,000 per vaccine, and fixed costs are $120,000,000 annually. If the discount rate is 12% and the tax rate is 30%, how many vaccines will the company produce annually? (Use either Excel's **Goal Seek** or its **Solver**—see Chapter 32.)

23. (Continuation of Exercise 22). The independent senator from Alaska, Michele Carey, has suggested that the government pay Long-Life $2,000,000 in exchange for the company guaranteeing that it will produce under the zero profit policy (that is, produce as long as NPV ≥ 0). How many vaccines will the company produce annually?

ISSUES IN CAPITAL BUDGETING

OVERVIEW

The capital budgeting decisions we examined in Chapter 7 were all pretty cut and dried: The NPV and IRR criteria always indicated which investment was worthwhile for the individual or the company. As you might expect, in real life the decisions of where and how to spend your investment dollars are not always so clear-cut.

In this chapter we expand on the discussion of capital budgeting started in Chapter 7 and examine a number of issues that often cause confusion.

Finance Concepts Discussed

- Problems with IRR as a decision criterion
    - IRR can't distinguish between borrowing and lending
    - Multiple IRRs
- Choosing between projects with different lifetimes
- Discounting cash flows that don't occur at year end ("midyear discounting")
- Incorporating tax considerations into the lease versus purchase problem
- Incorporating inflation into capital budgeting—discounting nominal versus real cash flows

Excel Functions Used

- **IRR, NPV**
- **Sum**
- **PMT**
- **If**
- **XNPV, XIRR**

8.1 A Problem With IRR: You Can't Always Tell Good Projects From Bad Ones

Sometimes it's hard to tell from the IRR whether a project is good or bad. Here's a simple example: You've decided to buy a car; the list price is $11,000, and the dealer has offered you two purchase options:

- You can pay the dealer cash and get a $1,000 discount, thus paying only $10,000.
- You can pay $5,000 now and pay $2,000 in each of the next three years. The dealer calls this his "zero-interest car loan" plan. The bank is giving car loans at 9% interest, so the dealer claims that his plan is much cheaper.

Which offer is better? Having learned a bit of finance, you set up the following Excel spreadsheet:

	A	B	C	D	E
1	**BUYING A CAR**				
2	List price of car	11,000.00			
3	Downpayment	5,000.00			
4	Cash cost of car	10,000.00			
5					
6	Year	**Payment in cash**	**Payment with credit**	**Cash spent or saved with credit plan**	
7	0	-10,000.00	-5,000.00	5,000.00	<-- =C7-B7
8	1		-2,000.00	-2,000.00	<-- =C8-B8
9	2		-2,000.00	-2,000.00	
10	3		-2,000.00	-2,000.00	
11					
12	Internal rate of return			9.70%	<-- =IRR(D7:D10)
13					
14	Bank rate of interest	9%			
15	NPV of cash saved	-62.59	<-- =D7+NPV(B14,D8:D10)		

The critical element in the spreadsheet is column D, which compares the annual cash outlays of the credit plan with those of the cash-payment plan. Column D shows that if you pay with the credit plan instead of paying cash, you'll spend $5,000 *less* in year 0. On the other hand, you'll spend $2,000 *more* in years 1, 2, and 3. The IRR of this column is 9.70%. Since the bank is lending money at 9%, you should take a bank loan instead of using the dealer's credit plan.

To understand this further, note that the pattern of the cash flows in column D is like the pattern of cash flows from taking a loan. When you take a loan, there is an initial positive cash flow (this is when you get the loan) and subsequent negative cash flows (the loan repayments). When you buy the car using the dealer's credit plan, the cash flow pattern is the same: There is an initial positive cash flow (the savings from paying only $5,000 instead of $10,000) and subsequent negative cash flows (the additional $2,000 annual cost of the credit plan). Thus, the IRR of 9.70% represents the *cost* of the dealer's credit plan. Since the bank lends at a cost of 9%, it is cheaper to borrow through the bank.

What if you don't have the $10,000 cash for the cash-payment plan? Then you should take a bank loan (read on for details).

Cell B15 discounts the differential payment flow of column D at the bank interest rate. This shows that this flow has a negative NPV, another indication that you shouldn't undertake this project: You should opt for the cash-payment plan.

How Will You Pay for the Car?

So you're better off paying the dealer cash. If you don't have the $10,000 cash, you could borrow $5,000 from the bank. This plan would have cash flows (assuming equal annual payments of principal and interest, calculated using Excel's **PMT** function) of:

	A	B	C	D	E
18	**Borrowing the money from the bank**				
19	Year	Payment in cash	Bank loan cash flows	Total cash flow to car owner	
20	0	-10,000.00	5,000.00	-5,000.00	
21	1		-1,975.27	-1,975.27	<-- =PMT(9%,3,C20)
22	2		-1,975.27	-1,975.27	
23	3		-1,975.27	-1,975.27	

The cash flows in cells D20 to D23 are an improvement over those in cells C7 to C10, which shows (again) that it's better to buy the car with cash and borrow the money from the bank than to take the dealer's financing offer.

The Dealer's Cash Flows

To see how confusing the IRR can be, consider the dealer's cash flows. He's offered you the choice of paying $10,000 in cash or $5,000 down with three equal payments of $2,000:

	A	B	C	D	E
1	**IRR VERSUS NPV--THE DEALER'S PROBLEM**				
2	List price of car	11,000.00			
3	Downpayment	5,000.00			
4	Cash cost of car	10,000.00			
5					
6	Year	Payment in cash	Payment with credit	Differential dealer cash flow	
7	0	10,000.00	5,000.00	-5,000.00	<-- =C7-B7
8	1		2,000.00	2,000.00	<-- =C8-B8
9	2		2,000.00	2,000.00	
10	3		2,000.00	2,000.00	
11					
12	Internal rate of return			9.70%	<-- =IRR(D7:D10)
13					
14	Bank rate of interest	9%			
15	NPV of cash saved	62.59	<-- =D7+NPV(B14,D8:D10)		

Column D shows that between the two plans, the dealer has a negative cash flow of $5,000 in year 0, but then has a positive cash flow of $2,000 in each of the three subsequent years. Effectively, the dealer is acting like a bank giving a loan, and the 9.70% represents the interest earned by the dealer on the loan; if he can borrow the $5,000 in cell D7 from the bank at 9%, he's better off—his NPV on the loan is $57.42.

What's the Point?

The dealer's IRR and your IRR are the same. But this turns out to mean that the payment plan is bad for you and good for the dealer: The IRR of the dealer's cash flows represents the interest he earns on the loan he's giving you; the IRR of your cash flows is the cost of the loan you're taking. To tell whether you're getting a good deal or a bad deal, use the NPV of the differential payments discounted at the bank's loan rate; this NPV clearly shows that the payment plan is bad for you (negative NPV of $57.42) and good for the dealer (positive NPV of $57.42).

8.2 Multiple Internal Rates of Return

A project has a "conventional cash flow pattern" when all the positive and negative cash flows are bunched together. If this condition is not met, then we'll call the cash flow pattern of the project "nonconventional." Here are some examples of conventional and nonconventional cash flows:

	A	B	C	D	E	F	G
1		CONVENTIONAL AND NON-CONVENTIONAL CASH FLOW PATTERNS					
2	Year	Cash flow Project A	Cash flow Project B	Cash flow Project C	Cash flow Project D	Cash flow Project E	Cash flow Project F
3	0	-100	-100	100	25	-25	-250
4	1	200	-50	55	35	80	35
5	2	500	60	35	-200	-100	145
6	3	50	80	50	33	200	330
7	4	60	99	-100	55	55	55
8	5	35	100	-35	155	-250	-250
9		↑ Conventional cash flow pattern	↑ Conventional cash flow pattern	↑ Conventional cash flow pattern	↑ Nonconventional cash flow pattern	↑ Nonconventional cash flow pattern	↑ Nonconventional cash flow pattern
10		Initial negative cash flow followed by positive cash flows	Two initial negative cash flows followed by positive cash flows	Initial positive cash flows followed by negative cash flows	Two positive cash flows, then negative, then three positive cash flows	Initial negative cash flow, then positive, then negative, positive, negative cash flows	Negative cash flows at beginning and end, other cash flows positive

In Section 7.4 of Chapter 7 we showed that for projects with conventional cash flows, the NPV and the IRR criteria give the same answers to the "yes–no" capital budgeting question (the question of whether a particular project is worthwhile). In this section we discuss the IRR of projects with nonconventional cash flows. Such projects often have multiple IRRs, which makes our analysis of nonconventional projects using the IRR confusing. We will ultimately conclude that NPV is a better decision tool.

Consider, the case of a company that operates sanitary landfills. A "landfill" is basically a big hole in the ground where lots of garbage is dumped until the hole is filled in.

Here are the cash flows anticipated by the company for a new landfill:

- The initial cost of the landfill is $800,000: This covers the expense of digging the hole, fencing it, and providing appropriate truck access.
- The annual net cash inflows from the landfill are $450,000. These represent the fees the company collects in return for giving trash collection companies the right to dump their trash in the landfill. These cash inflows are net of any costs incurred by the landfill company.
- After five years the landfill will be full. The costs of closing the land fill, incurred at the end of year 6, are $1,500,000. This includes the costs of abiding by various ecological regulations and so on.

In the spreadsheet below, the cash flows for the landfill are given in cells B3 to B9. In columns E and F we have created a table which computes the net present value of these cash flows at various discount rates. The graph shows that the cash flows have *two* internal rates of return: These are the two points at which the graph cuts the x-axis.

	A	B	C	D	E	F	G	H	I	J	K
1	SANITARY LANDFILL, INC.										
2	Year	Cash flow			Discount rate	NPV					
3	0	-800,000			0%	-50,000	<-- =NPV(E3,$B$4:$B$9)+$B$3				
4	1	450,000			2%	-10,900	<-- =NPV(E4,$B$4:$B$9)+$B$3				
5	2	450,000			4%	17,848	<-- =NPV(E5,$B$4:$B$9)+$B$3				
6	3	450,000			6%	38,123					
7	4	450,000			8%	51,465					
8	5	450,000			10%	59,143					
9	6	-1,500,000			12%	62,203					
10					14%	61,507					
11	Sum of cashflows	-50,000			16%	57,769					
12					18%	51,580					
13					20%	43,428					
14	First IRR	2.68%	<-- =IRR(B3:B9,0)		22%	33,721					
15	Second IRR	27.74%	<-- =IRR(B3:B9,25%)		24%	22,793					
16					26%	10,923					
17					28%	-1,658					
18					30%	-14,758					
19					32%	-28,219					
20					34%	-41,912					
21					36%	-55,727					

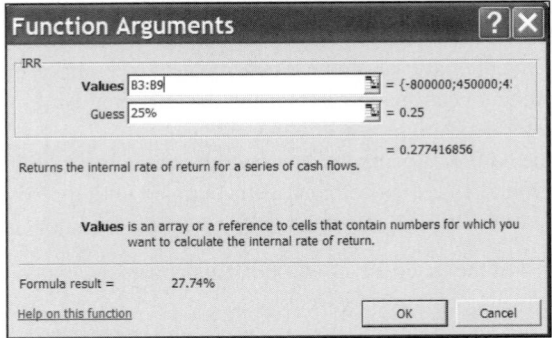

Sanitary Landfill, Inc.

In cells B14 and B15 we identify both of these IRRs, using Excel's **IRR** function. We have used the **Guess** option for this function. This option allows you to identify the *approximate* IRR (we used the graph to identify this number); Excel then computes an IRR close to this approximation. In the spreadsheet above we use 25% as a **Guess** in cell B15. Excel's **IRR** function then shows that the actual IRR that is close to this **Guess** is 27.74%.

EXCEL NOTE

DIALOG BOX FOR IRR FUNCTION, SHOWING USE OF **GUESS**

Function Arguments [?][X]

IRR

Values | B3:B9 | = {-800000;450000;4!

Guess | 25% | = 0.25

= 0.277416856

Returns the internal rate of return for a series of cash flows.

Values is an array or a reference to cells that contain numbers for which you want to calculate the internal rate of return.

Formula result =   27.74%

Help on this function   [OK]   [Cancel]

Note: If you enter a lower **Guess** (say, 0% or 3%), Excel finds the IRR of 2.68%. If you do not enter a **Guess,** Excel looks for the IRR closest to zero.

Two IRRs: What Does This Mean?

This business of two IRRs is confusing! Suppose we're trying to decide whether to undertake the landfill project. As you saw in Chapter 7, there are two traditional rules for accepting or rejecting a project:

- NPV rule: A project is acceptable if its NPV > 0. In the case of the sanitary landfill, the NPV rule says that the project is acceptable if the discount rate is larger than 2.68% and smaller than 27.74%.

- IRR rule: A project is acceptable if its IRR > appropriate discount rate. Because there are two IRRs in this case, the IRR rule is impossible to apply. In practical terms, this means that when a project has more than one IRR, you should determine its attractiveness only by the NPV rule.

How Many IRRs Are There?

For a given set of cash flows, there are potentially as many IRRs as there are changes in sign of the cash flow. The cash flow pattern of a conventional project has an initial negative cash flow and thereafter only positive cash flows; there is only one change of sign (from negative to positive) and hence only one possible IRR. The previous cash flow example has two changes in sign (and hence two possible IRRs): from −800,000 in year 0 to 450,000 in year 1 and then again from 450,000 in year 5 to −1,500,000 in year 6.[1]

8.3 Choosing Between Projects With Different Life Spans

Sometimes our capital budgeting choices involve projects with different life spans. Suppose your company is considering buying one of two tank trucks to haul high-tech liquid materials. The company is trying to decide between two alternatives:

- Truck A is a relatively cheap truck. It costs $100,000 and has a six-year life, during which it will produce an annual cash flow of $150,000.

- Truck B is much more expensive. It costs $250,000 and has only a three-year life, after which it has to be replaced. However, truck B is much more efficient than truck A, and during each of the three years of its life it produces a cash flow of $300,000.

If your company's discount rate is 12%, which truck should it choose? Here's a simple (and, as it turns out, misleading) way of doing the analysis.

	A	B	C	D
1	DIFFERENT LIFE SPANS			
2	Discount rate	12%		
3				
4	Year	Truck A	Truck B	
5	0	-100	-250	
6	1	150	300	
7	2	150	300	
8	3	150	300	
9	4	150		
10	5	150		
11	6	150		
12				
13	NPV	516.71	470.55	<-- =C5+NPV($B$2,C6:C11)

[1]Exercises 2 and 3 at the end of this chapter show examples with three IRRs.

Using this analysis you might conclude that truck A is preferable to truck B, since its NPV is higher. But because the two trucks have different life spans, there's a problem concluding that A is preferred to B. To make them comparable, we assume that at the end of year 3 we will replace truck B with another, similar truck. This makes the year 3 cash flow:

$$year\ 3\ cash\ flow = \underbrace{300}_{\substack{\text{Year-3 cash flow} \\ \text{from truck}}} - \underbrace{250}_{\substack{\text{Purchase price} \\ \text{of new truck}}} = 50$$

Once we've replaced truck B in year 3, the cash flows in years 4, 5, and 6 will be $300. We can put this into a spreadsheet:

	A	B	C	D
1		DIFFERENT LIFE SPANS at end of year 3, truck B is replaced		
2	Discount rate	12%		
3				
4	**Year**	**Cash flow (A)**	**Cash flow (B)**	
5	0	-100	-250	
6	1	150	300	
7	2	150	300	
8	3	150	50	<-- =300-250
9	4	150	300	
10	5	150	300	
11	6	150	300	
12				
13	NPV	516.71	805.48	<-- =C5+NPV($B$2,C6:C11)

As you can see in cells B13 and C13, the NPV from the two (now comparable) projects indicates that truck B is preferred to truck A.

There's another way to reach this same conclusion: Look at the following calculations:

$$NPV(A) = -100 + \frac{150}{(1.12)} + \frac{150}{(1.12)^2} + \frac{150}{(1.12)^3} + \frac{150}{(1.12)^4} + \frac{150}{(1.12)^5} + \frac{150}{(1.12)^6}$$

$$= 516.71$$

$$= \sum_{t=1}^{6} \frac{125.68}{(1.12)^t}$$

$$NPV(B) = -250 + \frac{300}{(1.12)} + \frac{300}{(1.12)^2} + \frac{300}{(1.12)^3} = 470.55$$

$$= \sum_{t=1}^{3} \frac{195.91}{(1.12)^t}$$

What these calculations show is that truck A is equivalent to getting a constant cash flow of $125.68 per year for each of the six years of its life, whereas truck B is equivalent to getting a constant cash flow of $195.91 for each of its three years of life. We call these cash flows the *equivalent annuity cash flow* (EAC). Since every time you buy truck B you get $195.91 per year and every time you buy truck A you get $125.68 per year, it is clear that truck B is preferred.

The EAC is easy to compute. It is defined as a constant future cash flow whose present value is equal to the net present value of the project:

$$NPV = CF_0 + \sum_{t=1}^{N} \frac{CF_t}{(1+r)^t}$$

$$= \sum_{t=1}^{N} \frac{\text{equivalent annuity cash flow (EAC)}}{(1+r)^t},$$

where N is the projectlife.

To compute the *EAC*, we rearrange this equation a bit and indicate the Excel functions that compute it:

$$EAC = \frac{CF_0 + \sum_{t=1}^{N} \frac{CF_t}{(1+r)^t}}{\sum_{t=1}^{N} \frac{1}{(1+r)^t}} = \frac{\mathbf{NPV}(r, CF_1:CF_N) + CF_0}{\mathbf{PV}(r, N, -1)}$$

$$\uparrow$$

Excel functions

If we go back to our example:

	A	B	C	D
		DIFFERENT LIFE SPANS		
1		**Computing the equivalent annuity cash flow (EAC)**		
2	Discount rate	12%		
3				
4	Year	Cash flow (A)	Cash flow (B)	
5	0	-100	-250	
6	1	150	300	
7	2	150	300	
8	3	150	300	
9	4	150		
10	5	150		
11	6	150		
12				
13	NPV	516.71	470.55	<-- =C5+NPV($B$2,C6:C11)
14	EAC--Equivalent annuity cash flow	125.68	195.91	<-- =C13/PV(B2,3,-1)
15				
16	=B13/PV(B2,6,-1)			

A Nontrivial Example of Different Life Spans: Choosing a Light Bulb

This business of the EAC may seem somewhat academic and ethereal, but it's not. In this section we offer a real-life example that can only be solved using the EAC.

You're considering replacing the light bulbs in a hotel you own. Currently, you're using 100 watt incandescent bulbs, which cost $1 each and have an average lifetime of 1000 hours. You're thinking of replacing them with compact fluorescent bulbs. These are much more expensive, costing $5 each. But they produce the same luminescence, use only 15 watts, and last 15,000 hours. Here are some additional facts:

- A kilowatt of electricity costs $0.10.
- You tend to burn a light bulb 250 hours per month.
- The interest rate is 8%. In the computations below we translate this to a monthly interest rate of $0.643\% = (1 + 8\%)^{1/12} - 1$.

Should you replace the bulbs? (See Figure 8.1.)

a   **b**

Figure 8.1 Standard bulb versus energy-saving fluorescent bulb.
a Standard incandescent bulb—cheap to buy, expensive to operate, short life. **b** Energy-saving fluorescent bulb—expensive to buy, cheap to operate, long life.

This problem can readily be solved using the equivalent annuity cash flow (EAC):

	A	B	C
1	**LIGHT BULBS** **Choosing between cheap incandescents and** **expensive fluorescents**		
2	Annual discount rate	8%	
3	Monthly discount rate	0.643%	<-- =(1+B2)^(1/12)-1
4	Electric cost per kilowatt (a kilowatt = 1000 watts)	$ 0.10	
5			
6	**Incandescent bulb**		
7	Watts	100	
8	Cost	$1.00	
9	Hours per month used	250	
10	Lifetime of bulb (hours)	1,000	
11	Lifetime in months	4	
12	Monthly cost	2.50	
13	NPV of lifetime use	$ 10.84	<-- =B8+PV(B3,B11,-B12)
14	Monthly equivalent annuity cash flow (EAC) for cheap incandescent	$ 2.75	<-- =B13/PV(B3,B11,-1)
15			
16	**Equivalent fluorescent bulb**		
17	Watts	15	
18	Cost	$5.00	
19	Hours per month used	250	
20	Lifetime of bulb (hours)	10,000	
21	Lifetime in months	40	
22	Monthly cost	0.38	
23	NPV of lifetime use	$ 18.19	<-- =B18+PV(B3,B21,-B22)
24	Monthly equivalent annuity cash flow (EAC) for expensive fluorescent	$ 0.52	<-- =B23/PV(B3,B21,-1)

This spreadsheet requires some additional explanation:

- An incandescent bulb costs $1.00 to buy and costs $2.50 per month to operate. As shown in cell B13, the NPV of buying and operating one incandescent bulb during its four-month life is

$$1.00 + \frac{2.50}{1+0.643\%} + \frac{2.50}{(1+0.643\%)^2} + \frac{2.50}{(1+0.643\%)^3} + \frac{2.50}{(1+0.643\%)^4} = 10.84$$

- A fluorescent bulb costs $5.00 to buy and costs $0.38 per month to operate. As shown in cell B23, the NPV of buying and operating one fluorescent bulb during its 40-month life is

$$5.00 + \frac{0.38}{1+0.643\%} + \frac{0.38}{(1+0.643\%)^2} + \cdots + \frac{0.38}{(1+0.643\%)^{40}} = 18.19$$

- To find the monthly equivalent annuity cash flow (EAC) of each bulb, we divide the NPV of the bulb's cost and operation by the appropriate PV factor:

$$\textit{incandescent EAC} = \frac{10.84}{\sum\limits_{t=1}^{4} \frac{1}{(1.00684)^t}} = \underbrace{\frac{1 + \text{PV}(0.643\%, 4, -2.50)}{\text{PV}(0.684\%, 4, -1)}}_{\text{Excel functions}} = 2.75/\text{month}$$

$$\textit{fluorescent EAC} = \frac{18.19}{\sum\limits_{t=1}^{40} \frac{1}{(1.00684)^t}} = \underbrace{\frac{1 + \text{PV}(0.643\%, 40, -0.38)}{\text{PV}(0.684\%, 40, -1)}}_{\text{Excel functions}} = 0.52/\text{month}$$

- As you can see, the monthly equivalent annuity cash flow of the incandescent light bulb is $2.75, whereas the monthly equivalent annuity cash flow of the fluorescent bulb is $0.52. The EAC tells you that it's *much cheaper* to switch to the fluorescent!

8.4 Lease Versus Purchase When Taxes Are Important

We dealt with leasing in Section 6.4, but there we assumed that taxes were not a factor. This is often true for individuals—when you're considering leasing a computer or buying one, the tax considerations are secondary, because you cannot usually subtract either your computer lease payment or any part of the purchase price of the computer from your taxes.

On the other hand, for a business tax considerations are very important. Firms can subtract depreciation from their pretax profits as a cost (as we showed in Section 7.7, this means that depreciation gives rise to a *tax shield*). Furthermore, firms that finance with debt can subtract their interest costs from their pretax profits; thus, the *after-tax* cost of an interest rate $r\%$ paid by a firm with a tax rate of T is $(1 - T) * r\%$.

In the example below we introduce tax considerations into the lease versus. purchase decision. We use the same example introduced in Chapter 6 (p. 139) but provide additional information about the firm's tax rate and depreciation policy.

An Example

Your business has decided that it needs another computer. Here are the facts:

- The business has a tax rate of 40% and can borrow from the bank at 15%.
- You can buy the computer for $4,000 and depreciate it on a straight-line basis over three years. This means annual depreciation of $4,000/3 = $1,333. Since you're taxed at a 40% rate, this depreciation will save you 40% * $1,333 = $533 per year in taxes. This *tax shield* is the cash savings from the depreciation deduction and must be taken into account in deciding between the lease and the purchase.
- You can lease the computer for $1,500 a year, payable in advance for four years. This means that if you lease the computer, you'll pay $1,500 today and $1,500 at the end of each of years 1, 2, and 3. The lease payment is an expense for tax purposes, so that its net after-tax cost to the firm is $(1 - 40\%) * \$1,500 = \$900$.

Here's a spreadsheet describing these cash flows:

	A	B	C	D	E	F
1	**LEASE OR PURCHASE?** **Costs are negative numbers and inflows positive numbers**					
2	Asset cost	4,000.00				
3	Annual depreciation if asset is purchased	1,333.33	<-- =B2/3			
4	Annual lease payment	1,500.00				
5	Bank rate	15%				
6	Tax rate	40%				
7						
8	Year	0	1	2	3	
9	**Purchase cash flows**					
10	Cost of machine	-4,000				
11	Depreciation tax shield		533	533	533	<-- =$B$3*$B$6
12	Total	-4,000	533	533	533	<-- =E11+E10
13						
14	**After-tax lease payments**	-900	-900	-900	-900	<-- =-$B$4*(1-$B$6)
15						
16	The lease saves	3,100	-1,433	-1,433	-1,433	<-- =-E12+E14
17						
18	IRR of lease savings	18.33%	<-- =IRR(B16:E16)			
19	Alternative cost (after-tax bank interest)	9.00%	<-- =B5*(1-$B$6)			
20						
21	Lease or purchase?	buy	<-- =IF(B18>B19,"buy","lease")			

Row 12 describes the after-tax cash flows associated with the purchase and row 14 the after-tax cash flows from the lease. In row 16 you can see that leasing the computer is like taking a loan of $3,100 with after-tax repayments of $1,433 in years 1–3. The IRR of this "loan" is 18.33%.

Should you lease or buy? If the bank is willing to lend you money at 15% and if interest costs are deductible expenses for tax purposes, then the after-tax cost of a bank loan is $(1 - 40\%) * 15\% = 9\%$. This means that the bank is a cheaper source of financing than the leasing company. The conclusion (cell B21): Buy the computer.

Another way to reach the conclusion that a purchase is better than a lease is to think of financing the machine with a three-year bank loan of $3,100:

	A	B	C	D	E	F
24	**Alternative: Borrow $3,100 from the bank and buy the computer**					
25	Year	0	1	2	3	
26	Loan at beginning of year		3,100.00	2,207.27	1,180.63	<-- =D26-D30
27	Payment at end of year		1,357.73	1,357.73	1,357.73	<-- =PMT(B5,3,-$C$26)
28	Of this payment					
29	Interest		465.00	331.09	177.10	<-- =$B$5*E26
30	Repayment of principal		892.73	1,026.64	1,180.63	<-- =E27-E29
31	Remaining principal at end of year		2,207.27	1,180.63	0.00	<-- =E26-E30
32						
33	After-tax interest		279.00	198.65	106.26	<-- =(1-$B$6)*E29
34	Net after-tax loan cash cost		1,171.73	1,225.29	1,286.89	<-- =E33+E30
35						
36	**Machine + loan**					
37	Cost of machine	-4,000.00				<-- =B10
38	Depreciation tax shield		533.33	533.33	533.33	<-- =E12
39	After-tax loan cash flow	3,100.00	-1,171.73	-1,225.29	-1,286.89	<-- =-E34
40	Total: Buy machine + take loan	-900.00	-638.40	-691.96	-753.56	<-- =SUM(E37:E39)
41						
42	Compare this to the after-tax lease payments	-900.00	-900.00	-900.00	-900.00	<-- =E14

Rows 26–31 are a standard loan table discussed in Chapter 5 (p. 112). Because interest is an expense for tax purposes, the after-tax interest cost to the firm is $(1 - 40\%) * interest$; in row 33 we compute this cost. The net after-tax cost of the loan to the firm (row 34) is the sum of the after-tax interest (row 33) and the annual repayment of principal (row 30).

In rows 37–40 we compute the total after-tax cash flows from buying the loan-financed machine. Comparing these to the after-tax lease payments (row 42 is just a copy of row 14)—you can see that buying with a loan is preferable to leasing.

What's the Maximum Lease Payment We'll Pay?

The above analysis shows that $1,500 per year is too much to pay for the lease. How much would you be willing to pay? To do this calculation, we use **Goal Seek** to find the lease payment for which the IRR of the differential cash flows (cell B18) is 9%. The **Goal Seek** screen for the spreadsheet looks like:

	A	B	C	D	E	F
		LEASE OR PURCHASE?				
1		**Costs are negative numbers and inflows positive numbers**				
2	Asset cost	4,000.00				
3	Annual depreciation if asset is purchased	1,333.33	<-- =B2/3			
4	Annual lease payment	1,500.00				
5	Bank rate	15%				
6	Tax rate	40%				
7						
8	Year	0	1			
9	**Purchase cash flows**					
10	Cost of machine	4,000				
11	Depreciation tax shield		-533			B$6
12	Total	4,000	-533			
13						
14	**After-tax lease payments**	-900	-900	-900	-900 <-- =-$B$4 (1-$B$6)	
15						
16	The lease saves	3,100	-1,433	-1,433	-1,433 <-- =E12+E14	
17						
18	IRR	18.33%	<-- =IRR(B16:E16)			
19	Alternative cost	9.00%	<-- =B5*(1-$B$6)			
20						
21	Lease or purchase?	buy	<-- =IF(B18>B19,"buy","lease")			

Goal Seek dialog:
Set cell: $B$18
To value: 9%
By changing cell: $B$4

The conclusion is that a lease payment of $1,250.72 is the largest lease payment the lessee should be willing to pay.

	A	B	C	D	E	F
		CORPORATE LEASING				
1		**Costs are negative numbers and inflows positive numbers**				
2	Asset cost	4,000.00				
3	Annual depreciation if asset is purchased	1,333.33	<-- =B2/3			
4	Annual lease payment	1,250.72				
5	Bank rate	15%				
6	Tax rate	40%				
7						
8	Year	0	1	2	3	
9	**Purchase cash flows**					
10	Cost of machine	4,000				
11	Depreciation tax shield		-533	-533	-533 <-- =-$B$3*$B$6	
12	Total	4,000	-533	-533	-533 <-- =E11+E10	
13						
14	**After-tax lease payments**	-750	-750	-750	-750 <-- =-$B$4*(1-$B$6)	
15						
16	The lease saves	3,250	-1,284	-1,284	-1,284 <-- =E12+E14	
17						
18	IRR	9.00%	<-- =IRR(B16:E16)			
19	Alternative cost	9.00%	<-- =B5*(1-$B$6)			

8.5 Capital Budgeting Principle: Think About Midyear Discounting

We could have called this section "Think about the timing of cash flows," but "midyear discounting" is catchier. To show what we mean, we present two examples. In our first example, a company's owner is thinking about spending $10,000 in order to produce an annual cash flow of $3,000 per year for the next five years. If the discount rate is 15%, and the cash flows occur at year end, then the NPV of the project is $56.47:

	A	B	C
1		NPV, CASH FLOWS OCCUR AT YEAR END	
2	Initial cost	10,000.00	
3	Annual cashflow	3,000.00	
4	Discount rate	15%	
5			
6	Year	Cash flow	
7	0	-10,000.00	
8	1	3,000.00	
9	2	3,000.00	
10	3	3,000.00	
11	4	3,000.00	
12	5	3,000.00	
13			
14	NPV of year-end cash flows	56.47	<-- =B7+NPV(B4,B8:B12)

The NPV of $56.47 assumes that the cash flow for each year occurs at the end of the year:

$$NPV = -10,000 + \frac{3,000}{(1.15)} + \frac{3,000}{(1.15)^2} + \frac{3,000}{(1.15)^3} + \frac{3,000}{(1.15)^4} + \frac{3,000}{(1.15)^5}$$
$$= 56.47$$

For many capital budgeting situations, this end-year cash flow assumption is not realistic. Think of a company buying a machine and getting cash flows by selling the machine's products—in this case the cash flows are likely to occur as a stream throughout the year rather than a single, end-year, cash flow. Since it's always better to get cash earlier, the NPV of the project will be higher than $56.47.

To get some feeling for whether this is important, suppose that the $3,000 annual cash flow is actually received as $750 at the end of each quarter. Then, as the spreadsheet below shows, the

NPV would increase significantly:

	A	B	C
1		**NPV, CASH FLOWS OCCUR EACH QUARTER**	
2	Initial cost	10,000.00	
3	Annual cashflow	3,000.00	
4	Discount rate	15%	
5	Quarterly discount rate	3.56%	<-- =(1+B4)^(1/4)-1
6			
7	**Quarter**	**Quarterly cash flow**	
8	0	-10,000.00	
9	1	750.00	
10	2	750.00	
11	3	750.00	
12	4	750.00	
13	5	750.00	
14	6	750.00	
15	7	750.00	
16	8	750.00	
17	9	750.00	
18	10	750.00	
19	11	750.00	
20	12	750.00	
21	13	750.00	
22	14	750.00	
23	15	750.00	
24	16	750.00	
25	17	750.00	
26	18	750.00	
27	19	750.00	
28	20	750.00	
29			
30	NPV, quarterly cash flows	605.68	<-- =B8+NPV(B5,B9:B28)

Notice that in calculating the NPV of the quarterly cash flows (cell E29), we've used the *quarterly discount rate,* which is equivalent to the annual discount rate of 15% (3.56%, cell E4). This quarterly discount rate is calculated by

$$(1 + \textit{quarterly discount rate}) = (1 + \textit{annual discount rate})^{1/4}$$

So far, the message of this section is clear and noncontroversial: When you discount, you should take the timing of the cash flows into account. The problem is that for many capital budgeting problems we project annual cash flows, even though the actual flows occur throughout the year.[2] In many cases it is difficult to project the precise timing of the cash flows throughout the year, even though our example shows that this timing is very important.

Midyear Discounting—An Elegant Compromise

On the one hand the timing of cash flows is important, but on the other hand it's difficult to deviate from end-year cash flow projections and project the precise timing of each cash flow. An

---

[2]This has a lot to do with most firms' accounting cycles, which are annual. (There we go again—blaming the accountants!)

elegant compromise is to project annual cash flow numbers but to assume that they occur in midyear. Here's how this looks in Excel:

	A	B	C	D
1		**MIDYEAR DISCOUNTING**		
2	Initial cost	10,000.00		
3	Annual cashflow	3,000.00		
4	Discount rate	15%		
5				
6	Year	Cash flow	Discounted value	
7	0	-10,000.00	-10,000.00	<-- =B7
8	1	3,000.00	2,797.51	<-- =B8/(1+$B$4)^(A8-0.5)
9	2	3,000.00	2,432.62	<-- =B9/(1+$B$4)^(A9-0.5)
10	3	3,000.00	2,115.32	
11	4	3,000.00	1,839.41	
12	5	3,000.00	1,599.49	
13				
14	NPV, midyear		784.36	<-- =SUM(C7:C12)
15			784.36	<-- =B7+NPV(B4,B8:B12)*(1+B4)^0.5

The spreadsheet shows two ways to do the calculation:

- In cells C8:C12, each cash flow has been discounted by a factor $(1+r)^{year-0.5}$. This is equivalent to calculating the following NPV:

$$NPV = -10,000 + \frac{3,000}{(1.15)^{0.5}} + \frac{3,000}{(1.15)^{1.5}} + \frac{3,000}{(1.15)^{2.5}} + \frac{3,000}{(1.15)^{3.5}} + \frac{3,000}{(1.15)^{4.5}} = \underbrace{784.36}_{\text{Cell B14}}$$

- In cell B15, we show a simple Excel formula that produces the same result: Simply take the Excel **NPV** formula and multiply by $(1+r)^{0.5}$.

Using the XNPV Function

We can also do the midyear NPV calculation by using Excel's **XNPV** function.[3] To use **XNPV** you have to indicate the dates on which the cash flows will be received. The spreadsheet below shows an implementation of the function to our problem.

	A	B	C
1		**CALCULATING THE MIDYEAR NPV WITH EXCEL'S XNPV FUNCTION**	
2	Annual discount rate	15%	
3			
4	Date	Cash flow	
5	1-Jan-02	-10,000	
6	1-Jul-02	3,000	
7	1-Jul-03	3,000	
8	1-Jul-04	3,000	
9	1-Jul-05	3,000	
10	1-Jul-06	3,000	
11			
12	NPV		788.43 <-- =XNPV(B2,B5:B10,A5:A10)

[3]If this function does not appear in your list of Excel functions, go to **Tools|Add-ins** on the Excel menu, and check **Analysis Toolpak**.

EXCEL NOTE

DIALOG BOX FOR THE **XNPV** FUNCTION

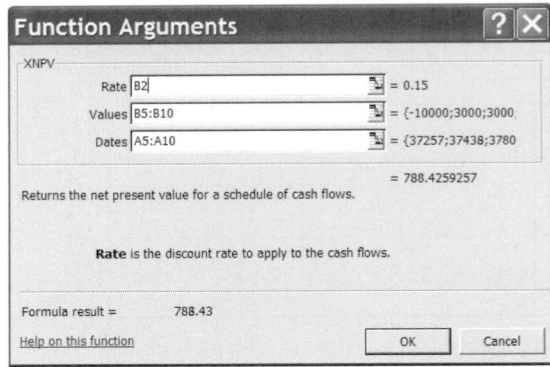

As the dialog box shows, **XNPV** requires you to input the *annual* discount rate, the values to be discounted, and the dates on which these values occur. The function then finds the net present value on the first date of the series (in our example: 1 Jan 02). The **XNPV** function differs from the **NPV** function in one very important aspect: In Chapter 5 (p. 94) we stressed that Excel's **NPV** calculates the present value of future cash flows; to calculate the true net present value, you have to add in the initial cash flow separately. The **XNPV** function has *all* the cash flows as inputs (including the initial cash flow) and has as output the true net present value.

The **XNPV** function and its cousin, the **XIRR** function (discussed later), are part of the standard Excel package, but they have to be installed separately as add-ins. Here's what you do:

Step 1: Tools|Add-Ins   **Step 2: Check Analysis ToolPak**

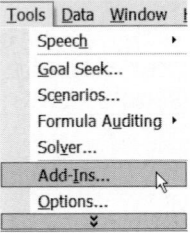   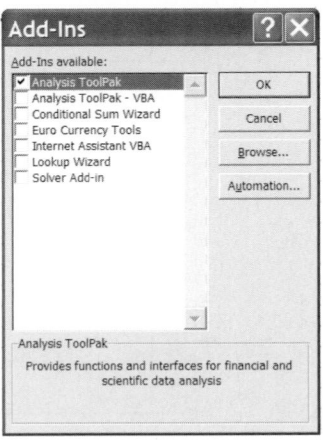

Calculating the Midyear IRR

What if you want to compute the IRR of the cash flows, taking into account the fact that they occur in midyear? The easiest way to do this is to use the Excel function **XIRR,** as shown below:

	A	B	C
1		**CALCULATING THE IRR OF MIDYEAR CASH FLOWS WITH EXCEL'S XIRR FUNCTION**	
2	**Date**	**Cash flow**	
3	1-Jan-02	-10,000	
4	1-Jul-02	3,000	
5	1-Jul-03	3,000	
6	1-Jul-04	3,000	
7	1-Jul-05	3,000	
8	1-Jul-06	3,000	
9			
10	IRR	19.06%	<-- =XIRR(B3:B8,A3:A8)

EXCEL NOTE

DIALOG BOX FOR THE **XIRR** FUNCTION

The **XIRR** function requires you to put in a list of dates at which the cash flows occur. The syntax of the function is given in the dialog box below:

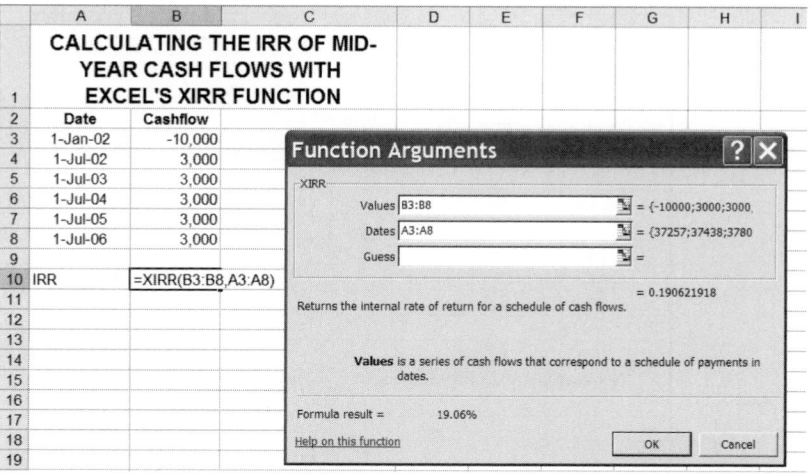

For cash flows with multiple IRRs, the **XIRR** function allows you to use a **Guess** (like Excel's **IRR** function discussed on p. 198).

Applying Midyear Cash Flows to Sally and Dave's Condo

In this section we have stressed the importance of cash flow timing in determining the NPV of a project. We have also suggested that, rather than try to determine the precise timing of each cash flow, it may be roughly equivalent to assume that the cash flows occur in midperiod.

The implementation of this simple idea can be complicated. Take Sally and Dave's condo, for example, which was discussed in Chapter 7 (p. 169). Recall that Sally and Dave's annual cash flow of $18,050 from the condo rental was computed as follows:

- The annual rent of $24,000 is taxable income, and the annual property taxes ($1,500) and maintenance ($1,000) are expenses for tax purposes. Since Sally and Dave's tax rate is 30%, these three items produce $(1 - 30\%) * (\$24,000 - \$1,000 - \$1,500) = \$15,050$ of after-tax income per year.
- The condo's annual depreciation of $10,000 produces a tax shield of $30\% * \$10,000 = \$3,000$. Adding this tax shield to the $15,050 gives Sally and Dave's annual cash flow of $18,050 in years 1–10.
- Sally and Dave plan to sell the condo for $100,000 after ten years. At this point the condo will be fully depreciated, so that all the money they receive from the sale will be income. Thus, the after-tax terminal value of the condo is $(1 - 30\%) * \$100,000 = \$70,000$. Adding this to the condo's year 10 cash flow produces a total year 10 cash flow of $88,050.

Our initial calculation gave us an IRR of 16.69% on Sally and Dave's investment (cell B37 below):

	A	B	C
1	**SALLY & DAVE'S CONDO** **Example from Section 7.7**		
2	Cost of condo	100,000	
3	Sally & Dave's tax rate	30%	
4			
5	Annual reportable income calculation		
6	Rent	24,000	
7	Expenses		
8	Property taxes	-1,500	
9	Miscellaneous expenses	-1,000	
10	Depreciation	-10,000	
11	Reportable income	11,500	<-- =SUM(B6:B10)
12	Taxes (rate = 30%)	-3,450	<-- =-B3*B11
13	Net income	8,050	<-- =B11+B12
14			
15	Annual cash flow	18,050	<-- =B13-B10
16			
17	Terminal value		
18	Estimated resale value, year 10	100,000	
19	Book value	0	
20	Taxable gain	100,000	<-- =B18-B19
21	Taxes	30,000	<-- =0.3*B20
22	Net after tax--cash flow from terminal value	70,000	<-- =B20-B21
23			
24	Year	Cash flow	
25	0	-100,000	
26	1	18,050	<-- =$B$15
27	2	18,050	
28	3	18,050	
29	4	18,050	
30	5	18,050	
31	6	18,050	
32	7	18,050	
33	8	18,050	
34	9	18,050	
35	10	88,050	<-- =$B$15+B22
36			
37	IRR	16.69%	

Incorporating the Timing of Cash Flows

Now suppose we try to incorporate the timing of the cash flows into our analysis of the condo IRR. We make the following assumptions:

- The annual rent of $24,000 occurs at midyear. This is an approximation to the fact that the renters pay their rent monthly.
- Miscellaneous expenses of $1,000 also occur at midyear.
- Property taxes and income taxes occur at the end of each year.
- The resale of the property (which produces a cash flow of $70,000) occurs at the end of year 10.

These assumptions lead to the cash flows given in cells E4 to E44 below. The IRR of these cash flows (9.59%, cell E46) is the *semiannual IRR* (remember that our cash flows are now semi-annual). The *annualized IRR* is $(1 + 9.59\%)^2 - 1 = 20.10\%$, which is significantly higher than the 16.69% we calculated above assuming that all cash flows occur at year-end. Since the IRR gets higher when positive cash flows occur earlier, this is not surprising.

	A	B	C	D	E	F
1				SALLY & DAVE'S CONDO--INCORPORATING MIDYEAR CASHFLOWS		
2	Tax rate	30%		Return on the condo--Taking into account midyear cash flows		
3				Year	Cash flow	
4	**Midyear cashflows**			0	-100,000	
5	Rent	24,000		0.5	23,000	<-- Rent + miscellaneous expenses
6	Miscellaneous expenses	-1,000		1	-4,950	<-- Property and income taxes
7	Sum of midyear cash flows	23,000	<-- =SUM(B5:B6)	1.5	23,000	
8				2	-4,950	
9	**End-year cash flows**			2.5	23,000	
10	Depreciation	10,000		3	-4,950	
11	Property taxes	-1,500		3.5	23,000	
12	Reported income	11,500		4	-4,950	
13	Income taxes	-3,450	<-- =-B2*B12	4.5	23,000	
14	Sum of end-year cash flows	-4,950	<-- =B11+B13	5	-4,950	
15				5.5	23,000	
16	Annual cash flow	18,050	<-- =B7+B14	6	-4,950	
17				6.5	23,000	
18				7	-4,950	
19				7.5	23,000	
20				8	-4,950	
21				8.5	23,000	
22				9	-4,950	
23				9.5	23,000	
24				10	-4,950	
25				10.5	23,000	
26				11	-4,950	
27				11.5	23,000	
28				12	-4,950	
29				12.5	23,000	
30				13	-4,950	
31				13.5	23,000	
32				14	-4,950	
33				14.5	23,000	
34				15	-4,950	
35				15.5	23,000	
36				16	-4,950	
37				16.5	23,000	
38				17	-4,950	
39				17.5	23,000	
40				18	-4,950	
41				18.5	23,000	
42				19	-4,950	
43				19.5	23,000	
44				20	65,050	<-- Sale of condo + taxes
45						
46				IRR (semiannual)	9.59%	<-- =IRR(E4:E44)
47				IRR (annualized)	20.10%	<-- =(1+E46)^2-1

Two "Reality" Notes

Note 1: The Sally–Dave condo example shows that getting the dates of the cash flows right is important, but it also shows that this can be cumbersome. As a compromise, perhaps we should have gone back to the midyear IRR. In the spreadsheet below we use the **XIRR** function in cell B37 to compute the IRR on the assumption that all the condo cash flows occur in midyear:

	A	B	C
1	SALLY & DAVE'S CONDO--MIDYEAR CASH FLOWS		
2	Cost of condo	100,000	
3	Sally & Dave's tax rate	30%	
4			
5	Annual reportable income calculation		
6	Rent	24,000	
7	Expenses		
8	Property taxes	-1,500	
9	Miscellaneous expenses	-1,000	
10	Depreciation	-10,000	
11	Reportable income	11,500	<-- =SUM(B6:B10)
12	Taxes (rate = 30%)	-3,450	<-- =-B3*B11
13	Net income	8,050	<-- =B11+B12
14			
15	Annual cash flow	18,050	<-- =B13-B10
16			
17	Terminal value		
18	Estimated resale value, year 10	100,000	
19	Book value	0	
20	Taxable gain	100,000	<-- =B18-B19
21	Taxes	30,000	<-- =0.3*B20
22	Net after tax--cash flow from terminal value	70,000	<-- =B20-B21
23			
24	Date	Cash flow	
25	1-Jan-02	-100,000	
26	1-Jul-02	18,050	<-- =$B$15
27	1-Jul-03	18,050	
28	1-Jul-04	18,050	
29	1-Jul-05	18,050	
30	1-Jul-06	18,050	
31	1-Jul-07	18,050	
32	1-Jul-08	18,050	
33	1-Jul-09	18,050	
34	1-Jul-10	18,050	
35	1-Jul-11	88,050	<-- =$B$15+B22
36			
37	IRR	18.69%	<-- =XIRR(B25:B35,A25:A35)

Note 2: In this book we often ignore midyear discounting—not because we don't believe it's important, but because it's cumbersome to explain this, along with all the other myriad capital budgeting problems. In this case our advice to you is: "Do as we say, don't do as we do."

8.6 Inflation: Real and Nominal Interest Rates and Cash Flows

Prices tend to rise and because they do, money loses its value over time. What else is new? This section discusses the terminology of inflation. When you finish the section, you should understand the difference between real and nominal interest rates and real and nominal cash flows. We illustrate these concepts with several "real world" examples, so that hopefully you'll have a better idea of the impact of inflation. In Section 8.7 we apply the concepts of this section to a number of capital budgeting problems.

First some facts. The spreadsheet below shows the purchasing power of $1 from 1980 through 2001. All the numbers in column B are in terms of 2001 dollars. As the spreadsheet shows, the goods you could buy with one U.S. dollar in 1980 would cost you $2.15 in 2001. Adjusting for inflation, one dollar in 1990 would be worth $1.355 at the end of 2001.

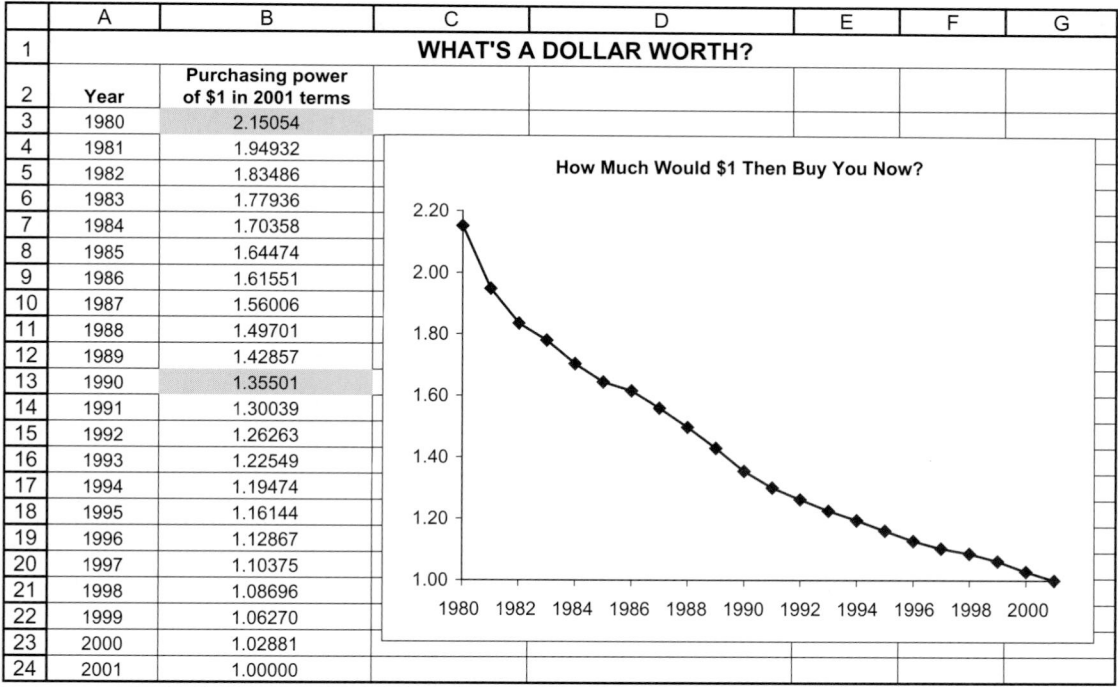

	A	B
1		**WHAT'S A DOLLAR WORTH?**
2	**Year**	**Purchasing power of $1 in 2001 terms**
3	1980	2.15054
4	1981	1.94932
5	1982	1.83486
6	1983	1.77936
7	1984	1.70358
8	1985	1.64474
9	1986	1.61551
10	1987	1.56006
11	1988	1.49701
12	1989	1.42857
13	1990	1.35501
14	1991	1.30039
15	1992	1.26263
16	1993	1.22549
17	1994	1.19474
18	1995	1.16144
19	1996	1.12867
20	1997	1.10375
21	1998	1.08696
22	1999	1.06270
23	2000	1.02881
24	2001	1.00000

Here's another way to understand this phenomenon. The table below gives the consumer price index (CPI) for the United States from 1980 to 2001.[4] The index has been normalized so that it is 100 in 1984. A basket of goods that cost $100 in 1984 would have cost $79.307 in 1980, $87.488 in 1981, and so on. The same basket would cost $170.452 in 2001.

---

[4]The consumer price index measures the market prices of a standard basket of goods. For (much) more information look at the website of the Bureau of Labor Statistics, http://www.bls.gov/cpi/, or the Minneapolis Federal Reserve Bank, http://minneapolisfed.org/Research/data/us/calc/index.cfm.

In column C we've used Excel to compute the *annual inflation rates* from this data:

$$\text{inflation rate in year } t = \frac{CPI_t}{CPI_{t-1}} - 1$$

As you can see from the graph, the inflation rate at the beginning of the 1980s was considerably higher than in the 1990s. Nevertheless, even throughout the relatively low inflation decade of the 1990s, the U.S. inflation rate has generally been between 2% and 4% per year. Through the period surveyed, the average inflation rate (cell C26) was 3.71%.

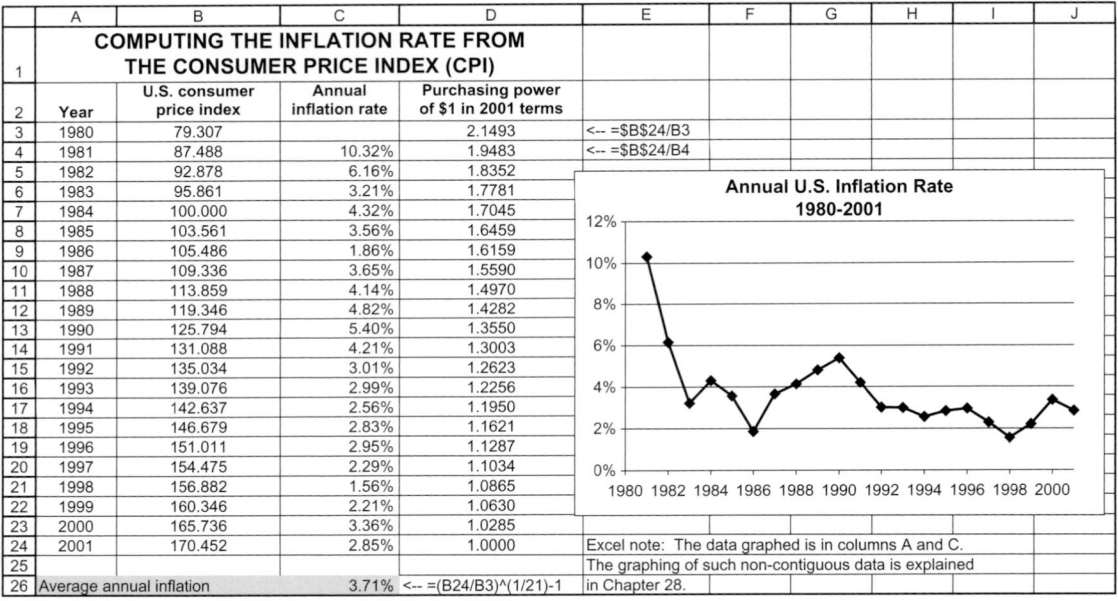

	A	B	C	D	E	F	G	H	I	J
1		COMPUTING THE INFLATION RATE FROM THE CONSUMER PRICE INDEX (CPI)								
2	Year	U.S. consumer price index	Annual inflation rate	Purchasing power of $1 in 2001 terms						
3	1980	79.307		2.1493	<-- =$B$24/B3					
4	1981	87.488	10.32%	1.9483	<-- =$B$24/B4					
5	1982	92.878	6.16%	1.8352						
6	1983	95.861	3.21%	1.7781		Annual U.S. Inflation Rate 1980-2001				
7	1984	100.000	4.32%	1.7045						
8	1985	103.561	3.56%	1.6459						
9	1986	105.486	1.86%	1.6159						
10	1987	109.336	3.65%	1.5590						
11	1988	113.859	4.14%	1.4970						
12	1989	119.346	4.82%	1.4282						
13	1990	125.794	5.40%	1.3550						
14	1991	131.088	4.21%	1.3003						
15	1992	135.034	3.01%	1.2623						
16	1993	139.076	2.99%	1.2256						
17	1994	142.637	2.56%	1.1950						
18	1995	146.679	2.83%	1.1621						
19	1996	151.011	2.95%	1.1287						
20	1997	154.475	2.29%	1.1034						
21	1998	156.882	1.56%	1.0865						
22	1999	160.346	2.21%	1.0630						
23	2000	165.736	3.36%	1.0285						
24	2001	170.452	2.85%	1.0000		Excel note: The data graphed is in columns A and C.				
25						The graphing of such non-contiguous data is explained				
26	Average annual inflation		3.71%	<-- =(B24/B3)^(1/21)-1		in Chapter 28.				

Inflation of 3.71% per year may not seem like much, but it adds up. Suppose, for example, that we had 3% inflation per year for ten years. As the Excel spreadsheet below shows, this means that the *cumulative inflation* over the decade would have been $(1+3\%)^{10} - 1 = 34.39\%$. Another way to think about this is that in every ten years, a dollar loses 26% of its value—an end-of-the-decade dollar is worth only $1/(1+3\%)^{10} = 0.7441$ in terms of a beginning-of-the-decade dollar:

	A	B	C
1	ANNUAL INFLATION RATES AND CUMULATIVE INFLATION		
2	Annual inflation rate	3%	
3	Cumulative inflation over 10 years	34.39%	<-- =(1+B2)^10-1
4	End-decade $ worth in terms of beginning of decade $	0.7441	<-- =1/(1+B2)^10

Putting this into a table:

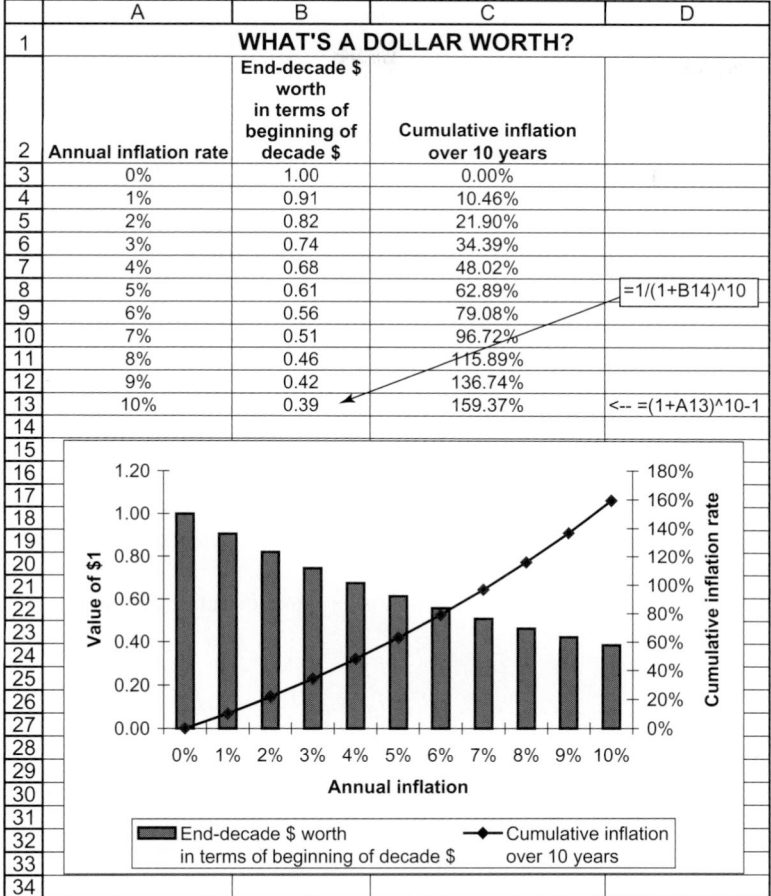

	A	B	C	D
1		WHAT'S A DOLLAR WORTH?		
2	Annual inflation rate	End-decade $ worth in terms of beginning of decade $	Cumulative inflation over 10 years	
3	0%	1.00	0.00%	
4	1%	0.91	10.46%	
5	2%	0.82	21.90%	
6	3%	0.74	34.39%	
7	4%	0.68	48.02%	
8	5%	0.61	62.89%	=1/(1+B14)^10
9	6%	0.56	79.08%	
10	7%	0.51	96.72%	
11	8%	0.46	115.89%	
12	9%	0.42	136.74%	
13	10%	0.39	159.37%	<-- =(1+A13)^10-1

Nominal and Real Interest Rates

Inflation affects not only the prices of goods—it also affects interest rates. Financial economists distinguish between *nominal* interest rates and *real* interest rates. The nominal interest rate is the rate quoted on a loan or a bank deposit and the real interest rate is the loan or bank deposit rate in purchasing-power terms (that is, after adjusting for inflation). In this section we explore and define these concepts.

Suppose you lend your friend Martha $100 with the agreement that she'll repay you next year. How much interest should you ask for? Martha suggests a 4% interest rate, but thinking about it, you realize that you anticipate 5% inflation over the year—meaning goods worth $100 today will cost $100 * (1.05) = $105 next year when the money is repaid. So if Martha repays you $100 * (1.04) = $104, she's not even repaying you the purchasing power of the loan. In this case,

$$\text{\begin{array}{c}\textit{next year's} \\ \textit{repayment in} \\ \textit{terms of this} \\ \textit{year's dollars}\end{array}} = \frac{\textit{amount repaid}}{1 + \textit{inflation}} = \frac{100 * (1 + \textit{interest})}{1 + \textit{inflation}} = \frac{104}{1.05} = 99.048$$

In the jargon of finance, the 4% interest rate is called the *nominal interest rate;* the word "nominal" indicates that the interest paid has not been adjusted for the effects of inflation. This is another way of saying that Martha will repay you $104 regardless of how much prices increase over the year. Quoted interest rates (whether on mortgages, credit cards, or government bonds) are almost always nominal interest rates ("lend me $100 today and I'll pay you back next year with 10% interest").

The *real interest rate* is defined as the interest rate in terms of purchasing power of money. In our example, you can see that you loan Martha $100 but get back (in purchasing power terms) $99.048. Thus the real interest paid by Martha is –0.952%:

$$\frac{\text{real interest}}{\text{on one-year loan}} = \frac{\text{purchasing power repaid}}{\text{purchasing power lent}} - 1 = \frac{99.048}{100} - 1 = -0.952\%$$

From the above formula, you can see that

$$real\ interest = \frac{1 + nominal\ interest}{1 + inflation} - 1 = \frac{1 + 4\%}{1 + 5\%} - 1 = -0.952\%$$

An equivalent and easier way to define the real interest rate is

$$1 + nominal\ interest = (1 + real\ interest) * (1 + inflation\ rate)$$

This equation is often called the Fisher equation, after the famous American economist Irving Fisher (1867–1947).

TERMINOLOGY REVIEW

Inflation: We almost always associate "inflation" with a decrease in the purchasing power of money (and an increase in the price level). Historically, there have also been periods of *deflation*—increases in the purchasing power of money caused by decreases in the price level.[5]

Nominal interest rate or nominal cash flow: An interest rate or cash flow that has not been adjusted for the effects of inflation. Example: You borrow $100 today and agree to repay $120 at the end of the year. The *nominal interest rate* is 20% and the $120 repayment (which will be in next year's dollars, irrespective of the inflation over the next year) is a *payment in nominal dollars.*

Real interest rate or real cash flow: An interest rate or cash flow adjusted for inflation. To calculate the real cash flow, decide on a base year, and compute all the cash flows in units of that base year. The cash flows so computed are *real cash flows* (cash flows in *constant dollars*) and the interest rates resulting from them are *real interest rates.*

---

[5]During the 1990s, Japan had prolonged periods of declining prices. See page 220.

Nominal and Real Cash Flows

In the previous subsection we showed the relation between the real and nominal interest rates. The nominal interest rate is the quoted interest rate, unadjusted for inflation, and the real interest rate is the interest rate adjusted for the change in the purchasing power of money.

In this section we show the relation between real and nominal cash flows. We start with a one-year example. You make an investment $100 in year 0 and get back $120 at the end of year 1; over this period the consumer price index increases from 131 to 138:

	A	B	C	D
1	**REAL AND NOMINAL CASH FLOWS**			
2		Year 0	Year 1	
3	Nominal cash flow	-100	120	
4	Consumer price index (CPI)	131	138	
5				
6	Inflation		5.34%	<-- =C4/B4-1
7				
8	Real cash flow in year 0 dollars	-100	113.913	<-- =C3*B4/C4
9				
10	Nominal return		20.00%	<-- =C3/-B3-1
11	Real return		13.91%	<-- =C8/-B8-1

The *real year 1 cash flow* (defined in this case as the year 1 cash flow in year 0 dollars) is computed as

$$year\ 1\ real\ cash\ flow = \frac{year\ 1\ cash\ flow}{1 + inflation\ rate\ over\ period}$$

$$= \frac{year\ 1\ cash\ flow}{\frac{CPI_{end-period}}{CPI_{beginning-period}}} = \frac{120}{(138/131)} = 113.913$$

To compute the real return on the investment:

$$1 + real\ investment\ return = \frac{year\ 1\ real\ cash\ flow}{year\ 0\ real\ cash\ flow} - 1$$

$$= \frac{113.913}{100} - 1 = 13.91\%$$

Equivalently, we can calculate the real return by using the *nominal rate of return* and deflating it by the inflation rate:

$$1 + real\ return = \frac{1 + nominal\ return}{1 + inflation\ rate} - 1 = \frac{\frac{end\text{-}period\ nominal\ cash\ flow}{beginning\text{-}period\ nominal\ cash\ flow}}{\frac{CPI_{end-period}}{CPI_{beginning-period}}}$$

$$= \frac{\frac{120}{100}}{\frac{138}{131}} - 1 = \frac{1 + 20\%}{1 + 5.34\%} = 1 + 13.91\%$$

Investment Analysis: How Much Did You *Really Earn*?

Suppose that at the end of 1995 you invested $1,000 in a security that subsequently paid you $150 at the end of each year from 1996, 1997, . . . , 2004. At the end of 2005, you sold the security for $1,150. Looking back you realize that the CPI went from 133 in 1995 to 195 in 2004. What was your real rate of return? To do this calculation, we translate each of the investment's nominal cash flows into real cash flows, using the cumulative inflation rate:

	A	B	C	D	E	F	G
1			**HOW MUCH DID YOU REALLY EARN?**				
2	Year	Nominal cash flow	CPI	Cumulative inflation rate		Real cash flow	< -- This is the cash flow in 1995 dollars
3	1995	-1,000	133			-1,000.00	
4	1996	150	138	3.76%	<-- =C4/$C$3-1	144.57	<-- =B4/(1+D4)
5	1997	150	142	6.77%	<-- =C5/$C$3-1	140.49	<-- =B5/(1+D5)
6	1998	150	145	9.02%	<-- =C6/$C$3-1	137.59	
7	1999	150	148	11.28%		134.80	
8	2000	150	153	15.04%		130.39	
9	2001	150	166	24.81%		120.18	
10	2002	150	172	29.32%		115.99	
11	2003	150	180	35.34%		110.83	
12	2004	150	191	43.61%		104.45	
13	2005	1,150	195	46.62%	<-- =C13/$C$3-1	784.36	
14							
15	Nominal IRR	15.00%	<-- =IRR(B3:B13)		Real IRR	10.93%	<-- =IRR(F3:F14)

As you can see, your 15% nominal rate of return was reduced by inflation to a 10.93% real rate of return (the rate of return adjusted for changes in the purchasing power of money).

Do Prices Always Go Up?

It seems like it, but the example below (Japan in the 1990s) shows that prices can also go down:

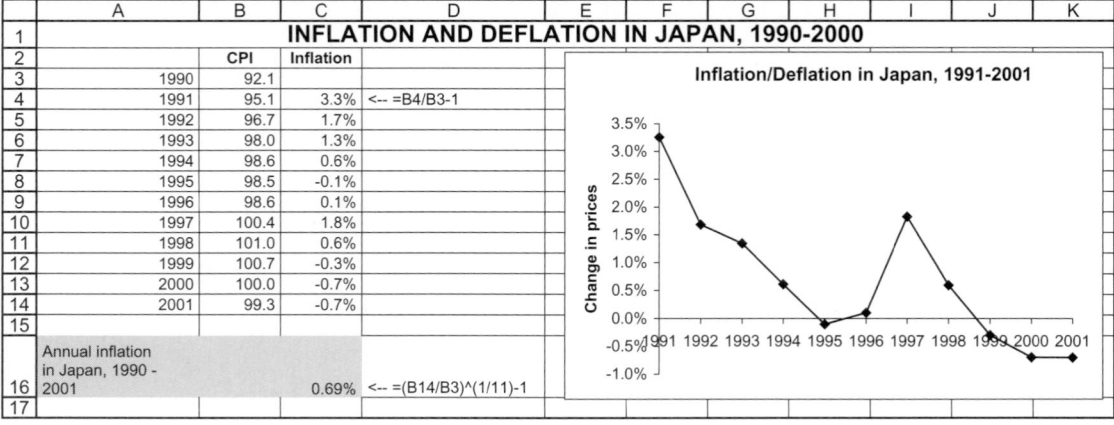

Even though Japan had deflation during four years of the period 1990–2001, the average annual inflation rate for the period was 0.69%.

Is Oil Cheap or Expensive?

In the 56 years between 1949 and 2005 the nominal price of a barrel of oil in the United States increased from \$2.54 in 1949 to \$70.00 per barrel in 2005. This is an annual increase of 6.10% per year: $(70.00/2.54)^{(1/56)} - 1 = 6.10\%$. The annual price increase in *real dollars* is much lower: The purchasing power, in terms of 2005 dollars, of the \$2.54 that a barrel of oil cost in 1949 is equivalent to \$17.54. Thus, the real price increase over the period was 2.10% per year:

	A	B	C
1	**NOMINAL AND REAL INCREASE IN U.S. OIL PRICES, 1949-2005**		
2	Nominal price increase		
3	1949 price per barrel	2.54	
4	2005 price per barrel	70.00	
5	Annual increase	6.10%	<-- =(B4/B3)^(1/56)-1
6			
7	Real price increase		
8	1949 price per barrel in 2005 dollars	17.54	
9	2005 price per barrel in 2005 dollars	70.00	
10	Annual increase	2.50%	<-- =(B9/B8)^(1/56)-1

Of course, comparing two points in time doesn't tell the whole story. Here's a chart of the real cost and nominal cost of oil throughout the period:

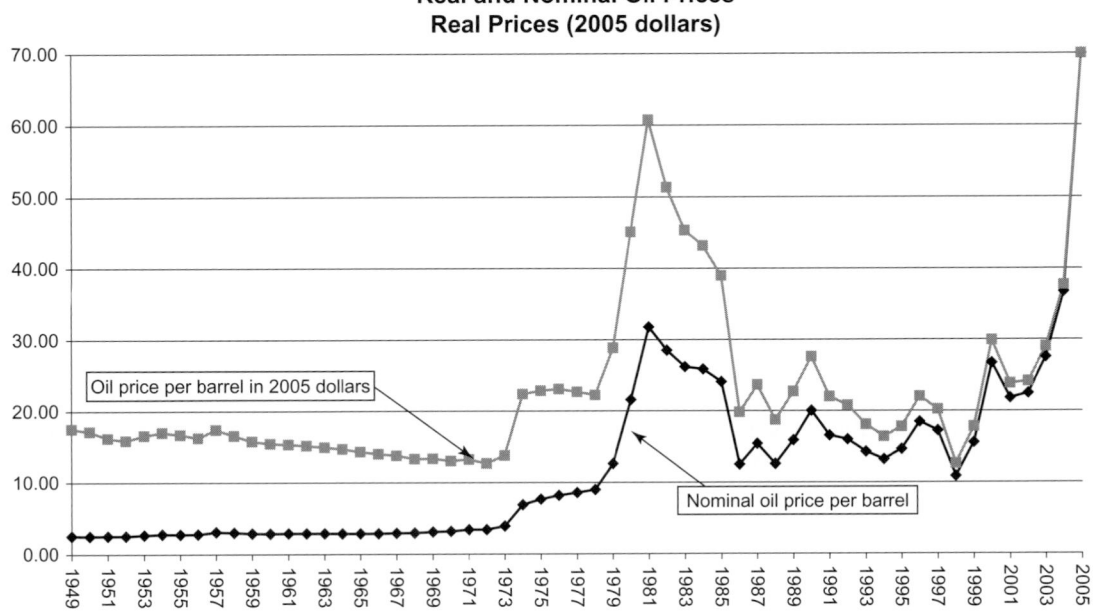

Real and Nominal Oil Prices
Real Prices (2005 dollars)

Data provided by James L. Williams of WTRG Economics
http://www.wtrg.com

Although the nominal increase in the oil price between 1949 and 2005 has been dramatic (from $2.54 per barrel in 1949 to $70.00 in 2005), the change in the real price has been much less remarkable. In terms of 2005 dollars, $2.54 in 1949 had a purchasing power of $17.54 (cell B8 above). The average annual real increase in the oil price has been 2.50% (cell B10).

8.7 Inflation-Adjusted Capital Budgeting

Now that we've got our concepts and terminology straight, we can apply inflation adjustments to typical capital budgeting problems. In this section we'll consider five typical capital budgeting problems that involve inflation. We start by comparing the new U.S. Treasury Inflation-Protected Security (TIPS) to more-familiar savings instruments (Problems 1–3). We then move on to analyze two capital budgeting problems involving the purchase of a machine.

Problem 1: Understanding a One-Year TIPS

The United States Treasury Department issues securities called Treasury Inflation-Protected Security (TIPS).[6] These securities promise a real rate of interest on your initial investment adjusted for increases in the consumer price index.

Here's an example to show how this works:

- You invest $1,000 today in a one year TIPS, which has a real interest rate of 4%. The consumer price index today is 120.
- In one year the Treasury will pay you $1,000 * $\dfrac{CPI_{1 \text{ year from now}}}{CPI_{today}} * (1 + 4\%)$

Your investment in TIPS is fully inflation protected. To see this, break up the TIPS repayment into two factors:

$$\underbrace{\$1,000 * \frac{CPI_{1 \text{ year from now}}}{CPI_{today}}}_{\substack{\uparrow \\ \text{Maintains the purchasing} \\ \text{power of \$1,000 today}}} * \underbrace{(1 + 4\%)}_{\substack{\uparrow \\ \text{Return of initial investment} \\ \text{adjusted for inflation} \\ \text{PLUS} \\ \text{Interest on the inflation–adjusted} \\ \text{investment}}}$$

To analyze this TIPS, suppose you think that the CPI will rise from 120 today to 126 in one year. As the spreadsheet below shows, you anticipate a repayment of $1,092.00.

---

[6]The U.S. Treasury website offers good explanations of these securities and current prices: http://www.publicdebt.treas.gov/sec/seciis.htm.

	A	B	C
1	**ANALYZING A 1-YEAR TREASURY INFLATION-PROTECTED SECURITY (TIPS)**		
2			
3	Initial investment	1,000.00	
4	TIPS real interest rate	4.00%	
5	Current CPI	120	
6	Anticipated CPI in one year	126	
7			
8	TIPS repayment in one year	1,092.00	<-- =B3*(B6/B5)*(1+B4)
9			
10	**Further analysis**		
11	Anticipated inflation rate	5.00%	<-- =B6/B5-1
12	TIPS repayment of inflation-adjusted investment	1,050.00	<-- =B3*(1+B11)
13	TIPS interest on inflation-adjusted investment	42.00	<-- =B4*B12
14	Total TIPS repayment in one year	1,092.00	<-- =B13+B12
15			
16	TIPS interest on inflation-adjusted investment (this is the *real* interest rate paid by the TIPS)	4.00%	<-- =B13/B12

In rows 11–16 we show an alternative analysis of the one-year TIPS repayment of $1,092.00:

- Your anticipated inflation rate is

$$\frac{CPI_{1\ year\ from\ now}}{CPI_{today}} - 1 = \frac{126}{120} - 1 = 5\%$$

- The TIPS always repays you the initial investment, adjusted for the inflation. In this case, this is $1,000 * (1 + anticipated\ inflation) = \$1,000 * (1.05) = \$1,050$.
- In addition, the TIPS pays you the real interest rate (4% in this case) on the inflation-adjusted initial investment. As you can see in cell B13, this is $42.

The result is that the TIPS *maintains the purchasing power of your investment* ($1,000 * (1.05) = \$1,050$) and *pays you interest on the inflation-adjusted investment* ($4\% * \$1,050 = \$42$).

Problem 2: Understanding a Ten-Year TIPS

Suppose you've got $1,000 to save, and you're considering buying a ten-year TIPS with the same conditions as above. What will be the nominal payment on the TIPS you can expect in ten years? In the spreadsheet below, we assume an annual inflation rate of 3%; this brings the total anticipated TIPS repayment to $1,989.32. A little analysis (rows 10–16) shows the breakdown of this payment into return of inflation-adjusted investment ($1,343.92) and interest ($645.41).

	A	B	C
1	**ANALYZING A 10-YEAR TREASURY INFLATION-PROTECTED SECURITY (TIPS)**		
2			
3	Initial investment	1,000.00	
4	TIPS real interest rate	4.00%	
5	Anticipated annual inflation rate	3.00%	
6			
7	TIPS repayment in 10 years	1,989.32	<-- =B3*(1+B5)^10*(1+B4)^10
8			
9	**Further analysis**		
10	Anticipated cumulative inflation rate over 10 years	34.39%	<-- =(1+B5)^10-1
11	TIPS repayment of inflation-adjusted investment	1,343.92	<-- =B3*(1+B10)
12	TIPS interest on inflation-adjusted investment	645.41	<-- =B11*((1+B4)^10-1)
13	Total TIPS repayment in one year	1,989.32	<-- =B12+B11
14			
15	TIPS interest on inflation-adjusted investment (this is the *real* interest rate paid by the TIPS)	48.02%	<-- =B12/B11
16	Annualized TIPS interest on inflation-adjusted investment	4.00%	<-- =(1+B15)^(1/10)-1
17			
18	Anticipated *nominal* return on TIPS	7.12%	<-- =(B7/B3)^(1/10)-1
19	Another way of computing the nominal return: (1+TIPS real rate)*(1+inflation rate)-1	7.12%	<-- =(1+B4)*(1+B5)-1

In cells B18 and B19 we calculate the TIPS anticipated nominal return. As suggested in the previous section,

$$1 + nominal\ interest = (1 + real\ interest) * (1 + inflation\ rate)$$
$$= (1 + 4\%) * (1 + 3\%) = 1.0712$$

Problem 3: Comparing TIPS and a Bank Certificate of Deposit

You have $1,000 extra cash which you don't think you'll need for the next five years. You're considering two alternatives:

- You can put the money in a bank certificate of deposit (CD). This is a security you buy from the bank (in this case for $1,000). The bank has agreed to pay you 8% per year, so that you anticipate receiving $1,000 * (1 + 8\%)^5 = $1,469.33$ in five years.
- On the other hand, you're considering buying a five-year TIPS. This security costs $1,000 and promises you 3.5% annual interest on your initial $1,000 investment, adjusted for the consumer price index (CPI).

How should you make your decision? The spreadsheet below shows the nominal payment made by the TIPS in five years. The graph compares these payments to the $1,469.33 you will get from the bank CD. As you can see from the table in cells A11:C19, if the anticipated inflation rate is more than 4.3478%, the TIPS will pay off more than the CD.

	A	B	C	D
1	COMPARING A 5-YEAR TIPS VERSUS A 5-YEAR BANK CERTIFICATE OF DEPOSIT (CD)			
2	Initial investment	1,000.00		
3	TIPS real interest rate	3.50%		
4	Anticipated annual inflation rate	3.00%		
5	Bank CD nominal interest rate	8.00%		
6				
7	TIPS repayment in 5 years	1,376.85	<-- =B2*(1+B4)^5*(1+B3)^5	
8	Bank CD repayment in 5 years	1,469.33	<-- =B2*(1+B5)^5	
9				
10	Anticipated annual inflation rate	CD payment in 5 years	TIPS payment in 5 years	
11	0%	1,469.33	1,187.69	<-- =$B$2*(1+$B$3)^5*(1+A11)^5
12	1%	1,469.33	1,248.27	
13	2%	1,469.33	1,311.30	
14	3%	1,469.33	1,376.85	
15	4.3478%	1,469.33	1,469.33	<-- Breakeven inflation rate
16	5%	1,469.33	1,515.82	
17	6%	1,469.33	1,589.39	
18	7%	1,469.33	1,665.79	
19	8%	1,469.33	1,745.10	

Nominal Return Certainty Versus Real Return Certainty: The comparison of the CD and TIPS in the above spreadsheet shows you that whereas the TIPS nominal return depends on the inflation rate, the CD nominal return is fixed. In some ways this might make it look as if the CD is preferred to the TIPS. But wait! In the spreadsheet below we compute the CD and TIPS real rate of return. This time the tables are turned: The TIPS always returns 3.5% in real terms, whereas the CD's real rate of return depends on the inflation rate.

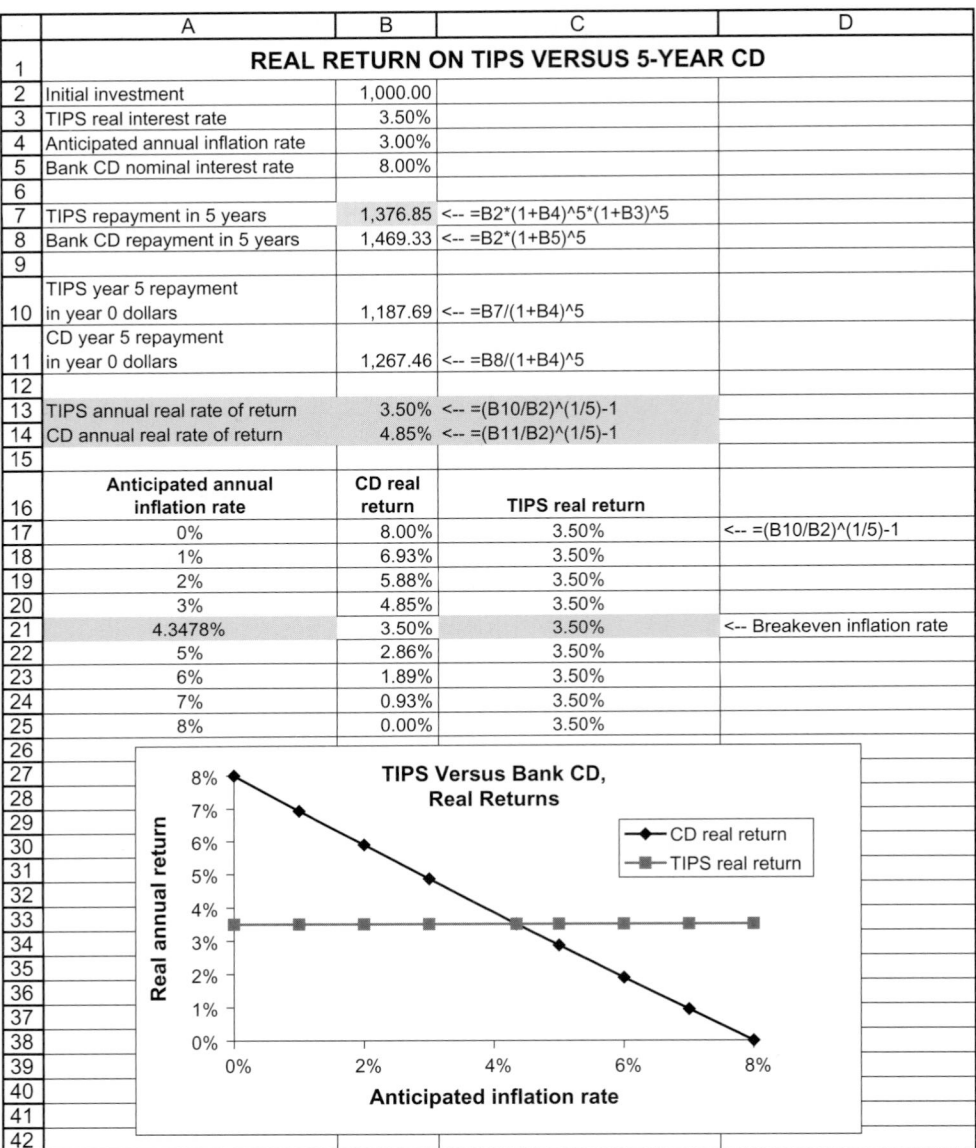

	A	B	C	D
1	**REAL RETURN ON TIPS VERSUS 5-YEAR CD**			
2	Initial investment	1,000.00		
3	TIPS real interest rate	3.50%		
4	Anticipated annual inflation rate	3.00%		
5	Bank CD nominal interest rate	8.00%		
6				
7	TIPS repayment in 5 years	1,376.85	<-- =B2*(1+B4)^5*(1+B3)^5	
8	Bank CD repayment in 5 years	1,469.33	<-- =B2*(1+B5)^5	
9				
10	TIPS year 5 repayment in year 0 dollars	1,187.69	<-- =B7/(1+B4)^5	
11	CD year 5 repayment in year 0 dollars	1,267.46	<-- =B8/(1+B4)^5	
12				
13	TIPS annual real rate of return	3.50%	<-- =(B10/B2)^(1/5)-1	
14	CD annual real rate of return	4.85%	<-- =(B11/B2)^(1/5)-1	
15				
16	**Anticipated annual inflation rate**	**CD real return**	**TIPS real return**	
17	0%	8.00%	3.50%	<-- =(B10/B2)^(1/5)-1
18	1%	6.93%	3.50%	
19	2%	5.88%	3.50%	
20	3%	4.85%	3.50%	
21	4.3478%	3.50%	3.50%	<-- Breakeven inflation rate
22	5%	2.86%	3.50%	
23	6%	1.89%	3.50%	
24	7%	0.93%	3.50%	
25	8%	0.00%	3.50%	

TIPS or CD? What's the Answer?   Like all good finance questions, the answer depends on your assumptions. If you believe that the inflation rate will be higher that 4.3478% per year, then the TIPS is preferred; otherwise, you should choose the CD.

Problem 4: Buying a Widget Machine

You're considering an investment in a new widget machine. The machine will cost $9,500 today; cells B9 to B14 give the widget sales forecasts for years 1–6. Widgets today sell for $15 each (cell B3), and the widget price in the future is expected to rise at the inflation rate of 4% (cell B2). Your nominal discount rate is 12% (cell B4).

	A	B	C	D	E	F	G
1			CAPITAL BUDGETING FOR THE WIDGET MACHINE				
2	Inflation rate	4.00%					
3	Widget price today	15.00					
4	Nominal discount rate	12.00%					
5	Equivalent real discount rate	7.69%	<-- =(1+B4)/(1+B2)-1				
6							
7	Year	Widgets sold	Anticipated nominal widget price	Anticipated nominal cash flow		Anticipated real cash flow in year 0 dollars	
8	0			-9,500.00		-9,500.00	
9	1	100	15.60	1,560.00	<-- =C9*B9	1,500.00	<-- =D9/(1+$B$2)^A9
10	2	125	16.22	2,028.00	<-- =C10*B10	1,875.00	<-- =D10/(1+$B$2)^A10
11	3	150	16.87	2,530.94		2,250.00	
12	4	160	17.55	2,807.66		2,400.00	
13	5	170	18.25	3,102.46		2,550.00	
14	6	200	18.98	3,795.96		3,000.00	
15							
16	NPV calculations			=$B$3*(1+$B$2)^A9			
17	Discounting nominal cash flows at nominal discount rates	778.93	<-- =NPV(B4,D9:D14)+D8				
18	Discounting real cash flows at real discount rates	778.93	<-- =NPV(B5,F9:F14)+F8				
19							
20	IRR calculations						
21	Nominal IRR	14.47%	<-- =IRR(D8:D14)				
22	Real IRR	10.06%	<-- =IRR(F8:F14)				
23	(1+nominal IRR)/(1+inflation)-1	10.06%	<-- =(1+B21)/(1+B2)-1				

- Assuming a nominal discount rate of 12%, an equivalent real discount rate is given in cell B5. This rate is computed by the formula

$$real\ discount\ rate = \frac{1 + nominal\ rate}{1 + inflation\ rate} - 1 = \frac{1 + 12\%}{1 + 4\%} - 1 = 7.69\%$$

- Column C of the spreadsheet shows the anticipated widget price in each of years 1–6. We've computed this price by computing the *nominal widget price* in each of years 1–6 using the formula

$$nominal\ time\text{-}t\ price = price\ today * (1 + inflation)^t$$

- Column D shows the anticipated nominal cash flow.[7] Discounting these cash flows at 12% gives the NPV of $778.93 in cell B17. Because the NPV is positive, you should invest in the new machine.

- Assuming that the increase in widget prices and the increase in general prices are the same, we can compute the real cash flows as in column F:

$$real\ cash\ flow,\ year\ t = (widgets\ sold) * (widget\ price\ today)$$

Column F actually shows a different formula, which gives the same result:

$$real\ cash\ flow,\ year\ t = \left(\frac{nominal\ value\ widgets\ sold}{(1 + inflation\ rate)^t} \right)$$

- The NPV of these real cash flows, computed in cell B18, is the same as the $778.93 computed in cell B17.

---

[7]We've assumed that it won't cost you anything to produce the widgets once you buy the machine. (Alternatively, you can assume that the widget price is net of production costs.)

Discounting nominal cash flows at a nominal discount rate and discounting real cash flows at a real discount rate gives the same net present value in year 0 dollars.

Computing the Real and Nominal IRR: We can compute the real and nominal IRR for the widget machine as follows:

- Taking the IRR of the nominal cash flows (cell B22) gives a nominal IRR of 14.47%. Because the nominal IRR is greater than the nominal discount rate of 12%, the widget machine is a good investment.
- Computing the IRR of the real cash flows (cell B23) gives a real IRR of 10.06%. The investment decision given by the real IRR is the same as the investment decision given by the nominal IRR: Because the real IRR is greater than the real discount rate of 7.69%, the machine is a good investment. Note that we've computed the real discount rate in cell B5 using the formula

$$real\ discount\ rate = \frac{1 + nominal\ discount\ rate}{1 + anticipated\ inflation\ rate} = \frac{1 + 12\%}{1 + 05\%} - 1 = 7.69\%$$

- The real IRR can also be computed by the formula

$$real\ IRR = \frac{1 + nominal\ IRR}{1 + inflation\ rate} - 1 = \frac{1 + 14.47\%}{1 + 4\%} - 1 = 10.06\%$$

TWO WAYS OF COMPUTING THE REAL IRR

The real IRR can be computed by either:

- Taking the IRR of the projected real cash flows (direct calculation of the real IRR).
- Taking the IRR of the nominal cash flows, dividing by (1 + inflation rate), and subtracting 1.

To see that these two are the same, notice that the nominal NPV is computed by

$$nominal\ NPV = CF_0 + \frac{CF_1(real) * (1 + inflation\ rate)}{(1 + real\ interest\ rate) * (1 + inflation\ rate)}$$
$$+ \frac{CF_2(real) * (1 + inflation\ rate)^2}{[(1 + real\ interest\ rate) * (1 + inflation\ rate)]^2}$$
$$+ \frac{CF_2(real) * (1 + inflation\ rate)^3}{[(1 + real\ interest\ rate) * (1 + inflation\ rate)]^3}$$
$$+ \cdots$$

Throughout this formula the (1 + inflation rate) term cancels out, so that

$$nominal\ NPV = CF_0 + \frac{CF_1(real)}{(1 + real\ interest\ rate)}$$
$$+ \frac{CF_2(real)}{(1 + real\ interest\ rate)^2} + \frac{CF_3(real)}{(1 + real\ interest\ rate)^3} + \cdots$$
$$= real\ NPV$$

Problem 5: Widget Prices Have a Different Inflation Rate Than the General Inflation Rate

In the previous problem the anticipated increase in widget prices was the same as the inflation rate. Suppose this isn't true. In the spreadsheet below, we assume that inflation (understood as the increase in the CPI) will be 4% per year, but that widget prices will increase at 8% per year. (Widget demand is expected to rise sharply, causing a big increase in prices.)

The analysis for this case is shown below. Though in principle it is not different from the analysis for Problem 4, the results, of course, are different—making widgets an even more profitable business.

	A	B	C	D	E	F	G
1	CAPITAL BUDGETING FOR THE WIDGET MACHINE widget prices increase at a different rate than the inflation rate						
2	Inflation rate	4.00%					
3	Widget price today	15.00					
4	Annual increase in widget prices	8.00%					
5	Nominal discount rate	12.00%					
6	Equivalent real discount rate	7.69%	<-- =(1+B5)/(1+B2)-1				
7							
8	Year	Widgets sold	Anticipated nominal widget price	Anticipated nominal cash flow		Anticipated real cash flow in year 0 dollars	
9	0			-9,500.00		-9,500.00	
10	1	100	16.20	1,620.00	<-- =C10*B10	1,557.69	<-- =D10/(1+$B$2)^A10
11	2	125	17.50	2,187.00	<-- =C11*B11	2,022.00	<-- =D11/(1+$B$2)^A11
12	3	150	18.90	2,834.35		2,519.73	
13	4	160	20.41	3,265.17		2,791.08	
14	5	170	22.04	3,746.79		3,079.59	
15	6	200	23.80	4,760.62		3,762.39	
16							
17	NPV calculations			=$B$3*(1+$B$4)^A10			
18	Discounting nominal cash flows at nominal discount rates	2,320.31	<-- =NPV(B5,D10:D15)+D9				
19	Discounting real cash flows at real discount rates	2,320.31	<-- =NPV(B6,F10:F15)+F9				
20							
21	IRR calculations						
22	Nominal IRR	18.87%	<-- =IRR(D9:D15)				
23	Real IRR	14.30%	<-- =IRR(F9:F15)				
24	(1+nominal IRR)/(1+inflation)-1	14.30%	<-- =(1+B22)/(1+B2)-1				

Compare this spreadsheet to the calculations we did in the previous example: Since widget prices increase faster than the inflation rate, both the nominal and the real anticipated cash flows are greater in every year. Thus, the project is more profitable, whether measured by real or nominal NPV or real or nominal IRR.

CONCLUSION

This chapter has dealt with a variety of issues in NPV and IRR analysis. Some of these issues dealt with problems associated with using the IRR: IRR may not always give you explicit answers (there can be multiple IRRs, and complicated cash flows can have IRRs that make it difficult to understand if you're borrowing or lending). We also examined the problem of choosing between short-lived and alternative long-lived assets, and we looked again at the lease/purchase problem first introduced in Chapter 6; this time we introduced taxes into the problem and discussed how corporations should choose between leasing and purchasing an asset.

Finally, we discussed how inflation should be incorporated into our analysis of capital budgeting.

EXERCISES

1. You are considering building a hotel in northern Alaska. Your plan is to build the hotel and then sell it. You've been offered an immediate planning grant of $500,000 from the Alaskan Tourist Authority, and you estimate that to complete the hotel you'll need to make an investment next year of $1,700,000. Once built, you think you can sell the hotel at the end of year 2 for $1,400,000, so that your cash flow pattern looks like:

	A	B
1	**ALASKAN HOTEL PROJECT**	
2	**Year**	**Cash flow**
3	0	500,000
4	1	-1,700,000
5	2	1,400,000

    (a)   Identify the two IRRs of this project.

    (b)   If the discount rate is 28%, should you undertake the project?

2. Here's an example of a cash flow with three changes in sign.

    (a)   Graph the NPV of the cash flows using discount rates between 0% and 100%. Use this graph to approximately identify the three internal rates of return.

    (b)   Use Excel's **IRR** function with its **Guess** option to identify the three IRRs exactly.

    (c)   Can you "spin" a story about why a project might have such a complicated cash flow pattern?

	A	B
1	**CASH FLOW WITH 3 IRRs**	
2	**Year**	**Cash flow**
3	0	-350,000
4	1	2,500,000
5	2	-3,000,000
6	3	500,000
7	4	500,000
8	5	500,000
9	6	500,000
10	7	-14,000,000
11	8	3,500,000
12	9	3,500,000
13	10	3,500,000
14	11	3,500,000
15	12	3,500,000
16	13	3,500,000
17	14	3,500,000
18	15	-11,000,000

3.   You are considering a project with the following cash flows:

	A	B
2	Year	Cash flow
3	0	-300
4	1	5,000
5	2	-20,000
6	3	8,000
7	4	6,000
8	5	3,500

(a)   What is the NPV of the project when the discount rate is 0% ?

(b)   What is the NPV of the project when the discount rate grows to infinity?

(c)   Find all the project IRRs.

4.   Your firm is considering two projects with the following cash flows:

	A	B	C
2	Year	Project A	Project B
3	0	22,500	50,000
4	1	-6,000	-15,000
5	2	-6,000	-15,000
6	3	-6,000	-15,000
7	4	-6,000	-15,000
8	5	-6,000	-15,000
9	6	-6,000	-15,000

In which discount rate range will the company prefer project A, in which discount rate range project B, and in which discount rate range will the company not invest?

5.   You bought a house in January 1996 for $100,000, and you sold the house at the end of 2002 for $185,000. The CPI rose in the period from 118 to 155.

(a)   What was your annualized nominal rate of return?

(b)   Calculate your annualized real rate of return.

6.   The bank is offering you a new saving, which will give you a 2% real annual interest rate. If the inflation rate is 5% annually, how long will it take you to double your money both in nominal and real terms?

7.   You are considering purchasing a machine to produce golf balls. The cost of the machine is $100,000 and its expected life span in eight years. The machine will have an annual production of 550,000 balls. The price of a golf ball today is $0.20, and it's expected to rise by 10% each year. The material used to produce a golf ball costs $0.08 and it's expected to rise by 2% a year. In order to operate the machine, you'll need two workers, each of them earning an annual salary of $30,000; according to their contracts their salaries will rise by 7% a year starting in the third year.

The real discount rate is 4%, the expected inflation is 5%, and the corporate tax rate is 40%.

(a)   Calculate the NPV of the project using nominal values.

(b)   Repeat the calculation using real values.

8.   A soft drink company is considering whether to use television or radio in its campaign for the new line of products. According to the company's estimates, the TV campaign will cost initially

(at $t = 0$) $205,000 and another $100,000 annually. The campaign will generate an annual income of $300,000 for three years.

The radio campaign will cost $48,000 and an additional cost of $20,000 annually. The radio campaign will generate an annual income of $150,000 for three years. The company's discount rate is 18% and the tax rate is 30%.

(a)   Calculate the NPVs of the television and the radio campaigns.

(b)   Repeat your calculations using midyear discounting and explain the difference in results.

9. A factory is considering purchasing a new machine. It has two alternatives:

	A	B	C
1	Discount rate	8%	
2	Tax rate	30%	
3			
4		**Machine A**	**Machine B**
5	Cost	15,000	50,000
6	Annual costs	3,000	1,000
7	Life span	3	7

Whichever machine is chosen, the factory will have to continue to choose the same machine forever. Which machine should the factory choose if the interest rate is 8% and the corporate tax is 30%? Assume straight-line depreciation to zero salvage value over the life of each machine.

10. Your firm has to replace one of its fender-bender machines. One of your financial wizards has determined that the appropriate discount rate for the machine cash flows is 10%. Your firm has two alternatives:

(a)   Fender-bender machine A costs $400,000 and produces annual cash flows of $200,000 at the end of each of its six years of life.

(b)   Fender-bender machine B costs $200,000 but has only a two-year life. However, it produces a $300,000 annual cash flow at the end of each of these two years.

	A	B	C
		Cash flow	Cash flow
3	Year	(A)	(B)
4	0	-400	-200
5	1	200	300
6	2	200	300
7	3	200	
8	4	200	
9	5	200	
10	6	200	

Calculate the equivalent annuity cash flow (EAC) and determine which machine is preferable.

11. You are the owner of a five-year-old taxi. Your doctor has advised you to quit driving due to a health problem. You are considering two alternatives:

(a)   Selling the taxi for $15,000. Because the taxi's book value is 0, you will have to pay tax.

(b)   Renting your taxi to your cousin. Your cousin will pay you $4,000 at *the beginning* of each year. You estimate that the taxi will be in working order for another five years and can then be sold for $300.

Which is the more profitable alternative if your tax bracket is 25% and your discount rate is 5%?

12. A firm is considering the purchase of a machine for one of its factories. The machine's cost is $300,000 and it is expected to save the factory $100,000 annually. The machine's life span is four years, the company discount rate is 15%, and the corporate tax rate is 35%.
    (a)   Under the above conditions, is it worth buying the new machine?
    (b)   Another supplier of the same machine suggested that instead of buying the machine the firm should lease it. If the leasing fee for the machine is $80,000 annually, and it is an expense for tax purposes, what is the NPV of the leasing offer?
    (c)   The original supplier suggested lending the firm $210,000 that will be returned in three equal payments without interest. What is the NPV of this offer?

13. In Section 8.2 we considered a project called Sanitary Landfill. Now consider a project called Stranger Sanitary Landfill, which has the following cash flows:

	A	B
4	Year	Cash flow
5	0	-800,000
6	1	450,000
7	2	450,000
8	3	450,000
9	4	450,000
10	5	450,000
11	6	-1,500,000

Show that you would accept this project for a suitably *low* or a suitably *high* discount rate, but not for discount rates in the middle. Explain.

14. You have a factory that produces light bulbs. Your old machine is costing a lot of money lately in repairs and you are considering replacing it. You have two offers:

	A	B	C
1	Discount rate	12%	
2	Corporate tax rate	40%	
3			
4	Annual production	1,000,000	
5	Price of light bulbs	0.40	
6			
7		Machine A	Machine B
8	Cost	500,000	200,000
9	Variable cost per light bulbs	0.12	0.25
10	Fixed costs	100,000	75,000
11	Life span	10	4

You sell each light bulb for $0.40, the discount rate is 12%, and the corporate tax rate 40%.
    (a)   Which machine would you prefer to buy if your annual production is 1,000,000 light bulbs?
    (b)   At what level of production will you change your answer?

15. ABC Corp. is trying to decide whether to buy or lease a new egg scrambling machine. Here are some relevant facts:
    •   The new machine costs $120,000 and will be depreciated over a five-year horizon to zero salvage value on a straight-line basis.
    •   ABC Corp. has a 30% corporate tax rate.
    •   The company can lease the machine from a reputable lessor for $29,941 per year; payments will be made on dates 0, 1, 2, . . . , 5 (in other words, six payments).

- ABC Corp. has a line of credit at its local bank. The bank is currently offering loans up to six years at 12%.

(a) Should ABC Corp. lease or buy the machine? Justify your answer.

(b) Suppose that the leasing company offers to sell the machine to ABC for $1 at the end of the lease term. The company feels that the machine can profitably be sold at this point for $25,000. Will this make the lease more or less attractive? (Give a qualitative, not numerical, answer.)

16. Wharton Waste Disposal (WWD) is trying to decide whether to replace its aged trash compactor with a new, more efficient, model. Here are the relevant facts:

- The new trash compactor costs $400,000. If introduced, the company estimates that it will save $60,000 annually on a before-tax basis (assume that this cash flow occurs at year-end).

- The old trash compactor has a book value of $100,000. Its market value is $50,000. The remaining book value of the old compactor is being depreciated on a straight-line basis to zero salvage value at the rate of $20,000/year.

- WWD has a corporate tax rate of 40% and is wildly profitable. The company uses a 15% discount rate for all cash flows.

- Trash compactors never die—they have an essentially infinite life. However, the new compactor will be straight-line depreciated on a ten-year life to zero salvage value.

- In order to encourage the replacement of smelly old trash compactors with new shiny ones, the state Environmental Protection Agency (EPA) is offering a *replacement subsidy*. The subsidy is paid one year after the new compactor is put in use.

What is the minimum subsidy that will make the replacement of the old compactor a break-even proposition?

17. Hunter Brothers, Inc. needs to buy printers for its offices. It can buy expensive laser printers or much cheaper (but shorter-lived) inkjets. Here are some relevant facts:

- A laser printer costs $1,000 and an inkjet costs $250.

- A laser printer has an anticipated life of six years, but an inkjet has an anticipated life of only two years. Printers are assumed to have a zero market value at the end of their lives.

- The cost per page for a laser printer is $0.03, whereas the cost per page for an inkjet is $0.10.

- Each printer purchased is anticipated to print 10,000 pages per year.

If Hunter Brothers has a discount rate of 12% and a tax rate of zero, which printers should it buy? Assume that the whole year's cost of printing falls at year-end.

18. Torreo Coffee Roaster is considering replacing one of its existing machines with a new, more automated and efficient machine. Torreo bought the machine four years ago for $87,500. It is being depreciated on a straight-line basis over a fourteen-year life. The machine could be sold today, January 1, 2006 for $20,000.

The new machine costs $95,000. The new machine's depreciable life is ten years with a salvage value of $13,000 in real terms. However, in accordance with U.S. tax law, the asset will be depreciated to zero over ten years via the straight-line method.

In 1999, Torreo's current coffee roasting machine accounted for annual revenues of $50,000 and has annual costs of $25,000. The new machine will increase this revenue to $65,000 per year (in real terms, that is, in 1999 dollars). The machine will also increase operating costs by $3,000 per year in real terms.

The nominal discount rate is 14% per annum. The corporate tax rate for both operating income and capital gains is 40%. The annual anticipated inflation rate is 5%. All cash flows are riskless and they occur at the end of the year. Taxes are also paid at the end of the same year. Torreo has profitable ongoing operations that can be used to offset losses.

Should Torreo Coffee Roaster replace the old machine with the new machine?

19. One Stop Golf, Inc. is thinking of building a plant to manufacture a child's putter. The initial outlay for the plant will be made today (31 December 2005) and will be $5 million. On 31 December 2006, a further outlay of $1 million is required. The plant will be ready for production on 1 January 2007 and will start production then. It is expected to produce and sell 1 million putters in 2007, 1.2 million in 2008, and 0.8 million in 2009. Each putter can be sold for $30 in 2007 and is expected to increase at a rate of 6% per year. The raw materials required for each putter are expected to cost $15 on average for those putters produced in 2007 and to increase at a rate of 3% per year. The cost of labor for each putter produced in 2007 is $5 and is expected to increase at the rate of 5% per year. Advertising the new putters will cost $500,000 in 2007, $220,000 in 2008, and $50,000 in 2009. No other inputs are required for the production of the child's putter.

    The plant will be built on land that could otherwise be rented out from 1 January 2006 to 31 December 2009 for $500,000 per year, before taxes.

    The firm uses straight-line depreciation and depreciates the total $6 million of plant costs over the three years the plant is used. The firm can offset any losses against other profitable ongoing projects. The salvage value of the plant is $250,000 on 31 December 2009. The appropriate discount rate for the project is 12%. Assume all cash flows occur at the end of the year. The corporate tax rate, t_c, is 34%.

    (a)   Calculate the project's incremental cash flows.

    (b)   Calculate the net present value as of 31 December 2005.

    (c)   Should One Stop Golf, Inc. start the production of children's putters?

20. Grandma Helen was reminiscing with her grandson Noah. "When I married Grandpa in 1937," she recalled, "his monthly salary was $300. We had to scrimp and save. Now here it is 2005, and you're telling me that your first job out of college is going to pay you $3,000 per month. Why, that's *ten times* as much as Grandpa made!"

    To compare the two salaries, Noah went to the Minneapolis Federal Reserve website and dug out CPI figures for 1913–2005. Whose salary was larger—in inflation-adjusted terms—Noah's or Grandpa's?

	A	B	C
1	**CPI AND INFLATION RATES** **1913-2005** **Source: Minneapolis Federal** **Reserve Bank** http://minneapolisfed.org/Research/data/us/calc/hist1913.cfm		
2	Year	Consumer price index	Annual inflation rate
25	1935	13.7	2.24%
26	1936	13.9	1.46%
27	1937	14.4	3.60%
28	1938	14.1	-2.08%
29	1939	13.9	-1.42%
30	1940	14	0.72%
31	1941	14.7	5.00%
32	1942	16.3	10.88%
91	2001	177.1	2.85%
92	2002	179.9	1.58%
93	2003	183.8	2.17%
94	2004	188.9	2.70%
95	2005	194.6	3.00%

(Note: The whole data series from 1913 to 2005 is on the disk with this book.)

21. The Minneapolis Federal Reserve Bank also published a CPI series for 1800–2005. The series is given on the disk with this book.

    (a) In 1803 the administration of President Thomas Jefferson purchased 800,000 square miles of North American territory from the French government for $15,000,000. The "Louisiana Purchase" doubled the size of the United States. Use the CPI series to adjust this price to 2005 dollars.[8]

    (b) There are 640 acres per square mile. What was the price of the Louisiana Purchase per acre in 2005 dollars?

    Some perspective: A random search of the Internet in 2004 reveals the following land prices in the area of the Louisiana Purchase:

    - A 32-acre farm in LaClede County, Missouri: $297,500
    - A 2.7-acre lot in the Ozarks (Missouri): $19,452
    - A 9,000-acre property in Kansas: $4,500,000
    - 37 acres in Shreveport, Louisiana: $151,540

22. (a) On 1 January 2004, the Fluffy Finance Company made a $1,000,000 loan to one of its clients. The loan interest was 12%, to be paid monthly (meaning, 1% per month), with full repayment of the loan on 1 January 2005. Because the client anticipated significant cash flow problems during July and August, Fluffy Loan agreed to forego interest payments during these months. Use Excel's **XIRR** to compute the annualized rate of return earned by Fluffy Finance on the loan.

    (b) Another Fluffy Finance client has asked for a similar loan but has asked to forego interest payments in May and June. If Fluffy can make only one of the loans, which should it make?

23. For each of the projects below, compute all the IRRs:

	A	B	C	D	E	F	G
1	CONVENTIONAL AND NONCONVENTIONAL CASH FLOW PATTERNS						
2	Year	Cash flow Project A	Cash flow Project B	Cash flow Project C	Cash flow Project D	Cash flow Project E	Cash flow Project F
3	0	-100	-100	100	25	-25	-250
4	1	200	-50	55	35	80	35
5	2	500	60	35	-200	-100	145
6	3	50	80	50	33	200	330
7	4	60	99	-100	55	55	55
8	5	35	100	-35	155	-250	-250
9		↑ Conventional cash flow pattern	↑ Conventional cash flow pattern	↑ Conventional cash flow pattern	↑ Nonconventional cash flow pattern	↑ Nonconventional cash flow pattern	↑ Nonconventional cash flow pattern
10		Initial negative cash flow followed by positive cash flows	Two initial negative cash flows followed by positive cash flows	Four initial positive cash flows followed by negative cash flows	Two positive cash flows, then negative, then three positive cash flows	Signs of cash flows change several times	Negative cash flows at beginning and end, other cash flows positive

---

[8]For historical details and a map, access http://gatewayno.com/history/LaPurchase.html.

CHOOSING A DISCOUNT RATE

OVERVIEW

When you use either NPV or IRR to make investment decisions, you have to choose a discount rate r. Just to remind you:

- In the case of the NPV, the discount rate r is used to discount the future cash flows of the investment. If the NPV is positive when cash flows are discounted at r, then the investment is a good one. An investment with a negative NPV should be rejected.

	"Yes or No": **Choosing Whether to** **Undertake a Single Project**	**"Project Ranking":** **Comparing Two Mutually** **Exclusive Projects**
NPV criterion	The project should be undertaken if its NPV > 0.	Project A is preferred to project B if NPV(A) > NPV(B)
IRR criterion	The project should be undertaken if its IRR > r, where r is the appropriate discount rate.	Project A is preferred to project B if IRR(A) > IRR(B).

Figure 9.1 Summarizing the use of NPV and IRR for investment decisions. The critical question discussed in this chapter is, "How do we determine the appropriate discount rate r?"

- In the case of the IRR, the discount rate r is the standard for comparison of the investment choices. If the rate r is less than the IRR of the investment, the investment is a good one; if r > IRR, you should reject the investment.[1]

As you can see, the choice of a discount rate is very important! This chapter discusses how to choose the discount rate. The main principles stressed are as follows:

- The rate you choose should be appropriate to the riskiness of the cash flows being discounted. The riskier the cash flows being discounted, the higher should be the discount rate used in the NPV or IRR computations.

- In many cases, the "funding cost" is a good choice for the discount rate. The funding cost is the rate of return demanded by the provider of the funds for the project.

- In a large number of cases involving investments by firms, the appropriate discount rate is the weighted average cost of capital (WACC). The WACC is the *average funding cost* for a firm. The bulk of this chapter is devoted to defining the WACC and showing you how to use it to value a firm.

Figure 9.1 summarizes the uses of NPV and IRR to make investment decisions. Despite the extensive discussions of Chapters 5–8, there are two NPV/IRR questions we haven't answered:

- What is the meaning of the cash flows that are discounted in the NPV and IRR computations? Suppose we're considering an investment that costs $100 today and promises $120 in one year. What does this promise of a future cash flow actually mean?
    - One possibility is that the $120 is *riskless*: In this case there is no doubt that the $120 will be paid one year from now. The $120 future cash flow is *certain*. Government bonds and bank accounts are two examples of investments that offer riskless cash flows.

    - Another possibility is that the $120 is an *anticipated* or *expected* cash flow but is not riskless. In this case the $120 is *risky* or *uncertain*. For example, it could be that the investment's cash flow one year from now is determined by the flip of a coin: If the coin comes up "heads," the cash flow will be $140, and if it comes up "tails," the cash flow will be $100. The average future cash flow is $120, but the actual cash flow is uncertain.

- How do we pick the proper discount rate r for the investment? In the NPV and IRR calculations of Chapters 5 – 8, r is the rate of return that we require from the investment (Figure 9.2).

---

[1]Recall from Chapter 8 that the IRR is not always the appropriate rule to use (for example, when there are multiple IRRs). In these cases, we should use the NPV.

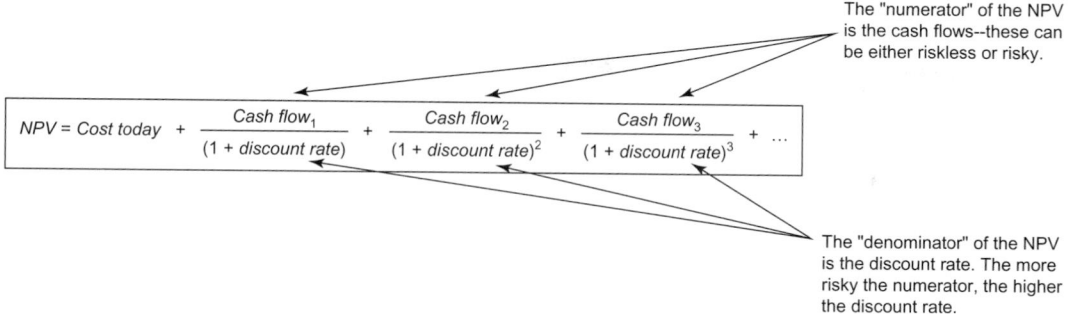

The "numerator" of the NPV is the cash flows--these can be either riskless or risky.

$$NPV = Cost\ today\ +\ \frac{Cash\ flow_1}{(1 + discount\ rate)} + \frac{Cash\ flow_2}{(1 + discount\ rate)^2} + \frac{Cash\ flow_3}{(1 + discount\ rate)^3} + \ ...$$

The "denominator" of the NPV is the discount rate. The more risky the numerator, the higher the discount rate.

Figure 9.2 The "numerator" and the "denominator" of the NPV. The cash flow in the numerator is the anticipated investment cash flow; the discount rate in the denominator is adjusted for the riskiness of the cash flow in the numerator. This chapter discusses the determination of the discount rate.

Once you realize that the cash flow figures you're quoted mask the uncertainty behind the numbers, you'll agree that r should be *risk-adjusted:* Investors dislike risk; therefore, the *greater the uncertainty* about the cash flows, the *higher* the rate of return r investors demand. To go back to the investment considered in the previous bullet:

- If the $120 is a *riskless* cash flow, then the appropriate discount rate r is the *riskless interest rate*. Good examples of riskless interest rates are the interest rates on government bonds or bank accounts.
- If the $120 is a *risky* cash flow, then the return investors will demand will be higher. This means that the appropriate discount rate r is a *risk-adjusted discount rate*.

Risk: At a later point in the book (Chapters 11–16), we give more formal definitions of risk and how to measure it. For the moment we'll rely on your intuitive understanding of risk. You understand that investing in a government bond is less risky than investing in stocks. You also understand that a real estate investment is more risky than putting your money in a savings account (but perhaps less risky than buying a race horse).

The main characteristic of the riskiness of a cash flow is its future variability: Some cash flows are known almost with certainty; if your bank promises you 6% interest, you can be certain that $100 today will grow to $106 in one year. Other kinds of cash flows are much more uncertain; past experience shows that a $1,000 investment in stocks gives an average annual return of 12%, but you also know that in some years this return has been as low as -20% and in other years it has been as high as 35%. In general, the higher the variability of an investment's return, the higher is its risk.

TERMINOLOGY

The finance literature is full of synonyms for discount rates. Here are some terms you're likely to encounter; all of them are sometimes used to denote the appropriate discount rate for a series of cash flows:

- Discount rate
- Cost of capital
- Opportunity cost
- Interest rate
- Risk-adjusted discount rate (RADR)

Finance Concepts Discussed

- Funding cost
- Cost of capital
- Cost of equity, r_E
- Cost of debt, r_D
- Free cash flow (FCF)
- Gordon dividend model
- Midyear discounting

Excel Functions Used

- **NPV**
- **IRR**
- **PMT**

9.1 Funding Cost as the Discount Rate

The *funding cost* is the cost of raising the money needed for an investment. The funding cost is often the appropriate candidate to be the discount rate. The idea behind using the funding cost as a discount rate is that we identify the cost of the funds used and use this cost to discount the future investment cash flows. We start with an example that illustrates the proper use of the funding cost as discount rate.

Example 1: Taking Money Out of a Savings Account to Buy a Bank Certificate of Deposit (CD)

You've got $10,000 in a savings account at the bank, which earns 4% per year, and you have no intention of using this money for the next couple of years. Your bank has offered you an alternative investment: a two-year certificate of deposit that earns 5%. This CD is like a bond issued by the bank: You pay the bank $10,000 today and the CD will pay you $500 in one year ($500 = 5% * $10,000) and $10,500 in two years.

The CD looks like a good investment—instead of earning 4%, you'll now earn 5%. Another way to think about this investment is that it will cost you 4% (the foregone interest rate on your savings account) to earn the 5% interest on the CD. Using the 4% rate as the appropriate discount rate, the NPV of the CD is $188.61:

	A	B	C
1		**BANK CD**	
2	Savings account interest rate	4.00%	
3	CD rate	5.00%	
4			
5	Year	CD cash flow	
6	0	-10,000.00	
7	1	500.00	
8	2	10,500.00	
9			
10	NPV	188.61	<-- =B6+NPV(B2,B7:B8)

The meaning of the $188.61 is that this is the additional wealth you will gain from taking your money out of the savings account and putting it into the CD.

Warning: Markets aren't stupid, so you have to ask yourself why the bank is offering you 5% on the CD and only 4% on the savings account. What are the *risks* involved in taking your money out of the savings account and putting it into the CD?

- Lock-in risk: The money in the CD is locked in and is not available for two years, whereas the money in the savings account is available at any time.

- Interest rate risk: If interest rates go up, the bank will probably raise the interest rate on the savings account (other banks will raise their savings interest rate and competitive pressure will probably force your bank to raise its interest rate). On the other hand, the CD is a two-year contract between you and the bank during which the interest rate will not change. (Of course, there's another aspect to the interest rate risk: If interest rates go down, then the savings account interest will decrease, but not the interest paid on the CD.)

- Default risk: It is possible that the bank will not be able to keep the promises it made with the CD. Most American bank CDs are guaranteed by the United States government, so that this is not really a factor.

The bottom line on this example is that if you think the riskiness of the bank savings account and the CD are not substantially different, you should use the savings bank rate of 4% to discount the investment in the CD. The funding cost is an appropriate discount rate.

Example 2: When Is the Funding Cost Not a Good Discount Rate?

In the previous example the riskiness of a bank savings account is not substantially different from the riskiness of a CD. This makes the savings account interest rate a good discount rate for evaluating the purchase of the CD. When the risks of funding finance differ substantially from the risks of the investment, the funding cost is not a good choice for a discount rate. Suppose you're thinking about buying a one-year Evelyn Wyer lipstick franchise. This franchise allows you to sell the prestigious Evelyn Wyer lipsticks on your campus for one year. Evelyn's lipstick comes in all colors, but this year's favorite among college students is vomit yellow. The franchise costs $1,000 and is good for one year. At the end of this year, you expect to earn $1,500 from the franchise.

If you make the investment, you'll have to take this $1,000 out of your savings account, which pays 4% interest. The 4% is thus the funding cost for the Evelyn Wyer franchise.

If you use the 4% as a discount rate, then the lipstick franchise is a very good investment. It has NPV = $442 and an IRR of 50%:

	A	B	C
1	EVELYN WYER LIPSTICK FRANCHISE		
2	Year	Franchise cash flow	
3	0	-1,000	
4	1	1,500	
5			
6	Discount rate	4%	
7	NPV	442	<-- =B3+B4/(1+B6)
8	IRR	50%	<-- =IRR(B3:B4)

However, to decide if the 4% funding cost is really the appropriate discount rate, you have to consider the relative risks of the lipstick franchise and the bank savings account.

- If you are certain that you will earn $1,500 from the lipstick franchise, then 4% (the funding cost) is the appropriate discount rate.
- If, on the other hand, the $1,500 is uncertain and hence risky, then the 4% rate is *too low* a discount rate. In this case you have to decide whether the 50% IRR is large enough to compensate you for the riskiness of the investment.[2]

Example 3: If Taxes Are a Factor, Use the After-Tax Funding Cost

Your company needs a new computer. The alternatives are to buy the computer for $4,000 or lease it. A leasing company has offered you a lease that involves a payment of $1,500 now and $1,500 at the end of each of years 1–3. An alternative financing method is to borrow the money from the bank, which is charging 15%. Your company has a tax rate of 40%; if it buys the computer it can depreciate it over three years, giving an annual depreciation tax shield of ($4,000/3) * 40\% = \$533.33. If the company leases the computer instead of buying it, the $1,500 annual cost of leasing can be deducted from its taxable income. The annual *after-tax cost* of the lease payment is thus $(1 - 40\%) * \$1500 = \$900$.

Here's the solution we offered to this problem in Chapter 7:

	A	B	C	D	E	F	G
1				**LEASE VERSUS PURCHASE WITH TAXES**			
2	Asset cost	4,000.00					
3	Annual lease payment	1,500.00					
4	Bank rate	15%					
5	After-tax bank rate	9%	<-- =B4*(1-B6)	This is the depreciation tax shield			
6	Tax rate	40%		if you buy the computer.			
7							
8	Year	Purchase cash flows		Lease cash flows		The differential cash flows: Lease minus purchase	
9	0	-4,000.00		-900.00	<-- =-$B$3*(1-$B$6)	3,100.00	<-- =D9-B9
10	1	533.33	<-- =$B$2/3*$B$6	-900.00		-1,433.33	
11	2	533.33		-900.00		-1,433.33	
12	3	533.33		-900.00		-1,433.33	
13	NPV	-2,649.98		-3,178.17	<-- =D9+NPV(B5,D10:D12)	18.33%	<-- =IRR(F9:F12)
14							
15	Explanation: The lease is like a loan--an inflow of $3,100.00 in year 0, and an after-tax outflow of $1,433.33 in year 1, $1,433.33 in year 2, and $1,433.33 in year 3. The IRR of these cash flows is 18.33%. Thus the lease is more expensive than borrowing the money from the bank, since the after-tax cost of a bank loan is 9.00%.						

Leasing instead of purchasing the asset saves you $3,100 in year 0 but costs you an additional $1,433.33 in years 1–3. The IRR of the differential cash flows (column F) is 18.33%.

Choosing a Discount Rate: In this case we can still use the alternative funding cost as the discount rate. However, we have to take into account the fact that the interest on the bank loan is an expense for tax purposes. Assuming that the riskiness of the lease and purchase cash flows is similar to the riskiness of a bank loan, the appropriate discount rate is the after-tax bank discount rate: $(1 - 40\%) * 15\% = 9\%$.

It now follows that we should purchase the asset instead of leasing it, since the IRR of the lease minus purchase cash flows is higher than the after-tax cost of a bank loan. Another way to see this is to compare the cash flows of a $3,100 bank loan to the cash flows saved by purchasing.

---

[2]At this point in the book, we use only an intuitive concept of risk. In Chapters 11–16 we define risk more formally and show how the discount rate and risk are related.

As you can see below, the bank loan costs substantially less in each of years 1–3 than the lease minus purchase cash flows:

	A	B	C	D
17	**What if you borrowed $3,100 from the bank?**			
18	Year	After-tax money saved by leasing	Same amount from bank	
19	0	3,100.00	3,100.00	
20	1	-1,433.33	-1,224.67	<-- =PMT(B5,3,C19)
21	2	-1,433.33	-1,224.67	
22	3	-1,433.33	-1,224.67	
23				
24	IRR	18.33%	9.00%	<-- =IRR(C19:C22)

Funding Cost as a Discount Rate—Summing up

The leasing example illustrates the use of the *funding cost* as a way to find the discount rate: Since your alternative financing for the computer is a bank loan (rather than the lease), we've used the cost of the bank loan as a discount rate.

You have to be careful in applying this method: The funding cost is only an appropriate discount rate if the cash flows being funded have the same riskiness as the source of the funding.

• If you use a bank loan to finance a set of *almost certain* cash flows, then the bank loan rate can be the discount rate. You *know* that you'll repay the loan, and you're convinced that the cash flows being financed will occur with certainty. This is the case for the lease discussed in this section.

• For corporations, the cost of bank loans is an expense for tax purposes; in this case the *after-tax funding cost* should be used as a discount rate.

• If you use a bank loan to finance the purchase of a race horse, then the riskiness of the cash flows is much greater than the loan cash flows (you're almost certain to repay the loan, but you're much less certain about the cash flows from the race horse).

9.2 The Weighted Average Cost of Capital as the Firm's Funding Cost

In the previous section we illustrated why the funding cost—the cost of raising the money for a given project—is often a good choice for the discount rate. The funding cost is a good choice for a project's discount rate when it is commensurate with the project's risk.

The funding cost for a company is often called the company's *weighted average cost of capital* (WACC). Companies raise funds in two primary ways: by raising funds from their shareholders or by raising funds from their bondholders. The WACC is determined by averaging the funding costs of these two methods.

• A company can raise funds from its shareholders either by selling additional shares on the stock market or by using earnings to finance new projects instead of paying shareholders dividends. The *funding cost* of a company's raising money from its shareholders is called the *cost of equity.* Symbolized by r_E, the cost of equity is the rate of return demanded by a company's shareholders. In Section 9.3 we show you how to compute r_E.

- A company can raise funds either by borrowing from banks or by selling bonds. The funding cost of borrowing, symbolized by r_D, is called the *cost of debt* and is the interest rate charged by lenders, be they banks or the purchasers of a company's bonds. A company's borrowing is an expense for tax purposes; denoting the corporate tax rate by T_C, the *after-tax cost of borrowing* is $(1 - T_C) * r_D$.

The *weighted average cost of capital* (WACC) is the *average funding cost of a company's equity and debt*. Another way of putting this is that the WACC is the *average return shareholders and debtholders expect to receive from the company*.[3] The definition of the WACC is

$$WACC = r_E * \underbrace{\frac{E}{E+D}}_{\substack{\text{The percentage}\\\text{of equity used to}\\\text{finance the firm}}} + r_D(1 - T_C) * \underbrace{\frac{D}{E+D}}_{\substack{\text{The percentage}\\\text{of debt used to}\\\text{finance the firm}}}$$

where

r_E = *the firm's cost of equity—the return required by the firm's shareholders*

r_D = *the firm's cost of debt—the return required by the firm's debtholders*

E = *market value of the firm's equity*

D = *market value of the firm's debt*

T_C = *the firm's tax rate*

Here's a simple example to show what we mean: United Transport, Inc. has 3 million shares outstanding; the current market price per share is $10. The company thinks its shareholders want an annual return on their investment of 20%; this 20% return is the company's cost of equity r_E.[4] The company has also borrowed $10 million from its banks at a rate of 8%; this is the company's cost of debt r_D. United Transport has a tax rate of $T_C = 40\%$.[5] To compute United Transport's WACC we use the formula

$$WACC = r_E * \frac{E}{E+D} + r_D(1 - T_C) * \frac{D}{E+D}$$

$$= 20\% * \frac{30}{30+10} + 8\% * (1 - 40\%) * \frac{10}{30+10} = 16.20\%$$

where

$r_E = 20\%$

$r_D = 8\%$

$E = 3{,}000{,}000$ shares each worth $10 = \$30{,}000{,}000$

$D = \$10{,}000{,}000$

$T_C = 40\%$

---

[3]In finance the *expected return*, the *required return*, the *cost of capital* (be it *cost of equity* or *cost of debt*), and the *required rate of return* are all synonyms. They all represent the market-adjusted rate that investors get (or demand) on various investments or securities.

[4]How did United Transport come to the conclusion that its shareholders want a 20% return? This is *the* question in the computation of the WACC, and we will spend a lot of this chapter discussing the answer. So be patient!

[5]We use the symbol T_C to indicate the *corporate* tax rate.

In a spreadsheet:

	A	B	C
1		**UNITED TRANSPORT--WACC**	
2	Number of shares	3,000,000	
3	Market price per share	10	
4			
5	E, market value of equity	30,000,000	<-- =B3*B2
6	D, market value of debt	10,000,000	
7			
8	r_E, cost of equity	20%	
9	r_D, cost of debt	8%	
10	T_C, firm's tax rate	40%	
11			
12	WACC, weighted average cost of capital: WACC=r_E*E/(E+D)+r_D*(1-TC)*D/(E+D)	16.20%	<-- =B8*B5/(B5+B6)+B9*(1-B10)*B6/(B5+B6)

The United Transport WACC computation shows you that the WACC depends on five critical variables.

- r_E, the cost of equity. r_E is the return required by the firm's shareholders. Of the five parameters in the WACC calculation, r_E is the most difficult to calculate. A model for calculating r_E is given in Section 9.3.

- E, the market value of a firm's equity. We will usually take E to equal the number of shares of the firm times the market price per share.

- r_D, the cost of debt. r_D is the cost of borrowing for the firm. In most cases we will take r_D to be the firm's marginal interest rate—the interest rate at which the firm could borrow additional funds either from its banks or by selling bonds. Alternatively, we will sometimes take r_D to be the company's average borrowing rate on its current debt. A detailed example of the calculation of r_D for an actual firm is given in Section 9.5.

- D, the market value of the firm's debt. In most cases we will take D to be the total value of the firm's financial obligations. An actual example of a calculation for D is given in Section 9.5.

- T_C, the firm's tax rate. Most often we calculate T_C by computing the average tax rate of the firm; see Section 9.5 for an example.

The Weighted Average Cost of Capital

The weighted average cost of capital (WACC) is the average rate of return the firm has to pay its shareholders and its lenders. The WACC is the funding cost for a company's projects, and it is widely used as the appropriate risk-adjusted discount rate for a company's investment cash flows. Two of the three examples that follow illustrate the use of the WACC in evaluating investments. The third example shows when the WACC is not an appropriate discount rate for a corporate investment.

- White Water Rafting Corporation is considering buying a new type of raft. The raft is more expensive than the existing rafts operated by the company because it is self-sealing—holes in the raft are automatically and permanently fixed by a new technology. During the rafting season, White Water's existing rafts spend a considerable amount of downtime having their punctures fixed, and the company anticipates that the new self-sealing rafts will improve its profitability by increasing efficiency and decreasing costs. By being the first rafting company on the river to have the self-sealing rafts, White Water hopes to attract business away from other rafting companies—customers naturally hate to have their trips interrupted by "flat rafts" (the rafting equivalent of a "flat tire"), and when they hear of White Water's new rafts, they will prefer White Water over its competitors.

The White Water financial analyst has derived the set of anticipated cash flows for the new raft. To complete the NPV analysis, the company needs to decide on an appropriate discount rate. Here's where the WACC comes in: Since the riskiness of the cash flows from the new rafts is similar to the riskiness of White Water Rafting's existing cash flows, the WACC is an appropriate discount rate.

- Gorgeous Fountain Water Company (GF) sells bottled water from the Gorgeous Fountain natural spring. The company is considering buying Dazzling Cascade Water Company. Dazzling Cascade (DC) operates in a neighboring area to that dominated by GF, and its operations, sales, and anticipated cash flows have been thoroughly analyzed by the Gorgeous Fountain financial analysis staff.

In order to value DC, GF has to decide on an appropriate discount rate for the anticipated DC cash flows. Here's where the weighted average cost of capital comes in. GF's WACC is the average rate of return demanded by its investors; assuming that the riskiness of DC's cash flows is similar to that of GF, the WACC is an appropriate discount rate for the GF cash flows. Discounting the DC cash flows at GF's WACC allows Gorgeous Fountain to establish a bid price for Dazzling Cascade.

- We conclude with an example where the WACC is not an appropriate discount rate. Delicious Licorice (DL) is a candy company whose WACC is $WACC_{DL} = 22\%$. In order to diversify, Delicious Licorice is considering the purchase of Cheap Talk, a regional cell phone operator. The cash flows of the potential purchase have been carefully analyzed by the Delicious Licorice financial staff. They realize that the WACC of Delicious Licorice is not the appropriate rate for analyzing the purchase of Cheap Talk—the risks included in the DL weighted average cost of capital are entirely different from the risks of the Cheap Talk cash flows. In order to use the WACC as a discount rate, it must be appropriate to the riskiness of the cash flows being evaluated.

Some Important Terminology Before We Start

When we talk about "firms" in this book we generally mean corporations, companies that have shareholders and debtholders.[6] Recall from Chapter 2 that a typical firm is *incorporated*, which means that it is a legal entity separate from its shareholders and debtholders. The income of a corporation is taxed at the corporate income tax rate.

The shareholders own stock in the firm. When the firm is profitable, management may decide to pay dividends to the shareholders, but these dividend payments are not guaranteed. Shareholders can also sell their shares and in doing so may make a profit (called a "capital gain") or experience a loss. As you can see, the cash flows of a shareholder in a firm are uncertain. The shareholders in the firm have *limited liability;* they are not responsible for repaying the debtholders if the firm cannot do so out of its cash flows.

The *cost of equity*, denoted r_E, is the discount rate applied by shareholders to their expected future cash flows from the firm. It goes without saying that this cost of equity depends on the

---

[6]Equivalent terminology for shareholders is stockholders, equity owners; equivalent terminology for debtholders is lenders, bondholders.

riskiness of the shareholder cash flows. The higher the riskiness of the shareholder's expected future cash flows, the higher the cost of equity r_E.

The firm's *debtholders* are its lenders. Debtholders are promised a fixed return (interest) on their lending to the firm. The debtholders may be banks, who have lent money to the firm, or they may be individuals or pension funds who have bought the firm's bonds. The interest payments to the firm's debtholders are expenses for tax purposes. The interest payments on the firm's debt and the firm's tax rate determine the *after-tax cost of debt* for the firm, which we denote $r_D(1 - T)$.

9.3 The Gordon Dividend Model: Discounting Anticipated Dividends to Derive the Firm's Cost of Equity r_E

In this section we present a formula for computing the firm's cost of equity r_E. This formula is called the *Gordon dividend model*, in honor of Myron Gordon who first set out the model in 1959.[7] This section has two subsections:

- In the first subsection, we derive a model for calculating the value of a firm's shares based on their future anticipated dividends.

- In the second subsection, we use the share valuation model of the first section to derive the cost of equity r_E.

Valuing the Firm's Shares as the Present Value of the Future Anticipated Dividends

We start by computing the fair market value of a stock that pays a growing dividend stream. Here is an example that presents most of the logic of our model: It is March 2, 2000, and you are thinking of purchasing a share of XYZ Corporation. Here are some facts about the company and its stock:

- XYZ is a steady payer of dividends; in the past it has paid dividends annually, and these dividends have tended to grow at an annual rate of 7%.

- The company just paid a dividend of $10 per share. This dividend was paid on March 1, the company's traditional dividend payment date.

You want to value XYZ shares by discounting the stream of future anticipated dividends. In predicting the future dividends of XYZ Corp., you assume that the dividends will grow at a rate of 7% per year. Then the future anticipated dividends per share are

$$
\begin{aligned}
dividend\ today = Div_0 &= \$10.00 \\
dividend\ next\ year = Div_1 &= Div_0(1 + g) = \$10 * (1 + 7\%) = \$10.70 \\
Div_2 &= Div_1(1 + g) = Div_0(1 + g)^2 = \$10 * (1 + 7\%)^2 = \$11.45 \\
Div_3 &= Div_2(1 + g) = Div_0(1 + g)^3 = \$10 * (1 + 7\%)^3 = \$12.25 \\
&\ \ \vdots \qquad\qquad \vdots \\
Div_t &= Div_0(1 + g)^t
\end{aligned}
$$

---

[7]The model is sometimes simply called the Gordon model; others call it the dividend discount model.

The three dots $\cdots$ indicate that you think the dividend stream is *very long* (when we write down the actual model, we will assume that the dividend stream goes on forever).

Suppose you think that the appropriate discount rate for the dividend stream is XYZ's cost of equity $r_E = 15\%$. Using r_E to discount the future anticipated dividends, you get the fair value of the XYZ Corp. stock today (we will denote this by P_0):

$$\text{fair share value today, } P_0 = \frac{Div_1}{(1 + r_E)} + \frac{Div_2}{(1 + r_E)^2} + \frac{Div_3}{(1 + r_E)^3} + \cdots$$

$$= \frac{Div_0(1 + g)}{(1 + r_E)} + \frac{Div_0(1 + g)^2}{(1 + r_E)^2} + \frac{Div_0(1 + g)^3}{(1 + r_E)^3} + \cdots$$

$$= \frac{Div_0(1 + g)}{r_E - g}$$

The last line of the above formula uses a formula for the present value of a constant-growth annuity developed in Chapter 5 (pp. 126–127): The present value of the cash flows $Div_0(1 + g)$, $Div_0(1 + g)^2$, $Div_0(1 + g)^3$, ... at the discount rate r_E is

$$P_0 = \sum_{t=1}^{\infty} \frac{Div_0(1 + g)^t}{(1 + r_E)^t} = \frac{Div_0(1 + g)}{r_E - g}, \quad \text{when}[8] \ |g| < |r_E|$$

Applying the valuation model to XYZ stock gives

$$\text{fair share value today, } P_0 = \frac{10(1.07)}{(1.15)} + \frac{10(1.07)^2}{(1.15)^2} + \frac{10(1.07)^3}{(1.15)^3} + \cdots$$

$$\text{This is } Div_0(1+g)$$
$$\downarrow$$
$$= \frac{\overbrace{10(1.07)}}{\underbrace{0.15 - 0.07}} = 133.75$$
$$\uparrow$$
$$\text{This is } r_E - g$$

Here's a spreadsheet implementation of the Gordon dividend model:

	A	B	C
1	**VALUING XYZ CORP. SHARES**		
2	Current dividend, D_0	10	
3	Dividend growth rate, g	7%	
4	Cost of equity, r_E	15%	
5	Share value	133.75	<-- =B2*(1+B3)/(B4-B3)

Using the Gordon Dividend Model to Calculate the Cost of Equity r_E

In the previous subsection we derived the value of a share P_0 based on the current dividend per share Div_0, the anticipated growth rate of dividends g, and the cost of equity r_E. In this section we turn this formula around: We derive the cost of equity r_E based on the current value of a share P_0, the current dividend per share Div_0, and the anticipated growth rate of dividends g.

---

[8]The condition $|g| < |r_E|$ means that the absolute value of g is less than the absolute value of r_E. If a firm's dividends have positive growth, then this is the same as assuming that $0 < g < r_E$.

According to the Gordon dividend model of the previous subsection, the stock price is given by $P_0 = [Div_0(1+g)]/(r_E - g)$. Turning this formula around to solve for the cost of equity r_E gives

$$r_E = \frac{Div_0(1+g)}{P_0} + g$$

This is the *Gordon dividend model cost of equity formula*. In the Gordon dividend model the cost of equity r_E—the discount rate to be applied to equity cash flows—is the sum of two terms:

- $[Div_0(1+g)]/P_0$. This is the *anticipated dividend yield* of the stock. Suppose you buy the stock today, paying P_0. Then you anticipate getting a next-period dividend of $Div_0(1+g)$, where g is the anticipated future growth rate of dividends. The term $[Div_0(1+g)]/P_0$ is the anticipated next period dividend return.
- g. This is the *anticipated growth rate of all future dividends paid on the stock.*

Applying the Gordon Dividend Model Cost of Equity Formula—A Simple Example

Consider a firm for which the current share price is $P_0 = \$25.00$ and which has just paid a per-share dividend of $Div_0 = \$3.00$. Shareholders of the firm believe that dividends will grow at a rate $g = 8\%$ per year. In this case the Gordon model cost of equity is $r_E = 20.96\%$:

	A	B	C
1	**USING THE GORDON MODEL TO COMPUTE THE COST OF EQUITY r_E**		
2	Current dividend, Div_0	3.00	
3	Current share price, P_0	25.00	
4	Anticipated dividend growth rate, g	8%	
5	Gordon model cost of equity, r_E	20.96%	<-- =B2*(1+B4)/B3+B4

Notice that the Gordon model's cost of equity r_E is very sensitive to the parameter values. If, for example, the dividend growth rate in the above example is 5%, then $r_E = 17.60\%$:

	A	B	C
1	**USING THE GORDON MODEL TO COMPUTE THE COST OF EQUITY r_E**		
2	Current dividend, Div_0	3.00	
3	Current share price, P_0	25.00	
4	Anticipated dividend growth rate, g	5%	
5	Gordon model cost of equity, r_E	17.60%	<-- =B2*(1+B4)/B3+B4

9.4 Applying the Gordon Cost of Equity Formula: Courier Corporation

Courier Corporation (stock symbol CRRC) is a book manufacturer that has experienced rapid growth of sales and profits. Courier's financial year ends September 30. We use the Gordon dividend model to calculate Courier's cost of equity at the end of September 2002.

Here's a spreadsheet that gives the relevant data and the calculations:

	A	B	C
1	\multicolumn{3}{c} **COURIER CORPORATION (CRRC)** **Calculation of cost of equity using Gordon model**	
2	**Year ended 30 Sept**	**Dividend per share**	
3	1998	0.2533	
4	1999	0.2667	
5	2000	0.3200	
6	2001	0.3700	
7	2002	0.4000	
8			
9	g, growth rate of dividends	12.10%	<-- =(B7/B3)^(1/4)-1
10	Div_0, current dividend	0.40	<-- =B7
11	Div_0*(1+g), dividend anticipated in 2003	0.45	<-- =B10*(1+B9)
12	P_0, stock price, 30 Sept. 2002	37.99	
13			
14	r_E, Gordon dividend model cost of equity	13.28%	<-- =B11/B12+B9

In order to use the Gordon model to calculate the cost of equity in cell B14, we need the following assumptions:

- **The price of the share, P_0, is known.** In this case P_0 is the stock price on the date of the calculation (30 September 2002). On this date $P_0 = \$37.99$.
- **The current dividend per share, Div_0, is known.** By "current dividend" we mean the last dividend paid by the firm, which in this case is the year 2002 Courier dividend $Div_0 = \$0.40$ per share.
- **The average growth rate of the dividends, g, can be derived.** We derive this below from the dividend series in cells B3 to B8. Our assumption is that

$$Div_{1998} = 0.2533$$
$$Div_{1999} = Div_{1998}(1 + g)$$
$$Div_{2000} = Div_{1999}(1 + g)^2$$
$$Div_{2001} = Div_{2000}(1 + g)^3$$
$$Div_{2002} = Div_{2001}(1 + g)^4 = 0.4000$$

This means that

$$g = \sqrt[4]{\frac{Div_{2002}}{Div_{1998}}} - 1 = \sqrt[4]{\frac{0.4000}{0.2533}} - 1 = 12.10\%$$

Given these assumptions, the cost of equity, r_E, for Courier is given by

$$r_E = \frac{Div_0(1 + g)}{P_0} + g = \frac{0.40 * (1 + 12.10\%)}{37.99} + 12.10\% = 13.28\%$$

This is the calculation performed in cell B14.

Alternative Calculations of the Growth Rate

The implementation of the Gordon model illustrated above uses the geometric growth rate $g = \sqrt[4]{D_{2002}/D_{1998}} - 1$ to calculate the g in the Gordon model. Here are two alternative ways to compute the growth rate g:

- *Alternative 1: Use a different time period.* In the example above, we've assumed that the future expected growth rate of dividends is predicted by the dividends between 1998 and 2002. However, we could—after some thought—decide that the dividends are better predicted by the period 1997–2002. In this case the dividend growth rate is

$$g = \sqrt[5]{\frac{Div_{2002}}{Div_{1997}}} - 1 = \sqrt[5]{\frac{0.40}{0.21}} - 1 = 13.75\%$$

This changes the cost of equity. Since anticipated dividend growth g is higher with this alternative than before, the cost of equity,

$$r_E = \frac{Div_0(1 + g)}{P_0} + g$$

will be higher as shown below:

	A	B	C
	COURIER CORPORATION (CRRC)		
1	**Alternative 1: Using a different base year**		
2	**Year ended 30 Sept**	**Dividend per share**	
3	1997	0.2100	
4	1998	0.2533	
5	1999	0.2667	
6	2000	0.3200	
7	2001	0.3700	
8	2002	0.4000	
9			
10	g, growth rate of dividends	13.75%	<-- =(B8/B3)^(1/5)-1
11	Div$_0$, current dividend	0.40	<-- =B8
12	Div$_0$*(1+g), dividend anticipated in 2001	0.46	<-- =B11*(1+B10)
13	P$_0$, stock price, 30 Sept. 2000	37.99	
14			
15	r$_E$, Gordon dividend model cost of equity	14.95%	<-- =B12/B13+B10

- *Alternative 2: Ignore historical dividends altogether.* You might decide that the past history of Courier dividends is not indicative of its future dividend payouts. In this case, you might want to use a different number altogether for the anticipated dividend growth rate g. In the example below you've decided that the growth rate for Courier's future dividends is 15%. This gives a cost of equity of 16.21%.

	A	B	C
1	**COURIER CORPORATION (CRRC)** **Alternative 2: Making up a future growth rate of dividends**		
2	g, growth rate of dividends	15.00%	
3	Div_0, current dividend	0.40	
4	$Div_0*(1+g)$, dividend anticipated in 2001	0.46	<-- =B3*(1+B2)
5	P_0, stock price, 30 Sept. 2000	37.99	
6			
7	r_E, Gordon dividend model cost of equity	16.21%	<-- =B4/B5+B2

A Final Alternative to Computing the Cost of Equity r_E: Using the Total Equity Payout Instead of Per-Share Data

In some of the years 1998–2002, Courier purchased stock from its shareholders in open-market repurchase transactions. In many ways a share repurchase is like a dividend—both dividends and repurchases represent money paid by the firm to its shareholders. The Excel spreadsheet below computes the total dividends plus share repurchases in each of the years 1998–2002 and uses this "total equity payout" to compute the Gordon dividend model cost of equity r_E:

	A	B	C	D	E	F	G
1	**COURIER CORPORATION (CRRC)** **Computing the total equity payout**						
2	Year ended 30 Sept	Dividend per share	Total dividends	Share repurchases	Total equity payout: Dividends + repurchases	Annual growth of total dividend payout	
3	1998	0.2533	1,205,000	0	1,205,000		
4	1999	0.2667	1,354,000	455,000	1,809,000	50.12%	<-- =E4/E3-1
5	2000	0.3200	1,572,000	114,000	1,686,000	-6.80%	<-- =E5/E4-1
6	2001	0.3700	1,824,000	0	1,824,000	8.19%	<-- =E6/E5-1
7	2002	0.4000	2,086,000	0	2,086,000	14.36%	<-- =E7/E6-1
8							
9	Stock price, 30 Sept. 2002	37.99					
10	Number of shares, 30 Sept. 2002	5,215,000					
11	Market value of equity, 30 Sept. 2002	198,117,850	<-- =B10*B9				
12							
13	2002 total dividend	2,086,000	<-- =E7				
14	Anticipated dividend growth rate	11.27%	<-- =AVERAGE(F6:F7)				
15							
16	Gordon model cost of equity, r_E	12.45%	<-- =B13*(1+B14)/B11+B14				

The data in column C are for the total dividend paid out by Courier (*total dividend = dividend per share * number of shares*); in column D we see the amount of cash paid out to shareholders for the repurchase of their shares. Column E gives the *total equity payout:* the sum of the dividends + repurchases. In column F we compute the year-on-year growth rates of total equity payouts. As you can see, these are quite variable, especially when compared to the relatively smooth growth of the cash dividends (columns B and C). In cell B14, we've decided to use the average of the last two years of total cash payout growth rates as our prediction of the future growth rate g. This gives us a cost of equity r_E of 12.45% (cell B16):

Gordon dividend model for cost of equity using all payouts
to equity holders

$$
r_E = \frac{\left(\begin{array}{c} \text{total current} \\ \text{equity payout} = \\ \text{total dividends} + \\ \text{repurchases of stock} \end{array}\right)\left(1 + \underbrace{g}_{\substack{\uparrow \\ \text{The anticipated} \\ \text{growth rate} \\ \text{of total equity} \\ \text{payouts}}}\right)}{\text{total equity value today}} + g
$$

$$
= \frac{2,086,000 * (1 + 11.27\%)}{198,117,850} + 11.27\% = 12.45\%
$$

Although there is some controversy attached to the use of total equity payouts to compute the cost of equity r_E, we think it is the correct method. In the examples for Courier Corporation which follow, we will assume that the r_E for Courier is 12.45%.

WHY DO FIRMS REPURCHASE STOCK?

In recent years share buybacks have exceeded dividends as a form of distribution to shareholders. Firms repurchase stock instead of paying extra dividends for several reasons:

- Repurchases are used to "soak up" extra cash and keep dividend growth predictable. Most dividend-paying firms think their shareholders want to see a steady pattern of dividend growth. So if they have extra cash, they'll use it to buy back shares instead of increasing the dividend paid to shareholders.

- Repurchases help reduce shareholder taxes on cash paid out to shareholders. When a dividend is paid, all the shareholders receiving the dividend pay taxes on it at their ordinary income tax rate. Stock repurchases are voluntary (you don't have to sell your stock back to the company). If you let your stock be repurchased, the gain in most cases is taxed at your capital gains tax rate (lower than the ordinary income tax rate).

- Stock repurchases benefit both the shareholder who is bought out and the shareholder who does not let his/her shares be repurchased. Why? When some of the shares of the firm are repurchased, those shareholders who "stay in" the firm will get a larger share of its income and dividend payments in the future. So all parties gain.

9.5 Calculating the WACC for Courier

So far we've calculated Courier's cost of equity as $r_E = 12.45\%$. This is the return demanded by the company's shareholders, taking into account their expectations of cash dividend growth and stock repurchases. Now we want to calculate Courier's weighted average cost of capital:

$$WACC = r_E \frac{E}{E + D} + r_D(1 - T_C)\frac{D}{E + D}$$

Before we can do this, however, we need to compute the values of the following variables:

- E, the market value of Courier's equity. As you can see from the previous spreadsheet, on 30 September 2002, Courier had 5,215,000 shares worth \$37.99 per share. This gives $E = 5,215,000 * \$37.99 = \$198,117,850$.

- D, the value of Courier's debt. On 30 September 2002, Courier had debt of \$752,000. This information comes from the company's annual report (see Figure 9.3). Courier's **debt** includes both the *current portion of long-term debt* and the *long-term debt* itself.[9] Note that Courier's debt has declined significantly from the previous year: 2001 debt for the company was \$16,577,000.

- r_D, the cost of Courier's borrowing. In theory r_D ought to be the marginal cost of debt—the borrowing rate of the company for additional debt. However, this rate is usually difficult to derive. A plausible alternative is to use information about the current borrowing rate of the company. In Figure 9.3 you can see what the company reports about its debt, and from Courier's profit and loss statement (Figure 9.4) you can learn about its interest paid. We use

	September 28, 2002	September 29, 2001
Liabilities and Stockholders' Equity		
Current liabilities:		
Current maturities of long-term debt	\$ 78,000	\$ 76,000
Accounts payable	6,708,000	11,933,000
Accrued payroll	7,642,000	6,652,000
Accrued taxes	6,965,000	6,092,000
Other current liabilities	6,362,000	6,789,000
Total current liabilities	27,755,000	31,542,000
Long-term debt	674,000	16,501,000
Deferred income taxes	4,658,000	2,801,000
Other liabilities	2,652,000	2,446,000
Total liabilities	35,739,000	53,290,000

Figure 9.3 Courier's liabilities from its balance sheet. The financial debt items are marked. The company repaid significant amounts of debt during the financial year.

---

[9]The calculation of the WACC actually calls for the *market value* of the firm's debt. However, this is a number that is very difficult to calculate; instead, it is standard practice to use the book value of the debt as illustrated.

For the Years Ended	September 28, 2002	September 29, 2001	September 30, 2000
Net sales	$202,184,000	$211,943,000	$192,226,000
Cost of sales	137,991,000	150,572,000	144,132,000
Gross profit	64,193,000	61,371,000	48,094,000
Selling and administrative expenses	39,602,000	39,258,000	31,406,000
Amortization of goodwill	—	1,410,000	596,000
Interest expense	480,000	1,899,000	325,000
Other income	—	(1,230,000)	(119,000)
Income before taxes	24,111,000	20,034,000	15,886,000
Provision for income taxes	7,936,000	6,817,000	5,249,000
Net income	$ 16,175,000	$ 13,217,000	$ 10,637,000

Figure 9.4 Courier's income statements, showing interest of $480,000 paid in 2002. Computing the interest paid on the average debt outstanding over the year (see Figure 9.3) gives $r_D = 480,000/[(752,000 + 16,577,000)/2] = 5.54\%$. By dividing the company's year 2002 taxes of $7,936,000 by its income before taxes, we arrive at a tax rate of $T_C = 7,936,000/24,111,000 = 32.91\%$.

the average borrowing rate of 5.54% (the rate applicable to most of the debt) as the company's cost of debt r_D.

	A	B	C	D
	COURIER CORPORATION (CRRC)			
1	Analysis of interest paid			
2	Year ending 30 September	2002	2001	
3	Total debt	752,000	16,577,000	
4	Interest paid	480,000		
5				
6	Average interest rate, r_D	5.54%	<-- =B4/AVERAGE(B3:C3)	

- T_C, Courier's tax rate. We can calculate Courier's tax rate from its provision for income taxes. Courier's provision for income taxes in 2002 was $T_C = 7,936,000/24,111,000 = 32.91\%$. We use this as an estimate for the firm's tax rate T_C.

	A	B	C	D
	COURIER CORPORATION (CRRC)			
1	Analysis of taxes paid			
2	Year ending 30 September	2002	2001	2000
3	Income before taxes	24,111,000	20,034,000	15,886,000
4	Provision for income taxes	7,936,000	6,817,000	5,249,000
5				
6	Average tax rate	32.91%	34.03%	33.04%

So What's Courier's WACC?

Here's our calculation for Courier's WACC:

	A	B	C
1	**COURIER CORPORATION (CRRC)** **Calculating the WACC, Sept. 2002**		
2	Cost of equity, r_E	12.45%	<-- Computed from total equity payouts
3	Cost of debt, r_D	5.54%	<-- From Courier Corp. financial statements
4			
5	Sept. 2002 equity value, E	198,117,850	<-- Number of shares times current share price
6	Sept. 2002 debt value, D	752,000	<-- From Courier Corp. financial statements
7	Total: Equity + Debt, E+D	198,869,850	<-- =SUM(B5:B6)
8			
9	Percentage of equity, E/(E+D)	99.62%	<-- =B5/B7
10	Percentage of debt, D/(E+D)	0.38%	<-- =B6/B7
11			
12	Tax rate, T_C	32.91%	<-- From Courier Corp. financial statements
13			
14	WACC	12.41%	<-- =B2*B9+B3*(1-B12)*B10

In the next section we use the WACC of 12.41% for Courier to value the company's equity.

9.6 Two Uses of the WACC

The weighted average cost of capital (WACC) is the weighted average rate of return required by a company's shareholders and debtholders. We presume that this rate of return reflects the average risk of shareholder and debtholder future cash flows. This is plausible, since we have derived the cost of equity r_E from anticipated future payouts to shareholders, and we have derived the cost of debt r_D from the rate demanded on the firm's debts by its lenders. Thus, the WACC represents a weighted average of the riskiness of shareholder and debtholder cash flows.

When the riskiness of a stream of cash flows is similar to the riskiness of the cash flows received by shareholders and debtholders, the WACC is the appropriate risk-adjusted discount rate. There are two important cases where this is often true:

- In capital budgeting situations. When a company is considering investing in a project whose risk is comparable to the riskiness of the company as a whole, the WACC is an appropriate discount rate for the project's cash flows. We previously illustrated this use of the WACC in the White Water Rafting example of Section 9.2.
- To value the company as a whole. Below we define the concept of *free cash flow* (FCF). The value of Courier is the discounted value of its future anticipated FCFs, where the WACC is the discount rate. The Gorgeous Fountain Water Company example of Section 9.2 gave a preliminary discussion of this use of the WACC.

In this section we illustrate both these uses of the WACC for Courier.

Using the WACC as a Discount Rate for Projects

The WACC of Courier Corporation is 12.41%—this is the weighted average return demanded by the firm's shareholders and bondholders. Recall that Courier is in the book printing business.

Suppose the company is thinking of investing in a project whose riskiness is like the riskiness of its current business. This could be something as simple as another printing press to print more books or a warehouse to house them, but it could also be something much more complicated—like the acquisition of another printing company.

In all these cases, the WACC is the natural starting point as a discount rate. What we mean by "starting point" is that—in discounting the cash flows of the project—Courier should assume as initial discount rate of 12.41% and then "tweak" the discount rate a bit to adjust for perceived risks.

Let's say that the company is considering buying a machine that will allow it to print more books. The cash flows, NPV, and IRR of the machine are given below. If the riskiness of the machine's cash flows is similar to the riskiness of Courier's overall cash flows, then the WACC is a reasonable discount rate. The analysis below shows that Courier should not undertake the investment—the investment's NPV is negative (−$11,777) and its IRR (7.80%) is less than the WACC of 12.41%:

	A	B	C
1	**COURIER CORPORATION (CRRC)** **Using the WACC as a discount rate**		
2	WACC	12.41%	
3			
4	**Year**	**Cash flows**	
5	0	-100,000	
6	1	15,000	
7	2	22,000	
8	3	33,000	
9	4	44,000	
10	5	12,000	
11			
12	NPV	-11,777	<-- =NPV(B2,B6:B10)+B5
13	IRR	7.80%	<-- =IRR(B5:B10)
14			
15	**Extreme case: Cash flows are riskless**		
16	Cost of debt	5.54%	
17	Courier tax rate	32.91%	
18	After-tax cost of debt	3.72%	<-- =(1-B17)*B16

Of course, there's always room for adjustment, since some of the assumptions we made may not be as accurate as we thought. Suppose, for example, that the machine's cash flows are perceived to be much less risky than the overall cash flows of Courier. As an extreme case we might consider the case where the machine cash flows are only as risky as Courier's debt. Since the company's after-tax cost of debt is $5.54\% * (1 - 32.91\%) = 3.72\%$, this would then be an appropriate discount rate for the project and the company should accept it (since the IRR of 7.80% is higher than 3.72%).

Valuing Courier Corporation Using Its WACC and Predicted Free Cash Flows (FCFs)

In the previous subsection we used the weighted average cost of capital (WACC) to value a typical project of the firm. The second major use of the WACC is to value companies. A complete explanation of this use of the WACC will have to wait until Chapter 10, where we explain the use of free cash flow (FCF) in detail. For our purposes in this chapter, the **free cash flow** (FCF) is the amount of cash generated by the company's business activities, by its operations as opposed to its financing activities. The FCF is "free" in the sense that it can be used to provide cash to the firm's shareholders and debtholders in the form of dividends and share repurchases (payments to shareholders) and interest payments (to debtholders).

To accurately define the FCF, you need some knowledge of accounting. If the following table gives you problems, you should read the accounting refresher in Chapter 3.

Here's the definition of the FCF:

Defining the Free Cash Flow (FCF)

Profit after taxes	This is the basic measure of the profitability of the business, but it is an accounting measure that includes financing flows (such as interest), as well as noncash expenses such as depreciation. Profit after taxes does not account for either changes in the firm's working capital or purchases of new fixed assets, both of which can be important cash drains on the firm. The FCF definition takes changes in working capital and purchases of new fixed assets into account separately.
+ Depreciation	This noncash expense is added back to the profit after tax.

The sum of the next two items is the *change in net working capital*, often denoted by ΔNWC

− Increase in current assets related to the firm's operations	When the firm's sales increase, more investment is needed in inventories, accounts receivable, and so on. This increase in current assets is not an expense for tax purposes (and is therefore ignored in the profit after taxes), but it is a cash drain on the company. For purposes of calculating the FCF, the increase in current assets does not include changes in cash and marketable securities.
+ Increase in current liabilities related to the firm's operations	An increase in the sales often causes an increase in financing related to sales (such as accounts payable or taxes payable). This increase in current liabilities—when related to sales—provides cash to the firm. The FCF includes all current liability items related to operations; it does not include financial items such as short-term borrowing, the current portion of long-term debt, and dividends payable.
− Capital expenditures (CAPEX)	An increase in fixed assets (the long-term productive assets of the company) is a use of cash, which reduces the firm's free cash flow.
+ After-tax interest payments (net)	FCF measures the cash produced by the business activity of the firm. The FCF should not include any items related to the firm's financing. In particular, we need to neutralize the effect of interest payments that appear in the firm's profit after taxes. We do this by: • Adding back the after-tax cost of interest on debt (*after-tax* since interest payments are taxdeductible) • Subtracting out the after-tax interest payments on cash and marketable securities

FCF = sum of the above

In 2002 Courier Corporation had a free cash flow (FCF) of $22,519,493. Cell B9 below shows how this number is derived by using the company's consolidated statement of cash flows:

	A	B	C
1	**COURIER CORPORATION** **Calculation of free cash flow for 2002**		
2	Profit after taxes	16,175,000	<-- =E11
3	Add back depreciation	10,687,000	<-- =B16
4	Changes in working capital		
5	Subtract increases in current assets	4,515,000	<-- =SUM(B17:B19)
6	Add increases in current liabilities	-2,411,000	<-- =B22+B21+B23
7	Subtract out capital expenditures	-6,739,000	<-- =B27+B28
8	Add back after-tax interest	292,493	<-- =(1-B50)*B44
9	**Free cash flow (FCF)**	**22,519,493**	<-- =SUM(B2:B8)
10			
11			
12	**CONSOLIDATED STATEMENT OF CASH FLOWS**	**2002**	
13	**Operating activities**		
14	Net income	16,175,000	
15	Adjustments to reconcile net income to cash provided from operating activities		
16	Depreciation and amortization	10,687,000	
17	Change in accounts receivable	2,914,000	
18	Change in inventory	728,000	
19	Change in accrued taxes	873,000	
20			
21	Change in accounts payable	-5,225,000	
22	Deferred income taxes	1,531,000	
23	Other changes in current liabilities	1,283,000	
24	Cash provided from operating activities	28,966,000	
25			
26	**Investment activities**		
27	Capital expenditures	-4,918,000	
28	Prepublication costs	-1,821,000	
29	Cash used for investment activities	-6,739,000	
30			
31	**Financing activities**		
32	Scheduled long-term debt repayments	-76,000	
33	Repayments of debt, net	-15,750,000	
34	Cash dividends	-2,058,000	
35	Stock repurchases	0	
36	Proceeds from stock plans	1,114,000	
37	Cash provided from financing activities	-16,770,000	
38			
39	Increase (decrease) in cash and equivalents	5,457,000	
40	Cash and equivalents at beginning of period	173,000	
41	Cash and equivalents at end of period	5,630,000	
42			
43	Supplemental information		
44	Interest paid	436,000	
45			
46	Income before taxes	24,111,000	
47	Provision for income taxes	7,936,000	
48	Net income	16,175,000	
49			
50	Tax rate =B47/B46	32.91%	

Using FCFs and WACC to Value Courier

In finance theory, the *enterprise value* of a company's debt and equity is the value of its free cash flows discounted at its weighted average cost of capital:

enterprise value = present value of future FCFs, discounted at WACC

The enterprise value represents the value today of the cash flows produced by the firm's future business activities. Suppose that you've performed a careful analysis of Courier Corporation and that you think the future growth of Courier's FCF is 4% per year. Since Courier's WACC is 12.41%, its enterprise value is

$$Courier\ enterprise\ value = PV(FCFs,\ discounted\ at\ WACC)$$

$$= \sum_{t=1}^{\infty} \frac{FCF_t}{(1 + WACC)^t}$$

$$= \sum_{t=1}^{\infty} \frac{FCF_{2002} * (1 + FCF\ growth\ rate)^t}{(1 + WACC)^t}$$

$$= \sum_{t=1}^{\infty} \frac{22{,}519{,}493 * (1 + 4\%)^t}{(1 + 12.41\%)^t}$$

$$= \frac{22{,}519{,}493 * (1 + 4\%)}{12.41\% - 4\%}$$

$$= 278{,}376{,}871$$

Notice that this valuation—like the Gordon dividend model of Section 9.3—makes use of the constant-growth annuity formula developed in Chapter 5:

$$\sum_{t=1}^{\infty} \frac{FCF_{2002} * (1 + FCF\ growth\ rate)^t}{(1 + WACC)^t} = \frac{FCF_{2002} * (1 + FCF\ growth\ rate)}{WACC - FCF\ growth\ rate}$$

To get from this enterprise valuation to a valuation of the company's shareholder equity, we have to make two additional adjustments:

- We add in the cash and marketable securities balances of $5,630,000 that Courier has on hand in 2002. The enterprise value measures the value today of Courier's future FCFs. The cash and marketable securities that the company has on hand today are not part of these future FCFs, but they belong to the company, so they must be added. In cell B8 of the next spreadsheet, you can see that adding in the cash balances gives an estimated asset value of $284,006,871.
- We subtract out the company's debt of $752,000 in 2002. In cell B10 below, you can see that subtracting out the debt value gives an estimated equity valuation of $283,254,871.

Here's our valuation with these two adjustments:

	A	B	C
1		**VALUING COURIER**	
2	Year 2002 FCF	22,519,493	
3	Anticipated FCF growth	4%	
4	WACC	12.41%	
5			
6	Enterprise value	278,376,871	<-- =B2*(1+B3)/(B4-B3)
7	Initial cash and marketable securities	5,630,000	From 2002 balance <-- sheet
8	Asset value	284,006,871	<-- =B6+B7
9	Debt value	752,000	
10	Equity value	283,254,871	<-- =B8-B9
11			
12	Number of shares	5,215,000	
13	Per-share valuation	54.32	<-- =B10/B12

Our per-share valuation of Courier is $54.32: Since there are 5,215,000 shares, each share is worth $283,254,871/5,125,000 = $54.32. This compares favorably with the current share price of Courier, $37.99, so this makes Courier (in the parlance of stock market analysts) a "buy" recommendation.

Valuing Courier Using Midyear Discounting

We introduced this topic in Chapter 8 (p. 207). The idea was that because most cash flows occur throughout the year, the appropriate discounting process should discount them as if they occur in midyear. In terms of the computation just done for Courier, instead of calculating

$$enterprise\ value = \frac{FCF_{2002}(1 + FCF\ growth)}{(1 + WACC)} + \frac{FCF_{2002}(1 + FCF\ growth)^2}{(1 + WACC)^2} + \cdots$$

$$= \frac{FCF_{2002}(1 + FCF growth)}{WACC - FCF\ growth}$$

we should be calculating

$$enterprise\ value_{midyear\ discounting} = \frac{FCF_{2002}(1 + FCF\ growth)}{(1 + WACC)^{0.5}} + \frac{FCF_{2002}(1 + FCF\ growth)^2}{(1 + WACC)^{1.5}} + \cdots$$

$$= \left(\frac{FCF_{2002}(1 + FCF\ growth)}{WACC - FCF\ growth} \right) * (1 + WACC)^{0.5}$$

As explained in Chapter 8 (p. 207), midyear discounting raises our valuation of cash flows, since the earlier a cash flow occurs, the more it is worth. If we implement midyear discounting for Courier, then our valuation of Courier's shares increases from $54.32 to $56.45:

	A	B	C
1	**VALUING COURIER** **Using midyear discounting**		
2	Year 2000 FCF	22,519,493	
3	Anticipated FCF growth	4%	
4	WACC	12.41%	
5			
6	Enterprise value	295,149,271	<-- =(1+B4)^0.5*B2*(1+B3)/(B4-B3)
7	Initial cash and marketable securities	5,630,000	From 2002 balance <-- sheet
8	Asset value	300,779,271	<-- =B6+B7
9	Debt value	752,000	
10	Equity value	294,397,271	<-- =B6-B9
11			
12	Number of shares	5,215,000	
13	Per-share valuation	56.45	<-- =B10/B12

One Further Note: Doing Some Sensitivity Analysis

No valuation is complete without doing some sensitivity analysis on the main parameters. For example, what happens to the per-share valuation if Courier's WACC is 15% instead of the 12.41% we have used? What happens to the per-share valuation if Courier's FCF growth rate is 5% instead of the 4% we used? With Excel this is easy:

	A	B	C
1	**VALUING COURIER** **Sensitivity analysis** **Still using midyear discounting**		
2	Year 2000 FCF	22,519,493	
3	Anticipated FCF growth	5%	<-- 5% instead of 4%
4	WACC	15.00%	<-- 15% instead of 12.41%
5			
6	Enterprise value	253,569,392	<-- =(1+B4)^0.5*B2*(1+B3)/(B4-B3)
7	Initial cash and marketable securities	5,630,000	From 2002 balance <-- sheet
8	Asset value	259,199,392	<-- =B6+B7
9	Debt value	752,000	
10	Equity value	252,817,392	<-- =B6-B9
11			
12	Number of shares	5,215,000	
13	Per-share valuation	48.48	<-- =B10/B12

A more extensive sensitivity analysis can be performed by using the **Data Table** feature of Excel explained in Chapter 30. In cells C19:H28 below you can see the valuation of Courier for various combinations of WACC and FCF growth. The highlighted cells are those combinations of WACC and FCF growth for which the per-share valuation exceeds the current market value of $37.99.

	A	B	C	D	E	F	G	H
1		**Courier Valuation--Sensitivity Analysis**						
2	Year 2000 FCF	22,519,493						
3	Anticipated FCF growth	5%						
4	WACC	15.00%						
5								
6	Enterprise value	253,569,392	<-- =(1+B4)^0.5*B2*(1+B3)/(B4-B3)					
7	Initial cash and marketable securities	5,630,000						
8	Asset value	259,199,392	<-- =B6+B7					
9	Debt value	752,000						
10	Equity value	252,817,392	<-- =B6-B9					
11								
12	Number of shares	5,215,000						
13	Per-share valuation	48.48	<-- =B10/B12					
14	Current share value	37.99						
15								
16	=IF(B4>B3,B13,"nmf")		**Data table: share value of Courier for various assumptions on WACC and FCF growth rates**					
17			FCF growth rate ↓					
18		48.48	**0%**	**2%**	**4%**	**6%**	**8%**	**10%**
19		6%	73.95	113.23	231.04	nmf	nmf	nmf
20	WACC -->	8%	55.95	76.15	116.53	237.70	nmf	nmf
21		10%	45.15	57.60	78.36	119.87	244.42	nmf
22		12%	37.94	46.47	59.27	80.59	123.24	251.20
23		14%	32.79	39.05	47.81	60.95	82.85	126.65
24		16%	28.92	33.74	40.16	49.15	62.64	85.12
25		18%	25.92	29.76	34.70	41.29	50.52	64.35
26		20%	23.51	26.66	30.60	35.67	42.43	51.89
27		22%	21.54	24.18	27.41	31.45	36.65	43.58
28		24%	19.89	22.15	24.86	28.17	32.31	37.64
29								
30			**Note**: The valuation formula in cell B6 is correct only when the WACC (cell B4) > growth rate (cell B3). Therefore we've put a formula into cell B18 which indicates that when B3 exceeds B4, the data table prints out "no meaningful figure" (nmf).					
31								
32			**Note**: The highlighted cells are combinations of WACC and FCF growth for which the Courier valuation exceeds the current share value of $37.99. We've used Excel's **Conditional Formatting** (see Chapter 33) to color these cells.					

CONCLUSION

In this chapter we have calculated the firm's weighted average cost of capital (WACC). The WACC is the risk-adjusted discount rate for the firm's free cash flows. It is often used to value projects whose riskiness is similar to the riskiness of the firm's existing activities, and it is also used to derive the value of the firm. Both of these uses have been illustrated in this chapter.

The WACC is defined as

$$WACC = r_E \frac{E}{E+D} + r_D(1-T_C)\frac{D}{E+D}$$

In the table below we summarize how we derived each of the elements of this formula:

Cost of equity, r_E	We used the Gordon model to determine the cost of equity: $$r_E = \frac{Div_0(1+g)}{P_0} + g$$ where Div_0 = total dividends + stock repurchases of the current year g = anticipated growth rate of dividends + repurchases P_0 = total equity value on current date
Cost of debt, r_D	In principle, this should be the firm's marginal borrowing rate, but this is often difficult to determine. For Courier, we used a number representative of the firm's cost of borrowing. An alternative is to use the firm's average borrowing cost over the previous year: $$r_D = \frac{interest\ paid\ in\ current\ year}{average\ debt,\ this\ year\ and\ last}$$
Market value of equity, E	(Current number of shares) $*$ (current market price per share)
Market value of debt, D	The market value of a firm's debt is difficult to calculate. We almost always substitute the *book value* of the firm's debt for this number. In the Courier example we showed how to determine this book value from the firm's balance sheets.
Firm's tax rate, T_C	T_C ought to be the firm's *marginal tax rate*. In practice we usually use either: (1) The firm's average tax rate, measured by $$average\ tax\ rate = \frac{taxes\ from\ Profit\ and\ Loss\ statement}{profit\ before\ taxes} = 33.04\%$$ (2) The firm's *statutory tax rates*. Courier's statutory federal tax rate is 34%. State taxes are another 2.98% of its income. Another estimate of its tax rates might thus be 36.98%.

A Final Warning

Cost-of-capital calculations are critical for valuations. Because cost-of-capital calculations involve a mixture of theory and judgment, they are quite often controversial. Almost every number in the WACC calculation above can be determined in several ways. In many cases, professionals do extensive sensitivity analysis on the WACC and the FCF growth to establish a *price range*—the range of valuations that appears to be reasonable, given the variation in plausible assumptions.

The most important modification you might want to make to the WACC calculation above involves the cost of equity, r_E. An important competing model to the Gordon model is the capital asset pricing model (CAPM). In Chapter 16 we will show you how to use this model to calculate the cost of equity.

EXERCISES

1. Compute the weighted average cost of capital (WACC) for a company having:

Market value of debt	$200,000
Market value of equity	$300,000
Cost of equity, r_E	13%
Cost of debt, r_D	7.5%
Tax rate, T_C	40%

2. Calculate the cost of equity r_E for a company having:

Market value of debt	$2,500,000
Market value of equity	$1,000,000
Cost of debt, r_D	5%
Tax rate, T_C	25%
Weighted average cost of capital, WACC	10%

3. Abbudy Corporation's stock price is currently $22.00 per share. The company has just paid a dividend of $0.55 per share, and shareholders anticipate that this dividend will grow in the future at a rate of 6% per year. Use the Gordon model to calculate the company's cost of equity r_E.

4. You wish to estimate the share price of Softy, your favorite underwear company. You know that tomorrow the company will pay its annual dividend of $1.50 per share, and you anticipate that the company's future dividends will grow at a rate of 4% per year. As an experienced investor, you demand a yield of 12% on your investment in the company. What should be the company's share price?

5. (a) XYZ Corp. has just paid a dividend of $5 per share. You think this dividend will grow at 8% per year. If you think the correct discount rate for the dividend stream of XYZ is 25%, how much should you be willing to pay for the stock?

   (b) Show in an Excel graph the share's price as a function of the XYZ dividend growth rate (let the growth rate be 0%, 2%, 4%, . . . , 20%).

6. You just bought a share of ABC Corp. for $28. The company has just paid a dividend of $2 per share, and you anticipate that this dividend will grow at a rate of 12% per year. What is your implied cost of equity for ABC?

7. Gradcom's anticipated next-year dividend is $1.20. Analysts anticipate that this dividend will grow at a 4% annual rate.

   (a) If the stock's current share price is $30, what is its cost of equity r_E according to the Gordon Model?

   (b) Show in an Excel graph the cost of equity as a function of the dividend growth rate (let the growth rate be 0%, 2%, 4%, . . . , 20%).

8. You are considering purchasing a stock of ABC Corp., which has just paid a $3 annual dividend per share. The company does not repurchase any of its shares. You anticipate that the company's dividends will grow at a rate of 20% per year for the next five years. After this time, you think that the growth of the annual dividends will slow to 5% per year. If your cost of equity for ABC is 10%, what price should you be prepared to pay for the stock?

9. Assume that Gradcom Company (from Exercise 7) has changed its dividend growth forecasts, and now assume that the growth in the first year will be 6%, 4% in the second and third year, and 3% from year 4 onward. If Gradcom's the cost of equity is 10%, what will be it's share price?

10. Consider the following data regarding Cinema Company.

	A	B	C	D	E	F
1			**Cinema Company**			
2	Year	Dividend per share	Total dividends	Number of share repurchases	Payments from share repurchases	Total
3	1995	0.25	???	0	0	???
4	1996	0.25	???	115,000	140,000	???
5	1997	0.3	???	0	0	???
6	1998	0.31	???	200,000	260,000	???
7	1999	0.35	???	120,000	180,000	???
8	2000	0.37	???	0	0	???
9	2001	0.39	???	0	0	???
10	2002	0.42	???	120,000	220,000	???
11						
12	Stock price, end of 2002	1.83				
13	Number of shares, January 1995	4,300,000				

(a) Complete the ??? in the spreadsheet above (assume that the dividend payment was before the share repurchase).

(b) Find the cost of equity r_E of Cinema using the Gordon dividend model for the total equity payout.

(c) What would be Cinema's cost of equity if we consider only the dividend payments without the share repurchases?

11. It is 1 January 2006, and you are interested in finding the cost of equity r_E of your company. After a quick search you have found the following data:
- The company currently has 1,600,000 shares outstanding. The current share price is $3.
- The company's earnings for 2005 were $2,000,000. The company has just paid out $300,000 in dividends, and it intends to continue this 15% dividend payout from earnings in the future.
- During 2005 the company spent $600,000 on share repurchases. It is the company's intention to increase the amount spent on share repurchases at the same growth rate as the amount spent on dividends.
- Projected earnings growth is 2% per year.

Using the Gordon model for the total equity payout, what is the company's cost of equity r_E?

12. Suppose that a firm is financed with 70% equity and 30% debt. The interest rate on debt is 8%, and the expected return on the common stock is 17%. The firm's tax rate is 40%. What is the firm's weighted average cost of capital?

13. Your boss asked you to find the WACC of Welcome to Paradise Company, based on the following data:
- The company has 1,600,000 shares, currently selling for $2 per share.
- The company's debt is $2,500,000. The interest paid last year by the company was $300,000.
- The corporate tax rate is 40%.
- The cost of capital requested by the investors is 13%.

What is the WACC for the company?

14. You are interested in calculating the cost of capital of Lion Company, based on the average WACC of its industry, which is 11%. You know that the company stock price is $11, and it has 5,500,000 shares. The company cost of debt is 9%, its debt is $4,000,000 and the company's tax rate is 40%. What is the company cost of capital?

15. You want to compute the WACC of ABC Company. The company's stock price is $8, and it has a debt to equity ratio of 1. ABC's cost of debt is 9%, its cost of equity is 12%, and the company's tax rate is 40%. What is the company's WACC?

16. Assume the following data concerning ZZZ Company and use it to compute the company's WACC:
   - The company has 2,000,000 shares, currently selling for $2.5 per share.
   - The company's debt is 3,000,000 from the company market value. The interest paid last year by the company was $250,000.
   - The company paid total dividends of $600,000 last year, and its expected dividend growth is 3%. In addition, the company repurchases 150,000 of its shares.
   - The corporate tax rate is 30%.

17. You have come up with the following data concerning Zion Company.
   - The company has 2,500,000 shares.
   - The company's debt is 90% from the company market value. The interest paid last year by the company was $500,000.
   - The company paid total dividends of $800,000 last year, which is 25% of its pretax profit, and its expected growth next year is $50,000 more.
   - The company paid taxes of $950,000.
   - The cost of capital requested by the investors is 13%.

   What is the company's WACC?

18. You have come up with the following data concerning your sister's company.
   - The company market value is $6,000,000.
   - The company's debt is 75% from the company market value. The interest paid last year by the company was $450,000.
   - The company paid total dividends of $600,000 last year, which is 20% of its pretax profit, and its expected growth next year is $45,000 more.
   - The company paid tax in the amount of $1,200,000.

   What is the company's WACC?

19. You are considering a new project for your firm. This project requires investment of $500,000 and generates cash flow of $70,000 for the next ten years. You think that these cash flows are completely riskless. You know that your company's WACC is 14%, and that the risk-free rate is 6%.
   (a) Should you take on this project?
   (b) Should you take on the project if its risk is comparable to the overall riskiness of the company's other activities?

20. "Sauce," a well-known pizza factory, has asked you to evaluate the factory's free cash flow (FCF). You estimate that the FCF of the factory is $4,500,000, its WACC is 12.5%, and its estimated growth is 5% each year.
   (a) If you know that Sauce's debt is $19,000,000 and it has 6,500,000 outstanding shares, what should be its share price?
   (b) Repeat the question by using midyear discounting.

21. You are given the following information for Twin, Inc.

Long-term debt outstanding	$300,000
Current yield to maturity (r_D)	8%
Number of shares of common stock	10,000
Price per share	$50
Book value per share	$25
Expected rate of return on stock (r_E)	15%

   (a) Calculate Twin's weighted average cost of capital (assuming that the firm pays no taxes).
   (b) How would r_E and the weighted average cost of capital change if Twin's stock price falls to $25 due to declining profits? Assume that business risk is unchanged.

CHAPTER 10

USING FINANCIAL PLANNING MODELS FOR VALUATION

OVERVIEW

This chapter explains how to build spreadsheet models that allow you to predict the future performance of a firm. These models are called *financial planning models* or *pro forma models*. Recall that accounting statements—the firm's profit and loss statement, its balance sheet, and its consolidated statement of cash flows—report what *happened* to the firm in the past. On the other hand, a financial planning model *predicts* what the firm's accounting statements will look like in the future. In accounting jargon, something that looks like an accounting statement but that is *forward looking* is sometimes called a "pro forma" statement.

Financial planning models have a variety of uses:

- Projecting future financing needs of the firm: Building a financial planning model helps you predict whether the firm will need financing in the future. It also helps you tie the firm's financing needs to its future performance. For example, does an increase in the growth rate of sales create cash or use cash? The answer is not always clear: More sales produce more profits (and hence produce more cash). However, an increase in the growth rate of sales may also require more capital investment (machines, land, etc.) and may require greater working capital (inventories, credit to clients, etc.). A financial planning model can help you sort out these two opposing trends.

- Creating business plans: When you make a business plan (which you then take to investors to get financing or to a bank to explain why you need a loan and can pay it back), you'll often need to build a pro forma model of your firm. The model you build illustrates your assumptions about the financial and business environment in which your firm will operate in the future.

- Valuing a firm: Financial planning models can be used to predict the future free cash flows, dividends, and profits of a firm. This chapter shows how to use the pro forma prediction of future cash flows to value a firm. The valuation technique employed—called *discounted cash flow* (DCF) *valuation*—is the valuation technique universally favored by the finance profession. When a financial planning model is used to do a DCF valuation, it is also used to do much of the sensitivity analysis, which helps determine if the valuation is reasonable.

Finance Concepts Used

- Present value and net present value
- Free cash flow
- Gordon model
- Terminal value
- Midyear valuation

Excel Functions Used

- **NPV**
- **Sum**
- **If**
- Relative versus absolute copying
- Circular references
- **Data Tables**

10.1 Initial Accounting Statements for a Financial Planning Model

Financial planning models are predictions of what a firm's *future* financial statements will look like. To build such a model we start with the *present*—the firm's current financial statements. To illustrate the process by which financial planning models are constructed, in the next section we project five years of financial statements for Whimsical Toenails (WT), a company that runs a chain of toenail-painting parlors. Whimsical's management and bankers want to project the firm's future performance, and we will help them by constructing a financial planning model.

Our starting point is Whimsical Toenail's current income statement and balance sheet for year-end 2004:

Whimsical Toenails Income Statement
31 December 2004

Sales	10,000,000
Cost of goods sold	−5,000,000
Depreciation	−1,000,000
Interest payments on debt	−320,000
Interest earned on cash	64,000
Profit before tax	3,744,000
Taxes (40% tax rate)	−1,497,600
Profit after tax	2,246,400
Dividends	−898,560
Retained earnings	1,347,840

Whimsical Toenails Balance Sheet 31 December 2004

Assets		Liabilities and Equity	
Cash	800,000	Current liabilities	800,000
Current assets	1,500,000	Debt	3,200,000
Fixed assets			
Fixed assets at cost	10,700,000	Equity	
Accumulated depreciation	−3,000,000	Stock (paid-in capital)	4,500,000
Net fixed assets	7,700,000	Accumulated retained earnings	1,500,000
Total assets	**10,000,000**	**Total liabilities and equity**	**10,000,000**

Accounting Versus Financial Planning Model Concepts

In the next section we build the Whimsical Toenails financial planning model. However, before we do this, it is important to point out some differences between certain concepts used by accountants and their adaptation to financial modeling. While most of the terminology in this chapter follows the standard accounting classification, some changes are necessary to accommodate the structure of financial planning models. For example, while accountants use "current assets" to denote both operating current assets (like inventories and accounts receivable—as yet unpaid customer bills) and financial short-term assets (like cash and marketable securities), financial planning models use "current assets" to mean only operating short-term assets. To emphasize this point, the terminology "operating current assets" is sometimes used. Similarly, in the accounting framework "current liabilities" include both operational items (like accounts payable—bills that are as yet unpaid by the firm) and financial items (like short-term debt and current portion of long-term debt). Financial planning models use "current liabilities" to denote operational items only. To emphasize this point, we sometimes use the terminology "operating current liabilities."

The next two subsections discuss these differences between accounting and financial concepts of current assets and current liabilities in more detail.

Current Assets—What's Included in the Financial Planning Model and What's Not?

In financial planning models the "current assets" category contains only items that are related to the operations of the firm. Here are several typical items that would be included in the financial planning model definition of current assets.

- Accounts receivable: These are payments due from customers and are generated by the operations of the firm. Since accounts receivable are generated by the firm's sales, they are included in the operating current assets of the financial planning model.
- Inventories: Inventories include both raw materials to be used for production and unsold finished products. Inventories are part of the operating current assets of the financial planning model.
- Prepaid expenses: Prepaid expenses are costs that the firm pays before it actually receives the associated services. An example might be rent paid by the firm for future periods: If the firm pays this rent in advance (for example, not month-by-month, but six months in advance), then this prepayment of the rent is recorded by the accountant as a prepaid expense, which is part of current assets. For our financial planning model, we assume that prepaid expenses are part of *operating* current assets.

Two important examples of accounting current assets that are not included in the financial planning model definition of current assets are cash and marketable securities:

- Cash: The "cash" item on the balance sheet refers to money kept in the firm's bank accounts. Sometimes the accounting line item is called "cash and equivalents," with the second term denoting assets like certificates of deposit and money market accounts, which can easily be converted into cash. "Cash" is an operating current asset to the extent that it is needed by the firm for its daily operations. In most cases, however, the cash accounts on the balance sheets simply refer to nonoperating assets that are kept in liquid form by the firm.
- Marketable securities: This item on the balance sheet refers to other financial assets—such as stocks and bonds—bought by the firm. Marketable securities are not needed for the firm's operations and thus are not an operating current asset.

The distinction between cash as an operating asset and cash as a store of value is usually obvious once you understand the business of the firm. A taxi driver needs to keep some cash on hand in order to make change for customers, and a supermarket needs to keep some cash in the till for the same reason; in these cases at least some of the cash is an operating current asset (although even for a taxi or supermarket, most of the cash is likely to be a financial, nonoperating current asset). On the other hand, in March 2003, Microsoft reported having $4.3 billion in cash and another $41.9 billion in marketable securities. It is unlikely that almost any of this $46.2 billion is needed for daily operations. It is not an operating current asset, but rather a financial current asset. In a financial planning model, financial current assets—cash and marketable securities not needed for the operations of the firm—are not included in the "current assets."

Current Liabilities

For purposes of the financial planning model, the "current liabilities" category contains only items that are related to the operations of the firm. Here are two typical items that would be included in the current liabilities of our financial planning model:

- Accounts payable: These are unpaid bills owed to the firm's suppliers. Since this item is related to the operations of the firm, we include it in the financial planning model definition of current liabilities.
- Taxes payable: When a firm's payment of taxes does not coincide with the accounting period, the taxes owed are entered into the balance sheet as a current liability. For example, for the year ending 31 December 2005, XYZ Corp. owes $2,000 in taxes, but it won't pay this tax bill until 15 January 2006. The financial statements of XYZ Corp. for 2005 will report taxes of $2,000 in the profit and loss statement; the firm's balance sheet will report taxes payable of $2,000 in the current liabilities. Taxes payable relate to the firm's operations and are included in the financial planning model definition of current liability.

Accounting current liability items that are not included in the financial planning model definition of current liabilities are typically financial items. Here are two examples:

- Short-term debt: These are borrowings by the firm that are due within one year. A bank overdraft (a credit line on a business's checking account) is a good example of a short-term debt. Accountants include this item in current liabilities, but financial planning models include them as *debt*.
- Current portion of long-term debt: This is the portion of the firm's debt that is due for payment within the current financial year. Accountants include this item in current liabilities; financial planning models include the current portion of long-term debt in the *debt* category.

10.2 Building a Financial Planning Model

Now that we have our terminology straight, we can build our financial planning model for Whimsical Toenails. A typical financial planning model has three major components:

- The model parameters. Also called the *value drivers,* a financial planning model's parameters include the major assumptions of the model. For example, we might assume that the *sales growth* parameter is 10% per year. Or we might assume that the *current assets to sales* parameter is 15%—meaning that an increase of $1,000 in sales requires an additional $150 of current assets. Typically, financial statement models are *sales driven;* this term means that many of the most important financial statement value drivers are assumed to be functions of the firm's sales.
- The financial policy assumptions. We will make assumptions about how the firm finances itself in the future. What is the mix between debt and new equity issued? Does excess cash produced by the firm go toward repaying debt or does it end up in the firm's cash

balances? These assumptions are important determinants of the firm's future financial statements.

- The pro forma financial statements. Once we decide on the financial model's parameters, we will build the pro forma financial statements for the firm we are modeling—the income statement, balance sheets, and free cash flows.

When we've used the model's parameters and the financing assumptions to project the future financial statements of the firm, we can then use the model. By varying the model's assumptions, we can use the financial planning model to build different scenarios of how the firm will perform in the future. In Sections 10.6–10.8 we use the financial planning model to project the future free cash flows of the firm in order to value the firm. We might also want to use the model to evaluate the ability of the firm to repay its debts (there's an end-of-chapter exercise that illustrates this use).

The Model's Parameters—The Value Drivers

The *sales growth* parameter is usually the most important parameter of the financial planning model. In our example, Whimsical Toenails's current (year 0) level of sales is $10,000,000. Over the five-year horizon of the financial planning model, the firm expects its sales to grow at a rate of 10% per year.

Other model parameters are derived from the following financial statement relations.[1]

- Current assets: We assume that Whimsical's end-year current assets on the balance sheet will be 15% of the annual firm sales.
- Current liabilities: We assume that Whimsical's end-year current liabilities on the balance sheet will be 8% of the annual firm sales.
- Net fixed assets: End-year net fixed assets are assumed to be 77% of annual sales.
- Depreciation: The annual depreciation charge is 10% of the average value of the fixed assets on the books during the year.
- Cost of goods sold: Assumed to be 50% of sales.
- Interest rate on debt: 10%.
- Interest earned on cash: Whimsical Toenails earns 8% on the average balances of cash.
- Tax rate: 40% of the firm's profit before taxes.
- Dividends paid: We assume that Whimsical Toenails pays out 40% of its profits after taxes as dividends to shareholders.

The Model's Financial Policy Assumptions

The second component of a financial planning model is the model's financial policy assumptions. In this initial financial planning model, we make the following assumptions:

- Debt: Whimsical currently has debt of $3,200,000 on its balance sheet. The company's agreement with the bank specifies that it will repay $800,000 of this debt in each of the next four years. Once the debt is fully repaid, the company intends to stay debt-free.

---

[1]In practice, the model's parameters are often derived from an analysis of the company's historical financial statements.

- Stock: Company management does not intend either to issue new stock or to repurchase stock over the five-year model horizon. The stock item in the firm's balance sheets thus remains at its 2004 level of $4,500,000.
- Cash: In our model this item is the *plug*—the cash item is defined so that the left-hand side of the balance sheet always equals the right-hand side of the balance sheet:

$$cash = total\ liabilities\ and\ equity - current\ assets - net\ fixed\ assets$$

The "plug" is the balance sheet item that guarantees the equality of the future projected total assets and the future projected total liabilities and equity. Every financial planning model has a plug, and the plug is almost always either cash (as in this case) or debt or stock.

To see how the plug fits into our model, consider the projected future balance sheets:

Whimsical Toenails Balance Sheet Model Assumptions

Assets	Liabilities and Equity
Cash [plug]	Current liabilities [8% of sales]
Current assets [15% of sales]	Debt [repaid by $800,000/year until zero]
Fixed assets	Equity
Fixed assets at cost	Stock (paid in capital) [constant]
−Accumulated depreciation	Accumulated retained earnings
[10% of average assets]	[previous year's accumulated retained
Net fixed assets [77% of sales]	+ this year's retained from income
	statement]
Total assets	**Total liabilities and equity**

The "plug" assumption has two meanings:

1. The *mechanical* meaning of the plug: By defining cash to equal the total liabilities and equity minus current assets and minus net fixed assets, we guarantee that future projected assets and liabilities will always be equal. This is important, since the two sides of the balance sheet must always be equal. As mentioned earlier, cash is not the only candidate to "plug" the financial model; we could also use stock or debt (there are some examples of this in the end-of-chapter exercises). However, no matter what the plug, its "mechanical" function is the same—to guarantee that the two sides of the financial model's balance sheet are equal.

2. The *financial* meaning of the plug: Whimsical Toenails sells no additional stock and is locked into a debt repayment schedule. By defining the plug to be cash, we are also making a statement about how the firm finances itself. For the case of Whimsical Toenails, this means that all incremental financing (if needed) for the firm will come from the cash; it also means that if the firm has additional cash, it will go into this account.

Projecting the 2005 Balance Sheet and Income Statement

Given Whimsical Toenails's financial statements and our assumptions, we can now develop the pro forma model and project the financial statements for 2005:

	A	B	C	D
1	**WHIMSICAL TOENAILS** **SETTING UP THE FINANCIAL STATEMENT MODEL** **for 2005**			
2	Sales growth	10%		
3	Current assets/Sales	15%		
4	Current liabilities/Sales	8%		
5	Net fixed assets/Sales	77%		
6	Costs of goods sold/Sales	50%		
7	Depreciation rate	10%		
8	Interest rate on debt	10.00%		
9	Interest earned on cash balances	8.00%		
10	Tax rate	40%		
11	Dividend payout ratio	40%		
12				
13	**Year**	**2004**	**2005**	
14	**Income statement**			
15	Sales	10,000,000	11,000,000	<-- =B15*(1+$B$2)
16	Costs of goods sold	(5,000,000)	(5,500,000)	<-- =-C15*$B$6
17	Depreciation	(1,000,000)	(1,166,842)	<-- =-$B$7*(C30+B30)/2
18	Interest payments on debt	(320,000)	(280,000)	<-- =-$B$8*(B36+C36)/2
19	Interest earned on cash and marketable securities	64,000	57,595	<-- =$B$9*(B27+C27)/2
20	Profit before tax	3,744,000	4,110,753	<-- =SUM(C15:C19)
21	Taxes	(1,497,600)	(1,644,301)	<-- =-C20*$B$10
22	Profit after tax	2,246,400	2,466,452	<-- =C21+C20
23	Dividends	(898,560)	(986,581)	<-- =-$B$11*C22
24	Retained earnings	1,347,840	1,479,871	<-- =C23+C22
25				
26	**Balance sheet**			
27	Cash	800,000	639,871	<-- =C39-C28-C32
28	Current assets	1,500,000	1,650,000	<-- =C15*$B$3
29	Fixed assets			
30	At cost	10,700,000	12,636,842	<-- =C32-C31
31	Depreciation	(3,000,000)	(4,166,842)	<-- =B31-$B$7*(C30+B30)/2
32	Net fixed assets	7,700,000	8,470,000	<-- =C15*$B$5
33	**Total assets**	10,000,000	10,759,871	<-- =C32+C28+C27
34				
35	Current liabilities	800,000	880,000	<-- =C15*$B$4
36	Debt	3,200,000	2,400,000	<-- =B36-800000
37	Stock	4,500,000	4,500,000	<-- =B37
38	Accumulated retained earnings	1,500,000	2,979,871	<-- =B38+C24
39	**Total liabilities and equity**	10,000,000	10,759,871	<-- =SUM(C35:C38)

EXCEL NOTE

RELATIVE VERSUS ABSOLUTE COPYING

The dollar signs within a formula indicate that when the formulas are copied the cell references to the model parameters should not change. The technical jargon for this in Excel is *absolute copying* as opposed to the *relative copying* when variables are indicated without dollar signs. The distinction between absolute and relative copying is critical for financial

contd.

planning models—if you fail to put the dollar signs correctly in the model, it will not copy correctly when you project year 2 and beyond.

Two cells in the previous spreadsheet have been highlighted to stress this important distinction:

- Cell C15: Sales in 2005 equal sales in the previous year times (1 + sales growth rate). Because we want to copy this definition to subsequent cells, cell C15's formula is **=B15*(1+$B$2)**. "$B$2" is the sales growth rate parameter, which stays the same as we copy the cell contents.
- Cell C16: Costs of goods sold in 2005 equal 50% of 2005 sales. The 50% parameter is in cell B6 and will stay the same as we copy the cell C16 formula to subsequent cells. Therefore, we write the formula in cell B16 as **=C15*$B$6**.

The use of relative versus absolute copying is explained in Chapter 27.

Income Statement Equations

Here are the relations for our financial planning model, with model parameters in boldface. These relations will end up as formulas in the cells of our Excel model.

- $\text{Sales}(t) = \text{Sales}(t-1) * (1 + \textbf{Sales growth})$
- Costs of goods sold = Sales * **Costs of goods sold/Sales**

  We assume that Whimsical's only expenses related to sales are costs of goods sold. Most companies also book an expense item called selling, general, and administrative (SG&A) expenses. Exercise 3 at the end of this chapter illustrates how you would introduce SG&A expenses into the model.

- Interest payments on debt = **Interest rate on debt** * Average debt over the year. We use this formula to estimate Whimsical's interest payments on the debt. For example, if the company's debt at the end of 2004 is $3,200,000 and its debt at the end of 2005 is $2,400,000, the financial planning model estimates its 2005 interest payments as:

$$10\% * \frac{3,200,000 + 2,400,000}{2} = 10\% * \underbrace{2,800,000}_{\substack{\uparrow \\ \text{Whimsical's} \\ \text{average debt} \\ \text{in year 1}}} = 280,000$$

- Interest earned on cash = **Interest rate on cash** * Average cash over the year. This is the same logic used for the interest payments on debt. Whimsical earns 8% on its average cash balances over the year. If end-2004 cash balances are $800,000 and end-2005 cash balances are $639,871, then the firm earned $57,595 on its cash balances:

$$8\% * \frac{800,000 + 639,871}{2} = 8\% * \underbrace{719,935}_{\substack{\uparrow \\ \text{Whimsical's} \\ \text{average cash} \\ \text{in year 1}}} = 57,595$$

- Depreciation = **Depreciation rate** * Average fixed assets at cost over the year. This assumes that all new fixed assets are purchased during the year. We also assume that there is no disposal of fixed assets. Looking at the financial model may help you understand the calculation of the depreciation: Whimsical's 2004 fixed assets at cost are $10,700,000 and its projected fixed assets at cost for 2005 are $12,636,842. Since the company's depreciation rate is 10%, its year 1 depreciation in the income statement is

$$10\% * \frac{10,700,000 + 12,636,842}{2} = 10\% * \underbrace{11,668,411}_{\substack{\uparrow \\ \text{Average fixed} \\ \text{assets at cost} \\ \text{in year 1}}} = 1,166,842$$

- Profit before taxes = Sales − Costs of goods sold − Interest payments on debt + Interest earned on cash and marketable securities – Depreciation.
- Taxes = **Tax rate** ∗ Profit before taxes.
- Profit after taxes = Profit before taxes − Taxes.
- Dividends = **Dividend payout ratio** ∗ Profit after taxes. Whimsical Toenails has a policy of paying out a fixed percentage of its profits as dividends. In the exercises for this chapter, we explore some alternative dividend policies.
- Retained earnings = Profit after taxes − Dividends.

Balance Sheet Equations

- Cash = Total liabilities − Current assets − Net fixed assets. As explained earlier, this definition means that cash is the balance sheet plug.
- Current assets = **Current assets/Sales** ∗ Sales.
- Net fixed assets = **Net fixed assets/Sales** ∗ Sales.
- Accumulated depreciation = Previous year's accumulated depreciation + **Depreciation rate** ∗ Average fixed assets at cost over the year.
- Fixed assets at cost = Net fixed assets + Accumulated depreciation. Note that this model does not distinguish between plant, property, and equipment (PP&E) and other fixed assets such as land.
- Current liabilities = **Current liabilities/Sales** ∗ Sales.[2]
- Debt is assumed to decrease by $800,000 per year. This means that Whimsical Toenails will repay all of its debt by the end of the fourth year of the financial model. An alternative model, which assumes that debt is the balance sheet plug, is the subject of one of the end-of-chapter exercises.
- Stock is assumed to be unchanged. The company is assumed to issue no new stock nor repurchase any existing stock.
- Accumulated retained earnings = Previous year's accumulated retained earnings + Current year's additions to retained earnings.

---

[2]Some modelers prefer to model current liabilities as a percentage of the firm's costs of goods sold (COGS). The thinking here is that—because current liabilities include the firm's accounts payable (which in turn include the firm's unpaid bills for inventories and the like)—current liabilities are largely dependent on the level of the firm's costs of goods sold. While it is easy to incorporate this assumption in our model, it doesn't make much difference: If COGS are a percentage of sales and current liabilities are a percentage of sales, then the current liabilities are also a percentage of the COGS.

EXCEL NOTE

SOLVING CIRCULAR REFERENCES IN EXCEL

Financial statement models in Excel always involve cells that are mutually dependent. In our model, for example, the interest earned on cash depends on the profits of the firm, but the profits depend on the interest earned on cash. Another example of mutual dependence in our model involves the fixed asset accounts: Fixed assets at cost are the sum of net fixed assets plus accumulated depreciation, but accumulated depreciation is a function of the fixed assets at cost.

As a result of these inevitable mutual dependencies, the solution of the model depends on the ability of Excel to solve circular references. To make sure your spreadsheet recalculates, you have to go to the **Tools|Options|Calculation** box and click **Iteration**. If you open a spreadsheet that involves iteration, and if this box is not clicked, you will see the following Excel error message:

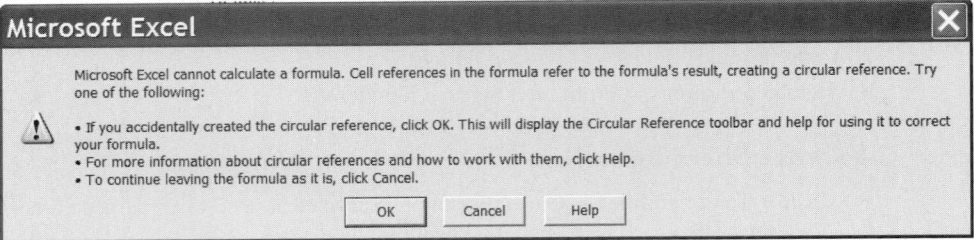

Depending on where you are in Excel when you open the file with the circular references, you may get a slightly different version of the above message. Whatever message you see, get out of it by pressing **Cancel** and go to **Tools|Options|Calculation|Iteration**. In this dialog box click the box labeled **Iteration**:

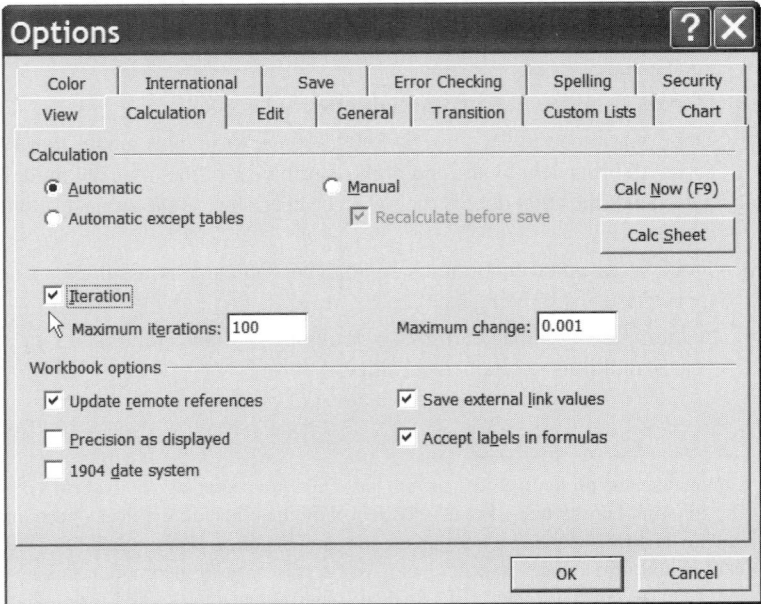

Notice that we have also clicked the **Automatic** button—this guarantees that the spreadsheet will recalculate every time a new entry is made. If your spreadsheet is very large or your computer somewhat aged, automatic recalculation can really slow you down. In this case it may be wise to click the **Manual** button and recalculate the spreadsheet manually by pressing the **F9** key.

10.3   Extending the Model to Year 2 and Beyond

Now that you have the model set up, you can extend it by copying the columns:

	A	B	C	D	E	F	G
1	WHIMSICAL TOENAILS--FINANCIAL MODEL						
2	Sales growth	10%					
3	Current assets/Sales	15%					
4	Current liabilities/Sales	8%					
5	Net fixed assets/Sales	77%					
6	Costs of goods sold/Sales	50%					
7	Depreciation rate	10%					
8	Interest rate on debt	10.00%					
9	Interest earned on cash balances	8.00%					
10	Tax rate	40%					
11	Dividend payout ratio	40%					
12							
13	Year	2004	2005	2006	2007	2008	2009
14	Income statement						
15	Sales	10,000,000	11,000,000	12,100,000	13,310,000	14,641,000	16,105,100
16	Costs of goods sold	-5,000,000	-5,500,000	-6,050,000	-6,655,000	-7,320,500	-8,052,550
17	Depreciation	-1,000,000	-1,166,842	-1,374,773	-1,613,102	-1,885,879	-2,197,668
18	Interest payments on debt	-320,000	-280,000	-200,000	-120,000	-40,000	0
19	Interest earned on cash and marketable securities	64,000	57,595	47,355	42,349	42,755	80,609
20	Profit before tax	3,744,000	4,110,753	4,522,582	4,964,248	5,437,376	5,935,491
21	Taxes	-1,497,600	-1,644,301	-1,809,033	-1,985,699	-2,174,950	-2,374,196
22	Profit after tax	2,246,400	2,466,452	2,713,549	2,978,549	3,262,426	3,561,295
23	Dividends	-898,560	-986,581	-1,085,420	-1,191,419	-1,304,970	-1,424,518
24	Retained earnings	1,347,840	1,479,871	1,628,130	1,787,129	1,957,455	2,136,777
25							
26	Balance sheet						
27	Cash	800,000	639,871	544,001	514,730	554,145	1,461,078
28	Current assets	1,500,000	1,650,000	1,815,000	1,996,500	2,196,150	2,415,765
29	Fixed assets						
30	At cost	10,700,000	12,636,842	14,858,615	17,403,417	20,314,166	23,639,190
31	Depreciation	-3,000,000	-4,166,842	-5,541,615	-7,154,717	-9,040,596	-11,238,263
32	Net fixed assets	7,700,000	8,470,000	9,317,000	10,248,700	11,273,570	12,400,927
33	Total assets	10,000,000	10,759,871	11,676,001	12,759,930	14,023,865	16,277,770
34							
35	Current liabilities	800,000	880,000	968,000	1,064,800	1,171,280	1,288,408
36	Debt	3,200,000	2,400,000	1,600,000	800,000	0	0
37	Stock	4,500,000	4,500,000	4,500,000	4,500,000	4,500,000	4,500,000
38	Accumulated retained earnings	1,500,000	2,979,871	4,608,001	6,395,130	8,352,585	10,489,362
39	Total liabilities and equity	10,000,000	10,759,871	11,676,001	12,759,930	14,023,865	16,277,770

The most common Excel mistake to make in the transition between the two-columned financial model and this one is the failure to mark the model parameters with dollar signs. We discussed this critical point in the Excel note on page 275. If you commit this error, you will get zeros in places where there should be numbers.[3]

---

[3]If this paragraph is mysterious to you, change the model by putting in the following mistake: In cell C28, write the formula **=C15*B3** (instead of the correct formula **=C15*$B$3**). Then copy cell C28 to D28:G28. Now you will understand the importance of *dollarizing* the correct cell references!

Understanding the Model by Changing Some of the Value Drivers

The financial model we've built shows that our firm's profits after tax will grow from $2,246,400 in 2004 to $3,561,295 in 2009. The balances of cash grow from $800,000 to $1,461,078, the firm's total assets grow to $16,277,770, and so on. . . .

What would happen if we changed some of the value drivers in the model? For example, what would happen to profits if the growth rate of sales were to be 8% instead of 10% and if the costs of goods sold were to be 55% of sales instead of the 50% currently in the model? Given our Excel model, we simply have to make the relevant changes in the parameters in cells B2 and B6. Our intuition is that these performance changes will make the firm's financial results worse, and this is indeed confirmed in the model, as shown below:

	A	B	C	D	E	F	G
1	**WHIMSICAL TOENAILS MODEL WITH SOME CHANGES**						
2	Sales growth	8%	<-- Changed from 10%				
3	Current assets/Sales	15%					
4	Current liabilities/Sales	8%					
5	Net fixed assets/Sales	77%					
6	Costs of goods sold/Sales	55%	<-- Changed from 50%				
7	Depreciation rate	10%					
8	Interest rate on debt	10.00%					
9	Interest earned on cash balances	8.00%					
10	Tax rate	40%					
11	Dividend payout ratio	40%					
12							
13	**Year**	**2004**	**2005**	**2006**	**2007**	**2008**	**2009**
14	**Income statement**						
15	Sales	10,000,000	10,800,000	11,664,000	12,597,120	13,604,890	14,693,281
16	Costs of goods sold	(5,500,000)	(5,940,000)	(6,415,200)	(6,928,416)	(7,482,689)	(8,081,304)
17	Depreciation	(1,000,000)	(1,158,737)	(1,348,145)	(1,562,886)	(1,806,057)	(2,081,118)
18	Interest payments on debt	(320,000)	(280,000)	(200,000)	(120,000)	(40,000)	-
19	Interest earned on cash and marketable securities	64,000	55,181	39,185	26,432	16,813	42,050
20	Profit before tax	3,244,000	3,476,444	3,739,840	4,012,250	4,292,956	4,572,909
21	Taxes	(1,297,600)	(1,390,578)	(1,495,936)	(1,604,900)	(1,717,182)	(1,829,163)
22	Profit after tax	1,946,400	2,085,866	2,243,904	2,407,350	2,575,774	2,743,745
23	Dividends	(778,560)	(834,347)	(897,562)	(962,940)	(1,030,309)	(1,097,498)
24	Retained earnings	1,167,840	1,251,520	1,346,342	1,444,410	1,545,464	1,646,247
25							
26	**Balance sheet**						
27	Cash	800,000	579,520	400,102	260,691	159,629	891,628
28	Current assets	1,500,000	1,620,000	1,749,600	1,889,568	2,040,733	2,203,992
29	Fixed assets						
30	At cost	10,700,000	12,474,737	14,488,162	16,769,550	19,351,589	22,270,768
31	Depreciation	(3,000,000)	(4,158,737)	(5,506,882)	(7,069,767)	(8,875,824)	(10,956,942)
32	Net fixed assets	7,700,000	8,316,000	8,981,280	9,699,782	10,475,765	11,313,826
33	**Total assets**	10,000,000	10,515,520	11,130,982	11,850,042	12,676,128	14,409,446

If you compare the model above to our previous version of the model, you'll see that the firm's sales growth has slowed (from 10% to 8%) and that its sales have become more expensive (costs of goods sold are 55% of sales instead of 50%). The result is that profits after taxes (row 22) are lower than before. Cash balances (row 27) are also lower than in the previous version of the model.

10.4 Free Cash Flow (FCF): Measuring the Cash Produced by the Firm's Operations

In this section we use our model to measure the firm's projected *free cash flow* (FCF). We have previously discussed the concept of free cash flow in Chapters 3 and 9. A good way to think of FCF is that it is the amount of cash the firm would produce if it had no debt whatsoever. This is equivalent to the amount of cash produced by the firm if the shareholders have to finance *all* of the operations of the firm. For short, we'll say that the FCF is a measure of the *cash produced by the firm's operations*.

The FCF is the measure on which we base our valuation of the firm. We gave an example of this in Chapter 9 (pp. 260–262, where we used the future predicted FCFs of Courier Corporation to value the company). In Section 10.6 we return to this topic and show how a financial planning model's predictions of FCFs can be used to value a company.

In this section we merely use the financial planning model to project the firm's future free cash flows. Before we do so, however, let's recap the definition and the terminology we use.

The definition of the free cash flow is:

Defining the Free Cash Flow (FCF)

Profit after taxes	This is the basic measure of the profitability of the business, but it is an accounting measure that includes financing flows (such as interest), as well as noncash expenses such as depreciation. Profit after taxes does not account for changes in the firm's working capital or purchases of new fixed assets, both of which can be important cash drains on the firm.
+ Depreciation	This noncash expense is added back to the profit after taxes.
− Increase in current assets	When the firm's sales increase, more investment is needed in inventories, accounts receivable, and so on. This increase in current assets is not an expense for tax purposes (and is therefore ignored in the profit after taxes), but it is a cash drain on the company. Note that our use of the term "current assets" is slightly different from the standard accounting usage—see the discussion in Section 10.1.
+ Increase in current liabilities	An increase in the sales often causes an increase in financing related to sales (such as accounts payable or taxes payable). This increase in current liabilities—when related to sales—provides cash to the firm. Since it is directly related to sales, we include this cash in the FCF calculations. Note that our use of the term "current liabilities" is slightly different from the standard accounting usage—see the discussion in Section 10.1.
− Increase in fixed assets at cost (also called "capital expenditures"—CAPEX)	An increase in fixed assets (the long-term productive assets of the company) is a use of cash, which reduces the firm's FCF.
+ After-tax interest payments (net)	FCF is an attempt to measure the cash produced by the business activity of the firm. To neutralize the effect of interest payments on the firm's profits, we: • Add back the after-tax cost of interest on debt (*after-tax* since interest payments are tax deductible) • Subtract out the after-tax interest payments on cash
FCF = sum of the above	The FCF measures the cash produced by the firm's operations.

Here is the FCF calculation for Whimsical Toenails. Note that we have returned to the initial model (sales growth = 10%, costs of goods sold = 50% of sales):

	A	B	C	D	E	F	G
42	**Free cash flow calculation**						
43	**Year**	**2004**	**2005**	**2006**	**2007**	**2008**	**2009**
44	Profit after tax		2,466,452	2,713,549	2,978,549	3,262,426	3,561,295
45	Add back depreciation		1,166,842	1,374,773	1,613,102	1,885,879	2,197,668
46	Subtract increase in current assets		-150,000	-165,000	-181,500	-199,650	-219,615
47	Add back increase in current liabilities		80,000	88,000	96,800	106,480	117,128
48	Subtract increase in fixed assets at cost		-1,936,842	-2,221,773	-2,544,802	-2,910,749	-3,325,025
49	Add back after-tax interest on debt		168,000	120,000	72,000	24,000	0
50	Subtract after-tax interest on cash		-34,557	-28,413	-25,410	-25,653	-48,365
51	**Free cash flow**		1,759,895	1,881,136	2,008,739	2,142,733	2,283,085

The FCFs in row 51 are substantially lower than the firm's profits after taxes in row 44. The major reason for this is the large capital expenditure (row 48) in each year which outweighs the cash effect of the depreciation (row 45).

The FCF calculations are sensitive to the model assumptions. Suppose that Whimsical Toenails's sales growth is 8% (instead of 10%) and that its costs of goods sold are 55% of sales (instead of 50%). You might suspect that these negative changes in the model assumptions will make Whimsical's future projected FCFs substantially lower, and you're right:

	A	B	C	D	E	F	G
1	**WHIMSICAL TOENAILS MODEL WITH SOME CHANGES**						
2	Sales growth	8%	<-- Changed from 10%				
3	Current assets/Sales	15%					
4	Current liabilities/Sales	8%					
5	Net fixed assets/Sales	77%					
6	Costs of goods sold/Sales	55%	<-- Changed from 50%				
7	Depreciation rate	10%					
8	Interest rate on debt	10.00%					
9	Interest earned on cash balances	8.00%					
10	Tax rate	40%					
11	Dividend payout ratio	40%					
41							
42	**Free cash flow calculation**						
43	**Year**	**2004**	**2005**	**2006**	**2007**	**2008**	**2009**
44	Profit after tax		2,085,866	2,243,904	2,407,350	2,575,774	2,743,745
45	Add back depreciation		1,158,737	1,348,145	1,562,886	1,806,057	2,081,118
46	Subtract increase in current assets		(120,000)	(129,600)	(139,968)	(151,165)	(163,259)
47	Add back increase in current liabilities		64,000	69,120	74,650	80,622	87,071
48	Subtract increase in fixed assets at cost		(1,774,737)	(2,013,425)	(2,281,388)	(2,582,040)	(2,919,179)
49	Add back after-tax interest on debt		168,000	120,000	72,000	24,000	0
50	Subtract after-tax interest on cash		(33,108)	(23,511)	(15,859)	(10,088)	(25,230)
51	**Free cash flow**		1,548,758	1,614,633	1,679,670	1,743,160	1,804,266

EXCEL NOTE

HIDING AND GROUPING ROWS IN EXCEL

In the above example we've hidden rows 12–40 in order to make more room on the screen. To hide rows in Excel:

- Mark the rows you want to hide.
- Right-click on the mouse and click on **Hide**.

Here's what the screen looks like:

	A	B	C	D	E	F	G
8	Interest rate on debt	10.00%					
9	Interest earned on cash balances	8.00%					
10	Tax rate	40%					
11	Dividend payout ratio	40%					
12							
13	Year	2004	2005	2006	2007	2008	2009
14	Income statement						
15	Sales	10,00	1,664,000	12,597,120	13,604,890	14,693,281	
16	Costs of goods sold	(5,50	6,415,200)	(6,928,416)	(7,482,689)	(8,081,304)	
17	Depreciation	(1,00	1,348,145)	(1,562,886)	(1,806,057)	(2,081,118)	
18	Interest payments on debt	(32	(200,000)	(120,000)	(40,000)	-	
19	Interest earned on cash and marketable securities	64	39,185	26,432	16,813	42,050	
20	Profit before tax	3,24	3,739,840	4,012,250	4,292,956	4,572,909	
21	Taxes	(1,29	1,495,936)	(1,604,900)	(1,717,182)	(1,829,163)	
22	Profit after tax	1,94	2,243,904	2,407,350	2,575,774	2,743,745	
23	Dividends	(77	(897,562)	(962,940)	(1,030,309)	(1,097,498)	
24	Retained earnings	1,16	1,346,342	1,444,410	1,545,464	1,646,247	
25							
26	Balance sheet						
27	Cash	80	400,102	260,691	159,629	891,628	
28	Current assets	1,500,000	1,620,000	1,749,600	1,889,568	2,040,733	2,203,992
29	Fixed assets						
30	At cost	10,700,000	12,474,737	14,488,162	16,769,550	19,351,589	22,270,768
31	Depreciation	(3,000,000)	(4,158,737)	(5,506,882)	(7,069,767)	(8,875,824)	(10,956,942)
32	Net fixed assets	7,700,000	8,316,000	8,981,280	9,699,782	10,475,765	11,313,826
33	Total assets	10,000,000	10,515,520	11,130,982	11,850,042	12,676,128	14,409,446
34							
35	Current liabilities	800,000	864,000	933,120	1,007,770	1,088,391	1,175,462
36	Debt	3,200,000	2,400,000	1,600,000	800,000	0	0
37	Stock	4,500,000	4,500,000	4,500,000	4,500,000	4,500,000	4,500,000
38	Accumulated retained earnings	1,500,000	2,751,520	4,097,862	5,542,272	7,087,736	8,733,984
39	Total liabilities and equity	10,000,000	10,515,520	11,130,982	11,850,042	12,676,128	14,409,446
40							
41							
42	Free cash flow calculation						
43	Year	2004	2005	2006	2007	2008	2009
44	Profit after tax		2,085,866	2,243,904	2,407,350	2,575,774	2,743,745
45	Add back depreciation		1,158,737	1,348,145	1,562,886	1,806,057	2,081,118

Marking the rows and clicking **Unhide** reverses the action.

Another slightly more sophisticated way to accomplish the same result is to **Group** the rows. To do this, first mark the rows as before. Then go to **Data|Group and Outline|Group** as shown below:

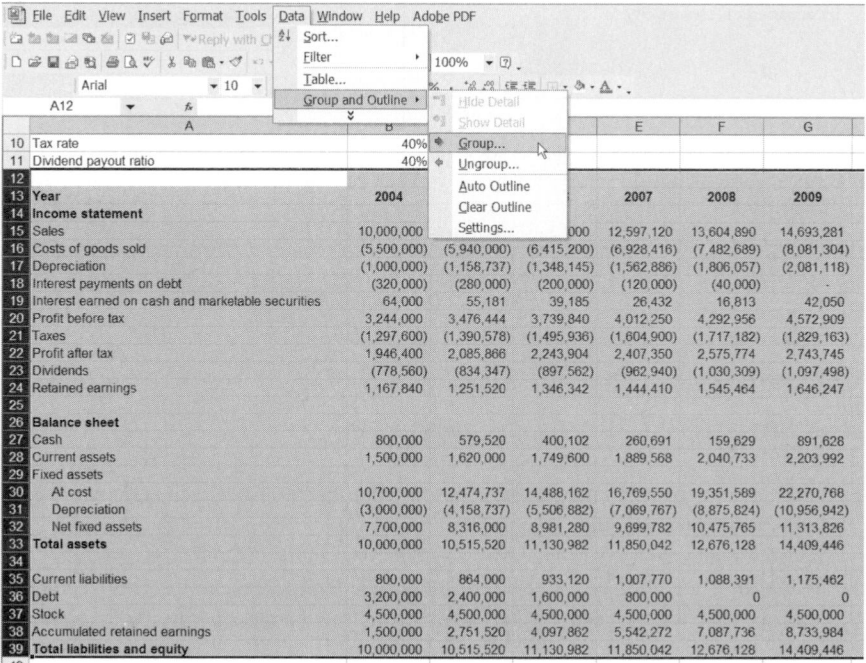

contd.

The result is a marker in the left-hand margin of the spreadsheet, which allows you to hide or unhide the rows:

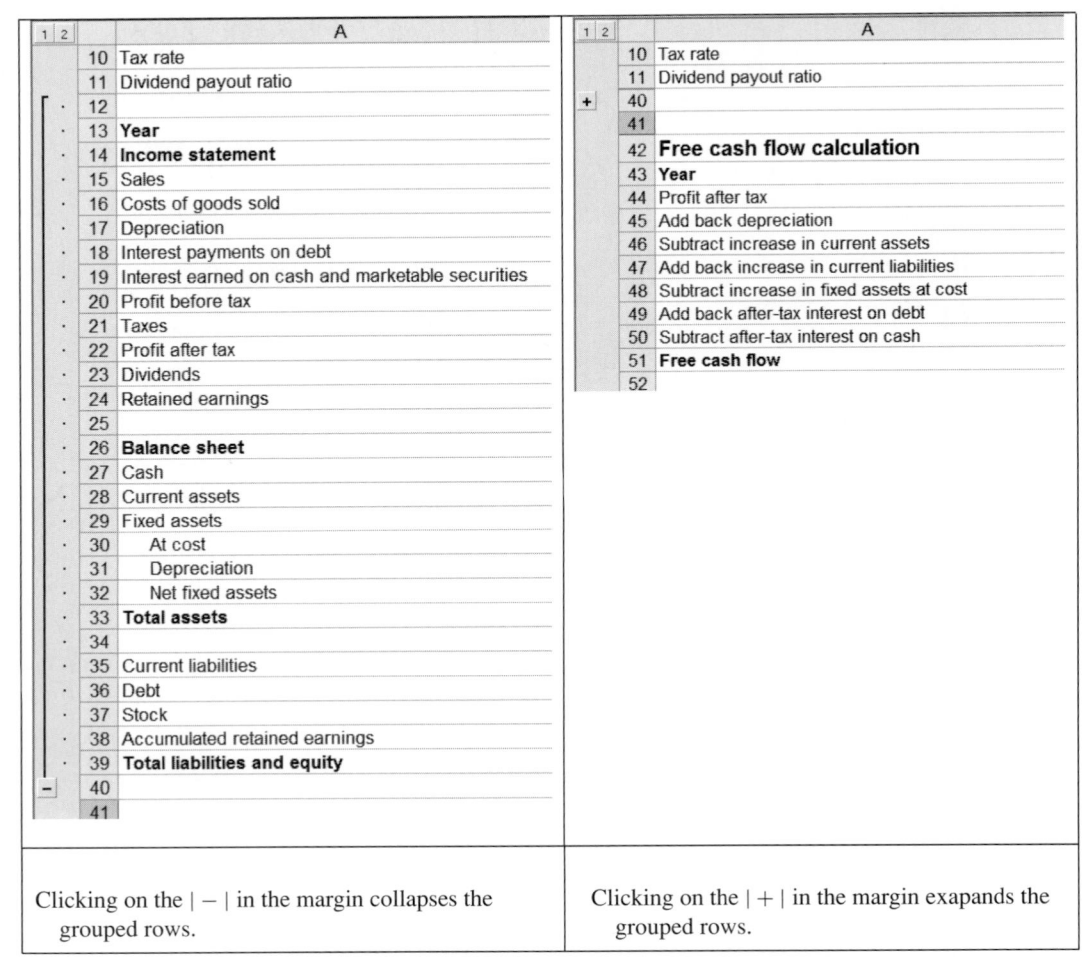

Clicking on the | − | in the margin collapses the grouped rows.

Clicking on the | + | in the margin exapands the grouped rows.

10.5 Reconciling the Cash Balances: The Consolidated Statement of Cash Flows

The free cash flow calculation is different from the "consolidated statement of cash flows" that is a part of every accounting statement (see Chapter 3, pp. 40–42). The FCF calculation shows you how much cash is produced by the firm's operations. On the other hand, the purpose of the accounting statement of cash flows is to explain the increase in the cash accounts in the balance sheet as a function of the cash flows from the firm's operating, investing, and financing activities. Here's the consolidated statement of cash flows for our model:

	A	B	C	D	E	F	G
1	WHIMSICAL TOENAILS--RECONCILING THE CASH BALANCES						
	Note that the profit and loss statement and FCF statement have been hidden						
2	Sales growth	10%					
3	Current assets/Sales	15%					
4	Current liabilities/Sales	8%					
5	Net fixed assets/Sales	77%					
6	Costs of goods sold/Sales	50%					
7	Depreciation rate	10%					
8	Interest rate on debt	10.00%					
9	Interest earned on cash balances	8.00%					
10	Tax rate	40%					
11	Dividend payout ratio	40%					
12							
25							
26	**Balance sheet**						
27	Cash	800,000	639,871	544,001	514,730	554,145	1,461,078
28	Current assets	1,500,000	1,650,000	1,815,000	1,996,500	2,196,150	2,415,765
29	Fixed assets						
30	At cost	10,700,000	12,636,842	14,858,615	17,403,417	20,314,166	23,639,190
31	Depreciation	(3,000,000)	(4,166,842)	(5,541,615)	(7,154,717)	(9,040,596)	(11,238,263)
32	Net fixed assets	7,700,000	8,470,000	9,317,000	10,248,700	11,273,570	12,400,927
33	**Total assets**	10,000,000	10,759,871	11,676,001	12,759,930	14,023,865	16,277,770
34							
35	Current liabilities	800,000	880,000	968,000	1,064,800	1,171,280	1,288,408
36	Debt	3,200,000	2,400,000	1,600,000	800,000	0	0
37	Stock	4,500,000	4,500,000	4,500,000	4,500,000	4,500,000	4,500,000
38	Accumulated retained earnings	1,500,000	2,979,871	4,608,001	6,395,130	8,352,585	10,489,362
39	**Total liabilities and equity**	10,000,000	10,759,871	11,676,001	12,759,930	14,023,865	16,277,770
40							
41							
54	CONSOLIDATED STATEMENT OF CASH FLOWS--RECONCILING THE CASH BALANCES						
55	Cash flows from operating activities						
56	Profit after tax		2,466,452	2,713,549	2,978,549	3,262,426	3,561,295
57	Add back depreciation		1,166,842	1,374,773	1,613,102	1,885,879	2,197,668
58	Adjust for changes in net working capital:						
59	Subtract increase in current assets		(150,000)	(165,000)	(181,500)	(199,650)	(219,615)
60	Add back increase in current liabilities		80,000	88,000	96,800	106,480	117,128
61	Net cash from operating activities		3,563,294	4,011,322	4,506,950	5,055,135	5,656,475
62							
63	Cash flow from investing activities						
64	Aquisitions of fixed assets--capital expenditures		(1,936,842)	(2,221,773)	(2,544,802)	(2,910,749)	(3,325,025)
65	Purchases of investment securities		0	0	0	0	0
66	Proceeds from sales of investment securities		0	0	0	0	0
67	Net cash used in investing activities		(1,936,842)	(2,221,773)	(2,544,802)	(2,910,749)	(3,325,025)
68							
69	Cash flow from financing activities						
70	Net proceeds from borrowing activities		-800,000	-800,000	-800,000	-800,000	0
71	Net proceeds from stock issues, repurchases		0	0	0	0	0
72	Dividends paid		(986,581)	(1,085,420)	(1,191,419)	(1,304,970)	(1,424,518)
73	Net cash from financing activities		(1,786,581)	(1,885,420)	(1,991,419)	(2,104,970)	(1,424,518)
74	=C73+C67+C61						
75	Net increase in cash and cash equivalents		-160,129	-95,870	-29,271	39,415	906,933
76	Cash balances at end of previous year	=C27	800,000	639,871	544,001	514,730	554,145
77	Cash balances at end of current year		639,871	544,001	514,730	554,145	1,461,078
78							
79	=C75+C76. This number should						
80	be equal to cell C27.						

Row 77 checks that the ending balances in the cash accounts derived through the consolidated statement of cash flows match those derived in row 27 of the balance sheets (which use cash as a plug). The fact that row 77 is the same as row 27 shows that our model correctly accounts for all the accounting relations. To see this, look at cells C75, C76, and C77:

- C76 shows that at the end of year 0 the firm's cash balances were $800,000.

- C75 shows that *everything the firm did during the year*—sales, costs of sales, interest paid, new financing through debt and equity, . . .—*everything*—produced a net decrease in cash of $160,129.

- C77 is the sum of the previous two cells: If the firm started off the year with $800,000 in cash and if its total activities produced −$160,129 in cash, then the ending cash balances should be $639,871. And so they are—this is the cash listed in cell C27. Our model accounts for all the firm's activities!

What's More Useful—The Consolidated Statement of Cash Flows or the Free Cash Flow?

What's more useful—the cash increment in row 75 of the consolidated statement of cash flows or the free cash flow we derived in Section 10.4? Although they both have their purposes, there's no doubt that, for finance purposes, the FCF is a more useful and more widely used number. The FCF measures the cash produced by the firm's business activities. It is the relevant finance measure for the effectiveness of the firm at doing what it was founded to do—make something and sell it. The cash increment in row 75 is also important, however. First of all, it allows us to check that we've done our calculations correctly by giving a check and balance on the cash line in the balance sheet. Second, it shows us why the cash line in the balance changed.

10.6 Valuing Whimsical Toenails by Using a DCF Model

The terms "value of a company" or "value of a firm" are often used interchangeably by finance professionals. Even finance professionals, however, can use a confusing variety of meanings for these terms. In finance the definition most often used for "firm value" is the following:

> **The finance definition of firm value:** The value of a firm is the market value of the firm's equity plus the market value of the firm's financial debt.

The finance definition of firm value, which we use in this chapter, is not the only definition of firm value that is in use. Often when individuals discuss the *firm value,* they really mean the *value of its shares*. It is better to use the term *equity value* for the value of a company's shares and to use the term *firm value* (or *company value*) to denote the market value of the firm's equity plus its debt. In our calculations on page 292, we also show you how to compute the value of a firm's shares.

Sometimes the term *firm value* is used to denote the *accounting value* of the firm. Also known as the *book value*, this value is based on the firm's balance sheets. Because accounting statements are based on historical values, people in finance generally prefer not to use this definition. At the end of this section we illustrate why we do not like this valuation method.

In this section we illustrate three methods of computing the finance definition of firm value.

- The simplest valuation method is to value the firm's equity (its shares) using the firm's share price in the market, and to add to this the value of the firm's debt.

- A second valuation method, the DCF method, is based on discounted cash flows. This is the method preferred by finance professionals; it is the main method illustrated in this section. In a DCF valuation, firm value equals the present value of the firm's future FCFs *plus* the value of its currently available liquid assets. The discount rate is the firm's weighted average cost of capital (WACC), which we previously discussed in Chapter 9.

- A third valuation method values the firm by using the book value of a firm's assets.

The Share Price Valuation Method: Valuing Whimsical Toenails by Using Current Share Price

The simplest way to value Whimsical Toenails (WT) is to look at its share price. WT has one million shares, which were trading on 31 December 2004 at $10 per share. Thus, the market value of the firm's equity is $10 million. In addition, the company's balance sheet shows that it has debt of $3.2 million; we use these balance sheet values (also called book values) of the debt as an approximation of the debt's market value.[4]

Using the current share price, the *firm value* of Whimsical Toenails is $13,200,000:

	A	B	C
1	**WHIMSICAL TOENAILS** **Valuation using share price**		
2	Number of shares	1,000,000	
3	Current share price	10.00	
4	Market value of equity	10,000,000	<-- =B2*B3
5			
6	Debt	3,200,000	
7			
8	**Firm value: Market Value of Equity + Debt**	**13,200,000**	<-- =B4+B6

The Discounted Cash Flow (DCF) Valuation Method: Valuing WT by Discounting Its Future Free Cash Flows

The advantage of the share-price valuation method illustrated above is that it is very simple: The firm value equals the market value of the firm's shares plus the book value of its debt. Valuing the company at its current price of $10 per share is perfectly acceptable for someone considering buying a few shares of the company, but it makes less sense if Whimsical Toenails is selling a controlling block of shares. In this case, the purchaser would probably have to take the following considerations into account:

- If the purchaser tried to buy a big block of shares of Whimsical on the open market, he/she might have to offer more than the current market price per share. As the buyer bought more and more shares, the price would go up; in addition, the announcement that someone was trying to take over Whimsical Toenails would—in many cases—force the share price up.

- There are benefits to controlling a company that are not included in the market price per share. The market price of a share reflects the value of a company's future dividends to a *passive* shareholder who has no control over the company. In general, the value of a controlling block of shares is larger than the market value, since the controlling shareholder can actually decide what the company will do. He/she can also derive considerable *private benefits* from running the company.[5]

---

[4]This is common practice. Most company debt is not traded on financial markets, and therefore there is no easily available market value for the debt. As a first approximation, most finance professionals use the book value of a firm's debt as a proxy for the debt's market value.

[5]Economists use the term *private benefits* to denote all kinds of financial and nonfinancial benefits associated with firm ownership. The big car with a driver that the company gives its president is a private benefit of ownership, and so is the feeling of ownership—a psychological benefit, perhaps, but nonetheless valuable.

To deal with these problems, we use the *discounted cash flow* (DCF) valuation method to value the shares. DCF valuations are a standard finance methodology, which defines the value of the firm as the present value of the firm's future free cash flows (FCFs), discounted at the weighted average cost of capital (WACC), plus the firm's initial cash and marketable securities. Section 10.9 discusses the theory behind this method of valuation, but for the moment we skip all the theory and simply present the formula:

$$DCF \text{ firm value} = \frac{\text{market value}}{\text{of firm's debt}} + \frac{\text{market value}}{\text{of firm's equity}}$$

$$= \underbrace{PV \left(\frac{\text{all future FCFs}}{\text{discounted at WACC}} \right)}_{\substack{\uparrow \\ \text{Often called the "enterprise value"} \\ \text{of the firm}}} + \frac{\text{today's cash and}}{\text{marketable securities}}$$

As you can see in the equation, the present value of the firm's future FCFs is often called the firm's *enterprise value*. By using the financial planning model for Whimsical Toenails, we conclude that when the WACC is 14%, a share of Whimsical is worth $20.11:

	A	B	C	D	E	F	G
1		WHIMSICAL TOENAILS--DCF VALUATION					
2	Year	2005	2006	2007	2008	2009	
3	Estimated free cash flow	1,759,895	1,881,136	2,008,739	2,142,733	2,283,085	
4	Terminal value					30,250,880	<-- =F3*(1+B8)/(B7-B8)
5	Total	1,759,895	1,881,136	2,008,739	2,142,733	32,533,966	
6							
7	Weighted average cost of capital, WACC	14.00%					
8	Long-term FCF growth	6.00%					
9							
10	Enterprise value, PV of future FCFs + terminal value	22,512,874	<-- =NPV(B7,B5:F5)				
11	Add current cash & marketable securities	800,000					
12	Firm value	23,312,874	<-- =B11+B10				
13							
14	Subtract out debt	-3,200,000					
15	Estimated value of equity	20,112,874	<-- =B12+B14				
16							
17	Number of shares	1,000,000					
18	Estimated value per share	20.11	<-- =B15/B17				

There are a few things to explain about this valuation:

- We have used the financial planning model of Section 10.4 to project five years of future FCFs. At the end of the five years, we have projected a *terminal value* for the company. The DCF methodology requires us to estimate the present value of all the future free cash flows: *PV (all future FCFs discounted at WACC)*. However, instead of estimating all future FCFs, we estimate five years of FCFs and then estimate the *terminal value*, the value of Whimsical at the end of year 5:

$$\text{enterprise value} = PV \left(\frac{\text{all future FCFs}}{\text{discounted at WACC}} \right)$$

$$= \frac{FCF_{2005}}{(1 + WACC)} + \frac{FCF_{2006}}{(1 + WACC)^2} + \cdots + \frac{FCF_{2009}}{(1 + WACC)^5}$$

$$+ \frac{\text{terminal value}}{(1 + WACC)^5}$$

- The terminal value is estimated by assuming that the 2009 FCF of $2,283,085 will grow in years 2010, 2011, . . . at a long-term FCF growth rate of 6% (cell B8). This means that the terminal value is

$$
\begin{aligned}
\text{terminal value} \atop \text{at end of 2009} &= \frac{FCF_{2010}}{(1+WACC)} + \frac{FCF_{2011}}{(1+WACC)^2} + \frac{FCF_{2012}}{(1+WACC)^3} + \cdots \\
&= \frac{FCF_{2009}*(1+LT\ growth)}{(1+WACC)} + \frac{FCF_{2009}*(1+LT\ growth)^2}{(1+WACC)^2} \\
&\quad + \frac{FCF_{2009}*(1+LT\ growth)^3}{(1+WACC)^3} + \cdots \\
&= \frac{FCF_{2009}*(1+LT\ growth)}{WACC - LT\ growth} \\
&= \frac{\$2,283,085*(1.06)}{14\% - 6\%} = \$30,250,880
\end{aligned}
$$

The theory behind this is explained further in Section 10.9.

- If the weighted average cost of capital (WACC) is 14%, the enterprise value—the present value of the FCFs and the terminal value—is $22,512,874 (cell B10 in the previous spreadsheet).[6]

- Adding current balances of cash and marketable securities to the present value of the FCFs and subtracting out the value of the firm's debts gives an *equity valuation* of $20,112,874 (cell B15). Since there are one million shares outstanding, this values each share at $20.11 (cell B18).

Thus, the conclusion from this DCF valuation is that each share of Whimsical Toenails is worth $20.11, more than double the current market value of $10.

Valuation by Using the Firm's Book Value—A Definition We'd Rather Not Use

There's another valuation method that is sometimes used to value a firm: The *accounting definition* of the firm value uses the balance sheet to arrive at the value of the firm. For the case of Whimsical Toenails, the balance sheet at the end of 2004 looks like:

	A	B	C	D	E	F
1	WHIMSICAL TOENAILS, BALANCE SHEET 31 December 2004					
2	Assets			Liabilities and equity		
3	Cash and marketable securities	800,000		Current liabilities	800,000	
4	Current assets	1,500,000		Debt	3,200,000	
5	Fixed assets at cost	10,700,000				
6	Accumulated depreciation	-3,000,000		Common stock	4,500,000	
7	Net fixed assets	7,700,000		Accumulated retained earnings	1,500,000	
8	Total assets	10,000,000	<-- =B3+B4++B7	Total liabilities and equity	10,000,000	<-- =SUM(E3:E7)

---

[6]See Chapters 9 and 16 for two techniques to compute the WACC.

By the accounting definition of firm value, the firm is worth

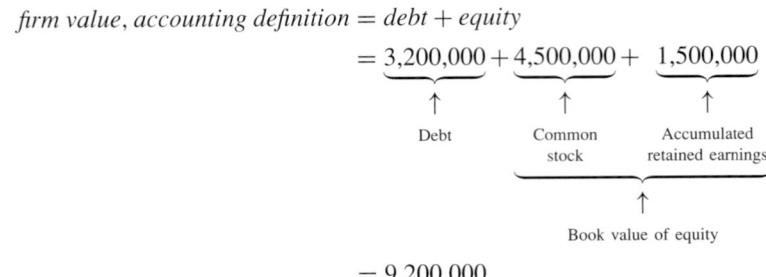

$$\text{firm value, accounting definition} = \text{debt} + \text{equity}$$

$$= \underbrace{3,200,000}_{\text{Debt}} + \underbrace{4,500,000}_{\text{Common stock}} + \underbrace{1,500,000}_{\text{Accumulated retained earnings}}$$

$$\underbrace{\hspace{4cm}}_{\text{Book value of equity}}$$

$$= 9,200,000$$

The accounting definition of firm value relies on *book values,* the value of the firm's debt and equity as listed in the firm's balance sheet. Recall from Chapter 3 that the accounting definition, which is based on historical values, is a *backward-looking* definition. The finance definition of firm value is a *forward-looking* definition (it discounts the future anticipated values of the cash flows). In general, the accounting definition gives an inappropriate firm valuation.[7] In the case of Whimsical Toenails, the forward-looking DCF valuation of the firm is $23,312,874, whereas the backward-looking accounting definition is $9,200,000.

10.7 Using the DCF Valuation: A Summary

The DCF valuation of a firm is based on discounting the firm's future expected free cash flows (FCFs), using the weighted average cost of capital (WACC) as the discount rate. In this section we summarize the steps for implementing this valuation.

Step 1: Estimate the Weighted Average Cost of Capital

The WACC is the discount rate for the future FCFs. We discussed the WACC in Chapter 9 and gave an example of how to estimate it.[8] In this chapter we do not go into the details of estimating the WACC; calculating the WACC entails many assumptions and in many cases the calculation itself becomes a topic of controversy among the parties involved in the valuation. For this example, we assume that the WACC is 14%. In Section 10.8 we perform a sensitivity analysis (using an Excel **Data Table**, discussed in Chapter 30) to show how changes in the WACC affect the valuation.

Step 2: Project a Reasonable Number of FCFs

A financial planning model's predictions of future FCFs are based on the assumption that the parameters of the model will not change by too much. Most financial analysts define "reasonable" to mean number of periods over which this basic assumption is not too silly.[9] Everyone recognizes that a firm's environment is dynamic and that the model parameters will change over time,

---

[7]This is not meant to disparage accounting (very important) or accountants (most of whom would readily agree that book values are an inappropriate approximation to market values).

[8] Later in the book, Chapter 16 gives another approach to estimating the WACC.

[9]The author defines "not too silly" as something he can explain to his mother with a straight face.

a fact that is usually addressed by doing a sensitivity analysis (see Section 10.8). In our valuation we assumed that we can reasonably project the next five years of cash flows.

Step 3: Project the Long-Term FCF Growth Rate and the Terminal Value

Valuation using the DCF method in principle requires us to project an *infinite number* of future FCFs, but in a standard financial planning model we project only a limited number of FCFs. A solution to this problem is to define the firm's terminal value as the firm value at the end of year 5. The definition we use is illustrated in Figure 10.1.

$$DCF\ firm\ value = PV\left(\begin{array}{c} all\ future\ FCFs \\ discounted\ at\ WACC \end{array}\right) + \begin{array}{c} current\ cash\ and \\ marketable\ securities \end{array}$$

$$= \frac{FCF_1}{(1+WACC)} + \frac{FCF_2}{(1+WACC)^2} + \frac{FCF_3}{(1+WACC)^3} + \cdots + \begin{array}{c} Current\ cash\ and \\ marketable\ securities \end{array}$$

$$= \frac{FCF_1}{(1+WACC)} + \frac{FCF_2}{(1+WACC)^2} + \frac{FCF_3}{(1+WACC)^3} + \frac{FCF_4}{(1+WACC)^4} + \frac{FCF_5}{(1+WACC)^5}$$
← *Line* 1: We estimate these FCFs with a financial planning model

$$+ \frac{FCF_6}{(1+WACC)^6} + \frac{FCF_7}{(1+WACC)^7} + \cdots$$
← *Line* 2: We use the terminal value in place of these numbers:

$$\frac{1}{(1+WACC)^5} \underbrace{\frac{FCF_5 * (1 + long\text{-}term\ FCF\ growth)}{WACC - long\text{-}term\ FCF\ growth}}$$
↑
This is the "terminal value"

$$+ \begin{array}{c} today's\ cash\ and \\ marketable\ securities \end{array}$$
← *Line* 3: The last term in the valuation

Figure 10.1　A DCF valuation.

As you can see, there are three parts to this valuation equation:

- Line 1 is the present value of the first five years of free cash flows. We projected these cash flows one-by-one, using our financial planning model.
- Instead of projecting the present value of each of the cash flows in years 6, 7, 8, . . ., infinity, we summarized them in the *present value of the terminal value*. In Line 2 this is given as

$$\frac{1}{(1+WACC)^5} \underbrace{\frac{FCF_5 * (1 + long\text{-}term\ FCF\ growth)}{WACC - long\text{-}term\ FCF\ growth}}$$
↑
This is the "terminal value"

Terminal value is what we project the firm to be worth at the end of the projection horizon. In Section 10.9 we explain how this expression for the terminal value is derived.
- Line 3 gives the value of the cash and marketable securities.

The terminal value formula requires us to estimate the long-term FCF growth rate. In the financial planning model for the Whimsical Toenails FCFs, this long-term growth rate is different from the sales growth rate projected for the company's next five years. As you saw in Section 10.2, we project a growth rate of sales of 10% for Whimsical over the five-year horizon of the planning model. Our criterion for choosing the long-term FCF growth rate of the company is that a company's cash flows cannot grow forever at a rate greater than the economy in which it operates. The long-term rate of 6% for Whimsical Toenails is meant to represent an estimate of the company's sustainable FCF growth rate.

Using this model, we estimate that Whimsical's year 5 FCF is $2,283,085. Using the WACC of 14% and the long-term FCF growth rate of 6%, the company's terminal value is $30,250,880:

$$terminal\ value = \frac{FCF_5 * (1 + long\text{-}term\ FCF\ growth)}{WACC - long\text{-}term\ FCF\ growth} = \frac{\$2,283,085 * (1 + 6\%)}{14\% - 6\%}$$
$$= \$30,250,880$$

Step 4: Determine the Value of the Firm

At this point all the elements of the firm valuation formula are in place:

- WACC: the discount rate for the FCFs and the terminal value
- Five years of FCFs projected from the financial planning model
- The terminal value of the firm
- The firm's initial (year 0) balances of cash and marketable securities
  We can now value the firm:

	A	B	C	D	E	F	G
1	WHIMSICAL TOENAILS--DCF VALUATION						
2	Year	2005	2006	2007	2008	2009	
3	Estimated free cash flow	1,759,895	1,881,136	2,008,739	2,142,733	2,283,085	
4	Terminal value					30,250,880	<-- =F3*(1+B8)/(B7-B8)
5	Total	1,759,895	1,881,136	2,008,739	2,142,733	32,533,966	
6							
7	Weighted average cost of capital, WACC	14.00%					
8	Long-term FCF growth	6.00%					
9							
10	Enterprise value, PV of future FCFs + terminal value	22,512,874	<-- =NPV(B7,B5:F5)				
11	Add current cash & marketable securities	800,000					
12	Firm value	23,312,874	<-- =B11+B10				
13							
14	Subtract out debt	-3,200,000					
15	Estimated value of equity	20,112,874	<-- =B12+B14				
16							
17	Number of shares	1,000,000					
18	Estimated value per share	20.11	<-- =B15/B17				

The value of the firm is $23,312,874 (cell B12). In cells B15 and B18 we've added two more steps, detailed below.

Step 5: Value the Firm's Equity by Subtracting the Value of the Firm's Debt Today From the Firm Value

The firm value is the value of the firm's debt + equity. We are often interested in valuing only the firm's equity—our estimate of the market value of the firm's shares:

$$firm\ value = debt + equity = \$23,312,874$$

This means that

$$equity = firm\ value - debt = \$23,312,874 - \$3,200,000 = \$20,112,874$$

Stock market analysts often use the estimate of a firm's equity value to arrive at a per-share valuation of the firm. They then compare this estimated per-share value to the current market price to come up with a buy or sell recommendation for the stock. Since Whimsical Toenails has 1,000,000 shares outstanding, the estimated market value per share is $20,112,874/1,000,000 = 20.11.

This share valuation is much higher than the current market value per share of $10. If the DCF valuation analysis were being used to make recommendations about the stock, we would expect the analyst would make a "buy" recommendation for the shares of Whimsical Toenails.

Step 6: Adding Midyear Valuation

In Chapter 8 (pp. 207–209) we discussed *midyear valuation* of cash flows. The idea was that, when cash flows occur over the course of the year and not at the end of the year, we should take the standard present value formula and multiply it by $(1 + WACC)^{0.5}$. For Whimsical Toenails, midyear valuation makes sense, since the company's sales occur throughout the year and not just at year-end. In the spreadsheet below you can see how midyear valuation affects the value of the firm and projected share valuation: Cell B10 shows that the present value of future cash flows and terminal value of the firm value increases to $24 million. In cell B18 you can see that the projected share value increases to $21.64 from the $20.11 computed without the midyear valuation.

	A	B	C	D	E	F	G
1	WHIMSICAL TOENAILS--DCF VALUATION using mid-year discounting (see cell B10)						
2	Year	2005	2006	2007	2008	2009	
3	Estimated free cash flow	1,759,895	1,881,136	2,008,739	2,142,733	2,283,085	
4	Terminal value					30,250,880	<-- =F3*(1+B8)/(B7-B8)
5	Total	1,759,895	1,881,136	2,008,739	2,142,733	32,533,966	
6							
7	Weighted average cost of capital, WACC	14.00%					
8	Long-term FCF growth	6.00%					
9							
10	PV of future FCFs + terminal value	24,037,172	<-- =NPV(B7,B5:F5)*(1+B7)^0.5				
11	Add current cash & marketable securities	800,000					
12	Firm value	24,837,172	<-- =B11+B10				
13							
14	Subtract out debt	-3,200,000					
15	Estimated value of equity	21,637,172	<-- =B12+B14				
16							
17	Number of shares	1,000,000					
18	Estimated value per share	21.64	<-- =B15/B17				

Step 7: Don't Trust Anything! Do a Sensitivity Analysis

Valuations are based on a formidable number of assumptions! Performing a sensitivity analysis helps us evaluate the effect of changing values of the main variables on the value of the firm. Our "weapon of choice" for sensitivity analysis is the **Data Table** feature of Excel (see Chapter 30). In the next section we demonstrate the use of sensitivity analysis in the DCF valuation of Whimsical Toenails.

10.8 Sensitivity Analysis

Given the full-blown financial planning model, there are obviously many sensitivity analyses we can perform. Below we show two data tables. The first table analyzes the effect of the sales growth assumption (cell B2 of the model) on the share valuation. In our initial model we estimated sales growth of 10% annually for the next five years. In rows 81–90, we use the **Data Table** feature of Excel to explore the effect of different rates of sales growth on the share valuation of Whimsical Toenails.

	A	B	C	D	E	F	G	H	I
1			WHIMSICAL TOENAILS--FINANCIAL MODEL						
2	Sales growth	10%							
3	Current assets/Sales	15%							
4	Current liabilities/Sales	8%							
5	Net fixed assets/Sales	77%							
6	Costs of goods sold/Sales	50%							
7	Depreciation rate	10%							
8	Interest rate on debt	10.00%							
9	Interest earned on cash balances	8.00%							
10	Tax rate	40%							
11	Dividend payout ratio	40%							
12									
13	**Year**	**2004**	**2005**	**2006**	**2007**	**2008**	**2009**		
14	**Income statement**								
15	Sales	10,000,000	11,000,000	12,100,000	13,310,000	14,641,000	16,105,100		
16	Costs of goods sold	-5,000,000	-5,500,000	-6,050,000	-6,655,000	-7,320,500	-8,052,550		
17	Depreciation	-1,000,000	-1,166,842	-1,374,773	-1,613,102	-1,885,879	-2,197,668		
18	Interest payments on debt	-320,000	-280,000	-200,000	-120,000	-40,000	0		
19	Interest earned on cash and marketable securities	64,000	57,595	47,355	42,349	42,755	80,609		
20	Profit before tax	3,744,000	4,110,753	4,522,582	4,964,248	5,437,376	5,935,491		
21	Taxes	-1,497,600	-1,644,301	-1,809,033	-1,985,699	-2,174,950	-2,374,196		
22	Profit after tax	2,246,400	2,466,452	2,713,549	2,978,549	3,262,426	3,561,295		
23	Dividends	-898,560	-986,581	-1,085,420	-1,191,419	-1,304,970	-1,424,518		
24	Retained earnings	1,347,840	1,479,871	1,628,130	1,787,129	1,957,455	2,136,777		
25									
26	**Balance sheet**								
27	Cash	800,000	639,871	544,001	514,730	554,145	1,461,078		
28	Current assets	1,500,000	1,650,000	1,815,000	1,996,500	2,196,150	2,415,765		
29	Fixed assets								
30	At cost	10,700,000	12,636,842	14,858,615	17,403,417	20,314,166	23,639,190		
31	Depreciation	-3,000,000	-4,166,842	-5,541,615	-7,154,717	-9,040,596	-11,238,263		
32	Net fixed assets	7,700,000	8,470,000	9,317,000	10,248,700	11,273,570	12,400,927		
33	**Total assets**	10,000,000	10,759,871	11,676,001	12,759,930	14,023,865	16,277,770		
34									
35	Current liabilities	800,000	880,000	968,000	1,064,800	1,171,280	1,288,408		
36	Debt	3,200,000	2,400,000	1,600,000	800,000	0	0		
37	Stock	4,500,000	4,500,000	4,500,000	4,500,000	4,500,000	4,500,000		
38	Accumulated retained earnings	1,500,000	2,979,871	4,608,001	6,395,130	8,352,585	10,489,362		
39	**Total liabilities and equity**	10,000,000	10,759,871	11,676,001	12,759,930	14,023,865	16,277,770		
40									
41									
42	**Free cash flow calculation**								
43	**Year**	**2004**	**2005**	**2006**	**2007**	**2008**	**2009**		
44	Profit after tax		2,466,452	2,713,549	2,978,549	3,262,426	3,561,295		
45	Add back depreciation		1,166,842	1,374,773	1,613,102	1,885,879	2,197,668		
46	Subtract increase in current assets		-150,000	-165,000	-181,500	-199,650	-219,615		
47	Add back increase in current liabilities		80,000	88,000	96,800	106,480	117,128		
48	Subtract increase in fixed assets at cost		-1,936,842	-2,221,773	-2,544,802	-2,910,749	-3,325,025		
49	Add back after-tax interest on debt		168,000	120,000	72,000	24,000	0		
50	Subtract after-tax interest on cash		-34,557	-28,413	-25,410	-25,653	-48,365		
51	**Free cash flow**		1,759,895	1,881,136	2,008,739	2,142,733	2,283,085		
52									
53									
54	**Valuing the firm**								
55	Weighted average cost of capital, WACC	14%							
56	Long-term growth rate of FCFs, g	6%							
57									
58	Year 5 FCF	2,283,085							
59	Terminal value	30,250,880	<-- =B58*(1+B56)/(B55-B56)						
60									
61	**Year**	**2004**	**2005**	**2006**	**2007**	**2008**	**2009**		
62	FCF		1,759,895	1,881,136	2,008,739	2,142,733	2,283,085		
63	Terminal value						30,250,880	<-- =B59	
64	Total		1,759,895	1,881,136	2,008,739	2,142,733	32,533,966		
65									
66	PV of row 64	22,512,874	<-- =NPV(B55,C64:G64)						
67	Add in initial (year 0) cash and mkt. securities	800,000	<-- =B27						
68	Firm value	23,312,874	<-- =B67+B66						
69	Subtract out value of firm's debt today	-3,200,000	<-- =-B36						
70	Equity value	20,112,874	<-- =B68+B69						
71	Per-share equity valuation	20.11	<-- =B70/1000000						
72									
73	**Valuing the firm using midyear valuation**								
74	PV of row 64, with mid-year adjustment	24,037,172	<-- =NPV(B55,C64:G64)*(1+B55)^0.5						
75	Add in initial (year 0) cash and mkt. securities	800,000	<-- =B27						
76	Firm value	24,837,172	<-- =B75+B74						
77	Subtract out value of firm's debt today	-3,200,000	<-- =-B36						
78	Equity value	21,637,172	<-- =B76+B77						
79	Per-share equity valuation	21.64	<-- =B78/1000000						
80									
81	**Data table: effect of sales growth on share value**	**Sales growth**	21.64	<-- =B79					
82		0%	20.25						
83		2%	20.70						
84		3%	20.89						
85		6%	21.36						
86		8%	21.55						
87		10%	21.64						
88		12%	21.60						
89		15%	21.30						
90		20%	19.98						
91									

Sales Growth and Share Value

The sales growth assumption produces a surprising result: Up to a point, larger sales growth rates produce large share valuations. But very large growth rates actually reduce the value of the shares.[10]

EXCEL NOTE

DATA TABLES

This may be the appropriate place for you to read Chapter 30, which discusses **Data Tables**. What may be confusing in the data table on page 294 is the "21.64" in cell C81. This is a reference to the share price calculation in cell B79 in the initial model. The data table asks Excel to redo this calculation for the sales growths in cells B82 to B90.

A second sensitivity analysis examines the effect of the weighted average cost of capital and the long-term growth rate (cells B55 and B56) on the per-share valuation. Notice that these two parameters affect the valuation in two ways:

- The terminal value calculation in cell G63 is

$$\frac{FCF_5 * (1 + \text{long-term FCF growth})}{WACC - \text{long-term FCF growth}}$$

This computation is affected by both the long-term growth and the WACC parameters.

- The present value calculation in cell B66 is affected by the WACC.

To examine the effect of these two parameters, we build a two-dimensional data table:

	A	B	C	D	E	F	G
95	=IF(B55>B56,B78,"nmf")						
96			**WACC**				
97		21,637,172	**10%**	**14%**	**20%**	**22%**	**24%**
98		**0%**	20,381,232	13,905,234	9,073,530	8,053,685	7,205,794
99	**Long-term FCF growth**	**2%**	24,469,956	15,623,442	9,743,593	8,571,101	7,613,120
100		**4%**	31,284,495	18,028,934	10,581,171	9,203,499	8,101,912
101		**6%**	44,913,574	21,637,172	11,658,057	9,993,996	8,699,323
102		**8%**	85,800,810	27,650,902	13,093,905	11,010,349	9,446,088
103		**10%**	nmf	39,678,362	15,104,092	12,365,487	10,406,214
104		**12%**	nmf	75,760,741	18,119,373	14,262,680	11,686,382
105		**14%**	nmf	nmf	23,144,842	17,108,469	13,478,617
106		**16%**	nmf	nmf	33,195,778	21,851,451	16,166,970
107							
108			**Note**: Data tables are discussed in Chapter 30				

The results produced by this sensitivity analysis are not surprising:

- *Going across rows* shows that as the WACC increases, the value per share decreases. Since a larger WACC means that the present value of a future cash flow is less, this is to be expected.
- *Going down columns* shows that the larger the long-term growth rate expected from Whimsical Toenails, the more the shares are worth. Again, this is not a surprise, since larger long-term growth rates mean higher FCFs after the year 5 model horizon. As noted in the box

---

[10]The reason for this is probably that large sales growth rates require large amounts of new fixed assets. This reduces the free cash flows by enough to also reduce share value.

below, our terminal value model only works when the long-term growth rate is less than the WACC. When this assumption is not true (meaning the long-term growth $\geq$ WACC), we've had Excel write "nmf" ("no meaningful figure"). The technique for doing this is explained below.

EXCEL/FINANCE NOTE

Notice our use of the **If** function in cell B97 of the data table above. The terminal value formula is

$$terminal\ value = \frac{FCF_5 * (1 + long\text{-}term\ FCF\ growth\ rate)}{WACC - long\text{-}term\ FCF\ growth\ rate}$$

As noted in Chapter 9, this formula is only valid when *WACC > long-term FCF growth*. Since some of the combinations of growth and WACC in the data table violate this condition, we've used the **If** function to isolate them. As used in cell B97, this function says

$$If(B55 > B56, \quad \underbrace{B78} \quad , \quad \underbrace{\text{"nmf"}} \quad)$$

↑	↑
If WACC > long-term FCF growth, put in the valuation as performed in cell B78	If WACC $\leq$ long-term FCF growth, write "no meaningful figure"

10.9 Advanced Section: The Theory Behind the DCF Model

In this section we explain some theoretical points about the valuation model illustrated in the previous section. Not all of this is easy, and you may (understandably) want to skip this section.[11]

Why Is the Firm's Value Related to the PV of the Future FCFs?

Our basic valuation formula is

$$firm\ value = debt + equity$$
$$= \begin{array}{c} initial\ cash \\ and\ marketable \\ securities \end{array} + \frac{FCF_1}{(1 + WACC)^1} + \frac{FCF_2}{(1 + WACC)^2} + \frac{FCF_3}{(1 + WACC)^3} + \cdots$$

The *enterprise value* of the firm is defined to be the value of the firm's operations. In financial theory, the enterprise value is the present value of the firm's future anticipated cash flows. In this section we explain these concepts.

---

[11] Why would an author put a section like this in the book? Our experience is that ultimately almost all finance professionals are called upon to do valuations. At some point in every valuation, someone is going to question your techniques and theory. That's the time to come back to this section.

The Valuation Process

One way of viewing valuation is through the use of the accounting paradigm, but using market values. We rewrite the balance sheet by moving the current liabilities from the liabilities/equity side to the asset side of the balance sheet:

USING THE BALANCE SHEET AS AN ENTERPRISE VALUATION MODEL		
ORIGINAL BALANCE SHEET		
Assets	**Liabilities**	
Cash and marketable securities	Operating current liabilities	
Operating current assets	Debt	
Net fixed assets	Equity	
Goodwill		
Total assets	**Total liabilities and equity**	
THE ENTERPRISE VALUATION "BALANCE SHEET"		
Assets	**Liabilities**	
Cash and marketable securities		
Operating current assets	Debt	
- Operating current liabilities		
= Net working capital		=PV(FCFs discounted at WACC)
Net fixed assets	Equity	
Goodwill		
Firm value	**Firm value**	

To value a company, we set

$$firm\ value = initial\ cash\ balances + \sum_t \frac{FCF_t}{(1+WACC)^t}$$

$$= initial\ cash\ balances + enterprise\ value$$

If we are valuing the equity of the firm, we subtract the value of the debt:

$$equity\ value = firm\ value - debt$$

$$= initial\ cash\ balances + \sum_t \frac{FCF_t}{(1+WACC)^t} - debt$$

$$= \sum_t \frac{FCF_t}{(1+WACC)^t} - (debt - initial\ cash)$$

Note that this means we can write the enterprise balance sheet in a slightly different form:

THE ENTERPRISE VALUATION "BALANCE SHEET" A slight variation (cash netted out from debt)		
Assets	**Liabilities**	
Operating current assets	Debt - cash & Mkt. securities	
- Operating current liabilities	= Net debt	
= Net working capital		=PV(FCFs discounted at WACC)
Net fixed assets	Equity	
Goodwill		
Enterprise Value	**Enterprise Value**	
Note that both variations on the enterprise valuation "balance sheet" give the same equity value.		

We can use the FCF projections and a cost of capital to determine the enterprise value of the firm. Suppose we have determined that the firm's weighted average cost of capital (WACC) is 20%.[12] Then the *enterprise value* of the firm is the discounted value of the firm's projected FCFs plus its terminal value:

$$\text{enterprise value} = \frac{FCF_1}{(1 + WACC)^1} + \frac{FCF_2}{(1 + WACC)^2} + \cdots + \frac{FCF_5}{(1 + WACC)^5}$$
$$+ \frac{\text{year 5 terminal value}}{(1 + WACC)^5}$$

In this formula, the *year 5 terminal value* is a proxy for the present value of all FCFs from year 6 onward.[13]

Terminal Value: In determining the terminal value, we use a version of the Gordon model described in Chapter 9. We have assumed that—after the year 5 projection horizon—the cash flows will grow at a long-term FCF growth of 6%. This gives the terminal value as

$$\text{terminal value at end of year } 5 = \sum_{t=1}^{\infty} \frac{FCF_{t+5}}{(1 + WACC)^t} = \sum_{t=1}^{\infty} \frac{FCF_5 * (1 + LT\ FCF\ growth)^t}{(1 + WACC)^t}$$
$$= \frac{FCF_5 * (1 + LT\ FCF\ growth)}{WACC - growth}$$

The last equality is derived in a manner similar to the dividend valuation of shares (the Gordon model) discussed in Chapter 9.

CONCLUSION

In this chapter we used Excel to construct financial planning models. These models, also called pro forma models or financial planning models, have a variety of uses in finance. Financial planning models are at the heart of most business plans, the financial projections that firms use to persuade banks to loan them money and to persuade investors to buy their shares. Financial planning models are used to value firms (see Chapter 11) and to build scenarios showing how the firm will perform under various operating and financial assumptions.

Building a financial planning model is a powerful intellectual exercise: It forces you to combine accounting statements, the firm's operational parameters, and the firm's financing into one integrated model of the firm.

To do a DCF valuation you have to understand almost all facets of the business:

• How the business works. This affects the financial parameters used in the financial planning model. The composition of the firm's current assets and current liabilities (meaning its net working capital needed to do its business) and the amount of fixed assets (buildings and equipment and land) needed to do this business—all of these factors affect a firm's valuation.

---

[12]In Chapter 9 we introduced the topic of the WACC and showed you how to calculate this using the Gordon dividend model. In Chapter 15 we show an alternative calculation of the WACC, which uses the security market line. In this chapter we simply assume a value for the WACC.

[13]We don't actually project these cash flows. We determine the terminal value based on year 5 FCF.

- How to compute the cost of capital. The weighted average cost of capital (WACC) is the discount rate used to value the future FCFs of the firm. In this chapter we have not discussed its computation (Chapters 9 and 16 give different methods of computing the WACC).
- How to use Excel to do the relevant computations.

EXERCISES

1. Assume the following data describe the activity of your firm in the previous year:
   - The company's cash at the end of the year was $105,000.
   - The company owes $20,000 to its suppliers.
   - The company bought securities in the amount of $22,000.
   - The company's income during the year was $170,000. Of this amount only 70% was paid.
   - The company was forced to pay damages of $40,000 to one of its clients. This amount has still not been paid.
   - The company had materials inventory of $7,500 and product materials of $5,000 at the end of the year.
   - The company has to pay $12,000 to its bank in the following year.
   - The company tax payment is $45,000. Half of the taxes remain unpaid and are due in the current year.
   - The company rented a store for three years at the beginning of the year, paying $14,000 for each year in advance for the entire period.

   Calculate the firm's operating current assets and its operating current liabilities.

2. Here's a basic exercise that will help you understand what's going on in the modeling of financial statements. Replicate the model in Section 10.2. That is, enter the correct formulas for the cells and see that you get the same results as the book. (This turns out to be more of an exercise in accounting than in finance. If you're like many financial modelers, you'll see that there are some aspects of accounting you've forgotten!)

3. The model of Section 10.2 includes costs of goods sold but not selling, general and administrative (SG&A) expenses. Suppose that the firm has $200 of these expenses each year, irrespective of the level of sales.
   (a) Change the model to accommodate this new assumption. Show the resulting profit and loss statements, balance sheets, the free cash flows, and the valuation.
   (b) Do a data table in which you show the sensitivity of the equity value to the level of SG&A expenses. Let SG&A expenses vary from $0 per year to $500 per year.

4. Suppose that in the model of Section 10.2 the fixed assets *at cost* for years 1–5 are 100% of sales (in the current model, it is *net* fixed assets which are a function of sales). Change the model accordingly. Show the resulting profit and loss statements, balance sheets, and free cash flows for years 1–5. (Assume that in year 0, the fixed assets accounts are as shown in Section 10.2. Note that since year 0 is given—it is the current situation of the firm, whereas years 1–5 are the predictions for the future—there is no need for the year 0 ratios to conform to the predicted ratios for years 1–5.)

Note: The CD-ROM that comes with Principles of Finance with Excel contains an Excel notebook entitled **pfe_chap10template.xls**. Except for Exercise 1, this template can be used as the basis for almost all the problems (although you may have to make some changes in the template).

5. Back to the model of Section 10.2 as given in the book. Suppose that the fixed assets at cost follow the step function

$$\text{fixed assets at cost} = \begin{cases} 100\% * sales & \text{if } sales \leq 1200 \\ 1200 + 90\% * (sales - 1200) & 1200 < sales \leq 1400 \\ 1{,}380 + 80\% * (sales - 1400) & sales > 1400 \end{cases}$$

Incorporate this function into the model.

6. Consider the model in Section 10.2. Make two changes in the model: (1) Let debt be the plug and keep cash constant at its year 0 level. (2) Suppose that the firm has 1000 shares and that it decides to pay, in year 1, a dividend per share of 15 cents. In addition, suppose that it wants this dividend per share to grow in subsequent years by 12% per year.
   (a) Incorporate these changes into the pro forma model.
   (b) Do a sensitivity analysis in which you show the effect on the debt/equity ratio of the annual growth rate of dividends. Vary this rate from 0% to 18%, in steps of 2%.

7. The following sheet presents a firm's balance sheet and profit and loss statement:

	A	B
1	**Balance Sheet and P&L statement**	
2	Year	**0**
3	**Income statement**	
4	Sales	50,000
5	Costs of goods sold	(25,000)
6	Depreciation	(20,000)
7	Interest earned on cash	7,000
8	Profit before tax	12,000
9	Taxes (40%)	(4,800)
10	Profit after tax	7,200
11	Retained earnings	7,200
12		
13	**Balance sheet**	
14	Cash	140,000
15	Accounts receivable	10,000
16	Fixed assets	
17	At cost	400,000
18	Depreciation	(240,000)
19	Net fixed assets	160,000
20	**Total assets**	310,000
21		
22	Current liabilities	20,000
23	Debt	-
24	Stock	275,000
25	Accumulated retained earnings	15,000
26	**Total liabilities and equity**	310,000

Assume the following:
- The firm expects its sales growth rate to be 10% per year.
- The current assets at the end of each year are 20% of the annual firm sales.
- The current liabilities at the end of each year are 15% of the annual firm sales.
- The net fixed assets at the end of each year are 320% of annual sales.
- The annual depreciation is 5% of the average of the fixed assets value during the year.

- The costs of goods sold are 50% of sales.
- Interest earned on cash is 5% on the average balances of cash.
- The tax rate is 40%.

Use the above data to project the financial statements for year 1.

8. (a) Extend the model of Exercise 7 to five years.

   (b) The model in part (a) contains the COGS (costs of goods sold) but doesn't contain SG&A (selling, general and administrative) expenses. Assume that these costs are $4,000 in year 0 and have a growth rate of 7.5%. Make the appropriate adjustment to the model of part (a).

9. The following sheet presents a firm's balance sheet and income statement:

	A	B	C	D	E
1	**BALANCE SHEET AND INCOME STATEMENT**				
2	**Assets**			**Liabilities and Equity**	
3	**Current assets**			**Current liabilities**	
4	Cash	10,000		Accounts payable	2,000
5	Prepaid expenses	1,500		**Total current liabilities**	2,000
6	**Total current assets**	11,500			
7				**Long-term liabilities**	
8				Debt	10,000
9	**Fixed assets**				
10	At cost	30,000		**Equity**	
11	Accumulate depreciation	-14,000		Equity	10,500
12	**Net Fixed assets**	16,000		Accumulated retained earnings	5,000
13					
14	**Total assets**	27,500		**Total liabilities and equity**	27,500
15					
16	**Income statement**				
17	Sales	20,000			
18	Cost of Goods Sold (COGS)	-12,000			
19	Depreciation	-2,000			
20	Interest on cash	300			
21	Interest payments on debt	-400			
22	Profit before tax	5,900			
23	Tax (40%)	-2,360			
24	Profit after tax	3,540			
25	Dividend	-708			
26	Retained Earnings	2,832			

(a) You believe that these financial statements are representative of the firm's *value drivers*. (For example, if the sales are $20,000 and the COGS are $12,000, then the COGS to sales parameter is 60%.) Find and calculate the *value drivers* that can be derived from the firm's balance sheet and P&L statement.

(b) Use the following data to project the financial statements for year 1:
- The sales growth is 12%.
- The depreciation is 10% of the average of the fixed assets value during the year.
- The interest rate earned on cash is 5% on the average cash balances.
- The debt payments are $2,000 each year.
- The interest rate on debt is 8%.

(c) Show in a graph the change in the firm's profit relative to the change in the COGS.

10 (a) Extend the project in Exercise 9 to six years.

(b) The model we are dealing with doesn't contain advertising and marketing costs (these usually are a part of the SG&A expenses). Assume that these costs are $800 in year 0, and 5% of sales in years 1–6. Furthermore, assume that the firm has to pay each year for a license at a fixed cost of $1500. Adjust the model in part (a) to these new assumptions.

(c) Show in a graph the change in the firm's profit relative to the change in the license fee.

11. Compute the FCF for the firm model in Exercise 8(a) and in Exercise 10(a).

12. Compute the consolidated statements of cash flow for the firm model in Exercise 8(a) and in Exercise 10(a).

13. The following sheet contains data concerning Donna Company's balance sheet, income statement, and value drivers.

	A	B	C	D	E	F	G
1	**DONNA'S BALANCE SHEET AND INCOME STATEMENT**						
2	**Value Drivers**						
3	Sales growth	15%					
4	Current assets/sales	20%					
5	Current liabilities/sales	14%					
6	Net fixed assets/sales	80%					
7	Costs of goods sold/sales	45%					
8	Depreciation rate	10%					
9	Interest rate on debt	8%					
10	Interest earned on average cash balances	5%					
11	Tax rate	36%					
12	Dividend payout ratio	30%					
13	Annual debt repayments	6,000					
14							
15	**Income statement**						
16	**Year**	**0**	**1**	**2**	**3**	**4**	**5**
17	Sales	45,000					
18	Cost of goods sold (COGS)	-33,000					
19	Depreciation	-4,000					
20	Interest on cash	80					
21	Interest payments on debt	-150					
22	Profit before tax	7,930					
23	Tax (36%)	-2,855					
24	Profit after tax	5,075					
25	Dividend	-1,523					
26	Retained earnings	3,553					
27							
28	**Balance sheet**						
29	**Assets**						
30	Cash	10,000					
31	Current assets	4,700					
32	Fixed assets						
33	At cost	47,000					
34	Accumulate depreciation	-14,000					
35	Net Fixed assets	33,000					
36	**Total assets**	47,700					
37							
38	**Liabilities and Equity**						
39	Current liabilities	4,000					
40	Debt	30,000					
41	Equity						
42	Equity	10,000					
43	Accumulated retained earnings	3,700					
44	**Total liabilities and equity**	47,700					

You know that Donna Company pays $6,000 of its debt every year and that the interest rate, paid and earned, is on the average debt and cash balances, respectively, and the depreciation is on the average fixed assets.

Make a model of Donna's balance sheet, profit and loss statement, and FCF for the following five years based on these data.

14. Consider the following changes in the assumptions regarding the Donna Company from Exercise 13:

   • Assume the debt remains at its current level and the loan is paid back only at the end of year 5.

   • The dividend has a constant growth of 15%, irrelevant of the increase in the company sales.

   • The company pays a bonus of 5% from sales to its employees if the sales are more than $70,000.

   Combine these changes to the pro forma model and the FCF evaluation.

15. How will your answer to Exercise 13 change, if you know that Donna Company intends to increase its debt by 6% each year for the next five years, and that the current liabilities are 25% of COGS?

16. Assume the following sheet presents the balance sheet of your firm:

	A	B	C	D	E
1		**BALANCE SHEET**			
2	**Assets**			**Liabilities and Equity**	
3	**Current assets**			**Current liabilities**	
4	Cash	72,000		Accounts payable	40,000
5	Marketable securities	80,000		Tax payable	35,000
6	Accounts receivable	42,000		Short-term debt	32,000
7	Prepaid expenses	15,000		**Total current liabilities**	107,000
8	**Total current assets**	209,000			
9				**Long-term liabilities**	
10				Debt	420,000
11	**Fixed assets**				
12	At cost	500,000		**Equity**	
13	Accumulated depreciation	-25,000		Equity	120,000
14	**Net fixed assets**	475,000		Accumulated retained earnings	37,000
15					
16	**Total assets**	684,000		**Total liabilities and equity**	684,000

What is the firm's value according to the share price valuation model, if the share price in the market is $5.50 and there are 90,000 outstanding shares?

17. What is the value of the firm in Exercise 16 using the book value? What is the share valuation?

18. The Yahoo profile for PepsiCo Company (PEP) is given below. What is PEP's firm value according to the share price valuation model? What is the PEP book value?

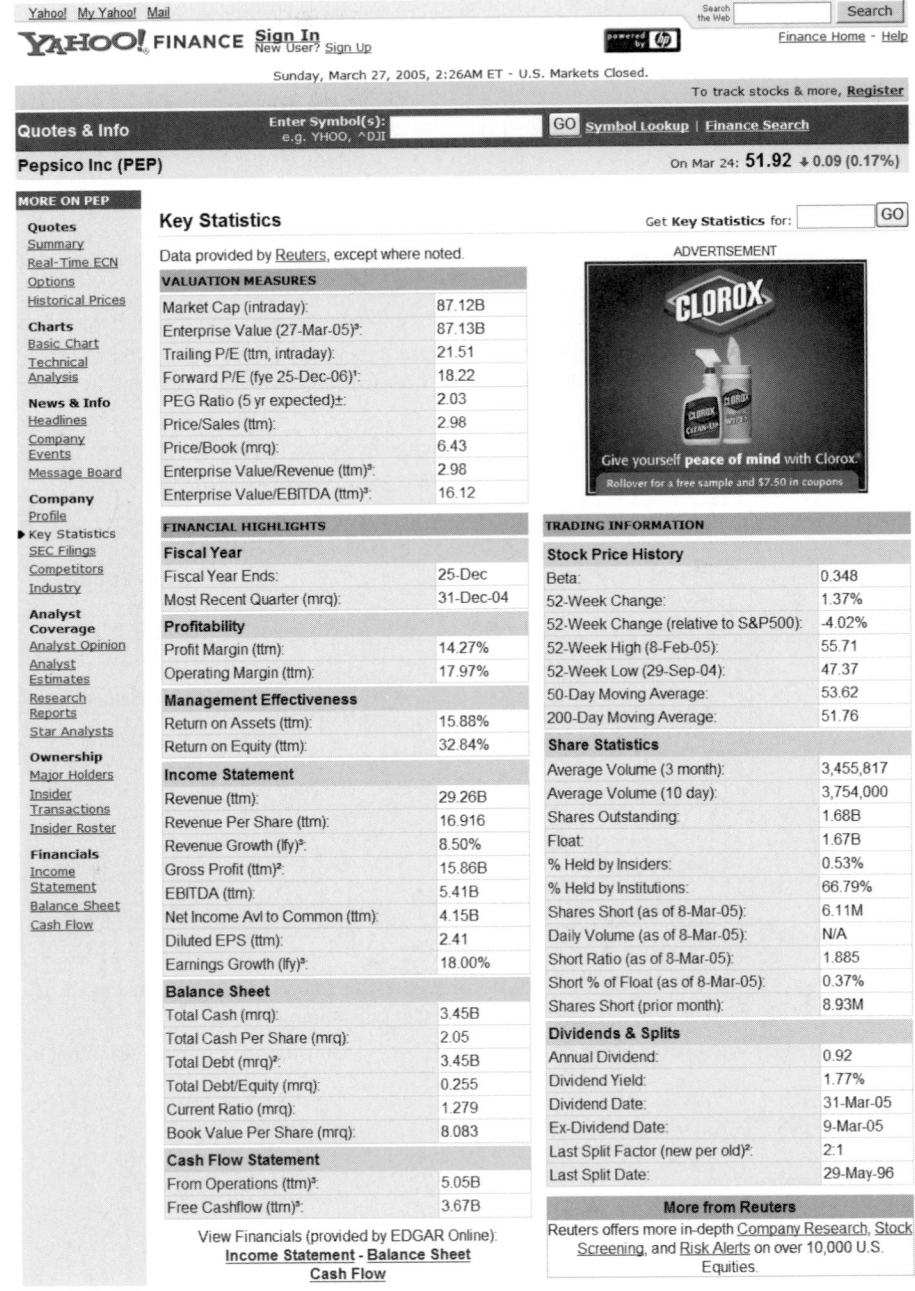

Quotes & Info   Enter Symbol(s): [   ] e.g. YHOO, ^DJI   [GO] **Symbol Lookup** | **Finance Search**

Pepsico Inc (PEP)   On Mar 24: **51.92** ↓0.09 (0.17%)

MORE ON PEP

Quotes
Summary
Real-Time ECN
Options
Historical Prices

Charts
Basic Chart
Technical
Analysis

News & Info
Headlines
Company
Events
Message Board

Company
Profile
▶ Key Statistics
SEC Filings
Competitors
Industry

Analyst
Coverage
Analyst Opinion
Analyst
Estimates
Research
Reports
Star Analysts

Ownership
Major Holders
Insider
Transactions
Insider Roster

Financials
Income
Statement
Balance Sheet
Cash Flow

Key Statistics   Get **Key Statistics** for: [   ] [GO]

Data provided by Reuters, except where noted.

VALUATION MEASURES

Market Cap (intraday):	87.12B
Enterprise Value (27-Mar-05)[3]:	87.13B
Trailing P/E (ttm, intraday):	21.51
Forward P/E (fye 25-Dec-06)[1]:	18.22
PEG Ratio (5 yr expected)±:	2.03
Price/Sales (ttm):	2.98
Price/Book (mrq):	6.43
Enterprise Value/Revenue (ttm)[3]:	2.98
Enterprise Value/EBITDA (ttm)[3]:	16.12

FINANCIAL HIGHLIGHTS

Fiscal Year

Fiscal Year Ends:	25-Dec
Most Recent Quarter (mrq):	31-Dec-04

Profitability

Profit Margin (ttm):	14.27%
Operating Margin (ttm):	17.97%

Management Effectiveness

Return on Assets (ttm):	15.88%
Return on Equity (ttm):	32.84%

Income Statement

Revenue (ttm):	29.26B
Revenue Per Share (ttm):	16.916
Revenue Growth (lfy)[3]:	8.50%
Gross Profit (ttm)[2]:	15.86B
EBITDA (ttm):	5.41B
Net Income Avl to Common (ttm):	4.15B
Diluted EPS (ttm):	2.41
Earnings Growth (lfy)[3]:	18.00%

Balance Sheet

Total Cash (mrq):	3.45B
Total Cash Per Share (mrq):	2.05
Total Debt (mrq)[2]:	3.45B
Total Debt/Equity (mrq):	0.255
Current Ratio (mrq):	1.279
Book Value Per Share (mrq):	8.083

Cash Flow Statement

From Operations (ttm)[3]:	5.05B
Free Cashflow (ttm)[3]:	3.67B

View Financials (provided by EDGAR Online):
Income Statement - Balance Sheet
Cash Flow

TRADING INFORMATION

Stock Price History

Beta:	0.348
52-Week Change:	1.37%
52-Week Change (relative to S&P500):	-4.02%
52-Week High (8-Feb-05):	55.71
52-Week Low (29-Sep-04):	47.37
50-Day Moving Average:	53.62
200-Day Moving Average:	51.76

Share Statistics

Average Volume (3 month):	3,455,817
Average Volume (10 day):	3,754,000
Shares Outstanding:	1.68B
Float:	1.67B
% Held by Insiders:	0.53%
% Held by Institutions:	66.79%
Shares Short (as of 8-Mar-05):	6.11M
Daily Volume (as of 8-Mar-05):	N/A
Short Ratio (as of 8-Mar-05):	1.885
Short % of Float (as of 8-Mar-05):	0.37%
Shares Short (prior month):	8.93M

Dividends & Splits

Annual Dividend:	0.92
Dividend Yield:	1.77%
Dividend Date:	31-Mar-05
Ex-Dividend Date:	9-Mar-05
Last Split Factor (new per old)[2]:	2:1
Last Split Date:	29-May-96

19. The Yahoo profile for Boeing (BA) is given below. What is BA's firm value according to the share price valuation model? What is Boeing's book value?

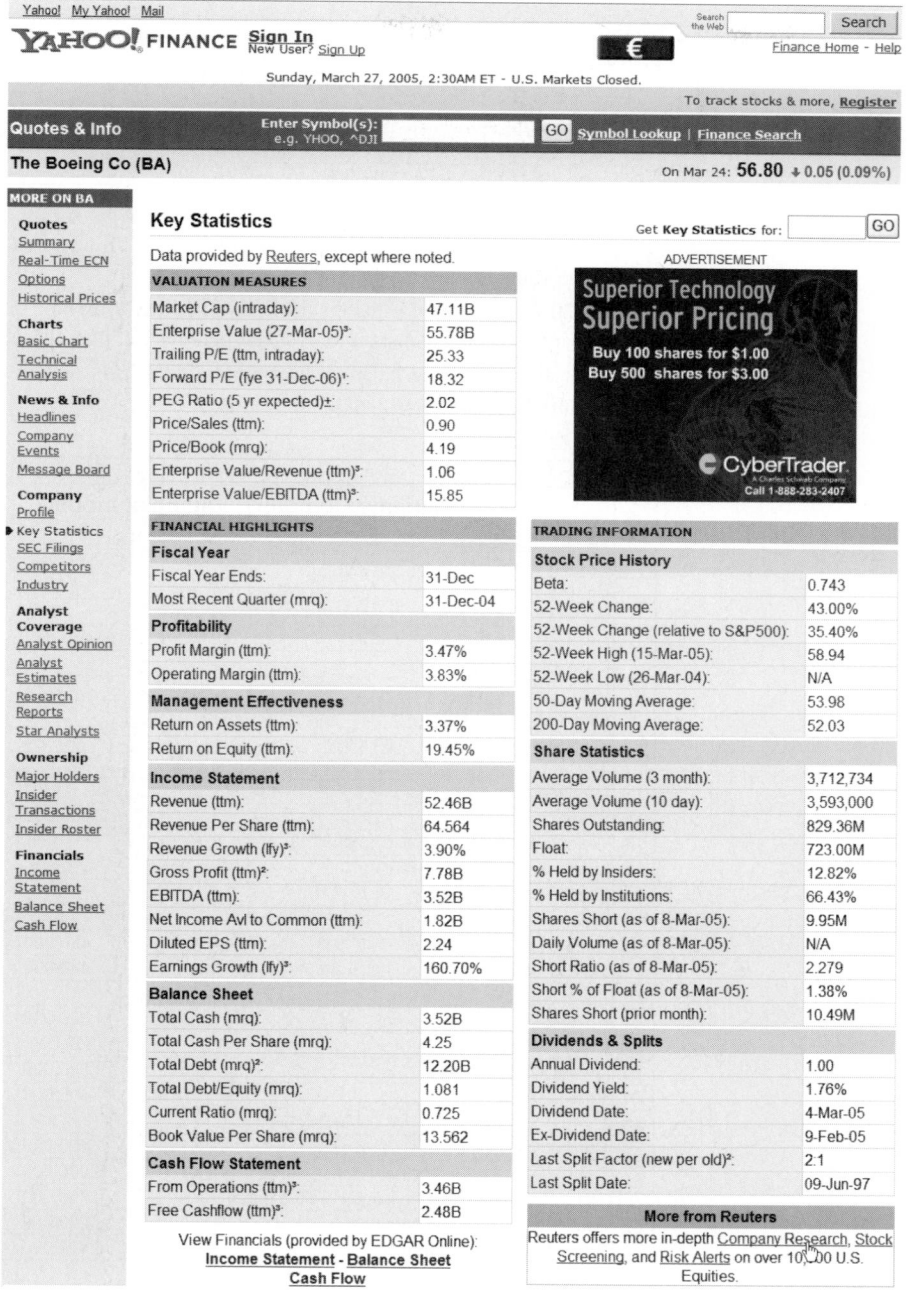

20. Go back to the firm in Exercise 16. In the firm's board meeting it was decided to evaluate the firm using the DCF evaluation, and after performing the evaluation you came up with the data described in the following sheet:

	A	B	C	D	E	F
1	DCF VALUATION					
2	Year	1	2	3	4	5
3	Estimated free cash flow	220,115	232,150	274,410	315,145	316,000
4	Terminal value					750,456
5	Total	220,115	232,150	274,410	315,145	1,066,456

What is the firm's equity value, assuming the firm's WACC is 18% and using the firm's balance sheet? What is the equity value per share?

21. Repeat Exercise 20, but instead of using the firm's terminal value, assume that the FCF of the firm from the sixth year will remain constant forever (perpetuity cash flow). Use midyear discounting.

22. The following sheet presents the balance sheet and value drivers of Yummy Company, which manufactures a very special tomato sauce:

	A	B	C
1	Yummy Company, Financial model		
2	Value drivers:		
3	Sales growth	12%	
4	Current assets/Sales	22%	
5	Current liabilities/Sales	20%	
6	Net fixed assets	5%	
7	Costs of goods sold/Sales	45%	
8	Depreciation rate	20%	
9	Interest rate on debt	8.00%	
10	Interest earned on cash balances	4.00%	
11	Tax rate	36%	
12	Dividend payout ratio	25%	
13	Sales	2,000,000	
14	Weighted average cost of capital	16%	
15	Long-term FCF growth rate	4%	
16			
17	Balance sheet		
18	Cash	460,000	
19	Current assets	440,000	
20	Fixed assets		
21	At cost	4,000,000	
22	Depreciation	(500,000)	
23	Net fixed assets	3,500,000	
24	Total assets	4,400,000	
25			
26	Current liabilities	400,000	
27	Debt	3,000,000	
28	Stock (1,500,000 shares, issued at $0.5 each)	750,000	
29	Accumulated retained earnings	250,000	
30	Total liabilities and equity	4,400,000	
31			

Additional model assumptions are:
- The FCF evaluation is for a five-year period. In addition, a terminal value should be determined using the long-term FCF growth rate.

- The debt principal repayments are $300,000 each year.
- Cash is a plug in the model.

Make a pro forma model for Yummy and compute the firm value using a DCF valuation model with year-end discounting.

23. Compute the following while referring to the Yummy Company in Exercise 22:
    (a) Show how the company value and its share value change if you use midyear discounting.
    (b) Show in a graph the sensitivity of the enterprise value (of the end-year calculation) to the growth in sales.
    (c) Show in a graph the sensitivity of the enterprise value (of the end-year calculation) to the company's WACC.

24. The following sheet presents the balance sheet and value drivers of Little India—a company that operates Indian food restaurants:

	A	B	C
1	**Little India, Financial model**		
2	**Value drivers:**		
3	Sales growth	25%	
4	Current assets/Sales	10%	
5	Current liabilities/Sales	30%	
6	Net fixed assets	15%	
7	Costs of goods sold/Sales	35%	
8	Depreciation rate	5%	
9	Interest rate on debt	8.00%	
10	Interest earned on cash balances	3.00%	
11	Tax rate	40%	
12	Dividend payout ratio	20%	
13	Sales	1,100,000	
14	Weighted average cost of capital	12%	
15	Long-term FCF growth rate	3%	
16			
17	**Balance sheet**		
18	Cash	370,000	
19	Current assets	110,000	
20	Fixed assets		
21	At cost	2,000,000	
22	Depreciation	(500,000)	
23	Net fixed assets	1,500,000	
24	**Total assets**	1,980,000	
25			
26	Current liabilities	330,000	
27	Debt	1,000,000	
28	Stock (500,000 shares, issued at $1 each)	500,000	
29	Accumulated retained earnings	150,000	
30	**Total liabilities and equity**	1,980,000	
31			

Additional model assumptions are:

- The FCF evaluation is for a five-year period. In addition, a terminal value should be determined using the long-term FCF growth rate.
- The debt principal repayments are $200,000 each year.
- Cash is a plug in the model.

Make a pro forma model including a DCF valuation to determine the company value and its estimated share value using midyear discounting.

PART III

PORTFOLIO ANALYSIS AND THE CAPITAL ASSET PRICING MODEL

In Part 3 we discuss how portfolio composition affects the risk of the combined assets. Most individuals hold investment portfolios composed of multiple stocks and bonds. This means that the risk of the investment portfolio is related to the combined riskiness of the securities in the portfolio, as opposed to the riskiness of the individual portfolio assets.

Chapter 11 starts by introducing and illustrating the concept of financial risk. This chapter examines the three components of an asset's risk: horizon, safety, and liquidity. Using illustrations from the stock and bond markets, we show how even safe assets can be risky. We also show how risk can be measured.

In order to discuss portfolio risks, you will need some statistical background. Chapter 12 develops the statistical concepts that you need to analyze portfolios. Although many readers of *Principles of Finance with Excel* have had a statistics course, Chapter 12 assumes virtually no background. Of course Excel—with its many mathematical and statistical functions—is extraordinarily helpful in doing portfolio statistics.

Chapters 13 and 14 combine the statistical analysis of portfolios with some basic economics. The result is the capital asset pricing model (CAPM). This model relates portfolio returns to portfolio risks (a concept summarized in the capital market line, the CML). The CAPM also relates the risks of individual assets to their returns, a concept known as the security market line (SML).

Chapters 15 and 16 show how the SML can be used. In Chapter 15 we examine the uses of the SML to measure portfolio performance: How well do portfolio managers perform, given the riskiness of their portfolios? Chapter 16 returns to the concept of the weighted average cost of capital (WACC) first discussed in Chapter 9; this chapter shows how the SML can be used to compute the cost of equity and the WACC.

WHAT IS RISK?

OVERVIEW

Risk is the magic word in finance. Whenever finance people can't explain something, they try to look confident and say "it must be the risk." If you want to appear intelligent when hearing a financial presentation, look skeptical and say, "Have you considered the risks?" Usually that's enough to score a point or two.[1]

Our intuition usually relates financial risks to *unpredictability*. A financial asset like a savings account is thought to be not risky because its future value is known, whereas a financial asset like a stock is risky because we do not know what it will be worth in the future. Financial assets of different types have different gradations of risk: Our intuitions tell us that a savings account is less risky than a share in a company, and a share in a high-tech start-up is more risky than a share in a well-established blue-chip company.

The intuition that ties unpredictability and risk together is valid but can have some surprising aspects. For example, in Section 11.2 we show that a Treasury bill ("T-bill"), a certain kind of bond issued by the United States government, can sometimes be risky, even though it is completely safe. The T-bill becomes risky if you need to sell it before it matures. We illustrate this risk with an example. We also look at the risk of holding a share and show that it can be quantified statistically. This is an important insight for Chapters 12–14, where we use a statistical description of stock price risk to talk about choosing portfolios of stocks.

We have tried to make the chapter unstatistical and nonmathematical. However, inevitably the measurement of risk involves some calculations.[2]

Finance Concepts Discussed

- Ex-post and ex-ante returns
- Holding-period returns
- Treasury bond returns
- Return statistics—mean, variance, and standard deviation

Excel Functions Used

- **Month**
- **Sqrt**
- **Average**
- **Varp**
- **Frequency**

---

[1]I give my students the following hint about taking finance exams: Suppose you have to answer a question to which you absolutely don't know the answer ("What is the zeta function of the annual returns?" "How do you explain the difference between XYZ Corp.'s annual returns over time?"). If you know nothing about the question, make up a meaningless sentence that includes the word "risk" ("The zeta function of the annual returns relates to the riskiness of the returns." "XYZ's annual returns vary because of the changing risk of the company.") You're bound to get a point or two.

[2]Students reading this book will generally have had a statistics course. This chapter assumes some familiarity with basic statistical concepts and the next chapter reviews these concepts in the context of financial assets. In this sense Chapters 11 and 12 are twins.

11.1 The Risk Characteristics of Financial Assets: Some Introductory Blather

In the course of your life you'll be exposed to many financial assets. You've already been exposed to them, even if you didn't know that they were "financial assets": When you were small, your parents might have opened a savings account for you at the local bank, or your grandparents bought you a few shares of stock. Now that you're a student, you're stuck with student loans, and each month you're trying to decide whether to pay off your credit card balances or let them ride for another month and pay interest on them. Once you finish school, you'll be taking a car loan, buying a house and taking a mortgage, buying stocks and bonds, and so on.

All financial assets have different characteristics of *horizon, safety,* and *liquidity.* All three of these terms are in some basic sense indicative of the asset's riskiness. In this section we briefly review these concepts.

Horizon

Some assets are *short-term* and others *long-term.* Money deposited in a checking account is a good example of a *very short-term* financial asset; the money can be withdrawn at any time. On the other hand, many savings accounts require you to deposit the money for a given period of time. Look at Figure 11.1, which shows the rates offered on certificates of deposit (CDs) by Metropolitan Bank of Chicago. A CD is a time deposit at a bank—a deposit that cannot be withdrawn for a certain period of time.[3] Not surprisingly, longer-term CDs offer higher interest rates.

You're not always "locked in" to a financial asset with a long horizon. Many long-horizon assets can be sold in the open market. Suppose, for example, that you buy a ten-year government bond. You can "cash out" of the bond at almost any time by selling the bond in the open market, but selling the bond before its ten-year maturity exposes you to the riskiness of an unknown market price. This subject is explored in detail in Section 11.2.

Some assets have a long and indeterminate horizon. A share of stock in a company is a good example. Holding a share of McDonald's stock, for example, entitles you to whatever dividends the company pays its shareholders for as long as you hold the stock and the company exists. You can, of course, sell the stock in the stock market, but this exposes you to the risks of stock price fluctuations. In Section 11.3 we discuss how to analyze the riskiness of stock holding; this is a topic to which we return in much greater detail in Chapters 12–15.

Safety

Financial assets differ in the certainty with which you get back your money. The Metropolitan Bank CDs in Figure 11.1 are guaranteed by the Federal Deposit Insurance Corporation, an agency of the United States government, up to a limit of $100,000. Up to this limit, the purchaser of a Metropolitan Bank CD will get his/her money back (including interest), even if the Metropolitan Bank fails to meet its obligations.

CDs issued by the Millenium Bank and Trust (MB&T) of St. Vincent (a small Caribbean country) pay much higher interest rates (see Figure 11.2) but are not guaranteed by the U.S. government. The return on the MB&T CDs is less certain and consequently the interest rates offered by the bank are higher.

---

[3]Most banks will allow you to withdraw your money from a CD before the horizon date, but only if you pay a penalty.

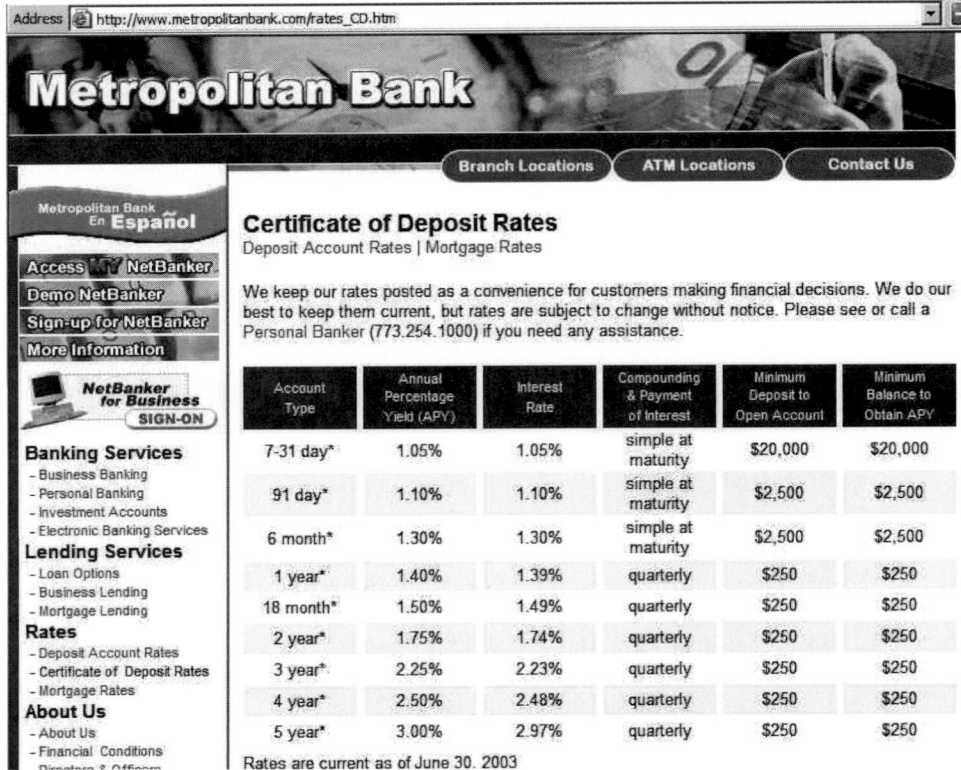

Figure 11.1 Certificate of deposit (CD) rates offered by the Metropolitan Bank of Chicago on June 30, 2003. Metropolitan Bank offers a variety of CDs, which differ by interest rate and by the amount of time the money is locked up. CDs with longer lock-up times offer higher interest rates. APY is Metropolitan Bank's terminology for the effective annual interest rate (EAIR) discussed in Chapter 6. For example, the five-year CD pays 2.97% quarterly. This makes the EAIR 3.00%:
$$EAIR = (1 + 2.97\%/4)^4 - 1 = 3.00\%.$$

The issuer of a CD announces the interest rate to be paid on the CD and will, presumably, keep this promise if possible. The same holds for a bond issued by a company or a government. On the other hand, the issuer of a stock does not give any undertaking about either the stock's dividends or the market price of the stock. In this sense the safety of a stock is much less than the safety of a CD or a bond.

In general, the less safe an asset, the greater the return investors will demand and expect from the asset. Thus, for example, if Metropolitan Bank's CDs pay interest between 1% and 3%, intelligent holders of McDonald's stock (less safe and more uncertain than a CD) should expect a return greater than 1–3%.

This business of "expected return" is complicated:

- If you buy a Metropolitan Bank five-year CD, you are promised an annual return of 3%. You will get this annual return with absolute certainty (well, *almost absolute:* There's always the remote possibility of a catastrophe that prevents both Metropolitan and the U.S. government from honoring their obligations). For the Metropolitan Bank five-year CD, the *expected return* and the *realized return* (by which we mean the actual return received) are the same. In economists'

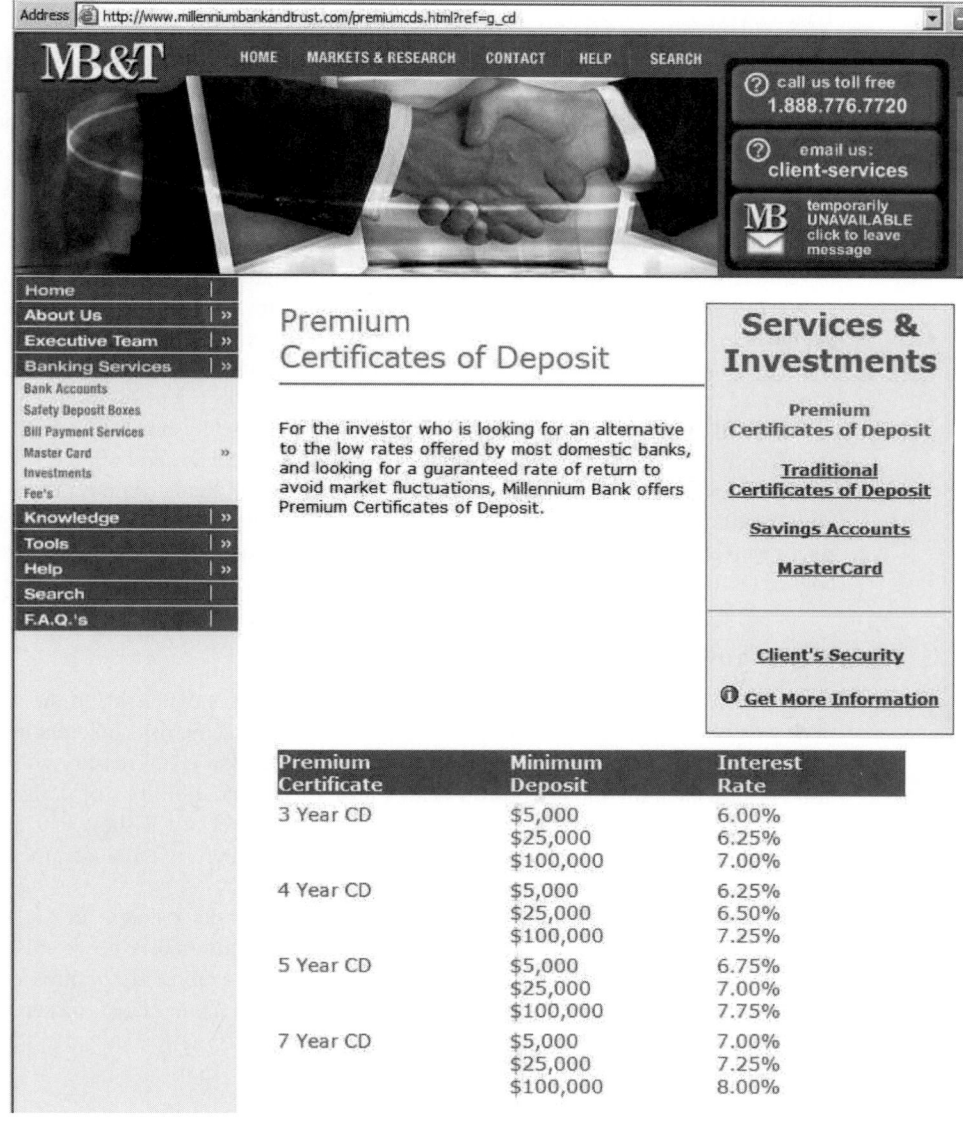

Figure 11.2 CD rates offered by the Millenium Bank and Trust (St. Vincent). In many respects the Millenium Bank CDs are similar to those offered by Metropolitan Bank (Figure 11.1). However, Millenium Bank CDs are not guaranteed by an agency of the United States federal government. The rates reflect this risk and are higher than those offered by Metropolitan Bank.

jargon, the expected return is often called the *ex-ante return* and the realized return is often called the *ex-post* return (this terminology is derived from Latin words for "before" and "after").

- If you buy a share of McDonald's stock, you will *expect* to get more than 3% annual return. However, in this case this *expectation* is merely an *anticipated average future return*. In other words, you would be disappointed but not too surprised if the actual annual return on the stock after five years was less than 3%.

Liquidity

The *ease* with which an asset can be bought or sold is the asset's *liquidity*. In general, the more liquid an asset, the easier it is to "get rid of" and the less its risk.

Listed stocks of major American companies have very high liquidity. For the period 1990–1999, the average daily number of McDonald's shares traded (meaning shares bought and sold) on the New York Stock Exchange was 1.5 million shares. This is the average; the highest number of shares traded daily was almost 12 million and the lowest number of shares was 63,000. If you want to buy or sell a single share of stock (or even several thousand shares), you'll have no trouble doing so: McDonald's stock is very liquid.

Liquidity has another aspect, which financial economists call *price impact*. Suppose you decided to sell the 1,000 shares of McDonald's stock your father gave you. You'll have no trouble selling the stock, but will your sale affect the market price? For McDonald's stock the answer is "no."

Not all stocks are equally liquid: Aladdin Knowledge Systems is a small company that trades on the NASDAQ Stock Exchange. On an average day around 60,000 shares of Aladdin are bought and sold, but this number has been as low as 100 shares per day. You would have relatively little trouble buying or selling several thousand shares of Aladdin stock, but your action might well affect the market price of the stock. Aladdin is not nearly as liquid as McDonald's and consequently has greater liquidity risk.

What Now?

Horizon, safety, and *liquidity* all determine the *risk* of a financial asset. In the succeeding sections we give some concrete examples. We start by looking at the risks inherent in holding a U.S. Treasury bill. A T-Bill is completely *safe,* in the sense that the U.S. Treasury will keep its obligation to pay back the money borrowed. It's also very *liquid*—billions of dollars of T-bills are bought and sold every day in the financial market. However, we'll show that the *horizon* of a T-bill means that it is *somewhat risky*—if you try to sell it before it matures, the market price is unpredictable.

From the T-bill we move on to an analysis of the risks inherent in McDonald's stock. McDonald's stock is *not safe* in the sense that the company makes no promises about either dividends or the future market price of the stock. We'll analyze the returns on McDonald's stock over the decade 1990–2000 and we'll try to make some statistical sense out of these returns.

IS IT RISK OR UNCERTAINTY?

Frank H. Knight (1885–1972) wrote a dissertation in 1921 called *Risk, Uncertainty and Profit*. Knight used *risk* to mean *randomness with knowable probabilities* and *uncertainty* to mean *randomness that is unmeasurable*. In finance the distinction between these two concepts is often blurred and the words "risk" and "uncertainty" are used interchangeably.

11.2 A Safe Security Can Be Risky Because It Has a Long Horizon

Finance people use the words "risk-free" and "riskless" to describe an asset whose value in the future is known with certainty. One classic textbook example of a risk-free asset is a bank savings account. If you deposit $100 in your bank savings account, which currently earns 10%, then you *know* that one year from now there will be $110 in the account. It's risk-free and it's safe.

A United States Treasury bill is an example of a safe asset that is not riskless. Treasury bills are short-term bonds issued by the government of the United States.[4] Unlike bank CDs, Treasury bills do not have an explicit interest rate. Instead they are sold at a discount—a bill with a face value of $1,000 which matures one year from now might be sold today for $953.04. In this case the purchaser of the bill who holds the bill to maturity would be paid $1,000 by the U.S. Treasury and would thus earn a rate of return of $1,000/953.04 - 1 = 4.93\%$ Since Treasury bills are issued by the U.S. government, at least one kind of risk—default risk—is absent from these instruments: Since the government owns the printing machines that produce dollar bills, it can always run off a few dollars to make good on its promises.

While Treasury bills are free of default risk, however, they may have elements of *price risk*. The rest of this section illustrates this.

Suppose that on 1 January 2001 you buy a one-year $1,000 U.S. Treasury bill, intending to hold the bill until its maturity on 1 January 2002. As we said, a Treasury bill doesn't pay any interest; instead, it is bought at a discount—that is, for less than its face value. In the case at hand, suppose you buy the bill for $953.04; since it matures in one year after the purchase, you anticipate getting interest of 4.93%:

	A	B	C
1	**INTEREST ON THE TREASURY BILL**		
2	Purchase price	953.04	
3	Payoff on maturity	1,000.00	<-- This is the Treasury bill's face value
4			
5	Interest	4.93%	<-- =B3/B2-1

Now before we start doing fancier calculations, let's make one thing perfectly clear: *If you hold the Treasury bill from 1 January 2001 until its maturity one year later, you will absolutely, definitely earn 4.93% interest.* T-bills are obligations of the United States government and it has never defaulted on them.

In finance jargon the *ex-ante* return (sometimes called the *anticipated* or *expected* return) is the return you *think* you're going to get. The *ex-post* return (also called the *realized* return) is the *actual* return that you get when you sell the asset. For the Treasury bill illustrated here, the ex-ante return equals the ex-post return *if you hold the bill until maturity*. This is always true for riskless bonds.

---

[4]There are many different kinds of bonds. For a more complete discussion, see Chapter 18.

The Price Risk of Treasury Bills

Out of curiosity, you track the market price of the bill on the first of each month during the year. Here's what you find:

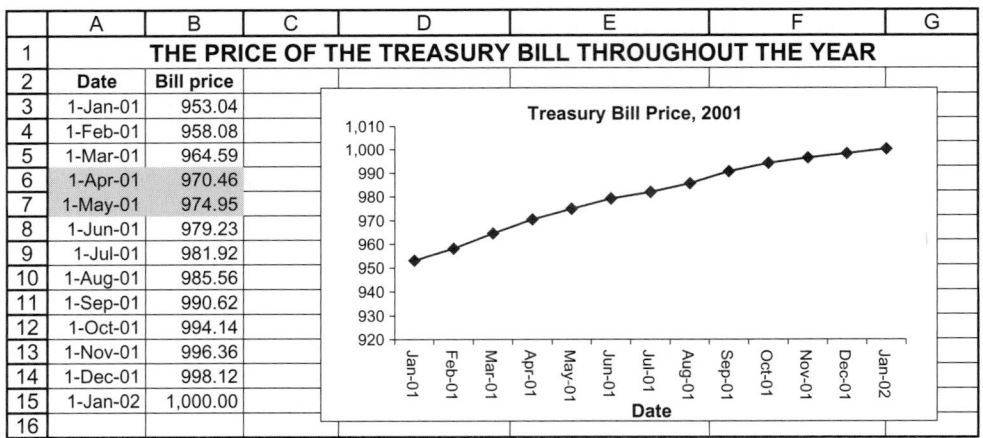

	A	B	C	D	E	F	G
1	**THE PRICE OF THE TREASURY BILL THROUGHOUT THE YEAR**						
2	Date	Bill price					
3	1-Jan-01	953.04					
4	1-Feb-01	958.08					
5	1-Mar-01	964.59					
6	1-Apr-01	970.46					
7	1-May-01	974.95					
8	1-Jun-01	979.23					
9	1-Jul-01	981.92					
10	1-Aug-01	985.56					
11	1-Sep-01	990.62					
12	1-Oct-01	994.14					
13	1-Nov-01	996.36					
14	1-Dec-01	998.12					
15	1-Jan-02	1,000.00					
16							

We use this monthly price data to compute some returns.

What Ex-Post Rate of Return Would You Have Earned If You'd Sold the Treasury Bill Early?

Suppose you had sold the T-bill on 1 May 2001 for $974.95. What would you have earned? A relatively simple calculation provides the answer. The monthly rate of return—the *ex-post* return—is defined by

$$1 + \textit{ex-post monthly rate of return} = \left(\frac{\textit{price on , 1 May 01}}{\textit{initial price on 1 Jan 01}} \right)^{1/4}$$
$$= \left(\frac{974.95}{953.04} \right)^{1/4} = 1.0057$$

The exponent of 1/4 is there because of the four-month interval between January and May. If we raise this to the 12th power, we will get an annual rate of return of 7.06%:

	A	B	C
1	**ANNUALIZED EX-POST RETURN, JAN-MAY**		
2	Bought, 1 January 2001	953.04	
3	Sold, 1 May 2001	974.95	
4	Monthly return	0.57%	<-- =(B3/B2)^(1/4)-1
5	Annualized return	7.06%	<-- =(1+B4)^12-1

If, instead, you had sold the Treasury bill on April 1, one month earlier, you would have made 7.51% in annual terms:

	A	B	C
1	**ANNUALIZED EX-POST RETURN, JAN-APRIL**		
2	Bought, 1 January 2001	953.04	
3	Sold, 1 April 2001	970.46	
4	Monthly return	0.61%	<-- =(B3/B2)^(1/3)-1
5	Annualized return	7.51%	<-- =(1+B4)^12-1

We can do this exercise for each of the months from February to December. In the spreadsheet below we calculate the ex-post, annualized return from selling the Treasury bill at the beginning of February, March, . . . , December:

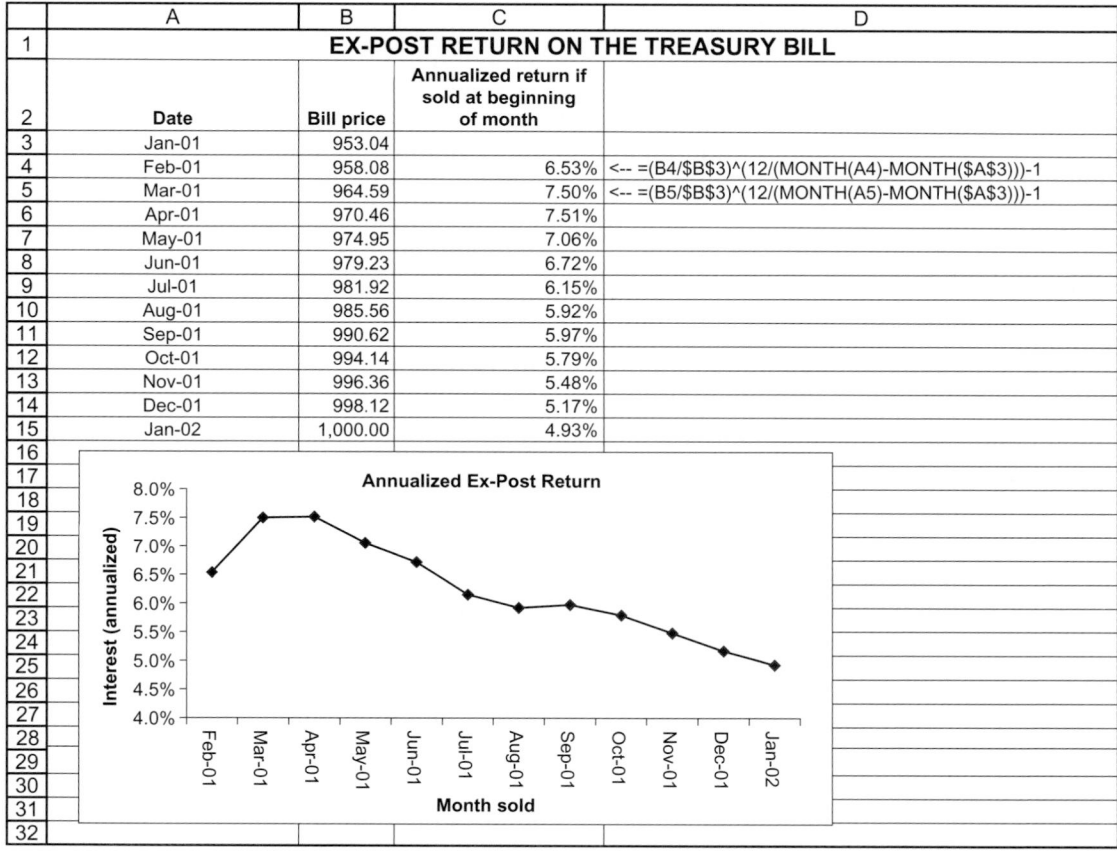

	A	B	C	D
1	**EX-POST RETURN ON THE TREASURY BILL**			
2	Date	Bill price	Annualized return if sold at beginning of month	
3	Jan-01	953.04		
4	Feb-01	958.08	6.53%	<-- =(B4/$B$3)^(12/(MONTH(A4)-MONTH($A$3)))-1
5	Mar-01	964.59	7.50%	<-- =(B5/$B$3)^(12/(MONTH(A5)-MONTH($A$3)))-1
6	Apr-01	970.46	7.51%	
7	May-01	974.95	7.06%	
8	Jun-01	979.23	6.72%	
9	Jul-01	981.92	6.15%	
10	Aug-01	985.56	5.92%	
11	Sep-01	990.62	5.97%	
12	Oct-01	994.14	5.79%	
13	Nov-01	996.36	5.48%	
14	Dec-01	998.12	5.17%	
15	Jan-02	1,000.00	4.93%	

As you can see, if the T-bill is sold before its maturity, there is a considerable amount of risk—defined here as the possible variation in the ex-post rate of return. The Treasury bill—a completely safe security in the sense that the U.S. Treasury will always make good on its obligation—has price risk, which translates to risky returns if sold before maturity.

EXCEL NOTE

The interest rate calculations above use the following formula:

$$r_{monthly} = 1 + monthly\ interest\ rate = \left(\frac{T\text{-}bill\ price,\ month\ t}{T\text{-}bill\ purchase\ price} \right)^{1/(number\ of\ months\ held)}$$

$$r_{annual} = 1 + annual\ interest\ rate = (1 + r_{monthly})^{12}$$

In order to calculate the number of months the T-bill has been held, we use the Excel function **Month**. This function, when applied to a date, identifies the month by a number (January = 1, February = 2, ...):

	A	B	C
1	**USING EXCEL'S MONTH FUNCTION**		
2	Date	Month	
3	3-Jan-03	1	<-- =MONTH(A3)
4	16-Sep-06	9	<-- =MONTH(A4)

What Ex-Ante Rate of Return Would You Have Earned If You'd Bought the Treasury Bill During the Year?

In the previous exercise we calculated the ex-post rate of return that you would have earned if you had bought the T-bill on 1 January 2001 and had sold it before the bill's maturity on 1 January 2002. There's a second "game" we can play with the T-bill prices. Suppose you had bought the bill at the beginning of May for 974.95 and suppose you intended to hold it until the end of the year. What's the annualized ex-ante return you could expect? We can compute this by first computing the monthly ex-ante return and then annualizing this return in a manner similar to our computation for the ex-post returns:

$$1 + ex\text{-}ante\ monthly\ rate\ of\ return = \left(\frac{1,000}{price\ on\ 01\ May\ 01} \right)^{1/8}$$

$$= \left(\frac{1,000}{974.95} \right)^{1/8}$$

$$= 1.0032$$

$$annualized\ ex\text{-}ante\ return = (1.0032)^{12} - 1$$

$$= 3.88\%$$

If we do this for each of the months, we'll see that throughout 2001 the ex-ante rate on Treasury bills fell:

	A	B	C	D	E	F
1				THE EX-ANTE RATE THROUGHOUT 2001 Using Treasury-bill prices		
2	Date	Bill price	Months till maturity	Implied monthly interest ex-ante rate	Ex-ante rate annualized	=($B$15/B3)^(1/C3)-1
3	Jan-01	953.04	12	0.40%	4.93%	<-- =(1+D3)^12-1
4	Feb-01	958.08	11	0.39%	4.78%	
5	Mar-01	964.59	10	0.36%	4.42%	
6	Apr-01	970.46	9	0.33%	4.08%	
7	May-01	974.95	8	0.32%	3.88%	
8	Jun-01	979.23	7	0.30%	3.66%	
9	Jul-01	981.92	6	0.30%	3.72%	
10	Aug-01	985.56	5	0.29%	3.55%	
11	Sep-01	990.62	4	0.24%	2.87%	
12	Oct-01	994.14	3	0.20%	2.38%	
13	Nov-01	996.36	2	0.18%	2.21%	
14	Dec-01	998.12	1	0.19%	2.29%	
15	Jan-02	1,000.00	0			
16						

Implied Annual Interest Rate

What's the Message?

This example, which illustrates the riskiness of a "riskless" U.S. Treasury bill, illustrates that financial risk depends on horizon: A financial asset can be riskless over one horizon and risky over another. In our example, buying the Treasury bill at any point during the year and holding it until maturity *guarantees* that the *ex-ante* return will equal the *ex-post* return. On the other hand, selling the bill before its maturity involves risk—in this case the realized return (the ex-post return) varies.

A Final Word: What Caused the Riskiness of the Treasury Bills?

We've shown that holding a T-bill during 2001 could have been pretty risky—if you were thinking of selling the bill before maturity. The cause of all this uncertainty was the Federal Reserve

Bank's Open Market Committee. This powerful committee sets short-term interest rates, which have a dramatic effect on the value of all bonds, but especially on short-term bonds like Treasury bills. In an effort to shore up the flagging U.S. economy, the Fed's Open Market Committee reduced interest rates *eleven times* during the course of 2001! These changes in interest rate caused the changes in the ex-post and ex-ante returns, which we've documented in this section.

11.3 Risk in Stock Prices: McDonald's Stock

A U.S. Treasury bill is a relatively simple security: The issuer is very well-known and has never defaulted, the *ex-ante* return can be derived from the price, and this return is guaranteed if you hold the bill until maturity. A stock has none of these properties and is thus in every sense riskier. The problem is how to quantify this risk.

Here's an example—Figure 11.3 shows how the stock price of McDonald's varied over the decade of the 1990s.

The fact that the stock's price goes up and down is an indication of the stock's riskiness.[5] If we calculate the daily returns, we see a different kind of risk. Below we calculate the *daily return* from holding McDonald's stock—this is, what you would earn in percentages if you bought the stock at its closing price on day t and sold it at its closing price on day $t + 1$:

$$daily\ return,\ day\ t = \frac{P_{t+1}}{P_t} - 1$$

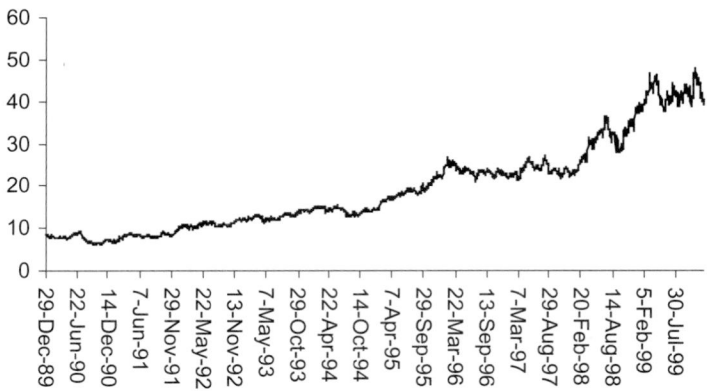

Figure 11.3 The stock price of McDonald's, 29 December 1989 to 31 December 1999.

If you plot the daily returns for one month, you get a very spiky pattern:

---

[5]A technical note that you can ignore but that may make your finance professor happy: The prices of McDonald's stock have been adjusted to include dividends.

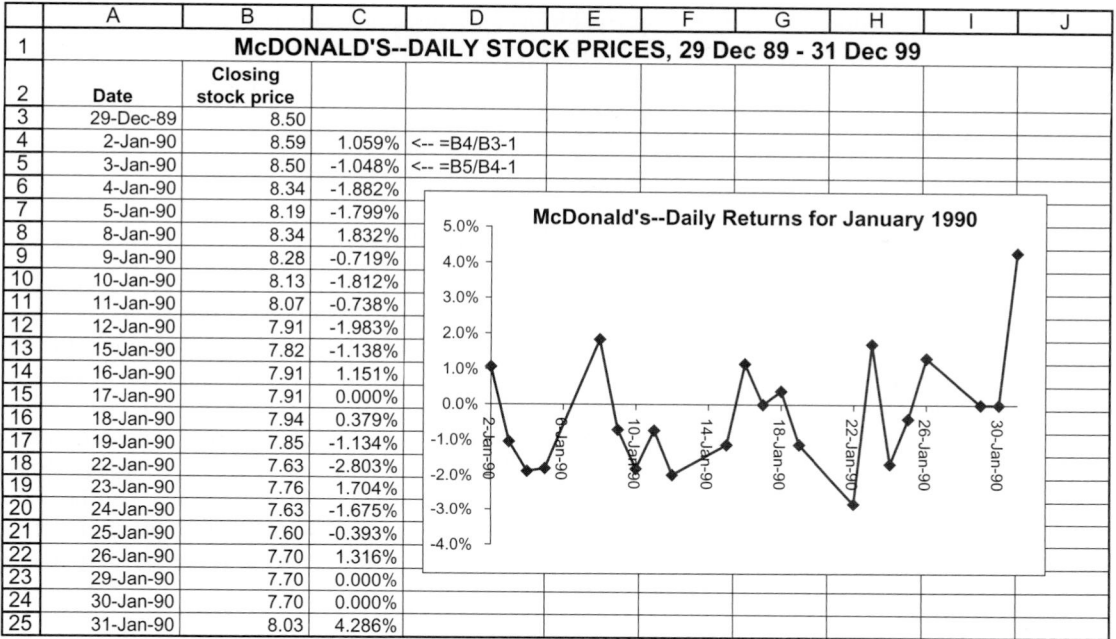

	A	B	C	D	E	F	G	H	I	J
1			McDONALD'S--DAILY STOCK PRICES, 29 Dec 89 - 31 Dec 99							
2	Date	Closing stock price								
3	29-Dec-89	8.50								
4	2-Jan-90	8.59	1.059%	<-- =B4/B3-1						
5	3-Jan-90	8.50	-1.048%	<-- =B5/B4-1						
6	4-Jan-90	8.34	-1.882%							
7	5-Jan-90	8.19	-1.799%							
8	8-Jan-90	8.34	1.832%							
9	9-Jan-90	8.28	-0.719%							
10	10-Jan-90	8.13	-1.812%							
11	11-Jan-90	8.07	-0.738%							
12	12-Jan-90	7.91	-1.983%							
13	15-Jan-90	7.82	-1.138%							
14	16-Jan-90	7.91	1.151%							
15	17-Jan-90	7.91	0.000%							
16	18-Jan-90	7.94	0.379%							
17	19-Jan-90	7.85	-1.134%							
18	22-Jan-90	7.63	-2.803%							
19	23-Jan-90	7.76	1.704%							
20	24-Jan-90	7.63	-1.675%							
21	25-Jan-90	7.60	-0.393%							
22	26-Jan-90	7.70	1.316%							
23	29-Jan-90	7.70	0.000%							
24	30-Jan-90	7.70	0.000%							
25	31-Jan-90	8.03	4.286%							

If you plot the daily returns for all 2,528 data points, you get a very "noisy" pattern:

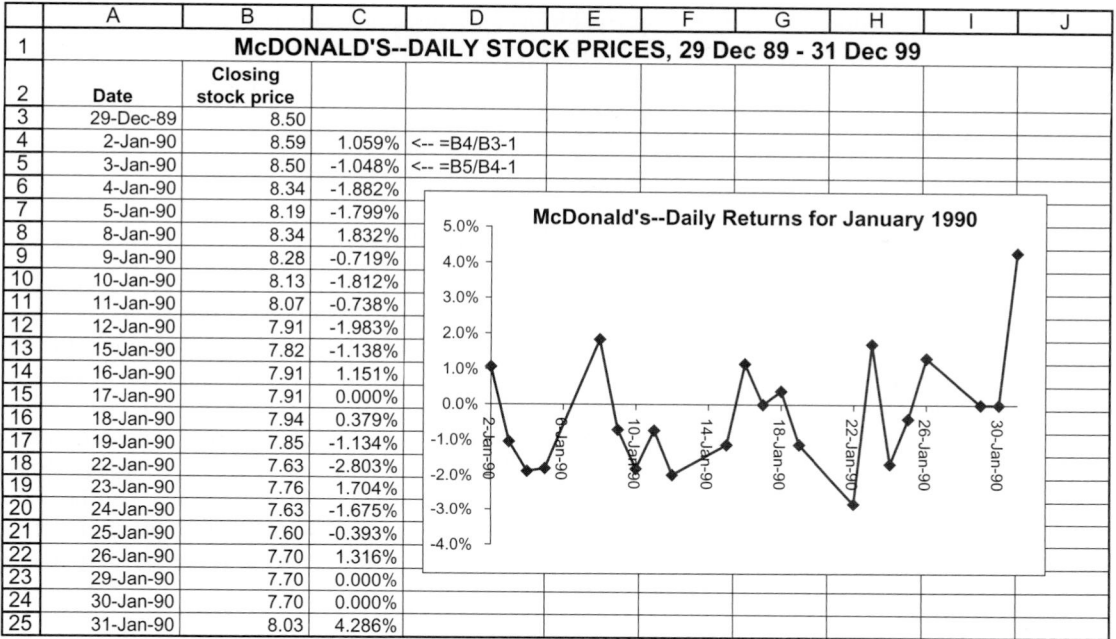

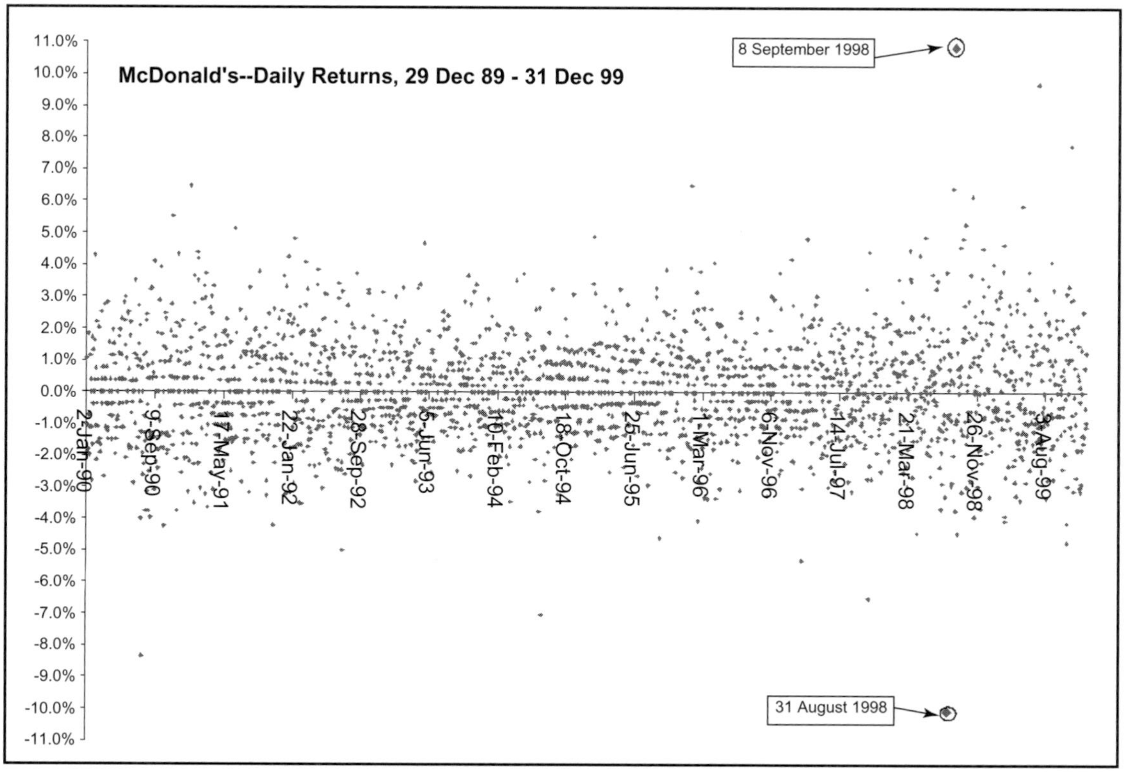

Each dot represents the return on McDonald's stock on a particular day. Although there are dots all over the place, there seem to be slightly more dots above the *x*-axis than below it, indicating that on average the return on McDonald's stock was positive. The two circled returns represent the highest and lowest daily returns over the period: On 31 August 1998 the price of McDonald's stock went down by 10.071% and eight days later, on 8 September 1998, the price increased by 10.863%.

The Distribution of McDonald's Stock Returns

The previous two graphs show the return on McDonald's stock on each specific date. These graphs clearly show that the stock is risky—the returns vary from day to day—but they don't give much insight into the statistical nature of the riskiness of the stock. A different way to think about the riskiness of McDonald's stock is to look at the frequency distribution of the daily returns: Of the 2,528 daily returns, how many were between 0.40% and 1.09%? The answer turns out to be 416, which is 16.456% of the total number of returns. As another example: A total of 36 of the returns (1.424% of the total), were between -3.80% and -3.10%. In the spreadsheet below we've used Excel's **Frequency** function to calculate the whole frequency distribution of the returns (see the Excel Note on page 326 for more on how to use this function). A plot of the returns looks very much like the normal distribution (the "bell curve") you've probably studied in a statistics course.

McDONALD'S--DAILY STOCK PRICES, 29 Dec 89 - 31 Dec 99

Date	Stock price	C	D
29-Dec-89	8.50		
2-Jan-90	8.59	1.059%	<-- =B4/B3-1
3-Jan-90	8.50	-1.048%	<-- =B5/B4-1
4-Jan-90	8.34	-1.882%	
5-Jan-90	8.19	-1.799%	
8-Jan-90	8.34	1.832%	
9-Jan-90	8.28	-0.719%	
10-Jan-90	8.13	-1.812%	
11-Jan-90	8.07	-0.738%	
12-Jan-90	7.91	-1.983%	
15-Jan-90	7.82	-1.138%	
16-Jan-90	7.91	1.151%	
17-Jan-90	7.91	0.000%	
18-Jan-90	7.94	0.379%	
19-Jan-90	7.85	-1.134%	
22-Jan-90	7.63	-2.803%	
23-Jan-90	7.76	1.704%	
24-Jan-90	7.63	-1.675%	
25-Jan-90	7.60	-0.393%	
26-Jan-90	7.70	1.316%	
29-Jan-90	7.70	0.000%	
30-Jan-90	7.70	0.000%	
31-Jan-90	8.03	4.286%	
1-Feb-90	8.16	1.619%	
2-Feb-90	8.19	0.368%	
5-Feb-90	8.25	0.733%	
6-Feb-90	8.16	-1.091%	
7-Feb-90	8.34	2.206%	
8-Feb-90	8.16	-2.158%	
9-Feb-90	8.13	-0.368%	
12-Feb-90	8.00	-1.599%	
13-Feb-90	8.03	0.375%	
14-Feb-90	7.94	-1.121%	
15-Feb-90	8.10	2.015%	
16-Feb-90	7.97	-1.605%	
20-Feb-90	7.85	-1.506%	
21-Feb-90	7.70	-1.911%	
22-Feb-90	7.70	0.000%	
23-Feb-90	7.57	-1.688%	
26-Feb-90	7.76	2.510%	

Computing the frequency distribution of MCD returns

Largest daily return	10.86%	<-- =MAX(C4:C2531)
Smallest daily return	-10.07%	<-- = MIN(C4:C2531)

Bin	How many?	Percentage
-10.08%	0	0.000%
-9.38%	1	0.040%
-8.68%	0	0.000%
-7.99%	1	0.040%
-7.29%	0	0.000%
-6.59%	1	0.040%
-5.89%	1	0.040%
-5.19%	1	0.040%
-4.49%	3	0.119%
-3.80%	11	0.435%
-3.10%	36	1.424%
-2.40%	68	2.690%
-1.70%	138	5.459%
-1.00%	337	13.331%
-0.30%	471	18.631%
0.40%	457	18.078%
1.09%	416	16.456%
1.79%	265	10.483%
2.49%	162	6.408%
3.19%	75	2.967%
3.89%	48	1.899%
4.59%	18	0.712%
5.29%	8	0.316%
5.98%	3	0.119%
6.68%	4	0.158%
7.38%	0	0.000%
8.08%	1	0.040%
8.78%	0	0.000%
9.48%	0	0.000%
10.17%	1	0.040%
10.87%	1	0.040%

Note: We've used the Excel **Frequency** function (see Excel Note).
To understand the numbers: there is 1 daily return between -10.08% and -9.38%.
There are 0 daily returns between -9.38% and-8.68%, etc.

McDonald Stock Returns Look Like the Normal Distribution "Bell Curve"

The highlighted data in the table on the left is shown as larger data points in the graph.

EXCEL NOTE

THE FREQUENCY FUNCTION

The frequency distribution that gave rise to the "bell curve" for McDonald's stock returns was calculated with an Excel function called **Frequency**. To use this function, consider the following example, which gives the monthly returns on Ford stock between January 2001 and January 2003:

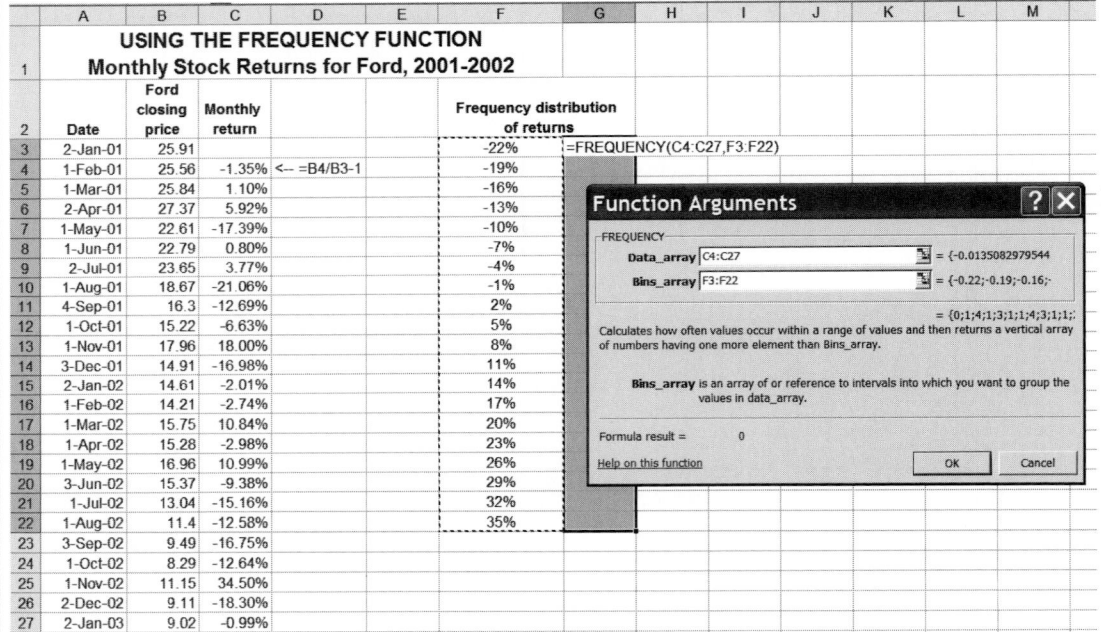

	A	B	C	D	E	F	G	H	I	J	K	L	M
1	**USING THE FREQUENCY FUNCTION** **Monthly Stock Returns for Ford, 2001-2002**												
2	Date	Ford closing price	Monthly return			Frequency distribution of returns							
3	2-Jan-01	25.91				-22%	=FREQUENCY(C4:C27,F3:F22)						
4	1-Feb-01	25.56	-1.35%	<-- =B4/B3-1		-19%							
5	1-Mar-01	25.84	1.10%			-16%							
6	2-Apr-01	27.37	5.92%			-13%							
7	1-May-01	22.61	-17.39%			-10%							
8	1-Jun-01	22.79	0.80%			-7%							
9	2-Jul-01	23.65	3.77%			-4%							
10	1-Aug-01	18.67	-21.06%			-1%							
11	4-Sep-01	16.3	-12.69%			2%							
12	1-Oct-01	15.22	-6.63%			5%							
13	1-Nov-01	17.96	18.00%			8%							
14	3-Dec-01	14.91	-16.98%			11%							
15	2-Jan-02	14.61	-2.01%			14%							
16	1-Feb-02	14.21	-2.74%			17%							
17	1-Mar-02	15.75	10.84%			20%							
18	1-Apr-02	15.28	-2.98%			23%							
19	1-May-02	16.96	10.99%			26%							
20	3-Jun-02	15.37	-9.38%			29%							
21	1-Jul-02	13.04	-15.16%			32%							
22	1-Aug-02	11.4	-12.58%			35%							
23	3-Sep-02	9.49	-16.75%										
24	1-Oct-02	8.29	-12.64%										
25	1-Nov-02	11.15	34.50%										
26	2-Dec-02	9.11	-18.30%										
27	2-Jan-03	9.02	-0.99%										

Function Arguments

FREQUENCY

Data_array `C4:C27` = {-0.0135082979544

Bins_array `F3:F22` = {-0.22;-0.19;-0.16;-

= {0;1;4;1;3;1;1;4;3;1;1;

Calculates how often values occur within a range of values and then returns a vertical array of numbers having one more element than Bins_array.

Bins_array is an array of or reference to intervals into which you want to group the values in data_array.

Formula result =   0

Help on this function   OK   Cancel

When you finish putting in range C4:C27 and F3:F22 as shown above, *don't click on* **OK**! Instead, simultaneously press the keys [Ctrl]+[Shift]+[Enter]. This will put the frequency in the spreadsheet as shown on the next page:

	F	G
2	**Frequency distribution of returns**	
3	-22%	0
4	-19%	1
5	-16%	4
6	-13%	1
7	-10%	3
8	-7%	1
9	-4%	1
10	-1%	4
11	2%	3
12	5%	1
13	8%	1
14	11%	2
15	14%	0
16	17%	0
17	20%	1
18	23%	0
19	26%	0
20	29%	0
21	32%	0
22	35%	1

This table shows that in the period January 2001 to January 2003, there was one month when Ford stock had a return between –22% and –19%, four months when Ford stock had a return between –19% and –16%, and so on.

Computing the Average and Standard Deviation of the McDonald's Returns

In the spreadsheet below we look at the end-year prices of McDonald's between 1989 and 1999. Using these data, we can compute the average annual return of 18.86%. On average, a McDonald's shareholder got an annual return of 18.86% per year over the period 1990–1999. The standard deviation of the annual returns is 23.28%. The standard deviation is a statistical measure of the variation of the stock's returns—the greater the standard deviation, the greater the riskiness of the stock.

	A	B	C	D	E	F	G	H
1			McDONALD'S--End-Year Stock Prices, 1989–1999					
2	Date	Stock price	Return					
3	29-Dec-89	8.50				Statistics		
4	31-Dec-90	7.17	-15.647%	<-- =B4/B3-1		Largest annual return	60.88%	<-- =MAX(C4:C13)
5	31-Dec-91	9.36	30.544%	<-- =B5/B4-1		Smallest annual return	-15.65%	<-- =MIN(C4:C13)
6	31-Dec-92	12.01	28.312%					
7	31-Dec-93	14.04	16.903%			Average annual return	18.86%	<-- =AVERAGE(C4:C13)
8	30-Dec-94	14.41	2.635%			Variance of annual returns	0.0542	<-- =VARP(C4:C13)
9	29-Dec-95	22.23	54.268%			Standard deviation of annual returns	23.28%	<-- =STDEVP(C4:C13)
10	31-Dec-96	22.35	0.540%					
11	31-Dec-97	23.52	5.235%					
12	31-Dec-98	37.84	60.884%					
13	31-Dec-99	39.71	4.942%					
14								
15			STATISTICAL REVIEW					
16		McDonald's return	Return minus average, squared			This statistical review shows you how to compute the average, variance, and standard deviation using the formulas described in the text and (hopefully) learned in your statistics course.		
17	31-Dec-90	-15.65%	11.908%	<-- =(B17-$B$28)^2		See the "Excel and Statistical Review" box in the text for more details.		
18	31-Dec-91	30.54%	1.365%	<-- =(B18-$B$28)^2				
19	31-Dec-92	28.31%	0.893%					
20	31-Dec-93	16.90%	0.038%					
21	30-Dec-94	2.64%	2.633%					
22	29-Dec-95	54.27%	12.536%					
23	31-Dec-96	0.54%	3.357%					
24	31-Dec-97	5.23%	1.857%					
25	31-Dec-98	60.88%	17.659%					
26	31-Dec-99	4.94%	1.938%					
27								
28	Average	18.86%	<-- =SUM(B17:B26)/10					
29	Variance	0.0542	<-- =SUM(C17:C26)/10					
30	Standard deviation	23.28%	<-- =SQRT(B29)					

EXCEL NOTE

EXCEL AND STATISTICAL REVIEW

We delve deeper into statistics in Chapter 12. Here's a reminder of the meanings of the terms:

- The *average* (also called the *mean*) annual return for McDonald's is computed by summing the annual returns and dividing by 10, the number of returns. In cell G7 we've computed the average by using the Excel function **Average**; in cell B28 we compute the average by using **=Sum(B17:B26)/10**.

- The *variance* of McDonald's annual returns is computed in three steps: (1) Subtract each return from the average. Then (2) square the result; these "squared deviations from the average" are shown in cells C17:C26. (3) Average the sum of the squared deviations. This is illustrated in cell B29. Cell G8 shows that the Excel function **Varp** gives the same result.

- Since the returns are in percent, the variance has units "percent squared." This is a bit difficult to understand. The *standard deviation* of the returns is the square root of the variance (this has units that are percent). Informally, you can think of the standard deviation as representing the average percentage variability of the individual returns. Cell B30 used the Excel function **Sqrt** to derive the standard deviation, and cell G9 uses the Excel function **Stdevp**.

How Risky Are Other Assets?

To give you some feel for how risky different assets are, here is a table of the annualized returns and standard deviations for various assets:

AVERAGE RETURN VERSUS STANDARD DEVIATION OF RETURNS A Somewhat Arbitrary List of Assets, 1990-1999						
	Average return	Standard deviation			Average return	Standard deviation
Abbott	17.12%	19.27%	Marriott		7.15%	39.81%
Airproducts	12.73%	27.05%	McGraw- Hill		17.96%	19.52%
Alcoa	19.03%	27.59%	Microsoft		62.72%	37.99%
AmericanAirlines	9.26%	29.34%	NASDAQ		23.00%	20.17%
ATT	6.76%	27.96%	Nicor		9.15%	16.50%
Boeing	7.57%	25.57%	Nordstrom		5.44%	38.21%
Cisco	67.31%	38.80%	Northrop		14.76%	34.40%
Coke	10.18%	24.29%	PPG		14.42%	23.02%
Dell	69.86%	55.48%	Procter & Gamble		19.41%	20.91%
Duke	11.07%	15.43%	Safeway		25.65%	33.53%
Exxon	12.42%	13.96%	Standard & Poor's 500 Index		15.09%	13.18%
Ford	9.12%	29.11%	Teva		26.57%	36.17%
GM	11.37%	27.63%	U.S. Steel		4.17%	32.80%
Hershey	13.17%	20.74%	UST		10.39%	22.89%
IBM	14.89%	29.57%	Vanguard Long-Term Treasury Fund		2.43%	7.94%
Kellogg	8.92%	23.16%	Walmart		25.84%	25.45%
Magellan Fund	17.82%	14.40%	WR Grace		8.73%	31.20%
Manpower	9.93%	33.32%				

A closer look at the four highlighted financial assets can give you some better intuitions on the relation between financial risk and return:

- Vanguard's Long-Term Treasury Fund is a mutual fund that invests in long-term U.S. Treasury bonds. As you saw in Section 11.2, the absence of default risk in these bonds does not mean that they are riskless: Their prices can vary considerably, and as a result the holder of the Vanguard Long-Term Treasury Fund may experience uncertainty in his/her returns. Nevertheless, our intuition tells us (correctly, as you'll see in the succeeding bullets) that this fund ought to be less risky than most stocks. During the decade of 1990–1999, the Vanguard Long-Term Treasury Fund gave an average annual return of 2.43% and this return had a standard deviation of 7.94%.

- The Standard & Poor's 500 Index is a broad-based index of the largest U.S. stocks and is often used as a measure of the performance of the U.S. stock markets. During the decade of the 1990s, the S&P 500 Index had an average annual return of 15.09% and a standard deviation of 13.18%. As you might expect, there's a clear trade-off between the average return of the S&P 500 and the Vanguard Long-Term Treasury Fund: The S&P 500 gives more return, but you pay for this return with greater variability (measured by the standard deviation):

$$Treasury\ Fund\ average\ return = 2.43\% < 15.09\% = S\&P\ 500\ average\ return$$

$$Treasury\ Fund\ standard\ deviation = 7.94\% < 13.18\% = S\&P\ 500\ standard\ deviation$$

- The riskiest asset in our table is Dell stock. This stock performed spectacularly over the decade, giving an annual average return of 69.86%.[6] On the other hand, Dell was also the riskiest stock in the table, with a standard deviation of return of 55.48%.

- After the fact (or, as economists like to say, *ex-post*) some assets were clearly inferior to other assets. Manpower's stock turned out to have lower average return and higher risk (measured by standard deviation) than the S&P 500.

Over this period there seems to be a positive relation between the standard deviation of the returns and the annualized return of the assets, although a closer look at the graph will show you that there is a large group of assets with different standard deviations and roughly the same average returns. The graph should be taken as somewhat indicative of a possible relation between risk (as measured here by the standard deviation of returns) and average returns. From this graph you might be tempted to conclude that when an asset's standard deviation of returns increases, the return expected from the asset increases. This is not far from the truth—but in Chapter 14 we define another measure of asset risk, called *beta*, which works better.[7]

11.4 Using Continuously Compounded Returns to Compute Annualized Return Statistics (Advanced Topic)

We discussed continuous compounding in Chapter 6 (p. 150). As explained there, the continuously compounded return is calculated using the **Ln** function. For reasons that are beyond the scope of this book, the continuously compounded return is often a better method of computing return statistics (by "better" we mean two things: there's a theory behind the numbers, and this theory gives the same results whether you're computing the annual statistics from daily, weekly, or monthly data). In the spreadsheet below, we've computed the continuously compounded return statistics for McDonald's.

---

[6]This number deserves some thought and admiration: If you'd invested $100 in Dell stock in 1990, it would have grown to $100 * (1 + 69.86\%)^{10} = \$19,955$ by the end of the decade!

[7]Actually, if you look really carefully at the trendline in the graph, you'll see it's mostly influenced by the three rightmost points (these are for Microsoft, Cisco, and Dell). Without these points, there would be no relation between the return and the standard deviation of the returns—we need a better measure of asset risk, which we develop in the following chapters.

	A	B	C	D	E	F	G	H
1			**McDONALD'S--DAILY STOCK PRICES, 29 Dec 89 - 31 Dec 99**					
			This spreadsheet uses the continuously compounded return					
2	**Date**	**Closing stock price**				**Statistics**		
3	29-Dec-89	8.50				**Daily returns**		
4	2-Jan-90	8.59	1.053%	<-- =LN(B4/B3)		Largest daily return	10.31%	<-- =MAX(C4:C2531)
5	3-Jan-90	8.50	-1.053%	<-- =LN(B5/B4)		Smallest daily return	-10.62%	<-- =MIN(C4:C2531)
6	4-Jan-90	8.34	-1.900%					
7	5-Jan-90	8.19	-1.815%			Average daily return	0.0610%	<-- =AVERAGE(C4:C2531)
8	8-Jan-90	8.34	1.815%			Variance of daily returns	0.0257%	<-- =VARP(C4:C2531)
9	9-Jan-90	8.28	-0.722%			Standard deviation of daily returns	1.6039%	<-- =SQRT(G8)
10	10-Jan-90	8.13	-1.828%					
11	11-Jan-90	8.07	-0.741%			**Annualized**		
12	12-Jan-90	7.91	-2.003%			Average annual return	15.43%	<-- =G7*253
13	15-Jan-90	7.82	-1.144%			Variance of annual returns	6.51%	<-- =G8*253
14	16-Jan-90	7.91	1.144%			Standard deviation of annual returns	25.51%	<-- =SQRT(G13)
15	17-Jan-90	7.91	0.000%					
16	18-Jan-90	7.94	0.379%					
17	19-Jan-90	7.85	-1.140%					
18	22-Jan-90	7.63	-2.843%					
19	23-Jan-90	7.76	1.689%					
20	24-Jan-90	7.63	-1.689%					
21	25-Jan-90	7.60	-0.394%					
22	26-Jan-90	7.70	1.307%					
23	29-Jan-90	7.70	0.000%					
24	30-Jan-90	7.70	0.000%					
25	31-Jan-90	8.03	4.196%					
26	1-Feb-90	8.16	1.606%					

The average daily continuously compounded return (cell G7) is 0.0610%. To *annualize* this return, we multiply by 253, the average number of business days per year.[8] The annualized average continuously compounded return is 15.43% (cell G12). Similarly, the annualized return variance is 6.51% (cell G13), and the annualized standard deviation of returns is 25.51% (cell G14).[9]

11.5 Risk and Return Depend on the Unit of Account[10]

As we've shown in earlier examples, risk and return depend on the kind of security you're considering. Returns can also depend on *what currency you're calculating in*. Investors these days are putting their money in many stock markets around the world, and their returns are affected by fluctuations in both stock prices and rates of exchange.

In the example below we calculate the return—in euros and in dollars—from holding the Amsterdam Stock Exchange index (symbol: AEX). In the table below we use the continuously compounded returns. As shown in Section 11.4, using continuously compounded returns makes it much easier to go from monthly data to annual data. For example:

- The average *monthly* euro return on the AEX index is −0.14% (cell C41). To compute the average *annual* return, we simply multiply this number by 12: $12*(-0.14\%) = -1.67\%$ (cell C44).
- The *monthly* standard deviation of AEX euro returns is 5.10% (cell C42). To compute the average *annual* standard deviation, we multiply this number by $\sqrt{12}$: $\sqrt{12}*5.10\% = 17.68\%$ (cell C44).

---

[8]Over the ten-year period 1990–1999, there were 2528 days on which McDonald's stock was transacted. This averages out to 253 days per year.

[9]Note that the continuously compounded average return of 15.43% is less than the discretely compounded return of 18.86% computed in the previous subsection. One reason for this is that continuous compounding builds up faster than discretely compounded interest. As noted in Chapter 6, there are legitimate alternative ways to compute returns. To compare the returns of two assets, make sure that the basis of the computation is the same.

[10]This section uses continuously compounded returns, so you might want to consider it an advanced topic section.

	A	B	C	D	E	F	G	H
1				**AMSTERDAM STOCK EXCHANGE INDEX (AEX)**				
				In euros and dollars				
2	Date	Index price in euros	Monthly return in euros		Euro/$ exchange rate	Index price in $	Monthly return in $	
3	January-99	532.09			1.161	617.76		
4	February-99	536.12	0.75%	<-- =LN(B4/B3)	1.121	600.99	-2.75%	<-- =LN(F4/F3)
5	March-99	536.93	0.15%	<-- =LN(B5/B4)	1.088	584.18	-2.84%	<-- =LN(F5/F4)
6	April-99	573.52	6.59%		1.070	613.67	4.92%	
7	May-99	554.06	-3.45%		1.063	588.97	-4.11%	
8	June-99	561.19	1.28%		1.038	582.52	-1.10%	
9	July-99	552.77	-1.51%		1.035	572.12	-1.80%	
10	August-99	572.42	3.49%		1.060	606.77	5.88%	
11	September-99	547.45	-4.46%		1.050	574.82	-5.41%	
12	October-99	571.82	4.36%		1.071	612.42	6.34%	
13	November-99	602.11	5.16%		1.034	622.58	1.65%	
14	December-99	671.41	10.89%		1.011	678.80	8.64%	
15	January-00	612.38	-9.20%		1.014	620.95	-8.91%	
16	February-00	664.28	8.14%		0.983	652.99	5.03%	
17	March-00	662.29	-0.30%		0.964	638.45	-2.25%	
18	April-00	661.38	-0.14%		0.947	626.33	-1.92%	
19	May-00	655.50	-0.89%		0.906	593.88	-5.32%	
20	June-00	672.14	2.51%		0.949	637.86	7.14%	
21	July-00	668.18	-0.59%		0.940	628.09	-1.54%	
22	August-00	689.52	3.14%		0.904	623.33	-0.76%	
23	September-00	661.52	-4.15%		0.872	576.85	-7.75%	
24	October-00	680.56	2.84%		0.855	581.88	0.87%	
25	November-00	649.92	-4.61%		0.856	556.33	-4.49%	
26	December-00	637.60	-1.91%		0.897	571.93	2.76%	
27	January-01	639.98	0.37%		0.938	600.30	4.84%	
28	February-01	597.33	-6.90%		0.922	550.74	-8.62%	
29	March-01	558.36	-6.75%		0.910	508.11	-8.06%	
30	April-01	593.09	6.03%		0.892	529.04	4.04%	
31	May-01	585.15	-1.35%		0.874	511.42	-3.39%	
32	June-01	573.50	-2.01%		0.853	489.20	-4.44%	
33	July-01	548.72	-4.42%		0.861	472.45	-3.48%	
34	August-01	523.63	-4.68%		0.900	471.27	-0.25%	
35	September-01	453.87	-14.30%		0.911	413.48	-13.08%	
36	October-01	460.33	1.41%		0.906	417.06	0.86%	
37	November-01	492.67	6.79%		0.888	437.49	4.78%	
38	December-01	506.78	2.82%		0.892	452.05	3.27%	
39								
40	**Return statistics**		In euros				In dollars	
41	Monthly average		-0.14%				-0.89%	<-- =AVERAGE(G4:G38)
42	Monthly standard deviation		5.10%				5.15%	<-- =STDEVP(G4:G38)
43								
44	Annual average		-1.67%				-10.71%	<-- =12*G41
45	Annual standard deviation		17.68%				17.83%	<-- =SQRT(12)*G42

A "euro investor"—someone living in Euro-land and who thinks in euros—would have lost 1.67% per year (cell C44) on his/her investment in the AEX over the two years surveyed. Over the same time period a "dollar investor"—say, an American investing in the Amsterdam AEX—would have lost almost 10.71% per year (cell G44).

Why do the euro returns and the dollar returns differ so radically? Take a look at what happened between 1 January 1999 and 1 February 1999. A euro investor who bought the AEX index on 1 January 1999 would have paid €532.09; if the investor sold the index one month later, he/she would have gotten €536.12. This is a euro return of $Ln(€536.12/€532.09) = 0.75\%$ (cell C4).

On the other hand, a dollar investor who bought the Amsterdam index on 1 January 1999 would have paid $617.76 (at the point the investor purchased the index, $1 was worth €1.161, so that the dollar price of the index becomes $€532.09 * 1.161 = \$617.76$). When this dollar investor sold the index after one month, it was at €536.12 and the value of a dollar had fallen to $1 = €1.121, so that the dollar price of the index was $€536.12 * 1.121 = \$600.99$. As a result the investor's dollar return was $Ln(\$600.99/\$617.76) = -2.75\%$ (cell G4).

The conclusion: Whether the Amsterdam Stock Exchange index was just a bad or a very bad investment depends very much on whether you were a euro investor (in which case it was a bad investment) or a dollar investor (much worse).

The unit of account (dollar or euro) matters.

CONCLUSION

In this chapter we tried to give you some intuitions into the nature of financial risk by a series of examples. Risk—the variability of returns from an asset over time—depends on a number of factors. Broadly speaking, the characteristics of an asset's risk are its *horizon*, its *safety*, and its *liquidity*. As shown, even default-free assets like U.S. Treasury bills can be risky because their prices can change over the asset's horizon. With our example of McDonald's stock we showed that some statistical sense can be made of the variability of the stock's return over time—by using Excel's **Frequency** function, we were able to show that McDonald's stock returns look very much like the familiar statistical "bell curve." Finally, with our example of the Amsterdam Stock Exchange index, we showed that risks can differ depending on who's measuring them: The dollar investor in Amsterdam stocks did much worse than the euro investor.

Risk is the most important concept in finance: The variability of financial asset returns is the main fact of financial life, but this risk is not easy to define or measure. In Chapters 13–16 we develop a model to *price risks;* by this we mean a model that will help us determine the risk-adjusted discount rate. The important innovation of this model is that risk depends on a *portfolio context*—it is not just the asset's returns by themselves that determine the asset's riskiness, but the asset's returns in the context of the portfolio of all the assets held by the investor.

Before we can develop this model, however, you might need a brush-up on your statistics skills. This is the task we set ourselves in the next chapter.

EXERCISES

1. Professor Smith was bragging about her abilities as an investor in the stock market: "In the last month, I earned 8% on my portfolio," she told her friends. "That's nothing special," commented Mr. Jackson. "Last month I made 20% on my portfolio, without studying 15 years at university." Did Mr. Jackson really outperform Professor Smith?

2. Can a corporate bond have a lower expected return than a government bond? Can it have lower ex-post return?

3. It's 1 January 2007 and you're considering buying a $1,000 face-value U.S. Treasury bill that matures in one year. The interest rate is 7% annually.
   (a) If you buy the T-Bill now, how much will you pay?
   (b) If the interest rate remains 7% annually, how much will the bill be worth on 1 February 2007? 1 March? 1 April? . . . 1 December?

4. Diana bought bonds issued by the ZZZ Company, a small high-tech company from Newfoundland. The bond is zero-coupon, has a face value of $1,000, and matures in two years. Diana intends to keep the bond until maturity.
   (a) If the price of the bond is $756.14, what is the annual expected return of Diana's bond?
   (b) A day after Diana bought her bond, ZZZ was purchased by the electronic giant ABA Company, which has a very low default probability. Investors demand only a 6.5% annual return on ABA's bonds. What will be the new price of the ZZZ bonds and how much will Diana gain from the takeover?

5. On 15 March 2002, you purchased a two-year Treasury bond with face value $10,000 and a 4% coupon (payable semiannually). The price of the bond was $9,750. The bond promises a coupon of $200 on 15 September 2002, 15 March 2003, 15 September 2003, and 15 March 2004 (on this last date the bond will repay its face value).

  (a) Based on the following, compute the annualized IRR of the bond purchase:

	A	B	C
1	**Date**	**Cash flows**	
2	15-Mar-02	-9,750	
3	15-Sep-02	200	
4	15-Mar-03	200	
5	15-Sep-03	200	
6	15-Mar-04	10,200	
7			
8	Semiannual IRR	2.67%	<-- =IRR(B2:B6)

  (b) Immediately after receiving the $200 bond interest payment on 15 September 2002, you sold the bond for $10,000. What was your ex-post annualized yield? What was the ex-ante annualized yield of the buyer of the bond?

6. During a stamp collector convention, the chairman spoke about the profitability of investing in rare stamps. "Last year I invested $150,000 in rare stamps. These stamps are now worth $200,000 according to the catalog, meaning an annual return of 33%. For comparison the average return in the stock market in the last 30 years was only 16%." Find (at least) three problems with the chairman's argument.

7. A basic assumption of economics is that investors are risk averse, meaning when they view asset A as riskier than asset B they will demand a higher expected return.

  A "fair bet" is a bet whose expected return is zero. Here's an example of a fair bet: Pay $1 to get $2 if a coin flip yields heads or to get $0 if the coin flip yields tails. Notice that this bet has expected return of zero:

$$expected\ payoff = \underbrace{0.5}_{\substack{\uparrow \\ \text{Probability} \\ \text{of heads}}} * \underbrace{\$2}_{\substack{\uparrow \\ \text{Payoff} \\ \text{if heads}}} + \underbrace{0.5}_{\substack{\uparrow \\ \text{Probability} \\ \text{of tails}}} * \underbrace{\$2}_{\substack{\uparrow \\ \text{Payoff} \\ \text{if tails}}} = \$1$$

$$expected\ return = \frac{expected\ payoff}{cost\ of\ bet} - 1 = \frac{\$1}{\$1} - 1 = 0\%$$

Will a risk-aversive investor agree to a fair bet?

8. A risk-neutral investor is willing to make bets with expected return of zero. Suppose a risk-neutral investor is offered the chance to participate in a die-toss game. If the die comes up 1, the payoff is $1, if the die comes up 2, the payoff is $2, and so on. What is the maximum price the risk-neutral investor is willing to pay to play this game.

9. On planet Apathy all investors are indifferent to risk. The annual expected returns on government bonds are 5%. Does that mean that the average stock returns should be 5%?

10. One of the ways in which the United States helps foreign countries is to guarantee their bank loans. Explain (briefly) the benefits for foreign countries in getting those guaranties. (Footnote 1 is a good place to start your answer.)

11. During a finance lecture Professor Johnson explained to his students the relation between higher risk and higher expected returns. At the end of the lecture one of the students asked: "Yesterday I read in the paper that the U.S. stock markets earned higher returns than 15 African stock markets in the last decade. How is that fact consistent with high risk equaling higher returns?" How would you advise Professor Johnson to respond to his students? (Your answer should include the worlds ex-ante and ex-post.)

12. On 1 January 2007, the U.S. government is issuing two series of bonds. The two series are completely identical except for the fact that the volume of trade in the first series is anticipated to be much higher than the volume in the second series. What do you expect will be the relation between the prices of the two series?

13. DEF is a firm that is traded on NASDAQ. On 1 January 2010 the company will issue 10,000 zero-coupon bonds. Each bond will have a face value of $100 and will mature on 1 January 2015. The bonds will be the only debt of the company. A bond rating company estimates the total value of DEF's assets on 1 January 2015 as follows:

Probability	Value of DEF assets on 1 Jan 15
0.2	2,000,000
0.3	1,750,000
0.4	1,200,000
0.1	750,000

Two years after the bond issue, on 1 January 2012, the bond rating agency expects to reexamine the DEF Company and estimates the total value of the firm's assets as follows:

Probability	Value of DEF assets on 1 Jan 15
0.05	2,000,000
0.25	1,750,000
0.65	1,200,000
0.05	750,000

(a) What will be the influence of the new estimation on the expected return on DEF bonds?

(b) What influence will the new estimation have on the DEF stock price?

14. Can you think of a risk-based explanation for the following finding? Over the last forty years "small" stocks—defined as shares of firms with a low market value—had higher returns than big stocks.

15. A well-known finance professor published a paper in which he argued that due to the high volume of stock trade in the Internet he expects stock returns to decline in future years. What is the basis for the professor's argument?

16. At the end of 1999 an investor bought 10,000 shares of Yakuna Corporation for ¥456 each in the Japanese stock market (¥ is the symbol for Japanese yen). At that time $1 U.S. was worth ¥128.35. The investor sold all the shares at the beginning of 2003 when the stock was worth ¥448 and $1 U.S. was worth ¥108.33. Calculate the annual return in dollar terms and yen terms.

17. On 1 January 2006 an American investor bought $1,000,000 worth of Swiss francs (SFr) and put it in a savings account for one year. The annual interest rate in Swiss francs was 6%. During that period the interest rate in the United States was 2%. On the 1 January 2006 the exchange rate was $1 = SFr 1.56.

(a) One year after the start of the savings in Switzerland, the exchange rate was SFr 1.45 = U.S. $1. If the investor turned his savings back into dollars, what *dollar rate of return* did he earn?

(b) What should be the exchange rate on 1 January 2007 in order for the investment in Swiss francs to be better than investment in U.S. dollars?

18. The disk that comes with this book has daily prices for AMD Corporation's stock from 1 July 1994 through 26 July 2004.

(a) Compute the daily stock returns and graph them.

(b) Use **Frequency** to build a frequency distribution of the stock returns and graph this distribution.

19. The disk that comes with this book contains data on annual stock prices for Ford Motor Company for 1987–2003. Compute the average annual return and the standard deviation of annual returns for Ford.

	A	B
1	**FORD MOTOR COMPANY** annual stock prices	
2	**Date**	**Closing price**
3	2-Jan-87	0.5900
4	4-Jan-88	0.8900
5	3-Jan-89	1.3600
6	2-Jan-90	1.3500
7	2-Jan-91	1.1900
8	2-Jan-92	1.5600
9	4-Jan-93	2.6800
10	3-Jan-94	4.3000
11	3-Jan-95	3.4800
12	2-Jan-96	4.4100
13	2-Jan-97	5.2100
14	2-Jan-98	8.8700
15	4-Jan-99	25.9000
16	3-Jan-00	22.3100
17	2-Jan-01	25.1400
18	2-Jan-02	14.1800
19	2-Jan-03	8.7600
20	2-Jan-04	14.4500

20. The disk that comes with this book contains data on annual stock prices for Kellogg for 1987–2003. Compute the average annual return and the standard deviation of annual returns for Kellogg.

	A	B
1	**KELLOGG** annual stock prices	
2	**Date**	**Closing price**
3	2-Jan-87	5.68
4	4-Jan-88	5.48
5	3-Jan-89	7.66
6	2-Jan-90	8.27
7	2-Jan-91	11.26
8	2-Jan-92	17.91
9	4-Jan-93	20.37
10	3-Jan-94	18.47
11	3-Jan-95	19.90
12	2-Jan-96	29.03
13	2-Jan-97	27.59
14	2-Jan-98	38.01
15	4-Jan-99	34.14
16	3-Jan-00	20.93
17	2-Jan-01	23.52
18	2-Jan-02	28.70
19	2-Jan-03	32.00
20	2-Jan-04	37.35

21. Graph the annual stock returns of Kellogg and Ford on the same graph. Is one of the companies more risky than the other? Explain.

STATISTICS FOR PORTFOLIOS

OVERVIEW

In order to understand and work through Chapters 13–16, you will need to know some statistics. If you're like a lot of finance students, you've had a statistics course and forgotten much of what you learned there. This chapter is a refresher—it show you exactly what you need in order to proceed with the succeeding chapters, using Excel to do all the calculations. (Excel is a great statistical toolbox—someday all business-school statistics courses will use it. In the meantime you're stuck with this chapter.)

Finance Concepts Discussed

- How to calculate stock returns and adjust them for dividends and stock splits
- Return mean, variance, and standard deviation for an asset
- Return mean and variance for a portfolio of two assets
- Regressions

Excel Functions Used

- **Average**
- **Var** and **Varp**
- **Stdev** and **Stdevp**
- **Covar** and **Correl**
- **Trendlines** (Excel's term for regressions)
- **Slope, Intercept, Rsq**

12.1 Basic Statistics for Asset Returns: Mean, Standard Deviation, Covariance, and Correlation

In this section you learn to calculate the return on a stock and its statistics: the *mean* (interchangeably referred to as the *average* or *expected* return), the *variance,* and the *standard deviation.*

General Motors Stock and Its Returns

The following spreadsheet shows data for General Motors (GM) stock during the decade of the 1990s. For each year, we've given the closing price of GM stock and the dividend the company paid during the year.[1] We've also calculated the annual returns and their statistics; these calculations are explained after the table:

---

[1]The "closing price" is the price of the stock at the end of the day.

	A	B	C	D	E
1		PRICE AND DIVIDEND DATA FOR GENERAL MOTORS (GM)			
2	Date	Closing Price	Dividend	Annual return	
3	29-Dec-89	42.2500	-		
4	31-Dec-90	34.3750	3.00	-11.54%	<-- =(C4+B4)/B3-1
5	31-Dec-91	28.8750	1.60	-11.35%	<-- =(C5+B5)/B4-1
6	31-Dec-92	32.2500	1.40	16.54%	
7	31-Dec-93	54.8750	0.80	72.64%	
8	30-Dec-94	42.1250	0.80	-21.78%	
9	29-Dec-95	52.8750	1.10	28.13%	
10	31-Dec-96	55.7500	1.60	8.46%	
11	31-Dec-97	60.7500	5.59	19.00%	
12	31-Dec-98	71.5625	2.00	21.09%	
13	31-Dec-99	72.6875	14.15	21.34%	
14					
15	Average return, $E(r_{GM})$			14.25%	<-- =AVERAGE(D4:D13)
16	Variance of return, σ^2_{GM}			0.0638	<-- =VARP(D4:D13)
17	Standard deviation of return, σ_{GM}			25.25%	<-- =STDEVP(D4:D13)

Suppose you had bought a share of GM at the end of December 1989 for $42.25 and sold it a year later, at the end of December 1990, for $34.375. During this year, GM paid a per-share dividend of $3.[2] Your return from holding GM throughout 1990 would have been

$$r_{GM,1990} = \frac{P_{GM,1990} + Div_{GM,1990} - P_{GM,1989}}{P_{GM,1989}} = \frac{34.375 + 3.00 - 42.25}{42.25} = -11.54\%$$

Several notes:

- We use $r_{GM,1990}$ to denote the return on GM stock in 1990 and we use $Div_{GM,1990}$ to denote GM's dividend in 1990.

- The numerator of $r_{GM,1990}$ is

$$P_{GM,1990} + Div_{GM,1990} - P_{GM,1989} = 34.375 + 3.00 - 42.25 = -4.875$$

This is the gain on holding GM during the year (in this case it's a negative "gain": a loss of $4.875). The denominator of $r_{GM,1990}$ is the initial investment from buying GM stock at the beginning of the year.

- In cell D4 of the spreadsheet we've written $r_{GM,1990}$, the return for 1990, in a slightly different form as **(C4+B4)/B3−1**:

$$r_{GM,1990} = \frac{P_{GM,1990} + Div_{GM,1990} - P_{GM,1989}}{P_{GM,1989}} = \frac{P_{GM,1990} + Div_{GM,1990}}{P_{GM,1989}} - 1$$

Cells D15, D16, and D17 give the return statistics for GM.

- Cell D15: The average return over the decade is 14.25% per year. This number is also called the *mean return* and it's calculated with the Excel function =**Average(D4:D13)**. We often use the past returns to predict future returns. When we make this use of the data, we also call the mean the *expected return*, meaning that we use the historic average of GM's stock returns as a prediction of what the stock will return in the future. We sometimes use the notations.

---

[2]Actually, the company paid four quarterly dividends of $0.75, but we've added these together to get the annual dividend.

$E(r_{GM})$ or $\bar{r}_{GM}$. In this book, the terms mean, average, and expected return are used almost interchangeably. The formal definition is

$$mean\ GM\ return = E(r_{GM}) = \bar{r}_{GM} = \frac{r_{GM,1990} + r_{GM,1991} + \cdots + r_{GM,1999}}{10}$$

You might wonder at the number of expressions (mean, average, expected return) and the number of symbols ($E(r_{GM})$, $\bar{r}_{GM}$) for the same idea. We introduce them all for convenience and because, in your further finance studies, you're likely to see them used synonymously.

- Cell D16: The variance of the annual returns is 6.38%. Variance and standard deviation are statistical measures of the variability of the returns. The variance is calculated with the Excel function **=Varp(D4:D13)**. (See the Excel Note box further on for more information about this function and its cousin, **=Var(D4:D13)**.) The variance is often denoted by the Greek symbol σ^2_{GM} (pronounced "sigma squared of GM"); sometimes it's written as $Var(r_{GM})$. The formal definition of the variance is

$$Var(r_{GM}) = \sigma^2_{GM} = \frac{\left(r_{GM,1990} - \bar{r}_{GM}\right)^2 + \left(r_{GM,1991} - \bar{r}_{GM}\right)^2 + \cdots + \left(r_{GM,1999} - \bar{r}_{GM}\right)^2}{10}$$

- Cell D17: The standard deviation of the annual returns is the square root of the variance: $\sqrt{0.0638} = 25.25\%$. Excel has two functions, **Stdevp** and **Stdev**, to do this calculation directly. Since we usually use **Varp** for the variance, we will use **Stdevp** for the standard deviation. It is common to use the Greek letter sigma for the standard deviation, writing σ_{GM} (pronounced "sigma of GM").

EXCEL NOTE

EXCEL AND STATISTICS (SKIP UNTIL LATER, OR PERHAPS FOREVER, IF YOU LIKE)

Excel has two variance functions, **Varp** and **Var**. The former measures the "population variance," and the latter measures the "sample variance." Similarly, Excel has two functions for the standard deviation, **Stdevp** and **Stdev**. In this book we use only the functions **Varp** and **Stdevp**. This box is a reminder but not an explanation of the difference between the two concepts.

If you have return data $\{r_{stock,1}, r_{stock,2}, \ldots, r_{stock,N}\}$ for a *stock,* then the mean return is

$$\bar{r}_{stock} = \frac{1}{N} \sum_{t=1}^{N} r_{stock,t}$$

The definitions of the two variance functions are

$$Varp(\{r_{stock,1}, r_{stock,2}, \ldots, r_{stock,N}\}) = \frac{1}{N} \sum_{j=1}^{N} (r_{stock,j} - \bar{r}_i)^2$$

$$Var(\{r_{stock,1}, r_{stock,2}, \ldots, r_{stock,N}\}) = \frac{1}{N-1} \sum_{j=1}^{N} (r_{stock,j} - \bar{r}_i)^2$$

There's a long story about the difference between these two concepts, which we leave for someone else (like your statistics instructor) to explain. Suffice it to say that in the examples covered in this book we use **Varp** and its standard deviation equivalent **Stdevp.**

Finally, you might wonder why there are two expressions—the variance and the standard deviation—that measure the variability. The answer has to do with the units of these expressions. Each term in the variance is squared in order to make everything positive. But this means that the units of the variance are "percent squared," which is a bit difficult to understand. The standard deviation, the square root of the variance, reduces the squared percentages of the variance back to "percent." This way the mean and the standard deviation have the same units.

Microsoft Stock and Its Returns

The GM example earlier illustrated the adjustment of the stock return data to include dividends. We now use Microsoft stock to show you how stock returns are affected by stock splits. A *stock split* occurs when stockholders get multiple shares of stock for each share they own. The most typical stock split is a "2-for-1" split, in which shareholders get one additional share for each share they already own (see Figure 12.1 for a Microsoft stock split announcement in 1996).

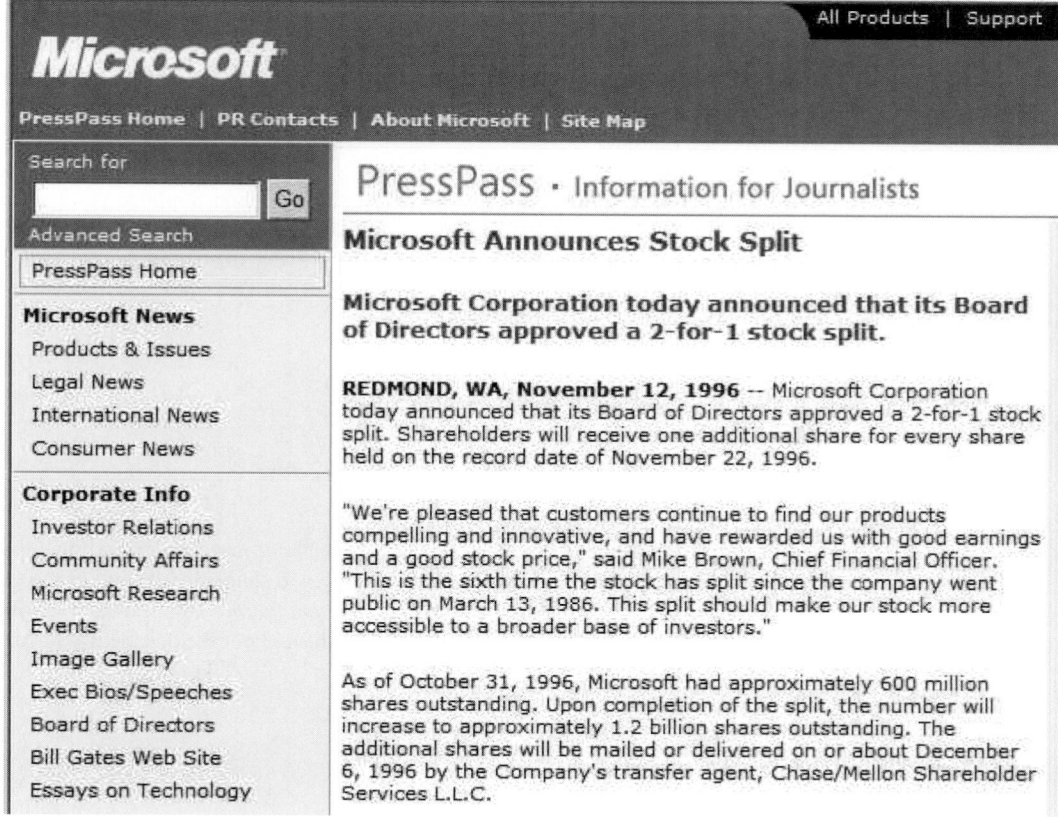

Figure 12.1 On 12 November 1996, Microsoft announced a 2-for-1 stock split. Shareholders owning one share on 22 November 1996 would be mailed an additional share of stock. This increased the number of shares of the company from 600 million to 1.2 billion. The Microsoft statement hints at the company's reasoning for the split: With its stock trading at almost $150 per share before the split, Microsoft used the split to reduce the price of the share in order to put it into a range that would make it "more accessible to a broader base of investors."

Microsoft (MSFT) paid no dividends in the 1990–1999 decade, but the stock split several times. Here are some data:

	A	B	C
	PRICE AND STOCK SPLIT DATA FOR MICROSOFT (MSFT)		
1			
2	Date	Closing Price	Stock split during year?
3	29-Dec-89	87.0000	
4	31-Dec-90	75.2500	2.0 for 1
5	31-Dec-91	111.2500	1.5 for 1
6	31-Dec-92	85.3750	1.5 for 1
7	31-Dec-93	80.6250	no
8	30-Dec-94	61.1250	2.0 for 1
9	29-Dec-95	87.7500	no
10	31-Dec-96	82.6250	2.0 for 1
11	31-Dec-97	129.2500	no
12	31-Dec-98	138.6875	2.0 for 1
13	31-Dec-99	116.7500	2.0 for 1

Here's what these stock splits mean for Microsoft shareholders: Suppose you had bought one share of MSFT on 29 December 1989 for $87.00 and held it throughout 1990. During 1990, Microsoft *split* its stock, giving shareholders two shares for every one share they owned. At the end of 1990, each of these (split) shares was worth $75.25, so that your $87 investment had grown to $150.25! The return for the year is therefore

$$r_{MSFT,1990} = \frac{(P_{MSFT,31Dec90}) * 2}{P_{MSFT,29Dec89}} - 1$$

$$= \frac{150.50}{87} - 1 = 72.99\%$$

The "2" in the formula above is the stock split *adjustment factor,* which shows that one share of Microsoft owned at the beginning of 1990 became two shares by the end of the year. In the spreadsheet below we calculate the *cumulative adjustment factor.* This shows you how your end-1989 $87.00 investment in MSFT would have grown throughout the decade if you correctly account for the stock splits.

	A	B	C	D	E	F	G
16	Date	Closing Price	Stock split during year?	Cumulative adjustment factor	Adjusted price	Annual return	
17	29-Dec-89	87.0000		1	87.00		
18	31-Dec-90	75.2500	2.0 for 1	2	150.50	72.99%	<-- =E18/E17-1
19	31-Dec-91	111.2500	1.5 for 1	3	333.75	121.76%	<-- =E19/E18-1
20	31-Dec-92	85.3750	1.5 for 1	4.5	384.19	15.11%	
21	31-Dec-93	80.6250	no	4.5	362.81	-5.56%	
22	30-Dec-94	61.1250	2.0 for 1	9	550.13	51.63%	
23	29-Dec-95	87.7500	no	9	789.75	43.56%	
24	31-Dec-96	82.6250	2.0 for 1	18	1,487.25	88.32%	
25	31-Dec-97	129.2500	no	18	2,326.50	56.43%	
26	31-Dec-98	138.6875	2.0 for 1	36	4,992.75	114.60%	
27	31-Dec-99	116.7500	2.0 for 1	72	8,406.00	68.36%	
28							
29	Average return, $E(r_{MSFT})$					62.72%	<-- =AVERAGE(F18:F27)
30	Variance of return, σ^2_{MSFT}					14.43%	<-- =VARP(F18:F27)
31	Standard deviation of return, σ_{MSFT}					37.99%	<-- =SQRT(F30)
32							
33							

The cumulative adjustment factor is the product of all the splits: 72 = 2*1.5*1.5*2*2*2

Taking into account the stock splits, your $87.00 investment in MSFT would have grown to $8,406 by the end of the decade! During the 1990s, MSFT gave an average annual return of 62.72%; this return had a standard deviation of 37.99%.[3]

STOCK SPLITS AND THE CUMULATIVE ADJUSTMENT FACTOR

On 31 January 2002, you bought one share of XYZ stock for $50. One year minus one day later, on 30 January 2003, your share of XYZ stock is trading at $80. At the end of the day the stock *splits:* For every share you own, you now have *two* shares. In a logical world, this would mean that the price of the share should fall by 50%, so that on 31 January 2003, XYZ trades at $40 per share.[4]

Now suppose you're trying to calculate your return on the stock. Is it $40/$50 − 1 = −20% or is the return (2 ∗ $40)/$50 − 1 = 60%? The latter, of course! *You adjusted the stock price by the adjustment factor.*

Suppose that in July 2003 XYZ splits 1.5 for 1 and that on 31 January 2004 the price per share is $25. Then your return since you bought the stock is

$$\frac{2 * 1.5 * \$25}{\$50} - 1 = \frac{3 * \$25}{\$50} - 1 = 50\%$$

The cumulative adjustment factor is the product of all the splits since you bought the stock.

---

[3]Adding or subtracting the standard deviation from the average gives a plausible range for Microsoft stock returns. Roughly speaking, the 37.99% standard deviation indicates that with a 68% probability, the Microsoft stock returns are in the range between 24.73% and 100.71%. These two numbers are computed by 24.73% = 62.72% − 37.99% and 100.71% = 62.72% + 37.99%.

[4]The world is not all that logical, but this in fact usually happens—when a stock splits 2 for 1, its post-split price is usually very close to half its pre-split price. If the stock splits on a 1.5 for 1 basis, the post-split price is close to two-thirds (2/3 = 1/1.5) its pre-split price.

12.2 Downloaded Data From Commercial Sources Is Adjusted for Dividends and Splits

The author's two favorite data sources for information about stock prices, dividends, and stock splits are Yahoo, which is free, and the Center for Research in Security Prices (CRSP), a database that originates from the University of Chicago (many universities subscribe to CRSP—ask your data manager).[5] When you download data from these sources, they automatically adjust the price data to account for dividends and splits. So you don't have to do all the adjustment calculations illustrated in the previous section.[6]

It is important to note, however, that the adjustments made by Yahoo and CRSP may look different from the ones we made above. For example, here's the adjusted Microsoft data from Yahoo:

	A	B	C	D
1	DOWNLOADED ADJUSTED DATA FROM YAHOO FOR MICROSOFT			
2	Date	MSFT adjusted price		
3	29-Dec-89	1.2083		
4	31-Dec-90	2.0903	73.00%	<-- =B4/B3-1
5	31-Dec-91	4.6354	121.76%	<-- =B5/B4-1
6	31-Dec-92	5.3359	15.11%	<-- =B6/B5-1
7	31-Dec-93	5.0391	-5.56%	<-- =B7/B6-1
8	30-Dec-94	7.6406	51.63%	<-- =B8/B7-1
9	29-Dec-95	10.9688	43.56%	<-- =B9/B8-1
10	31-Dec-96	20.6562	88.32%	<-- =B10/B9-1
11	31-Dec-97	32.3125	56.43%	<-- =B11/B10-1
12	31-Dec-98	69.3438	114.60%	<-- =B12/B11-1
13	31-Dec-99	116.7500	68.36%	<-- =B13/B12-1
14				
15	Average return, $E(r_{MSFT})$		62.72%	<-- =AVERAGE(C4:C13)
16	Variance of return, σ^2_{MSFT}		14.43%	<-- =VARP(C4:C13)
17	Standard deviation of return, σ_{MSFT}		37.99%	<-- =STDEVP(C4:C13)

The annual return statistics are the same, but the method of price adjustment is different: Yahoo has adjusted the stock prices so that the stock price on the last date ($116.75) is the same as the market price on that date. All previous prices have been adjusted accordingly. For example, the 29 December 1989 Yahoo price for MSFT of $1.2083 is 1/72 times the actual market price on this date—this adjustment is made since the stock split 72 times in the period 1990–1999.

---

[5]For penniless students, Yahoo is especially useful. Appendix 12.1 shows you how to download financial data from Yahoo.

[6]If it's all in the downloaded data, why the heck did we do all the work in this section? The answer, of course, is that it helps to understand what the numbers are telling you.

THE BOTTOM LINE ON DOWNLOADED DATA

Don't worry too much about how the adjustment is done. Calculate your returns from the adjusted stock price data given by your data provider. They usually do the corrections right.

12.3 Covariance and Correlation: Two Additional Statistics

So far we've looked at statistics—mean, variance, standard deviation—that relate to the returns of an individual stock. In this section we examine two statistics—*covariance* and *correlation*—that relate the returns of two stocks to each other. We continue to use our data for GM and MSFT. In the following spreadsheet, we've put the returns for both stocks on one spreadsheet and calculated the covariance and correlation (cells B17:B19):

	A	B	C	D
1	GM AND MSFT, ANNUAL RETURN DATA			
2	Date	GM return	MSFT return	
3	31-Dec-90	-11.54%	72.99%	
4	31-Dec-91	-11.35%	121.76%	
5	31-Dec-92	16.54%	15.11%	
6	31-Dec-93	72.64%	-5.56%	
7	30-Dec-94	-21.78%	51.63%	
8	29-Dec-95	28.13%	43.56%	
9	31-Dec-96	8.46%	88.32%	
10	31-Dec-97	19.00%	56.43%	
11	31-Dec-98	21.09%	114.60%	
12	31-Dec-99	21.34%	68.36%	
13				
14	Average return, $E(r_{GM})$ and $E(r_{MSFT})$	14.25%	62.72%	
15	Variance of return, σ^2_{GM} and σ^2_{MSFT}	6.38%	14.43%	
16	Standard deviation of return, σ_{GM} and σ_{MSFT}	25.25%	37.99%	
17	Covariance of returns, $Cov(r_{GM}, r_{MSFT})$	-0.0552		<-- =COVAR(B3:B12,C3:C12)
18	Correlation of returns, $\rho_{GM,MSFT}$	-0.5755		<-- =CORREL(B3:B12,C3:C12)
19		-0.5755		<-- =B17/(B16*C16)

The *covariance* between two series is a measure of how much the series (in our case, the returns on GM and MSFT) move up or down together. The formal definition is

$$Cov(r_{GM}, r_{MSFT}) = \sigma_{GM,MSFT}$$

$$= \frac{1}{10} \left\{ \begin{array}{l} (r_{GM,1} - \bar{r}_{GM})(r_{MSFT,1} - \bar{r}_{MSFT}) + (r_{GM,2} - \bar{r}_{GM})(r_{MSFT,2} - \bar{r}_{MSFT}) \\ + \cdots + (r_{GM,10} - \bar{r}_{GM})(r_{MSFT,10} - \bar{r}_{MSFT}) \end{array} \right\}$$

The idea behind the formula is to measure the deviations of each data point from its average and to multiply these deviations. As you can see from cell B17, Excel has a function **Covar**, which, when applied directly to the returns in columns B and C, calculates the covariance. Notice that the covariance is sometimes written as $\sigma_{GM,MSFT}$.

Calculating the covariance the long way using the formal definition may give you some more insight into what the covariance measures and what Excel's **Covar** function does.

	A	B	C	D	E	F	G	H
1		**CALCULATING THE COVARIANCE THE LONG TEDIOUS WAY**						
2	Date	GM return	MSFT return		GM return minus average	MSFT return minus average	=C3-$C$14 ▼ Product	
3	31-Dec-90	-11.54%	72.99%	=B3-$B$14-->	-25.79%	10.27%	-0.0265	<-- =E3*F3
4	31-Dec-91	-11.35%	121.76%		-25.60%	59.04%	-0.1511	
5	31-Dec-92	16.54%	15.11%		2.28%	-47.61%	-0.0109	
6	31-Dec-93	72.64%	-5.56%		58.38%	-68.28%	-0.3987	
7	30-Dec-94	-21.78%	51.63%		-36.03%	-11.09%	0.0400	
8	29-Dec-95	28.13%	43.56%		13.88%	-19.16%	-0.0266	
9	31-Dec-96	8.46%	88.32%		-5.79%	25.60%	-0.0148	
10	31-Dec-97	19.00%	56.43%		4.74%	-6.29%	-0.0030	
11	31-Dec-98	21.09%	114.60%		6.84%	51.88%	0.0355	
12	31-Dec-99	21.34%	68.36%		7.09%	5.64%	0.0040	
13								
14	Average return	14.25%	62.72%	<-- =AVERAGE(C3:C12)		Covariance	-0.0552	<-- =AVERAGE(G3:G12)
15						Covariance	-0.0552	<-- =COVAR(B3:B12,C3:C12)
16						Correlation	-0.5755	<-- =CORREL(B3:B12,C3:C12)
17						Correlation	-0.5755	<-- =G14/(STDEVP(B3:B12)*STDEVP(C3:C12))

In cell E3, we've subtracted GM's 1990 return of -11.54% from its decade average return of 14.25% (cell B14); the resulting number indicates that in 1990 GM stock underperformed its average by -25.79%. During the same year, MSFT overperformed its average by 10.27%. The covariance takes the product of these two numbers ($-25.79\% * 10.27\% = -0.0265$) and similar numbers for each of the other years and averages them (cell G14). As you can see, Excel's **Covar** function gives the same result (cell G15) and saves a lot of work. The covariance of -0.0552 for GM and MSFT tells us that, on average, when GM exceeded its mean, MSFT was below its mean, and vice versa.

Another common measure of how much two data series move up or down together is the *correlation coefficient*. The correlation coefficient is always between -1 and $+1$, which—as you'll see in the next subsection—makes it possible for us to be more precise about how the two sets of returns move together. Roughly speaking, two sets of returns that have a correlation coefficient of -1 vary *perfectly inversely,* by which we mean that when one return goes up (or down), we can perfectly predict how the other return goes down (or up). A correlation coefficient of $+1$ means that the returns vary in *perfect tandem,* by which we mean that when one return goes up (or down), we can perfectly predict how the other return goes up (or down). A correlation coefficient between -1 and $+1$ means that the two sets of returns vary together less than perfectly.

The correlation coefficient is defined as

$$Correlation(r_{GM}, r_{MSFT}) = \rho_{GM,MSFT} = \frac{Cov(r_{GM}, r_{MSFT})}{\sigma_{GM}\sigma_{MSFT}}$$

The Greek letter ρ (pronounced "rho") is often used as a symbol for the correlation coefficient. In the spreadsheet above, we calculate the correlation coefficient in two ways: In cell G16 of the previous spreadsheet, we use the Excel function **Correl** to compute the correlation. Cell G17 applies the formula $Cov(r_{GM}, r_{MSFT})/\sigma_{GM}\sigma_{MSFT}$ (and, of course, gets the same result).

Some Facts About Covariance and Correlation

Here are some facts about covariance and correlation. We state them without much attempt at elaborate explanation or proof.

Fact 1: Covariance is affected by units; correlation isn't. Here's an example. In the spreadsheet below, we've presented the annual returns as whole numbers instead of percentages (writing GM's 1990 return as -11.54 instead of -11.54%). The covariance (cell B18) is now -552.10, which is 10,000 times our previous calculation. But the correlation coefficient (B19) remains the same as before, -0.5755.

	A	B	C	D
1	GM AND MSFT, ANNUAL RETURN DATA Percentages presented as whole numbers			
2	Date	GM annual return	MSFT annual return	
3	29-Dec-89			
4	31-Dec-90	-11.54	72.99	
5	31-Dec-91	-11.35	121.76	
6	31-Dec-92	16.54	15.11	
7	31-Dec-93	72.64	-5.56	
8	30-Dec-94	-21.78	51.63	
9	29-Dec-95	28.13	43.56	
10	31-Dec-96	8.46	88.32	
11	31-Dec-97	19.00	56.43	
12	31-Dec-98	21.09	114.60	
13	31-Dec-99	21.34	68.36	
14				
15	Average return, $E(r_{GM})$ and $E(r_{MSFT})$	14.25	62.72	
16	Variance of return, σ^2_{GM} and σ^2_{MSFT}	637.80	1442.92	
17	Standard deviation of return, σ_{GM} and σ_{MSFT}	25.25	37.99	
18	Covariance of returns, $Cov(r_{GM}, r_{MSFT})$	-552.10		<-- =COVAR(B4:B13,C4:C13)
19	Correlation of returns, $\rho_{GM,MSFT}$	-0.5755		<-- =CORREL(B4:B13,C4:C13)
20		-0.5755		<-- =B18/(B17*C17)
21				
22	Correlation is symmetric, $\rho_{MSFT,GM}$	-0.5755		<-- =CORREL(C4:C13,B4:B13)

STATISTICAL NOTE: WHY DOES COVARIANCE DEPEND ON THE UNITS OF MEASUREMENT WHEREAS CORRELATION DOESN'T?

Why is the covariance measured in whole numbers 10,000 times bigger than the covariance measured in percentages? Since we've represented percentages as whole numbers, we've essentially multiplied each percentage return by 100. This is how −11.54% becomes −11.54. Since the covariance multiplies the percentages for GM and MSFT together, this means that we've multiplied our previous calculations by $100 * 100 = 10,000$.

The correlation coefficient divides the covariance by the product of the standard deviations,

$$Correlation(r_{GM}, r_{MSFT}) = \frac{Cov(r_{GM}, r_{MSFT})}{\sigma_{GM}\sigma_{MSFT}}$$

In our new calculation, the covariance is 10,000 times bigger, but each standard deviation is 100 times bigger, so that the denominator is also 10,000 times bigger. The result is that the correlation is the same, no matter if the data is measured in percentages or whole numbers.

Fact 2: The correlation between GM and MSFT is the same as the correlation between MSFT and GM. The same holds for the covariance: $Cov(r_{GM}, r_{MSFT}) = Cov(r_{MSFT}, r_{GM})$. The technical jargon for this is that "correlation and covariance are symmetric." To see this in Excel, note that cells B19 (**=Correl(B4:B13,C4:C13)**) and B22 (**=Correl(C4:C13,B4:B13)**) are equal in the above spreadsheet.

Fact 3: The correlation will always be between +1 and −1. The higher the correlation coefficient is in absolute value, the more the two series move together. If the correlation is either

−1 or +1, then the two series are *perfectly correlated*, which means that knowing one series allows you to predict completely the value of the second series. If the correlation coefficient is between −1 and +1, then the two series move in tandem less than perfectly.

Fact 4: If the correlation coefficient is either +1 or −1, this means that the two returns have a linear relation between them. Since this is not easy to understand, we illustrate with a numerical example. Adams Farm and Morgan Sausage are two shares listed on the Farmers Stock Exchange. For reasons that are difficult to determine, each Morgan Sausage's stock return is equal to 60% of that of Adams Farm plus 3%. We can thus write $r_{Morgan\ Sausage,t} = 3\% + 0.6 * r_{Adams\ Farm,t}$. This means that the return on Morgan Sausage stock is *completely predictable* given the return on Adams Farm stock. Thus, the correlation is either −1 or +1. Since, when Adams Farm's return moves up, so does the return of Morgan Sausage, the correlation is +1.[7]

The Excel spreadsheet that follows confirms that the correlation is +1.

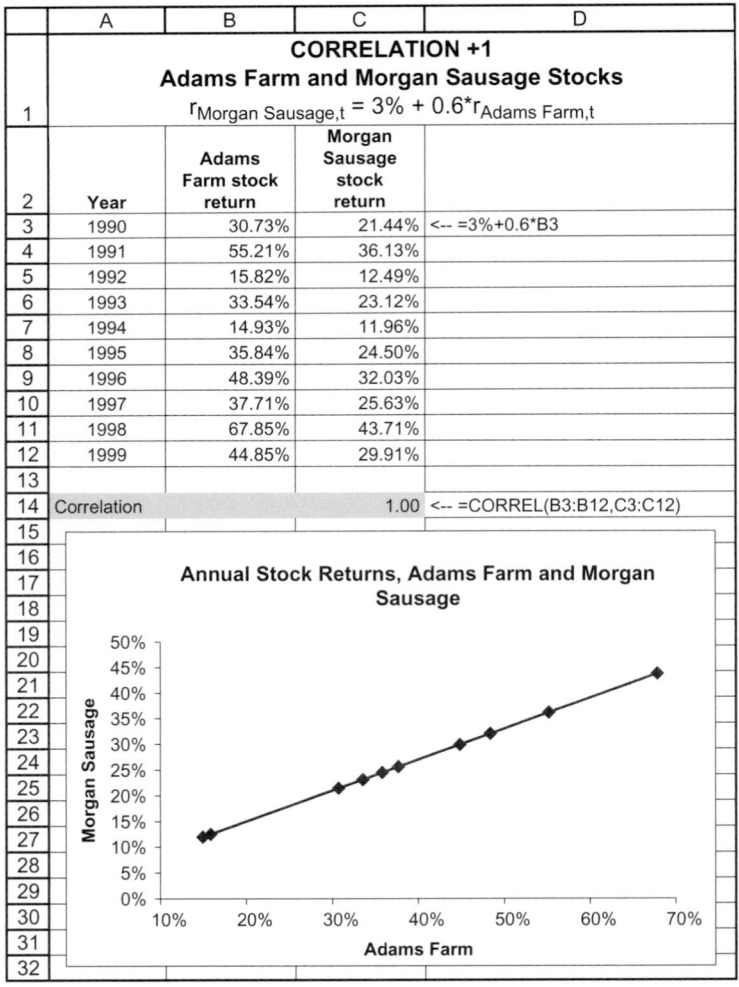

	A	B	C	D
1			**CORRELATION +1** **Adams Farm and Morgan Sausage Stocks** $r_{Morgan\ Sausage,t} = 3\% + 0.6*r_{Adams\ Farm,t}$	
2	Year	**Adams Farm stock return**	**Morgan Sausage stock return**	
3	1990	30.73%	21.44%	<-- =3%+0.6*B3
4	1991	55.21%	36.13%	
5	1992	15.82%	12.49%	
6	1993	33.54%	23.12%	
7	1994	14.93%	11.96%	
8	1995	35.84%	24.50%	
9	1996	48.39%	32.03%	
10	1997	37.71%	25.63%	
11	1998	67.85%	43.71%	
12	1999	44.85%	29.91%	
13				
14	Correlation		1.00	<-- =CORREL(B3:B12,C3:C12)

---

[7]The Farmers Stock Exchange has two other stocks whose returns are related by the equation $r_{Chicken\ Feed,t} = 50\% − 0.8 * r_{Poultry\ Delight,t}$. In this case, the negative coefficient (−0.8) tells us that the correlation between the two sets of returns is −1. (See end-of-chapter Exercise 11.)

Fact 4 can be written mathematically as follows: Suppose Stock 1 and Stock 2 are *perfectly correlated* (meaning that the correlation is either +1 or −1). Then

$$r_{Stock1,t} = a + b * r_{Stock2,t}, \ \text{where} \begin{cases} b > 0 \text{ if the correlation} = +1 \\ b < 0 \text{ if the correlation} = -1 \end{cases}$$

12.4 Portfolio Mean and Variance for a Two-Asset Portfolio

A *portfolio* is a set of stocks or other financial assets. Most people who own stock own more than one stock; they own portfolios of stocks, and the risks they bear relate to the riskiness of their portfolio. In the next chapter we'll start our economic analysis of portfolios. In this section we show you how to compute the mean and variance of a portfolio composed of two stocks. Suppose that between 1990 and 1999 you held a portfolio invested 50% in GM and 50% in MSFT. Column E of the spreadsheet below shows what the annual returns would have been on this portfolio. For example, holding 50% of your portfolio in GM and 50% in Microsoft would have given you a portfolio return of 30.73% in 1990:

$$30.73\% = \underbrace{50\%}_{} * \underbrace{(-11.54\%)}_{} + \underbrace{50\%}_{} * \underbrace{72.99\%}_{}$$

Proportion of GM stock in portfolio   Return on GM stock in 1990   Proportion of MSFT stock in portfolio   Return on MSFT stock in 1990

In cells E17 to E21 we calculate the portfolio return statistics in the same way we calculated the return statistics for the individual assets GM and MSFT.

	A	B	C	D	E	F
1		**CALCULATING PORTFOLIO RETURNS**				
		AND THEIR STATISTICS				
2	Proportion of GM	0.5				
3	Proportion of MSFT	0.5	<-- =1-B2			
4						
5	Date	**General Motors GM**	**Microsoft MSFT**		**Portfolio return**	
6	Dec-90	-11.54%	72.99%		30.73%	<-- =$B$2*B6+$B$3*C6
7	Dec-91	-11.35%	121.76%		55.21%	
8	Dec-92	16.54%	15.11%		15.82%	
9	Dec-93	72.64%	-5.56%		33.54%	
10	Dec-94	-21.78%	51.63%		14.93%	
11	Dec-95	28.13%	43.56%		35.84%	
12	Dec-96	8.46%	88.32%		48.39%	
13	Dec-97	19.00%	56.43%		37.71%	
14	Dec-98	21.09%	114.60%		67.85%	
15	Dec-99	21.34%	68.36%		44.85%	
16						
17	Mean	14.25%	62.72%		38.49%	<-- =AVERAGE(E6:E15)
18	Variance	6.38%	14.43%		2.44%	<-- =VARP(E6:E15)
19	St. dev.	25.25%	37.99%		15.62%	<-- =STDEVP(E6:E15)
20	Covariance		-0.0552			
21	Correlation		-0.5755			
22						
23	Direct calculation of portfolio mean and variance					
24	Portfolio mean	38.49%	<-- =B2*B17+B3*C17			
25	Portfolio variance	2.44%	<-- =B2^2*B18+B3^2*C18+2*B2*B3*C20			
26	Portfolio st. dev.	15.62%	<-- =SQRT(B25)			

Cells B24 to B26 show that these portfolio statistics can be calculated directly from the statistics for the individual assets. To calculate the portfolio mean using these shortcuts, we first need some notation: Let x_{GM} stand for the proportion of GM stock in the portfolio and let x_{MSFT} denote the proportion of MSFT stock in the portfolio. In our example, $x_{GM} = 0.5$ and $x_{MSFT} = 0.5$ and the portfolio mean return is given by

$$portfolio\ mean\ return = E(r_p) = x_{GM}E(r_{GM}) + x_{MSFT}E(r_{MSFT})$$
$$= x_{GM}E(r_{GM}) + (1 - x_{GM})E(r_{MSFT})$$

Notice the second line of the formula: If we only have two assets in the portfolio, then the proportion of the second asset is "one minus" the proportion of the first asset: $x_{MSFT} = 1 - x_{GM}$.

The formula for the portfolio variance is given by

$$portfolio\ variance = Var(r_p)$$
$$= x_{GM}^2 Var(r_{GM}) + x_{MSFT}^2 Var(r_{MSFT}) + 2x_{GM}x_{MSFT}Cov(r_{GM}, r_{MSFT})$$

In the spreadsheet below we built a table of the portfolio statistics using the formulas. In the table we vary the proportion of GM stock in the portfolio from 0% to 100% (which means, of course, that the proportion of MSFT stock goes from 100% to 0%).

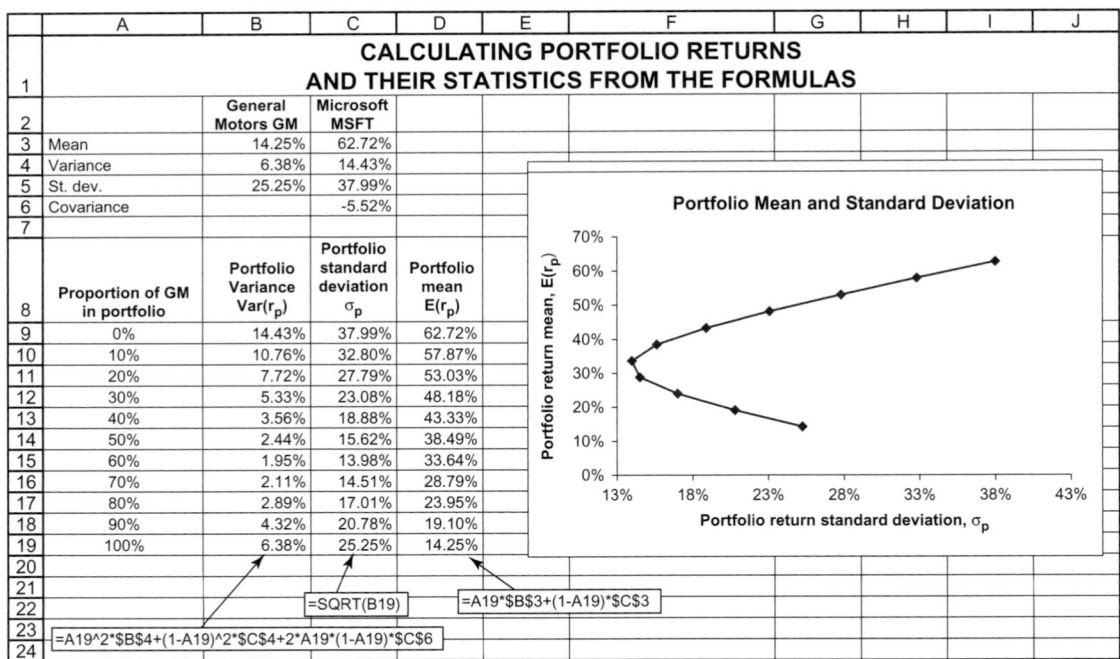

The graph is one that you will see again (lots!) in Chapters 13 and 14. It plots the portfolio standard deviation σ_p on the x-axis and the portfolio mean return $E(r_p)$ on the y-axis. The parabolic shape of the graph is the subject of much discussion in finance, but this is a purely technical chapter—the finance part of the discussion will have to wait until the following chapters.

EXCEL NOTE

TWO NOTES ABOUT THE GRAPH

Note 1: The graph above is an Excel XY (scatter) plot of the data in the range C9:D19. Notice that we've put the data in a somewhat "unnatural" order: We first compute the variance (cells B9 to B19), then the standard deviation (cells C9 to C19), and only then the expected return (D9 to D19). All this is done to make it easier to use Excel's XY charts, which by default use the leftmost data column as the data for the x-axis and data in columns to the right for y-axis data. (There are other work-arounds, but they're too cumbersome to explain here.)

Note 2: When we originally made this graph, the x-axis went from 0% to 40%.

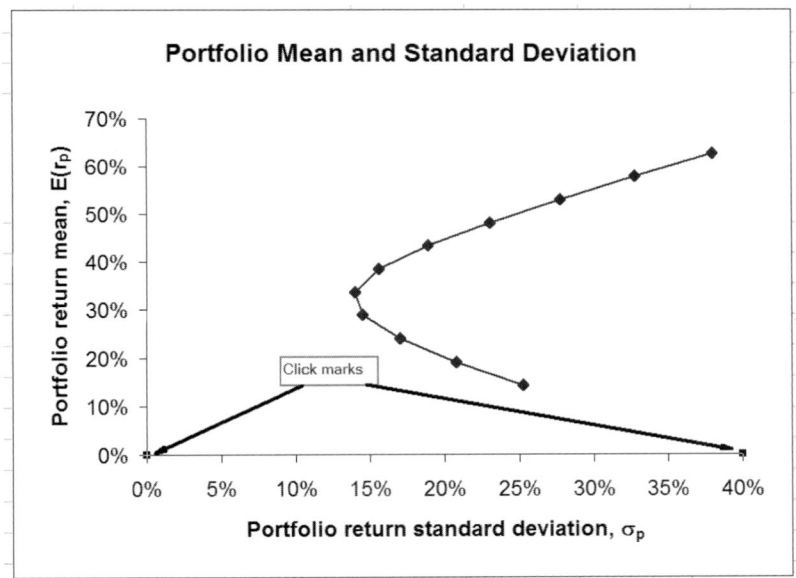

We "shortened" the x-axis by (1) clicking on the axis (you can see the "click marks" on the x-axis above), (2) right-clicking the mouse and bringing up the menu for **Format axis**, and (3) changing the **Minimum** and the **Maximum** settings to the following:

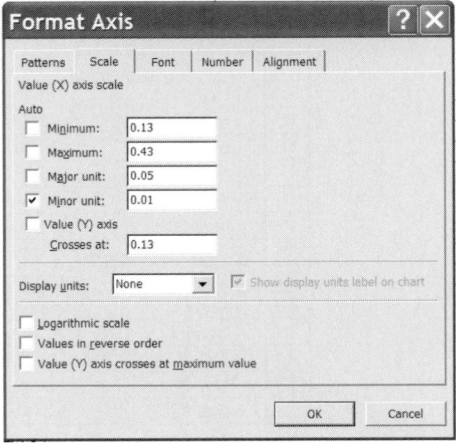

12.5 Using Regressions

Linear regression (for short: regression) is a technique for fitting a line to a set of data. Regressions are used in finance to examine the relation between data series. In the chapters that follow we often need to use regressions; we introduce the basic concepts here. We do not discuss the statistical theory behind regressions, but instead we show you how to run a regression and how to use it.

We've divided the discussion into three subsections: First we discuss the mechanics of doing a regression in Excel, then we discuss the meaning of the regression, and finally we discuss alternative ways of doing the regression.

The Mechanics of Doing a Regression in Excel

In this subsection we discuss a simple regression example and make little attempt to explain the economic meaning of the regression. Instead, we focus on the mechanics of doing the regression in Excel and leave the economic interpretation for the next subsection.

The table below gives the monthly returns for the S&P 500 Index (stock symbol SPX) and for Mirage Resorts (stock symbol MIR) for 1997 and 1998. The S&P 500 Index includes the 500 largest stocks traded on U.S. stock exchanges, and its performance is roughly indicative of the performance of the U.S. stock market as a whole. We use the regression analysis to see if we can understand the relation between the SPX's returns and MIR's returns—that is, if we can understand the effect of the U.S. stock market on the returns of MIR stock.

Here's the data we examine:

	A	B	C
1	**SIMPLE REGRESSION EXAMPLE**		
2	**Date**	**S&P 500 Index SPX**	**Mirage Resorts MIR**
3	Jan-97	6.13%	16.18%
4	Feb-97	0.59%	0.00%
5	Mar-97	-4.26%	-15.42%
6	Apr-97	5.84%	-5.29%
7	May-97	5.86%	18.63%
8	Jun-97	4.35%	5.76%
9	Jul-97	7.81%	5.94%
10	Aug-97	-5.75%	0.23%
11	Sep-97	5.32%	12.35%
12	Oct-97	-3.45%	-17.01%
13	Nov-97	4.46%	-5.00%
14	Dec-97	1.57%	-4.21%
15	Jan-98	1.02%	1.37%
16	Feb-98	7.04%	-0.54%
17	Mar-98	4.99%	5.99%
18	Apr-98	0.91%	-9.25%
19	May-98	-1.88%	-5.67%
20	Jun-98	3.94%	2.40%
21	Jul-98	-1.16%	0.88%
22	Aug-98	-14.58%	-30.81%
23	Sep-98	6.24%	12.61%
24	Oct-98	8.03%	1.12%
25	Nov-98	5.91%	-12.18%
26	Dec-98	5.64%	0.42%

We now use Excel to produce an XY scatter plot of these returns. We use the command **Insert|Chart**, and then the **Chart Wizard** to produce the desired graph:

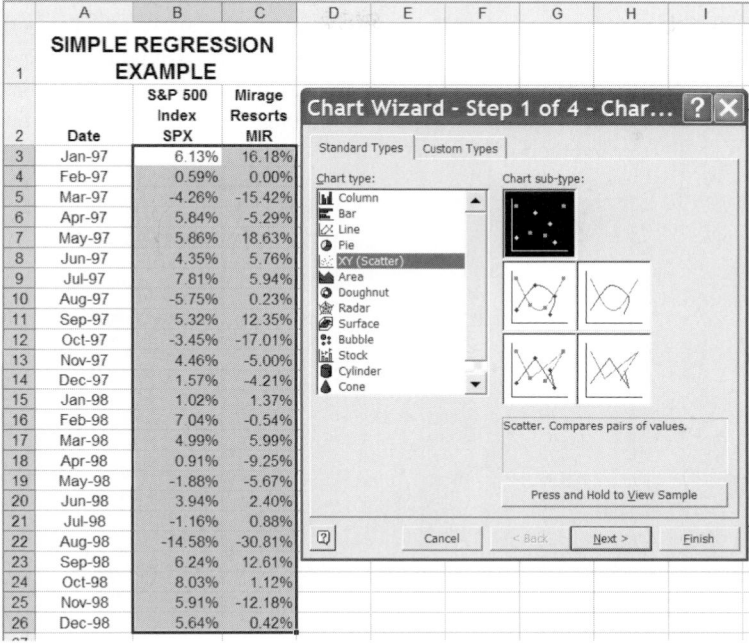

Here's what the chart looks like. As described in Chapter 28 on graphs in Excel, we've gotten rid of the grey background, which is the Excel default.

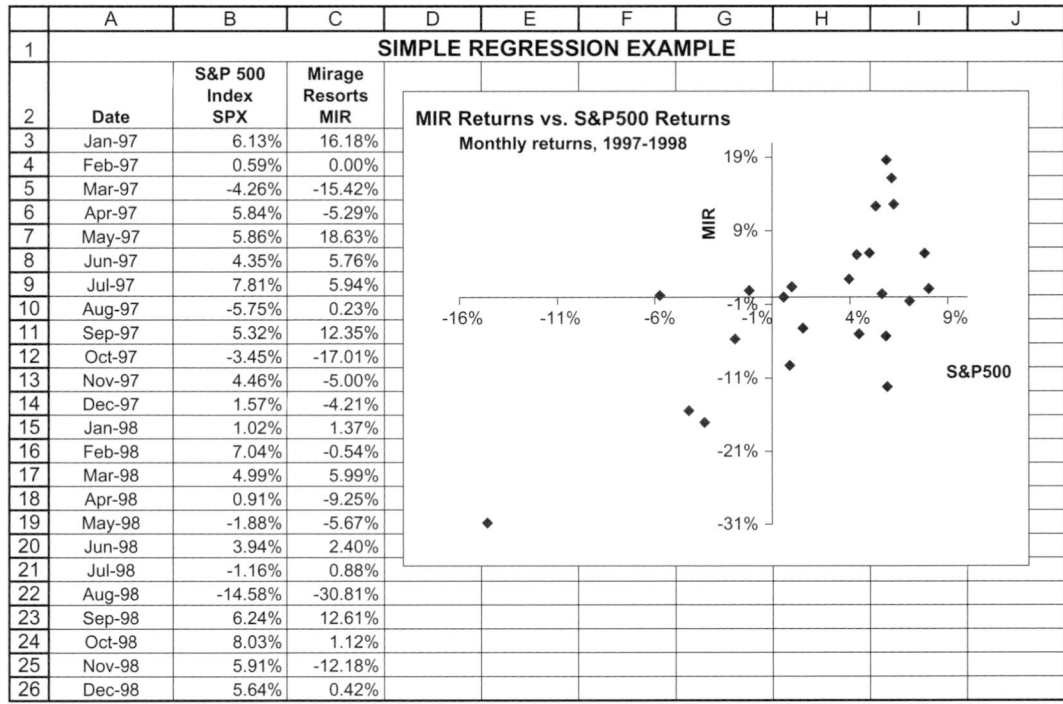

	A	B	C	D	E	F	G	H	I	J
1					SIMPLE REGRESSION EXAMPLE					
2	Date	S&P 500 Index SPX	Mirage Resorts MIR							
3	Jan-97	6.13%	16.18%							
4	Feb-97	0.59%	0.00%							
5	Mar-97	-4.26%	-15.42%							
6	Apr-97	5.84%	-5.29%							
7	May-97	5.86%	18.63%							
8	Jun-97	4.35%	5.76%							
9	Jul-97	7.81%	5.94%							
10	Aug-97	-5.75%	0.23%							
11	Sep-97	5.32%	12.35%							
12	Oct-97	-3.45%	-17.01%							
13	Nov-97	4.46%	-5.00%							
14	Dec-97	1.57%	-4.21%							
15	Jan-98	1.02%	1.37%							
16	Feb-98	7.04%	-0.54%							
17	Mar-98	4.99%	5.99%							
18	Apr-98	0.91%	-9.25%							
19	May-98	-1.88%	-5.67%							
20	Jun-98	3.94%	2.40%							
21	Jul-98	-1.16%	0.88%							
22	Aug-98	-14.58%	-30.81%							
23	Sep-98	6.24%	12.61%							
24	Oct-98	8.03%	1.12%							
25	Nov-98	5.91%	-12.18%							
26	Dec-98	5.64%	0.42%							

We want to draw a line through the points above, and we want this line to be the "best" line in the sense that it is the closest line you could draw through the points.[8] There are several ways to do this in Excel (as usual . . .). Here's what we do:

- Click on the points of the graph so that Excel marks all of them. If you have a lot of data points, Excel may mark only some of the points; just ignore this and proceed to the next step. After you do this, you'll see a graph like the one below (notice that Excel shows us the coordinates of the point we happened to point at—in this case the point where the SPX return is 0.91% and the MIR return is −9.25%):

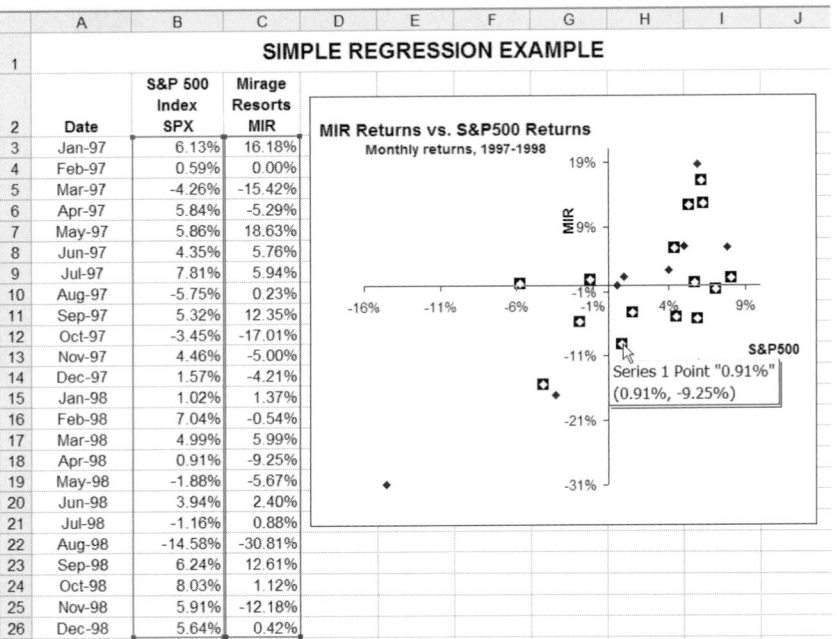

- With the points marked, right-click the mouse and choose **Add Trendline**.

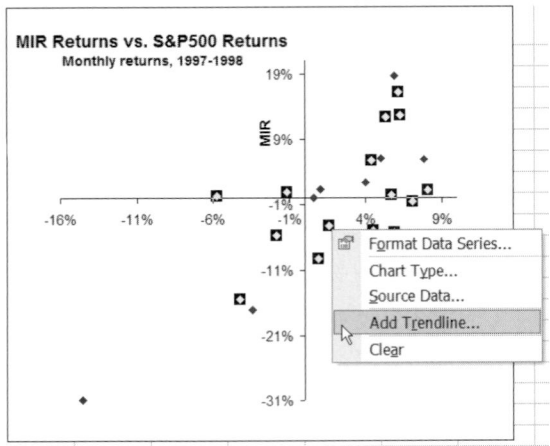

---

[8]There's a formal statistical definition of "best" and "closest," but we leave that to another course.

- **Add Trendline** brings up the following box, in which we leave the choice **Linear** regression.

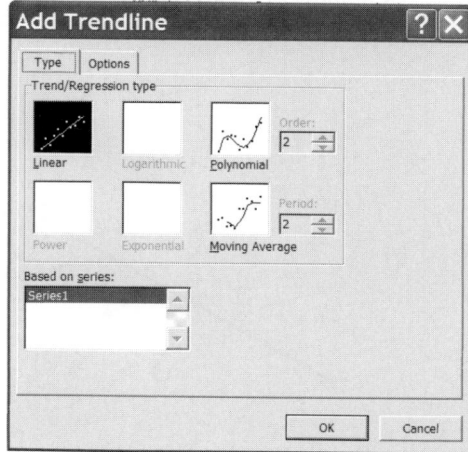

- Before clicking **OK**, we move to the **Options** tab and mark **Display equation on chart** and **Display R-squared value on chart**.

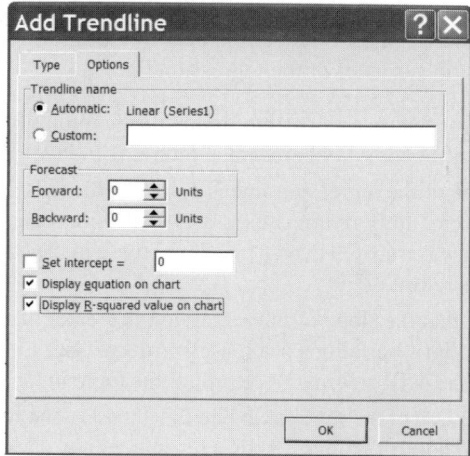

- Now you can click **OK**.

Excel displays the following chart:

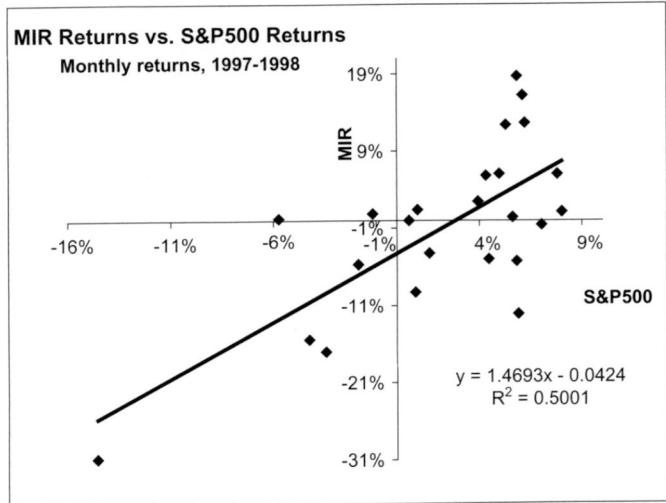

The box with the regression results can be moved with the mouse. The text inside the box can be formatted to the font and the size you desire.

What Does the Regression Mean?

The graph above shows the regression line as $y = 1.4693x - 0.0424$, $R^2 = 0.5001$. Since we're trying to understand the effect of the S&P 500 Index on MIR stock, we can attach the following meaning to the variables of the regression line:

- The "y" of the regression line stands for the monthly percentage return of MIR and the "x" stands for the monthly percentage return of the S&P 500 Index.

- The *slope* of the regression line is 1.4693. This tells us that, on average, a 1% increase in the S&P 500 monthly return caused a 1.4693% increase in the MIR monthly return. Of course, the reverse is true: On average a 1% decrease in the S&P 500 is related to a 1.4693% decrease in MIR's return.

- The fact that the slope of the regression is greater than 1 means that MIR is very sensitive to the S&P 500: Variations (increases or decreases) in the S&P 500 return cause larger variations in the MIR return. We return to this topic in Chapter 14.

- The *intercept* of the regression line is -0.0424. The intercept tells us that in months when the S&P 500 doesn't "move," MIR's return tends to decrease by 4.24%.

- The R^2 (pronounced "r squared") of the regression line says that 50.01% of the variability in the MIR returns is explained by the variability of the S&P 500 returns. This may seem sort of low but it's actually quite respectable: The R^2 of 50% says that half of MIR's return variability is explained by the variability of the S&P 500 Index. The other 50% of the return variability is presumably explained by factors that are unique to MIR. You wouldn't expect much more: If for some strange reason the R^2 were 100%, this would mean that *all* of MIR's returns are explained by the S&P 500 returns, which is clearly nonsense.

The regression line thus allows you to make some interesting predictions about the MIR return based on the S&P 500 return. Suppose you're a financial analyst and you think that this month the S&P 500 Index will go up by 20%. Then based on the regression, you'd expect MIR to increase by $1.4693 * 20\% - 0.0424 = 25.146\%$. Knowing that the R^2 is approximately 50%, only about half of the variability in MIR stock returns is explained by the S&P 500 stock return, and you would thus attach some degree of skepticism to this prediction.

Other Ways of Doing a Regression in Excel

As you might expect, in Excel there are other methods for calculating the slope, intercept, and R^2 of the regression equation. Excel has functions called **Slope**, **Intercept**, **Rsq**. These functions are illustrated below in cells B28, B31, B34. Note that in these functions, the MIR returns come before the S&P 500 returns, so that we write, for example, **Slope(MIR returns,S&P returns)**.

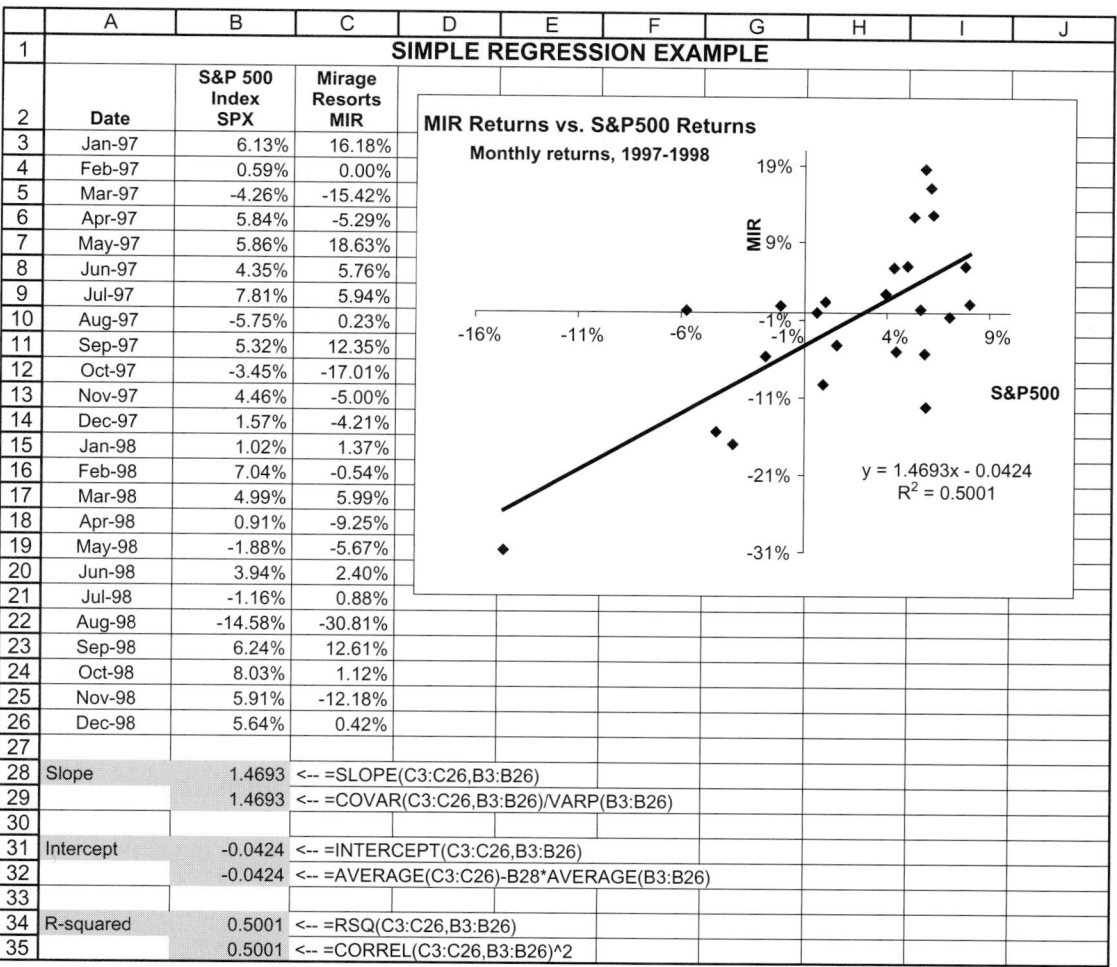

	A	B	C	D	E	F	G	H	I	J
1					SIMPLE REGRESSION EXAMPLE					
2	Date	S&P 500 Index SPX	Mirage Resorts MIR							
3	Jan-97	6.13%	16.18%							
4	Feb-97	0.59%	0.00%							
5	Mar-97	-4.26%	-15.42%							
6	Apr-97	5.84%	-5.29%							
7	May-97	5.86%	18.63%							
8	Jun-97	4.35%	5.76%							
9	Jul-97	7.81%	5.94%							
10	Aug-97	-5.75%	0.23%							
11	Sep-97	5.32%	12.35%							
12	Oct-97	-3.45%	-17.01%							
13	Nov-97	4.46%	-5.00%							
14	Dec-97	1.57%	-4.21%							
15	Jan-98	1.02%	1.37%							
16	Feb-98	7.04%	-0.54%							
17	Mar-98	4.99%	5.99%							
18	Apr-98	0.91%	-9.25%							
19	May-98	-1.88%	-5.67%							
20	Jun-98	3.94%	2.40%							
21	Jul-98	-1.16%	0.88%							
22	Aug-98	-14.58%	-30.81%							
23	Sep-98	6.24%	12.61%							
24	Oct-98	8.03%	1.12%							
25	Nov-98	5.91%	-12.18%							
26	Dec-98	5.64%	0.42%							
27										
28	Slope		1.4693	<-- =SLOPE(C3:C26,B3:B26)						
29			1.4693	<-- =COVAR(C3:C26,B3:B26)/VARP(B3:B26)						
30										
31	Intercept		-0.0424	<-- =INTERCEPT(C3:C26,B3:B26)						
32			-0.0424	<-- =AVERAGE(C3:C26)-B28*AVERAGE(B3:B26)						
33										
34	R-squared		0.5001	<-- =RSQ(C3:C26,B3:B26)						
35			0.5001	<-- =CORREL(C3:C26,B3:B26)^2						

MIR Returns vs. S&P500 Returns
Monthly returns, 1997-1998

$y = 1.4693x - 0.0424$
$R^2 = 0.5001$

The slope, intercept, and R^2 can also be calculated using **Average**, **Covar**, **Varp**, and **Correl** (cells B29, B32, B35). Look at the alternative definitions of each of the regression variables:

- The regression slope can be computed with the **Slope** function (cell B28), but as shown in cell B29 it is also equal to $Covariance(S\&P, MIR)/Var(S\&P)$.
- The regression intercept can be computed with the **Intercept** function (cell 31), but as shown in cell B32 it is also equal to $Average(MIR) - slope * Average(S\&P)$.
- The regression R^2 can be computed with the **Rsq** function (cell B34), but as shown in cell B35 it is also equal to the squared correlation between the S&P and MIR: $[Correlation (S\&P, MIR)]^2$.

12.6 Portfolio Statistics for Multiple Assets (Advanced Topic)

This section discusses a slightly more advanced topic, which is used only in Appendix 13.2 of Chapter 13. You can skip it on first reading. In Section 12.4, we discussed the calculation of the portfolio mean and variance for a two-asset portfolio. In this section we discuss the calculation for a portfolio composed of more than two assets.

In order to set the scene, we introduce some notation. Suppose that we have *three* stocks, and that for each stock i ($i = 1, 2, 3$) we have computed the mean $E(r_i)$ and the variance $\sigma_i^2 = Var(r_i)$ of the stock's returns. Furthermore, suppose that for each pair of stocks i and j, we have calculated the covariance of the returns $Cov(r_i, r_j)$. Here's an example:

	A	B	C	D	E
1		PORTFOLIO RETURNS FOR A THREE-STOCK PORTFOLIO			
2	Year ending	General Motors GM	Microsoft MSFT	Heinz HNZ	
3	Dec-90	-11.54%	72.99%	2.46%	
4	Dec-91	-11.35%	121.76%	14.54%	
5	Dec-92	16.54%	15.11%	16.89%	
6	Dec-93	72.64%	-5.56%	-15.95%	
7	Dec-94	-21.78%	51.63%	6.55%	
8	Dec-95	28.13%	43.56%	39.81%	
9	Dec-96	8.46%	88.32%	11.56%	
10	Dec-97	19.00%	56.43%	45.89%	
11	Dec-98	21.09%	114.60%	14.11%	
12	Dec-99	21.34%	68.36%	-27.44%	
13					
14	Average	14.25%	62.72%	10.84%	<-- =AVERAGE(D3:D12)
15	Variance	0.0638	0.1443	0.0440	<-- =VARP(D3:D12)
16	Sigma	25.25%	37.99%	20.98%	<-- =STDEVP(D3:D12)
17					
18	**Covariances**				
19	Cov(r_{GM},r_{MSFT})	-0.0552	<-- =COVAR(B3:B12,C3:C12)		
20	Cov(r_{GM},r_{HNZ})	-0.0096	<-- =COVAR(B3:B12,D3:D12)		
21	Cov(r_{MSFT},r_{HNZ})	0.0092	<-- =COVAR(C3:C12,D3:D12)		

Now suppose we form a portfolio composed of the following proportions of each of the stocks: $x_{GM} = 20\%$, $x_{MSFT} = 50\%$, $x_{HNZ} = 1 - x_{GM} - x_{MSFT} = 30\%$. Cells G3 to G12 in the spreadsheet below show you the returns of this portfolio, and cells G14 to G16 compute the portfolio's mean return, variance, and standard deviation:

	A	B	C	D	E	F	G	H
1		PORTFOLIO RETURNS FOR A THREE-STOCK PORTFOLIO						
2	Year ending	General Motors GM	Microsoft MSFT	Heinz HNZ			Portfolio return	
3	Dec-90	-11.54%	72.99%	2.46%			34.92%	<-- =0.2*B3+0.5*C3+0.3*D3
4	Dec-91	-11.35%	121.76%	14.54%			62.97%	<-- =0.2*B4+0.5*C4+0.3*D4
5	Dec-92	16.54%	15.11%	16.89%			15.93%	
6	Dec-93	72.64%	-5.56%	-15.95%			6.96%	
7	Dec-94	-21.78%	51.63%	6.55%			23.42%	
8	Dec-95	28.13%	43.56%	39.81%			39.35%	
9	Dec-96	8.46%	88.32%	11.56%			49.32%	
10	Dec-97	19.00%	56.43%	45.89%			45.78%	
11	Dec-98	21.09%	114.60%	14.11%			65.75%	
12	Dec-99	21.34%	68.36%	-27.44%			30.22%	
13								
14	Average	14.25%	62.72%	10.84%	<-- =AVERAGE(D3:D12)	Average	37.46%	<-- =AVERAGE(G3:G12)
15	Variance	0.0638	0.1443	0.0440	<-- =VARP(D3:D12)	Variance	0.0331	<-- =VARP(G3:G12)
16	Sigma	25.25%	37.99%	20.98%	<-- =STDEVP(D3:D12)	Sigma	18.21%	<-- =STDEVP(G3:G12)
17								
18	Covariances						Alternative calculation of portfolio statistics	
19	Cov(r_{GM},r_{MSFT})	-0.0552	<-- =COVAR(B3:B12,C3:C12)			Average	37.46%	<-- =0.2*B14+0.5*C14+0.3*D14
20	Cov(r_{GM},r_{HNZ})	-0.0096	<-- =COVAR(B3:B12,D3:D12)			Variance	0.0331	<-- =0.2^2*B15+0.5^2*C15+0.3^2*D15 +2*0.2*0.5*B19+2*0.2*0.3*B20+2*0.5*0.3*B21
21	Cov(r_{MSFT},r_{HNZ})	0.0092	<-- =COVAR(C3:C12,D3:D12)			Sigma	18.21%	<-- =SQRT(G20)

If you look at cells G19 to G21, you'll see that there is a more straightforward way of doing the same calculations, based on the following formulas:

$$\text{average portfolio return (cell G19)} = E(r_p) = x_{GM}E(r_{GM}) + x_{MSFT}E(r_{MSFT}) + x_{HNZ}E(r_{HNZ})$$

$$\text{portfolio variance (cell G20)} = Var(r_p) = x_{GM}^2 Var(r_{GM}) + x_{MSFT}^2 Var(r_{MSFT}) + x_{HNZ}^2 Var(r_{HNZ})$$
$$+ 2x_{GM}x_{MSFT}Cov(r_{GM}, r_{MSFT}) + 2x_{GM}x_{HNZ}Cov(r_{GM}, r_{HNZ})$$
$$+ 2x_{MSFT}x_{HNZ}Cov(r_{MSFT}, r_{HNZ})$$

$$\text{portfolio standard deviation (cell G21)} = \sqrt{\text{portfolio variance(cell G20)}}$$

These formulas generalize to any number of assets: If we have a portfolio composed of N assets, and we know all the expected returns, variances, and covariances, then:

- The portfolio's expected return is the weighted average of the individual asset returns. Denoting the portfolio weights by $\{x_1, x_2, \ldots, x_N\}$, the portfolio expected return is

$$E(r_p) = x_1 E(r_1) + x_2 E(r_2) + \cdots + x_N E(r_N)$$
$$= \sum_{i=1}^{N} x_i E(r_i)$$

- The portfolio's variance of return is the sum of the following two expressions:
  - The sum of each asset's variance, weighted by the *square* of the asset's portfolio proportion: $x_1^2 Var(r_1) + x_2^2 Var(r_2) + \cdots + x_N^2 Var(r_N)$.

- The sum of twice each of the covariances, weighted by the *product* of the asset proportions:

$$2x_1x_2Cov(r_1, r_2) + 2x_1x_3Cov(r_1, r_3) + \cdots + 2x_1x_NCov(r_1, r_N)$$
$$+ 2x_2x_3Cov(r_2, r_3) + \cdots + 2x_2x_NCov(r_2, r_N)$$
$$+ \cdots + 2x_{N-1}x_NCov(r_{N-1}, r_N)$$

CONCLUSION

Information about stocks—their prices, dividends, and returns—produces mounds of data. Statistics is a way of dealing with these large masses of data. This chapter has given you the necessary statistical techniques to do typical finance computations related to stocks. We've shown how to compute stock returns from basic data about stock prices, dividends, and stock splits. We've also shown how to compute the mean return (also called the average return), the variance and standard deviation of returns, and the covariance between the returns of two different stocks.

Stocks are most often combined into portfolios, and this chapter has shown you how to compute the mean and standard deviation of a portfolio's return. It also introduced you to regression analysis, which allows you to relate the returns of two stocks to each other.

In succeeding chapters we will use these statistical techniques to do financial analysis of individual stocks and stock portfolios.

EXERCISES

1. Here is the stock price history of HighTech Corp. and LowTech Corp.

	A	B	C
1		**HighTech Corp.** Stock price	**LowTech Corp.** Stock price
2	31-Dec-91	75.00	40.00
3	31-Dec-92	86.25	45.20
4	31-Dec-93	125.32	55.60
5	31-Dec-94	91.64	48.37
6	31-Dec-95	100.80	32.88
7	31-Dec-96	145.93	61.64
8	31-Dec-97	151.21	75.82
9	31-Dec-98	196.57	97.05
10	31-Dec-99	226.05	109.66
11	31-Dec-00	89.00	122.99

Calculate the following:
(a) The annual returns for each stock.
(b) The mean (average) return for the ten-year period for each firm. Which stock has the higher average return?
(c) The variance and the standard deviation of returns, for the ten-year period for each firm. Which stock is riskier?

Note: Data for these exercises can be found on the disk that accompanies this book.

(d)   The covariance and correlation of the returns for each firm. Use two formulas to compute the correlation: The Excel formula **Correl** and the definition

$$Correlation(r_A, r_B) = \frac{Cov(r_A, r_B)}{\sigma_A \sigma_B}$$

(e)   If you had to choose between the two stocks, which would you choose? Explain briefly.

2.   Below are price data for three mutual funds:

	A	B	C	D
1	DATA ON THREE MUTUAL FUNDS			
2	Date	Scudder Development Fund	Value Line Leveraged Growth Fund	Fidelity Fund
3	4-Jan-93	24.34	17.47	9.47
4	3-Jan-94	24.2	20.32	11.39
5	3-Jan-95	20.87	19.15	11.19
6	2-Jan-96	30.35	24.45	15.25
7	2-Jan-97	30.94	26.95	18.46
8	2-Jan-98	31.28	32.08	23.44
9	4-Jan-99	33.32	47.19	31.04
10	3-Jan-00	36.06	49.12	35.36
11	2-Jan-01	33.89	47.23	33.82
12	2-Jan-02	20.01	37.31	28.46
13	2-Jan-03	13.79	26.87	21.55

(a)   Compute the annual returns on the funds for the period.

(b)   Compute the mean, variance, and standard deviation of the fund returns.

(c)   Graph the fund returns and the dates.

(d)   Calculate the correlations of the fund returns.

(e)   If the historical information correctly predicts future returns (is this reasonable?), which fund would you choose?

3.   Here are the monthly stock price data for Ford Corporation and GM Corporation:

	A	B	C	D
1	PRICES FOR FORD AND GM STOCK			
2	Date	Ford	GM	
3	8-Nov-99	24.44	66.08	
4	1-Dec-99	25.79	65.09	
5	3-Jan-00	24.32	72.14	
6	1-Feb-00	20.35	68.54	
7	1-Mar-00	22.45	74.63	
8	3-Apr-00	27.00	84.37	
9	1-May-00	23.95	64.02	
10	1-Jun-00	22.08	52.63	
11	3-Jul-00	24.17	51.61	
12	1-Aug-00	21.95	63.97	
13	1-Sep-00	23.14	59.40	
14	2-Oct-00	23.98	56.77	
15	1-Nov-00	20.89	45.64	
16	1-Dec-00	21.52	46.96	
17	2-Jan-01	26.16	49.51	
18	1-Feb-01	25.30	51.77	

Calculate the following:

(a)   Monthly returns for each firm.

(b)   Covariance between returns of Ford Corporation and GM Corporation.

(c)   Correlation between returns of Ford Corporation and GM Corporation.

4.   By using the returns of Ford Corp. and GM Corp. that you calculated in Exercise 3, perform a regression of Ford's returns versus GM's returns. Report:

- The slope of the regression.

- The value of the intercept.

- The R^2 of the regression.

Is the mutual impact of the two company's sales (one on the other) large or small? Explain.

5.   Here are the stock price and dividend data for Kellogg Co.:

	A	B	C
1	**KELLOGG PRICE AND DIVIDEND DATA**		
2		Price	Dividend during year
3	31-Dec-89	64.62	
4	31-Dec-90	78.00	1.44
5	31-Dec-91	56.75	2.15
6	31-Dec-92	62.12	1.16
7	31-Dec-93	53.75	1.32
8	31-Dec-94	55.00	1.40
9	31-Dec-95	76.62	1.50
10	31-Dec-96	69.62	1.62
11	31-Dec-97	46.38	1.28
12	31-Dec-98	40.62	0.90
13	31-Dec-99	24.25	0.98
14	31-Dec-00	26.20	1.00
15	31-Dec-01	30.86	1.00
16	31-Dec-02	33.40	1.00

(a)   Calculate the dividend-adjusted returns for each of the years, their mean, and their standard deviation.

(b)   Stock analysts like to talk about the *dividend yield*—the dividend divided by the stock price. Compute the annual dividend yield for Kellogg (define it as *(dividends over the year)/(stock price at begining of year)*) and compute its statistics (mean and standard deviation) over the period.

(c)   If you bought Kellogg stock and had no intention of ever selling it, why might you be interested in the stock's dividend yield?

6.   Below are the stock price, dividend, and split data for IBM. Calculate the dividend and split-adjusted returns for each of the years, their mean, and their standard deviation.

	A	B	C	D
1			IBM PRICE, DIVIDEND AND SPLIT DATA	
2		Closing price	Dividend during year	Other information
3	31-Dec-89	98.62		
4	31-Dec-90	126.75		
5	31-Dec-91	90.00		
6	31-Dec-92	51.50		
7	31-Dec-93	56.50		
8	31-Dec-94	72.12		
9	31-Dec-95	108.50		
10	31-Dec-96	156.88		
11	31-Dec-97	98.75		2 for 1 split (May 97)
12	31-Dec-98	183.25		
13	31-Dec-99	112.25		2 for 1 split (May 99)
14	31-Dec-00	112.00		
15	31-Dec-01	107.89		
16	31-Dec-02	78.20	0.30	

7. Compute the covariance and correlation coefficient between Kellogg and IBM (Exercises 5 and 6). Are there any advantages to diversifying between Kellogg and IBM?

8. Here are the stock price and split data for HeavySteel Corporation.

	A	B	C
1		HEAVYSTEEL CORPORATION	
2		Closing stock price	Stock splits
3	31-Dec-90	11.24	
4	31-Dec-91	11.98	
5	31-Dec-92	10.23	
6	31-Dec-93	11.02	2 for 1
7	31-Dec-94	12.56	
8	31-Dec-95	13.45	
9	31-Dec-96	15.36	1.5 for 1
10	31-Dec-97	16.01	
11	31-Dec-98	17.23	
12	31-Dec-99	15.23	

(a) Calculate the split-adjusted returns for each year and its statistics (mean and standard deviation).

(b) If you bought 100 shares of this stock in the beginning of 1990 and during the period of ten years never sold or bought additional shares, how many shares would you have by the end of 2000?

9. A *reverse split* is just like a split, but only in a reverse direction. For example, in a 1 for 2 reverse split, you receive 1 share for every 2 shares you hold. How would your answers to the previous question change if you learned that in 1999 the firm did a 3 for 4 reverse split?

10. Consider two companies: Young Corporation and Mature Corporation. Young Corporation grows very rapidly, does not pay any dividends, and retains all its profits. Mature Corporation stopped growing a long time ago, generates sizable cash flows, and pays out dividends.

	A	B	C	D
1		**Young Corp.**	**Mature Corp.**	
2		Share price	Share price	Dividend per share
3	31-Dec-90	32.56	78.50	0.00
4	31-Dec-91	34.50	82.50	0.00
5	31-Dec-92	38.98	84.50	1.00
6	31-Dec-93	44.50	81.60	0.00
7	31-Dec-94	40.20	79.60	1.50
8	31-Dec-95	39.50	80.96	1.50
9	31-Dec-96	38.45	82.65	0.00
10	31-Dec-97	37.50	83.69	2.00
11	31-Dec-98	43.58	82.79	2.00
12	31-Dec-99	50.30	81.97	0.00

(a) Calculate Young's yearly returns.

(b) Calculate Mature's yearly returns.

(c) Which is the better investment of the two? Give a brief explanation.

11. Chicken Feed and Poultry Delight are two stocks traded on the Farmers Stock Exchange. A statistician has determined that the returns on the two stocks are related by the equation $r_{Chicken\ Feed,t} = 50\% - 0.8 * r_{Poultry\ Delight,t}$. Show that the correlation between the two sets of returns is -1. Use the following template:

	A	B	C
2	Year	Poultry Delight stock return	Chicken Feed stock return
3	1990	30.73%	
4	1991	55.21%	
5	1992	15.82%	
6	1993	33.54%	
7	1994	14.93%	
8	1995	35.84%	
9	1996	48.39%	
10	1997	37.71%	
11	1998	67.85%	
12	1999	44.85%	
13			
14	Correlation		

12. Below are the annual returns of two assets. Fill in the blanks and graph the returns of the portfolios (rows 13–27).

	A	B	C
1		**Asset 1**	**Asset 2**
2	31-Dec-90	12.56%	7.56%
3	31-Dec-91	13.50%	8.56%
4	31-Dec-92	14.23%	4.56%
5	31-Dec-93	15.23%	2.12%
6	31-Dec-94	14.23%	1.23%
7	31-Dec-95	12.23%	0.26%
8	31-Dec-96	10.23%	3.25%
9	31-Dec-97	5.26%	4.89%
10	31-Dec-98	4.25%	5.56%
11	31-Dec-99	2.23%	6.45%
12			
13	Average return		
14	Return variance		
15	Covariance		
16	**Proportion of asset 1**	**Portfolio standard deviation**	**Portfolio mean return**
17	0		
18	0.1		
19	0.2		
20	0.3		
21	0.4		
22	0.5		
23	0.6		
24	0.7		
25	0.8		
26	0.9		
27	1		

13. Here are data on the stock prices and returns of General Electric, Boeing, and S&P 500 Index.

	A	B	C	D	E	F	G
1	MONTHLY RETURNS ON GE, BOEING, S&P500, 2000						
2	Date	GE	GE Return	Boeing	Boeing return	S&P500	S&P return
3	Jan-02	37.15		40.22		1130.20	
4	Feb-02	38.50	3.63%	45.33	12.71%	1106.73	-2.08%
5	Mar-02	37.40	-2.86%	47.59	4.99%	1147.39	3.67%
6	Apr-02	31.55	-15.64%	43.99	-7.56%	1076.92	-6.14%
7	May-02	31.14	-1.30%	42.23	-4.00%	1067.14	-0.91%
8	Jun-02	29.05	-6.71%	44.55	5.49%	989.82	-7.25%
9	Jul-02	32.20	10.84%	41.11	-7.72%	911.62	-7.90%
10	Aug-02	30.15	-6.37%	36.87	-10.31%	916.07	0.49%
11	Sep-02	24.65	-18.24%	33.95	-7.92%	815.28	-11.00%
12	Oct-02	25.25	2.43%	29.59	-12.84%	885.76	8.64%
13	Nov-02	27.12	7.41%	34.05	15.07%	936.31	5.71%
14	Dec-02	24.35	-10.21%	32.99	-3.11%	879.82	-6.03%
15							
16	Average return						
17	Standard deviation						
18	Covariances						
19	Cov(GE,Boeing)						
20	Cov(GE,SP)						
21	Cov(Boeing,SP)						
22							
23	Correlations						
24	Correlation(GE,Boeing)						
25	Correlation(GE,SP)						
26	Correlation(Boeing,SP)						
27							
28	Portfolio proportions						
29	GE	0.5					
30	Boeing	0.3					
31	S&P	0.2	<-- =1-B30-B29				
32							
33	Portfolio return						
34	Portfolio standard deviation						

Calculate the highlighted cells.

14. Go to http://finance.yahoo.com. Download monthly adjusted stock price data for Oracle Corporation (ORCL), Microsoft Corporation (MSFT), Dell Corporation (DELL), and Gateway Corporation (GTW) for 1998 and 1999. Also, download the same data for S&P 500 Index (SPX) for the same period.[9] Answer the following questions:

   (a) What is the mean return, variance, and standard deviation of a portfolio consisting of the four stocks, where wealth is allocated equally among each stock?

   (b) On average, would you be better off by investing in this portfolio or by investing in S&P 500 Index, during the period of two years?

   (c) What is the sensitivity of your portfolio to the movements of S&P 500 Index? You will have to perform a regression of the portfolio returns versus S&P 500 returns and report the results.

---

[9]Recall that when you download data from Yahoo into Excel, it is already adjusted for stock splits and dividends.

15. By using information provided in Exercise 14, perform a regression of the portfolio returns versus. S&P 500 Index returns for the period of 24 months. Report the slope of the regression, its intercept, and R^2. Explain what each of these numbers tell you.

16. (This is a hard question!) On the disk that comes with this book, you will find two years of monthly unadjusted and adjusted stock price data for AT&T Corporation (symbol: T).

   (a) Calculate the cumulative adjustment factor for AT&T stock.

   (b) What two interesting things happened in November 2002 and what happened to the cumulative adjustment factor in this month? Can you explain?

   Here's the data:

	A	B	C	D	E	F	G	H	I
1	Date	Open	High	Low	Close	Volume	Adj. Close*	Cumulative Adjustment factor	
2	Dec 02			$0.19 Cash Dividend					
3	Dec 02	28.54	28.88	25.11	26.11	4,932,428	26.11		
4	Nov 02			$8.48 Cash Dividend					
5	Nov 02			1:5 Stock Split					
6	Nov 02	12.94	28.25	12.84	28.04	13,146,915	28.04		<-- AT&T Spins Off AT&T Broadband To Shareowners And Completes AT&T Broadband Merger With Comcast
7	Oct 02	12.1	13.64	10.45	13.04	14,453,869	65.2		1 to 5 Reverse Split
8	Sep 02			$0.04 Cash Dividend					
9	Sep 02	11.95	13.79	11.2	12.01	15,095,745	60.05		
10	Aug 02	10.12	12.85	8.69	12.22	17,147,918	61.1		
11	Jul 02	10.5	10.55	8.2	10.18	18,639,136	50.9		
12	Jun 02			$0.04 Cash Dividend					
13	Jun 02	11.85	12.4	9.09	10.7	29,520,930	53.5		
14	May 02	13.2	14.3	11.76	11.97	17,814,400	59.85		
15	Apr 02	15.74	15.85	12.66	13.12	15,936,609	65.6		
16	Mar 02			$0.04 Cash Dividend					
17	Mar 02	15.8	16.48	15	15.7	11,042,700	78.5		
18	Feb 02	17.55	17.91	14.18	15.54	16,401,442	77.7		
19	Jan 02	18.48	19.25	16.65	17.7	11,919,185	88.5		
20	Dec 01			$0.04 Cash Dividend					
21	Dec 01	17.35	18.75	15.8	18.14	14,846,490	90.7		
22	Nov 01	15.33	17.85	14.75	17.49	10,987,857	87.45		
23	Oct 01	19.15	20	15.17	15.25	15,015,643	76.25		
24	Sep 01			$0.04 Cash Dividend					
25	Sep 01	19.01	19.64	16.5	19.3	15,798,733	96.5		
26	Aug 01	20.32	20.95	18.66	19.04	7,457,491	95.2		
27	Jul 01			$5.52 Cash Dividend					
28	Jul 01	21.75	23	18.1	20.21	16,556,647	101.05		
29	Jun 01			$0.04 Cash Dividend					
30	Jun 01	21.16	22.16	19.82	22	11,332,052	110		
31	May 01	22.58	23.1	20.48	21.17	15,562,513	105.85		
32	Apr 01	21.3	23.27	19.85	22.28	12,075,000	111.4		
33	Mar 01			$0.04 Cash Dividend					
34	Mar 01	22.8	24.6	20.6	21.3	12,662,459	106.5		
35	Feb 01	23.95	24.53	20.2	23	12,220,989	115		
36	Jan 01	17.37	25.15	17.25	23.99	20,407,609	119.95		
37	Dec 00			$0.04 Cash Dividend					
38	Dec 00	19.44	22.69	16.5	17.25	23,385,210	86.25		
39	Nov 00	22.62	22.94	18.25	19.62	20,863,095	98.1		
40	Oct 00	29	30	21.25	23.19	24,254,945	115.95		
41	Sep 00			$0.22 Cash Dividend					
42	Sep 00	31.62	32.94	27.25	29	19,280,690	145		
43	Aug 00	30.94	32.94	29.62	31.62	17,828,760	158.1		
44	Jul 00	31.81	35.19	30.5	30.94	19,562,070	154.7		
45	Jun 00			$0.22 Cash Dividend					
46	Jun 00	34.94	37.75	31.25	31.81	20,312,436	159.05		
47	May 00	46.31	49	33.63	34.94	25,649,081	174.7		
48	Apr 00	56.69	58.81	45.88	45.88	12,616,194	229.4		
49	Mar 00			$0.22 Cash Dividend					
50	Mar 00	49.38	61	47.5	56.31	13,692,547	281.55		
51	Feb 00	52.75	53	44.31	49.38	10,648,485	246.9		
52	Jan 00	50.81	56	47.5	52.75	11,964,045	263.75		
53	Dec 99			$0.22 Cash Dividend					
54	Dec 99	55.88	58.69	49.88	50.81	9,812,559	254.05		
55	Nov 99	47.13	61	44.94	55.88	13,277,338	279.4		
56	Oct 99	43.5	49.06	41.5	46.75	11,850,266	233.75		
57	Sep 99			$0.22 Cash Dividend					
58	Sep 99	45.38	48.81	41.81	43.5	10,775,514	217.5		
59	Aug 99	52.13	52.81	44.25	45	12,892,813	225		
60	Jul 99	55.94	59	51.75	52.13	9,257,600	260.65		
61	Jun 99			$0.22 Cash Dividend					
62	Jun 99	55.5	56.88	52.38	55.81	10,673,172	279.05		
63	May 99	51	63	50.88	55.5	14,542,265	277.5		
64	Apr 99			3:2 Stock Split					
65	Apr 99	79.81	89.5	50.06	50.5	13,690,428	252.5		
66	Mar 99			$0.33 Cash Dividend					
67	Mar 99	82.12	89	75.87	79.81	9,906,500	266.03		
68	Feb 99	91.94	95.12	82.12	82.12	8,755,210	273.73		
69	Jan 99	76.5	96.12	76.5	90.75	10,024,863	302.5		

17. Explain why each of the following statements is correct or incorrect:
   (a) Diversification reduces risk because prices of stocks do not usually move exactly together.
   (b) The expected return on a portfolio is a weighted average of the expected returns on the individual securities.
   (c) The standard deviation of returns on a portfolio is equal to the weighted average of the standard deviations on the individual securities if these returns are completely uncorrelated.

18. Suppose that the annual returns on two stocks (A and B) are perfectly negatively correlated, and that $r_A = 0.05$, $r_B = 0.15$, $\sigma_A = 0.1$, $\sigma_B = 0.4$. Assuming that there are no arbitrage opportunities, what must the one-year interest rate be?

19. Assume that an individual can either invest all of her resources in one of two securities A or B; or alternatively, she can diversify her investment between the two. The distribution of the returns are as follows:

	A	B	C	D
1	Security A		Security B	
2	Return	Probability	Return	Probability
3	-10%	0.5	-20%	0.5
4	50%	0.5	60%	0.5

Assume that the correlation between the returns from the two securities is zero.
   (a) Calculate each security's expected return, variance, and standard deviation.
   (b) Calculate the probability distribution of the returns on a *mixed portfolio* comprised of equal proportions of securities A and B. Also calculate the expected return, variance, and standard deviation.
   (c) Calculate the expected return and the variance of a mixed portfolio comprised of 75% of security A and 25% of security B.

20. The correlations between the returns of three stocks A, B, and C are given in the following table:

	A	B	C	D
1	**Stock**	A	B	C
2	A	1.00	0.80	0.10
3	B		1.00	0.15
4	C			1.00

The expected rates of return on A, B, and C are 16%, 12%, and 15%, respectively. The corresponding standard deviations of the returns are 25%, 22%, and 25%.
   (a) What is the standard deviation of a portfolio invested 25% in stock A, 25% in stock B, and 50% in stock C?
   (b) You plan to invest 50% of your money in the portfolio constructed in part (a) of this exercise and 50% in the risk-free asset. The risk-free interest rate is 5%. What is the expected return on this investment? What is the standard deviation of the return on this investment?

21. You believe that there is a 15% chance that stock A will decline by 10% and an 85% chance that it will increase by 15%. Correspondingly, there is a 30% chance that stock B will decline by 18% and a 70% chance that it will increase by 22%. The correlation coefficient between the two stocks is 0.55. Calculate the expected return, the variance, and the standard deviation for each stock. Then calculate the covariance between their returns.

22. Outdoorsy people know that the crickets chirp faster when the temperature is warmer. Some evidence for this can be found in a book published in 1948 by Harvard physics professor George W. Pierce.[10] Pierce's book includes the table below, which relates the average number of cricket chirps per minute to the temperature at which the data was recorded. Plot the data in an Excel graph and use regression to determine the (approximate) relation between the number of chirps per second and the temperature. If you detect 19 chirps per second, what would you guess the temperature to be? What about 22 chirps per second? (We know this problem has nothing to do with finance, but it's interesting!)

	A Chirps per second	B Temperature in Farenheit
4		
5	20.0	88.60
6	16.0	71.60
7	19.8	93.30
8	18.4	84.30
9	17.1	80.60
10	15.5	75.20
11	14.7	69.70
12	17.1	82.00
13	15.4	69.40
14	16.2	83.30
15	15.0	79.60
16	17.2	82.60
17	16.0	80.60
18	17.0	83.50
19	14.4	76.30

23. Economists have long believed that the more money printed, the higher will be long-term interest rates. Evidence for this view can be found in the table below, which gives long-term government bond rates for 31 countries and the corresponding growth rate of money supply for each country.[11]

    (a) Plot the data and use a regression to find the relation between the money growth and the long-term bond interest rate.

    (b) If a country has zero money growth, what is its predicted long-term bond interest rate?

    (c) The monetary authorities in your country are considering increasing the money growth rate by 1% from its current level. Predict by how much this will increase the long-term bond interest rate.

    (d) Do you find the evidence in the table convincing? (Discuss briefly the R^2 of the regression.)

---

[10]Additional facts: Cricket chirping is produced by the rapid sliding of the cricket's wings one over the other. The higher the temperature, the faster the crickets slide their wings. George W. Pierce's book is called *The Songs of Insects* and was published by Harvard University Press.

[11]The data was first presented in an article entitled "Money and Interest Rates," by Cyril Monnet and Warren Weber in the *Federal Reserve Bank of Minneapolis Quarterly Review,* Fall 2001. My thanks to the authors for providing me with an Excel version of their data.

	A	B	C	D	E	F	G
38	**MONEY GROWTH AND BOND INTEREST RATES**						
39	**Country**	**Average mone growth**	**Average long-term bond interest rate**		**Country**	**Average money growth**	**Average long-term bond interest rate**
40	US	5.65%	7.40%		New Zealand	10.29%	8.81%
41	Austria	6.82%	7.80%		South Africa	14.14%	11.11%
42	Belgium	5.20%	8.22%		Honduras	16.20%	15.57%
43	Denmark	9.43%	10.36%		Jamaica	19.88%	15.35%
44	France	8.15%	8.49%		Netherlands Antilles	4.36%	9.40%
45	Germany	8.00%	7.20%		Trinidad & Tobago	12.14%	9.10%
46	Italy	12.07%	10.66%		Korea	15.12%	16.53%
47	Netherlands	7.89%	7.31%		Nepal	15.55%	8.59%
48	Norway	10.64%	8.00%		Pakistan	12.79%	7.88%
49	Switzerland	5.53%	4.54%		Thailand	10.86%	10.62%
50	Canada	8.99%	8.52%		Malawi	20.80%	17.62%
51	Japan	9.07%	6.16%		Zimbabwe	13.49%	12.01%
52	Ireland	9.43%	10.38%		Solomon Islands	15.89%	12.12%
53	Portugal	12.91%	10.79%		Western Samoa	12.90%	13.17%
54	Spain	10.38%	12.72%		Venezuela	28.47%	28.92%
55	Australia	9.15%	8.95%				

24. Mabelberry Fruit and Sawyer's Jam are two competing companies. An MBA student has done a calculation and found that the return on Sawyer's Jam stock is completely predictable once the return on Mabelberry Fruit stock is known:

$$r_{Sawyer's,t} = 40\% - 1.5 * r_{Mabelberry,t}$$

(a)   Given the Mabelberry Fruit stock returns below, compute the Sawyer's Jam returns.

(b)   Regress Mabelberry Fruit stock returns on those for Sawyer's Jam. Can you explain the R^2?

	A	B
2	Year	**Mabelberry Fruit stock return**
3	1990	30.73%
4	1991	15.00%
5	1992	-9.00%
6	1993	12.00%
7	1994	13.00%
8	1995	22.00%
9	1996	30.00%
10	1997	12.00%
11	1998	43.00%
12	1999	16.00%

APPENDIX 12.1: DOWNLOADING DATA FROM YAHOO[12]

Yahoo provides free stock price data, which can be used to calculate returns. In this appendix we show you how to access this data and download it into Excel.

Step 1: Go to http://www.yahoo.com and click on Finance:

---

[12]Yahoo occasionally changes its interface; the information in this appendix is correct as of July 2006.

Step 2: In the "Enter symbol" box, put in the symbol for the stock you want to look up (we've put in MRK for Merck). You see that you can also look up symbols or put in multiple symbols. When you have put in the symbols, click on **Go**.

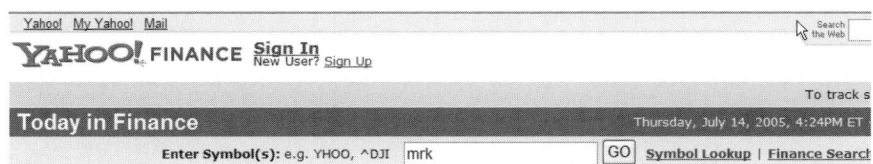

Step 3: This brings up the screen below. We choose **Historical Prices** to get Merck's price history.

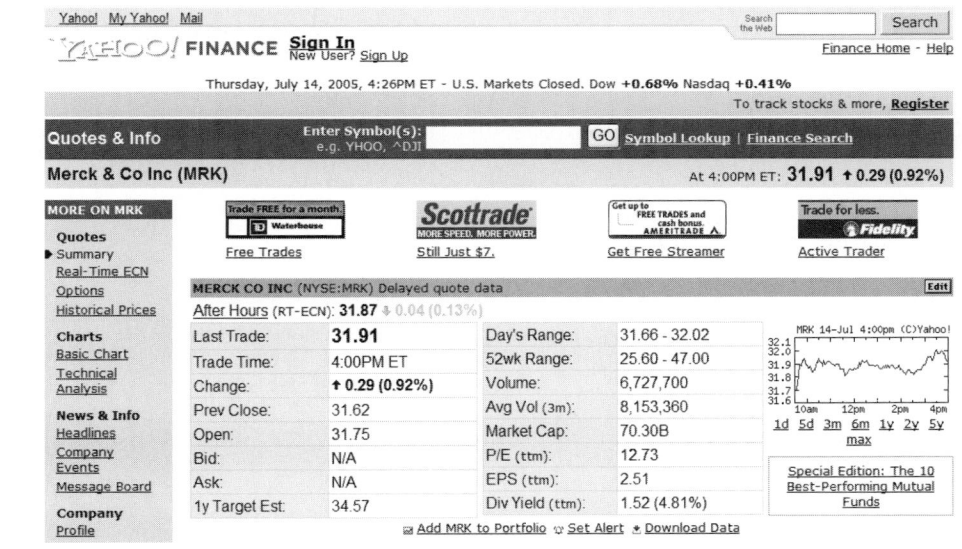

Step 4: In the next screen, we indicated the time period and frequency for the data we want. Yahoo provides a table with stock prices, dividends, and an **Adjusted Closing Stock Price** that accounts for dividends and stock splits:

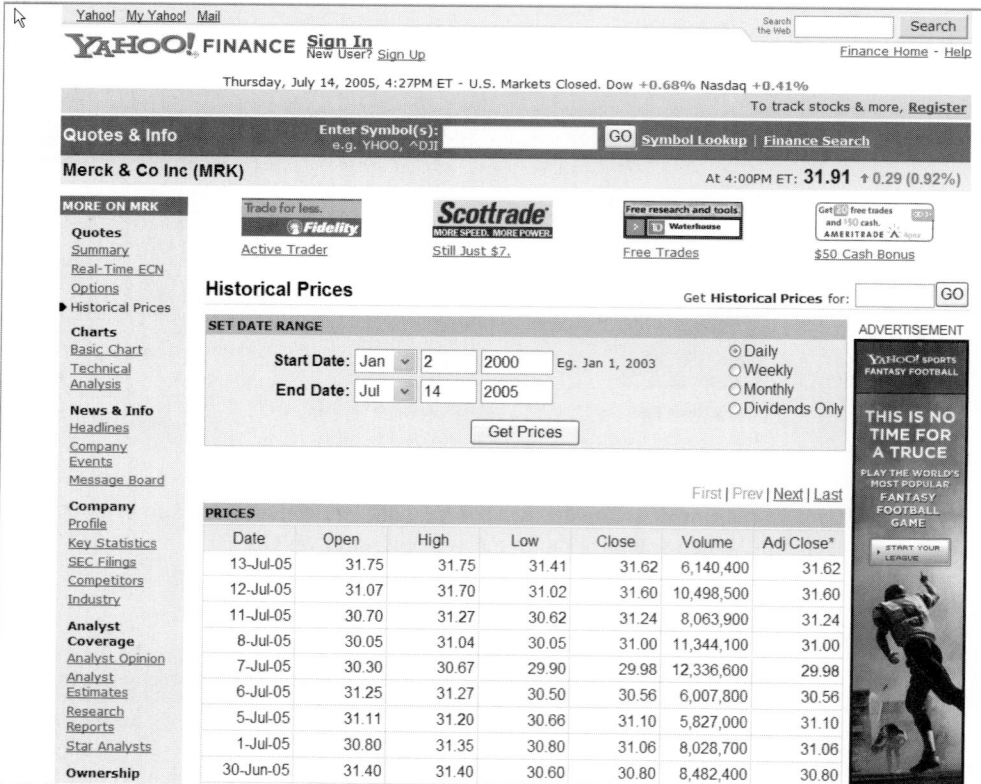

Step 5: The bottom of the above table allows you to download the data in spreadsheet format. In most browsers the Excel spreadsheet opens automatically (see results in Step 6):

21-Apr-05	34.97	34.98	33.95	34.28	9,455,100	33.88
20-Apr-05	34.40	34.56	33.60	34.07	8,629,800	33.67
19-Apr-05	34.65	34.83	34.13	34.68	8,203,800	34.27
18-Apr-05	34.75	34.75	34.00	34.43	10,407,000	34.03
15-Apr-05	35.24	36.26	34.76	34.80	19,490,900	34.39
14-Apr-05	34.60	34.97	34.53	34.78	14,166,500	34.37
13-Apr-05	33.81	35.30	33.52	34.52	25,685,600	34.12
12-Apr-05	33.05	33.82	32.95	33.81	7,908,000	33.41
11-Apr-05	33.45	33.59	33.05	33.14	4,930,800	32.75

* Close price adjusted for dividends and splits.

First | Prev | Next | Last

⬆ Download To Spreadsheet

Step 6: In the author's browser Yahoo offers to save a file called **Table.csv**. We changed the name of this file to **Merck.csv** and saved it on our hard disk.

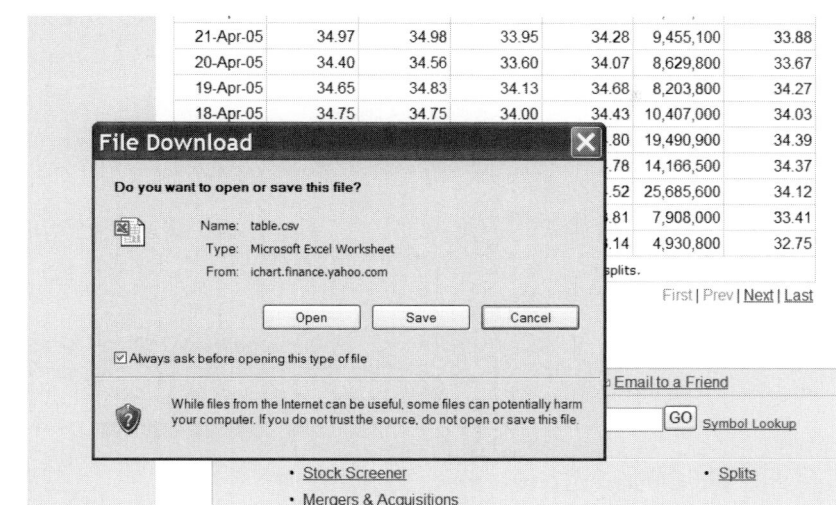

Step 7: The author's browser offered to open the file immediately (it will open as an Excel file). Here's the way opened Excel file looks. Note that only the adjusted stock prices are given.

	A	B	C	D	E	F	G
1	Date	Open	High	Low	Close	Volume	Adj. Close*
2	13-Jul-05	31.75	31.75	31.41	31.62	6140400	31.62
3	12-Jul-05	31.07	31.7	31.02	31.6	10498500	31.6
4	11-Jul-05	30.7	31.27	30.62	31.24	8063900	31.24
5	8-Jul-05	30.05	31.04	30.05	31	11344100	31
6	7-Jul-05	30.3	30.67	29.9	29.98	12336600	29.98
7	6-Jul-05	31.25	31.27	30.5	30.56	6007800	30.56
8	5-Jul-05	31.11	31.2	30.66	31.1	5827000	31.1
9	1-Jul-05	30.8	31.35	30.8	31.06	8028700	31.06
10	30-Jun-05	31.4	31.4	30.6	30.8	8482400	30.8
11	29-Jun-05	31	31.04	30.7	30.83	6737900	30.83
12	28-Jun-05	30.78	31.12	30.6	30.97	7471900	30.97
13	27-Jun-05	30.4	30.88	30.4	30.5	7233700	30.5
14	24-Jun-05	31.13	31.22	30.45	30.55	10039000	30.55
15	23-Jun-05	31.91	31.91	31.22	31.25	9680100	31.25
16	22-Jun-05	32.24	32.24	31.91	31.98	6514700	31.98
17	21-Jun-05	32.2	32.28	31.88	31.99	5628000	31.99
18	20-Jun-05	32	32.29	31.92	32.11	5925300	32.11
19	17-Jun-05	32.5	32.5	31.87	32.22	11040800	32.22

Step 8: It is advisable to use the Excel command **File|Save As** to save the file as a standard Excel file:

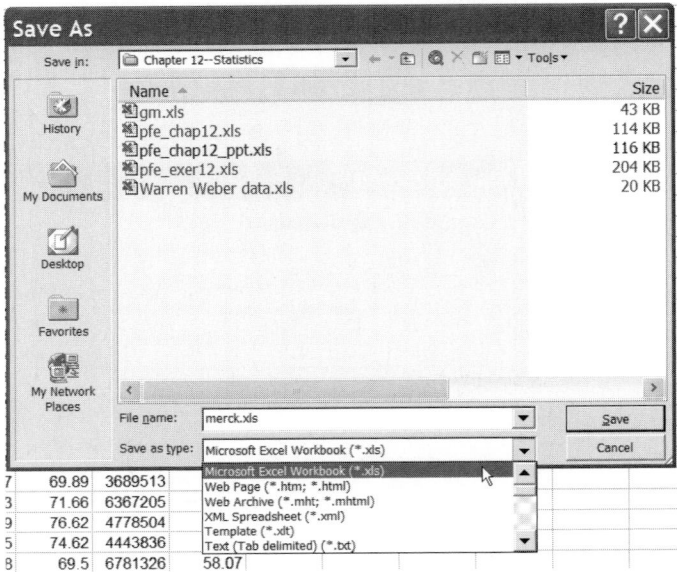

APPENDIX 12.2: WHY VARP INSTEAD OF VAR?

Throughout *Principles of Finance with Excel* we use the Excel functions **Varp** and **Stdevp** instead of their cousins **Var** and **Stdev**. This appendix briefly discusses this choice.

Recall that the definitions of these two functions relate to whether the data is taken from a *sample* or whether the data is the *whole population*. Suppose we have return data $\{r_1, r_2, \ldots, r_N\}$ for a stock. Then **Varp** is the population variance and **Var** is the sample variance:

$$\text{population variance} = Varp = \frac{1}{N} \sum_{t=1}^{N} (r_t - \bar{r})^2$$

$$\text{sample variance} = Var = \frac{1}{N-1} \sum_{t=1}^{N} (r_t - \bar{r})^2$$

There are two reasons why we choose **Varp** instead of **Var**: The first reason is that in most introductory statistics courses students are taught **Varp** (that is, divide by N) instead of **Var** (divide by $N - 1$). Thus, the choice made in *Principles of Finance with Excel* corresponds with what students have previously been taught.

The second reason for choosing **Varp** is that this choice makes the Excel **Slope** function consistent with the definition of β that we teach,

$$\beta_i = \frac{Covariance(r_{it}, r_{Mt})}{Variance(r_{Mt})}$$

To see this, reconsider the following example from Section 12.5 in which we calculate the β_{Mirage} for Mirage Resorts from monthly data for Mirage and for the S&P 500 Index:

	A	B	C	D
1		WHY VARP INSTEAD OF VAR?		
2	Date	S&P 500 Index SPX	Mirage Resorts MIR	
3	Jan-97	6.13%	16.18%	
4	Feb-97	0.59%	0.00%	
5	Mar-97	-4.26%	-15.42%	The S&P index represents the market returns
6	Apr-97	5.84%	-5.29%	
7	May-97	5.86%	18.63%	
8	Jun-97	4.35%	5.76%	
9	Jul-97	7.81%	5.94%	
10	Aug-97	-5.75%	0.23%	
11	Sep-97	5.32%	12.35%	
12	Oct-97	-3.45%	-17.01%	
13	Nov-97	4.46%	-5.00%	
14	Dec-97	1.57%	-4.21%	
15	Jan-98	1.02%	1.37%	
16	Feb-98	7.04%	-0.54%	
17	Mar-98	4.99%	5.99%	
18	Apr-98	0.91%	-9.25%	
19	May-98	-1.88%	-5.67%	
20	Jun-98	3.94%	2.40%	
21	Jul-98	-1.16%	0.88%	
22	Aug-98	-14.58%	-30.81%	
23	Sep-98	6.24%	12.61%	
24	Oct-98	8.03%	1.12%	
25	Nov-98	5.91%	-12.18%	
26	Dec-98	5.64%	0.42%	
27				
28	Mirage β using **VarP**	1.4693	<-- =SLOPE(C3:C26,B3:B26)	
29		1.4693	<-- =COVAR(C3:C26,B3:B26)/VARP(B3:B26)	
30				
31	Mirage β using **Var**	1.4693	<-- =SLOPE(C3:C26,B3:B26)	
32		1.4080	<-- =COVAR(C3:C26,B3:B26)/VAR(B3:B26)	
33				
34	Market β using **Var**	1.0000	<-- =SLOPE(C3:C26,C3:C26)	
35		1.0000	<-- =COVAR(B3:B26,B3:B26)/VARP(B3:B26)	
36		0.9583	<-- =COVAR(B3:B26,B3:B26)/VAR(B3:B26)	
37				
38			The beta of the market should = 1. But using Covar(r_M,r_{Mirage})/Var(r_M) produces a beta < 1.	
39				
40				
41				

In cells B28 and B29 we compute the β_{Mirage} using the Excel function **Slope(C3:C26, B3:B26)** and the Excel functions **Covar(C3:C26,B3:B26)/VarP(B3:B26)**. These two definitions give the same (and the correct) answer. In cells B31 and B32 we compare the Excel **Slope** function to the answer given by **Covar(C3:C26,B3:B26)/Var(B3:B26)**. Note that the answers are different (the second answer is *incorrect*).

To drive home this point, we compute β_M in cells B34 to B36. The **Slope** function gives the correct answer, as does the definition **Covar(B3:B26,B3:B26)/VarP(B3:B26)**. However, using the function **Var** in cell B36 gives the *wrong* answer.

Conclusion: Best use **VarP** instead of **Var**![13]

---

[13]There's a slightly more cynical answer to the difference between **Var** and **Varp**. "If the difference between N and $N - 1$ ever matters to you, then you are probably up to no good anyway—e.g., trying to substantiate a questionable hypothesis with marginal data." This wonderful quote is from the book *Numerical Recipes* by William H. Press, Brian P. Flannery, Saul A. Teukolsky, and William T. Vettering (Cambridge University Press, 1986, page 456).

CHAPTER 13

PORTFOLIO RETURNS AND THE EFFICIENT FRONTIER

OVERVIEW

How should you invest your money? What's the best investment portfolio? How do you maximize your return without losing money? People often ask these knotty questions, and you may even be reading this book in order to answer them. In this and the next chapter we explore some of the answers to these questions. You will see that—although no one can tell you exactly how

Figure 13.1 Vanguard Funds is a major manager of stock and bond funds. Here's how the Vanguard website defines *diversification*.
Source: http://flagship.vanguard.com/web/siteservices/SiteSvcsGlossDiversification.html
http://flagship2.vanguard.com/web/planret/AdvicePTIBOverview.html

to invest—we can shed considerable light on some important general investment principles. We can also show you some rules of thumb about how *not to invest*.

Let's go back to the questions with which we started the previous paragraph.

- How should you invest your money? Finance can't tell you *in what* to invest, but it can give you some guidelines. The most important of these is: You should *diversify* your investment—spread it out among many assets in order to lower the risk. Using simple examples with only two stocks, this chapter shows you how diversification can lower investment risk (Figure 13.1).

- What's the best investment portfolio? It won't surprise you that the finance answer to this question tells you that there is no single best investment portfolio. It all depends on your willingness to trade off *return* for *additional risk*.[1] What may surprise you, however, is that we can say a lot about how not to invest. In this chapter we develop the notion of the *efficient frontier*—this is the set of all portfolios that you would consider as investment portfolios. Inherent in the concept of the efficient frontier is that there are many portfolios that are not good investments, and that these portfolios can be described statistically.

- How do you maximize your return without losing money? To some extent the efficient frontier answers this question: It shows us which portfolios are so bad that you can improve both the return and the risk. Once we've gotten on the efficient frontier, however, the risk–return trade-off begins to operate, and higher returns mean larger risks.[2]

In most of this chapter we examine the risk and return of portfolios composed of two financial assets. By choosing a combination of the two assets, you can achieve significant reductions in risk.[3] Much of the chapter relies on the statistics for portfolios discussed in the previous

---

[1] As you learned in Chapter 11, nearly all the interesting finance questions involve the word "risk." Portfolio choice is no different!

[2] As the author's father used to say: "It is better to be rich and healthy than poor and sick." The investment interpretation of this is that we would all like to *have more return* and *risk less*. The efficient frontier represents the set of difficult investment choices: Once you're on the efficient frontier, it is impossible to get more return without taking on more risk.

[3] Of course, in the real world there are many investment assets. We use the two-asset case to develop the requisite intuitions and ask you to take it on faith that the multiasset case is similar.

chapter. Even our main example, which considers portfolios of General Motors (GM) and Microsoft (MSFT) stock, is one we started in Chapter 12.

The close links in the materials of this chapter and the materials in Chapter 12 should not blind you to their differences. Whereas Chapter 12 develops the statistical concepts necessary for portfolio choice, this chapter looks at portfolio choice as an economic choice. In this chapter we develop concepts that help us think more precisely about acceptable and unacceptable portfolios. In the next chapter we carry this line of thought further.

Finance Concepts Discussed

- Mean and standard deviation of portfolio of two assets
- Portfolio risk and return
- Minimum variance portfolio
- The efficient frontier
- Mean–variance calculations for three-asset portfolios

Excel Concepts and Functions Used

- **Average, Varp, Stdevp**
- **Regression**
- Sophisticated graphing
- **Solver**

13.1 The Advantage of Diversification: A Simple Example

In this section we give an example that illustrates the benefits of diversification. In finance jargon, diversification means investing in several different assets as opposed to putting all of your money in one single asset. In our examples you will see when diversification pays off (and when it doesn't). The examples are much simpler than the real world examples that follow in the next sections, but they embody many of the intuitions of why investors invest in portfolios. In particular, you will see how the correlation between asset returns is important in determining the amount of risk reduction you can get through portfolio formation.

In each of the following examples you can invest in two assets. The return on each asset is uncertain and is determined by the flip of a coin: If the coin comes up heads, the asset returns 20% and if the coin comes up tails, the asset returns −8%. In dollar terms: If you invest $100 in one of the two assets, you'll get back $120 if the coin comes up heads and $92 if it comes up tails.

In terms of the sequence of coin flips, here's what the asset returns look like:

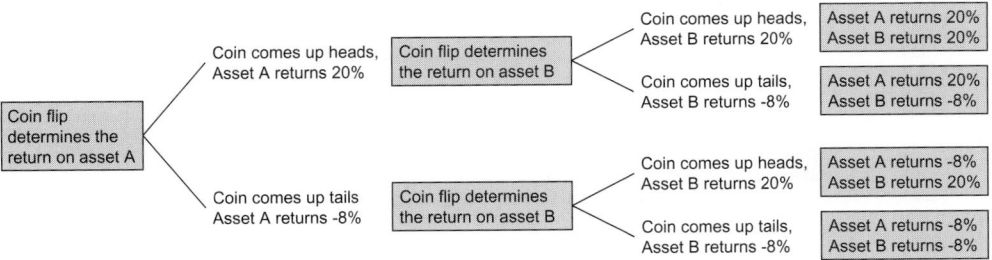

Case 1: Investing in a Single Risky Asset

Suppose you decide to invest your $100 wholly in asset A. If the coin comes up heads, you'll earn 20% on your investment, and if it comes up tails you will lose 8%. Your $100 investment in asset A will have the following cash flow and return pattern:

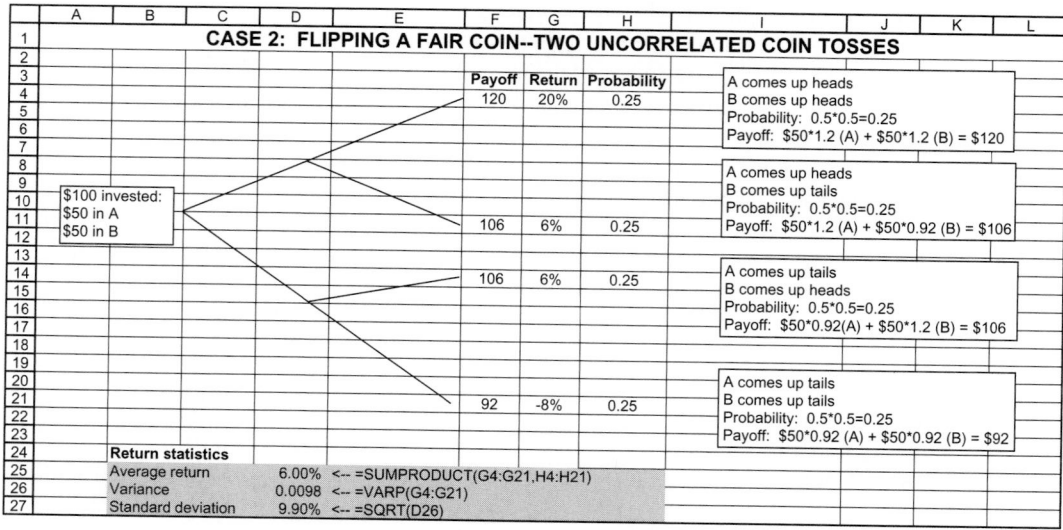

	A	B	C	D	E	F	G	H	I	J
1	CASE 1: MEAN AND STANDARD DEVIATION OF RETURN FROM A SINGLE COIN FLIP									
2	Coin flip:									
3	heads		**Cash flow**		**Return**			**Return statistics**		
4			120		20%	<-- =C4/A6-1		Average return	6.00% <-- =AVERAGE(E4,E8)	
5								Variance	0.0196 <-- =VARP(E4,E8)	
6	100							Standard deviation	14.00% <-- =SQRT(I5)	
7										
8			92		-8%	<-- =C8/A6-1				
9	Coin flip:									
10	tails									
11										

Notice the return statistics in column I: Asset A has an average return of 6% and a return standard deviation of 14%.[4]

Case 2: The Case of the "Fair" Coin: Splitting Your Investment Between the Assets

In Case 1 you invested in only one asset. In Cases 2–5 you will invest in both assets A and B.

In Case 2 we suppose that the coin determining the returns on asset A and the coin determining the returns on asset B are *uncorrelated*. In simple terms you can think of a single coin that is flipped twice—once to determine the return of A and the second time to determine the return of B. If the coin flip is "fair," then the results of the first coin flip have no influence on the results of the second coin flip.

Now here's the question we want to answer: Should you invest all your money in A, all in B, or should you split your investment between the two? The answer has to do with the effects of diversification. To examine this question more closely, let's assume that you have decided to invest $50 in each asset. Your final outcomes are given below:

	A	B	C	D	E	F	G	H	I	J	K	L
1	CASE 2: FLIPPING A FAIR COIN--TWO UNCORRELATED COIN TOSSES										
2												
3						**Payoff**	**Return**	**Probability**				
4						120	20%	0.25	A comes up heads			
5									B comes up heads			
6									Probability: 0.5*0.5=0.25			
7									Payoff: $50*1.2 (A) + $50*1.2 (B) = $120			
8												
9									A comes up heads			
10	$100 invested:								B comes up tails			
11	$50 in A								Probability: 0.5*0.5=0.25			
12	$50 in B					106	6%	0.25	Payoff: $50*1.2 (A) + $50*0.92 (B) = $106			
13												
14						106	6%	0.25	A comes up tails			
15									B comes up heads			
16									Probability: 0.5*0.5=0.25			
17									Payoff: $50*0.92(A) + $50*1.2 (B) = $106			
18												
19												
20									A comes up tails			
21						92	-8%	0.25	B comes up tails			
22									Probability: 0.5*0.5=0.25			
23									Payoff: $50*0.92 (A) + $50*0.92 (B) = $92			
24		**Return statistics**										
25		Average return		6.00%	<-- =SUMPRODUCT(G4:G21,H4:H21)							
26		Variance		0.0098	<-- =VARP(G4:G21)							
27		Standard deviation		9.90%	<-- =SQRT(D26)							

---

[4]You'll notice that we used the Excel function **Varp** to compute the portfolio variance and *not* the function **Var.** The reasons for this choice—which we make throughout the book—were given in Chapter 12, page 340. Similarly, we would use **Stdevp** to compute the standard deviation and not **Stdev.** We can also calculate the standard deviation by taking the square root of the variance, which is what we've done in the current example.

As you can see, the average return from the investment in two assets (6%) is the same as the average return in Case 1, where we invested in only one asset. Note, however, that the standard deviation went down from 14% to 9.9%—you earn the same but incur less risk.

Message: Diversification in uncorrelated assets improves your investment returns.

This message—that diversification pays off because it reduces risk—can be explored further. In the next example we explore the returns when you have *correlated* assets.

Case 3: The Case of the Counterfeit Coin: A Correlation of +1

Now suppose you have the same situation as above; only this time your coin is counterfeit. You do not know if you will get heads or tails but you do know that whatever the result of the "A" coin, the result of the "B" coin will be the same. In statistical terms this is a correlation of +1. Will diversification improve your returns in this situation?

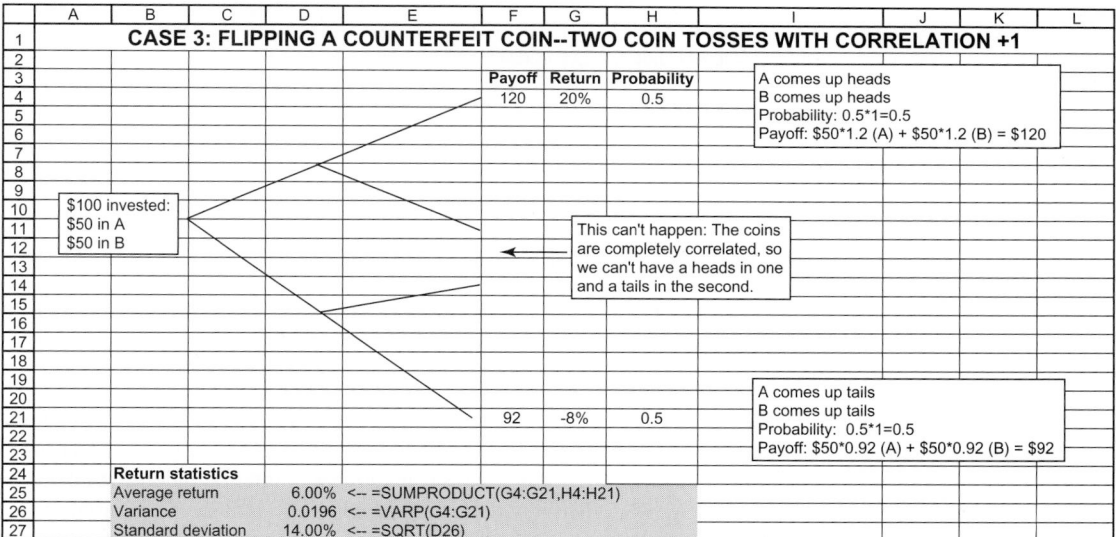

As you can see, the returns from splitting your investment between two assets are identical to the return of only investing in one asset (cells D25 to D27). Both the average return and the return standard deviation are the same as in Case 1, where we flipped only one coin.

Message: When the asset returns are perfectly positively correlated, diversification will not reduce your risk.

Case 4: The Case of the Counterfeit Coin: A Correlation of −1

We're still on the same example, and our coin is still counterfeit. But this time it's counterfeit with a perfectly negative correlation (−1): If coin "A" comes up heads, coin "B" will come up tails. In statistical terms, the correlation between the two coins is −1. For this case we can find a portfolio that completely eliminates all risk: By splitting our investment between assets

A and B, we get 6% expected return without any standard deviation:

	A	B	C	D	E	F	G	H	I	J	K	L
1				CASE 4: FLIPPING A COUNTERFEIT COIN--TWO COIN TOSSES WITH CORRELATION -1								
2												
3						Payoff	Return	Probability	This can't happen: The coins			
4									are completely correlated, so			
5									we can't have a heads in one			
6									and a heads in the second.			
7												
8									A comes up heads			
9									B comes up tails			
10		$100 invested:							Probability: 0.5*1=0.5			
11		$50 in A				106	6%	0.5	Payoff: $50*1.2 (A) + $50*0.92 (B) = $106			
12		$50 in B										
13									A comes up tails			
14						106	6%	0.5	B comes up heads			
15									Probability: 0.5*1=0.5			
16									Payoff: $50*0.92 (A) + $50*1.2 (B) = $106			
17												
18												
19									This can't happen: The coins			
20									are completely correlated, so			
21									we can't have a tails in one and			
22									a tails in the second.			
23												
24		Return statistics										
25		Average		6.00%	<-- =SUMPRODUCT(G5:G20,H5:H20)							
26		Variance		0	<-- =VARP(G5:G20)							
27		Standard deviation		0.00%	<-- =SQRT(D26)							

Message: When the asset returns are perfectly negatively correlated, diversification can completely eliminate all risk.

Case 5: The Partially Counterfeit Coin (the Real World?)

In the real world there's often a connection between the stock prices of one company and those of another. In the most general handwaving[5] way, stock prices reflect two elements:

- How well a particular business is doing: In some industries this element leads to *negative correlation*. For example, if Procter & Gamble (a major manufacturer of toothpastes, laundry soaps, and so on) is gaining market share, it is likely to be at the expense of Unilever (another company in the same industry). This isn't always true though: If Intel (a major manufacturer of computer chips) is doing well, then it may be that the computer industry is expanding and that AMD (another player in the same industry) is also doing well.

- How well the economy is doing: Stock prices are heavily affected by the performance of the economy. This factor tends to be an across-the-board factor, leading to *positive correlation*: When the stock market as a whole is up, most stock prices tend to be up, and vice versa. For stock prices, this factor tends to dominate the first: In general, stock prices move together, though their correlation is far from complete.

Notice how careful we've been here in our language: We've used words like "tend to go up"—stock prices are only partially, not perfectly, correlated.[6]

---

[5] The website http://c2.com defines "handwaving" as "what people do when they don't want to tell you the details, either because they don't want to get bogged down, they don't know, nobody knows, or they have sinister ulterior motives."

[6] Negative correlation in stock returns can also happen: Our General Motors–Microsoft example in Chapter 12—to which we return in Section 13.2—is an illustration.

In order to model partial correlation with our coin toss example, we'll assume that the "A" coin result influences the result of the "B" coin, but not completely. If the "A" coin comes up heads (this happens with a probability of 0.5), the probability of the "B" coin coming up heads is 0.7. If the "A" coin comes up tails (probability 0.5), the probability that the "B" coin also comes up tails is 0.7. Here's the spreadsheet that summarizes the returns:

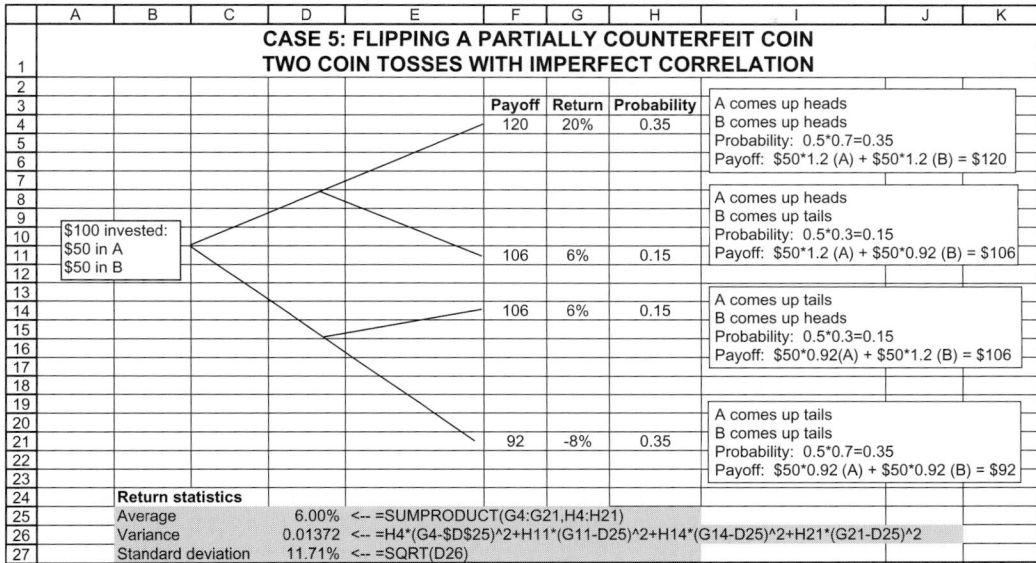

Message: When the asset returns are partially correlated, diversification will reduce risk but not completely eliminate it.

What's the Point?

Though the two-asset, two-coin examples are simple and farfetched, the lessons you learn from these examples also apply in the "real world" cases of asset diversification:

- If the correlation between asset returns is +1, then diversification will not reduce portfolio risk.

- If the correlation between asset returns is −1, then we can create a risk-free asset—an asset with no uncertainty about its returns (a bank savings account is an example)—using a portfolio of the two assets.

- In the real world asset returns are almost never fully correlated. When asset returns are partially, but not completely, correlated (meaning that the correlation is between −1 and +1), diversification can lower risk, though it cannot completely eliminate it.

13.2 Back to the Real World: Microsoft and General Motors

In Chapter 12 we calculated the data for the annual returns on General Motors (GM) stock and on Microsoft (MSFT) stock for the ten years between 1990 and 1999. Here are our calculations:

	A	B	C	D
1	GM AND MSFT RETURN STATISTICS, 1990-1999			
2	Date	GM return	MSFT return	
3	31-Dec-90	-11.54%	72.99%	
4	31-Dec-91	-11.35%	121.76%	
5	31-Dec-92	16.54%	15.11%	
6	31-Dec-93	72.64%	-5.56%	
7	30-Dec-94	-21.78%	51.63%	
8	29-Dec-95	28.13%	43.56%	
9	31-Dec-96	8.46%	88.32%	
10	31-Dec-97	19.00%	56.43%	
11	31-Dec-98	21.09%	114.60%	
12	31-Dec-99	21.34%	68.36%	
13				
14	Average, $E(r_{GM})$ and $E(r_{MSFT})$	14.25%	62.72%	<-- =AVERAGE(C3:C12)
15	Variance, $Var(r_{GM})$ and $Var(r_{MSFT})$	0.0638	0.1443	<-- =VARP(C3:C12)
16	Standard deviation, σ_{GM} and σ_{MSFT}	25.25%	37.99%	<-- =STDEVP(C3:C12)
17	Covariance of returns, $Cov(r_{GM}, r_{MSFT})$	-0.0552	<-- =COVAR(B3:B12,C3:C12)	
18	Correlation of returns, $\rho_{GM,MSFT}$	-0.5755	<-- =B17/(B16*C16)	

You can see that the average return of holding GM stock (14.25% per year) is much lower than the average return of holding MSFT stock (62.73%). On the other hand, the risk of holding Microsoft—measured by either the variance or the standard deviation of the return—is higher than the risk of General Motors: This is the trade-off we would expect—GM has lower return and lower risk than MSFT. Note also that GM and MSFT returns are *negatively correlated* (cell B18): On average, an increase in MSFT returns was accompanied by a decrease in GM returns. If you use Excel to plot GM returns on the *x*-axis and MSFT returns on the *y*-axis, you can detect a slight "northwest to southeast" pattern in the returns.

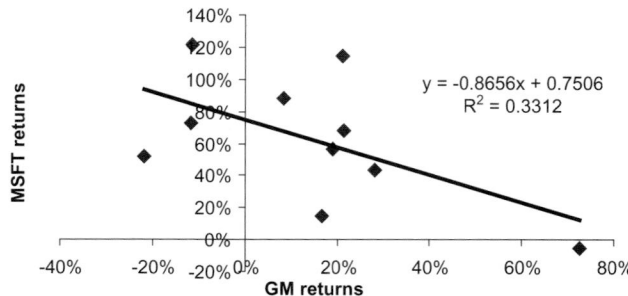

MSFT Versus GM Returns

$y = -0.8656x + 0.7506$
$R^2 = 0.3312$

The trendline (which illustrates the regression of MSFT on GM) shows this trend.[7]

---

[7]As explained in Chapter 12, the regression R^2 indicates the percentage MSFT's return variability explained by the variability in GM's returns. R^2 is the correlation coefficient squared: $R^2 = 0.3312 = [Correlation (Return_{GM}, Return_{MSFT})]^2 = (-0.5755)^2$. While this R^2 may seem low, it is typical for the relation between two stocks.

13.3 Graphing Portfolio Returns

In this section we graph the returns available to the investor from an investment in a portfolio composed of GM and MSFT stock. We start by showing you several individual portfolios and end the section by graphing the curve representing all the possible portfolio returns.

Deriving the Risk–Return of an Individual Portfolio

Suppose we form a portfolio composed of 50% GM and 50% MSFT stock. Cells E8 to E17 in the spreadsheet below show the annual returns of this portfolio:

	A	B	C	D	E	F
1	A PORTFOLIO OF GM AND MSFT STOCK					
2	Portfolio proportions					
3	Percentage in GM	50%				
4	Percentage in MSFT	50%	<-- =1-B3			
5						
6	Date	Stock returns			Portfolio returns	
7		GM	MSFT			
8	Dec-90	-11.54%	72.99%		30.73%	<-- =$B$3*B8+$B$4*C8
9	Dec-91	-11.35%	121.76%		55.21%	
10	Dec-92	16.54%	15.11%		15.82%	
11	Dec-93	72.64%	-5.56%		33.54%	
12	Dec-94	-21.78%	51.63%		14.93%	
13	Dec-95	28.13%	43.56%		35.84%	
14	Dec-96	8.46%	88.32%		48.39%	
15	Dec-97	19.00%	56.43%		37.71%	
16	Dec-98	21.09%	114.60%		67.85%	
17	Dec-99	21.34%	68.36%		44.85%	
18						
19	Average, E(r$_{GM}$) and E(r$_{MSFT}$)	14.25%	62.72%		38.49%	<-- =AVERAGE(E8:E17)
20	Variance, Var(r$_{GM}$) and Var(r$_{MSFT}$)	6.38%	14.43%		2.44%	<-- =VARP(E8:E17)
21	Standard deviation, σ$_{GM}$ and σ$_{MSFT}$	25.25%	37.99%		15.62%	<-- =STDEVP(E8:E17)
22	Covariance of returns, Cov(r$_{GM}$,r$_{MSFT}$)	-5.52%	<-- =COVAR(B8:B17,C8:C17)			

As discussed in Chapter 12, the portfolio return statistics in cells E19 to E21 can be derived using formulas that involve only information about the individual asset returns, their variances, and the covariance. There's no need to do the extensive calculation in cells E19 to E21:

- The average portfolio return of 38.49% is the *weighted* average of the GM and the MSFT return. Write the percentage weight of GM stock as w_{GM} and the percentage weight of MSFT stock as w_{MSFT}; it follows, of course, that $w_{MSFT} = 1 - w_{GM}$, since the portfolio proportions must sum to 100%. The formula for the average portfolio return is

$$average\ portfolio\ return,\ E(r_p) = w_{GM}E(r_{GM}) + w_{MSFT}E(r_{MSFT})$$
$$= w_{GM}E(r_{GM}) + (1 - w_{GM})E(r_{MSFT})$$

- The variance of the portfolio return, 2.44%, is a more complicated function of the two variances and the portfolio weights:

$$\text{variance of portfolio return,} \quad Var(r_p)$$
$$= w_{GM}^2 Var(r_{GM}) + w_{MSFT}^2 Var(r_{MSFT}) + \underbrace{2w_{GM}w_{MSFT}Cov(r_{GM}, r_{MSFT})}$$

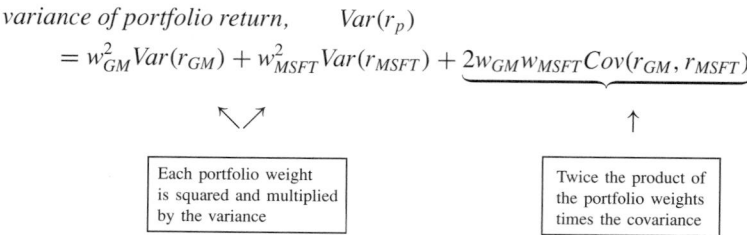

| Each portfolio weight is squared and multiplied by the variance | Twice the product of the portfolio weights times the covariance |

By using these two formulas, you avoid the need for the long calculation of the portfolio return, variance, and standard deviation in cells E8 to E21. In the spreadsheet below we incorporate these formulas for the portfolio mean, variance, and standard deviation in cells B12 to B14:

	A	B	C	D
1	**PORTFOLIO STATISTICS FOR A GM-MSFT PORTFOLIO**			
2		**GM**	**MSFT**	
3	Average, $E(r_{GM})$ and $E(r_{MSFT})$	14.25%	62.72%	
4	Variance, $Var(r_{GM})$ and $Var(r_{MSFT})$	6.38%	14.43%	
5	Sigma, σ_{GM} and σ_{MSFT}	25.25%	37.99%	
6	Covariance of returns, $Cov(r_{GM}, r_{MSFT})$	-5.52%	<-- =COVAR(B9:B18,C9:C18)	
7				
8	**Portfolio return and risk**			
9	Percentage in GM	50%		
10	Percentage in MSFT	50%		
11				
12	Expected portfolio return, $E(r_p)$	38.49%	<-- =B9*B3+B10*C3	
13	Portfolio variance, $Var(r_p)$	2.44%	<-- =B9^2*B4+B10^2*C4+2*B9*B10*B6	
14	Portfolio standard deviation, σ_p	15.62%	<-- =SQRT(B13)	
15				
16				

Portfolio Returns: Expected Return $E(r_p)$ and Standard Deviation σ_p

Portfolio standard deviation (15.62%) and expected return (38.49%) from a portfolio invested 50% in GM and 50% in MSFT.

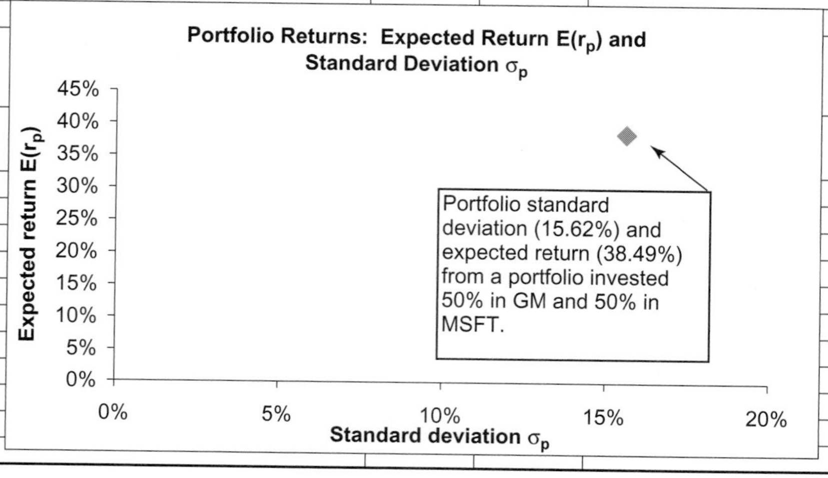

The point here is that you don't need to do an extensive calculation of annual portfolio returns—it's enough to know the return statistics for each stock, the portfolio proportions, and the covariance of the stock returns.

Another Portfolio—Increasing the Weight of MSFT, Decreasing GM

Now suppose we graph another portfolio—this time a portfolio invested 25% in GM and 75% in Microsoft:

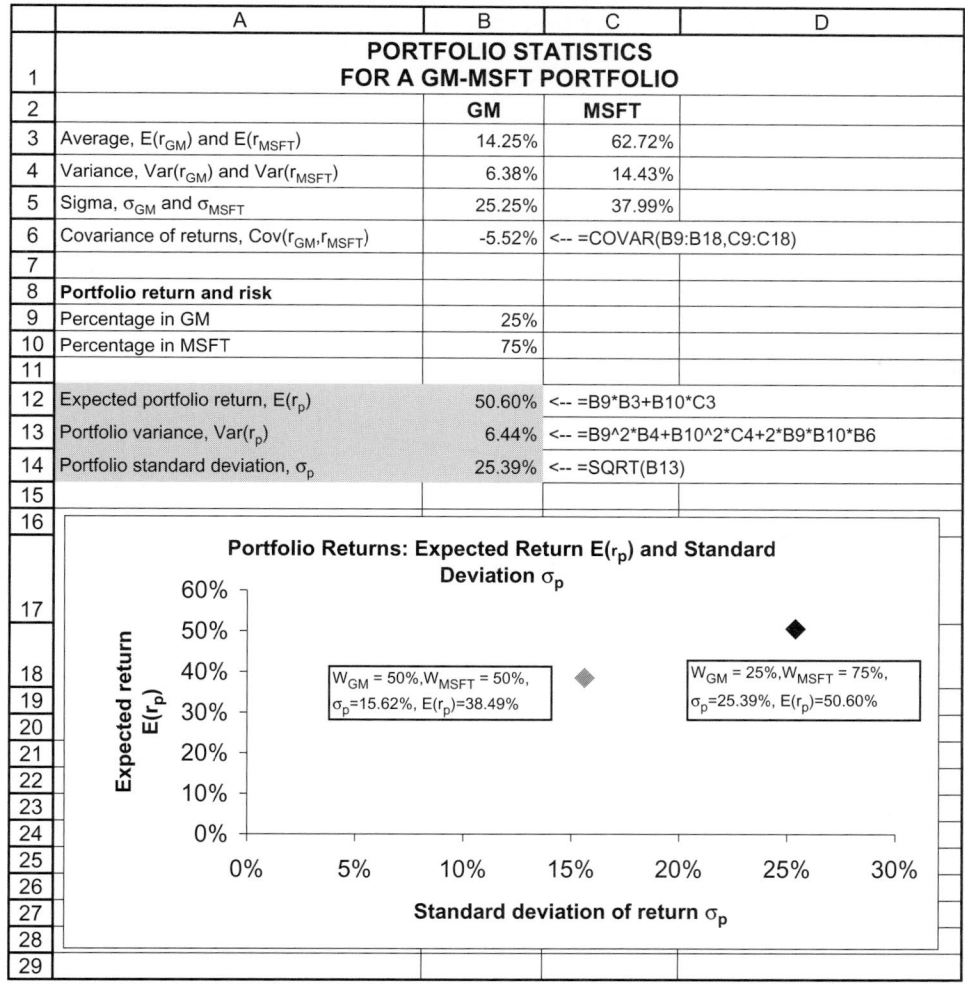

	A	B	C	D
1	PORTFOLIO STATISTICS FOR A GM-MSFT PORTFOLIO			
2		GM	MSFT	
3	Average, $E(r_{GM})$ and $E(r_{MSFT})$	14.25%	62.72%	
4	Variance, $Var(r_{GM})$ and $Var(r_{MSFT})$	6.38%	14.43%	
5	Sigma, σ_{GM} and σ_{MSFT}	25.25%	37.99%	
6	Covariance of returns, $Cov(r_{GM},r_{MSFT})$	-5.52%	<-- =COVAR(B9:B18,C9:C18)	
7				
8	**Portfolio return and risk**			
9	Percentage in GM	25%		
10	Percentage in MSFT	75%		
11				
12	Expected portfolio return, $E(r_p)$	50.60%	<-- =B9*B3+B10*C3	
13	Portfolio variance, $Var(r_p)$	6.44%	<-- =B9^2*B4+B10^2*C4+2*B9*B10*B6	
14	Portfolio standard deviation, σ_p	25.39%	<-- =SQRT(B13)	
15				
16				

Notice that the new portfolio's performance is to the "northeast" of the first portfolio—it has both higher returns and higher standard deviation. The new portfolio gives you greater expected return but has higher risk. This is what you would expect—higher return is achieved at the price of higher risk. As you will see in the next subsection, this may not always be the case.

Varying the Portfolio Composition—Graphing All Possible Portfolios

Suppose we vary the composition of the portfolio, letting the percentage of GM vary from 0% to 100%. In cells G19:H29 below we generate a table of portfolio returns $E(r_p)$ and standard deviations σ_p.

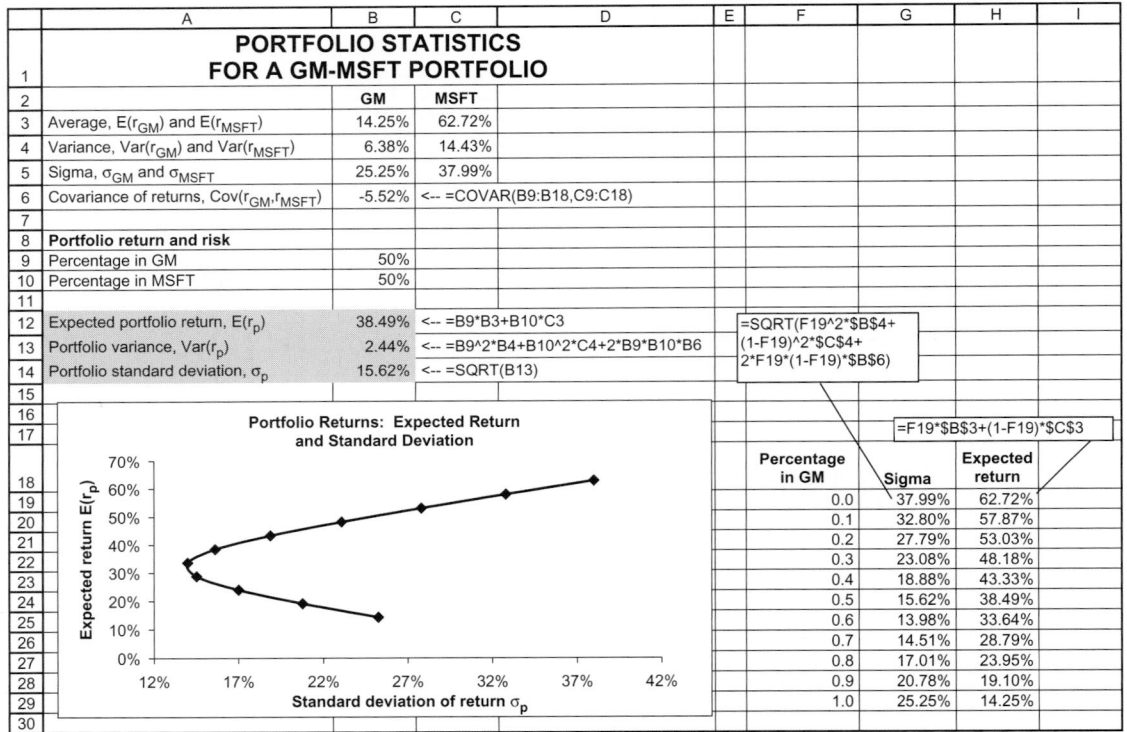

	A	B	C	D	E	F	G	H	I
1	**PORTFOLIO STATISTICS** **FOR A GM-MSFT PORTFOLIO**								
2		GM	MSFT						
3	Average, $E(r_{GM})$ and $E(r_{MSFT})$	14.25%	62.72%						
4	Variance, $Var(r_{GM})$ and $Var(r_{MSFT})$	6.38%	14.43%						
5	Sigma, σ_{GM} and σ_{MSFT}	25.25%	37.99%						
6	Covariance of returns, $Cov(r_{GM}, r_{MSFT})$	-5.52%	<-- =COVAR(B9:B18,C9:C18)						
7									
8	**Portfolio return and risk**								
9	Percentage in GM	50%							
10	Percentage in MSFT	50%							
11									
12	Expected portfolio return, $E(r_p)$	38.49%	<-- =B9*B3+B10*C3			=SQRT(F19^2*$B$4+			
13	Portfolio variance, $Var(r_p)$	2.44%	<-- =B9^2*B4+B10^2*C4+2*B9*B10*B6			(1-F19)^2*$C$4+			
14	Portfolio standard deviation, σ_p	15.62%	<-- =SQRT(B13)			2*F19*(1-F19)*$B$6)			
15									
16									
17								=F19*$B$3+(1-F19)*$C$3	
18							**Percentage in GM**	**Expected return**	
19							0.0	Sigma 37.99%	62.72%
20							0.1	32.80%	57.87%
21							0.2	27.79%	53.03%
22							0.3	23.08%	48.18%
23							0.4	18.88%	43.33%
24							0.5	15.62%	38.49%
25							0.6	13.98%	33.64%
26							0.7	14.51%	28.79%
27							0.8	17.01%	23.95%
28							0.9	20.78%	19.10%
29							1.0	25.25%	14.25%
30									

Chart (cells A16:D29): **Portfolio Returns: Expected Return and Standard Deviation** — Expected return $E(r_p)$ (y-axis, 0% to 70%) plotted against Standard deviation of return σ_p (x-axis, 12% to 42%).

EXCEL NOTE

USING DATA TABLE TO SIMPLIFY THE CALCULATIONS

The table in cells G19:H29 above were generated using formulas for the standard deviation and expected return. Each cell contains a formula (note the use of absolute and relative cell references in these formulas). You can simplify the building of the table by using the **Data Table** technique discussed in Chapter 30. **Data Table** is not an easy technique to master, but it makes building tables much easier. Here's an example:

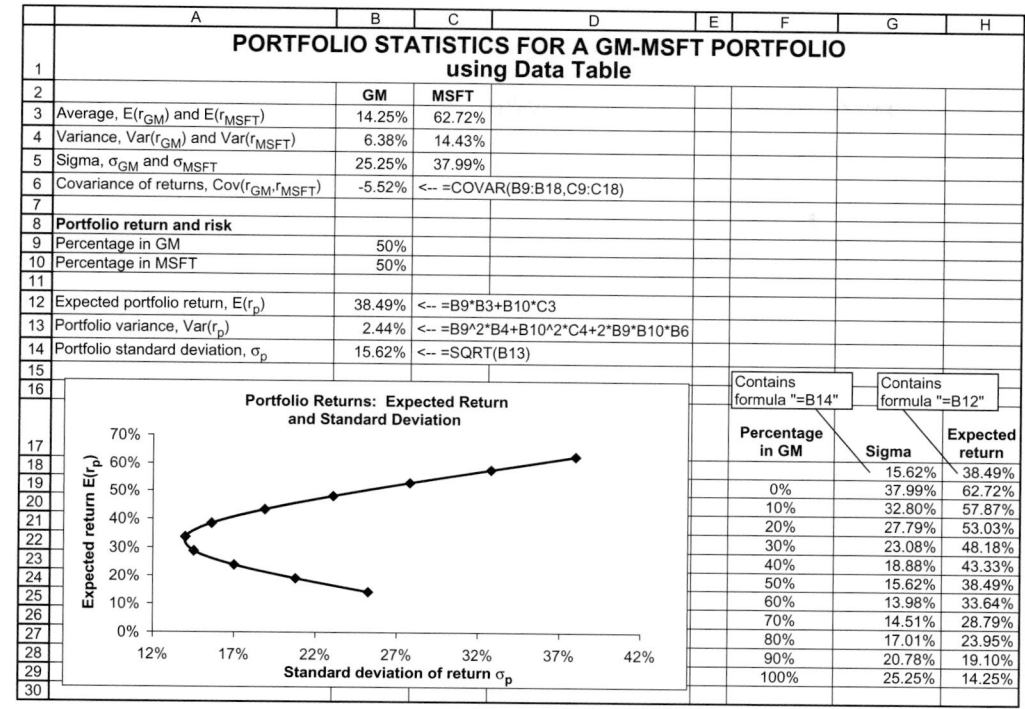

PORTFOLIO STATISTICS FOR A GM-MSFT PORTFOLIO using Data Table

	GM	MSFT	
Average, $E(r_{GM})$ and $E(r_{MSFT})$	14.25%	62.72%	
Variance, $Var(r_{GM})$ and $Var(r_{MSFT})$	6.38%	14.43%	
Sigma, σ_{GM} and σ_{MSFT}	25.25%	37.99%	
Covariance of returns, $Cov(r_{GM},r_{MSFT})$	-5.52%	<-- =COVAR(B9:B18,C9:C18)	
Portfolio return and risk			
Percentage in GM	50%		
Percentage in MSFT	50%		
Expected portfolio return, $E(r_p)$	38.49%	<-- =B9*B3+B10*C3	
Portfolio variance, $Var(r_p)$	2.44%	<-- =B9^2*B4+B10^2*C4+2*B9*B10*B6	
Portfolio standard deviation, σ_p	15.62%	<-- =SQRT(B13)	

Contains formula "=B14"   Contains formula "=B12"

Percentage in GM	Sigma	Expected return
	15.62%	38.49%
0%	37.99%	62.72%
10%	32.80%	57.87%
20%	27.79%	53.03%
30%	23.08%	48.18%
40%	18.88%	43.33%
50%	15.62%	38.49%
60%	13.98%	33.64%
70%	14.51%	28.79%
80%	17.01%	23.95%
90%	20.78%	19.10%
100%	25.25%	14.25%

You create the data table by marking the cells F18:H29. The command **Data|Table** brings up the dialog box to which you add the appropriate cell reference:

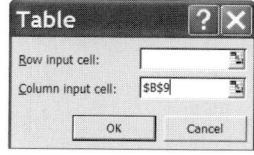

Better Portfolios . . . Worse Portfolios . . .

Take a careful look at the graph in the above spreadsheet—it shows the standard deviation σ_P of the portfolio returns on the x-axis and the corresponding expected portfolio return $E(r_p)$ on the y-axis. Looking at the graph, it is easy to see that some portfolios are better than others. Consider, for example, the portfolio invested 90% in GM and 10% in MSFT (this portfolio is circled in the graph below). By investing in the portfolio indicated by the arrow, you can improve the expected return without increasing the riskiness of the return. Thus, the circled portfolio is not optimal. In fact, none of the portfolios on the bottom part of the graph are optimal: Each is dominated by a portfolio on the top part of the graph, which has the same standard deviation σ_P and higher expected return $E(r_p)$.

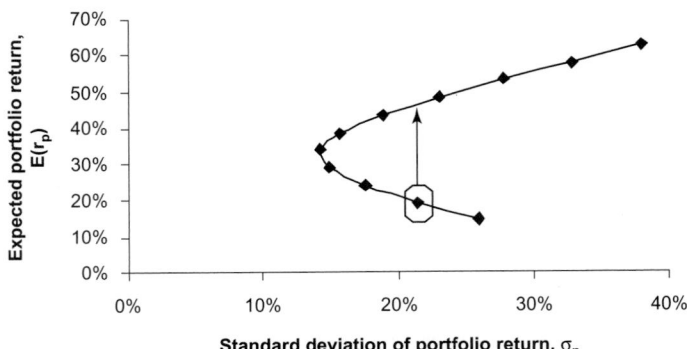

On the other hand, consider the two portfolios circled below:

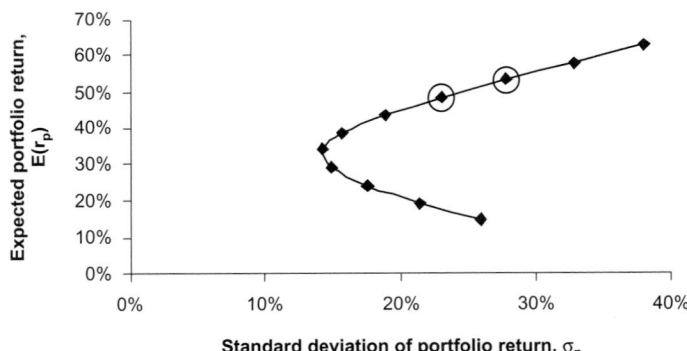

There is a clear risk–return trade-off between these two portfolios—it is impossible to say that one is unequivocally better than the other. The portfolio with the higher return also has the higher standard deviation of returns. All of the portfolios on the top part of the graph have this property. This top part of the graph is called the *efficient frontier*. The efficient frontier is the area of hard portfolio choices—along the efficient frontier, portfolios with greater expected return require you to undertake greater risk.

The efficient frontier slopes upward from left to right. What this means is that the choice between any two portfolios on the efficient frontier involves a trade-off between higher expected portfolio return, $E(r_p)$, and higher risk as indicated by a higher standard deviation of the return, σ_P. An investor choosing only risky portfolios would choose a portfolio on the efficient frontier.

In the next section we investigate some of the properties of the efficient frontier.

13.4 The Efficient Frontier and the Minimum Variance Portfolio

The *efficient frontier* is the set of all portfolios that are on the upward-sloping part of the graph above. "Upward-sloping" means that portfolios on the efficient frontier involve difficult choices—increasing expected portfolio return $E(r_p)$ has the cost of increasing portfolio standard deviation σ_P. If you are choosing investment portfolios that are a mix of GM and MSFT stock, then clearly the only portfolios you would be interested in are those on the efficient frontier. These portfolios are the only ones that have a "northeast" risk–return relation.

In order to calculate the efficient frontier, we have to find its starting point, the portfolio with the minimum standard deviation of returns. In the jargon of finance, this portfolio is (somewhat confusingly) called the *minimum variance portfolio;* just recall that if the portfolio has minimum variance it also has minimum standard deviation. The minimum variance portfolio is the portfolio on the left-hand corner of the efficient frontier; the graph below indicates its approximate location:

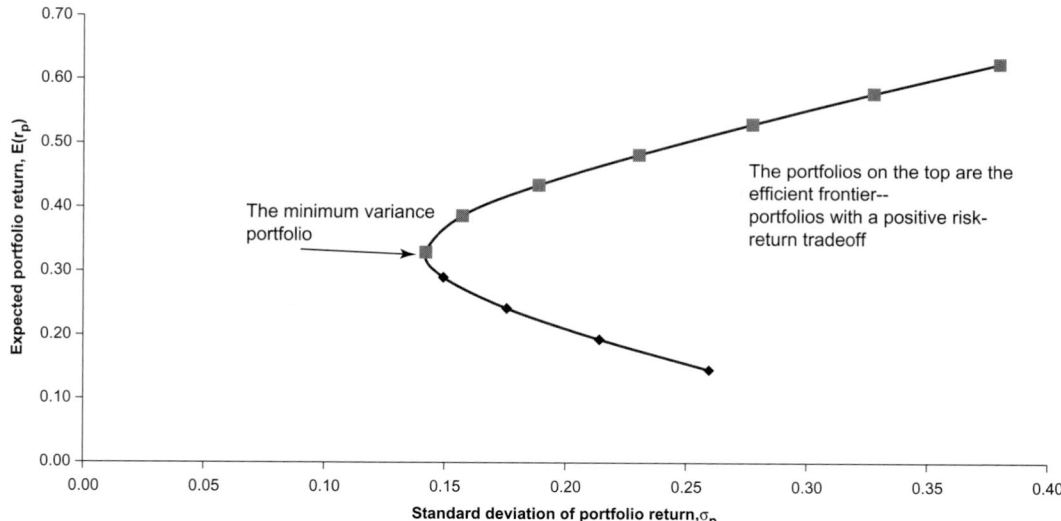

We can find the minimum variance portfolio in two ways—either by using the **Solver** or by using a bit of mathematics. We illustrate both methods.

The Minimum Variance Portfolio Using Excel's Solver

By using the **Solver** (see Chapter 32), we can calculate the percentage of GM in a portfolio which has minimum variance. The screen below shows the **Solver** dialog box. In this box, we've asked **Solver** to minimize the portfolio variance (cell B13) by changing the percentage of GM stock in the portfolio (cell B9):

	A	B	C	D	E	F
1	CALCULATING THE MINIMUM VARIANCE PORTFOLIO					
2			GM	MSFT		
3	Average, E(r_{GM}) and E(r_{MSFT})		14.25%	62.72%		
4	Variance, Var(r_{GM}) and Var(r_{MSFT})		6.38%	14.43%		
5	Sigma, σ_{GM} and σ_{MSFT}		25.25%	37.99%		
6	Covariance of returns, Cov(r_{GM},r_{MSFT})		-5.52%			
7						
8	**Portfolio return and risk**					
9	Percentage in GM	40.00%				
10	Percentage in MSFT	60.00%	<-- =1-B9			
11						
12	Expected portfolio return, E(r_p)	43.33%	<-- =B9*C3+B10*D3			
13	Portfolio variance, Var(r_p)	0.0356	<-- =B9^2*C4+B10^2*D4+2*B9*B10*C6			
14	Portfolio standard deviation, σ_p	18.88%	<-- =SQRT(B13)			
15						

Solver Parameters   ? X

Set Target Cell: $B$13

Equal To: ⚬ Max   ⦿ Min   ⚬ Value of: 0

By Changing Cells:

$B$9

Subject to the Constraints:

[Solve] [Close] [Guess] [Options] [Add] [Change] [Reset All] [Delete] [Help]

Clicking on **Solve** gives:

	A	B	C	D	E	F
1	CALCULATING THE MINIMUM VARIANCE PORTFOLIO					
2			GM	MSFT		
3	Average, E(r_{GM}) and E(r_{MSFT})		14.25%	62.72%		
4	Variance, Var(r_{GM}) and Var(r_{MSFT})		6.38%	14.43%		
5	Sigma, σ_{GM} and σ_{MSFT}		25.25%	37.99%		
6	Covariance of returns, Cov(r_{GM},r_{MSFT})		-5.52%			
7						
8	**Portfolio return and risk**					
9	Percentage in GM	62.64%				
10	Percentage in MSFT	37.36%	<-- =1-B9			
11						
12	Expected portfolio return, E(r_p)	32.36%	<-- =B9*C3+B10*D3			
13	Portfolio variance, Var(r_p)	0.0193	<-- =B9^2*C4+B10^2*D4+2*B9*B10*C6			
14	Portfolio standard deviation, σ_p	13.90%	<-- =SQRT(B13)			

Thus, the minimum variance portfolio has 62.64% in GM and 37.36% in MSFT.[8]

Minimum Variance Portfolios Using Calculus

There's actually a formula for the minimum variance portfolio:

$$w_{GM} = \frac{Var(r_{MSFT}) - Cov(r_{GM}, r_{MSFT})}{Var(r_{GM}) + Var(r_{MSFT}) - 2Cov(r_{GM}, r_{MSFT})}$$

---

[8] Although—as explained in Chapter 32—**Solver** and **Goal Seek** are in many cases interchangeable, this is a calculation that **Solver** does easily but that cannot be done in **Goal Seek.**

Using this formula, which is derived in Appendix 13.1 (p. 401), is simpler than using **Solver**. Implementing the formula in Excel gives the same answer as that given by **Solver**:

	A	B	C	D	E	F
1	CALCULATING THE MINIMUM VARIANCE PORTFOLIO WITH A FORMULA					
2			GM	MSFT		
3	Average, $E(r_{GM})$ and $E(r_{MSFT})$		14.25%	62.72%		
4	Variance, $Var(r_{GM})$ and $Var(r_{MSFT})$		6.38%	14.43%		
5	Sigma, σ_{GM} and σ_{MSFT}		25.25%	37.99%		
6	Covariance of returns, $Cov(r_{GM}, r_{MSFT})$		-5.52%			
7						
8	**Minimum variance portfolio--analytic formula**					
9	Percentage in GM	62.64%	<-- =(D4-C6)/(C4+D4-2*C6)			
10	Percentage in MSFT	37.36%	<-- =1-B9			
11						
12	Expected portfolio return, $E(r_p)$	32.36%	<-- =B9*C3+B10*D3			
13	Portfolio variance, $Var(r_p)$	0.0193	<-- =B9^2*C4+B10^2*D4+2*B9*B10*C6			
14	Portfolio standard deviation, σ_p	13.90%	<-- =SQRT(B13)			

The Efficient Frontier and the Minimum Variance Portfolio

Now that we know the minimum variance portfolio, we can plot the efficient frontier, the set of all portfolios with an economically meaningful risk–return trade-off. "Economically meaningful risk–return trade-off" means that along the efficient frontier additional portfolio return $E(r_p)$ is achieved at the cost of additional portfolio standard deviation σ_p. The efficient frontier is all portfolios that are to the right of the minimum variance portfolio.

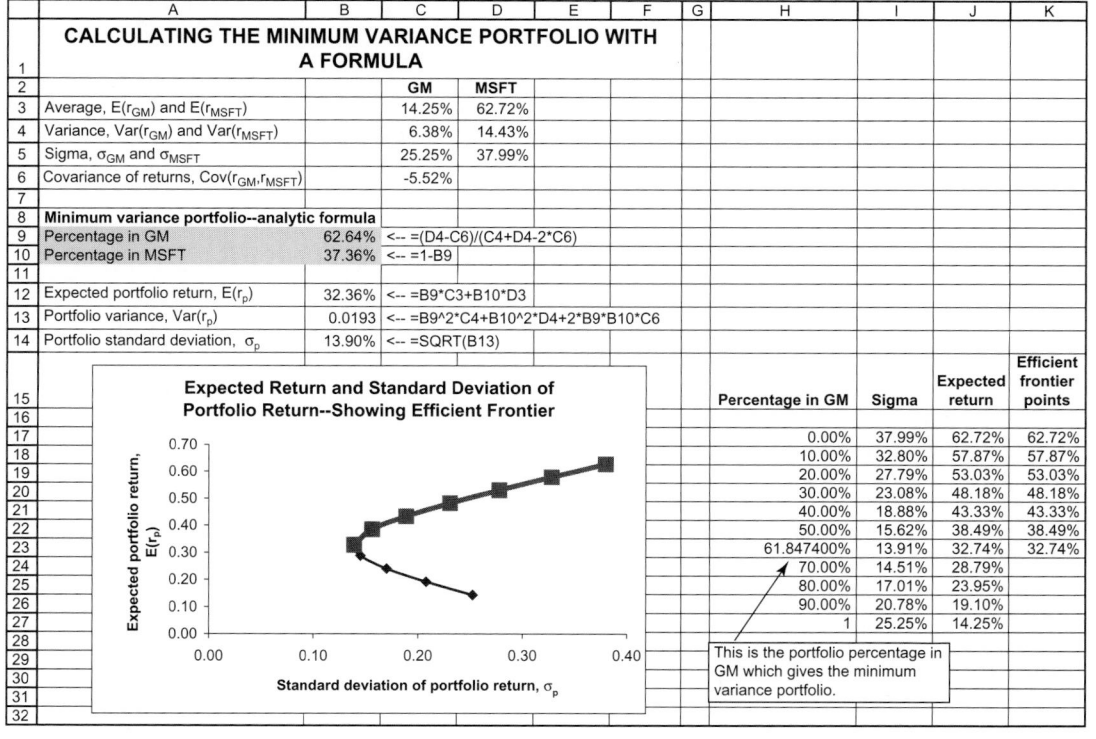

	A	B	C	D	E	F	G	H	I	J	K
1	CALCULATING THE MINIMUM VARIANCE PORTFOLIO WITH A FORMULA										
2			GM	MSFT							
3	Average, $E(r_{GM})$ and $E(r_{MSFT})$		14.25%	62.72%							
4	Variance, $Var(r_{GM})$ and $Var(r_{MSFT})$		6.38%	14.43%							
5	Sigma, σ_{GM} and σ_{MSFT}		25.25%	37.99%							
6	Covariance of returns, $Cov(r_{GM}, r_{MSFT})$		-5.52%								
7											
8	**Minimum variance portfolio--analytic formula**										
9	Percentage in GM	62.64%	<-- =(D4-C6)/(C4+D4-2*C6)								
10	Percentage in MSFT	37.36%	<-- =1-B9								
11											
12	Expected portfolio return, $E(r_p)$	32.36%	<-- =B9*C3+B10*D3								
13	Portfolio variance, $Var(r_p)$	0.0193	<-- =B9^2*C4+B10^2*D4+2*B9*B10*C6								
14	Portfolio standard deviation, σ_p	13.90%	<-- =SQRT(B13)								
15								Percentage in GM	Sigma	Expected return	Efficient frontier points
16											
17								0.00%	37.99%	62.72%	62.72%
18								10.00%	32.80%	57.87%	57.87%
19								20.00%	27.79%	53.03%	53.03%
20								30.00%	23.08%	48.18%	48.18%
21								40.00%	18.88%	43.33%	43.33%
22								50.00%	15.62%	38.49%	38.49%
23								61.847400%	13.91%	32.74%	32.74%
24								70.00%	14.51%	28.79%	
25								80.00%	17.01%	23.95%	
26								90.00%	20.78%	19.10%	
27								1	25.25%	14.25%	
28											
29								This is the portfolio percentage in GM which gives the minimum variance portfolio.			
30											
31											
32											

EXCEL NOTE

EXCEL TRICK

The graph of the efficient frontier shown above is an **XY Scatter plot.** The x-data is the data for sigma in cells I17 to I27. Cells J17 to J27 give the data for the portfolio expected returns, and cells K17 to K27 give data for the expected returns *only for efficient portfolios.* The two data series, cells J17 to J27 and cells K17 to K27, constitute the y-data for the XY scatter plot. Where they coincide, Excel superimposes them, creating the effect seen in the graph.

To create the graph, mark the three columns I17:K27. Then go to the chart wizard and pick **XY (Scatter)** as shown below. Proceed from there to build the graph.

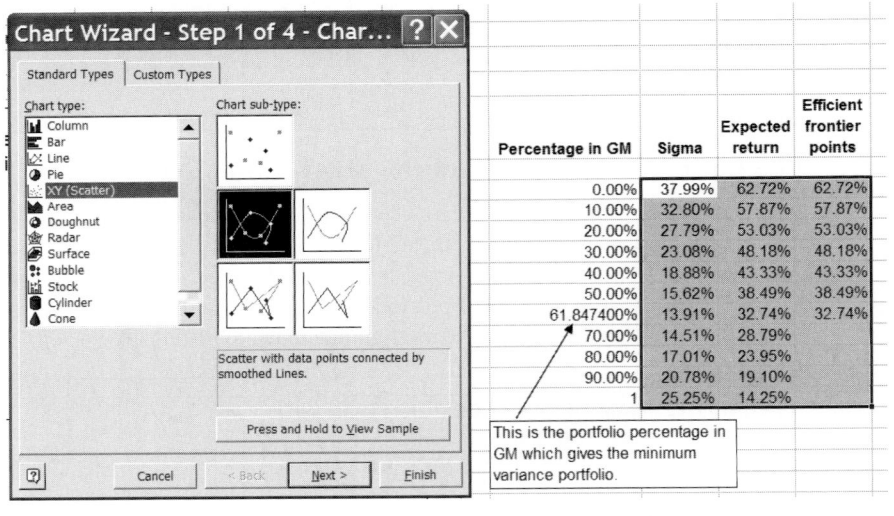

Percentage in GM	Sigma	Expected return	Efficient frontier points
0.00%	37.99%	62.72%	62.72%
10.00%	32.80%	57.87%	57.87%
20.00%	27.79%	53.03%	53.03%
30.00%	23.08%	48.18%	48.18%
40.00%	18.88%	43.33%	43.33%
50.00%	15.62%	38.49%	38.49%
61.847400%	13.91%	32.74%	32.74%
70.00%	14.51%	28.79%	
80.00%	17.01%	23.95%	
90.00%	20.78%	19.10%	
1	25.25%	14.25%	

This is the portfolio percentage in GM which gives the minimum variance portfolio.

13.5 The Effect of Correlation on the Efficient Frontier

When we looked at the "coin flip" economy of Section 13.1, we concluded that the correlation between asset returns made a big difference. In this section we examine the effect of stock return correlation on portfolio returns, repeating the correlation experiment of Section 13.1 for a more "real world" example.

First, recall what we concluded in Section 13.1:

- When the two coins have a perfectly negative correlation of −1, we can create a risk-free asset using combinations of the two assets. In this section you'll see that a similar conclusion is true for stock portfolios: Perfectly negatively correlated stock returns allow you to create a risk-free asset.
- When the two coins have a perfectly positive correlation of +1, it's impossible to diversify away any risk. You will see that a similar conclusion holds for stock portfolios.
- When the two coins have correlation between −1 and +1, some of the risk can be eliminated through diversification. Again this is true for stock portfolios.

In our example we use some of the same numbers used in our GM–MSFT example, but we'll allow the correlation between the returns on the two stocks to vary. We start with the following example, in which the correlation coefficient between GM and MSFT is $\rho_{GM,MSFT} = 0.5$ (cell B6).

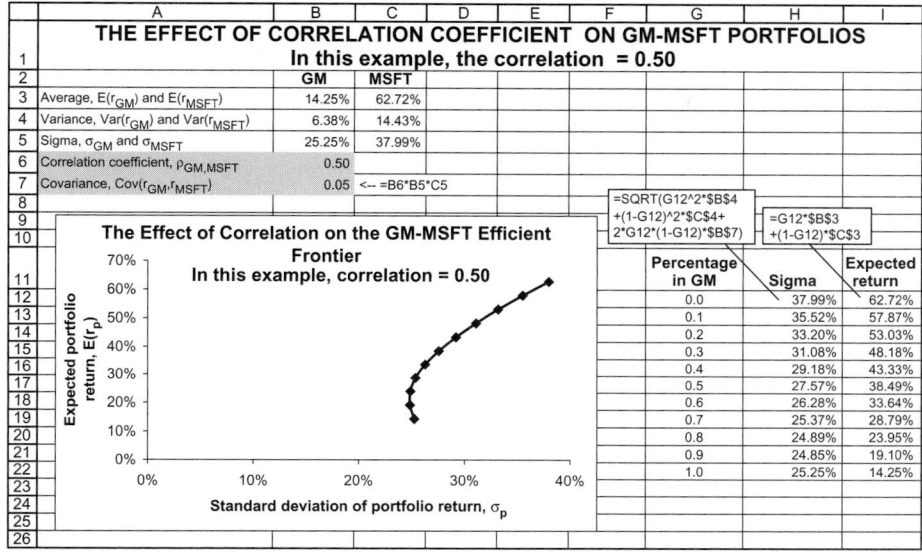

Correlation Coefficient = −1: Perfectly Negative Correlation

When the correlation coefficient $\rho_{GM,MSFT} = -1$, we can use our portfolio to create a riskless asset. This was the message in the simple "coin toss" example with which we started this chapter (Section 13.1), and it is still true here:

> Perfectly negative correlation between two risky assets allows the creation of a portfolio that is risk-free.

Here's our example in Excel:

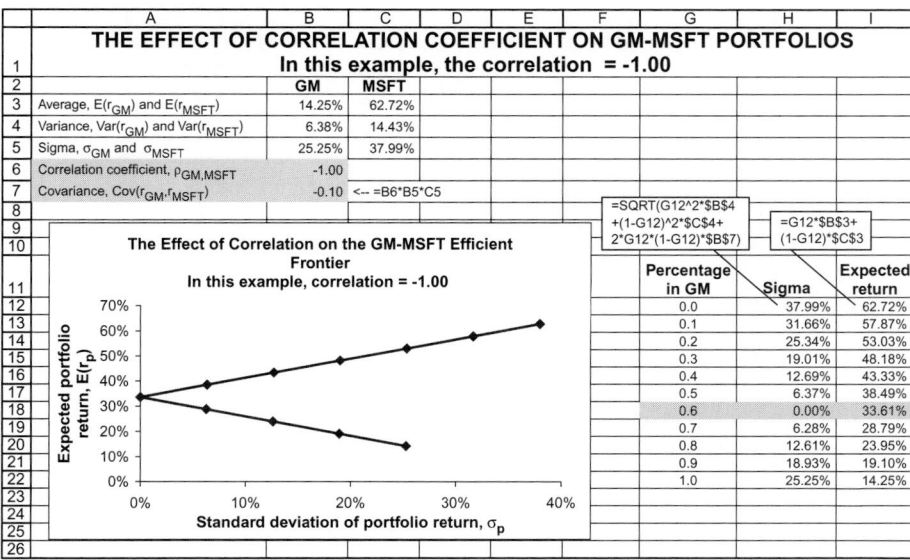

The minimum variance portfolio (highlighted in cells G18:I18) is achieved when the proportion in GM is 60.066%. When the correlation between the two stocks is -1, the minimum variance portfolio is riskless—the portfolio's return of 33.61% is achieved with zero standard deviation.

A little mathematics explains this result. The portfolio variance for this case can be written

$$Var(r_p) = w_{GM}^2 Var(r_{GM}) + w_{MSFT}^2 Var(r_{MSFT}) + 2w_{GM}w_{MSFT}\rho_{GM,MSFT}\sigma_{GM}\sigma_{MSFT}$$
$$= w_{GM}^2 \sigma_{GM}^2 + w_{MSFT}^2 \sigma_{MSFT}^2 - 2w_{GM}w_{MSFT}\sigma_{GM}\sigma_{MSFT}$$
$$= w_{GM}^2 \sigma_{GM}^2 + (1 - w_{GM})^2 \sigma_{MSFT}^2 - 2w_{GM}(1 - w_{GM})\sigma_{GM}\sigma_{MSFT}$$
$$= (w_{GM}\sigma_{GM} - (1 - w_{GM})\sigma_{MSFT})^2$$

This means that we can—by choosing the appropriate weights w_{GM} and w_{MSFT}—set the portfolio variance equal to zero:

$$Var(r_p) = (w_{GM}\sigma_{GM} - (1 - w_{GM})\sigma_{MSFT})^2 = 0$$
$$\text{when} \quad w_{GM} = \frac{\sigma_{MSFT}}{\sigma_{MSFT} + \sigma_{GM}}$$

In our case, this means that

$$w_{GM} = \frac{\sigma_{MSFT}}{\sigma_{MSFT} + \sigma_{GM}} = \frac{62.72\%}{62.72\% + 14.25\%} = 0.60066$$

This value is given in cell G18.

Correlation Coefficient $= +1$: Perfectly Positive Correlation

When the correlation coefficient $\rho_{GM,MSFT} = +1$, diversification does not reduce risk.

Perfectly positive correlation between two risky assets means that risk is not reduced in a portfolio context.

Here's our example in Excel:

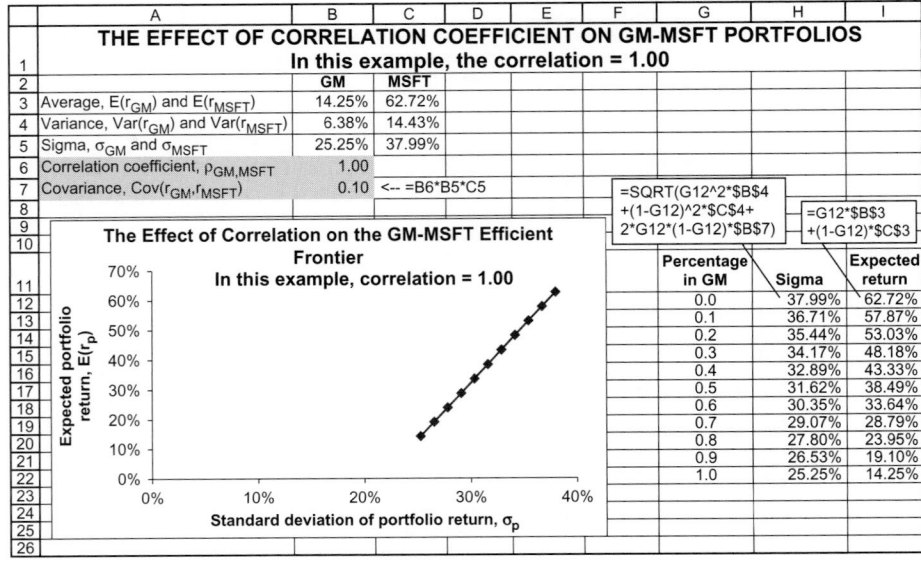

	A	B	C	D	E	F	G	H	I
1	THE EFFECT OF CORRELATION COEFFICIENT ON GM-MSFT PORTFOLIOS								
	In this example, the correlation = 1.00								
2		GM	MSFT						
3	Average, $E(r_{GM})$ and $E(r_{MSFT})$	14.25%	62.72%						
4	Variance, $Var(r_{GM})$ and $Var(r_{MSFT})$	6.38%	14.43%						
5	Sigma, σ_{GM} and σ_{MSFT}	25.25%	37.99%						
6	Correlation coefficient, $\rho_{GM,MSFT}$	1.00							
7	Covariance, $Cov(r_{GM},r_{MSFT})$	0.10	<-- =B6*B5*C5						
8							=SQRT(G12^2*$B$4		
9							+(1-G12)^2*$C$4+	=G12*$B$3	
10							2*G12*(1-G12)*$B$7)	+(1-G12)*$C$3	
11							Percentage in GM	Sigma	Expected return
12							0.0	37.99%	62.72%
13							0.1	36.71%	57.87%
14							0.2	35.44%	53.03%
15							0.3	34.17%	48.18%
16							0.4	32.89%	43.33%
17							0.5	31.62%	38.49%
18							0.6	30.35%	33.64%
19							0.7	29.07%	28.79%
20							0.8	27.80%	23.95%
21							0.9	26.53%	19.10%
22							1.0	25.25%	14.25%

The Effect of Correlation on the GM-MSFT Efficient Frontier
In this example, correlation = 1.00

Expected portfolio return, $E(r_p)$
Standard deviation of portfolio return, σ_p

Notice what we mean by "diversification does not reduce risk": The risk–return combinations for this case are on a straight line. In the previous two cases (correlation = 0.50 and correlation = −1), the portfolio frontier had a "northwest" portion; on a "northwest" portion of the frontier, we reduce risk and increase return. For this case the frontier only has a "northeast" portion—there is no way to reduce risk and increase return.

When the correlation between the two assets' returns is +1, the standard deviation of the portfolio return for this case is the weighted average of the asset standard deviations. A little mathematics explains this result. The portfolio variance for this case can be written

$$Var(r_p) = w_{GM}^2 Var(r_{GM}) + w_{MSFT}^2 Var(r_{MSFT}) + 2w_{GM}w_{MSFT}\rho_{GM,MSFT}\sigma_{GM}\sigma_{MSFT}$$

$$= w_{GM}^2\sigma_{GM}^2 + w_{MSFT}^2\sigma_{MSFT}^2 \underbrace{+2w_{GM}w_{MSFT}\sigma_{GM}\sigma_{MSFT}}_{}$$

$$\uparrow$$

The correlation coefficient
$\rho_{GM,MSFT}=1$

$$= (w_{GM}\sigma_{GM} + (1 - w_{GM})\sigma_{MSFT})^2$$

This means that the standard deviation of the portfolio is the weighted average of the asset standard deviations:

$$\sigma(r_p) = w_{GM}\sigma_{GM} + (1 - w_{GM})\sigma_{MSFT}$$

Thus, there is no real gain from diversification.

CONCLUSION

In this chapter we have discussed the importance of diversification for portfolio returns and risks. We showed how to calculate the mean and variance and standard deviation of a portfolio's return. The *efficient frontier* is the set of those portfolios that offer the highest expected return for a given standard deviation. We discussed this frontier and how it is affected by the correlation between the asset returns.

EXERCISES

1. The table below presents the year-end prices for the shares of Ford and PPG from 1989 to 2001:

	A	B	C
1	PRICES FOR FORD AND PPG STOCK		
2	Date	Ford stock price	PPG stock price
3	31-Dec-89	11.813	14.024
4	31-Dec-90	7.210	17.229
5	31-Dec-91	7.617	19.138
6	31-Dec-92	11.612	25.721
7	31-Dec-93	17.469	30.518
8	31-Dec-94	15.100	30.736
9	31-Dec-95	15.642	38.980
10	31-Dec-96	17.472	49.007
11	31-Dec-97	26.310	51.040
12	31-Dec-98	31.807	53.172
13	31-Dec-99	28.895	58.626
14	31-Dec-00	22.470	44.867
15	31-Dec-01	15.720	51.720

Note: Data for these exercises can be found on the disk that accompanies this book.

(a)   Calculate the following statistics for these two shares: average return, variance of returns, standard deviation of returns, covariance of returns, and correlation coefficient.

(b)   If you invested in a portfolio composed of 50% Ford and 50% PPG, what would be the portfolio expected return? The standard deviation?

(c)   Comment on the following statement: "Ford has lower returns and higher standard deviation of returns than PPG. Therefore, any rational investor would invest only in PPG and would leave Ford out of the portfolio."

2.   You invest $500 in a stock for which the return is determined by a coin flip. If the coin comes up heads the stock returns 10%, and if it comes up tails the investment returns −10%. What is the average return, the return variance, and the return standard deviation of this investment, if you flip the coin one time?

3.   You have $500 to invest. You decide to split it into two parts. The return on each $250 will be determined by a coin toss, and the results of the two tosses are not correlated. If the coin comes up heads the investment will return 10%, and if the coin comes up tails it will return −10%. What is the average return, the return variance, and the return standard deviation of this investment?

4.   Exercise 3 assumes that the correlation between the coin flips in 0. Repeat this exercise with the following correlations:

(a)   If the first coin flip is heads, then the second coin flip will be heads as well, and vice versa (correlation of +1).

(b)   If the first coin flip is heads, then the second coin flip will be tails, and vice versa (correlation of −1).

(c)   If the first coin flip is heads, then the second coin flip will be heads with a probability of 0.8. If the first coin flip is tails, then the second coin flip will be tails with a probability of 0.6.

(d)   What can you conclude about the connection between the variance of the return from the coin flips and the correlation between the flips?

5.   Calculate the average return and the variance of a portfolio composed of 30% GM and 70% MSFT stocks, using the data from page 385.

6.   Consider the following statistics for a portfolio composed of shares of Companies A and B:

	A	B	C	D	E	F
1		Company A stock	Company B stock			
2	Average return	25%	48%			
3	Variance	0.0800	0.1600			
4	Sigma	28.28%	40.00%			
5						
6	Covariance of returns	0.00350				
7	Correlation of returns	0.03094	<-- =B6/(B4*C4)			
8						
9	Portfolio					
10	Proportion of A	0.9				
11	Proportion of B	0.1				
12	Portfolio average return	27.30%	<-- =B10*B2+C2*B11			
13	Portfolio standard deviation	25.89%	<-- =SQRT(B10^2*B3+B11^2*C3+2*B10*B11*B6)			

(a)   Suggest a portfolio combination that improves return while maintaining the same level of risk.

(b)   Calculate the minimum variance portfolio for the portfolio composed of the two assets described above.

7.   Consider the monthly returns for Ford and General Motors stock given below. Were there advantages to diversifying between these two stocks? Explain.

	A	B	C
1	MONTHLY RETURNS FOR FORD AND GM STOCK		
2	Date	Ford	GM
3	1-Dec-99	5.52%	-1.50%
4	3-Jan-00	-5.70%	10.83%
5	1-Feb-00	-16.32%	-4.99%
6	1-Mar-00	10.32%	8.89%
7	3-Apr-00	20.27%	13.05%
8	1-May-00	-11.30%	-24.12%
9	1-Jun-00	-7.81%	-17.79%
10	3-Jul-00	9.47%	-1.94%
11	1-Aug-00	-9.18%	23.95%
12	1-Sep-00	5.42%	-7.14%
13	2-Oct-00	3.63%	-4.43%
14	1-Nov-00	-12.89%	-19.61%
15	1-Dec-00	3.02%	2.89%
16	2-Jan-01	21.56%	5.43%
17	1-Feb-01	-3.29%	4.56%
18			
19	Average	0.85%	-0.79%
20	Standard deviation	11.23%	12.58%
21	Correlation	0.4056	

8. The following spreadsheet presents data for stocks A and B.

	A	B	C
1	RETURN STATISTICS OF A AND B STOCK		
2		Stock A	Stock B
3	Average return	34%	25%
4	Variance	0.12	0.07
5	Standard deviation	34.64%	26.46%
6			
7	Covariance of return, $Cov(r_A, r_B)$	0.0160	
8	Correlation of return	0.1746	<-- =B7/(B5*C5)

(a) What are the return and the standard deviation of a portfolio composed of 30% stock A and 70% stock B?

(b) What are the return and the standard deviation of an equally weighted portfolio of stocks A and B?

9. Suppose that the return statistics for stocks A and B are given below. What is the standard deviation of the minimum variance portfolio? (The answer requires only one calculation.)

	A	B	C
1	RETURN STATISTICS OF A AND B STOCK		
2		A	B
3	Average return	25%	15%
4	Variance	0.1600	0.0484
5	Standard deviation	40.00%	22.00%
6			
7	Covariance of return	-0.0880	

10. ABC and XYZ are two stocks with the following return statistics:

	A	B	C
1		**Expected return**	**Standard deviation of return**
2	ABC	15%	33%
3	XYZ	25%	46%
4	Covariance(ABC,XYZ)	0.0865	
5	Correlation(ABC,XYZ)	0.5698	

   (a) Compute the expected return and standard deviation of a portfolio composed of 25% ABC and 75% XYZ.

   (b) Compute the returns of all portfolios that are combinations of ABC and XYZ with the proportion of ABC being 0%, 10%, ..., 90%, 100%. Graph these returns.

   (c) Compute the minimum variance portfolio.

11. Melissa Jones wants to invest in a portfolio composed of stocks ABC and XYX (from Exercise 10) that will yield a return of 19%. What is the weight of each stock in such a portfolio, and what is the portfolio's standard deviation? Answer the question both by using Excel's **Goal Seek** or **Solver** and by using the formulas for $E(r_p)$ and $Var(r_p)$ on pages 385–386.

12. Your client asks you to create a two-asset portfolio having an expected return of 15% and return standard deviation of 12%. The client specifies that the portfolio include 60% of the stock "Merlyn" (named for her beloved mother . . .), which has an expected return of 13% and a standard deviation of 10%.

   (a) What should be the return statistics of the second stock you'll combine in this portfolio, assuming the stocks have zero correlation?

   (b) What should be the return statistics of the second stock you'll combine in this portfolio, assuming the stocks have a covariance of 0.01?

13. What will be the weights, the expected return, the variance, and the standard deviation of a minimum variance portfolio combining the stocks below, using the mathematical way:

	A	B	C	D
1	**RETURN STATISTICS OF X AND Y STOCK**			
2		**X**	**Y**	
3	Mean return	21.00%	14.00%	
4	Variance	0.11	0.045	
5	Sigma	33.17%	21.21%	
6				
7	Covariance of returns	-0.0020		
8	Correlation of returns	-0.0284		

14. This exercise relates to the data in Exercise 13.

   (a) Calculate and graph the efficient frontier of the stock portfolios composed of stocks X and Y in Exercise 13.

   (b) Calculate and graph the efficient frontier of the stock portfolios composed of stocks X and Y in Exercise 13, assuming the correlation between the two stocks is −1.

15. Let's go again to the data of GM and Microsoft stocks on page 384. A portfolio composed of 90% GM and 10% Microsoft stocks has expected return of 19.1% and standard deviation of 20.78%. Find another portfolio with the same standard deviation and a higher return. (You can do this by trial and error, but you can also use **Solver**.)

16. John and Mary are considering investing in a combination of ABC stock and XYZ stock. The return on ABC is determined by a coin flip: If the coin is heads the return on ABC is 35%, and if

the coin is tails the return on ABC is 10%. The return on XYZ stock is similarly determined, but by a *separate coin flip*.

(a) Compute the mean, variance, and standard deviation of the returns on ABC and XYZ.

(b) What is the correlation of the returns? (Nothing to compute here, just think!)

(c) John has decided to invest in a portfolio composed of 100% XYZ stock. Mary, on the other hand, is investing in a portfolio composed of 50% ABC and 50% XYZ. Whose portfolio is better? Why?

17. Elizabeth and Sandra are considering investing in a combination of ABC stock and XYZ stock. The return on both stocks is determined by a single coin flip: If the coin is heads the return on both stocks is 35%, and if the coin is tails the return is 10%.

(a) Compute the mean, variance, and standard deviation of the returns on ABC and XYZ.

(b) What is the correlation of the returns? (Nothing to compute here, just think!)

(c) Elizabeth has decided to invest in a portfolio composed of 100% XYZ stock. Sandra, on the other hand, is investing in a portfolio composed of 50% ABC and 50% XYZ. Whose portfolio is better?

APPENDIX 13.1: DERIVING THE FORMULA FOR THE MINIMUM VARIANCE PORTFOLIO

In this appendix we derive the formula for the minimum variance portfolio. Recall the formula for variance of the portfolio:

$$Var(r_p) = w_{GM}^2 Var(r_{GM}) + w_{MSFT}^2 Var(r_{MSFT}) + 2w_{GM}w_{MSFT}Cov(r_{GM}, r_{MSFT})$$

Substituting $w_{MSFT} = 1 - w_{GM}$ in this equation, we have

$$Var(r_p) = w_{GM}^2 Var(r_{GM}) + (1 - w_{GM})^2 Var(r_{MSFT}) + 2w_{GM}(1 - w_{GM})Cov(r_{GM}, r_{MSFT})$$

Setting the derivative of this equation equal to zero will give the formula for the minimum variance portfolio:

$$\frac{d\,Var(r_p)}{dw_{GM}} = 2w_{GM}Var(r_{GM}) - 2(1 - w_{GM})Var(r_{MSFT}) + Cov(r_{GM}, r_{MSFT})(2 - 4w_{GM}) = 0$$

$$\Rightarrow w_{GM} = \frac{Var(r_{MSFT}) - Cov(r_{GM}, r_{MSFT})}{Var(r_{GM}) + Var(r_{MSFT}) - 2Cov(r_{GM}, r_{MSFT})}$$

APPENDIX 13.2: PORTFOLIOS WITH THREE AND MORE ASSETS

In this appendix we look at portfolios and their efficient frontiers when there are more than two assets. The main points we make are:

• In the multiasset context we can still calculate the efficient frontier, and it still has its characteristic shape.

- The more risky assets there are, the more the portfolio variance is influenced by the covariances between the assets.

We start by considering a three-asset problem. To describe three assets, we need to know the expected return, the variance, and all the *pairs* of covariances. This data is described below.

	A	B	C	D	E
1	**A THREE-ASSET PORTFOLIO PROBLEM**				
2		**Stock A**	**Stock B**	**Stock C**	
3	Mean	10%	12%	15%	
4	Variance	15%	22%	30%	
5					
6	Cov(r_A,r_B)	0.03			
7	Cov(r_B,r_C)	-0.01			
8	Cov(r_A,r_C)	0.02			

Suppose we form a portfolio of risky assets composed of proportion x_A in asset A, x_B in asset B, and x_C in asset C. Since the portfolio is fully invested in risky assets, it follows that $x_C = 1 - x_A - x_B$.

Portfolio Return Statistics: The expected return of the portfolio is given by

$$E(r_p) = x_A E(r_A) + x_B E(r_B) + x_C E(r_C)$$

The calculation of the portfolio's variance of return requires both the variances and the covariances:

$$Var(r_p) = x_A^2 Var(r_A) + x_B^2 Var(r_B) + x_C^2 Var(r_C) + 2x_A x_B Cov(r_A, r_B)$$
$$+ 2x_A x_C Cov(r_A, r_C) + 2x_B x_C Cov(r_B, r_C)$$

Notice that there are three *variances* and three *covariances*. When—at the end of this section—we show you the formula for a four-asset problem, there will be four variances and six covariances. As the number of assets grows, so does the number of covariances (in fact, their number grows much faster than the number of variances). This is the meaning of the second bullet at the beginning of this section—for multiasset portfolio problems, the portfolio variance is increasingly influenced by the covariances.

Here's an example of the mean return and variance calculation for our three-asset portfolio. The portfolio statistics are calculated in cells B16 to B18:

	A	B	C	D	E	F	G	H	I	J
1	**A THREE-ASSET PORTFOLIO PROBLEM**									
2		**Stock A**	**Stock B**	**Stock C**						
3	Mean	10%	12%	15%						
4	Variance	15%	22%	30%						
5										
6	Cov(r_A,r_B)	0.03								
7	Cov(r_B,r_C)	-0.01								
8	Cov(r_A,r_C)	0.02								
9										
10	**Portfolio proportions**									
11	x_A	0.4370								
12	x_B	0.3151								
13	x_C	0.2479	<-- =1-B12-B11							
14										
15	**Market portfolio statistics**									
16	Mean	0.1187	<-- =B11*B3+B12*C3+B13*D3							
17	Variance	0.0800	<-- =B11^2*B4+B12^2*C4+B13^2*D4+2*B11*B12*B6+2*B11*B13*B8+2*B12*B13*B7							
18	Sigma	0.2828	<-- =SQRT(B17)							

CALCULATING THE EFFICIENT FRONTIER WITH THREE ASSETS

We can use Excel to calculate and graph the efficient frontier for this case.[9] We'll make use of Excel's **Solver**.

Step 1: We use **Solver** to find the minimum variance portfolio:

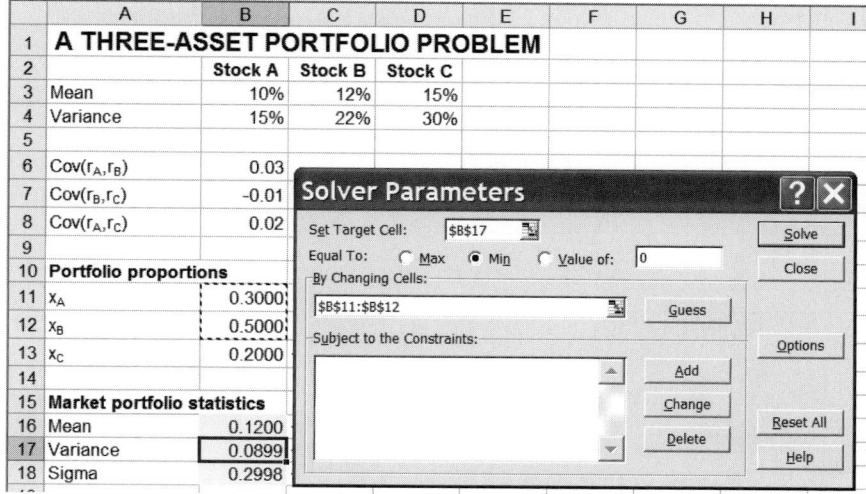

Here's the result:

	A	B	C	D	E	F	G	H	I	J
1	**A THREE-ASSET PORTFOLIO PROBLEM**									
2		**Stock A**	**Stock B**	**Stock C**						
3	Mean	10%	12%	15%						
4	Variance	15%	22%	30%						
5										
6	Cov(r_A, r_B)	0.03								
7	Cov(r_B, r_C)	-0.01								
8	Cov(r_A, r_C)	0.02								
9										
10	**Portfolio proportions**									
11	x_A	0.4370								
12	x_B	0.3151								
13	x_C	0.2479	<-- =1-B12-B11							
14										
15	**Market portfolio statistics**									
16	Mean	0.1187	<-- =B11*B3+B12*C3+B13*D3							
17	Variance	0.0800	<-- =B11^2*B4+B12^2*C4+B13^2*D4+2*B11*B12*B6+2*B11*B13*B8+2*B12*B13*B7							
18	Sigma	0.2828	<-- =SQRT(B17)							

---

[9]The procedure we're about to explain is somewhat long-winded—for a much shorter and efficient procedure, see the author's book *Financial Modeling* (MIT Press, 2000).

Step 2: We now specify sigma and use **Solver** to find a portfolio with the maximum return. We do this by first adding a cell ("Target sigma," cell B20) to the spreadsheet:

	A	B	C	D	E	F	G	H	I	J
1	A THREE-ASSET PORTFOLIO PROBLEM									
2		Stock A	Stock B	Stock C						
3	Mean	10%	12%	15%						
4	Variance	15%	22%	30%						
5										
6	Cov(r_A,r_B)	0.03								
7	Cov(r_B,r_C)	-0.01								
8	Cov(r_A,r_C)	0.02								
9										
10	Portfolio proportions									
11	x_A	0.4370								
12	x_B	0.3151								
13	x_C	0.2479	<-- =1-B12-B11							
14										
15	Market portfolio statistics									
16	Mean	0.1187	<-- =B11*B3+B12*C3+B13*D3							
17	Variance	0.0800	<-- =B11^2*B4+B12^2*C4+B13^2*D4+2*B11*B12*B6+2*B11*B13*B8+2*B12*B13*B7							
18	Sigma	0.2828	<-- =SQRT(B17)							
19										
20	Target sigma	0.3000								
21										
22	TABLE OF SIGMA VERSUS MEAN									
23	Target sigma	Mean								
24	0.2828	0.1187	<-- This is the minimum sigma portfolio							

Notice that—starting from row 24—we've begun to build a table of the results. The first row of this table is the minimum sigma portfolio. Now we'll use **Solver** to add another row to this table.

We do this by adding a *constraint* to **Solver**:

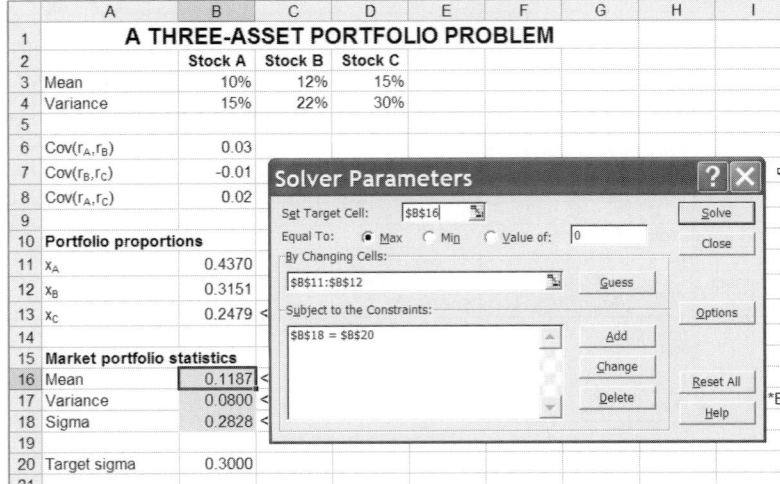

The constraint was added by pressing **Add** in the lower portion of the **Solver** dialog box:

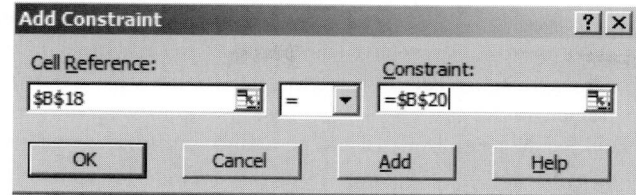

Here's the result:

	A	B	C	D	E	F	G	H	I	J	K
1	**A THREE-ASSET PORTFOLIO PROBLEM**										
2		**Stock A**	**Stock B**	**Stock C**							
3	Mean	10%	12%	15%							
4	Variance	15%	22%	30%							
5											
6	$Cov(r_A,r_B)$	0.03									
7	$Cov(r_B,r_C)$	-0.01									
8	$Cov(r_A,r_C)$	0.02									
9											
10	**Portfolio proportions**										
11	x_A	0.2533									
12	x_B	0.3544									
13	x_C	0.3923	<-- =1-B12-B11								
14											
15	**Market portfolio statistics**										
16	Mean	0.1267	<-- =B11*B3+B12*C3+B13*D3								
17	Variance	0.0900	<-- =B11^2*B4+B12^2*C4+B13^2*D4+2*B11*B12*B6+2*B11*B13*B8+2*B12*B13*B7								
18	Sigma	0.3000	<-- =SQRT(B17)								
19											
20	Target sigma	0.3000									

If we repeat this calculation many times for many Target sigmas, we get the efficient frontier:

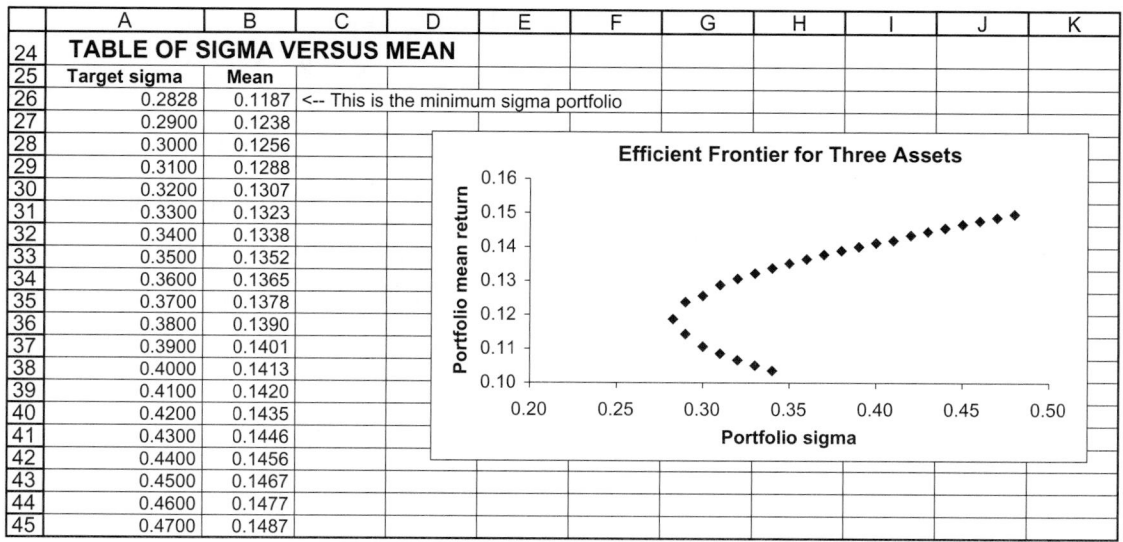

	A	B	C	D	E	F	G	H	I	J	K
24	**TABLE OF SIGMA VERSUS MEAN**										
25	**Target sigma**	**Mean**									
26	0.2828	0.1187	<-- This is the minimum sigma portfolio								
27	0.2900	0.1238									
28	0.3000	0.1256									
29	0.3100	0.1288									
30	0.3200	0.1307									
31	0.3300	0.1323									
32	0.3400	0.1338									
33	0.3500	0.1352									
34	0.3600	0.1365									
35	0.3700	0.1378									
36	0.3800	0.1390									
37	0.3900	0.1401									
38	0.4000	0.1413									
39	0.4100	0.1420									
40	0.4200	0.1435									
41	0.4300	0.1446									
42	0.4400	0.1456									
43	0.4500	0.1467									
44	0.4600	0.1477									
45	0.4700	0.1487									

FOUR ASSETS

The discussion so far has gone into depth about how to calculate returns and variances for a three-asset portfolio. If we have four assets, we can do the same kinds of calculations (we leave this as an exercise). What you have to know for this case is how to calculate the portfolio return and variance.

Call the assets A, B, C, D, and denote the portfolio weights by x_A, x_B, x_C, x_D.

Portfolio Return Statistics: The expected return of the portfolio is given by

$$E(r_p) = x_A E(r_A) + x_B E(r_B) + x_C E(r_C) + x_D E(r_D)$$

The calculation of the portfolio's variance of return requires both the variances and the covariances:

$$\begin{aligned}
Var(r_p) = {} & x_A^2 Var(r_A) + x_B^2 Var(r_B) + x_C^2 Var(r_C) + x_D^2 Var(r_D) \\
& + 2x_A x_B Cov(r_A, r_B) + 2x_A x_C Cov(r_A, r_C) + 2x_A x_D Cov(r_A, r_D) \\
& + 2x_B x_C Cov(r_B, r_C) + 2x_B x_D Cov(r_B, r_D) \\
& + 2x_C x_D Cov(r_C, r_D)
\end{aligned}$$

Notice that there are now four *variances* and six *covariances*.

EXERCISES FOR APPENDIX 13.2

All three problems relate to the following statistics for stocks ABC, QPD, and XYZ:

	A	B	C	D
1	**RETURN STATISTICS FOR THREE STOCKS**			
2		ABC	QPD	XYZ
3	Average return .	22.00%	17.50%	30.00%
4	Variance	0.2	0.05	0.17
5	Standard deviation	44.72%	22.36%	41.23%
6				
7	Correlations			
8	Corr(ABC,QPD)	0.05		
9	Corr(ABC,XYZ)	-0.1		
10	Corr(QPD,XYZ)	0.5		

A.1. Find the average return and standard deviation of a portfolio composed of 50% stock ABC, 20% stock QPD, and 30% stock XYZ.

A.2. Find the minimum variance portfolio and its statistics.

A.3. Find the portfolio having maximum return given that the portfolio standard deviation is 30%.

CHAPTER 14

THE CAPITAL ASSET PRICING MODEL (CAPM) AND THE SECURITY MARKET LINE (SML)

OVERVIEW

In this chapter we discuss two powerful results about returns and risks in capital markets. One result, termed the *capital market line* (CML), gives investors advice about how to invest. The CML says that the best investment portfolio for any investor is a combination of two assets—a risk-free asset such as a savings account and a risky asset representative of the risks of the overall stock market (the S&P 500 Index is often used as an example). The choice about which proportion to invest in the risk-free asset and which proportion to invest in the risky asset depends on the investor's willingness to bear risks.

A second result, called the *security market line* (SML), links the return of any asset to its risk. The SML states that the expected return of any asset depends on the asset's sensitivity to the market. This sensitivity is termed beta and is often written with the Greek letter β. Assets with higher βs have higher risks and will earn higher expected returns.

In this chapter we develop the concepts of the CML and SML. In Chapter 13 we discussed the risk and return combinations offered by a portfolio of risky assets. In this chapter we add a risk-free asset to the portfolio problem discussed in Chapter 13. Adding this asset gives investors new possibilities, since it allows them to buy an asset that gives a nonrisky return: They can invest either in stocks, or in the risk-free asset, or in some combination of the two. A portfolio composed of risky assets and the risk-free asset allows investors to achieve returns that are greater than the returns offered by a portfolio of only risky assets.

The addition of a risk-free asset to the portfolio of risky assets leads to four new concepts:

- The *market portfolio* (denoted by the letter M) is the best portfolio of risky assets available to all investors.
- The *capital market line* (CML) is the set of all optimal investment portfolios for an investor. The CML contains an important piece of investment advice: It tells us that every investor's optimal investment portfolio should be a combination of the risk-free asset and the market portfolio.
- The *beta* of a stock (denoted by the Greek letter β) is a measure of the stock's risk.
- The *security market line* (SML) describes the relation between the expected returns of any stock and its beta.

Because the material in this chapter is not easy, we start the chapter with a summary of its main results. At some point you may want to skip ahead to Chapters 15 and 16 to see how the concepts are used in practice.

Finance Concepts Used

- Portfolios, risk-free asset
- Capital market line (CML)
- Beta, security market line (SML)
- Sharpe ratio

Excel Functions Used

- **Varp, Stdevp, Sqrt**
- Sophisticated graphing
- **Solver**

14.1 Summarizing the Chapter

Much of the material in this chapter is technical and somewhat harder than other chapters in this book. To ease your understanding of the chapter materials, we start with a summary of the chapter's main results.

The big "takeaways" from this chapter are two concepts: the capital market line (CML) and the security market line (SML). The CML tells us how an investor should optimally split an investment between risky and nonrisky assets. The SML tells us how the expected return of any asset is related to its risk and how this risk should be measured. In the next two subsections we give examples of the use of the CML and the SML.

In discussing the CML and the SML it is helpful to have two pieces of notation. We denote by r_f the return of a risk-free asset; you can think of this as the interest rate paid by banks on their savings accounts or as the interest paid by money market funds.[1] We denote by $E(r_m)$ the *expected return on the market*, the rate of return on a portfolio of stocks which is representative of the riskiness of the whole stock market. For example, as this chapter is written (mid 2005), the risk-free rate in the United States—a representative rate paid by banks on savings is $r_f = 3\%$. At the same time, the consensus of stock market analysts is that over the next five years the U.S. stock market will have an annual return of $E(r_M) = 8\%$.

The Capital Market Line (CML)

The CML says that an investor's optimal investment strategy is to split his/her capital between two assets: a risk-free asset earning r_f and a risky asset representing the risks of the overall market. The CML states that the expected return of such a portfolio is given by the following equation:

CML: Expected return of an optimal portfolio

$$E(r_p) = r_f + (\% \text{ invested in market portfolio}) * [E(r_M) - r_f]$$

Here's how you might use the CML: Suppose your friend Benjamin says to you: "I've got $10,000 to invest. You're a finance major. Help me pick some stocks."

You should start by telling Benjamin not even to try to pick stocks! Much financial research has shown that stock picking is largely futile; on average, even experienced "stock pickers" do not earn superior returns. Instead of picking stocks, the CML advises you to ask Benjamin what proportion of his money he wants to put at risk and what proportion he needs to keep absolutely safe. There's a trade-off here: The risky part of his investment will, on average, earn more than the risk-free part.

Suppose Benjamin answers that he's willing to put 30% of his money at risk and wants the remaining 70% in a safe investment. At that point you can give him the following good advice, based on the CML:

- Invest $7,000 in a money market fund such as the Fidelity Cash Reserves Fund. Money market funds invest in very short-term bonds and earn interest virtually without risk. They are very liquid (meaning you can withdraw your money at any time), and they are very safe.

- Invest $3,000, which he's willing to put at risk, in a mutual fund that represents the average risk of the market. A typical fund might be Fidelity's Spartan Index 500 Fund. This fund

---

[1]A money market fund is a mutual fund that invests in a highly diversified portfolio of very short-term bonds issued by the United States Treasury or by U.S. corporations that have high credit ratings. The bonds bought by a money market fund typically mature within 7–20 days, meaning that the fund is lending out its money for a very short time in a highly liquid market. The return of a money market fund is representative of the risk-free interest rate in the economy. For a more in-depth explanation, look at http://www.fool.com/savings/shortterm/03.htm.

invests only in the stocks of the S&P 500 Index—an index broadly representative of the riskiness of the American stock market.[2]

The CML states that Benjamin's expected portfolio return is related to the risk-free rate r_f and to the percentage of his investment in the market. Suppose that $r_f = 3\%$ and suppose that $E(r_m) = 8\%$. Then Benjamin can expect an annual portfolio return of 5%:

CML: Expected return of an optimal portfolio

$$E(r_p) = r_f + (\% \ invested \ in \ market \ portfolio) * [E(r_M) - r_f]$$
$$= 3\% + 30\% * [8\% - 3\%]$$
$$= 4.5\%$$

Benjamin's 70%–30% strategy shows that he's fairly risk averse. His risk aversion leads Benjamin to an investment strategy that puts most of his money in a risk-free investment and puts only a small part in a risky investment. Benjamin will not be putting much of his money at risk, but on the other hand he will earn less than he would if he undertook more risk.

Now suppose your parents ask you how to invest their $1,000,000 of savings. They suggest to you that they're investing for the long term and can bear more risks. Since they can bear more risk than Benjamin, you might ask them what they think of a 20%–80% investment strategy. You might suggest to them that they invest $200,000 in Fidelity Cash Reserves and the remaining $800,000 in the Spartan Index 500 Fund. In the long run they will earn more from their investments, but they will undertake more risks. The CML predicts that your parents will earn 10%:

CML: Expected return of an optimal portfolio

$$E(r_p) = r_f + (\% \ invested \ in \ market \ portfolio) * [E(r_M) - r_f]$$
$$= 3\% + 80\% * [8\% - 3\%]$$
$$= 7\%$$

As you can see, the CML simplifies investment strategies by concentrating only on the split between a risk-free and a risky investment asset. It also predicts the expected return of the portfolio.[3] To sum up the investment advice contained in the CML:

- The *best* investment portfolios involve a simple split between the risk-free asset and the market portfolio. These portfolios, whose return/risk configuration is given by the CML, are the best portfolios available to the investor: Beyond the portfolios on the CML, there are no portfolios that offer a superior return/risk combination.

- Beyond the simple choice of the investor's split between a risk-free asset and the market portfolio, there's *no point* in thinking further! Investors cannot improve the performance of their investment portfolios by the judicious picking of stocks. Neither can investment managers.

---

[2]The relevant URLs for the two funds mentioned can be found at the Fidelity website: http://www. fidelity.com. Note that almost all mutual fund companies have money market and index funds, so that the use of Fidelity funds is merely illustrative.

[3]Anticipating the results of Section 14.3: The CML also suggests that the standard deviation of the returns of the optimal investment strategy are given by $\sigma_p = (\% \ invested \ in \ market \ porrtfolio) * \sigma_M$.

The Security Market Line (SML)

The CML deals only with the composition of optimal investment portfolios. But there are many assets in the market—what about them? The SML says that the expected return of *any stock or portfolio* is related to three factors:

1. The risk-free rate in the market r_f.
2. The stock's market risk. A stock's risk is measured by a number called beta (β), which measures the sensitivity of the stock's return to the return of the market. If a stock has a high beta, then when the market goes up, the stock goes up even more (and, of course, the opposite—when the market goes down, the stock goes down even more). The price movements of a low beta stock are less sensitive to variations in the market.
3. The expected return of the market, $E(r_M)$.

The SML states that the expected return of any asset is determined by the following equation:

SML: Expected return of any asset

$$E(r_{Asset}) = r_f + \beta_{Asset} * [E(r_M) - r_f]$$

Here are two examples of the use of the SML. Suppose that the risk-free rate $r_f = 3\%$ and that the market expected return is $E(r_M) = 8\%$. What are the expected returns of Microsoft (stock symbol MSFT) and of Merck (stock symbol MRK) stocks? A look at Yahoo (see Figure 14.1) shows that Microsoft's beta is $\beta_{MSFT} = 1.28$ and that Merck's beta is $\beta_{MRK} = 0.405$. Applying the SML shows that the market expects Microsoft's return to be 9.40% and Merck's return to be 5.08%:

$$
\begin{aligned}
\text{Microsoft's expected return, } E(r_{MSFT}) &= r_f + \beta_{MSFT} * [E(r_M) - r_f] \\
&= 3\% + 1.28 * [8\% - 3\%] \\
&= 9.40\% \\
\text{Merck's expected return, } E(r_{MRK}) &= r_f + \beta_{MRK} * [E(r_M) - r_f] \\
&= 3\% + 0.405 * [8\% - 3\%] \\
&= 5.03\%
\end{aligned}
$$

You might ask yourself whether Microsoft's higher expected return means that Microsoft is a better investment than Merck. The answer is "no"—Microsoft has a higher expected return because it is riskier than Merck.

Where Do We Go From Here?

This section has summarized the main results from this chapter. In the two succeeding chapters we discuss the uses of these results for evaluating investments (Chapter 15) and for measuring the cost of capital (Chapter 16). In the remainder of this chapter, we derive the CML and the SML. The discussion is (unavoidably) somewhat technical, and you may decide to skip ahead to Chapters 15 and 16.

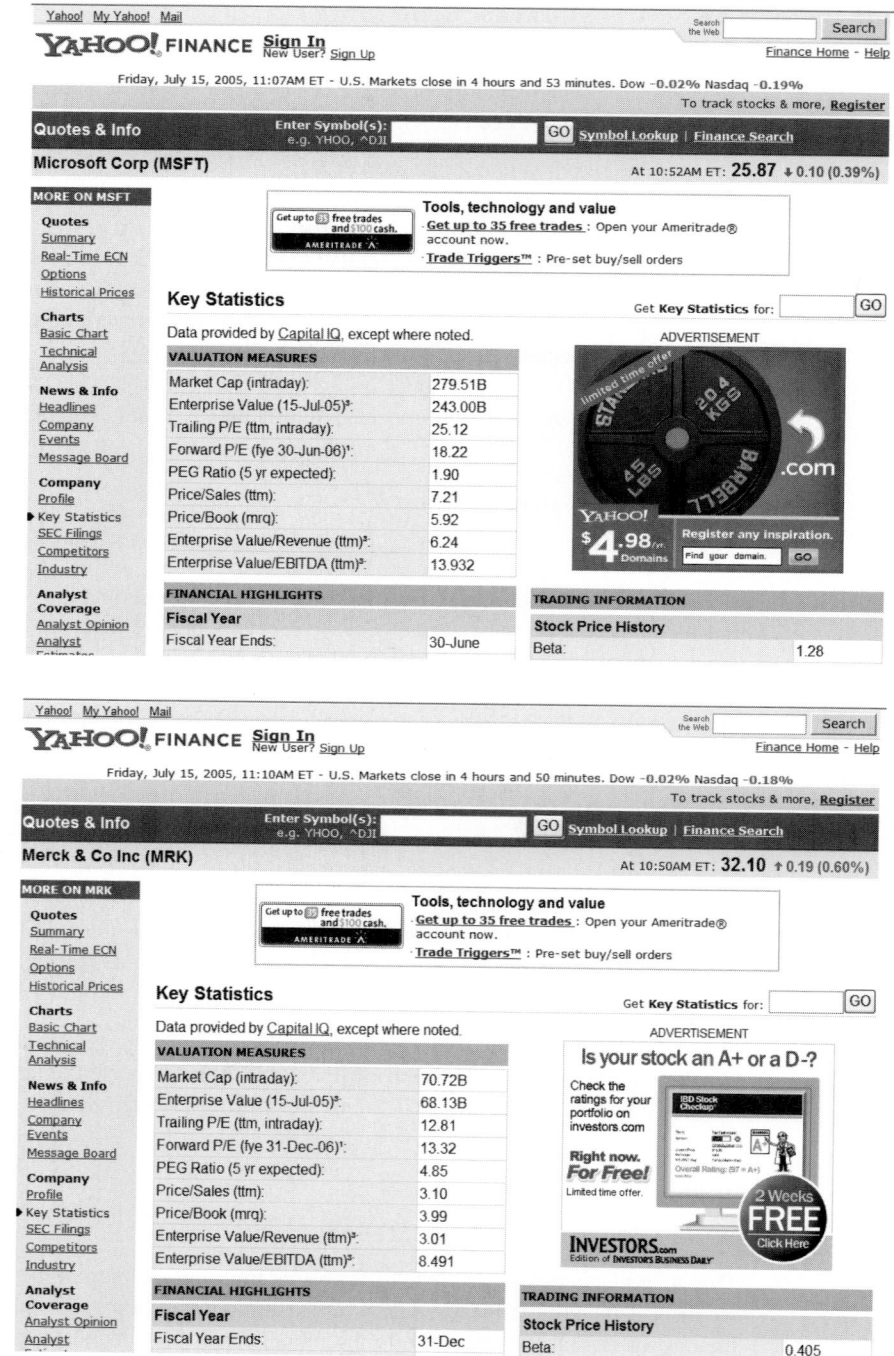

Figure 14.1 Screen clips from Yahoo showing beta (β) for Microsoft and Kellogg. The results can be obtained by going to http://finance.yahoo.com, choosing the stock, and then going to **Key statistics**.

14.2 Risky Portfolios and the Risk-free Asset

Now that we've reviewed the main results of the chapter, here's the nitty-gritty. We start by considering a portfolio problem of the kind dealt with in Chapter 13. We assume that there are two risky assets, stock A and stock B, and also a *risk-free asset*—an asset that gives an annual interest payment with *certainty*. You can think of this asset as being a savings account in a bank, a government bond, or a money market fund. In the examples of this section, we suppose that the risk-free asset gives a 2% annual return, and we denote the return on the risk-free asset by r_f. The first few lines of the following spreadsheet give you all the details:

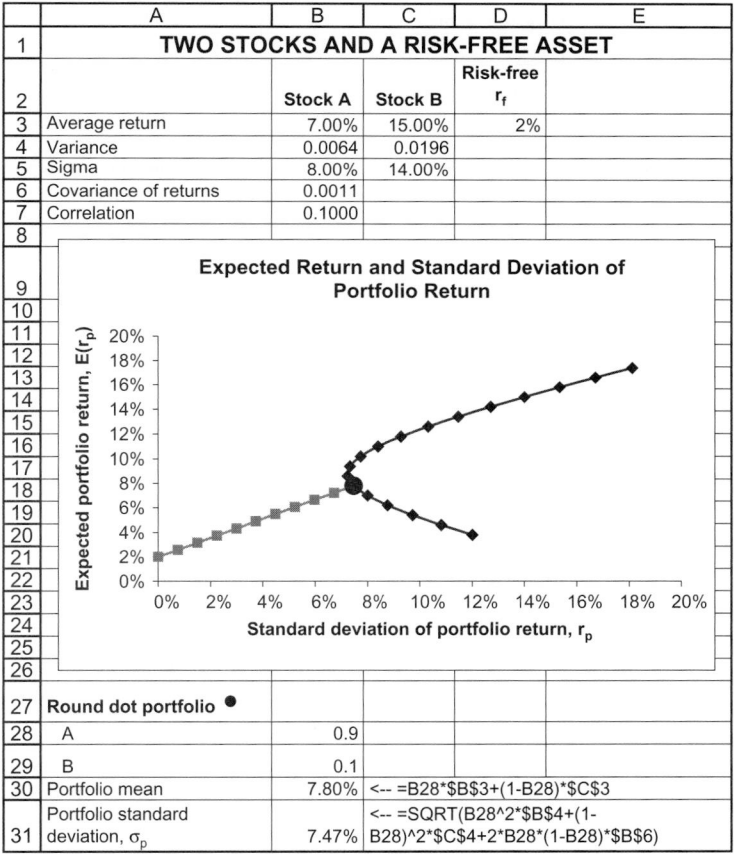

	A	B	C	D	E
1	**TWO STOCKS AND A RISK-FREE ASSET**				
2		**Stock A**	**Stock B**	**Risk-free** r_f	
3	Average return	7.00%	15.00%	2%	
4	Variance	0.0064	0.0196		
5	Sigma	8.00%	14.00%		
6	Covariance of returns	0.0011			
7	Correlation	0.1000			
8					

Expected Return and Standard Deviation of Portfolio Return

27	Round dot portfolio ●				
28	A	0.9			
29	B	0.1			
30	Portfolio mean	7.80%	<-- =B28*$B$3+(1-B28)*$C$3		
31	Portfolio standard deviation, σ_p	7.47%	<-- =SQRT(B28^2*$B$4+(1-B28)^2*$C$4+2*B28*(1-B28)*$B$6)		

The curved line shows the portfolio mean $E(r_p)$ and standard deviation ("sigma-p") σ_p of combinations of stock A and stock B.[4] The straight line shows the mean and standard deviation of portfolio combinations of the risk-free asset (which returns $r_f = 2\%$) and a specific portfolio of risky assets, denoted by a round dot (●).

Rows 28–31 give information about the round dot portfolio ●: It is composed of 90% stock A and 10% stock B, and it has expected return $E(r_p) = 7.8\%$ and standard deviation of return $\sigma_p = 7.47\%$.

---

[4]This was illustrated in Chapters 12 and 13.

Computing a Point on the Straight Line

In the spreadsheet below we indicate two points on the straight line that connects the risk-free rate r_f and the round dot portfolio •. Each point represents an investment portfolio that is invested partly in the risk-free asset and partly in the portfolio •. Take a look, and then after the spreadsheet we'll show you how to calculate the mean and standard deviation of the points on the line.

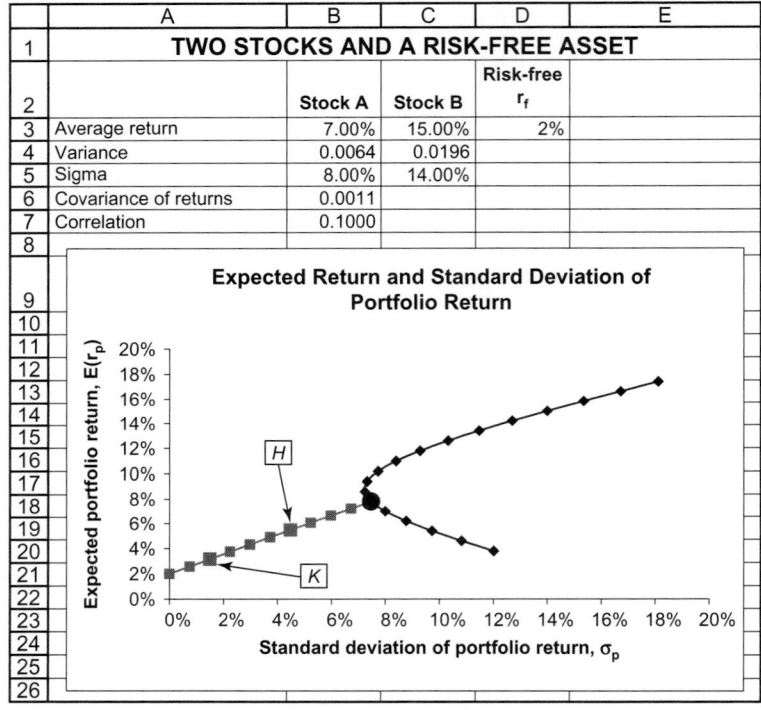

	A	B	C	D	E
1		**TWO STOCKS AND A RISK-FREE ASSET**			
2		**Stock A**	**Stock B**	**Risk-free** r_f	
3	Average return	7.00%	15.00%	2%	
4	Variance	0.0064	0.0196		
5	Sigma	8.00%	14.00%		
6	Covariance of returns	0.0011			
7	Correlation	0.1000			
8					

Expected Return and Standard Deviation of Portfolio Return

The round dot portfolio • is composed of an investment of 90% A and 10% B. What about portfolio H? H is a portfolio invested 60% in the round dot portfolio and 40% in the risk-free asset. To compute the returns of this portfolio, we use the following equations:

$$E(r_H) = \underbrace{x}_{\substack{\uparrow \\ \text{Percent in} \\ \text{round dot} \\ \text{portfolio}}} E(r_{round\ dot}) + \underbrace{(1-x)}_{\substack{\uparrow \\ \text{Percent in} \\ \text{risk-free asset}}} * r_f = 60\% * 7.8\% + 40\% * 2\% = 5.48\%$$

$$\sigma_H = \underbrace{x}_{\substack{\uparrow \\ \text{Percent in} \\ \text{round dot} \\ \text{portfolio}}} \sigma_{round\ dot} = 60\% * 7.47\% = 4.48\%$$

In a similar fashion portfolio K—invested 20% in the round dot portfolio and 80% in the risk-free asset—has statistics

$$E(r_K) = \underbrace{x}_{\substack{\uparrow \\ \text{Percent in} \\ \text{round dot} \\ \text{portfolio}}} E(r_{round\ dot}) + \underbrace{(1-x)}_{\substack{\uparrow \\ \text{Percent in} \\ \text{risk-free asset}}} * r_f = 20\% * 7.8\% + 80\% * 2\% = 3.16\%$$

$$\sigma_K = \underbrace{x}_{\substack{\uparrow \\ \text{Percent in} \\ \text{round dot} \\ \text{portfolio}}} \sigma_{round\ dot} = 20\% * 7.47\% = 1.49\%$$

A STATISTICAL NOTE

The equations used in the last calculation follow from our lessons in portfolio statistics in Chapter 12. Suppose the investor invests a percentage of her wealth x in a portfolio A of risky assets, which has expected return $E(r_A)$ and standard deviation of return σ_A. Suppose she invests the rest of her wealth $1 - x$ in a risk-free asset that has expected return r_f and standard deviation of return 0. By the formula given in Chapter 13, the portfolio's expected return is its weighted average return:

$$E(r_p) = x\,E(r_A) + (1-x)r_f$$

The portfolio's return variance is

$$Var(r_p) = x^2 Var(r_A) + (1-x)^2 \underbrace{Var(r_f)}_{\substack{\uparrow \\ = 0, \text{ since} \\ \text{the risk-free} \\ \text{asset is risk-free} \\ \text{(duh!)}}} + 2 * x * (1-x) * \underbrace{Cov(A, r_f)}_{\substack{\uparrow \\ = 0, \text{ since} \\ \text{the risk-free} \\ \text{asset is} \\ \text{risk-free} \\ \text{(duh!)}}}$$

$$= x^2 Var\,(r_A) = x^2 \sigma_A^2$$

This means that the standard deviation of the portfolio's return is $\sigma_p = \sqrt{Var(r_p)} = x\sigma_A$.

Improving the Risk–Return Relation

We can choose portfolios that have a better risk–return relation than those on the line connecting r_f and the round dot portfolio ● by choosing another portfolio on the efficient frontier. The line connecting the risk-free asset and the "big square" portfolio below is an improvement on the line of the previous section:

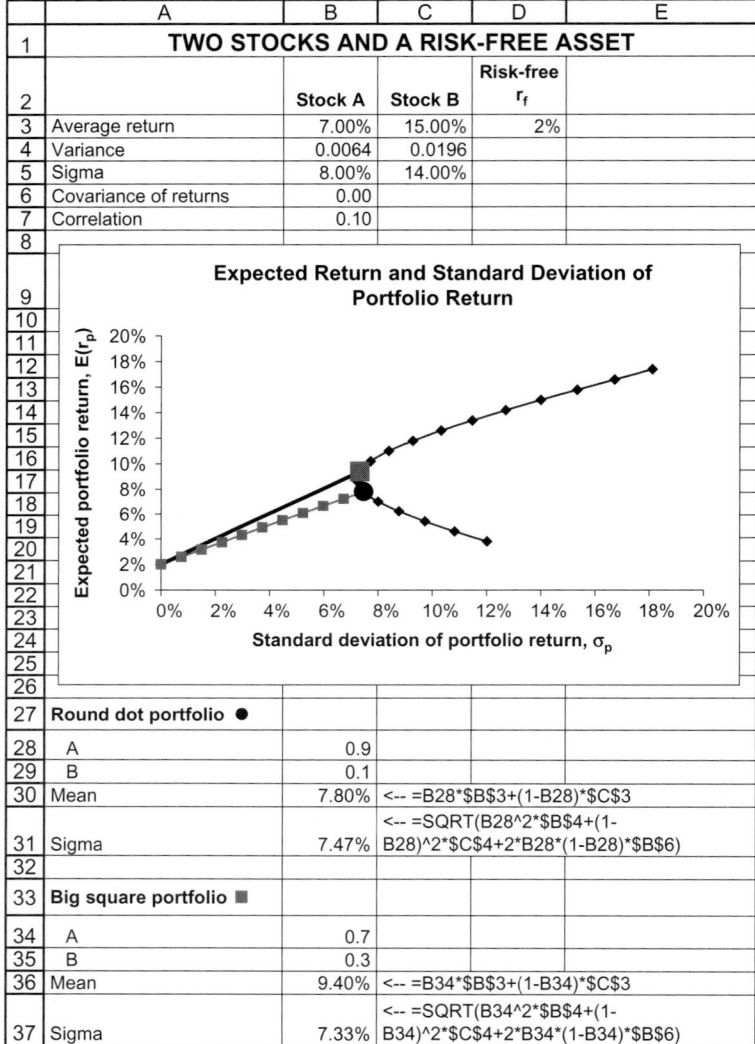

	A	B	C	D	E
1	TWO STOCKS AND A RISK-FREE ASSET				
2		Stock A	Stock B	Risk-free r_f	
3	Average return	7.00%	15.00%	2%	
4	Variance	0.0064	0.0196		
5	Sigma	8.00%	14.00%		
6	Covariance of returns	0.00			
7	Correlation	0.10			
8					
27	**Round dot portfolio ●**				
28	A	0.9			
29	B	0.1			
30	Mean	7.80%	<-- =B28*$B$3+(1-B28)*$C$3		
31	Sigma	7.47%	<-- =SQRT(B28^2*$B$4+(1-B28)^2*$C$4+2*B28*(1-B28)*$B$6)		
32					
33	**Big square portfolio ■**				
34	A	0.7			
35	B	0.3			
36	Mean	9.40%	<-- =B34*$B$3+(1-B34)*$C$3		
37	Sigma	7.33%	<-- =SQRT(B34^2*$B$4+(1-B34)^2*$C$4+2*B34*(1-B34)*$B$6)		

Since the new line is higher than the old line, all the points on the line to the big square ■ are better than the points on the line to the black circle ●. For any point on the round dot line there's always a point on the big square line that gives a higher return but has the same portfolio standard deviation σ_p.

There must be a *best* line, which starts off from the point 2% on the y-axis. This best line, shown below, connects the risk-free rate $r_f = 2\%$ to a point ■ on the efficient frontier. It is shown below:

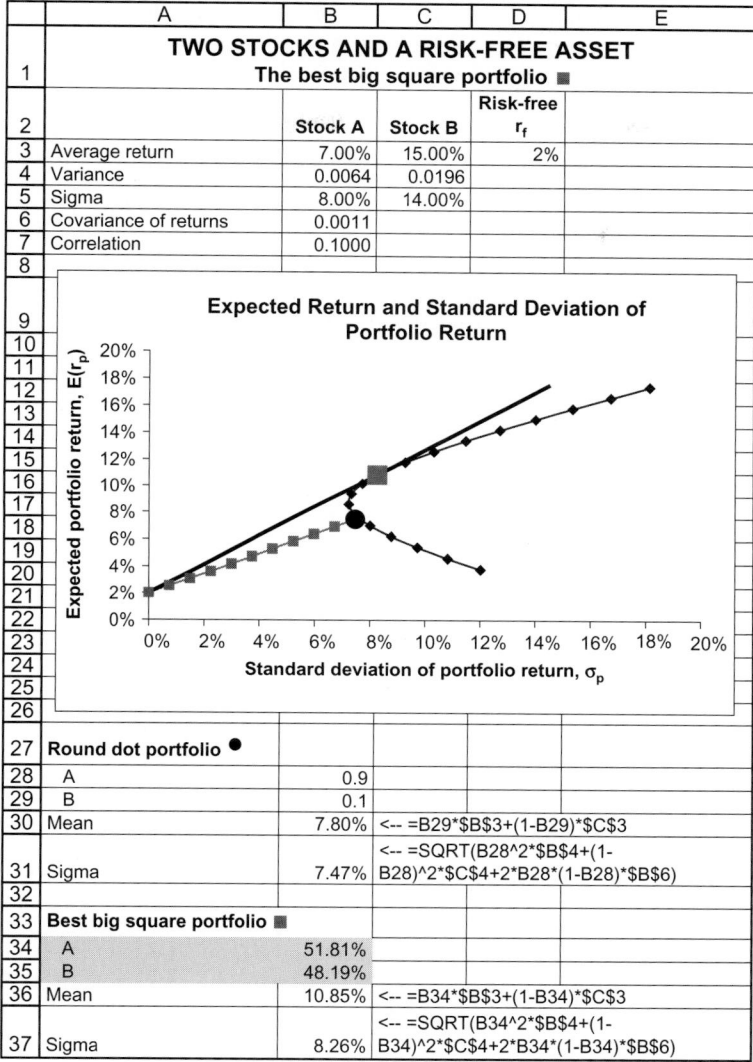

	A	B	C	D	E
1	\multicolumn{5}{c}{**TWO STOCKS AND A RISK-FREE ASSET**}				
	\multicolumn{5}{c}{**The best big square portfolio ■**}				
2		**Stock A**	**Stock B**	**Risk-free** r_f	
3	Average return	7.00%	15.00%	2%	
4	Variance	0.0064	0.0196		
5	Sigma	8.00%	14.00%		
6	Covariance of returns	0.0011			
7	Correlation	0.1000			
8					
9					
10					
11					
12					
13					
14					
15					
16					
17					
18					
19					
20					
21					
22					
23					
24					
25					
26					
27	**Round dot portfolio ●**				
28	A	0.9			
29	B	0.1			
30	Mean	7.80%	<-- =B29*$B$3+(1-B29)*$C$3		
31	Sigma	7.47%	<-- =SQRT(B28^2*$B$4+(1-B28)^2*$C$4+2*B28*(1-B28)*$B$6)		
32					
33	**Best big square portfolio ■**				
34	A	51.81%			
35	B	48.19%			
36	Mean	10.85%	<-- =B34*$B$3+(1-B34)*$C$3		
37	Sigma	8.26%	<-- =SQRT(B34^2*$B$4+(1-B34)^2*$C$4+2*B34*(1-B34)*$B$6)		

The line as drawn has several properties:

- It starts from the risk-free rate (2%) on the *y*-axis.
- It goes to (and through) a stock portfolio ■ on the efficient frontier market by the big square. As you can see in cells B35 to B37, this portfolio is composed of 51.81% stock A and 48.19% stock B. It has an expected return of 10.85% and a standard deviation of 8.26%. In Section 14.4 we describe how we computed this portfolio.
- It is tangent to the efficient frontier—meaning the line touches the efficient frontier only at the big square portfolio and nowhere else. This means that with the exception of the big square portfolio ■, every portfolio on the efficient frontier is below the line.

- Finally (and this is the most important point), since the big square line is above the efficient frontier (except for the one point ■ at which it touches the frontier), all the best investment portfolios are on the line. This point is so important that we explore it in a separate subsection.

The big square portfolio ■ is called the *market portfolio*. The market portfolio is the portfolio of risky assets which allows investors to achieve maximal returns.

The Capital Market Line

To emphasize the optimality take another look at the "big square line." Notice that the line is above the efficient frontier *everywhere* (except at the point of tangency, which we now call the *market portfolio M*). We call this line the *capital market line* (CML):

The capital market line is the set of optimal investment portfolios. Each point on the line is (1) a combination of some percentage invested in the risk-free asset and (2) another percentage invested in the market portfolio *M*.

In Section 14.4 we show how to compute the market portfolio *M*. In the next section we explore the practical meaning of the CML.

14.3 Three Points on the Capital Market Line (CML): Exploring Optimal Investment Combinations

What do portfolios on the CML—the line connecting the risk-free rate r_f and the market portfolio *M*—look like? What does the CML mean for an investor? To get a feel for this, we explore two portfolios on the CML.

Portfolio 1: Investing in the Market Portfolio *M* and in the Risk-free Asset

Suppose you have $1,000 to invest. You can choose any combination of three assets—the risk-free asset, stock A, or stock B. In Portfolio 1, you choose to invest $500 in the risk-free asset and $500 in the market portfolio *M*—the portfolio composed of 51.81% stock A and 48.19% stock B.

	A	B	C	D	E
1	**PORTFOLIO ON THE CAPITAL MARKET LINE (CML)**				
2	**The market portfolio, M**	Percent			
3	Stock A	51.81%			
4	Stock B	48.19%			
5	Expected return of market portfolio M	10.85%	<-- =B3*G19+B4*H19		
6	Standard deviation of market portfolio M	8.26%	<-- =SQRT(B3^2*G20+B4^2*H20+2*B3*B4*G22)		
7					
8	**Investor portfolio**				
9	Invested in risk-free	50%			
10	Invested in market portfolio M	50%			
11					
12	**Portfolio return statistics--point on the CML**				
13	Expected portfolio return	6.43%	<-- =B9*I19+B10*B5		
14	Portfolio standard deviation	4.13%	<-- =B10*B6		

This looks a little complicated, but it's really a version of the portfolio calculations we did in Chapter 13. The investment is divided 50% into the risk-free asset and another 50% into portfolio M, which has an expected return of 10.85% (cell B5) and a standard deviation of 8.26% (cell B6). According to the formula given in Section 14.2, the expected return and the standard deviation of returns are calculated by

$$E(r_p) = xE(r_M) + (1 - x)r_f$$
$$\sigma_p = x\sigma_M$$

As you can see in cells B13 and B14, this gives $E(r_p) = 6.43\%$ and $\sigma_p = 4.13\%$. This portfolio is indicated in the graph below:

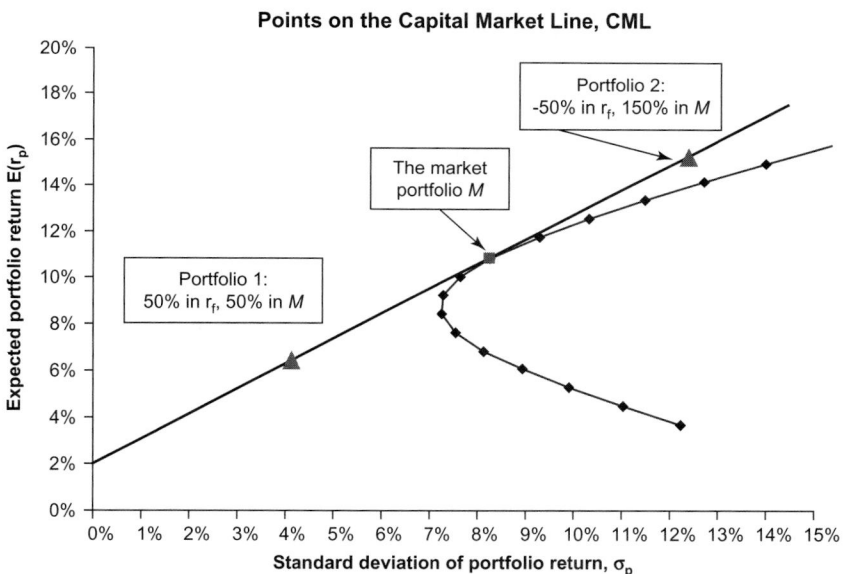

Portfolio 2: Borrowing at the Risk-free Rate r_f to Buy More of the Market Portfolio M

In Portfolio 1 you split your investment of $1,000 between the risk-free asset and the market portfolio M. In Portfolio 2 we investigate an investment strategy in which you borrow money at the risk-free rate and invest *more than $1,000* in the risky portfolio M. You do this by using borrowed funds to increase your investment in M.

As before, you have $1,000 to invest, and as before you choose to invest some of your money in the risk-free asset and the rest in the market portfolio M, composed of 51.81% stock A and 48.19% stock B. However, in Portfolio 2 you choose to *borrow* $500 at the risk-free rate and invest $1,500 in the portfolio of stock A and stock B. As you can see in cells B13 and B14 below, this is a riskier portfolio (it has a standard deviation of 12.40%), but it also has a higher expected return (15.28%):

	A	B	C	D	E
1	**PORTFOLIO ON THE CAPITAL MARKET LINE (CML)**				
2	**The market portfolio, M**	Percent			
3	Stock A	51.81%			
4	Stock B	48.19%			
5	Expected return of market portfolio M	10.85%	<-- =B3*G19+B4*H19		
6	Standard deviation of market portfolio M	8.26%	<-- =SQRT(B3^2*G20+B4^2*H20+2*B3*B4*G22)		
7					
8	**Investor portfolio**				
9	Invested in risk-free	-50%			
10	Invested in market portfolio M	150%			
11					
12	**Portfolio return statistics--point on the CML**				
13	Expected portfolio return	15.28%	<-- =B9*I19+B10*B5		
14	Portfolio standard deviation	12.40%	<-- =B10*B6		

Comparing Portfolio 1 and Portfolio 2

Which portfolio is better—Portfolio 1 or Portfolio 2? Comparing their returns with their standard deviations shows that neither portfolio is better. Portfolio 2 has much higher expected return than Portfolio 1, but it also has higher risk. The choice between the portfolios depends on how much risk the investor is willing to take.

	Expected Return $E(r_p)$	Return Standard Deviation σ_p
Portfolio 1	6.43%	4.13%
Portfolio 2	15.28%	12.40%

All the portfolios on the CML incorporate this choice: Each CML portfolio is a combination of an investment in the risk-free asset r_f and the market portfolio M. Any portfolio on the CML is optimal in the sense that it could possibly be a rational investor's choice of the best investment portfolio. Figure 14.2 shows some other points on the CML and their return/risk trade-off.

The CML: Summing Up

The capital market line (CML) indicates that all optimal investment portfolios should be split between a percentage investment in the risk-free asset and a percentage investment in the market portfolio M. Suppose we denote these percentages by x_M and $x_{r_f} = 1 - x_M$. Then the investor's portfolio will have:

- Expected return $E\left(r_p\right) = x_M E\left(r_M\right) + (1 - x_M)r_f$
- Standard deviation of return $\sigma_p = x_M \sigma_M$

Percentage invested in market portfolio M	$E(r_p) = (\% \ in \ risk\text{-}free) * r_f$ $+ \ (\% \ in \ market) * E(r_M)$	$\sigma_p = (\% \ in \ market) * \sigma_M$
0% (invest all your wealth in risk-free asset r_f)	$E(r_p) = 100\% * r_f = 2\%$	$\sigma_p = 0\% * \sigma_M = 0$
50% (invest 50% of your wealth in market portfolio M and 50% in risk-free asset)	$E(r_p) = 50\% * r_f + 50\% * E(r_M)$ $= 50\% * 2\% + 50\% * 10.85\%$ $= 6.43\%$	$\sigma_p = 50\% * \sigma_M$ $= 50\% * 8.26\% = 4.13\%$
100% (invest all your wealth in market portfolio M)	$E(r_p) = 0\% * r_f + 100\% * E(r_M)$ $= 100\% * 10.85\%$ $= 10.85\%$	$\sigma_p = 100\% * \sigma_M$ $= 100\% * 8.26\% = 8.26\%$
125% (borrow 25% of your wealth to increase investment in risky assets M)	$E(r_p) = -25\% * r_f + 125\% * E(r_M)$ $= -25\% * 2\% + 125\% * 10.85\%$ $= -0.5\% + 13.57\% = 13.06\%$	$\sigma_p = 125\% * \sigma_M$ $= 125\% * 8.26\% = 10.33\%$
150% (borrow 50% of your wealth to increase investment in risky assets M)	$E(r_p) = -50\% * r_f + 150\% * E(r_M)$ $= -50\% * 1\% + 150\% * 10.85\%$ $= -1\% + 16.28\% = 15.28\%$	$\sigma_p = 150\% * \sigma_M$ $= 150\% * 8.26\% = 12.39\%$
200% (borrow 100% of your wealth to increase investment in risky assets M)	$E(r_p) = -100\% * r_f + 200\% * E(r_M)$ $= -100\% * 2\% + 200\% * 10.85\%$ $= -2\% + 21.70\% = 19.70\%$	$\sigma_p = 200\% * \sigma_M$ $= 200\% * 8.26\% = 16.52\%$

Figure 14.2 Portfolio proportions and investment returns on the CML, for different combinations of an investment in the risk-free asset and the market portfolio M. As the proportion in the risk-free asset decreases, the proportion invested in the market portfolio M increases. Increasing the proportion invested in M increases the portfolio's expected return $E(r_p)$ but also increases the portfolio's risk σ_p. The calculations assume that $E(r_M) = 10.85\%$, $r_f = 2\%$, and $\sigma_M = 8.26\%$.

Portfolios on the CML are optimal in the sense that investors cannot find investment combinations that have a higher portfolio return $E(r_p)$ given the portfolio risk σ_p.

14.4 The Sharpe Ratio and the Market Portfolio M (Advanced Topic)

In this section we show how to compute the market portfolio M. In the process we introduce a concept called the *Sharpe ratio*—this is one of the standard *return/risk* measures used in capital markets. As you'll see, the portfolio M is the portfolio that maximizes the Sharpe ratio.

To get some intuitions, look at the spreadsheet below. It continues our example of stocks A and B and the risk-free rate of 2%. In cells B9 and B10 we're looking at a portfolio invested 30% in stock A and 70% in stock B. The expected return of this portfolio is 12.60% and its standard deviation is 10.32% (cells B12 and B13):

	A	B	C	D	E
1	PORTFOLIO RETURNS WITH A RISK-FREE ASSET THE SHARPE RATIO				
2		Stock A	Stock B	Risk-free r_f	
3	Average return	7.00%	15.00%	2.00%	
4	Variance of return	0.64%	1.96%		
5	Sigma of return	8.00%	14.00%		
6	Covariance of returns	0.0011			
7					
8	**Portfolio return and risk**				
9	Percentage in stock A	30.00%			
10	Percentage in stock B	70.00%			
11					
12	Expected portfolio return	12.60%	<-- =B9*B3+B10*C3		
13	Portfolio standard deviation	10.32%	<-- =SQRT(B9^2*B4+B10^2*C4+2*B9*B10*B6)		
14					
15	Risk premium	10.60%	<-- =B12-D3		
16					
17	Sharpe ratio	1.0271	<-- =(B12-D3)/B13		
18					
19	The Sharpe ratio is [E(r_p) - r_f]/σ_p. It denotes the ratio of portfolio *risk premium* to portfolio *risk*.				

The portfolio's *risk premium* (sometimes called the portfolio *excess return*) is defined as the difference between its expected return and the return of the risk-free asset:

$$portfolio\ risk\ premium = portfolio\ expected\ return - risk\text{-}free\ rate$$
$$= E(r_p) - r_f$$
$$= 12.60\% - 2.00\% = 10.60\%$$

The ratio of this risk premium to the portfolio's standard deviation is called the *Sharpe ratio:*

$$Sharpe\ ratio = \frac{E(r_p) - r_f}{\sigma_p}$$
$$= \frac{12.60\% - 2.00\%}{10.32\%} = 1.0271$$

The Sharpe ratio (named after William Sharpe, one of the developers of modern portfolio theory and winner of the Nobel prize in economics in 1990) is a "return/risk" ratio: The numerator is the extra return (over the risk-free rate) you get from your portfolio, and the denominator is the cost of this extra return—its standard deviation.

If you play a bit with the spreadsheet, you'll see that there are other portfolios with higher Sharpe ratios. Here's an example:

	A	B	C	D	E
8	**Portfolio return and risk**				
9	Percentage in stock A	40.00%			
10	Percentage in stock B	60.00%			
11					
12	Expected portfolio return	11.80%	<-- =B9*B3+B10*C3		
13	Portfolio standard deviation	9.28%	<-- =SQRT(B9^2*B4+B10^2*C4+2*B9*B10*B6)		
14					
15	Risk premium	9.80%	<-- =B12-D3		
16					
17	Sharpe ratio	1.0557	<-- =(B12-D3)/B13		

Calculating the Market Portfolio *M*—The Portfolio With the *Highest Attainable* Sharpe Ratio

We can use Excel's **Solver** (see Chapter 32) to calculate the portfolio that gives the highest Sharpe ratio. This portfolio is the *market portfolio M*.

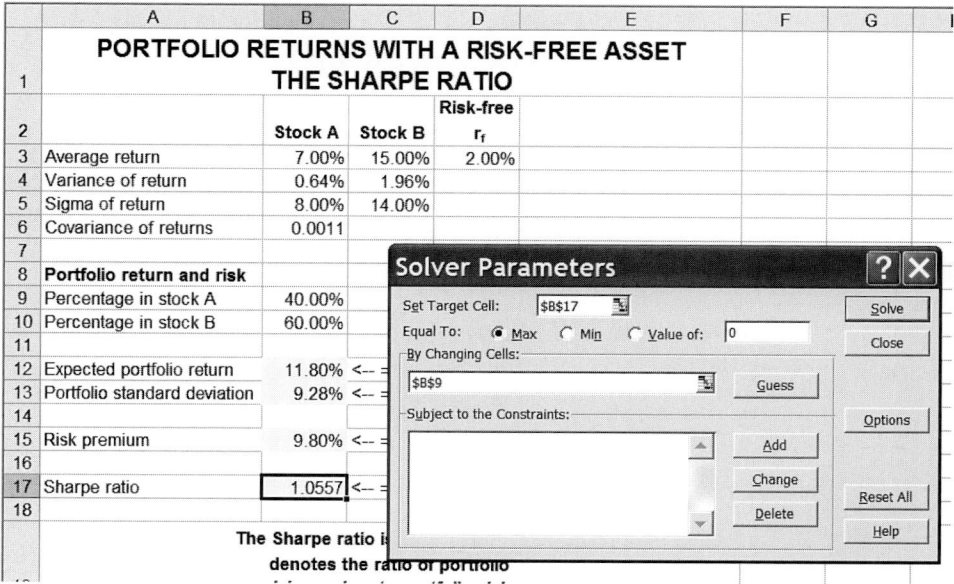

Pressing **Solve** yields the answer:

	A	B	C	D	E
1	PORTFOLIO RETURNS WITH A RISK-FREE ASSET THE SHARPE RATIO				
2		Stock A	Stock B	Risk-free r_f	
3	Average return	7.00%	15.00%	2.00%	
4	Variance of return	0.64%	1.96%		
5	Sigma of return	8.00%	14.00%		
6	Covariance of returns	0.0011			
7					
8	**Portfolio return and risk**				
9	Percentage in stock A	51.81%			
10	Percentage in stock B	48.19%			
11					
12	Expected portfolio return	10.85%	<-- =B9*B3+B10*C3		
13	Portfolio standard deviation	8.26%	<-- =SQRT(B9^2*B4+B10^2*C4+2*B9*B10*B6)		
14					
15	Risk premium	8.85%	<-- =B12-D3		
16					
17	Sharpe ratio	1.0716	<-- =(B12-D3)/B13		

From now on, we'll denote the portfolio with the maximum Sharpe ratio by *M*:

Given a risk-free asset and a set of risky assets (in the current example there are only two such assets), the market portfolio *M* is the portfolio that maximizes the Sharpe ratio: $[E(r_M) - r_f]/\sigma_M$. The portfolio *M* is the best combination of risky assets available to the investor.

14.5 The Security Market Line (SML)

The capital market line shows investors the return/risk relation for their optimal portfolios. The risk/return relation for individual assets is described by a line called the *security market line* (SML). The SML states that the expected return of an asset or portfolio is determined by the asset's risk (called β), the risk-free rate, and the portfolio that maximizes the Sharpe ratio.

Summing Up the SML First

The SML says that *the expected return of any asset i is related to the risk-free rate and the market risk-premium through the following relation:*

$$E(r_i) = r_f \; + \; \frac{Cov(r_i, r_M)}{Var(r_M)} * [E(r_M) - r_f]$$

$$\uparrow \qquad\qquad\qquad \uparrow \qquad\qquad\qquad \uparrow$$

Risk-free rate β_i $E(r_M)$ is the return on the portfolio that maximizes the Sharpe ratio

Note that in the above equation "asset i" (represented by the letter "i") can be a lot of things:

- Asset i can be just *one* risky asset. $E(r_i)$ can stand for the return of stock A or $E(r_i)$ can stand for the return of stock B.
- Asset i can be the combination of two risky assets. $E(r_i)$ can stand for the return of a portfolio such as 60% in stock A and 40% in stock B.
- Asset i can be a combination of the risk-free asset and the two stocks; for example, 25% in the risk-free, 30% in stock A, and 45% in stock B is a portfolio.

In short, the SML defines the risk/return relation *for all assets in the market*. The SML is an important tool in investment management, and in the next two chapters we examine the uses of the SML for evaluating the performance of portfolio managers (Chapter 15) and for computing the cost of capital for a firm (Chapter 16). In this section we illustrate why the SML holds.

In order to illustrate the SML, we use a few examples.

Example 1: The SML Works When Asset i Is Only Stock A

Lines 3–14 of the spreadsheet below repeat facts we've already given. In row 24 we compute the covariance between asset i (in this case stock A) and the market portfolio M. We use a general fact about covariance: Suppose that i is composed of a percentage x_{iA} of stock A and a percentage $1 - x_{iA}$ of stock B, and suppose that the market portfolio is composed of a percentage x_{MA} of stock A and a percentage $1 - x_{MA}$ of stock B. Then the covariance between r_i and r_M is

$$Cov(r_i, r_M) = Cov(x_{iA}r_A + x_{iB}r_B, x_{MA}r_A + x_{MB}r_B)$$
$$= x_{iA}x_{MA}Var(r_A) + x_{iB}x_{MB}Var(r_B) + (x_{iA}x_{MB} + x_{iB}x_{MA}) * Cov(r_A, r_B)$$

Now suppose that $x = 1$, so that i refers to stock A.

- Cell B22 indicates that $E(r_i) = 7.00\%$. This is the left-hand side of the SML.
- Cell B24 shows that $Cov(r_i, r_M) = 0.0039$.
- In cell B25 we divide $Cov(r_i, r_M)$ by $Var(r_M)$ to get

$$\beta_i = \frac{Cov(r_i, r_M)}{Var(r_M)} = 0.5647$$

- Cell B26 shows that $r_f + \beta_i * \left[E(r_M) - r_f\right] = 2\% + 0.5647 * [10.85\% - 2\%] = 7.00\%$.

The equality between cells B22 and B26 shows that the SML works for the case where i is only stock A.

	A	B	C	D	E
1	THE SECURITY MARKET LINE (SML) ILLUSTRATION				
2		Stock A	Stock B	Risk-free r_f	
3	Average return	7.00%	15.00%	2.00%	
4	Variance of return	0.0064	0.0196		
5	Sigma of return	8.00%	14.00%		
6	Covariance of returns	0.0011			
7					
8	**Market portfolio M--this is the portfolio that maximizes the Sharpe ratio**				
9	Proportion of stock A, x_{MA}	51.81%			
10	Proportion of stock B, x_{MB} = 1- x_{MA}	48.19%	<-- =1-B9		
11					
12	Expected market portfolio return, E(r_M)	10.85%	<-- =B9*B3+B10*C3		
13	Market portfolio return variance, σ^2_M=Var(r_M)	0.0068	<-- =B9^2*B4+B10^2*C4+2*B9*B10*B6		
14	Market portfolio standard deviation σ_M=standard deviation(r_M)	8.26%	<-- =SQRT(B13)		
15					
16	Market excess return E(r_M)-r_f	8.85%	<-- =B12-D3		
17					
18	**"Proof" of SML: E(r_i) = r_f + β_i *[E(r_M) - r_f]**				
19	Asset i				
20	Percentage in stock A, x_{iA}	100.00%			
21	Percentage in stock B, x_{iB} = 1- x_{iA}	0.00%	<-- =1-B20		
22	Expected portfolio return E(r_i)=x_{iA}*E(r_A)+x_{iB}*E(r_B) SML, left-hand side	7.00%	<-- =B20*B3+B21*C3		
23					
24	Cov(r_i,r_M)	0.0039	<-- =B20*B9*B4+B21*B10*C4+(B20*B10+B21*B9)*B6		
25	Beta β_i	0.5647	<-- =B24/B13		
26	r_f+β_i *[E(r_M)-r_f] SML,right-hand side	7.00%	<-- =D3+B25*B16		

Though computed in different ways, cells B22 and B26 give the same result. This is the SML:

$$E(r_A) = r_f + \underbrace{\beta_A}_{\frac{Cov(r_A,r_M)}{Var(r_M)}} * [E(r_M) - r_f]$$

$$\underbrace{7\%}_{\substack{\text{SML,} \\ \text{left-hand} \\ \text{side} \\ \text{cell B22}}} = \underbrace{2\% + 0.5647 * [12\% - 2\%]}_{\substack{\text{SML,} \\ \text{right-hand side} \\ \text{cell B26}}}$$

Example 2: The SML Works for a Portfolio Composed Only of Stock B

We can repeat the calculations for the case where "i" is stock B. As you can see in cell B25 below, stock B has β_B = 1.4681. The equality of cells B22 and B26 means that the SML also works for stock B:

$$E(r_B) = r_f + \underbrace{\beta_B}_{\frac{Cov(r_A, r_M)}{Var(r_M)}} * [E(r_M) - r_f]$$

$$\underbrace{15\%}_{\substack{\text{SML,} \\ \text{left-hand} \\ \text{side} \\ \text{cell B22}}} = \underbrace{2\% + 1.4681 * [12\% - 2\%]}_{\substack{\text{SML,} \\ \text{right-hand side} \\ \text{cell B26}}}$$

	A	B	C	D	E
18	"Proof" of SML: E(r_i) = r_f + β_i *[E(r_M) - r_f]				
19	Asset i				
20	Percentage in stock A, x_{iA}	0.00%			
21	Percentage in stock B, x_{iB}	100.00%			
22	Expected portfolio return E(r_i)=x_{iA}*E(r_A)+x_{iB}*E(r_B) SML, left-hand side	15.00%	<-- =B20*B3+B21*C3		
23					
24	Cov(r_i,r_M)	0.0100	<-- =B20*B9*B4+B21*B10*C4+(B20*B10+B21*B9)*B6		
25	Beta β_i	1.4681	<-- =B24/B13		
26	r_f+β_i*[E(r_M)-r_f] SML,right-hand side	15.00%	<-- =D3+B25*B16		

Example 3: The SML Works for Portfolios

In this section asset *i* is a portfolio composed of 80% stock A and 20% stock B. As in the previous examples, the equality between cells B22 and B26 means that the SML correctly describes the return/risk relation for the asset:

	A	B	C	D	E
18	"Proof" of SML: E(r_i) = r_f + β_i *[E(r_M) - r_f]				
19	Asset i				
20	Percentage in stock A, x_{iA}	80.00%			
21	Percentage in stock B, x_{iB}	20.00%			
22	Expected portfolio return E(r_i)=x_{iA}*E(r_A)+x_{iB}*E(r_B) SML, left-hand side	8.60%	<-- =B20*B3+B21*C3		
23					
24	Cov(r_i,r_M)	0.0051	<-- =B20*B9*B4+B21*B10*C4+(B20*B10+B21*B9)*B6		
25	Beta β_i	0.7453	<-- =B24/B13		
26	r_f+β_i*[E(r_M)-r_f] SML,right-hand side	8.60%	<-- =D3+B25*B16		

Betas Add Up

Another way to have done the previous calculation is to use the *portfolio beta*:

The portfolio beta is the weighted average of the individual betas, $\beta_p = x_A \beta_A + x_B \beta_B$.

For example, suppose we want to know the expected return from a portfolio invested 80% in stock A and 20% in stock B. This portfolio will have a β_p of

$$\beta_p = x_A \beta_A + x_B \beta_B = 0.8 * 0.5647 + 0.2 * 1.4681 = 0.7453$$

Consequently, its expected return should be determined by the SML using the β_p:

	A	B	C
1	**BETAS ADD UP**		
2	β_A	0.5647	
3	β_B	1.4681	
4			
5	Expected return of market, $E(r_M)$	10.85%	
6	Risk-free rate, r_f	2.00%	
7			
8	**Portfolio composition**		
9	Percentage A	80%	
10	Percentage B	20%	
11	Portfolio beta, β_p	0.7453	<-- =B9*B2+B10*B3
12			
13	**Portfolio expected return, using SML = $r_f + \beta_p * [E(r_m)-r_f]$**	8.60%	<-- =B6+B11*(B5-B6)

CONCLUSION

The capital asset pricing model (CAPM) is a model of portfolio formation and asset pricing. The model shows:

- How the expected return and standard deviation of portfolios are affected by the portfolio composition.
- How the addition of a risk-free asset to the choices available to investors changes their risk–return opportunity set.
- How to compute the *market portfolio M*. This is the portfolio that maximizes the Sharpe ratio: $[E(r_p) - r_f]/\sigma_p$.
- How to choose an *optimal portfolio* when you can invest in risky and risk-free assets. This is the *capital market line* (CML), which states that all optimal portfolios are combinations of the risk-free asset and the market portfolio.
- How to compute the *beta* for a stock or portfolio. Beta (β) is a *risk measure* for an asset. For a portfolio p, β_p is defined as $\beta_p = Cov(r_p, r_M)/Var(r_M)$. (Recall that "portfolio" includes the case of individual assets.)
- How the *expected return of any portfolio* is related to the risk-free rate and the portfolio's beta. This is the *security market line* (SML):

$$E(r_i) = r_f + \beta_i [E(r_m) - r_f]$$

In succeeding chapters we explore the implications of this model, using it to examine the performance of portfolio managers and to calculate a firm's cost of capital.

EXERCISES

1. Walking down the street of Spartanburg (your hometown), you encounter two street hustlers. John, the first hustler, is running a coin-toss game, which works like this: You pay John $0.80. He flips a coin. If the coin comes up heads, he pays you $2, and if the coin comes up tails, you pay him $1.

   (a)   What is your expected return from this game?

   (b)   What is the standard deviation of your return from playing this game?

2. Still in Spartanburg, you encounter a street hustler named Mary. Her game is more complicated: After you pay Mary $0.80, she throws a die. If the die comes up "1," you pay Mary $2. If it comes up "2," you pay nothing and win nothing. If it comes up "3, 4, 5, 6," Mary pays you $2.

Mary's Die Toss Game

Event	Probability	Winnings
1	0.1667	−2
2	0.1667	0
3	0.1667	2
4	0.1667	2
5	0.1667	2
6	0.1667	2

Picture downloaded from http://www.turbosquid.com

   (a)   What are the expected returns from playing this game?

   (b)   What is the standard deviation of the returns?

   (c)   Which game is riskier—Mary's die throw or John's coin toss (previous exercise)?

   (d)   Which game would you prefer to play? Why?

3. What do Exercises 1 and 2 have to do with investing in stocks?

4. Consider a stock with an expected return of 13% and standard deviation of return of 15%, and a risk-free asset with return of 1%. What will be the average return and standard deviation of a portfolio composed of 20% the risk-free asset and 80% stock?

5. You're considering investing in a combination of a stock and a risk-free asset. The stock has an expected return of 17% and standard deviation of return of 11%, and the risk-free asset has a return of 3%.

   (a)   Complete the table below, and graph the expected portfolio return as a function of the portfolio standard deviation.

   (b)   Suppose you're investing $1,000. What is the meaning of a portfolio invested 150% in the risky asset?

Note: Data for these exercises can be found on the disk that accompanies this book.

	A	B	C
1	Expected stock return	17%	
2	Stock standard deviation	11%	
3	Risk-free rate	3%	
4			
5			
6	Proportion of stock in portfolio	Portfolio standard deviation	Portfolio expected return
7	0%		
8	10%		
9	20%		
10	30%		
11	40%		
12	50%		
13	60%		
14	70%		
15	80%		
16	90%		
17	100%		
18	110%		
19	120%		
20	130%		
21	140%		
22	150%		

6. Consider the following data of X and Y stocks and a risk-free asset:

	A	B	C
1	**RETURNS OF X AND Y STOCKS**		
2		X	Y
3	Average return	19.00%	13.00%
4	Variance	0.09	0.015
5	covariance of return	0.01	
6			
7	Risk-free return	3.00%	

(a) What is the return and standard deviation of the minimum variance portfolio of X and Y stocks?

(b) What is the return and standard deviation of a portfolio composed of 30% minimum variance portfolio and 70% risk-free asset? Repeat this question with weights of 50% each for the risk-free asset and the minimum variance portfolio.

(c) Mary Jones asks you to create a portfolio composed of the risk-free asset and the minimum variance portfolio. Mary wants an expected return of 9%. What will be the percentage of the portfolio invested in the risk-free asset and in the minimum variance portfolio?

(d) Keith Benforth wants a portfolio composed of the risk-free asset and the minimum variance portfolio. Find a portfolio for Keith that has a standard deviation of returns of 5%.

7. What is the Sharpe ratio of the minimum variance portfolio of Exercise 6? Show another portfolio composed of stocks X and Y that has a better Sharpe ratio.

8. Compute the Sharpe ratio for the following portfolios, assuming the risk-free asset is 4%. What is the best portfolio according to Sharpe ratio?

	A	B	C
1	**Portfolio statistics**		
2		**Average return**	**Return standard deviation**
3	**Portfolio 1**	19.00%	9.00%
4	**Portfolio 2**	13.00%	1.50%
5	**Portfolio 3**	25.00%	10.00%
6	**Portfolio 4**	32.00%	15.00%
7	**Portfolio 5**	14.00%	2.10%
8	**Portfolio 6**	22.00%	3.20%
9	**Portfolio 7**	17.00%	5.50%
10	**Portfolio 8**	12.00%	0.96%
11	**Portfolio 9**	40.00%	20.00%
12	**Portfolio 10**	23.00%	23.00%
13			
14	**Risk-free return**	4.00%	

9. Below are given the end-year prices of the shares of IBM and Coca-Cola. Answer the following questions:

   (a) For the years 1991–2002, calculate the following statistics for the two shares: annual return, average return for the entire period, variance and standard deviation of returns, covariance of returns, and correlation coefficient.

   (b) Calculate the returns and standard deviations for portfolios composed of these two stocks.

   (c) Find the market portfolio using the Sharpe ratio, assuming the risk-free asset return is 5%. Is it the minimum variance portfolio? If not, calculate the Sharpe ratio of the minimum variance portfolio as well.

	A	B	C
1	**Prices of IBM and Coca-Cola Stock**		
2	**Date**	**Coke**	**IBM**
3	31-Dec-90	13.43	28.02
4	31-Dec-91	14.91	22.07
5	31-Dec-92	14.11	12.5
6	31-Dec-93	29.23	14.01
7	30-Dec-94	22.01	18.23
8	29-Dec-95	30	22.66
9	31-Dec-96	42.65	37.58
10	31-Dec-97	61.61	51.9
11	31-Dec-98	52.17	91.47
12	31-Dec-99	43.78	107.03
13	29-Dec-00	35.84	84.34
14	31-Dec-01	36.75	120.02
15	31-Dec-02	63.94	77.21

10. In the Golkoland stock market there are only two listed stocks, Xirkind and Yirkind. The risk-free rate of return in Golkoland is 5% and the portfolio of Xirkind and Yirkind stocks which has the

highest Sharpe ratio is given below:

	A	B	C
2		**Xirkind**	**Yirkind**
3	Average return	19.84%	15.38%
4	Variance of returns	0.1575	0.1378
5	Standard deviation	39.68%	37.12%
6	Covariance of returns	-1.10%	
7	Correlation	-7.47%	
8	Risk-free return	5.00%	
9			
10	**Highest Sharpe ratio**		
11	Weight of Xirkind	0.546	
12	Weight of Yirkind	0.454	
13			
14	Portfolio return	17.81%	
15	Portfolio variance	6.99%	
16	Portfolio standard deviation	26.43%	
17	Sharpe ratio	0.485	

(a) What is the market portfolio, M, in Golkoland?

(b) What is the equation of the capital market line (CML) in Golkoland?

(c) What does the CML mean and why are we interested in it?

(d) What is the expected return and standard deviation of a portfolio composed of 30% risk-free asset and 70% market portfolio?

(e) Suppose an investor wants the same return as the above portfolio, but invests only in a portfolio composed of Xirkind and Yirkind stocks. What will be the standard deviation of the returns of his portfolio? How do you explain the difference in standard deviations between this question and question 10(d)?[5]

11. Some data for the market portfolio and the risk-free rate of return on the Tierra del Fuego stock market is given below.

(a) What is the equation of the Tierra del Fuego CML?

(b) Compute the following CML portfolios:

- A portfolio composed of 35% risk-free asset and 65% market portfolio
- A portfolio composed of 120% market portfolio
- A portfolio that yields a return of 15%
- A portfolio that yields a return of 23%
- A portfolio with standard deviation of 35%
- A portfolio with standard deviation of 5%

12. Find the equation of the capital market line (CML) for a stock market that has only two stocks:

	A	B	C
1	**RETURN STATISTICS OF A AND Z STOCKS**		
2		**A**	**Z**
3	Average return	31.00%	15.00%
4	Variance	0.3	0.08
5	Covariance of returns	-0.05	
6			
7	Risk-free return	5.00%	

---

[5]Remember our hint from Chapter 13: Use the word "risk" in your explanation, even if you don't have the vaguest idea what you're doing.

13. Will the market portfolio of Exercise 12 change if the risk-free asset return is 3%? If yes, explain why and calculate the new market portfolio. Answer this question again assuming the market portfolio is 0%.

14. Below are given the return statistics of X and Y stocks (of Exercise 4):

	A	B	C
1	**RETURN STATISTICS OF X AND Y STOCKS**		
2		**X**	**Y**
3	Average return	19.00%	13.00%
4	Variance	0.09	0.015
5	Covariance of returns	0.01	
6			
7	Risk-free return	3.00%	

(a) Calculate the CML line using this data.

(b) Find the difference in standard deviation between a portfolio on the CML and a portfolio on the efficient frontier, both with average return of 19%. What will be the weight of the risk-free asset in the CML portfolio?

15. (Challenge exercise) The Northern Peninsula stock market has only two listed stocks, Big Mining and Shallow Mining. The market portfolio is composed of 40% Big Mining and 60% Shallow Mining. Using the data below, find the β of each of the two stocks.

	A	B	C	D
1	**NORTHERN PENINSULA STOCK MARKET**			
2		**Big Mining**	**Shallow Mining**	
3	Expected return	15%	25%	
4	Return standard deviation	25%	40%	
5	Covariance of returns	0.05		

16. Formula and Dormula are two stocks listed on the Chitango stock market. Their βs are 1.8 and 2.6, respectively. What is the beta of a portfolio invested 20% in Formula and 80% in Dormula?

17. Consider the following data: $E(r_m) = 0.18$, $\beta_i = 1.05$, and $R_f = 0.07$. What is the expected return of stock i?

18. Consider the following data: $E(r_m) = 0.22$, $E(r_i) = 0.33$, and $R_f = 0.09$. What is the β of stock i?

19. Consider the following data: $E(r_m) = 0.25$, $\beta_i = 0.85$, and $E(r_i) = 0.22$. What is the return of the risk-free asset?

20. Consider the following data: $E(r_m) = 0.2$, $Cov(r_i, r_m) = 0.1$, $r_f = 0.06$, and $\sigma_M^2 = 0.15$. What is the expected return of stock i?

21. Consider the following data: $E(r_i) = 0.15$, $Cov(r_i, r_m) = 0.067$, $r_f = 0.02$, and $\sigma_M^2 = 0.089$. What is the market return?

22. Consider the following data: $E(r_m) = 0.22$, $Cov(r_i, r_m) = 0.27$, $E(r_i) = 0.14$, and $\sigma_M^2 = 0.09$. What is the return of the risk-free asset?

23. Suppose that there are only two stocks, Company A and Company B. The relevant statistics for the portfolio are given below:

	A	B	C	D
1		**Company A**	**Company B**	
2	Expected return	8.00%	25.00%	
3	Variance of return	0.0200	0.0900	
4	Standard deviation of return	14.14%	30.00%	<-- =SQRT(C3)
5				
6	Covariance of returns	-0.03500		
7	Correlation of returns	-0.82496	<-- =B6/(B4*C4)	
8				
9	Portfolio proportions			
10	Company A	80%		
11	Company B	20%		
12				
13	Portfolio expected return	11.400%	<-- =B10*B2+B11*C2	
14	Portfolio variance	0.0052	<-- =B10^2*B3+B11^2*C3+2*B10*B11*B6	
15	Portfolio standard deviation	7.21%	<-- =SQRT(B14)	

(a) Show that a portfolio invested 40% in Company A and 60% in Company B is not optimal by showing a better portfolio.

(b) Calculate the minimum variance portfolio for the portfolio composed of the two assets described above.

24. Using the data provided in Exercise 23, calculate the market portfolio M, when the risk-free rate of return is 8%. (Recall that the M portfolio maximizes the Sharpe ratio.)

25. On the occasion of your birthday, your wealthy Aunt Hilda sends you a check for $5,000, under the express condition that you invest the money in either (or all) of the following: Government Bonds, Hilda's Hybrids, Inc., and/or Hilda's Hubby, Inc. The relevant statistics on each of these investments are provided below.

	A	B	C	D
1		**Hilda's Hybrids**	**Hilda's Hubby**	**Government bond**
2	Expected return	30.00%	16.25%	10.00%
3	Variance	28.58%	2.30%	
4	Sigma	53.46%	15.17%	
5				
6	Covariance of returns	0.0343		
7	Correlation of returns	0.4224	<-- =B6/(B4*C4)	

(a) Show the capital market line, that is, all the combinations of investment in the risk-free asset and the two companies. Provide results in both chart and graph form. Assume that the market portfolio M is composed of equal proportions of the two risky assets.

(b) Suppose you decide to invest in the following proportions: 40% government bonds and 60% in the M portfolio. Calculate the expected return and variance of returns for this portfolio.

26. With reference to Exercise 25, you are feeling lucky and decide to take on a riskier portfolio. In particular, in addition to your $5,000 gift, you are able to borrow another $1,000 at the risk-free rate of 10%. You decide to invest this total of $6,000 in a portfolio containing a mix of Hilda's Hybrids and Hilda's Hubby.

(a) In what proportion will you invest your $6,000 if your objective is to create the "best combination" of these risky assets?

(b) What will be the expected return and the expected risk for this more daring portfolio?

27. (a)   Consider the data below. Compute the expected return and standard deviation of returns for a portfolio composed of 75% stock A and 25% stock B.

	Asset A	Asset B
Mean return	30%	13%
Return sigma σ	40%	10%
Correlation ρ_{AB}	0.5	

(b)   Stock C has a β_C of 1.3 and a portfolio P of 75% C and 25% D has a $\beta_P = 1.8$. What is the β of stock D?

28. You have $1,000 to invest. The risk-free rate is $r_f = 6\%$. The market portfolio has expected return $E(r_M) = 15\%$ and $\sigma_M = 20\%$.

(a)   What are the mean and standard deviation of your investment if you invest $500 in the risk-free asset and $500 in the market portfolio?

(b)   Your sister also has $1,000 to invest but wants to borrow another $1,000 in order to make an investment of $2,000 in the market portfolio M. What will be the mean and standard deviation of her portfolio return?

(c)   Which portfolio is better, yours or your sister's?

29. The table below provides the annual rates of return on ABC Corp., XYZ Corp. and the market portfolio M.

	A	B	C	D
		Market	ABC	XYZ
3	Year	Portfolio	Corp.	Corp.
4	1	11.90%	14.40%	121.20%
5	2	0.40%	-22.20%	-33.90%
6	3	26.90%	47.50%	3.70%
7	4	-8.60%	7.70%	3.10%
8	5	22.80%	42.80%	17.20%
9	6	16.50%	30.70%	-16.90%
10	7	12.50%	11.40%	-32.80%
11	8	-10.06%	-32.50%	-30.40%
12	9	23.90%	30.50%	114.00%
13	10	11.10%	1.80%	-3.70%
14	11	-8.50%	-6.20%	-33.00%
15	12	3.90%	22.30%	-33.20%
16	13	14.30%	4.30%	21.60%
17	14	19.10%	6.50%	17.80%
18	15	-14.70%	-37.80%	7.50%
19	16	-26.50%	-27.60%	-62.30%
20	17	37.30%	97.10%	65.40%
21	18	23.80%	45.85%	-28.02%
22	19	-7.15%	-11.25%	-6.33%
23	20	12.16%	-4.70%	26.67%

(a)   Calculate the β_{XYZ} and the β_{ABC}. Use the formulas:

$$\beta_{ABC} = \frac{Covariance(ABC\ returns,\ market\ returns)}{Variance(market\ returns)}$$

$$\beta_{XYZ} = \frac{Covariance(XYZ\ returns,\ market\ returns)}{Variance(market\ returns)}$$

(b)   Which company's returns is better explained by the market's returns? Explain by regressing each company's returns on the market returns (see Chapter 12).

30. Anders Smith proposes to invest in a portfolio of two stocks, X and Y. Information about the two stocks is given below.

	A	B	C
2		**Stock X**	**Stock Y**
3	Expected return	20%	14%
4	Sigma of return	25%	15%
5	Correlation	0.4	
6			
7	**General X-Y portfolio**		
8	**Percentage of X**	**Sigma**	**Mean**
9	0%		
10	10%		
11	20%		
12	30%		
13	40%		
14	50%		
15	60%		
16	70%		
17	80%		
18	90%		
19	100%		

(a)   Fill in the highlighted box and compute the mean and standard deviation of each of the indicated portfolios.

(b)   Plot the portfolios on a mean–standard deviation plot.

(c)   Suppose that Mr. Smith can also borrow and lend at an interest rate of 6%. Discuss how this alters his investment opportunities. Calculate the portfolio M that maximizes the Sharpe ratio and discuss briefly why Smith will always invest in this portfolio.

31. Assume that there are only three stocks in the market, and that the optimal investment proportions in each stock A, B, and C is 1/3. Also assume that variance of stock A is 10%, the variance of stock B is 8%, and the variance of stock C is 20%. The covariance between stocks A and B is 0.08, the covariance between stocks B and C is −0.10, and the covariance between stocks A and C is 0.04.

(a)   Calculate the covariance between each stock and the market portfolio.

(b)   Calculate the systematic risk (beta) for each of the three stocks.

APPENDIX 14.1: THE CAPM WITH THREE OR MORE ASSETS[6]

This appendix generalizes the CAPM and SML discussion in this chapter. The first part of the appendix discusses portfolios of three assets. It will then be clear how to apply this to portfolios of more than three assets. This appendix is meant to confirm that all of the "messages" of Chapter 14 still hold, even if there are more than two risky assets.

---

[6]This appendix relates to Appendix 13.2 of Chapter 13. It can easily be skipped—its purpose is to demonstrate that all of the results of this chapter hold in a more general setting. If you believe this already, go on to the next chapter.

- Calculation of the efficient frontier.
- Calculation of the Sharpe ratio.
- Calculating the *market portfolio*—the portfolio of risky assets for which the Sharpe ratio is maximized. This calculation also requires the risk-free rate r_f.
- Calculating the SML—this is a relation between the *expected return of any asset,* the *risk-free rate* r_f, and the *expected return on the market portfolio* $E(r_M)$:

$$\underbrace{E(r_i)}_{\substack{\text{The expected} \\ \text{return of some} \\ \text{asset } i. \text{ This can} \\ \text{be a single asset} \\ \text{or a portfolio.}}} = r_f + \underbrace{\beta_i}_{\substack{\text{The asset's } beta \\ \text{is defined as} \\ \beta_i = \frac{Cov(r_i, r_M)}{Var(r_M)}}} * \underbrace{[E(r_M) - r_f]}_{\substack{\text{The market} \\ \text{risk premium}}}$$

EXAMPLE

We start by considering a three-asset problem. To describe three assets, we need to know the expected return (or mean return—should standardize on one terminology), the variance, and all the *pairs* of covariances. This data is described below.

	A	B	C	D	E
1	\multicolumn{5}{c|}{**A THREE-ASSET PORTFOLIO PROBLEM**}				
2		**Stock A**	**Stock B**	**Stock C**	
3	Mean	10%	12%	15%	
4	Variance	15%	22%	30%	
5	Risk-free return	6%			
6					
7	Cov(r_A,r_B)	0.03			
8	Cov(r_B,r_C)	-0.01			
9	Cov(r_A,r_C)	0.02			

Suppose we form a portfolio of risky assets composed of proportion x_A in asset A, x_B in asset B, and x_C in asset C. Since the portfolio is fully invested in risky assets, it follows that $x_C = 1 - x_A - x_B$.

Portfolio Return Statistics: The expected return of the portfolio is given by

$$E(r_p) = x_A E(r_A) + x_B E(r_B) + x_C E(r_C)$$

The calculation of the portfolio's variance of return requires both the variances and the covariances:

$$Var(r_p) = x_A^2 Var(r_A) + x_B^2 Var(r_B) + x_C^2 Var(r_C) + 2x_A x_B Cov(r_A, r_B)$$
$$+ 2x_A x_C Cov(r_A, r_C) + 2x_B x_C Cov(r_B, r_C)$$

Here's an example: The portfolio statistics are calculated in cells B17 to B19:

	A	B	C	D	E
1	A THREE-ASSET PORTFOLIO PROBLEM				
2		Stock A	Stock B	Stock C	
3	Mean	10%	12%	15%	
4	Variance	15%	22%	30%	
5	Risk-free return	6%			
6					
7	Cov(r_A,r_B)	0.03			
8	Cov(r_B,r_C)	-0.01			
9	Cov(r_A,r_C)	0.02			
10					
11	Portfolio proportions				
12	x_A	0.6000			
13	x_B	0.3000			
14	x_C	0.1000	<-- =1-B13-B12		
15					
16	Portfolio statistics				
17	Mean	0.1110	<-- =B12*B3+B13*C3+B14*D3		
18	Variance	0.0894	<-- =B12^2*B4+B13^2*C4+B14^2*D4 +2*B12*B13*B7+2*B12*B14*B9+2*B13*B14*B8		
19	Sigma	0.2990	<-- =SQRT(B18)		
20					
21	Sharpe ratio	0.1706	<-- =(B17-B5)/B19		

Cell B21 calculates the Sharpe ratio, $[E(r_p) - r_f]/\sigma_p$, for the particular portfolio. In Section 14.4, we used Excel's **Solver** to find the portfolio with the maximum Sharpe ratio. We repeat this procedure here:

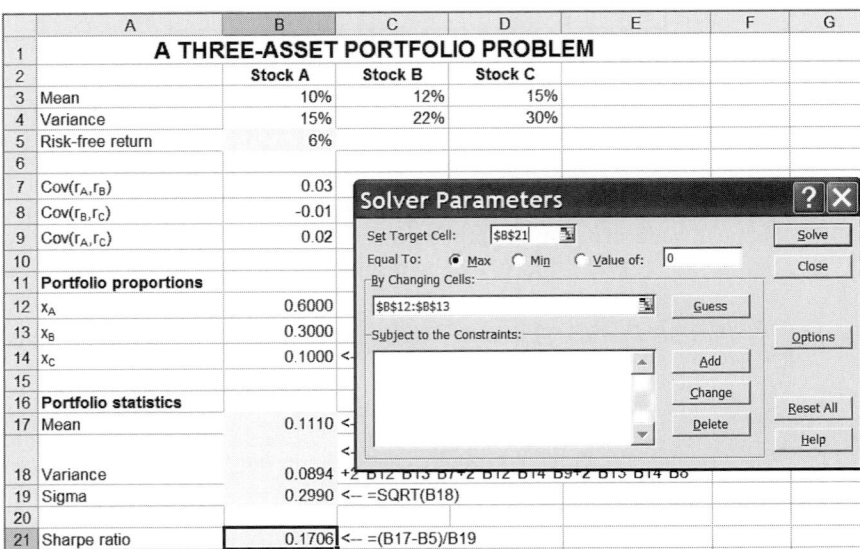

Pressing **Solve** gives the solution—the portfolio that maximizes the Sharpe ratio. Given a risk-free rate $r_f = 6\%$, this portfolio is the market portfolio M.

	A	B	C	D	E
1	\multicolumn{5}{c}{**A THREE-ASSET PORTFOLIO PROBLEM**}				
2		**Stock A**	**Stock B**	**Stock C**	
3	Mean	10%	12%	15%	
4	Variance	15%	22%	30%	
5	Risk-free return	6%			
6					
7	Cov(r_A,r_B)	0.03			
8	Cov(r_B,r_C)	-0.01			
9	Cov(r_A,r_C)	0.02			
10					
11	**Portfolio proportions**				
12	x_A	0.2378			
13	x_B	0.3575			
14	x_C	0.4047	<-- =1-B13-B12		
15					
16	**Portfolio statistics**				
17	Mean	0.1274	<-- =B12*B3+B13*C3+B14*D3		
18	Variance	0.0918	<-- =B12^2*B4+B13^2*C4+B14^2*D4 +2*B12*B13*B7+2*B12*B14*B9+2*B13*B14*B8		
19	Sigma	0.3030	<-- =SQRT(B18)		
20					
21	Sharpe ratio	0.2224	<-- =(B17-B5)/B19		

THE SECURITY MARKET LINE AND β

In Section 14.5 we showed that the asset's β, defined as $\beta_i = Cov(r_i, r_M)/Var(r_M)$, relates the asset's expected return and the risk-free rate:

$$E(r_i) = r_f + \frac{Cov(r_i, r_M)}{Var(r_M)}[E(r_M) - r_f]$$

In the spreadsheet below, you can see that this is also true for our example. You need to know how to compute the covariance for a combination of assets. In the equation below, we compute the covariance between the market portfolio, composed of proportions x_A, x_B, and x_C of stocks A, B, and C and any generic portfolio (here composed of proportions y_A, y_B, and y_C of these same stocks):

$$Cov(r_p, r_M) = x_A y_A \sigma_A^2 + x_B y_B \sigma_B^2 + x_C y_C \sigma_C^2 + \sigma_{AB}(x_A y_B + x_B y_A)$$
$$+ \sigma_{BC}(x_B y_C + x_C y_B) + \sigma_{AC}(x_A y_C + x_C y_A)$$

Now you can implement this, as shown in the spreadsheet:

	A	B	C	D	E	F
1	THE SML WORKS FOR PORTFOLIOS OF THREE ASSETS!					
2		Stock A	Stock B	Stock C		
3	Mean	10%	12%	15%		
4	Variance	15%	22%	30%		
5	Risk-free return	6%				
6						
7	$Cov(r_A,r_B)$	0.03				
8	$Cov(r_B,r_C)$	-0.01				
9	$Cov(r_A,r_C)$	0.02				
10						
11	Portfolio proportions					
12	x_A	0.2378				
13	x_B	0.3575	<-- Now called the Market portfolio			
14	x_C	0.4047				
15						
16	Market portfolio statistics					
17	Mean	12.74%	<-- =B12*$B$3+B13*$C$3+B14*$D$3			
18	Variance	0.0918	<-- =B12^2*B4+B13^2*C4+B14^2*D4 +2*B12*B13*B7+2*B12*B14*B9+2*B13*B14*B8			
19	Sigma	0.3030	<-- =SQRT(B18)			
20						
21	Market risk premium, $E(r_M)-r_f$	0.0674	<-- =B17-B5			
22						
23	"Proof" of SML					
24	Any portfolio, p					
25	y_A	0.3				
26	y_B	0.4				
27	y_C	0.3				
28						
29	Mean, $E(r_p)$	12.30%	<-- =B25*$B$3+B26*$C$3+B27*$D$3			
30	Covariance(p,M)	0.0858	<-- =B12*B25*B4+B13*B26*C4+B14*B27*D4+B7*(B12*B26+B13* B25)+B9*(B12*B27+B14*B25)+B8*(B13*B27+B26*B14)			
31	Portfolio beta, Cov(p,M)/Var(M)	0.9349	<-- =B30/B18			
32						
33	$E(r_p)$ by SML $=r_f+\beta_p*[E(r_M)-r_f]$	12.30%	<-- =B5+B31*B21			
34						
35	When we say that the SML "works," we mean					
36	that the expected portfolio return is					
37	determined by the beta for *any* portfolio.					
38						

In cells B30 and B31, we do the calculation for the β of any arbitrary portfolio. In cell B33 we show that the $r_f + \beta[E(r_M)-r_f]$ calculates the expected return of the portfolio. Here are some other examples, which show that the SML relation always holds:

	A	B
24	Any portfolio, p	
25	y_A	0
26	y_B	1
27	y_C	0
28		
29	Mean, E(r_p)	12.00%
30	Covariance(p,M)	0.0817
31	Portfolio beta, Cov(p,M)/Var(M)	0.8904
32		
33	E(r_p) by SML =r_f+β_p*[E(r_M)-r_f]	12.00%

	A	B
24	Any portfolio, p	
25	y_A	-0.5
26	y_B	1.3
27	y_C	0.2
28		
29	Mean, E(r_p)	13.60%
30	Covariance(p,M)	0.1035
31	Portfolio beta, Cov(p,M)/Var(M)	1.1278
32		
33	E(r_p) by SML =r_f+ β_p*[E(r_M)-r_f]	13.60%

We conclude that:

Given the market portfolio M (defined as the Sharpe ratio maximizing portfolio), then for any other asset or portfolio p, the following relationship holds:

$$E(r_p) = r_f + \frac{Cov(r_p, r_M)}{Var(r_M)} [E(r_M) - r_f]$$
$$\uparrow$$
$$\beta_p$$

PORTFOLIOS WITH MORE THAN THREE ASSETS

We've repeated the calculations of this chapter for a portfolio of three assets. The primary result which we've demonstrated is the SML:

If M maximizes the Sharpe ratio $[E(r_p) - r_f]/\sigma_p$, then for any asset or portfolio, the security market line—which relates the asset's expected return to its risk β—holds:

$$E(r_{asset}) = r_f + \frac{Cov(r_{asset}, r_M)}{Var(r_M)} [E(r_M) - r_f]$$
$$\uparrow$$
$$\beta_{asset}$$

What if there are more than three risky assets? Everything we've said is still true—but unfortunately the computations involved require techniques beyond the scope of this book.[7]

---

[7]*Financial Modeling* by Simon Benninga (MIT Press, 2000) contains details on how to do these calculations for the general case with many assets.

CHAPTER 15

USING THE SECURITY MARKET LINE (SML) TO MEASURE INVESTMENT PERFORMANCE

OVERVIEW

This and the next chapter show how to use the security market line (SML), which was introduced in Chapter 14. This chapter discusses investment performance, and the next chapter discusses the use of the model to measure the cost of capital.

"Investment performance" is finance jargon for the question: "How well did an asset—either a stock or a portfolio—perform?" Often the underlying question is really: "How well did my investment manager (or mutual fund manager) do in managing my money?" To determine the investment performance of an asset, we have to account for the asset's risk. Since we anticipate that riskier assets should have higher returns to compensate for their risk, true investment performance measures should take account of the returns that investors earn *in excess* of the returns warranted by the asset risks.

The security market line (SML) provides us with one of the standard methods of measuring investment performance. By using the SML to measure *risk-adjusted performance,* we can determine whether a particular asset provided performance in excess of its risks (overperformance) or not (underperformance).

In this chapter we show how to use the SML to measure investment performance.

- We show how to compute the β ("beta") of a security by regressing the security's excess returns on those of the market portfolio. We often use the S&P 500 as the "market portfolio." β measures the riskiness of the security.
- We show how to compute the α ("alpha") of a security. α measures the security's risk-adjusted performance.
- We discuss the difference between *nondiversifiable risk* (also called *market risk*) and *diversifiable risk* (also called *idiosyncratic risk*) and show that combining stocks in a portfolio reduces the diversifiable risk.

Finance Concepts Discussed

- Security market line (SML)
- α, β, R^2
- Systematic (nondiversifiable, market) risk
- Nonsystematic (diversifiable) risk
- Performance evaluation

Excel Functions Used

- **Average, Stdevp, Varp, Covar**
- **Intercept, Slope, Rsq**
- **Trendline** (Excel's regression tool)

15.1 Jack and Jill's Investment Argument

To understand the issues behind performance measurement, we start with the story of Jack and Jill. Sometime in August 2003, Jack and Jill were arguing about their investment strategies. They had been together a long time, and like many couples they often had the same argument/ discussion. The one about investment strategies was one they'd replayed many times.

Jill started off. "I invested in the NASDAQ in May 1990," she said to Jack. "If you'd followed my advice and invested in the NASDAQ instead of investing in that stodgy Fidelity Puritan Fund, you'd be a lot better off. For every dollar I put into the NASDAQ, I've now got $3.60, whereas you've only got $2.70 for each dollar you put into Puritan. The NASDAQ simply *out- performs* Puritan."

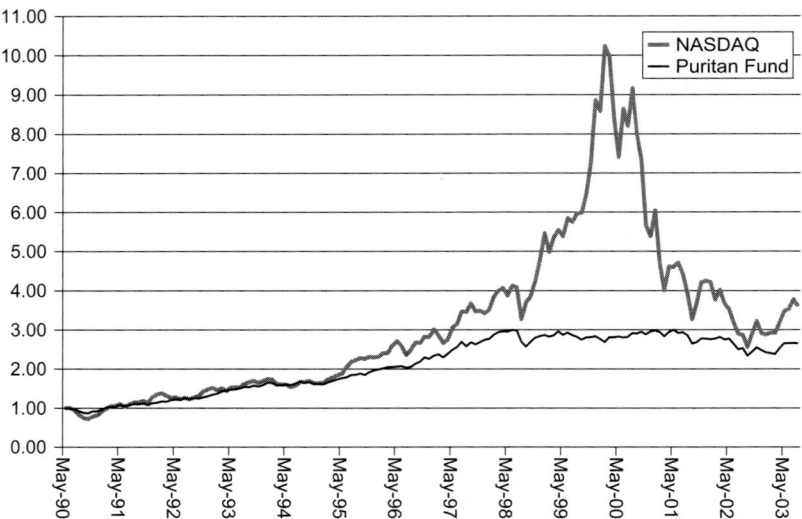

Figure 15.1 The growth of $1 invested in the NASDAQ and the Puritan Fund in the period from May 1990 to August 2003. $1 invested in the NASDAQ grew over the period to $3.60, whereas $1 invested in Fidelity's Puritan Fund grew to $2.70.

This line of argument infuriated Jack. Ever since he'd met Jill in their MBA program at Squash Hill College, she'd insisted—in her typical incautious way—that she was much better with money than he. It risked spoiling their otherwise lovely relationship. She claimed to be able to pick investments that outperform the market, even though she had a difficult time defining this concept.[1]

If you consider the whole period from 1990 to 2003 (Figure 15.1), Jill had indeed done better than Jack. Even though the NASDAQ was subject to bigger fluctuations than Puritan, an investor like Jill who'd stuck with the NASDAQ throughout the period would have been ahead of an investor like Jack who'd stuck with Puritan. An investor who had invested $1 in the NASDAQ in May 1990 would have had $3.60 in August 2003, whereas an investor who had invested $1 in the Puritan Fund in May 1990 would have ended up with $2.70 in August 2003.

But Jack also had a valid point. "Listen, dear," he said snootily to Jill. "Look what a bumpy ride the NASDAQ took you on. Remember how cocky you were in late 1999 and what a bundle of nerves you were in 2001? This overperformance stuff is a crock of spam. He showed Jill the wild gyrations of the NASDAQ between May 1999 and May 2001 (Figure 15.1).

"Also," he reminded her, "the supposed overperformance of the NASDAQ hasn't always held. When we got our bonuses in December 1999, you put yours in the NASDAQ and I—OK, I'm more conservative than you—put mine in Puritan. Then the market took a downward turn and we both lost money, but in the downturn you lost a lot more than I." He showed her Figure 15.2. "For every dollar I put in at the end of 1999, I've now got 94 cents, whereas you've got only 41 cents per dollar."

---

[1]She hadn't read this chapter!

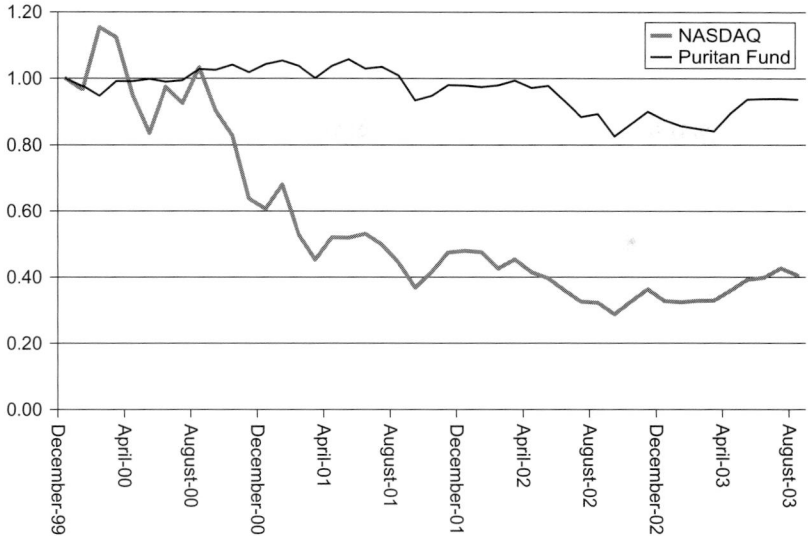

Figure 15.2 The growth of $1 invested in the NASDAQ and the Puritan Fund in the period from December 1999 to August 2003. Actually "growth" is a euphemism—both investments went down over the period. $1 invested in the NASDAQ was worth $0.41 by August 2003, and $1 in the Puritan was worth $0.94.

"What comes down will go up again," said Jill, ever the optimist.[2] "I'll bet you a Philadelphia steak sandwich that sometime in the future I'll be ahead."

"Of course you'll be ahead once in a while—the NASDAQ is riskier than Puritan. It bounces around more, so at some point you're bound to be ahead. But 'slow and steady' is my motto. The Puritan Fund isn't as risky, and since I'm not into risk, I'm happy with its lower return. Remember how Professor Simons at Squash Hill College was always hammering home the relation between risk and return?"

At this point Jill got tired of the argument. Both she and Jack had made their points, and Jill sat back to read that day's *Wall Street Journal*.

The Real Question

Jack and Jill's argument about risk, return, performance, and overperformance is typical of the pointless discussions in which many investors engage. Their discussion is misfocused because they've ignored the risks of their investments. In finance we believe that investment performance is related to the riskiness of the assets invested in—assets that are riskier should, on average, provide greater returns to compensate investors for their risk. Thus, we are not surprised that Jill did better with the NASDAQ (a risky investment) and that Jack had to settle for lower returns with his Puritan Fund (a much less risky asset). The real question is whether the NASDAQ returns were commensurate with the riskiness of the NASDAQ and the Puritan returns were commensurate with the riskiness of Puritan.

So the problem with Jack and Jill's argument is that they're not asking the right question. Let's start with Jill's argument that she's made more money than Jack since 1990. She's right,

---

[2]One of the lessons of market efficiency is that past stock price performance doesn't predict future stock prices. Perhaps Jill should read Chapter 17 in which this is explained.

of course, but a glance at Figure 15.1 will show you that the NASDAQ was much riskier than the Puritan Fund—the variations in returns are much greater for the NASDAQ than for Puritan. If the NASDAQ is riskier, then Jill's greater earnings could just be her reward for undertaking more risk.

The same point can be made about Figure 15.2. If the NASDAQ is riskier than the Puritan Fund, it's not surprising that in periods when the market goes down, the NASDAQ goes down even more. When Jack says that he's done better with the Puritan Fund in a down period, we're also not surprised.

So neither Jack nor Jill is asking the right question: The real question is *whether the NASDAQ performance is commensurate with the NASDAQ risk and whether Puritan Fund performance is commensurate with Puritan Fund risk.* In the language of the CAPM, the question is whether a security has *risk-adjusted underperformance or overperformance.*

This chapter shows you how to answer this question. We use the security market line (SML) to answer questions about performance versus risk. In Section 15.5 we return to Jack and Jill and answer the question about who actually did better.

15.2 Measuring the Investment Performance of General Electric Stock

In this section we illustrate the use of the SML for measuring investment performance by using it to measure the investment performance of General Electric (GE) stock. We show that over the decade 1990–1999, GE stock outperformed the market on a risk-adjusted basis.

We start by summarizing the security market line (SML). The SML shows the relation between an asset's risk and its expected return. An asset's risk is measured by its beta (β), which shows how sensitive the asset's return is to changes in the market return. The higher the asset's β, the higher the return investors expect from the asset.

In equation form the SML states that an asset's expected return $E(r_i)$ is given by

$$E(r_i) = r_f + \beta_i[E(r_M) - r_f]$$
$$\text{where } \beta_i = \frac{Cov(r_i, r_M)}{\sigma_M^2}$$

The letter "i" is used in $E(r_i)$ to indicate that the SML is a risk/return relation for *all* risky assets. Thus, the "i" can stand for any asset, whether a stock, a bond, or a portfolio. In this chapter we use "i" to represent either stocks or mutual funds (large diversified portfolios of stocks or bonds).

The following spreadsheet contains the data necessary to measure the performance of GE:

- Annual return data for the S&P 500 Index (cells B3 to B12) and General Electric (cells C3 to C12) for the ten-year period from 1990 to 1999.[3] The returns include dividends; the annual return in year t is calculated by assuming that the investor bought the stock at the end of year $t - 1$ and held it until the end of year t:

$$return_t = \frac{stockprice_t - stockprice_{t-1} + dividend_t}{stockprice_{t-1}}$$

---

[3]Most of the stock data in this chapter comes from Yahoo; the dividend-adjusted returns for the S&P 500 come from the Vanguard website http://www.vanguard.com.

- Annual risk-free rate data (cells D3 to D12). Because we are looking at annual data, the risk-free rate is taken to be the return on a one-year U.S. Treasury Bill.[4]
- Excess return data. The "excess return" is the difference between the return on the security (be it the S&P 500 or GE) and the risk-free rate for the same period. For example, someone who invested in the S&P 500 Index throughout 1990 would have lost 3.10% on the investment (cell B3); in the same period the investor could have earned 7.92% by holding a riskless U.S. Treasury security. Thus, over this period, the S&P 500 Index returned 11.02% *less* than the risk-free rate. This −11.02% is the *excess return* for the S&P 500 for the period. As you can see in columns F and G of the spreadsheet, 1990 was an exception—during most of this ten-year period both GE and the S&P 500 had hefty positive excess returns. In 1991, for example, the risk-free rate was 6.64%; the S&P 500 had a return of 30.47% (an excess return of 23.83%) and GE stock had a return of 33.34% (excess return of 26.70%).

	A	B	C	D	E	F	G	H
1			GE AND THE S&P500, 1990-1999					
2	Date	S&P 500 returns	GE returns	Risk-free rate		S&P 500 excess returns	GE excess returns	
3	Dec-90	-3.10%	-11.04%	7.92%		-11.02%	-18.96%	<-- =C3-D3
4	Dec-91	30.47%	33.34%	6.64%		23.83%	26.70%	
5	Dec-92	7.62%	11.77%	4.15%		3.47%	7.62%	
6	Dec-93	10.08%	22.67%	3.50%		6.58%	19.17%	
7	Dec-94	1.32%	-2.74%	3.54%		-2.22%	-6.28%	
8	Dec-95	37.58%	41.18%	7.05%		30.53%	34.13%	
9	Dec-96	22.96%	37.33%	5.09%		17.87%	32.24%	
10	Dec-97	33.36%	48.42%	5.61%		27.75%	42.81%	
11	Dec-98	28.58%	39.01%	5.24%		23.34%	33.77%	
12	Dec-99	21.04%	51.72%	4.51%		16.53%	47.21%	
13								
14	Average	18.99%	27.17%	5.33%	<-- =AVERAGE(C3:C12)			
15	Variance	1.80%	4.14%	0.02%	<-- =VARP(C3:C12)			
16	Sigma	13.43%	20.36%	1.42%	<-- =STDEVP(C3:C12)			
17								
18					Alpha	0.0277	<-- =INTERCEPT(G3:G12,F3:F12)	
19								
20					Beta	1.3952	<-- =SLOPE(G3:G12,F3:F12)	
21						1.3952	<-- =COVAR(F3:F12,G3:G12)/VARP(F3:F12)	
22								
23					R-squared	0.8029	<-- =RSQ(G3:G12,F3:F12)	

GE Versus S&P 500--Excess Returns

y = 1.3952x + 0.0277
R² = 0.8029

---

[4]Finance researchers often use monthly or even weekly return data, but annual data is often easier to visualize. When we return to Jack and Jill in Section 15.6, we use monthly data.

During the period 1990–1999 General Electric clearly had higher performance than the S&P 500: The average return on the S&P 500 was 18.99% (cell B14), whereas the average return on GE's stock was 27.17% (cell C14). The question we answer is whether GE had *risk-adjusted overperformance*.

To answer this question, we regress GE's excess returns on the excess returns of the S&P 500. To perform this regression, we estimate the best line that passes through the points on the graph.[5] In essence we are trying to explain the excess returns of GE as a linear function of the excess returns of the S&P 500:

$$\text{Regression line:} \quad \underbrace{r_{GE,t} - r_{f,t}}_{\substack{\text{GE's excess} \\ \text{return in period } t}} = \alpha_{GE} + \beta_{GE} * \underbrace{[r_{S\&P,t} - r_{f,t}]}_{\substack{\text{S\&P 500 excess} \\ \text{return in period } t}}$$

The actual regression line that we compute is

$$GE \text{ excess return} = \underbrace{2.77\%}_{\substack{\text{This is GE's} \\ \text{alpha } (\alpha_{GE})\text{—its} \\ \text{performance over} \\ \text{and above the S\&P} \\ \text{500 Index}}} + \underbrace{1.3952}_{\substack{\text{This is GE's} \\ \text{beta } (\beta_{GE})\text{—its} \\ \text{riskiness} \\ \text{versus the S\&P} \\ \text{500 Index}}} * S\&P \text{ excess return}, \quad \underbrace{R^2 = 80.29\%}_{\substack{\text{The "r-squared" is} \\ \text{a measure of how} \\ \text{well GE's excess} \\ \text{returns are explained} \\ \text{by the S\&P 500} \\ \text{excess returns}}}$$

The regression calculation requires three statistics:

Statistic 1, GE's β_{GE} ("Beta"): β_{GE} measures the sensitivity of GE's excess returns to the S&P 500's excess returns. β_{GE} is the most common measure of a security's market-related risk. In the spreadsheet β_{GE} is computed in three ways: in cells F20 and F21 and on the graph.[6] All three methods give $\beta_{GE} = 1.3952$.

The β is the most common *risk measure* for a stock. GE's $\beta_{GE} = 1.3952$ shows that GE's returns were very sensitive to the return on the S&P 500—on average a 1% increase in the S&P 500 excess return was accompanied by a 1.3952% increase in the excess return on GE stock. In the parlance of investment analysts, GE is an *aggressive* asset; when the market goes up, GE's stock return tends to go up by more, and vice versa. An asset whose $\beta < 1$ is termed a *defensive* asset.

Statistic 2, GE's α_{GE} ("Alpha"): α_{GE} is a measure of the extra performance of GE. GE's alpha, α_{GE}, is 2.77%. In the spreadsheet α_{GE} is computed in two ways: in cell F18 and on the graph. To understand the importance of α_{GE}, take another look at the regression line:

$$GE \text{ excess return} = \underbrace{2.77\%}_{\text{GE's alpha } (\alpha_{GE})} + \underbrace{1.3952}_{\text{GE's beta } (\beta_{GE})} * S\&P \text{ excess return}$$

---

[5]For details on how to perform a regression in Excel, see the discussion in Chapter 12 (p. 352) or the Excel Note that follows this section.

[6]See the Excel Note below for a further explanation of how to compute β.

Suppose that in a particular year the S&P 500 returns 10% in excess of the risk-free rate. Then the regression predicts that GE would return 16.72%:

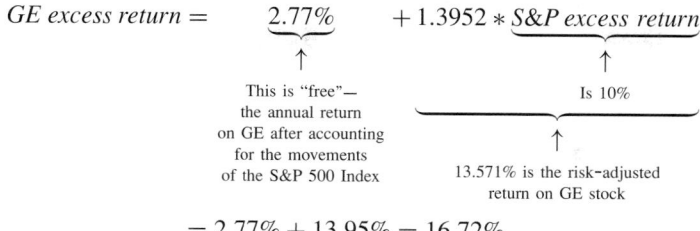

$$= 2.77\% + 13.95\% = 16.72\%$$

α_{GE} tells you that if GE's stock returns behave as predicted by this equation, you will earn 2.77% *more* than the market risk-adjusted return. Naturally, what this is telling you is that GE is a great stock![7]

This is a remarkable fact. It means that GE has a positive net return in excess of its risk. This explains why α measures the risk-adjusted overperformance or underperformance of a stock. In Section 15.5 we return to α and show how it can be used to measure the performance of mutual fund managers.[8]

Statistic 3, GE's R^2 ("R-Squared"):   The GE returns were very highly correlated with the S&P 500 returns: 80.29% of the variability in the GE returns was explained by variations in the S&P 500. This number (known as the R^2–pronounced "r-squared"—of the regression) is calculated by the Excel function **Rsq(y-range,x-range)** in cell F23 and also appears on the graph.[9] Another interpretation of R^2 is that it measures the degree to which the stock "tracks" the S&P 500.

GE tracks the S&P 500 highly, but most stocks don't track the market index nearly as well. In Sections 15.3 and 15.4 we show that a diversified portfolio's tracking of the market index is generally much better than the tracking of the individual portfolio components.

EXCEL NOTE

COMPUTING THE THREE STATISTICS α, β, R^2

The previous spreadsheet shows several ways of computing each of the statistics α, β, and R^2:

- You can use an Excel XY chart and then use the Excel regression function **Trendline** (see Chapter 12). The trendline equation (printed on the Excel chart) is *GE annual return* $= 1.3952 * S\&P$ *annual return* $+ 0.0277, R^2 = 0.8029$. 1.3952 is GE's beta (β_{GE}) and 2.77% is GE's alpha (α_{GE}).

contd.

---

[7]Or *was a great stock*—we're making the strong assumption here that historical performance over the 1990–1999 period will predict future performance.

[8]α is often called "Jensen's α," after Professor Michael Jensen of Harvard, who introduced the term.

[9]As you will see in some of the other chapter examples, an R^2 of 80% is unusually high for a regression of the SML type, when the data in question describes a single stock. It is much more usual for the R^2 of a single stock to be around 20–30%.

- You can use the Excel functions **Intercept(y-range,x-range)**, **Slope(y-range, x-range)**, and **Rsq(y-range,x-range)** to compute α_{GE}, β_{GE}, and R^2, respectively. This is illustrated in cells B18, B20, and B23.
- You can use the Excel functions **Covar** and **Varp** to compute the β_{GE}:
  $$\beta_{GE} = Covar(r_{GE}, r_{S\&P})/Varp(r_{S\&P}).$$

Advanced Excel Hint

In the cell formulas below, the three statistics α, β, and R^2 are calculated directly, without computing the excess returns. For example, the Excel expression B3:B12-D3:D12 can be written in the formulas for the excess return of the S&P 500. Similarly, C3:C12-D3:D12 is understood by Excel to be the excess returns for GE. We use this method in the next section.

	A	B	C	D	E
1			**GE AND THE S&P500, 1990-1999** computing the regression coefficients without a direct computation of the excess returns		
2	**Date**	**S&P 500 returns**	**GE returns**	**Risk-free rate**	
3	Dec-90	-3.10%	-11.04%	7.92%	
4	Dec-91	30.47%	33.34%	6.64%	
5	Dec-92	7.62%	11.77%	4.15%	
6	Dec-93	10.08%	22.67%	3.50%	
7	Dec-94	1.32%	-2.74%	3.54%	
8	Dec-95	37.58%	41.18%	7.05%	
9	Dec-96	22.96%	37.33%	5.09%	
10	Dec-97	33.36%	48.42%	5.61%	
11	Dec-98	28.58%	39.01%	5.24%	
12	Dec-99	21.04%	51.72%	4.51%	
13					
14	Alpha	0.0277	<-- =INTERCEPT(C3:C12-D3:D12,B3:B12-D3:D12)		
15	Beta	1.3952	<-- =SLOPE(C3:C12-D3:D12,B3:B12-D3:D12)		
16	R-squared	0.8029	<-- =RSQ(C3:C12-D3:D12,B3:B12-D3:D12)		

15.3 Diversification Pays

In the previous section we measured the risk-adjusted performance of GE stock by regressing the excess returns of GE on the excess returns of the S&P 500. In this section we repeat this exercise for a portfolio and regress the excess returns from a portfolio of stocks on the excess returns of the S&P 500. Doing this enables us to make two points:

- First, we can use the regression to measure the risk-adjusted underperformance or overperformance of a portfolio. This is similar to what we did for GE stock in Section 15.2.
- Second, we can use the regression to show that diversification pays by increasing the R^2 of the regression—meaning that there is less "noise" in a diversified portfolio: More of the returns are explained by the market portfolio (in this case, the S&P 500).

In the example below we present annual return data for the S&P 500, Dupont (DD), Heinz (HNZ), and Kimberly-Clark (KMB). Using the Excel functions described earlier, we calculate the α and β for each of the stocks and the R^2 of the regression that determines them (rows 15–17). Note that the R^2 for each of the stocks is in the 20–30% range (much lower than the R^2 for GE); this range is typical when we regress individual stock returns on the market portfolio. As you will see, one of the benefits of portfolio diversification is that, in general, a portfolio has a higher R^2 than the assets composing it.

	A	B	C	D	E	F	G
1					**ANNUAL RETURN DATA FOR S&P 500, DUPONT, HEINZ, AND KIMBERLY-CLARK**		
2	Date	S&P 500	Dupont DD	Heinz HNZ	Kimberly-Clark KMB	Risk-free rate	
3	Dec-90	-3.10%	-6.34%	2.46%	18.74%	7.92%	
4	Dec-91	30.47%	31.86%	14.54%	24.71%	6.64%	
5	Dec-92	7.62%	4.62%	16.89%	19.88%	4.15%	
6	Dec-93	10.08%	6.14%	-15.95%	-9.08%	3.50%	
7	Dec-94	1.32%	20.11%	6.55%	0.28%	3.54%	
8	Dec-95	37.58%	28.65%	39.81%	69.15%	7.05%	
9	Dec-96	22.96%	38.33%	11.56%	17.75%	5.09%	
10	Dec-97	33.36%	30.31%	45.89%	5.52%	5.61%	
11	Dec-98	28.58%	-9.78%	14.11%	12.84%	5.24%	
12	Dec-99	21.04%	26.90%	-27.44%	22.31%	4.51%	
13							
14	Regression of stock excess returns on S&P						
15	Alpha		0.0308	-0.0493	0.0399	<-- =INTERCEPT(E3:E12-$F$3:$F$12,$B$3:$B$12-$F$3:$F$12)	
16	Beta		0.6346	0.7647	0.6511	<-- =SLOPE(E3:E12-$F$3:$F$12,$B$3:$B$12-$F$3:$F$12)	
17	R-squared		0.2618	0.2412	0.2032	<-- =RSQ(E3:E12-$F$3:$F$12,$B$3:$B$12-$F$3:$F$12)	
18							
19	Note: The computations of alpha, beta, and R-squared use the advanced Excel hint						
20	described in the box on page000.						
21							
22	**COMPUTING PORTFOLIO RETURNS AND PORTFOLIO ALPHA, BETA, AND R-SQUARED**						
23	Portfolio weights						
24	Dupont	25.00%					
25	Heinz	35.00%					
26	Kimberly-Clark	40.00%					
27							
28	Portfolio excess returns						
29	Date	S&P 500 excess return	Portfolio excess return		This is the weighted average of portfolio weights times the individual asset excess returns.		
30	Dec-90	-11.02%	-1.15%	<-- =($B$24*C3+$B$25*D3+$B$26*E3)-F3			
31	Dec-91	23.83%	16.30%	<-- =($B$24*C4+$B$25*D4+$B$26*E4)-F4			
32	Dec-92	3.47%	10.87%				
33	Dec-93	6.58%	-11.18%				
34	Dec-94	-2.22%	3.89%				
35	Dec-95	30.53%	41.71%				
36	Dec-96	17.87%	15.64%				
37	Dec-97	27.75%	20.24%				
38	Dec-98	23.34%	2.39%				
39	Dec-99	16.53%	1.54%				
40							
41	Regression of portfolio excess returns on S&P						
42	Alpha	0.0064	<-- =INTERCEPT(C30:C39,B30:B39)				
43	Beta	0.6867	<-- =SLOPE(C30:C39,B30:B39)				
44	R-squared	0.4224	<-- =RSQ(C30:C39,B30:B39)				
45							
46	Weighted average of individual parameters						
47	Avg. alpha	0.0064	<-- =$B$24*C15+$B$25*D15+$B$26*E15				
48	Avg. beta	0.6867	<-- =$B$24*C16+$B$25*D16+$B$26*E16				
49	Avg. R-sq.	0.2311	<-- =$B$24*C17+$B$25*D17+$B$26*E17				

Now suppose we form a portfolio composed of 25% Dupont, 35% Heinz, and 40% Kimberly-Clark. The portfolio proportions are described in cells B24 to B26, and the portfolio returns appear in cells C30 to C39.

In cells B42 to B44 we compute the regression of the portfolio excess returns on the S&P 500 excess returns. The portfolio returns are described by the regression

$$portfolio\ excess\ return_t = \underbrace{0.0064}_{\substack{\uparrow \\ \text{This is the} \\ \text{portfolio } \alpha_P}} + \underbrace{0.6867}_{\substack{\uparrow \\ \text{This is the} \\ \text{portfolio } \beta_P}} * S\&P\ excess\ return_t, \quad R^2 = 0.4224$$

Here are some things to note about this regression:

- The portfolio α_P and β_P are the weighted average alpha and beta of the individual stock αs and βs. In the spreadsheet the beta is calculated twice: In cell B43 the portfolio β_P is calculated using Excel's **Slope** function, and in cell B48 β_P is calculated using the weighted average of each of the individual stock βs. If we denote the portfolio weights by x_{DD}, x_{HNZ}, and x_{KMB}, then, for example, the portfolio beta (either cell B43 or cell B48), β_P, is given by $\beta_P = x_{DD}\beta_{DD} + x_{HNZ}\beta_{HNZ} + x_{KMB}\beta_{KMB}$. In the particular example illustrated, this formula gives a portfolio beta $\beta_P = 0.6867$:

$$\beta_P = \underbrace{0.25}_{\substack{\uparrow \\ \text{Portfolio} \\ \text{weight of} \\ \text{Dupont,} \\ x_{DD}}} * 0.6346 + \underbrace{0.35}_{\substack{\uparrow \\ \text{Portfolio} \\ \text{weight of} \\ \text{Heinz,} \\ x_{HNZ}}} * 0.7647 + \underbrace{0.40}_{\substack{\uparrow \\ \text{Portfolio} \\ \text{weight of} \\ \text{Kimberly-Clark,} \\ x_{KMB}}} * 0.6511 = 0.6867$$

  The same goes for α_P, which can be calculated either by using Excel's **Intercept** function (cell B42) or as an average of the individual stock αs (cell B47).

- Whereas a portfolio's alpha (α_P) and beta (β_P) are the weighted average of individual asset αs and βs, the portfolio R^2 is *larger* than the average R^2. In our example, the R^2 of the three-asset portfolio, computed using the **Rsq** function in cell B44, is 42.24%, whereas the portfolio weighted average R^2 of the three stocks (cell B49) is 23.11%. This is almost always true: *The R^2 of a well-diversified portfolio is higher than the weighted average R^2 of the portfolio assets.* What this means is that much more of the return of a well-diversified portfolio is explained by the market return than is the return of the individual portfolio components. In other words, diversification pays by reducing the *nonmarket risks* associated with a portfolio (Figure 15.3). (After the next section of this chapter, you can say that diversification decreases the *idiosyncratic* or *nonsystematic* risk of the portfolio.)

Volatility Measures

as of 08/31/2003

Beta: 1.26   R²: 0.86   Standard Deviation: 24.96

Top

Holdings

Top Ten Holdings [4] as of 06/30/2003	Geographical Diversification[4]	
MOTOROLA INC	as of 07/31/2003	
LENNAR CORP CL A	USA	80.2%
NOKIA CORP SPON ADR	Japan	9.0%
LIBERTY MEDIA CORP NEW CL A	Grand Cayman	
AOL TIME WARNER INC	(UK Overseas	4.0%
MICROSOFT CORP	Ter)	
UNIVISION COMMUNICATIONS CL A	Finland	3.2%
JOHNSON & JOHNSON	Korea (South)	1.8%
DELL COMPUTER CORPORATION		
VIACOM INC CL B NON-VTG		
32.70% of the portfolio		
Total Holdings 177		

Figure 15.3 Fidelity's Capital Appreciation Fund has 177 stocks in its portfolio. The fund's $\beta = 1.26$, which indicates that the fund is very sensitive to the returns of the S&P 500; on average a 1% increase in the S&P 500 excess return was accompanied by a 1.26% increase in the Fidelity Capital Appreciation Fund's excess return (and, of course, a 1% decrease in the S&P 500 excess return meant a 1.26% decrease in the Capital Appreciation Fund). The Capital Appreciation Fund's R^2 is 86%, which means that 86% of the variability in the Fund's returns is explained by the S&P 500. Fidelity's website does not give information about the Capital Appreciation Fund's α.
Source: http://personalmro.fidelity.com/products/funds/mfl_frame.shtml?316066109.

15.4 Diversifiable Versus Nondiversifiable Risk

By looking at the regressions we illustrated in the previous two sections, we can distinguish between two kinds of risk.

Market risk: Also called *nondiversifiable* or *systematic* risk. This is the risk measured by the β—the sensitivity of an asset's returns to the returns of the market portfolio. In the case of General Electric we saw that its $\beta_{GE} = 1.3952$, meaning that GE's stock returns were very sensitive to the excess returns on the S&P 500. The $R^2 = 80.29\%$ indicates that 80% of the variability in GE's stock returns is due to variability in the returns of the S&P 500. Since most stocks are correlated with the market (meaning when the market goes up, the general tendency of most stock returns is also to rise and vice versa), market risk is well-nigh inevitable. In the case of Dupont, Heinz, and Kimberly-Clark, the relatively low R^2 of all three stocks (in row 17 of the previous spreadsheet) means that only about one-quarter of the risk of the stocks is attributable to the market risk. But when we form an equally weighted portfolio of the three stocks, we find that the portfolio's β_P accounts for 45% of its riskiness.

Idiosyncratic stock risk: Also called *diversifiable* or *nonsystematic* risk. This is the return riskiness that is not attributable to the market return. GE's idiosyncratic risk is very low, (80% of its return variation comes from the market), but the idiosyncratic risk for DD, HNZ, and KMB is much higher: For these individual stocks the R^2 is fairly low, which means that the nonmarket components of return riskiness are much higher. Because the portfolio R^2 of the equally weighted portfolio is much higher than the average R^2, the portfolio's idiosyncratic risk is much lower than the average idiosyncratic risk of the three individual assets. This is one of the benefits of diversification—the portfolio returns "track" much better on the market return, meaning that much more of the portfolio's return is predictable by the market than is the case for the individual asset returns.

What our three-stock example shows is that when you diversify (that is, invest in a portfolio of three stocks instead of one stock), the portion of returns due to market risk increases and the idiosyncratic portfolio risk of the portfolio becomes less than that for the individual stocks. To put this another way: For a well-diversified portfolio, the portfolio β_P is a good description of the portfolio riskiness, *even if* the individual stocks' βs do not describe their riskiness.

Another Diversification Example

In Section 15.3 we showed how a portfolio of three assets could lead to a significant decrease in the nonsystematic risk. We finish this section by giving another diversification example that illustrates how diversification pays. Our portfolio this time is larger (it includes eight stocks instead of the three stocks in the Section 15.3 example); however, it is still not very large. The message: Diversification over even small portfolios can lead to a huge decrease in the nonsystematic risk.

In the example below rows 3–12 show the annual return data for the S&P 500, eight stocks, and the risk-free rate. Rows 22–31 show the returns on an equally weighted portfolio of these stocks.

Now look at the portfolio's α_P, β_P, and R^2.

- The portfolio α_P is a weighted average of the individual asset αs. Cells D35 and D36 show two ways of computing the portfolio α_P.
- The portfolio β_P is a weighted average of the individual asset βs. Cells D39 to D41 show three ways of computing the portfolio β_P.
- The portfolio R^2 (cell D44) is much larger than the weighted average of the R^2 of the individual assets (cell D45). Whereas the individual assets do a relatively poor job of tracking the S&P 500, the weighted average portfolio does a very good job of tracking the S&P 500.

The payoff to diversification is the improved R^2. Combining the stocks into a portfolio means that many of the idiosyncratic risks have been diversified away.

HOW BIG IS A WELL-DIVERSIFIED PORTFOLIO?

For a portfolio of stocks to be well-diversified, it should be composed of many stocks with relatively small proportions for each stock. How many? Usually 20–30 stocks suffice to give a high R^2. When the R^2 is high (say, above 70%), most of the portfolio's risk is market risk.

	A	B	C	D	E	F	G	H	I	J	K
1			ANNUAL RETURN DATA FOR 8 STOCKS AND S&P 500								
2		S&P 500	General Motors GM	Dupont DD	Microsoft MSFT	Heinz HNZ	Kimberly-Clark KMB	General Electric GE	Caterpillar CAT	Ford F	Risk-free rate
3	Dec-90	-3.10%	-12.47%	-6.34%	73.00%	2.46%	18.74%	-11.04%	-16.86%	-38.96%	7.92%
4	Dec-91	30.47%	-13.29%	31.86%	121.76%	14.54%	24.71%	33.34%	-4.21%	5.64%	6.64%
5	Dec-92	7.62%	16.10%	4.62%	15.11%	16.89%	19.88%	11.77%	23.74%	52.45%	4.15%
6	Dec-93	10.08%	73.36%	6.14%	-5.56%	-15.95%	-9.08%	22.67%	67.45%	50.44%	3.50%
7	Dec-94	1.32%	-22.00%	20.11%	51.63%	6.55%	0.28%	-2.74%	24.93%	-13.56%	3.54%
8	Dec-95	37.58%	28.70%	28.65%	43.56%	39.81%	69.15%	41.18%	8.78%	3.59%	7.05%
9	Dec-96	22.96%	8.65%	38.33%	88.32%	11.56%	17.75%	37.33%	31.08%	11.69%	5.09%
10	Dec-97	33.36%	19.38%	30.31%	56.43%	45.89%	5.52%	48.42%	31.31%	50.59%	5.61%
11	Dec-98	28.58%	21.32%	-9.78%	114.60%	14.11%	12.84%	39.01%	-3.05%	20.89%	5.24%
12	Dec-99	21.04%	26.11%	26.90%	68.36%	-27.44%	22.31%	51.72%	4.67%	-9.16%	4.51%
13											
14	Alpha		0.02	0.03	0.44	-0.05	0.04	0.03	0.12	-0.02	
15	Beta		0.51	0.63	0.97	0.76	0.65	1.40	-0.04	0.76	
16	R-squared		0.06	0.26	0.12	0.24	0.20	0.80	0.00	0.11	
17											
18			GM	DD	MSFT	HNZ	KMG	GE	CAT	F	
19	Portfolio weights of the 8 assets		0.125	0.125	0.125	0.125	0.125	0.125	0.125	0.125	
20											
21	Date	Portfolio return									
22	Dec-90	1.06%	<-- =$C$19*C3+$D$19*D3+$E$19*E3+$F$19*F3+$G$19*G3+$H$19*H3+$I$19*I3+$J$19*J3								
23	Dec-91	26.79%	<-- =$C$19*C4+$D$19*D4+$E$19*E4+$F$19*F4+$G$19*G4+$H$19*H4+$I$19*I4+$J$19*J4								
24	Dec-92	20.07%									
25	Dec-93	23.68%									
26	Dec-94	8.15%									
27	Dec-95	32.93%									
28	Dec-96	30.59%									
29	Dec-97	35.98%									
30	Dec-98	26.24%									
31	Dec-99	20.43%									
32											
33	The 3 statistics, α_P, β_P, R^2 for the portfolio										
34	Alpha										
35	Using **Intercept** function			0.0762	<-- =INTERCEPT(B22:B31-K3:K12,$B$3:$B$12-K3:K12)						
36	Using portfolio average of stock alphas			0.0762	<-- =$C$19*C14+$D$19*D14+$E$19*E14+$F$19*F14+$G$19*G14+$H$19*H14+$I$19*I14+$J$19*J14						
37											
38	Beta										
39	Using **Slope** function			0.7062	<-- =SLOPE(B22:B31-K3:K12,$B$3:$B$12-K3:K12)						
40	Using **Covar** and **Varp** functions			0.7062	<-- =COVAR($B$3:$B$12-K3:K12,B22:B31-K3:K12)/VARP($B$3:$B$12-K3:K12)						
41	Using portfolio average of stock betas			0.7062	<-- =$C$19*C15+$D$19*D15+$E$19*E15+$F$19*F15+$G$19*G15+$H$19*H15+$I$19*I15+$J$19*J15						
42											
43	R-squared										
44	Using **Rsq** function			0.7875	<-- =RSQ(B22:B31-K3:K12,$B$3:$B$12-K3:K12)						
45	Using portfolio average of stock r-squareds			0.2253	<-- =$C$19*C16+$D$19*D16+$E$19*E16+$F$19*F16+$G$19*G16+$H$19*H16+$I$19*I16+$J$19*J16						
46											
47	**Note**: As you can see above:										
48	* The portfolio alpha is the weighted average alpha of the assets in the portfolio.										
49	* The portfolio beta is the weighted average beta of the assets in the portfolio.										
50	* The R^2 of the portfolio returns regressed on the S&P returns is *much higher* than the weighted										
51	average of the R^2's of the individual regressions. Diversification reduces non-market risks!										

15.5 Measuring the Investment Performance of Mutual Funds

Thus far in this chapter we have used the capital asset pricing model (CAPM) to measure investment performance. By regressing a stock's excess returns on the excess returns of a market index, we are able to estimate the performance (α) and the risk (β). We are also able to estimate the intensity of the systematic risk of the stock—the R^2 of the regression.

In the case of General Electric, for example, we estimated the following regression:

$$GE \text{ excess return} \; = \; \underbrace{2.77\%}_{\uparrow} \; + \; \underbrace{1.3952}_{\uparrow} \; * \; S\&P \text{ excess return}, \quad R^2 = 80.29\%$$

This is GM's alpha (α)—its performance over and above the S&P 500 Index

This is GM's beta (β)—its riskiness versus the S&P 500 Index

As explained in Section 15.2, GE's α_{GE} = 2.77% indicates significant overperformance, since it shows we expect GE to earn 2.77% per year in excess of the performance of the S&P 500. On average, however, the results for GE (a positive α) cannot be generally true for all stocks—for the average stock, α must be zero. Some stocks will have positive α (indicating risk-adjusted overperformance), and others will have negative α (underperformance), but on average there will be neither underperformance nor overperformance. The average β of all stocks will be 1—like the β of the S&P 500.

For mutual funds things are somewhat more complicated, as you'll see shortly. But first, here's the same exercise for a mutual fund that we did for GE: The mutual fund in question is Vanguard's Growth and Income Fund. As you can see in the spreadsheet that follows, this fund's sensitivity to the market is almost 1—its β is 0.9786, meaning that the fund closely tracks the S&P 500.

	A	B	C	D	E	F	G	H	I
1	PERFORMANCE MEASUREMENT: VANGUARD GROWTH AND INCOME FUND AND THE S&P500, 1990-1999								
2	Date	Risk-free		S&P500 Return	S&P excess return		Growth-Income Fund return	Fund excess return	
3	Dec-90	7.92%		-3.10%	-11.02%		-2.44%	-10.36%	<-- =G3-B3
4	Dec-91	6.64%		30.47%	23.83%		30.29%	23.65%	<-- =G4-B4
5	Dec-92	4.15%		7.62%	3.47%		7.01%	2.86%	
6	Dec-93	3.50%		10.08%	6.58%		13.83%	10.33%	
7	Dec-94	3.54%		1.32%	-2.22%		-0.61%	-4.15%	
8	Dec-95	7.05%		37.58%	30.53%		35.93%	28.88%	
9	Dec-96	5.09%		22.96%	17.87%		23.06%	17.97%	
10	Dec-97	5.61%		33.36%	27.75%		35.59%	29.98%	
11	Dec-98	5.24%		28.58%	23.34%		23.94%	18.70%	
12	Dec-99	4.51%		21.04%	16.53%		26.04%	21.53%	
13									
14									

Performance Measurement
Growth and Income Fund Versus S&P 500

y = 0.98x + 0.0055
R^2 = 0.9586

Fund excess return

S&P 500 excess return

The α of the Growth and Income Fund is 0.0055, which is about 0.5%. This seems to indicate a slight overperformance. Actual overperformance might be even larger than indicated by the Growth and Income Fund's α:

- Vanguard charges a fee for managing your money. For the Growth and Income Fund, the annual fee is 0.40% of the assets managed, so that, all other things being equal, you would expect that the fund's $\alpha = -0.40\%$, reflecting the annual cost of the Vanguard fee.
- On the other hand, perhaps the managers of the Fund are able to outperform the market—meaning that they are able to make better investments than the average investor and thus bring excess returns to their fund holders. If this were the case with the Fund, we would expect to see a positive α. The Growth and Income Fund's α is *slightly* positive ($\alpha = 0.55\%$), so there must be some excess performance, since the Fund charges a management fee.[10]

Too Good to Be True? Vanguard's Windsor II Fund

The examples of GE (with its positive α) and of Vanguard's Growth and Income Fund (with its $\alpha \approx 1/2\%$) may be somewhat misleading. The average α of stocks in the market should be zero, and the α of a mutual fund is—as indicated at the end of the last section—the result of two factors: On the one hand, the fees charged by a fund tend to depress its α, but if the fund managers are able to provide superior investment performance, this would tend to increase the fund's α.

Before telling you what financial research says on this matter, let's look at another Vanguard fund:

	A	B	C	D	E	F	G	H	I
1	PERFORMANCE MEASUREMENT: VANGUARD WINDSOR II FUND AND THE S&P 500, 1990-1999								
2	Date	Risk-free		S&P 500 Return	Excess return		Windsor II return	Excess return	
3	Dec-90	7.92%		-3.10%	-11.02%		-9.98%	-17.90%	<-- =G3-B3
4	Dec-91	6.64%		30.47%	23.83%		28.70%	22.06%	<-- =G4-B4
5	Dec-92	4.15%		7.62%	3.47%		11.99%	7.84%	
6	Dec-93	3.50%		10.08%	6.58%		13.60%	10.10%	
7	Dec-94	3.54%		1.32%	-2.22%		-1.16%	-4.70%	
8	Dec-95	7.05%		37.58%	30.53%		38.83%	31.78%	
9	Dec-96	5.09%		22.96%	17.87%		24.18%	19.09%	
10	Dec-97	5.61%		33.36%	27.75%		32.37%	26.76%	
11	Dec-98	5.24%		28.58%	23.34%		16.36%	11.12%	
12	Dec-99	4.51%		21.04%	16.53%		-5.81%	-10.32%	

Performance Measurement Windsor II Versus S&P 500

$y = 0.9645x - 0.036$
$R^2 = 0.6687$

Windsor II excess return

S&P 500 excess return

---

[10]On the other hand, only 79% of the Fund's performance is explained by the S&P 500, so perhaps the slightly positive α is just statistical "noise."

As you can see, the Windsor II Fund's risk is roughly equivalent to that of the S&P 500 (its β is almost 1). The R^2 tells us that 67% of the Fund's return variability can be attributed to the variability of the S&P 500. The negative α of Windsor II means that *on average* in each year the investor *started* with a 3.6% *disadvantage* in returns; for the period 1990–1999, the Windsor II Fund has *negative risk-adjusted performance*.[11]

What Does Academic Financial Research Tell Us About Investment Performance?

The *efficient markets hypothesis* (Chapter 17) tells us that it's very difficult to make money using only publicly available information. Thus, there's no reason to believe that investment managers can provide better investment performance than you would get in an otherwise well-diversified portfolio put together by someone (like yourself) with no "investment expertise." In fact, there are two reasons for believing that investment managers may provide worse results:

- They charge fees. (To be fair—investing on your own also involves the payment of brokerage fees, not to mention the opportunity costs of the time you would need to spend gathering information.) In the case of the two Vanguard funds we researched in this chapter, the fees are 0.40%, but mutual fund fees can go from as low as 0.05% to as high as 1.5% or even 2%.

- Many investment managers like to turn over their portfolios. This, in turn, incurs costs for the mutual fund investors and lowers returns.

For these reasons, many knowledgeable academics (and a lot of other "streetwise" types) prefer investing in index funds like the Vanguard Index 500 Fund, which we've used as an example in this chapter. The aim of these index funds is to closely match the composition of a market index like the S&P 500. These funds are able to provide a highly diversified portfolio with low costs and with minimal interference in the investment decision by a portfolio manager.

A considerable amount of academic research bears out our conclusions. The average α of mutual funds is negative, and there is little evidence that mutual funds are able to provide superior investment performance.[12]

Other Index Funds

Lest this chapter sound too much like an advertisement for Fidelity and Vanguard Funds, we hasten to point out that the American investor has many index funds available. Figure 15.4 gives a few examples (a search in Yahoo finds at least 75 such funds):

---

[11] Windsor II's annual management fee is 0.40%, which doesn't explain the negative α.

[12] For a good academic reference on this topic, try reading "Returns from Investing in Equity Mutual Funds 1971–1991," by Burton G. Malkiel, *Journal of Finance,* June 1995.

Provider	Fund Name	Annual Expenses	Assets Under Management (end 2001)	Minimum Initial Investment
Vanguard	500 Index Fund	0.18%	$67.36 billion	$3,000
Fidelity	Spartan 500 Index	0.19%	$8.47 billion	$10,000
American Advantage	S&P 500 Index	0.55%	$31.6 million	$2,500
Scudder	S&P 500 Index	0.40%	$384.99 million	$2,500
Dreyfus	Basic S&P 500 Stock Index	0.20%	$1.4 billion	$10,000
Paine-Webber	Brinson S&P 500 Index A	0.60%	$33.18 million	$1,000
Morgan-Stanley	S&P 500 Index	0.69%	$165.04 million	$1,000

Note: Vanguard has two index funds, the one listed and another—the Index 500 Admiral Fund—for bigger investors (minimum investment, $250,000). The latter fund has $12.14 billion of assets and annual expenses of 0.12%, so that Vanguard has almost $80 billion in S&P 500 Index funds.

Figure 15.4 Some S&P 500 Index funds available to the investor. *Source:* Information source—Yahoo/Morningstar, as of 21 January 2002.

15.6 Back to Jack and Jill—Who's Right?

In the preceding sections we've shown how we can measure under- or overperformance by regressing an asset's excess returns on the market's excess returns. Now let's go back to Jack and Jill. Recall that Jack was investing in the "stodgy" Puritan Fund, whereas Jill was a "go-go" investor in the NASDAQ. Over the period 1990–2003, Jill has done better than Jack, but over the period 1999–2003, she's done a lot worse.

Who's done better? Who's right?

Running the regressions of the monthly excess returns of each portfolio on the S&P 500 shows that each portfolio has earned returns commensurate with its risks. The Puritan Fund is much less risky than the NASDAQ (($\beta_{NASDAQ} = 1.4346$, $\beta_{Puritan} = 0.5632$). However, neither investment has an α that is significantly different from zero, so that there is no under- or overperformance (Figures 15.5 and 15.6).

Both Jack and Jill are getting what they're paying for—the correct risk-adjusted return. That's the nature of capital markets.

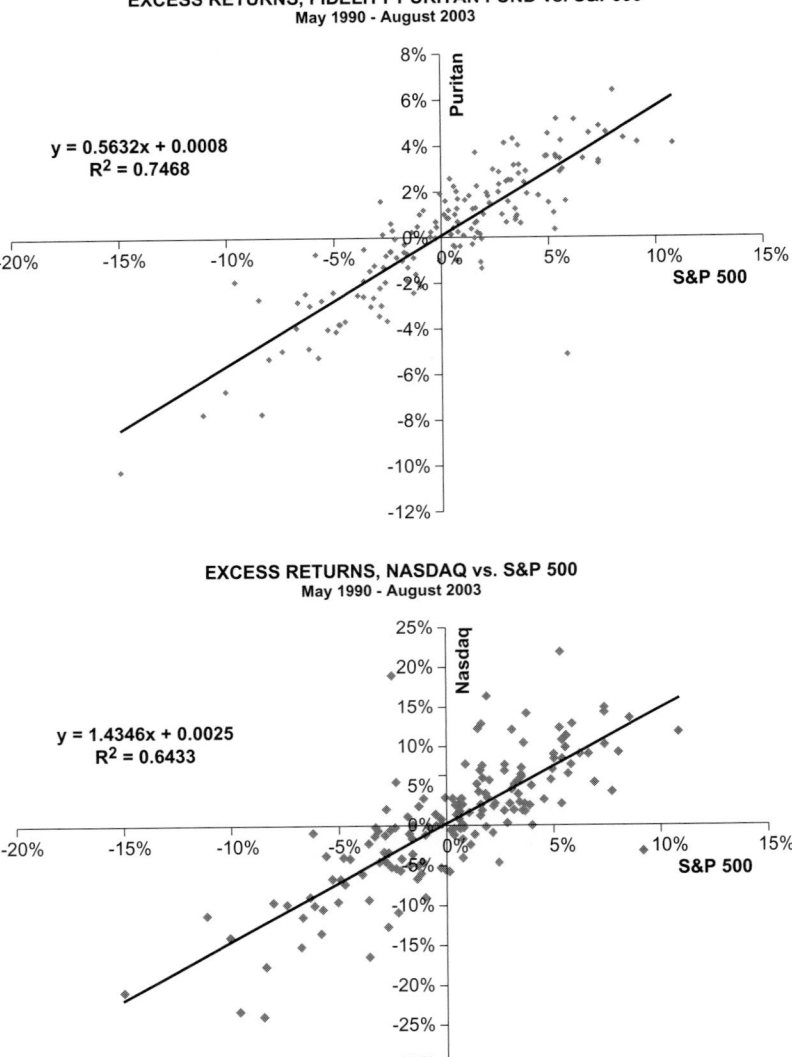

Figure 15.5 Analyzing the excess returns on the Puritan Fund and the NASDAQ reveals that over the period 1990–2003, the NASDAQ is almost three times as risky as Puritan ($\beta_{NASDAQ} = 1.4346$, $\beta_{Puritan} = 0.5632$). Neither regression reveals αs that are significantly different from zero. In other words, both Jack and Jill are getting returns commensurate with the risk they're undertaking. There is no excess performance in either of these investments. The lower R^2 for the NASDAQ as opposed to Puritan (64% versus 75%) indicates that the NASDAQ has somewhat more idiosyncratic risk.

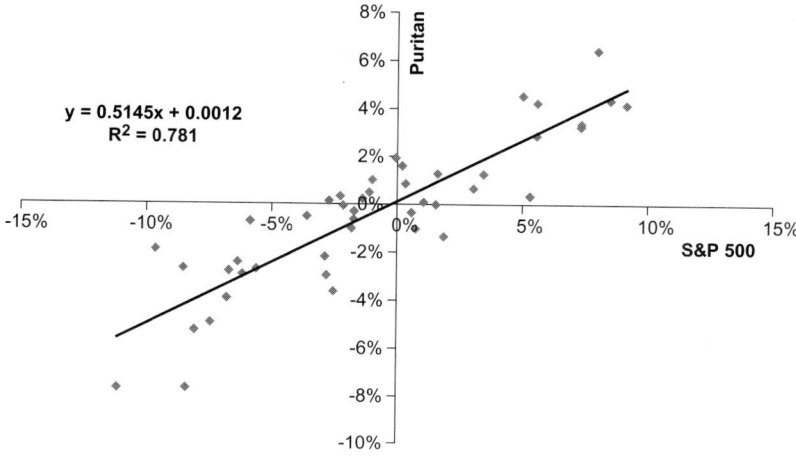

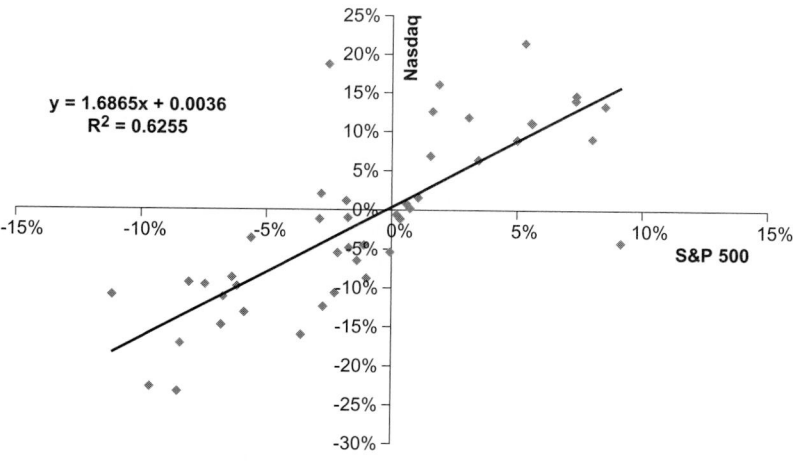

Figure 15.6 An analysis of the excess returns on the Puritan Fund and the NASDAQ over the period 1999–2003 reveals no substantial change in our previous conclusion. Although there are minor changes in β and α, neither investment exhibits overperformance or underperformance.

CONCLUSION

In this chapter we showed how to find the beta (β) and the alpha (α) of a security and of a portfolio. We defined the concepts of market risk (nondiversifiable risk) and idiosyncratic risk (diversifiable risk), and we showed how forming a portfolio reduces the idiosyncratic risk.

Using the α to measure the investment performance, we explored the performance of various mutual funds and related this important issue to fund fees and the efficient markets hypothesis. In Chapter 16, we show how the SML can be used to compute the cost of capital for a firm.

EXERCISES

1. Find the β_i for stock i based on the following data: $E(r_M) = 15\%$, $E(r_i) = 12\%$, $r_f = 7\%$.
2. Suppose that for asset i, $\beta_i = 1$, $E(r_i) = 21\%$. What is the market return $E(r_M)$?
3. Suppose that for asset i, $E(r_M) = 21\%$, $\beta_i = 0.7$, $E(r_i) = 25\%$. What is the return of the risk-free asset?
4. Consider the following data: $E(r_M) = 25\%$, $Cov(r_i, r_M) = 0.07$, $r_f = 8\%$, $Var(r_M) = 0.1$. What is the expected return of stock i, $E(r_i)$?
5. Consider the following data: $E(r_i) = 15\%$, $Cov(r_i, r_M) = 0.06$, $\sigma_M^2 = 0.06$. What is $E(r_M)$, the expected market return?
6. Consider the following data: $E(r_M) = 10\%$, $Cov(r_i, r_M) = 0.2$, $E(r_i) = 18\%$, $Var(r_M) = 0.09$. What is the return of the risk-free asset, r_f?
7. Consider the following data concerning the S&P 500, FedEx Company, and the returns on one-year U.S. Treasury bills.

	A	B	C	D
1	\multicolumn{4}{c|}{FEDEX AND S&P 500}			
2	Year	S&P Total return	FedEx return	1-year T-bill
3	1990	-3.10%	-4.46%	7.89%
4	1991	30.47%	24.18%	5.86%
5	1992	7.62%	9.19%	3.89%
6	1993	10.08%	10.67%	3.43%
7	1994	1.32%	-3.61%	5.32%
8	1995	37.58%	24.04%	5.94%
9	1996	22.96%	8.76%	5.52%
10	1997	33.36%	25.95%	5.63%
11	1998	28.58%	14.01%	5.05%
12	1999	21.04%	30.89%	5.08%
13	2000	-9.10%	-4.26%	6.11%
14	2001	-11.89%	-7.20%	3.49%
15	2002	-22.10%	-21.27%	2.00%

(a) Compute the excess returns for the S&P 500 and for FedEx.
(b) Show by a graph the excess returns of FedEx versus the S&P 500. Use Excel to compute the regression line and the R^2.
(c) Is FedEx stock an aggressive or defensive stock?

8. Consider the following data concerning the S&P 500, IBM Company, and the returns on one-year U.S. Treasury bills:

Note: Data for these exercises can be found on the disk that accompanies this book.

	A	B	C	D
1		**IBM AND S&P500**		
2	Year	S&P Total return	IBM Return	1-year T-bill
3	1990	-3.10%	17.46%	7.89%
4	1991	30.47%	-23.87%	5.86%
5	1992	7.62%	-56.85%	3.89%
6	1993	10.08%	11.40%	3.43%
7	1994	1.32%	26.33%	5.32%
8	1995	37.58%	21.75%	5.94%
9	1996	22.96%	50.59%	5.52%
10	1997	33.36%	32.28%	5.63%
11	1998	28.58%	56.67%	5.05%
12	1999	21.04%	15.71%	5.08%
13	2000	-9.10%	-23.83%	6.11%
14	2001	-11.89%	35.28%	3.49%
15	2002	-22.10%	-44.11%	2.00%

(a)   Compute the excess returns for the S&P 500 and for IBM.

(b)   Show by a graph the excess returns of IBM versus the S&P 500. Use Excel to compute the regression line and the R^2.

(c)   Does IBM have excess performance over the S&P 500?

(d)   Is IBM an aggressive or defensive stock?

9. Using the data from Exercises 7 and 8, assume you invested in an equally weighted portfolio composed of IBM and FedEx stocks.

(a)   Compute the excess return of the portfolio.

(b)   Compute the portfolio β_P. Show three different ways to calculate the portfolio β_P:
- By using Excel's **Slope** function.
- By using the formula $\beta_P = Cov(r_P, r_M)/Var(r_M)$.
- By averaging the βs of the two portfolio components IBM and FedEx.

(c)   Compute the portfolio α_P. Show two different ways to calculate the portfolio α_P:
- By using Excel's **Intercept** function.
- By taking the weighted average of the αs of the two portfolio components IBM and FedEx.

10. Consider the data of another stock—3M Corporation.

	A	B	C	D
1		**3M AND S&P500**		
2	Year	S&P Total return	3M return	1-year T-bill
3	1990	-3.10%	11.03%	7.89%
4	1991	30.47%	14.04%	5.86%
5	1992	7.62%	8.81%	3.89%
6	1993	10.08%	10.85%	3.43%
7	1994	1.32%	1.49%	5.32%
8	1995	37.58%	25.03%	5.94%
9	1996	22.96%	25.04%	5.52%
10	1997	33.36%	1.20%	5.63%
11	1998	28.58%	-11.70%	5.05%
12	1999	21.04%	34.43%	5.08%
13	2000	-9.10%	20.79%	6.11%
14	2001	-11.89%	-1.92%	3.49%
15	2002	-22.10%	4.22%	2.00%

(a)   Does 3M have excess performance?

(b)   Graph the excess returns of 3M against those of the S&P 500. Use Excel to compute the regression line and the R^2.

11. Using the data for the S&P 500, FedEx, IBM, and 3M from Exercises 7, 8, and 10, compute the portfolio alpha, α_P, and the portfolio beta, β_P, of a portfolio composed of 30% 3M stock, 50% FedEx stock, and 20% IBM stock. Explain the diversification advantages of this portfolio.

12. Consider the following data regarding ten stocks, the S&P 500, and the annual risk-free rate. Your friend who works in an investment bank tells you that an equally weighted portfolio composed of these ten stocks yields risk-adjusted excess returns when compared to the S&P 500. Check if she's right.

	A	B	C	D	E	F	G	H	I	J	K	L	M
1	ANNUAL RETURN DATA FOR TEN STOCKS, S&P 500 AND RISK-FREE RATE												
2	Year	Johnson & Johnson	Apple	Bank of America	PepsiCo	Reebok	Kellogg	Gillette	FedEx	IBM	3M	S&P 500	1-year T-bill
3	1990	21.09%	19.90%	-66.07%	19.75%	-48.20%	11.50%	24.51%	-4.46%	17.46%	11.03%	-3.10%	7.89%
4	1991	48.39%	27.09%	61.57%	26.47%	106.99%	54.42%	58.11%	24.18%	-23.87%	14.04%	30.47%	5.86%
5	1992	-10.76%	5.82%	26.73%	20.29%	3.60%	2.09%	1.36%	9.19%	-56.85%	8.81%	7.62%	3.89%
6	1993	-9.34%	-71.48%	-1.44%	-1.51%	-11.53%	-16.23%	4.69%	10.67%	11.40%	10.85%	10.08%	3.43%
7	1994	22.27%	28.80%	-4.51%	-12.05%	28.36%	2.37%	22.80%	-3.61%	26.33%	1.49%	1.32%	5.32%
8	1995	46.47%	-20.16%	46.87%	43.30%	-32.59%	28.44%	33.10%	24.04%	21.75%	25.03%	37.58%	5.94%
9	1996	16.63%	-42.32%	36.74%	4.58%	40.34%	-16.30%	39.99%	8.76%	50.59%	25.04%	22.96%	5.52%
10	1997	29.51%	-46.31%	24.12%	21.46%	-37.53%	41.37%	25.60%	25.95%	32.28%	1.20%	33.36%	5.63%
11	1998	25.43%	113.64%	1.29%	12.02%	-66.07%	-37.45%	-4.92%	14.01%	56.67%	-11.70%	28.58%	5.05%
12	1999	11.77%	92.07%	-15.09%	-14.82%	-59.71%	-10.20%	-14.90%	30.89%	15.71%	34.43%	21.04%	5.08%
13	2000	13.31%	-123.96%	-4.61%	34.07%	120.54%	-16.02%	-12.09%	-4.26%	-23.83%	20.79%	-9.10%	6.11%
14	2001	13.10%	38.65%	35.56%	-1.77%	-3.12%	13.69%	-5.59%	-7.20%	35.28%	-1.92%	-11.89%	3.49%
15	2002	-8.20%	-42.41%	13.59%	-14.26%	10.38%	12.97%	-7.50%	-21.27%	-44.11%	4.22%	-22.10%	2.00%

13. Consider the following annual data regarding Dreyfus Laurel Funds, Inc. (DSPIX), the S&P 500 Stock Index Fund, and the T-bill rate. Did the fund manager outperform the market?

	A	B	C	D	E	F	G
1	RETURN DATA FOR DSPIX FUND, S&P 500 AND THE RISK-FREE RATE						
2			DSPIX	S&P Total return	1-year T-bill		DSPIX excess return	S&P 500 excess return
3	1997	25.67%	33.36%	5.63%		20.04%	27.73%
4	1998	22.95%	28.58%	5.05%		17.90%	23.53%
5	1999	17.01%	21.04%	5.08%		11.93%	15.96%
6	2000	-10.74%	-9.10%	6.11%		-16.85%	-15.21%
7	2001	-14.07%	-11.89%	3.49%		-17.56%	-15.38%
8	2002	-26.70%	-22.10%	2.00%		-28.70%	-24.10%

CHAPTER 16

THE SECURITY MARKET LINE (SML) AND THE COST OF CAPITAL

OVERVIEW

This is the second of two chapters that show the use of the security market line (SML). In Chapter 15 we discussed the use of the SML for performance measurement, and in this chapter we discuss how to use the SML to calculate the cost of capital for a firm.[1]

---

[1]If you need a lightning review of the SML, look at the first section of Chapter 15.

The weighted average cost of capital (WACC) is the minimum return that a firm must earn in order to satisfy its shareholders and bondholders. As discussed in Section 9.6, the WACC has two major uses:

- Using WACC in capital budgeting: When evaluating a project whose risk is comparable to the riskiness of the company's current activities, the WACC is the appropriate discount rate for the project's cash flows.
- Using WACC to value a company: The value of a company is based on the present value of its future free cash flows discounted at the WACC.

We previously discussed the WACC in Chapter 9, where we used the Gordon model to calculate the cost of equity. In this chapter we use the SML to calculate the cost of equity. These two models—the Gordon model and the SML—are the major approaches to computing the cost of equity for a firm.

Finance Concepts Discussed

- The use of security market line (SML) to calculate the cost of equity r_E for a firm.
- Calculating the firm's weighted average cost of capital (WACC). Note that the computation of the WACC was also discussed in Chapter 9, where we used the Gordon model to calculate the firm's cost of equity r_E.
- Calculating the market value of the firm's debt and equity, the firm's tax rate T_C, and the firm's cost of debt r_D. Our discussion of these issues in this chapter is in many ways a repeat of a similar discussion in Chapter 9.
- The concept of *asset beta*, β_{Assets}, and its use as an alternative method to calculate the firm's WACC.

Throughout this chapter we assume that you know how to calculate the β of a stock (this issue was discussed in the previous chapter). In actual fact, you often don't have to compute the β of a firm's shares—the information is publicly available (in this chapter, for example, we use data on β provided by Yahoo).

Excel Functions Used

- **NPV**
- **Average**

16.1 The CAPM and the Firm's Cost of Equity: An Initial Example

Abracadabra, Inc. is considering a new project, which has the following free cash flows.[2]

---

[2]An extended discussion of the free cash flow (FCF) is given in Chapters 9 and 10. Figure 16.1 reviews the concept in tabular form.

	A	B
2	Year	FCF
3	0	-1,000
4	1	1,323
5	2	1,569
6	3	3,288
7	4	1,029
8	5	1,425
9	6	622
10	7	3,800
11	8	3,800
12	9	3,800
13	10	2,700

In order to decide whether to accept or reject the project, the company needs to calculate the risk-adjusted discount rate for these cash flows (Figure 16.1). It decides that the riskiness of the new project is very much like the riskiness of Abracadabra's current activities; the financing for

Profit after taxes	This is the basic measure of the profitability of the business, but it is an accounting measure that includes financing flows (such as interest), as well as non-cash expenses such as depreciation. Profit after taxes does not account for either changes in the firm's working capital or purchases of new fixed assets, both of which can be important cash drains on the firm.
+ Depreciation	This noncash expense is added back to the profit after tax.
+ After-tax interest payments (net)	FCF is an attempt to measure the cash produced by the business activity of the firm. To neutralize the effect of interest payments on the firm's profits, we: • Add back the after-tax cost of interest on debt (*after-tax* since interest payments are tax deductible). • Subtract out the after-tax interest payments on cash and marketable securities.
− Increase in current assets	When the firm's sales increase, more investment is needed in inventories, accounts receivable, and so on. This increase in current assets is not an expense for tax purposes (and is therefore ignored in the profit after taxes), but it is a cash drain on the company.
+ Increase in current liabilities	An increase in the sales often causes an increase in financing related to sales (such as accounts payable or taxes payable). This increase in current liabilities—when related to sales—provides cash to the firm. Since it is directly related to sales, we include this cash in the free cash flow calculations.
− Increase in fixed assets at cost	An increase in fixed assets (the long-term productive assets of the company) is a use of cash, which reduces the firm's free cash flow.
FCF = sum of the above	

Figure 16.1 The free cash flow (FCF) is the amount of cash generated by a firm's business activities. Discounting the FCFs at a firm's weighted average cost of capital (WACC) gives the enterprise value of the firm. The concept of FCF was introduced in Chapter 9. It appears in several other places in this book: In the context of accounting and financial planning models, we used the FCF in Chapter 10 to value a firm. In Chapter 19 we return to the concept of FCF in the context of stock valuation.

the project is also similar to that of the firm. In this case the appropriate discount rate is the *weighted average cost of capital* (WACC); this is the average cost of financing the firm's activities. Assuming that Abracadabra has both equity and debt, the formula for the WACC is given by

$$WACC = r_E * \frac{E}{E+D} + r_D * (1-T_C) * \frac{D}{E+D}$$

$$= \left(\begin{array}{c} \text{cost of} \\ \text{equity} \end{array}\right) * \left(\begin{array}{c} \text{proportion} \\ \text{of firm} \\ \text{financed by} \\ \text{equity} \end{array}\right) + \left(\begin{array}{c} \text{cost of} \\ \text{debt} \end{array}\right) * \left(\begin{array}{c} 1 - \text{corporate} \\ \text{tax rate} \end{array}\right) * \left(\begin{array}{c} \text{proportion} \\ \text{of firm} \\ \text{financed by} \\ \text{debt} \end{array}\right)$$

We can use the SML to calculate the cost of equity for Abracadabra. Here are our assumptions for this problem:

- The firm's stock has a beta of $\beta = 1.4$.
- The expected market return is $E(r_M) = 10\%$.
- The risk-free rate $r_f = 4\%$.
- Abracadabra's equity has a market value $E = \$10,000$.
- Abracadabra's debt has a market value $D = \$15,000$.
- Abracadabra can borrow new funds at a cost of $r_D = 6\%$.
- Abracadabra's corporate tax rate is $T_C = 40\%$.

The first three assumptions mean that Abracadabra's cost of equity r_E as given by the SML is 12.4%:

$$r_E = r_f + \beta * [E(r_M) - r_f]$$
$$= 4\% + 1.4 * [10\% - 4\%]$$
$$= 12.4\%$$

Then Abracadabra's weighted average cost of capital (WACC) is

$$WACC = r_E * \frac{E}{E+D} + r_D * (1-T_C) * \frac{D}{E+D}$$
$$= 12.4\% * \frac{10,000}{10,000 + 15,000} + 6\% * (1-40\%) * \frac{15,000}{10,000 + 15,000}$$
$$= 7.12\%$$

The WACC of 7.12% is the discount rate we will use to determine whether or not Abracadabra should undertake the project.

The following spreadsheet shows our calculations for the WACC (rows 20–36) and the NPV calculation for the project (rows 3–16).

	A	B	C
1	VALUING ABRACADABRA'S INVESTMENT we calculate the WACC using the SML to compute the cost of equity r_E		
2	Year	FCF	
3	0	-1,000	
4	1	1,323	
5	2	1,569	
6	3	3,288	
7	4	1,029	
8	5	1,425	
9	6	622	
10	7	3,800	
11	8	3,800	
12	9	3,800	
13	10	2,700	
14			
15	Weighted average cost of capital, WACC	7.12%	<-- =B36
16	Project NPV	14,424	<-- =NPV(B15,B4:B13)+B3
17			
18			
19	Computing Abracadabra's Weighted Average Cost of Capital (WACC)		
20	Market value of equity, E	10,000	
21	Market value of debt, D	15,000	
22	Market value of equity + debt, E+D	25,000	
23			
24	Corporate tax rate, T_C	40%	
25			
26	Abracadabra's stock beta, β	1.4	
27			
28	Facts about market		
29	$E(r_M)$	10%	
30	r_f	4%	
31			
32	Abracadabra's cost of capital		
33	Cost of equity using SML, r_E	12.40%	<-- =B30+B26*(B29-B30)
34	Cost of debt, r_D	6.00%	
35			
36	Weighted average cost of capital (WACC)	7.12%	<-- =B20/B22*B33+B21/B22*B34*(1-B24)

When the project free cash flows are discounted at the WACC, the net present value (NPV) is $14,424 (cell B16). Since the NPV is positive, Abracadabra should undertake the project.

Comparing the SML and the Gordon Model for Calculating the WACC

The weighted average cost of capital is the most widely used discount rate for computing the value of corporate projects and for computing the value of the firm. The WACC depends critically on the cost of equity r_E. In this chapter we compute the cost of equity using the security market line (SML), whereas in Chapter 9 we computed the cost of equity using the Gordon dividend model.

The Gordon dividend model and the SML are only two practical ways of calculating the cost of equity.[3] Both models have their advantages and disadvantages. The Gordon model is simple to calculate but is very sensitive to assumptions about the firm's equity payout—the total dividends plus stock repurchases of the firm. The SML requires relatively more calculations but is more widely used. The SML also requires us to make assumptions about the expected return on the market $E(r_M)$. This problem is discussed in the next section.

So which model should you use in practice? The best answer is to *use both models* and to compare the results. This way each model can serve as a "reality check" on the other. We apply this logic in Chapter 19, which discusses stock valuation. There we apply both models and compare the results to see if we have arrived at an appropriate WACC.

16.2   Using the SML to Calculate the Cost of Capital: Calculating the Parameter Values

The Abracadabra example of the previous section gives the broad outlines of calculating the cost of capital using the SML, but it leaves a number of questions unanswered:

- How do we calculate the market value of a firm's equity, E?
- How do we calculate the expected return on the market, $E(r_M)$?
- How do we calculate the risk-free rate, r_f?
- How do we calculate the market value of a firm's debt, D?
- How do we calculate a firm's borrowing rate, r_D?
- How do we calculate a firm's corporate tax rate, T_C?

We discuss each of these questions in turn. Although we occasionally provide an illustration, we save a full-blown example for Section 16.3.

Computing the Market Value of a Firm's Equity, E

This is easy: For a firm whose shares are sold on the stock market, the market value of the equity (E in our WACC equation) is the number of shares times the market value per share.

Computing the Expected Return on the Market, $E(r_M)$

There are two ways to calculate the expected return on the market: (1) We can use the *historical market return*, or (2) we can use a version of the Gordon dividend model to derive $E(r_M)$ from current market data. Neither method is perfect, though we prefer the latter.

$E(r_M)$ Using the Historical Returns: A standard technique is to use a broad-based index—usually the S&P 500 Index—to proxy for the market portfolio. To do this, you need some data. Below we show you the returns on Vanguard's 500 Index Fund. This is an index mutual fund that is invested in the S&P 500 index.[4] The average return on the S&P 500 is 14.13% for the period 1984–2004 (cell F25). This *historical average return* is often used as a proxy for the *expected market return* in the SML.

---

[3]The academic finance literature has come up with other models for calculating the cost of equity, but in practice these models are very difficult to apply and rarely used.
[4]We discussed index funds in Chapter 15, Section 15.5.

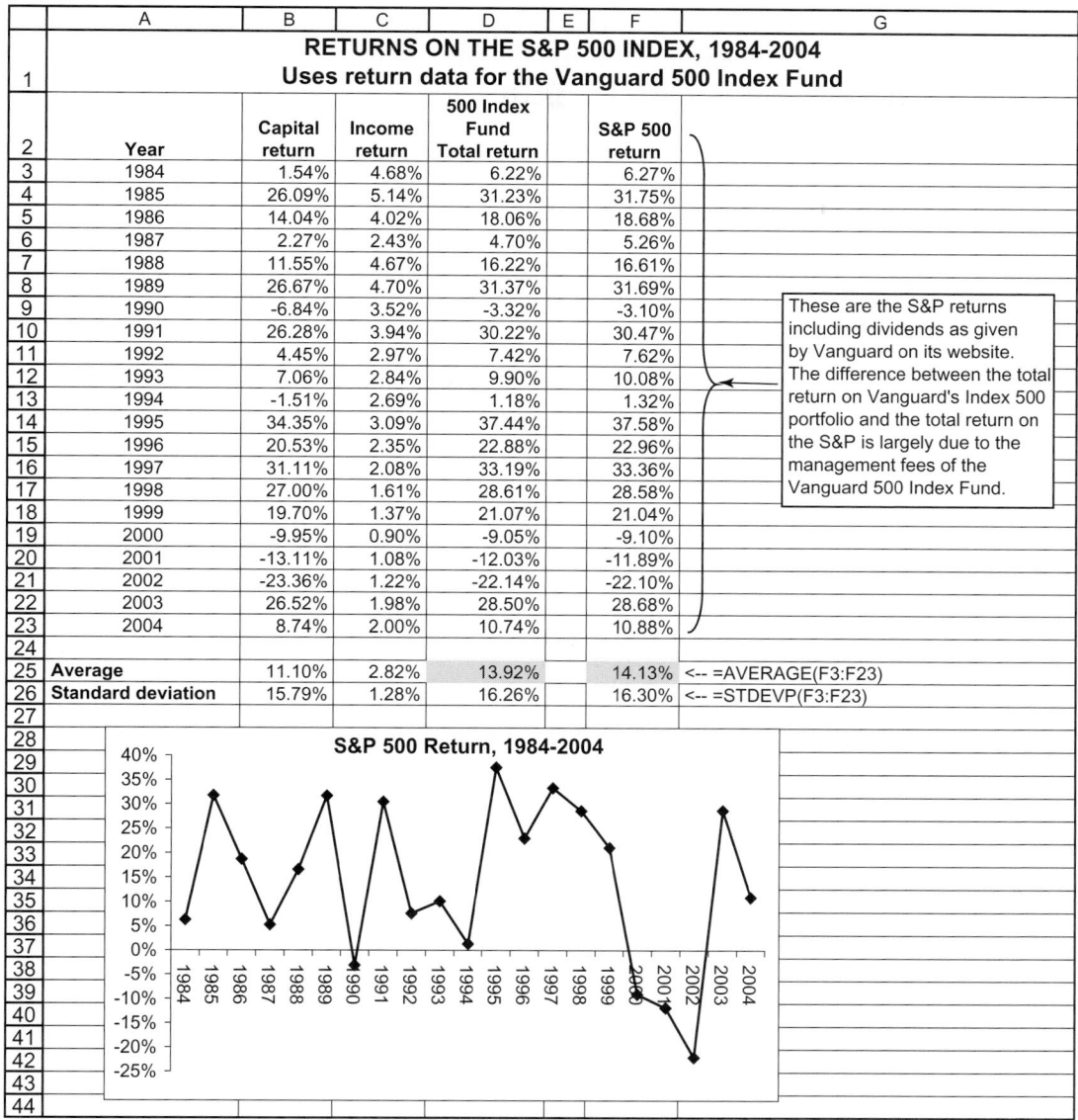

	A	B	C	D	E	F	G
1		**RETURNS ON THE S&P 500 INDEX, 1984-2004**					Uses return data for the Vanguard 500 Index Fund
2	**Year**	**Capital return**	**Income return**	**500 Index Fund Total return**		**S&P 500 return**	
3	1984	1.54%	4.68%	6.22%		6.27%	
4	1985	26.09%	5.14%	31.23%		31.75%	
5	1986	14.04%	4.02%	18.06%		18.68%	
6	1987	2.27%	2.43%	4.70%		5.26%	
7	1988	11.55%	4.67%	16.22%		16.61%	
8	1989	26.67%	4.70%	31.37%		31.69%	
9	1990	-6.84%	3.52%	-3.32%		-3.10%	
10	1991	26.28%	3.94%	30.22%		30.47%	
11	1992	4.45%	2.97%	7.42%		7.62%	
12	1993	7.06%	2.84%	9.90%		10.08%	
13	1994	-1.51%	2.69%	1.18%		1.32%	
14	1995	34.35%	3.09%	37.44%		37.58%	
15	1996	20.53%	2.35%	22.88%		22.96%	
16	1997	31.11%	2.08%	33.19%		33.36%	
17	1998	27.00%	1.61%	28.61%		28.58%	
18	1999	19.70%	1.37%	21.07%		21.04%	
19	2000	-9.95%	0.90%	-9.05%		-9.10%	
20	2001	-13.11%	1.08%	-12.03%		-11.89%	
21	2002	-23.36%	1.22%	-22.14%		-22.10%	
22	2003	26.52%	1.98%	28.50%		28.68%	
23	2004	8.74%	2.00%	10.74%		10.88%	
24							
25	Average	11.10%	2.82%	13.92%		14.13%	<-- =AVERAGE(F3:F23)
26	Standard deviation	15.79%	1.28%	16.26%		16.30%	<-- =STDEVP(F3:F23)

These are the S&P returns including dividends as given by Vanguard on its website. The difference between the total return on Vanguard's Index 500 portfolio and the total return on the S&P is largely due to the management fees of the Vanguard 500 Index Fund.

WHY USE VANGUARD INSTEAD OF YAHOO FOR S&P 500 RETURNS?

The usual data sources (for example, Yahoo) give only the *price data* for the S&P 500 Index. (This is somewhat strange, since Yahoo's data for individual stocks is adjusted for dividends.) Vanguard's website gives the *total return* data both for its 500 Index Fund and for the actual S&P 500 Index. The Vanguard 500 Index Fund's returns are slightly lower than those of the S&P 500. This is due primarily to the management fees paid by the 500 Index Fund to Vanguard.

E(r_M) Using Current Market Data: This technique is less widely used, though we prefer it.[5] It is based on the Gordon dividend model, which gives the expected return on a stock as a function of the stock's current equity payout Div_0, the current market value of the firm's equity P_0, and the expected growth rate of g of the equity payout. The equity payout is defined as the sum of the firm's dividends and its stock repurchases (see Chapter 9, p. 253 for a full explanation):

Gordon dividend model

$$r_E = \frac{Div_0(1+g)}{P_0} + g$$

where Div_0 = current equity payout of firm (total dividends + stock repurchases)

$\qquad\quad P_0$ = current market value of equity

$\qquad\quad g$ = anticipated equity payout growth rate

To use the Gordon model to calculate the expected return on the market, we restate the model in terms of the price–earnings (P/E) ratio: Assume that every year the firm pays out a percentage b of its earnings to its shareholders, both in the form of dividends and stock repurchases. Then we can rewrite the formula above as

$$r_E = \frac{Div_0(1+g)}{P_0} + g = \frac{b * EPS_0(1+g)}{P_0} + g$$

where EPS_0 is the firm,s current earnings per share.

Manipulating this formula a bit, we get

$$r_E = \frac{b * (1+g)}{\underbrace{P_0/EPS_0}_{\substack{\uparrow \\ \text{This is the firm's} \\ \text{P/E(price–earnings)} \\ \text{ratio}}}} + g$$

We now apply this logic to the market as a whole. We regard a market index such as the S&P 500 (symbolized by M) as a stock having its own payout ratio b and growth rate of equity payouts g. We then use the above formula to compute the expected market return $E(r_M)$.[6]

---

[5]It was first published in *Corporate Finance: A Valuation Approach,* by Simon Benninga and Oded Sarig (McGraw-Hill, 1997).

[6]A sensitive reader may note that there's some confusion of symbols here. The formula

$$r_E = \frac{b * (1+g)}{P_0/EPS_0} + g$$

uses r_E to stand for the cost of equity for a stock. Since the "cost of equity" is a synonym for the "expected return from equity," when we apply the formula to the market portfolio M (in this case, the S&P 500), we should by logic have called this r_M. Instead, we use $E(r_M)$. Our excuse is that the symbol $E(r_M)$ is so widely used that we cannot give it up.

Here's an example using data for the S&P 500 Index at the end of December 2004:

	A	B	C
1	**USING THE PRICE-EARNINGS RATIO TO COMPUTE E(r$_M$)**		
2	S&P 500 P/E on 31dec01	21	
3	Estimated growth of equity payout, g	6%	
4	Payout ratio, b	50%	
5			
6	E(r$_M$)	8.52%	<-- =B4*(1+B3)/B2+B3

The price–earnings (P/E) ratio for the S&P 500 is not that easy to find (see Figure 16.2 for the source of our data). We have had to "guesstimate" the estimated growth of dividends and the dividend payout ratio.

Dividend payout is defined as the total expended by firms on both cash dividends and repurchases of shares (we discussed this topic a bit in Chapter 9, when calculating the cost of equity for Courier Corporation using the Gordon model). While the cash dividends are a matter of record, the amount of repurchases is more debatable. Current estimates put the sum of dividends and repurchases at around 50% of corporate earnings. Figure 16.3, for example, is a graph showing the relation between share repurchases and dividends for the Standard & Poor's 500 Index through 1998. Notice that by the end of the data sample, repurchases outweighed dividends.

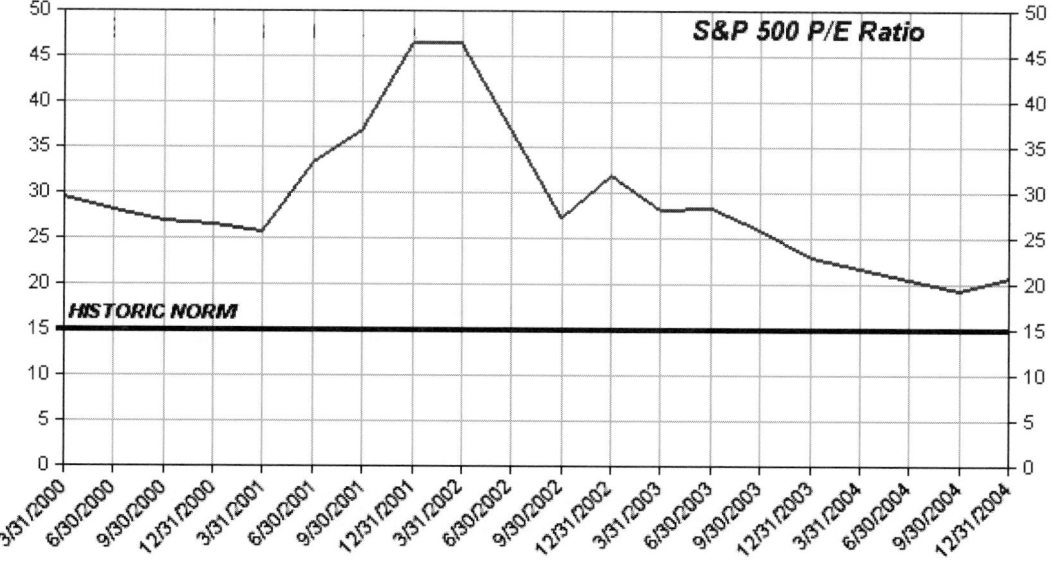

Figure 16.2 The price–earnings (P/E) ratio of the S&P 500 Index is not that easy to find. Here is a website that calculates the P/E ratio. The numerical example in this section uses the P/E ratio of 21 on 31 December 2004 to compute the expected return on the market $E(r_M)$. *Source:* http://www. bullandbearwise.com

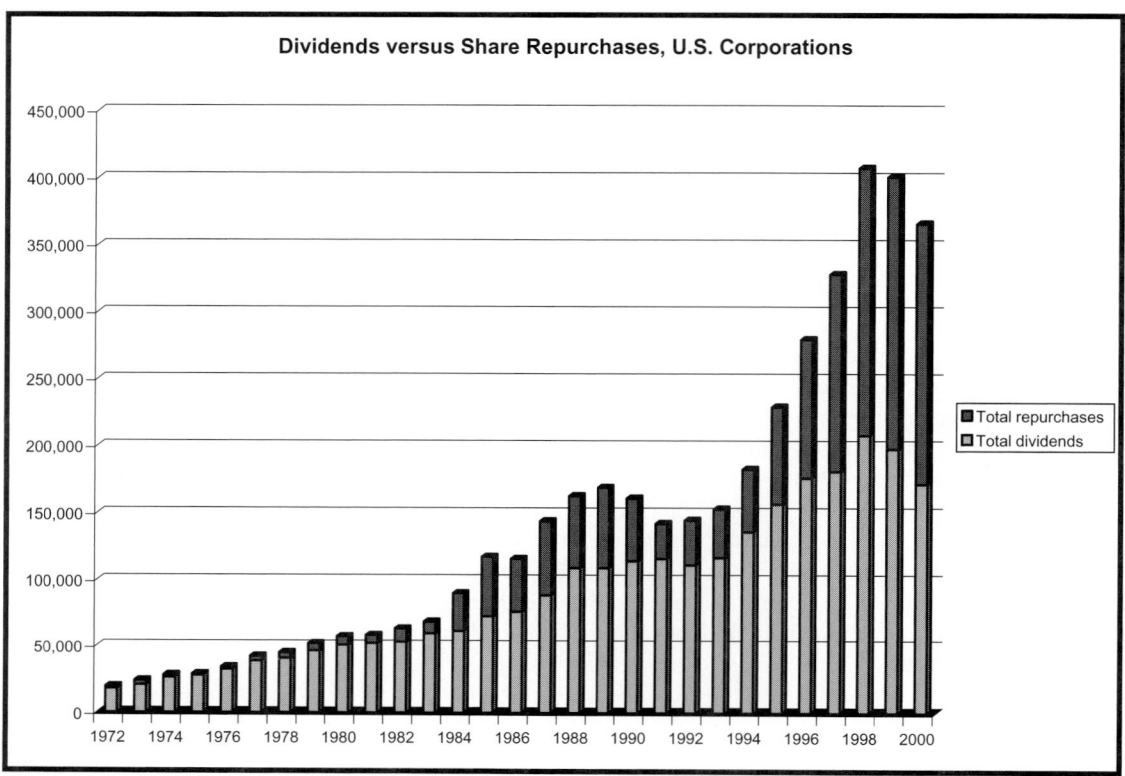

Figure 16.3 Share repurchases and dividends in the United States, 1972–2000. Whereas at the beginning of the period share repurchases were negligible compared to dividends, by the end of the period more cash was paid out to shareholders by corporations in the form of share repurchases than as dividends. *Source*: Gustavo Grullon and Rony Michaely, "Dividends, Share Repurchases, and the Substitution Hypothesis," Journal of Finance, August 2002.

Dividend growth is the market anticipation of the growth of total dividends (broadly defined as cash dividends plus repurchases) for the future. If we assume that dividends will grow at the rate of growth of the economy, 6% is a reasonable long-term estimate.

Computing the Risk-Free Rate, r_f

The risk-free rate r_f should be the short-term Treasury rate. This rate is available from a variety of places, including Yahoo (see example in Section 16.3).

Computing the Market Value of a Firm's Debt, D

In principle, D should be the *market value* of the firm's debt. However, in practice, this value is usually very difficult to calculate. Standard practice is to use the book value of the firm's debt *minus* the value of its cash reserves; we refer to this concept as *net debt*.

Computing a Firm's Borrowing Rate, r_D

The rate r_D used in the WACC formula ought to be the firm's *marginal cost of borrowing*, the rate at which it can borrow additional funds through sales of bonds or from banks. In many cases, however, the marginal cost of borrowing is very difficult to calculate. Two common "quick fixes" are:

- Compute r_D from the firm's average borrowing rate.
- Compute r_D by "eyeballing" the firm's current borrowing rate from information given in the financial statements.

    Both approaches are illustrated in Section 16.3.

Computing a Firm's Corporate Tax Rate, T_C

The tax rate T_C used in the WACC formula ought to be the firm's *marginal tax rate*, the rate the firm would have to pay on an additional dollar of income. This rate is very difficult to determine, and two "quick fixes" are common:

- In many cases a firm's average tax rate is an acceptable proxy for T_C . This is the case for Hilton Hotels in Section 16.3.
- In some cases we might prefer to use information about the average corporate tax rate in the economy. This rate is approximately 37%.[7] For a firm whose own historical tax rate is not a good predictor of its future tax rate, this number might be a preferable substitute.

16.3 A Fully-Worked-Out Example: Hilton Hotels

We illustrate the approach to calculating the WACC by using data for Hilton Hotels Corp. (symbol: HLT). As discussed earlier, we need eight parameters to calculate the WACC for this (or any other) company:

- E, the market value of the company's equity today. This is simply the number of shares times the current stock price.
- D, the market value of the company's debt today. We use the *book value* (that is, the accounting value) of the company's debt as a proxy for this number.
- r_E, the cost of equity for the company. In this chapter we use the SML to calculate the cost of equity. Using the SML means that the cost of equity is dependent on:
    - The β of the firm's equity. In the previous chapter we computed this β. In practice, it is often available without computation (as in this example, read on).
    - r_f, the risk-free rate.
    - $E(r_M)$, the expected return on the market.
- r_D, the cost of debt for the company. In principle, this should be the marginal cost (the company's cost of obtaining new debt). In practice, we often use the company's average cost of existing debt.

---

[7]The federal tax rate in the United States is 35% (see Chapter 2). Since companies also pay state and local taxes, the tax rate for most companies is some where between 35% and 40%.

Figure 16.4 The Yahoo screen, indicating the **Key Statistics.** This choice gives the updated financial information for the firm used below. (Yahoo's presentation of financial materials changes occasionally, so that you may have to look elsewhere for the financial profile.)

- T_C, the company's tax rate. In principle, this should be the company's marginal tax rate (the rate on an additional dollar of earnings). In practice, we often use the company's average tax rate.

Much of the data is available on Yahoo; Figure 16.4 shows the Yahoo screen leading to Hilton Hotel's "key statistics."

From Yahoo's profile, Figure 16.5, shows some data for Hilton Hotels as of 21 January 2005.

From this data we learn:

- Hilton's equity $\beta_E = 0.956$.
- The current value of a share of Hilton Hotels is $22.49. The number of shares outstanding is 386.03 million. The market value of Hilton's equity is the product of these two numbers, giving $E = \$8.68$ billion.
- The book value of Hilton's debt is $D = \$3.743$ billion. With a bit of work, this number can be calculated from Yahoo. According to Yahoo:
  - The book value of equity per share is $6.388.
  - The debt/equity ratio of Hilton Hotels is 1.518. This is the ratio of the book value of the firm's debt to the book value of its equity.

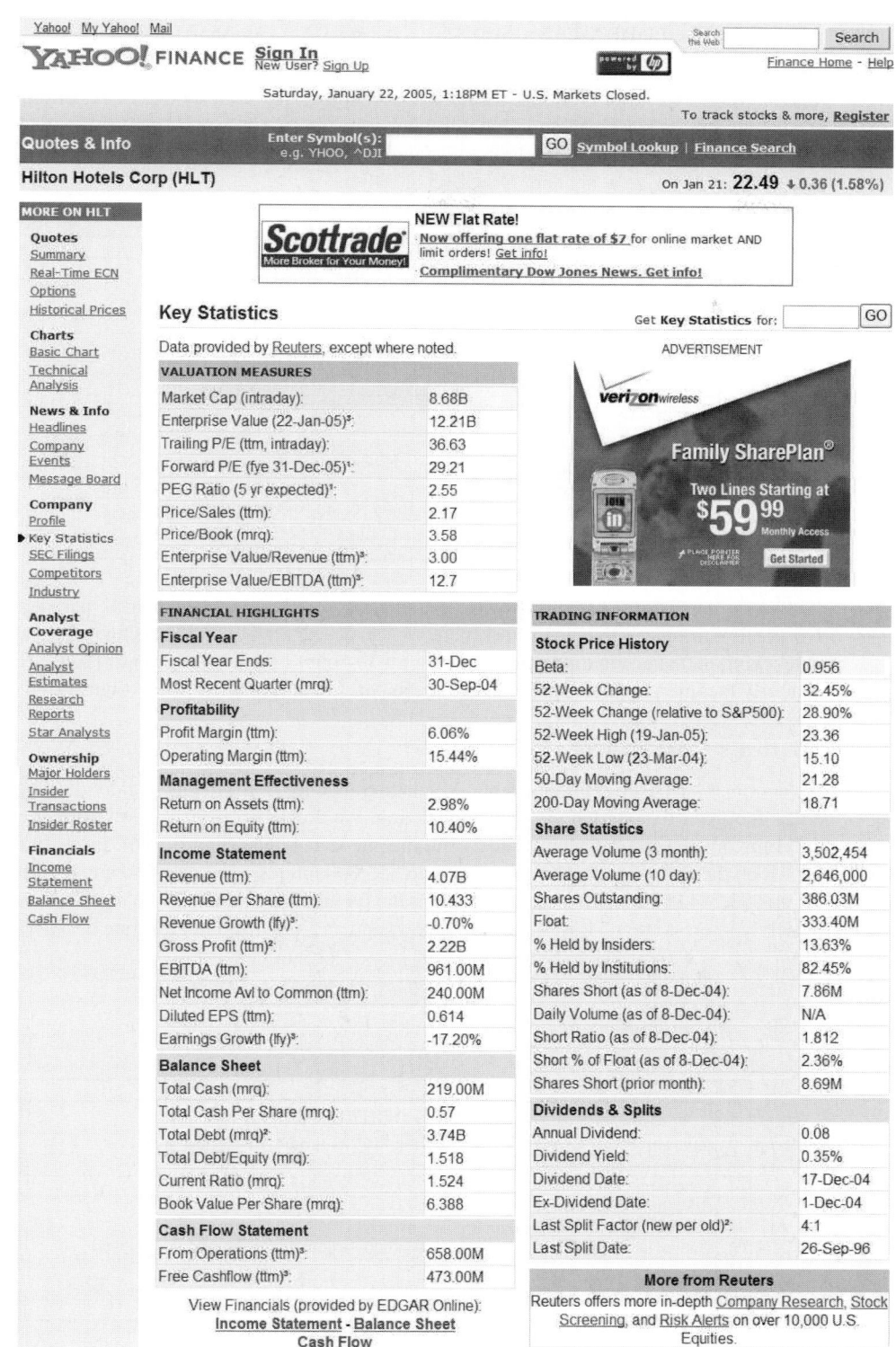

Figure 16.5 Yahoo's profile for Hilton Hotels. Highlighted numbers are used in the computation of Hilton's WACC.

Since Hilton has 386.03 million shares outstanding, its total book value of equity is: $386.03 * 6.388 = 2,466$. Multiplying this number by the debt/equity ratio gives the total debt of Hilton Hotels as \$3.743 billion . From this number we subtract the \$219 million in cash held by the company to arrive at net debt $D = \$3.524$ billion.[8]

	A	B	C
1	HILTON HOTELS CORPORATION (HLT) using Yahoo for much of the information		
2	Equity beta	0.956	<-- Yahoo
3			
4	Shares outstanding (million)	386.03	<-- Yahoo
5	Market value per share	22.49	<-- Yahoo
6	Market value of equity (\$ million), E	8,682	<-- =B5*B4
7			
8	Book value of equity per share	6.388	<-- Yahoo
9	Total book value of equity	2,466	<-- =B8*B4
10	Debt/Equity ratio	1.518	<-- Yahoo
11	Book value of debt	3,743	<-- =B10*B9
12	Cash on hand	219	<-- Yahoo
13	Net debt (\$ million), D	3,524	<-- =B11-B12

We still need the two firm-related parameters (r_D, T_C) and two market parameters $(r_f, E(r_M))$. For these, we'll have to work a bit. We can access the Hilton Hotels financial statements by clicking on the accounting information at the bottom of the first column of Figure 16.5. The quarterly income statements and balance sheets thus obtained are shown in Figure 16.6.

Hilton's Cost of Debt r_D Is 5.55%

We compute the cost of Hilton's debt r_D by taking its interest payments and dividing by the average debt over the quarter and then annualizing. We download from Yahoo information about the company's quarterly balance sheets and income statements (Figure 16.6). In the last quarter for which there are reports, the company paid \$53,000 interest. The debt at the end of this quarter was \$3,744,000 and the debt at the end of the previous quarter was \$4,058,000. This gives a quarterly interest rate of 1.36% (cell B8 below) and an annualized interest rate of 5.55%:

$$quarterly\ interest\ paid = \frac{53,000}{Average(3,744,000\ and\ 4,058,000)} = 1.36\%$$

$$annualized\ interest\ rate = r_D = (1 + 1.36\%)^4 - 1 = 5.55\%$$

	A	B	C	D	E
1	HILTON'S COST OF DEBT, r_D				
2	Quarter	30-Sep-04	30-Jun-04	31-Mar-04	
3	Interest expense	53,000	86,000	70,000	
4	Long term debt	3,730,000	3,720,000	3,801,000	
5	Short term debt and current portion of long term debt	14,000	338,000	338,000	
6	Debt at end of quarter	3,744,000	4,058,000	4,139,000	<-- =D5+D4
7					
8	Quarterly interest expense	1.36%	2.10%		<-- =C3/AVERAGE(C6:D6)
9	Annualized	5.55%	8.66%		<-- =(1+C8)^4-1

---

[8]Cash is subtracted from the firm's debt because Hilton Hotels could, in principle, use the cash to pay off some of its debt.

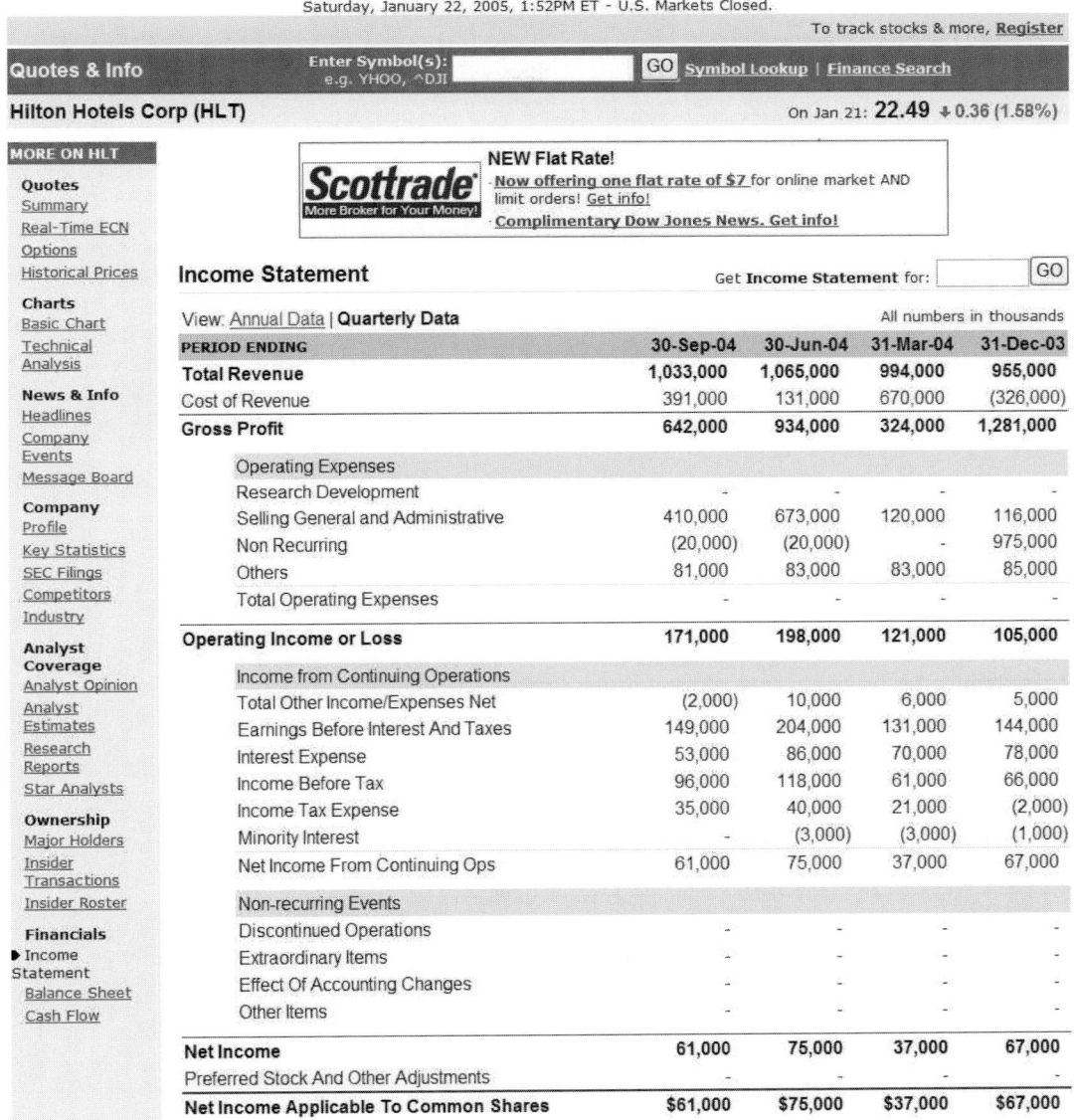

Figure 16.6 Income statement and balance sheet information for Hilton Hotels.

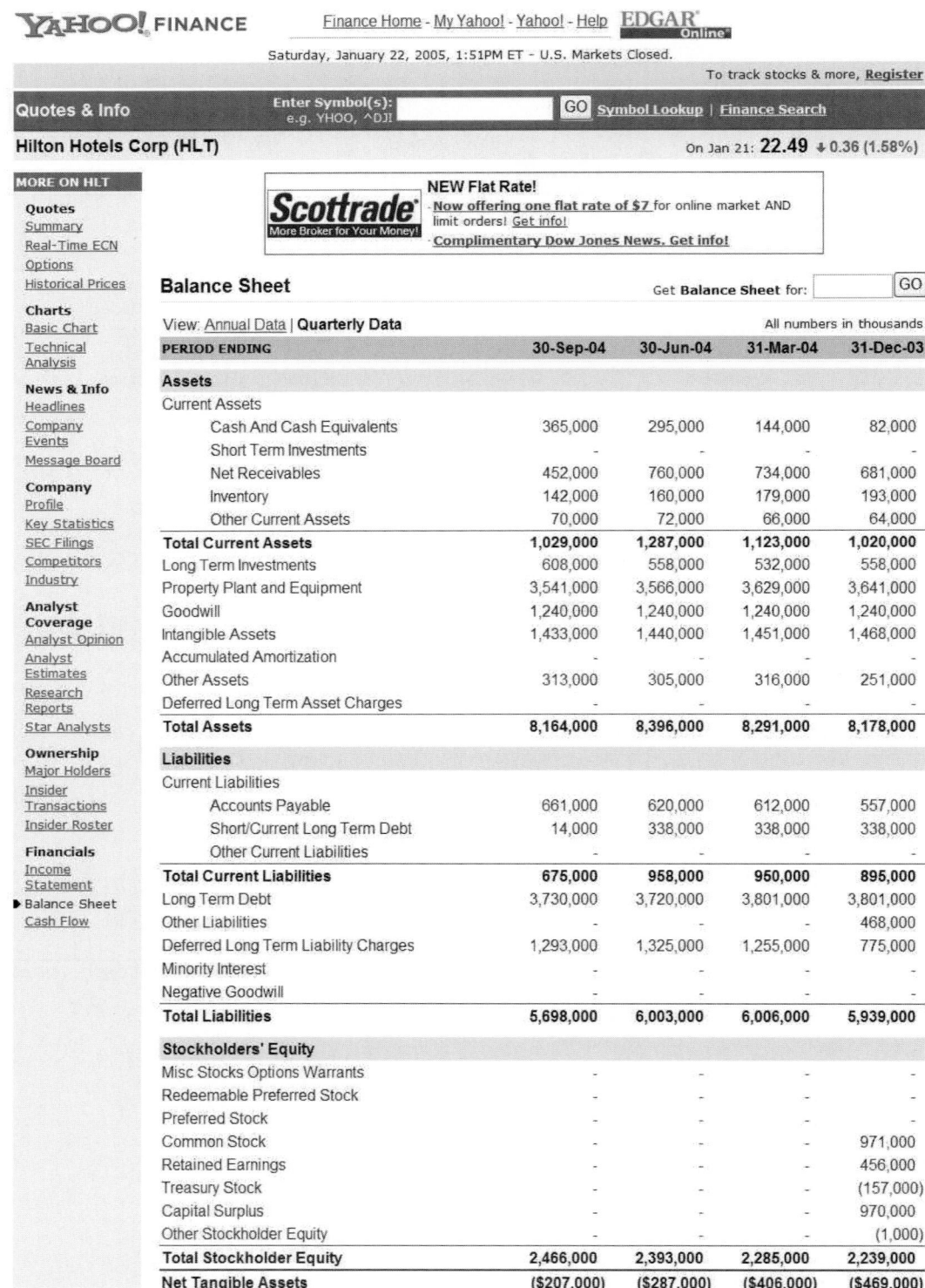

Figure 16.6 *Continued*

Notice that Hilton's interest rate has decreased from the previous quarter, in which the annualized interest rate was 8.66%. In the previous quarter the company had much more expensive short-term debt.

Hilton's Tax Rate T_C Is Approximately 35%

From the income statements in Figure 16.6 we can also compute the company's tax rate. The average quarterly tax rate for the last three quarters is 34.93%. This is the rate we will use for T_C.

	A	B	C	D	E
1	HILTON'S TAX RATE T_C				
2	Quarter	30-Sep-04	30-Jun-04	31-Mar-04	
3	Earnings before tax	96,000	118,000	61,000	
4	Provision for taxes	35,000	40,000	21,000	
5	Tax rate	36.46%	33.90%	34.43%	<-- =D4/D3
6					
7	Average tax rate, T_C		34.93%	<-- =AVERAGE(B5:D5)	

The Risk-Free Rate in the Economy r_f Is 2.21%

We get this number from Yahoo, as shown in Figure 16.7.

The Expected Return on the Market $E(r_M)$ Is Approximately 8.52%

This was illustrated on page 473.

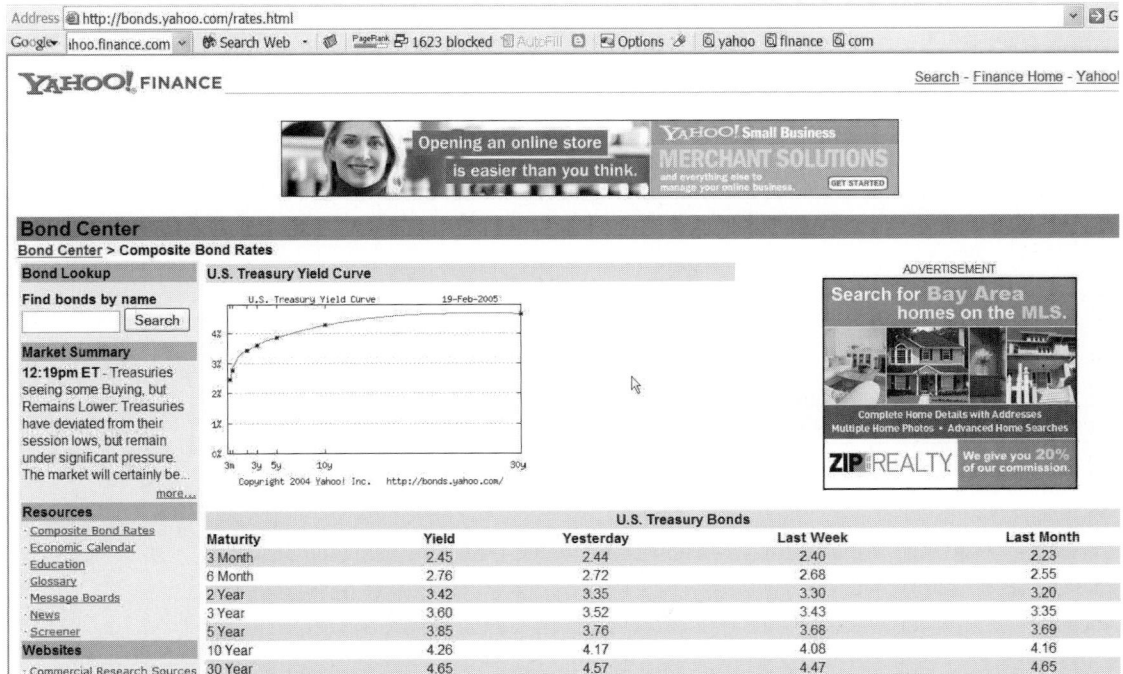

Figure 16.7 Yahoo screen with interest rates. The r_f for use in the SML is the short-term Treasury bond rate, 2.21%.

So What's Hilton's WACC?

The weighted average cost of capital for Hilton is 6.91%:

	A	B	C
1	**HILTON HOTELS CORPORATION (HLT)** **Using Yahoo for much of the information**		
2	Equity beta	0.956	<-- Yahoo
3			
4	Shares outstanding (million)	386.03	<-- Yahoo
5	Market value per share	22.49	<-- Yahoo
6	Market value of equity ($ million), E	8,682	<-- =B5*B4
7			
8	Book value of equity per share	6.388	<-- Yahoo
9	Total book value of equity	2,466	<-- =B8*B4
10	Debt/Equity ratio	1.518	<-- Yahoo
11	Book value of debt	3,743	<-- =B10*B9
12	Cash on hand	219	<-- Yahoo
13	Net debt ($ million), D	3,524	<-- =B11-B12
14			
15	Risk-free rate, r_f	2.21%	
16	Expected market return, $E(r_M)$	8.52%	
17			
18	**Computation of WACC**		
19	Percentage of equity, E/(E+D)	0.7113	<-- =B6/(B6+B13)
20	Percentage of debt, D/(E+D)	0.2887	<-- =1-B19
21	Cost of equity, r_E	8.25%	<-- =B15+B2*(B16-B15)
22	Cost of debt, r_D	5.55%	
23	Tax rate, T_C	34.93%	
24	WACC	6.91%	<-- =B19*B21+(1-B23)*B20*B22

16.4 Computing the WACC Using an Asset Beta, β_{Asset}

A somewhat different approach to computing the weighted average cost of capital (WACC) is to use the *asset beta* approach. In this approach we need both the equity beta β_E and the debt beta β_D for Hilton Hotels. The asset beta is defined as the weighted average β of the debt and equity betas:

$$\beta_{Asset} = \beta_E * \frac{E}{E+D} + \beta_D * (1-T_C) * \frac{D}{E+D}$$

$$= \left(\begin{array}{c}\text{equity}\\\text{beta}\end{array}\right) * \left(\begin{array}{c}\text{proportion}\\\text{of equity}\\\text{in firm}\\\text{value}\end{array}\right) + \left(\begin{array}{c}\text{debt}\\\text{beta}\end{array}\right) * \left(1 - \begin{array}{c}\text{corporate}\\\text{tax rate}\end{array}\right) * \left(\begin{array}{c}\text{proportion}\\\text{of debt}\\\text{in firm}\\\text{value}\end{array}\right)$$

Having computed β_{Asset}, we now compute the WACC by using the SML:

$$WACC = r_f + \beta_{Asset} * [E(r_M) - r_f]$$

In order to illustrate this approach for Hilton, we note that all the necessary calculations have been done in the previous section—with the exception of the computation of the debt beta β_D. We compute this beta by assuming that the SML holds for debt as well as equity:

$$cost\ of\ debt = r_D = r_f + \underbrace{\beta_D}_{\substack{\uparrow \\ \text{This is the} \\ \text{beta of} \\ \text{Hilton's debt}}} * [E(r_M) - r_f]$$

$$\Rightarrow \beta_D = \frac{r_D - r_f}{E(r_M) - r_f}$$

In the spreadsheet below you can see that Hilton's debt β is 0.528 (cell B8).[9] This means that its asset beta is 0.78 (cell B15), which gives the WACC as 7.13% (cell B17).

	A	B	C
1	**HILTON HOTELS CORPORATION (HLT)** **Computing the WACC with the asset beta**		
2	Equity beta, β_E	0.956	<-- Yahoo
3			
4	Risk-free rate, r_f	2.21%	
5	Expected market return, $E(r_M)$	8.52%	
6			
7	Cost of debt	5.55%	
8	Debt beta, β_D	0.528	<-- =(B7-B4)/(B5-B4)
9			
10	Corporate tax rate	34.93%	
11			
12	Percentage of equity, E/(E+D)	0.7113	
13	Percentage of debt, D/(E+D)	0.2887	
14			
15	Asset beta, β_{Asset}	0.78	<-- =B2*B12+(1-B10)*B13*B8
16			
17	WACC	7.13%	<-- =B4+B15*(B5-B4)

16.5 Don't Read This Section!

A final question that may have occurred to you: Why is it that we get a different cost of capital using the traditional WACC approach and using the asset beta (β_{Asset}) approach? We're going to answer this question in this section, but we warn you that reading the section may be bad for your health.[10]

Still here? The answer is that for cost of capital purposes, you should adjust the SML for corporate taxes. In addition, there are two SMLs—one for equity and one for debt. Here are the appropriate formulas:

Equity SML: $r_E = r_f * (1 - T_C) + \beta_E * [E(r_M) - r_f * (1 - T_C)]$

Debt SML: $r_D = r_f + \beta_D * [E(r_M) - r_f * (1 - T_C)]$

---

[9] Hilton's $\beta_D = 0.528$ may seem high, especially when compared to its equity beta, $\beta_E = 0.956$. Clearly, the market thinks that Hilton's debt is quite risky.

[10] And—in all honesty—the difference between the two calculations in the previous part of the chapter is not big enough to make much of a difference.

Note that the two SMLs have the same tax-adjusted market risk premium, $[E(r_M) - r_f * (1 - T_C)]$, but have different intercepts—the equity SML has intercept $r_f * (1 - T_C)$ whereas the debt SML has intercept r_f.[11]

If we apply this approach to Hilton Hotels, and if we assume that the cost of debt is $r_D = 6.81\%$, then we get the debt β_D as

$$
\begin{aligned}
\beta_D &= \frac{r_D - r_f}{E(r_M) - r_f * (1 - T_C)} \\
&= \frac{6.81\% - 1.60\%}{7.15\% - 1.60\%} \\
&= 0.8387
\end{aligned}
$$

Now, as you can see in the spreadsheet below, the WACC is the same, whether you compute it with the traditional method or with the asset β_{Asset}:

	A	B	C
1	**HILTON HOTELS CORPORATION (HLT)** **Using the two-SML model**		
2	Risk-free rate, r_f	2.21%	
3	Expected market return, $E(r_M)$	8.52%	
4	Corporate tax rate	34.93%	
5			
6	**WACC using traditional method**		
7	Equity beta	0.956	<-- Yahoo
8	Cost of equity	8.21%	<-- =B2*(1-B4)+B7*(B3-B2*(1-B4))
9	Cost of debt	5.55%	
10			
11	Percentage of equity, E/(E+D)	0.7113	
12	Percentage of debt, D/(E+D)	0.2887	
13	WACC	6.88%	<-- =B11*B8+B12*(1-B4)*B9
14			
15	**WACC using the asset beta and the two-SML model**		
16	Equity beta, β_E	0.956	
17	Debt beta, β_D	0.4708	<-- =(B9-B2)/(B3-B2*(1-B4))
18	Asset beta, β_{Asset}	0.7684	<-- =B11*B16+B17*(1-B4)*B12
19	WACC	6.88%	<-- =B2*(1-B4)+B18*(B3-B2*(1-B4))
20			
21	**Note**: In this method $r_E = r_f*(1 - T_C) + \beta_E*[E(r_M) - (1-T_C)*r_f]$ and $r_D = r_f + \beta_D*[E(r_M) - (1-T_C)r_f]$. The method is more theoretically correct; it also produces full agreement between the traditional WACC approach and the asset beta approach. However, for practical purposes the differences between this method and that illustrated in the first part of the chapter are usually not significant.		

---

[11]The two-SML model is fully explained in *Corporate Finance: A Valuation Approach*, by Simon Benninga and Oded Sarig (McGraw-Hill, 1997).

CONCLUSION

The computation of the weighted average cost of capital (WACC) is critical for corporate valuation. In this book we have already seen the importance of the WACC in Chapter 6.[12]

The WACC depends critically on our estimate of the cost of equity r_E. There are only two practical approaches for computing the cost of equity—the Gordon dividend model, discussed in Chapter 6, and the SML. This chapter dealt in great detail with using the SML to compute the cost of equity and the resulting WACC. We illustrated the use of the equity β_E for computing the cost of equity r_E. We also showed how you can use a combination of the equity beta β_E, the debt beta β_D, and the asset beta β_{Asset} to compute the WACC.

Through the use of a detailed example for Hilton Hotels, we showed where to get the data required to make all these calculations.

EXERCISES

1. Consider the following data, concerning ASAP Company:

$$Debt, D = 500,000$$
$$Equity, E = 300,000$$
$$Cost\ of\ debt, r_D = 6\%$$
$$Cost\ of\ equity, r_E = 11\%$$
$$Corporate\ tax, T_C = 25\%$$

Find ASAP's weighted average cost of capital, WACC.

2. Consider the following data, concerning Elizabeth Company:

$$E(r_m) = 21\%$$
$$Cost\ of\ debt, r_D = 8\%$$
$$Corporate\ tax\ rate, T_C = 25\%$$
$$\beta_{Elizabeth\ stock} = 0.7$$
$$Debt, D = 1,000,000$$
$$Value\ of\ equity, E = 1,000,000$$
$$Risk\text{-}free\ rate, r_f = 4\%$$

Find the company's weighted average cost of capital, WACC.

---

[12]The issue of stock valuation is discussed in somewhat more detail in Chapter 19, which sums up the various approaches to this important topic.

3. Consider the following data concerning Abby Company. Abby's stock is not currently listed on a stock exchange.

$$E(r_M) = 20\%$$
$$\text{Cost of debt, } r_D = 10\%$$
$$\text{Corporate tax rate, } T_C = 30\%$$
$$Cov(r_{Abby}, r_M) = 0.13$$
$$\text{Value of debt, } D = 1,500,000$$
$$r_f = 7\%$$
$$Var(r_M) = 0.11$$
$$\text{Value of equity, } E = 3,000,000$$

(a) Find Abby's WACC.

(b) Suppose Abby issues its stock in an initial public offering (IPO). After the IPO the company has 3,500,000 shares, worth $2.5 each. What is its WACC after the IPO.

4. Consider the following data, concerning Ever-Lasting Company:

$$E(r_M) = 18\%$$
$$\text{Cost of debt, } r_D = 7.5\%$$
$$\text{Corporate tax rate, } T_C = 30\%$$
$$\beta_{Ever\text{-}Lasting} = 1$$
$$\text{Market value of debt, } D = 1,250,000$$
$$\text{Market value of equity, } E = 2,000,000$$

Find the company's WACC.

5. Consider the following data:

$$EPS_0 = \$0.55$$
$$P_0 = \$22$$
$$g = 0.06$$
$$b = 45\% \text{ (dividend payout ratio)}$$

Find the price–earnings (P/E) ratio and the cost of equity using the Gordon model.

6. Consider the following data:

$$r_D = 10\%$$
$$T_C = 30\%$$
$$D = 2,500,000$$
$$E = 2,000,000$$
$$EPS_0 = \$2.5$$
$$P_0 = \$16$$
$$g = 0.075$$
$$b = 55\% \text{ (dividend payout ratio)}$$

Find the price–earnings (P/E) ratio and the company's WACC.

7. Use the following data to compute the WACC for Cobra, Inc. at year-end 2002:
   - Cobra has 1,500,000 shares. The share price at the end of 2002 was $12.00.
   - Cobra's debt at year-end 2002 was $44,500,000 and its debt at year-end 2001 was $35,000,000. The amount of interest paid in 2002 by the company was $400,000.
   - Cobra's corporate tax rate is 36%.
   - The risk-free rate of interest at the end of 2002 was $r_f = 3\%$.

   Data for the S&P 500 (the market portfolio in this case) and for Cobra returns are given below (data for this exercise can be found on the disk that accompanies this book):

	A	B	C	D
1	\multicolumn{4}{c}{**Calculating Cobra's WACC**}			
2	Year	**S&P 500 return**	**Cobra return**	**Risk-free rate**
3	1990	-3.10%	-16.00%	7.92%
4	1991	30.47%	89.12%	6.64%
5	1992	7.62%	25.33%	4.15%
6	1993	10.08%	28.95%	3.50%
7	1994	1.32%	-12.34%	3.54%
8	1995	37.58%	102.33%	7.05%
9	1996	22.96%	51.98%	5.09%
10	1997	33.36%	25.61%	5.61%
11	1998	28.58%	5.05%	5.24%
12	1999	21.04%	50.25%	4.51%
13	2000	-9.10%	-15.33%	6.12%
14	2001	-11.89%	-18.22%	4.81%
15	2002	-22.10%	-38.00%	2.16%

8. Use the Yahoo profile for Microsoft (MSFT) (given below).
   (a) What is Microsoft's price–earnings (P/E) ratio, its β, and its debt to equity ratio? (Use the trailing P/E ratio.[13])
   (b) Find MSFT's recent stock price and its number of shares and use them to compute MSFT's market equity value. Does this agree with the Yahoo computation?
   (c) Assume that $r_f = 3\%$ and the $E(r_M) = 8\%$. Compute MSFT's cost of equity r_E.

---

[13]The trailing P/E ratio is the ratio of today's price to the previous year's earnings per share. The "forward P/E" is the ratio of today's price to anticipated future earnings per share.

Quotes & Info	Enter Symbol(s): [ ] GO **Symbol Lookup** | **Finance Search**
	e.g. YHOO, ^DJI

Tyson Foods Inc (TSN)

On Mar 24: **17.00** ↑ 0.18 (1.07%)

Key Statistics

Get **Key Statistics** for: [   ] GO

Data provided by Reuters, except where noted.

VALUATION MEASURES

Market Cap (intraday):	6.00B
Enterprise Value (27-Mar-05)[3]:	9.03B
Trailing P/E (ttm, intraday):	15.32
Forward P/E (fye 2-Oct-06)[1]:	11.89
PEG Ratio (5 yr expected)±:	1.40
Price/Sales (ttm):	0.23
Price/Book (mrq):	1.37
Enterprise Value/Revenue (ttm)[3]:	0.34
Enterprise Value/EBITDA (ttm)[3]:	6.5

FINANCIAL HIGHLIGHTS

Fiscal Year

Fiscal Year Ends:	2-Oct
Most Recent Quarter (mrq):	31-Dec-04

Profitability

Profit Margin (ttm):	1.49%
Operating Margin (ttm):	3.38%

Management Effectiveness

Return on Assets (ttm):	3.79%
Return on Equity (ttm):	9.38%

Income Statement

Revenue (ttm):	26.39B
Revenue Per Share (ttm):	73.968
Revenue Growth (lfy)[3]:	7.70%
Gross Profit (ttm)[2]:	1.89B
EBITDA (ttm):	1.39B
Net Income Avl to Common (ttm):	395.00M
Diluted EPS (ttm):	1.11
Earnings Growth (lfy)[3]:	19.60%

Balance Sheet

Total Cash (mrq):	41.00M
Total Cash Per Share (mrq):	0.12
Total Debt (mrq)[2]:	3.07B
Total Debt/Equity (mrq):	0.707
Current Ratio (mrq):	1.377
Book Value Per Share (mrq):	12.266

Cash Flow Statement

From Operations (ttm)[3]:	1.09B
Free Cashflow (ttm)[3]:	621.00M

TRADING INFORMATION

Stock Price History

Beta:	0.413
52-Week Change:	-6.23%
52-Week Change (relative to S&P500):	-11.21%
52-Week High (6-Jul-04):	21.28
52-Week Low (26-Oct-04):	13.97
50-Day Moving Average:	17.19
200-Day Moving Average:	17.55

Share Statistics

Average Volume (3 month):	1,395,804
Average Volume (10 day):	1,266,000
Shares Outstanding:	353.10M
Float:	195.10M
% Held by Insiders:	44.75%
% Held by Institutions:	46.21%
Shares Short (as of 8-Mar-05):	7.81M
Daily Volume (as of 8-Mar-05):	N/A
Short Ratio (as of 8-Mar-05):	5.519
Short % of Float (as of 8-Mar-05):	4.00%
Shares Short (prior month):	7.13M

Dividends & Splits

Annual Dividend:	0.16
Dividend Yield:	0.94%
Dividend Date:	15-Jun-05
Ex-Dividend Date:	27-May-05
Last Split Factor (new per old)[2]:	3:2
Last Split Date:	18-Feb-97

More from Reuters

Reuters offers more in-depth Company Research, Stock Screening, and Risk Alerts on over 10,000 U.S. Equities.

View Financials (provided by EDGAR Online):
**Income Statement - Balance Sheet
Cash Flow**

9. Use the Yahoo profile for Tyson Food's (TSN) (given below). Compute Tyson's WACC using the company's β and other information you find on the profile. Assume that $r_f = 3\%$ and $E(r_M) = 8\%$. Last year the company paid \$186,000 in taxes on \$523,000 of pretax income. Its cost of debt $r_D = 7.76\%$.

10. Calculate General Electric's tax rate for 2002, 2003, and 2004, using the data below:

	A	B	C	D
1	**GENERAL ELECTRIC COMPANY** Income statements, 2002-2004			
2		**2002/12/31**	**2003/12/31**	**2004/12/31**
3	Total Operating Revenue	\$132,226,000,000	\$134,641,000,000	\$152,866,000,000
4	Cost of Goods Sold	\$52,856,000,000	\$51,206,000,000	\$61,759,000,000
5	Interest Expense	\$10,151,000,000	\$10,892,000,000	\$12,036,000,000
6	Income Before Tax	\$18,972,000,000	\$20,291,000,000	\$20,480,000,000
7	Net Income	\$14,167,000,000	\$15,236,000,000	\$16,819,000,000

11. Use the data below to calculate Amgen's weighted average cost fo capital (WACC) for end-2002. Assume that $E(r_M) = 8\%$ and $r_f = 4\%$.

	A	B
1	**Calculating Amgen's WACC**	
2	$E(r_M)$	8.00%
3	r_f	2.00%
4	Tax rate	44.74%
5	Beta	0.82
6	Stock price, end-2002	58.34
7		
8	Outstanding shares	1,290,000,000
9	Book value per share	14.70
10	Total book value of equity	18,963,000,000
11	Debt to equity ratio (book)	16.07%
12	Amgen's debt	3,047,700,000
13	Amgen's total value	3,047,700,058
14		
15	Interest paid, 2002	44,200,000
16	Debt, end-2002	3,047,700,000
17	Debt, end-2001	223,000,000

12. Use the data from question 12 to calculate Amgen's WACC using an asset β_{Asset}.

Wednesday, September 15, 2004, 7:24AM ET - U.S. Markets open in 2 hours and 6 minutes.

Welcome, Guest [Sign In]   To track stocks & more, **Register**

Quotes & Info	Enter Symbol(s): GO **Symbol Lookup** | **Finance Search**
	e.g. YHOO, ^DJI

Amgen Inc (AMGN)   On Sep 14: **58.34** 0.00 (0.00%) Reuters

MORE ON AMGN	
Quotes	
Summary	
Real-Time	
Mkt/ECN	
Options	
Historical Prices	
Charts	
Basic Chart	
Technical	
Analysis	
News & Info	
Headlines	
Company	
Events	
Message Board	
Company	
Profile	
▶ Key Statistics	
SEC Filings	
Competitors	
Industry	
Analyst	
Coverage	
Analyst Opinion	
Analyst	
Estimates	
Research	
Reports	
Star Analysts	
Ownership	
Major Holders	
Insider	
Transactions	
Insider Roster	
Financials	
Income	
Statement	
Balance Sheet	
Cash Flow	

Key Statistics

Get **Key Statistics** for: [   ] GO

Data provided by Reuters, except where noted.

VALUATION MEASURES

Market Cap (intraday):	73.86B
Enterprise Value (15-Sep-04)[3]:	72.16B
Trailing P/E (ttm, intraday):	29.77
Forward P/E (fye 31-Dec-05)[1]:	20.61
PEG Ratio (5 yr expected)[1]:	1.20
Price/Sales (ttm):	7.79
Price/Book (mrq):	3.80
Enterprise Value/Revenue (ttm)[3]:	7.61
Enterprise Value/EBITDA (ttm)[3]:	18.59

FINANCIAL HIGHLIGHTS

Fiscal Year

Fiscal Year Ends:	31-Dec
Most Recent Quarter (mrq):	30-Jun-04

Profitability

Profit Margin (ttm):	27.39%
Operating Margin (ttm):	37.41%

Management Effectiveness

Return on Assets (ttm):	10.03%
Return on Equity (ttm):	13.42%

Income Statement

Revenue (ttm):	9.48B
Revenue Per Share (ttm):	7.105
Revenue Growth (lfy)[3]:	51.30%
Gross Profit (ttm)[2]:	7.02B
EBITDA (ttm):	3.88B
Net Income Avl to Common (ttm):	2.60B
Diluted EPS (ttm):	1.96
Earnings Growth (lfy)[3]:	N/A

Balance Sheet

Total Cash (mrq):	4.26B
Total Cash Per Share (mrq):	3.37
Total Debt (mrq)[2]:	3.10B
Total Debt/Equity (mrq):	0.159
Current Ratio (mrq):	1.369
Book Value Per Share (mrq):	15.34

Cash Flow Statement

From Operations (ttm)[3]:	3.36B
Free Cashflow (ttm)[3]:	1.81B

View Financials (provided by EDGAR Online):
**Income Statement - Balance Sheet
Cash Flow**

TRADING INFORMATION

Stock Price History

Beta:	0.622
52-Week Change:	-15.44%
52-Week Change (relative to S&P500):	-23.78%
52-Week High (18-Sep-03):	70.14
52-Week Low (22-Jun-04):	52.15
50-Day Moving Average:	56.53
200-Day Moving Average:	58.87

Share Statistics

Average Volume (3 month):	7,968,409
Average Volume (10 day):	8,153,000
Shares Outstanding:	1.27B
Float:	1.14B
% Held by Insiders:	9.71%
% Held by Institutions:	69.42%
Shares Short (as of 9-Aug-04):	28.31M
Daily Volume (as of 9-Aug-04):	N/A
Short Ratio (as of 9-Aug-04):	3.306
Short % of Float (as of 9-Aug-04):	2.48%
Shares Short (prior month):	19.86M

Dividends & Splits

Annual Dividend:	N/A
Dividend Yield:	0.00%
Dividend Date:	19-Nov-99
Ex-Dividend Date:	22-Nov-99
Last Split Factor (new per old)[2]:	2:1
Last Split Date:	22-Nov-99

More from Reuters

Reuters offers more in-depth Company Research, Stock Screening, and Risk Alerts on over 10,000 U.S. Equities.

13. Compute Boeing's end-2002 weighted average cost of capital (WACC) using the following template.

	A	B	C
1	**Calculating Boeing's WACC**		
2	E(r_M)	7.50%	
3	r_f	3.00%	
4	Stock price	53.92	
5	Stock beta	0.72	
6	Market value of equity		
7			
8	Outstanding shares	840,900,000	
9	Book value per share	$8.28	
10	Book value of equity		
11	Debt to equity ratio	2.09	
12	Boeing's debt		
13	Market value, debt + equity		
14			
15		**2002**	**2001**
16	Income before tax	3,180,000,000	3,564,000,000
17	Income tax expense	861,000,000	738,000,000
18	Annual tax rate	27.08%	20.71%
19			
20	Interest paid, 2002	730,000,000	
21	Debt, end-year 2002	12,589,000,000	
22	Debt, end-year 2001	10,866,000,000	
23	Average debt, 2001-2002		
24	Boeing's cost of debt		
25			
26	Boeing's cost of equity		
27			
28	Boeing's WACC		

14. Use the data from question 13 to calculate Boeing's WACC using an asset beta β_{Asset}.

15. The current risk-free rate is $r_f = 4\%$ and the expected rate of return on the market portfolio is $E(r_M) = 10\%$. The BrandyWine Corporation has two divisions of equal market value. The debt to equity ratio of the company is 3/7, and the company's bonds are risk-free. For the last few years, the Brandy division has been using a discount rate of 12% in capital budgeting decisions and the Wine division a discount rate of 10%. You have been asked by their managers to report on whether these discount rates are properly adjusted for the risk of the projects in the two divisions.

   (a) What are the betas of typical projects implicit in the discount rates used by the two divisions?

   (b) You estimate that the stock beta of BrandyWine is $\beta = 1.6$. Is this consistent with the stock beta implicit in the discount rates used by the two divisions?

   (c) You estimate that the stock beta of the Korbell Brandy Corp. is 1.8. Korbell is purely in the brandy business, its debt to equity ratio is 2/3, and its bond beta is 0.2. Based on this information (and on your estimate of BrandyWine's stock beta), what discount rate would you recommend for projects in the Brandy and in the Wine divisions of BrandyWine?

16. Sun, Inc. has an equity beta of 0.5. Its capital structure consists of equal amounts of equity and risk-free debt. The debt has a pretax yield of 6% and the expected rate of return on the market index is 18%. Sun, Inc. is considering expanding into the Snow, Inc. business. This new business

is expected to generate an after-tax internal rate of return of 25%. Vacation, Inc. is already in this new business, and its equity beta is 2.0 and it uses a blend of 10% (risk-free) debt and 90% equity in its capital structure. If the new project is to be funded with 50% debt, should Sun, Inc. enter the Snow, Inc. business? Assume that both companies have a marginal tax rate of 50%, and that the business risk of Vacation, Inc. is comparable to the risk of Sun, Inc.'s venture.

17. A company is deciding whether to issue stock to raise money for an investment project that has the same risk as the market and an expected return of 15%. If the risk-free rate is 5%, and the expected return on the market is 12%, the company should:

    (a) Not take on this project—True or False?

    (b) Proceed with the investment regardless of the company's beta—True or False?

    (c) Proceed with the investment unless the company's beta is greater than 1.25—True or False?

    (d) Proceed with the investment unless the company's beta is less than 1.25—True or False?

18. The project whose cash flows are given below has a $\beta = 1.6$. If the market return $E(r_M) = 15\%$ and the risk-free rate $r_f = 7\%$, should the firm undertake the project?

	A	B
1	Year	Cash flow
2	0	-100
3	1	60
4	2	50
5	3	40

19. A share of a stock with a beta of 0.75 now sells for $50. Investors expect the stock to pay a year-end dividend of $3. The T-Bill rate is 4%, and the market risk premium is 8%. What is the investors' expectation of the price of the stock at the end of the year?

20. Reconsider the stock in Exercise 19. Suppose investors actually believe the stock will sell for $54 at year-end. Is the stock a good or bad buy? What will investors do? At what point will the stock reach an equilibrium at which it again is perceived as fairly priced?

PART IV

VALUING SECURITIES

Two of the three chapters of Part 4 of *Principles of Finance with Excel* look at how to value bonds (Chapter 18) and stocks (Chapter 19).

Chapter 17 examines market efficiency. Roughly speaking, market efficiency is a group of concepts that look at how information is incorporated in financial markets. Does the bundling of assets into one package affect their prices? This question concerns price additivity, and when you read Chapter 17, you'll see that the answer to this question is not trivial. Does the knowledge of the price history of a stock affect your ability to predict the future price of the stock (market efficiency says "no")?

The market efficiency discussed in Chapter 17 provides you with the necessary background for the valuation of bonds and stocks. Details specific to bond markets are given in Chapter 18; this chapter also discusses preferred stocks, which are very similar to bonds.

In Chapter 19 we apply the concepts of cash flow discounting and market efficiency to the valuation of stocks. Chapter 19 discusses and compares the four most commonly used techniques for stock valuation.

CHAPTER 17

Efficient Markets— Some General Principles of Security Valuation

OVERVIEW

Finance often requires a lot of calculation, which is why this book concentrates on solving financial problems with a powerful tool like Excel. But sometimes understanding the way that financial markets work requires only wisdom and very little calculation. This chapter discusses some general principles of valuation, which can save you from a lot of nonsense and in many cases require almost no calculation. Having discussed these very important general principles, we then move on to deal with the valuation of bonds (Chapter 18) and stocks (Chapter 19).

Here's an example of the kind of nonsense that you'll learn to avoid by reading and understanding this chapter: Your college roommate Clarence has just given you a "hot tip" on Federated Underwear (FU) stock: Clarence is sure that you should immediately buy the stock.

"It's going to go up. I know it," he says excitedly. "My pop says that FU has been fluctuating between $15 and $25 for the past year. Every time it gets close to $15, it goes up, and when it gets close to $25, it goes down again. Yesterday FU closed at $15.05. Buy it and wait—the stock is sure to go up, and then you'll sell it at $25 and make a killing."

After reading this chapter, you'll know to tell Clarence: "My friend, your advice is a perfect example of a *technical trading rule*. And Chapter 17 of my college finance textbook *Principles of Finance with Excel,* explains that these rules are a clear violation of the principle of weak-form market efficiency, which almost always holds. If you want to bet your money on such foolishness, go ahead. I'm going to spend my hard-earned cash on a night out at the Efficient Markets Disco."

In the broadest sense the general principles discussed in this chapter all deal with the role of information in determining asset prices. When translated into simple language, these principles sound pretty dumb. They say things like: "Information is important." "Transaction costs matter." "One plus one equals two." When applied to asset markets the valuation principles discussed in this chapter often enable you to make surprising statements about what things are worth.

Here are four basic principles of valuation discussed in this chapter.

Efficient Markets Principle 1: *Single price for a single good.* In financial markets, equivalent financial assets have the same price. Section 17.1 uses cross-listed stocks—stocks that trade on two financial markets, like IBM stock on the New York Stock Exchange and IBM stock on the Pacific Stock Exchange—as a nontrivial example of this principle.

Efficient Markets Principle 2: *Price additivity.* The price of a bundle of securities should be the sum of the prices of each of the securities. It is difficult to overestimate the importance of this principle. One of its predictions is that there are no "money machines"—it costs money to make money. Another prediction is that knowing the prices of the *components* of a financial asset will help you price the whole asset.

Efficient Markets Principle 3: *Information is critical.* Finding out previously unknown information can be a very profitable exercise. Conversely, it is difficult to make money from facts that everyone knows. The more widely information is known, the less you can make money from the information. Principle 3 is usually split into three parts:

- The principle of *weak-form efficiency* states that prices incorporate all current and past price information. If this principle holds (and almost all economists believe that it does), then it is not possible to make money based on the pattern of past prices of a traded security. This means that "money-making" rules that are based on price patterns—"buy a stock if it's gone up three days in a row, sell it if it's gone down three days running"—are futile. The weak-form version of the efficient markets hypothesis should make you skeptical about a lot of investment strategies. An example is investment advisors who claim to be able to tell market trends from price patterns. These so-called "technical traders" are giving advice that violates the weak-form efficient markets hypothesis, and this advice should be ignored.

- The principle of *semi-strong-form efficiency* states that prices incorporate all publicly known information. Financial markets are awash in publicly available information. Can you make money by carefully reading the financial statements of IBM? Probably not—IBM has many shareholders and is followed by hundreds of stock analysts. If the analysts are doing their jobs even moderately well, the information that can be gleaned from the IBM financial statements is already incorporated in the company's stock price. Most economists believe that markets are more-or-less semi-strong efficient. As you'll see in this chapter, it depends on how difficult it is to derive the information and how many investors carefully follow a particular stock.

- The principle of *strong-form efficiency* states that prices incorporate *all information* that exists (public or private) about a security. In addition to IBM's publicly available financial statements and the analyses of stock analysts, there's also lots of *private* information about the company. For example, people working for the company know a lot about the sales, production, and costs of their individual units. Is this information also incorporated in IBM's stock price? Almost no economists believe this. Meaning: Knowing privately available information can provide you with profits.[1] Markets are not strong-form efficient.

   Efficient Markets Principle 4: Transaction costs are important and can screw up everything. This is an important truth about markets. Transaction costs—by this we mean not just the costs of buying and selling securities, but also the cost of ferreting out information—make it more difficult to trade. And it's trade—the buying and selling of financial assets like stocks and bonds—that makes market prices reflect the true value of assets.

Finance Concepts Discussed

- Efficiency
- Additivity
- Short sales
- Open-end and closed-end mutual funds

Excel Functions Used

- This chapter has some Excel, but nothing sophisticated

17.1 Efficient Markets Principle 1: Competitive Markets Have a Single Price for a Single Good

A *competitive market* is a market with a large number of buyers and sellers, none of whom can influence the price of the goods bought and sold in the market. Financial markets are good examples of competitive markets: There are a large number of buyers and sellers for most stocks sold on major stock exchanges, there are many banks competing for your bank accounts and for your mortgage, and so on.

   The principle that *competitive markets have a single price for a single good* is basic to economics and is drilled home in most introductory economics courses. Under some circumstances, this principle seems to be ridiculously obvious. For example, in the Asheville, North Carolina, farmer's market (the author's hometown), there are many stands selling apples. Many of the vendors sell Granny Smith (GS) apples. The GS apples sold by the vendors are of approximately the same size and quality. The result: The price of apples of the same type is approximately the same at all the stands. Why? Suppose one vendor deviates from the equilibrium price of GS apples by selling below the price of the other vendors. Then he'll attract a lot of buyers. Being competitive, he will raise his price and the other GS vendors (also competitive) will lower their prices until, equilibrium being restored, the market price for GS apples is the same at all GS stands.

---

[1]Beware! Stock trading on the basis of insider information is also illegal.

Cross-Listed Stocks—An Application of the One-Price Principle

The one-good, one-price principle also has applications in stock markets. Here's an example. IBM stock is traded both on the New York Stock Exchange (NYSE) and on the Pacific Stock Exchange (PSE). When both exchanges are open, the price of IBM stock is basically the same in both exchanges. This isn't surprising: If the price of IBM in New York is $120 and its price is $118 in San Francisco, brokers would obviously try to *arbitrage* (that is, make money from unreasonable differences in prices) by buying IBM stock in San Francisco and selling it in New York. Since transaction costs are very low and since trade in stocks is instantaneous, this will drive the prices together.[2]

There's more to this than meets the eye: The NYSE opens before the PSE, but the PSE stays open later. This means that information about IBM that arrives late in the day will be incorporated in the PSE stock price but will hit the NYSE price only the next morning. In some cases this phenomenon is even more extreme. For example, there's a large group of Israeli shares that are traded both in Tel-Aviv and on the NASDAQ in the United States. The trading overlap between the two markets is only one hour per day (between 9:30 and 10:30 am Eastern time, both NASDAQ and Tel-Aviv are open—after this Tel-Aviv closes and all trading in the cross-listed stocks is on the NASDAQ). During this trading overlap, cross-listed stocks have the same price in both markets, but when only one market is open, this need not be so.

17.2 Efficient Markets Principle 2: Bundles Are Priced Additively

Prices are *additive* when the market price of A + B is equal to the market price of A plus the price of B. This sounds so obvious that it's hard to believe that it could be interesting (and, indeed, once you understand it, it's pretty boring!).

For an initial example, we go back to the Asheville farmer's market. Our previous example dealt with Granny Smith (GS) apples, but some of the vendors also sell Red Delicious (RD) apples. As we speak, the price of GS apples is $2 per pound and the price of RD apples is $3 per pound. Simon, a somewhat peculiar vendor, sells bags of apples containing both GS and RD apples: Each bag weighs 2 pounds and contains 1 pound of GS and 1 pound of RD apples. How should he price these bags? Obviously the answer is $5 per bag.

Why? Not so trivial, actually. Suppose Simon prices the bags at $4.50. Then anyone wanting 1 pound of GS and 1 pound of RD will obviously buy with Simon. If Simon is sensitive to supply and demand, he'll notice the demand for his mixed bags of apples and raise the price; at the same time, other apple stands—seeing their demand weaken—will lower the prices of their apples.

Furthermore, if Simon persists in selling his bags of apples at $4.50, Sharon—a sharp cookie (or should we say "sharp apple"?)—will buy bags of apples from Simon. She'll then take the apples out of the bag and sell them at her apple stand for the market price of $2 for GS and $3 for RD. In the language of finance—Sharon is *arbitraging the price*. In the language of her grandmother, Sharon is buying cheap and selling dear.

---

[2]Notice how we've already slipped in the importance of *transaction costs* ("Principle 4: Transaction costs are important"). The sentence in the text suggests that transaction costs may include not only the direct cost of buying and selling (commissions, computer time, etc.), but also the cost of the time involved in transporting a good from one market to another. Luckily for this example, stock markets have pretty low transaction costs, especially for brokers and dealers.

On the other hand, suppose Simon prices the bags at $5.50. People will probably stop buying with him, even if they want bags with equal combinations of GS and RD—they can buy them cheaper elsewhere. Eventually, Simon will have to lower his price. If, contrary to expectations, it turns out that Simon does a brisk business in the apple bags for $5.50, then other smart apple stand owners will start selling their own bags of apples; since they can put together a bag for less than what Simon charges, the price of the mixed bags will go back down.

There might actually be room for Simon to sell his apple bags for $5.05, since he's saving his customers the trouble of going to two apple stands. In the language of finance, he's saving them the *transaction cost* of buying the apples separately. They ought to be willing to pay him for this service.

The principle of price additivity is often summed up by the statement that *there are no money machines* in financial markets: You cannot simply make money by buying a complex financial asset (like Simon's bags of apples), taking it apart (separate bags of GS and RD), and selling the separate bags. The converse is also true: The "money machine" of combining GS and RD apples into one bag won't work.[3]

Now that you understand the principle of additivity as applied to the Asheville farmer's market, here are some nontrivial finance applications:

RICHARD GERE THE ARBITRAGEUR

In the movie *Pretty Woman* (1990), Richard Gere plays an "arbitrageur": Gere buys up companies and then breaks them up and sells off the parts for a profit. To quote a website that discusses this movie: "This is presented in the movie, as such things are in the press generally, as a useless, evil thing, that destroys jobs and wrecks business—the 'greed' of the 80's. In the movie, Julia Roberts even compares it to stealing cars and selling the parts. In fact, it is a useful thing, which easily creates jobs and increases production. A company can be broken up and sold for a profit only if it is worth less than what the sum of what its parts are worth individually. But if a company is worth less than the sum of its parts, then breaking up the company frees capital that can be used for other investment purposes, including creating jobs in other companies or industries." (http://www.friesian.com/trade.htm)

Additivity, Example 1: The Term Structure Prices Bonds

The principle of bundle pricing is often applied to the pricing of bonds. A bond gives you a series of payments over time. Each of these payments is a separate financial package. If we can price each financial package, then we should be able to price the bond. For the moment we confine ourselves to a simple bond example, saving more complicated ones for the next chapter.

Here's an example. Suppose there are two bonds in the financial market, Bond A and Bond B:

- Bond A sells today for $100 and pays off $110 in one year. The bond's IRR is $10.00\% = 110/100 - 1$.

- Bond B also sells today for $100. This bond has a payoff only at the end of two years, at which point it pays $125. The IRR of the bond is $11.80\% = (125/100)^{1/2} - 1$.

---

[3]In a broader sense, all of the efficient markets principles in this chapter say that there are no easy ways to make money on financial markets. If you want to make money, you'll have to do some meaningful work.

Now suppose that you're trying to price a Bond C, which has a payoff of $23 in one year and $1023 in two years. The price-additivity principle says that the way to price this bond is to apply the IRRs calculated above separately to each year's bond payment. In a formula,

$$bond\ price = \frac{23}{1.10} + \frac{1023}{(1.1180)^2} = 839.31$$

In this formula we've discounted the first bond payment of $23 by the market interest rate on the one-year bonds, and we've discounted the second bond payment of $1023 by the IRR derived from Bond B. Here's the spreadsheet:

	A	B	C	D
1		**PRICE ADDITIVITY IN BONDS**		
2	**Bond A: maturity in one year**			
3	Price today	100		
4	Payoff in one year	110		
5	IRR	10.00%	<-- =B4/B3-1	
6				
7	**Bond B: maturity in two years**			
8	Price today	100		
9	Payoff in one year	0		
10	Payoff in two years	125		
11	IRR	11.80%	<-- =(B10/B8)^(1/2)-1	
12				
13				
14	**Bond C: A bond with payments at end of year 1 and year 2**			
15	Date	Payment	Present value of payment	
16	1	23	20.91	<-- =B16/(1+B5)
17	2	1023	818.40	<-- =B17/(1+B11)^2
18	**Bond price?**		**839.31**	<-- =SUM(C16:C17)

Figure 17.1 presents the logic in a schematic.

To sum up: We've used market discount rates derived from bonds with only one payment to additively price a bond with multiyear payments.

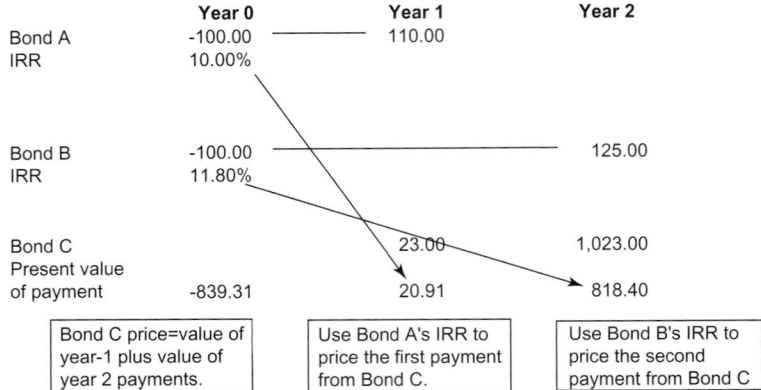

Figure 17.1 Pricing a bond by additivity. Bond C is priced by taking the IRR of Bond A and applying it to the first-year payment of Bond C and by taking the IRR of Bond B and applying it to the second-year payment of Bond C. In the jargon of bond markets, both Bond A and Bond B are known as *zero-coupon bonds*. A zero-coupon bond is a bond with only two cash flows: the initial price of the bond and the final payoff. See Chapter 18 for more details.

Additivity, Example 2: Open-End Mutual Funds

The webpage of the United States Securities and Exchange Commission (SEC) defines a *mutual fund* as:

> A mutual fund is a company that brings together money from many people and invests it in stocks, bonds or other assets. The combined holdings of stocks, bonds or other assets the fund owns are known as its *portfolio*. Each investor in the fund owns shares, which represent a part of these holdings.
> http://www.sec.gov/investor/tools/mfcc/mutual-fund-help.htm

Figure 17.2 gives some more information from the SEC about mutual funds.

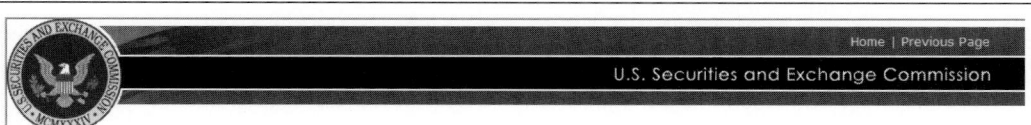

Mutual Funds

A mutual fund is a company that pools money from many investors and invests the money in stocks, bonds, short-term money-market instruments, or other securities. Legally known as an "open-end company," a mutual fund is one of three basic types of *investment company*. The two other basic types are *closed-end funds* and *Unit Investment Trusts (UITs)*.

Here are some of the traditional and distinguishing characteristics of mutual funds:

- Investors purchase mutual fund shares from the fund itself (or through a broker for the fund), but are not able to purchase the shares from other investors on a secondary market, such as the New York Stock Exchange or Nasdaq Stock Market. The price investors pay for mutual fund shares is the fund's per share *net asset value (NAV)* plus any *shareholder fees* that the fund imposes at purchase (such as sales loads).

- Mutual fund shares are "redeemable." This means that when mutual fund investors want to sell their fund shares, they sell them back to the fund (or to a broker acting for the fund) at their approximate NAV, minus any fees the fund imposes at that time (such as deferred sales loads or redemption fees).

- Mutual funds generally sell their shares on a continuous basis, although some funds will stop selling when, for example, they become too large.

- The investment portfolios of mutual funds typically are managed by separate entities known as "*investment advisers*" that are registered with the SEC.

Mutual funds come in many varieties. For example, there are *index funds, stock funds, bond funds, money market funds,* and more. Each of these may have a different investment objective and strategy and a different investment portfolio. Different mutual funds may also be subject to different risks, volatility, and *fees and expenses.*

All funds charge management fees for operating the fund. Some also charge for their distribution and service costs, commonly referred to as "*12b-1" fees.* Some funds may also impose *sales charge or loads* when you purchase or sell fund shares. In this regard, a fund may offer different "*classes*" of shares in the same portfolio, with each class having different fees and expenses.

Figure 17.2 Description of mutual funds from the SEC website. *Source:* http://www.sec.gov/answers/mutfund.htm.

Does it matter if you *bundle* securities together in a mutual fund? How should the price of such a fund be determined? The principle of pricing additivity gives us a way to handle this problem—it suggests that the price of a mutual fund should be determined by the market prices of all the fund's assets.

As a simple example, suppose you start a new company, the Super-Duper Fund, which sells a mutual fund of a very specific type.

- Super-Duper currently has 10,000 shareholders, each of whom has invested $100—so that the total assets of the company are $1,000,000.
- Super-Duper's money is currently invested 50% in shares of IBM (currently trading at $100) and 50% in shares of Intel (currently trading at $50). The Super-Duper Fund currently owns 5,000 shares of IBM and 10,000 shares of Intel.
- The number of shares in the fund is *flexible*.[4] Right now, there are 10,000 shares, but this number can go up or down:
  - If a shareholder wants to sell, you promise to liquidate his/her proportional part of the fund's assets. So if Uncle Joe from Winona, who owns one Super-Duper share worth $100, wants to sell his share in the company, Super-Duper will sell $1/2$ share of IBM and 1 share of Intel and repay him his $100. Now the fund will have $999,900 in assets, still invested 50% in IBM and 50% in Intel.
  - If any new shareholders want to join, Super-Duper will buy—per $100 of new funds that come into the company—$50 of IBM and $50 of Intel.[5]

Suppose that today no one sells or buys shares in the fund. The asset value of the Super-Duper Fund today is $1,000,000. Now suppose that tomorrow the price of IBM is $110 and the price of Intel is $48. Then the value of a fund share is $103 (cell C14 below):

	A	B	C	D
1		SUPER-DUPER OPEN END MUTUAL FUND		
2		Today	Tomorrow before new fundholders	
3	Number of shareholders	10,000	10,000	
4				
5	Portfolio			
6	Price of IBM	100	110	
7	Price of Intel	50	48	
8				
9	Portfolio composition			
10	Shares of IBM	5,000	5,000	
11	Shares of Intel	10,000	10,000	
12				
13	Total fund value	1,000,000	1,030,000	<-- =C10*C6+C11*C7
14	Value of 1 fund share	100	103	<-- =C13/C3
15				
16		Tomorrow: after new fundholders		New shares are created at the current fund share price, so the fund is now worth 10,500*$103=$1,081,500.
17	Number of shareholders	10,500		
18	Total fund value	1,081,500	<-- =B17*C14	
19				
20	Portfolio composition			
21	Shares of IBM	4,915.91	<-- =B18*50%/C6	
22	Shares of Intel	11,265.63	<-- =B18*50%/C7	

---

[4]In the jargon of mutual funds, this makes it an *open-end* fund. Our next example considers a closed-end fund.

[5]Actually, Super-Duper Fund does all this at the end of the day. So if Uncle Joe wants to sell his share and Aunt Maude wants to invest an additional $100, Super-Duper has a *wash,* and it can save on the transaction costs of buying and selling. Every penny helps!

Now suppose that at the close of the day tomorrow another 500 individuals buy shares of the fund. This means that they pay $500 * \$103 = \$51,500$ to buy shares in the fund. Assuming that the fund sticks to its current policy of splitting its investment equally between IBM and Intel, the total fund value of $1,081,500 (cell B18 above) will now be invested in 4,915.91 shares of IBM and 11,265.63 shares of Intel.

In an *open-end mutual fund* the number of shares is flexible. New shareholders buy into the fund at the per-share value of the fund, and shareholders in the fund who want to cash out cash out at the per-share value of the fund. At any point in time, the per-share value of the fund is given by the formula

$$
\begin{aligned}
\textit{open-end fund per-share value} &= \frac{\textit{fund net asset value (NAV)}}{\textit{number of shares in fund}} \\
&= \frac{\textit{market value of fund's portfolio} - \textit{fund expenses}}{\textit{number of shares in fund}}.
\end{aligned}
$$

Notice that we've introduced a new bit of jargon: A mutual fund's net asset value (NAV) is the market value of the fund's portfolio minus fund expenses.

The additivity principle applied to open-end mutual funds means that *an open-end mutual fund is priced at the sum of the values of the share portfolio held by the fund.*

Mutual Fund Costs: Some Technical Details: The fund has some expenses that are charged to the fund holders and deducted from the value of the fund. These include the costs of buying and selling shares. Another fund cost is the cost of paying the managers: Typically, fund managers charge their clients a percentage cost. If your fund charges 1% (in the U.S. this is typical), then this cost ($10,000 per year in our example) has to be taken out of the value of the fund.

Our Super-Duper Fund doesn't charge shareholders to buy or sell shares in the fund. However, an important class of mutual funds charge shareholders to buy shares in their funds. These so-called *front-end load* mutual funds are more expensive than *no-load* funds. Suppose, for example, that Super-Super-Duper were to charge a 7% front-end load. Then you would pay $107 (= \$100 + 7\%$ front-end load) to buy a share of the fund. Front-end loads are obviously expensive; mutual fund salespeople sometimes justify these extra charges as an appropriate price to pay for the expertise of better fund management, but there is almost no evidence to show that this is true.[6]

Additivity, Example 3: Closed-End Mutual Funds—When Additivity Fails

Value additivity doesn't always work. In this subsection we give an example of *closed-end mutual funds*. A closed-end mutual fund is an investment company with a fixed number of shares. Like open-end mutual funds, closed-end mutual funds invest in a portfolio of stocks. As opposed to an open-end mutual fund, however, where the number of shares can be expanded or contracted, a closed-end mutual fund has a fixed number of shares, which are sold on the stock market. The company issues no more new shares, and the market price fluctuates with supply

---

[6]Recall that in Chapter 12 we discussed a technique for judging mutual fund performance using the capital asset pricing model (CAPM). Finance researchers employing this and more sophisticated techniques find little evidence that front-end load mutual funds outperform no-load mutual funds.

and demand for the fund's shares. Closed-end funds are investment companies for which value additivity usually fails.

Here's an example. The Chippewa Fund is a closed-end fund that looks a lot like the Super-Duper Fund. Like Super-Duper, Chippewa has 10,000 shares. Chippewa's share portfolio currently consists of $500,000 of IBM stock and $500,000 of Intel stock, and its shares are registered on the Chippewa Stock Exchange. The fund has no other assets.

What should be the price of a Chippewa Fund share? It seems that it should be equal to the per-share value of the fund's assets—in our case $100 per share (as you saw in our discussion of open-end mutual funds, the finance jargon is the *net asset value* of the Chippewa Fund is $100 per share). But checking the newspapers, you find that the share price of the Chippewa Fund is $90, below its net asset value. A back-check of the prices of the Chippewa Fund shows you that Chippewa almost always sells for less than its net asset value. In fact, a finance-knowledgeable friend has told you that almost all closed-end funds sell for less than their net asset value.

The reasons why closed-end funds sell at a discount are not well-understood.[7] What is well-understood, however, is that it is difficult to arbitrage a closed-end fund discount—meaning that it is difficult for investors to make money out of the discount and, by making money, cause the discount to disappear. Suppose, for example, that shares of Chippewa Fund trade below the $100 net asset value, say, at $90. Then both existing and potential fund shareholders have a problem: On the one hand, the existing shareholders are holding $100 market-value shares worth only $90. If the closed-end fund were to break up, existing shareholders would get the net asset value of $100. So all the shareholders would in principle favor breaking up the fund, but no individual shareholder would want to sell his individual shares before such a breakup. A potential new shareholder is faced with the same problem: He gets $100 (market value) of shares for $90, but he has no guarantee that the value of the closed-end fund will ultimately get back to the market value.

This whole scenario may sound somewhat improbable, but in fact there are many closed-end mutual funds. Figure 17.3 gives an actual example: Tri-Continental Corporation is a closed-end fund registered on the New York Stock Exchange. On 23 November 2001, the fund's shares were worth 11.18% less than the market value of the fund's portfolio. This *closed-end fund discount* is pervasive throughout the closed-end fund industry.

Summing Up Additivity

As long as market participants can freely arbitrage, we expect value additivity to hold: The value of a basket of goods or financial assets should equal the sum of the values of the components. Arbitrage in this case means the ability of market participants to create and sell their own bundles of goods or assets, or to break up existing bundles and sell the components. This is true whether we're discussing the cost of a bag of apples in the Asheville farmers' market or the

---

[7]A readable survey of closed-end fund discounts is a paper by Elroy Dimson and Carolina Minua-Paluello, Closed-End Funds: A Survey, which is available on the Web. In their introduction, they write: "Closed-end funds are characterized by one of the most puzzling anomalies in finance: the closed-end fund discount. Shares in American funds are issued at a premium to net asset value (NAV) of up to 10 percent, while British funds are issued at a premium amounting to at least 5 percent. This premium represents the underwriting fees and start-up costs associated with the flotation. Subsequently, within a matter of months, the shares trade at a discount, which persists and fluctuates. . . . Upon termination (liquidation or 'open-ending') of the fund, share price rises and discounts disappear."

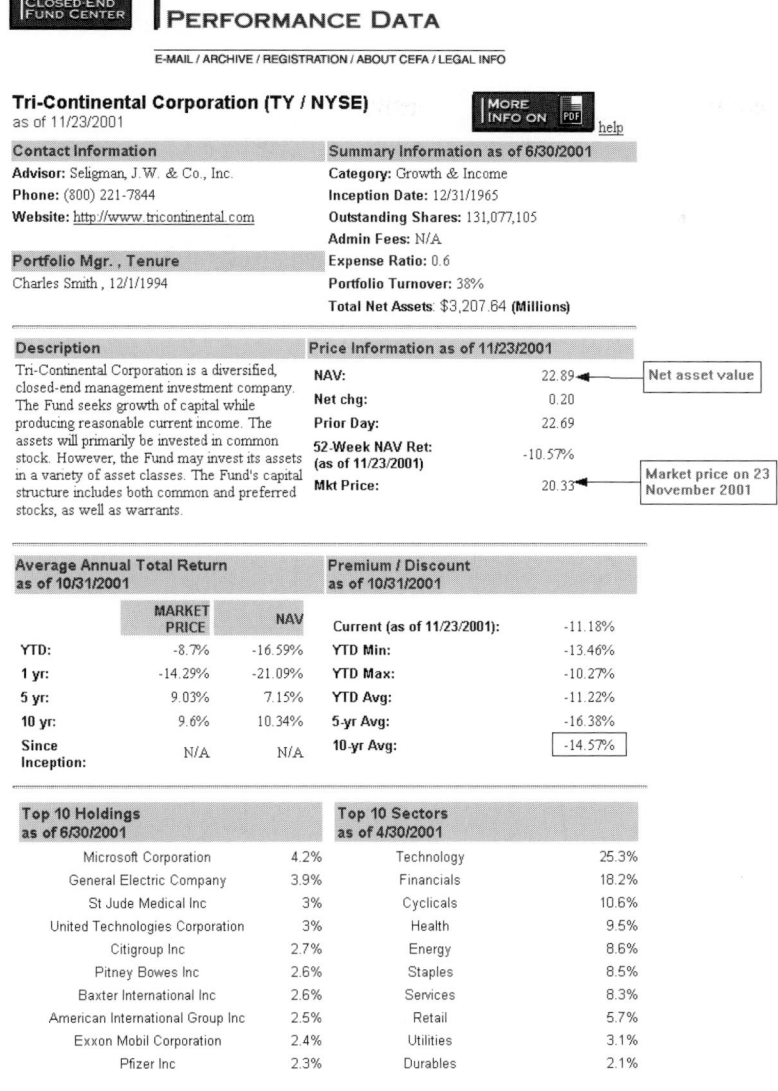

PERFORMANCE DATA

E-MAIL / ARCHIVE / REGISTRATION / ABOUT CEFA / LEGAL INFO

Tri-Continental Corporation (TY / NYSE)
as of 11/23/2001

MORE INFO ON [PDF] help

Contact Information

Advisor: Seligman, J.W. & Co., Inc.
Phone: (800) 221-7844
Website: http://www.tricontinental.com

Portfolio Mgr., Tenure

Charles Smith , 12/1/1994

Summary Information as of 6/30/2001

Category: Growth & Income
Inception Date: 12/31/1965
Outstanding Shares: 131,077,105
Admin Fees: N/A
Expense Ratio: 0.6
Portfolio Turnover: 38%
Total Net Assets: $3,207.64 **(Millions)**

Description

Tri-Continental Corporation is a diversified, closed-end management investment company. The Fund seeks growth of capital while producing reasonable current income. The assets will primarily be invested in common stock. However, the Fund may invest its assets in a variety of asset classes. The Fund's capital structure includes both common and preferred stocks, as well as warrants.

Price Information as of 11/23/2001

NAV:	22.89	← Net asset value
Net chg:	0.20	
Prior Day:	22.69	
52-Week NAV Ret: (as of 11/23/2001)	-10.57%	
Mkt Price:	20.33	← Market price on 23 November 2001

Average Annual Total Return as of 10/31/2001

	MARKET PRICE	NAV
YTD:	-8.7%	-16.59%
1 yr:	-14.29%	-21.09%
5 yr:	9.03%	7.15%
10 yr:	9.6%	10.34%
Since Inception:	N/A	N/A

Premium / Discount as of 10/31/2001

Current (as of 11/23/2001):	-11.18%
YTD Min:	-13.46%
YTD Max:	-10.27%
YTD Avg:	-11.22%
5-yr Avg:	-16.38%
10-yr Avg:	-14.57%

Top 10 Holdings as of 6/30/2001

Microsoft Corporation	4.2%
General Electric Company	3.9%
St Jude Medical Inc	3%
United Technologies Corporation	3%
Citigroup Inc	2.7%
Pitney Bowes Inc	2.6%
Baxter International Inc	2.6%
American International Group Inc	2.5%
Exxon Mobil Corporation	2.4%
Pfizer Inc	2.3%

Top 10 Sectors as of 4/30/2001

Technology	25.3%
Financials	18.2%
Cyclicals	10.6%
Health	9.5%
Energy	8.6%
Staples	8.5%
Services	8.3%
Retail	5.7%
Utilities	3.1%
Durables	2.1%

Figure 17.3 Tri-Continental Corporation is a closed-end fund whose shares are registered on the New York Stock Exchange. On 23 November 2001, Tri-Continental's assets—the market value of the shares contained in its portfolio—totaled $3,207,840,000. Since the fund has 131,077,105 shares, this works out to a *net asset value* (*NAV*) per share of $NAV = \$3,207,840,000/131,077,105 = \$22.89$. However, on the same date, the fund's shares sold for $20.33, *a discount* of 11.18%. The Tri-Continental discount is pervasive. In the last ten years the discount has averaged 14.57%. *Source:* http://www.closed-endfunds.com/

price of an open-end mutual fund. But there are also situations, like a closed-end fund, where arbitrage is difficult. For these cases, like the closed-end funds discussed above, we would not expect value additivity to hold.

We're not quite done with additivity: In the next section we discuss an interesting case where value additivity was clearly violated, but where—eventually—market prices came to reflect value additivity.

17.3 Additivity Is Not Always Instantaneous: The Case of Palm and 3Com

During the 1990s, 3Com developed the Palm Pilot, a handheld personal information manager, which became a raging success. In March 2000, 3Com sold 5.7% of its Palm subsidiary to the public. After this "equity carveout," there were separate stock market listings for Palm (still 94.3% owned by 3Com) and for the parent company 3Com. On 3 March 2000, the closing stock price for Palm was $80.25 per share and the closing stock price for 3Com was $83.06 per share. As you'll see, this situation represents an interesting violation of the principle of value additivity.

In the spreadsheet below we calculate the market value of Palm (cell B5) and of 3Com (cell B10).

	A	B	C
1	**3COM AND PALM** **This spreadsheet reflects market prices on** **3 March 2000, the day after the issue of 5.7%** **of Palm stock held by 3Com**		
2	**Palm**		
3	Price per share	80.25	
4	Number of shares outstanding	562,258,065	
5	Market value	45,121,209,716	<-- =B4*B3
6			
7	**3Com**		
8	Price per share	83.06	
9	Number of shares outstanding	349,354,000	
10	Market value	29,017,343,240	<-- =B9*B8
11			
12	Value of Palm stock held by 3Com (94.3%)	42,549,300,762	<-- =94.3%*B5
13	Value of non-Palm 3Com activities	-13,531,957,522	<-- =B10-B12

If you look at these numbers you'll see a startling *failure* of value additivity:

- 3Com owns most of Palm, but Palm's value is bigger than 3Com's! To be more precise, the 94.3% of Palm stock still owned by 3Com is worth $42.5 billion (cell B12), but all of 3Com is worth only $29.0 billion (cell B10).

- Using these numbers, the market seems to value all of the non-Palm activities of 3Com at a *negative* $13.5 billion!!!! The only way this would be possible is if these activities were big money losers (which wasn't the case).

Why did additivity fail in this big way? Why didn't market participants arbitrage the 3Com and Palm stock prices so that additivity would be restored (below we explain how such an arbitrage would work)? One possible reason is that markets are (temporarily) relatively stupid: The enthusiasm for the initial public offering (IPO) of Palm at the beginning of March 2000 was so overwhelming that investors (temporarily, as you'll see below) forgot that 3Com still owned most of Palm. So they mispriced the relative values of Palm and 3Com, producing the weird case shown above. If they had thought a bit, they would have realized that a share of 3Com should be worth at least 1.52 times the price of a share of Palm:

	A	B	C
16	**Minimum logical value of 3Com shares, compared to Palm**		
17	Number of shares of Palm held by 3Com	530,209,355	<-- =94.3%*B4
18	Number of 3Com shares	349,354,000	
19	Number of Palm shares per 3Com share	1.52	<-- =B17/B18

Actually, if they knew how to read a balance sheet, they would conclude that the price of a 3Com share should be even more. In 3Com's last quarterly statement, just one week before the Palm IPO, its balance sheet showed almost $3 billion in cash and short-term investments. Assuming that these items were not needed for production of 3Com's products, they are worth $8.53 per 3Com share:

	A	B	C
22	**On 25 Feb 2000, from 3Com's balance sheet**		
23	Cash and equivalents	1,812,503,000	
24	Short-term investments	1,166,026,000	
25		2,978,529,000	<-- =B24+B23
26			
27	Cash and investments per 3Com share	8.53	<-- =B25/B9

So the minimum value for a 3Com share should have been

$$3Com\ share\ price \geq 1.52 * Palm\ share\ price + \$8.53$$

Short-Selling as a Way of Correcting Market Mispricing

Short-selling is a technique of borrowing a stock, selling it, and repaying it later.[8] Suppose you could freely short-sell Palm stock. Then you could make money from the above situation by shorting Palm stock and buying 3Com stock. We'll explain the arbitrage technique in a second, but the logic is: Palm stock is overpriced (relative to 3Com stock) and 3Com stock is underpriced (relative to Palm stock); so you should buy the cheap stock (3Com) and sell the overpriced stock (Palm).

The arbitrage with which an investor could profit from the market mispricing is as follows:

- Borrow a share of Palm stock and sell it. Selling borrowed stock is called *short-selling*. In the example below, an arbitrageur short-sells 1 share of Palm for $80.25.
- Buy the equivalent value of 3Com stock. At the time of the arbitrage we explore below, 3Com was selling for $83.06 per share. The arbitrageur—having just shorted Palm for $80.25, spends this money to buy 0.966 share of 3Com (0.966 * $83.06 = $80.25).

If you're right about the mispricing of the Palm versus 3Com shares, you should make money under any price scenario. In the example below the arbitrageur shorted 1 share of Palm on

---

[8] The actual procedures for implementing a short sale are not simple. A well-written academic survey is a recent paper by Gene D'Avolio, "The Market for Borrowing Stock," http://papers.ssrn.com/sol3/papers.cfm?abstract_id=305479. There's also a wonderful article in the 1 December 2003 issue of the *New Yorker Magazine* by James Surowiecki. Entitled "Get Shorty," the article can be found on the Web at http://newyorker.com/talk/content/?031201ta_talk_surowiecki.

3 March and used the proceeds to buy 0.966 share of 3Com. Suppose that the arbitrageur undid his position on 10 March (meaning he bought 1 share of Palm and sold 0.966 share of 3Com). If on 10 March the prices of Palm and 3Com were in line with his additive valuation, then the arbitrageur would make money. In the example below, the share price of Palm on 10 March is $99 and the share price of 3Com is $159.01. As you can see, the arbitrageur makes $60.01:

	A	B	C
1	**3COM AND PALM: ARBITRAGING THE MISPRICING**		
2	3 March 2000--short-sell 1 Palm share and buy $80.25/$83.06 = 0.9662 3Com shares		
3	Cash flow	0.00	<-- =80.25-0.9662*83.06
4			
5	10 March 2000--buy 1 Palm share and sell $80.25/$83.06 = 0.9662 3Com shares		
6	Suppose Palm price is	99.00	
7	Logical *minimum* 3Com price	159.01	<-- =1.52*B6+8.53
8	Profit	60.01	<-- =B7-B6

If you play with the spreadsheet, you'll see that as long as you're right about the *price relation* between Palm and 3Com, you'll make money—whether the price of Palm goes up (as in the previous example) or down. For example, suppose that shares of Palm go down in price, and that they sell for $60 on 10 March:

	A	B	C
1	**3COM AND PALM: ARBITRAGING THE MISPRICING**		
2	3 March 2000--short-sell 1 Palm share and buy $80.25/$83.06 = 0.9662 3Com shares		
3	Cash flow	0.00	<-- =80.25-0.9662*83.06
4			
5	10 March 2000--buy 1 Palm share and sell $80.25/$83.06 = 0.9662 3Com shares		
6	Suppose Palm price is	60.00	
7	Logical *minimum* 3Com price	99.73	<-- =1.52*B6+8.53
8	Profit	39.73	<-- =B7-B6

As you can see from this arbitrage example, short-selling is essential to making the prices "behave" in an additive way. Since short-selling involves selling borrowed stock, one explanation of the lack of additivity in 3Com–Palm prices is that initially there were just too few Palm shares around for arbitrageurs to sell.

What Happened Later?

The graph below shows the relation between Palm's stock price and 3Com's (column C of the spreadsheet calculates the ratio (*3Com's stock price*)/(*Palm's stock price*)). As you can see, the ratio climbed in the days following the Palm IPO, reaching the 1.52 point on 9 May 2000. From then on until the end of July 2000, the ratio remained above this ratio—presumably the word had gotten out and enough investors understood the intricacies the 3Com–Palm relationship to force the prices into an appropriate pattern.

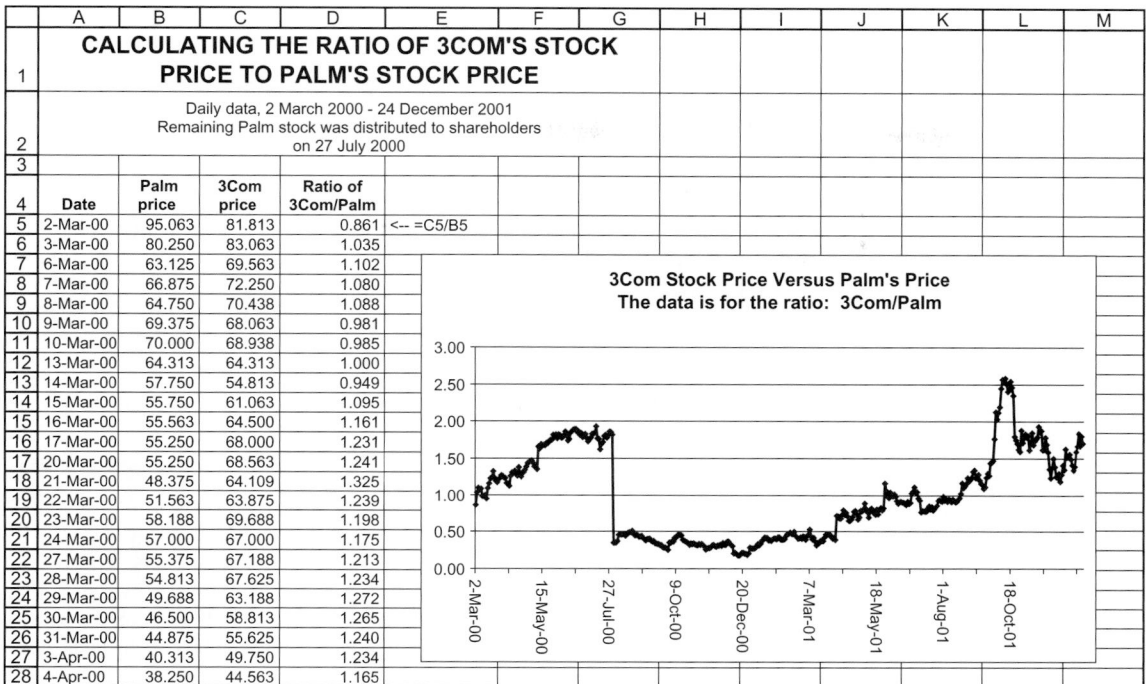

	A	B	C	D	E	F	G	H	I	J	K	L	M
1	**CALCULATING THE RATIO OF 3COM'S STOCK PRICE TO PALM'S STOCK PRICE**												
2	Daily data, 2 March 2000 - 24 December 2001 Remaining Palm stock was distributed to shareholders on 27 July 2000												
3													
4	**Date**	**Palm price**	**3Com price**	**Ratio of 3Com/Palm**									
5	2-Mar-00	95.063	81.813	0.861	<-- =C5/B5								
6	3-Mar-00	80.250	83.063	1.035									
7	6-Mar-00	63.125	69.563	1.102									
8	7-Mar-00	66.875	72.250	1.080									
9	8-Mar-00	64.750	70.438	1.088									
10	9-Mar-00	69.375	68.063	0.981									
11	10-Mar-00	70.000	68.938	0.985									
12	13-Mar-00	64.313	64.313	1.000									
13	14-Mar-00	57.750	54.813	0.949									
14	15-Mar-00	55.750	61.063	1.095									
15	16-Mar-00	55.563	64.500	1.161									
16	17-Mar-00	55.250	68.000	1.231									
17	20-Mar-00	55.250	68.563	1.241									
18	21-Mar-00	48.375	64.109	1.325									
19	22-Mar-00	51.563	63.875	1.239									
20	23-Mar-00	58.188	69.688	1.198									
21	24-Mar-00	57.000	67.000	1.175									
22	27-Mar-00	55.375	67.188	1.213									
23	28-Mar-00	54.813	67.625	1.234									
24	29-Mar-00	49.688	63.188	1.272									
25	30-Mar-00	46.500	58.813	1.265									
26	31-Mar-00	44.875	55.625	1.240									
27	3-Apr-00	40.313	49.750	1.234									
28	4-Apr-00	38.250	44.563	1.165									

On 28 July 2000, the ratio dropped precipitously, from 1.815 to 0.347. What happened? After markets closed on 27 July, 3Com *distributed all remaining Palm shares to its shareholders*. There was no longer any compelling reason for 3Com's share price to be related to Palm's. As you can see in the graph above, since then the ratio of the prices has been all over the place.

	A	B	C	D	E	F	G
1	**CALCULATING THE RATIO OF 3COM'S STOCK PRICE TO PALM'S STOCK PRICE**						
2	Daily data, 2 March 2000 - 24 December 2001 Note that remaining Palm stock was distributed to shareholders on 27 July 2000						
3							
4	**Date**	**Palm**	**3Com**	**Ratio of 3Com/Palm**			
99	17-Jul-00	39.500	66.813	1.691	Palm's stock price		
100	18-Jul-00	37.313	64.063	1.717			
101	19-Jul-00	34.875	62.750	1.799			
102	20-Jul-00	36.750	66.625	1.813	3Com's stock price		
103	21-Jul-00	38.313	68.000	1.775			
104	24-Jul-00	36.625	66.188	1.807	3Com sells for 1.815 times Palm		
105	25-Jul-00	36.563	67.938	1.858			
106	26-Jul-00	36.688	67.875	1.850			
107	27-Jul-00	35.563	64.563	1.815	<-- =C107/B107		
108	28-Jul-00	37.250	12.938	0.347	<-- =C108/B108		
109	31-Jul-00	39.000	13.563	0.348			
110	1-Aug-00	39.375	13.688	0.348			
111	2-Aug-00	39.125	14.438	0.369			

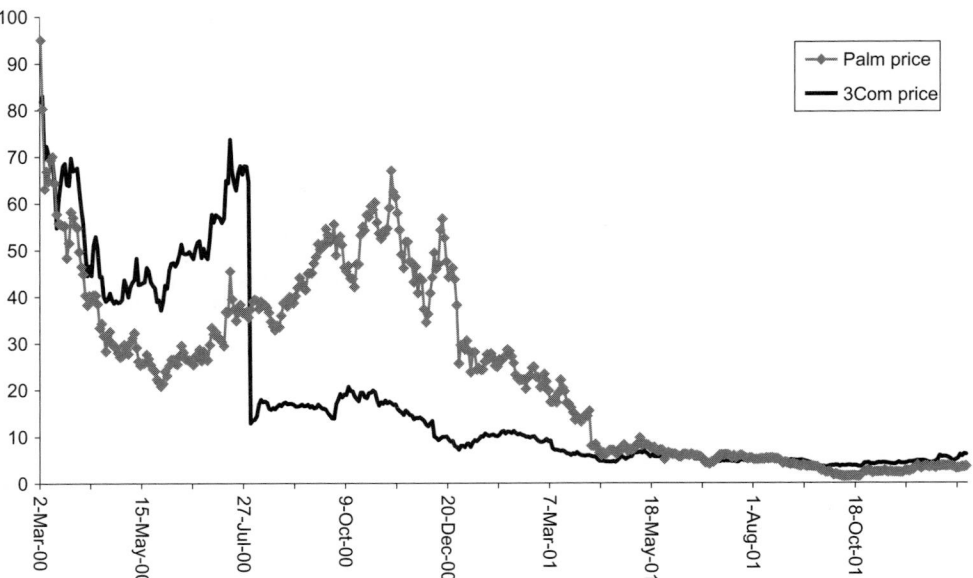

Figure 17.4   The prices of 3Com and Palm stock, 2 March 2000–24 December 2001. A partial spin-off of Palm was initiated by 3Com on 3 March 2000 and completed on 27 July 2000 (on this date there was a precipitous decline in 3Com's stock price).

What Happened on 27 July 2000?

After 27 July 2000 (the divestiture of all Palm stock by 3Com), the price of 3Com dropped dramatically. By that date investors—well informed about the coming divestiture of Palm—realized that the divestiture of the stock by 3Com would lower 3Com's value. And so it did (Figure 17.4).

Palm and 3Com—What's the Point?

Additivity is a basic efficiency feature of financial markets. As in the case of closed-end funds, it may not hold where the structural features of the funds make arbitrage difficult, or—as in the case of Palm and 3Com—it may take some time for markets to figure out what's happening and to initiate the arbitrage that will lead to additivity. Difficulties in short-selling can lead to failure of additivity.

17.4 Efficient Markets Principle 3: Cheap Information Is Worthless

Financial markets are awash in information, and it is important for you to have some opinions about how this information affects market prices. In this section we discuss three hypotheses that relate to how information is incorporated into financial markets. The finance jargon for these hypotheses is: weak-form efficiency, semi-strong-form efficiency, and strong-form efficiency.

In one form or another all three of these hypotheses state that information is important and that cheap and easily accessible information is likely to be worthless. The cheaper and more easily accessible the information, the less it's worth.

Read the previous paragraph again. It sounds contradictory!

- Information is important? This seems obvious. Whether it's the cost of a bank loan or information about whether Upward Slopes Ski Site is making money—the more informed you are about a financial asset, the more you should be able to judge its worth.

- Cheap and easily accessible information is likely to be worthless? If it's so important, why isn't it worth anything? The reason is that many people think it's important, and so they're all trying to figure out what the information is and how it affects the value of the asset. With so much energy expended on finding out the effect of the information and with the information so cheap, you're likely to find that the whole price impact of the information has already been extracted and is already reflected in the market price.

Weak-Form Efficiency: Almost Always True

The hypothesis of weak-form efficiency says that you cannot predict the future price of a financial asset by carefully examining the asset's past prices and its current price. Since *everyone* has easy and cheap access to the past prices of IBM stock, there's nothing left to be learned from these prices—all possible information contained in these prices is already incorporated in the *current market price* of IBM. Everyone knows past prices, and therefore, if you could make a profitable prediction based on a stock's price history, so could everyone else. In trying to implement this profitable information, you and other investors would drive its profitability out of existence. This sounds obvious (and it is), but it's a principle often overlooked by investors.

Technical Analysis—Do Previous Prices Predict Future Prices?

Its proponents claim that *technical analysis* is the art or science of using historical stock price patterns to predict the future stock price. Finance professors think that technical analysis is neither an art nor a science, but simply voodoo. They base this belief on the weak-form efficient markets hypothesis and on tons of academic research.

Here's a simple example of technical analysis. Based on an analysis of ABC's historical stock price, you've concluded that it fluctuates in a band between $25 and $35. When the price gets close to $25, it inevitably goes up, and when the price gets close to $35, the stock price goes down. This leads you to develop the following money-making strategy:

- Buy ABC when the price gets to $25.50; since this is very close to $25, the price will have a very high probability of moving up. In any case you'll have little to lose, since the price can't go below $25.

- Sell ABC when the price gets to $34.50; since this is very close to $35, the price has a very high probability of moving down. In any case at $34.50 you have very little to gain.

This sounds like a money-making strategy, but on the other hand it's self-defeating: If all investors try to implement this strategy (and why shouldn't they, since your analysis is based on publicly available information?), then the "price band" will narrow—no one will want to buy ABC stock when it gets close to $34.50 or $25.50.

But now everyone will try to implement a profit strategy based on the new price band. And so on and so on. . . .

The conclusion: There is no price band! It may be that ABC's share price has been between $25 and $35 in the past, but this says nothing about its share price in the future.

In fact you could make a broader conclusion: As long as there are many people trading in a market, a strategy based only on past and current prices cannot be profitable.

Technical Trading Rules—Another Violation of Weak-Form Efficiency

A technical trading strategy is a rule for buying and selling a stock based on the stock's previous price movements.[9] The weak-form efficiency hypothesis says that technical trading rules won't work.

The earlier ABC example (where ABC's stock was assumed to trade in a band between $25 and $35) is a simple example of a technical trading rule. Figure 17.5 gives a more sophisticated example.

The down trendline explains the downturn in Budget Group's stock price by connecting four "price peaks." The prediction and the associated trading rule are:

- When the stock price of Budget Group gets close to the down trendline, it will move down. To exploit this information, you should buy when the price is farther away from the trendline and sell when it is close to the line.

- *If* the stock price of Budget Group *breaks through* the down trendline, "a change of trend could be imminent." This is the technical analyst's escape hatch—the information contained in the prices is true except when it's not true.

Down Trendline
A down trendline has a negative slope and is formed by connecting two or more high points. The second high must be lower than the first for the line to have a negative slope. Down trendlines act as resistance and indicate that net-supply (supply less demand) is increasing even as the price declines. A declining price combined with increasing supply is very bearish and shows the strong resolve of the sellers. As long as prices remain below the down trendline, the downtrend is considered solid and intact. A break above the down trendline indicates that net-supply is decreasing and a change of trend could be imminent.

Figure 17.5   Technical analysis of Budget stock. *Source:* http://www.stockcharts.com:85/education/What/ChartAnalysis/trendlines.html.

---

[9]There are lots of good websites on technical trading. Here are a few: http://technicaltrading.com/, http://www.stockcharts.com/education/What/TradingStrategies/MurphysLaws.html.

Semi-strong-Form Efficiency: Sometimes True

Semi-strong-form efficiency predicts that not just past prices but all publicly available information are incorporated in current security prices. This suggests, for example, that the analysis of a firm's financial statements is not going to help you make better investment decisions.

Semi-strong market efficiency seems to be true . . . *occasionally*. It's a lot of work to understand *all* the publicly available information about a stock, and it's quite common to see cases where information existed, but it wasn't incorporated into the stock price. The 3Com–Palm story discussed in Section 17.3 is a case in point. Only after some rigorous analysis of the relation between 3Com and Palm and analysis of the cash reserves of 3Com could we conclude that Palm's price was overpriced relative to 3Com's price. There has to be a lot at stake to motivate investors to engage in this kind of research. If it's worthwhile, then we would expect semi-strong-form efficiency to prevail.

Strong-Form Efficiency: Usually Not True

The strong-form efficient markets hypothesis says that *all* information is incorporated into securities prices. Hardly anyone believes that this is true. In fact, it's often illegal, since *all* information includes proprietary information and inside knowledge—by law, insiders are forbidden to trade on their information if it hasn't been revealed to the public.

17.5 Efficient Markets Principle 4: Transaction Costs Are Important

Transaction costs are all the various costs of buying and selling a security and also the costs (monetary or otherwise) of *understanding* a security. When you buy a stock for $50, you pay a brokerage commission. In the United States this commission is typically 0.5%. So the purchase of a share of stock costs you $50.25 and its sale delivers you $49.75:

	A	B	C
3	Buy commission	0.50%	
4	Sell commission	0.50%	
5			
6	Stock price	$50.00	
7			
8	Purchase price	50.25	<-- =B6*(1+B3)
9	Selling price	49.75	<-- =B6*(1-B4)

The result: If you think that the stock is worth $50.15, it won't be worth your while to buy it: Even though the stock's price today is $50, less than what you think it's worth, transaction costs make it more expensive to buy the stock ($50.25) than you think it's worth.

Similarly, suppose you own a share of the stock and suppose you think it's worth only $49.80. In the absence of transaction costs, it would be logical to sell the stock, but with a 0.5% transaction cost, you would be getting less than you think the stock is worth.

Here's a more interesting example. Below are the prices of sugar in London and in New York on 25 July 2003.

	A	B	C
1	**COMPARING SUGAR PRICES IN LONDON AND NEW YORK**		
2	New York (dollars/pound)	0.0693	
3	London (dollars/tonne)	208.30	
4	pounds per tonne	2,200	
5	London (dollars/pound)	0.0947	<-- =B3/B4
6			
7	**One container of sugar**		
8	Contains 21 tons		
9	in pounds	46,200	<-- =21*B4
10	"Arbitrage profit"	1,172.64	<-- =(B5-B2)*B9

New York sugar is selling for 6.93 cents per pound, whereas sugar in London is selling for $208.30 per tonne. Could there be an opportunity here to make money? In comparing the prices, you have to make sure the units are the same; for example—a tonne is a *metric ton,* 1,000 kilograms (which equals 2,200 pounds). As you can see, the London price translates to 9.47 cents per pound.

It looks like there's an arbitrage opportunity here: If we buy sugar in New York and sell it in London, we can make over 2.5 cents per pound. Since a 20-foot container can hold 21 tons of sugar (or 46,200 pounds—see cell B9 above), it looks like we could make almost $1,173 profit per container. And since a ship can hold hundreds of containers . . . this must be a surefire way to get rich!

But hold on—this couldn't be. We must have forgotten the transaction costs:

- It *costs money* to ship sugar from New York to London. It costs approximately $1,000 to ship a container of sugar from New York to London. This alone would almost eliminate the arbitrage profit.

- It *takes time* to ship sugar from New York to London—somewhere between ten days and three weeks, depending on the availability of shipping. So even if the freight costs are less than $1,500, this isn't an arbitrage—it's a kind of educated gamble on the price differentials between the two cities.[10]

So there might be a profit here, but it's not certain. The transaction costs, the cost and the time needed to ship the sugar from New York to London, will eat up most of the profits. Of course, this is what you would expect in an efficient market: You can't make money from things that are easy to do.

---

[10]What we need is a forward or a futures contract: These are contracts that enable us to fix a price today for sugar delivered in London at some point in the future. Such contracts exist, but they're beyond the scope of this book. For a good text, see John Hull, *Options, Futures, and Other Derivatives,* 4th edition (Prentice-Hall, 2000).

CONCLUSION

Financial economists use the words "efficient markets" to describe a variety of rules about financial asset prices, which are so simple that they almost always have to be true. In this chapter we explored several of these asset pricing rules:

- One price for one asset. In an efficient financial market, assets that are the same ought to have the same value and price.
- Price additivity of asset bundles: In an efficient market, bundling two or more assets together—whether it's different kinds of apples in a bag or stocks in a mutual fund—doesn't change their value.
- Informational effects on prices: Generally known information cannot be worth much, and the more widely the information is known, the less it is worth. We explored three versions of this principle. The weak-form efficiency principle says that the future asset price cannot be predicted from knowledge of historical asset prices and the current asset price. The semi-strong-form efficiency principle says that publicly known information—not just prices, but published accounting data and other information that can be derived (with some work) from the information—is worthless. Economists believe that semi-strong form efficiency holds frequently but not always. The strong-form efficiency principle, which almost no one believes, says that *all* information—whether public or not—is worthless.
- Transaction costs: These pesky critters can screw up the previous three principles, because they interfere with arbitrage. Arbitrage, the buying and selling of assets with profit, is the mechanism by which the three above principles are forced to hold. Transaction costs, the cost of buying and selling an asset, or the cost of finding out information about the asset, can make it more difficult to arbitrage and hence cause market inefficiencies.

EXERCISES

1. One of the earliest tests of market efficiency was to examine the returns of stocks around the publication of their earnings reports. The graph below shows the price of XYZ stock seven days before and after the earnings announcement date (date = 0). Assume that the only new information during this period is the publication of the earnings report showing higher profits than expected. Does the price pattern of XYZ stocks support the concept of market efficiency?

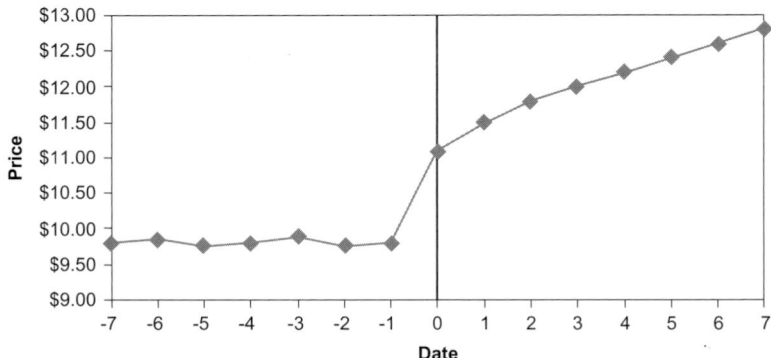

XYZ Price Around the Announcement Date

2. In the three graphs below, are the principles of market efficiency violated? If so, which principle and why?

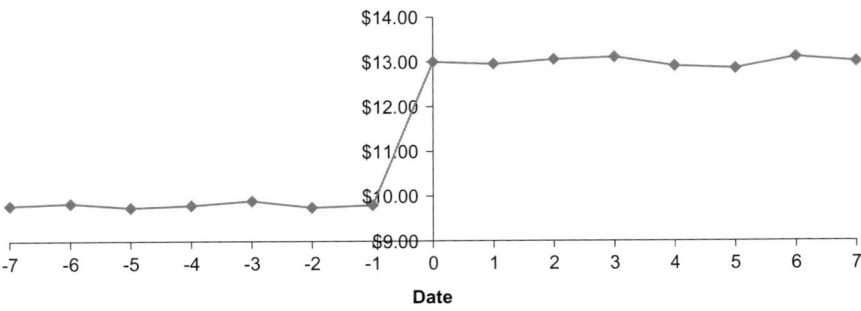

Cumin Stock Price Around Dividend Announcement Date

Tangerine Stock Price Around Earnings Announcement Date

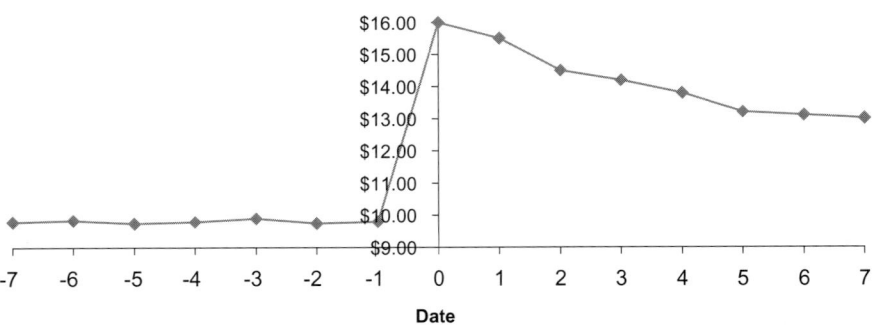

Persimmon Stock Price Around Annual Report Date

3. Which of the following results support/contradict market efficiency?
   (a) Stocks that perform best in January perform worst in February.
   (b) Only 35% of mutual funds earned higher returns than the S&P 500 Index.
   (c) Firms that announce a dividend cut continue to underperform similar stocks six months after the announcement date.

    (d)   When the founder of a company unexpectedly retires from his management position the firm's stock tends to go up.

    (e)   During the month of January stocks earn higher returns than in other months.

4. Are the following statements true or false? Explain.

    (a)   Studying a company is a waste of effort because all information is incorporated in the company's stock prices.

    (b)   A price drop of 60% in one day implies that the market is inefficient.

    (c)   Arbitrageurs are key players in preserving market efficiency.

    (d)   The higher the transactions costs, the more mispricing is expected.

5. On 27 October an arbitrageur in London was following the exchange rates in Asheville. At that time $1 was traded for €0.8051 and £0.4111 (you can't directly change pounds into euros and vice versa at Asheville). At the same time in London £1 was traded for €1.9608 and $2.4390.

    (a)   Show a strategy that will enable the arbitrageur to make arbitrage profits.

    (b)   Assume that the arbitrageur invests £100,000 in the strategy. How much money will she gain from implementing it?

6. Continuing with Exercise 5: If the transaction costs in London are 0.25% per transaction and 0.5% in Asheville, is the strategy still profitable? What are the maximum transaction costs (assuming they are twice as much in Asheville as in London) that will make the strategy break even?

7. Teva is a pharmaceutical company traded both on the Tel Aviv stock exchange and on the NASDAQ. At 9:30 am Eastern time (when both exchange markets are open) Teva was traded for $25.75 on the NASDAQ and for NIS 112 (new Israeli shekel) in Tel Aviv. At the same time $1 was traded for NIS 4.48. Show a strategy that enables arbitrageurs to earn profits. When do you think that the profit opportunities will cease to exist?

8. On 17 July 2004, ABC Corporation reported an increase of 2 cents in earnings per share (EPS). Nevertheless, the price of the stock dropped by $1.50. In contrast, on the same day, the DEF Company reported a decrease of 3 cents, in its EPS, but the stock price rose by $2.20. A journalist wrote that "since this is the only new information received on 17 July about ABC and DEF, this proves that the stock market is inefficient." Is the journalist's statement correct?

9. In February 2022 a messenger arrived in Lower Fantasia and gave the correct prices of all stocks that traded in the country. A journalist argued that the accurate price disclosure eliminates all risk in investing in stocks; hence their returns should be equal to the risk-free rate. Assume that the messenger did not know the future, but "only" the average future free cash flows (FCFs) and the appropriate discount rate. Is the journalist right in her assessment? Discuss.

10. The CEO of Monkey Business Corporation (MBC) and his nephew were arrested after it was found that the nephew bought $1,000,000 worth of MBC stocks shortly before the price of the stocks jumped by 45%. Assuming that the allegations are true, what type of market efficiency does the above contradict?

11. The workers at a large factory in Michigan received information according to which the price of the Monkey Business Corporation stock is about to rise by more than 50%. According to the rumors, the source of the information is the nephew (not the one that was arrested) of the CEO. Your sister is working in that factory and advised you to buy MBC stocks. Would you follow her advice? Explain.

12. Two years after MBC went public, it was found that the company tampered with the accounting reports. As a result of this finding, the price of the company's stock fell by 80% the next day. Does the sharp fall in price violate market efficiency?

13. One puzzling phenomenon of financial markets is the "weekend effect." According to this phenomenon, stock returns on Monday are lower than every other day of the week. The following graph presents the returns of the stock market dependent on the day of the week.

    (a)   Do the results contradict market efficiency?

    (b)   Do you have a reasonable explanation as to why the anomaly persists and does not disappear due to the arbitrageurs actions?

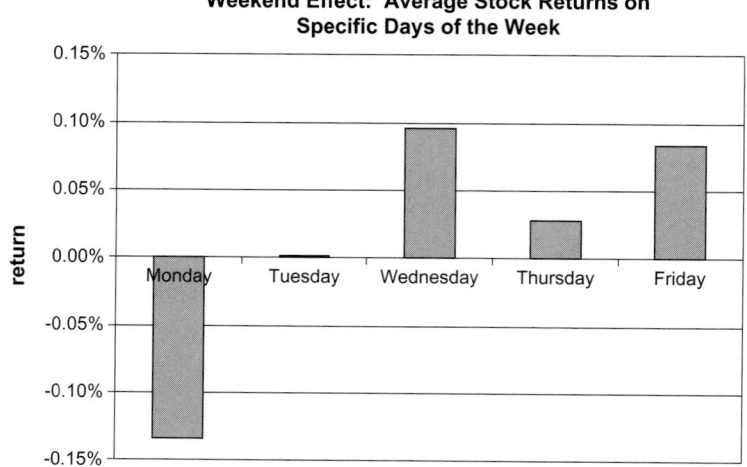

14. "Beat the Market" (BTM) is an open-end mutual fund. The fund's portfolio consists of 10,000 Yahoo, Inc. shares traded for $36.14, 15,000 shares of Goggle, Inc. traded for $191.94, and 20,000 shares of General Electric Co traded for $33.95. There are currently 32,000 BTM shares.

    (a)   If the price of a BTM share is $122.48, does the price-additivity rule hold?

    (b)   The following day the price of Goggle drops by 5%, the price of General Electric drops by 2%, and the price of Yahoo remains the same. The price of BTM was $117. Does the price-additivity rule hold?

15. The DEF Company recruited one of the best CEOs in the country to its service in an unanticipated move. However, the price of DEF stock fell once the company announced the change in management. Assume that the new CEO was the only new information about the company (and that he is indeed better than the old CEO). Does the fall of stock prices indicate market inefficiency?

16. Assume that markets are efficient. Do you expect that more or less than half of the mutual funds returns will be higher than the market?

17. "Due to the unexpected positive earnings report the price of GLZ shares rose on each trading day in the past week."

    (a)   Explain why this sentence contradicts market efficiency.

    (b)   What type of market efficiency does the sentence contradict? Try to distinguish between two possibilities.

    (c)   What should have been the market response if market efficiency holds?

18. In country A short-selling is allowed, whereas in country B it is illegal. If all other things are equal, where do you anticipate more frequent mispricing? Explain.

19. In Upper Fantasia a well-known professor showed that during the last 50 years stocks whose prices rose for three consecutive days will tend to go down on the fourth day. Assuming that the professor's finding is true, what do you expect will happen after the publication of this result?

20. The "new issue puzzle" is a phenomenon according to which the returns from investing in firms that issue stocks is lower than other stocks five years after the date of the issue. Ritter (who

originally reported the phenomenon) argues that it is because investors are too optimistic about the performance of issuing stocks.

(a)   Is Ritter's explanation consistent with market efficiency?

(b)   Can you think about an explanation that is consistent with market efficiency that will explain the new issue puzzle?

21. An entrepreneur is marketing new software that estimates the prices of stocks according to a new model.

(a)   Do you think that brokerage houses should buy the new software?

(b)   What would you advise the entrepreneur to do with her software?

22. One pound of apples is sold for $2.50 in Ashville and for $4.20 in Alaska. Does this fact violate the one price rule?

23. Recent research in Lower Fantasia found that companies whose stocks register a large increase in prices in a given quarter tend to have an increase in profits after six months. Does this fact contradict market efficiency?

24. The same research was also conducted in Upper Fantasia and found that stocks having a high increase in their profits tend to have low returns in the year after the announcement date. Try to give a reasonable explanation for this finding. Does your explanation contradict market efficiency?

25. One of the puzzling results of recent academic literature is that stocks with high beta values do not earn higher returns than stocks with low beta values. Does this fact contradict market efficiency?

26. A recent finding shows that low-rated bonds have earned lower returns in the last 60 years than government bonds. Does this fact contradict market efficiency?

BOND VALUATION

OVERVIEW

When businesses, governments, or municipalities borrow money, they often issue *bonds*. The fundamental characteristic that distinguishes a bond from other kinds of securities, such as stocks, preferred stock, and options, is that the borrower is very specific about the promised payments on the bond. All bonds specify the precise dates and the amounts which the issuer/borrower *promises* to repay to the bond's purchaser/lender.

In this chapter we apply the discounting techniques discussed in Chapters 5 and 6 to value bonds. In the remainder of this overview to Chapter 18 we show you some examples of various kinds of bonds and acquaint you with some basic bond terminology.

The XYZ Corporation Bond

To get the bond terminology straight, Figure 18.1 gives some details for an imaginary bond offering by XYZ Corporation, a highly reliable borrower.

The terminology (underlined in Figure 18.1) is as follows:

- The XYZ bond has a *face value* and a *coupon rate*. The $10 million of bonds issued by XYZ Corporation are issued as individual bonds of $1,000 face value; each such bond pays a coupon rate of 7%. The periodic interest payments are based on the product of the coupon rate and the face value. The XYZ bonds pay interest only once a year; since the coupon rate is 7% and the face value is $1,000, this means that the *coupon payments* are $70 annually. (As you will see in Section 18.1, most corporate bonds pay interest semiannually; if this were true for the XYZ bonds, they would pay $35 on 15 December and 15 June of each year.)

- The XYZ bond has a *principal repayment* on the last day of the bond's maturity (the bond's *maturity date*). On this day, 15 December 2007, a $1,000 face-value XYZ bond will pay its holder a final repayment of principal of $1,000 in addition to the interest payment of $70 due for 2007.

- The bond's *offer price* is the initial price at which it is sold to the public. The XYZ bonds are offered at *par value*, meaning that the initial sale price is equal to the bond's face value.

- *Tricky details, covenants, and other conditions:* XYZ promises to make a set of contractual payments in exchange for the loan of $1,000 made to it by the purchaser. Often the bond-issuing company agrees to abide by certain restrictions on its behavior; these restrictions, termed *bond covenants*, might specify that XYZ will pay no dividends until the bond issue is redeemed, or perhaps that it will refrain from certain other actions.[1] The *boilerplate* in which all these conditions are specified also specifies what happens if XYZ defaults, that is, if it fails to keep its promises. The boilerplate also specifies what constitutes default.[2]

XYZ CORPORATION
Offer to sell $10,000,000 of bonds

Date of sale: December 15, 2000
Offer price: $1,000 (bonds sold at *par value*)
Face value: $1,000
Bond *maturity date:* December 15, 2007
Coupon rate: 7%, paid annually on December 15
(meaning: *coupon payments* of $70 on December 15 of 2001,
    2002, . . . , 2007)
Principal repayment: December 15, 2007
Tricky details, covenants and other conditions: See *boilerplate*
on other side

Figure 18.1 On 15 December 2000, XYZ Corporation sold $10 million of bonds paying a 7% coupon. The underlined terms are explained in the text.

---

[1] A detailed example of covenants is given in Section 18.4 where we discuss the Giant Industries bonds.
[2] This is not as trivial as it might sound. If a coupon payment is late by two days, does this violation of the contract automatically mean bankruptcy? Suppose one of the bond covenants is violated? Do bondholders have recourse (can they do something if the covenants are violated)?

Some Other Corporate Bonds

Figure 18.2 shows you some of the corporate bonds issued in the week of 21 July 2003. By looking at the figure, you can learn the following facts about bonds:

- Not all the bonds are issued at par. The GMAC bonds, for example, are issued at $107.25 for every $100 of face value. In Section 18.1 we discuss the effect of issuance not at par on the analysis of the bond.

- Bonds differ in their *ratings*. Bonds are rated according to the credit worthiness of their issuers. Figure 18.3 shows you the ratings used by the two primary bond rating agencies, Moody's and Standard & Poor's. The ratings are based on the agency's estimation of the issuing company's ability to pay off the bonds and play an important role in determining the

Corporate Bond Watch

Investment Grade Bonds

Corporate Bonds rated BBB / Baa or higher. These bond will fluctuate in value and if sold prior to maturity may be worth more or less than their original cost.

Description	Rating	Coupon	Maturity	Price	YTM / YTC
GMAC	BBB	6.75	1/15/06	107.25	3.65
GE Capital	AAA	2.85	1/3/06	102.5	1.82
Sears Roebuck Acct	BBB	5.8	2/15/06	106.75	3.03
Bristol Myers	AA	4.75	10/1/06	108.5	1.98
Ford Motor Credit	BBB	6.5	1/25/07	106	4.62
Countrywide	A	5.5	2/1/07	110	2.51
John Deere Capital	A-	4.5	8/22/07	106.5	2.8
Merrill Lynch	A+	4	11/15/07	104.75	2.82
CIT Group	A	4	5/8/08	103.25	3.26
Household Finance	A	5.875	2/1/09	111	3.65
Morgan Stanley	A+	4.25	5/15/10	103.25	3.7
Credit Suisse FB	A+	6.125	11/15/11	111.925	4.39
Walt Disney	BBB+	6.375	3/1/12	113.375	4.48
Alcan	A-	4.5	5/15/13	100.325	4.45
GMAC	BBB	7.4	2/15/21	102.795	7.11 / 5.5
Household Finance	A	6	4/15/23	104.25	5.64 / 5
Bank of America	A	6.85	5/15/26	106.806	6.28 / 4.25
General Motors	BBB	8.375	7/15/2033	101.375	8.25

High Yield Bonds

Corporate Bonds rated below BBB / Baa. These bonds may have large fluctuations in value and if sold prior to maturity may be worth more or less thatn their original cost.

Description	Rating	Coupon	Maturity / Call	Price	YTM / YTC
Sprint Capital	BBB-	7.9	3/15/05	109.5	2.05
Royal Caribbean	BB+	8.25	4/1/05	106.25	4.13
Sprint Capital	BBB-	7.125	1/30/06	110.5	2.77
JC Penney	BB+	7.6	4/1/07	105.5	5.91
TXU Corp	BBB-	6.375	1/1/08	107.25	4.55
Williams Hld Del	B+	6.5	12/1/08	98.25	6.89
JC Penney	BB+	8	3/1/10	105.75	6.89
Xerox	B+	7.125	6/15/2010	100.5	7.03
Liberty Media	BBB-	5.7	5/15/13	99.25	5.8
Xerox	B+	7.625	6/15/13	100.5	7.55 / 7.53
Royal Caribbean	BB+	7.25	3/15/2018	96	7.7
Georgia Pacific	BB+	9.625	3/15/2022	101.25	9.47 / 9.4
Tyco International	BBB-	6.875	1/15/2029	102.5	6.66

Figure 18.2 A partial list of corporate bonds issued in the third week of July 2003.
Source: http://www.cfcplanners.com/newsclients/newsletters/CFD6-17-03A.pdf.

Long-Term Senior Debt Ratings					
Investment-Grade Ratings			Speculative-Grade Ratings		
S&P	Moody's	Interpretation	S&P	Moody's	Interpretation
AAA	Aaa	Highest Quality	BB+ BB BB-	Ba1 Ba2 Ba3	Likely to fulfill obligations; ongoing uncertainty
AA+ AA AA-	Aa1 Aa2 AA3	High Quality	B+ B B-	B1 B2 B3	High-risk obligations
A+ A A-	A1 A2 A3	Strong Payment Capacity	CCC+ CCC CCC-	Caa	Current vulnerability to default
BBB+ BBB BBB-	Baa1 Baa2 Baa3	Adequate Payment Capacity	C D	Ca D	In bankruptcy or default, or other marked shortcomings

Figure 18.3 Standard & Poor's and Moody's bond rating classifications.

interest rate that the company pays on its bonds. The "Investment Grade" bonds in the top half of Figure 18.2 are issued by companies whose ability to repay the funds borrrowed is highly regarded by the rating agencies. The "High Yield Bonds" (often called "junk bonds") in the bottom half of the figure are issued by companies whose credit ratings are lower.

- Some bonds are *callable*. A bond is callable if the issuer has the right to refund the bond's principal before maturity. For example, the Bank of America bonds in Figure 18.2 promise to pay 6.85% interest annually until 15 May 2026. However, these bonds are callable after 15 May 2006: After this date, Bank of America can refund the bonds by forcing bondholders to return their bonds to the company for their face value. We discuss callable bonds in Section 18.5.

- The price, coupon, and maturity of the bond affect the internal rate of return (IRR) of the bondholder. In bond markets the jargon for IRR is *yield to maturity* (YTM). If the bond is callable, we can also calculate a *yield to call* (YTC). These concepts are discussed in Sections 18.1 and 18.5.

United States Government Debt

The market for U.S. government debt is without question the largest and most important bond market in the world. In August 2003, the U.S. Treasury had $6.7 *trillion* of bonds outstanding (see Figure 18.4). Almost every week the Treasury sells stupendous amounts of debt to the public (see Figure 18.5 for a fairly standard weekly announcement, in which the government sells $34 billion of short-term debt).

   The U.S. Treasury classifies its debt into three main categories: bills, notes, and bonds.

- *Treasury bills* are short-term bonds sold by the government. Treasury bills (T-bills) have no explicit interest rate; they are sold at a discount. For example, a one-year Treasury bill with a $100 face value might be sold for $90. The Treasury bill has no explicit interest rate: The purchaser of this bill pays $90 today and gets back $100 in one year. We discuss the pricing of T-bills in Section 18.2.

The Debt to the Penny and Who Holds It

Current	Debt Held by the Public	Intragovernmental Holdings	Total
01/20/2005	4,421,475,089,169.44	3,191,740,523,158.93	7,613,215,612,328.37

Prior Fiscal Years	Debt Held by the Public	Intragovernmental Holdings	Total
09/30/2004	4,307,344,596,908.92	3,071,708,099,421.40	7,379,052,696,330.32
09/30/2003	3,924,090,106,880.88	2,859,140,955,862.74	6,783,231,062,743.62
09/30/2002	3,553,180,247,874.74	2,675,055,717,722.42	6,228,235,965,597.16
09/28/2001	3,339,310,176,094.74	2,468,153,236,105.32	5,807,463,412,200.06
09/29/2000	3,405,303,490,221.20	2,268,874,719,665.66	5,674,178,209,886.86
09/30/1999	3,636,104,594,501.81	2,020,166,307,131.62	5,656,270,901,633.43
09/30/1998	3,733,864,472,163.53	1,792,328,536,734.09	5,526,193,008,897.62
09/30/1997	3,789,667,546,849.60	1,623,478,464,547.74	5,413,146,011,397.34

Figure 18.4 The debt of the United States government. On 20 January 2005, the U.S. government had $4.4 trillion of debt outstanding in the form of bonds owned by the public. A further $3.1 trillion of debt was between government agencies. The total government debt was $7.6 trillion. *Source:* http://www.publicdebt.treas.gov/opd/opdpdodt.htm.

DEPARTMENT OF THE TREASURY

TREASURY NEWS

OFFICE OF PUBLIC AFFAIRS • 1500 PENNSYLVANIA AVENUE, N.W. • WASHINGTON, D.C. • 20220 • (202) 622-2960

```
EMBARGOED UNTIL 11:00 A.M.              CONTACT:    Office of Financing
March 6, 2003                                       202/691-3550

            TREASURY OFFERS 13-WEEK AND 26-WEEK BILLS

     The Treasury will auction 13-week and 26-week Treasury bills totaling $34,000
million to refund an estimated $27,010 million of publicly held 13-week and 26-week
Treasury bills maturing March 13, 2003, and to raise new cash of approximately $6,990
million.  Also maturing is an estimated $20,000 million of publicly held 4-week
Treasury bills, the disposition of which will be announced March 10, 2003.
```

Figure 18.5 On 6 March 2003, the U.S. Treasury announced the sale of $34 *billion* of Treasury bills. Similar sales are generally held weekly. Note that $27 billion of the proceeds will go toward refunding existing debt. *Source:* http://www.publicdebt.treas.gov/of/ofresults2003.htm.

- The U.S. Treasury uses the word *notes* to describe coupon bonds that have maturities up to ten years. It uses the word *bonds* to describe coupon bonds that have greater maturities. Since there is no analytical difference between U.S. Treasury notes and bonds—both refer to bonds that have coupon payments—we analyze them together in Section 18.3.

What Do We Do in This Chapter?

In this chapter you will learn to analyze a bond based on its yield to maturity (YTM). The YTM is a concept much like the internal rate of return discussed first in Chapters 5 and 6. You will learn to analyze the different kinds of bonds: Treasury bills, Treasury bonds, corporate bonds, and callable bonds. We end the chapter with a brief discussion of preferred stock, a security which—despite its name—is very much like a bond.

Finance Concepts Discussed

- Basic definitions, example of bond value and YTM
- U.S. Treasury markets: discussion of the types of bonds and yield conventions
    - Discussion of T-bills
    - Treasury bonds
    - Strips
- The U.S. Treasury yield curve
- Corporate bond markets: example of Giant Industries
- Callable bonds
- Preferred stock

Excel Functions Used

- **IRR**
- **XIRR**
- **Rate**
- **Yield**

18.1 Computing the Yield to Maturity (YTM) of a Bond

The most common tool for the analysis of bonds is the yield to maturity (YTM). YTM of the bond is the internal rate of return of the bond's cash flows. Suppose we observe the bond's market price P and we know its stream of future promised payments $C_1, C_2, \ldots, C_N$. Then the YTM is defined as the internal rate of return of the bond price and its future payments, which is the rate of return that sets the present value of the bond's future promised payments equal to its current price:

$$P = \frac{C_1}{(1 + YTM)} + \frac{C_2}{(1 + YTM)^2} + \frac{C_3}{(1 + YTM)^3} + \cdots + \frac{C_N}{(1 + YTM)^N}$$

In this section we illustrate how to compute the YTM. In addition to the **IRR** function, which you already know, Excel also has functions that allow you to compute the YTM in more complicated cases.[3] We use the XYZ Corp. bond from the previous section as our example.

Back to the XYZ Bond

Suppose that it's the morning of 15 December 2000, and that you have been asked to value the XYZ bond illustrated in the overview to this chapter (p. 521). Using Excel's **IRR** function you

---

[3]The author somewhat insincerely apologizes for the fact that yield to maturity (YTM) and internal rate of return (IRR) stand for *exactly the same concept* when applied to bonds.

determine that the YTM of the bond is 7.00%:

	A	B	C
1	**YIELD TO MATURITY**		
2	Market price of bond	1,000.00	
3			
4	Year	**Bond cash flow**	
5	0	-1,000.00	
6	1	70.00	
7	2	70.00	
8	3	70.00	
9	4	70.00	
10	5	70.00	
11	6	70.00	
12	7	1,070.00	
13			
14	YTM of bond	7.00%	<-- =IRR(B5:B12)

Are the XYZ bonds a good buy? This depends on whether the market interest rate on *equivalently risky* bonds is bigger or smaller than 7%. If the market is paying more than 7% for bonds of companies that—in terms of risk—are like XYZ Corp., then the XYZ bonds are not a good buy. On the other hand, if the market is paying less than 7%, they are a good buy.[4]

Just for the sake of argument, suppose that on 15 December 2000, the market interest rate for bonds like the XYZ Corp. bond is 6.5%. You can use the NPV of the future payments on the bond to determine how much you should be willing to pay for them:

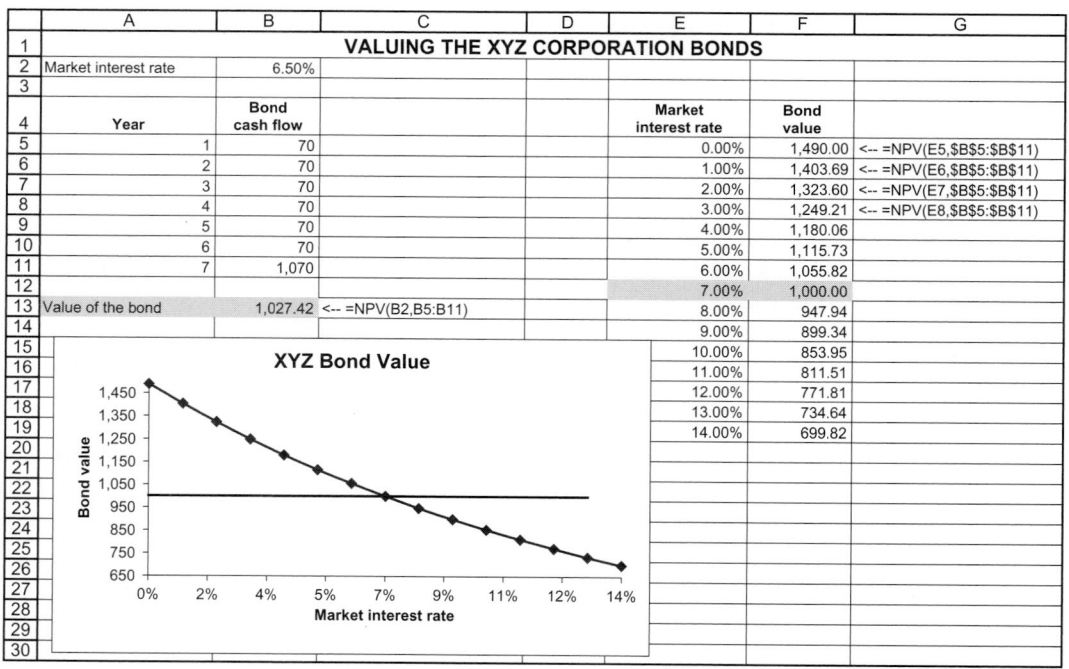

	A	B	C	D	E	F	G
1	**VALUING THE XYZ CORPORATION BONDS**						
2	Market interest rate	6.50%					
3							
4	Year	**Bond cash flow**			**Market interest rate**	**Bond value**	
5	1	70			0.00%	1,490.00	<-- =NPV(E5,$B$5:$B$11)
6	2	70			1.00%	1,403.69	<-- =NPV(E6,$B$5:$B$11)
7	3	70			2.00%	1,323.60	<-- =NPV(E7,$B$5:$B$11)
8	4	70			3.00%	1,249.21	<-- =NPV(E8,$B$5:$B$11)
9	5	70			4.00%	1,180.06	
10	6	70			5.00%	1,115.73	
11	7	1,070			6.00%	1,055.82	
12					7.00%	1,000.00	
13	Value of the bond	1,027.42	<-- =NPV(B2,B5:B11)		8.00%	947.94	
14					9.00%	899.34	
15					10.00%	853.95	
16					11.00%	811.51	
17					12.00%	771.81	
18					13.00%	734.64	
19					14.00%	699.82	

XYZ Bond Value

---

[4]Having read Chapter 17 on efficient markets, you naturally suspect that the market price pretty much reflects the risk-adjusted return on the XYZ bonds.

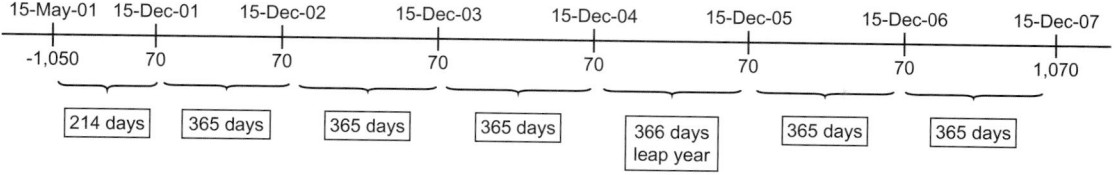

Payment pattern of XYZ bond purchased on 15 May 2001 and held to maturity

Figure 18.6 If you buy the XYZ bond on 15 May 2001, the first coupon payment will be received in 214 days. Subsequent coupon payments will be received with spacing of one year. Excel's **XIRR** function computes the YTM for the bond.

If the market values the bond using the 6.5% interest rate, then it would be worth $1,027.42. If you could buy the bond for $1,000, you should do so. Making a table (cells E5:F19) in Excel shows that the bond is worth more than $1,000 if the market interest rate is less than 7% and vice versa.

As you can see, the basics of bond analysis using the YTM are very similar to standard IRR analysis and quite simple. However, for bonds there are three factors that sometimes complicate the pricing calculations. In the rest of this section we discuss these complications.

Complicating Factor 1: Uneven Spacing of Bond Payments

The calculation of both the present value of the bond's future payments and the YTM can be complicated by the fact that the payments are not evenly spaced. Suppose, for example, that you buy the XYZ bond on 15 May 2001 and that its market price on that date is $1,050. In order to compute the YTM of the bond, we have to compute the IRR of its payments. But the problem is that the payments are not evenly spaced. As you can see in Figure 18.6, the time between the purchase date of the bond and the first coupon payment is 214 days, whereas all the other payments are 365 or 366 days.

Excel's **IRR** function will not correctly compute the YTM of this bond—**IRR** assumes that all the payments are spaced at equal intervals, whereas in our example the first interval (214 days) is very different from the subsequent payment intervals. Fortunately, Excel has a function called **XIRR,** which correctly computes the internal rate of return for uneven spacing of payments. The use of this function is discussed in a separate Excel Note on page 528.[5] Here is its implementation for our problem:

	A	B	C
1	**YIELD TO MATURITY** **For uneven date spacing**		
2	Market price of bond	1,050.00	
3			
4	**Date**	**Bond cash flow**	
5	15-May-01	-1,050.00	
6	15-Dec-01	70.00	
7	15-Dec-02	70.00	
8	15-Dec-03	70.00	
9	15-Dec-04	70.00	
10	15-Dec-05	70.00	
11	15-Dec-06	70.00	
12	15-Dec-07	1,070.00	
13			
14	YTM of bond	6.58%	<-- =XIRR(B5:B12,A5:A12)

---

[5]For more information on dates and date functions in Excel, see Chapter 29.

As you can see, when you buy the bond on 15 May 2001, the YTM is 6.58% annually.

EXCEL NOTE

THE **XIRR** FUNCTION

To use **XIRR,** you have to put in the dates on which the payments are received. In the previous example, cells B5 to B12 contain these dates. Once you've got the dates in, you can use **XIRR** as illustrated below:

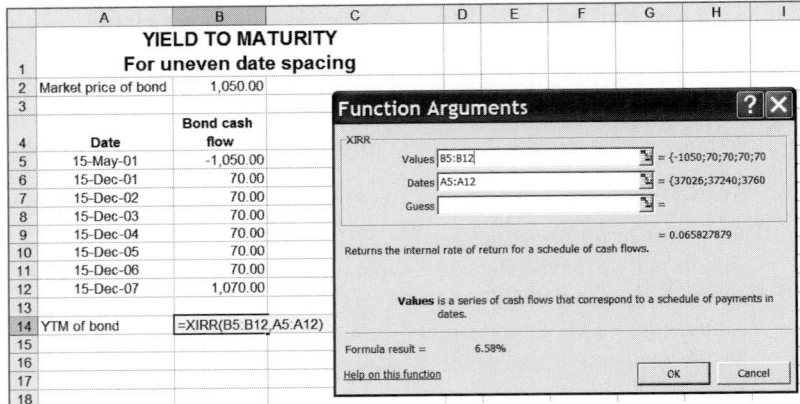

Note that the **XIRR** function computes the effective *annual* YTM. You may not see **XIRR** in your list of Excel functions. In this case go to **Tools|Add-ins** and click on the **Analysis ToolPak** box:

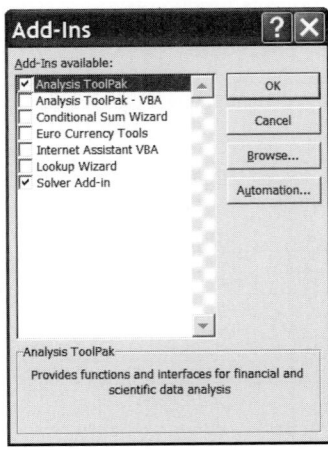

Complicating Factor 2: Semiannual Interest

Corporate and government bonds often pay interest twice a year and not annually. We are thus faced with a problem of *annualizing the interest rate on the bond*. This corresponds to the concept of effective annual interest rate (EAIR) discussed in Chapter 2.

Here is an example. Suppose that the ABC Corp. issues a bond at the same time as XYZ Corp. Like the XYZ bond, ABC's bond pays a 7% coupon on its face value of $1,000, is issued on 15 December 2000, and matures on 15 December 2007. The only difference between the two bonds is that ABC's interest payment is *semiannual:* Instead of paying $70 once a year, the ABC bond pays $35 twice a year, on 15 June and 15 December.

We can use either **IRR** or **XIRR** to compute the yield to maturity of the ABC bond:

	A	B	C	D	E	F	G
1		YTM WITH SEMIANNUAL COUPON PAYMENTS					
2	Market price of bond	1000.00					
3							
4	Period	ABC bond cash flow			Date	ABC bond cash flow	
5	0	-1,000.00			15-Dec-00	-1,000.00	
6	1	35.00			15-Jun-01	35.00	
7	2	35.00			15-Dec-01	35.00	
8	3	35.00			15-Jun-02	35.00	
9	4	35.00			15-Dec-02	35.00	
10	5	35.00			15-Jun-03	35.00	
11	6	35.00			15-Dec-03	35.00	
12	7	35.00			15-Jun-04	35.00	
13	8	35.00			15-Dec-04	35.00	
14	9	35.00			15-Jun-05	35.00	
15	10	35.00			15-Dec-05	35.00	
16	11	35.00			15-Jun-06	35.00	
17	12	35.00			15-Dec-06	35.00	
18	13	35.00			15-Jun-07	35.00	
19	14	1,035.00			15-Dec-07	1,035.00	
20							
21	Semiannual IRR	3.50%	<-- =IRR(B5:B19)				
22	Annualized IRR This is the YTM!	7.12%	<-- =(1+B21)^2-1		YTM using XIRR	7.12%	<-- =XIRR(F5:F19,E5:E19)

In cell B21 we use **IRR** to calculate the internal rate of return of the bond price and its payments. Because the basic period is a half-year, the annualized IRR is $(1 + 3.50\%)^2 - 1 = 7.12\%$ (cell B22). In columns E and F, we have listed the actual dates of the payments and used the **XIRR** function. Note that **XIRR** calculates the annualized YTM directly.

Complicating Factor 3: Accrued Interest

In U.S. bond markets the "price" quoted for a bond is usually not the amount you will be asked to pay for the bond because it doesn't include the interest that has accrued on the bond. Sound confusing? Here's an example.

Suppose you're going to buy the XYZ bond on 3 April 2001. You call a bond dealer, who quotes you a price of $1050 for the bond. To this quoted price is added the bond's *accrued interest,* the proportional part of the bond's annual coupon payment (see Figure 18.7).

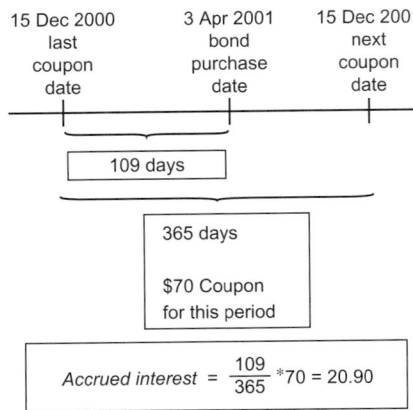

Figure 18.7 Computing the accrued interest. The *accrued interest* is jargon for the unpaid part of the bond coupon since the last interest payment. In U.S. bond markets, the accrued interest is added to the quoted bond price to compute the amount actually paid for the bond. In most European bond markets, the quoted bond price is the actual price paid for the bond and there is no separate accrued interest calculation.

	A	B	C	D	E
1	**ACCRUED INTEREST AND YTM COMPUTATIONS**				
2	Bond purchase date	3-Apr-01			
3	Previous coupon date	15-Dec-00	Number of days since last coupon	109	<-- =B2-B3
4	Next coupon date	15-Dec-01	Number of days between coupons	365	<-- =B4-B3
5	Coupon payment over the period	70.00			
6					
7	Quoted bond price	1050.00			
8	Accrued interest	20.90	<-- =B5*D3/D4		
9	Actual bond price paid	1070.90	<-- =B7+B8		
10					
11	**Year**	**Bond cash flow**			
12	3-Apr-01	-1,070.90			
13	15-Dec-01	70.00			
14	15-Dec-02	70.00			
15	15-Dec-03	70.00			
16	15-Dec-04	70.00			
17	15-Dec-05	70.00			
18	15-Dec-06	70.00			
19	15-Dec-07	1,070.00			
20					
21	YTM of bond, using **XIRR**	6.06%	<-- =XIRR(B12:B19,A12:A19)		
22	YTM of bond, using **Yield**	6.06%	<-- =YIELD(A12,A19,7%,105,100,1,3)		

In the spreadsheet above, the accrued interest is $20.90 (cell B8). This is computed as 109/365 times the annual bond coupon of $70. The actual price paid for the bond is $1,070.90 (cell B9), and using **XIRR** we can compute the bond's YTM as 6.06% (cell B21).

In cell B22 we illustrate **Yield,** yet another Excel function that computes the yield to maturity. This function is explained in the Excel Note on page 531. **Yield** is somewhat more complicated to use than **XIRR,** but its advantage is that it does the accrued interest calculation automatically.

EXCEL NOTE

THE **YIELD** FUNCTION

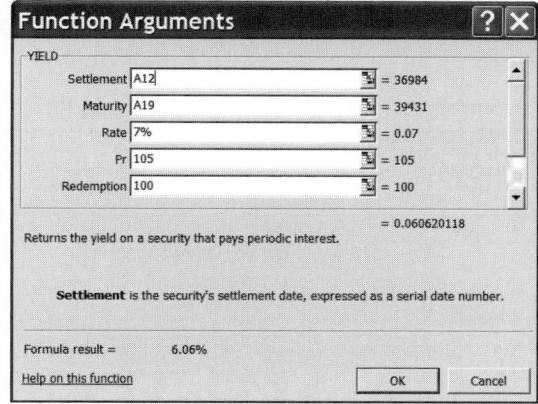
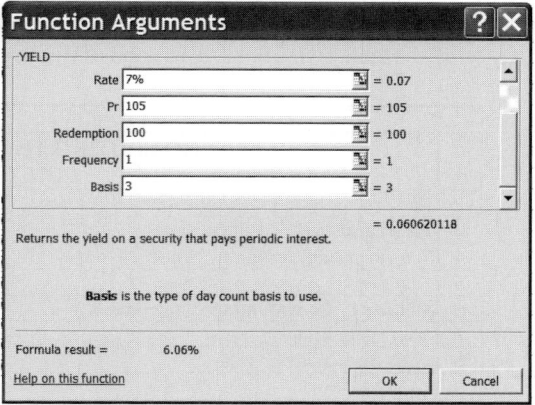

The **Yield** function contains seven cells to fill (**Settlement, Maturity, Rate, Pr, Redemption, Frequency, Basis**). Excel's dialogue box for this function can't accommodate all the arguments on one screen, so it includes a "slider" so you can navigate between the arguments. The two screens above show all the arguments.

For the **Yield** function used in cell B22:

- The **Settlement** is the date that the bond is purchased (cell A12). Notice that Excel translates this date to 36984; to understand this translation, refer to Chapter 29.
- **Maturity** is the maturity date of the bond.
- **Rate** is the *annual* coupon rate on the bond.
- **Pr** is the price per $100 face value. In our example a $1,000 face-value ABC bond is selling for $1,050; this is $105 for each $100 of face value.
- **Redemption** is the redemption value per $100 face value.
- **Frequency** is the number of coupon payments per year.
- **Basis** is the number of days in a year (sounds stupid, but there are different conventions). The answer of "3" used here tells Excel to use the actual number of days.

18.2 U.S. Treasury Bills

U.S. government bonds are variously defined as *Treasury bills, Treasury notes,* and *Treasury bonds.* In this section we analyze U.S. Treasury bills, and in the next section we examine U.S. Treasury bonds and notes.[6]

---

[6]There's a very good website operated by the U.S. government which explains more about Treasury securities: http://www.publicdebt.treas.gov/of/ofbasics.htm.

Treasury bills ("T-bills") are short-term securities sold by the U.S. Treasury. T-bills mature in one year or less from their issue date. They have no coupon payments. Instead, you pay less than the face value and get the face value at maturity. Here's an example: Suppose you purchase a 26-week T-bill with face value $10,000 for $9,750. In 26 weeks (182 days) you will get $10,000. The spreadsheet below illustrates two methods for computing the yield to maturity of the T-bill. (The discussion of these two methods follows the spreadsheet.) Remember that the YTM is nothing more than the annualized internal rate of return; thus, these calculations are very reminiscent of our discussion of the effective annual interest rate (EAIR) in Chapter 6.

	A	B	C
1	**COMPUTING THE YIELD TO MATURITY (YTM) ON TREASURY BILLS**		
2	Purchase price	9,750.00	
3	Face value	10,000.00	
4	Time to maturity (days)	182	<-- =26*7
5			
6	**Method 1: Compound the daily return**		
7	Daily interest rate	0.0139%	<-- =(B3/B2)^(1/B4)-1
8	YTM--the annualized rate	5.2086%	<-- =(1+B7)^365-1
9			
10	**Method 2: Calculate the continuously compounded return**		
11	Continuously compounded	5.0775%	<-- =LN(B3/B2)*(365/B4)
12			
13	**Future value *in one year* using each method**		
14	Method 1	10,257.84	<-- =B2*(1+B8)
15	Method 2	10,257.84	<-- =B2*EXP(B11)

Method 1: YTM of the Treasury Bill Is the Compounded Daily Return

One way to calculate the T-bill YTM is to compound the *daily interest rate* paid by the T-bill. To do this, we first find the daily interest rate paid by the T-bill: $10,000 = 9,750 * (1 + r_{daily})^{182}$. Solving this equation gives $1 + r_{daily} = \left(\frac{10,000}{9,750}\right)^{1/182}$, which results in $r_{daily} = 0.0139\%$. Compounding this rate to give an annual rate shows that the T-bill pays 5.2086% annually: $(1 + 0.0139\%)^{365} - 1 = 5.2086\%$.

Method 2: YTM of the Treasury Bill Is the Continuously Compounded Return

This is the method preferred by most finance academics and by many finance professionals.[7] We assume that the purchase price grows at continuously compound rate r:

$$10,000 = 9,750 * e^{0.5r}$$

$$\Rightarrow e^{0.5r} = \frac{10,000}{9,750}$$

$$\Rightarrow r = \frac{\ln\left(\frac{10,000}{9,750}\right)}{0.5} = 5.064\%$$

---

[7]Continuous compounding and discounting was explained in Section 6.6. If you're not comfortable with continuous discounting and compounding, just skip Method 2.

Which Method Is Correct?

Both methods are correct! We know this is confusing, but then so are many other things in life. The principle is that *any method that gives the same future value using the annualized interest* is a valid method. In the spreadsheet cells B14 and B15 you can see that both methods indeed give the same future value.

18.3 U.S. Treasury Bonds and Notes

Treasury bonds and notes have a coupon rate and a fixed maturity date at which time the bond's principal is repaid.[8] Here's an example. On 15 August 1999 the Treasury issued a ten-year, 6% Treasury note. Suppose you bought $1,000 face value of this security at issue for its par price of $1,000. Then you would expect to be paid a $30 coupon every half-year (15 February 2000, 15 August 2000, 15 February 2001, . . .) until, on the bond's maturity date of 15 August 2009, you would be paid $1030 (the repayment of the bond's principal plus the last half-year's coupon payment).

If you bought the bond at issue and intended to hold it until maturity, your anticipated cash flows would be:

	A	B	C
1	UNITED STATES TREASURY BOND, 6%, MATURING 15 AUGUST 2009		
2	Face value of bonds bought	1,000	
3	Coupon rate	6.00%	
4	Maturity date	15-Aug-09	
5	Issue date	15-Aug-99	
6			
7	Cash flows to purchaser at bond issue		
8	Date	Cash flow	
9	15-Aug-99	-1,000	<-- =-B2
10	15-Feb-00	30	<-- =$B$3*$B$2/2
11	15-Aug-00	30	<-- =$B$3*$B$2/2
12	15-Feb-01	30	
13	15-Aug-01	30	
14	15-Feb-02	30	
15	15-Aug-02	30	
16	15-Feb-03	30	
17	15-Aug-03	30	
18	15-Feb-04	30	
19	15-Aug-04	30	
20	15-Feb-05	30	
21	15-Aug-05	30	
22	15-Feb-06	30	
23	15-Aug-06	30	
24	15-Feb-07	30	
25	15-Aug-07	30	
26	15-Feb-08	30	
27	15-Aug-08	30	
28	15-Feb-09	30	
29	15-Aug-09	1,030	<-- =$B$3*$B$2/2+B2
30			
31	IRR (semiannual interest)	3.00%	<-- =IRR(B9:B29)
32	Annualizing the semiannual IRR	6.09%	<-- =(1+B31)^2-1
33	YTM using XIRR	6.08%	<-- =XIRR(B9:B29,A9:A29)

[8] The nomenclature for interest-paying Treasury securities distinguishes between "Treasury Notes" and "Treasury Bonds." Notes have an initial maturity of ten years or less, whereas "Treasury Bonds" have an initial maturity longer than ten years. Since there is no analytical difference between the two, we shall refer to them both as "bonds" (with a lowercase "b").

Cell B31 gives the semiannual IRR for the bond, 3%. When we annualize this semiannual IRR, we find the yield to maturity (cell B32).

$$YTM \ of \ T\text{-}bond = (1 + semiannual \ IRR)^2 - 1 = (1 + 3\%)^2 - 1 = 6.09\%$$

We can also compute the YTM on the T-bond directly by using **XIRR** (cell B33).[9]

Time Moves On—Purchasing the 6% T-Note on 12 February 2001

Suppose you purchased $1,000 face value of the bond on 12 February 2001. In this case you would have paid $1,089.42 for the bond.[10] Had you intended to hold the bond to maturity, you would anticipate getting:

- $30 on 15 February 2001, 15 August 2001, 15 February 2002, ... , 15 February 2009.
- $1030 on 15 August 2009.

In the spreadsheet that follows we calculate the YTM of the bond using three calculations (cells B31 to B33):

	A	B	C	D	E	F
1	UNITED STATES TREASURY BOND, 6%, MATURING 15 AUGUST 2009					
2	Face value of bonds bought	1,000.00				
3	Coupon rate	6.00%				
4				Today's date	12-Feb-01	
5	Market price	1,059.51		Last coupon date	15-Aug-00	
6	Accrued interest	29.51	<-- =E12	Next coupon date	15-Feb-01	
7						
8	Actual price paid	1,089.02		Days since last coupon	181	<-- =E4-E5
9				Days between coupons	184	<-- =E6-E5
10	**Date**	**Cash flow**				
11	12-Feb-01	-1,089.02	<-- =-B8	Semiannual coupon	30	<-- =B3/2*B2
12	15-Feb-01	30.00	<-- =$B$3*$B$2/2	Accrued interest	29.51	<-- =E8/E9*E11
13	15-Aug-01	30.00				
14	15-Feb-02	30.00				
15	15-Aug-02	30.00				
16	15-Feb-03	30.00				
17	15-Aug-03	30.00				
18	15-Feb-04	30.00				
19	15-Aug-04	30.00				
20	15-Feb-05	30.00				
21	15-Aug-05	30.00				
22	15-Feb-06	30.00				
23	15-Aug-06	30.00				
24	15-Feb-07	30.00				
25	15-Aug-07	30.00				
26	15-Feb-08	30.00				
27	15-Aug-08	30.00				
28	15-Feb-09	30.00				
29	15-Aug-09	1,030.00	<-- =$B$3*$B$2/2+B2			
30						
31	**XIRR** (annualized IRR)	5.193%	<-- =XIRR(B11:B29,A11:A29)			
32	Excel's **Yield** function	5.128%	<-- =YIELD(A11,A29,B3,B5/10,100,2,3)			
33	Excel's **Yield** annualized	5.193%	<-- =(1+B32/2)^2-1			

---

[9]**XIRR** gives a slightly different answer than the calculation in cell B32 because it takes account of the actual days between each payment. See Section 31.4.

[10]In a moment we show how this price was arrived at.

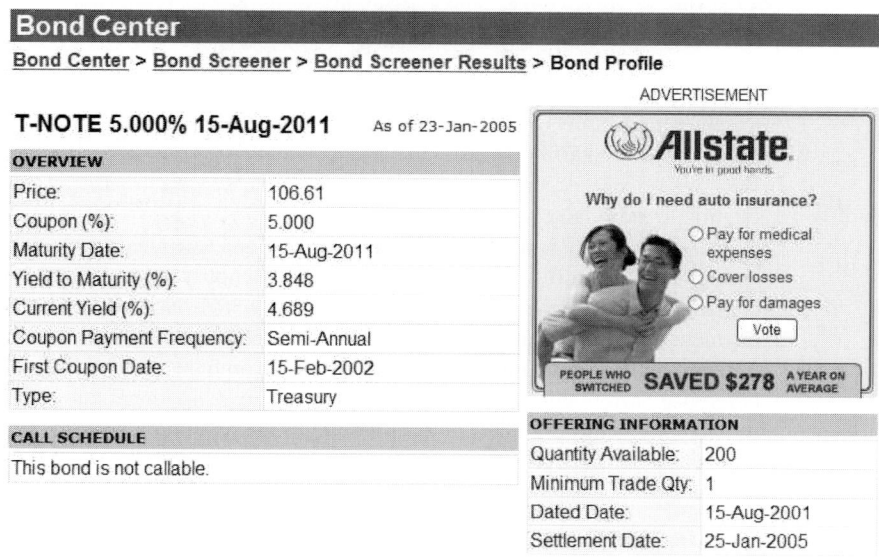

Figure 18.8 Much information about bonds is available on http://bonds.yahoo.com/ . The Treasury Note reported above pays $2.50 interest on 15 August and 15 February until the 15 August 2011 maturity date. The price of the bond of $106.61 does not include accrued interest. The *current yield* is the annual bond coupon divided by the bond price: $5/106.61 = 4.689\%$.

Cell B31 shows that the YTM computed with the **XIRR** function (discussed in Section 18.1, p. 528) is 5.193%. Cell B32 shows that Excel's **Yield** function computes the YTM as 5.128%. This is different from cell B31, because **Yield** follows the conventions of the U.S. bond markets in computing the *semiannual yield doubled*. To see what this means, look at cell B33, which shows you that, properly interpreted, **Yield** correctly calculates the YTM:

$$\text{Cell B33:} \quad \left(1 + \frac{\textit{Excel's }\textbf{Yield}\textit{ from cell B32}}{2}\right)^2 - 1 = \left(1 + \frac{5.128\%}{2}\right)^2 - 1 = 5.193\%$$

18.4 A Corporate Bond Example: Giant Industries

In this section we present a case example of a corporate bond. Giant Industries (stock symbol GI) is a petroleum refiner and marketer in the American Southwest. The firm's shares are listed on the New York Stock Exchange. Look at Figure 18.9 to see what the company had to say about the bonds in its 1999 annual report.

The Company's capital structure includes $150,000,000 of 9% senior subordinated notes due 2007 (the "9% Notes") and $100,000,000 of 9 3/4% senior subordinated notes due 2003 (the "9 3/4% Notes," and collectively with the 9% Notes, the "Notes"). The Indentures supporting the Notes contain restrictive covenants that, among other things, restrict the ability of the Company and its subsidiaries to create liens, to incur or guarantee debt, to pay dividends, to repurchase shares of the Company's common stock, to sell certain assets or subsidiary stock, to engage in certain mergers, to engage in certain transactions with affiliates or to alter the Company's current line of business. At December 31, 1999, the Company was in compliance with the restrictive covenants relating to these Notes.

The Company had been precluded from making restricted payments from the third quarter of 1998 until June 30, 1999, because it did not satisfy a financial ratio test contained in one of the covenants relating to the 9 3/4% Notes. This included the payment of dividends and the repurchase of shares of the Company's common stock. The terms of the Indenture also had restricted the amount of money the Company could otherwise borrow during this period. The Company is no longer subject to these restrictions, as the Company currently satisfies the requirements of the covenant's financial ratio test.

Lexicon:

Senior unsecured obligations: The debt in question has first claim on the company's assets in case of default. On the other hand, debt payment is not secured by a claim to a specific set of the company's assets (this would be the case if the company had borrowed money using one of its refiners as security).

Indenture: The terms under which the bond is issued. In the GI bond case, this will be a sizable document available from the company or its investment bankers.

Covenants: Restrictions on the company's actions.

Preferred stock: Corporate stock whose holders are guaranteed payment of dividends and a share of asset distribution before the holders of common stock. Preferred stock typically has a guaranteed annual dividend. It may be *cumulative preferred stock,* in which case the company has to make up any dividends missed.

Retirement of capital stock: The repurchase of stock (whether common or preferred) from shareholders.

Transactions with affiliates: Purchases or sales between subsidiaries of the company.

Interest in arrears: Interest payments missed by the company.

Figure 18.9 How Giant Industries reported its 9% senior subordinated notes. The two paragraphs (mildly edited) appeared in GI's 1999 annual report. The "Lexicon" explains some of the terminology.

Summarizing:

- The face value of the bonds is $150 million. The bonds were issued 1 September 1997. After deducting expenses, the company netted $146.8 million from the bond issue. The bonds mature on 1 September 2007.

- The coupon rate on the bonds is 9%. This interest is paid semiannually. Thus, the purchaser of $1,000 face value of bonds would get two payments per year of $(9\%/2) * 1,000 = 45.00$.

What Did the Bonds Cost the Company?

We start by considering the effective annual interest rate of the bond issue to GI. We do this by setting up a table of GI cash flows from the bonds:

	A	B	C
1	**GIANT INDUSTRIES 9% BONDS ISSUER PERSPECTIVE 1 Sept. 1997 (issue date)**		
2	Principal amount ($ million)	150.0	
3	Net received by Giant Industries	146.8	
4	Coupon rate	9.00%	
5	Maturity date	1-Sep-07	
6	Issue date	1-Sep-97	
7			
8	Date	**Cash flow to GI**	
9	1-Sep-97	146.8	<-- =B3
10	1-Mar-98	-6.75	<-- =-$B$4*$B$2/2
11	1-Sep-98	-6.75	<-- =-$B$4*$B$2/2
12	1-Mar-99	-6.75	
13	1-Sep-99	-6.75	
14	1-Mar-00	-6.75	
15	1-Sep-00	-6.75	
16	1-Mar-01	-6.75	
17	1-Sep-01	-6.75	
18	1-Mar-02	-6.75	
19	1-Sep-02	-6.75	
20	1-Mar-03	-6.75	
21	1-Sep-03	-6.75	
22	1-Mar-04	-6.75	
23	1-Sep-04	-6.75	
24	1-Mar-05	-6.75	
25	1-Sep-05	-6.75	
26	1-Mar-06	-6.75	
27	1-Sep-06	-6.75	
28	1-Mar-07	-6.75	
29	1-Sep-07	-156.75	<-- =-$B$4*$B$2/2-B2
30			
31	Semiannual IRR of payments	4.67%	<-- =IRR(B9:B29)
32	YTM--annualized semiannual IRR	9.55%	<-- =(1+B31)^2-1
33	YTM computed with **XIRR**	9.55%	<-- =XIRR(B9:B29,A9:A29)

We've written down the semiannual cash flows for the whole bond issue. Excel's **IRR** function shows that the internal rate of return (we could also call this the semiannual *yield to* *maturity*) of the bonds is 4.67% (cell B31). The *compounded effective annual cost* of the bonds to GI is given in cell B32: 9.55%. The yield to maturity as computed by Excel's **XIRR** function (cell B33) is the same.

The Bonds From the Buyer's Perspective

The previous subsection analyzed the GI bonds from the perspective of the issuing company and showed that when we account for the issuing costs of $3.2 million, the bonds cost the company 9.55% annually. We now examine the yield from the perspective of a buyer of the bonds. Suppose you had bought $1,000 face value of the bonds at issue.[11] As the next spreadsheet shows (cells B30 to B32), you would have expected to earn an annualized interest rate of 9.20% on your bonds, if (1) you anticipated holding them to maturity and (2) GI did not default on the bonds:

	A	B	C
1	**GIANT INDUSTRIES 9% BONDS** **BUYER PERSPECTIVE** **1 Sept. 1997 (issue date)**		
2	Face value of bonds bought	1,000.00	
3	Coupon rate	9.00%	
4	Maturity date	1-Sep-07	
5	Issue date	1-Sep-97	
6			
7	**Date**	**Cash flow**	
8	1-Sep-97	-1,000.00	<-- =-B2
9	1-Mar-98	45.00	<-- =$B$3*$B$2/2
10	1-Sep-98	45.00	<-- =$B$3*$B$2/2
11	1-Mar-99	45.00	
12	1-Sep-99	45.00	
13	1-Mar-00	45.00	
14	1-Sep-00	45.00	
15	1-Mar-01	45.00	
16	1-Sep-01	45.00	
17	1-Mar-02	45.00	
18	1-Sep-02	45.00	
19	1-Mar-03	45.00	
20	1-Sep-03	45.00	
21	1-Mar-04	45.00	
22	1-Sep-04	45.00	
23	1-Mar-05	45.00	
24	1-Sep-05	45.00	
25	1-Mar-06	45.00	
26	1-Sep-06	45.00	
27	1-Mar-07	45.00	
28	1-Sep-07	1,045.00	<-- =$B$3*$B$2/2
29			
30	Semiannual IRR of payments	4.50%	<-- =IRR(B8:B28)
31	YTM--annualized semiannual IRR	9.20%	<-- =(1+B30)^2-1
32	YTM computed with **XIRR**	9.20%	<-- =XIRR(B8:B28,A8:A28)

---

[11]Our example assumes that you paid no commissions or other transactions costs to buy the bonds. Typically, these costs would be $25 to $50 for a $1,000 bond purchase.

Note that there's a spread between what the bonds cost the company (9.55% YTM) and what they yield to the purchaser (9.20% YTM). The difference in the YTMs reflects the fact that it cost Giant Industries $3.2 million to issue the bonds, so that its costs are higher than the yield received by investors in the bonds.

Buying the Bonds on the Open Market After Issue

Thus far, we have only considered the purchase of the bonds at issue. We now suppose that the date is 7 December 2000, and that you purchase $1,000 (face value) of the bonds on the open market. Looking on a website that reports bond prices, you see that the price of the bond on this date is $932.50; to this price, we have to add the accrued interest:

$$actual\ price\ paid = 932.50 + accrued\ interest$$
$$= 932.50 + \frac{days\ between\ 1\ Sept.\ 2000\ and\ 7\ Dec.\ 2000}{days\ between\ 1\ Sept.\ 2000\ and\ 1\ Mar.\ 2001} * semiannual\ bond\ coupon$$
$$= 932.50 + \frac{97}{181} * 45.00$$
$$= 932.50 + 24.12$$
$$= 956.62$$

Because the time between the bond payments is unevenly spaced, the computation of the YTM requires the use of **XIRR**. Using this function shows that the YTM is 10.68% (cell B26 below).

	A	B	C	D	E	F
1		**GIANT INDUSTRIES 9% BONDS** **BUYER PERSPECTIVE** **7 Dec. 2000**				
2	Face value of bonds bought	1,000.00		**Accrued interest calculation**		
3	Coupon rate	9.00%				
4				Today's date	7-Dec-00	
5	Quoted price	932.50		Last coupon date	1-Sep-00	
6	Accrued interest	24.12	<-- =E12	Next coupon date	1-Mar-01	
7	Actual price paid	956.62				
8				Days since last coupon	97	<-- =E4-E5
9	Date	Cash flow		Days between coupons	181	<-- =E6-E5
10	12/7/2000	-956.62	<-- =-B7			
11	3/1/2001	45.00	<-- =$B$3*$B$2/2	Semiannual coupon	45.00	<-- =B3/2*B2
12	9/1/2001	45.00		Accrued interest	24.12	<-- =E8/E9*E11
13	3/1/2002	45.00				
14	9/1/2002	45.00				
15	3/1/2003	45.00				
16	9/1/2003	45.00				
17	3/1/2004	45.00				
18	9/1/2004	45.00				
19	3/1/2005	45.00				
20	9/1/2005	45.00				
21	3/1/2006	45.00				
22	9/1/2006	45.00				
23	3/1/2007	45.00				
24	9/1/2007	1,045.00	<-- =$B$3*$B$2/2+B2			
25						
26	YTM using XIRR	10.68%	<-- =XIRR(B10:B24,A10:A24)			
27	YTM using Excel's Yield function	10.41%	<-- =YIELD(A10,A24,B3,B5/10,100,2,3)			
28	Excel's Yield annualized	10.68%	<-- =(1+B27/2)^2-1			

Note that Excel's **Yield** function in cell B27 gives the doubled semiannual yield as it is often reported in U.S. bond markets. As in the Treasury bond example in Section 18.3, annualizing this yield (cell B28) gives the same answer as the YTM reported by **XIRR.**

18.5 Callable Bonds

Many bonds are *callable*. This means that the bond issuer has the right to refund the bonds after a given date. As an example of a callable bond, we consider the notes (remember that "note" is just another word for "bond") issued by General Electric, which are described in Figure 18.10.

The GE notes pay interest of 5.875%. This interest is paid quarterly, so that per $25 of par value, the bonds pay quarterly interest of $1.46875 (= (5.875% * $25)/4). The notes are callable at par on or after 20 February 2008. The notes mature on 18 February 2033.

Below we compute the internal rate of return on these bonds, assuming that they are sold on 18 August 2003 for $27.00 and held until maturity. (Note that the Excel clip hides rows 19–122; see Chapter 10, pp. 282–284, for instructions on how to do this.)

	A	B	C
1	**GENERAL ELECTRIC BONDS**		
2	Face value	25.00	
3	Coupon rate	5.875%	
4	Maturity date	18-Feb-33	
5	Current date	18-Aug-03	<-- The date the bonds are sold
6	First call	20-Feb-08	
7	Bond price on current date	27.00	
8			
9	**Computing the Yield to Maturity**		
10	Date	**Cash flow**	
11	18-Aug-03	-27.0000	<-- =-B7
12	18-Nov-03	0.3672	<-- =$B$3*$B$2/4
13	18-Feb-04	0.3672	<-- =$B$3*$B$2/4
14	18-May-04	0.3672	
15	18-Aug-04	0.3672	
16	18-Nov-04	0.3672	
17	18-Feb-05	0.3672	
18	18-May-05	0.3672	
123	18-Aug-31	0.3672	
124	18-Nov-31	0.3672	
125	18-Feb-32	0.3672	
126	18-May-32	0.3672	
127	18-Aug-32	0.3672	
128	18-Nov-32	0.3672	
129	18-Feb-33	25.3672	<-- =$B$3*$B$2/4+B2
130			
131	Using XIRR	5.44%	<-- =XIRR(B11:B129,A11:A129)
132	Annualizing the quarterly IRR	5.44%	<-- =(1+IRR(B11:B129,3%))^4-1
133			
134	Using Yield	5.34%	<-- =YIELD(B5,B4,B3,B7*4,B2*4,4,3)
135	4 times the YTM	5.34%	<-- =4*IRR(B11:B129,3%)

General Electric Capital Corp., 5.875% Notes due 2/18/2033
Ticker Symbol: GED   CUSIP: 369622493   Exchange: NYSE
Security Type: Exchange-Traded Debt Security

SECURITY DESCRIPTION: General Electric Capital Corp., 5.875% Notes due 2/18/2033, issued in $25 denominations, redeemable at the issuer's option on or after 2/20/2008 at $25 per share plus accrued and unpaid interest, maturing 2/18/2033, distributions of 5.875% ($1.46875) per annum are paid quarterly on 2/20, 5/20, 8/20 & 11/20 to holders of record on the business day prior to the payment date. Units are expected to trade flat, which means accrued interest will be reflected in the trading price and the purchasers will not pay and the sellers will not receive any accrued and unpaid interest. The Notes are senior obligations of the company and will rank equally with all existing and future unsecured and unsubordinated indebtedness of the company. See the IPO prospectus for further information on the notes by clicking on the 'Link to IPO Prospectus' provided below.

Stock Exchange	Cpn Rate Ann Amt	LiqPref CallPrice	Call Date Matur Date	Moodys/S&P Dated	Distribution Dates	15% Tax Rate
NYSE Chart	5.88% $1.46875	$25.00 $25.00	2/20/2008 2/18/2033	Aaa / AAA 7/06/04	2/20, 5/20, 8/20 & 11/20 Click for Ex-Div Date	No

Goto Parent Company's Record (GE)

Figure 18.10 A description of a callable bond issued by General Electric. *Source:* http://www.quantumonline.com.

The spreadsheet shows several ways of computing the notes' yield. Using the **XIRR** function (cell B131) gives a yield of 5.44%. Using the **Yield** function, the notes' yield is 5.34% (cell B134).

Each of these numbers can be derived using Excel's **IRR** function. Since the bond payments are quarterly, **IRR** computes the quarterly interest rate on the bonds. Cell B132 annualizes this quarterly rate by calculating $(1 + quarterly\ IRR)^4 - 1$; this is equivalent to the yield computed by **XIRR** in cell B131. Cell B135 multiplies the quarterly IRR by 4 to get the same number as computed by **Yield.**

Here are two comments on this spreadsheet:

1. The effective annual interest rate paid by the GE notes is the number computed by **XIRR** and not the number computed by **Yield.** So why do we use **Yield?** Because the *convention* in American bond markets is to compute annual rates of return by multiplying the periodic rates as is done in cell B135. If you're going to understand how bond rates are quoted in the United States, you have to understand the difference between the rates computed by **XIRR** and those computed by **Yield.**

2. The equivalence between cells B131 and B132 and between cells B134 and B135 works so nicely because our example starts on 18 August 2003, which is exactly the start of a quarter. For other starting dates, the equivalence would not work exactly. In this case **XIRR** always gives the correct effective annual interest rate.

To see the effect of the call provision of the bond, we calculate the *yield to first call*. This is the yield to maturity, assuming that the bond is actually called by GE at the first call date. The spreadsheet below shows the calculations.[12]

	A	B	C
9	\multicolumn{3}{c}{**Computing the Yield to First Call (YTC)**}		
10	Date	Cash flow	
11	18-Aug-03	-27.0000	<-- =-B7
12	18-Nov-03	0.3672	<-- =$B$3*$B$2/4
13	18-Feb-04	0.3672	<-- =$B$3*$B$2/4
14	18-May-04	0.3672	
15	18-Aug-04	0.3672	
16	18-Nov-04	0.3672	
17	18-Feb-05	0.3672	
18	18-May-05	0.3672	
19	18-Aug-05	0.3672	<-- =$B$3*$B$2/4
20	18-Nov-05	0.3672	
21	18-Feb-06	0.3672	
22	18-May-06	0.3672	
23	18-Aug-06	0.3672	
24	18-Nov-06	0.3672	
25	18-Feb-07	0.3672	
26	18-May-07	0.3672	
27	18-Aug-07	0.3672	
28	18-Nov-07	0.3672	
29	20-Feb-08	25.3672	
30			
31	Using XIRR	3.97%	<-- =XIRR(B11:B29,A11:A29)
32	Annualizing the quarterly IRR	3.99%	<-- =(1+IRR(B11:B29))^4-1
33			
34	Using Yield	3.93%	<-- =YIELD(B5,B6,B3,B7*4,100,4,3)
35	4 times the YTM	3.93%	<-- =4*IRR(B11:B29)

18.6 Preferred Stock

In addition to shares and bonds, companies sometimes issue preferred stock. Preferred stock is a security that promises a fixed payment to the shareholders. Although called "stock," preferred stock has many of the properties of a bond—the dividend is fixed and resembles the coupon payments on bonds. In addition, preferred stock can be callable.

In this section we analyze the preferred stock issued by Alabama Power Company (Figure 18.11). The 5.20% preferred stock issued by the Alabama Power Company has the following features:

- The par value of the stock is $25.00.
- The preferred stock's dividend is 5.20% of its par value, which is 5.20% * 25 = $1.30 annually. One-quarter of this annual dividend, $0.325, is paid four times a year, on 1 January, 1 April, 1 July, and 1 October.
- The preferred stock is listed on the New York Stock Exchange. The price varies with market interest rates and the market's estimation of Alabama Power's credit worthiness—its ability to make good its promise to pay the dividends on the preferred stock. The market price of the preferred stock on 1 July 2003 was $26.10.

---

[12]The slight difference between cell F31 and cell F32 has to do with the fact that **XIRR** is based on daily interest rates, whereas **IRR** assumes that all the quarters are of equal length.

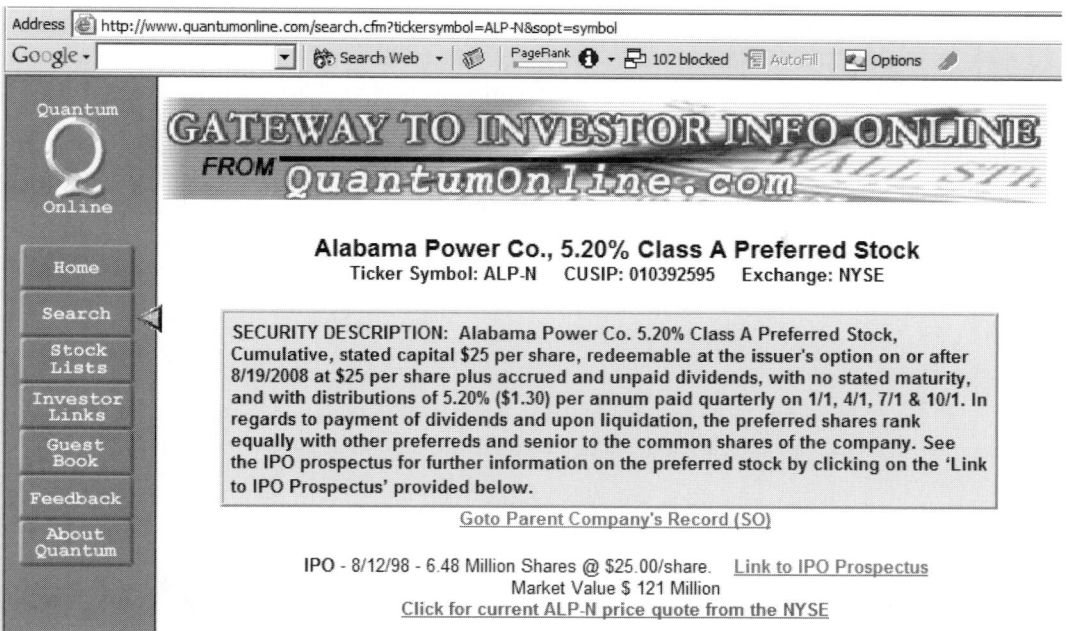

Figure 18.11 A description of Alabama Power Company's 5.20% preferred stock. *Source:* http://www.quantumonline.com.

Computing the Yield Assuming No Call

An investor who buys the Alabama Power preferred stock on 1 July 2003 pays the market price of $26.10 and gets a quarterly dividend of $0.325. If the investor assumes that the stock will never be called—that is, the dividend will be paid forever—then the annualized yield on the stock is 5.07%:

	A	B	C
1	**ALABAMA POWER PREFERRED STOCK** **annualized yield assuming no call**		
2	Annual dividend	1.30	<-- =5.2%*25
3	Quarterly dividend	0.325	<-- =B2/4
4	Market price, 1 July 2003	26.10	
5			
6	Quarterly yield	1.25%	<-- =B3/B4
7	Annualized yield	5.07%	<-- =(1+B6)^4-1

Cell B6 computes the quarterly yield of 1.25%. In cell B7 we annualize this yield as explained in Chapter 5.

Computing the Yield to First Call

Although in principle the preferred stock will pay its dividends indefinitely, Alabama Power Company can call the stock at any time after 19 August 2008. If the stock is called, the company is obliged to pay the preferred stock holders the par value of $25 plus the *accrued preferred dividend.* This concept is very much like the concept of the accrued interest discussed in Section 18.1 (p. 525). For example, if the Alabama Power Company calls the preferred stock on 19 August 2008, it has to pay the preferred stock holders $25.17:

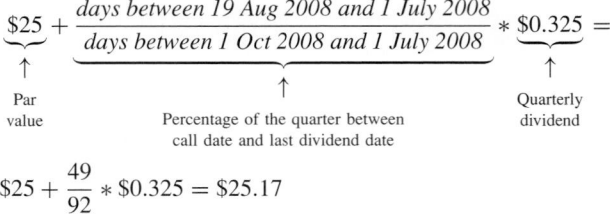

$$\underbrace{\$25}_{\substack{\uparrow \\ \text{Par} \\ \text{value}}} + \underbrace{\frac{\text{days between 19 Aug 2008 and 1 July 2008}}{\text{days between 1 Oct 2008 and 1 July 2008}}}_{\substack{\uparrow \\ \text{Percentage of the quarter between} \\ \text{call date and last dividend date}}} * \underbrace{\$0.325}_{\substack{\uparrow \\ \text{Quarterly} \\ \text{dividend}}} =$$

$$\$25 + \frac{49}{92} * \$0.325 = \$25.17$$

Suppose that the investor believes that Alabama Power will call the preferred stock at the first legal call date. Then the anticipated yield is 4.30%, as shown below in cell B37.

	A	B	C
1	**ALABAMA POWER PREFERRED STOCK** **computing the yield to first call**		
2	Call date	19-Aug-08	
3	Last dividend date	1-Jul-08	
4	Next dividend date	1-Oct-08	
5	Par value	25.00	
6	Quarterly dividend	0.325	<-- =(5.2%*25)/4
7			
8	Days since last dividend	49	<-- =B2-B3
9	Days between last dividend and next dividend	92	<-- =B4-B3
10	Accrued dividend on call date	0.173	<-- =B8/B9*B6
11	Paid by company to shareholders at call	25.17	<-- =B5+B10
12			
13	**Date**	**Cash flow**	
14	1-Jul-03	-26.10	
15	1-Oct-03	0.325	
16	1-Jan-04	0.325	
17	1-Apr-04	0.325	
18	1-Jul-04	0.325	
19	1-Oct-04	0.325	
20	1-Jan-05	0.325	
21	1-Apr-05	0.325	
22	1-Jul-05	0.325	
23	1-Oct-05	0.325	
24	1-Jan-06	0.325	
25	1-Apr-06	0.325	
26	1-Jul-06	0.325	
27	1-Oct-06	0.325	
28	1-Jan-07	0.325	
29	1-Apr-07	0.325	
30	1-Jul-07	0.325	
31	1-Oct-07	0.325	
32	1-Jan-08	0.325	
33	1-Apr-08	0.325	
34	1-Jul-08	0.325	
35	19-Aug-08	25.17	<-- =B11
36			
37	Yield to first call	4.30%	<-- =XIRR(B14:B35,A14:A35)

18.7 Deriving the Yield Curve From Zero-Coupon Bonds

A *zero-coupon* bond is a bond that makes no coupon payments between the time of the bond's issue and the bond's maturity. For example, the Treasury bills discussed in Section 18.2 of this chapter are zero-coupon bonds. Zero coupons have the pleasant property that they allow us to identify the time-specific discount for each payment. Here's an example similar to that given in Section 17.2.

	A	B	C	D
1	USING ZERO-COUPONS TO DETERMINE BOND DISCOUNT RATES			
2	Zero-coupon bond A: maturity in one year			
3	Price today	100		
4	Payoff in one year	105		
5	IRR	5.00%	<-- =B4/B3-1	
6				
7	Zero-coupon bond B: maturity in two years			
8	Price today	99		
9	Payoff in two years	110		
10	IRR	5.41%	<-- =(B9/B8)^(1/2)-1	
11				
12	Zero-coupon bond C: maturity in three years			
13	Price today	101		
14	Payoff in three years	122		
15	IRR	6.50%	<-- =(B14/B13)^(1/3)-1	
16				
17	Coupon bond D: A bond with payments at end of years 1, 2, 3			
18	Date	Payment	Present value of payment	
19	1	50	47.62	<-- =B19/(1+B5)
20	2	50	45.00	<-- =B20/(1+B10)^2
21	3	1,050	869.26	<-- =B21/(1+B15)^3
22	Bond price		961.88	<-- =SUM(C19:C21)

Bonds A, B, and C have no intermediate payments. The IRR of each bond is thus the discount rate for a specific payment at time *t*. For example, $100 paid out in two years would be discounted by 5.41%, the rate determined by bond B.

Now look at bond D. This bond is a regular coupon bond—it pays $50 at dates 1 and 2 and at date 3 it pays $1050 (the face value plus the interest). In cells A19:C22 we use the *zero-coupon yield curve* to determine the price of the bond as $961.88.

Suppose $961.88 is indeed the market price of bond D. Note that the bond's yield to maturity will be different from each of the pure-discount yields determined above:

	A	B	C
24	Determining the yield to maturity (YTM) of bond D		
25	Date	Payment	
26	0	-961.88	
27	1	50.00	
28	2	50.00	
29	3	1,050.00	
30	YTM	6.44%	<-- =IRR(B26:B29)

U.S. Treasury Strips

In the United States brokers often split up the payments on U.S. Treasury bonds and sell them off separately. The bonds created in this way are zero-coupon bonds and are referred to as *strips*. As an example, suppose a broker bought bond D from the previous example. She could sell off the year 1 coupon of $50 as a separate security, and the year 2 coupon of $50 as a separate security, and the year 3 payment of $1050 as a separate security. Each of these zero-coupon "strip securities" would have a separate price.

Zero-coupon strips allow customers with specialized payment needs to buy a security that makes a payment on a specific date. For example, if you know that you have to make a payment in two years, then you could buy two-year Treasury strips. This eliminates all intermediate interest rate risks.

We can use strip prices to identify a *yield curve*. This is a graph showing the zero-coupon interest rate on bonds for each date. Using Treasury strip data from August 2002, here's an example of a zero-coupon Treasury yield curve:

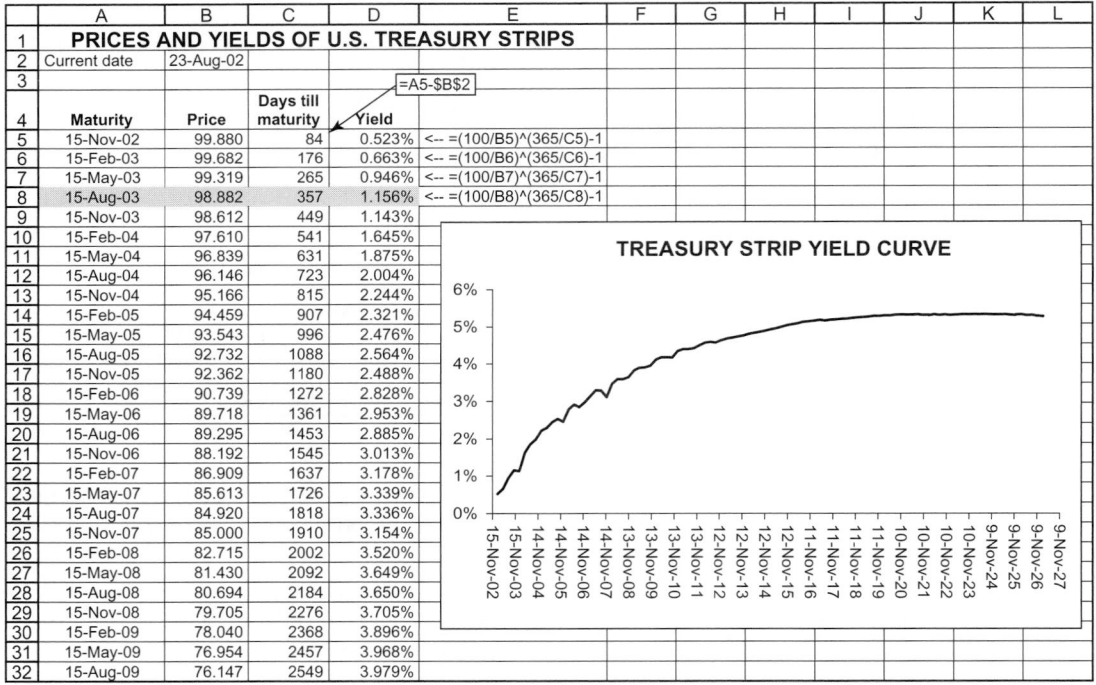

	A	B	C	D	E
1	**PRICES AND YIELDS OF U.S. TREASURY STRIPS**				
2	Current date	23-Aug-02			
3				=A5-$B$2	
4	**Maturity**	**Price**	**Days till maturity**	**Yield**	
5	15-Nov-02	99.880	84	0.523%	<-- =(100/B5)^(365/C5)-1
6	15-Feb-03	99.682	176	0.663%	<-- =(100/B6)^(365/C6)-1
7	15-May-03	99.319	265	0.946%	<-- =(100/B7)^(365/C7)-1
8	15-Aug-03	98.882	357	1.156%	<-- =(100/B8)^(365/C8)-1
9	15-Nov-03	98.612	449	1.143%	
10	15-Feb-04	97.610	541	1.645%	
11	15-May-04	96.839	631	1.875%	
12	15-Aug-04	96.146	723	2.004%	
13	15-Nov-04	95.166	815	2.244%	
14	15-Feb-05	94.459	907	2.321%	
15	15-May-05	93.543	996	2.476%	
16	15-Aug-05	92.732	1088	2.564%	
17	15-Nov-05	92.362	1180	2.488%	
18	15-Feb-06	90.739	1272	2.828%	
19	15-May-06	89.718	1361	2.953%	
20	15-Aug-06	89.295	1453	2.885%	
21	15-Nov-06	88.192	1545	3.013%	
22	15-Feb-07	86.909	1637	3.178%	
23	15-May-07	85.613	1726	3.339%	
24	15-Aug-07	84.920	1818	3.336%	
25	15-Nov-07	85.000	1910	3.154%	
26	15-Feb-08	82.715	2002	3.520%	
27	15-May-08	81.430	2092	3.649%	
28	15-Aug-08	80.694	2184	3.650%	
29	15-Nov-08	79.705	2276	3.705%	
30	15-Feb-09	78.040	2368	3.896%	
31	15-May-09	76.954	2457	3.968%	
32	15-Aug-09	76.147	2549	3.979%	

The graph gives actual prices and maturities for Treasury strips on 23 August 2002. The maturities (column C) are calculated in days. (There are another 70 rows of data which we haven't shown but which is on the CD-ROM that comes with this book.) Here's a sample calculation (cells A8:D8): On 23 August 2002 a zero-coupon Treasury strip with maturity 15 August 2003 sells for $98.882. This bond promises $100 on maturity. There are 357 days between 23 August 2002 and 15 August 2003. To compute the annualized yield for the bond, we find one plus the daily interest rate, $(100/98.882)^{1/357}$. Raising this number to the power 365 (the number of days per year) and subtracting 1 gives the annualized yield in cell D8:

$$yield\ to\ maturity = \left(\frac{100}{98.882}\right)^{365/357} - 1 = 1.156\%$$

CONCLUSION

This chapter discusses the pricing of bonds and the determination of bond yield to maturity. Pricing a bond is largely an exercise in applying the present value concepts discussed in Chapters 1–4. The yield on a bond is the annualized internal rate of return of its payments.

Bond pricing and yield computations are also applicable to callable bonds and to preferred stock. We have given examples of each of these securities. Finally, the chapter also discusses zero-coupon securities.

EXERCISES

1. On 1 August 2001, you are offered the following bond:
   - Face value: $1,000.00
   - Coupon rate: 12%
   - Coupon payments: once a year on 1 August 2002, 2003, . . . , 2012
   - Bond price: $1,252.00
   - Bond's face value repaid on last coupon date

   Use Excel's **IRR** function to compute the bond's yield to maturity (YTM).

2. On 10 September 2001, you are offered the following bond:
   - Face value: $1,000.00
   - Coupon rate: 12%
   - Coupon payments: once a year on 1 August 2002, 2003, ... , 2012
   - Bond price: $1,252.00
   - Bond's face value repaid on last coupon date

   Use Excel's **XIRR** function to compute the bond's yield to maturity (YTM).

3. Consider the following two bonds:

Bond A	Bond B
Term to maturity: ten years from today	Term to maturity: twenty years from today
Face value: $1,000	Face value: $1,000
Coupon: 10%, interest payments to be made in one year from today, two years from today, . . . , ten years from today	Coupon: 10%, interest payments to be made in one year from today, two years from today, . . . , twenty years from today
Repayment of bond: On last coupon date	Repayment of bond: On last coupon date

Make a table comparing the bond prices when the market interest rate varies from 5%, 6%, . . ., 17%. Use the template below, which is on the CD-ROM that accompanies *this book*. In the template you see that when the market interest rate is 10%, both bonds are valued at $1,000.

Can you conclude that "the longer-term bond's price is more sensitive to changes in the market interest rate"? Explain using a graph.

	A	B	C	D	E	F	G
1					**COMPARING TWO BONDS**		
2		Bond A	Bond B		Market interest rate	10%	
3	Coupon rate	10%	10%		Price of Bond A	$1,000.00	<-- =NPV(F2,B8:B17)
4	Maturity	10	20		Price of Bond B	$1,000.00	<-- =NPV(F2,C8:C27)
5	Face value	1,000.00	1,000.00				
6							
7	Year	**Bond A**	**Bond B**		**Data table: Effect of market interest rate on bond prices**		
8	1	100.00	100.00		**Interest rate**	**Bond A price**	**Bond B price**
9	2	100.00	100.00				
10	3	100.00	100.00		0%		
11	4	100.00	100.00		1%		
12	5	100.00	100.00		2%		
13	6	100.00	100.00		3%		
14	7	100.00	100.00		4%		
15	8	100.00	100.00		5%		
16	9	100.00	100.00		6%		
17	10	1,100.00	100.00		7%		
18	11		100.00		8%		
19	12		100.00		9%		
20	13		100.00		10%		
21	14		100.00		11%		
22	15		100.00		12%		
23	16		100.00		13%		
24	17		100.00		14%		
25	18		100.00		15%		
26	19		100.00		16%		
27	20		1,100.00		17%		

4. You have been offered a U.S. Treasury bill. The face value of the bill is $10,000 and the price is $8,925. The bill matures in six months. Compute the YTM of the bill using both discrete and continuously compounded interest.

5. You have been offered a U.S. Treasury bill. The bill has a face value of $10,000 and a price of $9,456. It matures in 210 days. Compute (a) the daily interest rate and the corresponding annualized interest rate, and (b) the continuously compounded interest rate.

6. On 20 February 2001 you are offered a U.S. Treasury note. Here are the terms of the note:

   • The note has a face value of $100,000 and a 6.5% coupon rate. The note matures on 15 October 2006.

   • The semiannual interest on the note (that is, $(6.5\% * 100,000)/2 = \$3,250$) is paid on 15 April and 15 October of each year. The last interest payment was 15 October 2000 and the next interest payment is on 15 April 2001.

   • Other interest payments are on 15 October 2001, 15 April 2002, . . . , 15 October 2006. On this last date the bond's principal of $100,000 is also returned.

   • On 20 February 2001 the bond was priced at $109,477.71. This price was computed as follows:

$$\underbrace{\$107,152.00}_{\substack{\uparrow \\ \text{In the jargon of} \\ \text{bond markets this is} \\ \text{called the "bond price"}}} + \text{ accrued interest of } \$2,285.71 = \underbrace{\$109,477.71}_{\substack{\uparrow \\ \text{In the jargon of} \\ \text{bond markets this is} \\ \text{called the "invoice price"}}}$$

   (a) Confirm the calculation of the accrued interest.

   (b) Use **XIRR** to calculate the annualized yield to maturity (IRR).

Use the following template:

	A	B	C
1		**TREASURY BOND CALCULATION**	
2	**Computing the accrued interest**		
3	Current date	20-Feb-01	
4	Previous interest payment date	15-Oct-00	
5	Next interest payment date	15-Apr-01	
6	Semiannual coupon	3,250.00	
7			
8	Days since last coupon date		
9	Days between last coupon date and next coupon date		
10			
11	Accrued interest		
12			
13	**Computing the YTM**		
14	Bond price	107,152.00	
15	Accrued interest		
16	Invoice price (bond price + accrued)		
17			
18	Date	**Bond cash flow**	
19	20-Feb-01		
20	15-Apr-01		
21	15-Oct-01		
22	15-Apr-02		
23	15-Oct-02		
24	15-Apr-03		
25	15-Oct-03		
26	15-Apr-04		
27	15-Oct-04		
28	15-Apr-05		
29	15-Oct-05		
30	15-Apr-06		
31	15-Oct-06		
32			
33			

7. On 26 February 2001, a UtilityCorp 8.2% bond maturing 15 January 2007 is priced at $103.790 per $100 of face value (this price does not include the accrued interest). The bond was originally issued in 1992. The bond pays interest semiannually, on 15 January and 15 July of each year. Compute the accrued interest and the yield to maturity of the bond.

8. You are given the following information on three traded bonds making annual coupon payments:

	A	B	C	D	E
1					
2	Bond	Face value	Coupon rate	Maturity	Yield to maturity
3	A	$1,000	0.00%	1	5.00%
4	B	$1,000	5.00%	2	5.85%
5	C	$1,000	10.00%	2	6.00%

(a) What are the prices of the above three bonds?

(b) What is the zero-coupon bond yield for a one-year bond. (This is a stupid question!)

(c)   What is the zero-coupon bond yield for a two-year bond based on the price of bond B? Of bond C? (This is not a stupid question.)

(d)   (Challenge exercise) Create an arbitrage strategy from buying and/or selling a combination of the three bonds.

9.   Use the data in the following table to create two graphs. (The data are on the disk that accompanies this book.)

(a)   Create a graph of the yields on bonds of each maturity during the period 1980–2002.

(b)   Create a graph of the risk-premium between Baa rated bonds and Aaa rated bonds for each year.

	A	B	C	D	E	F
1	Moody's Corporate Bond Yield Averages Long-Term Annual Averages (bonds with 20 years or more to maturity) 1980-2002					
2		Aaa	Aa	A	Baa	Avg. Corp
3	1980	11.9%	12.5%	12.9%	13.7%	12.7%
4	1981	14.2%	14.7%	15.3%	16.0%	15.1%
5	1982	13.8%	14.4%	15.4%	16.1%	14.9%
6	1983	12.0%	12.4%	13.1%	13.6%	12.8%
7	1984	12.7%	13.3%	13.7%	14.2%	13.5%
8	1985	11.4%	11.8%	12.3%	12.7%	12.0%
9	1986	9.0%	9.5%	9.9%	10.4%	9.7%
10	1987	9.4%	9.7%	10.0%	10.6%	9.9%
11	1988	9.7%	9.9%	10.2%	10.8%	10.2%
12	1989	9.3%	9.5%	9.7%	10.2%	9.7%
13	1990	9.3%	9.6%	9.8%	10.4%	9.8%
14	1991	8.8%	9.1%	9.3%	9.8%	9.2%
15	1992	8.1%	8.5%	8.6%	9.0%	8.5%
16	1993	7.2%	7.4%	7.6%	7.9%	7.5%
17	1994	8.0%	8.1%	8.3%	8.6%	8.3%
18	1995	7.6%	7.7%	7.8%	8.2%	7.8%
19	1996	7.4%	7.5%	7.7%	8.1%	7.7%
20	1997	7.3%	7.5%	7.5%	7.9%	7.5%
21	1998	6.5%	6.8%	6.9%	7.2%	6.9%
22	1999	7.0%	7.3%	7.5%	7.9%	7.4%
23	2000	7.6%	7.8%	8.1%	8.4%	8.0%
24	2001	7.1%	7.3%	7.7%	8.0%	7.6%
25	2002	6.5%	6.9%	7.2%	7.8%	7.1%
26						
27	Source: http://www.bondmarkets.com/research/C3.shtml					

10.   On 15 August 2006, Corporate Junk issues $100 million of ten-year bonds. The bonds have a coupon of 10%, payable semiannually on 15 February and 15 August of each year. They are issued at par. Corporate Junk's expenses related to the bond issue are $4 million. Compute the annualized yield to the bond investors and the annualized cost to the company.

11.   On 18 October 2006 the Corporate Junk bond issue (see Exercise 10) is selling for $103. Use **XIRR** to compute the investor's yield to maturity (YTM) of the bonds.

12. On 15 August 1996 the U.S. Treasury issued a bond maturing on 15 February 2026. The bond has a coupon rate of 6%, payable semiannually on 15 February and 15 August. If a $100 face-value bond is selling for $117.25 on 23 January 2005, compute the bond's yield to maturity.

13. On 15 May 1985 the U.S. Treasury issued a bond maturing 15 November 2014. The bond has a coupon rate of 11.75%, payable semiannually on 15 November and 15 May. On 23 January 2005 a $1,000 face-value bond was selling for $1356.20. This price does not include the accrued interest. The bond is callable at par starting 15 November 2009.

    (a)   Compute the bond's yield to maturity.

    (b)   Compute the bond's yield to first call.

    (c)   Why do you think the yield to first call is negative?

14. Consolidated Edison's 4.65% Series C cumulative preferred stock trades on the New York Stock Exchange. The stock has a face value of $100 and pays its dividend four times per year, on the first of February, May, July, and November. The stock is not redeemable. If the share price on 2 February 2005 is $85, what is the preferred stock's yield?

15. Reconsider the Consolidated Edison preferred stock in Exercise 14. Suppose that the stock trades for $87.50 on 3 January 2005. What is its yield? (Don't forget that the price does not include the accrued dividend.)

16. Genworth Financial's 5.25% Series A cumulative preferred stock has a par value of $50 and an interest rate of 5.25% payable quarterly on the first day of March, June, September, and December. The stock is callable at par from 1 June 2011. If the stock trades at $45.50 on 2 June 2005, what is its yield to first call?

Genworth Financial, 5.25% Series A Cumul Preferred Stock

Ticker Symbol: GNWTP   CUSIP: 37247D403   Exchange: PKSHT
Security Type: Preferred Stock

SECURITY DESCRIPTION: Genworth Financial Inc., 5.25% Series A Cumulative Preferred Stock, liquidation preference $50 per share, mandatorily redeemable on 6/01/2011 at $50 per share plus accrued and unpaid dividends with no provision for earlier redemption, maturing on 6/01/2011, and with distributions of 5.25% ($2.625) per annum paid quarterly on 3/1, 6/1, 9/1 & 12/1 to holders of record on the date fixed by the board, not more than 60 days or less than 10 days prior to the payment date. In regards to payment of dividends and upon liquidation, the preferred shares rank equally with other preferreds and senior to the common shares of the company. The prospectus (P306) states that the stock should be eligible for the 15% tax rate. See the IPO prospectus for further information on the preferred stock by clicking on the 'Link to IPO Prospectus' provided below.

Stock Exchange	Cpn Rate Ann Amt	LiqPref CallPrice	Call Date Matur Date	Moodys/S&P Dated	Distribution Dates	15% Tax Rate
PKSHT Chart	5.25% $2.625	$50.00 $50.00	6/01/2011 6/01/2011	Baa1 / BBB+ 11/13/04	3/1, 6/1, 9/1 & 12/1 Click for Ex-Div Date	Yes

Goto Parent Company's Record (GNW)

IPO - 5/25/2004 - 2.00 Million Shares @ $50.00/share.   **Link to IPO Prospectus**
Market Value $ 100 Million

17. On the disk that accompanies this book is the file below.
    (a) Complete the file to derive the continuous yields of the zero-coupon Treasury strips. Graph the yields to derive the yield curve on 21 January 2005.
    (b) Why do you think the yields of very short-term zero strips (the first two) are negative?

	A	B	C	D	E	F
1			**U.S. TREASURY STRIP DATA**			
			21 January 2005			
2						
3	Current date	21-Jan-05				
4	Price	Maturity	Yahoo yield	Days to maturity	Years to maturity	Continuous yield
5	100.17	15-Feb-05	-2.956%			
6	100.15	15-Feb-05	-2.642%			
7	99.57	15-May-05	1.421%			
8	99.56	15-May-05	1.457%			
9	98.8	15-Aug-05	2.188%			
10	98.85	15-Aug-05	2.087%			
11	98.04	15-Nov-05	2.481%			
12	98.04	15-Nov-05	2.477%			
13	97.33	15-Feb-06	2.572%			
14	97.35	15-Feb-06	2.554%			
15	97.34	15-Feb-06	2.563%			
16	96.52	15-May-06	2.736%			
17	96.57	15-May-06	2.696%			
18	95.73	15-Aug-06	2.820%			

18. Be ambitious! Go to Yahoo, download the zero-coupon data for a recent date, and repeat Exercise 17.

VALUING STOCKS

OVERVIEW

In Chapter 18 we discussed the valuation of bonds. This chapter deals with the valuation of stocks. Whereas the valuation of bonds is a relatively straightforward matter of computing yields to maturity, the valuation of stocks is much more difficult. The difficulty lies both in the greater uncertainty about the cash flows that need to be discounted in order to arrive at a stock valuation and in the computation of the correct discount rate.

In this chapter we discuss four basic approaches to stock valuation:

- **Valuation method 1, the efficient markets approach.** In its simplest form the *efficient markets* approach states that the current stock price is correct. A somewhat more sophisticated use of the efficient markets approach to stock valuation is that a stock's value is the sum of the values of its components. We explore the implications of these statements in Section 19.1.
- **Valuation method 2, discounting the future free cash flows (FCFs).** Sometimes called the *discounted cash flow* (DCF) approach to valuation, this method values the firm's debt and its equity together as the present value of the firm's future FCFs. The discount rate used is the weighted average cost of capital (WACC). This method is the valuation approach favored by most finance academics. We discuss this approach in Section 19.2 and discuss the computation of the WACC in Sections 19.5 and 19.6. In this chapter we do not discuss the concept or the computation of the free cash flow—this was done previously in Chapters 9 and 10.
- **Valuation method 3, discounting the future equity payouts.** A firm's shares can also be valued by *discounting the stream of anticipated equity payouts* at an appropriate cost of equity r_E. The concept of equity payout (the sum of a firm's total dividends plus its stock repurchases) was previously discussed in Chapter 9.
- **Valuation method 4, multiples.** Finally, we can value a firm's shares by a *comparative valuation based on multiples*. This very common method involves ratios such as the price–earnings (P/E) ratio, EBITDA multiples, and more industry specific multiples such as value per square foot of storage space or value per subscriber.

With the exception of the multiple method 4, almost all of the material in this chapter is also discussed elsewhere in this book. The efficient markets approach to valuation is also discussed in Chapter 17. Discounting free cash flows is discussed in Chapters 9 and 10. The Gordon dividend model (which values a firm's equity by discounting its anticipated dividend stream) is also discussed in Chapter 9. WACC computations are to be found in Chapters 9 and 16. The purpose of this chapter is to bring together these dispersed materials into a (hopefully coherent) whole.

Finance Concepts Discussed

- Discounted cash flows, free cash flows (FCFs)
- Cost of capital, cost of equity, cost of debt, weighted average cost of capital (WACC)
- Equity premium
- Beta, equity beta, asset beta
- Two-stage growth models

Excel Functions Used

- **Sum, NPV, If**
- **Data Table**

19.1 Valuation Method 1: The Current Market Price of a Stock Is the Correct Price (the Efficient Markets Approach)

The simplest stock valuation is based on the efficient markets approach (Chapter 17). This approach says that the *current market price of a stock is the correct price*. In other words, the market has already done the difficult job of stock valuation, and it's done this correctly, incorporating all of the relevant information. There's a lot of evidence for this approach, as you saw in Chapter 17.

This valuation method is very simple to apply:

- *Question:* "IBM looks a bit expensive to me—its price has been going up for the last three months. What do you think: Is IBM's stock price currently underpriced or overpriced?"

- *Answer:* "At Podunk U, we learned that markets with a lot of trading are in general efficient, meaning that the current market price incorporates all the readily available information about IBM. So—I don't think IBM is either underpriced or overpriced. It's actually correctly priced."

Here's another example of the use of this approach:

- *Question:* "I've been thinking of buying IBM, but I've been putting it off. The price has gone up lately, and I'm going to wait until it comes down a bit. It seems a bit high to me right now. What do you think?"

- *Answer:* "At Podunk U, we would call you a 'contrarian.' You believe that if the price of a stock has gone up, it will go back down (and the opposite). But this technical approach to stock valuation doesn't seem to work very well. So if you want to buy IBM, go ahead and do so now. There's nothing in the price runup of the last couple of months which indicates that there will now be a price rundown."

Some More Sophisticated Efficient Markets Methods

Efficient markets valuations don't always have to be as simplistic as the above examples. In Chapter 17 we looked at *additivity,* a fundamental principle of efficient markets. The principle of additivity says that the value of a basket of goods or financial assets should equal the sum of the values of the components. Additivity can often be used to value stocks.

Here's a very simple example. ABC Holding Corp., a publicly traded company, owns shares in two publicly traded companies (Figure 19.1). Besides owning these subsidiaries, ABC does little else.

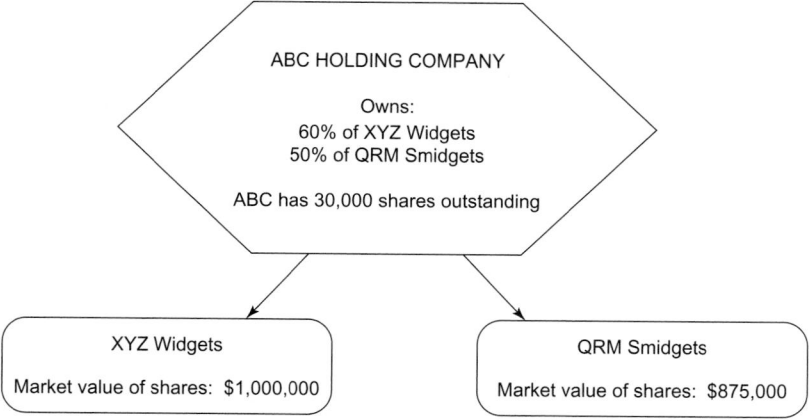

Figure 19.1 Ownership structure of ABC Holding Company.

What should be the value of a share of ABC Holding? The obvious way to do this is in the following spreadsheet, which computes the share value of ABC to be $34.58:

	A	B	C	D	E
1	ABC HOLDING COMPANY				
2	Number of ABC shares	30,000			
3					
4	ABC owns shares in	Percentage of shares owned by ABC	Market value	Market value of ABC holdings in company	
5	XYZ Widgets	60%	1,000,000	600,000	<-- =B5*C5
6	QRM Smidgets	50%	875,000	437,500	<-- =B6*C6
7	Total value of ABC holdings			1,037,500	<-- =D6+D5
8					
9	Per share value of ABC Holdings			34.58	<-- =D7/B2

Notice what this model *is* and *is not* telling you:

- *Is* telling you: If the market values of XYZ and QRM are correct, then the market value of ABC should be $34.58. The formula works out to be

$$ABC \ share \ price \ = \ \frac{60\% * [XYZ \ value] + 50\% * [QRM \ value]}{number \ of \ ABC \ shares}$$

- *Is not* telling you: The formula tells you a relation between the three share prices. It tells you if the share prices are *relatively correct,* but it does not tell you if they are *absolutely correct.* For example, after doing much work and research and applying the methods of the previous section, you come to the conclusion that, while the market valuation of QRM is correct, the market value of XYZ ought to $1,600,000. Then you would conclude that the share price of ABC ought to be $46.58.

	A	B	C	D	E
1	ABC HOLDING COMPANY				
2	Number of ABC shares	30,000			
3					
4	ABC owns shares in	Percentage of shares owned by ABC	Market value	Market value of ABC holdings in company	
5	XYZ Widgets	60%	1,600,000	960,000	<-- =B5*C5
6	QRM Smidgets	50%	875,000	437,500	<-- =B6*C6
7	Total value of ABC holdings			1,397,500	<-- =D6+D5
8					
9	Per share value of ABC Holdings			46.58	<-- =D7/B2

Note that if ABC has some of its own overheads and if it doesn't always pass through all the dividends of its subsidiaries, its market price will be *lower* than $34.58, since the market price of ABC will reflect not only the cost of the shares of its subsidiaries but also its own overheads. This looks a lot like the *closed-end fund* valuation problem discussed in Chapter 17.

19.2 Valuation Method 2: The Price of a Share Is the Discounted Value of the Future Anticipated Free Cash Flows

Valuation method 1 of the previous section says that there is nothing to be gained by second-guessing market valuations. In many cases, however, the finance expert (you!) will want to do a basic valuation of a company and derive the value of a share from the discounted value of the future anticipated free cash flows (FCFs). This method, often called the *discounted cash flow* (DCF) method of valuation, was discussed and illustrated in Chapter 10. Figure 19.2 reminds

Profit after taxes	This is the basic measure of the profitability of the business, but it is an accounting measure that includes financing flows (such as interest), as well as noncash expenses such as depreciation. Profit after taxes does not account for either changes in the firm's working capital or purchases of new fixed assets, both of which can be important cash drains on the firm.
+ Depreciation	This noncash expense is added back to the profit after tax.
+ After-tax interest payments (net)	FCF is an attempt to measure the cash produced by the business activity of the firm. To neutralize the effect of interest payments on the firm's profits, we: • Add back the after-tax cost of interest on debt (*after-tax* since interest payments are tax-deductible). • Subtract out the after-tax interest payments on cash and marketable securities.
− Increase in current assets	When the firm's sales increase, more investment is needed in inventories, accounts receivable, and so on. This increase in current assets is not an expense for tax purposes (and is therefore ignored in the profit after taxes), but it is a cash drain on the company.
+ Increase in current liabilities	An increase in the sales often causes an increase in financing related to sales (such as accounts payable or taxes payable). This increase in current liabilities—when related to sales—provides cash to the firm. Since it is directly related to sales, we include this cash in the free cash flow calculations.
− Increase in fixed assets at cost	An increase in fixed assets (the long-term productive assets of the company) is a use of cash, which reduces the firm's free cash flow.
FCF = sum of the above	

Figure 19.2 Defining the free cash flow. We previously discussed FCFs and their use in valuation in Chapters 9 and 10.

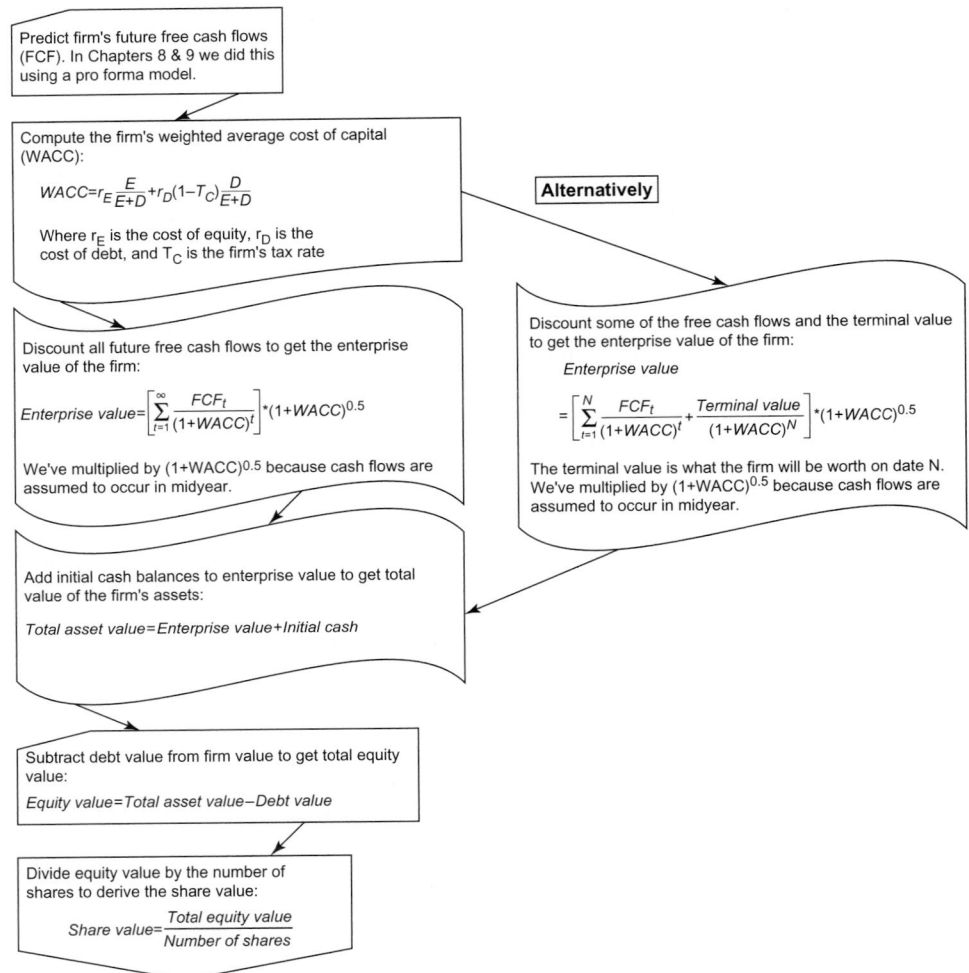

Figure 19.3 Flow diagram for a FCF valuation: calculating a firm's share value.

you of the definition of FCF and Figure 19.3 gives a flow diagram of the FCF valuation method.

Valuation 2: Example 1—A Basic Example

It is 31 December 2003 and you are trying to value Arnold Corp., which finished 2003 with a free cash flow of $2 million. The company has debt of $10 million and cash balances of $1 million. You estimate the following financial parameters for the company:

- The future anticipated growth rate of the FCF is 8%.
- The WACC of Arnold is 15%.

You can now estimate the value of Arnold:

- The *enterprise value* of Arnold is the present value of future anticipated FCFs discounted at the WACC:

$$enterprise\ value = \underbrace{\left[\sum_{t=1}^{\infty} \frac{FCF_t}{(1+WACC)^t} \right]}_{\substack{\uparrow \\ \text{This is the PV} \\ \text{formula, assuming that} \\ \text{FCFs occur at year-end}}} * \underbrace{(1+WACC)^{0.5}}_{\substack{\uparrow \\ \text{This factor ``corrects''} \\ \text{for the fact that FCFs occur} \\ \text{throughout the year}}}$$

$$= \underbrace{\left[\sum_{t=1}^{\infty} \frac{FCF_{2003}(1+g)^t}{(1+WACC)^t} \right]}_{\substack{\uparrow \\ \text{Future FCFs are expected} \\ \text{to grow at rate } g}} * (1+WACC)^{0.5} = \underbrace{\left[\frac{FCF_{2003}(1+g)}{WACC-g} \right]}_{\substack{\uparrow \\ \text{This formula was} \\ \text{given in Chapter 10}}} * (1+WACC)^{0.5}$$

Doing the computations in an Excel spreadsheet shows that the enterprise value of Arnold Corp. is $33,090,599 and that the estimated per-share value is $24.09:

	A	B	C
1	\multicolumn{3}{c}{**VALUING ARNOLD CORP.**}		
2	2003 FCF (base year)	2,000,000	
3	Future FCF growth rate	8%	
4	WACC	15%	
5	End-2003 debt	10,000,000	
6	End-2003 cash	1,000,000	
7	Number of shares outstanding	1,000,000	
8			
9	Enterprise value	33,090,599	<-- =B2*(1+B3)/(B4-B3)*(1+B4)^0.5
10	Add cash	1,000,000	<-- =B6
11	Subtract debt	-10,000,000	<-- =-B5
12	Value of equity	24,090,599	<-- =SUM(B9:B11)
13	Share value	24.09	<-- =B12/B7

Valuation Method 2: Example 2—Two FCF Growth Rates

In the valuation of Arnold Corp. in the previous subsection, we assumed a FCF growth rate that is unchanging over the future. This assumption is often suitable for a mature, stable company, but it may not be appropriate for a company that is currently experiencing very high growth rates. In this subsection we show how to perform a FCF valuation of a company for which we assume *two* FCF growth rates—a high FCF growth rate for a number of years followed by a subsequent lower FCF growth rate.

Xanthum Corp. has just finished its 2003 financial year. The company's 2003 FCF was $1,000,000. Xanthum has been growing very fast; you anticipate that for the coming five years the FCF growth rate will be 35%. After this time, you anticipate that the FCF growth will slow to 10% per year, because the market for Xanthum's products will become mature.

Xanthum has 3,000,000 shares outstanding and a WACC of 20%. It currently has $500,000 of cash on hand, which is not needed for operations; Xanthum also has $3,000,000 of debt. To value the company, we apply the same valuation scheme as before, but this time we use the two FCF growth rates:

$$enterprise\ value = \left[\underbrace{\sum_{t=1}^{5} \frac{FCF_t}{(1+WACC)^t}}_{\substack{\uparrow \\ \text{The PV of the "high} \\ \text{growth" FCFs}}} + \underbrace{\sum_{t=6}^{\infty} \frac{FCF_t}{(1+WACC)^t}}_{\substack{\uparrow \\ \text{The PV of the "normal} \\ \text{growth" FCFs}}} \right] * \underbrace{(1+WACC)^{0.5}}_{\substack{\uparrow \\ \text{This factor "corrects"} \\ \text{for the fact that FCFs occur} \\ \text{throughout the year}}}$$

There's a valuation formula that can be derived using techniques described in the appendix to Chapter 5:

$$enterprise\ value = \left[\underbrace{\frac{FCF_{2003}(1+g_{high})}{1+WACC} \left(\frac{1-\left(\frac{1+g_{high}}{1+WACC}\right)^5}{1-\frac{1+g_{high}}{1+WACC}} \right)}_{\uparrow} \right.$$

In the spreadsheet this is called "term 1" and $\frac{1+g_{high}}{1+WACC}$ is called "term 1 factor"

$$\left. + \underbrace{\frac{FCF_{2003}(1+g_{high})^5}{(1+WACC)^5} \left(\frac{1+g_{normal}}{WACC-g_{normal}} \right)}_{\uparrow} \right] * (1+WACC)^{0.5}$$

In the spreadsheet this is called "term 2"

The spreadsheet below shows that Xanthum's enterprise value is \$29,621,547 (cell B15) and that its per-share value is \$9.04 (cell B21):

	A	B	C
1	**VALUING XANTHUM CORP.**		
2	2003 FCF (base year)	1,000,000	
3			
4	High growth rate, g_{high}	35%	
5	Normal growth rate, g_{normal}	10%	
6	Number of high growth years	5	
7	Term 1 factor: $(1+g_{high})/(1+WACC)$	113%	<-- =(1+B4)/(1+B9)
8			
9	WACC	20%	
10	End-2003 debt	3,000,000	
11	End-2003 cash	500,000	
12			
13	Term 1: PV of high-growth cash flows	7,218,292	<-- =B2*B7*(1-B7^B6)/(1-B7)
14	Term 2: PV of normal-growth cash flows	19,822,357	<-- =B2*B7^B6*(1+B5)/(B9-B5)
15	Enterprise value	29,621,547	<-- =SUM(B13:B14)*(1+B9)^0.5
16	Add cash	500,000	<-- =B11
17	Subtract debt	-3,000,000	<-- =-B10
18	Value of equity	27,121,547	<-- =SUM(B15:B17)
19			
20	Number of shares, end 2003	3,000,000	
21	Share value	9.04	<-- =B18/B20

Valuation Method 2: Example 3—Using the Terminal Value in a Real Estate Project

In the previous two examples we discounted an infinite stream of cash flows. Sometimes it makes more sense to discount a finite number of cash flows and then attribute a terminal value to the project.

Here's an example. Your Aunt Sarah has quite a bit of money. She's been offered a share in a partnership that is being set up by a local real estate agent. The partnership will buy an existing building, called the Station Building, for $20 million. The agent is selling 25 shares, for $800,000 each ($800,000 = $20,000,000/25). Aunt Sarah has asked you to do some financial analysis to determine whether this is a fair price for a partnership share in the Station Building.

Here's what you discover:

- All income from the Station Building partnership will flow through to the shareholders, who will pay taxes on the income at their personal tax rates. Aunt Sarah's tax rate is 40%.
- Station Building will be depreciated over forty years, giving an annual depreciation of $500,000 per year.
- The building is fully rented out and brings in annual rents of $7 million. You do not anticipate that these rents will increase over the next ten years.
- Maintenance, property taxes, and other miscellaneous expenses for Station Building cost about $1 million per year.
- The agent who is putting together the partnership has proposed selling Station Building after ten years. He estimates that the market price of the building will not change much over this period—meaning that the market price of Station Building in year 10 is anticipated to be $20 million, like its price today.

In your valuation of the Station Building shares, you see that the annual free cash flow (FCF) to Aunt Sarah is $152,000 (cell B16 in the spreadsheet below). This FCF will be available to her in years 1–10 and is based on the building's profit before taxes of $5,500,000, which will be spread equally among the partners.

The terminal value of the building is $20,000,000, which on a per-share basis is $800,000 (cell B19). At the time the building is sold in year 10, its accumulated depreciation is $5,000,000, so that its book value is $15,000,000. To compute Aunt Sarah's cash flow from this terminal value, we deduct the per-share book value of the building ($600,000, cell B20) from the sale price to arrive at taxes of $80,000 on the profit from the sale of the building (cell B22). The cash flow from the sale is the $800,000 sale price minus the taxes—$720,000 as shown in cell B23.

Cells B26 to B35 show Aunt Sarah's anticipated free cash flows from the building partnership, including the terminal value. Discounting these cash flows at the WACC of 20% values a partnership share at $820,667.53. Conclusion: Aunt Sarah should invest in the building!

	A	B	C	D	E	F	G
1		STATION BUILDING PARTNERSHIP--SHARE VALUATION					
2	Building cost	20,000,000					
3	Depreciable life (years)	40					
4	Annual rents	7,000,000					
5	Annual expenses	1,000,000					
6	Annual depreciation	500,000	<-- =B2/B3		Profit and loss, Station Building as a whole		
7	Aunt Sarah's tax rate	40%			Annual rent	7,000,000	
8	WACC	18%			Minus annual expenses	-1,000,000	
9	Shares issued	25			Minus annual depreciation	-500,000	
10	Share price	800,000			Anticipated annual building profit before taxes	5,500,000	<-- =SUM(F7:F9)
11							
12	Profit and loss, Aunt Sarah's share						
13	Anticipated annual building profit before taxes	220,000	<-- =F10/B9		Terminal value, year 10, Station Building as a whole		
14	Profit after taxes	132,000	<-- =(1-B7)*B13		Anticipated building market price	20,000,000	<-- =B2
15	Building depreciation, per share	20,000	<-- =B6/B9		Accumulated depreciation, year 10	5,000,000	<-- =B6*10
16	Free cash flow	152,000	<-- =B14+B15		Book value of building, year 10	15,000,000	<-- =B2-F15
17							
18	Terminal value, year 10, Aunt Sarah's share						
19	Anticipated building market price	800,000	<-- =F14/B9				
20	Book value in year 10, per share	600,000	<-- =F16/B9				
21	Profit from sale of building	200,000	<-- =B19-B20				
22	Tax on profit	80,000	<-- =B7*B21				
23	Terminal value: cash flow from sale	720,000	<-- =B19-B22				
24							
25	Year	Aunt Sarah's anticipated FCF					
26	1	152,000	<-- =$B$16				
27	2	152,000					
28	3	152,000					
29	4	152,000					
30	5	152,000					
31	6	152,000					
32	7	152,000					
33	8	152,000					
34	9	152,000					
35	10	872,000	<-- =$B$16+B23				
36							
37	Share value: Present value of Aunt Sarah's free cash flows	$820,667.53	<-- =NPV(B8,B26:B35)				

Valuation Method 2: Example 4—Using the Terminal Value to Get Around Large FCF Growth Rates

Our second example of using the terminal value involves the Formanis Corporation. Formanis is in a growth industry and has had formidable FCF growth rates for the past several years, and you anticipate that these rates will continue for years 1–5. However, after year 5 you anticipate a big slowdown in Formanis's FCF growth, as its industry matures.

Here are the relevant facts about Formanis:

- The company's FCF for the current year is $1,000,000.
- You anticipate that the FCF for years 1–5 will grow at a rate of 25% per year.
- You anticipate a growth rate of FCFs of 6% per year for years 6, 7, . . . (termed the "long-term growth rate" in the spreadsheet below).
- The company has 5 million shares outstanding.

The valuation formula is

$$
Formanis\ value = \frac{FCF_1}{(1+WACC)} + \frac{FCF_2}{(1+WACC)^2} + \frac{FCF_3}{(1+WACC)^3}
$$
$$
+ \frac{FCF_4}{(1+WACC)^4} + \frac{FCF_5}{(1+WACC)^5}
$$
$$
+ \frac{1}{(1+WACC)^5} * \underbrace{\frac{FCF_5 * (1+long\text{-}term\ growth\ rate)}{(WACC - long\text{-}term\ growth\ rate)}}
$$

This is the terminal value:
an explanation is given in Chapter 10

To value Formanis, we first predict the FCFs for years 1–5 (cells B9 to B13 of the spread-sheet). The present value of these FCFs is $6,465,787 (cell B20). The terminal value represents the year-5 present value of the Formanis cash flows for years 6, 7, ... To compute the termi-nal value, we assume that Formanis's cash flows for these years grow at the long-term growth rate:

$$terminal\ value = year\text{-}5\ PV\ of\ Formanis\ FCFs,\ years\ 6,\ 7,\ldots$$

$$= \frac{FCF_6}{(1 + WACC)} + \frac{FCF_7}{(1 + WACC)^2} + \frac{FCF_7}{(1 + WACC)^2} + \cdots$$

$$= \frac{FCF_5 * (1 + long\text{-}term\ growth\ rate)}{(1 + WACC)} + \frac{FCF_5 * (1 + long\text{-}term\ growth\ rate)^2}{(1 + WACC)^2}$$

$$+ \frac{FCF_5 * (1 + long\text{-}term\ growth\ rate)^3}{(1 + WACC)^2} + \cdots$$

$$= \frac{FCF_5 * (1 + long\text{-}term\ growth\ rate)}{(WACC - long\text{-}term\ growth\ rate)}$$

In cell B17 below the terminal value—assuming a long-term FCF growth rate of 6%—is $17,025,596.

	A	B	C
1	**FORMANIS CORPORATION**		
2	Current FCF	1,000,000	
3	Anticipated growth rate, years 1-5	25%	
4	WACC	15%	
5	Long-term growth rate, after year 5	6%	
6	Number of shares outstanding	5,000,000	
7			
8	Year	**Anticipated FCF**	
9	1	1,250,000	<-- =$B$2*(1+$B$3)
10	2	1,562,500	<-- =B9*(1+$B$3)
11	3	1,953,125	<-- =B10*(1+$B$3)
12	4	2,441,406	
13	5	3,051,758	
14			
15	**Terminal value calculation**		
16	FCF in year 5	3,051,758	<-- =B13
17	Terminal value	17,025,596	<-- =B16*(1+B5)/(B3-B5)
18			
19	**Valuing Formanis Corporation**		
20	Present value of FCFs, years 1-5	6,465,787	<-- =NPV(B4,B9:B13)
21	Present value of terminal value	8,464,730	<-- =B17/(1+B4)^5
22	Value of Formanis	14,930,518	<-- =B21+B20
23	Per share value	$2.99	<-- =B22/B6

The value of Formanis (cell B22) is $14,930,518. The per-share value of Formanis is $2.99 (cell B23).

The terminal value method illustrated for Formanis is often used:

- It allows the stock analyst to distinguish between short-term growth and long-term growth. Often short-term growth is a function of market performance, whereas long-term growth is determined by macroeconomic factors. For example, in a new and rapidly developing market, we might anticipate high short-term growth rates. But we would also anticipate that as the market matures and becomes more saturated, the long-term growth rates would approximate the growth of the economy as a whole.

- From an Excel point of view, the terminal value method allows us to do interesting sensitivity analyses. For example, here is the per-share value of Formanis for a variety of long-term growth rates and WACCs; we use the **Data Table** technique described in Chapter 30:

	A	B	C	D	E	F
	Sensitivity analysis: Per-share value of Formanis with different WACC and long-term growth.					
26	**Year 1-5 growth rate = 25%.**					
27	=B23		Long-term growth rate ?			
28		$2.99	**0%**	**2%**	**4%**	**6%**
29	WACC ?	**15%**	2.51	2.64	2.80	2.99
30		**20%**	2.11	2.22	2.35	2.50
31		**25%**	1.80	1.89	1.99	2.12
32		**30%**	1.55	1.62	1.70	1.81

Varying the year 1–5 growth rate gives different values. In the table below, for example, we've assumed that year 1–5 growth is 20%:

	A	B	C	D	E	F
	Sensitivity analysis: Per-share value of Formanis with different WACC and long-term growth.					
26	**Year 1-5 growth rate = 20%.**					
27	=B23		Long-term growth rate ?			
28		$3.01	**0%**	**2%**	**4%**	**6%**
29	WACC ?	**15%**	2.38	2.54	2.75	3.01
30		**20%**	2.00	2.13	2.30	2.51
31		**25%**	1.70	1.81	1.95	2.12
32		**30%**	1.46	1.55	1.66	1.81

19.3 Valuation Method 3: The Price of a Share Is the Present Value of Its Future Anticipated Equity Cash Flows Discounted at the Cost of Equity

In the previous section we "backed into" the equity valuation of the firm, by first calculating the value of the firm's assets (the enterprise value plus initial cash balances), and then subtracting from this number the value of the firm's debts. In this section we present another method for calculating the value of the firm's equity—we directly discount the value of the firm's anticipated payouts to its shareholders.

As an example consider Haul-It Corp., which has a steady record of paying dividends and repurchasing shares. The company has 10 million shares outstanding. Here's a spreadsheet with the valuation model:

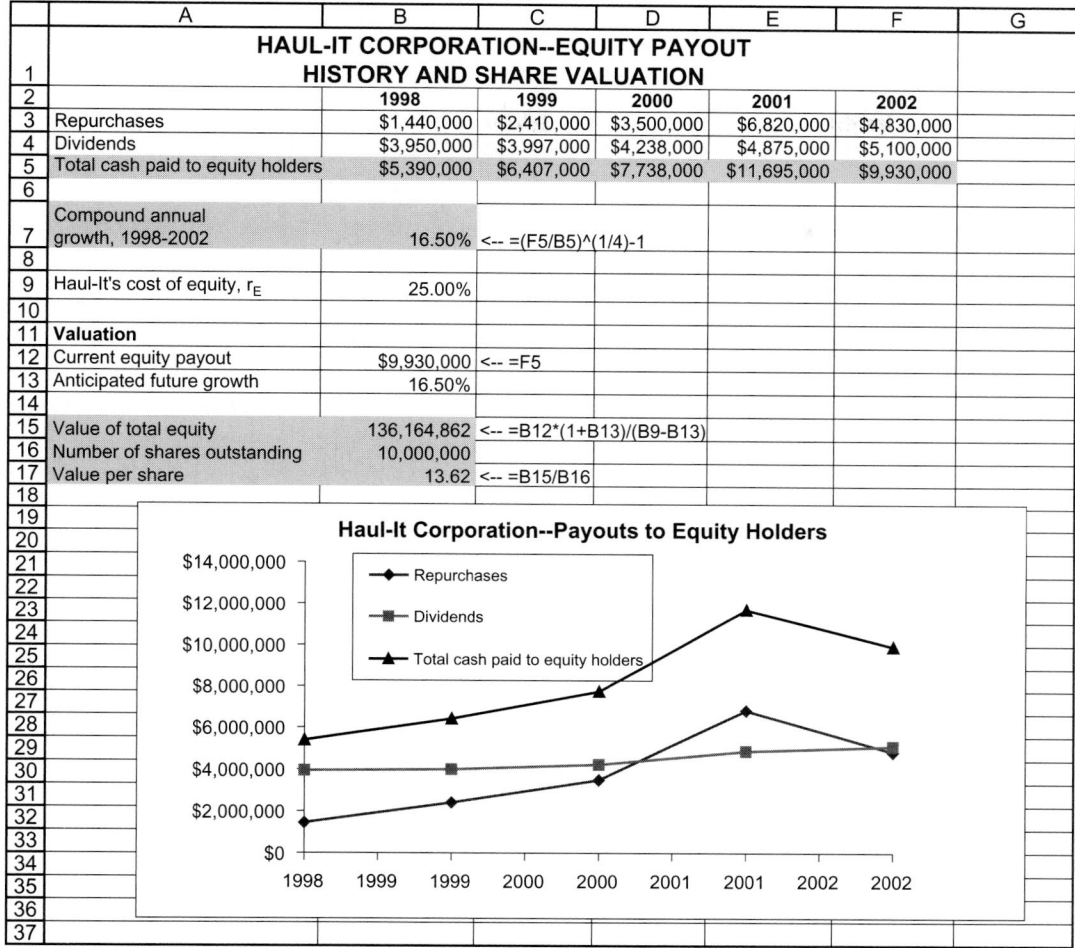

	A	B	C	D	E	F	G
1	HAUL-IT CORPORATION--EQUITY PAYOUT HISTORY AND SHARE VALUATION						
2		1998	1999	2000	2001	2002	
3	Repurchases	$1,440,000	$2,410,000	$3,500,000	$6,820,000	$4,830,000	
4	Dividends	$3,950,000	$3,997,000	$4,238,000	$4,875,000	$5,100,000	
5	Total cash paid to equity holders	$5,390,000	$6,407,000	$7,738,000	$11,695,000	$9,930,000	
6							
7	Compound annual growth, 1998-2002	16.50%	<-- =(F5/B5)^(1/4)-1				
8							
9	Haul-It's cost of equity, r_E	25.00%					
10							
11	**Valuation**						
12	Current equity payout	$9,930,000	<-- =F5				
13	Anticipated future growth	16.50%					
14							
15	Value of total equity	136,164,862	<-- =B12*(1+B13)/(B9-B13)				
16	Number of shares outstanding	10,000,000					
17	Value per share	13.62	<-- =B15/B16				
18							

Between 1998 and 2002, Haul-It's payouts to its equity holders have increased at an impressive rate of 16.50% per year (cell B7). The company's cost of equity r_E is 25% (cell B9).[1] Assuming that future equity payout growth equals historical growth, Haul-It is valued at $136 million (cell B15), which gives a per-share value of $13.62.

The equity value of the company is the discounted value of the future anticipated equity payouts:

$$
\begin{aligned}
equity\ value &= \frac{equity\ payout_{2003}}{1+r_E} + \frac{equity\ payout_{2004}}{(1+r_E)^2} + \frac{equity\ payout_{2004}}{(1+r_E)^3} + \cdots \\
&= \frac{equity\ payout_{2002}(1+g)}{1+r_E} + \frac{equity\ payout_{2002}(1+g)^2}{(1+r_E)^2} + \frac{equity\ payout_{2002}(1+g)^3}{(1+r_E)^3} + \cdots \\
&= \frac{equity\ payout_{2002}(1+g)}{r_E - g} = \frac{9,930,000(1.165)}{25.00\% - 16.50\%} = 136,164,862
\end{aligned}
$$

---

[1] At this point we do not discuss how we arrived at this cost of equity. For a recapitulation of cost of capital techniques, see Sections 19.6 and 19.7.

Dividing the equity value by the number of shares outstanding gives the estimated value per share:

$$value\ per\ share = \frac{equity\ value}{shares\ outstanding} = \frac{136,164,862}{10,000,000} = 13.62$$

Why Do Finance Professionals Shun Direct Equity Valuation?

Valuation method 3, the direct valuation of equity is so simple that it may surprise you that it is rarely used. There are several reasons for this, none of which we can fully explain at this point in the book:

- The direct equity valuation method depends on projected equity payouts (that is, dividends plus share repurchases), whereas method 2 depends on projected free cash flows. Whereas a firm's equity payouts are a function of management decisions about dividends and stock repurchases, FCFs are a function of the firm's operating environment—its sales, costs, capital expenditures, and so on. Because many components of the FCFs are determined by the firm's operating environment rather than management decisions about dividends, analysts are generally more comfortable predicting FCFs.
- The FCF method 2 discounts future FCFs at the firm's weighted average cost of capital (WACC). The equity payout method 3 discounts future equity payouts at the firm's cost of equity r_E. For reasons we will explain in Chapters 20 and 21, the cost of equity r_E is very sensitive to the firm's debt–equity ratio, whereas the WACC is not as sensitive to the debt–equity ratio.[2]

19.4 Valuation Method 4, Comparative Valuation: Using Multiples to Value Shares

The last valuation technique we discuss is based on a comparison of financial ratios for different companies. This valuation technique is often referred to as using "multiples." The technique is based on the logic that financial assets that are similar in nature should be priced the same way.

A Simple Example: Using the Price–Earnings (P/E) Ratio for Valuation

The *price–earnings ratio* is the ratio of a firm's stock price to its earnings per share:

$$P/E = \frac{stock\ price}{earnings\ per\ share}$$

When we use the P/E ratio for valuation, we assume that similar firms should have similar P/E ratios.

Here's an example. Shoes for Less (SFL) and Lesser Shoes (LS) are both shoe stores located in similar communities. Although SFL is bigger than LS, having double the sales and double the profits, the companies are in most relevant respects similar—management, financial structure,

---

[2]For reasons explained in Chapters 20 and 21, the WACC may in fact be completely invariant to a firm's leverage. If this is so, we can value a firm based on method 2 without worrying about its leverage.

and so on. However, the market valuation of the two companies does not reflect their similarity: The P/E ratio of SFL is significantly lower than that of LS, as can be seen in the spreadsheet below:

	A	B	C	D
1	SHOES FOR LESS (SFL) AND LESSER SHOES (LS) comparing P/E ratios			
2		SFL: Shoes for Less	LS: Lesser Shoes	
3	Sales	30,000	15,000	
4	Profits	3,000	1,500	
5	Number of shares	1,000	1,000	
6	Share price	24	18	
7	Equity value	24,000	18,000	<-- =C6*C5
8	EPS: Earnings per share		3	1.5	<-- =C4/C5
9	P/E: Price-earnings ratio	8.00	12.00	<-- =C6/C8

Based on the similarity between the two companies, SFL appears underpriced relative to LS—its P/E ratio is less. A market analyst might recommend that anyone interested in investing in the shoe store business should invest in SFL rather than LS.[3]

Kroger (KR) and Safeway (SWY)

Here's a slightly more involved example. Kroger and Safeway are both in the supermarket business. Some of the data for these two companies is in the spreadsheet below, which shows five multiples for these two firms.

	A	B	C	D	E	F
1	SAFEWAY (SWY) AND KROGER (KR)--COMPARISON BASED ON MULTIPLES Based on Yahoo Profiles, 12 September 2002					
2		KR	SWY		Who's more highly valued?	
3	Stock price	18.09	26.91	<-- Yahoo		
4	Earnings per share (EPS)	1.37	2.60	<-- Yahoo		
5	Price/Earnings (P/E) ratio	13.20	10.35	<-- =C3/C4	Kroger	<-- =IF(B5>C5,"Kroger","Safeway")
6						
7	Book value of equity per share	4.79	11.41	<-- Yahoo		
8	Equity market to book ratio	3.78	2.36	<-- =C3/C7	Kroger	<-- =IF(B8>C8,"Kroger","Safeway")
9						
10	Number of shares outstanding (million)	788.8	466.5	<-- Yahoo		
11	Market value of equity (billion)	14.27	12.55	<-- =C10*C3/1000		
12						
13	Debt/Equity (based on book values)	2.22	1.32	<-- Yahoo		
14	Debt (billion) this number is not in Yahoo	8.39	7.03	<-- =C10*C7*C13/1000		
15	Cash (billion)	0.185	0.051	<-- Yahoo		
16	Net debt	8.20	6.98	<-- =C14-C15		
17						
18	Book value of equity + debt (billion) - cash (book value of enterprise)	11.98	12.30	<-- =C10*C7/1000+C14-C15		
19	Market value of equity + debt (billion) - cash (market value of enterprise)	22.47	19.53	<-- =C11+C14-C15		
20	Enterprise value, market to book	1.88	1.59	<-- =C19/C18	Kroger	<-- =IF(B20>C20,"Kroger","Safeway")
21						
22	Earnings before interest, taxes, depreciation and amortization (EBITDA) in billion$	3.53	2.64	<-- Yahoo		
23	Market enterprise value to EBITDA	6.37	7.40	<-- =C19/C22	Safeway	<-- =IF(B23>C23,"Kroger","Safeway")
24						
25	Sales	50.7	34.7	<-- Yahoo		
26	Market enterprise value to Sales	0.44	0.56	<-- Yahoo	Safeway	<-- =IF(B26>C26,"Kroger","Safeway")

---

[3]A more radical strategy might be to *buy* shares of SFL and to *short* shares of LS. See Chapter 17 and its discussion of Palm and 3Com shares for a discussion of this strategy.

- **Price–earnings ratio:** This is the most common multiple used. Based on this ratio of the stock price to the earnings per share (EPS), KR is more highly valued than SWY. The problem with using this multiple is that it is influenced by many factors, including the firm's leverage. We prefer *enterprise value* ratios such as the next four.

- **Equity market to book ratio:** This is the ratio of the market value of the firm's equity to the book value (its accounting value). If the book value accurately measures the cost of the assets, then a higher equity market to book ratio reflects a greater valuation of the equity. However, the accounting numbers are heavily influenced by the age of the assets, the depreciation, and other accounting policies, so this ratio is not very accurate.

- **Enterprise value to book ratio:** The *enterprise value* is the value of the firm's equity plus its net debt (defined as book value of debt minus cash). Row 19 above measures the firm's net debt by subtracting the cash balances from the book value of the debt. The enterprise market to book ratio shows that Kroger is valued more highly than Safeway.

- **Enterprise value to EBITDA:** Earnings before interest, taxes, depreciation, and amortization (EBITDA) is a popular Wall Street measure of the ability of a firm to produce cash. In spirit it is similar to the free cash flow concept discussed in this chapter, though it ignores changes in net working capital and capital expenditures. The market enterprise value to EBITDA ratio shows that Safeway is actually more highly valued than Kroger.

- **Market enterprise value to sales ratio:** This is one of the many other ratios we could use to compare these two firms. As a percentage of its sales, Safeway is more highly valued than Kroger; this perhaps reflects Safeway's ability to extract more cash for its shareholders from each dollar of sales. Or perhaps it reflects greater shareholder optimism about the future sales growth rate.

Using Multiples to Value Firms—Summary

The multiple method of valuation is a highly effective way of comparing the values of several companies, *as long as the companies being compared are truly comparable*. Comparability is complicated, however, and you should be careful: Truly comparable firms will have similar operational characteristics such as sales and costs and also similar financing.[4]

19.5 Intermediate Summary

In Sections 19.1–19.4 we examined four stock valuation methods:

- Valuation method 1, the efficient markets approach, is based on the assumption that market prices are correct.

---

[4]We're getting ahead of ourselves, as we did in the previous footnote. The point is that it doesn't make sense to compare the stock price of two operationally similar firms if one is financed with a lot of debt and the other firm is financed primarily with equity. This point is a result of the discussion in Chapters 20 and 21. For more details see Chapter 10 of *Corporate Finance: A Valuation Approach,* by Simon Benninga and Oded Sarig (McGraw-Hill, 1997).

- Valuation method 2, the free cash flow (FCF) approach, values the firm by discounting the future anticipated FCFs at the weighted average cost of capital (WACC). Sections 19.6 and 19.7 show several methods of determining the WACC.
- Valuation method 3, the equity payout approach, values all of the firm's shares by discounting the future anticipated payouts to equity. The discount rate is the firm's cost of equity r_E .
- Valuation method 4, the multiples approach, gives a comparative valuation of firms based on ratios such as the price–earnings ratio.

In the next sections we discuss some issues related to valuation methods 2 and 3: We discuss the computation of the weighted average cost of capital (WACC) and the cost of equity r_E (Sections 19.6 and 19.7).

19.6 Computing Target's WACC: The SML Approach

Valuation method 2 depends on the weighted average cost of capital (WACC), which was previously discussed in Chapters 9 and 16. In this section we briefly repeat some of the things said in Chapter 16 and show how to compute the firm's WACC using the security market line (SML).

The basic WACC formula is

$$WACC = \frac{E}{E + D} r_E + \frac{D}{D + E} r_D (1 - T_C)$$

To estimate the WACC we need to estimate the following parameters:

$r_E =$ the cost of equity

$r_D =$ the cost of the firm's debt

$E =$ market value of the firm's equity

$\quad = $ *number of shares * current market value per share*

$D =$ market value of the firm's debt (this is usually approximated
    by the *book value* of the firm's debt)

$T_C =$ the firm's marginal tax rate

To illustrate the computation of the WACC, we use data for Target Corporation, a large discount retailer. Figure 19.4 gives the relevant financial information for Target. Using the Target data, we devote a short subsection to each of the WACC parameters, leaving the cost of equity r_E until last, since it is the most complicated.

Computing the Market Value of Target's Equity E

Target has 908,164,702 shares outstanding (cell B47, Figure 19.4). On 1 February 2003, the day of the company's annual report for its 2002 financial year, the stock price of Target was

	A	B	C	D	E
1	**TARGET CORPORATION**				
2	**Income statement**				
3		**2002**	**2001**		
4	Revenues	43,917	39,826		
5	Cost of sales	29,260	27,143		
6	Selling, general and administrative expenses	9,416	8,461		
7	Credit card expense	765	463		
8	Depreciation	1,212	1,079		
9	Interest expense	588	473		
10	Earnings before taxes	2,676	2,207		
11	Income taxes	1,022	839		
12	Net earnings	1,654	1,368		
13					
14	**Balance sheet**				
15	**Assets**	**2002**	**2001**		
16	Cash and cash equivalents	758	499		
17	Accounts receivable	5,565	3,831		
18	Inventory	4,760	4,449		
19	Other current assets	852	869		
20	Total current assets	11,935	9,648		
21					
22	Land, plant, property, and equipment				
23	At cost	20,936	18,442		
24	Accumulated depreciation	5,629	4,909		
25	Net land, plant, property and equipment	15,307	13,533		
26					
27	Other assets	1,361	973		
28	Total assets	28,603	24,154		
29					
30	**Liabilities and shareholder equity**				
31	Accounts payable	4,684	4,160		
32	Accrued liabilities	1,545	1,566		
33	Income taxes payable	319	423		
34	Current portion of long-term debt and notes payable	975	905		
35	Total current liabilities	7,523	7,054		
36					
37	Long-term debt	10,186	8,088		
38	Deferred income taxes	1,451	1,152		
39	Shareholders equity				
40	Common stock	1,332	1,173		
41	Accumulated retained earnings	8,111	6,687		
42	Total equity	9,443	7,860		
43	Total liabilities and shareholder equity	28,603	24,154		
44					
45					
46	**Other relevant information**				
47	Shares outstanding	908,164,702			
48	Stock beta	1.16			
49	Stock price, 1 February 2003	28.21			
50					
51	**Dividends and stock repurchases**				
52	**Year**	**Dividends**	**Repurchases**	**Total equity payout**	
53	1998	165	0	165	
54	1999	178	0	178	
55	2000	190	585	775	
56	2001	203	20	223	
57	2002	218	14	232	
58					
59	Growth rate	7.21%		8.89%	<-- =(D57/D53)^(1/4)-1

Figure 19.4 Financial information for Target Corp. We use this information to determine Target's cost of equity r_E and its weighted average cost of capital (WACC).

$28.21 per share. Thus, the market value of the company's equity is $908,164,702 * \$28.21 =$ $25,619,326,243. We will use this market value of equity in our computation of Target's weighted average cost of capital (next spreadsheet, p. 572).

Computing the Market Value of Target's Debt D

The Target balance sheets differentiate between short-term debt ("Current portion of long-term debt and notes payable"—row 34 of Figure 19.4) and long-term debt (row 37). For purposes of computing the debt for a WACC computation, both of these numbers should be added together. This gives debt for Target as:

	A	B	C	D
6		**2002**	**2001**	
7	Current portion of long-term debt and notes payable	975	905	
8	Long-term debt in 2002 and 2001 (columns B and C)	10,186	8,088	
9	Total debt, D	11,161	8,993	<-- =C8+C7

Estimating the Cost of Debt r_D

A simple method to compute the cost of debt r_D is to calculate the *average interest cost* over the year. In 2002 Target paid $588 interest (cell B9, Figure 19.4) on average debt of $10,077. This gives $r_D = 5.84\%$:

	A	B	C	D
13	Interest paid, 2002	588		
14	Average debt over 2002	10,077	<-- =AVERAGE(B9:C9)	
15	Interest cost, r_D	5.84%	<-- =B13/B14	

Target's Income Tax Rate T_C

In 2002 Target paid taxes of $1,022 on earnings of $2,676 (cells B11 and B10, respectively, of Figure 19.4). Its income tax rate was therefore 38.19%:

	A	B	C
17	Earnings before taxes, 2002	2,676	
18	Income taxes	1,022	
19	Corporate tax rate, T_C	38.19%	<-- =B18/B17

Computing Target's Cost of Equity r_E Using the SML

The SML equation for computing Target's cost of equity r_E is given by

$$r_E = r_f + \beta_E * [E(r_M) - r_f]$$

Yahoo gives Target's β as 1.16. In February 2003, the risk-free rate r_f was 2% and the expected return on the market $E(r_M)$ was 9.68%.[5] This gives Target's cost of equity as $r_E = 10.91\%$:

	A	B	C	D
21	Equity beta, β_E	1.16		
22	Risk-free rate, r_f	2%		
23	Expected market return, $E(r_M)$	9.68%	<-- See discussion below	
24	Cost of equity, r_E	10.91%	<-- =B22+B21*(B23-B22)	

Putting It All Together

Now that we've done all the calculations, we can compute Target's WACC:

$$WACC = \frac{E}{E+D}r_E + \frac{D}{D+E}r_D(1-T_C)$$
$$= \frac{25,619}{25,619+11,161}10.91\% + \frac{11,161}{25,619+11,161}5.84\%(1-38.19\%)$$
$$= 8.69\%$$

Here it is in a spreadsheet:

	A	B	C	D
1	**TARGET CORP.'S WACC USING** **SML FOR COST OF EQUITY**			
2	Number of shares (million)	908		
3	Market value per share, 1 February 2002	28.21		
4	Market value of equity 1 February 2002, E	25,619	<-- =B3*B2	
5				
6		**2002**	**2001**	
7	Current portion of long-term debt and notes payable	975	905	
8	Long-term debt in 2002 and 2001 (columns B and C)	10,186	8,088	
9	Total debt, D	11,161	8,993	<-- =C8+C7
10				
11	Market value of Target, E+D	36,780	<-- =B9+B4	
12				
13	Interest paid, 2002	588		
14	Average debt over 2002	10,077	<-- =AVERAGE(B9:C9)	
15	Interest cost, r_D	5.84%	<-- =B13/B14	
16				
17	Earnings before taxes, 2002	2,676		
18	Income taxes	1,022		
19	Corporate tax rate, T_C	38.19%	<-- =B18/B17	
20				
21	Equity beta, β_E	1.16		
22	Risk-free rate, r_f	2%		
23	Expected market return, $E(r_M)$	9.68%	<-- See discussion below	
24	Cost of equity, r_E	10.91%	<-- =B22+B21*(B23-B22)	
25				
26	WACC	8.69%	<-- =B4/B11*B24+(1-B19)*B9/B11*B15	

---

[5]To see how $E(r_M)$ was derived, see the boxed discussion on page 573.

Computing the Expected Return on the Market $E(r_M)$

The most controversial part of estimating the cost of capital using the CAPM is the estimation of the expected return on the market $E(r_M)$. We discussed this issue and some methods of estimation in Chapter 14. To recapitulate: We advocate using a P/E ratio multiple model for estimating the equity premium. This model, presented in Chapter 16 and briefly reviewed in the box below, gives us $E(r_M) = 9.68\%$.

P/E RATIO MULTIPLE MODEL FOR ESTIMATING $E(r_m)$

We start with the payout form of the Gordon dividend model:

$$r_E = \underbrace{\frac{D_0(1+g)}{P_0} + g}_{\substack{\text{Gordon dividend} \\ \text{model}}} = \underbrace{\frac{b * EPS_0(1+g)}{P_0} + g}_{\substack{b \text{ is the dividend payout} \\ \text{ratio, } EPS_0 \text{ is the current} \\ \text{firm earnings per share}}}$$

$$= \frac{b * (1+g)}{P_0/EPS_0} + g$$

This model is now used to measure the $E(r_M)$, using current market data:

$$E(r_M) = \frac{b * (1+g)}{P_0/EPS_0} + g$$

where

$b = market\ payout\ ratio$ (in U.S. around 50%)

$g = growth\ rate\ of\ market\ earnings$ (educated guess)

$P_0/EPS_0 = market\ price-earnings\ ratio$

Here's an Excel example:

	A	B	C
1	**ESTIMATING $E(r_M)$ USING THE P/E RATIO**		
2	Market P/E ratio	20.00	
3	Market dividend payout ratio, b	50%	
4	Estimated growth of market earnings, g	7%	
5			
6	$E(r_M)$	9.68%	<-- =B3*(1+B4)/B2+B4
7	Risk-free rate, r_f	2.00%	
8	Market risk premium, $E(r_M)$ - r_f	7.68%	<-- =B6-B7

We use these values—representative of market parameters in the United States in early 2003—in our determination of the Target Corp. cost of equity r_E.

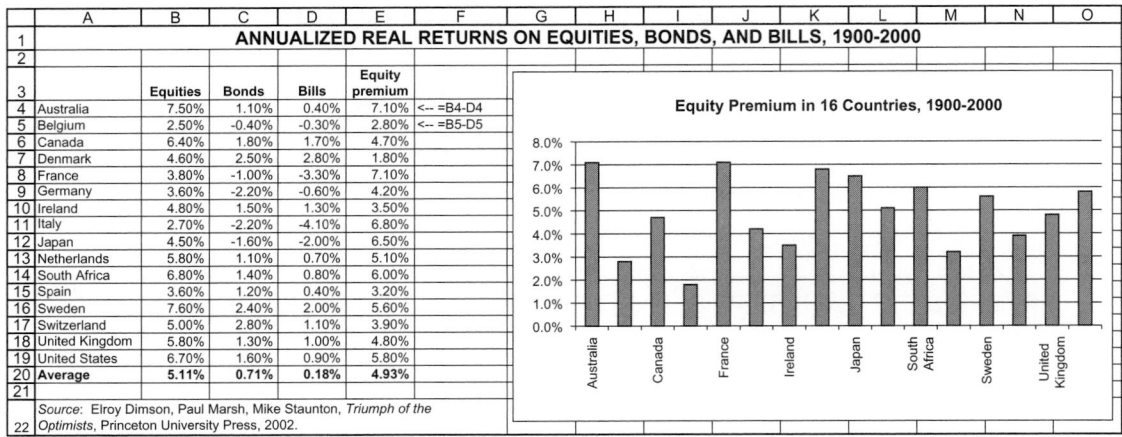

	A	B	C	D	E	F
1			ANNUALIZED REAL RETURNS ON EQUITIES, BONDS, AND BILLS, 1900-2000			
2						
3		**Equities**	**Bonds**	**Bills**	**Equity premium**	
4	Australia	7.50%	1.10%	0.40%	7.10%	<-- =B4-D4
5	Belgium	2.50%	-0.40%	-0.30%	2.80%	<-- =B5-D5
6	Canada	6.40%	1.80%	1.70%	4.70%	
7	Denmark	4.60%	2.50%	2.80%	1.80%	
8	France	3.80%	-1.00%	-3.30%	7.10%	
9	Germany	3.60%	-2.20%	-0.60%	4.20%	
10	Ireland	4.80%	1.50%	1.30%	3.50%	
11	Italy	2.70%	-2.20%	-4.10%	6.80%	
12	Japan	4.50%	-1.60%	-2.00%	6.50%	
13	Netherlands	5.80%	1.10%	0.70%	5.10%	
14	South Africa	6.80%	1.40%	0.80%	6.00%	
15	Spain	3.60%	1.20%	0.40%	3.20%	
16	Sweden	7.60%	2.40%	2.00%	5.60%	
17	Switzerland	5.00%	2.80%	1.10%	3.90%	
18	United Kingdom	5.80%	1.30%	1.00%	4.80%	
19	United States	6.70%	1.60%	0.90%	5.80%	
20	**Average**	**5.11%**	**0.71%**	**0.18%**	**4.93%**	
21						
22	Source: Elroy Dimson, Paul Marsh, Mike Staunton, *Triumph of the Optimists*, Princeton University Press, 2002.					

Figure 19.5 The equity premium is defined as the difference between the stock market rate of return and the return on risk-free bonds. In our SML-based computation of Target's weighted average cost of capital, we used the market P/E to compute the equity risk premium $E(r_M) - r_f$. The historic equity premium is often used instead of this market-based equity premium.

19.7 Computing Target's Cost of Equity r_E With the Gordon Model

An alternative to the CAPM for computing the cost of equity r_E is the Gordon model, which we previously discussed in Chapter 6. The Gordon model says that the equity value is the discounted value of future anticipated dividends. The standard version of the Gordon model is

$$r_E = \frac{Div_0(1 + g)}{P_0} + g$$

where

$$Div_0 = \text{current equity payout of firm (total dividends + stock repurchases)}$$

$$P_0 = \text{current market value of equity}$$

$$g = \text{anticipated equity payout growth rate}$$

For reasons explained in Chapter 6, we think the Gordon model should be used with the *total equity payout,* defined as total dividends plus stock repurchases. Below is the calculation for Target Corp.'s WACC using the Gordon model. The spreadsheet is the same as that of the previous section, except:

- Rows 32–36 show Target's equity payouts—the sum of its dividends and share repurchases—in each year from 1998 to 2002. The compound annual growth rate of the equity payouts is 8.89% per year (cell D38).

- Rows 22–25 show the Gordon model calculation of the cost of equity r_E. This is computed as

$$r_E = \frac{Div_0(1 + g)}{P_0} + g = \frac{232 * (1 + 8.89\%)}{25,619} + 8.89\% = 9.88\%$$

where

$$Div_0 = \text{current equity payout}$$
$$P_0 = \text{current market value of equity}$$
$$g = \text{anticipated equity payout growth rate}$$

	A	B	C	D	E
1		**TARGET CORP.'S WACC USING GORDON MODEL FOR COST OF EQUITY**				
2	Number of shares (million)	908			
3	Market value per share, 1 February 2002	28.21			
4	Market value of equity 1 February 2002, E	25,619	<-- =B3*B2		
5					
6		2002	2001		
7	Current portion of long-term debt and notes payable	975	905		
8	Long-term debt	7,523	7,054		
9	Total debt, D	8,498	7,959	<-- =C8+C7	
10					
11	Market value of Target, E+D	34,117	<-- =B9+B4		
12					
13	Interest paid, 2002	588			
14	Average debt over 2002	8,229	<-- =AVERAGE(B9:C9)		
15	Interest cost, r_D	7.15%	<-- =B13/B14		
16					
17		2002			
18	Earnings before taxes	2,676			
19	Income taxes	1,022			
20	Corporate tax rate, T_C	38.19%	<-- =B19/B18		
21					
22	Current equity value	25,619			
23	Current equity payout, Div_0	232	<-- =D36		
24	Growth rate of equity payout	8.89%	<-- =D38		
25	Cost of equity, r_E, using Gordon model	9.88%	<-- =B23*(1+B24)/B22+B24		
26					
27	WACC	8.52%	<-- =B4/B11*B25+(1-B20)*B9/B11*B15		
28					
29					
30		**Dividends and stock repurchases**				
31	Year	Dividends	Repurchases	Total equity payout	
32	1998	165	0	165	
33	1999	178	0	178	
34	2000	190	585	775	
35	2001	203	20	223	
36	2002	218	14	232	
37					
38			Growth rate	8.89%	<-- =(D36/D32)^(1/4)-1

Using the Gordon model estimate of the cost of equity, Target's WACC is 8.52% (cell B27).

CONCLUSION

This chapter discusses a grab-bag of share valuation methods. Three of these methods could be termed "fundamental valuations." Valuation method 1, the simplest of the fundamental valuation methods, is based on the assumption of market efficiency and says that a firm's stock is worth its current market price. Simple as it is, this approach has a lot of power and support in the academic community: If market participants have done their work, then the current price of a share reflects all publicly available information, and there's nothing else to do.

Valuation method 2, *discounted cash flow* (DCF) valuation, is preferred by most finance academics and many finance practitioners. This method is based on discounting the firm's projected future free cash flows (FCFs) at an appropriate weighted average cost of capital. The discounted value arrived at in this way is called the firm's *enterprise value*. To arrive at the valuation of the firm's equity, we add cash and marketable securities to the enterprise value and subtract the value of the firm's debt. Dividing by the number of shares gives the per-share valuation.

Valuation method 3, the *direct equity valuation,* discounts the projected payouts to equity holders (defined as the sum of dividends plus share repurchases) by the firm's cost of equity r_E. The resulting present value is the value of the firm's equity. Although it appears simpler and more direct than the FCF valuation, direct equity valuation is usually shunned by finance professionals. This is primarily because the cost of equity is heavily dependent on a firm's debt–equity financing mix, whereas the WACC is not nearly as dependent (and perhaps independent) of the debt–equity mix.

Valuation method 4, *multiple valuation,* is widely used. This method of valuation arrives at a relative valuation of the firm by comparing a set of relevant multiples for comparable firms. When used correctly, multiple valuations can be a powerful tool, but it is often difficult to arrive at a correct "peer group" for a particular firm.

EXERCISES

1. OwnItAll (OIA) is a holding company whose sole business is to own a portfolio of shares. The company has 200 million shares outstanding, list on the Portland Stock Exchange.
   (a) Given the current portfolio of OIA, what should be its share price? (There's a template on the disk that accompanies this book.)

	A	B	C
1	**OIA PORTFOLIO**		
2	**Stock**	**Number of shares**	**Share price**
3	IBM	1,500,000	92.89
4	Ahold	5,250,000	8.23
5	Kellogg	385,259	45.29
6	General Motors	12,000,000	36.64
7	Microsoft	1,000,000	26.18
8	AT&T	98,000,000	19.89
9	SBC	12,000,000	23.42
10	Merck	15,000,000	28.02
11	Nicor	2,000,000	36.42
12	Duke Power	25,000,000	26.14

   (b) The actual market price of OIA's shares is $25 per share. What can you conclude from this fact?

2. Walters, Inc. has an anticipated next-year free cash flow (FCF) of $10 million. This cash flow is anticipated to grow at an annual rate of 5%.
   (a) If the FCFs occur at year-end and if the WACC of Walters is 15%, what is the enterprise value of the company?
   (b) How would your answer change if the cash flows occur in midyear?

3. Houda Motors has just announced results showing the FCF for the past year is $23 million. An experienced analyst believes that the growth rate of the FCF for the next ten years will be 25% per year, and that after ten years the growth rate will be 7% annually. Houda's WACC is 18%, and the company has 100 million shares outstanding.

(a)   Value the shares assuming that the FCFs occur at year-end. Houda has no debt and no excess cash reserves.

(b)   Suppose that the FCFs occur in midyear. What would your answer be now?

4. You are considering buying a building in downtown Asheville. The building is selling for $10 million, and you anticipate an annual FCF of $1 million. At the end of ten years, the building will be half depreciated, and at this point you think you can sell the building for $15 million. If your cost of capital is 17%, does the building have positive NPV? Assume a 20% capital gains tax on the sale of the building in ten years; income taxes and depreciation tax shields have been included in the annual FCF of $1 million.

5. You are considering buying a 500 unit apartment complex in suburban Springfield. The current owner of the apartment complex is asking $25 million. Here are some facts:
   • On average, each unit produces $15,000 of pretax income per year.
   • The vacancy rate in Springfield averages 8%.
   • Operating expenses per unit are $2,000 annually. These expenses are incurred whether or not the units are occupied.
   • Income and expenses occur at year-end.
   • Your tax rate is 40% on pretax income and 20% on capital gains.
   • Your discount rate is 18%.
   • Real estate prices in the Springfield area have been increasing at 6% per year, and you anticipate that this rate will continue for the foreseeable future.

   Calculate the NPV.

6. Using the data in Exercise 5, suppose that the cash flows from rentals (including expenses and depreciation) occur in midyear. Suppose that the resale cash flow of the complex occurs at the end of ten years. Recalculate the NPV.

7. Consider the Springfield apartment complex once more (Exercises 5 and 6). Suppose that:
   • Cash flows from rentals (including expenses and depreciation) occur in midyear.
   • Next year's anticipated rental per unit is $15,000 and expenses are $2,000. In years 2–9 these numbers are expected to increase by 2% annually.
   • Other facts about the complex are unchanged.

   (a)   What is the NPV of the purchase?

   (b)   Create a data table for the NPV as a function of the annual rent/expense increase (0%, 1%, 2%, . . . , 5%) and the discount rate (8%, 10%, 12%, . . . , 24%).

8. Hectoritis Corp. currently has a free cash flow (FCF) of $13 million. A reputable analyst estimates that this FCF is anticipated to increase by 12% per year for the next five years. The analyst estimates that at the end of five years the company's terminal value will be based on the year-5 FCF and a long-term FCF growth rate of 4%. Suppose that for Hectoritis $\beta = 1.5, r_f = 3\%$, the market risk premium $E(r_M) - r_f = 14\%$, and Hectoritis has 8 million shares outstanding. How should the analyst value the shares of the company? Assume all cash flows occur at year-end.

9. (Challenge exercise) The last five year's results for Niccair Corp. are given below. Value the company's stock based on a model of FCF growth of your own design and the following additional facts. (This is not an easy problem, and it has no explicit answer—valuation is often like that!)
   • Niccair's 2003 year-end debt is $750 million.
   • Niccair's 2003 year-end cash is $50 million.
   • The company has a cost of debt of $r_D = 5\%$.
   • The company has 44,080,000 shares outstanding; the end-2003 share price is $37.
   • Niccair's share $\beta = 0.437, r_f = 3\%$, and $E(r_M) = 12\%$.

	A	B	C	D	E	F
1			NICCAIR CORPORATION, 1999 - 2003			
2		31-Dec-03	31-Dec-02	31-Dec-01	31-Dec-00	31-Dec-99
3	Net income	$105,300,000	$128,000,000	$122,100,000	$35,800,000	$116,300,000
4	Depreciation	$161,700,000	$155,000,000	$148,800,000	$145,100,000	$141,600,000
5	Changes in net working capital	(12,600,000)	268,300,000	491,300,000	233,000,000	213,400,000
6	Capital expenditures	(181,300,000)	(192,500,000)	(185,700,000)	(158,400,000)	(154,000,000)
7	Net interest paid before taxes	(41,100,000)	(34,600,000)	(46,900,000)	(50,600,000)	(45,500,000)
8	Tax rate	37.84%	31.03%	32.62%	16.94%	34.56%

10. Go to Yahoo and look up your two favorite drug store chains. Compare the following multiples for the two companies: P/E ratio and sales/market cap. Is one of the chains underpriced vis-à-vis the other?

11. (Challenge exercise) The table below (which appears on the disk that accompanies this book) shows price–earnings (P/E) ratios and other information for the retail industry.

   (a) In rows 25–27 use Excel to run a regression of the P/E ratio as y-variable versus each of the columns as x-variable. One of the regressions is shown:

$$P/E = a + b * market\ cap$$
$$= 21.390 + 0.009 * market\ cap,\ R^2 = 0.003$$

   Now run regressions of the P/E ratio on return on equity (ROE), long-term debt to equity, and so on.

   (b) Which regression has the most explanatory power? Do you have an explanation?

	A	B	C	D	E	F	G
1		P/E	Market cap (billion $)	ROE %	Long-Term Debt to Equity	Price to Equity Book Value	Year-on-year revenue growth (%)
2	Wal-Mart Stores, Inc. (WMT)	22.89	222	22.72	0.75	4.95	9.88
3	Target Corporation (TGT)	23.52	44.3	16.73	0.77	3.57	11.01
4	Kohl's Corporation (KSS)	23.75	15.7	15.26	0.31	3.34	14.62
5	(WMMVY.PK)	30.56	15	13.02	0	3.85	12.69
6	J.C. Penney Company, Inc. (JCP)	21.46	11.9	10.76	0.97	2.35	2.98
7	Sears, Roebuck & Co. (S)	30.74	10.8	5.97	0.73	1.77	-8.37
8	May Department Stores (MAY)	17	9.8	14.4	1.64	2.33	17.04
9	Federated Department Str. (FD)	14.25	9.3	12.24	0.7	1.68	0.14
10	Coles Myer Ltd. (ADR) (CM)	20.47	8.9	14.24	0.24	2.81	25.9
11	Kmart Holding Corporation (KMRT)	8.75	8.4	45.84	0.13	2.74	-13.75
12	Neiman-Marcus Group, (NMGA)	15.08	3.2	16.11	0.33	2.21	10.89
13	Dollar Tree Stores, Inc. (DLTR)	17.4	3	17.12	0.25	2.8	8.83
14	Dillard's, Inc. (DDS)	36.34	2.1	2.69	0.81	0.96	-3.59
15	Grupo Elektra S.A. de C.V (EKT)	11.12	2	30.85	2.78	3.09	22.21
16	Saks Incorporated (SKS)	41.19	1.9	2.37	0.77	0.99	0.99
17	Tuesday Morning Corporati (TUES)	19.68	1.2	45.22	0.51	7.39	7.04
18	ShopKo Stores, Inc. (SKO)	13.37	0.5282	6.72	0.76	0.88	-1.59
19	Bon-Ton Stores, Inc. (BONT)	14.15	0.2487	7.62	1.12	1.06	65
20	Retail Ventures, Inc. (RVI)	22.26	0.2252	4.74	1.8	1.04	2.81
21	Gottschalks Inc. (GOT)	19.73	0.1047	5.17	1.34	0.99	1.76
22	Duckwall-ALCO Stores, Inc (DUCK)	28.95	0.0832	2.61	0.2	0.74	1.32
23							
24	Regression: P/E = a + b*other						
25	a, intercept		21.390				
26	b, slope		0.009				
27	R^2		0.003				
28							
29	**Key**						
30	Market cap = (number of shares)*(price per share)						
31	ROE = Return on Equity = (Net income)/(Book value of Equity)						
32	Long-term debt to equity = (Book value of debt)/(Book value of equity)						
33	Price to equity book value = (Market cap)/(Book value of equity)						
34	Year-on-year revenue growth = growth rate of sales, most recent quarter versus same quarter one year ago						

PART V

CAPITAL STRUCTURE AND DIVIDEND POLICY

A company can finance itself either with money raised from its shareholders (equity) or with money borrowed from banks or financial markets (debt). Does the mix of financing affect the value of the company? Chapters 20 and 21 examine this thorny question, which has been the subject of much debate in the finance profession. As these chapters show, the valuation effects of capital structure depend primarily on the taxes that the company and its shareholders pay. Chapter 20 explores this question in detail, using a series of simple examples. Chapter 21 summarizes the results and tells you what to think.

Capital structure is closely related to a firm's dividend policies. When a firm pays more dividends, it uses shareholder cash and implicitly increases the debt to equity ratio of the firm. But there's more to dividends than just debt/equity. Many corporate mangers believe that their dividends impart important information to shareholders and the market about the health and the prospects of the company. Chapter 22 examines these questions to come up with an answer to the question: Does dividend policy matter?

CHAPTER 20

CAPITAL STRUCTURE AND THE VALUE OF A FIRM

OVERVIEW

"Capital structure" is finance jargon for how a firm should be financed—what mixture of debt and equity should be used by the shareholders of a firm to finance the firm's activities. To start you off thinking about this tricky question, we offer the example of Mortimer and Joanna, who are competing to buy the same supermarket.

The Fair City Supermarket—Does Financing Affect the Price?

Mortimer and Joanna live in Fair City. Each heads a group of investors who want to buy a supermarket located in the center of town. Both Mortimer and Joanna have superb records as supermarket managers. As manager of a supermarket, they're pretty much the same—meaning that the supermarkets they manage will have the same sales, costs of goods sold, and so on. However, while the management aspects of Mortimer's group and Joanna's group are pretty much the same, there's a big financial difference between the two competing groups: Mortimer's investors want to borrow 50% of the money needed to purchase the supermarket, whereas Joanna's investors hate debt and have decided to put up the whole cost of purchasing the supermarket without borrowing a penny.

The question: Which group of investors—Mortimer's or Joanna's—can afford to make the higher bid for the supermarket? This is the question examined in this chapter. At this point in the chapter we offer no answers to this question, but merely want to give you an insight into how possible answers might look.

Example 1: Both Groups Make the Same Bid

Suppose that both Mortimer and Joanna's groups bid $1 million for the supermarket. In this case the balance sheets would look like this:

Mortimer's Supermarket Group
Half equity (50%) and half debt (50%)

Supermarket	$1,000,000	Debt	$500,000
		Equity	$500,000
Total assets	**$1,000,000**	**Total debt and equity**	**$1,000,000**

Joanna's Supermarket Group
Only equity (100%)

Supermarket	$1,000,000	Debt	$0
		Equity	$1,000,000
Total assets	**$1,000,000**	**Total debt and equity**	**$1,000,000**

Why would both groups make a similar bid for the supermarket? The line of reasoning that might lead to this conclusion is the following:

> A supermarket is a supermarket is a supermarket, no matter how it's financed. If Mortimer's group thinks the supermarket is worth $1 million, then so will Joanna's group (and vice versa). The fact that one group finances with debt and equity whereas the other group finances only with equity is irrelevant to their valuation of the supermarket.

Example 2: Mortimer's Group Bids More

Is it possible that Mortimer's group should rationally decide that—because of the group's greater proportion of debt financing—the supermarket is worth more than what Joanna's group is willing to pay? One of Mortimer's investors thinks that their group can afford to bid more for the supermarket than Joanna. His line of reasoning:

> The fact that we're financing with debt means that it's cheaper for us to finance the supermarket. The interest paid on debt is an expense for tax purposes, which means that debt is cheaper than equity. In addition, since equity is more risky than debt, equity holders in any case want a higher return than debt holders. So our greater use of debt means that we can afford to pay more for the supermarket.

If this logic is correct, then it's possible that Mortimer's group would bid $1,200,000 for the supermarket, whereas Joanna's group would bid only $1,000,000. In this case the two balance sheets would look like this:

Mortimer's Supermarket Group
Half equity (50%) and half debt (50%)

Supermarket	$1,200,000	Debt	$600,000
		Equity	$600,000
Total assets	**$1,200,000**	**Total debt and equity**	**$1,200,000**

Joanna's Supermarket Group
Only equity (100%)

Supermarket	$1,000,000	Debt	$0
		Equity	$1,000,000
Total assets	**$1,000,000**	**Total debt and equity**	**$1,000,000**

Of course there's no question what would happen in this case: The sellers of the supermarket would prefer to sell to Mortimer's group, which is offering a higher price.

Which Example Is More Representative: Example 1 or Example 2?

As you'll see in the chapter, both examples could be representative of how things actually work in the world. In this chapter we frame the capital structure question (Example 1 versus Example 2) primarily in terms of the following two questions:

- Does the choice of financing affect the total cash that can be extracted from the firm? If Mortimer's group, with its higher proportion of debt financing, can extract more cash from the supermarket, then it might be logical for them to be willing to pay more for the supermarket.
- Should the choice of financing affect the discount rate the firm uses to evaluate projects? This is where *risk*, the magic word in finance, comes into play.[1] In simple words: Is the correct discount rate to be used for the supermarket by Mortimer's group different from that which should be used by Joanna's group? Does the choice of a financing mix affect the weighted average cost of capital (WACC)?

---

[1] Recall the opening words of Chapter 11: "Risk is the magic word in finance. Whenever finance people can't explain something, they try to look confident and say 'it must be the risk.'"

As you will see in this chapter, the answers to both these questions relate primarily to taxation. It will turn out that, depending on the tax system, either Example 1 or Example 2 could be a representation of how things work.[2]

Finance Concepts Discussed

- Debt versus equity financing
- Valuation effects of leverage
- Corporate versus personal taxation
- Modigliani–Miller model
- Miller's "Debt and Taxes"

Excel Functions Used

- **If**
- **NPV**

20.1 Capital Structure When There Are Corporate Taxes: ABC Corp.

We start our exploration of the effects of capital structure by examining the story of ABC Corp. This well-known company is located in Lower Fantasia. Lower Fantasia has an unusual tax code: In Lower Fantasia companies are taxed on their corporate income, but individuals are not taxed on their personal income.

Our hero, Arthur ABC, is trying to figure out (1) whether to buy ABC Corp., a well-known company in Lower Fantasia, and (2) if he buys the company, how to finance the purchase.

Buying ABC Corp. Using Only Equity

This turns out to be fairly simple. ABC has an expected annual free cash flow (FCF) of $1,000 per year; this FCF is anticipated to recur, year after year, at the same level. Arthur—who has an MBA from <u>E</u>astern <u>L</u>ower <u>F</u>antasia <u>S</u>tate University (their football team is called the "elfs")—has computed the cost of capital for the purchase as $r_U = 20\%$. The symbol "U" as a subscript for the discount rate r_U stands for "unlevered" and is meant to remind you that in this case r_U is the discount rate appropriate for the case where Arthur buys ABC Corp. with only equity (meaning his own money, without borrowing).

This $r_U = 20\%$ is a cost of capital that reflects only the business risks of ABC Corp. If purchased only with equity, therefore, the company is worth $\$1,000/20\% = \$5,000$.[3] In what follows we use the symbol V_U for the "unlevered value of the firm." V_U is what a company is worth if it is financed only with equity. In our case,

$$V_U = \sum_{t=1}^{\infty} \frac{FCF_t}{(1+r_U)^t} = \sum_{t=1}^{\infty} \frac{\$1,000}{(1+20\%)^t} = \frac{\$1,000}{20\%} = \$5,000$$

---

[2]It's even possible that another variant of Example 2 would hold in which Mortimer's group would bid less than Joanna's. This is pretty unlikely, as you'll see in the remainder of the chapter.

[3]The FCF is already *after* corporate taxes, and the discounted FCF value of the firm is thus

$$\sum_{t=1}^{\infty} \frac{FCF}{(1+20\%)^t} = \frac{FCF}{20\%}.$$

Buying ABC Corp. Using Debt

Arthur has a wonderful source of debt financing: his mother. This wealthy old lady is in fact his business partner, but their joint deals are structured so that she's always the lender and Arthur the equity owner. There's another unusual feature to the old lady's lending—she gives out *perpetual debt*—her loans require only an annual payment of interest, but no repayment of principal.[4] The cost of debt to Arthur, denoted by r_D, is the interest rate charged by his mother on her loans to him. In this case $r_D = 8\%$.

Together, Arthur and his Mom are exploring two alternative financing arrangements:

- In Alternative A, Arthur buys ABC Corp. for cash; immediately thereafter, the company borrows $3,000 from Mom and repays it to Arthur. (Corporate finance deals in Lower Fantasia are a bit complicated!) In this case ABC Corp. is a *levered* company. ("Leverage" in this context means that the company has debt on its balance sheets.)
- In Alternative B, Arthur borrows $3,000 from Mom and then buys ABC Corp. for cash. In this case, ABC Corp. is an *unlevered* "all-equity" company (no debt on its balance sheets) and Arthur is leveraged.

The fundamental difference between these two alternatives is that the Lower Fantasia tax code has a corporate income tax but no personal income tax. Under the tax code, interest paid by corporations is an expense for tax purposes, but this is not true for interest paid by individuals, who aren't taxed on their personal income.

From Figure 20.1 you can see that the *total family income* produced by Alternative A is more than that produced by Alternative B.

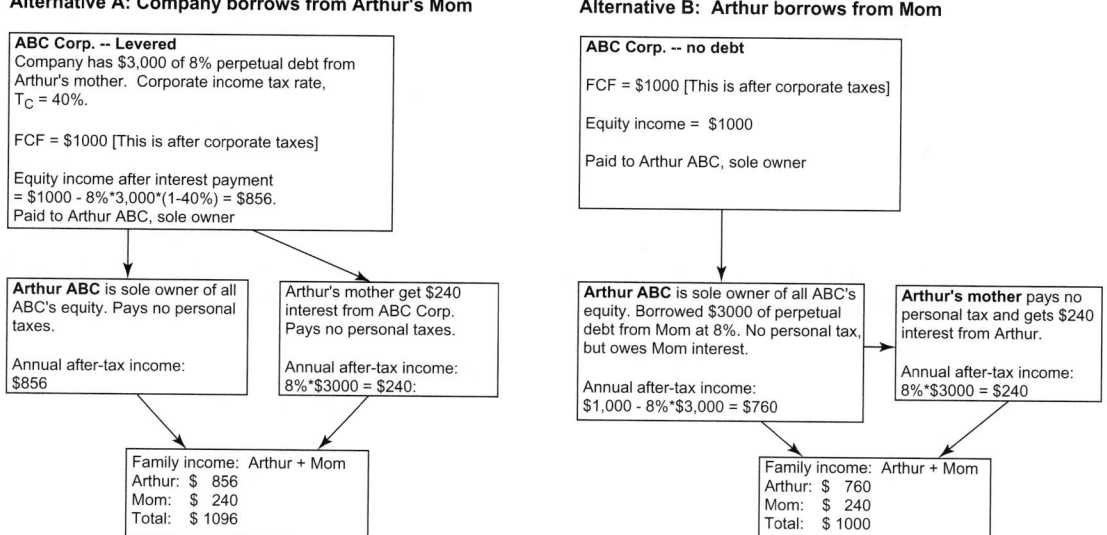

Figure 20.1 Financing Arthur's purchase of ABC Corp.: cash flows resulting from two methods of financing the purchase. The Lower Fantasia tax code includes a 40% corporate income tax, but no tax on personal incomes.

---

[4]Throughout this chapter you'll notice that we often assume that cash flows have infinite duration. This makes the valuations easier, but doesn't affect the principles.

From the family point of view, it is clear that the first alternative is better than the second. In this alternative the family (Arthur + Mom) has an annual income of $1,096, as opposed to the $1,000 in the second alternative. A little thought will reveal why the first alternative is preferable—ABC Corp. has a tax advantage over Arthur with respect to borrowing. It can deduct its interest expenses from its income taxes, so that its net income taxes are only $8\% * \$3,000 * (1 - 40\%) = \$144$. This compares with Arthur's cost for the same loan of $8\% * \$3,000 = \$240$.

To flesh this out a bit, let's write out some equations:

$$total\ family\ income\ from\ ABC\ (Arthur + Mom) = cash\ produced\ by\ firm$$

$$= FCF - \underbrace{r_D * debt * (1 - T_C)}_{\substack{\uparrow \\ \text{Cost of debt} \\ \text{to ABC Corp.}}} + \underbrace{r_D * debt}_{\substack{\uparrow \\ \text{Income from} \\ \text{debt to Mom}}} = FCF + r_D * debt * T_C$$

Thus, the total cash produced by the firm for its stockholders and bondholders increases with the amount of debt the firm has. Notice that the total cash produced by the firm does not increase if Arthur borrows the money from his mother.[5]

20.2 Valuing ABC Corp.: The Effect of Leverage When There Are Corporate Taxes

Recall that we stated in Section 20.1 that ABC Corp.'s FCFs are worth $5,000 if the company has no leverage:

$$V_U = unleveraged\ value\ of\ ABC$$

$$= PV\ (future\ FCFs,\ discounted\ @\ unlevered\ discount\ rate)$$

$$= \sum_{t=1}^{\infty} \frac{\$1,000}{(1.20)^t} = \frac{annual\ FCF}{r_U} = \frac{\$1,000}{20\%} = \$5,000$$

So how much is the leveraged version of ABC Corp. (this is the company that borrows $3,000 from Arthur's Mom) worth? We use the *additivity principle* explained in Chapter 17:

$$V_L = leveraged\ value\ of\ ABC$$

$$= unleveraged\ value\ of\ ABC + PV\ (additional\ debt\text{-}related\ CFs)$$

$$= \$5,000 + \sum_{t=1}^{\infty} \frac{8\% * \$3,000 * 40\%}{(1.08)^t} = \$5,000 + \frac{\$96}{0.08}$$

$$= \$5,000 + \$1,200 = \$6,200$$

---

[5]Looking at Figure 20.1, it's clear why this is so—when Arthur borrows from Mom, the interest is a *wash:* Arthur has an interest expense of $240 and Mom has interest income of $240, for a net $0. When the company borrows from Mom, the company has an interest expense of $(1 - 40\%) * 8\% * \$3,000 = \$144$, but Mom has interest income of $240, for a net of $96.

THE ADDITIVITY PRINCIPLE IN THIS CONTEXT

The additivity principle (Chapter 17) says that *the value of the sum of two cash flow streams is the sum of their values*. In the context of this problem, the two cash flow streams are: (1) the stream of FCFs deriving from the firm's business activities and (2) the stream of tax shields on the interest paid by the firm.

To value these streams using the additivity principle, we discount each at its appropriate risk-adjusted discount rate. The rate for the FCFs is r_U and the rate for the tax shields—which we assume to be riskless—is the interest rate on the debt r_D.

ABC Corp. is worth more as a levered firm than as an unlevered firm because it produces more cash for its owners. The additional cash produced—generated by the fact that the company can deduct the cost of its interest payments from its taxes, whereas Arthur cannot—is worth $1,200. In symbols:

$$V_L = V_U + PV \, (additional \; debt\text{-}related \; CFs)$$

$$= \begin{cases} V_U = \sum_{t=1}^{\infty} \dfrac{FCF_t}{(1+r_U)^t} = \sum_{t=1}^{\infty} \dfrac{\$1{,}000}{(1.20)^t} = \dfrac{\$1{,}000}{20\%} = \$5{,}000 \\[4pt] \text{The unleveraged value of the firm is} \\ \text{the present value of its free cash flows} \\ \text{discounted at an appropriate (unleveraged)} \\ \text{cost of capital } r_U \end{cases}$$

$$+ \begin{cases} PV \left(\begin{array}{c} interest \; tax \\ shields \end{array} \right) = \sum_{t=1}^{\infty} \dfrac{T_C * interest_t}{(1+r_D)^t} = \sum_{t=1}^{\infty} \dfrac{8\% * \$3{,}000 * 40\%}{(1.08)^t} = \dfrac{\$96}{8\%} = \$1{,}200 \\[4pt] \text{The tax shields created} \\ \text{by the debt are discounted at the interest} \\ \text{rate.} \end{cases}$$

$$= \$6{,}200$$

The Cost of Equity, $r_E(L)$, and the Weighted Average Cost of Capital, WACC, With Leverage

The *cost of equity* is the discount rate for the cash flows accruing to shareholders. In Chapters 9 and 16 we discussed the derivation of the cost of equity, stressing its relation to the riskiness of the equity cash flows. In this chapter we use the symbol $r_E(L)$, with the "L" showing that the cost of equity is related to the leverage of the firm. As you will see, greater leverage leads to a larger $r_E(L)$; the reason for this being that the equity cash flows are riskier when shareholders have promised larger amounts to debtholders.

We now proceed to the computation of $r_E(L)$ for ABC Corp. The leveraged version of ABC Corp. is worth $6,200, of which $D = \$3{,}000$ is debt. Thus, the equity of the company is worth $3,200. We denote the market value of the equity by E. In order to calculate the firm's cost of equity $r_E(L)$, we first compute the cash flows that the equity owners receive:

annual equity cash flow = FCF − after-tax interest paid by ABC

$$= \$1{,}000 - 8\% * \$3{,}000 * (1-40\%) = \$856$$

The discounted value of this annual equity cash flow of $856 is the value of the equity; this defines the cost of equity $r_E(L)$:

$$E = equity\ value = \sum_{t=1}^{\infty} \frac{equity\ cash\ flow_t}{(1+r_E)^t}$$

$$\$3,200 = \sum_{t=1}^{\infty} \frac{\$856}{(1+r_E)^t} = \frac{\$856}{r_E}$$

$$\Rightarrow r_E(L) = \frac{\$856}{\$3,200} = 26.75\%$$

With a little mathematical flimflammery, we can show that

$$r_E(L) = r_U + [r_U - r_D]\frac{D}{E}(1 - T_C)$$

$$= \underbrace{20\%}_{\substack{\uparrow}} + \underbrace{[20\% - 8\%]\frac{\$3,000}{\$3,200}(1 - 40\%)}_{\substack{\uparrow}} = 26.75\%$$

r_U is the discount rate for the FCFs, which represents the firm's business risk

When ABC borrows, it's shareholders bear an additional *financial risk*. The term above represents the financial risk premium for the equity holders

We can now compute the WACC:

$$WACC = r_E(L)\frac{E}{E+D} + r_D(1 - T_C)\frac{D}{E+D}$$

$$= 26.75\%\frac{\$3,200}{\$3,200 + \$3,000} + 8\%(1 - 40\%)\frac{\$3,000}{\$3,200 + \$3,000}$$

$$= 16.13\%$$

With a little more "flimflammery" we can show that discounting the FCFs at the WACC gives the total value of the firm:

$$\sum_{t=1}^{\infty} \frac{FCF_t}{(1 + WACC)^t} = \sum_{t=1}^{\infty} \frac{\$1,000}{(1 + 16.13\%)^t} = \frac{\$1,000}{16.13\%} = \$6,200$$

Here's all of this summarized in a spreadsheet. Note from the title of the spreadsheet that we've given this model a name; we've called it the "Modigliani–Miller Model With Only

Corporate Tax." To see why the name, refer to the box entitled "Some History of Finance (1)" on page 591.

	A	B	C
1	**COMPUTING THE WACC IN MODIGLIANI-MILLER MODEL WITH ONLY CORPORATE TAXES**		
2	Annual FCF	1,000	
3	r_U, unlevered cost of capital	20%	
4	D, debt (perpetual)	3,000	
5	r_D, the cost of debt (interest rate)	8%	
6	T_C, corporate tax rate	40%	
7			
8	**Value of firm**		
9	V_U, unlevered value = FCF/r_U	5,000.00	<-- =B2/B3
10	Value of tax shield on interest = T_C*r_D*D/r_D = T_C*D	1,200.00	<-- =B6*B4
11	V_L, levered value of firm = V_U + T_C*D	6,200.00	<-- =B10+B9
12			
13	E, value of equity = V_L - D	3,200.00	<-- =B11-B4
14			
15	Cash flow to equity = FCF - (1-T_C)*interest	856.00	<-- =B2-(1-B6)*B5*B4
16	Return on equity, r_E(L)= [FCF - (1-T_C)*interest]/E	26.75%	<-- =B15/B13
17			
18	WACC = r_E(L)*E/(E+D) + r_D*(1-T_C)*D/(E+D)	16.13%	<-- =B16*B13/B11+(1-B6)*B5*B4/B11
19			
20	**Two checks**		
21	Return on equity, r_E(L)= r_U + (r_U - r_D)*[D/E]*(1-T_C)	26.75%	<-- =B3+(B3-B5)*B4/B13*(1-B6)
22	Value of firm, V_L = FCF/WACC	6,200.00	<-- =B2/B18

We complete this section by restating its major conclusions. If only corporate income is taxed, leverage (borrowing) increases the value of the firm. This increase in value, represented by the present value of the tax shields on the debt, increases the cost of equity r_E, and decreases the WACC. The present value of the debt tax shields accrues to the firm's equity holders: In the above example, if the corporate tax rate were $T_C = 0\%$, debt of $3,000 would have decreased the value of the equity to $2,000. Instead, with $T_C = 40\%$, the value of the equity is decreased by the value of the debt but increased by the value of the debt tax shields:

$$Equity\ value\ of\ levered\ firm = V_L - D = V_U - D + T_C D$$

A summary table is given in Figure 20.2.

Item	Formula	Why
V_U = value of unlevered firm	$V_U = \sum_{t=1}^{\infty} \dfrac{FCF_t}{(1+r_U)^t}$	The value of the unleveraged firm is the PV of future FCFs discounted at r_U, the unlevered cost of capital.
	$V_L = V_U + PV\,(interest\ tax\ shields)$ $= V_U + \sum_{t=1}^{N} \dfrac{T_C * interest_t}{(1+r_D)^t}$	The value of the leveraged firm is V_U plus the present value of future interest tax shields. The cell to the left contains the formula for the value of the levered firm when there are N interest payments on the debt.
V_L = value of levered firm	$V_L = V_U + PV\,(interest\ tax\ shields)$ $= V_U + \sum_{t=1}^{\infty} \dfrac{T_C * interest}{(1+r_D)^t}$ $= V_U + T_C * D$	The cell to the left contains the formula for the leveraged firm when the firm issues perpetual debt.
E = value of equity	$V_U - (1 - T_C) * D$	The equity value of the levered firm is the value of the levered firm minus the value of the firm's debt: $E = V_L - D = V_U + D*T_C - D = V_U - (1 - T_C)D$
D = value of debt	D	The value of the debt is the value of the debt. (OK, this ain't so original!)
$r_E(L)$ = cost of equity of the leveraged firm	$r_E(L) = r_U + [r_U - r_D]\dfrac{D}{E}(1 - T_C)$	The cost of equity r_E is the discount rate for equity cash flows. In a leveraged firm it includes a *financial risk premium*: $[r_U - r_D]\dfrac{D}{E}(1 - T_C)$
WACC = weighted average cost of capital	$WACC = \dfrac{FCF}{V_L}$	You can correctly value the *whole firm* by discounting its FCFs at the WACC. This is the valuation principle employed in Chapters 6, 9, and 19.

Figure 20.2 Summary table of corporate valuation and cost of capital when only corporate income is taxed at rate T_C and when there are no personal taxes.

SOME HISTORY OF FINANCE (1)

The valuation model summarized in Figure 20.2 is often called the *Modigliani–Miller* model, after Professors Franco Modigliani and Merton Miller, both winners of the Nobel Prize in Economics. In two path-breaking articles published in 1958 and 1963, Modigliani and Miller showed that the value of a firm would not be affected by the method in which the firm was financed, except where the tax code explicitly favors one form of financing. In the example of ABC Corp. in Section 20.2, the tax code gives corporations a tax break on debt financing, whereas individuals (who are untaxed) get no such break; it is therefore optimal for the firm to finance with more debt and less equity.

Students of finance know this result as the "MM model." It has been widely studied and even more widely misunderstood.

In Section 20.7 we consider a variation of the MM model, which takes account not only of corporate taxes but also personal taxes. While the logic is the same, the conclusions are very different. This model—less widely studied and even more misunderstood—is known as the Miller model, after Merton Miller, who expounded it in a famous academic article that appeared in the *Journal of Finance* in 1977. (See the box entitled "Some History of Finance (2)" on page 604.

20.3 Why Debt Is Valuable in Lower Fantasia: Buying a Turfing Machine

It's easier to understand the theory of the previous section by looking at some numerical examples. In this and the following two sections we discuss several such examples. Each of these examples makes the point that under the Lower Fantasia tax regime—in which corporate income is taxed at a rate T_C, but in which there are no taxes on personal income—companies that finance with debt can increase their market value.

The tax regime in Lower Fantasia is characterized by a tax on corporate income but no other taxes. In the previous section we showed that this tax regime means that the value of a company in Lower Fantasia is increased when it levers itself.

We start with an example showing the effect of financing on a capital budgeting decision.

Buying a Machine

Wonderturf Corp., a company in Lower Fantasia, is considering purchasing a new turfing machine. The turfing machine costs $100,000; it has a ten-year life, during which it is straight-line depreciated to zero salvage value. In each of the ten years of the machine's life, it will produce sales of $40,000. These sales will cost $15,000 to produce. The result is that the machine has an annual free cash flow of $19,000 per year (see cell B10 below):

$$annual\ Wonderturf\ FCF = (1 - T_C) * (sales - expenses - Depreciation) + Depreciation$$
$$= (1 - 40\%) * (\$40,000 - \$15,000 - \$10,000) + 10,000$$
$$= \$19,000$$

	A	B	C
1	THE WONDERTURF TURFING MACHINE		
2	T_C, corporate tax rate	40%	
3			
4	Machine cost, year 0	100,000	
5			
6	Free cash flow (FCF) calculation		
7	Additional sales, annually	40,000	
8	Additional annual cost of sales	15,000	
9	Annual depreciation	10,000	<-- =B4/10
10	Annual FCF, years 1-10	19,000	<-- =(1-B2)*(B7-B8-B9)+B9
11			
12	r_U, discount rate for machine FCFs	15%	
13			
14	Year	Machine FCF	
15	0	-100,000	<-- =-B4
16	1	19,000	<-- =$B$10
17	2	19,000	
18	3	19,000	
19	4	19,000	
20	5	19,000	
21	6	19,000	
22	7	19,000	
23	8	19,000	
24	9	19,000	
25	10	19,000	
26			
27	Machine NPV	-4,643	<-- =B15+NPV(B12,B16:B25)

The Wonderturf financial wizards have determined that an appropriate risk-adjusted discount rate for the turfing machine's free cash flows is $r_U = 15\%$. Discounting the machine's FCFs at this rate shows that it has a negative NPV of $-\$4,643$ (cell B27). Thus, the conclusion is that Wonderturf should not acquire the turfing machine.

However, there's more to this story—read on!

Wonderturf Gets a Loan to Buy the Machine

Hearing from Wonderturf that it doesn't intend to buy the machine, the turfing machine's manufacturer offers the company a loan of $50,000. The loan's conditions are:

- Interest rate on the loan is $r_D = 8\%$. This is also the market interest rate.
- The loan's payments in years 1–9 consist of interest only: $8\% * \$50,000 = \$4,000$. This interest is an expense for tax purposes for Wonderturf, so that the after-tax cost of the interest to the company is $(1 - 40\%) * \$4,000 = \$2,400$.
- At the end of year 10, Wonderturf must repay the loan principal. In this year, the after-tax cost of the loan to the company is therefore $52,400 (the loan principal plus the after-tax interest).

The Excel table below shows that the loan to Wonderturf has a positive NPV of $10,736.

	D	E	F
12	Loan to buy machine	50,000	
13	r_D, loan interest rate	8%	
14		Loan CFs	
15		50,000	<-- =E12
16		-2,400	<-- =-(1-$B$2)*$E$13*$E$12
17		-2,400	
18		-2,400	
19		-2,400	
20		-2,400	
21		-2,400	
22		-2,400	
23		-2,400	
24		-2,400	
25		-52,400	<-- =-(1-$B$2)*$E$13*$E$12-E12
26			
27	Loan NPV	10,736	<-- =E15+NPV(E13,E16:E25)

The Wonderturf financial wizards now conclude that *it is worthwhile buying the turfing machine if Wonderturf takes the loan.* Their logic is

$$value(Wonderturf\ machine + financing) = value(Wonderturf\ machine) + value(financing)$$
$$= -\$4,643 + \$10,736$$
$$= \$6,093$$

Here's a spreadsheet showing their calculations:

	A	B	C	D	E	F
1	**THE WONDERTURF TURFING MACHINE**					
2	T_C, corporate tax rate	40%				
3						
4	Machine cost, year 0	100,000				
5						
6	Free cash flow (FCF) calculation					
7	Additional sales, annually	40,000				
8	Additional annual cost of sales	15,000				
9	Annual depreciation	10,000	<-- =B4/10			
10	Annual FCF, years 1-10	19,000	<-- =(1-B2)*(B7-B8-B9)+B9			
11						
12	r_U, discount rate for machine FCFs	15%		Loan to buy machine	50,000	
13				r_D, loan interest rate	8%	
14	Year	Machine FCF			Loan CFs	
15	0	-100,000	<-- =-B4		50,000	<-- =E12
16	1	19,000	<-- =$B$10		-2,400	<-- =-(1-$B$2)*$E$13*$E$12
17	2	19,000			-2,400	
18	3	19,000			-2,400	
19	4	19,000			-2,400	
20	5	19,000			-2,400	
21	6	19,000			-2,400	
22	7	19,000			-2,400	
23	8	19,000			-2,400	
24	9	19,000			-2,400	
25	10	19,000			-52,400	<-- =-(1-$B$2)*$E$13*$E$12-E12
26						
27	Machine NPV	-4,643	<-- =B15+NPV(B12,B16:B25)	Loan NPV	10,736	<-- =E15+NPV(E13,E16:E25)
28						
29	**NPV: Machine + Loan**	**6,093**	<-- =B27+E27			

As you can see in cell B29, the total value of the machine + loan combination is $6,093.

Where Does the Positive Loan NPV Come From?

The above analysis shows that the loan to Wonderturf has an NPV of $10,736. If we analyze this number, we see that this is exactly the *PV of the taxshields on the loan interest*:

$$NPV(loan) = \$50,000 - \frac{(1 - 40\%) * \$4,000}{1.08} - \frac{(1 - 40\%) * \$4,000}{(1.08)^2} - \cdots$$
$$- \frac{(1 - 40\%) * \$4,000}{(1.08)^9} - \frac{(1 - 40\%) * \$4,000 - \$50,000}{(1.08)^{10}}$$

We now split this expression into two parts:

$$NPV(loan) = \$50,000 - \frac{\$4,000}{1.08} - \frac{\$4,000}{(1.08)^2} - \cdots - \frac{\$4,000}{(1.08)^9} - \frac{\$4,000 - \$50,000}{(1.08)^{10}}$$
$$+ \frac{40\% * \$4,000}{1.08} + \frac{40\% * \$4,000}{(1.08)^2} + \cdots + \frac{40\% * \$4,000}{(1.08)^9} + \frac{40\% * \$4,000}{(1.08)^{10}}$$

The first line above has value 0 (recall from Chapter 6 that a loan and all its repayments have zero NPV when the discount rate is the loan borrowing rate). The second line above is the PV of the tax shields on the loan interest. Their value is $10,736:

$$NPV(loan) = \$10,736 = \frac{40\% * \$4,000}{1.08} + \frac{40\% * \$4,000}{(1.08)^2} + \cdots$$
$$+ \frac{40\% * \$4,000}{(1.08)^9} + \frac{40\% * \$4,000}{(1.08)^{10}}$$

Thus, the NPV of the loan is the *present value of the tax shields on the loan interest payments*.

The Wonderturf Result Is Not Surprising!

The second line of Figure 20.2 states that the value of a levered company is the sum of the value of the unleveraged company *plus* the value of the debt tax shields:

$$V_L = V_U + PV \, (interest \; tax \; shields)$$
$$= V_U + \sum_{t=1}^{\infty} \frac{T_C * interest_t}{(1 + r_D)^t}$$

This is precisely what we've done with our analysis of the Wonderturf turfing machine. For this machine,

$$V_L = value \; of \; the \; machine \; when \; purchased \; with \; a \; loan$$

$$= \underbrace{V_U}_{\substack{\uparrow \\ \text{Value of} \\ \text{the machine's} \\ \text{cash flows}}} + \underbrace{\sum_{t=1}^{\infty} \frac{T_C * interest_t}{(1 + r_D)^t}}_{\substack{\uparrow \\ \text{Value of the} \\ \text{tax shields from the} \\ \text{loan interest}}}$$

$$= -\$4,643 + \$10,736 = \$6,093$$

20.4 Why Debt Is Valuable in Lower Fantasia: Relevering Potfooler, Inc.

For our second example of the effect of financing on firm value, we use a question from a Finance 101 final exam at Eastern Lower Fantasia State University. As you'll see it's a fairly long question, with many interrelated parts.[6]

Here's the question: Potfooler, Inc. is a well-known Lower Fantasia company. Here are some facts about the company:

- Potfooler expects to have an annual free cash flow of $2 million at the end of years 1, 2, 3, . . . forever. Recall that the free cash flow is the after-tax amount of cash that the company generates from its business activities.

- Potfooler currently has 100,000 shares outstanding on the Lower Fantasia Stock Exchange. The Potfooler share price is $100 per share.

- Potfooler currently has no debt. However, a financial analyst has suggested that the company issue $3,000,000 of perpetual debt and use the proceeds to repurchase shares. The analyst explains that perpetual debt is debt that has only an annual interest payment and that has no return of principal.[7] The analyst suggests that this would be worthwhile for the company, because of the relation $V_L = V_U + T_C D$. The current interest rate on debt in Lower Fantasia is 8%, and the interest payments on the debt will be made annually.

Students on the finance exam were asked to answer the following questions.

Question 1: What is the current market value of Potfooler?

*Answer: Potfooler currently has 100,000 shares outstanding, each of which is worth $100. Thus, the company's equity value is currently $10,000,000 = $100 * 100,000. Since the company has no debt, this is also its market value. In short, $V_U = $ $10,000,000.*

Question 2: After Potfooler issues $3,000,000 of debt, what will be its market value?

*Answer: Since Lower Fantasia has only a corporate income tax, the relation $V_L = V_U + T_C D$ holds. This means that after the company issues its debt, its market value will be $V_L = V_U + T_C D = $10,000,000 + 40\% * $3,000,000 = $11,200,000.*

Question 3: After Potfooler issues debt of $3,000,000 and uses the proceeds to repurchase shares, what will be the company's total equity value, E?[8]

Answer: After Potfooler issues the debt and repurchases the shares, the total value of its equity, E, plus the total value of its debt, D, have to sum to the company's total market value, V_L. In short,

$$V_L = E + D = \$11,200,000$$

contd.

---

[6]The author's colleagues at Eastern Lower Fantasia State University love this question because it's easy to grade. If a student makes a mistake on any part of the question, then the answers on all subsequent parts of the question will also be wrong.

[7]Such debt is sometimes called a *consol*. Consols are easy to value, since a bond with a perpetual annual payment of C is worth C/r when the discount rate is r.

[8]Notice that upto this point in the exam, we haven't stated the price at which Potfooler repurchases the shares. This comes later.

But $D = \$3,000,000$, *and therefore*

$$E = V_L - D = \$11,200,000 - \$3,000,000 = \$8,200,000$$

Question 4: At what price will Potfooler repurchase its shares?

Answer: By issuing $3 million of debt, Potfooler has raised its total market value by $1,200,000 (from $10 million to $11.2 million). This increase in value belongs to all the shareholders. Since there are 100,000 shares outstanding before the share repurchase, this means that each share's price increases by $1,200,000/100,000 = $12. Thus, the answer to this question is that the share price for repurchase is $112: Of this amount, $100 is the share price before the repurchase, and $12 is the increase in the share price as a result of the debt issue.

Question 5: How many shares will Potfooler repurchase?

Answer: According to the previous question, Potfooler will repurchase its shares at $112 per share. Since the company has issued $3 million in debt to repurchase the shares, this means that it will repurchase $3,000,000/$112 = 26,785.71.

Question 6: What was Potfooler's cost of equity before the repurchase of shares?

Answer: Potfooler has an annual free cash flow (FCF) of $2,000,000. Thus, its unlevered cost of equity, $r_E(U) = FCF/V_U = 2,000,000/10,000,000 = 20\%$.

Question 7: What is Potfooler's cost of equity *after* the repurchase of the shares on the open market?

Answer: Potfooler issues $3 million in 8% debt in order to repurchase shares. Thus, its annual interest bill is 8% * $3,000,000 = $240,000. Since interest is an expense for tax purposes, the company's shareholders will have an annual expected cash flow of

$$\text{annual equity cash flow, after debt issuance} = FCF - (1 - T_C) * \text{interest}$$
$$= \$2,000,000 - (1 - 40\%) * \$240,000$$
$$= \$1,856,000$$

The value of the equity after the share repurchase is $8,200,000, so that the cost of equity of the leveraged company is

$$r_E(L) = \$1,856,000/\$8,200,000 = 22.63\%.$$

Question 8: What is Potfooler's weighted average cost of capital (WACC) *before* the repurchase of the shares?

Answer: Recall the definition of the WACC:

$$WACC = r_E * \frac{E}{E + D} + r_D * (1 - T_C) * \frac{D}{E + D}$$

The answer to question 8 is easy: Since Potfooler, before the share repurchase, has only equity, its $WACC = r_U = 20\%$.

Question 9: What is Potfooler's weighted average cost of capital (WACC) *after* the repurchase of the shares?

Answer:

$$WACC = r_E(L) * \frac{E}{E+D} + r_D * (1-T_C) * \frac{D}{E+D}$$

$$= 22.63\% * \frac{\$8,200,000}{\$8,200,000 + \$3,000,000}$$

$$+ 8\% * (1-40\%)\frac{\$3,000,000}{\$8,200,000 + \$3,000,000} = 17.86\%$$

Question 10: Why is $r_E(L) > r_U$?

Answer: Before Potfooler issued its bonds, the only risk borne by shareholders was the business risk inherent in the company's free cash flow. After the company issues its bonds, shareholders have to bear two kinds of risk: business risk and financial risk. Thus, r_E (L) represents a discount rate for cash flows that are riskier than the discount rate for the FCFs, r_U. Since riskier cash flows have higher discount rates, it follows that $r_E(L) > r_U$.

Question 11: Why does the market value of Potfooler increase after the issuance of the debt and repurchase of the equity?

Answer: By issuing the debt, the shareholders of Potfooler get an additional annual cash flow—the tax shield on the debt interest. This tax shield is riskless, and its value is

$$present\ value\ of\ interest\ tax\ shield = \sum_{t=1}^{\infty} \frac{T_C * (interest\ payment)}{(1+r_D)^t}$$

$$= \frac{T_C * (interest\ payment)}{r_D} = \frac{T_C * r_D * D}{r_D} = T_C * D$$

The present value of the tax shield accounts for the increase in Potfooler's market value:

$$V_L = \underbrace{V_U}_{} + \underbrace{T_C D}_{}$$

| Potfooler's value before the debt issuance | PV of additional interest tax shields |

Question 12: Why does the WACC *decrease* after the repurchase?

Answer: After the company issues its debt, it gains an additional cash flow (the tax shield on the interest). This cash flow is riskless. Thus, the average risk of the company's total cash flows—its FCF plus the interest tax shield—decreases. Since the WACC represents the average riskiness of the company, it decreases.

20.5 Potfooler Exam Question, Second Part

Having answered the long exam question of the previous section, students at Eastern Lower Fantasia State University were asked to put the calculations for questions 1–9 into an Excel spreadsheet. Here's the answer:

	A	B	C
1	**POTFOOLER--DEBT ISSUED TO REPURCHASE SHARES**		
2	**Unlevered company**		
3	Annual free cash flow (FCF)	$2,000,000	
4	Number of shares	100,000	
5	Price per share	$100	
6	Total equity value	$10,000,000	<-- =B5*B4
7			
8	Question 1: V_U, unlevered value of Potfooler	$10,000,000	<-- =B6
9			
10	**Levered company**		
11	Debt issued	$3,000,000	
12	Interest rate on debt	8%	
13	T_C, Lower Fantasia corporate tax rate	40%	
14	Question 2: V_L, levered value of Potfooler, $V_L = V_U + T_C*D$	$11,200,000	<-- =B8+B13*B11
15	Question 3: Equity value after share repurchase, $E = V_L - D$	$8,200,000	
16	Incremental firm value from exchanging equity by debt = $V_L - V_U = T_C*D$	$1,200,000	<-- =B13*B11
17	Incremental firm value on a per-share basis	$12	<-- =B16/B4
18	Question 4: New share value, after repurchase	$112	<-- =B5+B17
19			
20	Question 5: Number of shares repurchased = [debt used for repurchase]/[new share value]	26,785.71	<-- =B11/B18
21	Number of shares remaining after repurchase = original number of shares minus number of shares repurchased	73,214.29	<-- =B4-B20
22	**Check:** Market value of remaining shares = number of remaining shares * new share value	$8,200,000	<-- =B21*B18
23			
24	Question 6: Potfooler's cost of equity when unlevered, $r_U = FCF/V_U$	20.00%	
25			
26	Annual interest costs, before taxes	$240,000	<-- =B11*B12
27	Annual equity cash flow, after interest = FCF - (1-TC)*interest	$1,856,000	<-- =B3-(1-B13)*B26
28	Question 7: Potfooler's cost of equity when levered, $r_E(L)=[FCF-(1-T_C)*interest]/[value of equity, E]$	22.63%	<-- =B27/B22
29			
30	Question 8: Potfooler's WACC before the debt issuance = r_U	20.00%	
31			
32	Question 9: Potfooler's WACC after the debt issuance = $r_E(L)*E/(E+D)+r_D*(1-T_C)*D/(E+D)$		
33	Percentage of equity in Potfooler = E/(E+D)	73.21%	<-- =B22/B14
34	Percentage of debt in Potfooler = D/(E+D)	26.79%	<-- =B11/B14
35	WACC = $r_E(L)*E/(E+D)+r_D*(1-T_C)*D/(E+D)$	17.86%	<-- =B28*B33+B12*(1-B13)*B34

This spreadsheet enables us to do some interesting analysis.

What Happens If the Corporate Tax Rate $T_C = 0\%$?

When $T_C = 0$, leverage doesn't change the value of the firm. If you put $T_C = 0\%$ into cell B13 of the previous spreadsheet, you'll get a demonstration of this. The spreadsheet is given below, and the analysis follows after the spreadsheet:

	A	B	C
1	**POTFOOLER--DEBT ISSUED TO REPURCHASE SHARES, corporate tax rate = 0%**		
2	**Unlevered company**		
3	Annual free cash flow (FCF)	$2,000,000	
4	Number of shares	100,000	
5	Price per share	$100	
6	Total equity value	$10,000,000	<-- =B5*B4
7			
8	Question 1: V_U, unlevered value of Potfooler	$10,000,000	<-- =B6
9			
10	**Levered company**		
11	Debt issued	$3,000,000	
12	Interest rate on debt	8%	
13	T_C, Lower Fantasia corporate tax rate	0%	
14	Question 2: V_L, levered value of Potfooler, $V_L = V_U + T_C{}^*D$	$10,000,000	<-- =B8+B13*B11
15	Question 3: Equity value after share repurchase, $E = V_L - D$	$7,000,000	
16	Incremental firm value from exchanging equity by debt = $V_L - V_U = T_C{}^*D$	$0	<-- =B13*B11
17	Incremental firm value on a per-share basis	$0	<-- =B16/B4
18	Question 4: New share value, after repurchase	$100	<-- =B5+B17
19			
20	Question 5: Number of shares repurchased = [debt used for repurchase]/[new share value]	30,000.00	<-- =B11/B18
21	Number of shares remaining after repurchase = original number of shares minus number of shares repurchased	70,000.00	<-- =B4-B20
22	**Check:** Market value of remaining shares = number of remaining shares * new share value	$7,000,000	<-- =B21*B18
23			
24	Question 6: Potfooler's cost of equity when unlevered, $r_U=FCF/V_U$	20.00%	
25			
26	Annual interest costs, before taxes	$240,000	<-- =B11*B12
27	Annual equity cash flow, after interest = FCF - (1-TC)*interest	$1,760,000	<-- =B3-(1-B13)*B26
28	Question 7: Potfooler's cost of equity when levered, $r_E(L)=[FCF-(1-T_C){}^*interest]/[value\ of\ equity,\ E]$	25.14%	<-- =B27/B22
29			
30	Question 8: Potfooler's WACC before the debt issuance = r_U	20.00%	
31			
32	Question 9: Potfooler's WACC after the debt issuance = $r_E(L){}^*E/(E+D)+r_D{}^*(1-T_C){}^*D/(E+D)$		
33	Percentage of equity in Potfooler = E/(E+D)	70.00%	<-- =B22/B14
34	Percentage of debt in Potfooler = D/(E+D)	30.00%	<-- =B11/B14
35	WACC = $r_E(L){}^*E/(E+D)+r_D{}^*(1-T_C){}^*D/(E+D)$	20.00%	<-- =B28*B33+B12*(1-B13)*B34

- The total value of the company doesn't change (cell B14) when the amount of debt (cell B11) changes. In a formula,

$$V_L = V_U + \underbrace{T_C D}_{\substack{\uparrow \\ \text{When } T_C = 0\%, \\ \text{this term is zero}}} = V_U$$

- The company's equity becomes more risky. That is, $r_E(L) > r_U$. You can see this in cell B28: $r_E(L) = 25.14\%$ after the debt is issued as opposed to $r_U = 20\%$.

- The company's share price doesn't change. After the issuance of the debt and the repurchase of the equity, the share price is still $100 (cell B18).

- The company's WACC doesn't change. The *average riskiness* of the company's cash flows remains the same:

$$WACC = r_E(L) * \frac{E}{E+D} + r_D * (1 - T_C) * \frac{D}{E+D}$$

$$= 25.14\% * \frac{\$7,000,000}{\$7,000,000 + \$3,000,000}$$

$$+ 8\% * \underbrace{(1 - 0\%)}_{\uparrow} \frac{\$3,000,000}{\$7,000,000 + \$3,000,000}$$

Remember that
in this version of the
question $T_C = 0\%$

$$= 20\% = r_U$$

Relate the Company's Value to Different Levels of Debt

By using **Data Table** (see Chapter 30), we can make the following table and graph:

	B	C	D	E
38	**Debt issued**	**Value of levered firm, $V_L = V_U + T_C{*}D$**	**Cost of equity $r_E(L)$**	**WACC**
39				
40	0	10,000,000	20.00%	20.00%
41	1,000,000	10,400,000	20.77%	19.23%
42	2,000,000	10,800,000	21.64%	18.52%
43	3,000,000	11,200,000	22.63%	17.86%
44	4,000,000	11,600,000	23.79%	17.24%
45	5,000,000	12,000,000	25.14%	16.67%
46	6,000,000	12,400,000	26.75%	16.13%
47	7,000,000	12,800,000	28.69%	15.63%
48	8,000,000	13,200,000	31.08%	15.15%
49	9,000,000	13,600,000	34.09%	14.71%

Levered value V_L as a function of firm debt

20.6 Considering Personal as Well as Corporate Taxes: The Case of XYZ Corp.

In our story about ABC Corp. (Arthur and Mom), the capital structure decision mattered because Lower Fantasia taxes corporations but not individuals. The result is that shareholders (like Arthur) benefit from having companies borrow instead of doing the borrowing themselves. In this section we tell the story of Upper Fantasia, a country very much like Lower Fantasia, but with a somewhat different tax system. Upper Fantasia has three kinds of taxes:

- Corporations are subject to a 40% corporate tax rate. We denote this tax rate by T_C.
- Individual income derived from shares (this refers to dividends and capital gains on shares—in the jargon of the Upper Fantasia tax code, this is called "equity income") is subject to a 10% tax rate. The equity tax rate is denoted by T_E.
- All *ordinary income* (this term includes individual income derived from bonds; however, it does not include equity income) is subject to a 30% tax rate. We denote this tax rate by T_D. When individuals *pay interest*, they get to deduct the interest payments from their ordinary income.

As before, our mythical entrepreneur, Arthur XYZ, is trying to figure out how to finance his purchase of XYZ Corp. His Mom (bless her!) is always available to lend him money. The questions about the debt are the same as before:

- Should the purchase of the company be financed with debt?
- If so, who should borrow—the company or Arthur?

Figure 20.3 explains the cash flows.

When the company borrows the money, the total family income is $938.40. This compares to the total income of $900 when Arthur borrows the money from Mom. So it's better in this case for the company to borrow the money.

In order to understand what's happening, we create a spreadsheet. We'll have more to say about this spreadsheet (and the economics underlying it) below, but in the meantime, we stress its final conclusion.

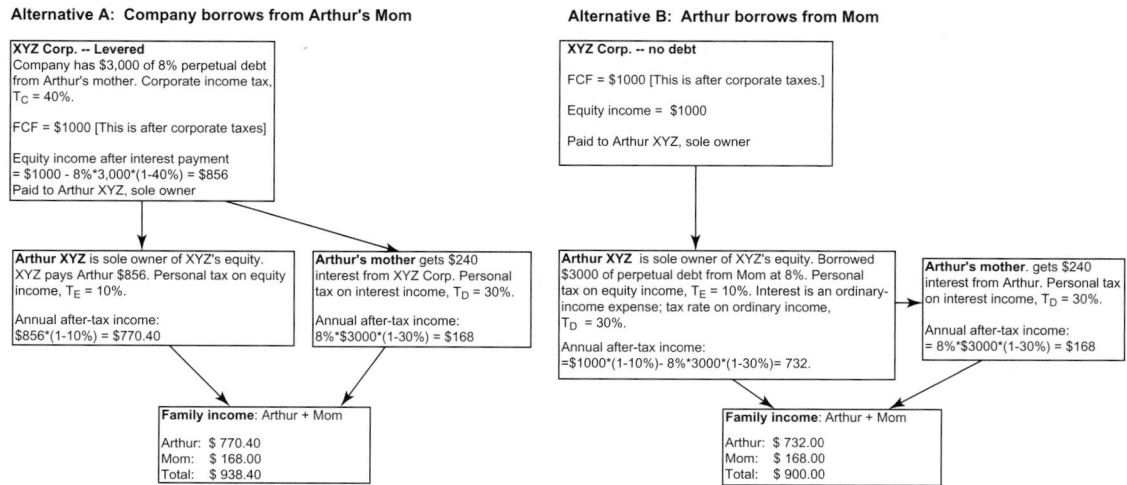

Figure 20.3 Financing Arthur's purchase of XYZ Corp.: The tax code in Upper Fantasia has a corporate income tax rate $T_C = 40\%$, a personal tax rate on equity income $T_E = 10\%$, and a personal tax rate on all other income $T_D = 30\%$.

- Since the total family income (the combined income of Arthur and his Mom) is larger when the company borrows than when Arthur borrows (cell B27 versus cell C27), the company should lever itself, and not Arthur.
- The advantages of corporate borrowing are considerably less in this case than in the previous case of ABC Corp. In the previous case corporate leverage of $3,000 added $96 to the family cash flows each year; in the current case it adds only $38.40. The difference, of course, is the fact that we now have taxes on personal income, which were absent in the ABC Corp. example.

	A	B	C	D
1	**FINANCING ARTHUR'S PURCHASE OF XYZ** Upper Fantasia tax code: Corporate income tax, T_C = 40%, Personal taxes: Tax on equity income, T_E = 10%, tax on all other income, T_D = 30%			
2	**Computing the family income**			
3	T_C, corporate tax rate	40%		
4	T_E, personal equity tax rate	10%		
5	T_D, personal debt tax rate on ordinary income	30%		
6	r_D, interest rate	8%		
7	D, Debt	3,000		
8	FCF, free cash flow (already after corporate taxes)	1,000		
9				
10		Company borrows	Arthur borrows	
11	FCF, after personal tax	1,000.00	1,000.00	
12	Corporate debt	3,000.00	0.00	
13	Corporate pre-tax interest payment	240.00	0.00	
14	Corporate after-tax interest payment	144.00	0.00	<-- =C13*(1-$B$3)
15	Payout to equity owners	856.00	1,000.00	<-- =C11-C14
16				
17	Arthur's income			
18	Pre-tax equity income from XYZ	856.00	1,000.00	<-- =C15
19	Post-tax equity income from XYZ	770.40	900.00	<-- =C18*(1-$B$4)
20	Arthur's debt	0.00	3,000.00	
21	Arthur's pre-tax interest payment	0.00	240.00	<-- =$B$6*C20
22	Arthur's after-tax interest payment	0.00	168.00	
23	Arthur's post-tax income	770.40	732.00	<-- =C19-C22
24				
25	Mom's pre-tax income	240.00	240.00	<-- =C20*B6
26	Mom's post-tax income	168.00	168.00	<-- =C25*(1-$B$5)
27	Total family income	938.40	900.00	<-- =C23+C26
28				
29	Who should borrow--Arthur or company?	Company	<-- =IF(B27>C27,"Company",IF(B27<C27,"Arthur","Indifferent"))	
30				
31	**Net advantage of corporate debt**			
32	$(1-T_D)-(1-T_E)*(1-T_C)$	0.16		

In order to understand this better, we need some equations:

$$total\ cash\ produced\ by\ firm = \underbrace{\underbrace{FCF - r_D * debt * (1 - T_C)}_{\substack{\downarrow \\ \text{Dividend to Arthur}}} * (1 - T_E)}_{\substack{\downarrow \\ \text{Arthur's after-tax dividend}}} + \underbrace{r_D * debt * (1 - T_D)}_{\substack{\downarrow \\ \text{Income from} \\ \text{debt to Mom}}}$$

$$= FCF + r_D * debt * \underbrace{[(1 - T_D) - (1 - T_E) * (1 - T_C)]}_{\substack{\downarrow \\ \text{Net corporate tax-advantage of debt}}}$$

$$In\ this\ case = (1 - T_D) - (1 - T_E) * (1 - T_C)$$
$$= (1 - 30\%) - (1 - 10\%) * (1 - 40\%) = 16\%$$

The term that makes all the difference is

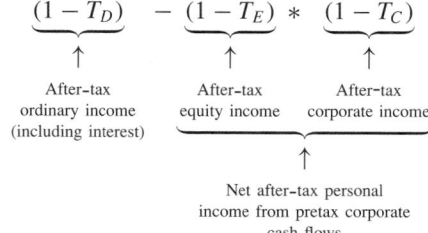

$$\underbrace{(1 - T_D)}_{} \quad - \quad \underbrace{(1 - T_E)}_{} \quad * \quad \underbrace{(1 - T_C)}_{}$$

After-tax ordinary income (including interest)   After-tax equity income   After-tax corporate income

Net after-tax personal income from pretax corporate cash flows

If this term is positive, as in the previous example (see cell B32), then XYZ Corp. should borrow; if it's negative—as in the next example (in which the corporate tax rate is $T_C = 20\%$), then Arthur should borrow and not the firm (Figure 20.4).

	A	B	C	D
1	**FINANCING ARTHUR'S PURCHASE OF XYZ** **Upper Fantasia tax code: Corporate income tax, T_C = 20%** **(instead of 40% in previous example)** **Personal taxes: Tax on equity income, T_E = 10%,** **Tax on all other income, T_D = 30%**			
2	**Computing the family income**			
3	T_C, corporate tax rate	20%		
4	T_E, personal equity tax rate	10%		
5	T_D, personal debt tax rate on ordinary income	30%		
6	r_D, interest rate	8%		
7	D, Debt	3,000		
8	FCF, free cash flow (already after corporate taxes)	1,000		
9				
10		Company borrows	Arthur borrows	
11	FCF, after personal tax	1,000.00	1,000.00	
12	Corporate debt	3,000.00	0.00	
13	Corporate pre-tax interest payment	240.00	0.00	
14	Corporate after-tax interest payment	192.00	0.00	<-- =C13*(1-$B$3)
15	Payout to equity owners	808.00	1,000.00	<-- =C11-C14
16				
17	Arthur's income			
18	Pre-tax equity income from XYZ	808.00	1,000.00	<-- =C15
19	Post-tax equity income from XYZ	727.20	900.00	<-- =C18*(1-$B$4)
20	Arthur's debt	0.00	3,000.00	
21	Arthur's pre-tax interest payment	0.00	240.00	<-- =$B$6*C20
22	Arthur's after-tax interest payment	0.00	168.00	
23	Arthur's post-tax income	727.20	732.00	<-- =C19-C22
24				
25	Mom's pre-tax income	240.00	240.00	<-- =C20*B6
26	Mom's post-tax income	168.00	168.00	<-- =C25*(1-$B$5)
27	Total family income	895.20	900.00	<-- =C23+C26
28				
29	Who should borrow--Arthur or company?	Arthur		<-- =IF(B27>C27,"Company",IF(B27<C27,"Arthur","Indifferent"))
30				
31	**Net advantage of corporate debt**			
32	$(1-T_D)-(1-T_E)*(1-T_C)$	-0.02		

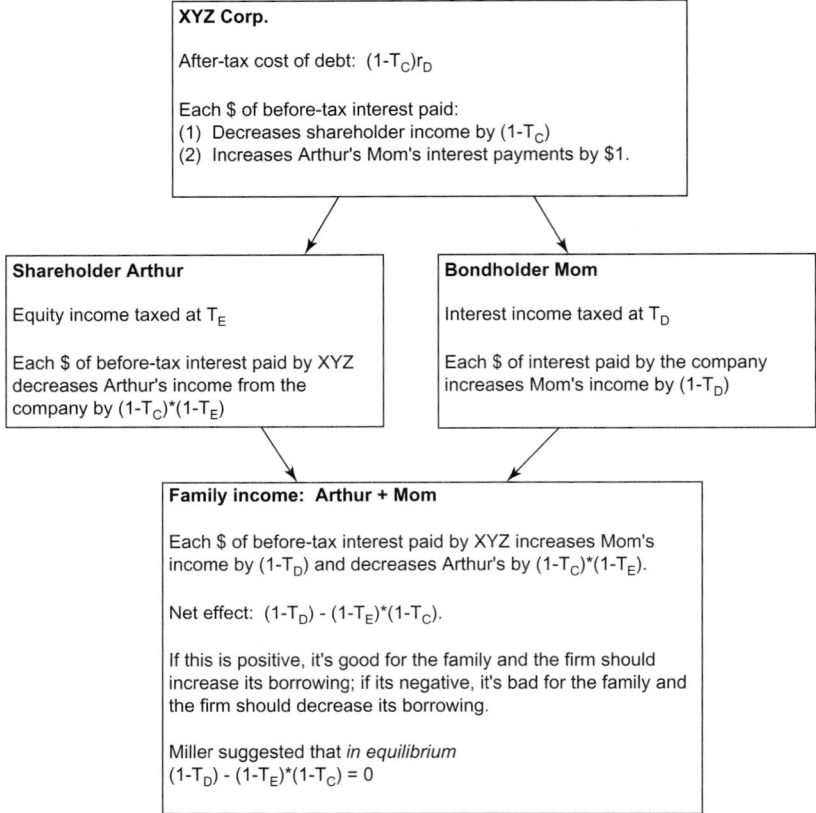

Figure 20.4 XYZ Corporation: cash flows of Arthur + Mom's family income. In this flow diagram, Arthur is the shareholder of XYZ Corp., and Mom is the bondholder of XYZ (meaning she lends the company money). Each $1 of interest income paid to Mom by XYZ Corp. changes the family income by $(1 - T_D) - (1 - T_E) * (1 - T_C)$. If this term is positive, then XYZ Corp.'s borrowing from Mom adds to the family income; if it is negative, then XYZ Corp.'s borrowing detracts from the family income.

SOME HISTORY OF FINANCE (2)

The Modigliani–Miller model dates from two articles published in 1958 and 1963. In 1977 Merton Miller (half of the MM team), reconsidered the problem of capital structure. He still focused on taxation, but this time considered the case where both corporate and personal incomes were taxed.

Miller's reasoning, incorporated in our example of XYZ Corp., was that the corporate tax rate T_C gives an advantage to corporations wishing to finance with debt. On the other hand, for individuals equity income is generally taxed at a lower rate T_E than the tax rate T_D on debt income. The primary reason for this is that the major part of income from equity is received by shareholders as capital gains; these are not only taxed at a lower tax rate, but the taxes on capital gains are also *postponable* (as a shareholder, you can decide when to sell your shares and realize your capital gains). This postponability lowers the T_E below the statutory rate (see some discussion in Chapter 21). Thus, Miller reasoned, there is a trade-off:

- On the corporate level, the deductibility of interest means that corporations produce higher before-personal-tax payouts to stakeholders (bondholders and shareholders) when they have more debt financing.

- On the personal level, giving stakeholders (bondholders and shareholders) more interest income instead of equity income means taxing them at higher personal rates.

This trade-off is summarized in the expression $(1 - T_D) - (1 - T_C) * (1 - T_E)$:

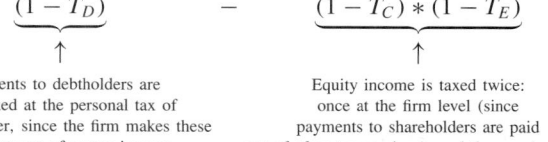

$$\underbrace{(1 - T_D)}_{\uparrow} \quad - \quad \underbrace{(1 - T_C) * (1 - T_E)}_{\uparrow}$$

Payments to debtholders are only taxed at the personal tax of the debtholder, since the firm makes these payments out of pretax income

Equity income is taxed twice: once at the firm level (since payments to shareholders are paid out of after-tax earnings), and then again at the personal level

On the other hand, $T_E < T_D$, so that there is a trade-off …

20.7 Valuing XYZ Corp.: The Effect of Leverage When There Are Corporate and Personal Taxes

We redo the calculations in Section 20.2, but this time use all the taxes—the corporate tax rate T_C, the personal tax rate on equity income T_E, and the personal tax rate on ordinary income (including interest) T_D. Without leverage, XYZ Corp.'s FCFs are worth \$5,000:

$$V_U = \textit{unleveraged value of XYZ}$$

$$= PV\,(\textit{future FCFs,discounted @ unlevered discount rate})$$

$$= \sum_{t=1}^{\infty} \frac{\$1,000}{(1.20)^t} = \frac{\textit{annual FCF}}{r_U} = \frac{\$1,000}{20\%} = \$5,000$$

We use the additivity principle to value the leveraged version of XYZ Corp.:

$$V_L = V_U + PV\,(additional\ debt\text{-}related\ CFs)$$

$$
= \begin{cases}
V_U = \displaystyle\sum_{t=1}^{\infty} \frac{FCF_t}{(1+r_U)^t} = \sum_{t=1}^{\infty} \frac{\$1,000}{(1.20)^t} = \frac{\$1,000}{20\%} = \$5,000 \\[4pt]
\text{The unleveraged value of the firm is} \\
\text{the present value of its free cash flows} \\
\text{discounted at an appropriate (unleveraged)} \\
\text{cost of capital } r_U
\end{cases}
$$

$$
+ \begin{cases}
PV\left(\begin{array}{c} interest\ tax \\ shields \end{array}\right) = \displaystyle\sum_{t=1}^{\infty} \frac{[(1-T_D)-(1-T_E)*(1-T_C)]*interest_t}{(1+(1-T_D)r_D)^t} \\[12pt]
\qquad\qquad\qquad\quad = \displaystyle\sum_{t=1}^{\infty} \frac{8\%*\$3,000*16\%}{(1+8\%*(1-30\%))^t} = \frac{\$38.4}{5.6\%} = \$685.71 \\[12pt]
\text{The tax shields created} \\
\text{by the debt are discounted at the} \\
\text{consumer's after-tax interest rate}
\end{cases}
$$

$$= \$5,685.71$$

XYZ Corp. is worth more as a levered firm than as an unleveraged firm because it produces more cash for its owners when it is levered. The additional cash produced—generated by the fact that the company has a cheaper cost of debt than Arthur—is worth \$685.71, which is the present value of the future tax shields on the interest:

$$
\begin{aligned}
PV\left(\begin{array}{c} interest\ tax \\ shields \end{array}\right) &= \sum_{t=1}^{\infty} \frac{[(1-T_D)-(1-T_E)*(1-T_C)]*interest}{(1+(1-T_D)r_D)^t} \\[8pt]
&= \frac{[(1-T_D)-(1-T_C)*(1-T_E)]}{(1-T_D)r_D} * interest \\[8pt]
&= \frac{[(1-T_D)-(1-T_C)*(1-T_E)]}{(1-T_D)} * \frac{interest}{r_D} \\[8pt]
&= \frac{[(1-T_D)-(1-T_C)*(1-T_E)]}{(1-T_D)} * D
\end{aligned}
$$

We use the letter T to denote the *debt-valuation factor*, the capitalized advantage of debt[9]:

$$T = \frac{[(1-T_D)-(1-T_E)*(1-T_C)]}{(1-T_D)}$$

---

[9]To relate this to the previous case with only corporate taxes, note that when $T_E = T_D = 0, T = T_C$.

What About the Cost of Capital—r_E and WACC With Leverage?

The leveraged version of XYZ Corp. is worth \$5,685.71, of which \$3,000 is debt. Subtracting the value of the debt from the total worth of the company, we see that the equity of the company is worth \$2,685.71. In order to calculate the firm's cost of equity r_E, we first compute the after-tax cash flows accruing to the equity owners:

$$annual\ after\text{-}corporate\text{-}tax\ equity\ cash\ flow = [FCF - after\text{-}tax\ interest\ paid\ by\ XYZ\,]$$
$$= [\$1{,}000 - 8\% * \$3{,}000 * (1 - 40\%)]$$
$$= \$856.00$$

The discounted value of this annual equity cash flow of \$856.00 is the value of the equity; this defines the cost of equity r_E:

$$equity\ value = \sum_{t=1}^{\infty} \frac{equity\ cash\ flow_t}{(1 + r_E)^t}$$

$$\$2{,}685.71 = \sum_{t=1}^{\infty} \frac{\$856.00}{(1 + r_E)^t} = \frac{\$856.00}{r_E}$$

$$\Rightarrow r_E = \frac{\$856.00}{\$2685.71} = 31.87\%$$

With a little mathematical flimflammery, we can show that

$$r_E = r_U + [r_U * (1 - T) - r_D * (1 - T_C)]\frac{D}{E}$$

$$= \underbrace{20\%}_{\substack{\uparrow \\ r_U \text{ is the discount} \\ \text{rate for the FCFs,} \\ \text{which represents} \\ \text{the firm's business} \\ \text{risk}}} + \underbrace{[20\%(1 - 22.86\%) - 8\%(1 - 40\%)]\frac{\$3{,}000}{\$2{,}685.71}}_{\substack{\uparrow \\ \text{When XYZ borrows, its shareholders} \\ \text{bear an additional } \textit{financial risk}. \text{ The} \\ \text{term above represents the financial risk} \\ \text{premium for the equity holders}}} = 31.87\%$$

We can now compute the WACC:

$$WACC = r_E \frac{E}{E + D} + r_D(1 - T_C)\frac{D}{E + D}$$

$$= 31.87\% \frac{\$2{,}685.71}{\$2{,}685.71 + \$3{,}000} + 8\%(1 - 40\%)\frac{\$3{,}000}{\$2{,}685.71 + \$3{,}000}$$

$$= 17.59\%$$

With a little more flimflammery we can show that discounting the FCFs at the WACC gives the total value of the firm:

$$\sum_{t=1}^{\infty} \frac{FCF_t}{(1 + WACC)^t} = \sum_{t=1}^{\infty} \frac{\$1,000}{(1 + 17.59\%)^t}$$

$$= \frac{\$1,000}{17.59\%} = \$5,685.71$$

Here's all of this summarized in a spreadsheet:

	A	B	C
1	**COMPUTING THE WACC IN THE MILLER MODEL** **with corporate and personal taxes**		
2	FCF, annual free cash flow (already after corporate taxes)	1,000	
3	r_U, unlevered cost of capital	20%	
4	D, Debt	3,000	
5	r_D, interest rate	8%	
6	T_C, corporate tax rate	40%	
7	T_E, personal equity tax rate	10%	
8	T_D, personal debt tax rate on ordinary income	30%	
9			
10	Tax advantage of debt, $(1-T_D)-(1-T_C)*(1-T_E)$	16.00%	<-- =(1-B8)-(1-B6)*(1-B7)
11	T= $[(1-T_D)-(1-T_C)*(1-T_E)]/(1-T_D)$, tax factor	22.86%	<-- =B10/(1-B8)
12			
13	**Value of firm**		
14	V_U, unlevered value	5,000.00	<-- =B2/B3
15	Value of tax shield on interest	685.71	<-- =B10*B5*B4/((1-B8)*B5)
16	V_L, levered value of firm	5,685.71	<-- =B15+B14
17			
18	E, value of equity	2,685.71	<-- =B16-B4
19			
20	Cash flow to equity	856.00	<-- =B2-(1-B6)*B5*B4
21	Return on equity, $r_E(L)$	31.87%	<-- =B20/B18
22			
23	WACC	17.59%	<-- =B21*B18/B16+(1-B6)*B5*B4/B16
24			
25	**Three checks**		
26	Return on equity, $r_E(L) = r_U + [r_U*(1-T) - r_D*(1-T_C)]*D/E$	31.87%	<-- =B3+(B3*(1-B11)-B5*(1-B6))*B4/B18
27	Value of firm, V_L = FCF/WACC	5,685.71	<-- =B2/B23
28	Value of firm, $V_L = V_U + T*D$	5,685.71	<-- =B14+B11*B4

Summarizing this Section

We complete this section by restating its major conclusions. If corporate income is taxed, and if the tax system differentiates between income derived from equity and ordinary income, then leverage (borrowing) may increase or decrease the value of the firm, depending on the sign of the tax factor $(1 - T_D) - (1 - T_E) * (1 - T_C)$.

A summary table is given in Figure 20.5.

Tax advantage of debt $= (1 - T_D) - (1 - T_C) * (1 - T_E)$; Tax factor $T = \dfrac{(1 - T_D) - (1 - T_C) * (1 - T_E)}{(1 - T_D)}$

Item	Formula	Why
V_U = value of unleveraged firm	$V_U = \displaystyle\sum_{t=1}^{\infty} \frac{FCF_t}{(1 + r_U)^t}$	The value of the unleveraged firm is the PV of future FCFs discounted at r_U, the unleveraged cost of capital.
V_L = value of the leveraged firm	$V_L = V_U + PV\,(net\ interest\ tax\ shields)$ $= V_U + \displaystyle\sum_{t=1}^{N} \frac{[(1 - T_D) - (1 - T_E)(1 - T_C)] * interest_t}{(1 + r_D(1 - T_D))^t}$ Another way to write this is $V_L = V_U + T * D$, where $T = \dfrac{(1 - T_D) - (1 - T_E) * (1 - T_C)}{1 - T_D}$	The value of the leveraged firm is V_U plus the present value of future interest tax shields. When there are both corporate and personal taxes, the PV of the tax shields is given by $\displaystyle\sum_{t=1}^{N} \frac{[(1 - T_D) - (1 - T_E)(1 - T_C)] * interest_t}{(1 + r_D(1 - T_D))^t}$
	$V_L = V_U + PV\,(net\ interest\ tax\ shields)$ $= V_U + \displaystyle\sum_{t=1}^{\infty} \frac{[(1 - T_D) - (1 - T_E)(1 - T_C)] * interest}{(1 + r_D(1 - T_D))^t}$ $= V_U + T * D,$ where $T = \dfrac{(1 - T_D) - (1 - T_E)(1 - T_C)}{(1 - T_D)}$	The cell to the left contains the formula for the value of the leveraged firm when the firm issues perpetual debt. This formula is the same as the parallel formula in Figure 20.2 for the case where $T_E = T_D = 0$. In the general case where personal taxes are perhaps not zero, $T = \dfrac{(1 - T_D) - (1 - T_E)(1 - T_C)}{(1 - T_D)}$ can be positive, negative, or zero.
E = value of equity	$E = V_U - (1 - T)D$	The equity value of the leveraged firm = $E = V_L - D = V_U - (1 - T)D$
D = value of debt	D	
$r_E(L)$ = cost of equity of the leveraged firm	$r_E(L) = r_U + [r_U(1 - T) - r_D(1 - T_C)]\dfrac{D}{E}$	
WACC = weighted average cost of capital	$WACC = \dfrac{FCF}{V_L}$	

Figure 20.5 Summary table of changing leverage when corporate income is taxed at rate T_C, personal ordinary income is taxed at rate T_D, and personal equity income is taxed at rate T_E.

20.8 Buying a Sturfing Machine in Upper Fantasia

In this section and the next we return to the examples of Sections 20.3 and 20.4. This time we do these examples for a company in Upper Fantasia, where, you will recall, there are three tax rates:

- In Upper Fantasia corporate income is taxed at the rate $T_C = 40\%$.
- Personal income from equity (meaning dividends and capital gains) is taxed at rate $T_E = 10\%$.
- Personal income from all other sources is taxed at rate $T_D = 30\%$.

Sonderturf Considers Buying a Sturfing Machine

Sonderturf Corp., a company in Upper Fantasia, is considering purchasing a new sturfing machine. The sturfing machine costs $100,000; it has a ten-year life, during which it is straight-line depreciated to zero salvage value. In each of the ten years of the machine's life, it will produce sales of $40,000. These sales will cost $15,000 to produce. The result is that the machine has an annual free cash flow of $19,000 per year.

The Sonderturf financial wizards have determined that an appropriate risk-adjusted discount rate for the sturfing machine's free cash flows is $r_U = 15\%$. Discounting the machine's FCFs at this rate shows that it has a negative NPV of −$4,643. Thus, the conclusion is that Sonderturf should not acquire the sturfing machine. (For details of these calculations, refer to Section 20.3.)

Sonderturf Gets a Loan to Buy the Machine

Having heard the bad news from Sonderturf, the sturfing machine's manufacturer offers the company a loan of $50,000. The loan's conditions are exactly the same as those of the loan in Section 20.3, which was offered to Wonderturf in Lower Fantasia: In years 1–9, Sonderturf will pay only interest ($4,000), and in year 10 it will pay interest of $4,000 as well as repay the loan principal.

It follows from the formula in Figure 20.5 that the value of the loan is

$$
PV \begin{pmatrix} \textit{loan in Upper Fantasia, where there are corporate income} \\ \textit{taxes } T_C, \textit{ taxes on equity income } T_E, \\ \textit{and taxes on ordinary income } T_D \end{pmatrix}
$$

$$
= PV\,(\textit{net interest tax shields}) = \sum_{t=1}^{10} \frac{[(1 - T_D) - (1 - T_E)(1 - T_C)] * interest_t}{(1 + r_D(1 - T_D))^t}
$$

$$
= \sum_{t=1}^{10} \frac{[(1 - 30\%) - (1 - 10\%)(1 - 40\%)] * \$4,000}{(1 + r_D(1 - 30\%))^t}
$$

$$
= \$4,801
$$

The Sonderturf financial wizards conclude that the company should now purchase the machine, taking the loan to finance part of the purchase. They calculate that

$$NPV(machine + loan) = NPV(machine) + NPV(loan)$$
$$= NPV(machine) + PV\ \underbrace{(loan\ interest\ tax\ shields)}$$

In Upper Fantasia the tax shield takes account of corporate as well as personal taxes:

$$\sum_{t=1}^{10} \frac{[(1-T_D)-(1-T_E)(1-T_C)]*interest_t}{(1+(1-T_D)*r_D)^t}$$

$$= -\$4,643 + \$4,801$$
$$= \$158$$

The calculations are shown in the following Excel spreadsheet:

	A	B	C	D	E	F
1			THE SONDERTURF STURFING MACHINE			
2	T_C, corporate tax rate	40%				
3	T_E, personal tax rate on equity	10%				
4	T_D, personal tax rate on debt	30%				
5						
6	Machine cost, year 0	100,000				
7						
8	Free cash flow (FCF) calculation					
9	Additional sales, annually	40,000				
10	Additional annual cost of sales	15,000				
11	Annual depreciation	10,000	<-- =B6/10			
12	Annual FCF, years 1-10	19,000	<-- =(1-B2)*(B9-B10-B11)+B11			
13						
14	Discount rate for machine FCFs	15%		Loan to buy machine	50,000	
15				r_D, loan interest rate	8%	
16				Net annual advantage of debt financing, (1-T_D)-(1-T_E)*(1-T_C)	16%	<-- =(1-B4)-(1-B3)*(1-B2)
17						
18	Year	Machine FCF			Tax advantage of interest	
19	0	-100,000	<-- =-B6			
20	1	19,000	<-- =$B$12		640	<-- =$E$16*$E$15*$E$14
21	2	19,000			640	<-- =$E$16*$E$15*$E$14
22	3	19,000			640	
23	4	19,000			640	
24	5	19,000			640	
25	6	19,000			640	
26	7	19,000			640	
27	8	19,000			640	
28	9	19,000			640	
29	10	19,000			640	
30						
31	Machine NPV	-4,643	<-- =B19+NPV(B14,B20:B29)	Loan NPV	4,801	<-- =E19+NPV(E15*(1-B4),E20:E29)
32						
33	NPV: Machine + Loan	158	<-- =B31+E31			

In Upper Fantasia Debt Is Not Always Valuable!

The Lower Fantasia tax system—which has only a corporate tax T_C but no other taxes on personal income—*always makes it more valuable to finance with debt.* You can see this from the following formula drawn from Figure 20.2, which holds in Lower Fantasia:

$$V_L^{Lower\ Fantasia} = V_U + PV\ (interest\ tax\ shields) = V_U + \sum_{t=1}^{\infty} \frac{T_C * interest_t}{(1+r_D)^t} > V_U$$

The same formula in Upper Fantasia—with its more complicated (but more realistic) tax system that combines a corporate income tax T_C with a personal tax on equity income T_E and a personal tax on ordinary income T_D—is given by

$$V_L^{Upper\ Fantasia} = V_U + PV\,(interest\ tax\ shields)$$

$$= V_U + \sum_{t=1}^{N} \frac{[(1 - T_D) - (1 - T_E) * (1 - T_C)] * interest_t}{(1 + (1 - T_D)r_D)^t}$$

The last expression need not always be positive. For example,

$$\sum_{t=1}^{N} \frac{[(1 - T_D) - (1 - T_E) * (1 - T_C)] * interest_t}{(1 + (1 - T_D)r_D)^t} > 0 \quad if \quad (1 - T_D) - (1 - T_E) * (1 - T_C) > 0$$

$$\sum_{t=1}^{N} \frac{[(1 - T_D) - (1 - T_E) * (1 - T_C)] * interest_t}{(1 + (1 - T_D)r_D)^t} = 0 \quad if \quad (1 - T_D) - (1 - T_E) * (1 - T_C) = 0$$

$$\sum_{t=1}^{N} \frac{[(1 - T_D) - (1 - T_E) * (1 - T_C)] * interest_t}{(1 + (1 - T_D)r_D)^t} < 0 \quad if \quad (1 - T_D) - (1 - T_E) * (1 - T_C) < 0$$

The conclusion is that in Upper Fantasia, financing with debt need not make a project more valuable. Suppose, for example, that $T_C = 40\%$, $T_E = 3\%$, and $T_D = 50\%$. Then the spreadsheet below shows that financing the sturfing machine with debt *decreases* the NPV:

	A	B	C	D	E	F
1			**THE SONDERTURF STURFING MACHINE** **different taxes make debt disadvantageous!**			
2	T_C, corporate tax rate	40%				
3	T_E, personal tax rate on equity	3%				
4	T_D, personal tax rate on debt	50%				
5						
6	Machine cost, year 0	100,000				
7						
8	Free cash flow (FCF) calculation					
9	Additional sales, annually	40,000				
10	Additional annual cost of sales	15,000				
11	Annual depreciation	10,000	<-- =B6/10			
12	Annual FCF, years 1-10	19,000	<-- =(1-B2)*(B9-B10-B11)+B11			
13						
14	Discount rate for machine FCFs	15%		Loan to buy machine	50,000	
15				r_D, loan interest rate	8%	
16				Net annual advantage of debt financing, (1-T_D)-(1-T_E)*(1-T_C)	-8%	<-- =(1-B4)-(1-B3)*(1-B2)
17						
18	Year	Machine FCF			Tax advantage of interest	
19	0	-100,000	<-- =-B6			
20	1	19,000	<-- =$B$12		-328	<-- =$E$16*$E$15*$E$14
21	2	19,000			-328	<-- =$E$16*$E$15*$E$14
22	3	19,000			-328	
23	4	19,000			-328	
24	5	19,000			-328	
25	6	19,000			-328	
26	7	19,000			-328	
27	8	19,000			-328	
28	9	19,000			-328	
29	10	19,000			-328	
30						
31	Machine NPV	-4,643	<-- =B19+NPV(B14,B20:B29)	Loan NPV	-2,660	<-- =E19+NPV(E15*(1-B4),E20:E29)
32						
33	NPV: Machine + Loan	-7,304	<-- =B31+E31			

20.9 Releveraging Smotfooler, Inc., an Upper Fantasia Company

In Section 20.4 we offered a question from a Finance 101 exam at Eastern Lower Fantasia State University. This section offers a similar question from an exam at Upper Fantasia University (their football team is called the Ufus).

Here's the question: Smotfooler, Inc. is a well-known Upper Fantasia company. Here are some facts about the company:

- Smotfooler expects to have an annual free cash flow of $2 million at the end of years 1, 2, 3, . . . forever. Recall that the free cash flow is the after-tax amount of cash that the company generates from its business activities.

- Smotfooler currently has 100,000 shares outstanding on the Upper Fantasia Stock Exchange. The Smotfooler share price is $100 per share.

- Smotfooler currently has no debt. However, a financial analyst has suggested that the company issue $3,000,000 of perpetual debt and use the proceeds to repurchase shares. The current interest rate on debt in Upper Fantasia is 8%, and the interest payments on the debt will be made annually.

- Tax rates in Upper Fantasia are $T_C = 40\%$, $T_D = 30\%$, and $T_E = 10\%$.

Students on the finance exam were asked to answer the following questions:

Question 1: What is the current market value of Smotfooler?

*Answer: Smotfooler currently has 100,000 shares outstanding, each of which is worth $100. Thus, the company's equity value is currently $10,000,000 = $100 * 100,000. Since the company has no debt, this is also its market value. In short, $V_U = \$10,000,000$.*

Question 2: After Smotfooler issues $3,000,000 of debt, what will be its market value?

Answer: Since Upper Fantasia has a corporate income tax, and personal income taxes the relation $V_L = V_U + TD$ holds, where

$$T = \frac{(1 - T_D) - (1 - T_C) * (1 - T_E)}{(1 - T_D)} = \frac{(1 - 30\%) - (1 - 40\%)(1 - 10\%)}{(1 - 30\%)} = 22.86\%$$

(See also cell B7 on the spreadsheet below).

   This means that after the company issues its debt, its market value will be

$$V_L = V_U + TD = \$10,000,000 + 22.86\% * \$3,000,000 = \$10,685,714$$

Question 3: After Smotfooler issues debt of $3,000,000 and uses the proceeds to repurchase shares, what will be the company's *total equity value, E*?

Answer: After Smotfooler issues the debt and repurchases the shares, the total value of its equity, E, plus the total value of its debt, D, have to sum to the company's total market value, V_L. In short,

$$V_L = \$10,685,714 = E + D$$

But $D = \$3,000,000$, and therefore

$$E = \$10,685,714 - \$3,000,000 = \$7,685,714$$

contd.

Question 4: At what price will Smotfooler repurchase its shares?

Answer: By issuing $3 million of debt, Smotfooler has raised its total market value by $685,714 (from $10 million to $10,685,714). This increase in value belongs to all the shareholders. Since there are 100,000 shares outstanding before the share repurchase, this means that each share's price increases by $685,714/100,000 = $6.86. Thus, the answer to this question is that the share price for repurchase is $106.86. Of this amount, $100 is the share price before the repurchase, and $6.86 is the increase in the share price as a result of the debt issue.

Question 5: How many shares will Smotfooler repurchase?

Answer: According to the previous question, Smotfooler will repurchase its shares at $106.86 per share. Since the company has issued $3 million in debt to repurchase the shares, this means that it will repurchase $3,000,000/$106.86 = 28,074.87.

Question 6: What was Smotfooler's cost of equity before the repurchase of shares?

Answer: Smotfooler has an annual free cash flow (FCF) of $2,000,000. Thus, its unleveraged cost of equity is

$$r_E(U) = r_U = \frac{FCF}{V_U} = \frac{2,000,000}{10,000,000} = 20\%$$

Question 7: What is Smotfooler's cost of equity *after* the repurchase of the shares on the open market?

Answer: Smotfooler issues $3 million in 8% debt in order to repurchase shares. Thus, its annual interest bill is 8% * $3,000,000 = $240,000. Since interest is an expense for tax purposes, the company's shareholders will have an annual expected cash flow of

$$\text{annual equity cash flow, after debt issuance} = FCF - (1 - T_C) * interest$$
$$= \$2,000,000 - (1 - 40\%) * \$240,000$$
$$= \$1,856,000$$

The value of the equity after the share repurchase is $7,685,714, so that the cost of equity of the leveraged company is

$$r_E(L) = \frac{\$1,856,000}{\$7,685,714} = 24.15\%$$

Note from Figure 20.5 that there's another way to do this calculation:

$$r_E(L) = r_U + [r_U(1 - T) - r_D(1 - T_C)]\frac{D}{E}$$
$$= 20\% + [20\%(1 - 22.86\%) - 8\%(1 - 40\%)]\frac{\$3,000,000}{\$7,685,714}$$
$$= 24.15\%$$

Question 8: What is Smotfooler's weighted average cost of capital (WACC) *before* the repurchase of the shares?

Answer: Recall the definition of the WACC:

$$WACC = r_E(L) * \frac{E}{E+D} + r_D * (1 - T_C) * \frac{D}{E+D}$$

The answer to question 8 is easy: Since Smotfooler, before the share repurchase, has only equity, its WACC = r_U = 20%.

Question 9: What is Smotfooler's weighted average cost of capital (WACC) *after* the repurchase of the shares?

Answer:

$$WACC = r_E(L) * \frac{E}{E+D} + r_D * (1 - T_C) * \frac{D}{E+D}$$

$$= 24.15\% * \frac{\$7,685,714}{\$7,685,714 + \$3,000,000} + 8\% * (1 - 40\%)\frac{\$3,000,000}{\$7,685,714 + \$3,000,000} = 18.72\%$$

Question 10: Why is $r_E(L) > r_U$?

Answer: Before Smotfooler issued its bonds, the only risk borne by shareholders was the business risk inherent in the company's free cash flow. After the company issues its bonds, shareholders have to bear two kinds of risk: business risk and financial risk. Thus, $r_E(L)$ represents a discount rate for cash flows that are riskier than the discount rate for the FCFs, r_U. Since riskier cash flows have higher discount rates, it follows that $r_E(L) > r_U$.

Question 11: Why does the market value of Smotfooler increase after the issuance of the debt and repurchase of the equity?

Answer: By issuing the debt, Smotfooler increases the amount of cash it produces by $[(1 - T_D) - (1 - T_C) * (1 - T_E)] * (interest payment)$ for every year that it has debt. This additional cash flow is riskless. Since the holders of riskless cash flows in Upper Fantasia use a discount rate of $(1 - T_D) * r_D$ to value the cash flows, it follows that

$$value\ of\ additional\ debt\text{-}related\ cash\ flows$$

$$= \sum_{t=1}^{\infty} \frac{[(1 - T_D) - (1 - T_C) * (1 - T_E)] * (interest\ payment)}{(1 + (1 - T_D)r_D)^t}$$

$$= \frac{(1 - T_D) - (1 - T_C) * (1 - T_E)}{(1 - T_D)r_D} * (interest\ payment)$$

$$= \frac{(1 - T_D) - (1 - T_C) * (1 - T_E)}{(1 - T_D)r_D} * r_D D = \underbrace{T}_{} \qquad * D$$

$$\uparrow$$
$$T =$$
$$\frac{(1 - T_D) - (1 - T_C) * (1 - T_E)}{(1 - T_D)}$$

contd.

The present value of the tax shield accounts for the increase in Smotfooler's market value:

$$V_L = \underbrace{V_U}_{} + \underbrace{TD}_{}$$

                ↑   ↑

       Smotfooler's value   PV of additional
       before the debt   debt−related cash
          issuance   flows

Question 12: Does debt always increase corporate value in Upper Fantasia?

Answer: No. It depends on the sizes of the three tax rates T_C, T_D, and T_E. In the example below, there is a net tax disadvantage to debt—by issuing debt, Smotfooler lowers its market value and raises its WACC:

Here's a spreadsheet that summarizes Questions 1–12:

	A	B	C
1	**SMOTFOOLER--DEBT ISSUED TO REPURCHASE SHARES** **Smotfooler is located in Upper Fantasia**		
2	**Upper Fantasia tax system**		
3	T_C, Upper Fantasia corporate tax rate	40%	
4	T_E, Upper Fantasia personal tax rate on equity income	10%	
5	T_D, Upper Fantasia personal tax rate on ordinary income	30%	
6	Annual debt advantage: $(1-T_D)-(1-T_E)^*(1-T_C)$	16%	<-- =(1-B5)-(1-B4)*(1-B3)
7	PV of debt advantage: $T = [(1-T_D)-(1-T_E)^*(1-T_C)]/(1-T_D)$	22.86%	<-- =B6/(1-B5)
8			
9	**Unlevered company**		
10	Annual free cash flow (FCF)	$2,000,000	
11	Number of shares	100,000	
12	Price per share	$100	
13	Total equity value	$10,000,000	<-- =B12*B11
14			
15	Question1: V_U, unlevered value of Smotfooler	$10,000,000	<-- =B13
16			
17	**Levered company**		
18	Debt issued	$3,000,000	
19	Interest rate on debt	8%	
20	Question 2: V_L, levered value of Smotfooler, $V_L = V_U + T^*D$	$10,685,714	<-- =B15+B7*B18
21	Question 3: Equity value after share repurchase, $E = V_L - D$	$7,685,714	
22	Incremental firm value from exchanging equity by debt $= V_L - V_U = T^*D$	$685,714	<-- =B20-B15
23	Incremental firm value on a per-share basis	$7	<-- =B22/B11
24	Question 4: New share value, after repurchase	$106.86	<-- =B12+B23
25			
26	Question 5: Number of shares repurchased = [debt used for repurchase]/[new share value]	28,074.87	<-- =B18/B24
27	Number of shares remaining after repurchase = original number of shares minus number of shares repurchased	71,925.13	<-- =B11-B26
28	**Check:** Market value of remaining shares = number of remaining shares * new share value	$7,685,714	<-- =B27*B24
29			
30	Question 6: Smotfooler's cost of equity when unlevered, $r_U=FCF/V_U$	20.00%	
31			
32	Annual interest costs, before taxes	$240,000	<-- =B18*B19
33	Annual equity cash flow, after interest = FCF - $(1-T_C)^*$interest	$1,856,000	<-- =B10-(1-B3)*B32
34	Question 7: Smotfooler's cost of equity when levered, $r_E(L)=[FCF-(1-T_C)^*$interest$]/[$value of equity, E$]$	24.15%	<-- =B33/B28
35	Note: See formula in row 44 below for another way to compute the levered cost of equity		
36			
37	Question 8: Smotfooler's WACC before the debt issuance = rU	20.00%	
38			
39	Question 9: Smotfooler's WACC after the debt issuance $= r_E(L)^*E/(E+D)+r_D^*(1-TC)^*D/(E+D)$		
40	Percentage of equity in Smotfooler = E/(E+D)	71.93%	<-- =B28/B20
41	Percentage of debt in Smotfooler = D/(E+D)	28.07%	<-- =B18/B20
42	WACC = $r_E(L)^*E/(E+D)+r_D^*(1-T_C)^*D/(E+D)$	18.72%	<-- =B34*B40+B19*(1-B3)*B41
43			
44	Additional formula: $r_E(L)=r_U+[r_U^*(1-T)-r_D^*(1-T_C)]^*D/E$	24.15%	<-- =B30+(B30*(1-B7)-B19*(1-B3))*B18/B21

20.10 Is There Really an Advantage to Debt?

In this chapter we laid out the theory of capital structure. We can answer the question of the importance of capital structure in several ways:

Method 1: What Are the Relevant Tax Rates T_C, T_D, T_E?

As you can see, the value of XYZ Corp. is critically dependent on two factors:

- r_U, the risk-adjusted rate of return for the free cash flows. This rate is unaffected by the capital structure, since the free cash flows are operating cash flows and do not depend on the financing of the firm.
- $(1 - T_D) - (1 - T_C)(1 - T_E)$—the relative after-tax costs of debt versus equity income.

Looking at this second parameter, we examine several cases. In the case below, the anticipated dividend yield of 2% is taxed at 40% while the anticipated capital gains yield of 6% is taxed at 10%. The equity tax rate is 17.5%, and the net tax advantage of debt over equity is 8.02%:

	A	B	C
1	**WHAT ARE THE RELATIVE TAX EFFECTS**		
2	Corporate tax rate, T_C	37%	
3			
4	Anticipated equity tax		**Tax rate**
5	Dividend yield	2.00%	40%
6	Capital gains yield	6.00%	10%
7			
8	Net after-tax yield	6.60%	<-- =B5*(1-C5)+B6*(1-C6)
9	Before tax yield	8.00%	<-- =B5+B6
10			
11	Personal tax rate on equity income, T_E	17.50%	<-- =1-B8/B9
12	Personal tax rate on ordinary income, T_D	40.00%	
13			
14	Tax advantage of debt over equity: $(1-T_D)-(1-T_C)*(1-T_E)$	8.02%	<-- =(1-B12)-(1-B2)*(1-B11)

With a somewhat different yield and tax configuration there is actually a net tax *disadvantage* to debt:

	A	B	C
1	**WHAT ARE THE RELATIVE TAX EFFECTS**		
2	Corporate tax rate, T_C	37%	
3			
4	Anticipated equity tax		**Tax rate**
5	Dividend yield	0.00%	40%
6	Capital gains yield	6.00%	0%
7			
8	Net after-tax yield	6.00%	<-- =B5*(1-C5)+B6*(1-C6)
9	Before tax yield	6.00%	<-- =B5+B6
10			
11	Personal tax rate on equity income, T_E	0.00%	<-- =1-B8/B9
12	Personal tax rate on ordinary income, T_D	40.00%	
13			
14	Tax advantage of debt over equity: $(1-T_D)-(1-T_C)*(1-T_E)$	-3.00%	<-- =(1-B12)-(1-B2)*(1-B11)

Below you will see a third case in which only corporate income is taxed. In this case, there is an overwhelming advantage to debt financing:

	A	B	C
1	**WHAT ARE THE RELATIVE TAX EFFECTS**		
2	Corporate tax rate, T_C	37%	
3			
4	Anticipated equity tax		**Tax rate**
5	Dividend yield	5.00%	0%
6	Capital gains yield	0.00%	0%
7			
8	Net after-tax yield	5.00%	<-- =B5*(1-C5)+B6*(1-C6)
9	Before tax yield	5.00%	<-- =B5+B6
10			
11	Personal tax rate on equity income, T_E	0.00%	<-- =1-B8/B9
12	Personal tax rate on ordinary income, T_D	0.00%	
13			
14	Tax advantage of debt over equity: $(1-T_D)-(1-T_C)*(1-T_E)$	37.00%	<-- =(1-B12)-(1-B2)*(1-B11)

Method 2: What's the Evidence in Firm Behavior?

Instead of asking whether tax rates support a net tax advantage, we can also look at different firms. We can ask whether in a particular industry there is a consistent behavior toward debt. The answer is no, as you will see in Chapter 21. In Chapter 21, we interpret this "inconsistent" behavior as evidence in favor of the argument that there is no net tax advantage to debt—that is, a firm's financial policy does not affect its market value.

Method 3: What Does Sophisticated Finance Research Say?

Chapter 21 looks at the latest academic research on the capital structure question. Our reading of this research is that the importance of debt over equity financing has been heavily overemphasized in finance textbooks. There may be a small advantage of debt over equity, but it is overwhelmed by the overall uncertainty of valuing a firm.

CONCLUSION: UNITED WIDGETS CORPORATION

United Widgets is a new company set up by John and Cindy, who are pondering the effect of the debt–equity financing mix. The question they have in mind is: Does it matter whether the company is financed with share capital (equity) or with money borrowed from a bank (debt)? The risk–return trade-off between the two financing alternatives is complex:

- The providers of equity financing are promised a share of the firm's profits (if there are any). If there are no profits, then shareholders will not get any dividends; although they will surely be disappointed, they cannot use the nonpayment of dividends to force the firm into bankruptcy.

- The providers of debt financing are promised a series of fixed payments. If United Widgets cannot keep the commitment of making the fixed payments, then the company may become insolvent. Bankruptcy will affect the shareholders of the company, denying them their share in United Widgets.

- Debt financing is generally cheaper than equity financing: The riskiness of the interest payments promised by United Widgets to its lenders is less than the riskiness of the dividend payments promised by the company to its shareholders. In addition, interest is a tax-deductible expense for United Widgets, whereas dividends have to be paid out of after-tax income. Shareholders, being at greater risk than lenders, will therefore demand a *higher expected return* than debtholders. The relative cheapness of debt versus equity appears to make debt preferable as a financing mechanism. But:

- Debt financing makes equity financing even more risky. The risky dividend stream that comes from the company is endangered even further when shareholders promise debtholders a series of future payments. The higher the amount of debt the firm has, the more risky the equity financing becomes.[10]

Realizing all these factors, John and Cindy ask themselves the following questions:

- Does the debt–equity mix affect the amount of cash that can be extracted from United Widgets?

- Does the mix of equity and debt affect the discount rate that United Widgets should use for discounting project cash flows? As we have seen in Chapters 6, 14, and 19, the relevant discount rate is the weighted average cost of capital (WACC).

- Does the debt–equity mix affect the cost of equity?

Figure 20.6 gives schematic answers to these questions.

Chapter 21 explores some empirical results and tries to give you a "take" on how to apply the theoretical answers developed in this chapter.

---

[10]John and Cindy briefly considered financing their firm with *only debt*. But this is impossible!

UNITED WIDGETS

John and Cindy set up a new company–United Widgets, Inc. They decide to buy a widget machine because financial analysis shows that the NPV of the machine's cash flows is positive.

United Widgets is financed with equity (meaning money put up by John and Cindy and their friends) and debt (money borrowed from the bank).

Does the debt–equity financing mix change the discount rate used to evaluate widget machines?

Does the debt–equity financing mix change the *total cash* extracted from the company?

EFFECT OF DEBT/EQUITY MIX ON WEIGHTED AVERAGE COST OF CAPITAL (WACC)

1. If there are no taxes, the debt–equity mix does not affect the widget machine discount rate.

2. If there are only corporate taxes and no personal taxes, then more debt means that the widget discount rate decreases.

3. If both personal and corporate incomes are taxed, widget machine discount rates can increase/decrease/stay the same when the debt–equity mix changes.

EFFECT OF DEBT/EQUITY MIX ON TOTAL CASH EXTRACTED FROM COMPANY

1. If there are no taxes, the debt/equity mix does not affect the total amount of cash extracted from the company.

2. If there are only corporate taxes and no personal taxes, then more debt means more cash extracted from the company; more debt means more cash extracted from the company; this happens because the tax system subsidizes debt (interest is an expense for tax purposes).

3. If both personal and corporate incomes are taxed, the cash extracted from the company can go up or down: Companies enjoy a tax subsidy on their interest payments (since interest is an expense for tax purposes). But shareholders pay lower taxes on earnings from equity (because of an advantageous capital gains tax) than on interest earnings from debt.

EFFECT OF DEBT/EQUITY MIX ON COST OF COST OF EQUITY AND WACC

More debt in the debt–equity mix *always* makes equity riskier! The equity owners have to pay debtholders before they pay themselves and this increases their risk.

The effect of capital structure on WACC depends on the mix of corporate and personal taxes:

1. If there are no taxes, WACC is unaffected by capital structure: the increase in the cost of equity as the debt–equity mix increases exactly offsets the savings of cheaper debt.

2. If there are only corporate taxes, WACC decreases when more debt is used to finance the firm.

3. If there are both corporate and personal taxes, WACC can increase/decrease/stay the same. Empirical evidence (Chapter 21) seems to indicate that it doesn't change much.

$$WACC = r_E(L) \frac{E}{E + D} + r_D(1 - T_C) \frac{D}{E + D}$$

where:

$r_E(L)$ = cost of equity (increase when debt–equity ratio ↑)

r_D = cost of debt

E = market value of firms equity

D = market value of firms debt

T_C = corporate tax rate

Figure 20.6 Financing United Widgets: Capital structure and its effects on the cost of capital and firm valuation.

EXERCISES

1. Go back to the supermarket example from the beginning of the chapter. Assume that the super-market after-tax operating income is $120,000 each year. If Mortimer's group took a $500,000 loan at 9% annual interest rate and its tax rate is 30%, what will be the return on equity (ROE) for Mortimer's group and Joanna's group. ($ROE = (profit\ after\ tax)/equity$)?

Mortimer's Supermarket Group Half equity (50%) and half debt (50%)			
Supermarket	$1,000,000	Debt	$500,000
		Equity	$500,000
Total assets	**$1,000,000**	**Total debt and equity**	**$1,000,000**

Joanna's Supermarket Group Only equity (100%)			
Supermarket	$1,000,000	Debt	$0
		Equity	$1,000,000
Total assets	**$1,000,000**	**Total debt and equity**	**$1,000,000**

2. (a) Repeat Exercise 1 with the following balance sheets (assume that the debt still bears a 9% interest rate):

Mortimer's Supermarket Group Half equity (50%) and half debt (50%)			
Supermarket	$1,200,000	Debt	$600,000
		Equity	$600,000
Total assets	**$1,200,000**	**Total debt and equity**	**$1,200,000**

Joanna's Supermarket Group Only equity (100%)			
Supermarket	$1,000,000	Debt	$0
		Equity	$1,000,000
Total assets	**$1,000,000**	**Total debt and equity**	**$1,000,000**

   (b) Show using **Data Table** and an Excel chart the sensitivity of the ROE to the debt–equity ratio.

3. You are interested in buying a warehouse for your firm. The warehouse costs $350,000 and using it will save the firm $50,000 annually forever. The firm can borrow any amount of money at an 8% annual interest rate; all money borrowed is "perpetual debt"—meaning that the firm pays only the annual interest payment and never returns the debt principal. The firm's tax rate is 40%.

   What will be the firm's additional annual income and its return on equity (ROE) on the investment in the following four cases?

   (a) The firm finances the purchase with equity only.

   (b) The firm finances the purchase with 75% equity and 25% debt.

   (c) The firm finances the purchase with 50% equity and 50% debt.

   (d) The firm finances the purchase with 20% equity and 80% debt.

4. (a) Repeat Exercise 3 and show the total annual amounts received by the firm's shareholders and debtholders.

   (b) Show using **Data Table** and an Excel chart the change in the total amount received by the firm's shareholders and debtholders as a function of the equity invested in the project.

5. Eddy is the sole owner of his firm. He now wishes to purchase the company next door for $600,000. His calculations show that the annual income before tax from the purchase is $80,000.

    He is considering two financing alternatives: The first is to ask for a personal loan of $300,000 and pay the remaining amount from his savings. The second alternative is to finance the purchase by having his firm take the $300,000 loan. Assuming the interest rate on the loan is 9% (for infinite duration) and the corporate tax rate is 40%, what will be the total amount received by the firm's shareholders and debtholders in each scenario, assuming that only the interest paid by Eddy's firm is an expense for tax purposes.

6. Returning to Exercise 5, what is the value of the firm Eddy wishes to buy under the two financing alternatives?

7. Annie owns a "shell firm"—this is a firm that is incorporated but has no activity whatsoever. Annie's shell firm is about to buy another firm for $900,000. The firm she is purchasing has an annual free cash flow (FCF) of $120,000 each year.

    (a) Annie's bank is willing to give her a perpetual loan equal to half of the purchase amount at 8% interest. Assuming Annie's firm has no debt and its tax rate is $T_C = 30\%$, what will be her firm's value after the purchase:
        • In case it will finance the purchase with equity only?
        • In case it takes the loan?

    (b) What will be the firm's value in case the loan is repaid in 20 equal repayments?

8. Section 20.3 gives two formulas for the cost of equity $r_E(L)$ of a leveraged firm for the case when there are only corporate taxes:

$$r_E(L) = \frac{annual\ equity\ cash\ flow}{value\ of\ equity}$$

$$r_E(L) = r_U + [r_U - r_D]\frac{D}{E}(1 - T_C)$$

    Use both these formulas to find the cost of equity $r_E(L)$ for the following cases:
    (a) The cost of equity $r_E(L)$ for the firm Eddy is buying in Exercise 5.
    (b) The cost of equity $r_E(L)$ of the supermarket in Exercise 1.
    (c) The cost of equity $r_E(L)$ of Annie's firm from Exercise 7.

9. Section 20.3 gives two formulas for the weighted average cost of capital (WACC) of a leveraged firm for the case when there are only corporate taxes:

$$WACC = r_E(L)\frac{E}{E+D} + r_D(1 - T_C)\frac{D}{E+D}$$

$$WACC = \frac{FCF}{V_L}$$

    Use both these formulas to find the WACC for the following cases:
    (a) The WACC for the firm Eddy is buying in Exercise 5.
    (b) The WACC of the supermarket in Exercise 1.
    (c) The WACC of Annie's firm from Exercise 7.

10. Sandy-Candy, a hot new chewing gum company, is for sale for $2,000,000. Henry is interested in buying the company and is exploring various financing alternatives. He knows that the interest rate on debt is $r_D = 9\%$, the corporate tax rate is $T_C = 36\%$, and the cost of capital of the purchase is $r_U = 12\%$. Henry estimates that Sandy-Candy has a free cash flow (FCF) of $300,000 each year.
    (a) What will be the market value of Sandy-Candy if Henry does not take a loan?
    (b) What will be the market value of Sandy-Candy if Henry takes a $1,200,000 loan? Assume that the loan is paid out of Sandy-Candy's earnings, and that the interest is an expense for tax purposes.

    (c)   What will be Sandy-Candy's cost of equity r_E for the two cases above?

    (d)   What will be Sandy-Candy's WACC for the two cases above?

11. Debby, the owner of Oxford Corporation, has decided that it's time to make some changes to the firm's capital structure. She estimates that Oxford's FCF is $150,000 each year and that this FCF can be expected to recur annually forever. The company has no debt and has 30,000 shares outstanding, each of which is currently worth $50.

       Debby wants Oxford to borrow $600,000 of perpetual debt and to use the proceeds to repurchase shares. Assuming the interest rate on debt is $r_D = 6\%$ and the corporate tax rate is $T_C = 30\%$, calculate the following changes.

    (a)   What is Oxford's market value before it issued debt?

    (b)   What is Oxford's market value after it issued debt?

    (c)   What will be Oxford's share price after the debt issuance?

    (d)   How many shares will be repurchased?

    (e)   What is Oxford's equity value after the repurchase of the shares?

    (f)   What is Oxford's cost of equity after the repurchase and dividend payment?

    (g)   What is Oxford's WACC after the repurchase and dividend payment?

12. XYZ Corp. is about to borrow $100,000. The terms of the loan specify an annual equal repayment of principal in each of the next eight years. The loan rate is $r_D = 8\%$, and XYZ has a corporate tax rate of $T_C = 40\%$. If the loan interest is an expense for tax purposes for XYZ, and if there are no other taxes besides corporate taxes, what will be the increase in XYZ's market value?

13. Go back to the example of buying the turfing machine (Section 20.3). Repeat the calculations assuming the loan is repaid in ten equal payments. What is the NPV of the investment now?

14. According to a recent tax reform in Lower Fantasia, the personal tax rate on all ordinary income except capital gains from stocks was changed from 0% to 25%. Capital gains will henceforth be taxed at 15%. The Lower Fantasia corporate tax rate remains unchanged at 40%.

    (a)   Assuming you plan to take a loan, what will be better—to borrow using your firm or take a personal loan? Show the net advantage of corporate debt in this case.

    (b)   Will your answer part (a) change if the corporate tax rate becomes 20%?

15. Eddy, from Exercise 5, needs your help again. He didn't purchase the firm since the bank didn't approve the loan, but now his dad is willing to step in and help him by loaning him the same amount ($300,000). In addition, after the recent elections he's now facing a personal tax rate of 40% (equal to the corporate tax rate) and a 15% tax on equity income.

    (a)   What should he do—finance the purchase using the firm or take a personal loan? Calculate the total amount received by the stakeholders (shareholders and debtholders).

    (b)   Assuming Eddy purchases the firm next door using his own firm, calculate the value of the firm, his cost of equity, and the WACC (assume his unleveraged discount rate is 12%).

16. Assume that the corporate tax rate is $T_C = 30\%$, and the equity income tax rate is $T_E = 10\%$. What is the ordinary income tax rate T_D for which an investor will be indifferent between choosing a personal loan and getting a loan using a firm?

17. (a)   Repeat Exercise 11 (Oxford Corporation) assuming the ordinary income tax rate is $T_D = 34\%$ and the personal equity tax rate is $T_E = 15\%$.

    (b)   For this case, calculate the "net advantage of corporate debt" and calculate the expression

$$T = \frac{(1 - T_D) - (1 - T_E)(1 - T_C)}{(1 - T_D)}$$

18. You are interested in buying a machine that will produce sales of $50,000 in each of the next six years. The machine costs $120,000 and has a six-year life. It is straight-line depreciated to a zero

salvage value. In addition, the machine activity costs $18,000 annually. The discount rate you decided to use for the machine's FCF is 12%.

You are considering taking a 9%, six-year loan to finance the purchase of the machine. The loan amount will be $70,000. The loan terms specify annual payments of interest only in years 1–5 and the repayment of the whole principal in year 6. Assuming that the corporate tax rate is $T_C = 40\%$, the personal tax rate (on ordinary income) is $T_D = 22\%$, and the equity tax rate is $T_E = 15\%$, answer the following:

(a)   What is the machine FCF?

(b)   What is the NPV of the machine if it is financed with equity only?

(b)   Calculate the "net advantage of corporate debt," T.

(c)   What is the NPV of the machine if it is financed with a mix of equity and debt?

19. (a)   Fill in the following Excel sheet:

	A	B	C
1	**FILL IN THE TAX EFFECTS**		
2	Corporate tax rate, T_C	36%	
3			
4	Anticipated equity tax		**Tax rate**
5	Dividend yield	2.50%	40%
6	Capital gains yield	5.00%	10%
7			
8	Net after-tax yield	??	
9	Before tax yield	??	
10			
11	Personal tax rate on equity income, T_E	??	
12	Personal tax rate on ordinary income, T_D	??	
13			
14	Tax advantage of debt over equity: $(1-T_D)-(1-T_C)*(1-T_E)$	??	

(b)   Show in a graph the change in "net advantage of corporate debt" as a function of the personal tax rate.

THE EVIDENCE ON CAPITAL STRUCTURE

OVERVIEW

In this chapter we discuss whether the capital structure of a company—the mix of equity and debt with which it finances itself—affects the company's weighted average cost of capital (WACC). Chapter 20 discussed the theory of capital structure, which concerns itself with the effects of financing on the valuation of assets. Capital structure theory asks, all other factors being the same, whether firms that are more highly leveraged are worth more than firms with less leverage.

In Chapter 20 we suggested that the importance of capital structure depends on how it affects the ability of the corporation to extract cash from its operating and financial activities. If, by increasing its leverage, a corporation can increase the total amount of cash it pays to its shareholders and bondholders, then it should do so. If, on the other hand, increasing leverage does not change the amount of cash paid to shareholders and bondholders, then increased leverage is not worthwhile.

In Chapter 20 we related the corporate ability to extract cash from a corporation's activities to the trade-off between personal and corporate taxation: Corporate borrowing is tax deductible (since interest is an expense for tax purposes); this tends to favor corporations with more rather than less debt in their capital structures. On the other hand, a corporation with more debt in its capital structure channels more of its income to bondholders rather than to shareholders, and bondholders have a higher tax rate on their interest income than do shareholders on their equity income.

To see why the Chapter 20 discussion of leverage is important, suppose for a moment that firms with more debt are worth more than similar but less-levered firms. Then we would suggest to corporate managers the following steps:

- Corporate managers should strive to increase the amount of debt used in financing corporate activities. If, for example, a firm builds a new plant, it should try to borrow the maximal amount it can to build the plant.

- Corporate managers should minimize the amount of cash they have on hand (subject, of course, to operational and safety considerations). If leverage (that is, paying interest on debt) adds to value, then holding cash (that is, having an asset earning interest) is a detriment to value.

- Corporate managers should increase the corporate dividend payments. By paying out dividends, managers decrease the amount of cash on hand and thus increase the effective leverage of the firm.

- For the same reason corporate managers should increase share repurchases, which decrease the amount of cash on hand and thus increase effective leverage.

The bullets above tell a manager how to operate if leverage is a positive value driver. If, on the other hand, leverage is a negative value driver—meaning that more leverage decreases corporate value—then the manager should take the opposite actions. And if—as we suggested at the end of Chapter 20—leverage is a neutral value driver because the tax benefits of corporate leverage are offset by the tax disadvantages of leverage at the personal taxation level, then none of the above matters.

As you can see, leverage theory can have significant operative implications.

WHAT'S THE CONCLUSION?

To anticipate the conclusions of this chapter: We see no evidence that leverage adds value to a firm. Nor do we find significant evidence that a firm's weighted average cost of capital (WACC) is affected by its financing mix of debt versus equity. The operative conclusions are:

- Firms should proceed as if the financing mix of their assets cannot add or subtract value.

- The WACC is unaffected by leverage.

- The best way to measure the WACC is by taking the *average WACC* of a firm's industry.

What Do We Do in This Chapter?

Chapter 20 was largely theoretical. In this chapter, on the other hand, we discuss the market evidence on capital structure. We ask whether we see—in market prices, cost of capital, and market risk measures—evidence for or against the positive effects of more debt on the value of firms. In Section 21.1 we summarize the results of Chapter 20. The upshot of these results is that the effects of financing on valuation depend largely on the tax system. Roughly speaking, if firms, by borrowing, can increase the total cash flow available to shareholders and bondholders, then the firms should move toward a more leveraged capital structure.

The remaining sections of this chapter present some empirical evidence of the effects of capital structure on the cost of capital. As you will see, the evidence seems to indicate that there is little significant effect of capital structure on the WACC.

Finance Concepts Discussed

- What are some facts about capital structure (how do firms capitalize)?
- Does capital structure affect the value of a firm?
- Does capital structure affect the cost of capital?
- Are there other important considerations—bankruptcy costs, control, and so on?
- How do you measure a firm's unleveraged cost of capital r_U?
- How do you compute the WACC for an *industry?*

Excel Functions Used

- **Average**
- **Stdev**
- **Regression (Trendline)**

21.1 Summarizing the Theory

The theory of capital structure outlined in the previous chapter says that the effect of capital structure on the value of a firm is primarily due to tax considerations. Very roughly speaking, if firms enjoy interest tax deductibility that is unavailable to their shareholders, then firms should borrow and increase their debt–equity ratios. This theory—the Modigliani–Miller theory (Chapter 20, Sections 20.3–20.5)—should be contrasted with the Miller model (Chapter 20, Sections 20.6–20.9), which postulates that the advantage of corporate debt is to some extent offset by the tax advantage of equity to investors.

These are complex concepts, which we illustrated with two simple examples (Arthur ABC and Arthur XYX) in the previous chapter. We sum up the conclusions of Chapter 20:

1. Leverage adds value to a firm if the *capitalized value of the interest tax shields* is positive:

$$V_L = V_U + PV(capitalized\ interest\ tax\ shields)$$

$$= PV(FCFs,\ discounted\ at\ r_U) + \sum_{t=1}^{\infty} \frac{[(1 - T_D) - (1 - T_E) * (1 - T_C)] * interest_t}{1 + (1 - T_D)r_D}$$

Here

T_C = *the corporate tax rate*

T_E = *the personal tax rate on equity income*

T_D = *the personal tax rate on ordinary income (including interest)*

2. Assuming that a firm is contemplating a permanent change $\Delta Debt$ in its capital structure, the value of the additional tax shields produced by the debt are given by the following equation:

PV (*capitalized interest tax shields*)

$$= \sum_{t=1}^{\infty} \frac{[(1 - T_D) - (1 - T_E) * (1 - T_C)] * interest}{1 + (1 - T_D)r_D}$$

$$= \frac{[(1 - T_D) - (1 - T_E) * (1 - T_C)] * r_D * \Delta Debt}{(1 - T_D)r_D}$$

$$= \frac{[(1 - T_D) - (1 - T_E) * (1 - T_C)] * \Delta Debt}{(1 - T_D)} = T * \Delta Debt$$

where

$$T = \frac{[(1 - T_D) - (1 - T_E) * (1 - T_C)]}{(1 - T_D)}$$

3. In the classic Modigliani–Miller theory, which invokes only corporate taxes, $T = T_C$, so that debt always adds to value. In Miller's more complex model, which takes into account both personal and corporate taxes, T can be positive, negative, or zero, depending on the sign of $(1 - T_D) - (1 - T_E)(1 - T_D)$. Miller hypothesized that $(1 - T_D) - (1 - T_E)(1 - T_D) = 0$; if this is so, then there would be no advantage to debt over equity financing.

4. Leverage affects both the weighted average cost of capital (WACC) and the cost of equity r_E. In the table below we give some formulas for the WACC, the cost of equity r_E, and the cost of capital of an unleveraged firm r_U:

Weighted average cost of capital, WACC	$WACC = \dfrac{E + D * (1 - T)}{E + D} * r_U$	If debt adds value (that is, $T > 0$), leverage decreases the WACC.
Cost of equity of a leveraged firm, r_E	$r_E = r_U + [r_U * (1 - T) - r_D * (1 - T_C)]\dfrac{D}{E}$	More debt *always* makes equity more risky and increases the cost of equity r_E. The amount by which the equity becomes more risky depends on the relative sizes of T and T_C.
Cost of unleveraged capital, r_U	$r_U = \dfrac{r_D * D * (1 - T_C) + r_E * E}{E + D * (1 - T)}$	Often we estimate a firm's cost of equity r_E; this formula lets you back out what would be the cost of capital r_U of the firm if it had no leverage.

5. Contrary to the formula in 2 above, the value of debt interest tax shields is not the only factor in determining the effect on a firm's value of a change in debt. Three other prominent factors discussed by academics and practitioners are bankruptcy costs, the costs of financial control (change name), and the option effects associated with debt.

These costs are difficult to quantify, but they certainly exist:

(a) Costs of financial distress ("bankruptcy costs"): Increasing a firm's leverage also makes it more likely that a firm will have a greater future probability of getting into financial trouble. The present value of the costs of getting out of this trouble (they should be called "costs of financial distress," but they are usually termed "bankruptcy costs") should be deducted from the benefits of additional leverage.[1]

(b) Costs of financial control: Borrowers will usually lend the firm more money only if they can exercise more control. Often this control involves debt covenants. These are restrictions imposed by the lender on the firm. For example, the Giant Industries bond issue discussed in Section 18.4 (p. 536) has the following covenants:

> The Indentures . . . contain restrictive covenants that, among other things, restrict the ability of the Company and its subsidiaries to create liens, to incur or guarantee debt, to pay dividends, to repurchase shares of the Company's common stock, to sell certain assets or subsidiary stock, to engage in certain mergers, to engage in certain transactions with affiliates or to alter the Company's current line of business.

(c) Option effects of debt: The shareholders in a heavily indebted firm have less to lose than those in a low-leverage firm. They may thus feel free to take more risks. Increased leverage may thus affect the riskiness of the firm's free cash flows (FCFs). An example: Bob and Jerry each own a similar building; the market value of each of their buildings is $100,000. The buildings are in need of a very expensive repair. Bob owns his building outright, whereas Jerry has a $99,000 mortgage on his building. Bob is much more likely to do the repairs, since he has more to lose; Jerry might well reason that in the worst case if something happens to his building, he'll default on his mortgage and let the bank take care of the problems.[2]

6. Finally, firms may be limited in their borrowing by the kinds of assets they own. If lenders require loan collateral, then firms with many fixed assets may be more easily able to borrow than firms with more "ephemeral" assets. Thus, even if Modigliani–Miller are right, and firms want to borrow as much as possible, it may be that software firms (with fewer tangible assets) are less able to borrow than real estate firms.

21.2 How Do Firms Capitalize?

One way to think about capital structure is to look at the actual capital structures for different companies and industries. As an example, consider Abbott Laboratories, a major American pharmaceutical firm: On 20 March 2002, Abbott's balance sheets showed debt of approximately $8.7 billion and equity of $10.7 billion. Using these book values of debt and equity, Abbott had a book value debt–equity ratio of 0.81:

$$\textit{Abbott Labs, book value, debt–equity ratio} = \frac{debt}{equity} = \frac{8.7}{10.7} = 0.81$$

---

[1] Empirical research in finance estimates bankruptcy costs as generally less than 10% of the face value of debt at the time of bankruptcy. If the Modigliani–Miller full tax shield on debt were to hold, it is unlikely that bankruptcy costs of this magnitude would retard corporate desires for more leverage. A recent paper (Timothy Fisher and M. Jocelyn Martel, "On Direct Bankruptcy Costs and the Firm's Bankruptcy Decision" (January 2001), http://ssrn.com/abstract=256128) gives interesting information of the size of bankruptcy and liquidation costs in Canada.

[2] Lenders know all about option effects. It causes them to restrict their lending and also to impose covenants on the borrowers.

The book value of Abbott's equity understates its market value. On 20 March 2002, Abbott had 1,563,436,372 shares outstanding; the market price per share was $51.80. Multiplying these two numbers together gives the market value of Abbott's equity as $81 billion, so that Abbott had a market value debt–equity ratio of 0.108:

$$Abbott\ Labs,\ market\ value,\ debt\text{–}equity\ ratio = \frac{debt}{equity} = \frac{8.7}{81.0} = 0.108$$

Finance professionals uniformly prefer market values to book values, so that this is our estimate for Abbott's debt–equity ratio.

The Debt-Equity Ratio of Pharmaceutical Firms

In the spreadsheet below we calculate the debt–equity ratio in both book and market values for major pharmaceutical companies.

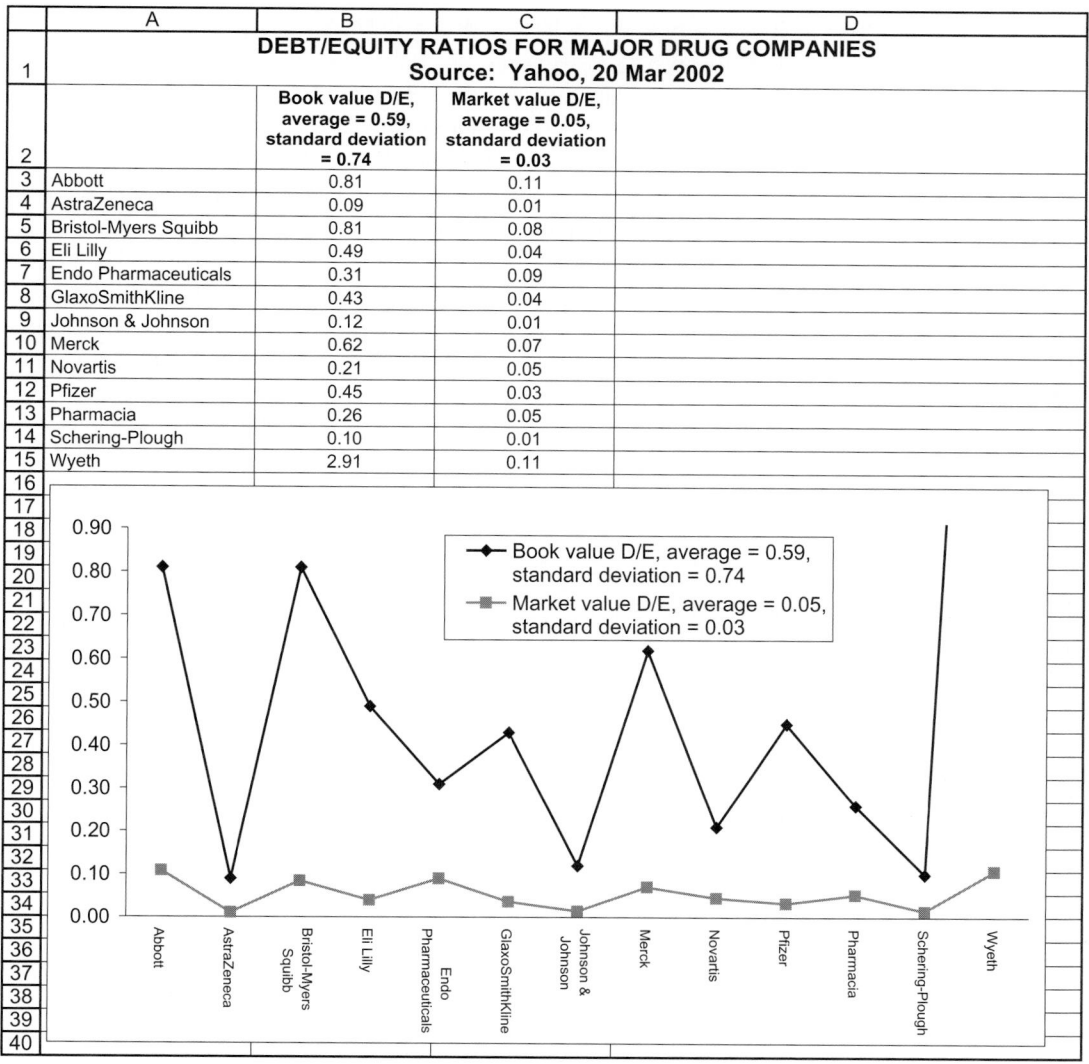

	A	B	C	D
1		DEBT/EQUITY RATIOS FOR MAJOR DRUG COMPANIES Source: Yahoo, 20 Mar 2002		
2		Book value D/E, average = 0.59, standard deviation = 0.74	Market value D/E, average = 0.05, standard deviation = 0.03	
3	Abbott	0.81	0.11	
4	AstraZeneca	0.09	0.01	
5	Bristol-Myers Squibb	0.81	0.08	
6	Eli Lilly	0.49	0.04	
7	Endo Pharmaceuticals	0.31	0.09	
8	GlaxoSmithKline	0.43	0.04	
9	Johnson & Johnson	0.12	0.01	
10	Merck	0.62	0.07	
11	Novartis	0.21	0.05	
12	Pfizer	0.45	0.03	
13	Pharmacia	0.26	0.05	
14	Schering-Plough	0.10	0.01	
15	Wyeth	2.91	0.11	
16				

Several things are clear from this data:

- The average market debt–equity ratio for these firms is approximately zero. If there is a value advantage to debt over equity, it appears that the pharmaceuticals have not realized this advantage.

- The variability in book debt–equity ratios is very large. It does not appear that drug companies appear to be striving for a common book debt–equity ratio.

Can we learn something from this data for pharmaceutical firms? To the author of this book, it appears that there is no evidence that pharmaceuticals are striving for any target debt–equity ratio. If, as we showed in Chapter 20 and Section 21.1, firm targeting of debt–equity ratios depends on the tax system, then the lack of a clear debt–equity pattern for pharmaceuticals indicates that the tax effects of debt–equity ratios are relatively neutral. In a word: The debt–equity ratios of the pharmaceutical sector are consistent with Merton Miller's hypothesis that $(1 - T_D) - (1 - T_C) * (1 - T_E) = 0$, so that there are no net tax benefits to either maximizing or minimizing the corporate debt–equity ratio.

The Debt-Equity Ratio of Other Industries

How does the pharmaceutical industry compare to retail grocery stores? As the graph below shows, grocery chains appear to have much higher debt–equity ratios than pharmaceutical firms. Having said this, the variation in debt–equity ratios for groceries is enormous. However, for grocery stores as for drug companies, there appears to be no evidence of a general trend:

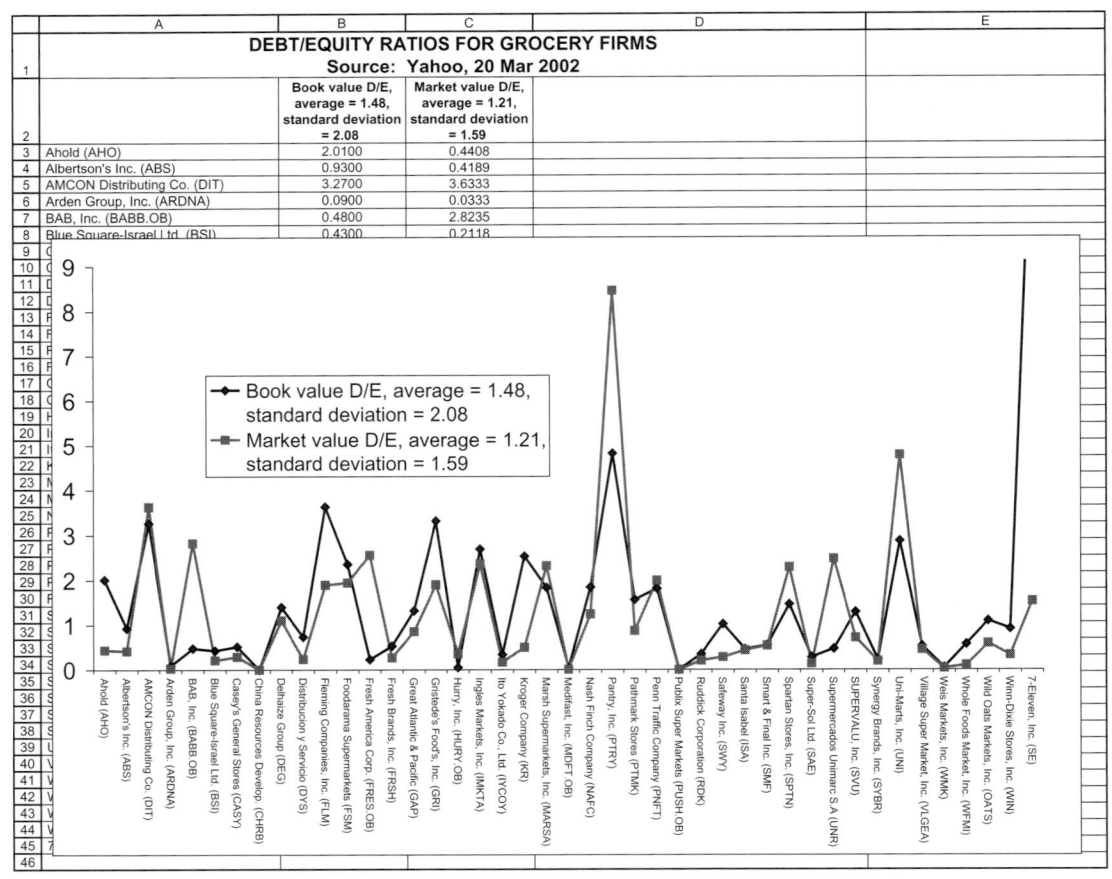

	A	B	C	D	E
1		**DEBT/EQUITY RATIOS FOR GROCERY FIRMS** Source: Yahoo, 20 Mar 2002			
2		Book value D/E, average = 1.48, standard deviation = 2.08	Market value D/E, average = 1.21, standard deviation = 1.59		
3	Ahold (AHO)	2.0100	0.4408		
4	Albertson's Inc. (ABS)	0.9300	0.4189		
5	AMCON Distributing Co. (DIT)	3.2700	3.6333		
6	Arden Group, Inc. (ARDNA)	0.0900	0.0333		
7	BAB, Inc. (BABB.OB)	0.4800	2.8235		
8	Blue Square-Israel Ltd. (BSI)	0.4300	0.2118		

Here's similar data for auto manufacturers:

	A	B	C	D
1	DEBT/EQUITY RATIOS FOR AUTO AND TRUCK MANUFACTURERS Source: Yahoo, 20 Mar 2002			
2		Book value D/E, average = 2.09, standard deviation = 3.12	Market value D/E, average = 1.76, standard deviation = 2.13	
3	Collins Industries (COLL)	0.6200	0.5905	
4	DaimlerChrysler(DCX)	2.3300	1.7007	
5	Featherlite (FTHR)	2.5600	6.9189	
6	Ford (F)	12.4500	5.1025	
7	General Motors (GM)	8.4400	4.8786	
8	Honda (HMC)	0.7600	0.6496	
9	Ingersoll-Rand (IR)	1.0000	0.4348	
10	Miller Industries (MLR)	0.9800	4.2609	
11	Monaco Coach (MNC)	0.3100	0.0845	
12	Navistar International (NAV)	2.4700	1.0292	
13	Oshkosh Truck (OTRKB)	0.9400	0.3345	
14	PACCAR (PCAR)	0.0600	0.0241	

In short: As viewed from the data, there does not appear to be a trend in debt–equity ratios, whether measured in book or market values. This is evidence in favor of *tax neutrality* with respect to debt–equity policy and against theories (like the Modigliani–Miller theory of capital structure with only corporate taxes) claiming debt is the preferred method of financing.

21.3 Measuring a Firm's Asset Beta (β_{Asset}) and WACC: An Example

In the previous section we concluded that there is little in actual firm financing patterns to indicate a preference for debt. This seeming indifference to debt raises doubts as to whether debt actually makes a difference in the valuation of a firm. Another way to measure the valuation effects is to look at a firm's *asset beta,* and to ask whether this β_{Asset} is affected by a firm's debt–equity ratio.

In this section we show how we measure β_{Asset} for Ford Motor Company. As discussed in Section 16.4, we use this β_{Asset} to compute the Ford's WACC using the formula

$$WACC = r_f + \beta_{Asset} * [E(r_M) - r_f]$$

Our primary interest in this section is not the WACC, however. Rather:

- We want to carefully show you how to use public sources of information (in this case Yahoo; see Figure 21.1) to compute a firm's debt beta, debt–equity ratio, and asset beta.
- We want to set the stage for the next section, in which we compute β_{Asset} for all the firms in the auto and truck industry in the United States. This enables us to ask whether β_{Asset} is affected by the debt–equity ratio, and to perform our own "homemade" test of the capital structure propositions of the previous chapter. The answer appears to be negative—for this industry we cannot find an effect of debt on β_{Asset}. Our conclusion is that the debt–equity mix does not affect the weighted average cost of capital (WACC).

For the moment we concentrate on the first bullet and compute some numbers for Ford. All the data come from Yahoo.

Ford's Cost of Debt and Debt Beta β_D

At the end of 2000, Ford reported income expense of $10.902 billion. Combined with the debts on the balance sheets for 2000 and 1999, we can conclude that Ford's interest rate was 6.62%:

	A	B	C
1		**FORD MOTOR COMPANY**	
2		**2000**	**1999**
3	Short-term debt	277,000,000	1,602,000,000
4	Long-term debt	169,503,000,000	158,150,000,000
5	Total debt	169,780,000,000	159,752,000,000
6			
7	Interest expense	10,902,000,000	
8	Implied interest rate	6.62% <-- =B7/AVERAGE(B5:C5)	

Yahoo gives Ford's equity β as 1.07 (Figure 21.2). In order to compute Ford's debt beta β_D, we use the following computation:

$$cost\ of\ debt = r_D = r_f + \beta_D * [E(r_M) - r_f]$$

This is the SML for debt. Since we know that $r_D = 6.62\%$, we can solve for β_D. To do this, we assume that $r_f = 4.80\%$ and that $E(r_M) - r_f = 5\%$:

$$\beta_D = \frac{r_D - r_f}{E(r_M) - r_f} = \frac{6.62\% - 4.80\%}{5\%} = 0.3633$$

	A	B	C
10	Risk-free rate	4.80%	
11	Market risk premium	5%	
12	Debt beta	0.3633 <-- =(B8-B10)/B11	

FORD MOTOR COMPANY FINANCIAL STATEMENTS		
Income statement	**31 Dec. 2000**	
Total revenue	170,064,000,000	
Cost of revenue	126,120,000,000	
Gross profit	43,944,000,000	
Selling, general and administrative expenses	14,855,000,000	
Other operating expenses	11,371,000,000	
Operating income	17,718,000,000	
Other income and net expenses	1,418,000,000	
Earnings before interest and taxes	19,136,000,000	
Interest expense	10,902,000,000	
Income before tax	8,234,000,000	
Income tax expense	2,705,000,000	
Minority interest	119,000,000	
Net income	5,410,000,000	
Balance sheet	**31 Dec. 2000**	**31 Dec. 1999**
Current assets		
Cash and cash equivalents	4,851,000,000	6,230,000,000
Short term investments	13,116,000,000	18,943,000,000
Net receivables	136,312,000,000	9,945,000,000
Inventory	7,514,000,000	6,435,000,000
Other current assets	5,318,000,000	4,126,000,000
Total current assets	167,111,000,000	45,679,000,000
Long term assets		
Long term investments	50,359,000,000	161,081,000,000
Property, plant and equipment	37,508,000,000	42,317,000,000
Other assets	26,101,000,000	24,336,000,000
Deferred long term asset charges	3,342,000,000	2,816,000,000
Total assets	**284,421,000,000**	**276,229,000,000**
Current liabilities		
Accounts payable	48,347,000,000	39,789,000,000
Short term and current long term debt	277,000,000	1,602,000,000
Total current liabilities	48,624,000,000	41,391,000,000
Long term debt	169,503,000,000	158,150,000,000
Other liabilities	37,981,000,000	40,022,000,000
Deferred Long term liability charges	9,030,000,000	8,454,000,000
Total liabilities	265,138,000,000	248,017,000,000
Equity		
Preferred stock	673,000,000	675,000,000
Common stock	19,000,000	1,222,000,000
Retained earnings	17,884,000,000	24,606,000,000
Capital surplus	6,174,000,000	3,632,000,000
Other stockholder equity	-5,467,000,000	-1,923,000,000
Total equity	19,283,000,000	28,212,000,000
Total liabilities and equity	**284,421,000,000**	**276,229,000,000**

Figure 21.1 The Ford computations in Section 21.3 are based on Ford's balance sheets and income statements above.

Ford's Debt–Equity Ratio

Yahoo gives Ford's debt–equity ratio as 12.45. However, this ratio is in book values, and we want the market value debt–equity ratio. Yahoo also gives Ford's "price–book" ratio as 2.45— by this is meant the ratio of the market price of Ford's shares to their book value. We can now

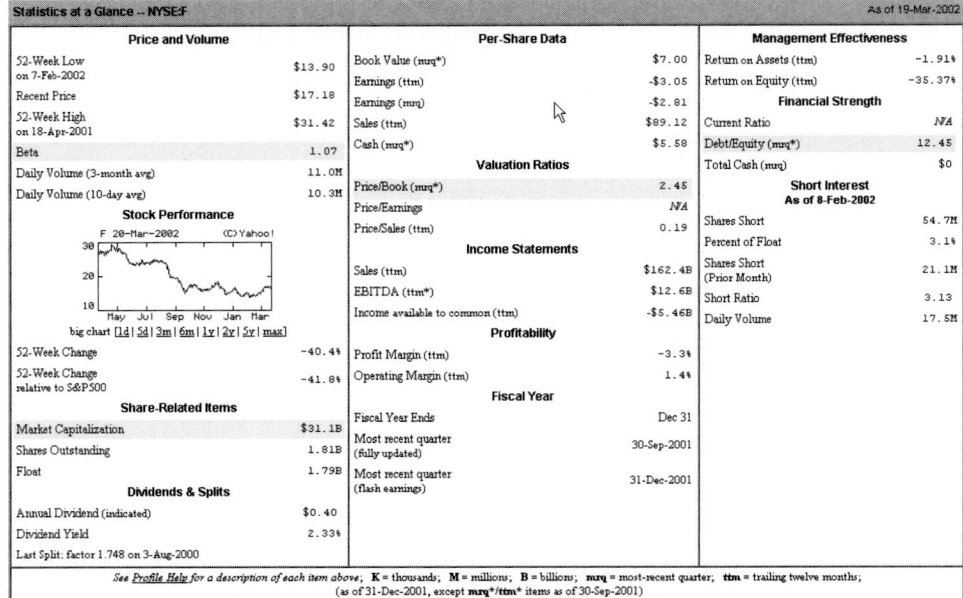

Figure 21.2 Financial profile of Ford, from Yahoo.

compute the market debt–equity ratio:

$$market\ debt–equity = \frac{book\ debt}{book\ equity} * \frac{1}{\underbrace{\dfrac{market\ equity}{book\ equity}}}$$

This is the "market–book"
ratio given in Yahoo

$$= 12.45 * \frac{1}{2.45} = 5.08$$

(Notice that we've assumed that the book value and market value of debt are equal. This is a very common assumption, which we previously discussed in Chapters 9 and 16.)

In our spreadsheet:

	A	B	C
14	Debt/Equity, book values	12.45	
15	Price/Book	2.45	
16	Debt/Equity, market values	5.08	<-- =B14/B15

Computing the Percentage of Debt in the Capital Structure, $D/(E + D)$

We now compute the ratio of the firm's debt to its total value of equity plus debt, $D/(E + D)$. From the previous calculation, we know that the debt–equity ratio in market values is 5.08. We use some algebra to compute $D/(E + D)$ from the D/E:

$$market\ value\ \frac{D}{E + D} = \frac{D}{E + D} * \frac{\frac{1}{E}}{\frac{1}{E}} = \frac{D/E}{1 + D/E} = \frac{5.08}{1 + 5.08} = 0.8356$$

We can now also compute

$$\frac{E}{E+D} = 1 - \frac{D}{E+D} = 0.1644$$

Computing Ford's Tax Rate T_C

To compute Ford's tax rate, we take its income tax expense and divide it into its pretax income:

	A	B	C
21	Income before tax	8,234,000,000	
22	Income tax expense	2,705,000,000	
23	Tax rate	32.85%	<-- =B22/B21

Computing Ford's Asset Beta β_{Asset}

The formula for β_{Asset} is

$$\beta_{Asset} = \beta_E * \frac{E}{E+D} + \beta_D * (1 - T_C) * \frac{D}{E+D}$$

where

$\beta_E = equity\ beta$

$\beta_D = debt\ beta$

$\dfrac{E}{E+D} = percent\ of\ equity; \quad \dfrac{D}{E+D} = percent\ of\ debt$

To do this computation, we use Yahoo's estimate of Ford's equity beta, $\beta_E = 1.07$, and we use our calculation of Ford's $T_C = 32.85\%$. Ford's asset beta is $\beta_{Asset} = 0.3798$:

	A	B	C
1	**FORD MOTOR COMPANY**		
2		**2000**	**1999**
3	Short-term debt	277,000,000	1,602,000,000
4	Long-term debt	169,503,000,000	158,150,000,000
5	Total debt	169,780,000,000	159,752,000,000
6			
7	Interest expense	10,902,000,000	
8	Implied interest rate	6.62%	<-- =B7/AVERAGE(B5:C5)
9			
10	Risk-free rate	4.80%	
11	Market risk premium	5%	
12	Debt beta	0.3633	<-- =(B8-B10)/B11
13			
14	Debt/Equity, book values	12.45	
15	Price/Book	2.45	
16	Debt/Equity, market values	5.08	<-- =B14/B15
17			
18	Debt/Assets, market values	0.8356	<-- =B16/(B16+1)
19	Equity/Assets, market values	0.1644	<-- =1-B18
20			
21	Income before tax	8,234,000,000	
22	Income tax expense	2,705,000,000	
23	Tax rate	32.85%	<-- =B22/B21
24			
25	Equity beta	1.07	
26	Asset beta	0.3798	<-- =B25*B19+B12*B18*(1-B23)

21.4 Repeating the Asset Beta (β_{Asset}) Calculation for an Industry

In the previous section we showed how to calculate β_{Asset} for Ford. Suppose we repeat this calculation for all American manufacturers of autos and trucks. The results are displayed on page 639. Here's the graph that relates the firms' debt–equity ratios and asset betas:

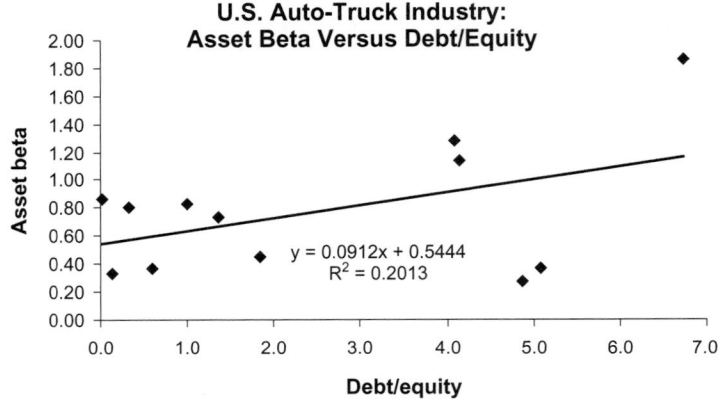

The graph shows a slight upward trend:

$$asset\ beta\ for\ autos = 0.5444 + 0.0912 * \frac{debt}{equity}, \quad R^2 = 20.13\%$$

Using this equation, we would conclude that the β_{Asset} for an unleveraged auto firm is 0.54, and that increased leverage adds to this β_{Asset}. A more careful analysis (not repeated here, but on the disk that accompanies this book) reveals that the positive slope is not statistically significant. Meaning: At least for this small sample, we can conclude that β_{Asset} is not affected by the capital structure. This is Miller's position:

- If the Modigliani–Miller results are representative, then the WACC will decrease when the amount of debt increases. The effect on β_{Asset} will be that β_{Asset} should decrease as leverage increases.
- If the Miller results are representative, then the WACC will be unaffected by the amount of debt. The effect on β_{Asset} will be that β_{Asset} should stay constant as leverage increases.

Overall, β_{Asset} seems to increase slightly with leverage for auto firms. The effect is not large and is statistically insignificant; if it were significant, it would be consistent with a *tax disadvantage* to debt. So—at least for the auto industry—Miller's theory seems to do better at explaining things than the MM theory.

One More Industry

The experiment we performed on the auto industry in the first part of this section is just that—a small experiment to see if we can find any effects of leverage on asset betas. To show that this experiment is not a fluke, we repeat it for the grocery industry:

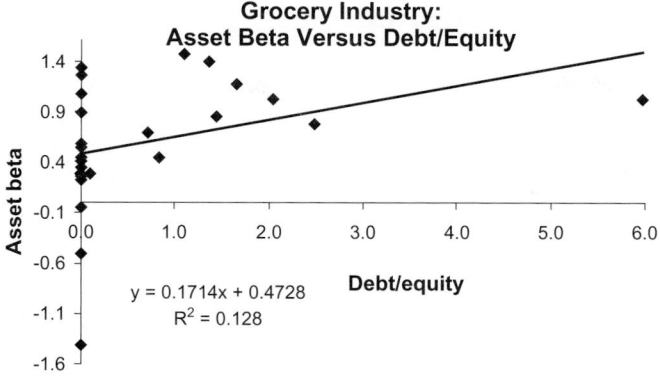

As for the auto industry, there seems to be a slight upward trend in the asset beta as a function of the debt–quity ratio of grocery firms. And, as for the auto industry, this upward slope, when subjected to more statistical scrutiny, is not significant. We conclude (again) that there is little evidence that leverage affects the asset beta and the WACC.

Several further notes about the grocery industry:

- The average equity β for grocery firms was 0.366 (with a standard deviation of 0.568—meaning that the equity beta was very widely dispersed).

- The average asset β for these firms was 0.594 (with a $\sigma = 0.638$).

- In a period (1999–2000) where the risk-free rate of interest was around 5%, these firms paid average interest rates of 16.75% (with $\sigma = 4.39\%$). Thus, while shareholders perceived these firms as having fairly low risk, lenders perceived them as having very high risks—the average $\beta_D = 2.39$ (with $\sigma = 0.88$).

	A	B	C	D	E	F	G	H	I	J	K
1		**ASSET BETAS FOR AMERICAN TRUCK AND AUTO COMPANIES**									
2		Equity beta	Debt beta	Tax rate	Market value of equity	Debt/Equity book values	Price/Book	Debt/Equity market values	Debt/Assets market values	Equity/Assets market values	Asset beta
3	Collins Industries (COLL)	0.150	1.134	35.31%	28.1	0.62	1.05	0.59	0.3713	0.6287	0.3667
4	Featherlite (FTHR)	0.800	2.162	6.87%	7.51	2.56	0.38	6.74	0.8707	0.1293	1.8569
5	Ford (F)	1.070	0.363	37.98%	31.1	12.45	2.45	5.08	0.8356	0.1644	0.3642
6	General Motors (GM)	1.120	0.147	33.40%	34	8.44	1.73	4.88	0.8299	0.1701	0.2715
7	Miller Industries (MLR)	1.560	1.811	33.03%	24.9	0.98	0.24	4.08	0.8033	0.1967	1.2809
8	Navistar International (NAV)	1.490	0.233	29.02%	2.65	2.47	2.47	1.00	0.5000	0.5000	0.8275
9	Oshkosh Truck (OTRKB)	0.930	0.674	37.25%	987.6	0.94	2.82	0.33	0.2500	0.7500	0.8032
10	PACCAR (PCAR)	0.880	0.627	33.57%	5.82	0.06	2.58	0.02	0.0227	0.9773	0.8695
11	Rush Enterprises (RUSH)	0.520	2.133	39.99%	49.4	2.53	0.61	4.15	0.8057	0.1943	1.1325
12	Spartan Motors (SPAR)	0.360	0.199	30.37%	86.6	0.36	2.53	0.14	0.1246	0.8754	0.3324
13	Supreme Industries (STS)	0.390	0.793	39.00%	65.9	2.27	1.23	1.85	0.6486	0.3514	0.4509
14	Wabash National (WNC)	0.910	0.984	39.04%	240.5	1.22	0.9	1.36	0.5755	0.4245	0.7316
15											
16	Average	0.848	0.938	32.90%							0.774
17	Standard deviation	0.437	0.733	0.089							0.473
18											
19											
20											
21											
22											
23											
24											
25											
26											
27											
28											
29											
30											
31											
32											
33											
34											

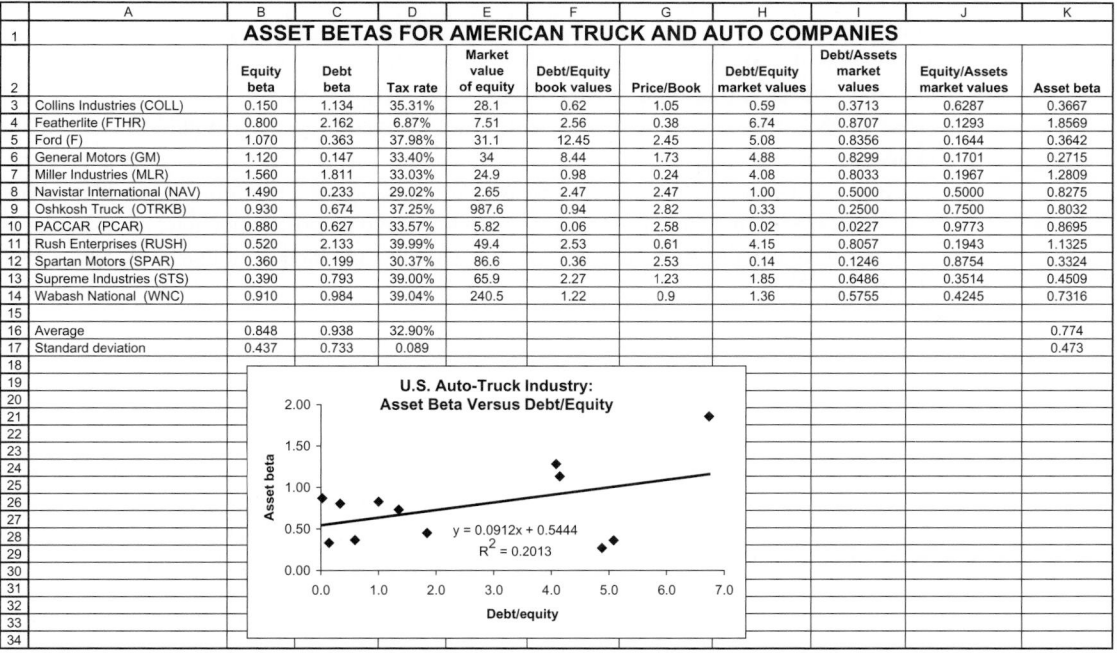

21.5 Academic Evidence

In the previous section we looked at a specific example—the U.S. auto–truck industry—to try to gauge whether capital structure affects the β_{Asset} of these firms. Our conclusion is that, for this industry, they don't: The β_{Asset}, and hence the WACC, is not affected by the capital structure.

Recent academic research seems to come to the same conclusion.[3]

- When Eugene Fama and Kenneth French regress firm value on leverage, they conclude that leverage doesn't matter.[4]

- John Graham, in a survey published in 2001, concludes that "at the margin the tax costs and tax benefits [of leverage] might be of similar magnitude."[5] To show you how confusing this is, Graham concludes that—using another method—the tax benefit of debt is approximately 9% for the years 1995–1999.[6] This probably represents the costs of bankruptcy.

- Ivo Welch, in a paper written in 2002, finds no evidence whatsoever that firms look for an optimal structure.[7] He finds that firms tend to make few changes in their debt, so that the actual capital structure (that is, the ratio of debt to the market value of equity) is largely driven by the market prices of the firm's shares. There is little evidence, according to Welch, of any optimizing in the debt decision.

CONCLUSION

The theory of capital structure suggests that the capital structure decision is driven largely by the differential taxation of debt and equity. The empirics of capital structure suggest that it doesn't matter very much in determining the value of the firm.

For practical purposes:

- You can assume that the weighted average cost of capital (WACC) of a firm is invariant to the firm's capital structure.

- This means that the WACC of a firm can be measured by taking the *average WACC* of the firm's industry. It also means that the asset beta (β_{Asset}) of a firm's industry is representative of the industry's overall risks and is not a function of the capital structure of the industry.

- The best way to value a firm is to use the WACC to discount the firm's anticipated future free cash flows (recall that these are operating cash flows and do not include interest and other financing). We have illustrated this approach in a number of chapters of this book: Chapters 9, 10, and 16.

---

[3]Be warned that this is still controversial. Every finance professor seems to have an opinion on this matter! If you want a good grade in the course, disagree with the book and not with your professor.

[4]"Taxes, Financing Decisions, and Firm Value," *Journal of Finance,* 1998, pp. 819–843.

[5]"Taxes and Corporate Finance: A Review," *Review of Financial Studies,* 2003, pp. 1075–1129.

[6]Ibid, pages 26–27.

[7]Ivo Welch, "Columbus' Egg: The Real Determinants of Capital Structure," Yale School of Management working paper, 2002.

A Final Example

We conclude with a final example, which shows our technique for using industry data to compute the WACC of a particular company. Suppose that we wish to compute the WACC for Duke Energy Corporation (DUK). After doing some research we decide that Duke's "peer group" is composed of the seven companies listed below. We use Yahoo to compute the equity capitalization E, equity β, cost of debt, tax rate T_C, and total debt D for each of the companies:

	A	B	C	D	E	F	G	H
1	COMPUTING THE WACC FOR DUKE ENERGY CORPORATION (DUK)							
2	$E(r_M)$	10.45%			6			
3	r_f	2.80%						
4	Company name (stock symbol)	Equity market capitalization (billion $)	Equity beta	Cost of equity	Cost of debt	Tax rate	Total debt (billion $)	WACC
5	American Electric Power (AEP)	14.10	0.400	6.48%	5.80%	40.68%	12.85	5.03%
6	CenterPoint Energy, Inc. (CNP)	3.70	0.697	9.21%	8.52%	32.53%	17.62	6.35%
7	Duke Energy Corporation (DUK)	26.00	0.626	8.56%	4.46%	24.44%	16.93	6.51%
8	Entergy (ETR)	0.91	0.311	5.66%	6.05%	37.61%	2.55	4.27%
9	FPL Group (FPL)	14.79	0.287	5.44%	4.33%	29.18%	9.74	4.50%
10	Progress Energy (PGN)	10.98	0.216	4.79%	5.81%	15.53%	10.66	4.85%
11	Wisconsin Energy Corporat (WEC)	4.10	0.058	3.33%	5.45%	35.62%	3.45	3.41%
12	XCel Energy (XEL)	7.37	0.664	8.91%	3.58%	23.65%	6.79	5.95%
13	Average		0.407	6.55%	5.50%	29.90%		5.11%

The Excel spreadsheet shows the current WACC for each of the companies. The *average* (5.11%) is the WACC we would use to value Duke Energy.[8]

---

[8]Computations are shown on the Excel notebook **pfe_chap21.xls,** which is on the CD-ROM accompanying this book.

DIVIDEND POLICY

OVERVIEW

When John started his college finance course in the fall semester of 2004, his grandmother gave him 100 shares of General Motors (GM) stock. "Owning shares is the best way to understand the stock market," she said to him. "When you own a stock, you'll start following the company." The succeeding months proved her right—stock ownership was very educational. John started to follow both the stock market and GM. Some of the fruits of his learning are in this introduction.

The present of 100 GM shares was a substantial gift: At the time his grandmother gave John the stock, a share of GM was trading for $41.10, so that Grandma's present was worth $4,110. During the months following the gift, GM's stock price went as high as $43.14 on

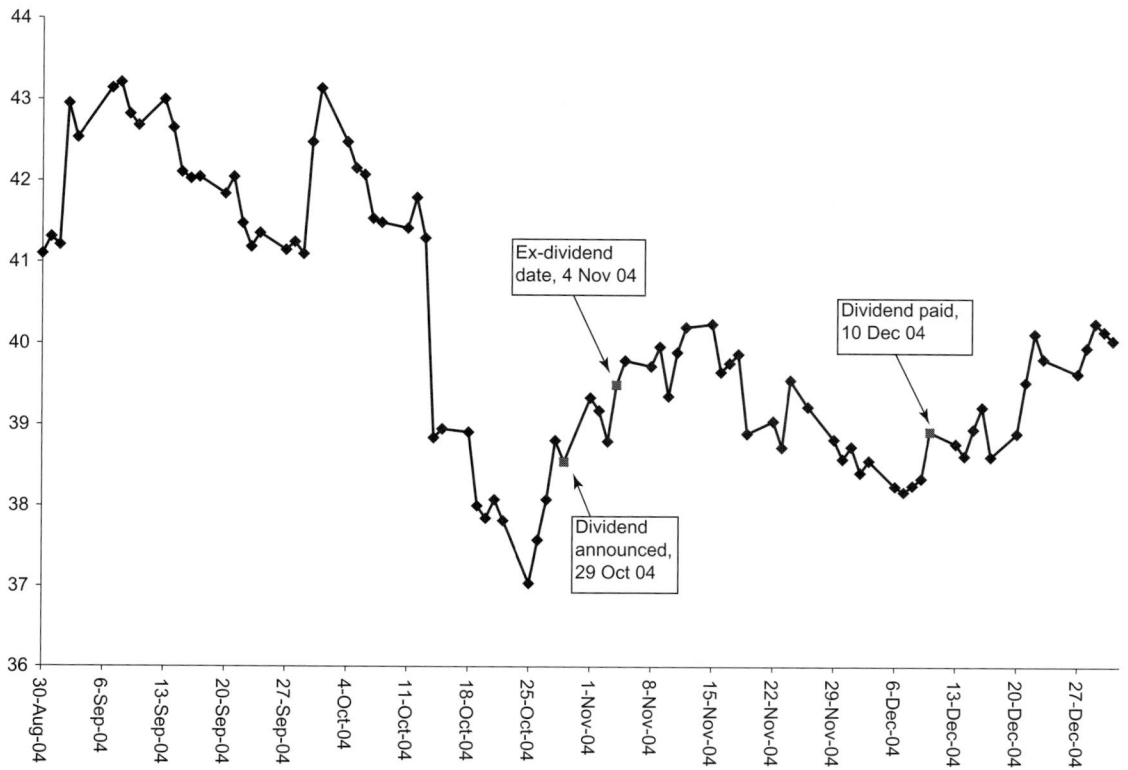

Figure 22.1 GM's stock price, 30 August 2004 to 31 December 2004.

8 September 2004 and as low as $37.04 on 25 October 2004 (Figure 22.1). John also followed the news about the company, which was mostly depressing (Figure 22.2).

Then on 29 October 2004, John read that GM had declared a $0.50 dividend per share (Figure 22.3). Since he owned 100 shares, he realized that this meant that he was about to get $50 from GM. Reading the announcement, John saw that he had to learn some new terminology:

- The *dividend payment date* was 10 December 2004. This is the date on which the dividend would actually be paid out to the GM shareholders.

- The dividend is payable to *holders of record* as of 8 November 2004. This means that only shareholders listed with GM on this date got the dividend.

- Because it takes two business days to register a change in ownership of a share, the dividend is actually only paid to shareholders who own the stock at the close of trading on 4 November 2004.[1] This date is referred to as the *ex-dividend date* of the stock.

John spent some time thinking about whether the dividend was a good thing or a bad thing. He soon realized that there were a considerable number of factors. In succeeding subsections we show John's thinking about the various factors affecting the dividend.

---

[1] 8 November 2004 was a Monday. Two business days before this Monday was Thursday 4 November 2004.

Cadillac: Better But Not Best Yet, **at Forbes.com** (Tue, Dec 14)

Ford, GM Earnings Outlooks Trimmed, **at Forbes.com** (Mon, Dec 13)

GM Signs up its One Millionth XM Satellite Radio Subscriber, **PR Newswire** (Mon, Dec 13)

Delphi Hurt By Lower GM Output, Troubled Suppliers, **at Forbes.com** (Fri, Dec 10)

General Motors bonds fall on word of job cuts, **at MarketWatch** (Thu, Dec 9)

GM to cut 12,000 jobs in Europe, **at MarketWatch** (Thu, Dec 9)

GM recalling 640 Saab 9-3 cars for free repair, **at Forbes.com** (Thu, Dec 9)

Open Letter to General Motors' CFO, **at RealMoney by TheStreet.com** (Thu, Dec 9)
GM should refinance at least half its 2005 and 2006 maturities while rates remain low. The company's future is threatened by any increase in bond yields.

GM's Desperation Gets Noisier, **Motley Fool** (Thu, Dec 9)
Yesterday, **General Motors** (NYSE: *GM - News*) beat its own previous personal best for crazy sales incentives (read about those *here*) and went for broke, instituting a *"Red Tag"* sale and bumping incentives on some 2004 models up to—better sit down for this—$7,500. And this is not just some gimmick to move the last few 2004 models off the lot, either. The company is apparently also offering rebates of up to $4,500 on select 2005 models as well—considerably more than the average $3,500 in incentives (on both 2004 and 2005 models) the company offered in *November*.

GM Sputters Toward 2005 Breakdown, **at RealMoney by TheStreet.com** (Thu, Dec 9)

GM Beefs Up Incentives After Poor Nov., **Associated Press** (Thu, Dec 9)

GM Europe Pledges to Avoid Plant Closures, **Associated Press** (Wed, Dec 8)

Saturn sees improved view, **at MarketWatch** (Wed, Dec 8)

Fiat may force GM to buy struggling unit, **at FT.com** (Mon, Dec 6)

Automakers Telling the Same Tale, **Motley Fool** (Fri, Dec 3)

SUV registrations slowing across country, **at MarketWatch** (Thu, Dec 2)

Ford, GM to Lower Production in 2005, **Associated Press** (Wed, Dec 1)

GM Sales Fall 13.1 Percent in November, **Associated Press** (Wed, Dec 1)

NEWS: Commentary: Sorry Detroit. The Garage Is Full **at BusinessWeek Online** (Wed, Dec 1)
Why the gloom? For the past three years, as auto makers have thrown ever better deals at buyers, sales have remained essentially flat at around 16.7 million vehicles. Even if sales hit about 16.8 million, as analysts expect, that won't be enough to help Detroit. Ford and General Motors (*GM*) are already having a tough time making money selling cars, while Chrysler (*DCX*) has only recently gotten a lift from some hot models.

GM to Lay Off About 1,000 at N.J. Plant, **Associated Press** (Tue, Nov 30)

2004 Was Record Year for Auto Recalls, **Associated Press** (Tue, Nov 30)

Junk Alert **at Forbes.com** (Mon, Nov 29)
The way things are trending lately, I believe that at least one rating agency will downgrade the auto giants to junk by this time next year. But don't let that stop you from buying Ford's and GM's bonds, with their nice yields. What's gone wrong with the big two car companies? Just about everything: loss of market share, humongous retiree costs, union difficulties, restructuring, rising raw materials prices, excessive inventory, lackluster new products. And what's right with them? They are big car companies, and they won't disappear. Ford and GM are two of the largest corporate bond issuers, with $168 billion and $284 billion, respectively, in consolidated debt (that is, with finance arms included). That means almost every sizable public pension fund and bond mutual fund holds their paper. A downgrade to junk would disqualify some of these investors, and they would have to sell their bonds eventually. But they will not be forced to do so suddenly. Prices, after a brief downdraft, will rebound. Someone buying now and holding for years (better still, to maturity) can afford to shrug off the downgrade.

Automakers Rein In Growth As Downgrades Loom, **at Forbes.com** (Wed, Nov 24)

GM prepares for healthcare cost inflation, **at FT.com** (Thu, Nov 11)

Figure 22.2 A selection of headlines about GM, September–December 2004. During the fall of 2004, most of the news about the company was bad. *Source:* http://finance.yahoo.com.

US carmakers set to launch new incentives, **at FT.com** (Mon, Nov 8)

Ford, GM October Sales Skid, **at TheStreet.com** (Wed, Nov 3)

GM Stuck in Reverse, **at TheStreet.com** (Thu, Oct 14)

Can't Ignore GM's Side of Economy, **at RealMoney by TheStreet.com** (Thu, Oct 14)
The national implications of the hapless auto industry must somehow get on the national agenda, pronto.
General Motors axes 12,000 jobs in Europe, **at FT.com** (Thu, Oct 14)

Big Autos Lag Other Transports, **RealMoney by TheStreet.com** (Tue, Oct 5)

Interest rates push US drivers into cheaper cars, **at FT.com** (Sun, Oct 3)

Auto Sales Mixed as Ford Raises Incentives, **at TheStreet.com** (Fri, Oct 1)

GM aims for further cost cuts across company, **at FT.com** (Wed, Sep 29)

Welcome to the Bankruptcy Economy, **at TheStreet.com** (Wed, Sep 22)
At General Motors . . . the average cost of providing health care and pension benefits is around $1,360 a car.
That's more per car than General Motors spends for steel. At Honda's U.S. operations, the health care and
pension-benefit cost is only $107 a car.

Ford, GM Have Low Reliability Ratings, **at RealMoney by TheStreet.com** (Wed, Sep 15)

Tough Month for Automakers, **at TheStreet.com** (Wed, Sep 1)

Figure 22.2 *Continued*

News   *General Motors*   GM Communications
                                                     media.gm.com

FOR RELEASE: 2004-10-29

CONTACTS

GM Declares Quarterly Dividend

DETROIT – General Motors Corp. (NYSE: GM) today announced a fourth-quarter dividend of
$0.50 per share on GM common stock. The dividend is payable Dec. 10, 2004, to holders of
record as of Nov. 8, 2004. The dividend rate is unchanged from the previous quarter.

General Motors, the world's largest vehicle manufacturer, designs, builds and markets cars
and trucks worldwide, and has been the global automotive sales leader since 1931. More
information on GM can be found at www.gm.com.

Figure 22.3 GM's dividend press release, 29 October 2004. *Source:* http://www.gm.com/
company/investor_information/div_info/div_hist.html.

The Dividend as Information

During the fall of 2004, the news about GM was almost unremittingly bad (see Figure 22.2). The
company's sales were dropping, its healthcare costs were ten times those of Honda, its bonds
were rumored to be downgraded, and it was forced to offer enormous rebates and incentives to
potential car buyers.

The dividend did not do much to counteract this pessimism about the company. Looking
back over the dividend history of GM, John saw that the company had paid a $0.50 per share
dividend each February, May, August, and November going back to 1997. Had GM raised its

dividend, perhaps John would have been able to interpret the dividend as a piece of positive information about GM. And had the company cut its dividend, this might have been interpreted as bad news. But keeping the dividend steady could hardly be interpreted as a meaningful signal about the company.

The Dividend and Ordinary Income Taxes

The GM dividend would be part of John's taxable income. As a relatively low-income student, John's income tax rate was only 15%, but still this meant that John would have to pay $15 * \$50 = \$7.50$ in taxes on the dividend, so that his net receipts from the dividend would be $42.50 instead of $50. John realized that for his grandmother, whose tax rate was 40%, the dividend would be much more costly—had she received the dividend, it would have cost her $20 in taxes, so that she would receive only $30 in net dividends.

On the other hand, John saw in Yahoo (Figure 22.4) that 77% of GM stock was owned by pension funds and mutual funds, which do not directly pay income taxes on their dividend income. So perhaps, he thought, the General Motors dividend policy is based on the assumption that, for most shareholders, taxes on dividends are irrelevant.

The Dividend and Capital Gains Taxes: Dividend Reinvestment Versus Retention by the Company

John actually planned to reinvest his dividends into GM stock. This meant that on receiving the dividend on 10 December 2004, he would spend his after-tax dividend of $42.50 on buying new shares of GM. Since the GM share price on 10 December was $38.93, John would buy $\$42.50/\$38.93 = 1.0917$ shares of GM stock.

John contrasted his reinvestment of dividends with the alternative of GM not paying out dividends at all. If GM had not paid out a dividend and retained the income, he assumed that the

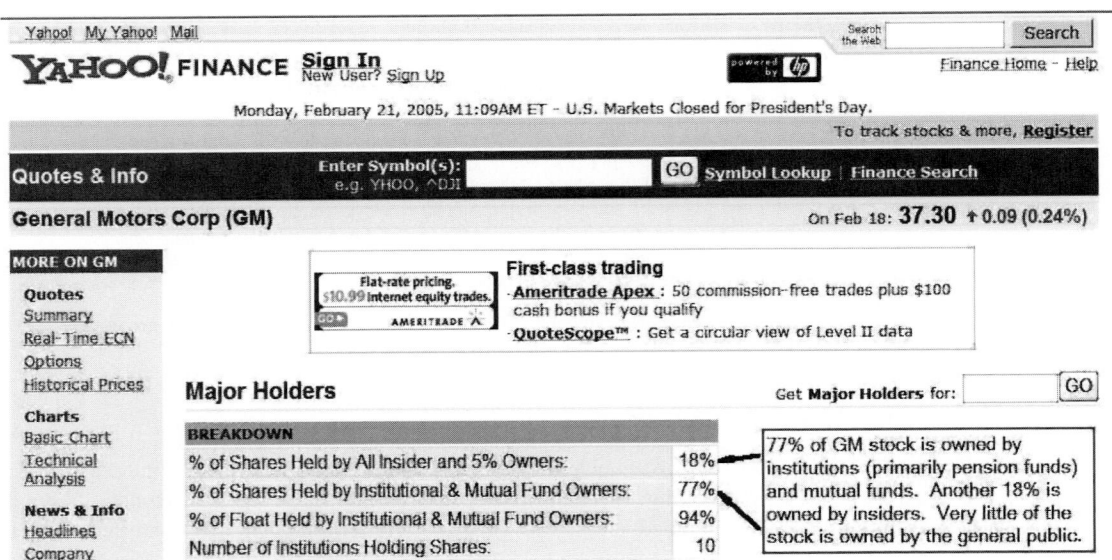

Figure 22.4 Note that 77% of GM stock is owned by pension funds and mutual funds, which do not directly pay taxes on their income, so that tax considerations in the payment of dividends by GM may not be critical.

stock price should increase by $0.50 per share. In this case he would have been better off in at least two ways:

- First of all, if the company had not paid out the dividend, John would have netted $0.50 per share instead of the $0.425 per share he actually got after income taxes. The company would have saved him the ordinary income taxes on his dividends.
- Had GM not paid out the dividends and had John ultimately sold his shares of GM, the gain of $0.50 per share would be taxed as a capital gain instead of as ordinary income. Since capital gains tax rates are lower than ordinary tax rates, John would have benefited a second way from the dividend retention.

Combining these three factors—information, income taxes, and capital gains taxes,—John realized that he needed some financial theory to help him understand dividends. The remainder of this chapter explores this theory.

Finance Concepts Discussed

- Dividends
- Retained earnings
- Capital gains versus ordinary income

Excel Functions Used

- We use a lot of Excel spreadsheets to put order in things, but truth to tell, this chapter uses hardly any sophisticated Excel concepts. The one function used is **Sum.**

22.1 The Financial Theory of Dividends

To help us consider the pure financial theory of dividends, we consider the story of John and Mary, both of whom own wholly identical taxi companies that differ only in their dividend policies. Each company owns the same number of taxis and has the same income and expenses. Here are the balance sheets for the two companies:

JOHN'S TAXI COMPANY, MARY'S TAXI COMPANY			
Assets		**Liabilities and equity**	
Cash	5,000	Debt	10,000
Taxis	20,000	Equity	
		Stock	5,000
		Accumulated retained earnings	10,000
Total assets	**25,000**	**Total liabilities and equity**	**25,000**

John Pays Himself a Dividend

Suppose that John wants some cash and decides to declare a dividend of $3,000. Here's the way his balance sheet looks (Mary's balance sheet is unchanged):

JOHN'S TAXI COMPANY--after dividend			
Assets		**Liabilities and equity**	
Cash	2,000	Debt	10,000
Taxis	20,000	Equity	
		Stock	5,000
		Accumulated retained earnings	7,000
Total assets	**22,000**	**Total liabilities and equity**	**22,000**

There are two changes in John's balance sheet:

- The cash balances decrease from $5,000 to $2,000, reflecting the dividend paid.
- The accumulated retained earnings decrease from $10,000 to $7,000. This is what is meant by the expression that "dividends are paid out of retained earnings." We don't like this expression, since dividends are paid out of cash; the decrease in retentions simply reflects the matching change made in the balance sheet.

Here are some questions you could ask about this situation:

Question 1: What are the valuation effects of the dividend?

Did the dividend paid by John change the value of his taxi business vis-à-vis Mary's business? Obviously not—they both still have the same number of taxis, and Mary has just kept her cash in the business instead of, as John did, pulling it out. A good way to see this is to write the balance sheets in terms of net debt—subtracting the cash from the debt:

JOHN'S or MARY'S TAXI COMPANY--net debt			
Assets		**Liabilities and equity**	
		Net debt = Debt - cash	5,000
Taxis	20,000	Equity	
		Stock	5,000
		Accumulated retained earnings	10,000
Total assets	**20,000**	**Total liabilities and equity**	**20,000**

JOHN'S TAXI COMPANY--after dividend			
Assets		**Liabilities and equity**	
		Net debt = Debt - cash	8,000
Taxis	20,000	Equity	
		Stock	5,000
		Accumulated retained earnings	7,000
Total assets	**20,000**	**Total liabilities and equity**	**20,000**

The asset side of the balance sheet is still worth the same, whether or not the dividend has been paid. On the other hand, the liabilities and equity side of the balance sheet is different—John has more debt and less equity than Mary.

Question 2: Perhaps it's just a capital structure question?

The above balance sheets for the two companies show that, while they are both the same on the asset side, the dividend has changed the capital structure of the companies. So perhaps the dividend question is related to the capital structure problem discussed in Chapters 20 and 21. If so, this suggests:

- *Dividends might matter if capital structure matters: An after-dividend company (like John's) will have a higher debt–equity ratio than a before-dividend company (like Mary's).*
- *If companies with a higher debt–equity ratio have a higher valuation, then companies should pay dividends.*

Now this book takes a definite stand on this question: In previous chapters we suggested that the capital structure question is ultimately a question of balancing personal against corporate taxation. We also suggested that the economic evidence suggests that on balance the taxes are pretty much of a wash, so that capital structure doesn't matter.

Though this argument suggests that dividends do not affect the valuation of a company, there's another tax aspect to this question—the trade-off between ordinary income taxes and capital gains taxes. We discuss this in the next section.

In the meantime, as long as Mary and John's taxi companies aren't taxed and as long as Mary and John aren't taxed on a personal level, the debt–equity aspects of the dividend decision shouldn't affect the valuation of their companies.

Question 3: Does the dividend affect the enterprise value?

Here's another way of thinking about this question: Suppose that both John and Mary are thinking about selling their taxi companies. Suppose that the "taxi part" of the business is valued at $40,000, which is, of course, more than its value on the balance sheet, and suppose that this valuation doesn't include the cash balances on the books. John and Mary have slightly different strategies about how to sell the business: John intends to first pay himself a dividend and then sell the business, whereas Mary intends to sell the business first without taking a dividend. Here are the calculations:

	A	B	C	D	E	F	G
1	Mary sells her taxi company for $40,000				John sells his taxi company for $40,000		
2	Sale price	40,000			Sale price	40,000	
3	Pay back net debt	5,000			Pay back net debt	8,000	
4	Net to equity	35,000	<-- =B2-B3		Net to equity	32,000	<-- =F2-F3
5	Book value of equity	15,000			Book value of equity	12,000	
6	Taxable gain	20,000	<-- =B4-B5		Taxable gain	20,000	<-- =F4-F5
7	Taxes on gain (0%)	0	<-- =0*B6		Taxes on gain (0%)	0	<-- =0*F6
8	Net to Mary from sale	35,000	<-- =B4-B7		Net to John from sale	32,000	<-- =F4-F7
9							
10	Add back dividend	0			Add back dividend	3,000	
11	Taxes on dividend (0%)	0	<-- =0%*B10		Taxes on dividend (0%)	0	<-- =0%*F10
12	Total	35,000	<-- =B8+B10-B11		Total	35,000	<-- =F8+F10-F11

The bottom line on these two calculations is the same—John and Mary each make a total of $35,000 on the sale, so that it doesn't matter whether they pay themselves a dividend or not.[2] Note the differences:

- Mary has less net debt to repay (John has taken out $3,000 in a dividend, so he has less cash left in the business).

- Mary's book value of equity is greater. When we add capital gains taxes (next example), this will mean that Mary has lower taxable gains. But with a 0% tax rate, it doesn't matter.

---

[2] Although, to anticipate the next section, the assumption that there are no taxes is critical to this argument.

WHO CARES WHERE THE MONEY IS AS LONG AS IT'S THERE?

This is really what it's all about—who cares whether the money is in the taxi company or in the individual bank account of the owner? Of course, you can think of several answers to this question which make it appear that it *does* matter:

- Taxes: If the company and its owners pay different tax rates, perhaps dividends are worthwhile. If capital gains taxes are lower than ordinary income taxes, perhaps—as suggested in the Overview to this chapter—companies should retain the dividend and not pay it out.

- Trust: If there are multiple owners of the company, maybe you want the money in *your hands* as opposed to leaving it in the company. Economists call this "agency costs"—an agent being someone you've hired to do your work for you (that is, the manager). The agency cost argument for paying dividends suggests that you and your manager may have different goals; if the manager's goal includes wasting your money, then maybe you should get the money out of the manager's hands by paying a dividend.

22.2   Taxes Can Make a Big Difference!

In Section 22.1 we looked at dividend policy in a world with no taxes. Using John and Mary's taxi businesses, we made two points:

- The value of the "taxi part" of the business—the enterprise value—is not affected by the dividend policy of John and Mary's taxi businesses.
- The proceeds—dividends plus gains from selling the business—to John and Mary are exactly the same, independent of their dividend policy.

Now look at the second point again, and suppose that we introduce taxes. We'll assume that dividends are taxed as "ordinary income" at a rate of 30% and that the gains from selling the business are taxed at a capital gains tax rate of 15%.

We'll start with Mary, who sells her taxi company for $40,000. As the calculation below shows, Mary's net from the sale of the company is $32,000:

	A	B	C	D
1	MARY'S TAXI COMPANY			
2	Assets		Liabilities and equity	
3			Net debt = Debt - cash	5,000
4	Taxis	20,000	Equity	
5			Stock	5,000
6			Accumulated retained earnings	10,000
7	Total assets	20,000	Total liabilities and equity	20,000
8				
9	Capital gains tax	15%		
10	Ordinary income tax rate	30%		
11				
12	Mary sells her taxi company for $40,000			
13	Sale price	40,000		
14	Pay back net debt	5,000		
15	Net to shareholders (Mary)	35,000	<-- =B13-B14	
16	Book value of equity	15,000	<-- =SUM(D5:D6)	
17	Taxable gain	20,000	<-- =B15-B16	
18	Taxes on capital gain (15%)	3,000	<-- =$B$9*B17	
19	Net to Mary from sale	32,000	<-- =B15-B18	
20				
21	Add back dividend	0		
22	Taxes on dividend (30%)	0	<-- =$B$10*B21	
23	Total	32,000	<-- =B19+B21-B22	

Now John: He also sells his company, but he has first paid himself a dividend. His net is lower:

	F	G	H	I
1	JOHN'S TAXI COMPANY--after dividend			
2	Assets		Liabilities and equity	
3			Net debt = Debt - cash	8,000
4	Taxis	20,000	Equity	
5			Stock	5,000
6			Accumulated retained earnings	7,000
7	Total assets	20,000	Total liabilities and equity	20,000
8				
9	Capital gains tax	15%		
10	Ordinary income tax rate	30%		
11				
12	John sells his taxi company for $40,000			
13	Sale price	40,000		
14	Pay back net debt	8,000		
15	Net to equity	32,000	<-- =G13-G14	
16	Book value of equity	12,000	<-- =SUM(I5:I6)	
17	Taxable gain	20,000	<-- =G15-G16	
18	Taxes on capital gain (15%)	3,000	<-- =$G$9*G17	
19	Net to John from sale	29,000	<-- =G15-G18	
20				
21	Add back dividend	3,000		
22	Taxes on dividend (30%)	900	<-- =$G$10*G21	
23	Total	31,100	<-- =G19+G21-G22	

The reason for the difference between John's net of $31,100 and Mary's net of $32,000 is that dividends are taxed. By not paying herself a dividend, Mary has saved herself $900 = 30% * 3,000 of taxes on her dividends.[3]

This analysis suggests that *dividends might matter* if there is both a dividend tax and a capital gains tax: In this case you shouldn't pay dividends.

What If John Really Needs the Money? Solution 1: Pay a Bonus

Suppose for some reason John really needs the money **now.** Then he should pay himself a bonus, which is a tax-deductible expense for the company. When John pays himself a bonus, it comes out of cash but gets tax deductibility. Here's what happens to the cash balances:

Initial cash balances	$5,000	
After-tax cost of bonus to company	$1,800	The company pays John a $3,000 bonus, which is an expense for tax purposes. At the company's 40% corporate tax rate, the after-tax cost of the bonus is $(1 - 40\%) * 3,000$.
Cash on hand after bonus	$3,200	

Figure 22.5 shows how the profits for John come out with a dividend and with a bonus. We've assumed that John pays a 25% ordinary income tax on both the dividend and on the bonus.

This little trick (the tax deductibility of the bonus) is actually more profitable than Mary's not paying a dividend at all (compare John's net of $32,450 to Mary's net of $32,000). However, whether a bonus is better than no bonus depends on the corporate versus the ordinary income tax rate. In the example below, John's ordinary income tax rate is 45%, which is more than his corporate tax rate. At these rates he'd be better off by not paying himself a bonus (or a dividend) and selling the company.

	A	B	C	D	E	F	G	H	I
1			JOHN'S TAXI COMPANY--after dividend				JOHN'S TAXI COMPANY--after bonus		
2	Assets		Liabilities and equity			Assets		Liabilities and equity	
3	Cash	2,000	Debt	10,000		Cash	3,200	Debt	10,000
4	Taxis	20,000	Equity			Taxis	20,000	Equity	
5			Stock	5,000				Stock	5,000
6			Accumulated retained earnings	7,000				Accumulated retained earnings	8,200
7	Total assets	22,000	Total liabilities and equity	22,000		Total assets	23,200	Total liabilities and equity	23,200
8									
9	Corporate tax rate	40%				Corporate tax rate	30%		
10	Capital gains tax	15%				Capital gains tax	15%		
11	Ordinary income tax rate	25%				Ordinary income tax rate	25%		
12									
13		John sells his taxi company for $40,000					John sells his taxi company for $40,000		
14	Sale price	40,000				Sale price	40,000		
15	Pay back net debt	8,000	<-- =D3-B3			Pay back net debt	6,800	<-- =I3-G3	
16	Net to equity	32,000	<-- =B14-B15			Net to equity	33,200	<-- =G14-G15	
17	Book value of equity	12,000	<-- =SUM(D5:D6)			Book value of equity	13,200	<-- =SUM(I5:I6)	
18	Taxable gain	20,000	<-- =B16-B17			Taxable gain	20,000	<-- =G16-G17	
19	Taxes on capital gain (15%)	3,000	<-- =$B$10*B18			Taxes on capital gain (15%)	3,000	<-- =$B$10*G18	
20	Net to John from sale	29,000	<-- =B16-B19			Net to John from sale	30,200	<-- =G16-G19	
21									
22	Add back dividend	3,000				Add back bonus	3,000		
23	Taxes on dividend (25%)	750	<-- =$B$11*B22			John's taxes on bonus (25%)	750	<-- =$G$11*G22	
24	Total	31,250	<-- =B20+B22-B23			Total	32,450	<-- =G20+G22-G23	

Figure 22.5 John's cash flow (cells B24 and G24) with a dividend and with a bonus. Because dividends, corporate income, and capital gains are taxed at different rates, John is better off paying himself a bonus instead of paying himself a dividend.

---

[3]In any case both John and Mary are going to pay the same capital gains taxes. This is because a dividend, paid out of cash, *reduces* the firm's equity and *increases* the firm's net debt. The result, as you can confirm from the examples, is that the capital gain to the firm's shareholders is independent of the dividend.

	F	G	H	I
1	JOHN'S TAXI COMPANY--after bonus			
2	Assets		Liabilities and equity	
3	Cash	3,200	Debt	10,000
4	Taxis	20,000	Equity	
5			Stock	5,000
6			Accumulated retained earnings	8,200
7	Total assets	23,200	Total liabilities and equity	23,200
8				
9	Corporate tax rate	30%		
10	Capital gains tax	15%		
11	Ordinary income tax rate	45%		
12				
13	John sells his taxi company for $40,000			
14	Sale price	40,000		
15	Pay back net debt	6,800	<-- =I3-G3	
16	Net to equity	33,200	<-- =G14-G15	
17	Book value of equity	13,200	<-- =SUM(I5:I6)	
18	Taxable gain	20,000	<-- =G16-G17	
19	Taxes on capital gain (15%)	3,000	<-- =$B$10*G18	
20	Net to John from sale	30,200	<-- =G16-G19	
21				
22	Add back bonus	3,000		
23	John's taxes on bonus (45%)	1,350	<-- =$G$11*G22	
24	Total	31,850	<-- =G20+G22-G23	

What If John Really Needs the Money? Solution 2: Repurchase Stock

Maybe John needs the money but can't, for some reason, pay himself a bonus. In this case, instead of paying himself a dividend, he should get the company to repurchase some stock from him. Suppose that John convinces the management of the company (himself!) to buy back $3,000 of stock. Suppose that after this repurchase of equity, John sells the company. Finally, suppose that all of the $3,000 repurchase of stock is taxed to John as a capital gain (this is very unlikely—read the Note that follows the spreadsheet). In this case, John would still be better off than if he had paid himself a dividend:

	F	G	H	I
1	JOHN'S TAXI COMPANY--after repurchase			
2	Assets		Liabilities and equity	
3	Cash after repurchase	2,000	Debt	10,000
4	Taxis	20,000	Equity	
5			Stock	5,000
6			Accumulated retained earnings	10,000
7	Total assets	22,000	Total liabilities and equity	25,000
8				
9	Corporate tax rate	30%		
10	Capital gains tax	15%		
11	Ordinary income tax rate	45%		
12				
13	John sells his taxi company for $40,000			
14	Sale price	40,000		
15	Pay back net debt	8,000	<-- =I3-G3	
16	Net to equity	32,000	<-- =G14-G15	
17	Book value of equity	15,000	<-- =SUM(I5:I6)	
18	Taxable gain	17,000	<-- =G16-G17	
19	Taxes on capital gain (15%)	2,550	<-- =$B$10*G18	
20	Net to John from sale	29,450	<-- =G16-G19	
21				
22	Add back repurchase of stock	3,000		
23	John's taxes on repurchase (15%)	450	<-- =$G$10*G22	
24	Total	32,000	<-- =G20+G22-G23	

Note: In order to minimize taxes, John should consult his accountant before repurchasing the stock. It is highly unlikely that the whole repurchase would be taxed as a dividend. It could be structured as a payout of capital (in which case there would be no taxes). The accountant might also be able to value John's *basis* in the stock (what he originally paid for it, plus the accumulated capital gains). Here's an example:

	F	G	H
27		**Accountant reasoning?**	
28	**Assets**		**Liabilities and equity**
29			Net debt
30	Enterprise value	40,000	Equity, market value
31	**Total assets**	40,000	**Total liabilities and equity**
32			
33	Amount spent on repurchase	3,000	
34	As a percent of market value of equity	8.57%	<-- =G33/I30
35			
36	Book value of equity	15,000	
37	basis = 8.57% of book equity	1,286	<-- =G34*G36
38			
39	Taxable gain on repurchase	1,714	<-- =G33-G37
40	Taxes on gain at capital gains tax	257	<-- =G10*G39
41	Net from repurchase	2,743	<-- =G33-G40
42			
43			
44		**John sells his taxi company for $40,000**	
45	Sale price	40,000	
46	Pay back net debt	8,000	<-- =I29+G33
47	Net to equity	32,000	<-- =G45-G46
48	Book value of equity	13,714	<-- =G36-G37
49	Taxable gain	18,286	<-- =G47-G48
50	Taxes on capital gain (274286%)	2,743	<-- =$B$10*G49
51	Net to John from sale	29,257	<-- =G47-G50
52			
53	Total: net from sale + net from repurchase	32,000	<-- =G51+G41

The accountant reckons as follows:

- Before the payout of cash, the company is worth $40,000, which makes the market value of the equity $35,000.
- By paying out $3,000 in cash for stock in the company, John has effectively repurchased 8.57% of the company's equity. Since the book value of the company's equity is $15,000, John has a capital gain of $1,714(= $3,000 − 8.57% * $15,000) on the repurchase. This capital gain will be taxed at 15%(= $257), so that John will net $2,743 from the repurchase.
- Now when John sells the company for $40,000, he will first have to pay off its net debt of $8,000 (the repurchase used $3,000 of cash and raised the net debt from $5,000 to $8,000). This leaves him with a market value of equity of $32,000, which has book value of $13,714(= $15,000 − 8.57% * $15,000). This gain also gets taxed at the capital gains tax rate of 15%.
- This leaves John with $32,000.

22.3 Dividends (Satisfaction Now) Versus Capital Gains (Enjoy Later)

Up to this point we've established that if you're going to sell your company, ordinary income taxes on dividends make it unwise to first pay yourself a dividend. But what if you're not going to sell the company right away? Should you leave the money in the company, for that golden day when you're going to sell it and benefit from the lowered capital gains taxes? Or should you pay yourself a dividend?

It all depends, of course, on the level of trust you have in the managers of your company. In the case of John and Mary, this is easy—they manage their own companies, and they wouldn't do anything to harm themselves. In this case they should leave the money in the company, where it can earn the same returns as if they paid it out.

22.4 Do Dividends Signal?

Sections 22.1 and 22.2 have developed the theory that from a pure financial point of view, dividends are unnecessary. For investors, the decision on whether a company should pay dividends or not is at best neutral and—given the gap between taxes on dividend income and taxes on corporate gains—usually leans toward, the nonpayment of dividends. There are two alternatives to dividends, both of which are more financially attractive than the dividend itself:

- The company can choose simply not to pay out the dividend. By retaining the income as cash on its own books, the company translates the potential dividend into a future capital gain for its investors. When ultimately realized by the investor, this capital gain is taxed at a lower rate than ordinary income.

- The company can choose to use the potential dividend cash flow to repurchase its own shares. This translates the dividends into immediate cash gains for those shareholders who sell their shares back to the company (cash gains that are taxed at a favorable capital gains tax rate). Shareholders who do not tender their shares gain an increased proportion of the firm's future earnings.

There remains the possibility that dividends are a signal to the investor about the health of the company. The *signaling theory of dividends* makes two assertions:

- All of other things being equal, higher dividends are a signal of more financial strength than lower dividends.

- Changes in dividends are indicative of the future financial health of the company. An increase in dividends is indicative that the future prospects of the firm are improved, and vice versa.

Is a Dividend Increase Always Good News?

On the other hand, not all increases in dividends seem to be good news. When Microsoft announced on 16 January 2003 that it would initiate a dividend, the stock price dropped the next day by 7%. According to a *Business Week* article:

> "That may have been mostly because management's outlook for the current quarter was weak, but it's also likely that some investors saw the dividend as a sign that Microsoft had run out of options for growth," says Don Luskin, chief investment officer at research boutique Trend Macrolytics. "The risk is that paying a dividend could signal that tech has matured and is no longer the racy growth sector it once was," says Paul Shread, an analyst at Internet.com.[4]

Current financial research indicates that dividend changes, whether they be increases or decreases, tend to be less informative than was once thought. Although stock market analysts interpret a decrease in a company's dividend as a bad signal about the company, and an increase in

---

[4]http://www.businessweek.com/technology/content/jan2003/tc20030128_1051.htm.

the dividend as a good signal, the actual behavior of profits after a dividend change does not follow this signaling interpretation.[5]

22.5 What Do Corporate Executives Think About Dividends?

A long line of financial research indicates that companies are extremely reluctant to change their dividend policy. Corporate executives apparently think that changing a firm's dividend policy is an important signal. In a recent survey of 384 corporate executives, researchers at Duke and Cornell found that they ranked the importance of maintaining the current dividend level on a par with other major corporate investment decisions. Share repurchases, on the other hand, were thought to come out of the residual cash flows after investment and dividend spending. However, the researchers report, "Many managers ... favor repurchases because they are viewed as being more flexible than dividends and can be used in an attempt to time the equity market or to increase EPS. Executives believe that institutions are indifferent between dividends and repurchases and that payout policies have little impact on their investor clientele. In general, management views provide little support for agency, signaling, and clientele hypotheses of payout policy. Tax considerations play a secondary role."[6]

The way that companies relate to their dividends bears this out. Notice the subhead on the Coca-Cola press release notifying the markets of an increase in dividend (Figure 22.6):

THE COCA-COLA COMPANY INCREASES ANNUAL DIVIDEND BY 12 PERCENT

43rd Consecutive Annual Increase

Atlanta, February 17, 2005 - The Board of Directors of The Coca-Cola Company today approved the Company's 43rd consecutive annual dividend increase, raising the quarterly dividend 12 percent from 25 cents to 28 cents per common share. This is equivalent to an annual dividend of $1.12 per share, up from $1 per share in 2004.

The dividend is payable April 1, 2005, to shareowners of record as of March 15, 2005.

This reflects the Board's confidence in the Company's long-term cash flow. In 2004, the Company generated $6 billion in cash from operations—a 9-percent increase over 2003. The Company returned more than $4 billion of that to shareowners, through $2.4 billion in dividends and $1.7 billion in share repurchase.

The Coca-Cola Company is the world's largest beverage company. Along with Coca-Cola, recognized as the world's most valuable brand, the Company markets four of the world's top five soft drink brands, including Diet Coke, Fanta and Sprite, and a wide range of other beverages, including diet and light soft drinks, waters, juices and juice drinks, teas, coffees and sports drinks. Through the world's largest beverage distribution system, consumers in more than 200 countries enjoy the Company's beverages at a rate exceeding 1 billion servings each day. For more information about The Coca-Cola Company, please visit our website at www.coca-cola.com.

Figure 22.6 When Coca-Cola announced a dividend increase on 17 February, 2005, the company cited its "confidence in its long-term cash flow." The company was using the dividends to send a signal to the financial markets, but it may not have worked: On the day of the announcement, Coke's stock price fell by 26 cents.

---

[5]See Chen, Shevlin, and Tong (2004). There is also some evidence that companies paying dividends outperform those that don't in down-markets. See Kathleen Fuller and Michael Goldstein, "Do Dividends Mean More in Declining Markets?" (http://papers.ssrn.com/sol3/papers.cfm?abstract_id=687067). This is discussed in http://www.forbes.com/2003/09/25/ cz_vj_0925soapbox.html by Vahan Janjigian.

[6]"Payout Policy in the 21st Century," by Alon Brav, John R. Campbell, John R. Graham, and Roni Michaeli. http://papers.ssrn.com/sol3/papers.cfm?abstract_id=358582.

Figure 22.7 Corporations consider dividend maintenance very important. When IBM announced its regular quarterly dividend, the company proudly noted that it had paid "357 consecutive quarterly dividends, starting in 1916."

"43rd Consecutive Annual Increase." Here are two more examples:

- IBM takes great pride in having paid quarterly dividends since 1916 (Figure 22.7). If the company were to change this policy, it would quite naturally be indicative of a major change at IBM.

- General Motors, with which we started this chapter, is quite reluctant to change its dividend policy, even though the financial health of the company is not good. The company evidently understands that a decrease in the quarterly dividend would be interpreted as bad news by the financial markets.

CONCLUSION

Dividends have a financial and an informational function. If we ignore their informational function, the payment of dividends presents a problem: Given a tax regime in which dividends are taxed at ordinary income tax rates whereas nonpayment of dividends or stock repurchases are taxed at lower capital gains tax rates—it is difficult to explain why firms pay dividends. Most shareholders would be better off if the dividend payment were either retained in the firm or diverted to share repurchases. As shown in Figure 22.8, this pure financial consideration perhaps explains the increasing role of share repurchases in firm dividend policies.

The informational role of dividends is more complicated. Firms are highly reluctant to change their dividend payout patterns—a company with no dividends tends to continue a no-payout policy, whereas companies with moderate dividend growth strive to continue their growth rates. Both corporate executives and financial markets tend to interpret a change in the dividend payout as having informational content. Most firms believe that dividend increases will be interpreted as good news about future firm prospects, and vice versa.

Volume 3, Number 9   SEPTEMBER 2002

FORBES
Growth Investor

ADVICE TO HELP YOU MANAGE YOUR GROWTH PORTFOLIO

www.forbesgrowthinvestor.com

Share Repurchases Substitute for Dividends

by Vahan Janjigian

The total return on equities is composed of two components: dividends and capital gains. Since the 1980s, however, the proportion coming from dividends has been shrinking. Furthermore, dividend yields (i.e., dividend per share divided by stock price) and payout ratios (i.e., dividend per share divided by earnings per share) have been falling steadily. Many experienced investors take this as prima facie evidence that stocks remain overvalued despite a tremendous two-year sell-off.

Value investors in particular believe that steadily rising cash dividends are an indication of financial health. These investors often shun stocks that lack a long history of dividend payments. But others, such as growth investors, believe dividends are not very meaningful.

A recent article in the Journal of Finance, a leading scholarly publication, provides evidence that the demise of the cash dividend is just an illusion. The authors, Gustavo Grullon and Roni Michaely, argue that focusing only on dividends ignores an increasingly important form of cash payout to stockholders: share repurchases. Cash dividends have been increasing at an annually compounded rate of only 6.3% since 1980. Yet cash spent on share repurchases has been rising at a much more rapid clip of 18.4% compounded annually. Furthermore, cash spent on share repurchases now exceeds that spent on dividends. And total cash paid out (i.e., dividends plus repurchases) as a percentage of earnings has actually been rising during the period studied.

Our tax code explains much of this behavior. When corporations pay dividends, investors are forced to pay taxes. In fact, dividends are taxed at the ordinary rate. But when corporations initiate share repurchases, investors can avoid taxes altogether by choosing not to sell. Yet if they do sell, they are taxed at the capital gains tax rate, which is much lower than the ordinary tax rate.

This was the case thirty years ago as well. So why weren't share repurchases as popular then? Grullon and Michaely argue that share repurchases didn't really start growing in popularity until a 1982 regulatory reform, which made it less likely that repurchasing firms would be accused by the SEC of trying to manipulate their stock prices.

There are a number of lessons to be drawn from this study. First, those who argue that stocks remain overvalued simply because dividend yields or dividend payout ratios are historically low are being shortsighted. They should instead focus on total cash payouts. Second, there should be no doubt that, good or bad, regulatory reforms affect firm behavior. Well-managed firms will do what is best for shareholders. As long as cash dividends are unfavorably taxed, investors will prefer capital gains. And as long as regulators allow it, good corporate boards will deliver what shareholders want.

Which brings us to a very important point. Dividends are paid from after-tax dollars. Taxing investors again for receiving those dividends imposes a very heavy burden. Regulators should eliminate this double taxation. Dividends should either be treated as a tax-deductible expense for corporations, or tax exempt income for individuals.

Figure 22.8 Since the 1980s, cash dividends have been increasing at a much slower rate than share repurchases. The explanation is in the much lower tax rates on capital gains versus ordinary income.

However, we have shown examples in this chapter where dividend changes have contrary effects to expectations: When Microsoft implemented a dividend, the markets interpreted this as a negative signal about the company's future prospects. When Coca-Cola increased its dividend, citing "confidence in its long-term cash flow," the stock price fell.

We can conclude from this that for firms whose shares are traded on stock markets, the dividend decision is a complicated, not totally understood, phenomenon that combines pure financial and tax considerations with complicated signaling and perhaps psychological motives.

EXERCISES

1. The following is the balance sheet for John's Supermarket. John is the sole owner of the supermarket.

	A	B	C	D
1			**JOHN'S SUPERMARKET**	
2	**Assets**		**Liabilities and equity**	
3	Cash	500,000	Debt	600,000
4				
5			Equity	
6	Supermarket	1,250,000	Stock	800,000
7			Accumulated retained earnings	350,000
8	**Total assets**	**1,750,000**	**Total debt and equity**	**1,750,000**

(a) Show the supermarket balance sheet in terms of net debt.

(b) Assuming John decides to pay himself a $250,000 dividend, show both the original balance sheet and the net debt balance sheet after the dividend payment.

2. John (from Exercise 1) needs your help again. After paying the dividend of $250,000, he decides to accept an offer to sell the supermarket for $1,800,000. The conditions of the sale are that John gets to keep the cash on the company's books, but that he is responsible for paying back the company's debt.

(a) Assuming no taxes of any kind, what will John net from his dividend and from his sale of the company?

(b) If John had sold the supermarket for $1,800,000 before the $250,000 dividend, what would have been his net gain?

(c) Back to the case of a $250,000 dividend: What will be John's net if there were a 30% tax on the dividend payment and a 20% tax rate on gains from the supermarket sale?

(d) With a 30% tax on dividends and a 20% capital gains tax, what would be John's net if he sold the supermarket without first paying a $250,000 dividend?

3. David has a cosmetics shop he's trying to sell for $200,000. The shop's balance sheet is given below. David has a 40% tax on ordinary income (including dividend payments), a 30% corporate tax rate, and a 25% tax rate on capital gains. Before selling the store, he wants to pay himself a dividend of $55,000, equal to his accumulated retained earnings. According to his belief, "My selling price is the same whether I pay the dividend (to myself) or not. So why not pay myself a dividend first? I'll have more money that way!"

Is David right? Present the calculations for both the dividend and the nondividend case.

	A	B	C	D
1			**David's Cosmetics Shop**	
2	**Assets**		**Liabilities and equity**	
3	Cash	60,000	Loan from bank	50,000
4	Inventory	25,000		
5			Equity	
6	Shop	100,000	Stock	80,000
7			Accumulated retained earnings	55,000
8	**Total assets**	**185,000**	**Total debt and equity**	**185,000**

4. (a) How will your answer to Exercise 3 change if instead of paying himself a dividend David pays himself a bonus of $55,000?

   (b) How will your answer to part (a) change if both the corporate tax rate and the ordinary income tax are 40%?

5. How will your answer to Exercise 3 change if instead of paying himself a dividend the shop repurchases shares from David for $55,000 (assume capital gains tax rate on stock repurchase)?

6. Mallory wants to sell her fishing business. She's trying to decide whether to sell the business as is, to pay herself a dividend of $5,000 combined with a bonus of $10,000, or to repurchase $15,000 of shares. Assuming Mallory will be paid $220,000 anyway, what will you recommend her to do?

   The balance sheet of the business is given below:

	A	B	C	D
1			**Mallory's Fishing Business**	
2	**Assets**		**Liabilities and equity**	
3	Cash	20,000	Loan from bank	25,000
4	Inventory	25,000		
5			Equity	
6	Ship	100,000	Stock	110,000
7	Warehouse	30,000	Accumulated retained earnings	40,000
8				
9	**Total assets**	**175,000**	**Total debt and equity**	**175,000**

7. HighTech.Com is a company whose sales and profits have been increasing steadily. The company has never paid a dividend. The company's management is trying to decide whether to use its large cash balances to pay a dividend to shareholders or to repurchase shares. Can you give them some advice?

8. Simon's Hotels is a company founded in 1995. The company owns a chain of hotels and has thus far not paid dividends, instead using its excess cash to pay down large levels of debt used to buy hotels. The company's debt has now reached acceptable levels. Can you advise management whether it should implement a dividend? How do you think a dividend will be interpreted by the market?

PART VI

OPTIONS AND OPTION VALUATION

The market for options has grown tremendously in the past two decades, and options form is an important component of many capital market investments. In addition *option concepts* are a critical component in the way markets work and investments are made. One example is the compensation given to managers in the form of stock options.

Part 6 gives an introduction to basic option concepts and valuation. A fuller treatment of these concepts will have to wait for a course dedicated to options, but Part 6 should give you the necessary background.

Chapter 23 introduces basic option concepts and terminology. Using a series of examples, this chapter tells you about option cash flows, buying and selling options, and the payoffs from option strategies.

Chapter 24 gives you some basic facts about option pricing. In more advanced textbooks these go by the name of "arbitrage restrictions" on option prices.

Chapters 25 and 26 discuss two option pricing models. Chapter 25 shows you how to use the Black–Scholes formula, the most famous option pricing model. The mathematics that underlie the Black–Scholes model can be daunting, but we keep things simple. As Chapter 25 shows, on a mechanical level, the Black–Scholes formula is easy to learn and use.

Chapter 26 discusses the other best-known option pricing model, the binomial model. The binomial model provides good intuitions about how options—as combinations of stocks and bonds—can be priced.

INTRODUCTION TO OPTIONS

OVERVIEW

The financial assets we have discussed so far in this book are bonds (Chapter 18) and stocks (Chapter 19). In Chapters 23–26 we discuss another kind of financial asset—options. As you will see in these chapters, an option is different in many respects from a stock or a bond:

- The value of an option is derived from the value of another asset, usually a stock. For this reason options are sometimes called *derivative assets*.

- The buyer of an option buys upside gains but has only limited downside losses.
- Options are more complicated than bonds or stocks. In order to understand options, you must learn some new terminology and some new ways of thinking about financial assets.

A Simple Example of an Option

In order to give some meaning to these somewhat mysterious statements, we start with a simple example.[1] It is 1 January 2006, and the price of an ounce of gold is $400. You have a very strong hunch that the price of gold will be $500 in three months. Your hunches have never failed you, so this must be a sure-fire way to make some money. Taking your total savings of $400, you go to your local jewelry mart to buy some gold. But with your paltry savings you can buy only one ounce of gold, and you can make a maximum of only $100—only a 25% return on your initial investment.

However, the jeweler has another offer for you: For $50, he is willing to sell you a contract that gives you the right to buy one ounce of gold in three months for $400. You realize that this contract—a *call option on gold*—gives you the opportunity of making much more money than actually buying gold (Figure 23.1).

Here's your calculation:

- Using your $400 savings, you can buy eight call options.
- In three months you can use the call options to buy eight ounces of gold for $400 per ounce. If your hunch is correct, the gold price in three months will be $500 per ounce, so that you can make $100 per ounce of gold purchased.
- Your total profit using the gold call options will be $800—a profit of 200% on your initial investment. This compares to the profit of 25% you will make if you use your $400 savings to buy one ounce of physical gold.

Downside: Suppose your hunch is wrong, and the price of gold in three months is $300. Now compare the profits of buying one ounce of physical gold to the profits of buying eight call options:

- If you bought one ounce of physical gold, you would have lost 25% of your initial $400 investment.
- If you bought eight options and the price of gold on 31 March 2006 is $300 per ounce, the *options will be worthless*. In this case you would have lost 100% of your initial $400 investment.

CALL OPTION ON ONE OUNCE OF GOLD

Price on 1 January 2006: $50

If presented at Asheville Jewelry Mart on or before 31 March 2006, this piece of paper gives you the right to buy one ounce of gold for $400. After 31 March 2006, this piece of paper is worthless.

The owner of this piece of paper can sell it to anyone else at any time.

Figure 23.1 The gold call option certificates sold by the Asheville Jewelry Mart.

---

[1]Even this simple example is nontrivial. Options are like that!

Peacemount Stock Options: An Example

Our gold example should convince you that options are an interesting way to make money. In this subsection we give an example of a stock option. Stock options give their holders the right to either buy or sell a stock in the future for a predetermined price. Stock options come in two flavors: A *call option* on a stock allows you to make money if the stock price goes up without losing too much if the stock price goes down. A *put option* on a stock allows you to make money if the stock's price goes down without losing too much if the stock's price goes up.

Take a look at Figure 23.2, which shows a call option (the right to buy a share of stock) on one share of a fictional company called Peacemount. On 26 November 2006 it would cost you $3 to buy this option. Having bought the option, you then have the right for the next three months to buy a share of Peacemount stock for $36.

Why buy this option? By spending $3 now, you lock in $36 as the maximum price Peacemount stock will cost you in the next three months. If the price of the stock goes up in the next

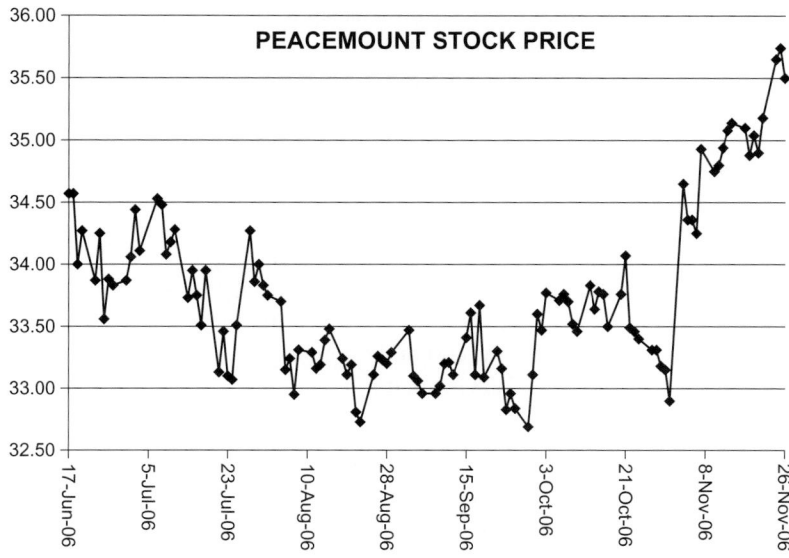

CALL OPTION ON PEACEMOUNT STOCK

Price on 26 November 2006: $3

If presented at the Asheville Stock Exchange on or before 26 February 2004, this piece of paper gives you the right to buy one share of Peacemount stock for $36. After 26 February 2007 this piece of paper is worthless.

The holder of this piece of paper can sell it to someone else at any time.

Some additional information:

- On 26 November 2006, shares of Peacemount stock sold for $35.50.
- Peacemount's stock price has experienced considerable variations during the past three months:

Figure 23.2 A call option on Peacemount stock. The option gives the holder the right to buy a share of Peacemount on or before 26 February 2007 for $36. The market price of the option on 26 November 2006 is $3.

PUT OPTION ON PEACEMOUNT STOCK

Price on 26 November 2006: $2.50

If presented at the Asheville Stock Exchange on or before 26 February 2007, this piece of paper gives you the right to sell one share of Peacemount stock for $36. After 26 February 2007 this piece of paper is worthless.

The holder of this piece of paper can sell it to someone else at any time.

Figure 23.3 A (hypothetical) put option on Peacemount stock. The option gives the holder the right to sell a share of Peacemount on or before 26 February 2007 for $36. The market price of the option on 26 November 2006 is $2.50.

three months, this will save you a lot of money. If, for example, Peacemount stock is selling on 26 February 2007 for $50, then by using your call option, you can buy the stock for $36. You will have a profit of $11 (buying the stock for $36 instead of $50 saves you $14; from this amount you have to deduct the $3 cost of the option). If, on the other hand, Peacemount stock declines below $36, then you will not exercise the option but you will only lose your $3 investment. In option market jargon: *The call option offers upside gains but only limited downside losses.*

There's another reason to buy the option: You might be able to sell it at some time during the next three months and make a profit. Suppose that in one week the price of Peacemount stock is $45. Then the price of the call option should be at least $9, since the owner of the option could immediately make a profit of $9 by exercising it.[2] Notice that in this example the price of the stock increases by 25% (from $36 to $45), whereas the price of the option increases by at least 300%. This makes the option a very interesting speculation. In option market jargon: *The call option's market price is very sensitive to the price of the underlying asset (in our case: the price of Peacemount stock).*

In addition to call options, this chapter also discusses *put options*. Whereas a call option is the right to buy a share of stock in the future, a put option is the right to sell a share of stock. An example is given in Figure 23.3: For $2.50 you could, on 26 November 2006 buy the right to sell one share of Peacemount stock for $36 during the next three months.

Why might you be interested in buying this put option? One reason is that, for holders of Peacemount stock, the put option places a *floor on your losses*. Suppose you own a share of Peacemount stock. On 26 November 2006 shares of Peacemount are selling for $35.50. If you buy the put option today for $2.50, you guarantee yourself that at any point during the next three months you will realize at least $33.50 from your stock.

To see this, suppose that on 26 February 2007 the price of Peacemount is $20. Instead of selling your share on the open market, you will use ("exercise") the put option to sell the share for $36. Accounting for the cost of the option, your net receipts will be $33.50 ($36 for the share minus the $2.50 cost of the put option).

---

[2]Whoever holds the option can purchase a share of Peacemount for $36. The stock price is now $45, so the immediate realizable profit is $9.

Name	Definition	Symbol
Call option	The right to buy a stock or other asset at a predetermined price on or before some future date	C
Put option	The right to sell a stock or other asset at a predetermined price on or before some future date	P
Exercise price	The predetermined price of the option—the price at which the stock/asset can be purchased in the future; also called the *strike price*	X
Exercise date	The last date on which the option can be exercised; past this date the option is worthless	T
Underlying asset	The stock or other asset that can be purchased with an option (in our previous examples, gold or one share of Peacemount stock)	S S_0: stock price today S_T: stock price on the exercise date T

Figure 23.4 Basic option terminology and symbols. More terminology is given in Figure 23.8.

What's Next?

This chapter gives you basic option definitions and introduces you to option cash flows (Figure 23.4). In addition, we show you how option strategies—the ability to combine options and stocks in portfolios—can change the payoff patterns available to investors. When you finish this chapter, you will understand why stock options are *really interesting* securities, and why you might want to invest in them.

Finance Concepts Discussed

- Call and put options
- Option strategies: protective puts, spreads, butterflies

Excel Functions Used

- **Max**
- **Min**

23.1 What's an Option?

A *call option on a stock* is the right to buy a stock on or before a given date at a predetermined price. Figure 23.5 gives prices for options on Cisco stock on 7 August 2002; we will use these prices in the examples that follow.

	A	B	C	D	E	F
1	CISCO OPTIONS, August 7, 2001 CLOSING PRICE ON CHICAGO BOARD OF OPTIONS EXCHANGE (CBOE)					
2	August 7, 2001, Cisco closing price	19.26				
3						
4	Stated expiration date	Exercise price, X	Call price	Put price	Actual expiration date	Days to maturity
5	Aug-01	7.50	11.90	0.05	17-Aug-01	10
6	Aug-01	10.00	9.60	0.20	17-Aug-01	10
7	Aug-01	12.50	6.50	0.10	17-Aug-01	10
8	Aug-01	15.00	4.20	0.10	17-Aug-01	10
9	Aug-01	17.50	2.10	0.40	17-Aug-01	10
10	Aug-01	20.00	0.65	1.45	17-Aug-01	10
11	Aug-01	22.50	0.15	3.40	17-Aug-01	10
12	Aug-01	25.00	0.05	5.00	17-Aug-01	10
13	Aug-01	27.50	0.10	7.50	17-Aug-01	10
14	Aug-01	30.00	0.10	11.90	17-Aug-01	10
15	Aug-01	32.50	0.05		17-Aug-01	10
16	Aug-01	35.00	0.05	16.20	17-Aug-01	10
17	Sep-01	10.00	9.50		21-Sep-01	45
18	Sep-01	12.50	6.30	0.15	21-Sep-01	45
19	Sep-01	15.00	4.50	0.40	21-Sep-01	45
20	Sep-01	17.50	2.75	0.90	21-Sep-01	45
21	Sep-01	20.00	1.35	2.00	21-Sep-01	45
22	Sep-01	22.50	0.55	3.80	21-Sep-01	45
23	Sep-01	25.00	0.20	5.50	21-Sep-01	45
24	Sep-01	27.50	0.10		21-Sep-01	45
25	Sep-01	30.00	0.05		21-Sep-01	45
26	Oct-01	10.00	10.00	0.10	19-Oct-01	73
27	Oct-01	12.50	6.90	0.25	19-Oct-01	73
28	Oct-01	15.00	5.00	0.65	19-Oct-01	73
29	Oct-01	17.50	3.20	1.40	19-Oct-01	73
30	Oct-01	20.00	1.80	2.55	19-Oct-01	73
31	Oct-01	22.50	0.95	4.10	19-Oct-01	73
32	Oct-01	25.00	0.45	6.00	19-Oct-01	73
33	Oct-01	27.50	0.20	7.50	19-Oct-01	73
34	Oct-01	30.00	0.15	10.70	19-Oct-01	73
35	Oct-01	35.00	0.05	16.30	19-Oct-01	73
36	Oct-01	40.00	0.05	21.50	19-Oct-01	73
37	Oct-01	45.00	0.05	29.50	19-Oct-01	73
38	Oct-01	50.00	0.05	31.12	19-Oct-01	73
39	Oct-01	55.00	0.10	37.50	19-Oct-01	73
40	Oct-01	60.00	0.05	36.75	19-Oct-01	73
41	Oct-01	65.00	0.05		19-Oct-01	73
42	Jan-02	10.00	9.50	0.30	18-Jan-02	164
43	Jan-02	12.50	8.20	0.60	18-Jan-02	164
44	Jan-02	15.00	5.70	1.20	18-Jan-02	164
45	Jan-02	17.50	4.10	2.00	18-Jan-02	164
46	Jan-02	20.00	2.90	3.40	18-Jan-02	164
47	Jan-02	22.50	1.85	4.90	18-Jan-02	164
48	Jan-02	25.00	1.20	7.00	18-Jan-02	164
49	Jan-02	26.25	0.95	7.50	18-Jan-02	164
50	Jan-02	27.50	0.80	9.80	18-Jan-02	164
51	Jan-02	30.00	0.45	11.30	18-Jan-02	164
52	Jan-02	32.50	0.45	13.10	18-Jan-02	164
53	Jan-02	35.00	0.15	15.00	18-Jan-02	164
54	Jan-02	37.50	0.20	20.10	18-Jan-02	164

Figure 23.5 Cisco stock option prices on 7 August 2001. A blank in the price (for example, the Oct 01 put price with exercise price 65) indicates that no options were traded. On 7 August 2001 Cisco options with maturities as far out as January 2004 were traded.

	A	B	C	D	E	F
4	Stated expiration date	Exercise price, X	Call price	Put price	Actual expiration date	Days to maturity
56	Jan-02	42.50	0.10	25.90	18-Jan-02	164
57	Jan-02	45.00	0.10	27.00	18-Jan-02	164
58	Jan-02	47.50	0.15	34.12	18-Jan-02	164
59	Jan-02	50.00	0.05	30.10	18-Jan-02	164
60	Jan-02	52.50	0.10	34.50	18-Jan-02	164
61	Jan-02	55.00	0.05	37.00	18-Jan-02	164
62	Jan-02	57.50	0.05	39.70	18-Jan-02	164
63	Jan-02	60.00	0.10	40.10	18-Jan-02	164
64	Jan-02	62.50	0.05	43.00	18-Jan-02	164
65	Jan-02	65.00	0.05	45.80	18-Jan-02	164
66	Jan-02	67.50	0.05	31.37	18-Jan-02	164
67	Jan-02	70.00	0.05	50.80	18-Jan-02	164
68	Jan-02	72.50	0.05	53.50	18-Jan-02	164
69	Jan-02	75.00	0.05	58.50	18-Jan-02	164
70	Jan-02	77.50	0.05	59.70	18-Jan-02	164
71	Jan-02	80.00	0.05	62.20	18-Jan-02	164
72	Jan-02	82.50	0.19	30.00	18-Jan-02	164
73	Jan-02	85.00	0.05	46.00	18-Jan-02	164
74	Jan-02	87.50	0.06	52.50	18-Jan-02	164
75	Jan-02	90.00	0.05	56.50	18-Jan-02	164
76	Jan-02	95.00	0.12	65.37	18-Jan-02	164
77	Jan-02	100.00	0.05	70.87	18-Jan-02	164
78	Jan-02	105.00	0.05	48.00	18-Jan-02	164
79	Jan-02	110.00	0.06	84.12	18-Jan-02	164
80	Jan-02	115.00	0.31	63.00	18-Jan-02	164
81	Jan-02	120.00	0.05	97.90	18-Jan-02	164
82	Jan-03	10.00	10.60	0.95	17-Jan-03	528
83	Jan-03	12.50	9.50	1.60	17-Jan-03	528
84	Jan-03	15.00	7.70	2.60	17-Jan-03	528
85	Jan-03	17.50	6.50	3.80	17-Jan-03	528
86	Jan-03	20.00	5.40	5.20	17-Jan-03	528
87	Jan-03	25.00	3.70	7.80	17-Jan-03	528
88	Jan-03	30.00	2.30	11.60	17-Jan-03	528
89	Jan-03	35.00	1.75	15.90	17-Jan-03	528
90	Jan-03	40.00	1.10	20.90	17-Jan-03	528
91	Jan-03	45.00	0.95	25.50	17-Jan-03	528
92	Jan-03	50.00	0.65	32.20	17-Jan-03	528
93	Jan-03	55.00	0.50	37.20	17-Jan-03	528
94	Jan-03	60.00	0.40	40.20	17-Jan-03	528
95	Jan-03	65.00	0.30	48.40	17-Jan-03	528
96	Jan-03	70.00	0.25	49.00	17-Jan-03	528
97	Jan-03	75.00	0.15	48.62	17-Jan-03	528
98	Jan-03	80.00	0.15	42.87	17-Jan-03	528
99	Jan-03	85.00	0.20	29.75	17-Jan-03	528
100	Jan-03	90.00	0.40	56.50	17-Jan-03	528
101	Jan-03	95.00	0.25	56.75	17-Jan-03	528
102	Jan-03	100.00	0.10	83.10	17-Jan-03	528
103	Jan-04	10.00	11.90	1.30	16-Jan-04	892
104	Jan-04	15.00	9.00	3.20	16-Jan-04	892
105	Jan-04	20.00	6.80	5.80	16-Jan-04	892
106	Jan-04	25.00	5.50	8.50	16-Jan-04	892
107	Jan-04	30.00	4.00	11.90	16-Jan-04	892

Figure 23.5 *Continued.*

Cisco Call Options

Row 21 of the Cisco spreadsheet tells you that on 7 August 2001, a call option on Cisco stock with an exercise price of $20.00 and an exercise date of 21 September 2001 was selling for $1.35:

	A	B	C	D	E	F
4	**Stated expiration date**	**Exercise price, X**	**Call price**	**Put price**	**Actual expiration date**	**Days to maturity**
20	Sep-01	17.50	2.75	0.90	21-Sep-01	45
21	Sep-01	20.00	1.35	2.00	21-Sep-01	45
22	Sep-01	22.50	0.55	3.80	21-Sep-01	45

Suppose you purchased this call option on 7 August. Figure 23.6 shows the option's cash flow pattern.

Now let's see what happens on 21 September:

- Suppose the Cisco stock price on 21 September is $35. In this case you get to buy one share of Cisco for $20. Your gain is $35 − $20 = $15.

- If the Cisco stock price on 21 September is $18, you would not exercise your call option to buy a share of Cisco for $20. (Why should you? You could buy it on the open market for less.) The option expires unexercised, and your gain is $0.

Cisco Put Options

What about the Cisco put option with an exercise price of $20? On 7 August 2001, it was selling for $2.00. The put option gives you the right to *sell* a share of Cisco on or before the terminal date for its exercise price. The put option's cash flow pattern is shown in Figure 23.7.

If Cisco's stock price on 21 September is $15, you will exercise your put option and sell a share of Cisco for $20, thus gaining $5.[3] On the other hand, if Cisco's share price on 21 September

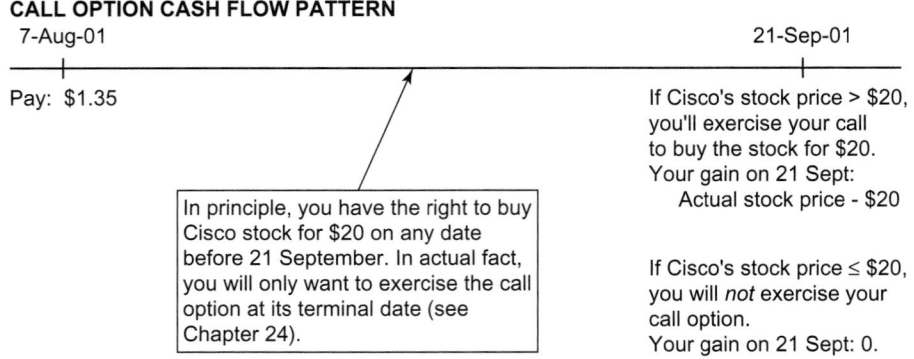

Figure 23.6 The cash flows from buying a Cisco call option on 7 August 2001 for $1.35 and possibly exercising it on 21 September 2001. The option has exercise price X = $20.

---

[3]What if you don't own a share of Cisco on 21 September? No problem: You buy a share on the open market for $15 and use your option to sell it for $20.

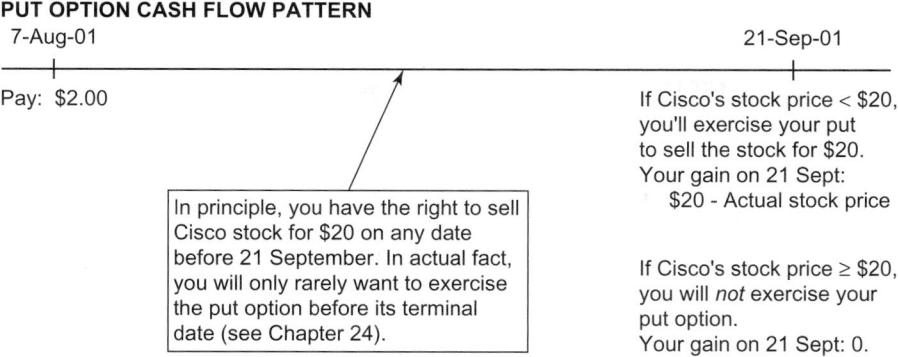

PUT OPTION CASH FLOW PATTERN

7-Aug-01

21-Sep-01

Pay: $2.00

If Cisco's stock price < $20, you'll exercise your put to sell the stock for $20. Your gain on 21 Sept:
    $20 - Actual stock price

In principle, you have the right to sell Cisco stock for $20 on any date before 21 September. In actual fact, you will only rarely want to exercise the put option before its terminal date (see Chapter 24).

If Cisco's stock price ≥ $20, you will *not* exercise your put option. Your gain on 21 Sept: 0.

Figure 23.7 The cash flows from buying a Cisco put option on 7 August 2001 for $2 and possibly exercising it on 21 September 2001. The option has exercise price $X = \$20$.

is $30, you will not exercise the put option. (Why sell a share using the option for $20 when you can sell it on the open market for $30?)

OPTION WEBSITES

All the data in this chapter were gathered from public sources on the Web. Many of these websites have superb data and also educational features. Here are some websites we especially enjoy.

- The website of the Chicago Board of Options Exchange (CBOE): http://www.cboe.com.
- Yahoo: http://biz.yahoo.com/opt/.

European Versus American Options

Cisco's stock options are *American* stock options—they can be exercised *on or before* the option maturity date T. A *European* stock option can be exercised *only on* its maturity date T. Clearly, an American stock option is worth at least as much as a European stock option: American options offer more flexibility than European options (Figure 23.8).

Two notes about American versus European stock options:

- The terminology has nothing to do with geography. Most traded options, whether in the United States, Europe, or Asia, are American and not European.
- A remarkable fact about American call options is the following: In many cases an American call option is worth *exactly* the same as an equivalent European call option. This happens if the stock on which the option is written does not pay a dividend before the option expiration date T. Since Cisco stock does not pay dividends, the "American" feature of Cisco stock call

Terminology	Definition
European option	The option is exercisable *only on* the exercise date T.
American option	The option is exercisable *on or before* the exercise date T. Most options traded on exchanges are American options. Although in principle an American option should be worth more than a European option, in many cases this is not true (see Chapter 24).
At-the-money option	An option whose exercise price X is equal to the underlying stock's current stock price S_0. "In-the-money" is often loosely used to describe an option whose exercise price X is approximately equal to the current stock price S_0.
In-the-money option	An option from which money can be made by immediate exercise. A call option is in the money if the current stock price S_0 is greater than the option's exercise price X. A put option is in the money if the current stock price S_0 is less than the option's exercise price X.
Out-of-the-money option	An option from which no money can be made by immediate exercise. A call option is out of the money if $X > S_0$. A put option is out of the money if $S_0 > X$.

Figure 23.8 More basic option terminology. Option pricing involves a lot of terminology.

options is worthless, and the call options on Cisco stock are worth the same as if they are European options. We discuss the reasons for this in Chapter 24.

In the Money, Out of the Money, at the Money

A call option is said to be "in the money" if the current stock price is larger than the option's exercise price. Look at the Cisco October calls in the spreadsheet below. The call with the exercise price of $12.50 (currently selling for $6.90) has an exercise price *less* than Cisco's current stock price of $19.26. Thus this call is *in the money*—the stock price is greater than the call's exercise price.

	A	B	C	D	E
1	**CISCO OCTOBER OPTIONS** **In or out of the money?**				
2	7, August 2001, Cisco closing price	19.26			
3					
4	**Expiration date**	**Exercise price, X**	**Call price**	**In or out of the money?**	
20	Oct-01	12.50	6.90	in the money	<-- =IF($B$2>B20,"in the money","out of the money")
21	Oct-01	15.00	5.00	in the money	<-- =IF($B$2>B21,"in the money","out of the money")
22	Oct-01	17.50	3.20	in the money	<-- =IF($B$2>B22,"in the money","out of the money")
23	Oct-01	20.00	1.80	out of the money	<-- =IF($B$2>B23,"in the money","out of the money")
24	Oct-01	22.50	0.95	out of the money	<-- =IF($B$2>B24,"in the money","out of the money")
25	Oct-01	25.00	0.45	out of the money	
26	Oct-01	27.50	0.20	out of the money	
27	Oct-01	30.00	0.15	out of the money	
28	Oct-01	35.00	0.05	out of the money	
29	Oct-01	40.00	0.05	out of the money	
30	Oct-01	45.00	0.05	out of the money	
31	Oct-01	50.00	0.05	out of the money	
32	Oct-01	55.00	0.10	out of the money	
33	Oct-01	60.00	0.05	out of the money	

The call with exercise price $50 (selling for $0.05) is *out of the money*—its exercise price is more than Cisco's current share price.

If the call's exercise price is equal to the current stock price, it is termed an *at-the-money* call. The call with an exercise price of $20 is almost at the money, and option traders would refer to it loosely as the at-the-money call.

A put is said to be *in the money* if the put's exercise price is greater than the current stock price. In the table below, showing Cisco's October put options, the $50 call (currently selling for $29.50) is *in the money* and the $12.50 put (selling for $0.10) is *out of the money*. There is no actual at-the-money put, but traders would refer to the $20 exercise put (selling for $1.40) as the *at-the-money* put.

	A	B	C	D	E
35		Exercise price, X	Put price	In or out of the money?	
36	Oct-01	12.50	0.10	out of the money	<-- =IF(B36>$B$2,"in the money","out of the money")
37	Oct-01	15.00	0.25	out of the money	<-- =IF(B37>$B$2,"in the money","out of the money")
38	Oct-01	17.50	0.65	out of the money	<-- =IF(B38>$B$2,"in the money","out of the money")
39	Oct-01	20.00	1.40	in the money	<-- =IF(B39>$B$2,"in the money","out of the money")
40	Oct-01	22.50	2.55	in the money	<-- =IF(B40>$B$2,"in the money","out of the money")
41	Oct-01	25.00	4.10	in the money	
42	Oct-01	27.50	6.00	in the money	
43	Oct-01	30.00	7.50	in the money	
44	Oct-01	35.00	10.70	in the money	
45	Oct-01	40.00	16.30	in the money	
46	Oct-01	45.00	21.50	in the money	
47	Oct-01	50.00	29.50	in the money	
48	Oct-01	55.00	31.12	in the money	
49	Oct-01	60.00	37.50	in the money	

23.2 Why Buy a Call Option?

Here are two simple reasons why you might want to buy a call option.

Reason 1: A Call Option Allows You to Delay the Purchase of a Stock

It's 7 August 2001, and you're thinking about buying a share of Cisco for its current market price of $19.26. As an alternative, you can buy a September call option with $X = 20. This option will cost you $1.35. Here's your thinking:

- If, on 21 September 2001, Cisco's stock price is >$20.00, you'll exercise the option and purchase the share for $20. If you're careful, you'll realize that there are several "subpossibilities":
  - Cisco's 21 September stock price = $35. Now you've made out like a bandit: You spent $1.35 for the option, but you bought the stock for $20, saving $15.00. Your net profit is $13.35($15.00 − $1.35 cost of the option).
  - If Cisco's 21 September stock price = $21.00, you'll still exercise the option and purchase the stock for $20.00. You've saved $1.00 on the purchase price of the stock, but this time you will have lost a bit of money, since the option cost you $1.35. Your net profit will be −$0.35.
- If on 21 September Cisco's stock is selling for < $20, you will not exercise your call option. If you still want to purchase the stock, you'll buy it on the open market. In all cases, you will be out only the $1.35 cost of the option.

Reason 2: A Call Option Allows You to Make a Bet on the Stock Price Going Up: This Bet is (a) Low Cost, (b) High Upside Potential, and (c) One-Sided

Suppose you buy the Cisco call option above: You spend $1.35 on 7 August 2001 to purchase an option which—on 21 September—gives you the right to purchase Cisco stock for $20. Your purpose is to bet on the price of Cisco stock in September. As you can see in the Figure 23.9:

- This bet has a low cost: You've put up only $1.35 to make it.
- You will never lose more than the $1.35. This is what we mean when we say that the bet is "one-sided": You can only lose a limited amount of money.

Price of Cisco on 21 September	Exercise the Option?	Your Profit or Loss	In Percentage
$15	No—the option gives you the right to buy Cisco for $20, but the market price is less, so you would *not* exercise the option.	−$1.35	$\dfrac{Profit/loss}{Option\ cost} = \dfrac{-\$1.35}{\$1.35} = -100\%$
$20	Yes/No—doesn't matter (you're buying the stock at its market price).	−$1.35	$\dfrac{Profit/loss}{Option\ cost} = \dfrac{-\$1.35}{\$1.35} = -100\%$
$21	Yes—the option lets you buy the stock for $20, but the market price is $21. So you should exercise (even though you've lost money—see next column).	$Profit\ on\ exercise - option\ cost$ $= (\$21 - \$20) - \$1.35$ $= -\$0.35$	$\dfrac{Profit\ on\ exercise - option\ cost}{option\ cost}$ $= \dfrac{(\$21 - \$20) - \$1.35}{\$1.35}$ $= \dfrac{-\$0.35}{\$1.35} = -26\%$
$25	Yes	$Profit\ on\ exercise - option\ cost$ $= (\$25 - \$20) - \$1.35$ $= \$3.65$	$\dfrac{Profit\ on\ exercise - option\ cost}{option\ cost}$ $= \dfrac{(\$25 - \$20) - 1.35}{\$1.35}$ $= \dfrac{\$3.65}{\$1.35} = 270\%$
$30	Yes	$Profit\ on\ exercise - option\ cost$ $= (\$30 - \$20) - \$1.35$ $= \$8.65$	$\dfrac{Profit\ on\ exercise - option\ cost}{option\ cost}$ $= \dfrac{(30 - 20) - 1.35}{1.35}$ $= \dfrac{8.65}{1.35} = 641\%$

Figure 23.9 Analyzing the profit from a call option. If the stock price is down on 21 September, your loss is limited to $1.35. However, if the price goes above $20, your percentage gains from the option are very large. The call option is a "one-sided" bet on the stock price going up—if the stock price goes up, you make money; if the stock price goes down, you lose a limited amount of money.

- The bet has very high upside potential: The profits, both in dollars and as a percentage of the money you put up, rise very rapidly when the stock price in September increases over $20.

You can summarize all of this in a spreadsheet:

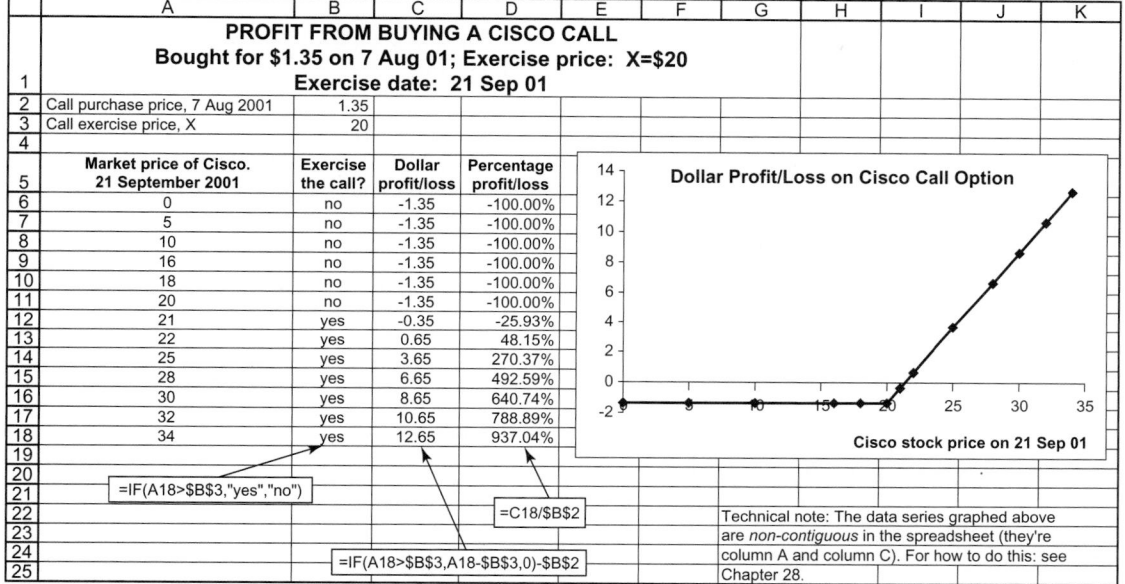

	A	B	C	D	E	F	G	H	I	J	K
1	PROFIT FROM BUYING A CISCO CALL — Bought for $1.35 on 7 Aug 01; Exercise price: X=$20 — Exercise date: 21 Sep 01										
2	Call purchase price, 7 Aug 2001	1.35									
3	Call exercise price, X	20									
4											
5	Market price of Cisco. 21 September 2001	Exercise the call?	Dollar profit/loss	Percentage profit/loss							
6	0	no	-1.35	-100.00%							
7	5	no	-1.35	-100.00%							
8	10	no	-1.35	-100.00%							
9	16	no	-1.35	-100.00%							
10	18	no	-1.35	-100.00%							
11	20	no	-1.35	-100.00%							
12	21	yes	-0.35	-25.93%							
13	22	yes	0.65	48.15%							
14	25	yes	3.65	270.37%							
15	28	yes	6.65	492.59%							
16	30	yes	8.65	640.74%							
17	32	yes	10.65	788.89%							
18	34	yes	12.65	937.04%							
19											
20											
21	=IF(A18>$B$3,"yes","no")										
22				=C18/$B$2				Technical note: The data series graphed above			
23								are non-contiguous in the spreadsheet (they're			
24								column A and column C). For how to do this: see			
25			=IF(A18>$B$3,A18-$B$3,0)-$B$2					Chapter 28.			

Dollar Profit/Loss on Cisco Call Option — Cisco stock price on 21 Sep 01

23.3 Why Buy a Put Option?

As in the case of the call, there are two simple reasons to buy a put.

Reason 1: The Put Option Allows You to Delay the Decision to Sell the Stock

It's 7 August 2001, and you own a share of Cisco stock. You're considering selling the stock; its current market price is $19.26. As an alternative, you can buy a September put option with $X = \$20$. This put option will cost you $2.00. Here's your thinking:

- If, on 21 September 2001, Cisco's stock price is <$20.00, you'll exercise the option and sell the share for $20. As in the case of the call option discussed earlier, there are several "subpossibilities":
  - Cisco's 21 September stock price = $5. Now you've made a lot of money: You spent $2 for the option, but you sold the stock for $20, which is $15.00 more than its market price. Your net profit is $13.00 ($15.00 − $2.00 cost of the option).
  - If Cisco's 21 September stock price = $19.00, you'll still exercise the option and sell the stock for $20.00. Compared to the market price, you've made $1.00 on the sale of the stock, but this time you will have lost a bit of money, since the option cost you $2.00. Your net profit will be −$1.00.

- If on 21 September Cisco's stock is selling for >$20, you will not exercise your put option. If you still want to sell the stock, you'll sell it on the open market. In all cases, you will be out only the $2.00 cost of the option.

Reason 2: A Put Option Allows You to Make a Bet on the Stock Price Going Down

If you buy a put for $2.00 and wait until 21 September to exercise, here are your profits:

$$
put\ profits = \begin{cases}
\$20.00 - S_T - \$2.00 & \begin{array}{l} \text{\textit{Cisco stock price, }} S_T, \text{\textit{ on 21-Sep-01}} \leq \$20 \\ \text{In this case you exercise the put and} \\ \text{make } S_T - \$20 \text{ minus the cost of the put} \end{array} \\[1em]
-\$2.00 & \begin{array}{l} \text{\textit{Cisco stock price, }} S_T, \text{\textit{ on 21-Sep-01}} > \$20 \\ \text{In this case you don't exercise the put;} \\ \text{your loss is the cost of the put} \end{array}
\end{cases}
$$

In a spreadsheet:

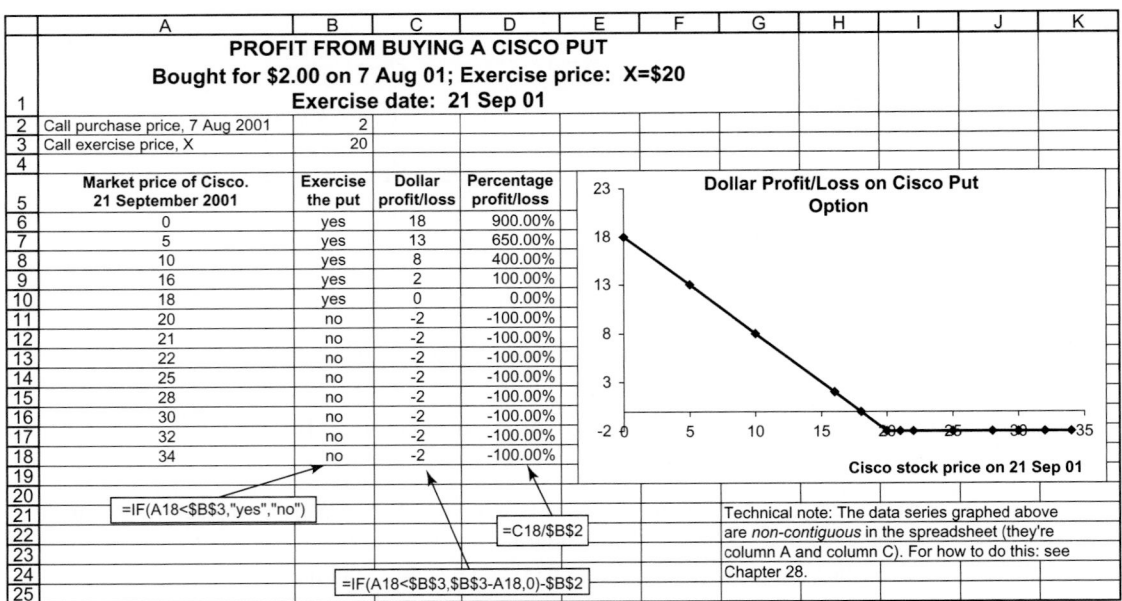

23.4 General Properties of Option Prices

In this section we review three general properties of option prices. We look at the effects of option time to maturity, exercise price, the stock price, interest rates, and risk on option prices. Our discussion is informal and intuitive.

Property 1: Options With More Time to Maturity Are Worth More

The longer you have to exercise an option, the more it should be worth. The intuition here is clear: Suppose you have a September call option to buy Cisco stock for $20 and also an October call option to buy Cisco for $20. Since Cisco options are American options, the October call gives you all the opportunities associated with the September call—and then some. Thus, the October call should be worth more than the September call.

Here's some data for the Cisco options. Notice that the prices of the options increase with maturity:

	A	B	C	D
1	**CISCO OPTIONS: THE EFFECT OF EXPIRATION DATE ON OPTION PRICE**			
2				
3	**Stated expiration date**	**Exercise price, X**	**Call price**	**Put price**
4	Aug-01	20.00	0.65	1.45
5	Sep-01	20.00	1.35	2.00
6	Oct-01	20.00	1.80	2.55
7	Jan-02	20.00	2.90	3.40
8	Jan-03	20.00	5.40	5.20
9	Jan-04	20.00	6.80	5.80
10				

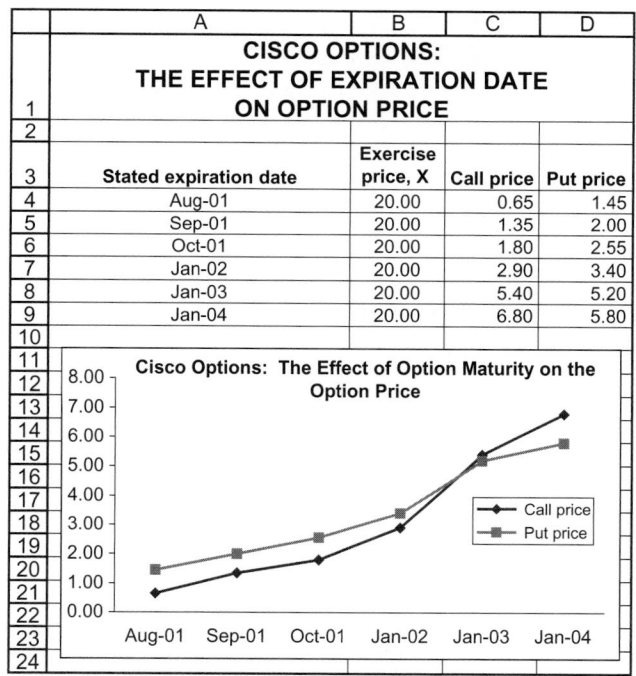

Property 2: Calls With Higher Exercise Prices Are Worth Less; Puts With Higher Exercise Prices Are Worth More

Suppose you had two October calls on Cisco: One call has an exercise price of $20 and the second call has an exercise price of $30. The second call is worth less than the first. Why? Think about calls as *bets* on the stock price: The first call is a bet that the stock price will go over $20, whereas the second call is a bet that the stock price will go over $30. You're always more likely to win the first bet (Cisco will go over $20) than the second bet.

From the table below you can see that Cisco's option prices conform to this property:

	A	B	C	D	E	F	G	H	I
1					**CISCO OCTOBER OPTIONS:**				
					THE EFFECT OF THE EXERCISE PRICE ON THE OPTION PRICE				
2	**Stated expiration date**	**Exercise price, X**	**Call price**	**Put price**					
3	Oct-01	10.00	10.00	0.10					
4	Oct-01	12.50	6.90	0.25					
5	Oct-01	15.00	5.00	0.65					
6	Oct-01	17.50	3.20	1.40					
7	Oct-01	20.00	1.80	2.55					
8	Oct-01	22.50	0.95	4.10					
9	Oct-01	25.00	0.45	6.00					
10	Oct-01	27.50	0.20	7.50					
11	Oct-01	30.00	0.15	10.70					
12	Oct-01	35.00	0.05	16.30					
13	Oct-01	40.00	0.05	21.50					
14	Oct-01	45.00	0.05	29.50					
15	Oct-01	50.00	0.05	31.12					
16	Oct-01	55.00	0.10	37.50					
17	Oct-01	60.00	0.05	36.75					
18	Oct-01	65.00	0.05						
19									

Here we've looked at all the options that expire on the same date (October 2001). As you can see, the higher the option exercise price, the lower the call price and the higher the put price. (There are a few exceptions; see paragraph below.)

The logic of this is clear:

- If an October 2001 Cisco call option with exercise price $10 (the right to buy a share of Cisco for $10) is worth $10, then an October 2001 call with exercise price $12.50 (the right to buy a share of Cisco for $12.50—more than $10) is worth less.

- If an October 2001 Cisco put option with exercise price $10 (the right to sell a share of Cisco in October for $10) is worth $0.10, then the right to sell a share of Cisco for $12.50 should be worth more. And so it is.

The graph and the table show what appear to be a few exceptions to this rule. For example, the Cisco put with $X = \$60$ traded for less than the put with $X = \$55$. If you see this kind of behavior it almost always has to do with the fact that the options in question are infrequently traded. In the example given here, the $65 and $60 calls only traded several times during the day in question. The result is that the option prices given in the table refer to options traded on Cisco stock at different times and with different prices. (Notice that one of the options—the October put with exercise price $65—didn't trade at all.)

Property 3: When the Stock Price Goes Up, Call Option Prices Go Up and Put Option Prices Go Down

The reason for this behavior is obvious, if you think of an option as a bet: Suppose you buy a Cisco $X = \$20$ October 2001 call option. We can view this option as a bet that Cisco's stock price in October will be above $20. The probability of your winning this bet is higher if Cisco's current stock price is higher, and hence so is the call option's price. Thus, for example, if you're willing to pay $1.80 for the $X = \$20$ October call when Cisco's current stock price is $19.26, you would be willing to pay more for the same call when Cisco's stock price is $22.

The logic for puts is the same, though the result is opposite: The higher the stock price, the lower the put option price.

23.5   Writing Options, Shorting Stock

Our discussion thus far has been from the point of view of the option purchaser. For example, in Section 23.2 we derived the profit pattern from buying a Cisco $20 call for $1.35 on 7 August 2001 and waiting until the call maturity on 21 September 2001. Similarly, in Section 23.3 we looked at the profit from buying a Cisco $20 put.

Writing Calls

There's another side to this story: When you buy a call, someone else sells the call. In the jargon of options markets, the call seller is *writing a call*.

Call buyer: On 7 August 2001 buys, for $1.35, the *right* to buy one share of Cisco stock for $20 on or before 21 September 2001.

Call writer: On 7 August 2001 sells, for $1.35, the *obligation* to sell one share of Cisco stock for $20—as per demand of the call option buyer—on or before 21 September.

Figure 23.10 shows the call writer's profit pattern.

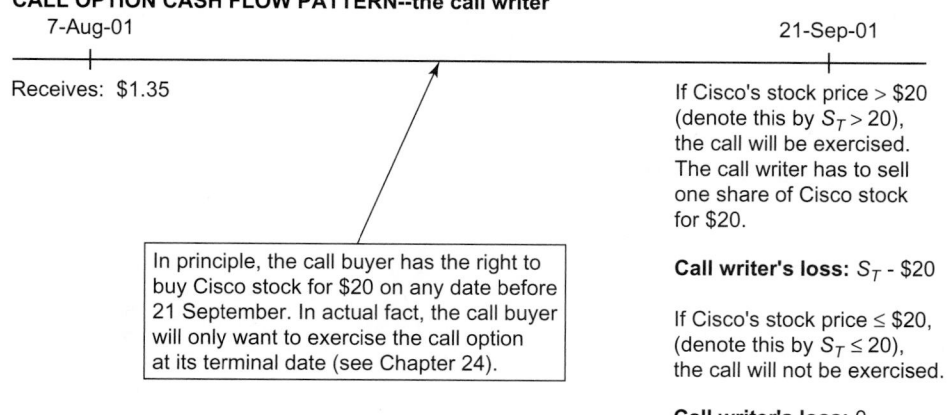

CALL OPTION CASH FLOW PATTERN--the call writer

7-Aug-01

Receives: $1.35

In principle, the call buyer has the right to buy Cisco stock for $20 on any date before 21 September. In actual fact, the call buyer will only want to exercise the call option at its terminal date (see Chapter 24).

21-Sep-01

If Cisco's stock price > $20 (denote this by $S_T > 20$), the call will be exercised. The call writer has to sell one share of Cisco stock for $20.

Call writer's loss: S_T - $20

If Cisco's stock price ≤ $20, (denote this by $S_T \le 20$), the call will not be exercised.

Call writer's loss: 0

Figure 23.10 The cash flows from writing a Cisco call option on 7 August 2001 for $1.35 and possibly having it exercised against the writer on 21 September 2001. The option has exercise price $X = \$20$.

Here's the profit graph from writing a call option:

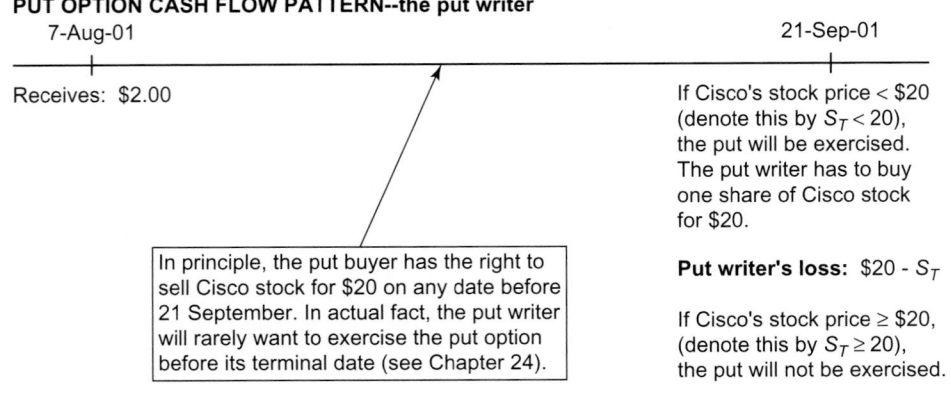

	A	B	C	D	E	F	G	H	I	J	K
1		**PROFIT FROM WRITING A CISCO CALL** Bought for $1.35 on 7 Aug 01; Exercise price: X=$20 **Exercise date: 21 Sep 01**									
2	Call price, 7 Aug 2001	1.35									
3	Call exercise price, X	20									
4											
5	S_T: Market price of Cisco, 21 September 2001	Will call buyer exercise the call?	Dollar profit/loss								
6	0	no	1.35								
7	5	no	1.35								
8	10	no	1.35								
9	16	no	1.35								
10	18	no	1.35								
11	20	no	1.35								
12	21	yes	0.35								
13	22	yes	-0.65								
14	25	yes	-3.65								
15	28	yes	-6.65								
16	30	yes	-8.65								
17	32	yes	-10.65								
18	34	yes	-12.65								
19											
20											
21		=IF(A18>$B$3,"yes","no")									
22								Technical note: The data series graphed above			
23								are *non-contiguous* in the spreadsheet (they're			
24			=$B$2-IF(A18>$B$3,A18-$B$3,0)					column A and column C). For how to do this: see			
25								Chapter 28.			

Writing Puts

There's a similar story for puts:

> **Put buyer:** On 7 August 2001 buys, for $2.00, the *right* to sell one share of Cisco stock for $20 on or before 21 September 2001.

> **Put writer:** On 7 August 2001 sells, for $2.00, the *obligation* to buy one share of Cisco stock for $20—as per demand of the put option buyer—on or before 21 September.

Figure 23.11 shows the call writer's profit pattern.

PUT OPTION CASH FLOW PATTERN--the put writer

7-Aug-01   21-Sep-01

Receives: $2.00

If Cisco's stock price < $20 (denote this by $S_T < 20$), the put will be exercised. The put writer has to buy one share of Cisco stock for $20.

Put writer's loss: $20 - S_T$

If Cisco's stock price ≥ $20, (denote this by $S_T ≥ 20$), the put will not be exercised.

Put writer's loss: 0

In principle, the put buyer has the right to sell Cisco stock for $20 on any date before 21 September. In actual fact, the put writer will rarely want to exercise the put option before its terminal date (see Chapter 24).

Figure 23.11 The cash flows from writing a Cisco put option on 7 August 2001 for $2.00 and possibly having it exercised against the writer on 21 September 2001. The option has exercise price $X = $20.

Here's a graph of the profit pattern from writing a put:

	A	B	C	D	E	F	G	H	I	J	K
1			**PROFIT FROM WRITING A CISCO PUT** **Bought for \$2.00 on 7 Aug 01; Exercise price: X=\$20** **Exercise date: 21 Sep 01**								
2	Put price, 7 Aug 2001		2								
3	Put exercise price, X		20								
4											
5	S_T: Market price of Cisco, 21 September 2001	Will put buyer exercise the put?	Dollar profit/loss to put writer								
6	0	yes	-18								
7	5	yes	-13								
8	10	yes	-8								
9	16	yes	-2								
10	18	yes	0								
11	20	no	2								
12	21	no	2								
13	22	no	2								
14	25	no	2								
15	28	no	2								
16	30	no	2								
17	32	no	2								
18	34	no	2								
19											
20											
21	=IF(A18<\$B\$3,"yes","no")						Technical note: The data series graphed above				
22							are *non-contiguous* in the spreadsheet (they're				
23			=\$B\$2-IF(A17<\$B\$3,\$B\$3-A18,0)					column A and column C). For how to do this: see				
24							Chapter 28.				

Put Writer: Dollar Profit/Loss on Cisco Put Option

S_T: Cisco stock price on 21 Sep 01

Profit = Put price - max(20-S_T,0)

Short-Selling a Stock

Short-selling a stock ("shorting") is the stock equivalent of writing an option. Here's how shorting a stock compares to buying a stock:

Stock buyer: On 7 August 2001 buys one share of Cisco stock, for \$19.26. When you sell the stock—call the date T—you'll get the stock price S_T. Of course, you will have also earned any dividends that Cisco will have paid up to and including date T.[4] Ignoring the time value of money, your profit from buying the stock is

$$S_T + Cisco\ dividends - 19.26$$

Stock shorter: On 7 August 2001 contacts his/her broker and borrows one share of Cisco stock, which he/she then sells, thus receiving \$19.26. At some future date T, the short-seller of the stock will purchase a share of Cisco on the open market, paying the then-current market price S_T. If along the way Cisco has paid any dividends, the short-seller will be obliged to pay these dividends to the person from whom the stock was borrowed. The short-seller's total profit will be

$$19.26 - (S_T + Cisco\ dividends)$$

(For more information, see the sidebar on the next page.)

---

[4]Not something you're likely to have to worry about: Cisco has never paid a dividend!

In the option chapters in this book, we will generally assume that stocks don't pay any dividends between the time you buy them and the time you sell them. This means that the profit from buying or shorting a stock can be represented as follows:

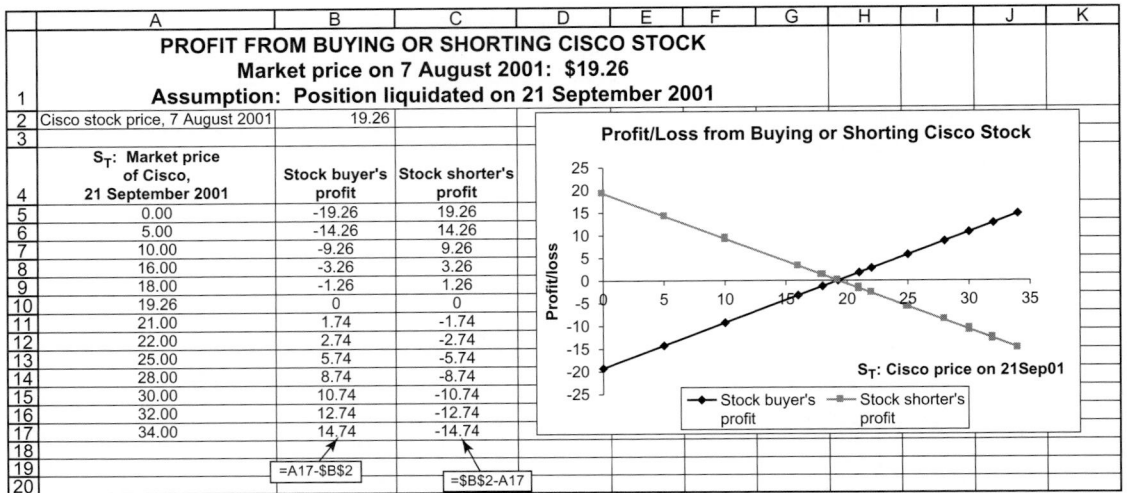

	A	B	C	D	E	F	G	H	I	J	K
1	**PROFIT FROM BUYING OR SHORTING CISCO STOCK** **Market price on 7 August 2001: $19.26** **Assumption: Position liquidated on 21 September 2001**										
2	Cisco stock price, 7 August 2001	19.26									
3											
4	S_T: Market price of Cisco, 21 September 2001	Stock buyer's profit	Stock shorter's profit								
5	0.00	-19.26	19.26								
6	5.00	-14.26	14.26								
7	10.00	-9.26	9.26								
8	16.00	-3.26	3.26								
9	18.00	-1.26	1.26								
10	19.26	0	0								
11	21.00	1.74	-1.74								
12	22.00	2.74	-2.74								
13	25.00	5.74	-5.74								
14	28.00	8.74	-8.74								
15	30.00	10.74	-10.74								
16	32.00	12.74	-12.74								
17	34.00	14.74	-14.74								
18											
19		=A17-$B$2									
20			=$B$2-A17								

SHORT SELLING

A *long* position in a stock involves buying the stock on a particular date and possibly selling the stock on a later date. When you have a long position in a stock, you can choose to hold on to the stock forever (in this case you will collect the dividends that the stock pays).

A *short* position in a stock involves selling borrowed stock on a particular date and buying the stock on a later date in order to give the shares back to the stock lender. Buying the stock in order to return the shares to the lender is called *closing out the short position*. When you have a short position in a stock you must close out the position at some future date.

The profits from short and a long position in a stock are diametrically opposite. When you take a long position in a stock, you will profit if the stock price goes up. When you take a short position in a stock, you profit if the stock price goes down. To see this, suppose that on 31 Oct 2006, You borrow 100 shares of DipseyDoodle (DD) stock. DD is currently selling for $100 and you anticipate that the share price will drop. Having borrowed the shares, you sell them for $10,000 (100 shares times the current price of $100). One month later, DD stock is selling for $80 a share, and you close out your short position: You purchase 100 shares of DD stock for $8,000 and return the shares to the lender. Your short-selling bet on DD stock's decline has paid off, and you've made $2,000. (Of course, if DD had gone up, you would have lost money.)

Two good articles describing short sales can be found at the following websites:

- Motley Fool: http://www.fool.com/FoolFAQ/FoolFAQ0033.htm
- James Surowiecki's article from the *New Yorker* on short selling: http://newyorker.com/talk/content/?031201ta_talk_surowiecki

23.6 Option Strategies: More Complicated Reasons to Buy Options

In the previous section we studied the profit and loss from buying and selling calls, puts, and shares. In this and the following two sections we look at the profit involved in more complicated option strategies. "Option strategy" refers to the profits that result from holding a combination of options and shares.

A Simple Option Strategy: Buy a Stock and Buy a Put

We begin with a very simple (but useful) strategy: Suppose we decide, on 7 August 2001, to purchase one share of Cisco stock *and* to purchase a put on the stock with exercise price $20 and expiration date September. The total cost of this strategy is $21.26: $19.26 for the share of Cisco and $2.00 for each put.

Such a strategy effective *insures* your stock returns by guaranteeing that on 21 September 2001 you will have at least $20 in hand. Your worst-case net profit will be a loss of $1.65:

Stock Price on 21 September	Strategy	Cash in Hand	Net Profit
Less than $20	Exercise put option and sell your share of Cisco for $20.	$20	$20 - (\$19.26 + \$2) = -\$1.65$
More than $20	Let the put option expire (don't use it).	Cisco stock price on 21 September, S_T	$S_T - (\$19.26 + \$2) =$ $S_T - \$21.26$

In a spreadsheet, here's the way this strategy looks:

	A	B	C	D	E	F
1	**STOCK + PUT: OPTION STRATEGY PROFITS**					
2	Stock price, 7 Aug 01	19.26				
3	Cost of put option	2				
4	Put exercise price, X	20	=IF(A7<$B$4,$B$4-A7,0)-$B$3			
5					=A7-$B$2	
6	**Market price of Cisco. 21 September 2001**	**Exercise the put**	**Profit/loss on the put**	**Profit/loss on the stock**	**Total profit/loss**	
7	0	yes	18	-19.26	-1.26	<-- =C7+D7
8	5	yes	13	-14.26	-1.26	
9	10	yes	8	-9.26	-1.26	
10	16	yes	2	-3.26	-1.26	
11	18	yes	0	-1.26	-1.26	
12	20	no	-2	0.74	-1.26	
13	21	no	-2	1.74	-0.26	
14	22	no	-2	2.74	0.74	
15	25	no	-2	5.74	3.74	
16	28	no	-2	8.74	6.74	
17	30	no	-2	10.74	8.74	
18	32	no	-2	12.74	10.74	
19	34	no	-2	14.74	12.74	

Profit/Loss: Stock + Put

Buying a stock or a portfolio *and* buying a put on the stock or portfolio is often called a *portfolio insurance* strategy. Portfolio insurance strategies are very popular among investors. They guarantee a minimum return on the investment in the shares (at an extra cost, of course: you have to buy the puts).

ANTICIPATING A BIT–PUT–CALL PARITY

You'll notice that the graph of the stock + put strategy looks a lot like the graph of a call (Section 23.2). This may lead you to surmise that the payoffs of the combination *stock + put* is somehow equivalent to the payoffs of a *call*. However, this isn't quite true, as you'll see in the next chapter. There we discuss the *put–call parity theorem* and show that, for a put and call written on the same stock and having the same exercise price X,

$$stock + put = call + PV(X)$$

A More Complicated Strategy: Stock + 2 Puts

Suppose you purchased one share of stock and bought 2 puts, each costing $2 and each having an exercise price of $20. Here's what your payoff pattern would look like:

Stock Price on 21 September	Strategy	Cash in Hand, 21 September	Net Profit
$S_T \leq \$20$	Exercise both put options. Give someone else your share of Cisco for $20. Buy an additional share in the market and give it to the put writer for S_T.	$2 * \$20 - S_T$	$2 * \$20 - S_T -$ ($\$19.26 + \$4$) = $\$16.74 - S_T$
$S_T > \$20$	Let the put options expire (don't use them)	Cisco stock price on 21 September, S_T	$S_T - (\$19.26 + \$4) =$ $S_T - \$23.26$

If we make an Excel table, here's what it looks like:

	A	B	C	D	E	F
1	\multicolumn{STOCK + 2 PUTS: OPTION STRATEGY PROFITS					
2	Stock price, 7 Aug 01	19.26				
3	Cost of put option	2.00	=2*(IF(A7<$B$4,$B$4-A7,0)-$B$3)			
4	Put exercise price, X	20.00				
5					=A7-$B$2	
6	Market price of Cisco 21 September 2001	Exercise the put	Profit/loss on the puts	Profit/loss on the stock	Total profit/loss	
7	0	yes	36	-19.26	16.74	<-- =C7+D7
8	5	yes	26	-14.26	11.74	
9	10	yes	16	-9.26	6.74	
10	16	yes	4	-3.26	0.74	
11	18	yes	0	-1.26	-1.26	
12	20	no	-4	0.74	-3.26	
13	21	no	-4	1.74	-2.26	
14	22	no	-4	2.74	-1.26	
15	25	no	-4	5.74	1.74	
16	28	no	-4	8.74	4.74	
17	30	no	-4	10.74	6.74	
18	32	no	-4	12.74	8.74	
19	34	no	-4	14.74	10.74	

Comparing Strategies

What's better as a strategy: buying a share of Cisco and buying 1 put, or buying a share of Cisco and buying 2 puts? Look at the graphs of the two strategies:

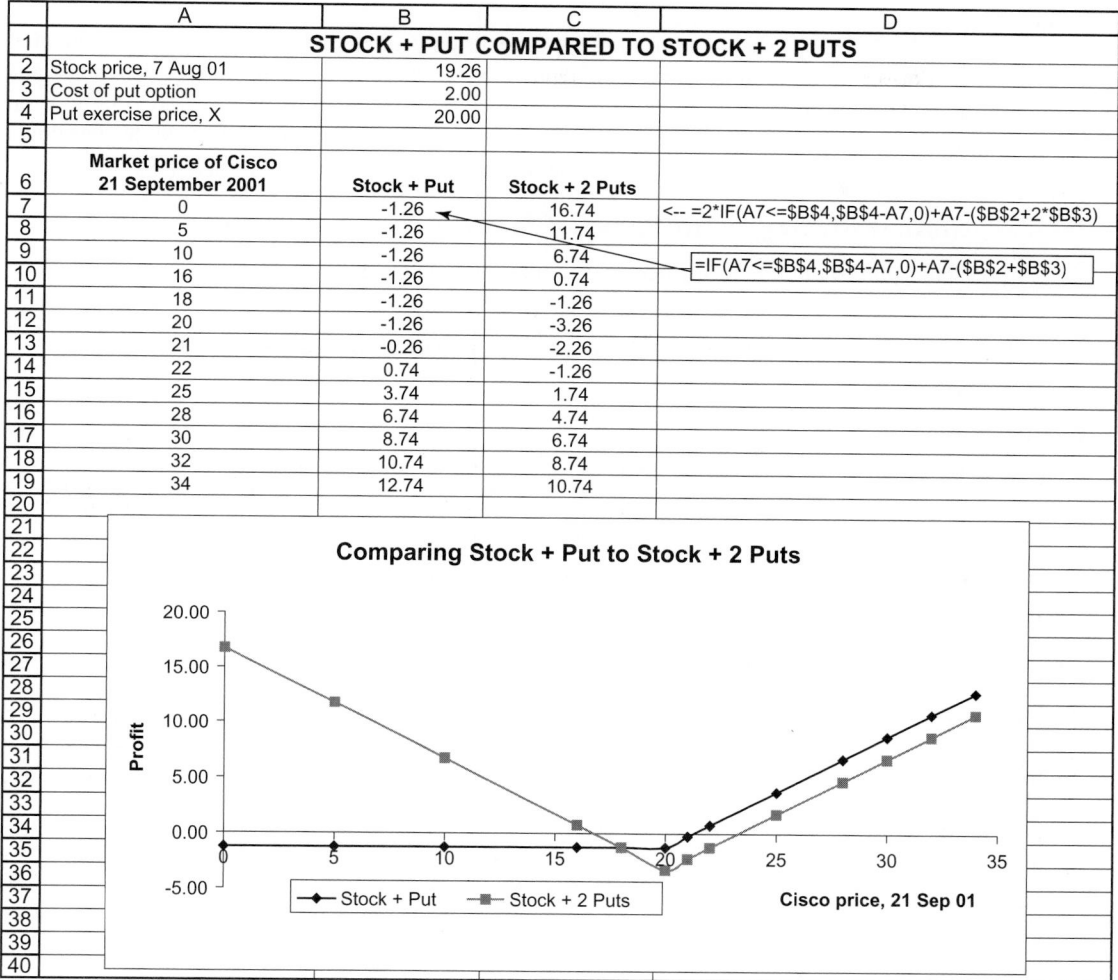

	A	B	C	D
1		**STOCK + PUT COMPARED TO STOCK + 2 PUTS**			
2	Stock price, 7 Aug 01	19.26		
3	Cost of put option	2.00		
4	Put exercise price, X	20.00		
5				
6	**Market price of Cisco 21 September 2001**	**Stock + Put**	**Stock + 2 Puts**	
7	0	-1.26	16.74	<-- =2*IF(A7<=$B$4,$B$4-A7,0)+A7-($B$2+2*$B$3)
8	5	-1.26	11.74	
9	10	-1.26	6.74	
10	16	-1.26	0.74	=IF(A7<=$B$4,$B$4-A7,0)+A7-($B$2+$B$3)
11	18	-1.26	-1.26	
12	20	-1.26	-3.26	
13	21	-0.26	-2.26	
14	22	0.74	-1.26	
15	25	3.74	1.74	
16	28	6.74	4.74	
17	30	8.74	6.74	
18	32	10.74	8.74	
19	34	12.74	10.74	

The choice between the two strategies involves *trade-offs* (that's the nature of market efficiency: in an efficient market no asset ever completely dominates another asset).

- The stock + put strategy has higher profit when the Cisco September stock price $\geq$ \$20, but it has a negative profit for Cisco $S_T \leq$ \$20.
- The stock + 2 put strategy costs more (you can see this by noting that its payoff when $S_T =$ \$20 is less than that of the stock + put strategy). On the other hand, it has positive profits both for very low and for high S_T.

Which strategy should you choose? It depends on your prediction of the future: If you think that Cisco is going to make a big move, up or down, then stock +2 puts is for you, since this strategy makes profits on "big moves" of the stock price (whether up or down). If you think, on the other hand, that Cisco might go up, but you want protection when and if its price goes down (that is, no bets for you), then stock +1 put is your choice.

Another Strategy: One Share of Stock + 1, 2, 3, or 4 Puts

There's almost nothing to say here, except to show you the graphs:

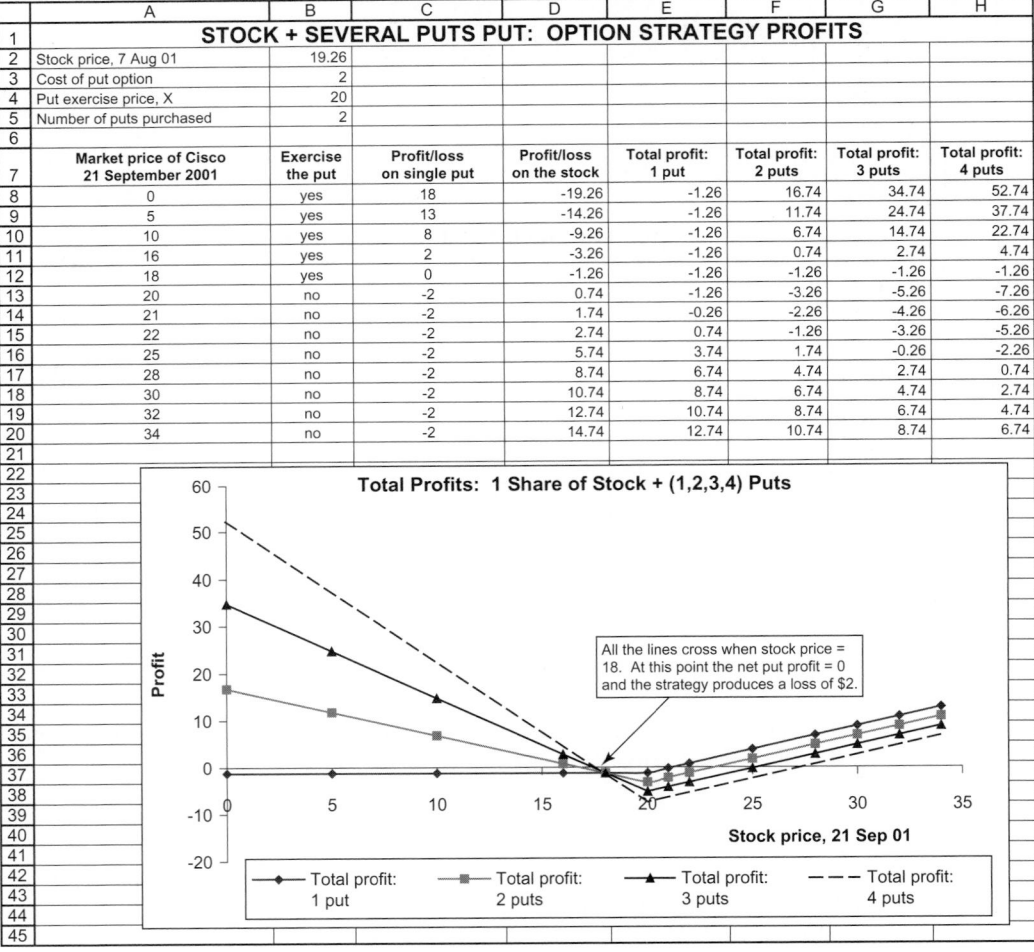

	A	B	C	D	E	F	G	H
1		**STOCK + SEVERAL PUTS PUT: OPTION STRATEGY PROFITS**						
2	Stock price, 7 Aug 01	19.26						
3	Cost of put option	2						
4	Put exercise price, X	20						
5	Number of puts purchased	2						
6								
7	**Market price of Cisco 21 September 2001**	**Exercise the put**	**Profit/loss on single put**	**Profit/loss on the stock**	**Total profit: 1 put**	**Total profit: 2 puts**	**Total profit: 3 puts**	**Total profit: 4 puts**
8	0	yes	18	-19.26	-1.26	16.74	34.74	52.74
9	5	yes	13	-14.26	-1.26	11.74	24.74	37.74
10	10	yes	8	-9.26	-1.26	6.74	14.74	22.74
11	16	yes	2	-3.26	-1.26	0.74	2.74	4.74
12	18	yes	0	-1.26	-1.26	-1.26	-1.26	-1.26
13	20	no	-2	0.74	-1.26	-3.26	-5.26	-7.26
14	21	no	-2	1.74	-0.26	-2.26	-4.26	-6.26
15	22	no	-2	2.74	0.74	-1.26	-3.26	-5.26
16	25	no	-2	5.74	3.74	1.74	-0.26	-2.26
17	28	no	-2	8.74	6.74	4.74	2.74	0.74
18	30	no	-2	10.74	8.74	6.74	4.74	2.74
19	32	no	-2	12.74	10.74	8.74	6.74	4.74
20	34	no	-2	14.74	12.74	10.74	8.74	6.74

Total Profits: 1 Share of Stock + (1,2,3,4) Puts

All the lines cross when stock price = 18. At this point the net put profit = 0 and the strategy produces a loss of $2.

Profit

Stock price, 21 Sep 01

— Total profit: 1 put   — Total profit: 2 puts   — Total profit: 3 puts   - - - Total profit: 4 puts

23.7 Another Option Strategy: Spread

A spread strategy involves buying one option on a stock and writing another option. In the example below on 7 August 2001:

- We buy one $X = \$15$ September call on Cisco. This option costs $4.50.
- We write one $X = \$20$ September call on Cisco. This option costs $1.35; since we're writing the option, this is income on 7 August.

In the spreadsheet below we examine this strategy's payoffs and graph them:

	A	B	C	D	E	F	G
1	**BULL SPREAD: A MODERATE BET ON STOCK PRICE INCREASE**						
2	Cost of September, X=15 call	4.5					
3	Number of X=15 calls purchased	1			=$B$6*(MAX(A9-20,0)-$B$5)		
4							
5	Cost of Sept. X=20 call	1.35	=$B$3*(MAX(A9-15,0)-$B$2)				
6	Number of X=20 calls purchased	-1				=C9+E9	
7							
8	**Market price of Cisco 21 September 2001**	**Exercise X=15 call?**	**Profit/loss on X=15 call**	**Exercise X=20 call?**	**Profit/loss on X=20 call**	**Total profit**	
9	0	no	-4.50	no	1.35	-3.15	
10	5	no	-4.50	no	1.35	-3.15	
11	10	no	-4.50	no	1.35	-3.15	
12	15	no	-4.50	no	1.35	-3.15	
13	18	yes	-1.50	no	1.35	-0.15	
14	20	yes	0.50	no	1.35	1.85	
15	21	yes	1.50	yes	0.35	1.85	
16	22	yes	2.50	yes	-0.65	1.85	
17	25	yes	5.50	yes	-3.65	1.85	
18	28	yes	8.50	yes	-6.65	1.85	
19	30	yes	10.50	yes	-8.65	1.85	
20	32	yes	12.50	yes	-10.65	1.85	
21	34	yes	14.50	yes	-12.65	1.85	
22							

Spread Strategy Profits

There's another way to think about the strategy profits: On 21 September 2001 (the option expiration date) we will have

$$-4.50 + \underbrace{Max[S_{CSCO,21Sep01} - 15, 0]}_{} + 1.35 \underbrace{-Max[S_{CSCO,21Sep01} - 20, 0]}_{}$$

This is the option payoff on 21Sep01 from buying a call with $X = \$15$ — This is the profit from buying the $X = \$15$ option

Writing an option means taking a loss if Cisco's stock price is > \$20 — This is the profit from writing the $X = \$20$ option

$$= -3.15 + \begin{cases} 0 & S_{CSCO,21Sep01} < \$15 \\ S_{CSCO,21Sep01} - 15 & 15 \le S_{CSCO,21Sep01} \le \$20 \\ 5 & S_{CSCO,21Sep01} > \$20 \end{cases}$$

In this case the spread is a not-too-risky bet on the stock price going up. If it goes up, you profit (moderately); if the stock price goes down, your loss is limited to \$3.15. This kind of a spread is called a *bull spread*—you're bullish on the stock (meaning that you think the stock price will go up).

Here's a *bear spread*: In this case we write the $X = \$15$ call and buy the $X = \$20$ call. As you can see from the graph below, the bear spread is a bet that the stock price will decline.

	A	B	C	D	E	F	G
1	BEAR SPREAD: A MODERATE BET ON STOCK PRICE DECLINE						
2	Cost of September, X=15 call	4.5					
3	Number of X=15 calls purchased	-1			=$B$6*(MAX(A9-20,0)-$B$5)		
4			=$B$3*(MAX(A9-15,0)-$B$2)				
5	Cost of Sept. X=20 call	1.35					
6	Number of X=20 calls purchased	1				=C9+E9	
7							
8	Market price of Cisco 21 September 2001	Exercise X=15 call?	Profit/loss on X=15 call	Exercise X=20 call?	Profit/loss on X=20 call	Total profit	
9	0	no	4.50	no	-1.35	3.15	
10	5	no	4.50	no	-1.35	3.15	
11	10	no	4.50	no	-1.35	3.15	
12	15	no	4.50	no	-1.35	3.15	
13	18	yes	1.50	no	-1.35	0.15	
14	20	yes	-0.50	no	-1.35	-1.85	
15	21	yes	-1.50	yes	-0.35	-1.85	
16	22	yes	-2.50	yes	0.65	-1.85	
17	25	yes	-5.50	yes	3.65	-1.85	
18	28	yes	-8.50	yes	6.65	-1.85	
19	30	yes	-10.50	yes	8.65	-1.85	
20	32	yes	-12.50	yes	10.65	-1.85	
21	34	yes	-14.50	yes	12.65	-1.85	
22							

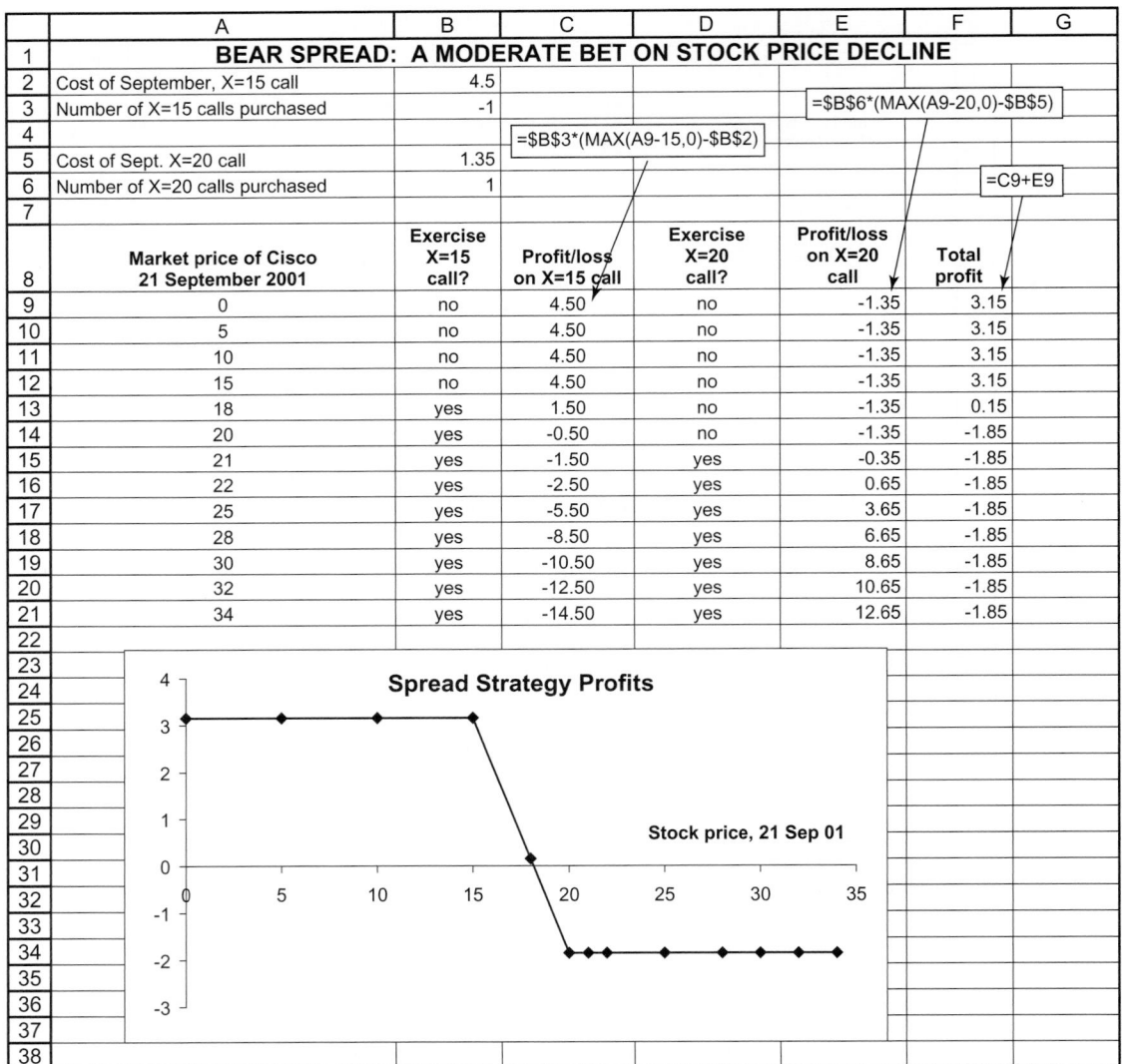

23.8 The Butterfly Option Strategy

The last option strategy we consider in this chapter is a *butterfly,* the combination of three options. In the butterfly illustrated below:

- We buy one Cisco, October $X = \$15$, call for $5.
- We write two Cisco, October $X = \$20$, calls for $1.80 each.

- We buy one Cisco, October $X = \$25$, call for $0.45.

Here's the resulting profit pattern:

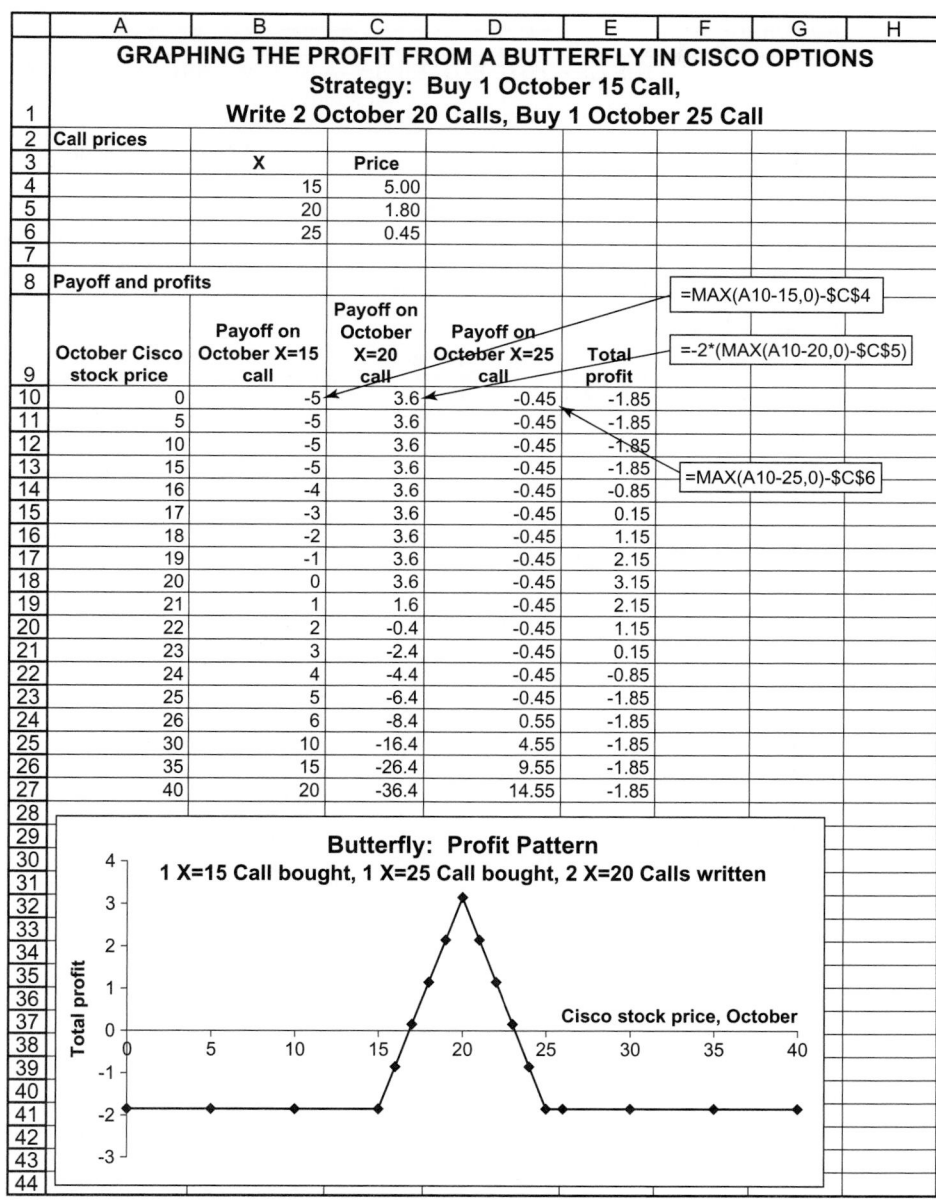

	A	B	C	D	E	F	G	H
1	GRAPHING THE PROFIT FROM A BUTTERFLY IN CISCO OPTIONS — Strategy: Buy 1 October 15 Call, Write 2 October 20 Calls, Buy 1 October 25 Call							
2	Call prices							
3		X	Price					
4		15	5.00					
5		20	1.80					
6		25	0.45					
7								
8	Payoff and profits					=MAX(A10-15,0)-$C$4		
9	October Cisco stock price	Payoff on October X=15 call	Payoff on October X=20 call	Payoff on October X=25 call	Total profit	=-2*(MAX(A10-20,0)-$C$5)		
10	0	-5	3.6	-0.45	-1.85			
11	5	-5	3.6	-0.45	-1.85			
12	10	-5	3.6	-0.45	-1.85			
13	15	-5	3.6	-0.45	-1.85	=MAX(A10-25,0)-$C$6		
14	16	-4	3.6	-0.45	-0.85			
15	17	-3	3.6	-0.45	0.15			
16	18	-2	3.6	-0.45	1.15			
17	19	-1	3.6	-0.45	2.15			
18	20	0	3.6	-0.45	3.15			
19	21	1	1.6	-0.45	2.15			
20	22	2	-0.4	-0.45	1.15			
21	23	3	-2.4	-0.45	0.15			
22	24	4	-4.4	-0.45	-0.85			
23	25	5	-6.4	-0.45	-1.85			
24	26	6	-8.4	0.55	-1.85			
25	30	10	-16.4	4.55	-1.85			
26	35	15	-26.4	9.55	-1.85			
27	40	20	-36.4	14.55	-1.85			

Why buy this butterfly? Looking at the graph you can see that it's a bet on the stock price not moving very much. If Cisco's October stock price is close to $20, we'll make money from our butterfly. If it deviates (up or down) by a lot, we'll lose money, but only moderately.

Of course, if we reverse the option positions in the butterfly, we'll get a bet on the stock price moving a lot (big movements either up or down will lead to profits, small movements in the stock price will lead to losses):

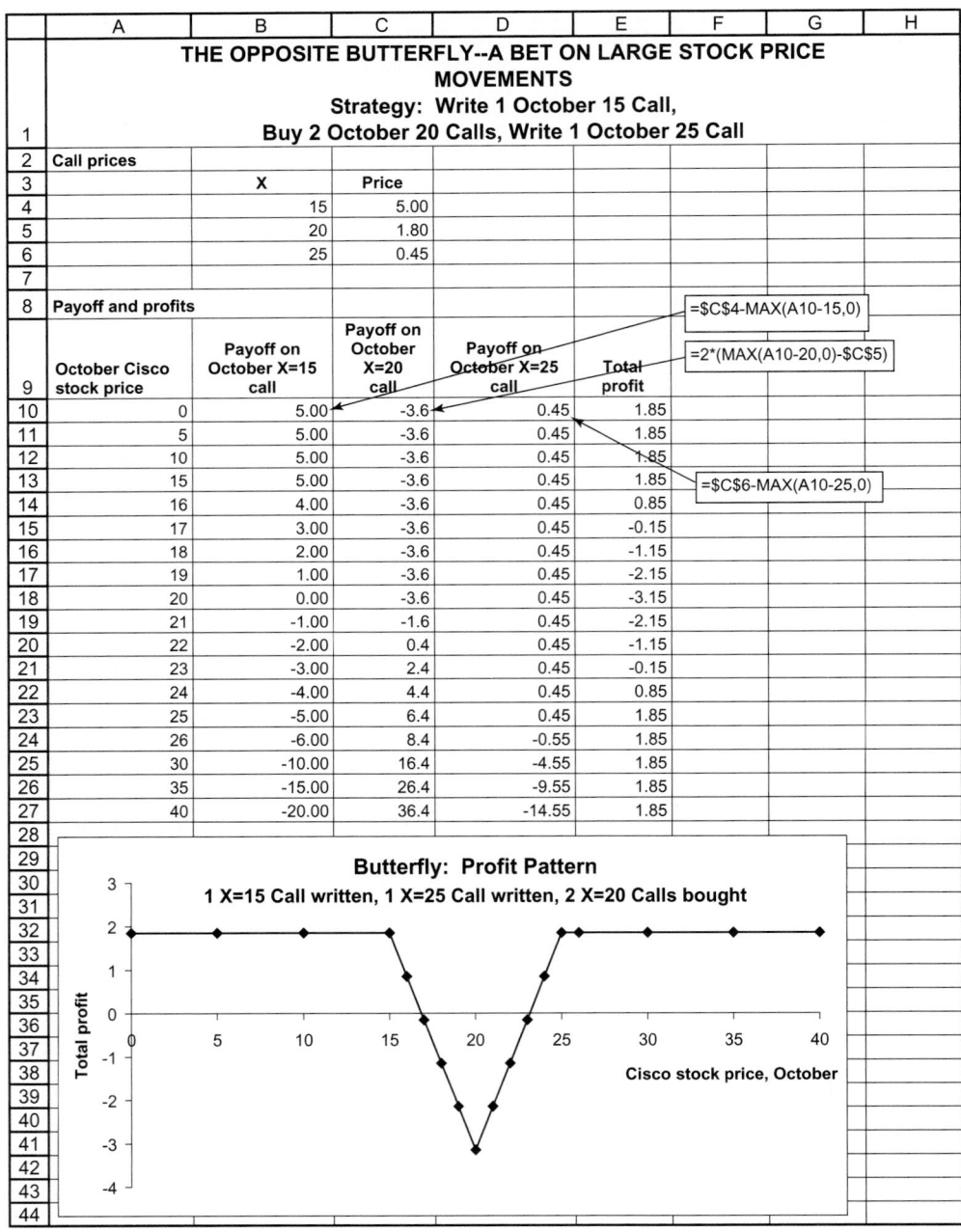

	A	B	C	D	E	F	G	H
1	THE OPPOSITE BUTTERFLY--A BET ON LARGE STOCK PRICE MOVEMENTS Strategy: Write 1 October 15 Call, Buy 2 October 20 Calls, Write 1 October 25 Call							
2	Call prices							
3		X	Price					
4		15	5.00					
5		20	1.80					
6		25	0.45					
7								
8	Payoff and profits					=$C$4-MAX(A10-15,0)		
9	October Cisco stock price	Payoff on October X=15 call	Payoff on October X=20 call	Payoff on October X=25 call	Total profit	=2*(MAX(A10-20,0)-$C$5)		
10	0	5.00	-3.6	0.45	1.85			
11	5	5.00	-3.6	0.45	1.85			
12	10	5.00	-3.6	0.45	1.85			
13	15	5.00	-3.6	0.45	1.85	=$C$6-MAX(A10-25,0)		
14	16	4.00	-3.6	0.45	0.85			
15	17	3.00	-3.6	0.45	-0.15			
16	18	2.00	-3.6	0.45	-1.15			
17	19	1.00	-3.6	0.45	-2.15			
18	20	0.00	-3.6	0.45	-3.15			
19	21	-1.00	-1.6	0.45	-2.15			
20	22	-2.00	0.4	0.45	-1.15			
21	23	-3.00	2.4	0.45	-0.15			
22	24	-4.00	4.4	0.45	0.85			
23	25	-5.00	6.4	0.45	1.85			
24	26	-6.00	8.4	-0.55	1.85			
25	30	-10.00	16.4	-4.55	1.85			
26	35	-15.00	26.4	-9.55	1.85			
27	40	-20.00	36.4	-14.55	1.85			
28								

Butterfly: Profit Pattern

1 X=15 Call written, 1 X=25 Call written, 2 X=20 Calls bought

Total profit

Cisco stock price, October

CONCLUSION

Stock options are securities that make it possible to bet on an increase in the stock price (calls) or a decrease in the price (puts). In this chapter we looked at the basics of option markets. We discussed definitions (calls, puts, American versus European options) and profit patterns of both individual options and combinations of options.

In the next chapter we discuss some facts about stock option prices.

EXERCISES

1. On 2 September 2004 Kellogg stock closed at $41.78. For $2.60 you can buy a call option on Kellogg with an exercise price of $40. The option expires 17 December 2004.
   (a) What right does this call option give you?
   (b) Suppose you buy the call option and hold it until the expiration date. If the price of Kellogg on 17 December 2004, is $52, will you exercise the option? What will be your profit?
   (c) If the price of Kellogg on 17 December 2004, is $38, will you exercise the option? What will be your profit?

2. It is mid-July 2008. Intel stock is currently trading at $30, and you think that the price of the stock will go down by 22 October 2008. For $3 you can buy a put on Intel stock that expires in October and that has an exercise price of $25.
   (a) What right does this put option give you?
   (b) What happens if the stock does not go below $25 by the time your option expires?
   (c) Suppose you buy the option and hold it until the expiration date. If the price of Intel on 22 October 2008 is $20, what will be your profit from the option? What if the price is $38?

3. It is 18 July 2006 and you've just bought one call option on ForeverYours stock. The option cost you $6, expires on 18 September 2004, and has an exercise price of $20.
   (a) Complete the following Excel table.
   (b) Make a graph showing the profit (column C) on the y-axis and the stock price on 18-Sep-04 (column A) on the x-axis.

	A	B	C
1	ForeverYours stock price, 18 Sep 04--S_T	Exercise the call option?	Profit
2	0		
3	5		
4	10		
5	15		
6	20		
7	25		
8	30		
9	35		
10	40		
11	45		
12	50		

Note: Templates for many of these problems are on the disk that accompanies this book.

4. It is 31 December 2007 and you've just bought one put option on ItStinks stock. The option cost you $3, expires on 13 March 2008, and has an exercise price of $35.
   (a) Complete the following Excel table.
   (b) Make a graph showing the profit (column C) on the *y*-axis and the stock price on 13-Mar-08 (column A) on the *x*-axis.

	A	B	C
1	ItStinks stock price, 13 Mar 08--S_T	Exercise the put option?	Profit
2	0		
3	5		
4	10		
5	15		
6	20		
7	25		
8	30		
9	35		
10	40		
11	45		
12	50		

5. On 1 September 2004 Ford's stock price was $13.90 per share.
   (a) Call options on Ford expiring on 17 September 2004 with an exercise price of $12.50 sold for $1.50. Should a call with an exercise price of $12.50 expiring on the 21 January 2005 sell for more than $1.50? Explain.
   (b) Look at the following table. Is there an option that is clearly mispriced?

Ford Call Options Expiring 21 Jan 05	
Exercise price X	Call option price
$ 2.50	$ 12.80
$ 5.00	$ 9.00
$ 7.50	$ 7.90
$ 10.00	$ 5.20
$ 12.50	$ 3.00
$ 15.00	$ 3.30
$ 17.50	$ 0.60
$ 20.00	$ 0.15
$ 22.50	$ 0.10
$ 25.00	$ 0.05

6. On 1 September 2004 GM's stock price was $41.21 per share.
   (a) Put options on GM expiring on 17 September 2004 with an exercise price of $40 sold for $1.80. Should a call with an exercise price of $40 expiring on the 21 January 2005 sell for more than $1.80? Explain.

(b)   Look at the following table. Is there an option that is clearly mispriced?

GM Put Options Expiring 21 Jan 05	
Exercise price X	Put option price
$ 5.00	$ 0.05
$ 10.00	$ 0.09
$ 15.00	$ 0.25
$ 20.00	$ 0.35
$ 30.00	$ 0.95
$ 35.00	$ 2.70
$ 40.00	$ 6.00
$ 45.00	$ 9.70
$ 50.00	$ 8.25
$ 55.00	$ 24.20
$ 60.00	$ 29.20
$ 65.00	$ 33.60
$ 70.00	$ 37.00

7. The price of IBM stock on 1 June 2004 was $88.00.
    (a)   If you purchased the stock on 1 June and sold it on 1 September 2004 for $84.05, what would have been your profit?
    (b)   If you shorted IBM stock on 1 June and closed out your short position on 1 September 2004, what would have been your profit?

8. It is 15 December 2006, and John is considering buying 100 shares of GoodLuck stock (the stock price is currently $40 per share). On the same date Mary is considering shorting 100 shares of GoodLuck stock. If both John and Mary intend to close out their positions on 1 April 2007, fill in the following table and graph their profits.

	A	B	C
1	GoodLuck stock price, 15 Dec 06	$ 40.00	
2			
3	GoodLuck stock price on 1 Apr 07	John's profit from buying 100 shares	Mary's profit from shorting 100 shares
4	$0.00		
5	$10.00		
6	$20.00		
7	$30.00		
8	$40.00		
9	$50.00		
10	$60.00		
11	$70.00		
12	$80.00		
13	$90.00		
14	$100.00		

9. You've decided to add 100 shares of ABC Corp. to your portfolio. ABC stock is currently trading at $50 a share. As an alternative to buying the shares now, you're considering buying 1,000 call options on ABC. Each option has an exercise price of $50 and expires in three months. The options cost $5 each.

(a) Compare the two strategies by filling in the following table and graphing the percentage profits of each strategy against the stock price S_T in three months.

(b) Which strategy is riskier?

	A	B	C	D	E
1	Investment today in buying 100 shares	$ 5,000			
2	Investment today in buying 1,000 call options	$ 5,000			
3					
4	ABC stock price in 3 months, S_T	Dollar profit from buying 100 shares	Dollar profit from buying 1,000 call options now	Percentage profit from buying 100 shares	Percentage profit from buying 1,000 call options now
5	0				
6	10				
7	20				
8	30				
9	40				
10	50				
11	60				
12	70				
13	80				
14	90				
15	100				

10. It is 14 February 2002 and Microsoft (MSFT) stock is trading at $48.30 per share. The price of a call option on MSFT expiring March 2003 is $1.45 for options with $X = \$47.50$ and $0.35 for options with $X = \$50$.

(a) You think that shares of MSFT will rise in price in the immediate future, and you want to speculate in the stock. Compare (graphically) the following two alternatives: purchasing 1,000 MSFT options with an exercise price of $47.5 versus purchasing 1,000 MSFT options with an exercise price of $50.

(b) Compare the two strategies. Which is preferable?

Use the following template:

	A	B	C
1	Exercise price	Call price	
2	47.5	1.45	
3	50	0.35	
4			
5	Investment		
6	A: 1000 options, X=47.5	1,450	<-- =B2*1000
7	B: 1000 options, X=50	350	<-- =B3*1000
8			
9	Stock price in 3 months, S_T	Percentage profit on strategy A	Percentage profit on strategy B
10	0.0		
11	10.0		
12	20.0		
13	30.0		
14	40.0		
15	42.5		
16	45.0		
17	47.5		
18	50.0		
19	55.0		
20	60.0		
21	70.0		
22	80.0		
23	90.0		
24	100.0		

11. It is 1 September 2004 and McDonald's (MCD) stock is trading at $27.19 per share. The price of a put option on MCD expiring 17 September 2004 is $0.10 for options with $X = \$25.00$ and $0.70 for options with $X = \$27.50$.

    (a) You think that shares of MCD will fall in price in the immediate future, and you want to speculate on the stock. Compare (graphically) the following two alternatives: purchasing 1,000 MCD options with an exercise price of $25 versus purchasing 1,000 MCD put options with a strike of $27.50.

    (b) Compare the two strategies. Which is preferable?

Use the following template:

Exercise price	Put price	
25	0.1	
27.5	0.7	
Investment		
A: 1000 options, X=25	100	<-- =B3*1000
B: 1000 options, X=27.50	700	<-- =B4*1000
Stock price in 3 months, S_T	Percentage profit on strategy A	Percentage profit on strategy B
0.0		
15.0		
20.0		
22.0		
24.0		
25.0		
26.0		
26.5		
27.0		
27.5		
28.0		
30.0		
32.5		
35.0		
40.0		

12. A put option written on ENERGY-R-US Corporation's stock is selling for $2.50. The option has an exercise price of $20 and six months to expiration. The current market price for a share of ENERGY-R-US is $26. Determine the profit from a strategy of buying the stock and buying the put; graph these profits. Use the following template.

	A	B	C	D
1	Energy-R-Us, stock	26.00		
2	Put price, X = 20	2.50		
3				
4	Stock price, S_T in 6 months	Profit from put	Profit from stock	Total profit
5	0			
6	5			
7	10			
8	15			
9	20			
10	25			
11	30			
12	35			
13	40			
14	45			
15	50			

13. Using the data from Exercise 12, compare the following three strategies:
    - Purchase one share of stock and one put on the stock.
    - Purchase one share of stock and two puts on the stock.
    - Purchase one share of stock and three puts on the stock.

14. Using the data and the template below, suppose you bought a GM call with exercise (strike) price $X = \$50$ and wrote a GM call with exercise price $X = \$45$. Graph the profit of this strategy at option expiration. Why might this be an attractive strategy?

	A	B	C	D
1	**Call Prices**			
2	**X**	**Price**		
3	45	4.10		
4	50	1.65		
5				
6	**GM stock price, S_T at option expiration**	**Profit on X=45 call (written)**	**Profit on X=50 call (bought)**	**Total profit**
7	20			
8	25			
9	30			
10	35			
11	40			
12	45			
13	50			
14	55			
15	60			
16	65			

15. Using the data from Exercise 14, compute and graph the profit from a strategy in which you buy a GM call with exercise price $X = \$45$ and write a call with exercise price $X = \$50$. Explain why this strategy might be attractive.

16. The following options are traded on WOW Corporation's stock. State which property of option prices is violated and show that you can design a strategy to profit from this mispricing.[5]

Option	Exercise Price	Expiration Date	Price
Call	40	1-Jan-04	$13.50
Call	40	1-Jul-04	$12.95

17. The following options are traded on Smow Corporation's stock. State which property of option prices is violated and show that you can design a strategy to profit from this mispricing.

Option	Exercise Price	Expiration Date	Price
Put	50	1-Mar-04	$4.25
Put	60	1-Mar-04	$4.00

---

[5]Such a strategy is called an *arbitrage strategy*. Such strategies are discussed at length in the next chapter.

18. David wants to buy a call option written on RAIDER Corp. stock. Patrick is willing to sell David a call option on RAIDER Corp. stock with an exercise price of $50 for $8.20. The option will mature in exactly one year. The current market price for RAIDER Corp. stock is $50.
    (a) Determine and graph the payoffs of both David and Patrick's respective positions.
    (b) For what stock price S_T is the profit of both David and Patrick zero?

Call price	8.20	
RAIDER stock price at option expiration, S_T	**Patrick's profit**	**David's profit**
0		
10		
20		
30		
40		
50		
60		
70		
80		
90		
100		

19. Portfolio insurance describes a position in which an investor buys put options to insure that the value of his/her portfolio does not fall below a certain point. Suppose Jo has a portfolio that consists of 100 shares of RTY stock. The current market price of RTY is $35 per share. The following options are also being traded on RTY stock:

Expiration date	Exercise price	Call price	Put price
1-Jun-04	20	$ 18.00	$ 0.10
1-Jun-04	25	$ 11.35	$ 0.45
1-Jun-04	35	$ 3.50	$ 3.20
1-Jun-04	40	$ 0.75	$ 5.65

    (a) What options must Jo buy if she wants to insure that the value of her portfolio will not drop below $2000?
    (b) How much will this cost?

20. A covered call position entails entering into a long position in stock and writing a call option with a high strike price. The purpose of such a position is to finance a portion of the stock purchase from the sale of the call option.

    Sam thinks that STF Corp. stock, currently priced at $80/share, will go up in price by about $15 in the next six months. He would like to buy 10,000 shares of STF today and cash in on his bullish sentiment. In order to cut the initial costs of his purchase, he would like to enter into a covered call position. The following options are being traded on STF Corp:

Expiration date	Exercise price	Call price
1-Aug-04	$ 70	$ 18.95
1-Aug-04	$ 80	$ 7.65
1-Aug-04	$ 90	$ 2.70
1-Aug-04	$ 100	$ 0.50

Suppose Sam writes 10,000 of the $90 calls. Show Sam's profit. Use the following template:

STF stock price	$ 80		
Number of shares purchased	10,000		
Stock price of STF in 6 months, S_T	**Profit from stock position**	**Profit from option position, 10,000 options with X = $90**	**Profit from covered call strategy**
50			
60			
70			
80			
90			
100			
110			
120			

21. Refer to the facts in Exercise 20:
    (a) Compare the profits from a covered call strategy using the $90 calls with one using the $100 calls.
    (b) Which of the two covered call strategies would you recommend?

22. Given the three calls below, design a butterfly strategy that pays off if the stock does not make a major move from its current value of $60. Graph the strategy profits. Use the following template.

Call prices			
	X	**Price**	
	50	22.00	
	60	15.00	
	70	10.00	
Payoff and profits			
Stock price at option expiration, S_T	**Payoff on X = 50 call**	**Payoff on X = 60 call**	**Payoff on X = 70 call**	**Total profit**
30.0				
35.0				
40.0				
45.0				
50.0				
52.5				
55.0				
57.5				
60.0				
62.5				
65.0				
67.5				
70.0				
72.5				
75.0				
80.0				
85.0				
90.0				

23. Given the data from Exercise 22, design a butterfly strategy that pays off if the stock price makes a large move from its current price of $60. Graph the strategy profits.

OPTION PRICING FACTS

OVERVIEW

In Chapter 23 we discussed basic option concepts: definitions of a call and a put, the reasons why you might want to buy or sell an option, and the profits resulting from various options strategies. In this chapter we discuss some basic facts about option pricing. Our emphasis is on a set of propositions known as *arbitrage restrictions* on option prices. These restrictions specify relations between the prices of puts and calls and the prices of either the stock underlying the options or a risk-free asset.

By understanding the option pricing restrictions in this chapter, you can often easily judge whether an option is mispriced. Here's an example: Suppose you're considering buying a call option on Microsoft stock, which is currently selling for $S_0 = \$63$ a share. Suppose the option expires in one year and has exercise price $X = \$60$. The interest rate is $r = 10\%$. The option is priced at $C_0 = \$7$. Is it a good buy or not? Our first option pricing fact (Section 24.1) will enable you to say that the option is *underpriced* and that it is definitely a good buy. As you will see in Section 24.1, the price of the option should be *at least* \$8.45.

NOTATION

Throughout the chapter we use the following notation:

S = Price of the stock. When we want to be precise about the price of the stock on a specific date, we will sometimes write S_0 for the price of the stock today (time 0) and S_T for the price of the stock on the option exercise date T.

X = Option exercise price.

r = Interest rate.

C = Call option price. When we want to be precise about the call price on a specific date, we will sometimes write C_0 for the price of the stock today (time 0) and C_T for the price of the stock on the option exercise date T. Occasionally, we will even use the full word, writing $Call_0$.

P = Put option price. When we want to be precise about the put price on a specific date, we will sometimes write P_0 for the price of the stock today (time 0) and P_T for the price of the stock on the option exercise date T. Occasionally, we will even use the full word, writing Put_0.

Throughout the chapter we assume that the stock on which the options are written does not pay dividends before the option maturity date. This is not an overly restrictive assumption: Stocks that pay dividends tend to do so at regular intervals (quarterly, semiannually, or annually). Holders of options on these stocks are thus reasonably sure when the stocks will pay a dividend. There are thus long periods of time when market participants can be assured that a stock will not pay a dividend.

For example, General Motors pays a regular quarterly dividend in February, May, August, and November. An investor who purchases an option on GM in March with an April maturity knows that in the intervening period no dividends will be paid on the stock.

Many other stocks have never paid a dividend and investors in these stocks' options can be reasonably assured that the dividend pricing restriction imposed in this chapter is not restrictive. Stocks falling into this category include many of the high-tech stocks whose options tend to attract the most investor interest.

Finance Concepts Discussed

- Option pricing restrictions
- No early exercise of calls
- Put–call parity

- Early exercise of American puts
- Option price convexity

Excel Functions Used

- **Max**
- **Sum**
- **If**

24.1 Fact 1: Call Price of an Option
$$C_0 > Max[S_0 - PresentValue(X), 0]$$

It's 15 August 2001, and you're considering buying a call option on Microsoft (MSFT). Currently, the MSFT share itself is selling for $S_0 = \$63$; you want to buy a call on MSFT with an exercise price $X = \$60$ and with time to maturity $T = 1$ year. Furthermore, we'll suppose that the option is an *American call option* and can be exercised at any time on or before T.

We examine Fact 1 in two stages. We start with a "dumb fact," something that is obvious once we say it, and then proceed to demonstrate Fact 1 for you.

Dumb Fact: For an American Call, *Call Price*, $C_0 \geq Max[S_0 - X, 0]$

Now it's probably clear to you that the Microsoft option should be selling for *at least* $\$3 = S - X = \$63 - \$60$. To see this, suppose that the option is selling for \$2. We'll devise an *arbitrage strategy*—a strategy that will make us money risklessly:

Arbitrage Strategy to Profit From Call Price $C_0 = \$2$ When Stock Price Is $S_0 = \$63$ and $X = \$60$

Action Taken Today	Cash Flow (Negative Numbers Indicate Costs)
Buy the option for price C_0	−$2
Immediately exercise the option, buying the stock for price S_0	−$60
Immediately sell the stock on the open market	+$63
Arbitrage profit	**+$1**

So the "dumb fact"—that an American call option should sell for more than the difference between the stock price and the exercise price—is pretty obvious.

DEFINITION: ARBITRAGE STRATEGY

An arbitrage strategy is a combination of assets—usually short or long positions in the stock, calls and puts on the stock, and a risk-free security—which produces nonnegative cash flows at all points in time. If you can design an arbitrage strategy for a given set of asset prices (as we do below), it shows that at least one of the prices is *wrong*.

Smart Fact: *Call Price, C_0 > Max $[S_0 - PV(X), 0]$*

This is a lot less obvious than the previous fact. It's also a lot more powerful.[1] The "dumb fact" above says that the option should sell for at least $3. As the spreadsheet below shows, the "smart fact" says much more; for example, if the interest rate is 10%, then the smart fact says that the option should sell for at least $8.45.

	A	B	C
1	**FACT 1: Lower bound on call price**		
2	Microsoft stock price, 15 August 2001, S	63	
3	Option exercise price, X	60	
4	Option exercise time, T (in years)	1	
5	Interest rate, r	10%	
6			
7	Lower bound on call price		
8	Dumb fact, call price, C_0 > Max$[S_0$ - X,0]	3	<-- =MAX(B2-B3,0)
9	Fact 1: call price, C_0 > Max$[S_0$ - PV(X),0]	8.45	<-- =MAX(B2-B3/(1+B5)^B4,0)

To prove the "smart fact," let's assume that you can buy the call for $5. We'll show that there exists an *arbitrage strategy,* and we will therefore conclude that the option price is too low.

The arbitrage strategy involves a set of actions at time 0 (today) and at time T (the option expiration date):

At time 0 (today):

- Short one share of the stock, get S_0.
- Invest in a riskless security paying off the call's exercise price at time T. This security will cost its present value, $PV(X)$.
- Buy a call on the option. This will cost C_0.

At time T:

- Purchase the stock on the open market at the time-T price, in order to close the short position. Closing the short position will cost S_T.
- Collect from the investment in the riskless security. This will give an inflow of X.
- Exercise the option if this is profitable. If the stock price $S_T > X$, this will give an inflow of $S_T - X$. If the stock price $S_T \le X$, it will not pay to exercise the option.

Here's an example, which assumes that the stock price at time 0 is $S_0 = \$63$, the interest rate is $r = 10\%$, the exercise price is $X = \$60$, and the time to maturity is $T = 1$. This specific example assumes that the call price at time 0 is $C_0 = 5$.

---

[1]How smart? Robert Merton, who first established this and lots of other facts about options, subsequently won the 1997 Nobel Prize in Economics, in part for his work on option pricing.

In the spreadsheet below we show the payoffs from the above strategy, assuming that the price of the stock at time T is $S_T = \$33$ (cell B17):

	A	B	C
1	**ARBITRAGE PROOF OF FACT 1**		
2	Microsoft stock price, 15 August 2001, S_0	63	
3	Option exercise price, X	60	
4	Option exercise time, T (in years)	1	
5	Interest rate, r	10%	
6			
7	**Call price at time 0 (today)**	5	Below examine if this price <-- violates the arbitrage restriction
8			
9	**ARBITRAGE STRATEGY**		
10	**Actions at time 0 (today)**		
11	Short the stock, get S_0	63	<-- =B2
12	Buy a bond which pays of X at time T, pay PV(X)	-54.55	<-- =-B3/(1+B5)^B4
13	Buy a call, pay C_0	-5	<-- =-B7
14	**Total cash flow at time 0**	3.45	<-- =SUM(B11:B13)
15			
16	**Cash flow at time T**		
17	S_T, stock price at time T	33	
18			
19	Repay the shorted stock, pay S_T	-33	<-- =-B17
20	Collect money from the bond, get X	60	<-- =B3
21	Exercise the call? Get Max(S_T - X,0)	0	<-- =MAX(B17-B3,0)
22	**Total cash flow at time T**	27	<-- =SUM(B19:B21)

In cells B19 to B22 we calculate the cash flow at time $T = 1$ from the strategy. In the example above, Microsoft stock at T is selling for $S_T = \$33$. In this case, we would have a positive time T cash flow of \$27 (cell B22).

In the example below, we assume that Microsoft stock at T is $S_T = \$90$. In this case you exercise the call (giving you a positive cash flow of \$30), but the total payoff from the strategy is now \$0.

	A	B	C
1	**ARBITRAGE PROOF OF FACT 1**		
2	Microsoft stock price, 15 August 2001, S_0	63	
3	Option exercise price, X	60	
4	Option exercise time, T (in years)	1	
5	Interest rate, r	10%	
6			
7	**Call price at time 0 (today)**	5	Below examine if this price <-- violates the arbitrage restriction
8			
9	**ARBITRAGE STRATEGY**		
10	**Actions at time 0 (today)**		
11	Short the stock, get S_0	63	<-- =B2
12	Buy a bond which pays of X at time T, pay PV(X)	-54.55	<-- =-B3/(1+B5)^B4
13	Buy a call, pay C_0	-5	<-- =-B7
14	**Total cash flow at time 0**	3.45	<-- =SUM(B11:B13)
15			
16	**Cash flow at time T**		
17	S_T, stock price at time T	90	
18			
19	Repay the shorted stock, pay S_T	-90	<-- =-B17
20	Collect money from the bond, get X	60	<-- =B3
21	Exercise the call? Get Max(S_T - X,0)	30	<-- =MAX(B17-B3,0)
22	**Total cash flow at time T**	0	<-- =SUM(B19:B21)

By changing the stock price S_T, you can see that our strategy always produces no worse than a zero cash flow at time T. This makes it an *arbitrage strategy*:

- At time 0, the cash flow is $3.45 > 0.
- At time T, the cash flow is either positive (if the stock price $S_T < 60$) or zero.

You can't lose from this strategy!! In a rational world this means that something is wrong with the asset prices. In this case, it's clear what's wrong—the call price is too low.

To see this, consider the case where the call price is $10. As you can see below (cell B14), this means that the initial cash flow from the arbitrage strategy is negative. If the stock price at time T is less than $60, say, $S_T = \$55$, then you will make a future profit (cell B22 below), but this profit is no longer an arbitrage profit (recall that arbitrage occurs when you can *never* lose money—with a $10 call price, you start off with an initial negative cash flow):

	A	B	C
7	Call price at time 0 (today)	10	Below examine if this price <-- violates the arbitrage restriction
8			
9	ARBITRAGE STRATEGY		
10	Actions at time 0 (today)		
11	Short the stock, get S_0	63	<-- =B2
12	Buy a bond which pays of X at time T, pay PV(X)	-54.55	<-- =-B3/(1+B5)^B4
13	Buy a call, pay C_0	-10	<-- =-B7
14	Total cash flow at time 0	-1.55	<-- =SUM(B11:B13)
15			
16	Cash flow at time T		
17	S_T, stock price at time T	55	
18			
19	Repay the shorted stock, pay S_T	-55	<-- =-B17
20	Collect money from the bond, get X	60	<-- =B3
21	Exercise the call? Get Max(S_T - X,0)	0	<-- =MAX(B17-B3,0)
22	Total cash flow at time T	5	<-- =SUM(B19:B21)

The cash flow at T (cell B22) is positive, but the initial cash flow (cell B14) is now negative. This makes more sense: Negative initial cash flows in this arbitrage strategy start when the call price is $> \$8.45$. If this is true, then you have to invest money today in order to have a nonnegative cash flow in the future. Note that $\$8.45 = S_0 - PV(X) = \$63 - \$60/1.10$.

We've proved our first option pricing fact: *Call price, $C_0 > Max[S_0 - PV(X), 0]$.*

24.2 Fact 2: It's Never Worthwhile to Exercise a Call Early[2]

Suppose that on 15 August 2001 you bought a Microsoft call option for $C_0 = \$12$ (note that this price does not violate Fact 1's price restriction). Furthermore, suppose that the option expires one year from that date, on 15 August 2002.

---

[2]To be completely accurate, Fact 2 holds whenever the call is written on a stock that does not pay a dividend before the option maturity date T.

Now suppose that after eight months (approximately 2/3 of a year), you want to get rid of the option. To make the problem interesting, we'll assume that the price of Microsoft has risen to $S_t = \$80$. You have two possibilities:

- You could exercise the option. In this case you would collect $\$20 = Max[S_t - X, 0] = Max[\$80 - \$60, 0]$.
- You could also *sell* the option on the open market. Of course, we don't know what the option's price would be, but Fact 1 tells us that in no case will the price be less than

$$Max[S_t - PV(X), 0] = Max\left[S_t - \frac{X}{(1+r)^{1/3}}, 0\right]$$
$$= Max\left[\$80 - \frac{\$60}{(1+10\%)^{1/3}}, 0\right]$$
$$= \$21.876$$

The present value $X/(1+r)^{1/3}$ expresses the fact that there is 1/3 of a year left before the option's exercise.

What should you do? Clearly, you should *sell* rather than *exercise* the call.

	A	B	C	D	E	F
1			**FACT 2: No early exercise of calls**			
2	Microsoft stock price, 15 August 2001, S_0	63				
3	Option exercise price, X	60				
4	Option exercise time, T (in years)	1				
5	Interest rate, r	10%				
6	Call price at time 0	12				
7						
8			**Time line**			
9	t=0			t=2/3		T=1
10						
11	Buy option for $12.00		Consider selling the option			
12			or exercising it.			
13						
14			Stock price, S_t	80.00		
15						
16			Payoff from option exercise	20.00	<-- =MAX(D14-B3,0)	
17			Minimum value of option			
18			according to Fact 1	21.88	<-- =MAX(D14-B3/(1+$B$5)^(1-2/3),0)	
19						
20			Exercise option or sell it?	sell	<-- =IF(D18>=D16,"sell","exercise")	

24.3 Fact 3: Put–Call Parity $Put_0 = Call_0 + PV(X) - S_0$

Put–call parity states that the put price is determined by the call price, the stock price, and the risk-free rate of interest.[3] Here's an example: Suppose that we're considering a one-year put option on the Microsoft stock we've been discussing throughout this chapter. Recall that Microsoft stock is currently selling for $S_0 = \$63$. What should be the put price on Microsoft—where we assume that the put has the same exercise price $X = \$60$ and the same time to maturity $T = 1$?

	A	B	C
1	**FACT 3: Put-Call Parity**		
2	Microsoft stock price, 15 August 2001, S_0	63	
3	Option exercise price, X	60	
4	Option exercise time, T (in years)	1	
5	Interest rate, r	10%	
6			
7	Call price, $Call_0$	15.00	
8	Put price, Put_0, by put-call parity	6.55	<-- =B7+B3/(1+B5)^B4-B2

Another interpretation of put–call parity is that the put price plus the stock price always equals the call price plus the present value of the exercise price:

$$Put_0 + S_0 = Call_0 + PV(X)$$

This means that given any three of the following four variables—put_0, S_0, $call_0$, X—the fourth variable is determined.

An Arbitrage Proof of Put–Call Parity (Can Be Skipped on First Reading)

We can prove put–call parity by using arbitrage, as specified in the spreadsheet below. We assume that the stock price is $S_0 = \$63$, the exercise price is $X = \$60$, the time to exercise is $T = 1$ year, the interest rate is $r = 10\%$, and the call price is $Call_0 = \$15$. Given these facts, put–call parity says that the put price should be $Put_0 = \$6.55$ (cell B8).

In cell B11 we suppose that the put price is $3, different from its put–call parity value; we then show that this makes an arbitrage profitable.

---

[3]Again, recall the assumption that the stock pays no dividends before the option maturity date T.

	A	B	C
1	**Arbitrage Proof of Put-Call Parity**		
2	Microsoft stock price, 15 August 2001, S_0	63	
3	Option exercise price, X	60	
4	Option exercise time, T (in years)	1	
5	Interest rate, r	10%	
6			
7	Call price, $Call_0$	15	
8	Put price, Put_0, by put-call parity	6.55	<-- =B7+B3/(1+B5)^B4-B2
9			
10	**Arbitrage proof of put-call parity**		
11	Put price today (t=0), Put_0	3	If this price differs from the price in cell B8, we will show that there is a profitable arbitrage strategy.
12			
13	**Actions at time 0 (today)**		
14	Buy stock, pay S_0	-63	<-- =-B2
15	Buy put, pay Put_0	-3	<-- =-B11
16	Write call, get $Call_0$	15	
17	Take a loan of PV(X) at risk-free interest, get PV(X)	54.55	<-- =B3/(1+B5)^B4
18	**Total cash flow at time 0**	3.55	<-- =SUM(B14:B17)
19			
20	**Cash flow at time T**		
21	S_T, stock price at time T	90	
22			
23	Sell stock, get S_T	90	<-- =B21
24	Exercise the put? Get Max(X - S_T,0)	0	<-- =MAX(B3-B21,0)
25	Cash flow from written call. Pay Max(S_T - X, 0)	-30	<-- =-MAX(B21-B3,0)
26	Repay loan. Pay X	-60	<-- =-B3
27	Total	0	<-- =SUM(B23:B26)

Here's the arbitrage strategy we designed.

At time 0 (today):

- Buy one share of Microsoft stock for $S_0 = \$63$.
- Buy one put with exercise price $X = \$60$ for $Put_0 = \$3$.
- Write one call with $X = \$60$, collecting (today) $Call_0 = \$15$.
- Take a loan of $PV(X) = \$54.55$; the loan has a one-year maturity (like the options). At the current interest rate of 10% you will have to pay off $X = \$60$ in one year.

At time T we close out all our positions:

- Sell our share of Microsoft at the prevailing market price S_T.
- Exercise the put, if this is profitable. Exercising the put gives you $Max(X - S_T, 0)$.

- Have the call exercised against us, if this is profitable for the call buyer. As the call writer, you can't make money from having the call exercised. The cash flow to the call writer is $-Max(S_T - X, 0)$.
- Repay the loan. This is a negative cash flow, $-X$.

Our example above shows that the cash flow at $T = 1$ will be zero if $S_T = \$90$. The cash flow will also be zero if $S_T = \$35$:

	A	B	C
20	**Cash flow at time T**		
21	S_T, stock price at time T	35	
22			
23	Sell stock, get S_T	35	<-- =B21
24	Exercise the put? Get Max(X - S_T,0)	25	<-- =MAX(B3-B21,0)
25	Cash flow from written call. Pay Max(S_T - X, 0)	0	<-- =-MAX(B21-B3,0)
26	Repay loan. Pay X	-60	<-- =-B3
27	Total	0	<-- =SUM(B23:B26)

As you can see, no matter what the Microsoft stock price is in one year, the cash flow at $T = 1$ from this strategy will be zero. However, the strategy has a positive initial cash flow of $3.55. Clearly, this is an arbitrage!

Symbolically, the future cash flow is given by

$$\underbrace{S_T}_{\text{Stock value}} + \underbrace{Max[X - S_T, 0]}_{\text{Put payoff}} - \underbrace{Max[S_T - X, 0]}_{\substack{\text{Cash flow to call} \\ \text{writer at } T = 1}} - \underbrace{X}_{\text{Loan repayment}}$$

$$= \begin{cases} S_T + X - S_T - X & \text{if } S_T < X \\ S_T - (S_T - X) - X & \text{if } S_T \geq X \end{cases}$$

$$= 0$$

A little thought will reveal that—given the stock price $S = \$60$, the interest rate $r = 10\%$, the exercise price $X = \$60$ of both the put and the call, and the call option price of $15—the put option price must be $6.55 to prevent arbitrage. This follows from the put–price parity relation:

$$Put = Call + PV(X) - S$$

$$= \$15 + \frac{\$60}{1.10} - \$63$$

$$= \$6.55$$

24.4 Fact 4: Bound on an American Put Option Price: $P_0 > Max [X - S_0, 0]$

Suppose you're contemplating buying an American put on Microsoft stock. The stock's price today is $S_0 = \$63$ and the option exercise price is $X = \$70$. Clearly, the option should sell for at least $7. If not, you could easily devise an arbitrage, as illustrated in the spreadsheet below:

	A	B	C
1	**FACT 4: Lower bound on _American put price_**		
2	Microsoft stock price, 15 August 2001, S_0	63	
3	Option exercise price, X	70	
4	Option exercise time, T (in years)	1	
5			
6	Fact 4: Lower bound of American put: $P_0 > Max[X - S_0, 0]$	7	<-- =MAX(B3-B2,0)
7			
8	**Arbitrage strategy**		
9	American put option price	3	
10	Buy option, pay P_0	-3	
11	Buy stock now, pay S_0	-63	
12	Exercise put option immediately: deliver stock and get X	70	
13	Immediate profit	4	<-- =SUM(B10:B12)

If the American put option is mispriced (that is, its price is less than $7), you can make money by buying the option, buying the stock, and exercising the option immediately. This arbitrage profit will not exist if the option's price is greater than $7.

24.5 Fact 5: Bounds on European Put Option Prices $P_0 > Max[PV(X) - S_0, 0]$

Fact 5 is the "put parallel" for Fact 1 about calls.[4]

	A	B	C
1	**FACT 5: Lower bound on _European_ put price**		
2	Microsoft stock price, 15 August 2001, S	63	
3	Option exercise price, X	70	
4	Option exercise time, T (in years)	1	
5	Interest rate, r	10%	
6			
7	Lower bound on call price		
8	Lower bound of American put: P > Max[X - S, 0]	7	<-- =MAX(B3-B2,0)
9	Fact 5: P > Max[PV(X) - S,0]	0.6364	<-- =MAX(B3/(1+B5)^B4-B2,0)

---

[4]There's a crucial difference in the parallel between Facts 1 and 5: Fact 1 applies to _all_ calls, whether European or American. Fact 5 applies _only_ to European puts. Of course, in both cases, the assumption is that the stock pays no dividends before option maturity.

We'll skip the proof of Fact 5. If you're interested, it's on the disk that accompanies this book.

AMERICAN VERSUS EUROPEAN PUTS

Fact 5 says that the price of a European put can actually be much lower than the price of an American put. Consider the example above, in which we look at the price of a put option on Microsoft stock with $T = 1$ and $X = \$70$. If our put was an American put, then it couldn't sell for less than \$7. On the other hand, a *European put,* which cannot be exercised until date T, can sell for anything more than \$0.6364.

24.6 Fact 6: You Might Find It Optimal to Early-Exercise an American Put on a Non-Dividend Paying Stock

Recall that you'll *never* find it optimal to early-exercise an American *call* on a non-dividend-paying stock. But this is not necessarily true for a put option. Here's an example.

Suppose that you're currently holding an option on PFE stock. You bought the option some time ago, when the PFE stock price was still healthy. However, at the current date, the stock has taken a plunge and is selling for \$1 per share. Your American put option has an exercise price of $X = \$100$ and expires in one year. The interest rate is 10%. If you exercise the option now, you'll have a net payoff of \$99 (\$100 minus the current value of the stock of \$1), which—if you invest it in bonds with an interest rate of 10%—will be $\$99 * 1.10 = \$108.90$ in one year. This is more than anyone would have if they waited a year to exercise the option.

Therefore, any rational holder of an American put option will choose to early-exercise the option if the current stock price is very low.

24.7 Fact 7: Option Prices Are Convex (Somewhat Advanced Topic)

Suppose we have three calls, each with a different exercise price but with the same time to exercise T, written on the same stock. Suppose that the exercise price of the first call is $X = \$15$, the exercise price of the second call is $X = \$20$, and the exercise price of the third call is $X = \$25$. Call price convexity says that for three such "equally spaced" calls, the middle call price must be less than the average of the two extreme call prices. In an equation,

$$Call\ price(X = 20) < \frac{Call\ price(X = 15) + Call\ price(X = 25)}{2}$$

To see the meaning of convexity, we return to the Cisco butterfly example from Chapter 23 (p. 690). Consider the three call options in rows 18, 20, and 22 of the next spreadsheet. The convexity relation says that

$$Call\,price(X=20) < \frac{Call\,price(X=15) + Call\,price(X=25)}{2} = \frac{\$4.50 + \$0.20}{2} = \$2.35$$

Since the Cisco call with $X = \$20$ is selling for $1.35 (cell C20), it fulfills the convexity relation.

	A	B	C	D	E	F
1	**CISCO OPTIONS, August 7, 2001 CLOSING PRICE ON CHICAGO BOARD OF OPTIONS EXCHANGE**					
2	August 7, 2001, Cisco closing price	19.26				
3	**Stated expiration date**	**Exercise price, X**	**Call price**	**Put price**	**Actual expiration date**	**Days to maturity**
4	Aug01	7.50	11.90	0.05	17 Aug01	10
5	Aug01	10.00	9.60	0.20	17 Aug01	10
6	Aug01	12.50	6.50	0.10	17 Aug01	10
7	Aug01	15.00	4.20	0.10	17 Aug01	10
8	Aug01	17.50	2.10	0.40	17 Aug01	10
9	Aug01	20.00	0.65	1.45	17 Aug01	10
10	Aug01	22.50	0.15	3.40	17 Aug01	10
11	Aug01	25.00	0.05	5.00	17 Aug01	10
12	Aug01	27.50	0.10	7.50	17 Aug01	10
13	Aug01	30.00	0.10	11.90	17 Aug01	10
14	Aug01	32.50	0.05		17 Aug01	10
15	Aug01	35.00	0.05	16.20	17 Sep01	41
16	Sep01	10.00	9.50		21 Sep01	45
17	Sep01	12.50	6.30	0.15	21 Sep01	45
18	Sep01	15.00	4.50	0.40	21 Sep01	45
19	Sep01	17.50	2.75	0.90	21 Sep01	45
20	Sep01	20.00	1.35	2.00	21 Sep01	45
21	Sep01	22.50	0.55	3.80	21 Sep01	45
22	Sep01	25.00	0.20	5.50	21 Sep01	45

Why Do Call Prices Have to Be Convex?

In this subsection we use a butterfly strategy (Chapter 23, p. 690) to show you why call prices always have to be convex. Recall that a *butterfly* strategy consists of buying one low-priced and one high-priced call and selling two medium-priced calls.

Suppose that the call option prices for Cisco were different from those actually seen in the market. In the example below, we show how our butterfly would have looked had the $X = \$20$ call been priced at $2.50 instead of $1.35:

	A	B	C	D	E	F	G	H
1	WHEN DOES A BUTTERFLY INDICATE AN ARBITRAGE OPPORTUNITY? Strategy: Buy 1 September X=15 Call, Write 2 September X=20 Calls, Buy 1 September X=25 Call							
2	Call prices							
3	X	Price						
4	15	4.50						
5	20	2.50	<-- The actual price is $1.35. To illustrate arbitrage, we assume $2.50					
6	25	0.20						
7								
8			Butterfly payoff and profits			=MAX(A10-15,0)-$B$4		
9	September Cisco stock price	Payoff on September X=15 call	Payoff on September X=20 call	Payoff on September X=25 call	Total profit	=-2*(MAX(A10-20,0)-$B$5)		
10	0	-4.5	5	-0.2	0.3	<-- =D10+C10+B10		
11	5	-4.5	5	-0.2	0.3			
12	10	-4.5	5	-0.2	0.3			
13	15	-4.5	5	-0.2	0.3	=MAX(A10-25,0)-$B$6		
14	16	-3.5	5	-0.2	1.3			
15	17	-2.5	5	-0.2	2.3			
16	18	-1.5	5	-0.2	3.3			
17	19	-0.5	5	-0.2	4.3			
18	20	0.5	5	-0.2	5.3			
19	21	1.5	3	-0.2	4.3			
20	22	2.5	1	-0.2	3.3			
21	23	3.5	-1	-0.2	2.3			
22	24	4.5	-3	-0.2	1.3			
23	25	5.5	-5	-0.2	0.3			
24	26	6.5	-7	0.8	0.3			
25	30	10.5	-15	4.8	0.3			
26	35	15.5	-25	9.8	0.3			
27	40	20.5	-35	14.8	0.3			
28								

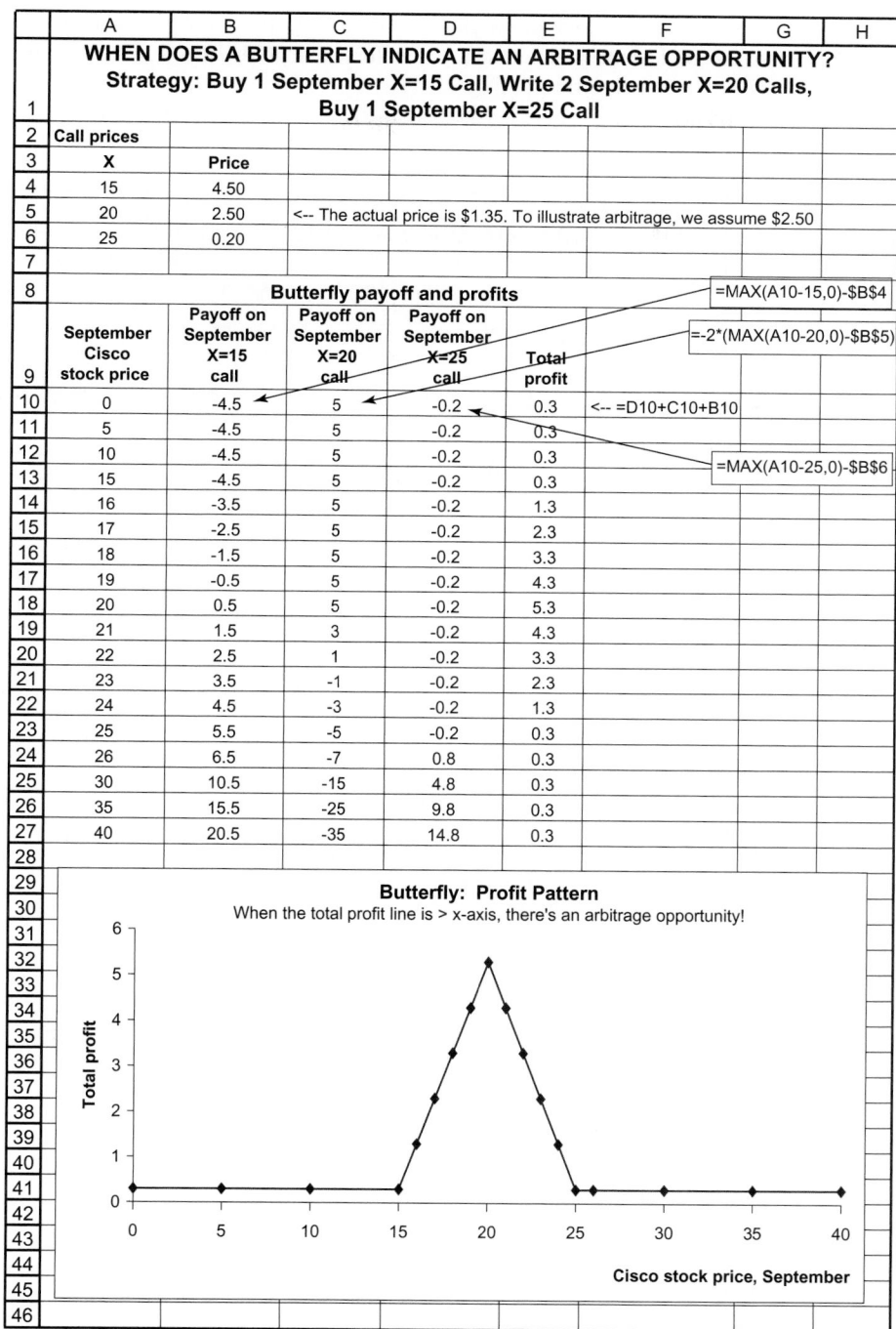

Butterfly: Profit Pattern
When the total profit line is > x-axis, there's an arbitrage opportunity!

Total profit

Cisco stock price, September

Notice that the total profit graph is *completely above the x-axis*. This means that no matter what the stock price in September, you will make a profit. This is clearly not logical—something is wrong with these prices!

You get the same thing if you assume that the $X = \$15$ call option is priced at $2.25 instead of $4.50:

	A	B	C	D	E	F	G	H
1	**WHEN DOES A BUTTERFLY INDICATE AN ARBITRAGE OPPORTUNITY?** Strategy: **Buy 1 September X=15 Call, Write 2 September X=20 Calls, Buy 1 September X=25 Call**							
2	Call prices							
3	X	Price						
4	15	2.25						
5	20	1.35	<-- The actual price is $4.50. To illustrate arbitrage, we assume $2.25					
6	25	0.20						
7								
8			**Butterfly payoff and profits**					
9	September Cisco stock price	Payoff on September X=15 call	Payoff on September X=20 call	Payoff on September X=25 call	Total profit			
10	0	-2.25	2.7	-0.2	0.25	<-- =D10+C10+B10		
11	5	-2.25	2.7	-0.2	0.25			
12	10	-2.25	2.7	-0.2	0.25			
13	15	-2.25	2.7	-0.2	0.25			
14	16	-1.25	2.7	-0.2	1.25			
15	17	-0.25	2.7	-0.2	2.25			
16	18	0.75	2.7	-0.2	3.25			
17	19	1.75	2.7	-0.2	4.25			
18	20	2.75	2.7	-0.2	5.25			
19	21	3.75	0.7	-0.2	4.25			
20	22	4.75	-1.3	-0.2	3.25			
21	23	5.75	-3.3	-0.2	2.25			
22	24	6.75	-5.3	-0.2	1.25			
23	25	7.75	-7.3	-0.2	0.25			
24	26	8.75	-9.3	0.8	0.25			
25	30	12.75	-17.3	4.8	0.25			
26	35	17.75	-27.3	9.8	0.25			
27	40	22.75	-37.3	14.8	0.25			
28								

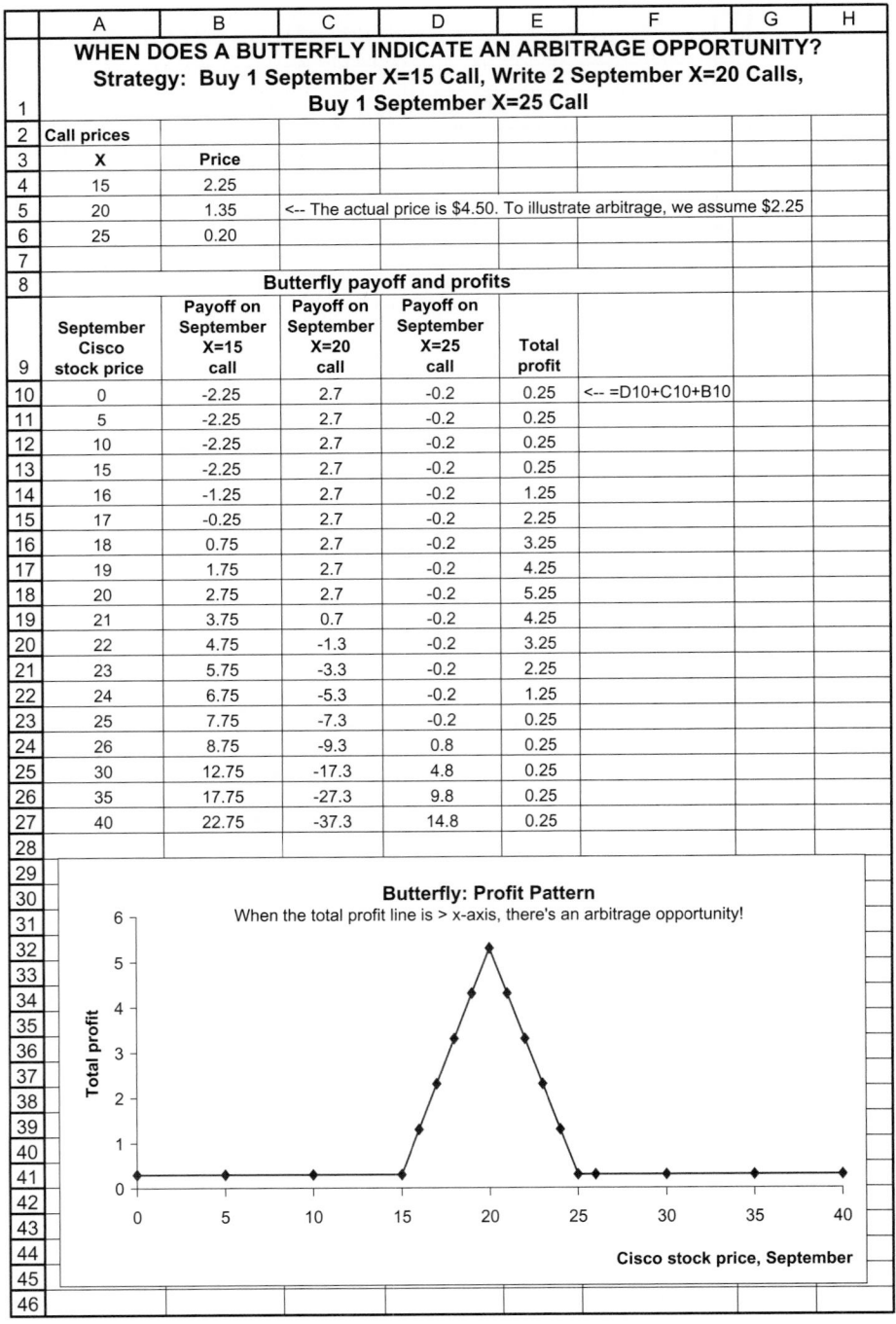

Butterfly: Profit Pattern
When the total profit line is > x-axis, there's an arbitrage opportunity!

Total profit (y-axis)

Cisco stock price, September (x-axis)

What's Wrong?

Playing around a bit with the numbers will convince you that a *condition necessary for the butterfly graph to straddle the x-axis* is

$$Call\, price(X_{Middle}) < \frac{Call\, price(X_{Low}) + Call\, price(X_{High})}{2}$$

where X_{Low}, X_{Middle}, X_{High} are three equally spaced exercise prices.

This condition—in the jargon of the options markets referred to as the *convexity property of call prices*—says that for three "equally spaced" calls, the middle call price must be less than the average of the two extreme call prices. Another way of saying this is that the line connecting two call prices always lies *above* the graph of the call prices (Figure 24.1).

Put prices are also convex.

$$Put\, price(X_{Middle}) < \frac{Put\, price(X_{Low}) + Put\, price(X_{High})}{2}$$

We leave put butterflies as an exercise and let you prove this on your own. Figure 24.2 shows how put prices look.

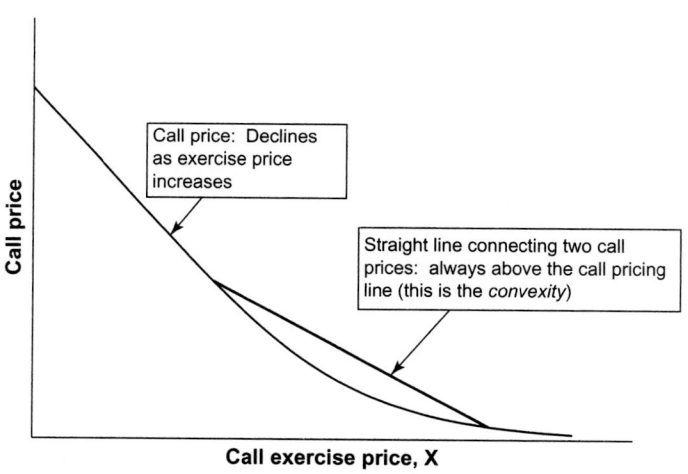

Figure 24.1 The convexity of call prices. The curved line illustrates the actual call prices for various exercise prices. Call price convexity means that the line connecting two call prices is always above the actual call pricing curve.

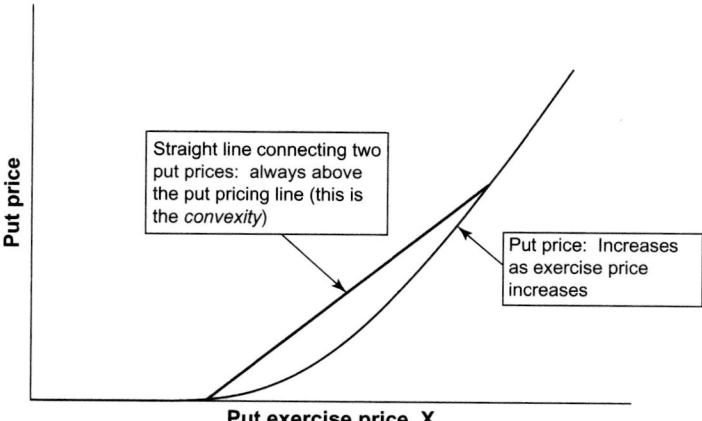

Figure 24.2 Put price convexity. The curved line illustrates the actual put prices for various exercise prices. Put price convexity means that the line connecting two put prices is always above the actual put pricing curve.

CONCLUSION

In this chapter we have derived restrictions on option prices, which stem from their being related to other securities in the market. These arbitrage restrictions help us bound option prices (that is, establish minimum prices for put and call options) as well as establish relations between the prices of various options and the underlying security (as in the case of the put–call parity theorem).

In this chapter we examined seven such option pricing restrictions, but there are many more that deal with cases involving dividends and transactions costs. Understanding the seven restrictions discussed in this chapter will help you understand not only the pricing of options (we will have more to say on this topic in the next chapter) but also the way option traders think—they are constantly busy trying to figure out how to arbitrage option prices.

EXERCISES

1. You want to buy one American call option on Dell Computer Corporation, expiring in six months, with a strike price of $25. The current stock price is at $24.80. Can the option price be lower than $0.60? Assume that the interest rate is 8%.

2. Assume that you can buy the call in Exercise 1 for $0.50 (which is less than the theoretical minimum). How can you exploit the mispricing to make a riskless gain?

3. Your generous uncle gives you 10,000 units of the option in Exercise 2 as a birthday gift. The stock price has risen to $28. Will you exercise the option early or sell it? Explain.

4. Cash dividends affect option prices through their effect on the underlying stock price. Because the stock price is expected to drop by the amount of the dividend on the ex-dividend date, high cash dividends imply lower call premiums. Suppose you own a call option with a strike price of $90 that expires in one week. The stock is currently trading at $100 and is expected to pay a $2.00 dividend tomorrow. The call option has a value of $10. What are you going to do: hold the option or exercise the option early?

5. The Fashion Corporation has stock outstanding that is currently selling for $83 per share. Both a put and call with a strike price of $80 and an expiration of six months are trading. The put option premium is $2.50, and the risk-free rate is 5%. If put–call parity holds, what is the call option premium?

6. The current market price of a two-month European put option on a non-dividend-paying stock with strike price of $50 is $4. The stock price is $47 and the risk-free interest rate is 6%.
   (a) If a two-month call option with the same strike price is currently selling for $1, what opportunities are there for an arbitrageur? How can she exploit arbitrage?
   (b) Would the above market prices still provide an arbitrage opportunity if the stock would be $46.8/per share in one month?

7. In general, what is the problem of using *Wall Street Journal* prices to search for violations of the put–call parity relationship?

8. Recall that a butterfly spread is an options strategy built on four trades at one expiration date and three different strike prices. For call options, one option each at the high and low strike prices are bought, and two options at the middle strike price are sold. A butterfly spread for ABC stock is created as follows: Sell 1 ABC Jun $180 Call for $20 and buy 2 ABC Jun $200 Call each at $10 and sell 1 ABC Jun $220 Call for $5 (net premium received: $20 - 2 * $10 + $5 = $5).

For put options, the trades are reversed: Sell 1 ABC Jun $180 Put, buy 2 ABC Jun $200 Put, and sell 1 ABC Jun $220 Put. Use put–call parity to show that the cost of a butterfly spread created from the European calls is identical to the cost of the butterfly spread created from European puts.

9. (Challenge exercise) You have the following information, 25 calendar days before the March 2004 option expiration day:

Strike	Put/Call	Price
1025	Call	$19.8
1025	Put	$14.5
1040	Call	$12.5
1040	Put	$22.17

   In the absence of arbitrage, what does the annualized risk-free rate have to be?

10. A European put and a call option both expire in a year and have the same exercise price of $20. The options are currently traded at the same market price of $3. Assume that the annual interest rate is 8%. What is the current stock price? In general, if a European put and a call have the same price and expire at the same time, what can you say about the relationships between the stock price and the exercise price: $S > X$? $S < X$? $S = X$?

11. You consider buying an American put option on Dell Computer Corporation, expiring in six months, with a strike price of $25. The current stock price is at $18. What is the minimum price the put will sell for? If you can buy the above put for $5 (which is less than the theoretical minimum), how can you exploit the mispricing to make a riskless gain?

12. ABC is a non-dividend-paying stock. Suppose that $S = \$17$, $X = \$20$, and $r = 5\%$ per annum.
   (a) Can a *European* put option that expires in six months trade at $2.50? Note that a European put option may sometimes be worth less than its intrinsic value.
   (b) Consider a situation where the European put option is traded at $2.40. Show how you can gain from arbitrage.

13. Suppose that you are currently holding an American put option on National Australia Bank that has an exercise price of $45. The option expires in six months. The share price is currently traded at $23.00.
   (a) Consider a situation where the American put option is traded at $21. Show how you can gain from arbitrage.
   (b) What is your net payoff if you exercise the put option today (assume that you invest your proceeds in bonds with an interest rate of 8%)?
   (c) What is your net payoff if you hold the option until its expiration date?

14. You need to weigh the benefits of early exercise of a put option you hold that expires in six months, $X = \$50$, $r = 20\%$, with profit you may be giving up by selling the stock today instead of later.
   (a) Assume $S = \$20$.
   (b) Assume $S = \$3$.
   In which case are you better off exercising the option?

15. Refer to the call options prices given in Exercise 8. Show that the convexity property of call prices holds.

16. A butterfly spread is created using the following put options: The investor buys a put option with a strike price of $55 and pays $15, buys a put with a strike price of $65 and pays $5, and sells two put options with an intermediate strike price of $60.

    (a) What is the upper bound for the $X = \$60$ put price, according to the convexity property?

    (b) Assume that the $X = \$60$ put price is $12. Draw the profit pattern at maturity for the butterfly using Excel (let the stock prices at maturity range between $40 and $80). Does the chart indicate an arbitrage opportunity?

17. At the expiration date the put–call parity $Put_0(X) = Call_0(X) + PV(X) - S_0$ has the following form: $Put_T(X) = Call_T(X) + X - S_T$ or $S_T = Call_T(X) - Put_T(X) + X$. Verify this equation using Excel: Let S_T range from $20 to $100 and the exercise price $X = \$60$. The option values at expiration are: $Put(X) = Max(S_T - X, 0)$ and $Call(X) = Max(X - S_T, 0)$.

18. Cisco (CSCO) stock sells for $25. The at-the-money CSCO April 24 call sells for $3\frac{3}{8}$ and the at-the-money CSCO April 24 put sells for $1\frac{3}{4}$. The call, put, and a Treasury bill all mature in four months. Today's price for a Treasury bill that pays off $100 in four months is $94.92. Assume that Cisco does not pay dividends in this period. Use the put–call parity relation to find the arbitrage profit today, if it exists.

CHAPTER 25

OPTION PRICING—THE BLACK–SCHOLES FORMULA

OVERVIEW

In the two previous chapters on option pricing, we discussed some facts about options, but we did not discuss *how to determine the price of an option*. In this chapter we show how to price options using the Black–Scholes formula. The Black–Scholes formula is the most important option pricing formula. The formula is in wide use in options markets. It has also achieved a certain degree of notoriety, in the sense that even nonfinance people (lawyers, accountants, judges, bankers, and so on) know that options are priced using the Black–Scholes formula. They may not know how to apply it, and they certainly wouldn't know why the formula is correct, but they know that it is used to price options.

In our discussion of the Black–Scholes model, we make no attempt whatsoever to give a theoretical background to the model. It's hopeless, unless you know a lot more math than 99% of all beginning finance students will ever know.[1]

The next chapter discusses the other major model for pricing options, the *binomial option pricing model*. The binomial model gives some insights into how to price an option, and it's also used widely (though not as widely as the Black–Scholes equation). Most books discuss the binomial model—which, in a theoretical sense, underlies the Black–Scholes formula—first and then discuss Black–Scholes. However, since we have no intention of making the theoretical connection between the binomial model and Black–Scholes model, we choose to reverse the order and deal with the more important model first.

What Does "Pricing an Option" Mean?

Suppose we're discussing a call option on Microsoft stock, which is sold on 8 February 2002. On this date, Microsoft's stock price is $S_0 = \$60.65$. Suppose that the call option has an exercise price $X = \$60$ and expires on 19 July 2002. Here's what you've learned so far:

- From Chapter 23, you know the basic option terminology. You know what an exercise price X is, you know the difference between a call and a put, and so on.

- From Chapter 23, you also know what the *payoff pattern* and *profit pattern* of the call option looks like—by itself and in combination with other assets.

- From Chapter 24, you know that there are some pricing *restrictions* on the call option. A simple restriction ("Fact 1" from Chapter 24, p. 704) says that $Call_0 > Max[S_0 - PV(X), 0]$. A more sophisticated restriction ("Fact 3," put–call parity, p. 708) says that once we know the price of Microsoft stock, the call price, and the interest rate, the put price is determined by the relation $Put_0 + S_0 = Call_0 + PV(X)$.

All of these facts are—by themselves—interesting. However, they don't tell us what the *price* of the call option should be. This is the subject of this chapter—the Black–Scholes formula tells us how what the market price of the option should be.

---

[1]A bitter truth, perhaps. But get this—your professor probably can't prove the Black–Scholes equation either (don't embarrass the professor by asking). On the other hand, you know how to drive a car but may not know how an internal combustion engine works; you know how to use a computer but can't make a central processing unit chip, ...

Chapter Notation

We recall the notation we're using throughout Chapters 23–26:

NOTATION

Throughout the chapter we use the following notation:

S = Price of the stock. When we want to be precise about the price of the stock on a specific date, we will sometimes write S_0 for the price of the stock today (time 0) and S_T for the price of the stock on the option exercise date T.

X = Option exercise price.

r = Interest rate.

C = Call option price. When we want to be precise about the call price on a specific date, we will sometimes write C_0 for the price of the stock today (time 0) and C_T for the price of the stock on the option exercise date T. Occasionally, we will even use the full word, writing $Call_0$.

P = Put option price. When we want to be precise about the put price on a specific date, we will sometimes write P_0 for the price of the stock today (time 0) and P_T for the price of the stock on the option exercise date T. Occasionally, we will even use the full word, writing Put_0.

Finance Concepts Discussed

- Black–Scholes formula
- Put–call parity
- Stock price volatility
- Implied volatility
- Real options

Excel Functions Used

- **Exp**
- **Date**
- **Ln**
- **Stdevp**
- **Varp**
- **Data Table**

25.1 The Black–Scholes Model

In 1973, Fisher Black and Myron Scholes proved a formula for pricing European call and put options on non-dividend-paying stocks. Their model is probably the most famous model of modern finance.[2] The Black–Scholes model uses the following formula to price calls on the stock:

$$C_0 = S_0 N(d_1) - Xe^{-rT} N(d_2)$$

where

$$d_1 = \frac{\ln(S_0/X) + (r + \sigma^2/2)T}{\sigma\sqrt{T}}$$

$$d_2 = d_1 - \sigma\sqrt{T}$$

Don't let this formula frighten you! We're going to show you how to use Excel to implement the Black–Scholes formula, and you won't really have to understand the mechanics or the math. However, if you want some explanations: C_0 denotes the price of a call, S_0 is the current price of the underlying stock, X is the exercise price of the call, T is the call's time to exercise, r is the interest rate, and σ is the standard deviation of the stock's return. $N(\ )$ denotes a value of the standard normal distribution. It is assumed that the stock will pay no dividends before date T.

The spreadsheet below prices an option on a stock whose current price is $S_0 = 100$. The option's exercise price is $X = \$90$ and its time to maturity is $T = 0.5$ (one-half year). The interest rate is $r = 4\%$, and sigma (σ, the stock's volatility—a measure of the stock's riskiness; more about this later) is $\sigma = 35\%$.

	A	B	C
1		**The Black-Scholes Option-Pricing Formula**	
2	S_0	100	Current stock price
3	X	90	Exercise price
4	T	0.50000	Time to maturity of option (in years)
5	r	4.00%	Risk-free rate of interest
6	Sigma	35%	Stock volatility
7			
8	d_1	0.6303	<-- (LN(S_0/X)+(r+0.5*sigma^2)*T)/(sigma*SQRT(T))
9	d_2	0.3828	<-- d_1-sigma*SQRT(T)
10			
11	N(d_1)	0.7357	<-- Uses formula NormSDist(d_1)
12	N(d_2)	0.6491	<-- Uses formula NormSDist(d_2)
13			
14	Call price, C_0	16.32	<-- S_0*N(d_1)-X*exp(-r*T)*N(d_2)
15	Put price, P_0	4.53	<-- call price - S_0 + X*Exp(-r*T): by Put-Call parity
16		4.53	<-- X*exp(-r*T)*N(-d_2) - S*N(-d_1): direct formula

By the put–call parity theorem (see Chapter 24, p. 708), a put with the same exercise date T and exercise price X written on the same stock will have price $P_0 = C_0 - S_0 + Xe^{-rT}$. We used this formula in cell B15. Cell B16 includes another version of put pricing—a direct formula that follows from the Black–Scholes formula.

---

[2]The 1997 Nobel Prize in Economics was awarded to Myron Scholes and Robert Merton for their role in developing the option pricing formula. Fisher Black, who died in 1995, would have undoubtedly shared in the prize had he still been alive.

What Do the Black–Scholes Parameters Mean?
How to Calculate Them?

The Black–Scholes option pricing model depends on five parameters:

- S_0, the *current price of the stock*. By this we always mean the stock price on the date we're calculating the option price.

- X, the *exercise price of the option* (this is also called the *strike price*).

- T, the *time to the option's expiration* (sometimes called the *option maturity*). In the Black–Scholes formula, T is always given in *annual terms*—meaning an option with three months to expiration has $T = 0.25$; an option with 51 days until expiration has $T = 51/365 = 0.1397$.

  You can use Excel's **Date** function (see Chapter 31) to compute the time T to option expiration. In the example below, the current date is 2 February 2002 and the option's expiration date is 19 July 2002. These two dates are entered using Excel's **Date** function (cells B2 and B3). Subtracting the two cells gives the number of days between the dates (cell B4). T is computed in cell B5:

	A	B	C
	COMPUTING T USING EXCEL		
1	**DATE FUNCTION**		
2	Current date	2/8/2002	<-- =DATE(2002,2,8)
3	Expiration date	7/19/2002	<-- =DATE(2002,7,19)
4	Days between dates	161	<-- =B3-B2
5	T, time in years to expiration	0.441096	<-- =B4/365
6			
7	Note: We formatted cell B4 to give a number, using **Format|Cells|Number|General**		

- r, the *risk-free interest rate*. This is also given in annual terms. If the interest rate is 6% per year and if an option has $T = 0.25$, then we write $r = 6\%$ in the Black–Scholes formula. We usually use the Treasury bill rate for a maturity that is closest to the option maturity.

- σ (*"sigma"*) is a measure of the *riskiness of the stock*. Sigma is an important variable in determining the option price, and it is not a simple concept to explain. We discuss it at length in Sections 25.2 and 25.3. However, here are some facts to help you get your bearings on sigma:
  - If the stock is riskless, then $\sigma = 0\%$. A stock is riskless if its future price is completely predictable.
  - An "average" U.S. stock has a σ value between 10% and 25%.
  - A risky stock may have a σ value as high as 80% or 100%.

25.2 Historical Volatility: Computing σ From Stock Prices

There are two main ways to compute sigma: (1) We can calculate sigma by looking at the series of past stock prices. This computation is sometimes called the *historical sigma* or the *historical volatility*. Alternatively, we can calculate the *implied sigma* by looking at options prices; this calculation is often called the *implied volatility*. This section describes the computation of the historical volatility, and the next section describes how to compute the implied volatility.

Below we show the annual prices for Microsoft for the decade from 1991 to 2001. Column C shows the *continuously compounded return* for the prices: $r_t^{continuous} = \ln(P_t/P_{t-1})$. (Continuously compounded interest was first discussed in Chapter 6; for a reminder see the box in this chapter on page 727.) Sigma is the standard deviation of these annual returns (cell C18). As you can see, the σ computed from these prices is $\sigma = 36.90\%$:

	A	B	C	D
1	**MICROSOFT STOCK PRICES--ANNUAL DATA**			
2	**Date**	**Closing stock price**	**Return**	
3	31-Dec-90	2.7257		
4	31-Dec-91	5.0104	60.88%	<-- =LN(B4/B3)
5	31-Dec-92	5.4062	7.60%	
6	31-Dec-93	5.3203	-1.60%	
7	31-Dec-94	7.4219	33.29%	
8	31-Dec-95	11.5625	44.33%	
9	31-Dec-96	25.5000	79.09%	
10	31-Dec-97	37.2969	38.02%	
11	31-Dec-98	87.5000	85.27%	
12	31-Dec-99	97.8750	11.21%	
13	31-Dec-00	61.0625	-47.18%	
14	31-Dec-01	66.2500	8.15%	
15				
16	Average return		29.01%	<-- =AVERAGE(C4:C14)
17	Return variance		13.61%	<-- =VARP(C4:C14)
18	Return standard deviation		36.90%	<-- =STDEVP(C4:C14)

In the world of option pricing it is not usual to compute σ from annual data. Most traders prefer daily, weekly, or monthly data. The use of nonannual data requires some adjustment to the calculations. We show these adjustments in the example below, where we calculate Microsoft's σ from monthly data; a discussion of what we did follows the spreadsheet.

	A	B	C	D
1	**MICROSOFT STOCK PRICES** **MONTHLY DATA FOR 2001**			
2	**Date**	**Close**		
3	29-Dec-00	43.3750		
4	31-Jan-01	61.0630	34.20%	<-- =LN(B4/B3)
5	28-Feb-01	59.0000	-3.44%	<-- =LN(B5/B4)
6	30-Mar-01	54.6880	-7.59%	<-- =LN(B6/B5)
7	30-Apr-01	67.7500	21.42%	
8	31-May-01	69.1800	2.09%	
9	29-Jun-01	73.0000	5.37%	
10	31-Jul-01	66.1900	-9.79%	
11	31-Aug-01	57.0500	-14.86%	
12	28-Sep-01	51.1700	-10.88%	
13	31-Oct-01	58.1500	12.79%	
14	30-Nov-01	64.2100	9.91%	
15	31-Dec-01	66.2500	3.13%	
16				
17	**Monthly return statistics**			
18	Average return		3.53%	<-- =AVERAGE(C4:C15)
19	Return variance		1.91%	<-- =VARP(C4:C15)
20	Return standard deviation		13.81%	<-- =STDEVP(C4:C15)
21				
22	**Annualized return statistics**			
23	Average return		42.36%	<-- =12*C18
24	Return variance		22.88%	<-- =12*C19
25	Return standard deviation		47.84%	<-- =SQRT(C24)

The standard deviation of the monthly returns is 13.81% (cell C20). The annualized standard deviation required for the Black–Scholes formula is 47.84% (cell C25). Notice that since

$$annual\ variance = 12 * monthly\ variance$$
$$annual\ standard\ deviation = \sqrt{12 * monthly\ variance}$$
$$= \sqrt{12} * monthly\ standard\ deviation$$

In general, if we're calculating from nonannual data:

$$\sigma,\ annual\ standard\ deviation = \sqrt{12} * monthly\ standard\ deviation$$
$$\sqrt{52} * weekly\ standard\ deviation$$
$$\sqrt{260} * daily\ standard\ deviation$$

(The use of 260 in calculating the annualized σ from weekly data may be a bit confusing: Since there are 52 weeks per year and 5 business days per week, many traders assume that there are 260 business days per year. However, others use 250 and 365.)

CONTINUOUS VERSUS DISCRETE RETURNS—A REMINDER

The Black–Scholes formula uses *continuously compounded* returns, whereas in most of this book we use *discretely compounded returns*. We discussed the difference between these two concepts in Chapter 6. Suppose you have an investment that is worth P_t at time t and worth P_{t+1} one period later. There are two ways to define the return on the investment. The *discrete return* is $r_t^{discrete} = (P_{t+1}/P_t) - 1$, and the *continuously compounded return* is $r_t^{continuous} = \ln(P_{t+1}/P_t)$. The example below shows the difference:

	A	B	C
1	**DISCRETE VERSUS CONTINUOUS RETURNS**		
2	Computing the returns from prices		
3	P_t	100	
4	P_{t+1}	120	
5			
6	Discrete return	20.00%	<-- =B4/B3-1
7	Continuously-compounded return	18.23%	<-- =LN(B4/B3)

25.3 Implied Volatility: Calculating σ From Option Prices

In the previous section we computed the annualized standard deviation of returns σ from historical stock prices. In this section we compute σ from option prices.

When we calculate the implied volatility from option prices, we use the Black–Scholes formula to *find which σ gives a specific options price*. Suppose, for example, that a share of ABC Corp. is currently selling for $S_0 = \$35$, and that a six-month at-the-money call option on ABC Corp. is selling for $C_0 = \$5.25$. (Recall that an "at-the-money" option has exercise price X equal to the current stock price S.) Suppose the interest rate is 6%. The spreadsheet below shows that

σ must be greater than 35% (since the call price increases with σ, and since $\sigma = 35\%$ gives a call price of \$3.94, we'll have to make σ larger to get a call price of \$5.25):

	A	B	C
1	**The Black-Scholes Option-Pricing Formula**		
2	S_0	35	Current stock price
3	X	35	Exercise price
4	T	0.50000	Time to maturity of option (in years)
5	r	6.00%	Risk-free rate of interest
6	Sigma	35.00%	Stock volatility
7			
8	d_1	0.2450	<-- (LN(S/X)+(r+0.5*sigma^2)*T)/(sigma*SQRT(T))
9	d_2	-0.0025	<-- d_1-sigma*SQRT(T)
10			
11	$N(d_1)$	0.5968	<-- Uses formula NormSDist(d_1)
12	$N(d_2)$	0.4990	<-- Uses formula NormSDist(d_2)
13			
14	Call price, C_0	3.94	<-- S*N(d_1)-X*exp(-r*T)*N(d_2)

Using **Goal Seek**, we can compute the σ that gives the market price; it turns out to be $\sigma = 48.71\%$. Here's the **Goal Seek** dialog box:

	A	B	C
1	**The Black-Scholes Option-Pricing Formula**		
2	S_0	35	Current stock price
3	X	35	Exercise price
4	T	0.50000	Time to maturity of option (in years)
5	r	6.00%	Risk-free rate of interest
6	Sigma	35%	Stock vol
7			
8	d_1	0.2450	<-- (LN(S
9	d_2	-0.0025	<-- d_1-sig
10			
11	$N(d_1)$	0.5968	<-- Uses
12	$N(d_2)$	0.4990	<-- Uses
13			
14	Call price, C_0	3.94	<-- S_0*N(d_1)-X*exp(-r*T)*N(d_2)

Goal Seek [?][X]

Set cell: \$B\$14

To value: 5.25

By changing cell: \$B\$6

[OK]   [Cancel]

And here's the final result:

	A	B	C
1	**The Black-Scholes Option-Pricing Formula**		
2	S_0	35	Current stock price
3	X	35	Exercise price
4	T	0.50000	Time to maturity of option (in years)
5	r	6.00%	Risk-free rate of interest
6	Sigma	48.71%	Stock volatility
7			
8	d_1	0.2593	<-- (LN(S/X)+(r+0.5*sigma^2)*T)/(sigma*SQRT(T))
9	d_2	-0.0851	<-- d_1-sigma*SQRT(T)
10			
11	$N(d_1)$	0.6023	<-- Uses formula NormSDist(d_1)
12	$N(d_2)$	0.4661	<-- Uses formula NormSDist(d_2)
13			
14	Call price, C_0	5.25	<-- S*N(d_1)-X*exp(-r*T)*N(d_2)

What's Used in Practice: Implied σ or σ From Historical Prices?

The answer is a bit of both. Smart traders compare the implied volatility with the historical volatility and try to form estimates of what the stock volatility actually is. There are whole websites devoted to this subject, and lots of proprietary software.

25.4 An Excel Black–Scholes Function

The spreadsheet **pfe_chap25.xls** that accompanies this chapter includes two Excel functions to compute the Black–Scholes call and put prices. These functions are not part of the original Excel package; they have been defined by the author. Here's an example of how to use them:

	A	B	C
1	**BLACK-SCHOLES OPTION FUNCTIONS**		
2	The functions in this spreadsheet--**Calloption** and **Putoption**--were defined by the author.		
3	S	100	Current stock price
4	X	90	Exercise price
5	T	0.50000	Time to maturity of option (in years)
6	r	4.00%	Risk-free rate of interest
7	Sigma	35%	Stock volatility
8			
9	Call price	16.32	<-- =calloption(B3,B4,B5,B6,B7)
10	Put price	4.53	<-- =putoption(B3,B4,B5,B6,B7)

The function **Calloption(stock price, exercise price, time to maturity, interest, sigma)** is a defined macro that is attached to the spreadsheet.[3] When you first open the spreadsheet, Excel will display the following message, which asks if you really want to open this macro. In this case the correct answer is **Enable macros**.

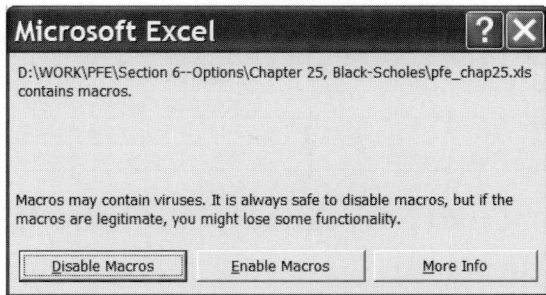

---

[3] As you can see in the spreadsheet, **Putoption** has the same format for the variables.

The dialog box for these functions is self-explanatory:

An Implied Volatility Function

The spreadsheet also comes with two functions to compute the implied volatility for a call and a put option. The function **CallVolatility(stock price, exercise price, option maturity, interest rate, target)** calculates the σ that gives the Black–Scholes price given the other parameters. The spreadsheet also includes a function called **PutVolatility**, which computes the implied volatility for a put option.[4] Both functions are illustrated below:

	A	B	C
1		**TWO IMPLIED VOLATILITY FUNCTIONS**	
2	**Using CallVolatility to compute the implied volatility for a call**		
3	S_0	35	Current stock price
4	X	35	Exercise price
5	T	0.50000	Time to maturity of option (in years)
6	r	6.00%	Risk-free rate of interest
7	Target	5.25	<-- This is the current call price we want to match
8	Implied call volatility	48.71%	<-- =CallVolatility(B3,B4,B5,B6,B7)
9			
10	**Using PutVolatility to compute the implied volatility for a call**		
11	S_0	35	Current stock price
12	X	35	Exercise price
13	T	1.00000	Time to maturity of option (in years)
14	r	6.00%	Risk-free rate of interest
15	Target	3.44	<-- This is the current put price we want to match
16	Implied put volatility	32.49%	<-- =putVolatility(B11,B12,B13,B14,B15)

25.5 Doing Sensitivity Analysis on the Black–Scholes Formula

We can use Excel to do a lot of Black-Scholes sensitivity analysis. In this section we give two examples, leaving other examples for the chapter exercises.

---

[4]In the spirit of this chapter, we do not explain how these functions work. For details, see the author's book *Financial Modeling,* 2nd edition (MIT Press, 2000).

Example 1: The Sensitivity of the Black–Scholes Call Price to the Current Stock Price S

The following **Data|Table** (see Chapter 30) shows the sensitivity of the Black–Scholes call value to the current stock price S. It compares the Black–Scholes call value to the call's intrinsic value $Max(S_0 - X, 0)$.

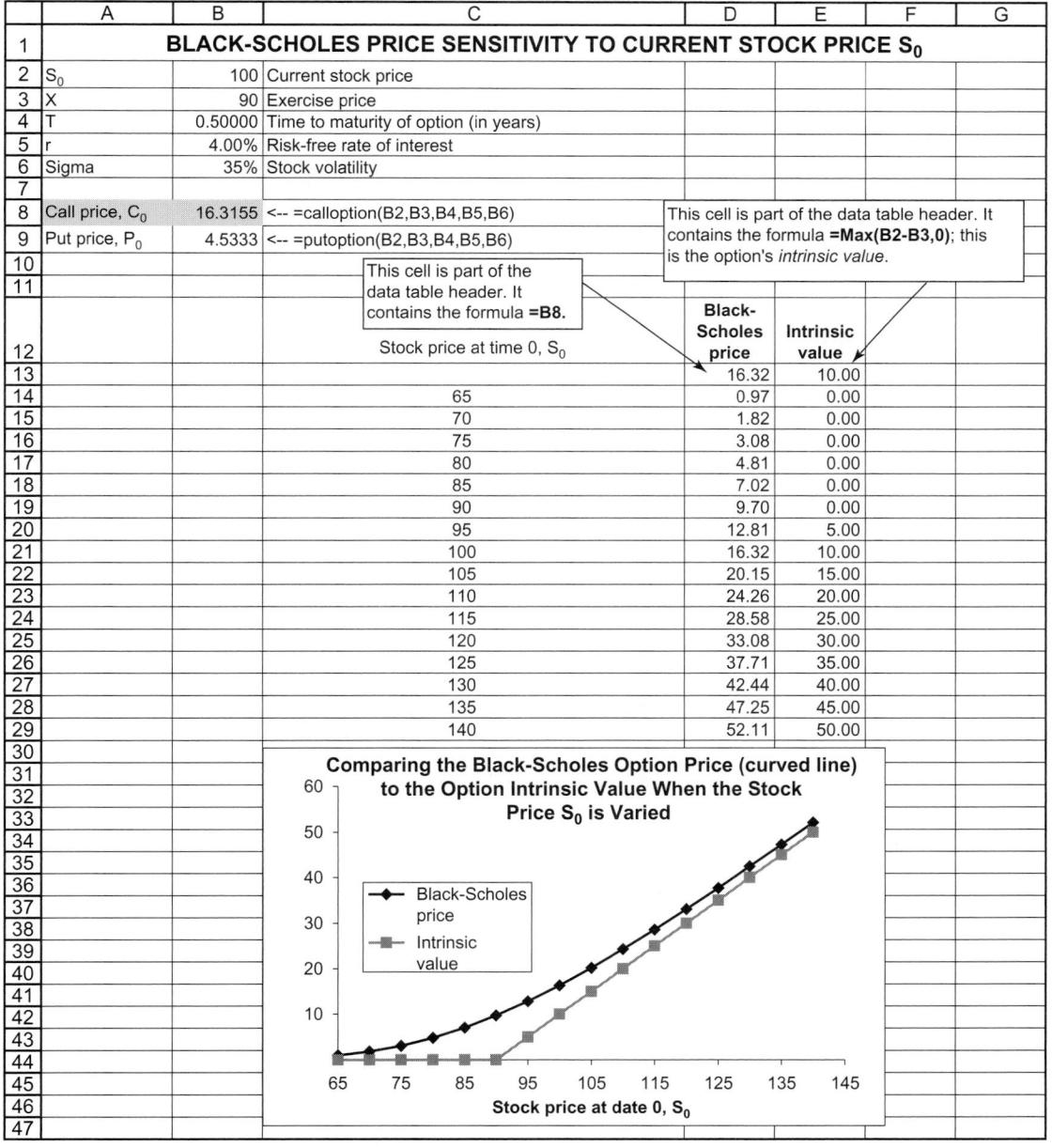

	A	B	C	D	E	F	G
1			**BLACK-SCHOLES PRICE SENSITIVITY TO CURRENT STOCK PRICE S_0**				
2	S_0	100	Current stock price				
3	X	90	Exercise price				
4	T	0.50000	Time to maturity of option (in years)				
5	r	4.00%	Risk-free rate of interest				
6	Sigma	35%	Stock volatility				
7							
8	Call price, C_0	16.3155	<-- =calloption(B2,B3,B4,B5,B6)		This cell is part of the data table header. It contains the formula **=Max(B2-B3,0)**; this is the option's *intrinsic value*.		
9	Put price, P_0	4.5333	<-- =putoption(B2,B3,B4,B5,B6)				
10			This cell is part of the data table header. It contains the formula **=B8.**				
11				Black-Scholes price	Intrinsic value		
12			Stock price at time 0, S_0				
13				16.32	10.00		
14			65	0.97	0.00		
15			70	1.82	0.00		
16			75	3.08	0.00		
17			80	4.81	0.00		
18			85	7.02	0.00		
19			90	9.70	0.00		
20			95	12.81	5.00		
21			100	16.32	10.00		
22			105	20.15	15.00		
23			110	24.26	20.00		
24			115	28.58	25.00		
25			120	33.08	30.00		
26			125	37.71	35.00		
27			130	42.44	40.00		
28			135	47.25	45.00		
29			140	52.11	50.00		
30							
31–47							

Comparing the Black-Scholes Option Price (curved line) to the Option Intrinsic Value When the Stock Price S_0 is Varied

Black-Scholes price

Intrinsic value

Stock price at date 0, S_0

The call option's intrinsic value $Max(S_0 - X, 0)$ shows what it would be worth if exercised immediately. The option's Black–Scholes price shows what the option would be worth. Notice that the Black–Scholes price for the call option is always greater than the intrinsic value—it is not worthwhile early-exercising the call option.

Example 2: The Sensitivity of the Black-Scholes Price to Different Estimates of σ

Here's the sensitivity analysis of the Black–Scholes price to σ.

	A	B	C	D	E	F
1			**BLACK-SCHOLES SENSITIVITY ON SIGMA**			
2	S_0	100	Current stock price			
3	X	90	Exercise price	This cell is part of the data table		
4	T	0.50000	Time to maturity of option (in years)	header. It contains the formula		
5	r	4.00%	Risk-free rate of interest	=calloption(B2,B3,B4,B5,50%).		
6						
7			This cell is part of the data table header; it contains the formula =calloption(B2,B3,B4,B5,20%). **Stock price, S_0**	**BS price, sigma = 20%**	**BS price, sigma = 50%**	
8				13.15	19.91	
9			10	0.00	0.00	
10			20	0.00	0.00	
11			30	0.00	0.01	
12			40	0.00	0.09	
13			50	0.00	0.53	
14			60	0.01	1.78	
15			70	0.24	4.25	
16			80	1.72	8.14	
17			90	5.96	13.41	
18			100	13.15	19.91	
19			110	22.14	27.38	
20			120	31.86	35.60	
21			130	41.80	44.37	
22			140	51.78	53.53	
23			150	61.78	62.96	
24			160	71.78	72.57	
25						
26			**Black-Scholes (BS) Options Price for Two Sigmas**			
27			**Higher Sigma gives a Higher BS Option Price**			

Black-Scholes (BS) Options Price for Two Sigmas Higher Sigma gives a Higher BS Option Price

The higher the stock's sigma σ, the higher the Black–Scholes option price.

25.6 Does the Black–Scholes Model Work? Applying It to Microsoft Options

In this section we do two experiments to examine whether and how well the Black–Scholes model works. First we compare the Black–Scholes option prices for a set of put and call options on Microsoft stock to the actual market prices. Then we compare the implied volatilities for the same options.

Our conclusion: The Black–Scholes model works pretty well!

Comparing Actual Market Prices to Black–Scholes Prices

The experiment we run here looks at options on Microsoft stock.

- On 8 February 2002 we look at the call and put options on Microsoft stock, which expire on 19 July 2002.
- We calculate the Black–Scholes price of these options and compare it to the actual market price.

We get our data from Yahoo, which allows us to look up the stock price of Microsoft on 8 February 2002 and also look up the prices of Microsoft options.[5]

Symbol	Last Trade		Change		Volume
MSFT	Feb 8	**60.65**	+0.85	+1.42%	30,642,600

Chart, Financials, Historical Prices, Insider, Messages, News, Options
Profile, Reports, Research, SEC Filings, Upgrades, **more...**

Get your tax refund fast. Use TurboTax® on Yahoo! Finance

The closing stock price of Microsoft stock on 8 February 2002 was $60.65. The stock was up 1.42% from the previous day's close, and the total volume of stock traded was 30,642,600 shares.

---

[5]See Appendix 25.1 for information about using Yahoo to get option prices.

We now look at the closing prices of options on Microsoft stock, which expire in July 2002. Clicking on **Options** in the above box leads us to the option prices:

Expires After: Fri 19-Jul-02

Options Center | Analyzer NEW | Most Actives | Symbology | Calendar

Options: Feb-02 | Mar-02 | Apr-02 | **Jul-02** | Jan-03 | Jan-04

Highlighted options are in-the-money

Calls							Strike Price	Puts						
Symbol	Last Trade	Chg	Bid	Ask	Vol	Open Int		Symbol	Last Trade	Chg	Bid	Ask	Vol	Open Int
MQFGE.X	**35.10**	0.00	35.70	36.10	0	166	**25**	MQFSE.X	**0.05**	0.00	0.00	0.15	0	70
MQFGF.X	**30.20**	0.00	30.80	31.20	0	99	**30**	MQFSF.X	**0.15**	0.00	0.00	0.15	0	171
MQFGG.X	**25.40**	0.00	25.90	26.30	0	53	**35**	MQFSG.X	**0.30**	0.00	0.15	0.30	0	1,644
MQFGH.X	**20.80**	0.00	21.20	21.60	0	161	**40**	MQFSH.X	**0.55**	0.00	0.40	0.55	0	451
MQFGI.X	**15.70**	-0.70	16.80	17.20	11	829	**45**	MQFSI.X	**1.00**	0.00	0.90	1.05	23	15,930
MSQGJ.X	**12.30**	0.00	12.70	13.10	3	1,086	**50**	MSQSJ.X	**2.00**	0.00	1.75	1.95	1,040	19,919
MSQGK.X	**8.70**	0.00	9.10	9.40	0	400	**55**	MSQSK.X	**3.30**	0.00	3.00	3.30	67	8,163
MSQGL.X	**5.60**	-0.20	6.00	6.30	81	2,444	**60**	MSQSL.X	**5.40**	0.00	5.00	5.30	39	14,609
MSQGM.X	**3.80**	+0.20	3.70	4.00	88	9,474	**65**	MSQSM.X	**8.30**	+0.10	7.60	7.90	32	8,441
MSQGN.X	**2.15**	+0.05	2.10	2.40	1,125	18,565	**70**	MSQSN.X	**12.30**	+0.70	11.00	11.40	15	9,112
MSQGO.X	**1.10**	0.00	1.10	1.30	86	19,073	**75**	MSQSO.X	**15.70**	0.00	14.90	15.30	0	692
MSQGP.X	**0.60**	0.00	0.50	0.65	35	14,770	**80**	MSQSP.X	**20.30**	0.00	19.40	19.80	0	757
MSQGQ.X	**0.35**	+0.10	0.20	0.35	23	8,636	**85**	MSQSQ.X	**25.10**	0.00	24.20	24.60	0	385
MSQGR.X	**0.20**	0.00	0.10	0.25	0	2,684	**90**	MSQSR.X	**30.10**	0.00	29.20	29.60	0	657
MSQGS.X	**0.15**	0.00	0.05	0.15	0	3,203	**95**	MSQSS.X	**35.10**	0.00	34.20	34.60	0	286
MSQGT.X	**0.10**	0.00	0.00	0.15	0	698	**100**	MSQST.X	**40.10**	0.00	39.20	39.60	0	6
MSQGA.X	**0.15**	0.00	0.00	0.15	0	306	**105**	MSQSA.X	**45.10**	0.00	44.20	44.60	0	10

Look carefully at the above box:

- Not all the options were traded on 8 February. For example, there was no "volume" (and hence no trading) of either calls or puts with exercise price ("strike price") of 25.
- Significant amounts of call options traded on 8 February were only for exercise prices $X = 60, 65, 70, 75, 80, 85$. Significant amounts of put options traded were only for exercise prices $X = 45, 50, 55, 60, 65, 70$.
- The price of the "last trade" is in boldface black. But where there is no volume for this day, the price refers to a previous day's price. (This means you have to be careful—in the jargon of finance, some of the prices are "stale.")

In the spreadsheet below we look at the Microsoft July call options, which actually traded on 8 February and compare the Black–Scholes price to the actual market price. We use the six-month Treasury bill rate of 1.7% as our risk-free rate.

	A	B	C	D	E	F	G	H
1			**MICROSOFT CALL OPTIONS: Comparing BS to actual prices**					
2	This spreadsheet computes the Black-Scholes value of the Microsoft July 2002 options on 8 February 2002 and compares the prices to the actual market prices. As you can see, the Black-Scholes formula works pretty well!							
3								
4						**Computing the time to maturity T**		
5	S_0		60.65	Microsoft stock, closing price 8 Feb 02		Current date	8-Feb-02	
6	T		0.44110	Time to maturity of option (in years)		Expiration date	19-Jul-02	
7	r		1.70%	Risk-free rate of interest		Time (days)	161	<-- =G6-G5
8	Sigma		31.66%	<-- =CallVolatility(B5,60,B6,B7,D13)		Time (% of year)	0.4411	<-- =G7/365
9								
10			**Exercise price**	**BS call price**	**Actual call market price**	**Market minus BS in dollars**	**Market minus BS in percentage**	
11			50	12.07	12.30	0.23	1.89%	<-- =(D11-C11)/D11
12			55	8.44	8.70	0.26	2.94%	<-- =(D12-C12)/D12
13			60	5.60	5.60	0.00	0.00%	
14			65	3.53	3.80	0.27	7.08%	
15			70	2.13	2.15	0.02	1.05%	
16			75	1.23	1.10	-0.13	-11.93%	
17			80	0.69	0.60	-0.09	-14.74%	
18			85	0.37	0.35	-0.02	-6.80%	
19								

BS Call Option Pricing
Microsoft July 2002 Call Options

We first use the function **CallVolatility** to compute the implied volatility of an at-the-money call (cell B8). We then use this volatility to price all the Microsoft calls using the Black–Scholes formula (cells C11 to C18). Columns E and F compare the Black–Scholes prices to the actual market prices in cells D11 to D18. The Black–Scholes model does a very good job of pricing the calls.

Below we repeat this exercise for Microsoft July puts.

	A	B	C	D	E	F	G	H
1			**MICROSOFT PUT OPTIONS: Comparing BS to actual prices**					
2	This spreadsheet computes the Black-Scholes value of the Microsoft July 2002 options on 8 February 2002 and compares the prices to the actual market prices. As you can see, the Black-Scholes formula works pretty well!							
3								
4						Computing the time to maturity T		
5	S$_0$		60.65	Microsoft stock, closing price 8 Feb 02		Current date	8-Feb-02	
6	T		0.44110	Time to maturity of option (in years)		Expiration date	19-Jul-02	
7	r		1.70%	Risk-free rate of interest		Time (days)	161	<-- =G6-G5
8	Sigma		37.35%	<-- =putVolatility(B5,60,B6,B7,D14)		Time (% of year)	0.4411	<-- =G7/365
9								
10			Exercise price	BS put price	Actual put market price	Market minus BS in dollars	Market minus BS in percentage	
11			45	0.67	1.00	0.33	32.72%	<-- =(D11-C11)/D11
12			50	1.60	2.00	0.40	19.79%	
13			55	3.16	3.30	0.14	4.27%	
14			60	5.40	5.40	0.00	0.00%	
15			65	8.30	8.30	0.00	0.00%	
16			70	11.77	12.30	0.53	4.31%	
17								

BS Put Option Pricing
Microsoft July 2002 Put Options

The Black–Scholes model works quite well for both puts and calls. The one problematic feature of the pricing is that the puts are priced at a higher implied volatility than the calls: The implied volatility of the at-the-money calls is 31.66% versus an implied volatility for at-the-money puts of 37.35%.

Does the Black–Scholes Model Work? Looking at Implied Volatilities

This is our second experiment. We take the Microsoft data above to calculate the implied volatility for each option (using the functions **CallVolatility** and **PutVolatility** discussed in Section 25.3). Here's our spreadsheet:

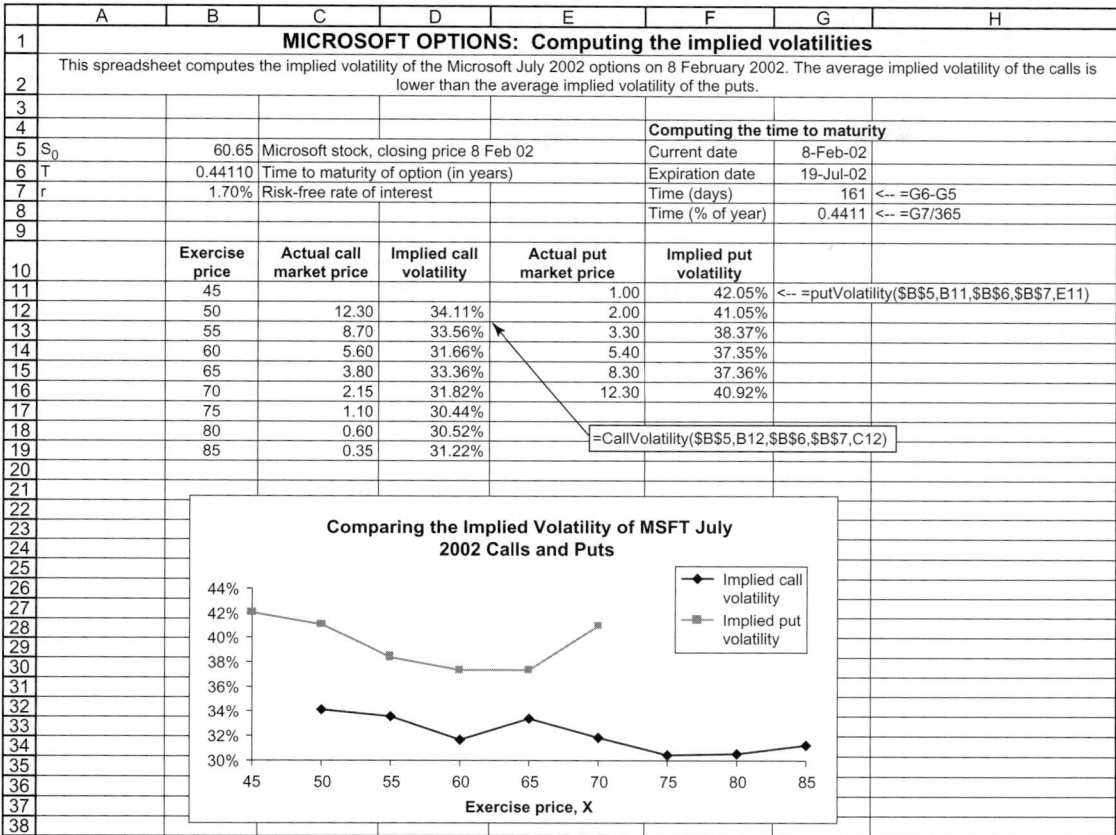

The results are both encouraging and discouraging:

- The implied volatilities for the calls are pretty close together, as are the implied volatilities for the puts. This is good news.

- On the other hand, the implied volatilities for the puts are uniformly larger than the implied volatilities for the calls. This is strange, since in the Black–Scholes formulation, the implied volatility refers to the volatility of the stock's return and hence has nothing to do with whether we're discussing a put or a call option.

- On the third hand,[6] the actual difference between the implied volatilities for the calls and the puts is not that great (only about 6%).

This is not the place to summarize the vast finance literature on implied volatilities. For our purposes, the Black–Scholes model works pretty well. That's enough!

---

[6]Harry Truman is reported to have gotten so sick of hearing economists say, "On the hand, ... But on the other hand, . . ." that he asked his chief of staff to get him a "one-handed economist." History does not record if he succeeded. The economist in this section's bullets has at least three hands. Harry Truman would not have liked him.

25.7 Real Options (Advanced Topic)

Thus far in this chapter we have discussed the use of the Black–Scholes model to price call or put options on shares. Such options are sometimes termed *financial options* because the option is written on a stock, which is a financial asset. A growing field in finance discusses *real options*. A real option is an option that becomes available as the result of an investment opportunity. Here are some examples of real options:

- Caulk Shipping is considering the purchase of a license to operate a ferry service from Philadelphia to Camden. The license requires the company to operate one boat on the ferry line but allows Caulk Shipping the possibility of operating as many as ten ferry boats on the line. This possibility—the *option to expand* the ferry service—should be taken into account when Caulk Shipping evaluates the economics of buying the license.

- Jones Oil is considering the purchase of a plot known to contain a large quantity of oil. Tom Shale, the company's financial analyst, has computed the NPV of the lease—he assumes that once the oil drilling equipment is in place, the company will pump the oil out of the ground at the maximum feasible rate. However, Tom also realizes that the financial analysis of the plot purchase should include an important *real option*: If the future oil price is low, Jones Oil can stop pumping the oil and wait until the price gets higher. This *option to delay* has obvious value.

- Merrill Widgets is considering the purchase of six new widget machines to replace machines currently in place. The new machines employ an innovative production technology and are much more sophisticated than the old machines. Simona Mba, the company's financial analyst, has determined that the NPV of replacing a single machine is negative and thus recommends against the replacement. Roberta Merrill, the company's owner, has a slightly different logic: She wants to purchase one widget machine in order to learn about the machine's possibilities; after a year she will then decide whether to buy the remaining five widget machines. The purchase of a single new widget machine gives Merrill Widgets the *option to learn*. The company's financial analysis should value this option. Below we return to this case and show how to value the option to learn.

A Simple Example of the Option to Learn

In the rest of this section we show how the Black–Scholes model can be used to value Merrill Widget's option to learn. Recall that the company is considering replacing each of its existing six widget machines with new machines. The new machines cost $1,000 each and have a five-year life. Simona Mba, the company's financial analyst, has estimated the expected per-machine cash flows; these flows are defined as the incremental cash flow of replacing a single old machine by a new machine and include the after-tax savings from introducing new machines, the tax shield on incremental depreciation from replacing an old by a new machine, and the sale of the old machine. It is important to emphasize that management does not know the exact realization of these annual cash flows, but only knows their expected values. The expected cash flows for the new machine are given below.

	A	B	C	D	E	F	G
3	Year	0	1	2	3	4	5
4	CF of single machine	-1000	220	300	400	200	150

Simona estimates the risk-adjusted cost of capital for the project as 12%. Using the expected cash flows and a cost of capital of 12% for the project; Simona has concluded that the replacement of a single old machine by a new machine is unprofitable, since the NPV is negative:

$$-1000 + \frac{220}{1.12} + \frac{300}{(1.12)^2} + \frac{400}{(1.12)^3} + \frac{200}{(1.12)^4} + \frac{150}{(1.12)^5} = -67.48$$

Now comes the (real options) twist. Roberta Merrill, the company's owner, says: "I want to try one of the new machines for a year and learn the true realization of its cash flows. At the end of the year, if the experiment is successful, I want to replace five other similar machines on the line with the new machines. If I do not try one of the new machines, I will never know their true cash flows."

Does this change our previously negative conclusion about replacing a single machine? The answer is "yes." To see this, we now realize that what we have is a package:

- Replacing a single machine today. This has a NPV of –67.48.
- The *option* of replacing five more machines in one year. We can view each such option as a call option on an asset that has current value of

$$S = \frac{220}{1.12} + \frac{300}{(1.12)^2} + \frac{400}{(1.12)^3} + \frac{200}{(1.12)^4} + \frac{150}{(1.12)^5} = 932.52$$

and an exercise price $X = \$1,000$. Of course, these call options can be exercised only if we purchase the first machine now; in effect, the real options model will be pricing the learning costs.

Let's suppose that the Black–Scholes option pricing model can price this call option. We further suppose that the risk-free rate is 6% and the standard deviation of the cash flows is $\sigma = 40\%$. The next figure shows that the value of each option to acquire one machine in one year is $143.98. It now follows that the value of the whole project is $652.39 (cell B11):

$$\textit{project value} = \textit{NPV of first machine} + 5 \textit{ options to acquire}$$
$$= -67.48 + 5 * 143.98 = 652.39$$

	A	B	C	D	E	F	G
1	MERRILL WIDGET--THE OPTION TO LEARN						
2	Year	0	1	2	3	4	5
3	CF of single machine	-1000	220	300	400	200	150
4							
5	Discount rate for machine cash flows	12%					
6	Riskless discount rate	6%					
7	NPV of single machine	-67.48					
8							
9	Number of machines bought next year	5					
10	Option value of single machine purchased in one more year	143.98	<-- =B24				
11	NPV of total project	652.39	<-- =B8+B10*B11				
12							
13	**Black-Scholes Option Pricing Formula**						
14	S_0		932.52	<-- =NPV(B5,C3:G3), PV of machine CFs			
15	X		1000.00	Exercise price = Machine cost			
16	r		6.00%	Risk-free rate of interest			
17	T		1	Time to maturity of option (in years)			
18	Sigma		40%	<-- Volatility			
19	d_1		0.1753	<-- (LN(S/X)+(r+0.5*sigma^2)*T)/(sigma*SQRT(T))			
20	d_2		-0.2247	<-- d_1 - sigma*SQRT(T)			
21	$N(d_1)$		0.5696	<--- Uses formula NormSDist(d_1)			
22	$N(d_2)$		0.4111	<--- Uses formula NormSDist(d_2)			
23	Option value = BS call price		143.98	<-- S*N(d_1)-X*exp(-r*T)*N(d_2)			

Thus, buying one machine today, and in the process acquiring the option to purchase five more machines in one year, is a worthwhile project.

One critical element here is the volatility. The lower the volatility (that is, the lower the uncertainty), the less worthwhile this project is. By building a data table we can examine the relation between the standard deviation σ and the project value:

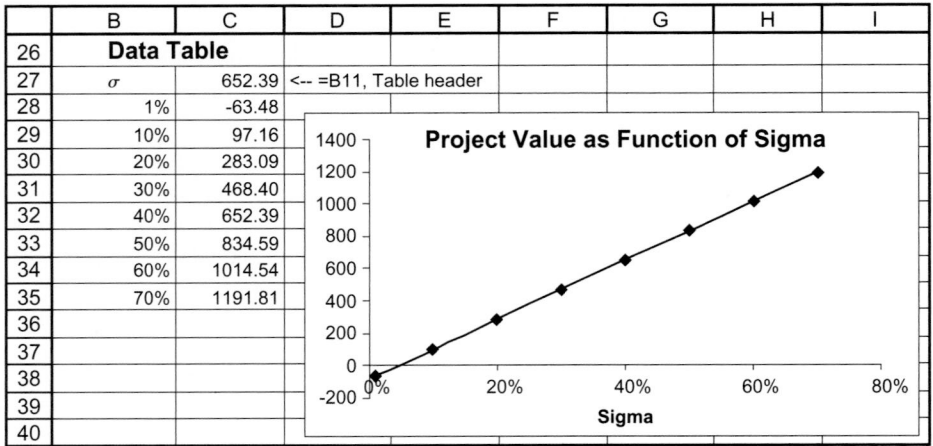

	B	C	D	E	F	G	H	I
26	**Data Table**							
27	σ	652.39	<-- =B11, Table header					
28	1%	-63.48						
29	10%	97.16						
30	20%	283.09						
31	30%	468.40						
32	40%	652.39						
33	50%	834.59						
34	60%	1014.54						
35	70%	1191.81						
36								
37								
38								
39								
40								

The value of the project as a whole comes from our uncertainty about the actual cash flows one year from now. The less this uncertainty is (measured by σ), the less valuable the project. In this particular example, a very low uncertainty ($\sigma \geq 4.75\%$) with respect to the machine cash flow returns is sufficient to justify its purchase.[7]

Real Options: Where Do We Go From Here?

Real options are increasingly used in finance to value corporate investments. The example of Merrill Widgets given above is only a small example of the use of the real options technique. For deeper discussions, we suggest you consult one of the books mentioned in footnote 7.

CONCLUSION

This chapter has given you a quick and hopefully practical insight into how to use the Black–Scholes model. The Black–Scholes model is remarkably good at pricing options and is widely used. It is also easy to use, provided you don't get too hung up on the details of where the formula comes from (in this chapter we left these hang-ups behind us and concentrated exclusively on implementational details).

EXERCISES

1. Use the Black–Scholes model to price the following:
   (a) A call option on a stock whose current price is $S = \$50$, with exercise price $X = \$50$, $T = 0.5, r = 10\%, \sigma = 25\%$.
   (b) A put option with the same parameters.

2. A call option on a stock is priced at \$5.35. The option has an exercise price of $X = \$40$. The current stock price $S = \$33$, the option's time to maturity is six months, and the interest rate $r = 6\%$. Use the Black–Scholes model to determine the implied volatility, the σ used to price the option. (Excel hint: Use **Goal Seek**, Chapter 32.)

3. A put option on a stock is priced at \$5. The option has an exercise price of $X = \$25$. The stock's current price is $S = \$25$, the option's time to maturity is one year, and the interest rate is $r = 5\%$. Use the Black–Scholes model to determine the option's implied volatility, the σ used to price the option. (Excel hint: Use **Solver**, Chapter 32.)

4. A call option with one-half year to maturity is written on a stock whose current price is \$40. The option's exercise price is \$38, the interest rate is 4%, and the stock's volatility is 30%.
   (a) Find the call option price using the Black–Scholes model.
   (b) Make a table showing the option's price for volatilities ranging from 10%, 20%, . . . , 60%. (Excel hint: By far the easiest way to do this is to use **Data Table**, explained in Chapter 30.)

---

[7]Estimating the σ for real option cash flows is problematic, since there is little market data (as there is for stocks) to guide us. Many authors use estimates in the range of 30–50% for the standard deviation of real option returns; this is somewhat higher than the average standard deviation of U.S. market returns for equity, which are in the range of 15–30%. To explore this issue, consult one of the three leading books in the area: Lenos Trigeorgis, *Real Options: Managerial Flexibility and Strategy in Resource Allocation* (MIT Press, 1996); Martha Amram and Nalin Kulik, *Real Options* (Harvard Business School, 1998); Tom Copeland and Vladimir Antikarov, *Real Options: A Practitioner's Guide* (Texere, 2001).

5. A put option with one-half year to maturity is written on a stock whose current price is $40. The option's exercise price is $38, the interest rate is 4%, and the stock's volatility is 30%.
   (a) Find the put option price using the Black–Scholes model.
   (b) Make a table showing the option's price for maturities ranging from $T = 0.2, 0.4, \ldots, 2.0$. (Excel hint: By far the easiest way to do this is to use **Data Table**, explained in Chapter 30.)

6. Use the data from Exercise 1 and **Data|Table** to produce graphs that show:
   - The sensitivity of the Black–Scholes call price to changes in the initial stock price S.
   - The sensitivity of the Black–Scholes put price to changes in σ.
   - The sensitivity of the Black–Scholes call price to changes in the time to maturity T.
   - The sensitivity of the Black–Scholes call price to changes in the interest rate r.
   - The sensitivity of the put price to changes in the exercise price X.

7. Produce a graph comparing a call's *intrinsic value* (defined as $Max(S - X, 0)$) and its Black–Scholes price. From this graph you should be able to deduce that it is never optimal to early-exercise a call priced by the Black–Scholes formula.

8. Produce a graph comparing a put's intrinsic value ($= Max(X - S, 0)$) and its Black–Scholes price. From this graph you should be able to deduce that it is may be optimal to early-exercise a put priced by the Black–Scholes formula.

9. Use the Excel **Solver** to find the stock price for which there is a maximum difference between the Black–Scholes call option price and the option's intrinsic value. Use the following values: $S = 45, X = 45, T = 1, \sigma = 40\%, r = 8\%$.

10. The table below gives June option prices for Pfizer (PFE) on March 4, 2005. On this date Pfizer's stock price was $26.85 and the interest rate was 2.60% annually. Compute the implied volatility for all traded puts and calls using the functions **Callvolatility** and **Putvolatility**. (If no price is given, the option was not traded.)

	A	B	C	D
	PFIZER (PFE) OPTION			
1	**PRICES, 4 MARCH 2005**			
2	Stock price	26.85		
3	Current date	4-Mar-05		
4	Interest rate	2.60%		
5				
6	**Expiration**	**Exercise**	**Call**	**Put**
7	17-Jun-05	22.50	4.70	0.25
8	17-Jun-05	25.00	2.55	0.65
9	17-Jun-05	27.50	1.00	1.60
10	17-Jun-05	30.00	0.30	3.50
11	17-Jun-05	32.50	0.05	
12	17-Jun-05	37.50		10.70

11. As shown in Chapter 23, the call option value is always greater than its immediate exercise value $(S - X)$ for $S > X$. However, the value of the European put is sometimes less than its intrinsic value $(X - S)$ for $S < X$. Use the put option pricing model to find such an example.

12. The probability that a European call option on the stock will be exercised is $N(d_2)$ (same expression as in Black–Scholes option pricing formula). What is the probability that a European call option on a stock with an exercise price of $40 and a maturity date in six months will be exercised? The current stock price is at $38, the interest rate is at 5%, stock return volatility is at 25%.

13. A stock price is currently $50 and the risk-free interest rate is 5%. Use the Black–Scholes model to translate the following table of European call options on the stock into a table of implied volatilities, assuming no dividends (Excel hint: Use **Solver**.)

Are the option prices consistent with Black–Scholes?

Exercise Price($)/ Maturity (months)	3	6	9
45	7	8.3	10.5
50	3.7	5.2	7.5
55	1.6	2.9	5.1

14. A put option with one year to maturity is written on a stock. The current underlying stock price is $20. The option's exercise price is $18, the interest rate is 3.74%, and the stock's volatility is 32.7%. The price of a call option written on the same stock with the same exercise price and time to maturity is $4.30. Use the Black–Scholes model to determine if put–call parity holds.

15. The stock price of ABC Corp. is currently $S = \$50$. What is the price of a European call option that expires in two months and that has an exercise price of $60? Assume the yearly interest rate is 5.5%, and the *monthly* volatility of the stock prices is 7.8%.

16. The price of a share of ABC-Corp. stock is currently $S = \$55$. Assume that the yearly interest rate is 2% and that the stock's volatility is 0.4.
    (a) Determine the prices of European call and put options with an exercise price of $55 and expiration in three months.
    (b) Verify put–call parity.

17. A one-month European call option is currently selling for $3.90. The exercise price of the option is $40, and the current stock price is $S = \$43$. The monthly interest rate is 0.5% and the monthly volatility of the stock return is at 7%. Does this price present an opportunity for arbitrage, according to the Black–Scholes model?

18. Consider an option trading on a stock with a year to maturity. The implied volatility of the option at the opening is 25% and at closing 22%. Assume that the stock prices haven't changed. What do you conclude about the price: has it increased or decreased?

19. If the volatility of a stock is 30% and assuming 250 trading days a year, what is the standard deviation of the return in one trading day?

APPENDIX 25.1: GETTING OPTION INFORMATION FROM YAHOO

Yahoo Finance (http://finance.yahoo.com) has excellent facilities for getting option prices.

1. Go to Yahoo Finance and put in the stock symbol for which you want prices. In the example below we've put in AT&T, whose symbol is T:

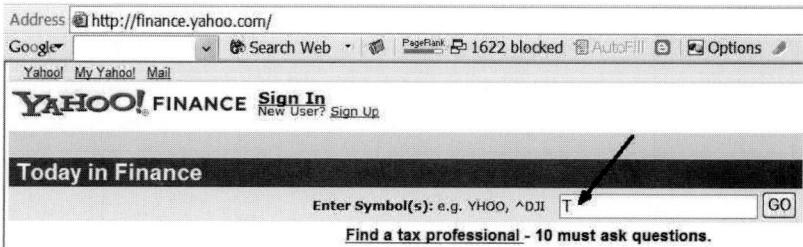

2.   When you're on the AT&T page, pick **Options**:

3.   Yahoo gives all the options by expiration date (note the exact expiration date, marked with the arrow):

THE BINOMIAL OPTION PRICING MODEL

OVERVIEW

In Chapter 25 we discussed the Black–Scholes formula, the most common method for pricing options. In this chapter we discuss the other major technique for determining option prices, the *binomial option pricing model*. This model gives some insights into how to price an option, and it's also used widely (though not as widely as the Black–Scholes formula).

The basis of the binomial model is a very simple description of stock price uncertainty. Here's an example. Suppose the current stock price of MicroDigits (MD) is $100. What can you say about the MD stock price one year from now? The *binomial model* assumes that the price of the stock in one year will either go *up* by a certain percentage or *down* by a certain percentage. Here's an example:

	A	B	C	D
1	**BINOMIAL MODEL FOR MICRODIGITS (MD) STOCK PRICE**			
2	Up	30%		
3	Down	-10%		
4				
5	**MD stock price one year from now**			
6			130	<-- =100*(1+B2)
7		100		
8			90	<-- =A7*(1+B3)
9				
10	**Date 0** **today**		**Date1** **one year** **from now**	
11				
12	**MD stock price *returns***			
13			0.3	<-- =C6/A7-1
14				
15			-0.1	<-- =C8/A7-1
16	**Date 0** **today**		**Date1** **one year** **from now**	

In the example above the MD stock price will either go up by 30% or down by 10% one year from today. This means that the *return* on the stock will be either 30% or −10% (cells C13 and C15).

It is difficult to believe that such a simple description of stock price uncertainty could be useful. However, if we extend the model to more periods, it turns out that the binomial model can describe a wide range of stock price behaviors. In the example below we assume that the price of MD stock goes up in each of the next two years by 30% or goes down by 10%. This means that there are three possible outcomes for the stock price at Date 2: It can be either $169, $117, or $81.

	A	B	C	D	E	F
1	**TWO-PERIOD BINOMIAL MODEL FOR MICRODIGITS (MD) STOCK PRICE**					
2	Up	30%				
3	Down	-10%				
4						
5					169	<-- =C6*(1+B2)
6			130			
7		100			117	<-- =C6*(1+B3)
8			90			
9					81	<-- =C8*(1+B3)
10	**Date 0** **today**		**Date 1** **one year** **from now**		**Date 2** **two years** **from now**	

If we extend the model to more periods, we get a wide range of possible prices and returns. In the spreadsheet below we look at stock prices after ten periods:

	A	B	C	D	E	F	G	H	I	J	K
1	MULTIPERIOD BINOMIAL MODEL FOR MICRODIGITS (MD) STOCK PRICE										
2	Up	30%									
3	Down	-10%									
4											
5	Date										
6	0	1	2	3	4	5	6	7	8	9	10
7											1378.58
8										1060.45	
9									815.73		954.40
10								627.49		734.16	
11							482.68		564.74		660.74
12						371.29		434.41		508.26	
13					285.61		334.16		390.97		457.44
14				219.70		257.05		300.75		351.87	
15			169.00		197.73		231.34		270.67		316.69
16		130.00		152.10		177.96		208.21		243.61	
17	100.00		117.00		136.89		160.16		187.39		219.24
18		117.00		105.30		123.20		144.15		168.65	
19			81.00		94.77		110.88		129.73		151.78
20				72.90		85.29		99.79		116.76	
21					65.61		76.76		89.81		105.08
22						59.05		69.09		80.83	
23							53.14		62.18		72.75
24								47.83		55.96	
25									43.05		50.36
26										38.74	
27											34.87

If you plot the stock return and the probabilities of the returns after ten years, you get a graph such as Figure 26.1.[1]

A Pedagogical Note

Most finance books first discuss the binomial option pricing model and then discuss the Black–Scholes model. Their reasoning is that this order is logical because in principle the Black–Scholes pricing formula can be derived from the binomial model. In this book we reversed the order, because we despair of telling you exactly how the Black–Scholes formula is derived from the binomial model. Instead, we treat the two models as entirely different topics with different pedagogical goals: Black–Scholes is the most commonly used option pricing model; as a finance person you should be familiar with this model and understand how to manipulate it (notice that we haven't said that you need to understand it!). The binomial model is more educational but less useful (at least on the level of this book): It gives some insights into how options are priced through a process of replication. It can also be used to understand topics such as the pricing of American options and real options.

---

[1]The mathematics required to produce such a graph are too much for this book. For further details see the author's book *Financial Modeling*, 2nd edition (MIT Press, 2000).

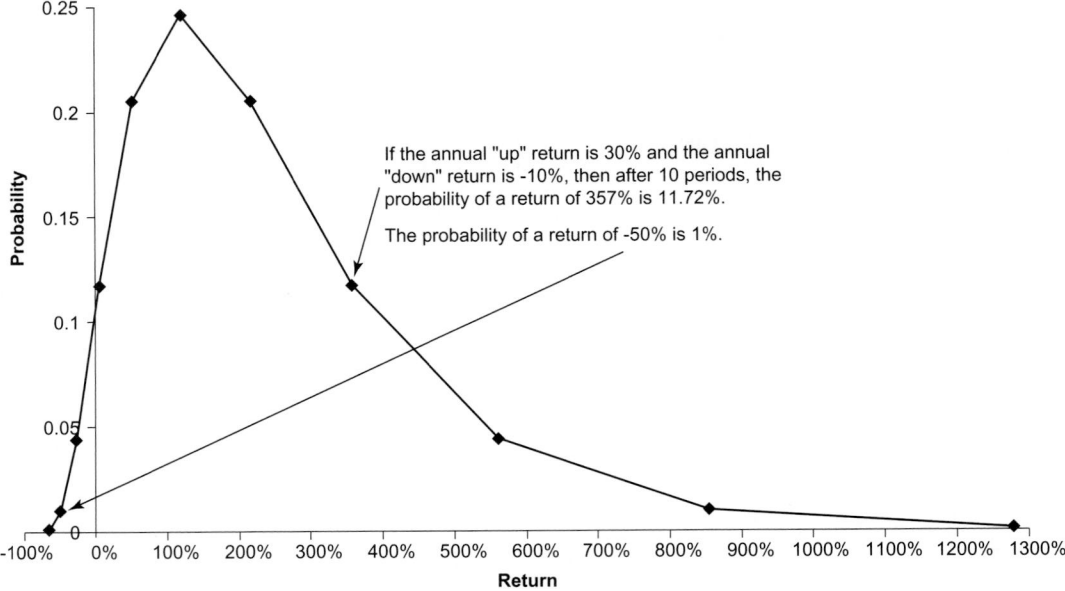

If the annual "up" return is 30% and the annual "down" return is -10%, then after 10 periods, the probability of a return of 357% is 11.72%.

The probability of a return of -50% is 1%.

Figure 26.1 Ten-date binomial model returns and probabilities.

One of the uses we show for the binomial option pricing model is to price American options (Section 26.4). These options cannot be priced using the Black–Scholes formula, which prices only European options. In an advanced options course you will learn to use the binomial option pricing model to price other, more complicated options.

Finance Concepts Discussed

- Binomial model
- Replicating portfolio

Excel Functions Used

- **Max**

26.1 The Binomial Pricing Model

To illustrate the use of the binomial model, we start with the following very simple example:

- You're trying to calculate the value of a call option on ABC stock. The option expires in one year and has an exercise price of $110.
- ABC stock sells today for $100. A wise person has informed you that in one year, the price of the stock will be either $130 or $90.[2] We will refer to these possibilities as the "up" and the "down" states.
- The one-year interest rate is 6%. You can borrow or lend at this rate.

---

[2]This wise person forgot to tell you the probabilities attached to these two events, but it turns out not to matter. Surprised? You should be. But read on.

Here's a spreadsheet picture that incorporates all this information (the spreadsheet also shows the payoffs on a put written on ABC stock—we'll get to that in a moment):

	A	B	C	D	E	F	G	H	I	J
1	PRICING OPTIONS ON ABC STOCK--THE BINOMIAL MODEL									
2	Up	30%								
3	Down	-10%								
4										
5	Initial stock price	100								
6	Interest rate	6%		ABC's stock price in the "up" state						
7	Exercise price	110								
8										
9		ABC's stock price					Bond price			
10				130	<-- =$B$11*(1+B2)				1.06	<-- =$G$12*(1+$B$7)
11		100					1			
12				90	<-- =$B$11*(1+B3)				1.06	<-- =$G$12*(1+$B$7)
13		ABC's stock price in the "down" state								
14					Call payoff in the "up" state					
15										
16		Call option payoffs					Put option payoffs			
17				20	<-- =MAX(D10-$B$7,0)				0	<-- =MAX($B$7-D10,0)
18		???					???			
19				0	<-- =MAX(D12-$B$7,0)				20	<-- =MAX($B$7-D12,0)
20										
21					Call payoff in the "down" state					
22										

We're going to price the call option by showing that there is a *combination of the bonds and stocks that gives exactly the same payoffs as the call option*. To show this, we use some basic high school algebra. Suppose we buy a portfolio of A shares of the stock and buy B bonds. Then the payoff of the portfolio in the "up" state is $130A + 1.06B$ and the payoff of the portfolio in the "down" state is $90A + 1.06B$. Now let's find A and B so that these two payoffs equal the call option payoffs:

$$130A + 1.06B = 20$$
$$90A + 1.06B = 0$$

This system of equations solves to give

$$130A + 1.06B = 20$$
$$90A + 1.06B = 0$$
$$A = \frac{20 - 0}{130 - 90} = 0.5, \quad B = \frac{0 - 90A}{1.06} = \frac{-90 * 0.5}{1.06} = -42.4528$$

So now we know that buying half a share of ABC (cost: $50) and borrowing $42.4528 will give you payoffs in one year which are exactly the same as the payoffs of the call option. The expenditure on this portfolio of {buy 1/2 share, borrow $42.4528} should be the same as the expenditure on the call option. Thus, the call option's price should be $7.5472:

$$call\ option\ price = \underbrace{0.5 * \$100}_{\substack{\text{The cost of the} \\ \text{stock in the} \\ \text{"replicating} \\ \text{portfolio"}}} - \underbrace{\$42.4528}_{\substack{\text{The financing} \\ \text{provided by} \\ \text{borrowing in the} \\ \text{"replicating} \\ \text{portfolio"}}} = \underbrace{7.5472}_{\substack{\text{The market price} \\ \text{of the call} \\ \text{option}}}$$

THE REPLICATING PORTFOLIO

The portfolio we derived above—$A = 0.5$ share and $B = -\$42.4528$ borrowed—gives the same payoffs as the call option. For this reason it is often called the *replicating portfolio*.

What's Going On?—Market Efficiency at Work

Option pricing in the binomial model is a wonderful example of the first two principles of efficient markets discussed in Chapter 17. The first principle ("Competitive markets have a single price for a single good") implies that the combination of the stock + borrowing (which in terms of payoffs has exactly the payoffs of the call option) should be priced like the call option. The second principle, price additivity ("The price of a bundle of securities should be the sum of the prices of each of the securities") is also illustrated here—the price of the call option is the cost of the stock (\$45) minus the borrowing to finance this cost.

For option pricing theorists this method of pricing options is an example of *arbitrage*—the principle that if you can construct an asset's payoffs in two ways, each of these ways should have the same market value (which is, of course, Chapter 17's first principle of efficiency).

Summing it all up:

	A	B	C	D	E	F	G	H	I	J
1				PRICING OPTIONS ON ABC STOCK--THE BINOMIAL MODEL						
2	Up	30%								
3	Down	-10%								
4										
5	Initial stock price	100								
6	Interest rate	6%		ABC's stock price						
7	Exercise price	110		in the "up" state						
8										
9		ABC's stock price					Bond price			
10				130	<-- =$B$11*(1+B2)				1.06	<-- =$G$12*(1+$B$7)
11		100						1		
12				90	<-- =$B$11*(1+B3)				1.06	<-- =$G$12*(1+$B$7)
13			ABC's stock price							
14			in the "down" state		Call payoff in					
15					the "up" state					
16		Call option payoffs					Put option payoffs			
17				20	<-- =MAX(D10-$B$7,0)				0	<-- =MAX($B$7-D10,0)
18		???					???			
19				0	<-- =MAX(D12-$B$7,0)				20	<-- =MAX($B$7-D12,0)
20										
21					Call payoff in the					
22					"down" state					
23	The call replicating portfolio									
24	Stock, *A*	0.5000	<-- =(D17-D19)/(D10-D12)							
25	Bonds, *B*	-42.4528	<-- =(D19-D12*B24)/(1+B6)							
26	Call price	7.5472	<-- =B24*B5+B25							

Using the Binomial Model to Price a Put on ABC Stock

We now use the binomial model to price a put on ABC with an exercise price of $110. The put payoffs are shown above:

	G	H	I	J
14				
15				Put payoff in the "up" state
16	Put option payoffs			
17			0	<-- =MAX($B$7-D10,0)
18		???		
19			20	<-- =MAX($B$7-D12,0)
20				
21				Put payoff in the "down" state
22				

The replicating portfolio is

$$130A + 1.06B = 0$$
$$90A + 1.06B = 20$$

These equations solve to give

$$A = \frac{-20}{130 - 90} = -0.5, \quad B = \frac{-130A}{1.06} = \frac{-130 * (-0.5)}{1.06} = 61.3208$$

The solution to the replicating portfolio indicates that short selling $A = -0.5$ share and investing in $B = \$61.3208$ of bonds gives the same payoffs as the put option. This means that the price of the put is $11.3208:

$$\textit{put option price} = \underbrace{-0.5 * \$100}_{\uparrow} + \underbrace{\$61.3208}_{\uparrow} = \underbrace{11.3208}_{\uparrow}$$

Cash provided by the short sale of stock in the "replicating portfolio"

Cash used to buy bonds in the "replicating portfolio"

The market price of the put option

Put–Call Parity: Another Way of Pricing the Put

In Chapter 24 we learned the put–call parity principle:

$$\textit{Put price} + \textit{Stock price} = \textit{Call price} + PV(\textit{Exercise price})$$

Applying this principle in our problem, we get

$$\textit{Put price} = \textit{Call price} + PV(\textit{Exercise price}) - \textit{Stock price}$$
$$= \$7.5472 + \frac{\$110}{1.06} - \$100 = \$11.3208$$

Here's the whole spreadsheet, one more time:

	A	B	C	D	E	F	G	H	I	J
1				PRICING OPTIONS ON ABC STOCK--THE BINOMIAL MODEL						
2	Up	30%								
3	Down	-10%								
4										
5	Initial stock price	100			ABC's stock price					
6	Interest rate	6%			in the "up" state					
7	Exercise price	110								
8										
9		ABC's stock price					Bond price			
10				130	<-- =$B$11*(1+B2)				1.06	<-- =$G$12*(1+$B$7)
11		100					1			
12				90	<-- =$B$11*(1+B3)				1.06	<-- =$G$12*(1+$B$7)
13										
14		ABC's stock price							Put payoff in the	
15		in the "down" state							"up" state	
16		Call option payoffs					Put option payoffs			
17				20	<-- =MAX(D10-$B$7,0)				0	<-- =MAX($B$7-D10,0)
18		???					???			
19				0	<-- =MAX(D12-$B$7,0)				20	<-- =MAX($B$7-D12,0)
20									Put payoff in the	
21									"down" state	
22										
23	The call replicating portfolio									
24	Stock, A	0.5000	<-- =(D17-D19)/(D10-D12)							
25	Bonds, B	-42.4528	<-- =(D19-D12*B24)/(1+B6)							
26	Call price	7.5472	<-- =B24*B5+B25							
27										
28	The put replicating portfolio									
29	Stock, A	-0.5000	<-- =(I17-I19)/(D10-D12)							
30	Bonds, B	61.3208	<-- =(I17-D10*B29)/(1+B6)							
31	Call price	11.3208	<-- =B29*B11+B30							
32										
33	Pricing the put by put-call parity									
34	Call price	7.5472	<-- =B26							
35	PV(exercise)	103.7736	<-- =B7/(1+B6)							
36	Stock price	100	<-- =B5							
37	Put price	11.3208	<-- =B34+B35-B36							

26.2 What Can You Learn From the Binomial Model?

The binomial option pricing model is very instructive. It is an easy way to price options, and it can also tell you something about more complicated option pricing models. Here are a few lessons you can learn from the binomial model.

- A call "looks like" a portfolio composed of the purchase of a stock and the short sale of a bond. The call's replicating portfolio is

$$A * S_{Up} + B * (1 + r) = Call\ payoff_{Up}$$
$$A * S_{Down} + B * (1 + r) = Call\ payoff_{Down}$$

where S_{Up} and S_{Down} are the stock prices in the "up" and "down" states, and $Call\ payoff_{Up}$ and $Call\ payoff_{Down}$ are the call payoffs.

In terms of the call's replicating portfolio, it turns out that A (the stock) is always positive and B (the bond) is always negative. This indicates the purchase of a stock financed by borrowing. In a sense the Black–Scholes (BS) formula has the same property:

$$BS\ call\ price = \underbrace{S * N(d_1)}_{\uparrow} \underbrace{-Xe^{-rT}N(d_2)}_{\uparrow}$$

Purchase of   Borrowing at

stock   the risk-free rate

(positive number)   (negative number)

- A put "looks like" a portfolio composed of the short sale of a stock and the purchase of a bond. The put's replicating portfolio is

$$A * S_{Up} + B * (1 + r) = Put\ payoff_{Up}$$
$$A * S_{Down} + B * (1 + r) = Put\ payoff_{Down}$$

where S_{Up} and S_{Down} are the stock prices in the "up" and "down" states, and $Put\ payoff_{Up}$ and $Put\ payoff_{Down}$ are the put payoffs.

In terms of the put's replicating portfolio, it turns out that A (the stock) is always negative and B (the bond) is always positive. This indicates the purchase of bonds financed by a short sale of the stock. In a sense the Black–Scholes formula has the same property:

$$BS\ put\ price = \underbrace{-S * N(-d_1)}_{\uparrow} \underbrace{+Xe^{-rT}N(-d_2)}_{\uparrow}$$

Short sale of   Investing at

stock   the risk-free rate

(negative number)   (positive number)

- The probabilities of the up and the down states don't appear explicitly in the calculation of the option price. To see what this means, look at the way we solved for the call option price at the beginning of this chapter:

$$130A + 1.06B = 20$$
$$90A + 1.06B = 0$$

These equations solve to give

$$A = \frac{20 - 0}{130 - 90} = 0.5, \quad B = \frac{0 - 90A}{1.06} = \frac{-90 * 0.5}{1.06} = -42.4528$$

The resulting call option price is

$$call\ option\ price = \underbrace{0.5 * \$100}_{\uparrow} - \underbrace{\$42.4528}_{\uparrow} = \underbrace{7.5472}_{\uparrow}$$

The cost of the   The financing   The market price

stock in the   provided by   of the call

"replicating   borrowing in the   option

portfolio"   "replicating

portfolio"

This calculation of the call option price when the option exercise price is $110 relies on three facts: (1) The current stock price is $100; (2) the stock price next period is either $130 or $90, and (3) the interest rate is 6%. Nowhere in this calculation have we made any reference to the *probabilities* that the stock price will be $130 or $90.[3]

- The binomial model is *extendible*—it can be used to price many options in a multiperiod setting. In the next section we show a multiperiod binomial model.

26.3 Multiperiod Binomial Model

The binomial model can be extended to multiple periods. Here's an example that extends the previous example:

	A	B	C	D	E	F	G	H	I	J	K	L
1					THREE-DATE BINOMIAL OPTION PRICING							
2	Up	30%										
3	Down	-10%										
4												
5	Initial stock price	100										
6	Interest rate	6%										
7	Exercise price	110										
8												
9	Stock price						Bond price					
10					169.00						1.1236	
11			130						1.06			
12		100			117.00		1				1.1236	
13			90						1.06			
14					81.00						1.1236	
15	Date 0		Date 1		Date 2		Date 0		Date 1		Date 2	
16												
17												
18	Call option price						Put option price					
19					59.00	<-- =MAX(E10-$B$7,0)					0.00	<-- =MAX($B$7-E10,0)
20			???-1						???-1			
21		???-0			7.00	<-- =MAX(E12-$B$7,0)	???-0				0.00	<-- =MAX($B$7-E12,0)
22			???-2						???-2			
23					0.00	<-- =MAX(E14-$B$7,0)					29.00	<-- =MAX($B$7-E14,0)
24	Date 0		Date 1		Date 2		Date 0		Date 1		Date 2	

In this example, the stock price goes up by 30% or down by 10% in each period. Starting with a stock price of $100 at Date 0, the stock price at Date 1 will be either $130 or $90, and the stock price at Date 2 will be either $169, $117, or $81.

- $169: This happens if it goes up twice—that is, $169 = $100 * (1.30)(1.30)$.
- $117: This happens if the stock price goes up once and down once—that is, $117 = $100 * (1.30) * (0.90)$. Notice that it doesn't matter if the stock price goes up first and then down or the reverse.
- $81: This happens if the stock price goes down twice—that is, $81 = $100 * (0.90)(0.90)$.

---

[3]Of course, you could quibble a bit and insist that the stock price today must incorporate these probabilities in some sense, and you'd be right. But even here you have to be careful—for example, it would be wrong to say that the stock price is the discounted expected future payoff of the stock. To explain this all would take us too far afield—suffice it to say that if investors are risk averse, they'll price the stock at *below* its expected future discounted payoff. The amount of this discount depends on the risk aversion.

In each period the risk-free interest rate is 6%, so that $1 invested in the bond will grow to $1.1236 at Date 2.

The Call Option's Terminal Payoffs

At the end of the second period, the option's payoffs are given by

$$Max(\text{stock price at Date 2} - 110, 0) = \begin{cases} Max(169 - 110, 0) = 59 \\ Max(117 - 110, 0) = 7 \\ Max(81 - 110, 0) = 0 \end{cases}$$

We now have to value the option. We proceed by doing three valuations—these are labeled in the diagram as "???-1," "???-2," and "???-0." The put option has the same labels—we'll figure out in a while how to price these.

Determining ???-1 for the Call

We proceed as we did for the one-period binomial option pricing model. Setting up the one-period stock and bond prices and option payoffs, we get:

	A	B	C	D	E	F	G	H
26	Finding ???-1 for the call							
27								
28		Stock price				Bond price		
29				169.00				1.1236
30		130				1.06		
31				117.00				1.1236
32								
33		Call option price						
34				59.00				
35		???-1						
36				7.00				

Setting up the equations (we use A to denote the number of shares and B to denote the bonds in the replicating portfolio):

$$169A + 1.1236B = 59$$
$$117A + 1.1236B = 7$$

Solution:

$$A = \frac{59 - 7}{169 - 117} = 1$$
$$B = \frac{7 - 117 * A}{1.1236} = -97.8996$$
$$\text{call option price} = 130 * A + 1.06 * B = 26.2264$$

These calculations are done in cells B39 to B41.

Determining ???-2 for the Call

Again we proceed as we did for the one-period binomial option pricing model. Setting up the one-period stock and bond prices and option payoffs, we get:

	A	B	C	D	E	F	G	H
44	Finding ???-2 for the call							
45								
46		Stock price				Bond price		
47				117.00				1.1236
48		90				1.06		
49				81.00				1.1236
50								
51		Call option price						
52				7.00				
53		???-2						
54				0.00				
55								
56	The call replicating portfolio							
57	Stock, A	0.1944	<-- =(D52-D54)/(D47-D49)					
58	Bonds, B	-14.0174	<-- =(D54-B57*D49)/H47					
59	Call price	2.6415	<-- =B57*B48+B58*F48					

Determining ???-0 for the Call

Once more we set up a simple binomial model, but this time we use the two values derived above—the prices of the call option at Date 1.

	A	B	C	D	E	F	G	H
62	Finding ???-0 for the call							
63								
64		Stock price				Bond price		
65				130.00				1.0600
66		100				1		
67				90.00				1.0600
68								
69		Call option price						
70				26.2264				
71		???-0						
72				2.6415				
73								
74	The call replicating portfolio							
75	Stock, A	0.5896	<-- =(D70-D72)/(D65-D67)					
76	Bonds, B	-47.5703	<-- =(D72-B75*D67)/H65					
77	Call price	11.3919	<-- =B75*B66+B76*F66					

The result—we've calculated the option price today as $11.3919.[4]

Pricing the Put—The Long Way

As you can see from the diagram, the put has Date 2 payoffs of:

	G	H	I	J	K	L
18	Put option price					
19					0.00	<-- =MAX($B$7-E10,0)
20			???-1			
21	???-0				0.00	<-- =MAX($B$7-E12,0)
22			???-2			
23					29.00	<-- =MAX($B$7-E14,0)
24	Date 0		Date 1		Date 2	

---

[4]You probably suspect that there's a more efficient way to do this, and you're right. A good starting place is *Financial Modeling,* Chapter 14.

We can use the same logic (and even the same equations) to price the put. The results (shown below with no explanations) show that the put price at Date 0 is $9.2916.

	A	B	C	D	E	F	G	H
80	**PRICING THE PUT**							
81	Finding ???-1 for the put							
82								
83		**Stock price**				**Bond price**		
84				169.00				1.1236
85		130				1.06		
86				117.00				1.1236
87								
88		**Put option price**						
89				0.00				
90		???-1				There's actually no need to do any calculations for ???-1: The price ???-1 is the value of a security which has <u>zero payoffs</u> one period hence. By any logic this price should be zero.		
91				0.00				
92								
93	**The put replicating portfolio**							
94	Stock, A	0.0000	<-- =(D89-D91)/(D84-D86)					
95	Bonds, B	0.0000	<-- =(D91-B94*D86)/H84					
96	Put price	0.0000	<-- =B94*B85+B95*F85					
97								
98								
99	Finding ???-2 for the put							
100								
101		**Stock price**				**Bond price**		
102				117.00				1.1236
103		90				1.06		
104				81.00				1.1236
105								
106		**Put option price**						
107				0.00				
108		???-2						
109				29.00				
110								
111	**The put replicating portfolio**							
112	Stock, A	-0.8056	<-- =(D107-D109)/(D102-D104)					
113	Bonds, B	83.8822	<-- =(D109-B112*D104)/H102					
114	Put price	16.4151	<-- =B112*B103+B113*F103					
115								
116								
117	Finding ???-0 for the put							
118								
119		**Stock price**				**Bond price**		
120				130.00				1.0600
121		100				1		
122				90.00				1.0600
123								
124		**Put option price**						
125				0.0000				
126		???-0						
127				16.4151				
128								
129	**The put replicating portfolio**							
130	Stock, A	-0.4104	<-- =(D125-D127)/(D120-D122)					
131	Bonds, B	50.3293	<-- =(D127-B130*D122)/H120					
132	Put price	9.2916	<-- =B130*B121+B131*F121					

Pricing the Put Using Put–Call Parity

We can also use put–call parity to price the put. As discussed in Section 24.3, put–call parity says

$$Put\ price + Stock\ price = Call\ price + PV(Exercise\ price)$$

Applying this principle to the two-date option, we get

$$Put\ price = Call\ price + PV(Exercise\ price) - Stock\ price$$

$$= \$11.3919 + \frac{\$110}{(1.06)^2} - \$100$$

$$= \$9.2916$$

	A	B	C	D	E	F
135	**Pricing the put with put-call parity**					
136	Initial stock price	100				
137	Interest rate	6%				
138	Exercise price	110				
139	Call price	11.3919				
140	Put price	9.2916	<-- =B139+B138/(1+B137)^2-B136			

26.4 Using the Binomial Model to Price an American Put (Advanced Topic)

The binomial model is cute and easy to understand. But why do we need it? The answer is complex and mostly beyond the scope of this book:

- Whereas the Black–Scholes formula prices only European options, the binomial model can be used to price American options. This use of the binomial model is illustrated in the next subsection.
- Properly implemented, the binomial model can help us prove the Black–Scholes formula. This use of the binomial model is too advanced for this book.
- The binomial model can be used to price more complex options than those priced with the Black–Scholes model, which prices only European options. For example, we can use the binomial model to price options where the exercise price changes over time, or where the interest rate varies.
- We can also use the binomial model to price options where the "up" and the "down" movements of the stock price vary over time. Many finance people believe, for example, that the volatility of the stock price return varies with the price itself—that the percentage "up" and "down" movements for a stock are larger when the stock price is small. This can be handled by the binomial model, but not by the Black–Scholes model.

"WEIRD" OPTIONS AND THE BINOMIAL MODEL

The binomial model is especially useful in determining the price of "weird" options. Here are two examples of such options.

An *Asian option* is an option whose payoff is determined by the average price of the stock over a certain period before the option's maturity. One specification of an Asian call option might be:

- On 29 January 2005 you buy an Asian call option on IBM with a maturity of one year. The option's payoff on 29 January 2006 is the difference between the average daily closing IBM stock price in the 30 days preceding the option's maturity and the option's exercise price $X = \$120$. This option cannot be priced using the Black–Scholes model, but it can be priced using the binomial model.

A *barrier option* is an option whose payoff depends on whether the stock price reaches a certain point during the life of the option. Here's an example:

- On 29 January 2005 you buy a one-year *knock-in barrier* option on IBM, which is currently selling at $93. The option specifies that you have the right to buy a share of IBM on 29 January 2006, provided that at some point during the year IBM's stock price exceeds $120 (this is the "knock-in barrier"). If the price of IBM during the coming year does not exceed $120, your option is worthless. Barrier options cannot be priced using the Black–Scholes model, but they can be priced using the binomial model.

There are many more of these "weird" options. A good place to start for some background is http://www.riskglossary.com.

Using the Binomial Model to Price American Options

To illustrate one more sophisticated use of the binomial model, we'll show you how it can be used to price an American option. Recall that American options can be exercised early. We go back to our two-date example and focus on the put price (highlighted):

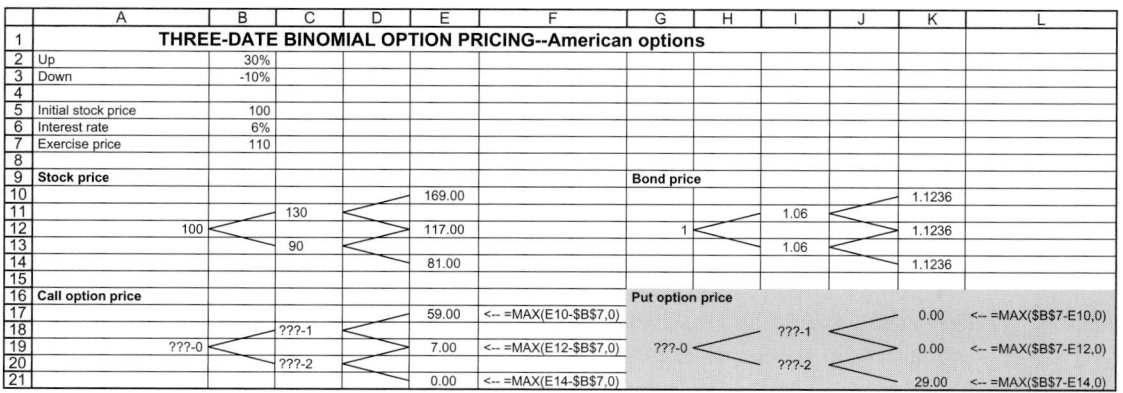

	A	B	C	D	E	F	G	H	I	J	K	L
1		THREE-DATE BINOMIAL OPTION PRICING--American options										
2	Up	30%										
3	Down	-10%										
4												
5	Initial stock price	100										
6	Interest rate	6%										
7	Exercise price	110										
8												
9	Stock price						Bond price					
10					169.00						1.1236	
11			130						1.06			
12		100			117.00		1				1.1236	
13			90						1.06			
14					81.00						1.1236	
15												
16	Call option price						Put option price					
17					59.00	<-- =MAX(E10-$B$7,0)					0.00	<-- =MAX($B$7-E10,0)
18			???-1						???-1			
19		???-0			7.00	<-- =MAX(E12-$B$7,0)	???-0				0.00	<-- =MAX($B$7-E12,0)
20			???-2						???-2			
21					0.00	<-- =MAX(E14-$B$7,0)					29.00	<-- =MAX($B$7-E14,0)

We'll price the put just as we did the call in the previous section. However, this time we assume that the put is an *American put*—meaning that it can be exercised early.

We start by pricing the put at the up-state of Date 1 (this is marked "???-1" in the spreadsheet). This is actually fairly simple: at ???-1 the put owner has future payoffs of zero, no matter what happens. This means that the put should be worth zero, and that's exactly what the spreadsheet tells us:

	A	B	C	D	E	F	G	H
24	**Finding ???-1 for the put**							
25								
26		**Stock price**				**Bond price**		
27				169.00				1.1236
28		130				1.06		
29				117.00				1.1236
30								
31		**Put option price**						
32				0.00		There's actually no need to do		
33		???-1				any calculations for ???-1: The		
34				0.00		price ???-1 is the value of a		
35						security which has <u>zero payoffs</u>		
36	**The put replicating portfolio**					one period hence. By any logic		
37	Stock, *A*	0.0000	<-- =(D32-D34)/(D27-D29)			this price should be zero.		
38	Bonds, *B*	0.0000	<-- =(D34-B37*D29)/H27					
39	Put price ???-1	0.0000	<-- =B37*B28+B38*F28					

At ???-2 the situation is more complicated. The put has a future payoff that is positive. We can use the binomial model to solve for the put price:

	A	B	C	D	E	F	G	H
42	**Finding ???-2 for the put**							
43								
44		**Stock price**				**Bond price**		
45				117.00				1.1236
46		90				1.06		
47				81.00				1.1236
48								
49		**Put option price**						
50				0.00				
51		???-2						
52				29.00				
53								
54	**The put replicating portfolio**							
55	Stock, *A*	-0.8056	<-- =(D50-D52)/(D45-D47)					
56	Bonds, *B*	83.8822	<-- =(D52-B55*D47)/H45					
57	European put price ???-2	16.4151	<-- =B55*B46+B56*F46					
58	American put price ???-2	20.0000	<-- =MAX(B7-B46,B55*B46+B56*F46)					

But now the early-exercise feature of the put comes in (remember—it's an American put). The put value of $16.4151 (cell B57 above) is the value of a put that has payoffs only next period. Instead of waiting until next period, we can exercise the put today: The stock price is $90 and the put exercise is $110, which means we can collect $20 immediately if we early-exercise the put. So the actual put value—given the early-exercise feature—is $20 and not $16.4151 (cell B58):

Using this value of $20, we can price the put at Date 0:

	A	B	C	D	E	F	G	H
60	Finding ???-0							
61								
62		Stock price				Bond price		
63				130.00				1.0600
64		100				1		
65				90.00				1.0600
66								
67		Put option price						
68				0.0000				
69		???-0						
70				20.0000				
71								
72	The put replicating portfolio							
73	Stock, A	-0.5000	<-- =(D68-D70)/(D63-D65)					
74	Bonds, B	61.3208	<-- =(D70-B73*D65)/H63					
75	American put price ???-0	11.3208	<-- =MAX(B7-B64,B73*B64+B74*F64)					

In Section 26.3 we priced a European put with the same exercise price $X = \$110$. There we concluded (p. 257) that the value of the European put is $9.2916. When we reprice the put as an American put, we see that its price is $11.3208, *higher* than the European put price. This happens because we will want to *early-exercise* the put at ???-2.

CONCLUSION

The binomial option pricing model can be used to price options under more general conditions than those which hold for the Black–Scholes model. This chapter has revealed only the tip of this financial iceberg, showing you how to implement the model in a one-date and two-date framework. We also indicated how the model can be used to price American options and "weird" options such as Asian options or barrier options.

EXERCISES

1. A stock selling for $25 today will, in one year, be worth either $35 or $20. If the interest rate is 8%, what is the value today of a one-year call option on the stock with exercise price $30? Use the simultaneous equation approach of Section 26.1 to price the option.

2. For the data of Exercise 1, calculate the value today of a one-year put option on the stock with exercise price $30. Show that put–call parity holds: That is, using your answer from this exercise and Exercise 1, show that

$$\text{call price} + \frac{X}{1+r} = \text{stock price today} + \text{put price}$$

3. In a binomial model a put option is written on a stock selling today for $30. The exercise price of the put option is $40. The put option's payoffs are $20 and $5. The price of the put is $12.25. What is the risk-free interest rate? Assume that the basic period is one year.

4. All reliable analysts agree that a share of ABC Corp., selling today for $50, will be priced at either $65 or $45 one year from now. They further agree that the probabilities of these events are 0.6 and 0.4, respectively. The market risk-free rate is 6%. What is the value of a call option on ABC whose exercise price is $50 and which matures in one year?

5. A stock is currently selling for $60. The price of the stock at the end of the year is expected either to increase by 25% or to decrease by 20%. The risk-free interest rate is 5%. Calculate the price of a European put on the stock with exercise price $55. Use the binomial option pricing model.

6. Fill in all the cells labeled ??? in the following spreadsheet:

THREE DATE BINOMIAL OPTION PRICING										
Up	35%									
Down	-5%	state prices								
		q_u	???							
Initial stock price	40	q_d	???							
Interest rate	25%									
Exercise price	40									
Stock price					**Bond price**					
			???					???		
		???								
	40		???			1		???		
		???								
			???					???		
Call option price					**European put option price**					
			???					???		
		???						???		
???			???			???			???	
		???						???		
			???					???		
American put option										
			???							
		???								
???			???							
		???								
			???							

7. Consider the following two-period binomial model, in which the annual interest rate is 9% and in which the stock price goes up by 15% per period or down by 10%:

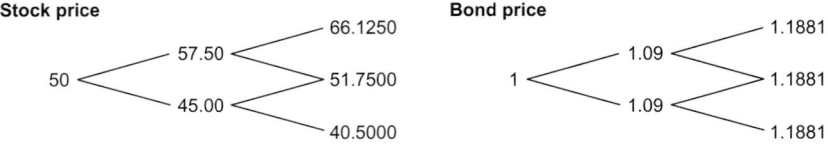

(a) Price a European call on the stock with exercise price $60.

(b) Price a European put on the stock with exercise price $60.

(c) Price an American call on the stock with exercise price $60.

(d) Price an American put on the stock with exercise price $60.

8. Consider the following three-date binomial model:
   - In each period the stock price either goes up by 30% or decreases by 10%.
   - The one-period interest rate is 25%.

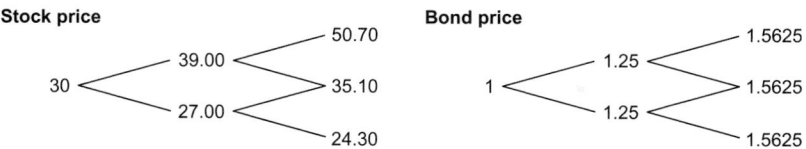

(a) Consider a European call with $X = \$30$ and $T = 2$. Fill in the blanks in the tree:

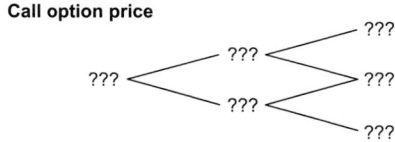

(b) Price a European put with $X = \$30$ and $T = 2$.
(c) Now consider an American put with $X = \$30$ and $T = 2$. Fill in the blanks in the tree:

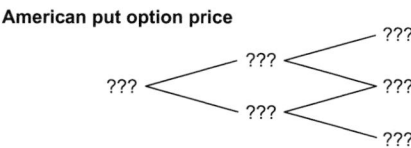

9. A prominent securities firm recently introduced a new financial product. This product, called "The Best of Both Worlds" (BOBOW for short), costs $10. It matures in five years, at which point it repays the investor the $10 cost *plus* 120% of any positive return in the S&P 500 Index. There are no payments before maturity.

   For example, if the S&P 500 is currently at 1500, and if it is at 1800 in five years, a BOBOW owner will receive back $12.40 = \$10 * [1 + 1.2 * (1800/1500 - 1)]$. If the S&P 500 is at or below 1500 in five years, the BOBOW owner will receive back $10.

   Suppose that the annual interest rate on a five year, continuously compounded, pure-discount bond is 6%. Suppose further that the S&P 500 is currently at 1500 and that you believe that in five years it will be at either 2500 or 1200. Use the binomial option pricing model to show that BOBOWs are worth more than their current price of $10.

10. A call option is written on a stock whose current price is $50. The option has a maturity of two years, and during this time the annual stock price is expected to increase by 25% or to decrease by 10%. The annual interest rate is constant at 6%. The option is exercisable at Date 1 at a price of $55 and at Date 2 for a price of $60. What is its value today? Will you ever exercise the option early?

11. A stock is currently selling for $60. A put option has a maturity of two years, and during this time the annual stock price is expected to increase by 30% or to decrease by 10%. The risk-free annual

interest rate is 6%. The put option is currently selling for $9. Is the option more likely an American or a European put option? Use the binomial option pricing model to determine.

12. A call option is written on a stock whose current price is $100. The option has a maturity of two years, and during this time the annual stock price is expected to increase by 30% or to decrease by 10%. The annual interest rate is constant at 6%. The option's exercise price is $110. Extend the binomial option pricing to incorporate a $3.00/share dividend that will be paid out in period 2. In other words, all of the period 2 stock prices will be reduced by $3.00. Determine the current prices of the call.

13. A two-year American put option is written on a stock whose current price is $42. You expect that in each year the stock price will either go up by 10% or decrease by 5%. The one-period interest rate is 5%. The option's exercise price is $45. Will you ever exercise the option early? Refer to Fact 6 of Chapter 24.

PART VII

EXCEL BACKGROUND

This book uses Excel throughout as the tool to understanding and implementing financial analysis. Part 7 serves two purposes:

- It serves as an introduction and reminder of the basics of Excel.
- It reviews the principal Excel techniques used in the book.

Part 7 starts off with Chapter 27, which reviews Excel basics. These are all the things that you probably knew all along but might have forgotten. Topics include opening Excel, saving your work, copying (both relative and absolute), and basic graphing.

Chapter 28 gets into more detail on graphs in Excel. After reading this chapter, you'll know how to make Excel charts look better, how to graph noncontiguous data, and how to make graph titles that change when the inputs change, and more.

Chapter 29 has brief discussions on most of the functions used in this book. (Some functions—for example, date functions and data functions—are discussed in Chapters 31 and 33.)

Excel's **Data Table**, the topic of Chapter 30, is a fabulous technique to do sensitivity analysis. **Data Table** is a bit complicated, but once you master it, you'll never understand how you functioned without it.

Chapter 31 discusses dates in Excel. Topics include the manipulation of dates and times in Excel and the use of Excel's date functions in financial analysis.

Chapter 32 discusses **Goal Seek** and **Solver**. These are two very useful Excel tools to find model solutions. Most students are aware of **Goal Seek**, but many Excel users are not aware that **Solver** is almost as easy to use and more useful. Chapter 32 shows you how to use both of these tools.

Excel has marvelous data manipulation abilities, discussed in Chapter 33. Topics include sorts, filters, more complicated functions such as **DSum** and **DAverage**, and importing text files.

Many Excel models end up in Word documents, and a lot of these documents are uglier than they need be. Chapter 34 provides some hints about how to move between these two powerful programs.

INTRODUCTION TO EXCEL

OVERVIEW

This chapter introduces you to Excel and shows you how to do the most important initial operations. Excel is not difficult to learn to use, provided you're willing to make many mistakes along the way, and you take an occasional look at the online Help (press function key F1).

Contents of This Chapter

- Turning Excel on
- Saving, creating a new directory
- Copying—relative versus absolute
- Formatting numbers
- Making a graph
- Fiddling with the default settings for Excel
- Using a few functions
- Printing

27.1 Getting Started

OK, you've started your computer and pressed on the Excel icon ^{Microsoft Excel} on your desktop (or

maybe it's not on your desktop—maybe you got there through the ⧉ *start* button . . .). You're facing a blank spreadsheet, and you want to play. Let's write a spreadsheet describing how $1,000 deposited in the bank at 15% will grow over time:

	A	B	C
1	**COMPOUND INTEREST**		
2	Year	Bank balance	
3	0	1000	
4	1		
5	2		
6	3		
7	4		
8	5		
9	6		
10	7		
11	8		
12	9		
13	10		

After you've finished typing in the above, put the cursor in cell B4. We're going to make a formula that describes how much money will be in the bank at the end of year 1. When you're in cell B4, type in the following formula and then hit [Enter] (no spaces, please!):

$$=B3*(1+15\%)$$

Here's what the spreadsheet should look like:

	A	B	C
1		**COMPOUND INTEREST**	
2	Year	Bank balance	
3	0	1000	
4	1	1150	
5	2		
6	3		
7	4		
8	5		
9	6		
10	7		
11	8		
12	9		
13	10		

If you put the cursor on cell B4 and look at the *formula bar* (next to the f_x symbol), you'll see what you've written in the spreadsheet:

			B4	▼	f_x =B3*(1+15%) I	

	A	B	C	Formula Bar
1		**COMPOUND INTEREST**		
2	Year	Bank balance		
3	0	1000		
4	1	1150		
5	2			
6	3			
7	4			
8	5			
9	6			
10	7			
11	8			
12	9			
13	10			

Copying the Formula

So, if you deposit $1,000 in the bank today and the bank gives you 15% interest, you'll have $1,150 at the end of year 1. If you've read Chapter 5 of this book, you know that at the end of year 2 you'll have $1,150 * (1 + 15\%)$ in the bank. Instead of typing in this formula, we'll use Excel's *copy* ability to put it in cell B5:

- The lower right-hand corner of the frame around cell B4 has a little black square; we call this the "handle" of the cell.

			B4	▼	f_x =B3*(1+15%)

	A	B	C
1		**COMPOUND INTEREST**	
2	Year	Bank balance	
3	0	1000	
4	1	1150	
5	2		
6	3		
7	4		The "handle"
8	5		
9	6		
10	7		
11	8		
12	9		
13	10		

- Put the cursor on the handle of cell B4. Press on the left mouse button, and drag down until you get to cell B13. At this point your spreadsheet will look like this:

	B	▼	*f*ₓ	=B3*(1+15%)

	A	B	C
1	**COMPOUND INTEREST**		
2	Year	Bank balance	
3	0	1000	
4	1	1150	
5	2		
6	3		
7	4		
8	5		
9	6		
10	7		
11	8		
12	9		
13	10		
14			

Release the left mouse button and:

	A	B	C
1	**COMPOUND INTEREST**		
2	Year	Bank balance	
3	0	1000	
4	1	1150	<-- =B3*(1+15%)
5	2	1322.5	<-- =B4*(1+15%)
6	3	1520.875	<-- =B5*(1+15%)
7	4	1749.00625	<-- =B6*(1+15%)
8	5	2011.357188	<-- =B7*(1+15%)
9	6	2313.060766	<-- =B8*(1+15%)
10	7	2660.01988	<-- =B9*(1+15%)
11	8	3059.022863	<-- =B10*(1+15%)
12	9	3517.876292	<-- =B11*(1+15%)
13	10	4045.557736	<-- =B12*(1+15%)

Notice how Excel copied the cell formulas.
- The formula in cell B4 says: "Take the contents of the cell above and multiply by (1+15%)."
- When we *drag down* the cell formula in B5 it says: "Take the contents of the cell above and multiply by (1+15%).

This kind of copying is called *relative copying* in Excel: The cell formulas change in the direction of the copy (that is, the direction in which you dragged the cell handle). There's also *absolute copying,* which we explain in Section 27.3.

EXCEL HINT

Instead of dragging cell B4, there's an even simpler way to copy. If you put your cursor on the handle and double-click with the left mouse button, the formula in cell B4 will be copied from cell B5 through B13.

Entering Formulas by Pointing (a Better Way)

So far we've written the formula in cell B4. But it's usually a better idea to use the mouse and *point* at the relevant cells. Pointing and clicking formulas avoids a lot of mistakes. In the previous example:

Put the cursor on cell B4	
Type in "="	
With the mouse, point at cell B3	
Write in the rest of the formula—*(1+15%). Click the left mouse button or hit [Enter].	

27.2 Formatting the Numbers

The spreadsheet we've constructed so far is cute but ugly. Why do we need so many decimal places? Why aren't there commas in the numbers? How about indicating that these are *dollar* amounts?

We can make all these changes by using Excel's extensive *formatting* facilities.

In other chapters we'll use the **Format|Cells** command to change the way dates and text and fonts appear in Excel. The important thing to note about this command is that *it changes the way cell contents appear, but not the actual cell contents.* For example, suppose your cell contents read 3287.65898992; now suppose that you made them look like dollars with a comma and two decimal places, so that the cell reads $3,287.66." The actual contents of the cell haven't changed—there are still eight decimal places, but it only shows two of them.

FORMATTING NUMBERS IN EXCEL

Before: Mark the numbers to be formatted.
Go to **Format|Cells|Number** on the menu bar
and choose something appropriate.

After: Here's what we chose:

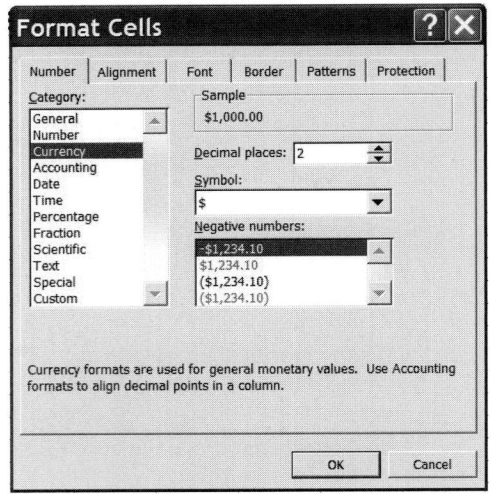

Here's how the spreadsheet looks now:

	A	B	C
1	**COMPOUND INTEREST**		
2	Year	Bank balance	
3	0	1000	
4	1	1150	
5	2	1322.5	
6	3	1520.875	
7	4	1749.00625	
8	5	2011.357188	
9	6	2313.060766	
10	7	2660.01988	
11	8	3059.022863	
12	9	3517.876292	
13	10	4045.557736	
14			

	A	B	C
1	**COMPOUND INTEREST**		
2	Year	Bank balance	
3	0	$1,000.00	
4	1	$1,150.00	
5	2	$1,322.50	
6	3	$1,520.88	
7	4	$1,749.01	
8	5	$2,011.36	
9	6	$2,313.06	
10	7	$2,660.02	
11	8	$3,059.02	
12	9	$3,517.88	
13	10	$4,045.56	

27.3 Absolute Copying: Building a More Sophisticated Model

The spreadsheet of the previous section is cute, but it doesn't allow us to change the interest rate at which the money accumulates. We fix this by writing the following spreadsheet; in this spreadsheet we've got a separate cell (B2) to indicate the interest rate. By changing this cell we'll change all the accumulations.

	A	B	C
1	**COMPOUND INTEREST**		
2	Interest	7%	
3			
4	Year		
5	0	$1,000.00	
6	1		
7	2		
8	3		
9	4		
10	5		
11	6		
12	7		
13	8		
14	9		
15	10		

Go to cell B6. Type the formula "=B5*(1+\$B\$2)" in this cell. The dollar signs on \$B\$2 indicate that when we copy this formula, this particular cell reference will not change. In the jargon of Excel: \$B\$2 is an *absolute reference,* whereas B5 is a *relative reference*—it will change to B6, B7, . . . as we go down the column.

	A	B	C
1	**COMPOUND INTEREST**		
2	Interest	7%	
3			
4	Year		
5	0	$1,000.00	
6	1	$1,070.00	<-- =B5*(1+$B$2)
7	2		
8	3		
9	4		
10	5		
11	6		
12	7		
13	8		
14	9		
15	10		

Copying as we did in the previous section (click on B6, put the cursor on the B6 handle and drag):

	A	B	C
1	**COMPOUND INTEREST**		
2	Interest	7%	
3			
4	Year		
5	0	$1,000.00	
6	1	$1,070.00	<-- =B5*(1+$B$2)
7	2		
8	3		Cursor

The result is a table much like that of the previous section:

	A	B	C
1	**COMPOUND INTEREST**		
2	Interest	7%	
3			
4	Year		
5	0	$1,000.00	
6	1	$1,070.00	<-- =B5*(1+$B$2)
7	2	$1,144.90	<-- =B6*(1+$B$2)
8	3	$1,225.04	<-- =B7*(1+$B$2)
9	4	$1,310.80	<-- =B8*(1+$B$2)
10	5	$1,402.55	<-- =B9*(1+$B$2)
11	6	$1,500.73	<-- =B10*(1+$B$2)
12	7	$1,605.78	<-- =B11*(1+$B$2)
13	8	$1,718.19	<-- =B12*(1+$B$2)
14	9	$1,838.46	<-- =B13*(1+$B$2)
15	10	$1,967.15	<-- =B14*(1+$B$2)

(We've formatted the numbers as currency.)

The difference between this spreadsheet and the previous one is that we can change the interest rate simply by changing the contents of cell B2. In this example the interest rate is 10%:

	A	B	C
1	**COMPOUND INTEREST**		
2	Interest	10%	
3			
4	Year		
5	0	$1,000.00	
6	1	$1,100.00	<-- =B5*(1+$B$2)
7	2	$1,210.00	<-- =B6*(1+$B$2)
8	3	$1,331.00	<-- =B7*(1+$B$2)
9	4	$1,464.10	<-- =B8*(1+$B$2)
10	5	$1,610.51	<-- =B9*(1+$B$2)
11	6	$1,771.56	<-- =B10*(1+$B$2)
12	7	$1,948.72	<-- =B11*(1+$B$2)
13	8	$2,143.59	<-- =B12*(1+$B$2)
14	9	$2,357.95	<-- =B13*(1+$B$2)
15	10	$2,593.74	<-- =B14*(1+$B$2)

EXCEL HINT

Never use a number if you can use a cell reference! Compare the previous example with this one: If, as in the previous section, you "hard-wire" the 15% interest rate in cells B6 to B15, you have to change each of these cells in order to change the interest rate assumption. On the other hand, if you put the interest rate in a cell (as in this section's example), you need only change the contents of that cell in order to recalculate the whole spreadsheet.

In Excel, numbers are always inferior to formulas!

Pointing and Using the F4 Key

Let's go back to the stage in this example where we were putting the formula "=B5*(1+$B$2)" into cell B5. We've already suggested that it's better to enter formulas by pointing and clicking than by typing. Now we'll teach you another little trick, the use of the F4 key to "dollarize" cell references—that is, to make them absolute references instead of relative references. Here's what you do:

- Put the cursor in cell B6. Type "=".

	A	B	C
1	**COMPOUND INTEREST**		
2	Interest	10%	
3			
4	Year		
5	0	$1,000.00	
6	1	=	
7	2		
8	3		

Now *point* at cell B5, the one that contains $1,000.00. You can point with either the mouse (clicking when you're on B5) or the arrow keys.

NPER   ▼ X ✓ *fx* =B5

	A	B	C
1	**COMPOUND INTEREST**		
2	Interest	10%	
3			
4	Year		
5	0	$1,000.00	
6	1	=B5	
7	2		
8	3		

- Now type a star, an opening parenthesis, a 1, and a + : *(1+ . Then point at cell B2 containing the interest rate:

NPER   ▼ X ✓ *fx* =B5*(1+B2

	A	B	C
1	**COMPOUND INTEREST**		
2	Interest	10%	
3			
4	Year		
5	0	$1,000.00	
6	1	=B5*(1+B2	
7	2		
8	3		

- Next hit function key **F4**. This puts the dollar signs into the cell reference B2 in cell B6.

NPER		▼ ✕ ✓ *fx* =B5*(1+$B$2
	A	**B**	**C**

	A	B	C
1	**COMPOUND INTEREST**		
2	Interest	10%	
3			
4	Year		
5		0	$1,000.00
6		1	=B5*(1+$B$2
7		2	
8		3	

- Finally, type a closing parenthesis by typing a ")". Hit [Enter].
- Copy cell B6 as before.

Correcting Errors—Editing the Cell

Suppose you made a mistake and forgot to "dollarize" the B2 cell reference, so that the contents of cell B6 are "=B5*(1+B2)." This isn't good—the cell contents should read "=B5*(1+$B$2)." To make the appropriate change, we edit the formula in cell B6 and we use the F4 key:

- Put the cursor on B6 and click the left mouse key twice. This opens the formula for editing.

NPER		▼ ✕ ✓ *fx* =B5*(1+B2)
	A	**B**	**C**

	A	B	C
1	**COMPOUND INTEREST**		
2	Interest	10%	
3			
4	Year		
5		0	$1,000.00
6		1	=B5*(1+B2)
7		2	
8		3	

- Move the cursor until it's somewhere on the B2 in the formula (it doesn't matter where). Hit the F4 key and your cell reference will be "dollarized."

NPER		▼ ✕ ✓ *fx* =B5*(1+$B$2)
	A	**B**	**C**

	A	B	C
1	**COMPOUND INTEREST**		
2	Interest	10%	
3			
4	Year		
5		0	$1,000.00
6		1	=B5*(1+$B$2)
7		2	

- Now hit [Enter] and copy as before.

THREE EXCEL HINTS ABOUT EDITING

1. You can also edit the cell contents by putting the cursor on the cell and hitting the **F2** function button.
2. If you can't edit the formula in the cell, someone may have changed the default settings on your Excel spreadsheet. Go to **Tools|Options**, click the **Edit** tab, and check the "Edit directly in cell" box:

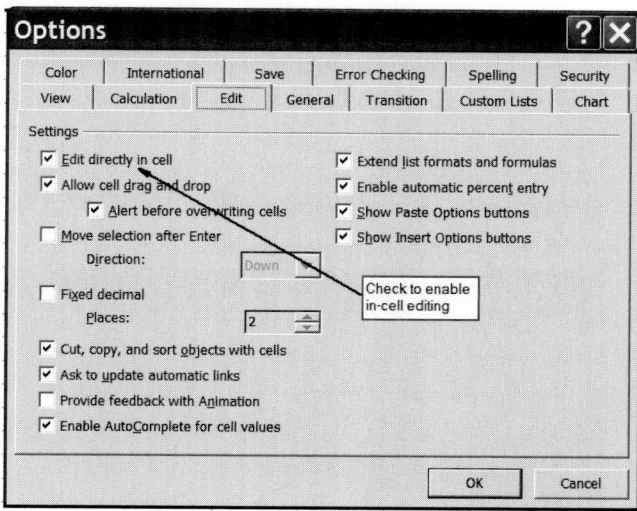

3. You can always edit a cell formula in the formula bar:

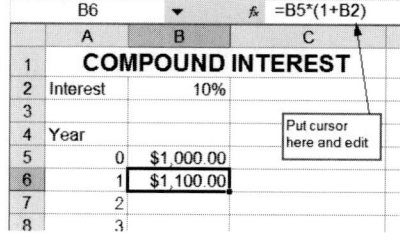

27.4 Saving the Spreadsheet

What's the next step? We suggest that you *save* the spreadsheet.[1] An appropriate place to save it is in the **Junk** directory that you're going to create right now.

---

[1] As a rule of thumb, we suggest that you save *all the time*. Someday, your computer is going to crash *right after* you've spent a long time working and *before* you've saved your work.

- Go to **File|Save**:

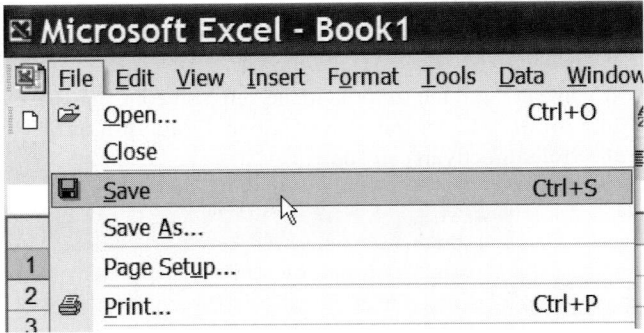

- Excel will probably suggest a directory called **My Documents**:

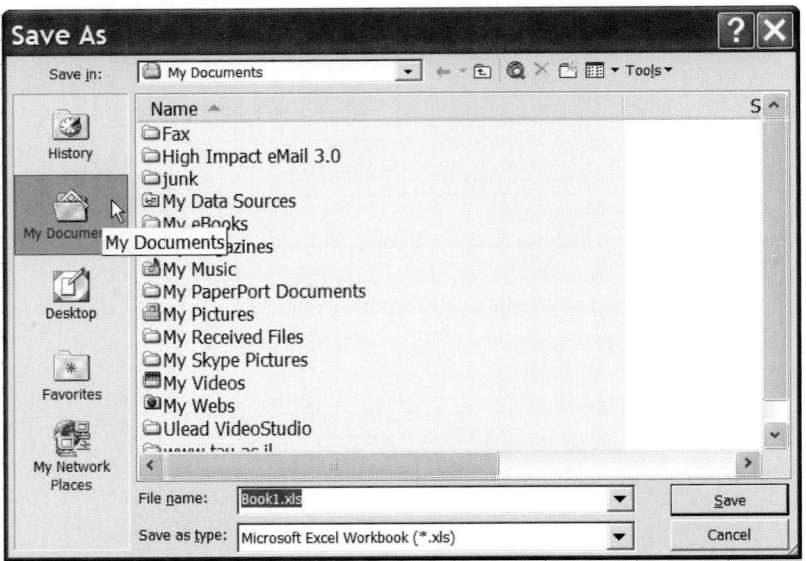

- Click on **My Documents**, and then click on the "Create New Folder" icon, which looks like this:

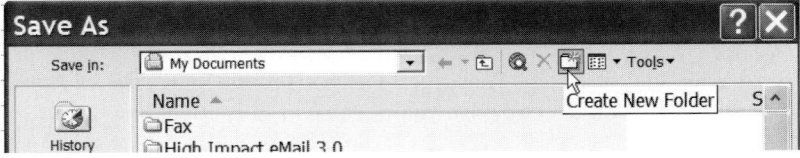

- When you click on the "Create New Folder" icon, you'll get a dialogue box:

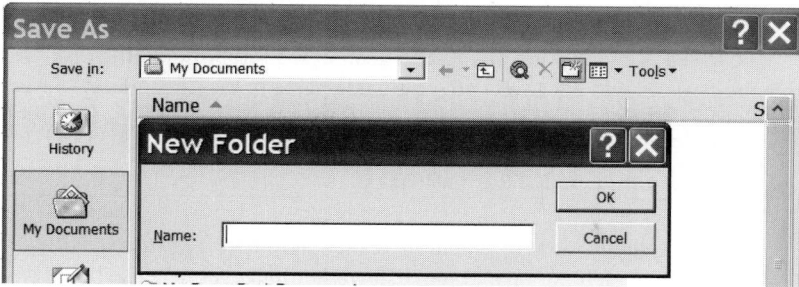

In the Name box, type "junk." The author's computer always has a directory called "junk"—it's the directory containing all the files that can be disposed of without thinking twice (a file called "junk" in the "junk" directory is a double whammy—absolutely worthless!). Now you'll find yourself in the **Junk** subdirectory:

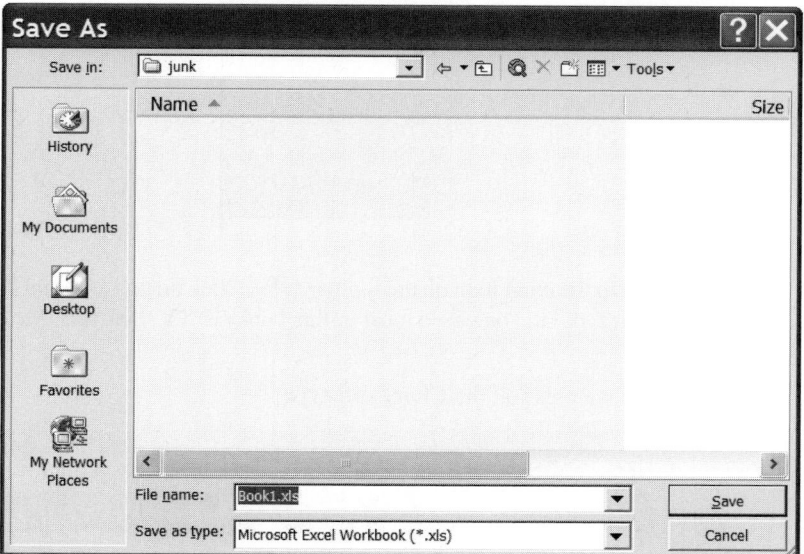

Type something clever in the box called **File Name**. We'll call our spreadsheet "garbage." Now you'll see the name of the spreadsheet in the upper left-hand corner of the sheet:

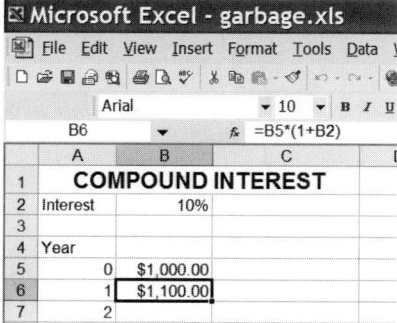

Every time you subsequently save the workbook (either by **File|Save** or by pressing [Ctrl]+S or by clicking on the save icon in the form of the little disk ▣), the workbook with all its changes will be saved under the same name in the same place.

27.5 Your First Excel Graph

You're going to want to graph the compound interest example. Take your mouse, put it in cell A5; push the left button and move down until you get to cell B15:

	A	B	C
1	**COMPOUND INTEREST**		
2	Interest	10%	
3			
4	Year		
5	0	$1,000.00	
6	1	$1,100.00	
7	2	$1,210.00	
8	3	$1,331.00	
9	4	$1,464.10	
10	5	$1,610.51	
11	6	$1,771.56	
12	7	$1,948.72	
13	8	$2,143.59	
14	9	$2,357.95	
15	10	$2,593.74	
16			

Now go to the chart icon on the toolbar (▦). Click on this icon and choose a chart type. Our favorite chart type (the one used most in this book) is **XY (Scatter)**. We also like the *connected*

XY chart, so we press on the **Chart sub-type** ⟨▧⟩ :

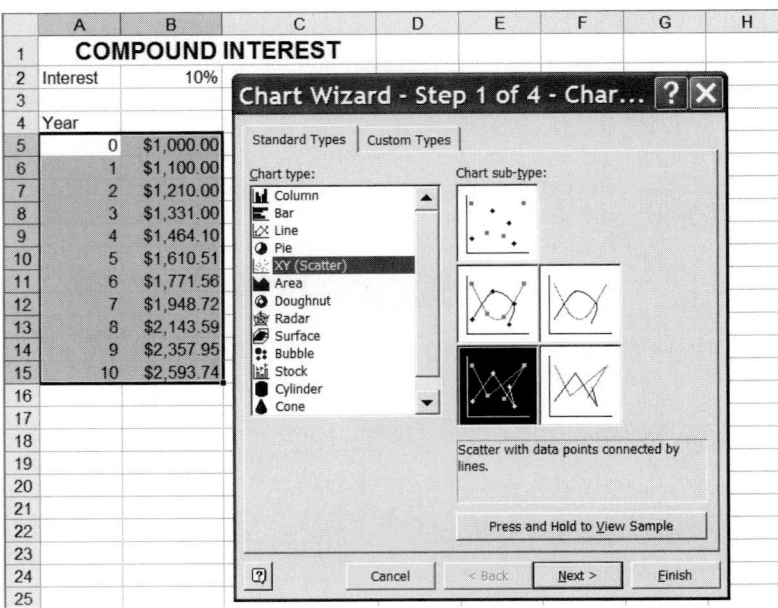

At this point there's lots we can do in terms of formatting the chart, but we explain that to you later in Chapter 28. Just press the **Finish** button at the bottom of the Chart Wizard, and you'll get a reasonable graph:

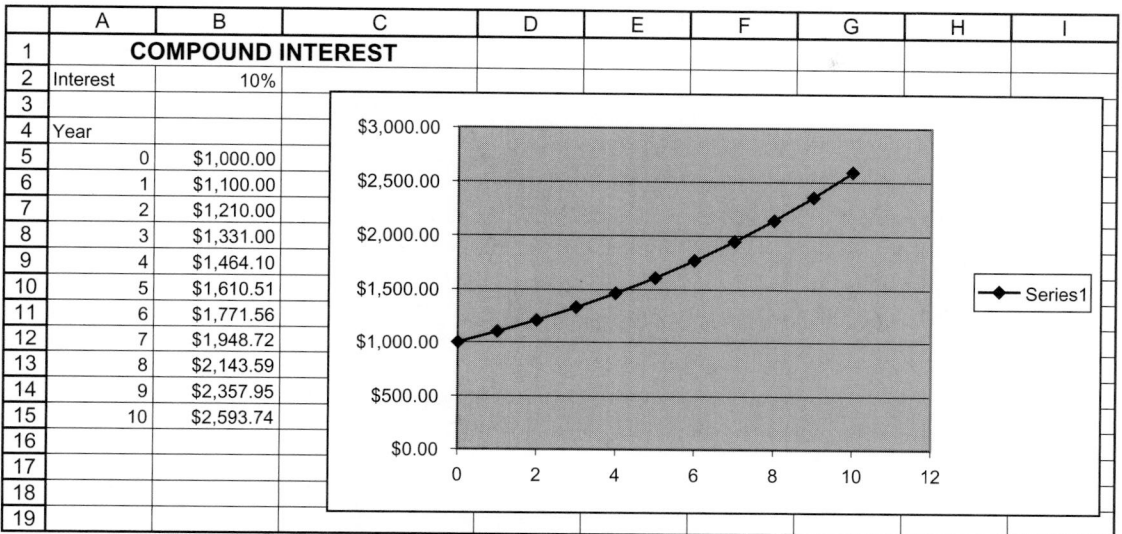

This graph has lots of features we don't like, but they can all be fixed (Chapter 28 again). Instead of fixing things, *play* with the spreadsheet—change the interest rate and see what happens:

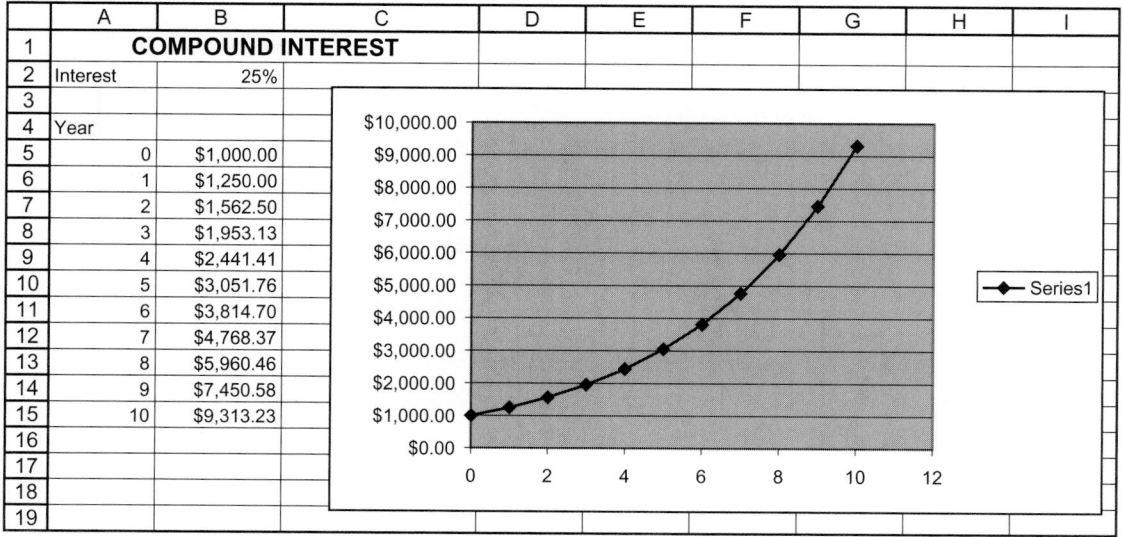

27.6 Initial Settings

Before you make intensive use of Excel, it's worthwhile to change a few of the initial settings to suit your needs and preferences. In this section we show you our suggestions (they're all reversible).

Make Excel Less Jumpy

The default installation of Excel has the cursor go down one cell each time you press [Enter].

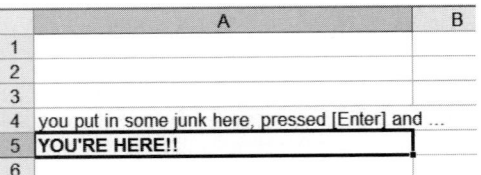

This is great for accountants, who have to enter lots of data. But we're finance people, and we make lots of mistakes! We want to stay on the cell we just entered, so we can correct it, and so we want to turn this feature off.

How? Press **Tools|Options** on the menu bar. Then go to the **Edit** tab and *unclick* the **Move selection after Enter** box. In the picture below, this box is still clicked (this is the default):

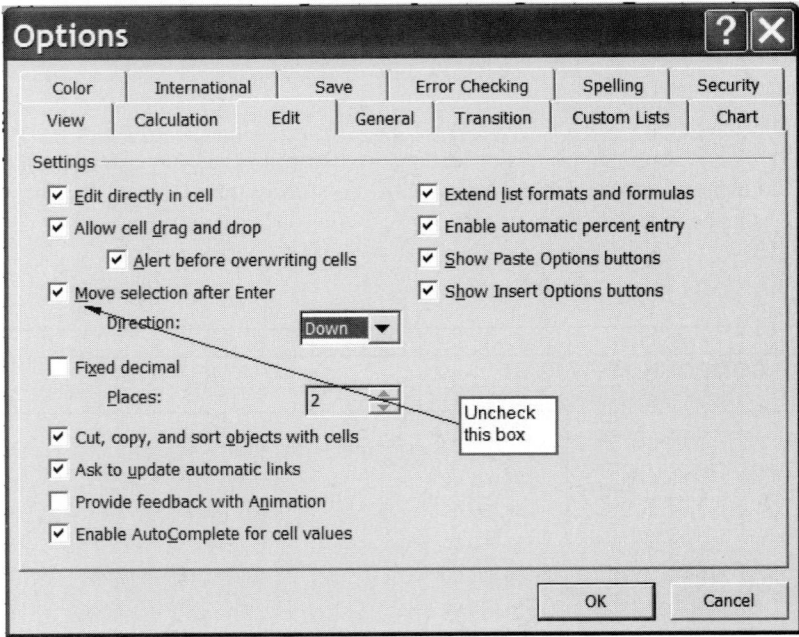

The Number of Sheets in a Workbook

The default installation for Excel starts each new workbook with three spreadsheets.[2] This means that the bottom of your screen looks like:

---

[2]Nomenclature: Microsoft calls an Excel file (the thing you saved as "Garbage.xls") a *workbook*. The individual sheets of the workbook are called *spreadsheets* or *worksheets*. Like many Excel users, we often mix up this nomenclature.

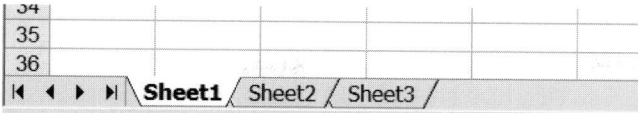

Each of these sheets can be programmed separately and also can be named separately (see below). But the fact remains that most users use only one sheet per workbook. We suggest that you change the defaults so that Excel starts a new workbook with only one spreadsheet (you can always add more). To do this, go to **Tools|Options** and click on the **General** tab:

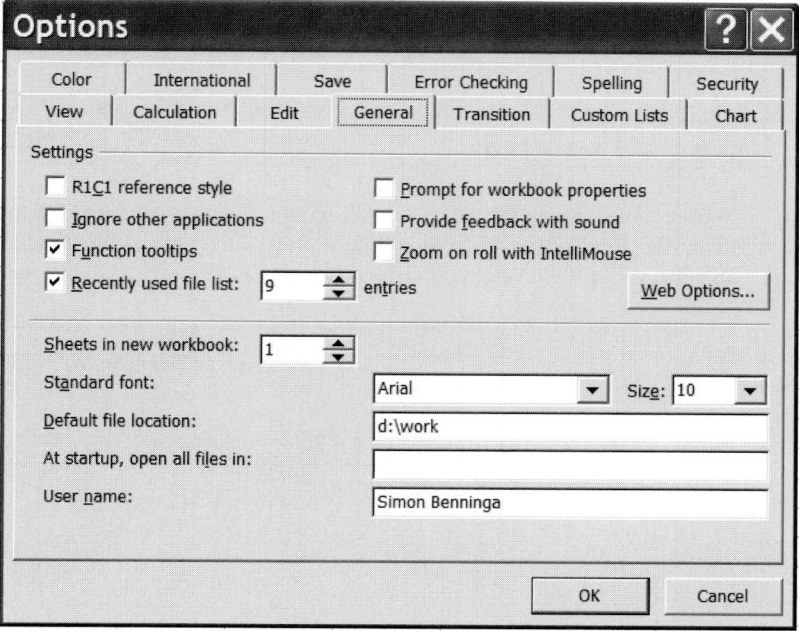

In the picture above we've changed the **Sheets in new workbook** to "1."

Naming a Sheet

To name a sheet, double click on the sheet tab. You can now type in the name you want for the sheet:

Before	After
34	34
35	35
36	36
⏮ ◀ ▶ ⏭ \Sheet1 /	⏮ ◀ ▶ ⏭ Compound interest /

Adding More Sheets

To add more sheets, go to **Insert|Worksheet**

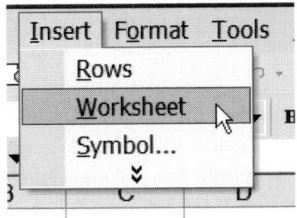

You can also delete a sheet (**Edit|Delete sheet**). This is an *irreversible* action, so we suggest you save the workbook before doing this.

27.7 Using a Function

Excel contains many functions. In this section we illustrate a few of these.[3] We go back to the spreadsheet in Section 27.5. In cell B17 we calculate the average value of the cells B5 to B15 (this has very little economic meaning). The final product will look like this:

	A	B	C
1	**COMPOUND INTEREST**		
2	Interest	7%	
3			
4	Year		
5	0	$1,000.00	
6	1	$1,070.00	<-- =B5*(1+$B$2)
7	2	$1,144.90	<-- =B6*(1+$B$2)
8	3	$1,225.04	<-- =B7*(1+$B$2)
9	4	$1,310.80	<-- =B8*(1+$B$2)
10	5	$1,402.55	<-- =B9*(1+$B$2)
11	6	$1,500.73	<-- =B10*(1+$B$2)
12	7	$1,605.78	<-- =B11*(1+$B$2)
13	8	$1,718.19	<-- =B12*(1+$B$2)
14	9	$1,838.46	<-- =B13*(1+$B$2)
15	10	$1,967.15	<-- =B14*(1+$B$2)
16			
17	Average	$1,434.87	<-- =AVERAGE(B5:B15)

To do this:

- In cell A17 we type "Average." This is known as "annotating the spreadsheet." In simple English—tell yourself what you're doing, because otherwise you'll forget.

  In cell B17, we type "**=average(**", and then hit the f_x sign on the toolbar:

---

[3]The discussion in this section is really preliminary and intended to give you a taste of how Excel functions work. In this book we use many Excel functions. Chapter 29 discusses most of the functions used in the book and Chapter 31 discusses Excel's date functions.

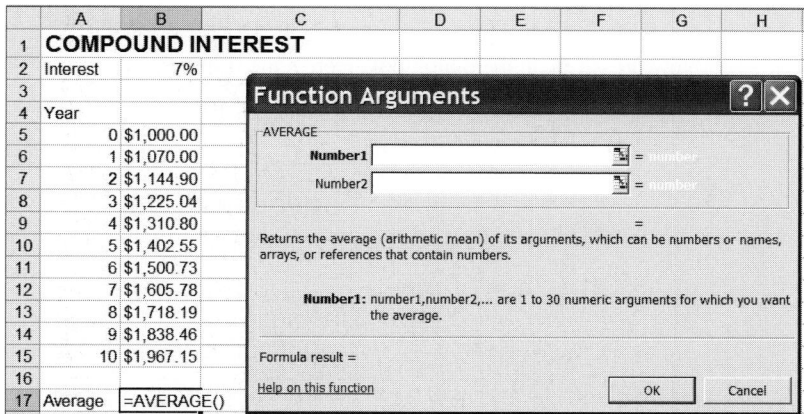

You'll see a *function dialog box:*

You cursor is already in a box labeled **Number1**. Put the mouse on cell B5, push down the left mouse button, and drag the cursor to B15. Here's what you'll see:

Now let the cursor go:

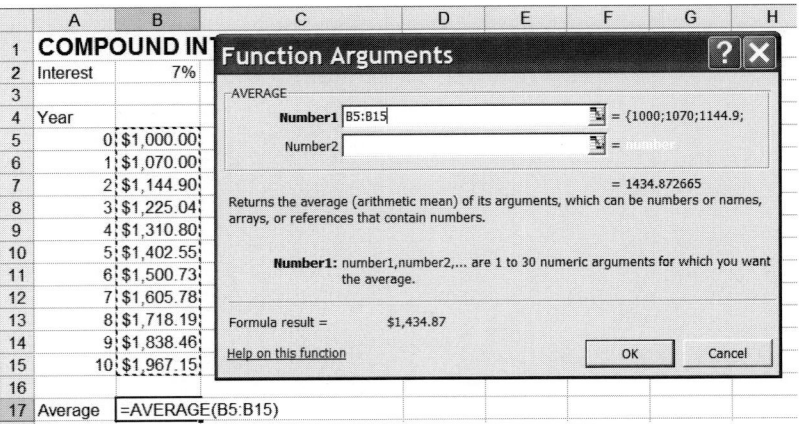

Now press **OK** in the dialog box. Here's the result:

	A	B	C
1		COMPOUND INTEREST	
2	Interest	7%	
3			
4	Year		
5	0	$1,000.00	
6	1	$1,070.00	
7	2	$1,144.90	
8	3	$1,225.04	
9	4	$1,310.80	
10	5	$1,402.55	
11	6	$1,500.73	
12	7	$1,605.78	
13	8	$1,718.19	
14	9	$1,838.46	
15	10	$1,967.15	
16			
17	Average	$1,434.87	<-- =AVERAGE(B5:B15)

Suppose you didn't want to average all the numbers, but only those from years 5–10. There are two ways to do this:

- You can double-click on cell B17, and change the range in the formula to **=Average(B10:B15)**.
- You can double-click on cell B17, and re-click the f_x sign on the toolbar. This reopens the dialog box. Now click on the ▦ next to the range currently being averaged:

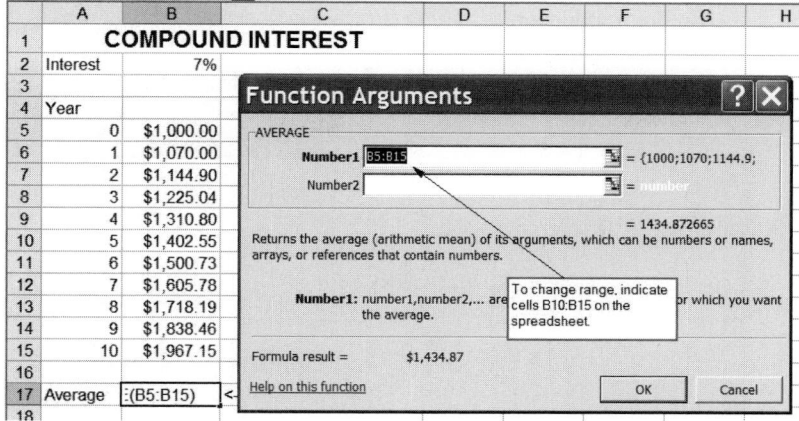

You can now indicate the range (B10:B15) you want to average. A couple of [Enters] should give you the result.

Practice Makes Perfect

The exercises to this chapter let you practice with a few functions that work like **Average**.

27.8 Printing

You've just completed your beautiful first spreadsheet and you want to print it. Press **File|Print**. This brings up the following screen:

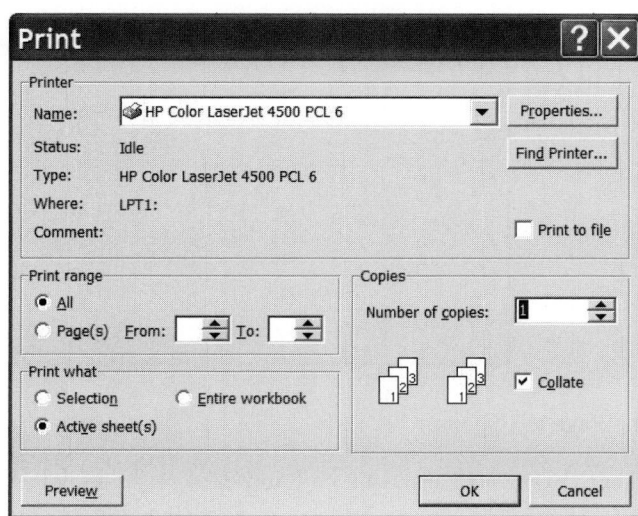

Before printing, press the **Preview** box:

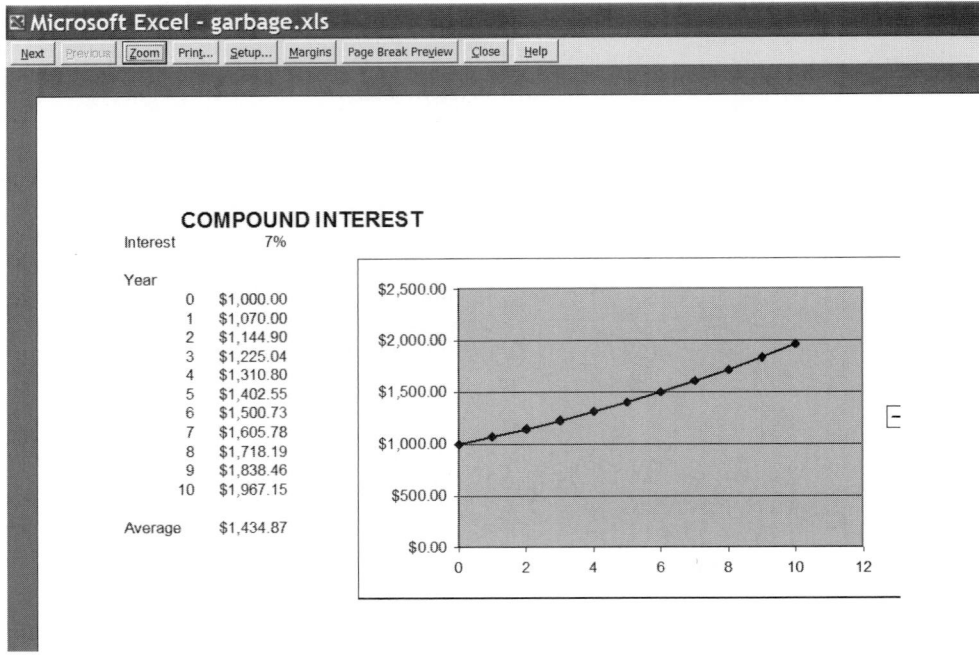

Notice that the graph is a bit cut off at the right edge. Press **Setup** and explore the various tabs:

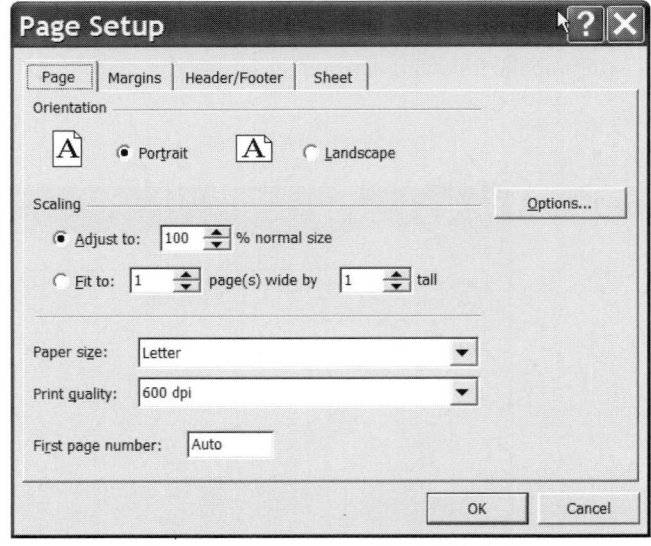

In the **Page** tab, choose to fit everything onto one sheet. (You could also put it on **Landscape** paper, using the button on the same tab.)

On the **Sheet** tab, you can choose to print the spreadsheet using **Gridlines** and **Row and column headings** (these are the settings we've used for most of the spreadsheets in this book).

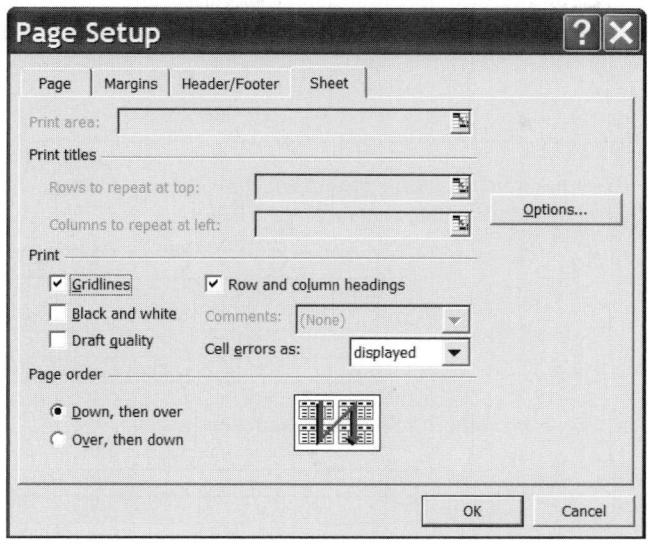

Now click on **OK** to see what the printing will look like:

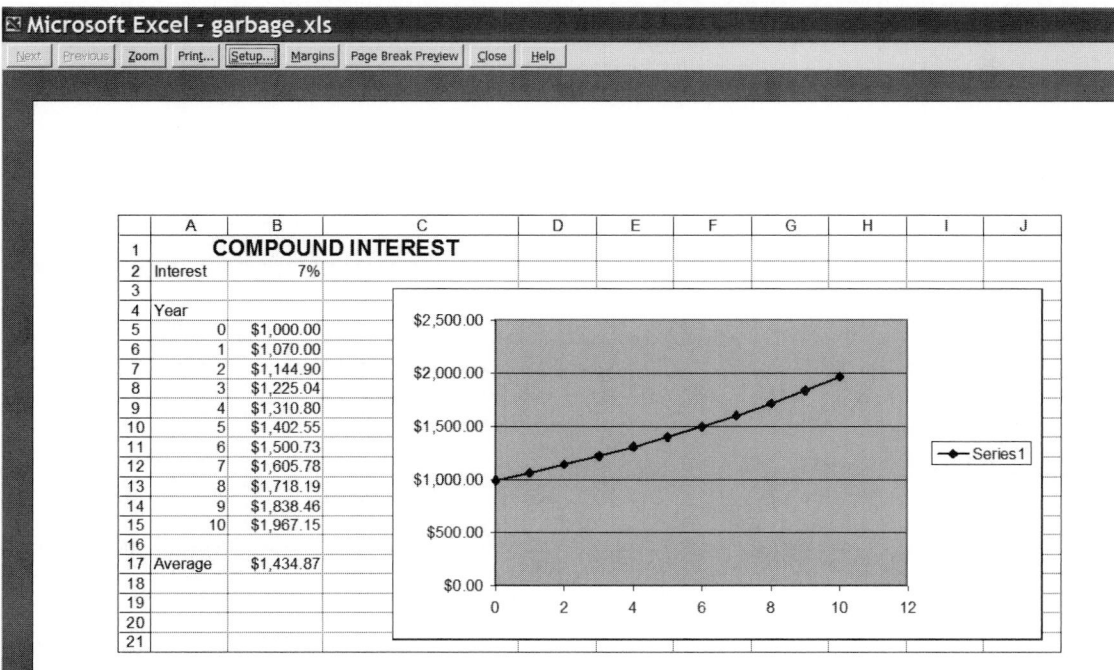

If this suits your purpose, press **Print**.

CONCLUSION

In this chapter we've explored the preliminaries of Excel—how to set up a spreadsheet, save it, type in a formula, use a function, and print your results. The following chapters explore more advanced Excel techniques.

EXERCISES

1. Excel has a function called **Sum**, which works like **Average**. Set up the spreadsheet below and use it to add the numbers in cells A1 to A3.

	A	B
1	28	
2	15	
3	22	
4		<-- Use **Sum** to add the numbers

2. In a new spreadsheet, follow the instructions below:

	A	B
1	28	
2	15	
3	22	
4		<-- Use **Sum(A1:A3)/3** to find the average

3. In another spreadsheet, show that you can use the function **Average** to get the same result:

	A	B
1	28	
2	15	
3	22	
4		<-- Use **Sum(A1:A3)/3** to find the average
5		
6		<-- Use **Average(A1:A3)**

4. The Excel function **Count** counts the number of cells containing numbers. Use this function in the spreadsheet below:

	A	B
1	15	
2	-11	
3	John	
4	23	
5		<-- Use **Count(A1:A4)**

5. The Excel function **CountA** counts the number of all the cells in a given range. Experiment with this function in the spreadsheet below:

	A	B
1	15	
2	-11	
3	John	
4	23	
5		<-- Use **CountA(A1:A4)**

6. Below are some statistics on the monthly rainfall in the city of Dunedin, New Zealand (the numbers are on the disk that accompanies this book). Use **Sum** and **Average** to compute the monthly rainfall.

	A	B	C	D	E	F	G	H	I	J	K	L	M	N	O
1				MONTHLY RAINFALL IN THE CITY OF DUNEDIN, NEW ZEALAND (in centimeters)											
2		Jan	Feb	Mar	Apr	May	Jun	Jul	Aug	Sep	Oct	Nov	Dec	Total	Average
3	1980	115	79	83	74	57	195	72	89	39	56	117	45		
4	1981	17	47	107	40	20	142	163	49	49	62	24	82		
5	1982	142	48	37	45	68	39	33	47	32	147	42	140		
6	1983	99	65	113	78	140	78	84	35	81	64	38	93		
7	1984	107	22	126	33	83	36	69	59	86	38	52	77		
8	1985	28	17	29	23	35	35	89	39	29	63	51	85		
9	1986	41	179	101	49	60	79	75	48	22	69	89	83		
10	1987	59	89	150	24	136	88	25	21	71	47	47	67		
11	1988	147	90	25	38	60	44	62	40	13	27	40	61		
12	1989	55	48	81	31	39	95	39	35	20	96	64	100		
13	1990	34	44	18	62	48	21	34	137	19	96	42	55		
14	1991	77	178	49	99	33	52	38	124	54	41	45	68		
15	1992	52	88	26	65	52	39	56	123	88	80	68	112		
16	1993	126	35	79	62	94	25	21	47	72	41	73	109		
17	1994	140	69	170	23	42	115	99	14	45	13	78	57		
18	1995	41	37	91	12	41	121	42	40	97	92	72	61		
19	1996	56	52	33	108	55	75	58	61	14	143	132	95		
20	1997	120	117	44	122	48	20	60	43	30	62	88	85		
21	1998	10	101	60	52	66	24	26	44	58	109	33	66		
22	1999	42	12	65	43	17	58	83	32	52	41	59	80		

7. Refer to the Dunedin rainfall data from Exercise 6.
   (a) Use the Excel function **Max** to compute the largest monthly rainfall in each of the years 1980–1999.
   (b) Compute the largest monthly rainfall for *all* the months in the table.

8. (a) Complete the following spreadsheet, showing how much will be in your bank account if you deposit an initial deposit (cell B2) today, and it draws annual interest given in cell B1.
   (b) Graph the results of the bank account.

	A	B
1	Interest	8%
2	Initial deposit	$155
3		
4	Year	In bank account
5	0	
6	1	
7	2	
8	3	
9	4	
10	5	

GRAPHS AND CHARTS IN EXCEL

OVERVIEW

Excel has extensive facilities to do graphs.[1] If you're like most Excel users and finance majors, you'll be using these facilities a lot.

In this short chapter, we discuss the basics of graphing, assuming that by and large you already know how to make a chart in Excel. We also discuss some less well-known techniques that have to do with charts:

- Making a graph with noncontiguous data series
- Changing the axis parameters of a chart
- Making a chart where the title changes when the data changes

---

[1]In "Excelese," graphs are called "charts." We use both words interchangeably.

28.1 The Basics of Excel Charts

Every Excel chart has its origins in the data on a spreadsheet:

	A	B	C	D
1	**MERCK & CO. 1991-2000**			
2		**Dividends**	**Purchase of treasury stock**	**Proceeds from exercise of stock options**
3	1991	893	184	48
4	1992	1,064	863	52
5	1993	1,174	371	83
6	1994	1,434	705	139
7	1995	1,540	1,571	264
8	1996	1,729	2,493	442
9	1997	2,040	2,573	413
10	1998	2,253	3,626	490
11	1999	2,590	3,582	323
12	2000	2,798	3,545	641

To create a graph that shows the dividends paid each year, we mark the relevant data:

	A	B	C	D
1	**MERCK & CO. 1991-2000**			
2		**Dividends**	**Purchase of treasury stock**	**Proceeds from exercise of stock options**
3	1991	893	184	48
4	1992	1,064	863	52
5	1993	1,174	371	83
6	1994	1,434	705	139
7	1995	1,540	1,571	264
8	1996	1,729	2,493	442
9	1997	2,040	2,573	413
10	1998	2,253	3,626	490
11	1999	2,590	3,582	323
12	2000	2,798	3,545	641

Clicking on the chart icon ▦ on the toolbar brings up the chart menu, which gives a bewildering variety of chart options. Being finance people, we're primarily interested in the XY (Scatter) chart option. We usually want to draw a connected line (shown here as the chosen "Chart sub-type"):

TWO OPTIONS FOR "CONNECTED" EXCEL XY CHARTS

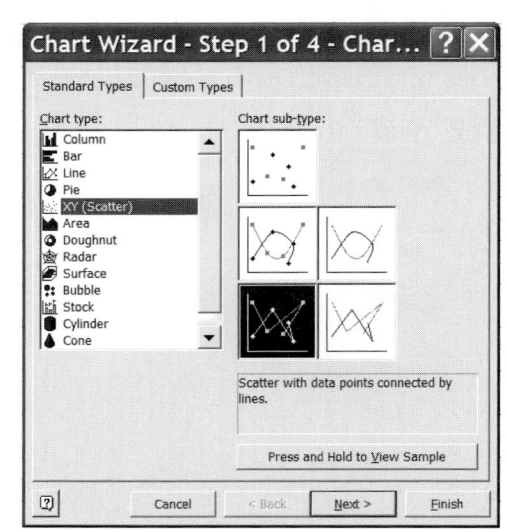

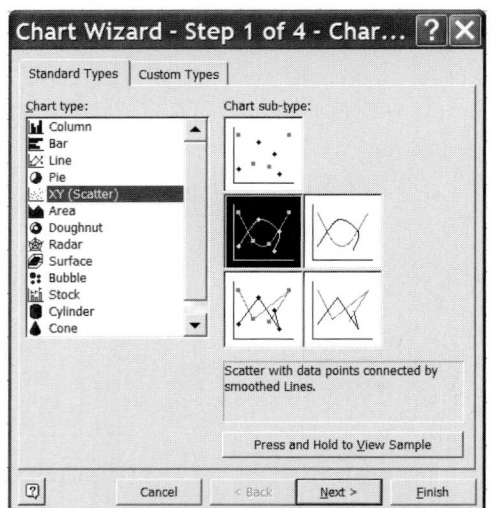

This creates a "jagged" XY chart (the points are connected by line segments). It is the option we generally use in this book

This smooths the lines connecting the points.

Going to the next step in the chart wizard, you'll see:

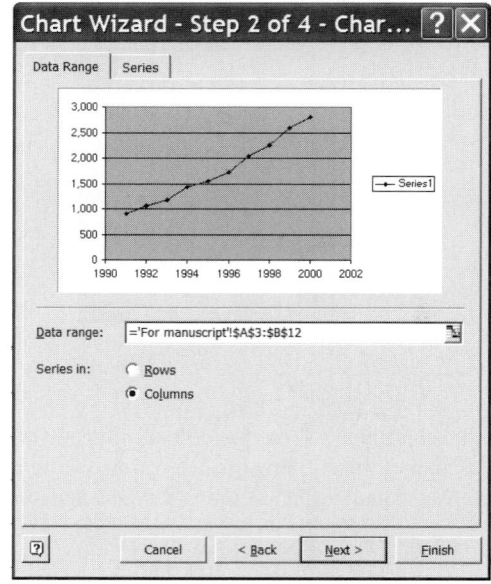

There's nothing much to do here, so press **Next** and go on to the next step, which allows you to annotate the graph with titles:

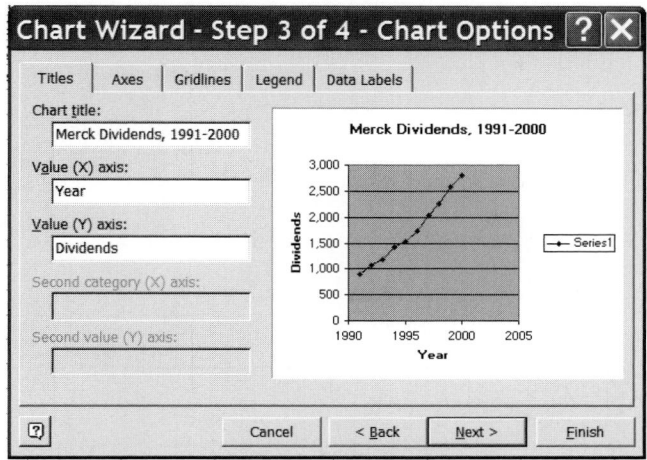

This author doesn't like gridlines of any sort!

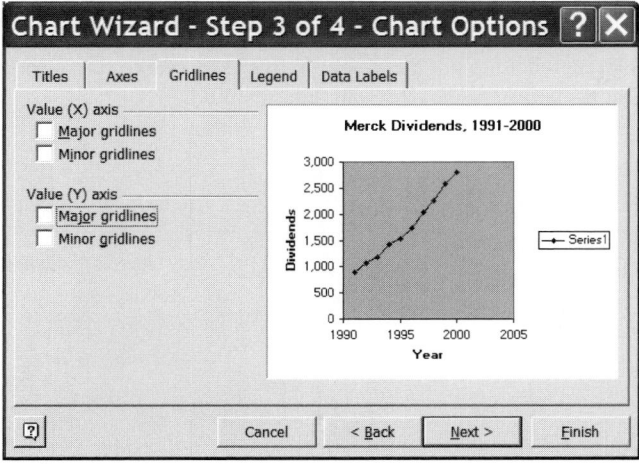

Nor does he like legends very much . . . though sometimes there's room for one (see Section 28.2):

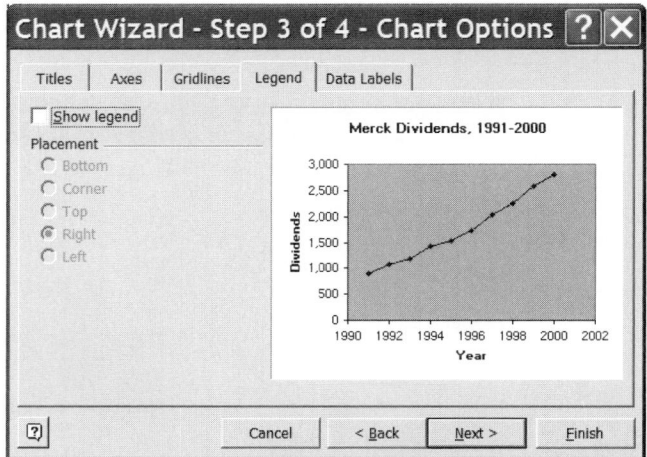

Pressing **Next** gets you to:

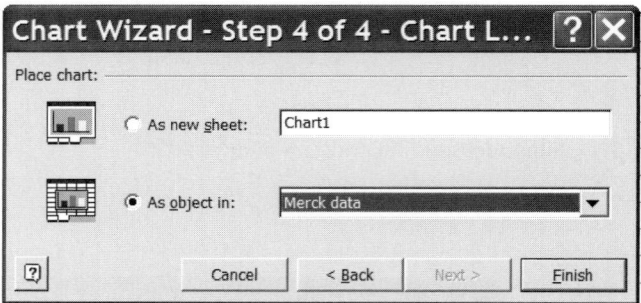

Tell Excel where to put the graph (in this case, on the spreadsheet labeled "Merck data," which is also the spreadsheet where our data is stored.

Pushing **Finish** gives the following graph:

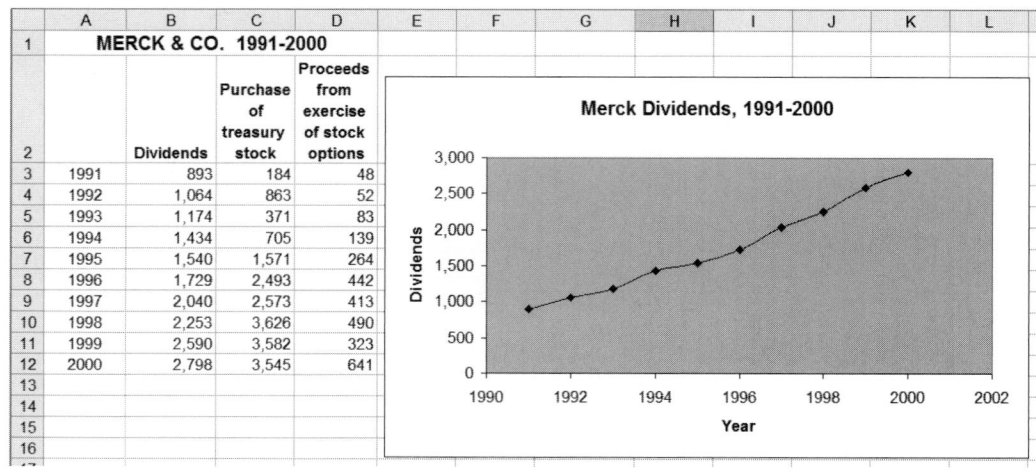

More Changes

Change 1: The Excel default graph has a murky gray area where the data is graphed. This looks alright on the screen, but it looks terrible when you print it. All the graphs in this book have this gray graph area blanked out. To do this, mark the graph area:

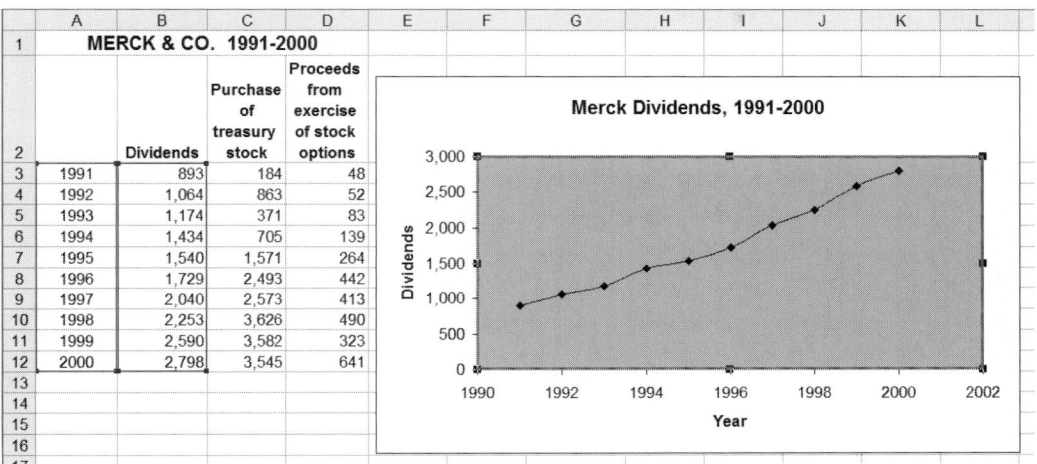

Now double-click on the graph area; this brings up the following box:

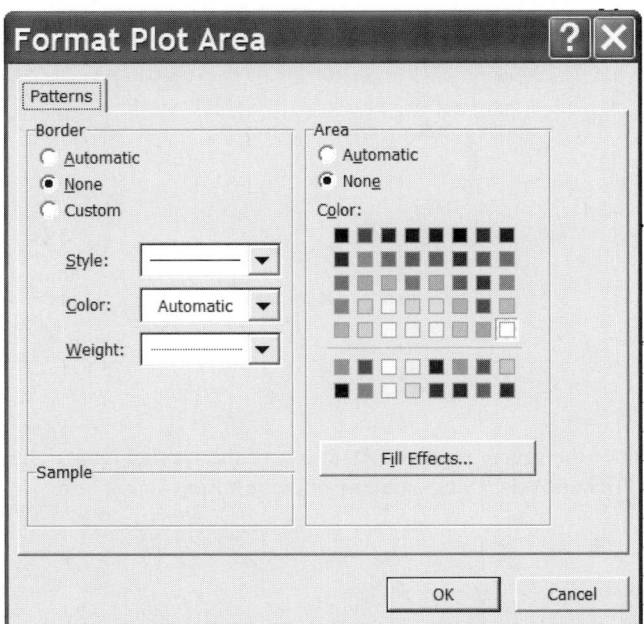

In the **Format Plot Area** box above, we always mark **Border—None** and **Area—None.** Here's the result:

	A	B	C	D	E	F	G	H	I	J	K	L
1	**MERCK & CO.　1991-2000**											
2		Dividends	Purchase of treasury stock	Proceeds from exercise of stock options								
3	1991	893	184	48								
4	1992	1,064	863	52								
5	1993	1,174	371	83								
6	1994	1,434	705	139								
7	1995	1,540	1,571	264								
8	1996	1,729	2,493	442								
9	1997	2,040	2,573	413								
10	1998	2,253	3,626	490								
11	1999	2,590	3,582	323								
12	2000	2,798	3,545	641								
13												
14												
15												
16												

Merck Dividends, 1991-2000 chart appears in cells E2 through L (plotting Dividends versus Year).

Change 2: Although our data only goes from 1991 to 2000, the *x*-axis on our chart goes from 1990 to 2002. To change this, mark the *x*-axis of the graph with a gentle click on the left mouse button:

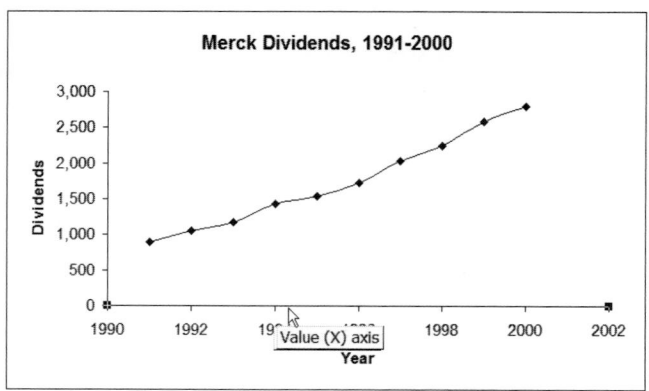

(Notice the square marks at either end of the *x*-axis.) Now right-click with the mouse and click on **Format Axis**. Click on **Scale** of the resulting dialog box.

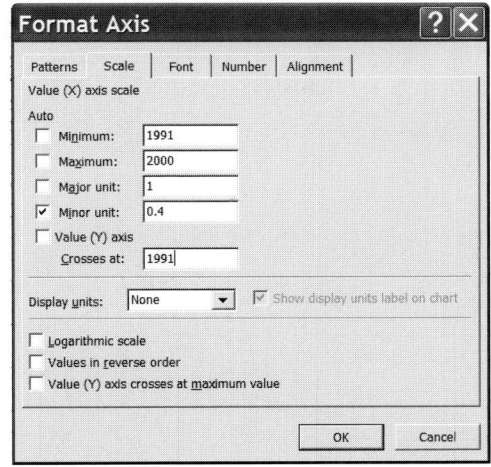

Before: A checked box indicates the Excel defaults. At this point the chart is set to show every other year on the *x*-axis (**Major unit** = 2). **Minor unit** indicates the number of ticks between the major units (not relevant here).

After: Note that we've changed both the **Minimum** and the **Maximum**, as well as the **Major unit**.

Here's the result:

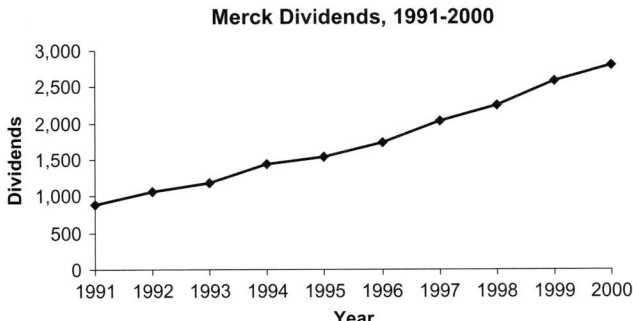

28.2 Creative Use of Legends

If you build your XY chart with data that includes legends, then Excel will generally transfer them in the proper way to the graph. Here's an example: We've marked the data to include the column headings:

	A	B	C	D
1	MERCK & CO. 1991-2000			
2		Dividends	Purchase of treasury stock	Proceeds from exercise of stock options
3	1991	893	184	48
4	1992	1,064	863	52
5	1993	1,174	371	83
6	1994	1,434	705	139
7	1995	1,540	1,571	264
8	1996	1,729	2,493	442
9	1997	2,040	2,573	413
10	1998	2,253	3,626	490
11	1999	2,590	3,582	323
12	2000	2,798	3,545	641

Here's the resulting graph:

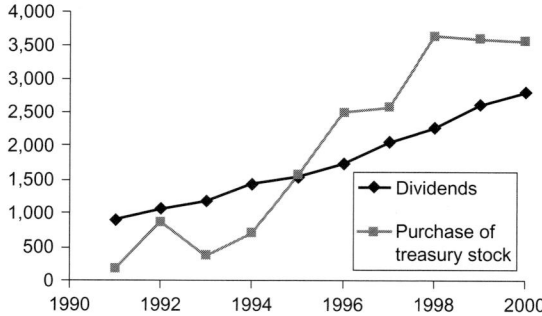

28.3 Graphing Noncontiguous Data

Suppose you want to make a graph of columns A, C, and D of the Merck data. To mark these three columns:

- Mark the first column (that is, press the left mouse button and "paint" cells A3 to A12).
- Press the [Ctrl] key and mark columns C and D (again, pressing the left mouse button).

At this point your spreadsheet looks like this:

	A	B	C	D
1	MERCK & CO. 1991-2000			
2		Dividends	Purchase of treasury stock	Proceeds from exercise of stock options
3	1991	893	184	48
4	1992	1,064	863	52
5	1993	1,174	371	83
6	1994	1,434	705	139
7	1995	1,540	1,571	264
8	1996	1,729	2,493	442
9	1997	2,040	2,573	413
10	1998	2,253	3,626	490
11	1999	2,590	3,582	323
12	2000	2,798	3,545	641

You can now follow the regular graphing procedure to create the following chart:

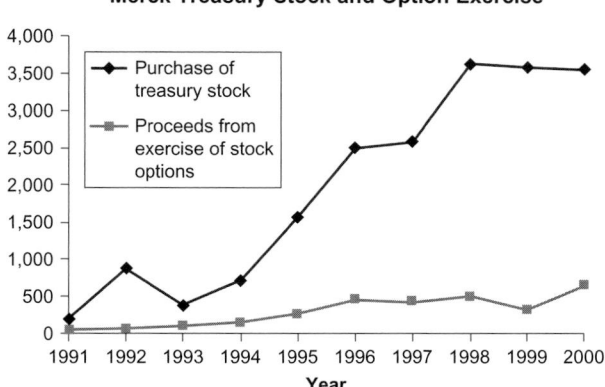

Fine-tuning—Changing Font Size So That the Axis Labels Fit

Sometimes when we use the **Format Axis** menu to change a chart axis, the labels don't fit properly. The example below is an illustration; the solution is given below the example.

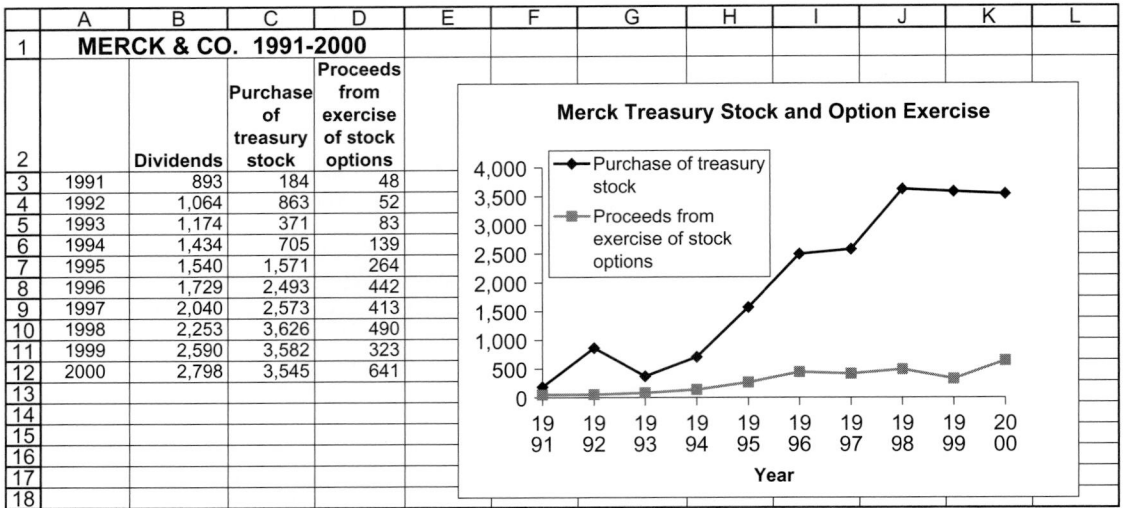

	A	B	C	D	E	F	G	H	I	J	K	L
1	**MERCK & CO. 1991-2000**											
2		Dividends	Purchase of treasury stock	Proceeds from exercise of stock options								
3	1991	893	184	48								
4	1992	1,064	863	52								
5	1993	1,174	371	83								
6	1994	1,434	705	139								
7	1995	1,540	1,571	264								
8	1996	1,729	2,493	442								
9	1997	2,040	2,573	413								
10	1998	2,253	3,626	490								
11	1999	2,590	3,582	323								
12	2000	2,798	3,545	641								
13												
14												
15												
16												
17												
18												

Go back into the dialog box and hit the **Font** tab to change the size of the *x*-axis font:

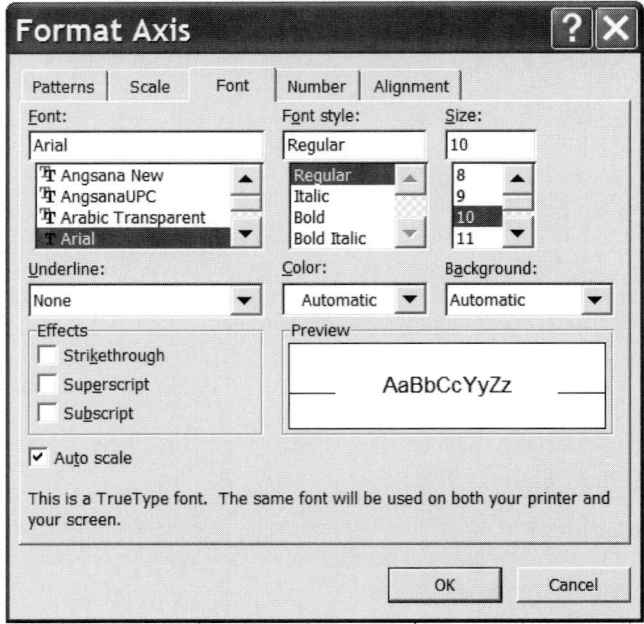

Now the graph looks fine:

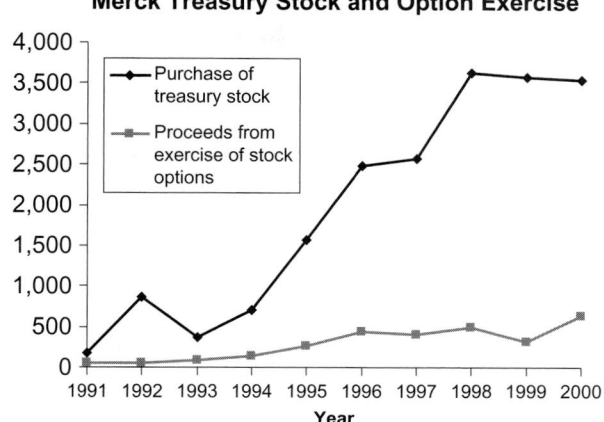

Merck Treasury Stock and Option Exercise

(There are other ways to accomplish this trick—if you make the chart bigger, for example.)

28.4 Line Charts With Titles on the *x*-Axis

Excel offers a bewildering variety of chart types. In this section we show you the **Line chart**, leaving other variations for you to explore. We use data for the average minimum and maximum temperatures in New York City:

	A	B	C	D	E	F	G	H	I	J	K	L	M
1	AVERAGE MONTHLY MAXIMUM AND MINIMUM TEMPERATURES--NEW YORK CITY												
2		Jan	Feb	Mar	Apr	May	Jun	Jul	Aug	Sep	Oct	Nov	Dec
3	Avg max temp (F)	38	40	50	61	72	80	85	84	76	65	54	43
4	Avg min temp (F)	25	27	35	44	54	63	68	67	60	50	41	31
5													
6													
7	Source: http://www.hm-usa.com/climate/ny.html												
8													
9													
10						NYC Temperatures							
11													
12													
13													
14													
15													
16													
17													
18									Avg max temp (F)				
19									Avg min temp (F)				
20													
21													
22													
23													
24													

To construct the chart, first mark the data you want to graph (here we have also indicated the legends in column A). *Do not* mark the *x*-axis labels, which appear in row 2. In the Chart

Wizard we choose the **Line** chart type:

	A	B	C	D	E	F	G	H	I	J	K	L	M
1	AVERAGE MONTHLY MAXIMUM AND MINIMUM TEMPERATURES--NEW YORK CITY												
2		Jan	Feb	Mar	Apr	May	Jun	Jul	Aug	Sep	Oct	Nov	Dec
3	Avg max temp (F)	38	40	50	61	72	80	85	84	76	65	54	43
4	Avg min temp (F)	25	27	35	44	54	63	68	67	60	50	41	31
5													
6													
7													

Chart Wizard - Step 1 of 4 - Char...

Standard Types | Custom Types

Chart type:
Column
Bar
Line
Pie
XY (Scatter)
Area
Doughnut
Radar
Surface
Bubble
Stock
Cylinder
Cone

Chart sub-type:

Line with markers displayed at each data value.

Press and Hold to View Sample

Cancel   < Back   Next >   Finish

Clicking **Next**, we get to the following screen. Follow the instructions to indicate the *x*-axis legend.

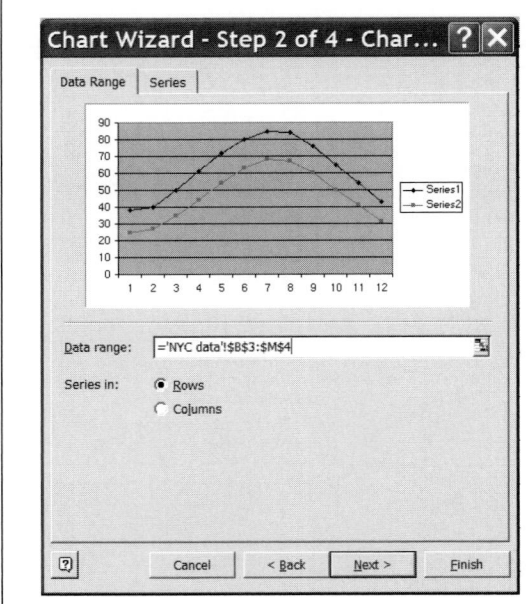

After marking the data in rows 3 and 4, this screen comes up in the Excel Chart Wizard.

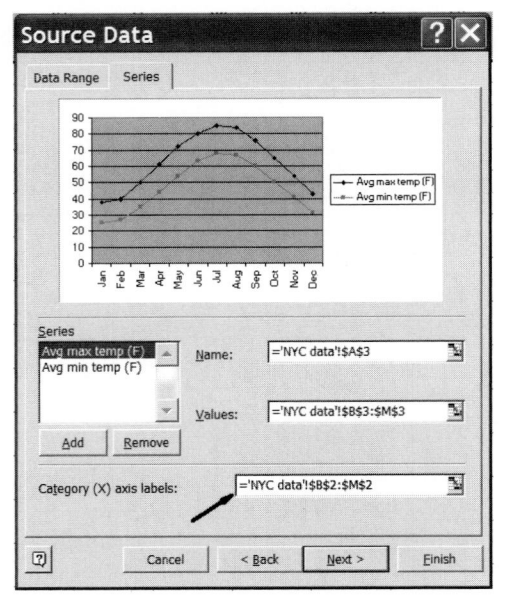

Clicking on the **Series** tab of this screen, we put in the data for the months (marked with an arrow).

What's the Difference Between a Line Chart and an XY (Scatter) Chart?

Line charts use equal spacing for the *x*-axis legend, whereas XY charts space the *x*-axis legend depending on the distance between the points. The following line chart example explains this perhaps obscure sentence:

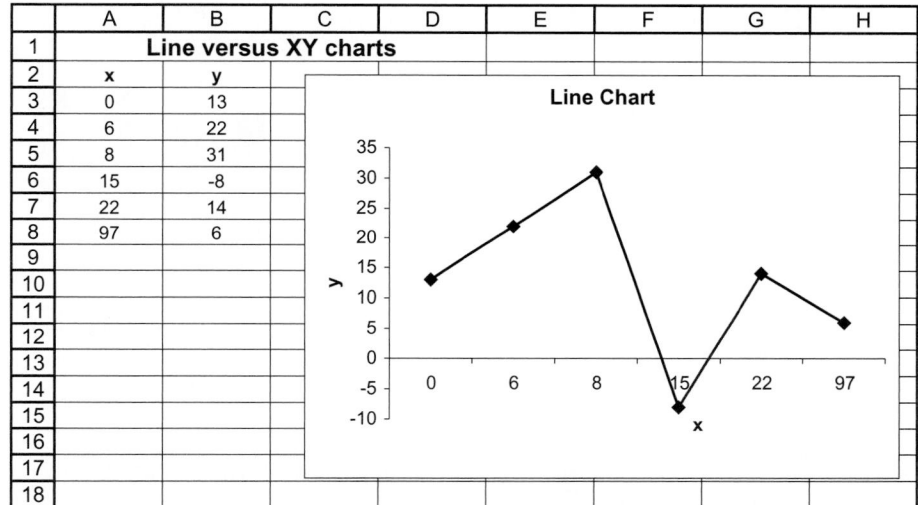

Notice that—even though the *x*-axis values are very unevenly spaced (0, 6, 8, 15, 22, 97)—the Line chart puts them at equal intervals on the *x*-axis. It is only the XY (Scatter) chart that spaces the *x*-axis labels according to their values.

28.5 Graph Titles That Update[2]

You want to have the graph title change when a parameter on the spreadsheet changes. For example, in the next spreadsheet, you want the graph title to indicate the growth rate.

---

[2]This section makes (largely self-explanatory) use of the **Text** function, which is discussed in Chapter 29.

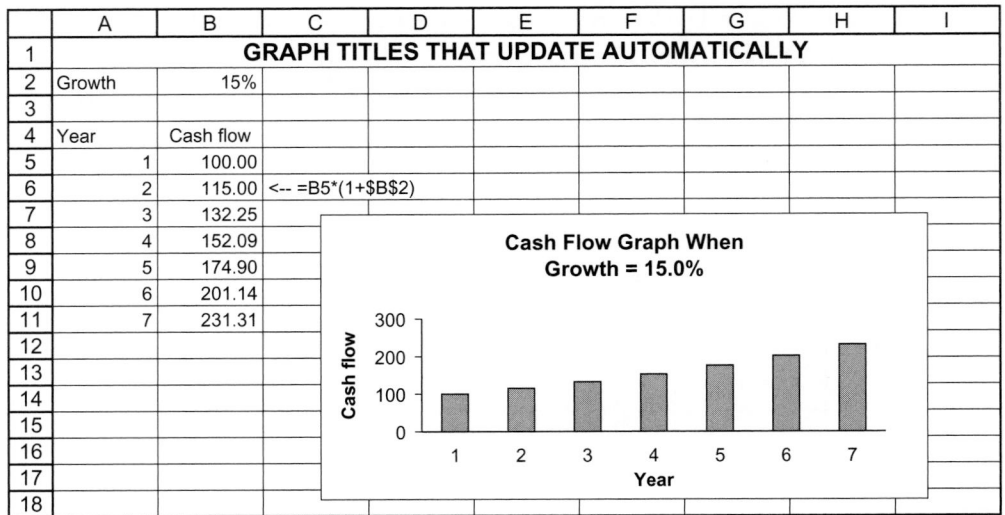

Once we have completed the necessary steps explained below, a change in the growth rate will change both the graph *and* its title:

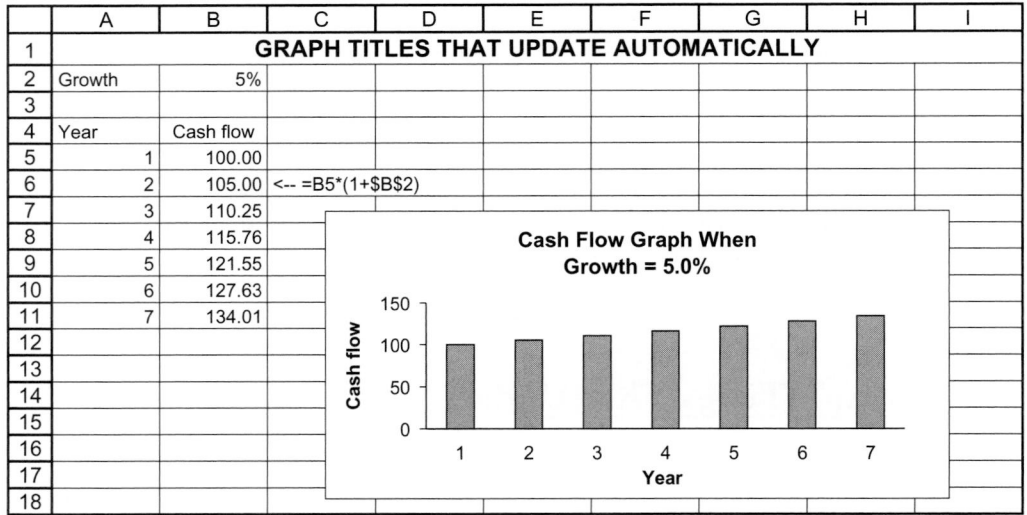

To make graph titles update automatically, carry out the following steps:

- Create the graph you want in the format you want it. Give the graph a "proxy title." (It makes no difference what, you're going to eliminate it soon.) At this stage your graph might look like:

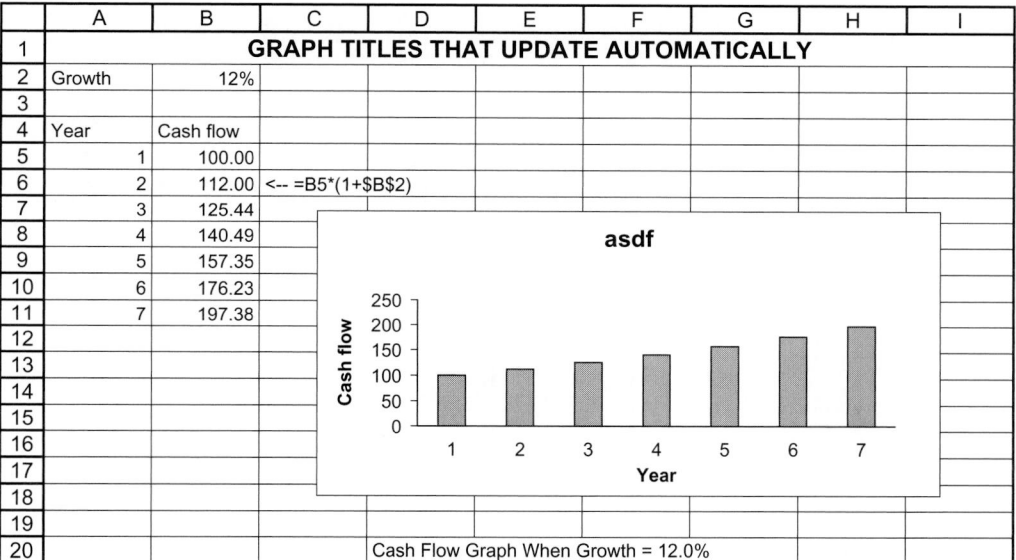

	A	B	C	D	E	F	G	H	I
1			**GRAPH TITLES THAT UPDATE AUTOMATICALLY**						
2	Growth	12%							
3									
4	Year	Cash flow							
5	1	100.00							
6	2	112.00	<-- =B5*(1+$B$2)						
7	3	125.44							
8	4	140.49							
9	5	157.35							
10	6	176.23							
11	7	197.38							
12									
13									
14									
15									
16									
17									
18									
19									
20			Cash Flow Graph When Growth = 12.0%						

- Create the title you want in a cell. In the example above, cell D20 contains the formula: ="Cash Flow Graph When Growth ="&TEXT(B2,"0.0%").
- Click on the graph title to mark it, and then go to the formula bar and insert an equal sign to indicate a formula. Then **point** at cell D20 with the formula and click [Enter]. In the picture below, you see the chart title highlighted and in the formula bar "=Titles that update!$D$20" indicating the title of the graph. Note that "Titles that update" is the name of the spreadsheet.

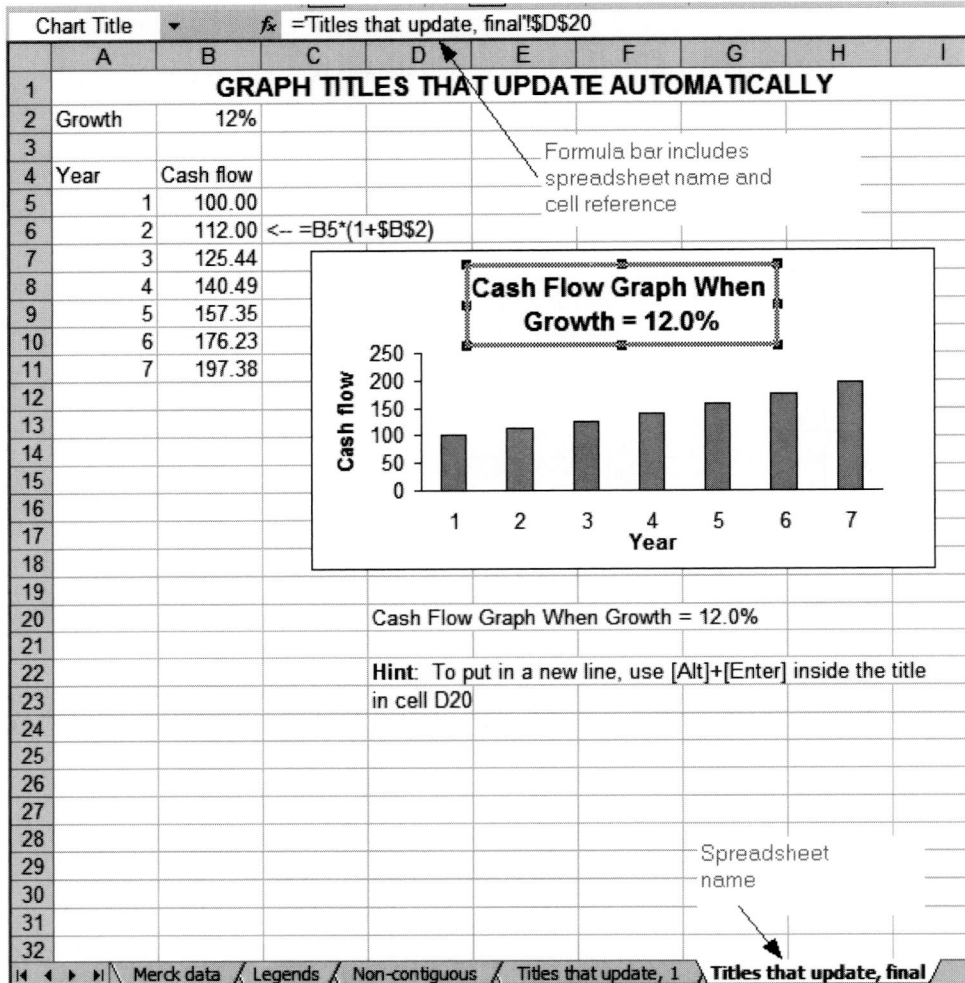

CONCLUSION

There's lots more you can do with Excel charts, but we've covered the essentials. The exercises to this chapter show you some more variations.

EXERCISES

1. The CD gives the monthly prices for the Dutch grocery chain Ahold from April 1991 through August 2004. Graph these prices.

Note: All the data for the exercises are on the disk that accompanies this book.

	A	B
1	**PRICE OF AHOLD STOCK** **April 1991 - August 2004**	
2	**Date**	**Stock price**
3	8-Apr-91	5.32
4	1-May-91	5.23
5	3-Jun-91	4.94
6	1-Jul-91	5.03
7	1-Aug-91	5.09
8	3-Sep-91	5.43
9	1-Oct-91	5.40
10	1-Nov-91	5.37
11	2-Dec-91	5.68
12	2-Jan-92	5.39

Your graph should look like this:

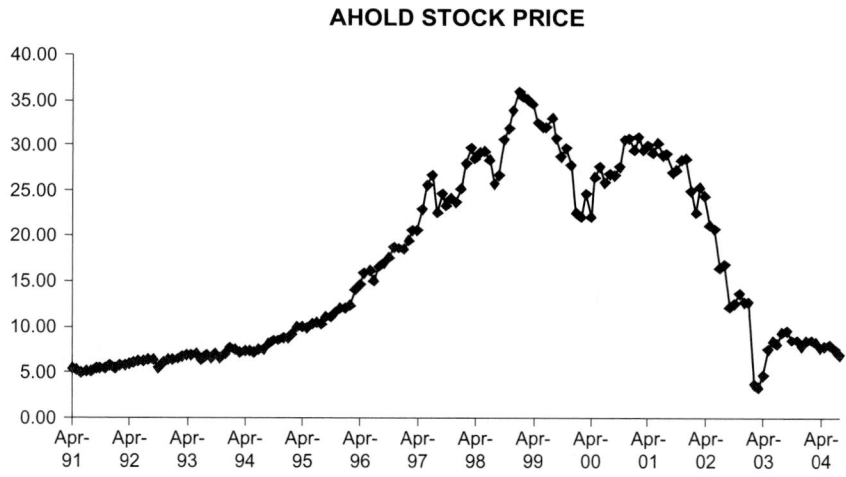

AHOLD STOCK PRICE

2. Using the data for Ahold from Exercise 1, determine the monthly stock returns and graph them. The monthly return for a stock that has price P_t in month t and price P_{t-1} in month $t-1$ is $(P_t/P_{t-1}) - 1$. (When you compute the returns, you'll have "noncontiguous data," so that you'll have to use the technique described in Section 28.3.)

	A	B	C	D
1	**RETURNS ON AHOLD STOCK** **April 1991 - August 2004**			
2	**Date**	**Stock price**	**Monthly return**	
3	8-Apr-91	5.32		
4	1-May-91	5.23	-1.69%	<-- =B4/B3-1
5	3-Jun-91	4.94	-5.54%	<-- =B5/B4-1
6	1-Jul-91	5.03	1.82%	<-- =B6/B5-1
7	1-Aug-91	5.09	1.19%	
8	3-Sep-91	5.43	6.68%	
9	1-Oct-91	5.40	-0.55%	

Your graph should look like this:

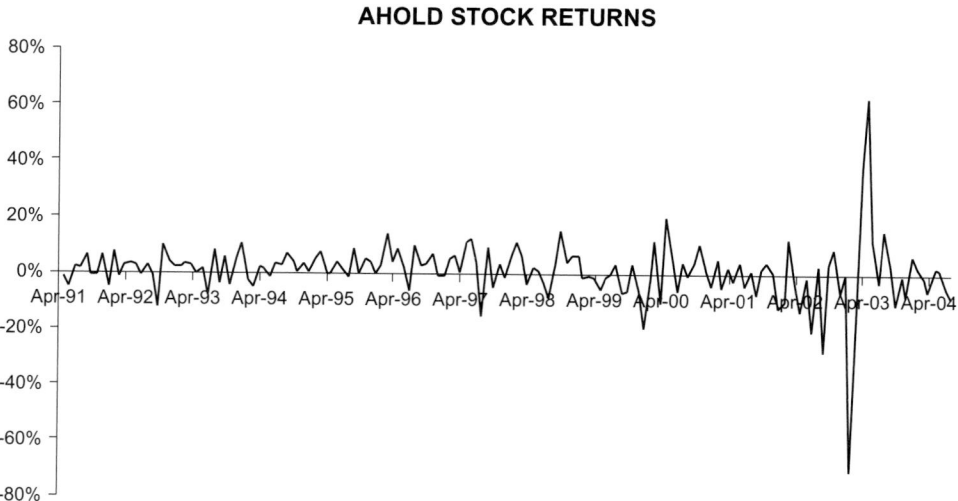

3. The disk that accompanies this book gives the prices for Ahold and for the S&P 500. Use this data to produce the following graph (see note following the graph):

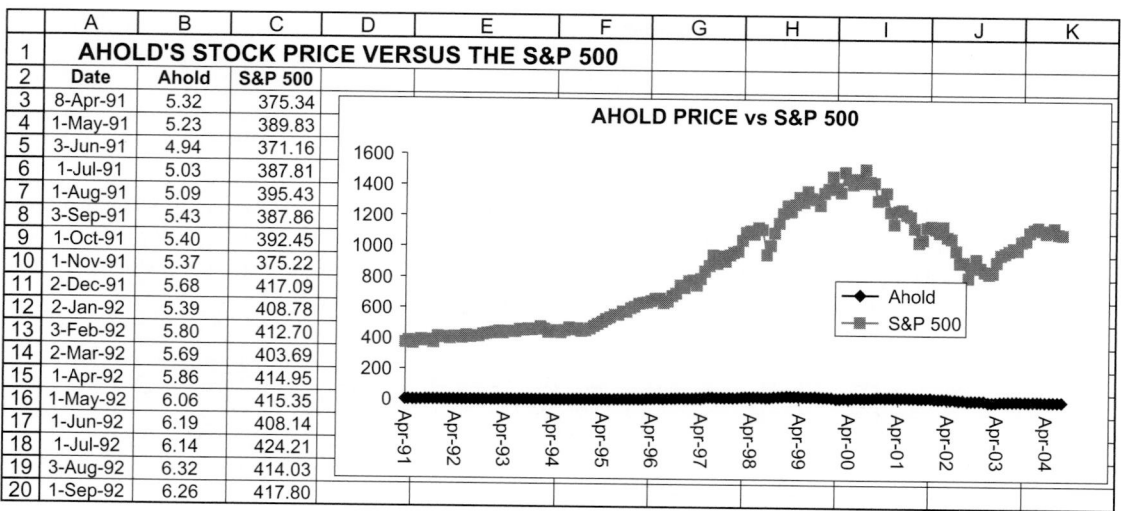

	A	B	C	D	E	F	G	H	I	J	K
1	AHOLD'S STOCK PRICE VERSUS THE S&P 500										
2	Date	Ahold	S&P 500								
3	8-Apr-91	5.32	375.34								
4	1-May-91	5.23	389.83								
5	3-Jun-91	4.94	371.16								
6	1-Jul-91	5.03	387.81								
7	1-Aug-91	5.09	395.43								
8	3-Sep-91	5.43	387.86								
9	1-Oct-91	5.40	392.45								
10	1-Nov-91	5.37	375.22								
11	2-Dec-91	5.68	417.09								
12	2-Jan-92	5.39	408.78								
13	3-Feb-92	5.80	412.70								
14	2-Mar-92	5.69	403.69								
15	1-Apr-92	5.86	414.95								
16	1-May-92	6.06	415.35								
17	1-Jun-92	6.19	408.14								
18	1-Jul-92	6.14	424.21								
19	3-Aug-92	6.32	414.03								
20	1-Sep-92	6.26	417.80								

Note: This graph is obviously unsatisfactory—Ahold's price is so much less than the S&P 500 price that the Ahold price series appears to be zero. See Exercise 4 for one solution to this problem.

4. Transform the S&P 500 and Ahold price data so that the beginning price of each is 100 and graph these series:

	A	B	C	D	E	F	G
1	AHOLD'S STOCK PRICE VERSUS THE S&P 500						
2	Date	Ahold	S&P 500		Ahold adjusted	S&P adjusted	
3	8-Apr-91	5.32	375.34		100.00	100.00	
4	1-May-91	5.23	389.83		98.31	103.86	<-- =F3*C4/C3
5	3-Jun-91	4.94	371.16		92.86	98.89	<-- =F4*C5/C4
6	1-Jul-91	5.03	387.81		94.55	103.32	<-- =F5*C6/C5
7	1-Aug-91	5.09	395.43		95.68	105.35	
8	3-Sep-91	5.43	387.86		102.07	103.34	

The final result should look like this:

AHOLD PRICE vs. S&P 500

5. You have been asked to graph the function $y = ax^3 - 2x^2 + x - 16$. The variable a can take on a variety of values (in the example below, $a = 0.4$). Make a graph of this function with a title that indicates the value of a, as illustrated below. (You may want to refer to Section 28.4.)

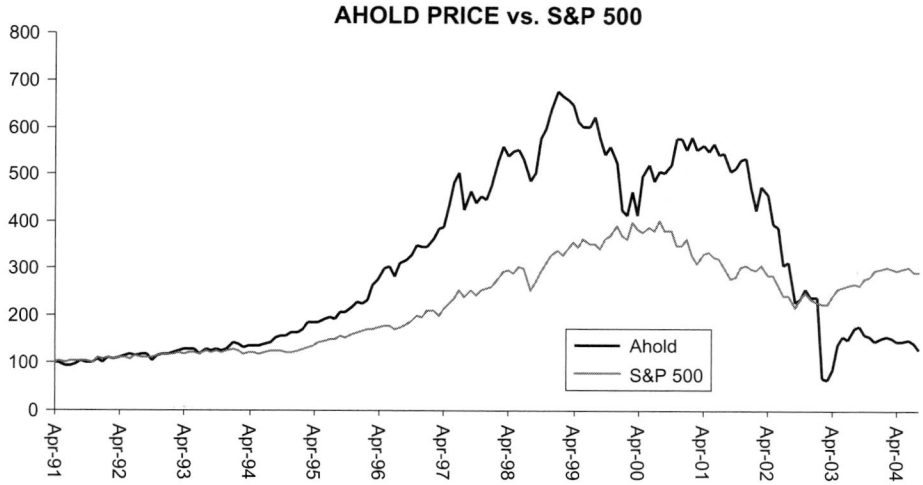

	A	B	C	D	E	F	G	H	I
1	a	0.4							
2									
3	x	y=a*x^3-2*x^2+x-16							
4	-6	-180.4	<-- =$B$1*A4^3-2*A4^2+A4-16						
5	-5	-121.0							
6	-4	-77.6							
7	-3	-47.8							
8	-2	-29.2							
9	-1	-19.4							
10	0	-16.0							
11	1	-16.6							
12	2	-18.8							
13	3	-20.2							
14	4	-18.4							
15	5	-11.0							
16	6	4.4							
17	7	30.2							
18	8	68.8							
19	9	122.6							
20									
21									
22									

Graph of y=a*x^3-2*x^2+x-16 when a = 0.40

6. The disk that accompanies this book contains a spreadsheet with the following data on rainfall in San Diego (the data go from 1964 to 2004—not all of which is shown below).

	A	B	C	D
1	**RAINFALL AT LINDBERGH FIELD SAN DIEGO COUNTY**			
2	Year	**Actual Rainfall (Inches)**	**Normal Rainfall (Inches)**	**% of Normal**
3	1964	5.15	10.41	
4	1965	8.81	10.41	
5	1966	14.76	10.41	
6	1967	10.86	10.41	
7	1968	7.86	10.41	
8	1969	11.48	10.41	
9	1970	6.23	10.41	
10	1971	8.03	10.41	
11	1972	6.12	10.41	
12	1973	10.99	10.41	
13	1974	6.59	10.41	
14	1975	10.64	10.41	
15	1976	10.14	10.41	
16	1977	9.18	10.41	
17	1978	17.3	10.41	
18	1979	14.93	10.41	
19	1980	15.62	10.41	

(a) Compute the annual rainfall as a percentage of the normal rainfall (column D).

(b) Use the data to produce the following graph:

San Diego Annual Rainfall

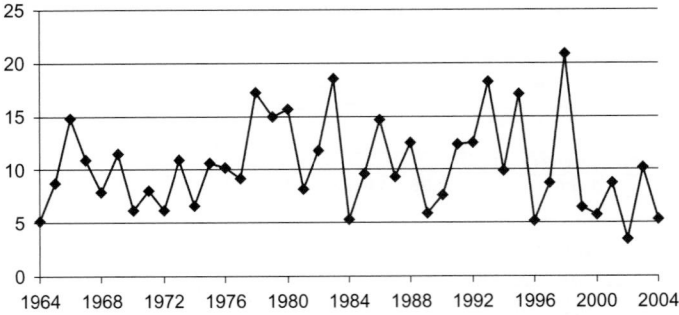

EXCEL FUNCTIONS

OVERVIEW

In this chapter we discuss the principal Excel functions a financial analyst needs to know. There is some overlap between the discussion here and in other chapters (for example, the **NPV** function is discussed in Chapter 5). We also discuss some functions that are not used in this book, but that are so handy that we include them for reference.

Here are the functions discussed in this book. Not all are in this chapter; the table below indicates the functions and where they are discussed (if not in this chapter).

Financial Functions	Date and Time Functions	Math Functions
FV	Discussed in Chapter 31	**LN**
IRR		**Exp**
NPV		**Round**
PMT		**RoundDown**
PV		**RoundUp**
Rate		**Truncate**
NPER		**Sqrt**
(**XIRR** and **XNPV** are		**Sum**
discussed in Chapter 31)		**SumIf**
		SumProduct

Statistical Functions	Lookup Functions	Database Functions
(All these functions are	**HLookup**	**DAverage**
discussed in Chapter 12)	**VLookup**	**DSum**
Average		**DCount**
Correl		**DStdev**
Count, CountA, CountIf		**DStdevp**
Covar		**DVar**
Frequency		**DVarp**
Intercept, Slope, Rsq		**DProduct**
Max, Min		
Median		
Stdev, Stdevp		
Var, Varp		(These functions are
Large( ) and **Rank( )**		discussed in Chapter 33)

Text Functions	Logical Functions	
Text	**If**	
Left, Right, Mid		
Combining text in cells		

A word about nomenclature: In order to differentiate an Excel function from the surrounding text, we usually denote it with boldface. Most Excel functions depend on some variable, but we do not always indicate these variables. For example, the variables for the **NPV** function are the interest rate and the range to be discounted; when we want to make this explicit, we write **NPV(interest,range)**.

One more note: The functions in each class are not always discussed alphabetically. Where there's a logical order, we use this (for example, we discuss **NPV** before **IRR**).

29.1 Financial Functions

NPV( )

This function is extensively discussed in Chapter 5. The Excel definition of **NPV( )** differs somewhat from the standard finance definition. In the finance literature, the net present value of a sequence of cash flows $C_0, C_1, C_2, \ldots, C_n$ at a discount rate r refers to the expression

$$\sum_{t=0}^{n} \frac{C_t}{(1+r)^t} \quad \text{or} \quad C_0 + \sum_{t=1}^{n} \frac{C_t}{(1+r)^t}$$

In many cases C_0 represents the cost of the asset purchased and is therefore negative.

The Excel definition of **NPV( )** always assumes that the first cash flow occurs after one period. The user who wants the standard finance expression must therefore calculate $NPV(r,\{C_1, \ldots, C_n\}) + C_0$. Here is an example:

	A	B	C	D	E	F	G
1			**EXCEL'S NPV FUNCTION**				
2	Discount rate	10%					
3	Year	0	1	2	3	4	5
4	Cash flow	-100	35	33	34	25	16
5							
6	NPV	$11.65	<-- =NPV(B2,C4:G4)+B4				

IRR( )

The internal rate of return (IRR) of a sequence of cash flows $C_0, C_1, C_2, \ldots, C_n$ is an interest rate r such that the net present value of the cash flows is zero:

$$\sum_{t=0}^{n} \frac{C_t}{(1+r)^t} = 0$$

The Excel syntax for the **IRR( )** function is **IRR(cash flows, guess)**. Here **cash flows** represents the whole sequence of cash flows, including the first cash flow C_0, and **guess** is a starting point for the algorithm that calculates the IRR.

First a simple example—consider the cash flows given above:

	A	B	C	D	E	F	G
8			**EXCEL'S IRR FUNCTION**				
9	Year	0	1	2	3	4	5
10	Cash flow	-100	35	33	34	25	16
11							
12	IRR	15.00%	<-- =IRR(B10:G10,0)				
13		15.00%	<-- =IRR(B10:G10)				

Note that **guess** is not necessary when there is only one IRR. Thus, in cell B13 (where we haven't indicated a **guess**) we get the same answer as in cell B12 (**guess** = 0).

The choice of **guess**, however, can make a difference when there is more than one IRR. Consider, for example, the following cash flows:

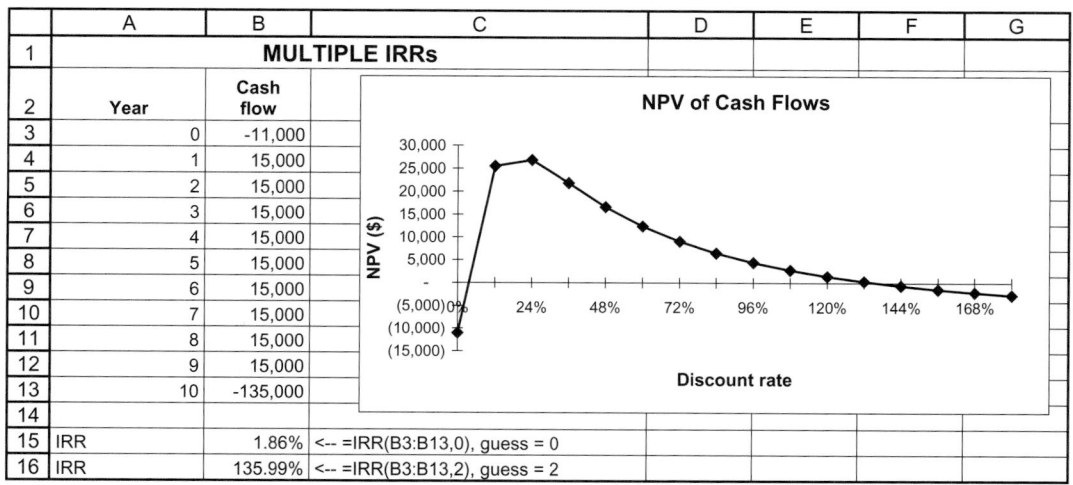

	A	B	C	D	E	F	G
1			**MULTIPLE IRRs**				
2	Year	Cash flow	**NPV of Cash Flows**				
3	0	-11,000					
4	1	15,000					
5	2	15,000					
6	3	15,000					
7	4	15,000					
8	5	15,000					
9	6	15,000					
10	7	15,000					
11	8	15,000					
12	9	15,000					
13	10	-135,000					
14							
15	IRR	1.86%	<-- =IRR(B3:B13,0), guess = 0				
16	IRR	135.99%	<-- =IRR(B3:B13,2), guess = 2				

The graph (created from a table that is not shown) shows that there are two IRRs, since the NPV curve crosses the *x*-axis twice. To find both these IRRs, we have to change the **guess** (though the precise value of guess is still not critical). In the example below we have changed both guesses but still get the same answer:

	A	B	C
15	IRR	1.86%	<-- =IRR(B3:B13,0.1)
16	IRR	135.99%	<-- =IRR(B3:B13,0.8)

Note: A given set of cash flows typically has more than one IRR if there is more than one change of sign in the cash flows. In the above example, the initial cash flow is negative, and CF_1–CF_9 are positive (this accounts for one change of sign); but then CF_{10} is negative—making a second change of sign. If you suspect that a set of cash flows has more than one IRR, the first thing to do is to use Excel to make a graph of the NPVs, as we did above. The number of times that the NPV graph crosses the *x*-axis identifies the number of IRRs (and also their approximate values).[1]

FV( )

The *future value* function, **FV**, calculates the future value of a series of deposits. Below we discuss several cases of this function. For a finance discussion of this function and the meaning of the numbers it produces, you should refer to Chapter 5.

The Future Value of a Series of Annual Investments: Using **FV** *and the Type Parameter:* Suppose you intend to make five annual deposits of $1,000 each to a 5% savings account. The first deposit is made today. How much will you have at the end of five years? In the spreadsheet below, we do this computation in two ways (cells C13 and C14):

	A	B	C	D
1	SAVING FOR THE FUTURE FV Type PARAMETER = 1			
2	Annual deposit to savings	1,000		
3	Interest rate	5%		
4				
5	Year	Deposit	Value at end of year 5	
6	0	1,000	1,276.28	<-- =B6*(1+$B$3)^(5-A6)
7	1	1,000	1,215.51	
8	2	1,000	1,157.63	
9	3	1,000	1,102.50	
10	4	1,000	1,050.00	
11	5			
12				
13	Total at end of 5 years		5,801.91	<-- =SUM(C6:C11)
14			5,801.91	<-- =FV(B3,5,-B2,,1)

In the table in cells A6:C11, we take each annual deposit of $1,000 and compute its future value at the end of year 5. Summing these values (cell C13) gives $5,801.91.

---

[1] For more examples of multiple IRRs, see Chapter 8.

In cell C14 we use the **FV** function. Here's the dialog box, with an explanation of the use of **Type**:

Notice that we've set **Type** equal to 1: The five payments are made *at the beginning of the period:* today and in each of years 1, 2, 3, 4.

The **FV** function allows **Type** to be 0 when the payments are made at the end of the period. To illustrate this, suppose you intend to make five annual deposits of $1,000 each to a 5% savings account, with the *first deposit to be made one year from now.* How much will you have at the end of five years? In the spreadsheet below, we again do this computation in two ways (cells C13 and C14):

	A	B	C	D
1		SAVING FOR THE FUTURE FV Type PARAMETER = 0		
2	Annual deposit to savings	1,000		
3	Interest rate	5%		
4				
5	Year	Deposit	Value at end of year 5	
6	0	0	0.00	<-- =B6*(1+$B$3)^(5-A6)
7	1	1,000	1,215.51	<-- =B7*(1+$B$3)^(5-A7)
8	2	1,000	1,157.63	
9	3	1,000	1,102.50	
10	4	1,000	1,050.00	
11	5	1,000	1,000.00	
12				
13	Total at end of 5 years		5,525.63	<-- =SUM(C6:C11)
14			5,525.63	<-- =FV(B3,5,-B2,,0)

To end this discussion, here are two additional points:

- If you don't enter a value for the **Type** in the **FV** function, Excel assumes that **Type** equals 0 (meaning the deposits are made at the end of the period).

- It is easy to confuse the "beginning" and "end" of period distinction and blind use of the **FV** function can lead to errors. The obvious way to avoid such errors is to build an extensive Excel table as illustrated above.

One final note: The **FV** function also allows for an optional **PV** parameter. This parameter allows you to use the **FV** function to compute loan payments. We prefer not to use this parameter—if we need to compute loan payments, we use the **PMT** function illustrated later.[2]

PV( )

The Excel **PV** function calculates the present value of an annuity (a series of fixed periodic payments). For example:

	A	B	C
1	**THE PV FUNCTION**		
2	**Payments made at the end of the period**		
3	Rate	10%	
4	Number of periods	10	
5	Payment	100	
6	Present value	(614.46)	<-- =PV(B3,B4,B5)

Thus, $\$614.46 = \sum_{t=1}^{10} [\$100/(1.10)^t]$. Here are two things to note about the **PV( )** function:

- Writing **PV(B3,B4,B5)** assumes that payments are made at dates 1, 2, . . ., 10. If the payments are made at dates 0, 1, 2, . . ., 9, you should write:

	A	B	C
8	**Payments made at the beginning of the period**		
9	Rate	10%	
10	Number of periods	10	
11	Payment	100	
12	Present value	(675.90)	<-- =PV(B9,B10,B11,,1)

- Irritatingly, when the payments are positive as in the above example, the **PV( )** function (and the **PMT( )** function—see below) gives the present value as a negative number (there is a logic here, but it's not worth explaining). To get a positive present value in cell B12, we would either write **-PV(B3,B4,B5)** or let the payment be negative by writing **PV(B3,B4,-B5)**.

PMT( )

This function calculates the payment necessary to pay off a loan with equal payments over a fixed number of periods. For example, the first calculation below shows that a loan of $1,000, to be paid off over ten years at an interest rate of 8% will require equal annual payments of interest and principal of $149.03. The calculation performed is the solution of the following equation:

$$\sum_{t=1}^{n} \frac{X}{(1+r)^t} = initial\ loan\ principal$$

where X is the payment.

---

[2] The use of the **PV** parameter of the **FV** function is nicely illustrated in a note by Linda Johnson on the following website: http://pubs.logicalexpressions.com/pub0009/LPMArticle.asp?ID=385.

	A	B	C
1		THE PMT FUNCTION	
2	Payments made at the end of the period		
3	Rate	8%	
4	Number of periods	10	
5	Principal	1000	
6	Payment	($149.03)	<-- =PMT(B3,B4,B5)
7			
8	Payments made at the beginning of the period		
9	Rate	8%	
10	Number of periods	10	
11	Principal	1000	
12	Payment	($137.99)	<-- =PMT(B9,B10,B11,,1)

Loan tables can be calculated using the **PMT( )** function. These tables—explained in detail in Chapter 5—show what part of each payment is interest and what part is repayment of the loan principal. In each period, the payment on the loan (calculated with **PMT( )**) is split:

- We first calculate the interest owing for that period on the principal outstanding at the beginning of the period. In the table below, at the end of year 1, we owe $80(= 8\% * \$1,000)$ of interest on the loan principal outstanding at the beginning of the year.
- The remainder of the payment (for year 1: $69.03) goes to reduce the principal outstanding.

	A	B	C	D	E
1		LOAN TABLE			
2	Interest	8%			
3	Number of periods	10			
4	Principal	1,000			
5	Annual payment	149.03	<-- =-PMT(B2,B3,B4)		
6					
7				Split of payment between	
8	Year	Principal at beginning of year	Payment	Interest	Repayment of principal
9	1	1,000.00	149.03	80.00	69.03
10	2	930.97	149.03	74.48	74.55
11	3	856.42	149.03	68.51	80.52
12	4	775.90	149.03	62.07	86.96
13	5	688.95	149.03	55.12	93.91
14	6	595.03	149.03	47.60	101.43
15	7	493.60	149.03	39.49	109.54
16	8	384.06	149.03	30.73	118.30
17	9	265.76	149.03	21.26	127.77
18	10	137.99	149.03	11.04	137.99

Note that the repayment of principal at the end of year 10 is exactly equal to the principal outstanding at the beginning of the year (that is, the loan has been paid off).

Using the* FV *Parameter of the* PMT *Function: The **PMT** function can also compute the periodic payment necessary to achieve a given *future* value. Here's an example. Suppose you want make ten annual payments into your savings account so that you have $10,000 in ten years.

Suppose the interest rate is 6%. What should your annual payment be? In the spreadsheet below we show two ways of solving this problem:

	A	B	C	D
1		**SAVING FOR THE FUTURE**		
		Using the PMT function to compute a <u>future</u> value		
2	Annual deposit to savings account	$ 715.74		
3	Interest rate	6%		
4				
5	Year	**Deposit to account**	**Total in account**	
6	0	$ 715.74	$ 715.74	<-- =B6
7	1	$ 715.74	$ 1,474.42	<-- =B7+C6*(1+$B$3)
8	2	$ 715.74	$ 2,278.63	<-- =B8+C7*(1+$B$3)
9	3	$ 715.74	$ 3,131.09	
10	4	$ 715.74	$ 4,034.69	
11	5	$ 715.74	$ 4,992.51	
12	6	$ 715.74	$ 6,007.81	
13	7	$ 715.74	$ 7,084.01	
14	8	$ 715.74	$ 8,224.79	
15	9	$ 715.74	$ 9,434.02	
16	10	$ -	$ 10,000.06	<-- =B16+C15*(1+$B$3)
17				
18	Using PMT to do the calculation		$715.74	<-- =PMT(B3,10,,-10000,1)

The table in cells A6:C16 shows you exactly what's happening: You deposit $715.74 today and in each of the next nine years. With 6% interest, this will accumulate to $10,000 after ten years.[3]

The **PMT** function in cell B18 can do the same calculation. Here's the way the dialog box for this function looks. Note the use of **Type** = 1, because the payments are made at the beginning of each year. Note also that we haven't put any entry into the **Pv** box:

Function Arguments   [?][X]

PMT

Rate B3   = 0.06

Nper 10   = 10

Pv   = number

Fv   -10000   = -10000

Type 1   = 1

= 715.7354549

Calculates the payment for a loan based on constant payments and a constant interest rate.

Type is a logical value: payment at the beginning of the period = 1; payment at the end of the period = 0 or omitted.

Formula result = $715.74

Help on this function   [OK]   [Cancel]

---

[3]You can compute the $715.74 in cell B2 by using **Goal Seek** or trial and error.

Rate( )

Rate calculates the internal rate of return of a series of constant payments. In the example below **Rate(B4,B5,-B3)** in cell B6 computes 10.56%, which is the internal rate of return:

$$-600 + \frac{100}{(1.1056)} + \frac{100}{(1.1056)^2} + \cdots + \frac{100}{(1.1056)^{10}} = 0$$

	A	B	C	D
		THE RATE FUNCTION		
1		**Compare to IRR**		
2	**RATE used for payments made at the end of the period**			
3	Initial payment	600		
4	Number of periods	10		
5	Annual payment	100		
6	Rate of return	10.56%	<-- =RATE(B4,B5,-B3)	
7				
8	**RATE used for payments made at the beginning of the period**			
9	Initial payment	600		
10	Number of periods	10		
11	Annual payment	100		
12	Rate of return	13.70%	<-- =RATE(B10,B11,-B9,,1,20%)	
13				
14	**What does RATE do? Computing the IRR**			
15	**Year**	**Payment at end of period**	**Payment at beginning of period**	
16	0	-600	-500	
17	1	100	100	
18	2	100	100	
19	3	100	100	
20	4	100	100	
21	5	100	100	
22	6	100	100	
23	7	100	100	
24	8	100	100	
25	9	100	100	
26	10	100		
27				
28	**IRR**	10.56%	13.70%	<-- =IRR(C16:C26)

Like **PV** and **PMT, Rate** gives the possibility of specifying whether the cash flows occur at the end of the period (the default) or its beginning. If you look in cell B12, **Rate(B10,B11, -B9,,1,20%)** computes 13.70%; this is the internal rate of return of an initial payment of $600 and ten payments of $100 *made at the beginning of the period* (the beginning of the period is indicated by the "1" at the end of the formula). The **20%** in the function is a **guess** like that which is also allowed in the IRR function.

Here's the dialog box that created this result:

Think for a second what this means for an internal rate of return:

$$-600 + \underbrace{100}_{\substack{\uparrow \\ \text{First payment} \\ \text{made at "beginning"} \\ \text{of period–meaning,} \\ \text{made at time 0}}} + \frac{100}{(1.1370)} + \frac{100}{(1.1370)^2} + \frac{100}{(1.1370)^3} + \cdots + \frac{100}{(1.1370)^9} = 0$$

Effectively, **Rate(B10,B11,-B9,,1,20%)** refers to an initial payment of $500 and nine subsequent payments of $100.

Rate Versus IRR

If you look at the above example, you will see (rows 16–28) that **IRR** and **Rate** give the same values. There are, of course, trade-offs:

- **Rate** is shorter; **IRR** requires you to specify all the cash flows.
- On the other hand, **IRR** can handle cash flows that vary over time.

NPER( )

This function calculates the number of periods to repay a loan given a fixed amount. For example, you borrow $1,000 from the bank, which charges you a 10% annual interest rate. You intend to repay the loan with $250 per year. How long will it take you to repay the loan?

	A	B	C	D	E
1	**HOW LONG TO PAY OFF THIS LOAN?**				
2	Loan amount	1,000.00			
3	Interest rate	10%			
4	Annual payment	250			
5	How long to pay off the loan?	5.3596	<-- =NPER(B3,B4,-B2)		
6					
7	Year	Principal at beginning of year	Payment at end of year	Interest	Repayment of principal
8	1	1,000.00	250.00	100.00	150.00
9	2	850.00	250.00	85.00	165.00
10	3	685.00	250.00	68.50	181.50
11	4	503.50	250.00	50.35	199.65
12	5	303.85	250.00	30.39	219.62
13	6	84.24	250.00	8.42	241.58

As you can see from the loan table, it takes somewhere between five and six years to repay the loan.[4] **NPER(B3,B4,-B2)** gives the exact number of periods as 5.3596.

29.2 Math Functions

Using Exp to Calculate Future Values

Suppose you invest $100 at 10% for three years. As explained in Chapter 5, if interest is compounded annually, the future value after three years will be

	A	B	C
1	**ANNUAL COMPOUNDING**		
2	Initial investment	100	
3	Years invested, t	3	
4	Interest rate, r	10%	
5	Future value, FV	133.1	<-- =B2*(1+B4)^B3

Suppose the 10% is compounded semiannually (meaning you get 5% each half-year). Then there will be six compounding periods—3 years $*$ 2 periods/year. Your future value will be *Initial investment* $* (1 + 5\%)^6 = 134.0096$:

	A	B	C
7	Initial investment	100	
8	Years invested, t	3	
9	Compounding periods per year, n	2	
10	Interest rate, r	10%	
11	Future value, FV	134.0096	<-- =B7*(1+B10/B9)^(B8*B9)

Denote the number of years by t, the interest rate by r, and the number of compounding periods per year by n. As the number of compounding periods increases, the future value tends

---

[4] Why? At the end of year 5 (which is also the beginning of year 6), there's still $84.24 of principal outstanding. But if you pay back $250 at the end of year 6, then you've paid back too much.

toward $100e^{rt}$, where e is the number 2.71828.[5] In Excel this is written as $100 * \mathbf{Exp(r*t)}.$ This is illustrated in the table and graph below:

	A	B	C	D	E	F
15	Years invested, t	3				
16	Interest rate, r	10%				
17						
18	**Number of compounding periods per year, n**	**Future value**				
19	1	133.100	<-- =$B$14*(1+$B$16/A19)^($B$15*A19)			
20	2	134.010	<-- =$B$14*(1+$B$16/A20)^($B$15*A20)			
21	3	134.327	<-- =$B$14*(1+$B$16/A21)^($B$15*A21)			
22	4	134.489				
23	5	134.587				
24	6	134.653				
25	7	134.700				
26	8	134.735				
27	9	134.763				
28	10	134.785				
29	20	134.885				
30						
31						
32						
33						
34						
35						
36						
37						
38						
39						
40	**As n gets large, this converges to**	134.9859	<-- =B14*EXP(B16*B15)			

Future Value as Function of Number of Compounding Periods per Year

Nomenclature: When the number of compounding periods becomes infinite, the investment is said to be *continuously compounded*. Otherwise (that is, when there are a finite number of compounding periods per year), the investment is said to be *discretely compounded*.

Using Exp to Calculate Present Values

Above we illustrated how $100 grows to $100*\mathbf{Exp(r*t)}$ when it is compounded continuously for t years at interest rate r. Suppose you're going to get $100 in three years. What is the present value of this $100 if the relevant interest rate is r? The answer depends on the number of compounding periods:

- If the investment is discretely compounded n times per year, then its present value is

$$\frac{100}{\left(1+\frac{r}{n}\right)^{nt}} = 100\left(1+\frac{r}{n}\right)^{-nt}$$

- If the investment will be continuously compounded, then its present value is

$$\frac{100}{\exp(rt)} = 100\exp(-rt)$$

---

[5]In mathematical notation: $\lim_{n\to\infty}(1+r/n)^{nt} = e^{rt}$.

In Excel:

	A	B	C
43	**Discounting--discrete versus continuous**		
44	Future value	100	
45	What year received, t	3	
46	Compounding periods per year, n	2	
47	Interest rate, r	10%	
48			
49	Present value, discrete discounting	74.62154	<-- =B44/(1+B47/B46)^(B46*B45)
50			
51	Present value, continuous discounting	74.08182	<-- =B44*EXP(-B47*B45)

You can use the above spreadsheet to show that as *n* gets very large, the two values in B49 and B51 converge. For example, when $n = 100$:

	A	B	C
43	**Discounting--discrete versus continuous**		
44	Future value	100	
45	What year received, t	3	
46	Compounding periods per year, n	100	
47	Interest rate, r	10%	
48			
49	Present value, discrete discounting	74.09293	<-- =B44/(1+B47/B46)^(B46*B45)
50			
51	Present value, continuous discounting	74.08182	<-- =B44*EXP(-B47*B45)

LN

This function (the "natural logarithm" to differentiate it from the "logarithm base 10" that you learned in high school) is often used to calculate continuously compounded rates of return.[6] Suppose you invest in a stock that is worth \$25 and suppose that one year later the stock is worth \$40. What rate of return *r* have you earned? If you use *discrete compounding*, the rate of return is $r = P_1/P_0 - 1 = 40/25 - 1 = 60\%$.

Now suppose that your alternative is to earn *continuously compounded interest r*. Then the rate of return has to solve the equation

$$P_0 \exp(r) = P_1 \Rightarrow \exp(r) = \frac{P_1}{P_0}$$

The function that solves this equation is the natural logarithm ln:

$$r = \ln\left(\frac{P_1}{P_0}\right)$$

---

[6]In this book we used it extensively in the option chapters, Chapters 23–26.

In Excel:

A	B	C
USING LN TO COMPUTE CONTINUOUSLY		
1 **COMPOUNDED RATES OF RETURN**		
2 Price of stock, t=0	25	
3 Price of stock, t=1	40	
4 Discretely compounded rate of return, r	60.00%	<-- =B3/B2-1
5 Continously compounded rate of return, r	47.00%	<-- =LN(B3/B2)

When $t \neq 1$, the problem looks like this:

$$P_0 \exp(rt) = P_t \Rightarrow \exp(rt) = \frac{P_t}{P_0}$$

has solution

$$r = \frac{1}{t} \ln\left(\frac{P_t}{P_0}\right)$$

For example, suppose you invested in Intel stock on 25 October 1999, buying the stock for its closing price of \$38.6079, and suppose you sold it at the end of the day, 24 July 2000, for \$64.4379. As the calculation below shows, you would have earned a continuously compounded return of 68.49% on your stock.

A	B	C	D
7 **Intel stock**			
8 Purchase date and price	25-Oct-99	38.6079	
9 Sale date and price	24-Jul-00	64.4379	
10			
11 Elapsed time, t	0.7479	<-- =(B9-B8)/365	
12 Continuously compounded rate of return, r	68.49%	<-- =1/B11*LN(C9/C8)	

Note that this calculation is easier than the calculation of the *annualized daily return*—it has one less step:

A	B	C	D
14 **Daily return, annualized**			
15 Purchase date and price	25-Oct-99	38.6079	
16 Sale date and price	24-Jul-00	64.4379	
17			
18 Elapsed days	273	<-- =(B16-B15)	
19 Daily return	0.1878%	<-- =(C16/C15)^(1/B18)-1	
20 Annualized	98.35%	<-- =(1+B19)^365-1	

A Short Finance Note

We can't resist a short finance note on the difference between the continuously compounded annual return of 68.49% and the discretely compounded annual return of 98.35%.

- Both of these returns cause \$38.6079 to grow over a period of 273 days to \$64.4379. So they're both—in an economic sense—the same number.
- The *daily* returns are very close: The continuously compounded daily return is calculated by

$$\frac{annual\ continuously\ compounded\ return}{365}$$

and the discretely compounded daily return is calculated by

$$\left(\frac{Stock\ price,\ day\ 273}{Stock\ price,\ day\ 0}\right)^{1/273} - 1$$

These numbers are very close:

	A	B	C
22	Note		
23	Daily, continuously-compounded return	0.1876%	<-- =B12/365
24	Daily, discretely-compounded return	0.1878%	<-- =B19

However, when you compound them for 365 days, the differences are very large.

Round, RoundDown, RoundUp, Trunc

The Excel functions **Round, RoundDown,** and **RoundUp** do exactly what they say. All three of these functions require you to specify the number of decimal places to which you want to round off the number. The function **Trunc** cuts off a number after a specified number of places (if you do not specify, **Trunc** gives you the integer part of a number). Here are examples using the Excel function **Pi** as a basis:

	A	B	C
1	**ROUNDING NUMBERS IN EXCEL**		
2	Number	3.1415926535898	<-- =PI()
3			
4	Round, no decimal places	3.00000000	<-- =ROUND(B2,0)
5	Round, 3 decimal places	3.14200000	<-- =ROUND(B2,3)
6			
7	RoundDown, no decimal places	3.00000000	<-- =ROUNDDOWN(B2,0)
8	RoundDown, 3 decimal places	3.14100000	<-- =ROUNDDOWN(B2,3)
9			
10	RoundUp, no decimal places	4.00000000	<-- =ROUNDUP(B2,0)
11	RoundUp, 4 decimal places	3.14160000	<-- =ROUNDUP(B2,4)
12			
13	Truncate, no decimal places	3.00000000	<-- =TRUNC(B2)
14	Truncate, 5 decimal places	3.14159000	<-- =TRUNC(B2,5)

There's a difference between using these functions and merely formatting a number so that it looks rounded or truncated. Here's an example:

	A	B	C
16	Number	4.5632	
17	Rounded to 2 decimals	4.56	<-- =ROUND(B16,2)
18	Formatted to 2 decimals	4.56	<-- =B16
19			
20	10 times cell B20	45.6	<-- =10*B17
21	10 times cell B21	45.632	<-- =10*B18

In cell B18 we used the "decrease decimal" button ⎯⎯| Decrease Decimal |⎯ to change the representation of the number. However, as you can see in cell B21, this button does not change the number, whereas **Round** actually changes the number.

Sqrt

This function calculates the square root of a number. In this book, we used square roots to calculate the standard deviation (see Chapter 12) of returns.

	A	B	C
1		**SQRT**	
2	Number	3	
3	Square root	1.732051	<-- =SQRT(B2)
4	Equivalent way	1.732051	<-- =B2^(1/2)

Note that you can use the carat (^) as an alternative way of calculating the square root. In Excel's notation, a^b raises a to the power b (meaning $a\hat{}\,b = a^b$). Since a square root is equivalent to the power 1/2, you can also use this notation (see cell B4 above).

Sum

The Excel function **Sum** adds numbers in a range of cells:

	A	B
1		**SUM**
2	1	
3	2	
4	3	
5	4	
6	5	
7	15	<-- =SUM(A2:A6)

SumIf

SumIf allows you to add only numbers that fulfill some specific condition. Here's an example in which we add only those scores that are greater than 30:

	A	B
9	**Score**	
10	30	
11	50	
12	80	
13	90	
14	20	
15	220	<-- =SUMIF(A10:A14,">30")

The function **SumIf** also allows you to have the conditional column some other place. In the following example, we add the numbers in D10 to D14 for which the corresponding number in E10 to E14 is greater than 40 (highlighted here):

	D	E	F
9	**Score 1**	**Score 2**	
10	30	55	
11	50	89	
12	80	22	
13	90	65	
14	20	35	
15	170	<-- =SUMIF(E10:E14,">40",D10:D14)	

The function wizard really helps when you use this function. Here it is for the above example. You'll notice that **Range** is the column of criteria ("Score 2") and **Sum_range** is the column to be added. If you don't specify **Sum_range**, Excel assumes that it's the same as **Range**:

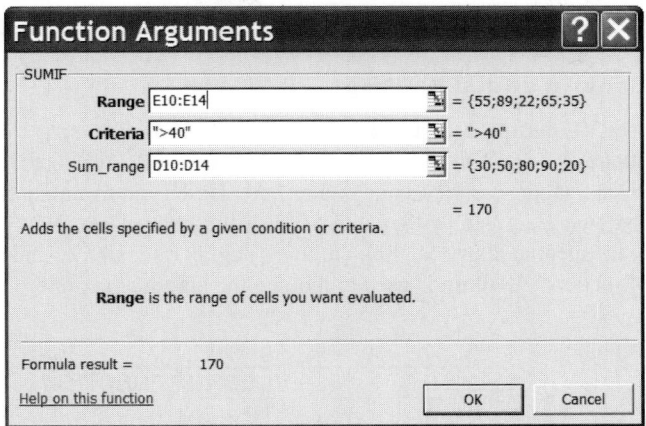

Sumproduct

This function pairwise multiplies the entries in two columns and adds the results. It's sometimes useful in statistics. Here's a simple example that calculates the expected return of a portfolio. There are four assets, each with a different expected return. To calculate the expected portfolio return, we have to multiply the expected return in column B by the portfolio proportion of each asset (column C). **Sumproduct** does this nicely:

	A	B	C	D	E	F
18	**Asset**	**Expected return**	**Portfolio proportion**			
19	1	20%	15%			
20	2	8%	22%			
21	3	15%	38%			
22	4	12%	25%			
23						
24		Expected portfolio return	13.46%	<-- =SUMPRODUCT(B19:B22,C19:C22)		

29.3 Conditional Functions

If( ), **VLookup( )**, and **HLookup( )** are three functions that allow you to put in conditional statements.

The syntax of Excel's **If** statement is: **If(condition,output if condition is true, output if condition is false)**. In the example below, if the initial number in B3 $\leq$ 3, then the desired output is 15. If B3 > 3, then the output is 0:

	A	B	C
1		**THE IF FUNCTION**	
2	Initial number	2	
3	If statement	15	<-- =IF(B2<=3,15,0)

You can make **If** print text also, by enclosing the desired text in double quotes:

	A	B	C
5	Initial number	2	
6	If statement	Less than or equal to 3	<-- =IF(B5<=3,"Less than or equal to 3","More than 3")

VLookup and HLookup

Since **VLookup( )** and **HLookup( )** both have the same structure, we concentrate on **VLookup( )** and leave you to figure out **HLookup( )** for yourself. **VLookup( )** is a way to introduce a table search in your spreadsheet. Here is an example. Suppose the marginal tax rates on income are given by the table below—for income less than $8,000, the marginal tax rate is 0%; for income above $8,000, the marginal tax rate is 15%, and so on. Cell B9 illustrates how the function **VLookup** is used to look up the marginal tax rate.

	A	B	C
1		**VLOOKUP FUNCTION**	
2	**Income**	**Tax rate**	
3	0	0%	
4	8,000	15%	
5	14,000	25%	
6	25,000	38%	
7			
8	Income	15,000	
9	Tax rate	25%	<-- =VLOOKUP(B8,A3:B6,2)

The syntax of this function is **VLookup(lookup_value,table,column).** The first column of the lookup table, A3 to A6, must be arranged in ascending (increasing) order. The **lookup_value** (in this case the income of 15,000) is used to determine the applicable row of the **table.** The row is the first row whose value is ≤ **lookup_value**; in this case, this is the row that starts with 14,000. The **column** entry determines from which column of the applicable row the answer is taken; in this case the marginal tax rates are in column 2.

Here's the Excel function wizard for this table:

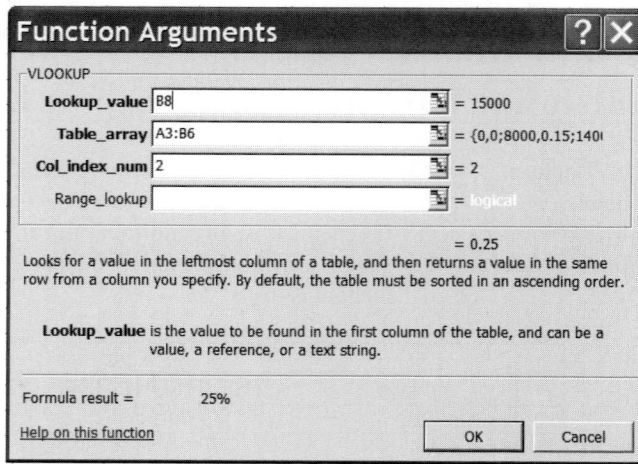

The First Column of VLookup Must Be Sorted

The first column of the **VLookup** table must be *sorted,* meaning it must be in increasing order (either numerical or alphabetical). To see what this means, we have a slightly complicated example. The data in columns A and B below were imported from a database; column A gives the date and column B gives an interest rate on a particular date.

	A	B	C	D	E	F
1	**FIRST COLUMN OF VLOOKUP MUST BE SORTED**					
2	**Date**	**Interest rate**		**Month**	**Day**	**Year**
3	JAN. 07,1991	6.721		JAN	07	1991
4	FEB. 07,1991	6.145		Feb	07	1991
5	FEB. 11,1991	6.03		FEB	11	1991
6	MAR. 04,1991	6.287		MAR	04	1991
7	APR. 01,1991	5.985		APR	01	1991
8	JUN. 08,1991	5.777		JUN	08	1991
9	AUG. 15,1991	5.744		AUG	15	1991
10	OCT. 22,1991	5.868		OCT	22	1991
11						
12						
13		=LEFT(A10,3)		=MID(A10,6,2)		=RIGHT(A10,4)

We would like to give each date a standard Excel value. That is, instead of "Jan. 07, 1991," we'd like to write

	A	B
18	**Standard Excel date format**	**Number equivalent**
19	7-Jan-91	33245

If this is unclear, refer to Chapter 31.

In order to write the date in the standard Excel format, we use the functions **Left**, **Mid**, and **Right** to *parse* the dates in column A into month, day, and year (see next section). We now need to identify each month with its number (that is, Jan = 1, Feb = 2, etc.). We can use **VLookup** to do this, but only if the **VLookup table** has its left column in alphabetical order.

	A	B	C	D	E	F	G	H	I	J	K
1	**FIRST COLUMN OF VLOOKUP MUST BE SORTED**										
2	**Date**	**Interest rate**		**Month**	**Day**	**Year**		**Which month?**		**Date value**	
3	JAN. 07,1991	6.721		JAN	07	1991		1	<-- =VLOOKUP(D3,$J$6:$K$17,2)	1/7/1991	<-- =DATE(F3,H3,E3)
4	FEB. 07,1991	6.145		Feb	07	1991		2			
5	FEB. 11,1991	6.03		FEB	11	1991		2		**VLookup table**	
6	MAR. 04,1991	6.287		MAR	04	1991		3		Apr	4
7	APR. 01,1991	5.985		APR	01	1991		4		Aug	8
8	JUN. 08,1991	5.777		JUN	08	1991		6		Dec	12
9	AUG. 15,1991	5.744		AUG	15	1991		8		Feb	2
10	OCT. 22,1991	5.868		OCT	22	1991		10		Jan	1
11										Jul	7
12										Jun	6
13		=LEFT(A10,3)		=MID(A10,6,2)	=RIGHT(A10,4)					Mar	3
14										May	5
15										Nov	11
16										Oct	10
17										Sep	9

This gives a rather strange-looking table (cells J6:K17), but you can convince yourself that this works.

29.4 Text Functions

Excel distinguishes between numbers and *text*. To sound stupid: You can add, subtract, etc. numbers, but you can't do this for text. On the other hand, Excel allows you to *concatenate* text (if this sounds mysterious, read on).

Concatenation: Combining Text From Several Cells

Here's an example. In the table below, we've written "twelve" in cell A2 and "cows" in cell B2. In cell A4, we tried to write **=A3+B3;** we intended this to come out "Twelvecows" but Excel won't accept this, because neither the contents of A2 ("Twelve") nor those of B2 ("cows") is a number. We can combine the text as in cell A5, by writing **=A3&B3**.

	A	B
2	Twelve	cows
3		
4	#VALUE!	<-- =A2+B2
5	Twelvecows	<-- =A2&B2
6		
7	Twelve blue cows	<-- =A2&" blue "&B2

In cell A7, we've added the word "blue" plus some spaces, putting the additional text/spaces inside quotation marks.

Text

Now look at the example below:

	A	B	C
10	Number of cows	1200	
11			
12	Text	1200 cows	<-- =TEXT(B10,"0")&" cows"
13			
14		1200.00 cows	<-- =TEXT(B10,"0.00")&" cows"
15		1,200.0 cows	<-- =TEXT(B10,"0,000.0")&" cows"
16		120,000.00% cows	<-- =TEXT(B10,"0,000.00%")&" cows"

In cell B12 we want to create a text that contains the number of cows (cell B10) and the word " cows." The Excel function **Text(B10,"0")** turns the number 1200 into a text form, which can then be used in the formula in cell B12. The second part of the **Text** function—where we've currently written "0"—is used to indicate the appearance of the text. Cells B14 to B16 give some other examples.

Left, Right, Mid, Len

The first three functions allow you to pick out parts of texts. In the example below, we've used these functions to pick out parts of the text in cell A18:

	A	B
18	15 pink flamingos went to the zoo	
19		
20	15	<-- =LEFT(A18,2)
21	pink flamingos	<-- =MID(A18,4,14)
22	zoo	<-- =RIGHT(A18,3)
23	33	<-- =LEN(A18)

The function **=Left(A19,2)** picks out the 2 leftmost characters of cell A19. The function **=Mid(A19,4,14)** picks out the 14 characters of cell A19, starting with the 4th character. And the function **=Right(A19,3)**, well . . . you'll figure that one out yourself.

As illustrated in cell A23, the function **Len** tells you the number of characters in the text.

You might ask why a finance book needs to consider these functions. The data below gives prices for some options on General Motors and was downloaded from the website of the Chicago Board of Options Exchange (CBOE). When we downloaded the data, here's what it looked like:

	A	B	C	D
1	**GENERAL MOTORS OPTION DATA** Downloaded from Chicago Board of Options Exchange Web Site			
2	Calls	Last Sale	Puts	Last Sale
3	01 Aug 60.00 (GM HL-E)	3.5	01 Aug 60.00 (GM TL-E)	0.5
4	01 Aug 60.00 (GM HL-A)	3.4	01 Aug 60.00 (GM TL-A)	0.4
5	01 Aug 60.00 (GM HL-P)	3	01 Aug 60.00 (GM TL-P)	0.4
6	01 Aug 60.00 (GM HL-X)	2.9	01 Aug 60.00 (GM TL-X)	0.6
7	01 Aug 60.00 (GM HL-8)	3.4	01 Aug 60.00 (GM TL-8)	0.5
8	01 Aug 65.00 (GM HM-E)	0.45	01 Aug 65.00 (GM TM-E)	2.85
9	01 Aug 65.00 (GM HM-A)	0.45	01 Aug 65.00 (GM TM-A)	1.8
10	01 Aug 65.00 (GM HM-P)	0.45	01 Aug 65.00 (GM TM-P)	2.4
11	01 Aug 65.00 (GM HM-X)	1.15	01 Aug 65.00 (GM TM-X)	2.25
12	01 Aug 65.00 (GM HM-8)	0.4	01 Aug 65.00 (GM TM-8)	2.7
13	01 Aug 70.00 (GM HN-E)	0.05	01 Aug 70.00 (GM TN-E)	7.9
14	01 Aug 70.00 (GM HN-A)	0.05	01 Aug 70.00 (GM TN-A)	6.3
15	01 Aug 70.00 (GM HN-P)	0.05	01 Aug 70.00 (GM TN-P)	0
16	01 Aug 70.00 (GM HN-X)	0.2	01 Aug 70.00 (GM TN-X)	7.5
17	01 Aug 70.00 (GM HN-8)	0.05	01 Aug 70.00 (GM TN-8)	6.8
18				
19				
20			Other information	
21				
22	Option expiration year and month			
23			Option exercise price	

The contents of columns A and C give information about the option, including the expiration year and month, the exercise price, and a parenthetical item that shows you the stock on which the option is written, the option symbol, and the exchange on which the option traded. For example:

GM HN-E   is a General Motors call option with exercise price $70 expiring in August 2001 and trading on the Chicago Board of Options Exchange.

GM TL-A   is the stock symbol for a General Motors put option with exercise price $60, expiring in August 2001 and trading on the American Stock Exchange.

Now suppose we want to separate the dates, the option's symbol, and the exchange on which the option traded:

	C	D	E	F	G	H	I	J	K
2	Puts	Last Sale		Date	Symbol	Exchange			
3	01 Aug 60.00 (GM TL-E)	0.5		01Aug	TL	E			
4	01 Aug 60.00 (GM TL-A)	0.4							
5	01 Aug 60.00 (GM TL-P)	0.4							
6	01 Aug 60.00 (GM TL-X)	0.6							
7	01 Aug 60.00 (GM TL-8)	0.5		=LEFT(C3,2)&MID(C3,4,3)					
8	01 Aug 65.00 (GM TM-E)	2.85					=MID(C3,LEN(C3)-4,2)		
9	01 Aug 65.00 (GM TM-A)	1.8							
10	01 Aug 65.00 (GM TM-P)	2.4							
11	01 Aug 65.00 (GM TM-X)	2.25							
12	01 Aug 65.00 (GM TM-8)	2.7		=MID(C3,LEN(C3)-1,1)					
13	01 Aug 70.00 (GM TN-E)	7.9							

In Chapter 31 (which explains how to use times and dates in Excel), we use this information to design a function that gives us the option's expiration date.

29.5 Statistical Functions

Many of Excel's statistical functions have already been discussed in previous chapters:

Average	Finds the average of a range of cells	Chapter 12
Covar	The covariance of two sets of data	Chapter 12
Correl	The correlation coefficient of two sets of data	Chapter 12
Frequency	An array function that computes the frequency distribution	Chapter 11
Intercept, Slope, Rsq	Computes the intercept, slope, and R^2 of a regression	Chapters 12 and 15
Max, Min	The maximum and minimum of a set of numbers	Chapter 11, Chapters 23–26
Stdev, Stdevp	The standard deviation	Chapters 11 and 12
Var, Varp	The variance	Chapters 12 and 13

Median, Large, and Rank

In this subsection we discuss three more statistical functions: **Median, Large,** and **Rank.** We illustrate the following example, which gives the grades for 11 students:

	A	B	C
1		**Median, Large, Rank**	
2	**Student**	**Grade**	
3	1	100	
4	2	50	
5	3	75	
6	4	32	
7	5	98	
8	6	86	
9	7	72	
10	8	63	
11	9	41	
12	10	88	
13	11	92	
14			
15	Average	72.45	<-- =AVERAGE(B3:B13)
16	Median	75	<-- =MEDIAN(B3:B13)
17	Large	92	<-- =LARGE(B3:B13,3)
18	Rank	7	<-- =RANK(B9,B3:B13)

The median is the grade that splits the list in two: There are 5 grades higher than 75 and 5 lower. The median is different from the average, as you can see.

The Excel function **Large** tells you the *k*th largest number in the set of grades:

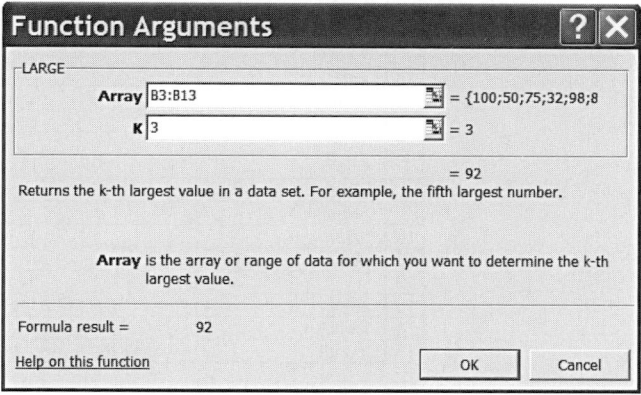

The Excel function **Rank** tells you where a particular number places in the range of grades. In the example given, the grade 72 is 7th among the set of grades in cells B3 to B13:

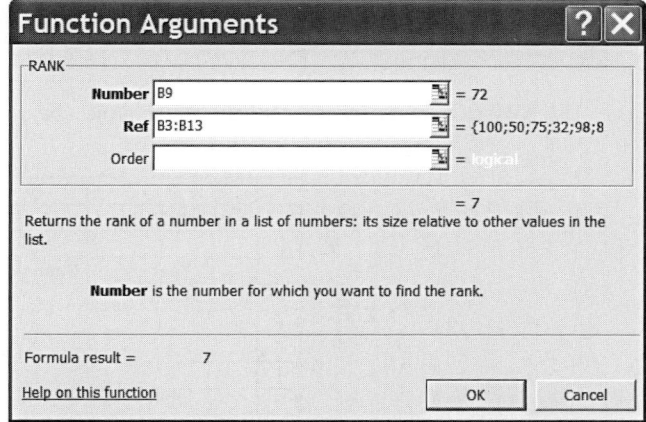

Count, CountIf, CountA

All three of these functions *count* cells. The difference is that:

- **Count** counts the number of cells that contain values and ignores the cells that contain text.
- **CountA** counts all nonblank cells in a range, whether they contain values or text.
- **CountIf** counts cells that fulfill a particular condition.

Now we illustrate:

	A	B	C
1	**COUNT, COUNTIF, COUNTA**		
2	List		
3	1		
4	2		
5	3		
6	4		
7	Terry		
8	Oliver		
9	Noah		
10	Sara		
11	Zvi		
12			
13	Count	4	<-- =COUNT(A3:A11)
14	CountA	9	<-- =COUNTA(A3:A11)
15	CountIf	2	<-- =COUNTIF(A3:A11,">2")

CONCLUSION

Excel has hundreds of functions. This chapter has illustrated the major functions used in this book (and then some). We rely on you, as an educated reader, to figure the rest out for yourself.

EXERCISES

1. (a) Use **NPV** to compute the present value of the project below:

	A	B
1	Discount rate	15%
2		
3	**Year**	**Cash flow**
4	1	100
5	2	200
6	3	300
7	4	400
8	5	500

   (b) Suppose the project costs $600. What is its net present value?

2. (a) Use **NPV** to compute the net present value for the project below:

	A	B
1	Discount rate	15%
2		
3	**Year**	**Cash flow**
4	0	-600
5	1	100
6	2	200
7	3	300
8	4	400
9	5	500

   (b) Use **Data Table** (see Chapter 30) to compute the present value of the project for discount rates of 0%, 4%, ... , 48%. Graph the results and estimate the project's internal rate of return.

3. Use the **IRR** function to compute the internal rate of return of the project in Exercise 2.

4. Use the **FV** function in the following exercises:
   (a) What is the value at the end of ten years of $200 deposited in the bank today and at the beginning of each of the next nine years at an annual interest rate of 3%?
   (b) What is the future value at the end of ten years of $200 deposited in the bank at the end of years 1, 2, . . ., 10? Assume a 3% interest rate.

5. You're 25 years old, and you want to save for the future. You intend to deposit $1,000 in the bank today.In each of the next 44 years you intend to make a similar deposit. If the interest rate is 5% annually, how much will you have when you reach the age of 70?

6. Your mom is 50 and wants to put away some money for retirement. She would like to make monthly deposits in the bank, starting today and at the beginning of every month between now and the month before her retirement at age 70. (To save you irritation: The total number of deposits is $15 * 20 = 300$.) If the interest rate is 6% annually (0.5% per month), how much should she save each month in order to have $200,000 on the day she retires? Use the **FV** function.

7. Your mom is 50 and wants to put away some money for retirement. She would like to make monthly deposits in the bank, starting today and at the beginning of every month between now and the month before her retirement at age 70. (To save you irritation: The total number of deposits is $15 * 20 = 300$.)
   (a) If the interest rate is 6% annually (0.5% per month), how much should she save each month in order to have $200,000 on the day she retires? Use the **PMT** function.
   (b) Use **Data Table** (Chapter 30) to repeat the above calculation for annual interest rates of 0%, 1%, . . . , 12%.

8. You've taken a $60,000, thirty-year mortgage to finance the purchase of your new house. The mortgage has an interest rate of 10% annually and requires monthly flat payments of interest and principal (by "flat" we mean that all the payments are equal).
   (a) Use **PMT** to compute the monthly payment.
   (b) Design a loan table showing that the payment you computed in the first part of this problem indeed pays off the mortgage.

9. You are considering buying a bond that pays $112.50 at the end of this and each of the subsequent ten years. The interest rate is 12%. Use the **PV** function to value the bond.

10. You've offered to finance Joe's purchase of a $20,000 car. Joe offers to repay you $500 per month for the next 48 months.
   (a) Use **Rate** to compute the monthly interest rate he's offering. Confirm your answer by using **IRR**.
   (b) What is the annual interest rate?

11. You are taking a $12,000 loan at 6%. If the maximum annual payment you can make is $2,000, how long will it take you to pay off the loan? (Hint: Use **NPER**.) Build a loan table that confirms your answer.

12. Your money market fund pays 3% interest annually, compounded continuously.
   (a) If you deposit $100,000 into the fund today, and if the 3% interest rate holds for the next ten years, how much will you have in ten years?
   (b) What is your effective annual interest rate (EAIR) on the fund? (Although you don't need it to answer this question, you may want to remind yourself what the EAIR is—Chapter 6.)

13. Your bank account pays 5.2% interest annually, compounded continuously. You have $25,000 in the account today, and you intend to withdraw this amount three years and four months from today. How much will you have in the account at that time?

14. Compute the continuously compounded present value of the following set of cash flows, using a discount rate of 15%.

	A	B
1	Continuously compounded discount rate	15%
2		
3	**Date**	**Cash flow**
4	1	15,000
5	2	22,000
6	3	14,750
7	4	3,222
8	5	6,333
9	6	18,000
10	7	280,000

15. Compute the continuously compounded present value of the following set of cash flows, using a discount rate of 15%. (This exercise requires some familiarity with dates in Excel—see Chapter 31.)

	A	B
1	Continuously compounded discount rate	15%
2	Date today	1-Jan-06
3	**Date**	**Cash flow**
4	31-Jan-06	15,000
5	31-Jan-07	22,000
6	17-Jul-07	14,750
7	31-Dec-07	3,222
8	14-Mar-08	6,333
9	11-Nov-08	18,000
10	13-Mar-09	280,000

16. You've been offered a financial asset that costs $1,000 today and pays back $1,100 in one year.
    (a) Compute the discretely compounded rate of return on the asset.
    (b) Compute the continuously compounded rate of return on the asset.

17. The disk that accompanies this book contains a spreadsheet with IBM stock prices and dividends from February 1990 through August 2004. Part of this spreadsheet is given below; note that column D of the spreadsheet shows the stock return for the period over which the dividend is paid (usually this period is a quarter). Use **SumIf** to find the total of all dividends paid during periods when the stock return was greater than 25%.

	A	B	C	D	E
1	Date	IBM Dividends	IBM Stock price	Stock return	
2	Feb-90		103.87		
3	May-90	1.21	120.00	15.53%	<-- =C3/C2-1
4	Aug-90	1.21	101.87	-15.11%	<-- =C4/C3-1
5	Nov-90	1.21	113.62	11.53%	<-- =C5/C4-1
6	Feb-91	1.21	128.75	13.32%	<-- =C6/C5-1
7	May-91	1.21	106.12	-17.58%	
8	Aug-91	1.21	96.87	-8.72%	
9	Nov-91	1.21	92.50	-4.51%	
10	Feb-92	1.21	86.87	-6.09%	

18. Use **SumProduct** to compute the return of the portfolio given below. The portfolio is composed of three stocks with weights as indicated.

	A	B	C
1	**Stock**	**Percentage of portfolio**	**Stock return**
2	A	40%	15%
3	B	25%	22%
4	C	35%	13%

19. The end-semester grades for Finance 101 are given below.

	A	B	C
1	**Student**	**Number grade**	**Letter grade**
2	Mary	85	
3	John	68	
4	Jennifer	72	
5	Mo	100	
6	Simon	57	
7	Noah	91	
8	Terry	78	
9	Sara	81	
10	Zvi	45	
11	George	93	

The professor for the course has to assign each student a letter grade based on his/her average. The professor's grading key is as follows:

Grade range	
≥ 0 and ≤ 50	F
≥ 50 and ≤ 60	D
≥ 60 and ≤ 70	C
≥ 70 and ≤ 85	B
≥ 85	A

Use **VLookup** to assign grades to each student.

20. On the disk that accompanies this book is a list of companies in the Dow Jones 30 Industrials (DJ30) and their share prices on 27 August 2004. Part of the list is given below.
   (a) What is the average price of a DJ30 stock?
   (b) What is the median price?
   (c) Use **Large** to determine the largest of the stock prices. Do the same using **Max**.
   (d) Use **Large** to determine the smallest of the stock prices. Do the same using **Min**.

(e)   Use **Rank** to determine the relative ranking of Microsoft's stock price among the DJ30.

	A	B
1	**DOW JONES 30 INDUSTRIALS** **Stock prices on 27 August 2004**	
2	3M Corporation	81.63
3	Alcoa Inc	32.99
4	Altria Group inc	49.15
5	American Express Company	50.07
6	American Intl Group Inc	70.96
7	Boeing Co.	52.08
8	Caterpillar Inc.	73.74
9	Citigroup, Inc.	46.75
10	E.I. du Pont de Nemours and Company	42.60

21. Using the list of DJ30 companies from Exercise 20:

(a)   Use **CountA** to determine the number of companies in the list in column A.

(b)   Use **Count** to determine the number of share prices in the list in column B.

(c)   Use **CountIf** to determine the number of companies whose share price is greater or equal to $30.

DATA TABLES

OVERVIEW

Data tables are Excel's most sophisticated way of doing sensitivity analysis. They are a bit tricky to implement, but the effort of learning them is well worth it!

30.1 A Simple Example

If we deposit $100 today and leave it in a bank drawing 15% interest for ten years, what will be its future value? As the example below shows, the answer is $404.56:

	A	B	C
1	**DATA TABLE EXAMPLE**		
2	Interest rate	15%	
3	Initial deposit	100	
4	Years	10	
5	Future value	$404.56	<-- =B3*(1+B2)^B4

Now suppose we want to show the sensitivity of the future value to the interest rate. In cells A10 to A16 we have put interest rates varying from 0% to 60%, and in cell B9 we have put **=B5**, which refers to the initial calculation of the future value.

	A	B	C
1	**DATA TABLE EXAMPLE**		
2	Interest rate	15%	
3	Initial deposit	100	
4	Years	10	
5	Future value	$404.56	<-- =B3*(1+B2)^B4
6			
7			
8	Interest rate		
9		$404.56	<-- =B5
10	0%		
11	10%		
12	20%		
13	30%		
14	40%		
15	50%		
16	60%		

To use the data table technique we mark the range A9:B16 and then use the command **Data|Table**. Here's the way the screen looks at this point:

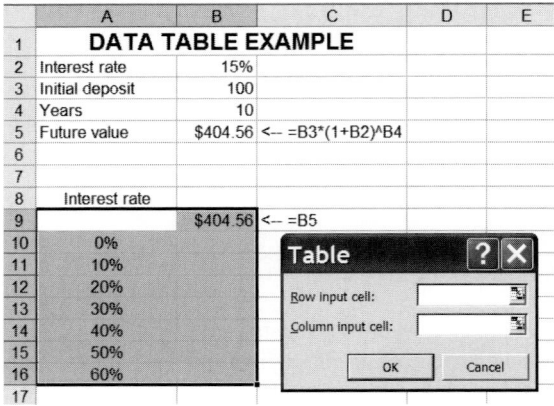

The dialog box asks whether the parameter to be varied is in a *row* or a *column* of the marked table. In our case, the interest rate to be varied is in column A of the table, so we move the cursor from **R**ow **input cell** to **C**olumn **input cell** and indicate *where in the original example the interest rate occurs:*

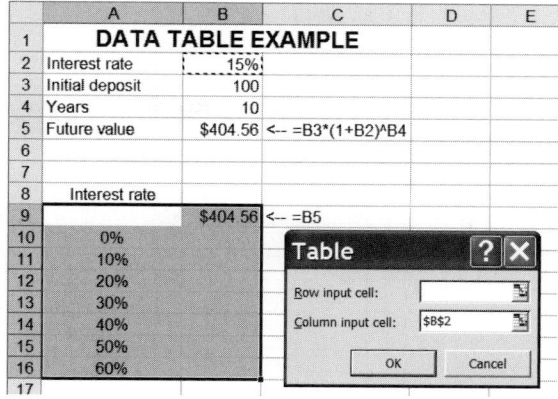

When you press **OK** you get the result:

	A	B	C
1	**DATA TABLE EXAMPLE**		
2	Interest rate	15%	
3	Initial deposit	100	
4	Years	10	
5	Future value	$404.56	<-- =B3*(1+B2)^B4
6			
7			
8	Interest rate		
9		$404.56	<-- =B5
10	0%	100	
11	10%	259.3742	
12	20%	619.1736	
13	30%	1378.585	
14	40%	2892.547	
15	50%	5766.504	
16	60%	10995.12	

30.2   Summary: How to Do a One-Dimensional Data Table

- Create an initial example.
- Set up a range with:
    - Some variable in the initial example that will be changed (like the interest rate in the above example).
    - A reference to the initial example (like the **=B5** in the above). Note that you will always have a *blank cell* next to this reference. Note the blank cells when the

variable is in a column:

	A	B	C	D
1	**DATA TABLE EXAMPLE**			
2	Interest rate	15%		
3	Initial deposit	100		
4	Years	10		
5	Future value	$404.56	<-- =B3*(1+B2)^B4	
6				
7			Blank cell when variable is in column	
8	Interest rate			
9			$404.56	<-- =B5
10	0%			
11	5%			
12	10%			
13	15%			
14	20%			
15	25%			
16	30%			

Here's the blank cell when the variable is in a row:

	E	F	G	H	I	J	K	L
6								
7		Blank cell when variable is in row						
8								
9		0%	5%	10%	15%	20%	25%	30%
10	$404.56							
11								
12	=B5							
13								

- Bring up the **Data|Table** command and indicate in the dialog box:
  - Whether the variable is in a column or a row.
  - Where in the initial example the variable occurs:

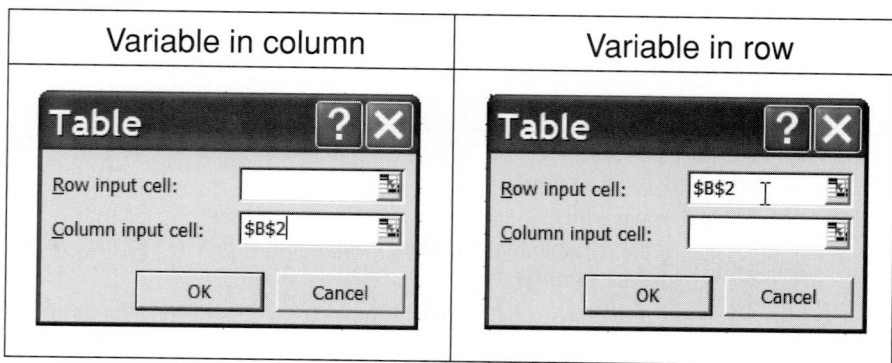

Either way the result will be a sensitivity table:

	A	B	C	D	E	F	G	H	I	J	K	L
1	DATA TABLE EXAMPLE											
2	Interest rate	15%										
3	Initial deposit	100										
4	Years	10										
5	Future value	$404.56	<-- =B3*(1+B2)^B4									
6												
7		Blank cell when variable is in column				Blank cell when variable is in row						
8	Interest rate											
9		$404.56	<-- =B5			0%	5%	10%	15%	20%	25%	30%
10	0%	100			$404.56	100	162.8895	259.3742	404.5558	619.1736	931.3226	1378.585
11	5%	162.8895										
12	10%	259.3742			=B5							
13	15%	404.5558										
14	20%	619.1736										
15	25%	931.3226										
16	30%	1378.585										

30.3 Some Notes on Data Tables

Data Tables Are Dynamic

Either you can change your initial example or the variables and the table will adjust. Here's an example where we've changed the interest rates we want to vary (compare to the previous example):

	A	B	C
1	DATA TABLE EXAMPLE		
2	Interest rate	15%	
3	Initial deposit	100	
4	Years	10	
5	Future value	$404.56	<-- =B3*(1+B2)^B4
6			
7			
8	Interest rate		
9		$404.56	<-- =B5
10	0%	100	
11	10%	259.3742	
12	20%	619.1736	
13	30%	1378.585	
14	40%	2892.547	
15	50%	5766.504	
16	60%	10995.12	

Here's another example. We change the function we're calculating, putting **=FV(B2,B4,−B3,,1)** in cell B5; as explained in Chapter 5, this function calculates the future value of ten annual $100 deposits starting today and accumulating interest at 15% for ten years.[1] Note that we've also changed the text in cell A5 from "initial deposit" to "annual deposit" to reflect what's now happening.

[1]As we also explained in Chapters 5 and 29, we put the minus sign before **B3** because otherwise—for reasons beyond logic—Excel produces a negative future value. Note that if we had typed **FV(B2,B4,-B3)** the assumption is that there are ten deposits starting one year from now.

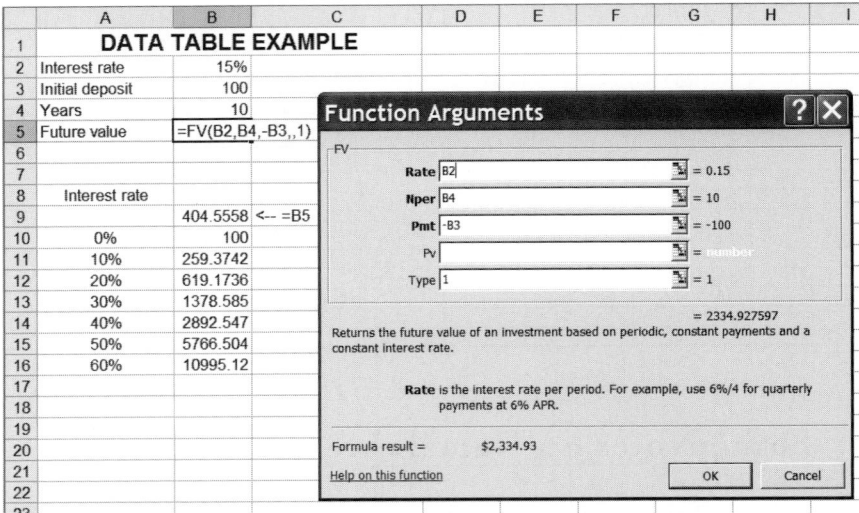

	A	B	C	D	E	F	G	H	I
1	**DATA TABLE EXAMPLE**								
2	Interest rate	15%							
3	Initial deposit	100							
4	Years	10							
5	Future value	=FV(B2,B4,-B3,,1)							
6									
7									
8	Interest rate								
9		404.5558	<-- =B5						
10	0%	100							
11	10%	259.3742							
12	20%	619.1736							
13	30%	1378.585							
14	40%	2892.547							
15	50%	5766.504							
16	60%	10995.12							
17									
18									
19									
20									
21									
22									
23									

When we press **OK**, both the example and the data table update:

	A	B	C
1	**DATA TABLE EXAMPLE**		
2	Interest rate	15%	
3	Initial deposit	100	
4	Years	10	
5	Future value	$2,334.93	<-- =FV(B2,B4,-B3,,1)
6			
7			
8	Interest rate		
9		2334.928	<-- =B5
10	0%	1000	
11	10%	1753.117	
12	20%	3115.042	
13	30%	5540.535	
14	40%	9773.913	
15	50%	16999.51	
16	60%	29053.64	

You Can Only Erase the Whole Table But You Cannot Erase Part of a Table

If you try to erase part of a data table, you'll get an error message. Below we've marked a few cells of data table and pressed the [Delete] key:

8	Interest rate		
9		2334.928	<-- =B5
10	0%	1000	
11	10%	1753.117	
12	20%	3115.042	
13	30%	5540.535	
14	40%	9773.913	
15	50%	16999.51	
16	60%	29053.64	

Microsoft Excel

⚠ Cannot change part of a table.

OK

You Can Hide the Cell Header But Not Erase It

The formula at the top of the table's second column (cell B9 in our case, containing the reference to cell B5) is called the "column header." This formula controls what the data table calculates. If you want to print a table, you often want to hide the column header. In the example below, we've put the cursor on cell B9. We then use the command **Format|Cells** and go to **Number|Custom**. Typing a semicolon in the **Type** box hides the cell:

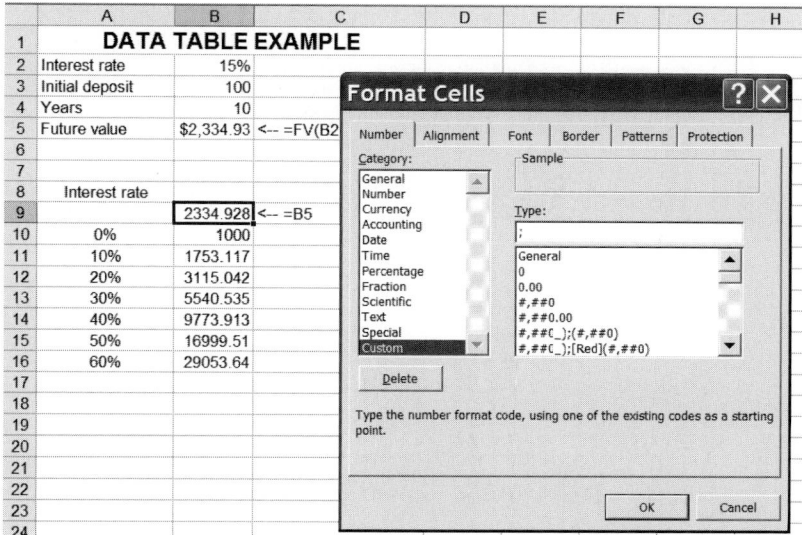

Here's the result:

	A	B	C
8	Interest rate		
9			<-- =B5
10	0%	1000	
11	10%	1753.117	
12	20%	3115.042	
13	30%	5540.535	
14	40%	9773.913	
15	50%	16999.51	
16	60%	29053.64	

30.4 Two-Dimensional Data Tables

In the example below we return to the **FV** example discussed earlier. We want to vary our initial example with respect to both the interest rate and the initial deposit. The data table is set up in cells B9:H15:

	A	B	C	D	E	F	G	H	I
1	**DATA TABLE EXAMPLE**								
2	Interest rate	15%							
3	Annual deposit	100							
4	Years	10							
5	Future value	$2,334.93	<-- =FV(B2,B4,-B3,,1)						
6									
7	Two-dimensional table, showing sensitivity of future value to both interest rate and deposit size								
8									
9		$2,334.93	0%	5%	10%	15%	20%	25%	
10		50							
11	=B5	100							
12		150							
13		200							
14		250							
15		300							

This time we indicate in the **Data|Table** command that there are two variables:

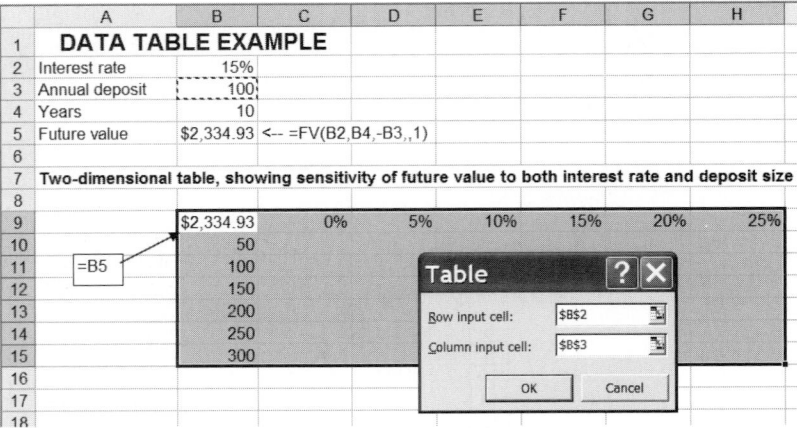

This creates a two-dimensional table:

	B	C	D	E	F	G	H
9	$2,334.93	0%	5%	10%	15%	20%	25%
10	50	500.00	660.34	876.56	1,167.46	1,557.52	2,078.31
11	100	1,000.00	1,320.68	1,753.12	2,334.93	3,115.04	4,156.61
12	150	1,500.00	1,981.02	2,629.68	3,502.39	4,672.56	6,234.92
13	200	2,000.00	2,641.36	3,506.23	4,669.86	6,230.08	8,313.23
14	250	2,500.00	3,301.70	4,382.79	5,837.32	7,787.60	10,391.53
15	300	3,000.00	3,962.04	5,259.35	7,004.78	9,345.13	12,469.84

EXERCISES

1. The spreadsheet below shows the value of the function $f(x) = x^2 + 3x - 16$ for $x = 3$. Create the indicated data table and use it to graph the function in the range $(-10, 14)$.

	A	B	C	D
3	x	3		
4	f(x)	2	<-- =B3^2+3*B3-16	
5				
6				
7	Data table			
8		2	<-- =B4	
9	-10			
10	-8			
11	-6			
12	-4			
13	-2			
14	0			
15	2			
16	4			
17	6			
18	8			
19	10			
20	12			
21	14			

2. The example below calculates the NPV and IRR for an investment.
   (a) Create a one-dimensional data table showing the sensitivity of the NPV and IRR to the year-1 cash flow (currently $10,000). Use a range of $9,000–12,000 in increments of $500.
   (b) Create a two-dimension data table showing the sensitivity of NPV to the year-1 cash flow and to the discount rate. Use the same range for the cash flow as in part (a) and use discount rates from 8% to 20%, with increments of 2%.

	A	B	C	D	E
3	Discount rate	15%			
4	Cost	50,000			
5	Cash flow growth	6%			
6					
7	Year	Cash flow			
8	0	(50,000.00)	<-- =-B4		
9	1	10,000.00			
10	2	10,600.00	<-- =B9*(1+$B$5)		
11	3	11,236.00	<-- =B10*(1+$B$5)		
12	4	11,910.16			
13	5	12,624.77			
14	6	13,382.26			
15	7	14,185.19			
16	8	15,036.30			
17	9	15,938.48			
18	10	16,894.79			
19					
20	NPV	11,925.54	<-- =NPV(B3,B9:B18)+B8		
21	IRR	20.41%	<-- =IRR(B8:B18)		

3. Project A and Project B cash flows are given in the spreadsheet below. Recreate the **Data Table** in cells A21:C37 and create the graph. Notice that the **Data Table** headers in cells B21:C21 have been hidden (see Section 30.3 for details on how to do this).

What is the crossover point of the two lines? (You can use the **Data Table** to do this, but you can also refer to Chapter 3 for a better solution.)

	A	B	C	D	E	F	G	H	I
1			TWO INVESTMENTS AND THEIR NPVs						
2	Discount rate	15%							
3									
4	Year	Project A cash flow	Project B cash flow						
5	0	-1,000	-1,000						
6	1	220	300						
7	2	220	300						
8	3	220	300						
9	4	220	300						
10	5	220	300						
11	6	220	100						
12	7	220	100						
13	8	220	100						
14	9	220	100						
15	10	220	100						
16									
17	NPV	104.13	172.31	<-- =NPV($B$2,C6:C15)+C5					
18	IRR	17.68%	20.64%	<-- =IRR(C5:C15)					
19									
20		NPV A	NPV B						
21				<-- The data table headers have been hidden; **see** Chapter 30 for details					
22	0%	1,200.00	1,000.00						
23	2%	976.17	840.95						
24	4%	784.40	701.45						
25	6%	619.22	578.48						
26	8%	476.22	469.55						
27	10%	351.80	372.61						
28	12%	243.05	285.98						
29	14%	147.55	208.23						
30	16%	63.31	138.18						
31	18%	-11.30	74.84						
32	20%	-77.66	17.37						
33	22%	-136.90	-34.95						
34	24%	-189.99	-82.74						
35	26%	-237.74	-126.51						
36	28%	-280.84	-166.71						
37	30%	-319.86	-203.73						
38									

4. Finance texts always have tables that give the present value factor for an annuity:

$$\frac{PV \text{ factor for annuity of \$1 for N years}}{\text{at interest } r} = \sum_{t=1}^{N} \frac{1}{(1+r)^t}$$

As illustrated below in Excel, these present value factors are created with the **PV** function:

	A	B	C	D	E	F	G	H	I	J	K
1					ANNUITY TABLE						
2	r, interest	9%									
3	N, number of periods	5									
4	PV factor	3.8897	<-- =PV(B2,B3,-1)								
5											
6											
7	Number of periods			PRESENT VALUE OF AN ANNUITY OF $1 FOR N PERIODS							
8		1%	2%	3%	4%	5%	6%	7%	8%	9%	10%
9	1										
10	2										
11	3										
12	4										
13	5										
14	6										
15	7										
16	8										
17	9										
18	10										

Use **Data Table** to create the table in the template above.

5. (Do this example only if you've studied Chapters 23–25 on option pricing.) The Black–Scholes option pricing model, defined in Chapter 25, prices call and put options based on five parameters:

- S, the stock price today
- X, the option's exercise price (also called the option's *strike price*)
- T, the option's expiration date
- r, the interest rate
- σ ("sigma"), the riskiness of the stock

These inputs and the resulting call and put prices are highlighted below.

   Your assignment: Use **Data Table** to create tables showing the sensitivity of the call and put prices to the various inputs. Here are some suggestions:

(a) Using the parameters shown below, what are the call and put prices given $\sigma = 10\%$, 15%, 20%, . . . , 80%?

(b) Using the parameters shown below, what are the call and put prices when $T = 0.1$, 0.2, 0.3, . . . , 1?

	A	B	C
1	**The Black-Scholes Option-Pricing Formula**		
2	S	100	Current stock price
3	X	90	Exercise price
4	T	0.50000	Time to maturity of option (in years)
5	r	4.00%	Risk-free rate of interest
6	Sigma	35%	Stock volatility
7			
8	d_1	0.6303	<-- (LN(S/X)+(r+0.5*sigma^2)*T)/(sigma*SQRT(T))
9	d_2	0.3828	<-- d_1-sigma*SQRT(T)
10			
11	N(d_1)	0.7357	<-- Uses formula NormSDist(d_1)
12	N(d_2)	0.6491	<-- Uses formula NormSDist(d_2)
13			
14	Call price	16.32	<-- S*N(d_1)-X*exp(-r*T)*N(d_2)
15	Put price	4.53	<-- call price - S + X*Exp(-r*T): by Put-Call parity

WORKING WITH DATES IN EXCEL

OVERVIEW

One of the most powerful features of Excel is its ability to work with dates. We made use of this feature in Chapter 18 on bond calculations and in Chapter 25 on the Black–Scholes model. In this short technical chapter we explain how to use dates in Excel.

Excel Concepts Discussed

- Entering dates and times into spreadsheets
- "Stretching out" dates and times over multiple cells
- Formatting cells for dates
- Functions: **Now, Today, Month, XNPV, XIRR, Date, Weekday, VLookup**

31.1 Typing Dates in a Spreadsheet

Read the quote from the Excel Help in Figure 31.1 and you will know almost everything you need to know about entering dates into your spreadsheet. The basic fact you need to know is that Excel translates a date into a number. Here's an example. Suppose you decide to type a date into a cell:

A2	▼ X ✓ *fx*	3Feb2001	
A	B	C	D
1			
2 3Feb2001			
3			

When you hit **Enter**, Excel decides that you've entered a date. Here's the way it appears:

A2	▼	*fx* 2/3/2001	
A	B	C	D
1			
2 3-Feb-01			
3			

Note that in the formula bar (indicated by the arrow above), Excel interprets the date entered as **2/3/2001**.[1] When you reformat the cell as **Format|Cells|Number|General**, you see that Excel interprets this date as the number 36925, the number 1 being 1 January 1900.

	A	B
1		
2	36925	
3		

Microsoft Excel stores dates as sequential numbers which are called serial values. By default, January 1, 1900 is serial number 1, and January 1, 2008 is serial number 39448 because it is 39,448 days after January 1, 1900. Excel stores times as decimal fractions because time is considered a portion of a day.

Because dates and times are values, they can be added, subtracted, and included in other calculations. You can view a date as a serial value and a time as a decimal fraction by changing the format of the cell that contains the date or time to General format.

Because the rules that govern the way that any calculation program interprets dates are complex, you should be as specific as possible about dates whenever you enter them. This will produce the highest level of accuracy in your date calculations.

Figure 31.1 Excel's Help explains dates and date systems.

---

[1]The way this appears and is interpreted depends on the Regional Settings entered in the Windows Control Panel. Our settings in this book follow the U.S. conventions.

Spreadsheet dates can be subtracted. In the spreadsheet below we've entered two dates and subtracted them to find the number of days between the dates:

	B	C	D	E
5		2-Dec-00		
6		8-Mar-99		
7	Days between	635	<-- =C5-C6	

(Cell C7 initially showed a date but was then reformatted with **Format|Cells|Number| General**.)

You can also add a number to a date to find another date. What, for example, was the date 165 days after 16 November 1947?

	C	D	E
11	16-Nov-47		
12	29-Apr-48	<-- =C11+165	

Stretching Out Dates

In the two cells below we've put in two dates and then "stretched" the cells out to add more dates with the same difference between them:

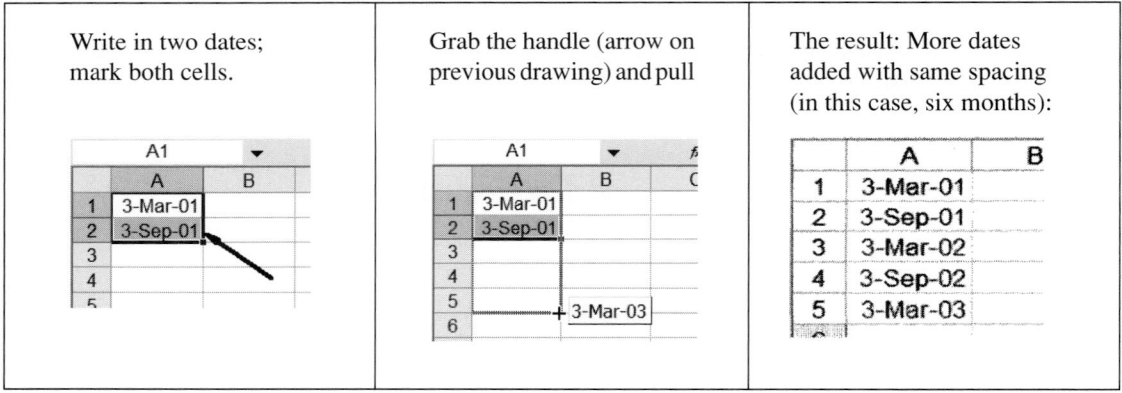

31.2 Times in a Spreadsheet

Hours, minutes, and so on can also be typed into a cell. In the cell below, we've typed in 8:22:

When we hit **Enter**, Excel interprets this as 8:22 am:

Excel recognizes 24 hour times and also recognizes the symbol **a** for am and **p** for pm:

As entered	When you hit **Enter**

As entered

	B4	▼ ✕ ✓ *fx*	3:58 p

	A	B	C	D
1				
2		8:22		
3				
4		3:58 p		
5				

Note that the **p** is separated from the time by a space. (Of course am is represented by an **a**.)

When you hit **Enter**

	B4	▼	*fx* 3:58:00 PM

	A	B	C	D
1				
2		8:22		
3				
4		3:58 PM		
5				

EXCEL RECOGNIZES 24-HOUR CLOCK

As entered

	B2	▼ ✕ ✓ *fx*	15:23

	A	B	C	D
1				
2		15:23		
3				

When you hit **Enter**

	B2	▼	*fx* 3:23:00 PM

	A	B	C	D
1				
2		15:23		
3				
4				

You can subtract times just like you subtract dates; cell B5 below tells you that 7 hours and 32 minutes have elapsed between the two times (ignore the "AM" in cell B5):

	B	C	D
3	3:48 PM		
4	8:16 AM		
5	7:32 AM	<-- =B3-B4	

When you reformat the cells above with **Format|Cells|Number|General**, you can see that times are represented in Excel as fractions of a day:

	B	C	D
3	0.658333		
4	0.344444		
5	0.313889	<-- =B3-B4	

If you type in a date and a time and reformat, you can also see this:

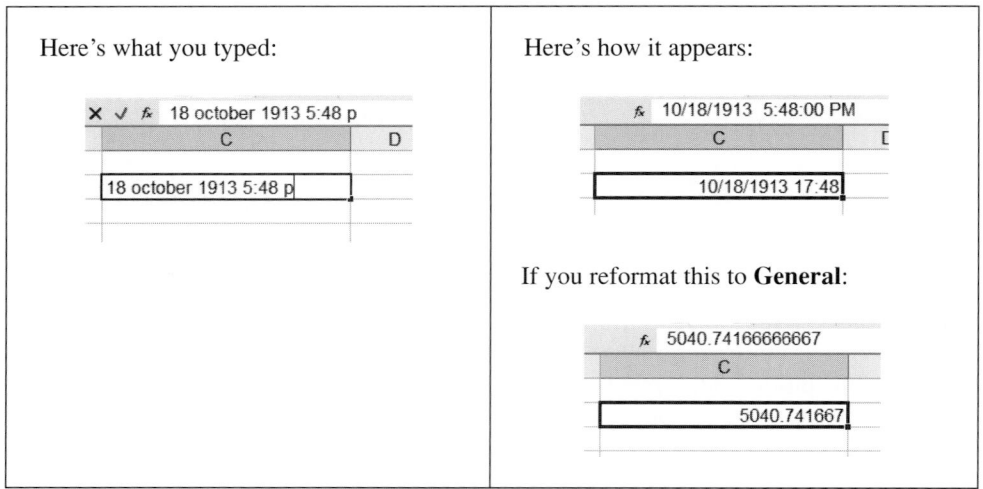

31.3 Time and Date Functions in Excel

Excel has a whole set of time and date functions. Here are several functions that we find useful. Note that several of these functions require empty parentheses:

- **Now( )** reads the computer clock and represents the date and the time.
- **Today( )** reads the computer's clock and prints the date.
- **Date(yyyy,mm,dd)** gives the date entered.
- **Weekday( )** gives the day of the week.
- **Month( )** gives the month.

Here are the first three functions in a spreadsheet:

	A	B	C	D	E
2	Serial representation	Date/time format			
3	36944.8493184028000	2/22/2001 20:23	<-- =NOW()		
4	36944	2/22/2001	<-- =TODAY()		
5	36245	3/26/1999	<-- =DATE(1999,3,26)		
6					
7	Different formatting of Now( )				
8		February 22, 2001	<-- =NOW()		
9		2/22/01 8:23 PM	<-- =NOW()		
10		8:23 PM	<-- =NOW()		
11					
12	When was day 1?				
13	1	<-- =DATE(1900,1,1)			

The use of **Weekday** and **Month** is self-explanatory:

	A	B	C
3	3-Nov-01	7	<-- =WEEKDAY(A3)
4		7	<-- =WEEKDAY("3nov2001")
5	In **Weekday**, 1=Sunday, 2=Monday, etc.		
6			
7		11	<-- =MONTH(A3)
8		12	<-- =MONTH("22dec2003")

Calculating the Difference Between Two Dates—The Function Datedif

This Excel function computes the difference between two dates in various useful ways:

	A	B	C
1		**DATEDIF COMPUTES DIFFERENCE BETWEEN TWO DATES**	
2	Date1	3-Apr-47	
3	Date2	22-Dec-02	
4			
5			**Explanation**
6	55	<-- =DATEDIF(B2,B3,"y")	Number of years between dates
7	668	<-- =DATEDIF(B2,B3,"m")	Number of months between dates
8	20352	<-- =DATEDIF(B2,B3,"d")	Number of days between dates
9	19	<-- =DATEDIF(B2,B3,"md")	Number of days in excess of full number of months
10	8	<-- =DATEDIF(B2,B3,"ym")	Number of months in excess of full number of years
11	263	<-- =DATEDIF(B2,B3,"yd")	Number of days in excess of full number of years

If Date1 is the author's birth date and Date2 is today, then the author is currently 55 years and 263 days old (cells A6 and A11).

31.4   The Functions XIRR( ) and XNPV( )

These two functions calculate the internal rate of return and the net present value for a series of cash flows received on specific dates. They are especially useful for calculating IRR and NPV when the dates are unevenly spaced.[2] If you do not have these functions, you will have to activate **Tools|Add-Ins** and then click on **Analysis ToolPak**:

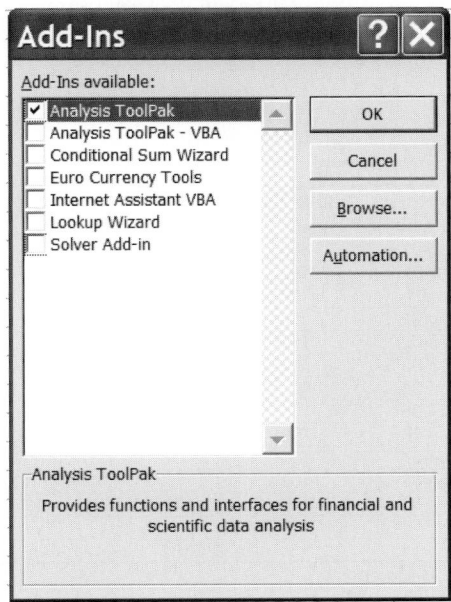

------

[2]Excel's **IRR** function assumes that the first cash flow occurs today, the next cash flow occurs one period hence, the following cash flow two periods hence, and so on. Excel's **NPV** function assumes that the first cash flow occurs one period from now, the next cash flow in two periods, and so on. We call this "even spacing of cash flows." When this is not the case, you'll need the **XIRR** and **XNPV** functions.

XIRR

Here's an example. You pay $600 on 16 February 2001 for an asset that repays $100 on 5 April 2001, $100 on 15 July 2001, and then $100 on every 22 September from 2001 until 2009. The dates are not evenly spaced, so you cannot use **IRR**. With **XIRR** (cell B16 below), you can compute the *annualized IRR* (the effective annual interest rate EAIR, as defined in Chapter 2).

	A	B	C
1	THE EXCEL FUNCTION XIRR		
2	Date	Payment	
3	16-Feb-01	-600	
4	05-Apr-01	100	
5	15-Jul-01	100	
6	22-Sep-01	100	
7	22-Sep-02	100	
8	22-Sep-03	100	
9	22-Sep-04	100	
10	22-Sep-05	100	
11	22-Sep-06	100	
12	22-Sep-07	100	
13	22-Sep-08	100	
14	22-Sep-09	100	
15			
16	XIRR	21.97%	<-- =XIRR(B3:B14,A3:A14)

XIRR works by discounting each cash flow at the daily rate. In our example the first cash flow of $100 occurs 48 days from now, the second in 149 days, ... **XIRR** transforms 21.97% to a daily rate and uses it to discount the cash flows:

$$-600 + \frac{100}{(1.2197)^{48/365}} + \frac{100}{(1.2197)^{149/365}} + \cdots + \frac{100}{(1.2197)^{3140/365}} = 0$$

	A	B	C	D	E
19			HOW DOES XIRR WORK?		
20	Date	Payment	Days from initial date	PV	
21	16-Feb-01	-600		-600	
22	05-Apr-01	100	48	97	<-- =B22/(1+$B$34)^(C22/365)
23	15-Jul-01	100	149	92	<-- =B23/(1+$B$34)^(C23/365)
24	22-Sep-01	100	218	89	
25	22-Sep-02	100	583	73	
26	22-Sep-03	100	948	60	
27	22-Sep-04	100	1314	49	
28	22-Sep-05	100	1679	40	
29	22-Sep-06	100	2044	33	
30	22-Sep-07	100	2409	27	
31	22-Sep-08	100	2775	22	
32	22-Sep-09	100	=H15-$H$4 ——▶ 3140	18	
33					
34	IRR?	21.97%	<-- =XIRR(B21:B32,A21:A32)	0	<-- =SUM(D21:D32)

XNPV

This function computes the NPV for unevenly spaced cash flows. In the example below, we use the function to compute the NPV on the same example we used for **XIRR**.

	A	B	C
1	THE EXCEL FUNCTION XNPV		
2	Date	Payment	
3	16-Feb-01	-600	
4	05-Apr-01	100	
5	15-Jul-01	100	
6	22-Sep-01	100	
7	22-Sep-02	100	
8	22-Sep-03	100	
9	22-Sep-04	100	
10	22-Sep-05	100	
11	22-Sep-06	100	
12	22-Sep-07	100	
13	22-Sep-08	100	
14	22-Sep-09	100	
15			
16	Discount rate	15%	
17	XNPV	97.29	<-- =XNPV(B16,B3:B14,A3:A14)

Notice that **XNPV** requires you to indicate all the cash flows (starting with the initial cash flow), as opposed to **NPV** which starts from the first cash flow.

XNPV and NPV Can Give Different Answers

The functions **XNPV** and **NPV** can give slightly different answers. Here's an example:

	A	B	C
1	XNPV VERSUS NPV		
2	Discount rate	12%	
3			
4	Date	Cash flow	
5	1-Jan-06	-1,000	
6	1-Jan-07	250	
7	1-Jan-08	250	
8	1-Jan-09	250	
9	1-Jan-10	250	
10	1-Jan-11	250	
11	1-Jan-12	250	
12	1-Jan-13	250	
13			
14	NPV	140.94	<-- =B5+NPV(B2,B6:B12)
15	XNPV	140.68	<-- =XNPV(B2,B5:B12,A5:A12)

In cell B14 we calculate the net present value using the **NPV** function and in cell B15 we do the same calculation using **XNPV**. Why the different answers? **XNPV** does the calculation using the daily interest rate $(1 + 12\%)^{(1/365)} - 1 = 0.03105\%$ and based on the number of days between each date. **NPV**, on the other hand, uses the annual interest rate of 12%. Since 2008 and 2012 are leap years, the **XNPV** calculation is slightly lower.[3]

---

[3]For the same reason, **IRR** and **XIRR** can give slightly different results.

31.5 A More Sophisticated Example: Calculating Option Expiration Dates

In this section we show how to use several Excel functions to compute the date on which an option expires (see Chapters 23–25 for why this might be important). The actual option expiration date is the third Friday of the month. The calendar below illustrates what we mean—the relevant day for each month is highlighted.

How do we find this day? We start with Excel's **Weekday** function. This function takes the text form of the date and tells you the day of the week. Here are two examples:

	A	B	C	D	E
3	3-Nov-01	7	<-- =WEEKDAY(A3)		
4					
5		7	<-- =WEEKDAY("3nov2001")		

In cell B3 we've referred to a serial number form of the date; in cell B5 we've written the date in text format. Both cells tell us that 3 November 2001 is the 7th day of the week, Saturday.

January 2001

S	M	Tu	W	Th	F	Sa
	1	2	3	4	5	6
7	8	9	10	11	12	13
14	15	16	17	18	19	20
21	22	23	24	25	26	27

February 2001

S	M	Tu	W	Th	F	Sa
				1	2	3
4	5	6	7	8	9	10
11	12	13	14	15	16	17
18	19	20	21	22	23	24

March 2001

S	M	Tu	W	Th	F	Sa
				1	2	3
4	5	6	7	8	9	10
11	12	13	14	15	16	17
18	19	20	21	22	23	24

April 2001

S	M	Tu	W	Th	F	Sa
1	2	3	4	5	6	7
8	9	10	11	12	13	14
15	16	17	18	19	20	21
22	23	24	25	26	27	28

May 2001

S	M	Tu	W	Th	F	Sa
		1	2	3	4	5
6	7	8	9	10	11	12
13	14	15	16	17	18	19
20	21	22	23	24	25	26

June 2001

S	M	Tu	W	Th	F	Sa
					1	2
3	4	5	6	7	8	9
10	11	12	13	14	15	16
17	18	19	20	21	22	23

July 2001

S	M	Tu	W	Th	F	Sa
1	2	3	4	5	6	7
8	9	10	11	12	13	14
15	16	17	18	19	20	21
22	23	24	25	26	27	28

August 2001

S	M	Tu	W	Th	F	Sa
			1	2	3	4
5	6	7	8	9	10	11
12	13	14	15	16	17	18
19	20	21	22	23	24	25

September 2001

S	M	Tu	W	Th	F	Sa
						1
2	3	4	5	6	7	8
9	10	11	12	13	14	15
16	17	18	19	20	21	22
23	24	25	26	27	28	29

October 2001

S	M	Tu	W	Th	F	Sa
	1	2	3	4	5	6
7	8	9	10	11	12	13
14	15	16	17	18	19	20
21	22	23	24	25	26	27
28	29	30	31			

November 2001

S	M	Tu	W	Th	F	Sa
				1	2	3
4	5	6	7	8	9	10
11	12	13	14	15	16	17
18	19	20	21	22	23	24
25	26	27	28	29	30	

December 2001

S	M	Tu	W	Th	F	Sa
						1
2	3	4	5	6	7	8
9	10	11	12	13	14	15
16	17	18	19	20	21	22
23	24	25	26	27	28	29

Now suppose we know the month and the year (as in cells B5 and C5 below). In cell D5 we included a text formula that creates "1Nov2001" from the combination of the month and the year (text formulas are discussed in Chapter 28 on graphs).

	A	B	C	D	E
1	**A FUNCTION THAT LOOKS UP THE OPTION EXPIRATION DATE**				
	Looks up the third Friday of the month				
2		**Month**	**Year**	**Month-Year**	
3		Nov	2001	1Nov2001	<-- ="1"&B3&TEXT(C3,0)
4					
5	Day of the week of the first day of month	5	<-- =WEEKDAY(D3)		
6	Key: 1=Sun, 2=Mon, ... 7= Sat				

In cell B5 we use **Weekday** to tell us that 1 November 2001 is a Thursday. Now it's only a matter of counting: If 1 November is a Thursday, so are 8 November and 15 November. So the first Friday after the third Thursday of November is 16 November. All of this is summarized in the following table:

	A	B	C
		Excel's **Weekday** function	Relevant Friday date
11	Day of the week		
12	Sunday	1	20
13	Monday	2	19
14	Tuesday	3	18
15	Wednesday	4	17
16	Thursday	5	16
17	Friday	6	15
18	Saturday	7	21

We can use the **VLookup** function (see Chapter 29) to give us the correct date (in cell B11):

	A	B	C	D	E
1	**A FUNCTION THAT LOOKS UP THE OPTION EXPIRATION DATE** **Looks up the third Friday of the month**				
2		Month	Year	Month-Year	
3		Nov	2001	1Nov2001	<-- ="1"&B3&TEXT(C3,0)
4					
5	Day of the week of the first day of month	5	<-- =WEEKDAY(D3)		
6	Key: 1=Sun, 2=Mon, ... 7= Sat				
7					
8	Date of option expiration	16	<-- =VLOOKUP(B5,B12:C18,2)		
9					
10	**Lookup table**				
11	Day of the week	Excel's **Weekday** function	Relevant Friday date		
12	Sunday	1	20		
13	Monday	2	19		
14	Tuesday	3	18		
15	Wednesday	4	17		
16	Thursday	5	16		
17	Friday	6	15		
18	Saturday	7	21		

EXERCISES

1. Enter a series of annual dates into Excel, starting with 31 January 2008 and ending with 31 January 2015. The final product should look like this:

	A
1	31-Jan-08
2	31-Jan-09
3	31-Jan-10
4	31-Jan-11
5	31-Jan-12
6	31-Jan-13
7	31-Jan-14
8	31-Jan-15

2. Enter a series of hourly times into Excel, starting with midnight and ending with 11 am. The final product should look like this:

	A
1	12:00 AM
2	1:00 AM
3	2:00 AM
4	3:00 AM
5	4:00 AM
6	5:00 AM
7	6:00 AM
8	7:00 AM
9	8:00 AM
10	9:00 AM
11	10:00 AM
12	11:00 AM

3. Professor Smith was born on 15 February 1964. Today is 18 March 2007.
   - (a) Subtract the two dates to compute Smith's age in days.
   - (b) Divided by 365 to compute Smith's age in years.
   - (c) Use **Weekday** to determine the day of the week when Smith was born.
   - (d) Use **Datedif** to determine the number of months of Smith's age.

4. (a) On 15 February 2005 a bond of XYZ Corp. is selling for $923. The bond has a $60 coupon payment on 15 May 2005 and each six months afterward until 15 November 2008, when it pays $1,000 plus the $60 coupon. Use **XIRR** to compute the bond's internal rate of return (IRR).

	A	B
1	Date	Bond cash flow
2	15-Feb-05	-923
3	15-May-05	60
4	15-Nov-05	60
5	15-May-06	60
6	15-Nov-06	60
7	15-May-07	60
8	15-Nov-07	60
9	15-May-08	60
10	15-Nov-08	1,060

(b) On 28 February 2005, the bond's price is $951. What is its IRR now?

5. A project whose discount rate is 13% has the cash flows indicated below. Use **XNPV** to compute the project's net present value.

	A	B
1	Discount rate	13.00%
2		
3	**Date**	**Project cash flow**
4	1-Nov-03	-1,000.00
5	13-Jan-04	-523.00
6	18-Jul-04	-1,500.00
7	31-Dec-04	1,500.00
8	17-May-05	2,200.00
9	19-Dec-05	1,200.00
10	22-Aug-05	-435.00
11	15-Jan-06	2,000.00

6. In this exercise you will show how **XNPV** is based on daily interest rates. In the spreadsheet below, fill in all the cells marked ??? and show that the sum of the entries E5 to E10 gives the same result as cell B12.

	A	B	C	D	E	F
1	Discount rate	8%				
2	Daily interest rate	???				
3						
4	**Date**	**Cash flow**		**Days between dates**	**Present value based on days from initial date**	
5	15-Mar-22	-1,500			???	
6	18-Apr-23	250		???	???	
7	22-Jun-23	155		???	???	
8	15-Nov-24	610		???	???	
9	16-Feb-25	222		???	???	
10	19-Oct-25	100		???	???	
11						
12	NPV	-380.076	<-- =XNPV(B1,B5:B10,A5:A10)		???	<-- =sum(E5:E10)

7. Use the number of days between dates to explain why the calculations of the IRR in cell B12 and in cell B13 are different.

	A	B	C
1		**IRR vs. XIRR**	
2	**Date**	**Cash flow**	
3	1-Jan-06	-1,000	
4	1-Jan-07	250	
5	1-Jan-08	250	
6	1-Jan-09	250	
7	1-Jan-10	250	
8	1-Jan-11	250	
9	1-Jan-12	250	
10	1-Jan-13	250	
11			
12	IRR	16.327%	<-- =IRR(B3:B10)
13	XIRR	16.317%	<-- =XIRR(B3:B10,A3:A10)

Using Goal Seek and Solver

OVERVIEW

Goal Seek and **Solver** are Excel tools to produce targeted results from your models (the technical jargon is "calibrate your model"). If this sentence sounds a bit dense, read on—you'll see that these tools are extremely useful.

   Although **Solver** is a much more sophisticated tool than **Goal Seek**, we don't use many of its more advanced capabilities. For our purposes, **Goal Seek** and **Solver** are thus largely interchangeable—they can both do most of the financial tasks that we require, and they are not difficult to use. When you get used to them, you'll probably find that **Solver** is preferable, because it "remembers" its arguments (at this stage you won't understand this, but read on).

32.1 Installing Solver

Both **Goal Seek** and **Solver** come with the standard Excel package, but **Solver** has to be installed. If it is not on your computer, do the following:

- Open Excel and go to **Tools|Add-Ins**:

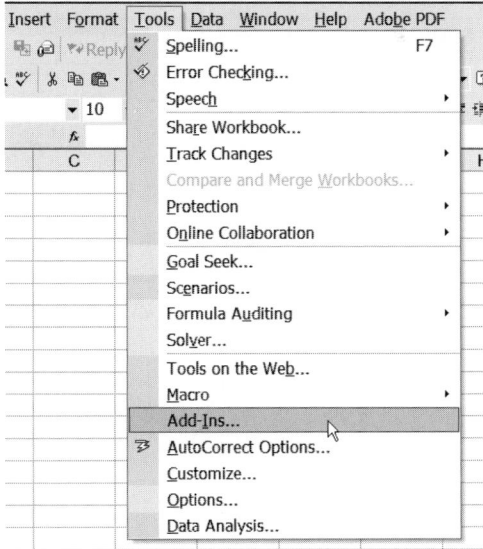

- After clicking **Add-Ins**, you'll get a drop-down menu; scroll down to **Solver Add-in** and click on the box. That should do it.

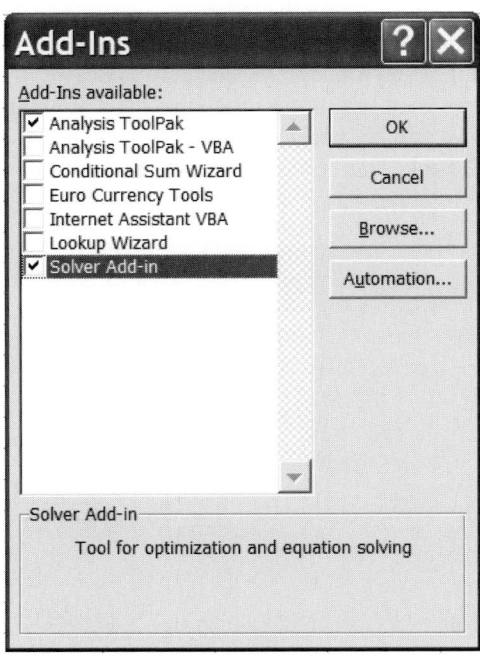

32.2 Using Goal Seek and Solver: A Simple Example

We start with a high-school algebra example. Suppose we're trying to graph the equation $y = -x^3 + 2x^2 - 3x + 121$. We can do this in Excel as follows:

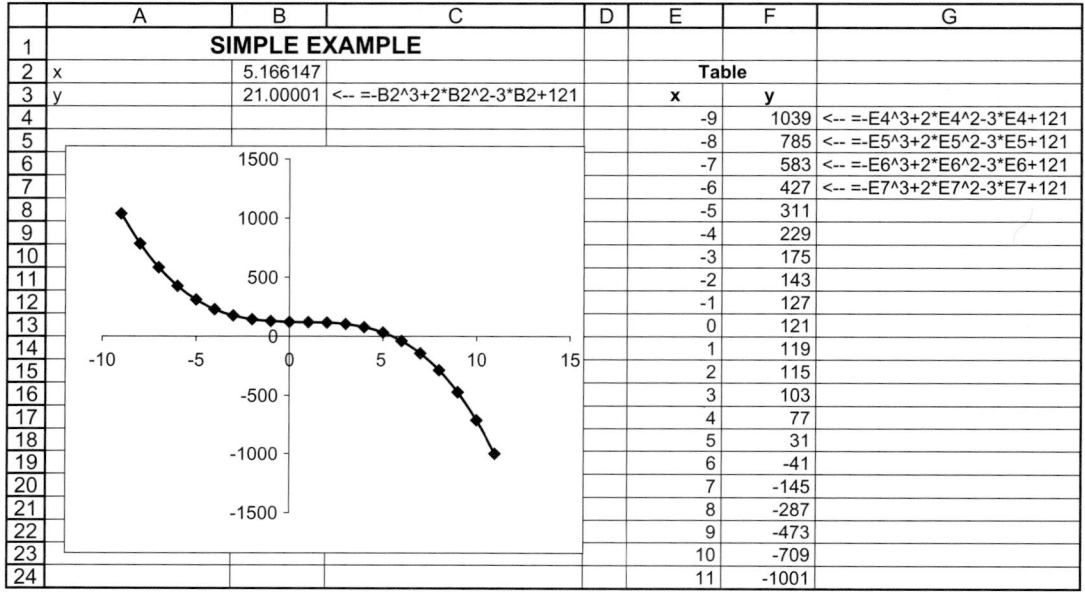

	A	B	C	D	E	F	G
1		**SIMPLE EXAMPLE**					
2	x	5.166147				Table	
3	y	21.00001	<-- =-B2^3+2*B2^2-3*B2+121		**x**	**y**	
4					-9	1039	<-- =-E4^3+2*E4^2-3*E4+121
5					-8	785	<-- =-E5^3+2*E5^2-3*E5+121
6					-7	583	<-- =-E6^3+2*E6^2-3*E6+121
7					-6	427	<-- =-E7^3+2*E7^2-3*E7+121
8					-5	311	
9					-4	229	
10					-3	175	
11					-2	143	
12					-1	127	
13					0	121	
14					1	119	
15					2	115	
16					3	103	
17					4	77	
18					5	31	
19					6	-41	
20					7	-145	
21					8	-287	
22					9	-473	
23					10	-709	
24					11	-1001	

Notice that we've put the function in twice: In cells B2 and B3, we've got a simple example of the function (one value of x and its corresponding y value); to the right, we've got the table for the graph (many values of x and many values of y).

Now we want to find the x such that the corresponding y is 21. You can tell from the table that the value will be somewhere between 5 and 6. To solve for it, we go to the Excel command **Tools|Goal Seek**. This brings up a dialog box, which we fill in as below:

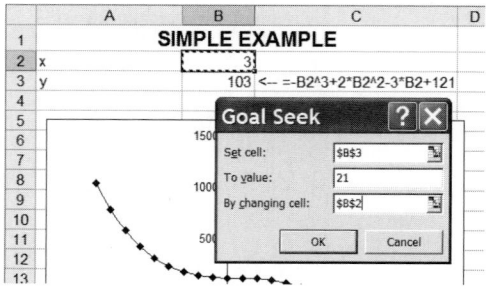

Hitting the **OK** box indicates that the answer is approximately 5.150067:

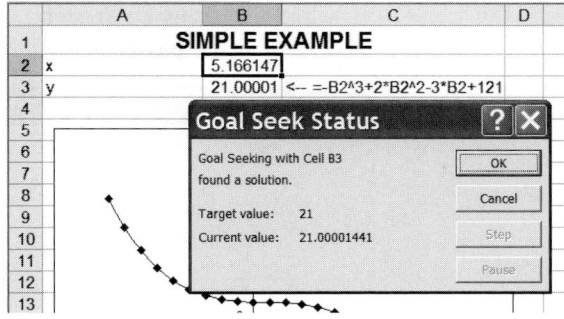

Hitting **OK** again, accepts this answer:

	A	B	C
1		SIMPLE EXAMPLE	
2	x	5.166147	
3	y	21.00001	<-- =-B2^3+2*B2^2-3*B2+121

Doing the Same Thing With Solver

We can do the same calculation with **Solver**. On the same spreadsheet, we go to the command **Tools|Solver**. This brings up a dialog box that we fill in as follows (note that we changed the question a bit—this time we're asking for the *x* value that gives a *y* = −58):

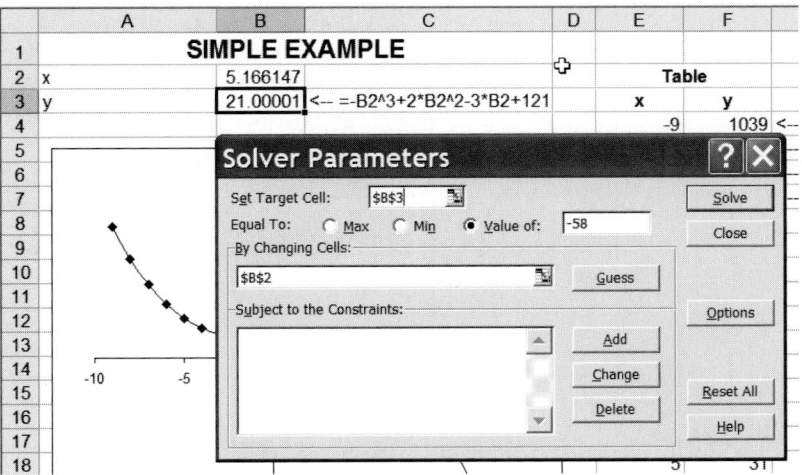

Hitting **Solve** gives the answer:

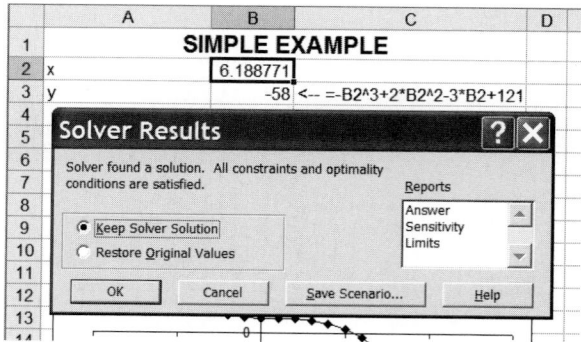

Hitting **OK** accepts the answer.

32.3 What's the Difference Between Solver and Goal Seek?

Solver and **Goal Seek** serve much the same purpose. Nevertheless, there are several differences between them.

Solver Remembers, Goal Seek Forgets

Suppose you've got another question: For which x will $y = 158$? If you use **Goal Seek** to answer this question, you'll have to reenter all the values into the dialog box. But if you use **Solver**, you'll see that it comes up with the previous set of values—you only have to change the entry in the **Value of** box:

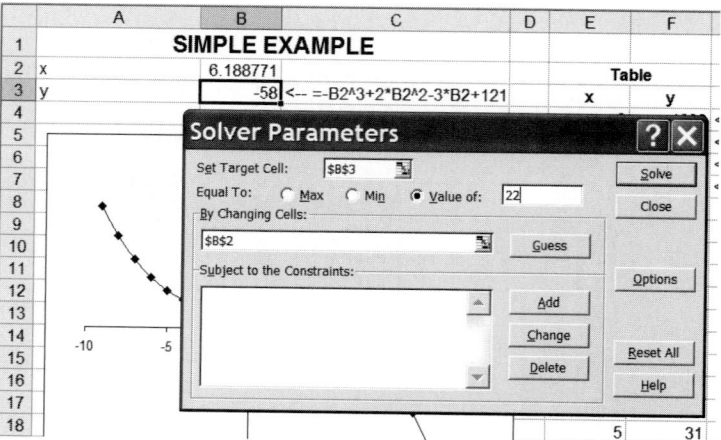

This "memory" of **Solver** carries over even if you save the file and reopen it later.

Solver Is More Flexible

Again we use an algebra example, but this time we use the function $y = x^2 - 7x - 14$. This function is a simple parabola:

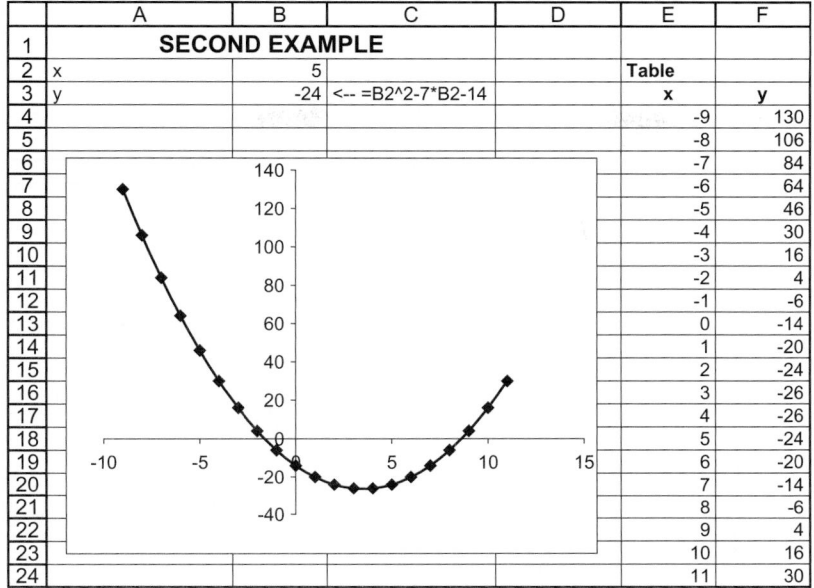

	A	B	C	D	E	F
1	**SECOND EXAMPLE**					
2	x	5			**Table**	
3	y	-24	<-- =B2^2-7*B2-14		**x**	**y**
4					-9	130
5					-8	106
6					-7	84
7					-6	64
8					-5	46
9					-4	30
10					-3	16
11					-2	4
12					-1	-6
13					0	-14
14					1	-20
15					2	-24
16					3	-26
17					4	-26
18					5	-24
19					6	-20
20					7	-14
21					8	-6
22					9	4
23					10	16
24					11	30

Now suppose we want to find x such that $y = 21$. As you can see above, there are two such x's: One is between –3 and –4, and the other is between 10 and 11. If you use **Goal Seek**, you cannot specify which x to find.

With **Solver**, however, you can specify *constraints* on the variables:

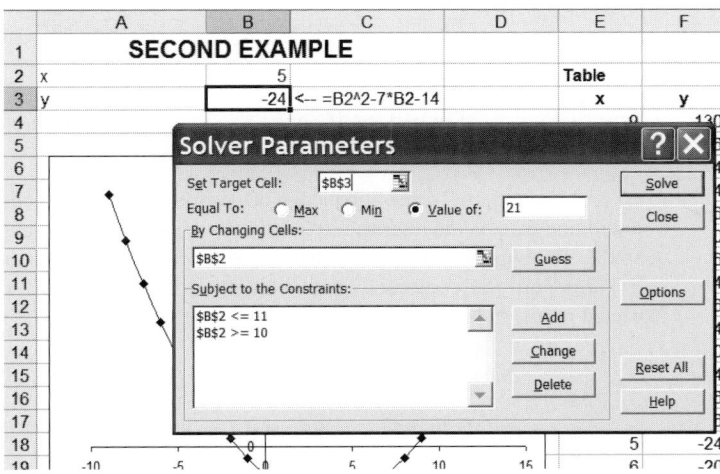

Here we've used **Add** to enter two constraints on x. Pressing **Solve** gives the correct answer:

	A	B	C
1	**SECOND EXAMPLE**		
2	x	10.37386	
3	y	21	<-- =B2^2-7*B2-14

EXERCISES

1. Consider the present value calculation of a financial asset whose cash flows are given below. Use **Goal Seek** to find the discount rate such that the present value of the asset's cash flows is $800.

	A	B	C
1	Discount rate	12.00%	
2			
3	**Year**	**Cash flow**	
4	1	100	
5	2	200	
6	3	300	
7	4	400	
8	5	500	
9			
10	Present value	$1,000.18	<-- =NPV(B1,B4:B8)

2. A financial asset costs $500 and produces cash flows in years 1, 2, . . . , 5. The year-1 cash flow is $100 and subsequent cash flows grow at a rate of 5%. As you can see below, the asset's internal rate of return (IRR) is 3.32%.

   Use **Solver** to find a growth rate such that the IRR is 10%.

	A	B	C
1	Year 1 cash flow	100.00	
2	Cash flow growth rate	5.00%	
3			
4	**Year**	**Cash flow**	
5	0	-500.00	
6	1	100.00	<-- =B1
7	2	105.00	<-- =B6*(1+$B$2)
8	3	110.25	<-- =B7*(1+$B$2)
9	4	115.76	
10	5	121.55	
11			
12	Internal rate of return	3.32%	<-- =IRR(B5:B10)

3. (This problem requires some knowledge of portfolio calculations covered in Chapter 12.) Below you will find data on the returns, $E(r_A)$ and $E(r_B)$, and standard deviations, σ_A and σ_B, of stocks A and B. The number ρ is the correlation coefficient of the returns of A and B.

   For a portfolio composed of proportion x_A of stock A and x_B of stock B, the portfolio expected return and standard deviation are given by

$$\text{expected portfolio return}, E(r_P) = x_A E(r_A) + x_B E(r_B)$$

$$\text{portfolio standard deviation}, \sigma_P = \sqrt{x_A^2 \sigma_A^2 + x_B^2 \sigma_B^2 + 2 x_A x_B \rho \sigma_A \sigma_B}$$

Because the portfolio proportions have to add to 100%, $x_B = 1 - x_B$.

   A sample calculation of a portfolio expected return and standard deviation is given in cells B15 and B16.

	A	B	C
1	**Stock A**		
2	Expected return, $E(r_A)$	12%	
3	Return standard deviation, σ_A	15%	
4			
5	**Stock B**		
6	Expected return, $E(r_B)$	22%	
7	Return standard deviation, σ_B	25%	
8			
9	Correlation of A and B returns, ρ	0.50	
10			
11	**Portfolio**		
12	Proportion of A, x_A	25%	
13	Proportion of B, x_B	75%	<-- =1-B12
14			
15	Portfolio expected return, $E(r_P)$	19.500%	<-- =B12*B2+B13*B6
16	Portfolio standard deviation, σ_P	20.88%	<-- =SQRT(B12^2*B3^2+B13^2*B7^2+2*B12*B13*B9*B3*B7)

(a) Use **Solver** to compute the proportions x_A and x_B for a portfolio that has the minimum standard deviation σ_P.

(b) Use **Solver** and a constraint to compute the proportions x_A and x_B for a portfolio that has the minimum standard deviation σ_P and a return of at least 18%.

4. (a) Graph the function $y = -2x^2 - 2x + 14$ for the $x = -4.0, -3.75, -3.50, \ldots, 3.0$. What are the approximate values of x for which $y = 0$?

(b) Using **Goal Seek** on the function, find x such that $y = 0$. Which of the two values of x does **Goal Seek** find?

(c) Use **Solver** with an appropriate constraint to find the second value of x for which the function $y = -2x^2 - 2x + 14$ has value 0.

DATA MANIPULATION IN EXCEL

OVERVIEW

When you use Excel to do finance, you'll often need to manipulate large amounts of data. For example, you've got a spreadsheet with lots of stock prices. When were the prices highest? Lowest? To do this, you'll have to sort the data using an Excel function. Another, more complicated question, concerns the relations between data sets. Suppose you have stock return data for two stocks, ABC Corp. and XYZ Corp. What's the average return on XYZ Corp. stock on days when ABC Corp.'s returns were over 3%?

These questions, and many more, can be answered using the data manipulation functions offered by Excel and discussed in this chapter. This chapter covers several sorts of data manipulation in Excel:

- Data sorts—rearranging the data (like alphabetizing, but more sophisticated)
- Data filter, which allows us to ask complicated questions of data
- Conditional formatting—painting or indicating cells according to criteria
- The **Dfunctions**—not simple, but very useful functions like **Dsum** and **Daverage**
- Importing data from text files

33.1 Example

Consider the following spreadsheet, which gives stock price data for ten stocks and the S&P 500 for the years 1992–2002:

	A	B	C	D	E	F	G	H	I	J	K	L
1	Price data											
2	Date	AMR	Boeing	Citigroup	Duke	Federated	Gillette	GM	MSFT	TXN	Exxon	S&P500
3	2-Jan-02	24.94	40.78	47.40	34.59	41.62	33.30	50.62	63.71	31.21	38.82	1130.20
4	2-Jan-01	39.09	57.46	55.12	35.31	44.56	30.93	51.20	61.06	43.68	40.93	1366.01
5	3-Jan-00	53.78	43.18	41.65	26.94	41.63	36.22	74.60	97.88	53.64	39.46	1394.46
6	4-Jan-99	58.72	33.34	27.08	27.73	41.81	56.32	66.94	87.50	24.55	33.09	1279.64
7	2-Jan-98	63.21	45.78	23.86	23.40	42.31	47.41	41.96	37.30	13.50	27.93	980.28
8	2-Jan-97	40.23	51.49	16.81	19.34	32.88	39.71	39.00	25.50	9.61	24.40	786.16
9	2-Jan-96	37.98	37.25	10.55	19.68	27.00	25.81	33.76	11.56	5.62	18.90	636.02
10	3-Jan-95	28.05	21.39	5.92	15.21	18.88	18.50	24.32	7.42	4.14	14.72	470.42
11	3-Jan-94	35.85	20.79	6.76	15.05	21.88	14.62	37.71	5.32	4.14	15.66	481.61
12	4-Jan-93	31.48	16.94	4.26	12.57	20.38	12.76	22.81	5.41	3.16	14.39	438.78
13	2-Jan-92	35.35	24.45	3.33	10.64	15.50	12.30	18.82	5.01	2.05	13.72	408.78

We want to sort the data so that the earlier dates come first. To do this, we put the cursor on any cell in the data to be sorted. We then use the command **Data|Sort**. Excel figures out what we want, marks the range to be sorted, and asks us which column should serve as a sort range, and in which order the rows should be sorted:

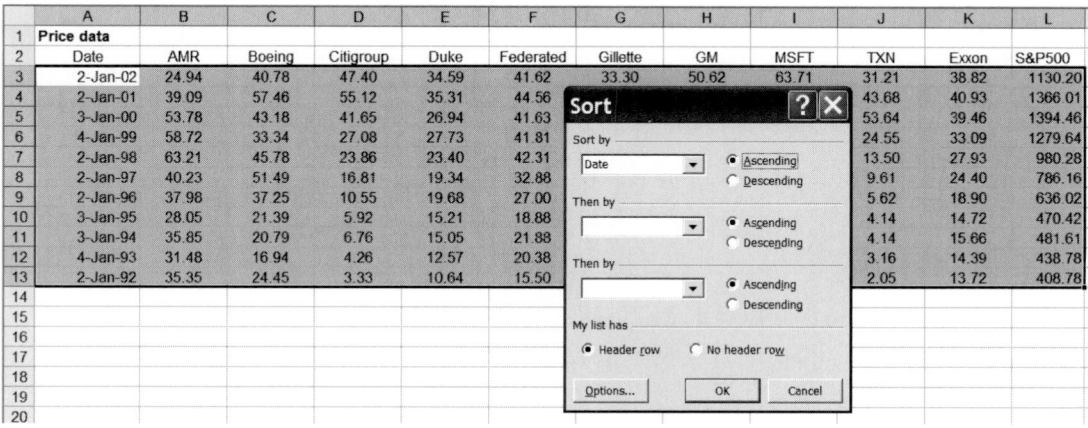

We want the data sorted in **Ascending** order. Marking the appropriate button and pressing **OK** sorts the data:

	A	B	C	D	E	F	G	H	I	J	K	L
1	Price data											
2	Date	AMR	Boeing	Citigroup	Duke	Federated	Gillette	GM	MSFT	TXN	Exxon	S&P500
3	2-Jan-92	35.35	24.45	3.33	10.64	15.50	12.30	18.82	5.01	2.05	13.72	408.78
4	4-Jan-93	31.48	16.94	4.26	12.57	20.38	12.76	22.81	5.41	3.16	14.39	438.78
5	3-Jan-94	35.85	20.79	6.76	15.05	21.88	14.62	37.71	5.32	4.14	15.66	481.61
6	3-Jan-95	28.05	21.39	5.92	15.21	18.88	18.50	24.32	7.42	4.14	14.72	470.42
7	2-Jan-96	37.98	37.25	10.55	19.68	27.00	25.81	33.76	11.56	5.62	18.90	636.02
8	2-Jan-97	40.23	51.49	16.81	19.34	32.88	39.71	39.00	25.50	9.61	24.40	786.16
9	2-Jan-98	63.21	45.78	23.86	23.40	42.31	47.41	41.96	37.30	13.50	27.93	980.28
10	4-Jan-99	58.72	33.34	27.08	27.73	41.81	56.32	66.94	87.50	24.55	33.09	1279.64
11	3-Jan-00	53.78	43.18	41.65	26.94	41.63	36.22	74.60	97.88	53.64	39.46	1394.46
12	2-Jan-01	39.09	57.46	55.12	35.31	44.56	30.93	51.20	61.06	43.68	40.93	1366.01
13	2-Jan-02	24.94	40.78	47.40	34.59	41.62	33.30	50.62	63.71	31.21	38.82	1130.20

Now suppose we compute the annual returns for each of the stocks. The spreadsheet fragment below shows a start on this:

	A	B	C	D	E	F	G	H	I	J	K	L
1	Price data											
2	Date	AMR	Boeing	Citigroup	Duke	Federated	Gillette	GM	MSFT	TXN	Exxon	S&P500
3	2-Jan-92	35.35	24.45	3.33	10.64	15.50	12.30	18.82	5.01	2.05	13.72	408.78
4	4-Jan-93	31.48	16.94	4.26	12.57	20.38	12.76	22.81	5.41	3.16	14.39	438.78
5	3-Jan-94	35.85	20.79	6.76	15.05	21.88	14.62	37.71	5.32	4.14	15.66	481.61
6	3-Jan-95	28.05	21.39	5.92	15.21	18.88	18.50	24.32	7.42	4.14	14.72	470.42
7	2-Jan-96	37.98	37.25	10.55	19.68	27.00	25.81	33.76	11.56	5.62	18.90	636.02
8	2-Jan-97	40.23	51.49	16.81	19.34	32.88	39.71	39.00	25.50	9.61	24.40	786.16
9	2-Jan-98	63.21	45.78	23.86	23.40	42.31	47.41	41.96	37.30	13.50	27.93	980.28
10	4-Jan-99	58.72	33.34	27.08	27.73	41.81	56.32	66.94	87.50	24.55	33.09	1279.64
11	3-Jan-00	53.78	43.18	41.65	26.94	41.63	36.22	74.60	97.88	53.64	39.46	1394.46
12	2-Jan-01	39.09	57.46	55.12	35.31	44.56	30.93	51.20	61.06	43.68	40.93	1366.01
13	2-Jan-02	24.94	40.78	47.40	34.59	41.62	33.30	50.62	63.71	31.21	38.82	1130.20
14												
15	Returns											
16	Date	AMR	Boeing	Citigroup	Duke	Federated	Gillette	GM	MSFT	TXN	Exxon	S&P500
17	4-Jan-93	-10.95%	<-- =B4/B3-1									
18	3-Jan-94	13.88%	<-- =B5/B4-1									
19	3-Jan-95											
20	2-Jan-96											
21	2-Jan-97											
22	2-Jan-98											
23	4-Jan-99											
24	3-Jan-00											
25	2-Jan-01											
26	2-Jan-02											

If you copy the formulas in cells B17 and B18, you will compute all the returns:

	A	B	C	D	E	F	G	H	I	J	K	L
15	Returns											
16	Date	AMR	Boeing	Citigroup	Duke	Federated	Gillette	GM	MSFT	TXN	Exxon	S&P500
17	4-Jan-93	-10.95%	-30.72%	27.93%	18.14%	31.48%	3.74%	21.20%	7.98%	54.15%	4.88%	7.34%
18	3-Jan-94	13.88%	22.73%	58.69%	19.73%	7.36%	14.58%	65.32%	-1.66%	31.01%	8.83%	9.76%
19	3-Jan-95	-21.76%	2.89%	-12.43%	1.06%	-13.71%	26.54%	-35.51%	39.47%	0.00%	-6.00%	-2.32%
20	2-Jan-96	35.40%	74.15%	78.21%	29.39%	43.01%	39.51%	38.82%	55.80%	35.75%	28.40%	35.20%
21	2-Jan-97	5.92%	38.23%	59.34%	-1.73%	21.78%	53.86%	15.52%	120.59%	71.00%	29.10%	23.61%
22	2-Jan-98	57.12%	-11.09%	41.94%	20.99%	28.68%	19.39%	7.59%	46.27%	40.48%	14.47%	24.69%
23	4-Jan-99	-7.10%	-27.17%	13.50%	18.50%	-1.18%	18.79%	59.53%	134.58%	81.85%	18.47%	30.54%
24	3-Jan-00	-8.41%	29.51%	53.80%	-2.85%	-0.43%	-35.69%	11.44%	11.86%	118.49%	19.25%	8.97%
25	2-Jan-01	-27.31%	33.07%	32.34%	31.07%	7.04%	-14.61%	-31.37%	-37.62%	-18.57%	3.73%	-2.04%
26	2-Jan-02	-36.20%	-29.03%	-14.01%	-2.04%	-6.60%	7.66%	-1.13%	4.34%	-28.55%	-5.16%	-17.26%

We use this return data to show:

- Data filtering
- Conditional formatting

Filtering the Data

Put the cursor anywhere in the return data and go to **Data|Filter|Autofilter**:

	A	B	C	D	E	F	G	H	I	J	K	L
1	Price data											
2	Date ▼	AMR ▼	Boeing ▼	Citigrou ▼	Duke ▼	Federate ▼	Gillette ▼	GM ▼	MSFT ▼	TXN ▼	Exxon ▼	S&P50(▼
3	2-Jan-02	24.94	40.78	47.40	34.59	41.62	33.30	50.62	63.71	31.21	38.82	1130.20
4	2-Jan-01	39.09	57.46	55.12	35.31	44.56	30.93	51.20	61.06	43.68	40.93	1366.01
5	3-Jan-00	53.78	43.18	41.65	26.94	41.63	36.22	74.60	97.88	53.64	39.46	1394.46
6	4-Jan-99	58.72	33.34	27.08	27.73	41.81	56.32	66.94	87.50	24.55	33.09	1279.64
7	2-Jan-98	63.21	45.78	23.86	23.40	42.31	47.41	41.96	37.30	13.50	27.93	980.28
8	2-Jan-97	40.23	51.49	16.81	19.34	32.88	39.71	39.00	25.50	9.61	24.40	786.16
9	2-Jan-96	37.98	37.25	10.55	19.68	27.00	25.81	33.76	11.56	5.62	18.90	636.02
10	3-Jan-95	28.05	21.39	5.92	15.21	18.88	18.50	24.32	7.42	4.14	14.72	470.42
11	3-Jan-94	35.85	20.79	6.76	15.05	21.88	14.62	37.71	5.32	4.14	15.66	481.61
12	4-Jan-93	31.48	16.94	4.26	12.57	20.38	12.76	22.81	5.41	3.16	14.39	438.78
13	2-Jan-92	35.35	24.45	3.33	10.64	15.50	12.30	18.82	5.01	2.05	13.72	408.78

The down arrows on the columns allow us to ask sophisticated data questions. For example, suppose we want to know what the returns of all stocks were in the years where Citigroup had a return of more than 20%. To do this, we click the down arrow next to Citigroup and specify a **Custom** filter. Then put in the appropriate query:

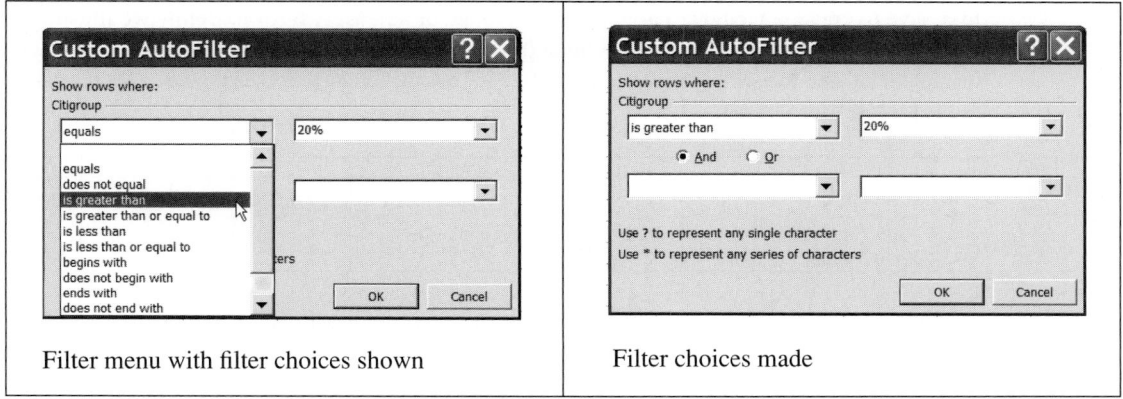

| Filter menu with filter choices shown | Filter choices made |

Here's what the data look like:

Returns											
Date	AMR	Boeing	Citigrou	Duke	Federate	Gillette	GM	MSFT	TXN	Exxon	S&P50(
4-Jan-93	-10.95%	-30.72%	27.93%	18.14%	31.48%	3.74%	21.20%	7.98%	54.15%	4.88%	7.34%
3-Jan-94	13.88%	22.73%	58.69%	19.73%	7.36%	14.58%	65.32%	-1.66%	31.01%	8.83%	9.76%
2-Jan-96	35.40%	74.15%	78.21%	29.39%	43.01%	39.51%	38.82%	55.80%	35.75%	28.40%	35.20%
2-Jan-97	5.92%	38.23%	59.34%	-1.73%	21.78%	53.86%	15.52%	120.59%	71.00%	29.10%	23.61%
2-Jan-98	57.12%	-11.09%	41.94%	20.99%	28.68%	19.39%	7.59%	46.27%	40.48%	14.47%	24.69%
3-Jan-00	-8.41%	29.51%	53.80%	-2.85%	-0.43%	-35.69%	11.44%	11.86%	118.49%	19.25%	8.97%
2-Jan-01	-27.31%	33.07%	32.34%	31.07%	7.04%	-14.61%	-31.37%	-37.62%	-18.57%	3.73%	-2.04%

You can do more complex filters by choosing multiple criteria. Here are all the rows for which Citigroup > 20% and Duke ≥ 18.14% (we leave you to figure this one out for yourself).

Returns											
Date	AMR	Boeing	Citigrou	Duke	Federate	Gillette	GM	MSFT	TXN	Exxon	S&P50(
3-Jan-94	13.88%	22.73%	58.69%	19.73%	7.36%	14.58%	65.32%	-1.66%	31.01%	8.83%	9.76%
2-Jan-96	35.40%	74.15%	78.21%	29.39%	43.01%	39.51%	38.82%	55.80%	35.75%	28.40%	35.20%
2-Jan-98	57.12%	-11.09%	41.94%	20.99%	28.68%	19.39%	7.59%	46.27%	40.48%	14.47%	24.69%
2-Jan-01	-27.31%	33.07%	32.34%	31.07%	7.04%	-14.61%	-31.37%	-37.62%	-18.57%	3.73%	-2.04%

Canceling a Filter

At some point you will want to get rid of all those annoying down arrows next to each column. If this is the case, put your cursor in the data and unclick **AutoFilter**:

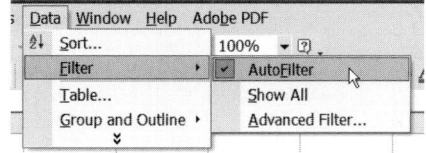

There's also a **ShowAll** option on the same menu—this doesn't cancel the filter arrows, but it does show you all the data.

Copying Filtered Data Elsewhere

Suppose you want to copy the filtered data to some other place on the spreadsheet. To do this, we first have to create a **Criteria range**. This is a range of at least two rows. Below we illustrate a two-row criteria range; the first row includes some or all of the column headings from our original data, and the second row contains ">20%" below Citicorp (this is the question we asked in the **Data|Filter** above).

	A	B	C	D	E	F	G	H	I	J	K	L
28	**Criteria range**											
29	Date	AMR	Boeing	Citigroup	Duke	Federated	Gillette	GM	MSFT	TXN	Exxon	S&P500
30				>20%								
31	**Output range**											
32	Date	Citigroup	Federated	GM	MSFT	S&P500						

Below the criteria range is our **Output range**, the place to which we want to copy the data. The output range includes some or all of the data headings. In our example it includes only five of the headings.

Notice that we've clicked the box **Copy to another location**, and that in the **Copy to** box we've indicated the headings below which the data will be copied.

Now click **OK**:

	A	B	C	D	E	F
31	**Output range**					
32	Date	Citigroup	Federated	GM	MSFT	S&P500
33	4-Jan-93	27.93%	31.48%	21.20%	7.98%	7.34%
34	3-Jan-94	58.69%	7.36%	65.32%	-1.66%	9.76%
35	2-Jan-96	78.21%	43.01%	38.82%	55.80%	35.20%
36	2-Jan-97	59.34%	21.78%	15.52%	120.59%	23.61%
37	2-Jan-98	41.94%	28.68%	7.59%	46.27%	24.69%
38	3-Jan-00	53.80%	-0.43%	11.44%	11.86%	8.97%
39	2-Jan-01	32.34%	7.04%	-31.37%	-37.62%	-2.04%

33.2 Conditional Formatting

We go back to the return data. We'd like to mark those data points between -10% and $+15\%$. We use the command **Format|Conditional Formatting** and indicate the appropriate values in the boxes:

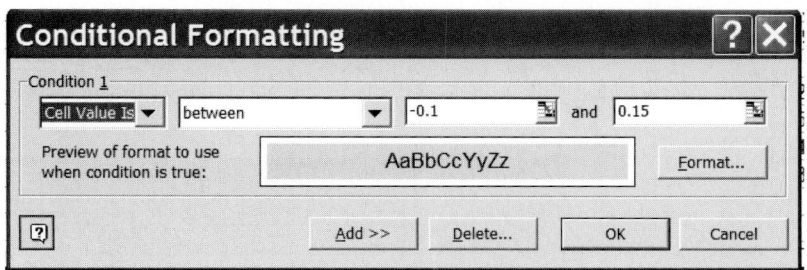

The **Format|Conditional Formatting** command with values filled in. The next box shows the **Format** command used to paint the cells.

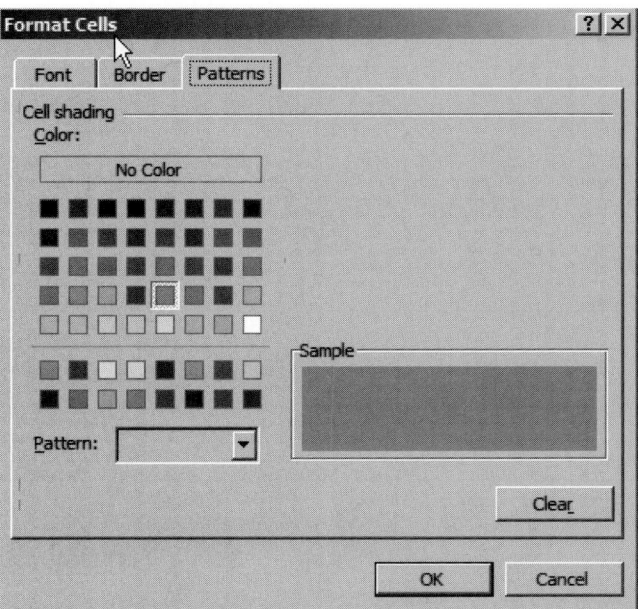

Notice that we could have chosen a **Border** or a **Font** for the cells that meet the criteria.

Here's the output:

	A	B	C	D	E	F	G	H	I	J	K	L
15	Returns											
16	Date	AMR	Boeing	Citigroup	Duke	Federated	Gillette	GM	Msft	TXN	Exxon	S&P500
17	4-Jan-93	-10.95%	-30.72%	27.93%	18.14%	31.48%	3.74%	21.20%	7.98%	54.15%	4.88%	7.34%
18	3-Jan-94	13.88%	22.73%	58.69%	19.73%	7.36%	14.58%	65.32%	-1.66%	31.01%	8.83%	9.76%
19	3-Jan-95	-21.76%	2.89%	-12.43%	1.06%	-13.71%	26.54%	-35.51%	39.47%	0.00%	-6.00%	-2.32%
20	2-Jan-96	35.40%	74.15%	78.21%	29.39%	43.01%	39.51%	38.82%	55.80%	35.75%	28.40%	35.20%
21	2-Jan-97	5.92%	38.23%	59.34%	-1.73%	21.78%	53.86%	15.52%	120.59%	71.00%	29.10%	23.61%
22	2-Jan-98	57.12%	-11.09%	41.94%	20.99%	28.68%	19.39%	7.59%	46.27%	40.48%	14.47%	24.69%
23	4-Jan-99	-7.10%	-27.17%	13.50%	18.50%	-1.18%	18.79%	59.53%	134.58%	81.85%	18.47%	30.54%
24	3-Jan-00	-8.41%	29.51%	53.80%	-2.85%	-0.43%	-35.69%	11.44%	11.86%	118.49%	19.25%	8.97%
25	2-Jan-01	-27.31%	33.07%	32.34%	31.07%	7.04%	-14.61%	-31.37%	-37.62%	-18.57%	3.73%	-2.04%
26	2-Jan-02	-36.20%	-29.03%	-14.01%	-2.04%	-6.60%	7.66%	-1.13%	4.34%	-28.55%	-5.16%	-17.26%

We can make the criteria flexible by indicating them in separate cells of the spreadsheet:

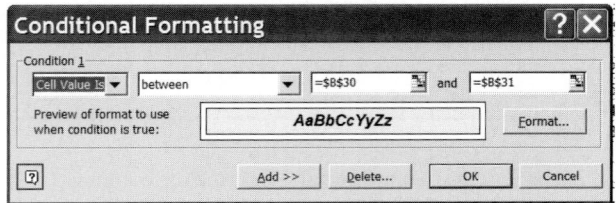

Here's the output. We leave it to you to play with the bounds in cells B30 and B31—you'll see that changing these bounds alters the cells selected.

	A	B	C	D	E	F	G	H	I	J	K	L
15	Returns											
16	Date	AMR	Boeing	Citigroup	Duke	Federated	Gillette	GM	MSFT	TXN	Exxon	S&P500
17	4-Jan-93	-10.95%	-30.72%	27.93%	18.14%	31.48%	3.74%	21.20%	7.98%	54.15%	4.88%	7.34%
18	3-Jan-94	13.88%	22.73%	58.69%	19.73%	7.36%	14.58%	65.32%	-1.66%	31.01%	8.83%	9.76%
19	3-Jan-95	-21.76%	2.89%	-12.43%	1.06%	-13.71%	26.54%	-35.51%	39.47%	0.00%	-6.00%	-2.32%
20	2-Jan-96	35.40%	74.15%	78.21%	29.39%	43.01%	39.51%	38.82%	55.80%	35.75%	28.40%	35.20%
21	2-Jan-97	5.92%	38.23%	59.34%	-1.73%	21.78%	53.86%	15.52%	120.59%	71.00%	29.10%	23.61%
22	2-Jan-98	57.12%	-11.09%	41.94%	20.99%	28.68%	19.39%	7.59%	46.27%	40.48%	14.47%	24.69%
23	4-Jan-99	-7.10%	-27.17%	13.50%	18.50%	-1.18%	18.79%	59.53%	134.58%	81.85%	18.47%	30.54%
24	3-Jan-00	-8.41%	29.51%	53.80%	-2.85%	-0.43%	-35.69%	11.44%	11.86%	118.49%	19.25%	8.97%
25	2-Jan-01	-27.31%	33.07%	32.34%	31.07%	7.04%	-14.61%	-31.37%	-37.62%	-18.57%	3.73%	-2.04%
26	2-Jan-02	-36.20%	-29.03%	-14.01%	-2.04%	-6.60%	7.66%	-1.13%	4.34%	-28.55%	-5.16%	-17.26%

When we change the numbers in B30 and B31, the results automatically change. For example, here are all the returns between −3% and 6%:

	A	B	C	D	E	F	G	H	I	J	K	L
15	Returns											
16	Date	AMR	Boeing	Citigroup	Duke	Federated	Gillette	GM	MSFT	TXN	Exxon	S&P500
17	4-Jan-93	-10.95%	-30.72%	27.93%	18.14%	31.48%	3.74%	21.20%	7.98%	54.15%	4.88%	7.34%
18	3-Jan-94	13.88%	22.73%	58.69%	19.73%	7.36%	14.58%	65.32%	-1.66%	31.01%	8.83%	9.76%
19	3-Jan-95	-21.76%	2.89%	-12.43%	1.06%	-13.71%	26.54%	-35.51%	39.47%	0.00%	-6.00%	-2.32%
20	2-Jan-96	35.40%	74.15%	78.21%	29.39%	43.01%	39.51%	38.82%	55.80%	35.75%	28.40%	35.20%
21	2-Jan-97	5.92%	38.23%	59.34%	-1.73%	21.78%	53.86%	15.52%	120.59%	71.00%	29.10%	23.61%
22	2-Jan-98	57.12%	-11.09%	41.94%	20.99%	28.68%	19.39%	7.59%	46.27%	40.48%	14.47%	24.69%
23	4-Jan-99	-7.10%	-27.17%	13.50%	18.50%	-1.18%	18.79%	59.53%	134.58%	81.85%	18.47%	30.54%
24	3-Jan-00	-8.41%	29.51%	53.80%	-2.85%	-0.43%	-35.69%	11.44%	11.86%	118.49%	19.25%	8.97%
25	2-Jan-01	-27.31%	33.07%	32.34%	31.07%	7.04%	-14.61%	-31.37%	-37.62%	-18.57%	3.73%	-2.04%
26	2-Jan-02	-36.20%	-29.03%	-14.01%	-2.04%	-6.60%	7.66%	-1.13%	4.34%	-28.55%	-5.16%	-17.26%

(Note that we've added more conditional formatting—the appropriate cells are now also italicized and boldfaced.)

33.3 Dsum, Daverage, and Similar Functions

Excel has functions that manipulate data subject to certain criteria. Here's an example. Suppose we want to know the average of all the Boeing returns for years in which Citigroup returned more than 20% and Duke returned less than 10%.[1]

To do this, we create a separate **Criteria range**—several rows of the spreadsheet in which the first row repeats the column headings of the data (below the criteria range is in cells A15:L16:

	A	B	C	D	E	F	G	H	I	J	K	L
1			**USING THE FUNCTIONS DSUM, DAVERAGE, ...**									
2	Date	AMR	Boeing	Citigroup	Duke	Federated	Gillette	GM	MSFT	TXN	Exxon	S&P500
3	4-Jan-93	-10.95%	-30.72%	27.93%	18.14%	31.48%	3.74%	21.20%	7.98%	54.15%	4.88%	7.34%
4	3-Jan-94	13.88%	22.73%	58.69%	19.73%	7.36%	14.58%	65.32%	-1.66%	31.01%	8.83%	9.76%
5	3-Jan-95	-21.76%	2.89%	-12.43%	1.06%	-13.71%	26.54%	-35.51%	39.47%	0.00%	-6.00%	-2.32%
6	2-Jan-96	35.40%	74.15%	78.21%	29.39%	43.01%	39.51%	38.82%	55.80%	35.75%	28.40%	35.20%
7	2-Jan-97	5.92%	38.23%	59.34%	-1.73%	21.78%	53.86%	15.52%	120.59%	71.00%	29.10%	23.61%
8	2-Jan-98	57.12%	-11.09%	41.94%	20.99%	28.68%	19.39%	7.59%	46.27%	40.48%	14.47%	24.69%
9	4-Jan-99	-7.10%	-27.17%	13.50%	18.50%	-1.18%	18.79%	59.53%	134.58%	81.85%	18.47%	30.54%
10	3-Jan-00	-8.41%	29.51%	53.80%	-2.85%	-0.43%	-35.69%	11.44%	11.86%	118.49%	19.25%	8.97%
11	2-Jan-01	-27.31%	33.07%	32.34%	31.07%	7.04%	-14.61%	-31.37%	-37.62%	-18.57%	3.73%	-2.04%
12	2-Jan-02	-36.20%	-29.03%	-14.01%	-2.04%	-6.60%	7.66%	-1.13%	4.34%	-28.55%	-5.16%	-17.26%
13												
14	**Criteria range**											
15	Date	AMR	Boeing	Citigroup	Duke	Federated	Gillette	GM	MSFT	TXN	Exxon	S&P500
16				>20%	<10%							
17												
18			33.871%	<-- =DAVERAGE(A2:L12,3,A15:L16)				13.48%	<-- =DAVERAGE(A2:L12,8,A15:L16)			
19			67.74%	<-- =DSUM(A2:L12,3,A15:L16)				26.96%	<-- =DSUM(A2:L12,8,A15:L16)			
20			2	<-- =DCOUNT(A2:L12,3,A15:L16)				2	<-- =DCOUNT(A2:L12,8,A15:L16)			
21			33.87%	<-- =DAVERAGE(A2:L12,3,A15:L16)				1.78%	<-- =DPRODUCT(A2:L12,8,A15:L16)			

The second row of the criteria range—in this case, row 16—lists the criteria. The functions in cells B19 to B24 show some uses of the **Dfunctions**. For example:

* The average of all Boeing returns for years in which Citigroup > 20% and Duke < 10% is 33.871% (cell C18). Note the way we write the **Daverage** function:

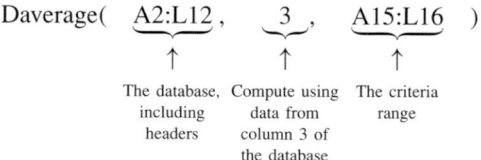

Daverage(A2:L12 , 3 , A15:L16)

The database, including headers | Compute using data from column 3 of the database | The criteria range

* The sum of GM returns that match the criteria (cell H19) is 26.96%. We write the function **=Dsum(A2:L12,8,A15:L16)**; A2:L12 is the database, GM is the eighth column of this database, and A15:L16 is the criteria range.

Other functions illustrated above are **Dproduct** (the product of all cells that match the criteria) and **Dcount** (the number of cells that match the criteria).

---

[1]Heaven only knows why we want to ask this question! But then spreadsheet users are a weird bunch of people. . . .

Matching Either–Or Criteria

In the example above, we manipulated Boeing returns for years in which *both* Citigroup > 20% *and* Duke < 10%. What if we want years in which *either* Citigroup > 20% *or* Duke < 10%? In this case we add an extra row to the criteria range and put each criterion in a separate row:

	A	B	C	D	E	F	G	H	I	J	K	L
23	Criteria range											
24	Date	AMR	Boeing	Citigroup	Duke	Federated	Gillette	GM	MSFT	TXN	Exxon	S&P500
25				>20%								
26					<10%							
27												
28			14.415%	<-- =DAVERAGE(A2:L12,3,A24:L26)								
29			129.74%	<-- =DSUM(A2:L12,3,A24:L26)								
30			34.44%	<-- =DSTDEV(A2:L12,3,A24:L26)								
31			9	<-- =DCOUNT(A2:L12,3,A24:L26)								
32			-0.0002%	<-- =DPRODUCT(A2:L12,3,A24:L26)								
33												
34						Note that the criteria range is A24:L26 (3 rows), and						
35						that each criterion (Citigroup > 20%, Duke < 10%) is						
36						in a separate row.						
37												

The average return on Boeing in periods where either the Citigroup return was > 20% or the Duke return was < 10% is 14.415% (cell C28). There are nine Boeing returns that match one of these two criteria (cell B31).

A List of Data Functions

Here's a list of all of Excel's data functions:

DATABASE AND LIST MANAGEMENT FUNCTIONS

Daverage	Returns the average of selected database entries
Dcount	Counts the cells that contain numbers in a database
Dcounta	Counts nonblank cells in a database
Dget	Extracts from a database a single record that matches the specified criteria
Dmax	Returns the maximum value from selected database entries
Dmin	Returns the minimum value from selected database entries
Dproduct	Multiplies the values in a particular field of records that match the criteria in a database
Dstdev	Estimates the standard deviation based on a sample of selected database entries
Dstdevp	Calculates the standard deviation based on the entire population of selected database entries
Dsum	Adds the numbers in the field column of records in the database that match the criteria
Dvar	Estimates variance based on a sample from selected database entries
Dvarp	Calculates variance based on the entire population of selected database entries

33.4 Importing a Text File into Excel

The disk that accompanies this book includes a small file called Wachovia.txt; this text file has a table from Wachovia's 2000 annual statement:

```
Period-End Loans                                                        Table 5
-
------------------------------------------------------------------------------------
(millions)


<TABLE>
<CAPTION>
                                          2000         1999        1998
                                          1997         1996
                                       ----------   ----------   ----------
                                       ----------   ----------
<S>                                      <C>          <C>          <C>        <C>
<C>
Loan Portfolio
Domestic borrowers:
  Commercial ....................      $ 17,661     $17,043     $14,328
$13,528        $10,341
  Tax-exempt ....................           605         690         973
1,607        2,016
  Direct retail .................         1,338       1,064       1,098
1,250        1,218
  Indirect retail ...............         4,220       3,741       3,240
3,028        3,082
  Credit card ...................         4,494       4,736       6,049
5,919        5,596
  Other revolving credit ........           835         667         537
460          424
  Construction ..................         3,370       2,311       2,044
1,780        1,247
  Commercial mortgages ..........         9,025       7,754       6,988
6,790        5,684
  Residential mortgages .........         9,234       7,757       7,490
8,099        7,132
  Lease financing, net ..........         2,840       2,597       1,879
1,094          831
                                       ---------    -------     -------
                                       -------      -------
      Total .....................        53,622      48,360      44,626
43,555        37,571
Foreign .........................         1,380       1,261       1,093
639          436
                                       ---------    -------     -------
                                       -------      -------
      Total loans ...............      $ 55,002     $49,621     $45,719
$44,194        $38,007
```

We want to import this file into Excel as a spreadsheet. To do this, we open a blank spreadsheet (**Insert|Worksheet** if you're already working in an Excel notebook; otherwise a new notebook entirely). Open this file into Excel by using the command **File|Open**; to see the file you may have to change the file type in the dialog box to "txt." [2]

Having found the text file and opened it, we see the following dialog box:

---

[2]In versions of Excel before Excel 2002, use the command **Data|Get External Data|Import Text File**.

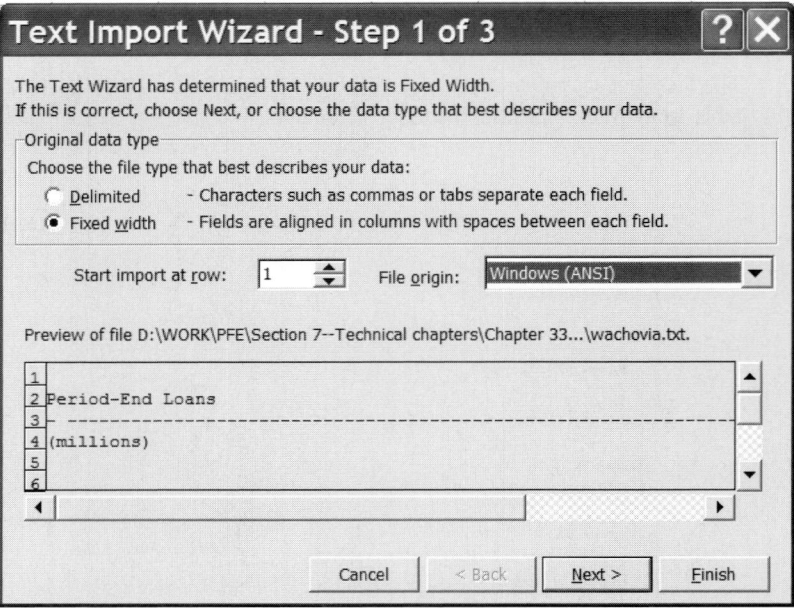

Excel tries to figure out whether the columns in the text file are of fixed width (the case for our file) or are separated by something else (commas, tabs—see example below). Clicking **Next** on the above box, we get to see where Excel will locate the column breaks (note the instructions at the top of this box about how to create, delete, or move column breaks):

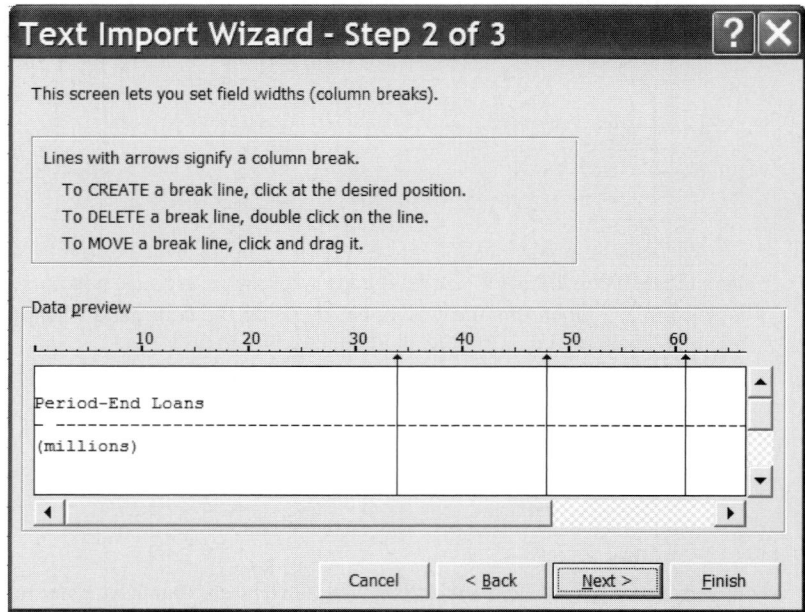

There is yet another page to this wizard, which allows us to choose the format for each column:

In our case, we click on **Finish** and accept the Excel choices. Here's the result, which needs only a bit of editing:

	A	B	C	D	E	F	G
1							
2	Period-End Loans			Table	5		
3	- --------------------------------	-------------	------------	------------	--------		
4	(millions)						
5							
6							
7							
8	<TABLE>						
9	<CAPTION>						
10		2000	1999	1998	1997	1996	
11		------------	----------	----------	----------	----------	
12	<S>	<C>	<C>	<C>	<C>	<C>	
13	Loan Portfolio						
14	Domestic borrowers:						
15	Commercial	$17,661	$17,043	$14,328	$13,528	$10,341	
16	Tax-exempt	605	690	973	1,607	2,016	
17	Direct retail	1,338	1,064	1,098	1,250	1,218	
18	Indirect retail	4,220	3,741	3,240	3,028	3,082	
19	Credit card	4,494	4,736	6,049	5,919	5,596	
20	Other revolving credit	835	667	537	460	424	
21	Construction	3,370	2,311	2,044	1,780	1,247	
22	Commercial mortgages	9,025	7,754	6,988	6,790	5,684	
23	Residential mortgages	9,234	7,757	7,490	8,099	7,132	
24	Lease financing, net	2,840	2,597	1,879	1,094	831	
25		--------	-------	-------	-------	-------	
26	Total	53,622	48,360	44,626	43,555	37,571	
27	Foreign	1,380	1,261	1,093	639	436	
28		--------	-------	-------	-------	-------	
29	Total loans	$55,002	$49,621	$45,719	$44,194	$38,007	
30							

Importing a Text File Separated by Commas, Tabs, or Spaces

Often the columns in text files are separated by commas, tabs, or spaces. On the disk that accompanies this book, there's another file labeled **Ecil.txt**:

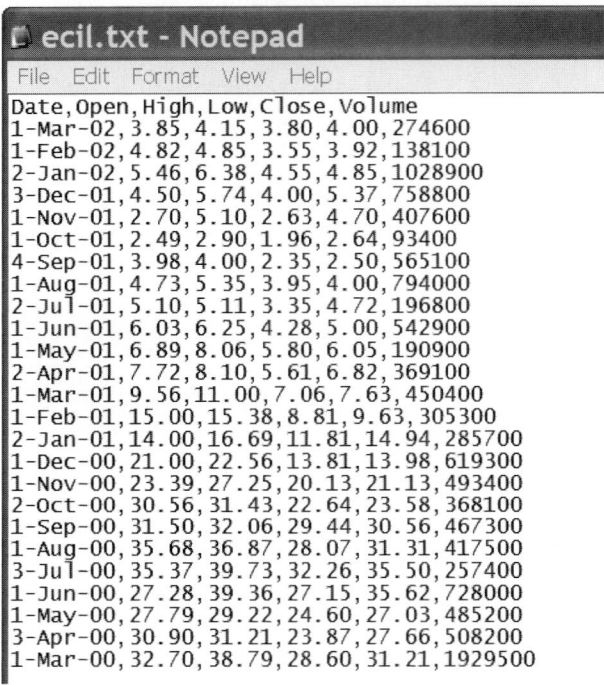

This file has some price and volume data for the stock of ECI, Inc. To import this into Excel, we again open a blank worksheet, and open the text file as we did in the previous example. This time, however, Excel identifies the file as having columns that are *delimited* by some character (which we know to be a comma):

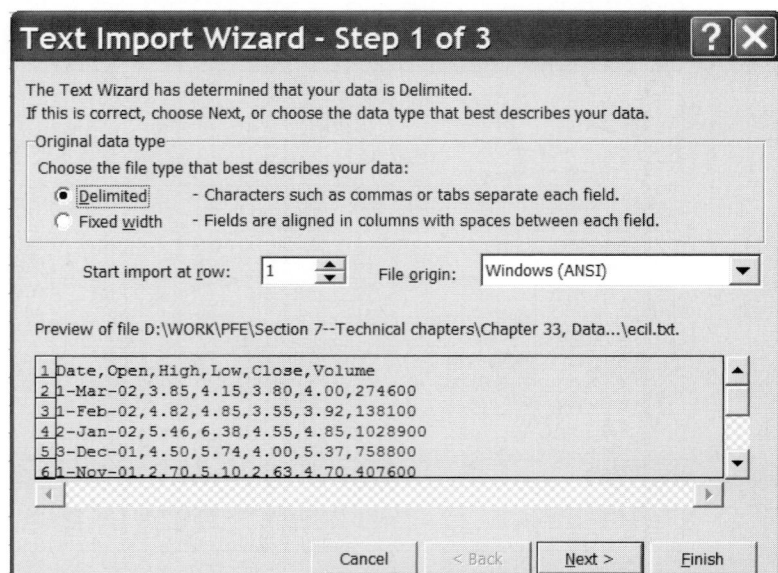

Going on to the next menu, we get a wrong signal—Excel thinks the columns are separated by tabs, whereas they're in fact separated by commas:

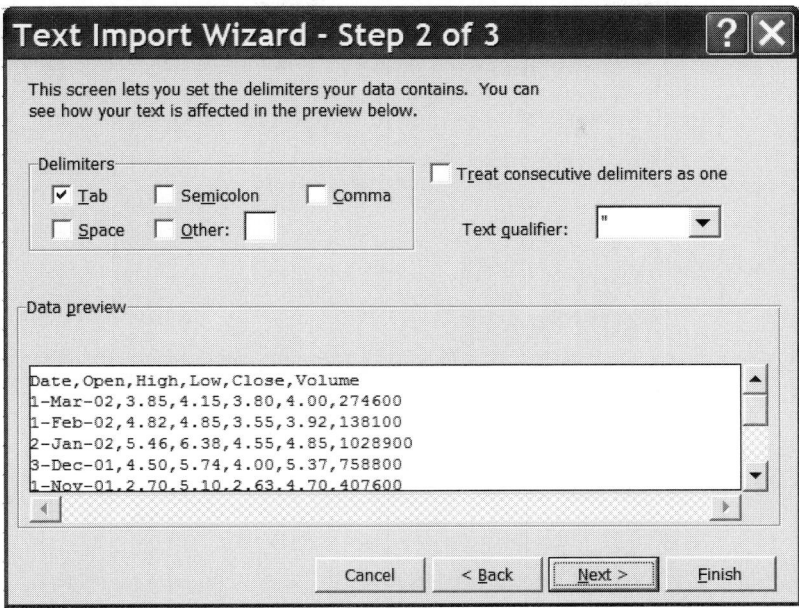

Unclick the **Tab** box and click the **Comma** box and see the column lines in the lower half of the box:

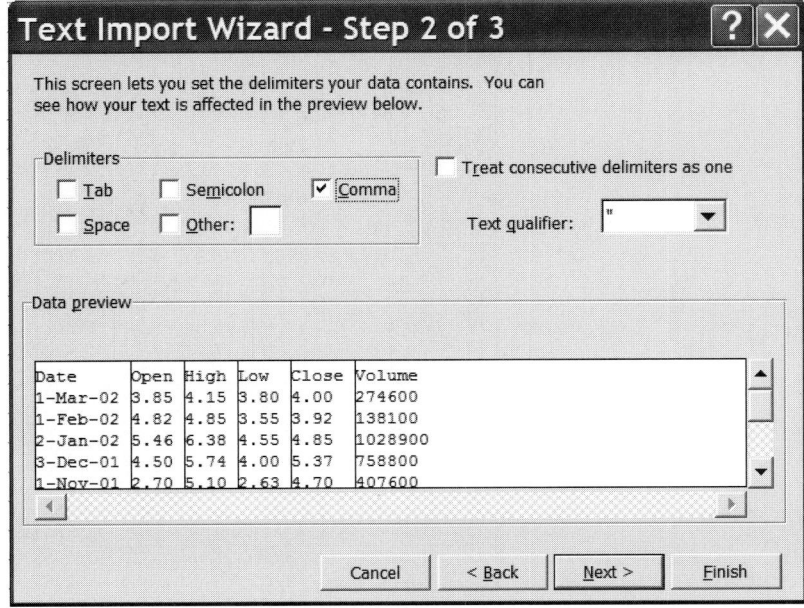

Clicking on **Next** we can make some further adjustments to the data (in this case, we've chosen to identify the first column as **Date**, leaving the other columns as **General**):

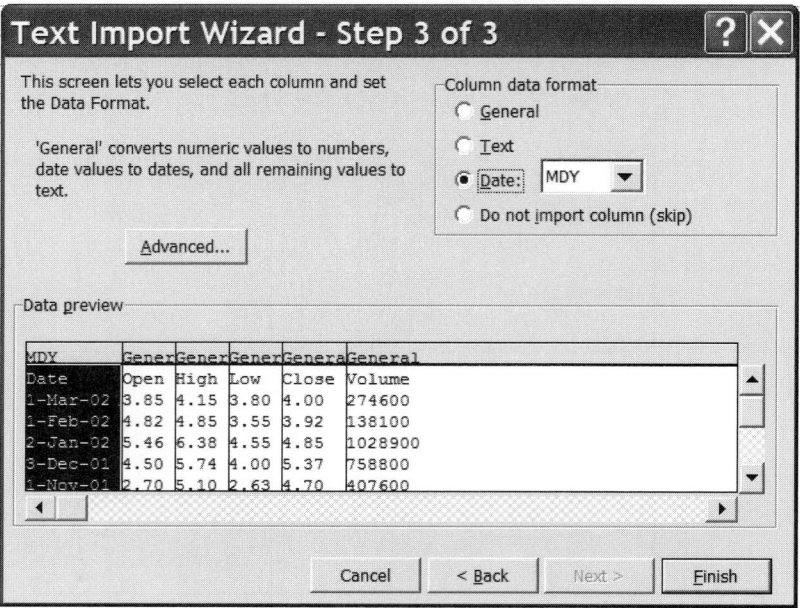

Clicking on **Finish** gives the desired result:

	A	B	C	D	E	F
1	Date	Open	High	Low	Close	Volume
2	1-Mar-02	3.85	4.15	3.8	4	274600
3	1-Feb-02	4.82	4.85	3.55	3.92	138100
4	2-Jan-02	5.46	6.38	4.55	4.85	1028900
5	3-Dec-01	4.5	5.74	4	5.37	758800
6	1-Nov-01	2.7	5.1	2.63	4.7	407600
7	1-Oct-01	2.49	2.9	1.96	2.64	93400
8	4-Sep-01	3.98	4	2.35	2.5	565100
9	1-Aug-01	4.73	5.35	3.95	4	794000
10	2-Jul-01	5.1	5.11	3.35	4.72	196800
11	1-Jun-01	6.03	6.25	4.28	5	542900
12	1-May-01	6.89	8.06	5.8	6.05	190900
13	2-Apr-01	7.72	8.1	5.61	6.82	369100
14	1-Mar-01	9.56	11	7.06	7.63	450400
15	1-Feb-01	15	15.38	8.81	9.63	305300
16	2-Jan-01	14	16.69	11.81	14.94	285700
17	1-Dec-00	21	22.56	13.81	13.98	619300
18	1-Nov-00	23.39	27.25	20.13	21.13	493400
19	2-Oct-00	30.56	31.43	22.64	23.58	368100
20	1-Sep-00	31.5	32.06	29.44	30.56	467300
21	1-Aug-00	35.68	36.87	28.07	31.31	417500
22	3-Jul-00	35.37	39.73	32.26	35.5	257400
23	1-Jun-00	27.28	39.36	27.15	35.62	728000
24	1-May-00	27.79	29.22	24.6	27.03	485200
25	3-Apr-00	30.9	31.21	23.87	27.66	508200
26	1-Mar-00	32.7	38.79	28.6	31.21	1929500

EXERCISES

1. This book's disk contains a spreadsheet with monthly stock prices for Boeing from January 1994 to August 2004. Part of the data is shown below.
   (a) Sort the stock prices by date in ascending order (that is, from January 1994 to August 2004).
   (b) Compute the monthly returns on the stock.

	A	B
1	**BOEING STOCK PRICE**	
2	**Date**	**Stock price**
3	2-Aug-04	51.99
4	1-Jul-04	50.55
5	1-Jun-04	50.88
6	3-May-04	45.62
7	1-Apr-04	42.32
8	1-Mar-04	40.71
9	2-Feb-04	42.99
10	2-Jan-04	41.23
11	1-Dec-03	41.61
12	3-Nov-03	37.91
13	1-Oct-03	37.84
14	2-Sep-03	33.75
15	1-Aug-03	36.76

2. On the disk that accompanies this book, you will find stock price data for seven U.S. companies (sample below).
   (a) Sort the data by date and create a table of monthly stock price returns.
   (b) Filter the data to show the returns on all the stocks for months when Boeing's return was greater than 10%.
   (c) Filter the data to show the returns on all the stocks for months when Boeing's return is negative and ATT's return is negative.
   (d) Filter the data to show the returns on all the stocks for months when Kellogg's return is greater than 5% or less than -3%.

3. The spreadsheet "Exercise 3 template" on the disk that accompanies this book contains the return data from Exercise 2.[3]
   (a) Use **Format|Conditional Formatting** to color all the cells in which the stock return is greater than 3% (sample below).

	A	B	C	D	E	F	G	H
1	**STOCK RETURN DATA FOR 7 U.S. COMPANIES**							
2	**Date**	**Boeing**	**Kellogg**	**ATT**	**Lucent**	**Sara Lee**	**Sears**	**JC Penney**
3	1-Feb-02	12.70%	12.79%	-12.20%	-14.66%	-0.41%	-0.08%	-21.42%
4	1-Mar-02	5.00%	-2.83%	1.09%	-14.98%	-0.77%	-2.49%	5.96%
5	1-Apr-02	-7.58%	7.00%	-16.44%	-2.85%	2.02%	2.89%	5.63%
6	1-May-02	-4.00%	2.87%	-8.77%	1.07%	0.25%	12.41%	12.54%
7	3-Jun-02	5.51%	-2.27%	-10.54%	-56.20%	-2.08%	-8.04%	-9.98%
8	1-Jul-02	-7.75%	-3.98%	-4.86%	5.42%	-9.22%	-13.14%	-19.60%
9	1-Aug-02	-10.29%	-5.88%	20.05%	-1.14%	-0.80%	-3.03%	-1.37%
10	3-Sep-02	-7.94%	3.39%	-1.66%	-56.07%	-0.86%	-14.30%	-8.32%
11	1-Oct-02	-12.82%	-4.20%	8.57%	61.84%	24.84%	-32.65%	20.71%
12	1-Nov-02	15.06%	5.55%	-50.82%	43.90%	2.88%	6.39%	24.56%
13	2-Dec-02	-3.13%	2.67%	-6.21%	-28.81%	-3.52%	-13.55%	-3.02%
14	2-Jan-03	-4.23%	-2.54%	-25.39%	47.62%	-11.43%	10.44%	-15.28%

---

[3]See the Excel Note at the end of the exercises for information on how we used **Copy|Paste Special** to create this spreadsheet.

(b) Use **Conditional Formatting** to color all cells whose monthly returns are between the value for **Low cutoff** and **High cutoff** as illustrated below. Make sure that you put the cells into the **Conditional Formatting** dialog box as formulas, so that you can vary the cell entries to see the effect (illustration below).

	A	B	C	D	E	F	G	H	I	J	K
1	STOCK RETURN DATA FOR 7 U.S. COMPANIES										
2	Date	Boeing	Kellogg	ATT	Lucent	Sara Lee	Sears	JC Penney			
3	1-Feb-02	12.70%	12.79%	-12.20%	-14.66%	-0.41%	-0.08%	-21.42%			
4	1-Mar-02	5.00%	-2.83%	1.09%	-14.98%	-0.77%	-2.49%	5.96%		Low cutoff	-2%
5	1-Apr-02	-7.58%	7.00%	-16.44%	-2.85%	2.02%	2.89%	5.63%		High cutoff	4%
6	1-May-02	-4.00%	2.87%	-8.77%	1.07%	0.25%	12.41%	12.54%			
7	3-Jun-02	5.51%	-2.27%	-10.54%	-56.20%	-2.08%	-8.04%	-9.98%			
8	1-Jul-02	-7.75%	-3.98%	-4.86%	5.42%	-9.22%	-13.14%	-19.60%			
9	1-Aug-02	-10.29%	-5.88%	20.05%	-1.14%	-0.80%	-3.03%	-1.37%			
10	3-Sep-02	-7.94%	3.39%	-1.66%	-56.07%	-0.86%	-14.30%	-8.32%			
11	1-Oct-02	-12.82%	-4.20%	8.57%	61.84%	24.84%	-32.65%	20.71%			
12	1-Nov-02	15.06%	5.55%	-50.82%	43.90%	2.88%	6.39%	24.56%			

Here's the way the dialog box looks:

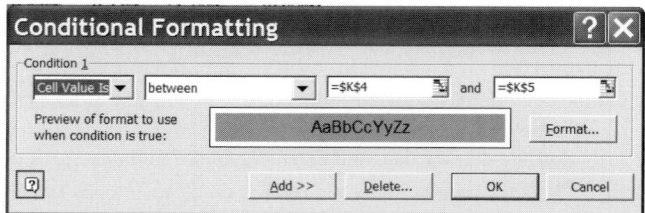

4. The disk that accompanies this book includes data on stock returns and stock volume (the number of shares traded each month) for six restaurant companies. A sample of the data is given below.[4]

	A	B	C	D	E	F	G	H	I	J	K	L	M
1	STOCK VOLUME TRADED AND MONTHLY STOCK RETURNS FOR 6 RESTAURANT STOCKS, JANUARY 1999 - AUGUST 2004												
2		McDonald's (MCD)		Yum! Brands (YUM)		Starbucks (SBUX)		Brinker (EAT)		Wendy's (WEN)		Outback (OSI)	
3	Date	OSI volume	OSI return	YUM volume	YUM return	SBUX volume	SBUX return	EAT volume	EAT return	WEN volume	WEN return	OSI volume	OSI return
4	1-Feb-99	2,222,515	7.86%	547,578	30.61%	1,686,368	1.54%	255,110	5.24%	492,215	1.07%	481,473	20.21%
5	1-Mar-99	2,190,015	6.86%	863,321	13.07%	1,121,584	6.13%	323,394	-10.37%	639,157	18.79%	1,084,447	11.97%
6	1-Apr-99	3,609,313	-6.47%	659,447	-8.36%	1,494,278	31.65%	267,269	7.46%	984,047	-4.83%	848,600	9.34%
7	3-May-99	3,428,928	-8.90%	878,295	-9.50%	1,814,457	-0.16%	245,742	0.70%	411,719	1.14%	876,490	0.17%
8	1-Jun-99	3,330,010	6.80%	702,700	-7.09%	1,753,525	1.84%	159,150	-2.03%	491,065	4.58%	510,360	9.59%
9	1-Jul-99	2,890,809	1.38%	998,354	-24.82%	1,820,500	-38.13%	179,022	2.07%	437,177	3.07%	562,545	-15.10%
10	2-Aug-99	2,912,914	-0.53%	1,025,547	-0.15%	7,656,961	-1.55%	140,028	-13.84%	540,661	-3.62%	507,190	-11.26%
11	1-Sep-99	2,655,895	4.54%	1,458,677	0.74%	2,847,604	8.30%	225,404	11.91%	287,700	-5.99%	736,304	-14.00%
12	1-Oct-99	2,413,995	-4.63%	972,752	-1.81%	2,547,385	9.77%	274,800	-14.30%	460,495	-9.91%	1,157,423	-9.71%
13	1-Nov-99	4,125,309	11.16%	681,366	3.24%	2,851,114	-2.35%	274,761	-2.46%	424,233	-7.12%	1,303,476	2.46%

(a) Compute the average monthly volume and return for each of the companies.

(b) What is the average monthly stock return for McDonald's for months in which the stock volume is greater than 6,000,000 shares?

---

[4]The stock volume and the stock return refer to the month before the date given. For example, in January 1999 (the month preceding 1 February 1999) McDonald's stock had a volume of 2,222,515 shares and a return of 7.86%.

(c)   What is the average monthly stock return for Outback for months when the Starbucks stock return is negative *and* the Wendy's stock return is greater than 3%?

(d)   What is the total of the monthly returns for Yum! for months when the Starbucks stock return is negative *or* the Wendy's stock return is greater than 3%?

5. The disk that accompanies this book contains a text file called **Dell.txt**, which contains Dell Computer's income statements for the years 2001–2003. Import this file into an Excel spreadsheet and "clean it up" so that it can be used for computations.

CONSOLIDATED STATEMENT OF INCOME
(in millions, except per share amounts)

	Fiscal Year Ended		
	January 31, 2003	February 1, 2002	February 2, 2001
Net revenue	$ 35,404	$ 31,168	$ 31,888
Cost of revenue	29,055	25,661	25,445
Gross margin	6,349	5,507	6,443
Operating expenses:			
Selling, general and administrative	3,050	2,784	3,193
Research, development and engineering	455	452	482
Special charges	–	482	105
Total operating expenses	3,505	3,718	3,780
Operating income	2,844	1,789	2,663
Investment and other income (loss), net	183	(58)	531

EXCEL NOTE

USING **EDIT|PASTE SPECIAL** TO GET RID OF FORMULAS

Sometimes we want to exhibit only the numerical values for a computation we've already done, getting rid of the formulas that "stand behind" the calculations. Here's a simple example. In a finance test with 15 questions, the number of questions answered correctly by the students is given in column B below:

	A	B	C	D
1	Number of questions	15		
2		Answered correctly	Percentage right	
3	Mary	15	100.00%	<-- =B3/$B$1
4	Anup	12	80.00%	<-- =B4/$B$1
5	Esther	8	53.33%	
6	Charley	10	66.67%	
7	Li Lei	14	93.33%	

Column C computes the percentage answered correctly using an obvious formula.

contd.

Now suppose we want to produce a spreadsheet with only the percentage figures, without the formula. Below we've copied the names and then copied column C using **Edit|Paste Special|Values**. Now there are just numbers, no formulas.

	A	B	C	D
9	Below: Formulas deleted with Edit|Paste Special|Values			
10		Percentage right		
11	Mary	100.00%	<-- No formula, just a number	
12	Anup	80.00%		
13	Esther	53.33%		
14	Charley	66.67%		
15	Li Lei	93.33%		

Here's the dialog box we used:

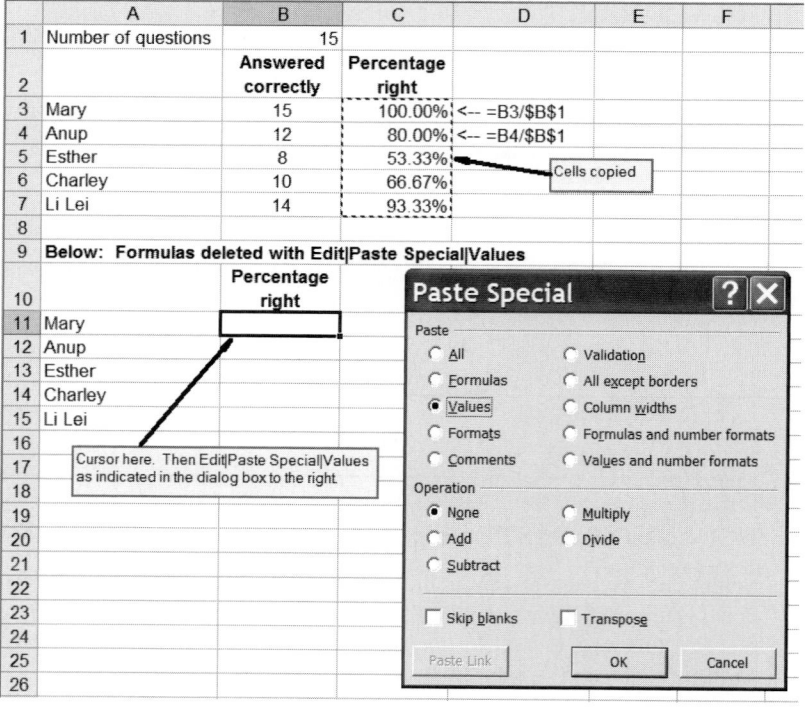

CHAPTER 34

USING EXCEL INFORMATION IN WORD DOCUMENTS

OVERVIEW

This short chapter discusses the incorporation of Excel information in Word documents. Properly speaking, this has absolutely nothing to do with finance, the subject of this book. On the other hand, finance people are always using Excel in their reports (and often doing it wrong!).

34.1 An Example

You've been working hard on preparing an Excel notebook for a presentation:

	A	B	C	D
1	**CALCULATING PRESENT VALUES WITH EXCEL**			
2	r, interest rate	9%		
3				
4	**Year**	**Payment at end of year**	**Present value**	
5	1	100	91.74	<-- =B5/(1+$B$2)^A5
6	2	200	168.34	<-- =B6/(1+$B$2)^A6
7	3	300	231.66	
8	4	400	283.37	
9	5	500	324.97	
10				
11	**Present value of all payments**			
12	Summing the present values		1,100.07	<-- =SUM(C5:C9)
13	Using Excel's NPV function		1,100.07	<-- =NPV($B$2,B5:B9)

Now you want to include the information in a Word document you're preparing. You've got a couple of options.

Option 1: Copy–Paste

This is the simplest way to copy:

- In Excel: Mark the area to be copied in the spreadsheet.
- Press [Ctrl]+C (or go to **Edit|Copy**).
- Go to your Word document: Press [Ctrl]+V (or **Edit|Paste**).

Here's the result:

CALCULATING PRESENT VALUES WITH EXCEL		
r, interest rate	9%	
Year	**Payment at end of year**	**Present value**
1	100	91.74 <-- =B5/(1+$B$2)^A5
2	200	168.34 <-- =B6/(1+$B$2)^A6
3	300	231.66
4	400	283.37
5	500	324.97
Present value of all payments		
Summing the present values	1,100.07	<-- =SUM(C5:C9)
Using Excel's NPV function	1,100.07	<-- =NPV($B$2,B5:B9)

This creates a table with text in the cells (thus you can edit the text). We have also shown the table gridlines by selecting the table and using the Word command **Format|Borders and Shading**:

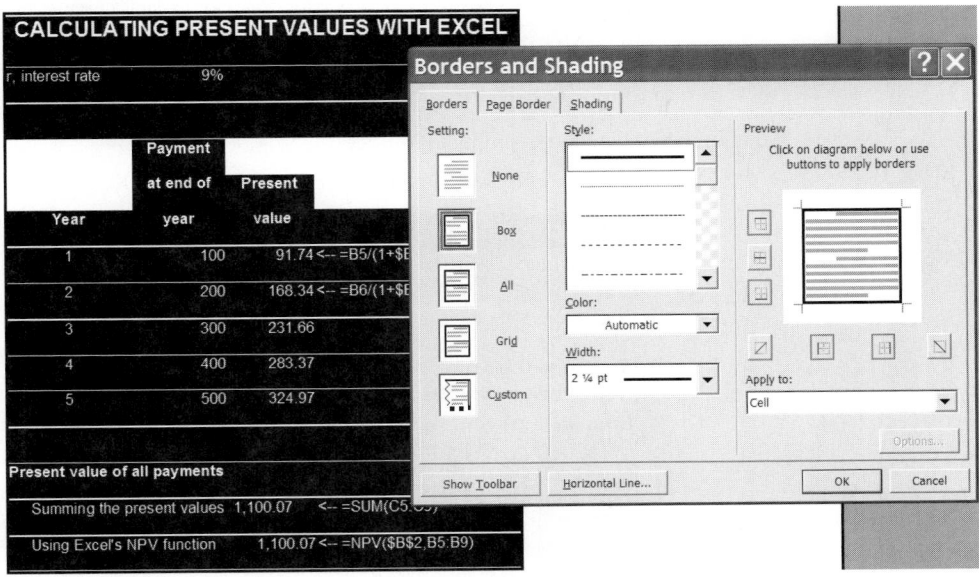

Option 2: Copy–Paste As a Picture

Before illustrating this method, we use the command **File|Page Setup|Sheet** to determine how Excel will print our spreadsheet. This command also affects the way the *copy–paste as a picture* works. In this example, we have chosen to print our spreadsheet showing both gridlines and row–column headings:

EXCEL HINT

The **File|Page Setup** command controls both the way the spreadsheet prints on a printer and the way it copies into Word.

We now repeat the **Copy** command in Excel:

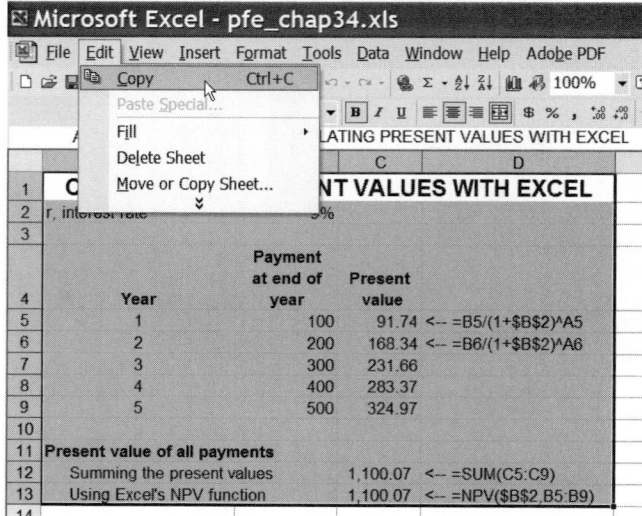

Returning to Word, we use the command **Edit|Paste Special|Picture**:

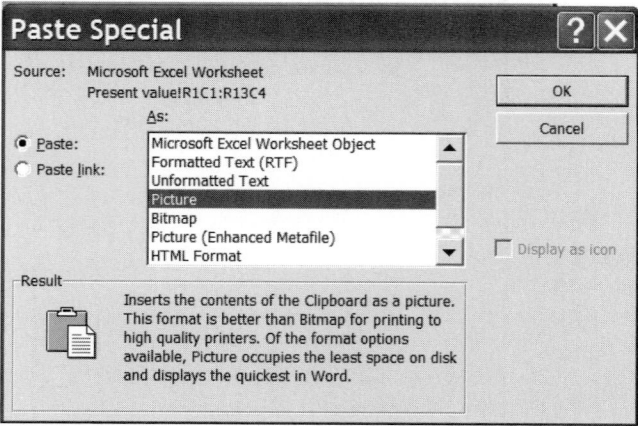

(Note that the **Paste link** button is not clicked. More about that later.) Here's the result:

	A	B	C	D
1	CALCULATING PRESENT VALUES WITH EXCEL			
2	r, interest rate	9%		
3				
4	Year	Payment at end of year	Present value	
5	1	100	91.74	<-- =B6/(1+$B$3)^A6
6	2	200	168.34	<-- =B7/(1+$B$3)^A7
7	3	300	231.66	
8	4	400	283.37	
9	5	500	324.97	
10				
11	Present value of all payments			
12	Summing the present values		1,100.07	<-- =SUM(C6:C10)
13	Using Excel's NPV function		1,100.07	<-- =NPV($B$3,B6:B10)

Option 3: Copy–Paste As a Picture, Another Way

Certain mixtures of symbols give Excel trouble when copied to Word. The spreadsheet below, for example, includes some Greek symbols in cells A2 and A3, which don't copy using the technique discussed in the previous subsection:

	A	B
1	DOESN'T COPY WELL THE REGULAR WAY	
2	α, alpha	
3	β, beta	
4	$E(r_M)$, market expected return	
5	The red dot ■	

To get them to copy press [**Shift**] and then **Edit**. This brings up the menu below:

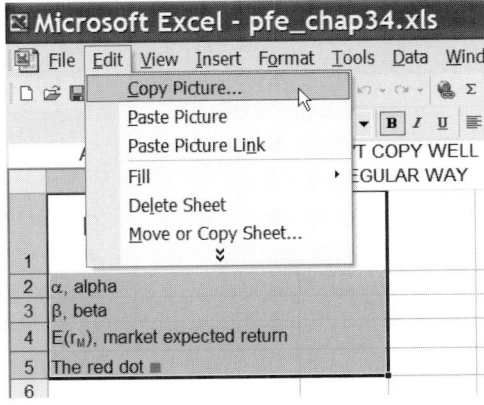

Using the **Copy Picture** option brings up the following menu:

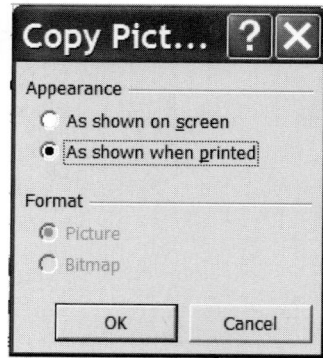

We've already indicated that the picture should be copied "As shown when printed." Now **Edit|Paste** (or [Ctrl]+V) works to copy the spreadsheet exactly as it would be printed.

	A	B
1	**DOESN'T COPY WELL THE REGULAR WAY**	
2	α, alpha	
3	β, beta	
4	E(r$_M$), market expected return	
5	The red dot ∎	

34.2 Linking Excel Notebooks and Word Documents

We can link our Excel notebook to our Word document. For example, in the previous example, we could have clicked the **Paste link** button—this would create a live link between the Excel notebook and the Word document. This has obvious advantages: Whenever you make a change in Excel, it will update the Word document.

CALCULATING PRESENT VALUES WITH EXCEL			
r, interest rate	9%		
Year	Payment at end of year	Present value	
1	100	91.74	<-- =B6/(1+$B$3)^A6
2	200	168.34	<-- =B7/(1+$B$3)^A7
3	300	231.66	
4	400	283.37	
5	500	324.97	
Present value of all payments			
Summing the present values		1,100.07	<-- =SUM(C6:C10)
Using Excel's NPV function		1,100.07	<-- =NPV($B$3,B6:B10)

However, linking also has a number of disadvantages:

- You may want to "play" with the Excel notebook and not have the results transferred to your document.

- Linking an Excel notebook and a Word document increases the size of the Word file.

INDEX